T0211789

Lecture Notes in Computer Science 11752

More information about this series at http://www.springer.com/series/7412

Elisa Ricci · Samuel Rota Bulò ·
Cees Snoek · Oswald Lanz ·
Stefano Messelodi · Nicu Sebe (Eds.)

Image Analysis and Processing – ICIAP 2019

20th International Conference
Trento, Italy, September 9–13, 2019
Proceedings, Part II

Springer

Editors
Elisa Ricci (ID)
University of Trento
Povo, Italy

Cees Snoek (ID)
University of Amsterdam
Amsterdam, The Netherlands

Stefano Messelodi (ID)
Fondazione Bruno Kessler
Povo, Italy

Samuel Rota Bulò (ID)
Mapillary Research
Graz, Austria

Oswald Lanz (ID)
Fondazione Bruno Kessler
Povo, Italy

Nicu Sebe (ID)
University of Trento
Povo, Italy

ISSN 0302-9743   ISSN 1611-3349   (electronic)
Lecture Notes in Computer Science
ISBN 978-3-030-30644-1   ISBN 978-3-030-30645-8   (eBook)
https://doi.org/10.1007/978-3-030-30645-8

LNCS Sublibrary: SL6 – Image Processing, Computer Vision, Pattern Recognition, and Graphics

This Springer imprint is published by the registered company Springer Nature Switzerland AG
The registered company address is: Gewerbestrasse 11, 6330 Cham, Switzerland

Preface

The International Conference on Image Analysis and Processing (ICIAP) is an established scientific meeting organized biennially and promoted by the Italian Association for Computer Vision, Pattern Recognition and Machine Learning (CVPL; ex-GIRPR) of the International Association for Pattern Recognition (IAPR). The conference traditionally covers topics related to computer vision, pattern recognition, and image processing, addressing both theoretical and applicative aspects.

The 20th International Conference on Image Analysis and Processing (ICIAP 2019), held in Trento, Italy, September 9–13, 2019 (https://event.unitn.it/iciap2019), was organized jointly by University of Trento and Fondazione Bruno Kessler.

The conference was located in the city center, at the Faculty of Law of University of Trento, nearby Piazza Duomo, namely the historical, main square of the city. ICIAP 2019 was endorsed by the International Association for Pattern Recognition (IAPR). This year the conference was co-located with the 13th International Conference on Distributed Smart Cameras (ICDSC 2019) (https://event.unitn.it/icdsc2019/), and a joint keynote speech and oral session was organized.

ICIAP is traditionally a venue to discuss image processing and analysis, computer vision, pattern recognition and machine learning, from both theoretical and applicative perspectives, promoting connections and synergies among senior scholars and students, universities, research institutes, and companies. ICIAP 2019 followed this trend, and the program was subdivided into nine main topics, covering a broad range of scientific areas, which were managed by two area chairs per each topic. They were: Video Analysis and Understanding, Pattern Recognition and Machine Learning, Deep Learning, Multiview Geometry and 3D Computer Vision, Image Analysis, Detection and Recognition, Multimedia, Biomedical and Assistive Technology, Digital Forensics, and Image Processing for Cultural Heritage.

ICIAP 2019 received 207 paper submissions from all over the world, including Algeria, Austria, Belgium, Brazil, Bulgaria, Canada, China, Czech Republic, Denmark, Egypt, Finland, France, Germany, Greece, India, Israel, Italy, Japan, Korea, Morocco, Mexico, Pakistan, Poland, Romania, Russia, Saudi Arabia, Slovenia, Spain, Sweden, Switzerland, Tunisia, Turkey, the United Kingdom, and the USA. To select papers from these submissions, 21 expert researchers were invited to act as areas chairs, together with the international Program Committee and an expert team of reviewers. A rigorous peer-review selection process was carried out where each paper received at least two reviews. This ultimately led to the selection of 117 high quality manuscripts, presented during the conference in the form of 18 orals, 18 spotlights, and 81 posters, with an overall acceptance rate of about 56%. Among oral papers selected at ICIAP 2019, four were selected as Brave New Ideas Paper, i.e. papers exploring highly innovative ideas, visionary applications, and theoretical paradigm shifts in the area of computer vision, pattern recognition, machine learning, multimedia analysis, and image processing. The ICIAP 2019 proceedings are published as volumes of the *Lecture Notes in Computer Science* (LNCS) series by Springer.

The program included four invited talks by experts in computer vision, pattern recognition, and robotics: Davide Scaramuzza, University of Zurich and ETH Zurich (Switzerland), Tal Ayellet, Technion Israel of Technology (Israel), Emanuele Rodolà, Sapienza University of Rome (Italy), and Alessandra Sciutti, Italian Institute of Technology (Italy), who addressed very interesting and recent research approaches and paradigms such as deep learning, 3D modeling and reconstruction, visual robot navigation, semantic scene understanding, human-robot interaction, visual cognition, computer graphics, and image enhancement. ICIAP 2019 also included several tutorials on topics of great relevance for the community: Vision, Language and Action: from Captioning to Embodied AI, Lorenzo Baraldi and Marcella Cornia (University of Modena Reggio Emilia); Transferring Knowledge Across Domains: an Introduction to Deep Domain Adaptation, Massimiliano Mancini (Sapienza University of Rome, FBK and Italian Institute of Technology) and Pietro Morerio (Italian Institute of Technology); High-Dynamic-Range Imaging: Improvements and Limits, Alessandro Rizzi (University of Milano); Anomaly Detection in Images, Giacomo Boracchi (Politecnico Milano) and Diego Carrera (ST Microelectronics); Fingerprint Presentation Attacks Detection: Lessons Learned and a Roadmap to the Future, Gian Luca Marcialis (University of Cagliari); and Probabilistic and Deep Learning for Regression in Computer Vision, Stephane Lathuilière (University of Trento) and Xavier Alameda-Pineda (Inria Grenoble). ICIAP 2019 also hosted the presentation of the results of the Challenge DAFNE (Digital Anastylosis of Frescoes challeNgE), an international competition in the artistic heritage sector designed to provide virtual solutions that ultimately add to the fresco restorer's toolkit.

ICIAP 2019 also hosted five satellite events: four workshops and one industrial session. The workshops were: BioFor Workshop on Recent Advances in Digital Security: Biometrics and Forensics, organized by Daniel Riccio, Francesco Marra, Diego Gragnaniello (University of Naples Federico II, Italy) and Chang-Tsun Li (Deakin University, Australia); the First International Workshop on eHealth in the Big Data and Deep Learning Era, organized by Tanmoy Chakraborty (Institute of Information Technology Delhi, India), Stefano Marrone (University of Naples "Federico II", Italy) and Giancarlo Sperl (CINI - ITEM National Lab, Naples, Italy); Deep Understanding of Shopper Behaviours and Interactions in Intelligent Retail Environment, organized by Emanuele Frontoni (Università Politecnica delle Marche), Sebastiano Battiato (University of Catania, Italy), Cosimo Distante (ISASI CNR, Italy), Marina Paolanti (Università Politecnica delle Marche, Italy), Luigi Di Stefano (University of Bologna, Italy), Giovanni Marina Farinella (University di Catania, Italy), Annette Wolfrath (GFK Verein, Germany) and Primo Zingaretti (Università Politecnica delle Marche, Italy) and the International Workshop on Pattern Recognition for Cultural Heritage (PatReCH 2019), organized by Francesco Fontanella, Mario Molinara (University of Cassino and Southern Lazio, Italy) and Filippo Stanco (University of Catania, Italy). The Industrial Session was organized with the purpose of bringing together researchers and practitioners in industrial engineering and computer science interested in industrial machine vision. The session was organized by Luigi di Stefano, Vittorio Murino, Paolo Rota, and Francesco Setti. In the industrial session we hosted

several companies as well as start-ups to show their activities while assessing them with respect to the cutting-edge research in the respective areas. The papers from the workshop and the industrial session were all collected in New Trends in Image Analysis and Processing – ICIAP 2019. We thank all the workshop and industrial session organizers and tutorial speakers who made possible such an interesting pre-conference program.

Several awards were conferred during ICIAP 2019. Two student support grants were provided by the International Association for Pattern Recognition (IAPR). The Eduardo Caianiello Award was attributed to the best paper authored or co-authored by at least one young researcher (PhD student, Post Doc, or similar). A Best Paper Award was also assigned after a careful selection made by an ad hoc appointed committee. The award was dedicated to Prof. Alfredo Petrosino, an eminent scientist and one of the most active members of the Italian Chapter of the IAPR, who passed away this year. During the conference an important moment was dedicated to commemorate the memory of Prof. Petrosino who will be greatly missed.

The organization and the success of ICIAP 2019 was made possible thanks to the cooperation of many people. First of all, special thanks should be given to all the reviewers and the area chairs, who made a big effort for the selection of the papers. Second, we also would like to thank the industrial, special session, publicity, publication, and Asia and US liaison chairs, who, operating in their respective fields, made this event a successful forum of science. Special thanks go to the workshop and tutorial chairs, as well as all workshop organizers and tutorial lecturers for making the conference program richer with notable satellite events. The communication services department of UNITN that supported all the communication, the registration process, and the financial aspects of the conference, among many other issues, should be acknowledged for all the work done. Last but not least, we are indebted to the local Organizing Committee (mainly colleagues from MHUG, University of Trento, and FBK-TeV) who covered almost every aspect of the conference when necessary and the day-to-day management issues of the ICIAP 2019 organization. Thanks very much indeed to all the aforementioned people, as without their support we would not have made it. We hope that ICIAP 2019 met its aim to serve as a basis and inspiration for future ICIAP editions.

August 2019

Elisa Ricci
Samuel Rota Bulò
Cees Snoek
Oswald Lanz
Stefano Messelodi
Nicu Sebe

Organization

General Chairs

Oswald Lanz   Fondazione Bruno Kessler, Italy
Stefano Messelodi   Fondazione Bruno Kessler, Italy
Nicu Sebe   University of Trento, Italy

Program Chairs

Elisa Ricci   University of Trento and Fondazione Bruno Kessler, Italy
Samuel Rota Bulò   Mapillary Research, Austria
Cees Snoek   University of Amsterdam, The Netherlands

Workshop Chairs

Marco Cristani   University of Verona, Italy
Andrea Prati   University of Parma, Italy

Tutorial Chairs

Costantino Grana   University of Modena e Reggio Emilia, Italy
Lamberto Ballan   University of Padova, Italy

Special Session Chairs

Marco Bertini   University of Florence, Italy
Tatiana Tommasi   Italian Institute of Technology, Italy

Industrial Chairs

Paul Chippendale   Fondazione Bruno Kessler, Italy
Fabio Galasso   OSRAM, Germany

Publicity/Web Chairs

Davide Boscaini   Fondazione Bruno Kessler, Italy
Massimiliano Mancini   Sapienza University of Rome, Fondazione Bruno Kessler and Italian Institute of Technology, Italy

Publication Chair

Michela Lecca   Fondazione Bruno Kessler, Italy

Local Chairs

Fabio Poiesi   Fondazione Bruno Kessler, Italy
Gloria Zen   University of Trento, Italy
Stéphane Lathuillère   University of Trento, Italy

Asia Liaison Chair

Ramanathan Subramanian   University of Glasgow, Singapore

USA Liaison Chair

Yan Yan   Texas State University, USA

Steering Committee

Virginio Cantoni   University of Pavia, Italy
Luigi Pietro Cordella   University of Napoli Federico II, Italy
Rita Cucchiara   University of Modena and Reggio Emilia, Italy
Alberto Del Bimbo   University of Firenze, Italy
Marco Ferretti   University of Pavia, Italy
Gian Luca Foresti   University of Udine, Italy
Fabio Roli   University of Cagliari, Italy
Gabriella Sanniti di Baja   ICAR-CNR, Italy

Invited Speakers

Davide Scaramuzza   University of Zurich and ETH Zurich, Switzerland
Tal Ayellet   Technion Israel of Technology, Israel
Emanuele Rodolà   Sapienza University of Rome, Italy
Alessandra Sciutti   Italian Institute of Technology, Italy

Area Chairs

Video Analysis and Understanding

Andrea Cavallaro   Queen Mary University of London, UK
Efstratios Gavves   University of Amsterdam, The Netherlands

Pattern Recognition and Machine Learning

Battista Biggio   University of Cagliari, Italy
Marcello Pelillo   University of Venice, Italy

Deep Learning

Marco Gori   University of Siena, Italy
Francesco Orabona   Boston University, USA

Multiview Geometry and 3D Computer Vision

Andrea Fusiello   University of Udine, Italy
Alessio Del Bue   Istituto Italiano di Tecnologia, Italy
Federico Tombari   Technische Universität München, Germany

Image Analysis, Detection and Recognition

Barbara Caputo   Politecnico di Torino and Italian Institute of
                                 Technology, Italy
Jasper Uijlings   Google AI, USA

Multimedia

Xavier Alameda-Pineda   Inria, France
Francesco De Natale   University of Trento, Italy

Biomedical and Assistive Technology

Giovanni Maria Farinella   University of Catania, Italy
Roberto Manduchi   University of California Santa Cruz, USA

Digital Forensics

Giulia Boato   University of Trento, Italy
Fernando Pérez-González   University of Vigo, Spain

Image Processing for Cultural Heritage

Andreas Rauber   TU Wien, Austria
Lorenzo Seidenari   University of Florence, Italy

Brave New Ideas

Michele Merler   IBM T. J. Watson Research Center, USA
Concetto Spampinato   University of Catania, Italy

Program Committee

Aladine Chetouani	Université d'Orléans, France
Albert Ali Salah	University of Utrecht, The Netherlands
Alberto Pedrouzo Ulloa	University of Vigo, Italy
Aleksandr Ermolov	University of Trento, Italy
Alessandro Ortis	University of Catania, Italy
Alessandro Piva	University of Florence, Italy
Alfredo Petrosino	Uniparthenope, Italy
Aliaksandr Siarohin	University of Trento, Italy
Anders Hast	Uppsala University, Sweden
Andrea Pilzer	University of Trento, Italy
Andrea Simonelli	Mapillary Research, Austria
	Fondazione Bruno Kessler and University of Trento, Italy
Andrea Torsello	Ca' Foscari University, Italy
Angelo Marcelli	University of Salerno, Italy
Antonino Furnari	University of Catania, Italy
Beatrice Rossi	ST Microelectronics, Italy
Benedetta Tondi	University of Siena, Italy
Bogdan Smolka	Silesian University of Technology, Poland
Brian Reily	Colorado School of Mines, USA
Carla Maria Modena	Fondazione Bruno Kessler, Italy
Carlo Colombo	University of Florence, Italy
Carlo Sansone	University of Salerno, Italy
Cecilia Pasquini	University of Innsbruck, Austria
Christian Riess	Friedrich-Alexander University Erlangen-Nuremberg, Germany
Christian Micheloni	University of Udine, Italy
Dan Popescu	CSIRO, Australia
Daniel Riccio	University of Naples Federico II, Italy
David Fofi	Université Bourgogne Franche-Comte, France
Davide Boscaini	Fondazione Bruno Kessler, Italy
Désiré Sidibé	Université de Bourgogne, France
Diego Carrera	Politecnico di Milano, Italy
Edoardo Ardizzone	University of Palermo, Italy
Eleonora Maset	University of Udine, Italy
Elisabetta Binaghi	University of Insubria, Italy
Enver Sangineto	University of Trento, Italy
Eyasu Zemene	Qualcomm, USA
Fabio Ganovelli	ISTI-CNR, Italy
Fabio Bellavia	University of Florence, Italy
Fabio Poiesi	Fondazione Bruno Kessler, Italy
Federica Arrigoni	University of Udine, Italy
Federico Becattini	University of Firenze, Italy
Federico Iuricich	Clemson University, South Carolina, USA

Filippo Stanco	University of Catania, Italy
Florian Bernard	Max Planck Institute, Germany
Francesco Banterle	CNR Pisa, Italy
Francesco Camastra	University of Naples Parthenope, Italy
Francesco Isgro	University of Naples, Italy
Francesco Turchini	University of Florence, Italy
Gianluigi Ciocca	University of Milano-Bicocca, Italy
Giosuè Lo Bosco	University of Palermo, Italy
Giovanni Fusco	Smith-Kettlewell Eye Research Institute, USA
Giovanni Gallo	University of Catania, Italy
Giuseppe Boccignone	University of Milan, Italy
Gloria Zen	University of Trento, Italy
Huiyu Zhou	University of Leicester, UK
Irene Amerini	University of Florence, Italy
Ismail Elezi	Ca' Foscari University of Venice, Italy
Levi Osterno Vasconcelos	Istituto Italiano di Tecnologia, Italy
Lorenzo Baraldi	University of Modena and Reggio Emilia, Italy
Lorenzo Porzi	Mapillary Research, Austria
Loretta Ichim	Polytechnic University of Bucharest, Romania
Lucia Maddalena	National Research Council, Italy
Luigi Di Stefano	University of Bologna, Italy
Luisa Verdoliva	University Federico II of Naples, Italy
Manuele Bicego	University of Verona, Italy
Marcel Worring	University of Amsterdam, The Netherlands
Marco Fiorucci	Italian Institute of Technology, Italy
Marco La Cascia	University of Palermo, Italy
Maria De Marsico	Sapienza University of Rome, Italy
Maria Giulia Preti	EPFL, Switzerland
Massimiliano Mancini	Sapienza University of Rome, Fondazione Bruno Kessler and Istituto Italiano di Tecnologia, Italy
Massimo Tistarelli	University of Sassari, Italy
Massimo Piccardi	University of Technology Sydney, Australia
Michal Kawulok	Silesian University of Technology, Poland
Michele Nappi	University of Salerno, Italy
Modesto Castrillon-Santana	University of Las Palmas de Gran Canaria, Spain
Mohamed Lakhal	Queen Mary University of London, UK
Pablo Mesejo	Universidad de Granada, Spain
Paolo Napoletano	University of Milano-Bicocca, Italy
Paul Gay	Insa-Rouen, France
Pier Luigi Mazzeo	CNR, Italy
Pietro Pala	University of Florence, Italy
Simone Marina	University of Florence, Italy
Richard Jiang	Lancaster University, UK
Richard Wilson	University of York, UK
Ruggero Pintus	Center for Advanced Studies, Research and Development in Sardinia, Italy

Endorsing Institutions

Institutional Patronage

Contents – Part II

Multimedia

Biomedical and Assistive Technology

Contents – Part I

Video Analysis and Understanding

Pattern Recognition and Machine Learning

Deep Learning

Multiview Geometry and 3D Computer Vision

Image Analysis, Detection and Recognition

Label Propagation Guided by Hierarchy of Partitions for Superpixel Computation

Carolina Stephanie Jerônimo de Almeida[2]([⊠]), Jean Cousty[1], Benjamin Perret[1], Zenilton Kleber G. Patrocínio Jr.[2], and Silvio Jamil F. Guimarães[1,2]

[1] Université Paris-Est, LIGM, CNRS - ENPC - ESIEE Paris - UPEM, Noisy-le-Grand, France
[2] Computer Science Department, Pontifical Catholic University of Minas Gerais, Belo Horizonte, MG, Brazil
carolinajeronimo@gmail.com, sjamil@pucminas.br

Abstract. Superpixel computation can be seen as a process of grouping similar pixels trying to preserve image boundaries. In this work, we propose a label propagation method guided by hierarchy of partitions in the context of the marked (supervised) segmentation problem. The main idea of the proposed method is to propagate labels on a tree modelling a hierarchical representation of the image. We propose several criteria to decide, in the case of a conflict, which of the competing labels must be propagated into a neighbor region of the tree. According to our experiments, the proposed method outperforms the baseline provided by the SLIC method.

Keywords: Hierarchy of partitions · Superpixel · Label propagation

1 Introduction

Superpixel computation is the process of grouping similar pixels trying to preserve image boundaries. Some of the methods to compute superpixels can be seen as image segmentation methods and can be done by hierarchical strategies [11]. A hierarchical image segmentation is a set of image segmentations at different detail levels that preserves spatial and neighboring information among the segmented regions. Hierarchies of partitions have been used in many approaches in the context of image and video segmentation [3,10,12,20–23,25]. Following the idea of [27], we propose a supervised image segmentation based on the label propagation guided by hierarchies of partitions taking into account information about the values extracted from the hierarchy as area and level value. The seminal idea for label propagation on a hierarchy of segmentations was proposed in [27], and later used for hierarchical segmentation assessment in [21,22]: in this approach, the labels from the background and from the foreground compete with each other in order to label the undefined regions. Differently of [21,22,27], in this work, we propose a method for label propagation in which different criteria are used to decide which label must be propagated. The general strategy can

© Springer Nature Switzerland AG 2019
E. Ricci et al. (Eds.): ICIAP 2019, LNCS 11752, pp. 3–13, 2019.
https://doi.org/10.1007/978-3-030-30645-8_1

be divided into three main steps: (i) automatically generate seeds (or markers); (ii) compute a hierarchy of partitions taking into account a specific attribute, such as the area or the volume, in which the pixels are represented on the leaves; and (iii) from leaves to root on the hierarchy, the labels are propagated considering a competition strategy. To decide which of the competing labels must be propagated into a neighbor region in the case of conflict, we have devised two different strategies: (i) the label that is related to a region with the highest attribute value is propagated; or (ii) the label that is related to the region with the smallest attribute value is propagated. It is worth to mention that some attribute values may directly be extracted from the hierarchy such as the hierarchy level, but others must be dynamically computed, *i.e.* the area of the regions.

This work is organized as follows. In Sect. 2, we present some important concepts related to superpixels computation and hierarchies. The proposed label propagation guided by hierarchy of partitions is described in Sect. 3. Some experimental results obtained for tests performed on four databases are detailed in Sect. 4. Finally, in Sect. 5, some conclusions are drawn and further works are discussed.

2   Fundamental Concepts

2.1   Graphs

A *graph* is as a pair (V, E) such that V is a finite set and E is composed of unordered pairs of distinct elements in V, *i.e.*, E is a subset of $\{\{x, y\} \subseteq V \mid x \neq y\}$. In the following, the pair $G = (V, E)$ denotes a connected graph. Each element of V is called a *vertex or a pixel*, and each element of E is called an *edge*. The *graph* G is used to model the image domain, *e.g.*, V will represent a regular 2D grid of pixels, and E encoded the 4 adjacency for every pixel. We denote by W a function from E to $\mathbb{R}$ that weights the edges of G. Therefore, the pair (G, W) is an *edge-weighted graph*, and, for any $u \in E$, the value $W(u)$ represents the *weight* of u.

2.2   Hierarchies

A partition, also called a segmentation, $\mathbf{P}$ of V is a family of subsets of V such that: (i) the intersection of any two distinct elements of $\mathbf{P}$ is empty; and (ii) the union of the elements of $\mathbf{P}$ is equal to V. Each element of a partition $\mathbf{P}$ is called a region of the partition $\mathbf{P}$. Given two partitions $\mathbf{P}_1$ and $\mathbf{P}_2$, we say that $\mathbf{P}_2$ is a refinement of $\mathbf{P}_1$ if every region of $\mathbf{P}_2$ is included in a region of $\mathbf{P}_1$.

A hierarchy (of partitions) $H = (\mathbf{P}_0, ..., \mathbf{P}_n)$ is a sequence of partitions of V such that $\mathbf{P}_0$ is the single region partition $\mathbf{P}_0 = \{V\}$, the partition $\mathbf{P}_n$ contains every singletons of V, *i.e.*, $\mathbf{P}_n = \{\{x\} \mid x \in V\}$, and $\mathbf{P}_i$ is a refinement of $\mathbf{P}_{i-1}$ for all i in $\{1, ..., n\}$. It is usually represented as a tree or a dendrogram and can be visualized as a saliency map, which is a contour map in which the grey level represents the strength of the contour: i.e., its level of disappearance in the hierarchy. The reader may refer to [7] for more details about the hierarchy of partitions.

The Quasi-Flat Zones (QFZ) hierarchy is a classical structure that is constructed by considering the connected components of the level sets of the dissimilarity function [7,16,17]. More precisely, we say that two pixels are λ-connected if they can be joined by a path such that the dissimilarity between any two successive pixels of this path is lower than λ. For a given λ in $\mathbb{R}$, the equivalence classes of the relation "is λ-connected" form the λ-partition of the image into its λ-connected components also called λ-flat zones. The set of all λ-partitions for every λ in $\mathbb{R}$ forms the QFZ hierarchy.

Watershed (WS) hierarchies are constructed by considering the watershed segmentation of an image that is iteratively flooded under the control of an attribute [4,6,8,15,18,19,21]. For example, the watershed segmentations of the area closings of size k of an image for every positive integer k form the WS hierarchy by area of the image. In this article, we consider 2 possible attributes: (i) area (WSArea); and (ii) volume (WSVol).

2.3   Seed Location and Superpixel Computation

According to [28], in order to really develop a superpixel approach one should address some requirements such as being a partition of the image, representing connected sets of pixels, preserving image boundaries, being generated efficiently and with a controllable number of generated superpixels. Usually, the methods for superpixel computation are classified in six different types: (i) Watershed-based [14]; (ii) Density-based [1]; (iii) Graph-based [24]; (iv) Contour evolution [5]; (v) Clustering-based [1]; and (vi) Boundary-aware.

In the context of superpixels, computer vision applications have come to rely increasingly attention on superpixels computation mainly due to the SLIC method [1]. The SLIC algorithm groups pixels into regions which can be used to replace the rigid structure of the pixel grid. Firstly, seeds are distributed throughout the image taking into account uniform regions, each one containing a centroid seed. The approximate size of each superpixel is N/K pixels, where N is the size of the image and K is the number of regions (or superpixels). Thus, seeds are equally spaced in the range of $S = \sqrt{N/K}$. During the execution of the SLIC algorithm, the centers of the superpixels are moved to the lowest gradient position in a 3×3 neighborhood to avoid starting at a very noisy pixel. Next, in the assignment step, each pixel is associated to the nearest cluster center according to a distance measure D. Thereafter, an update step, based on the K-means clustering algorithm, to compute the centers of the superpixels is done. The assignment and update steps are then repeated until stability or up to the maximum number of iterations. The strategy of seed location based on the SLIC method is so-called **grid sampling**. Despite the good results obtained by this sampling strategy, we can use a **random sampling** in order to randomly put seed on the image.

3   Label Propagation Guided by a Hiearchy of Partitions

The seminal idea for label propagation on a hierarchical watershed, was proposed in [27] in which labels from background and foreground compete with each other in order to be assigned to undefined regions. Differently of [27], in this work, we propose a method for label propagation in which distinct criteria may be used to decide which label must be propagated. The proposed strategy may be divided into three main steps: (i) seed generation; (ii) computation of the hierarchy of partitions; and (iii) label propagation.

In the first step, seed generation, seeds (or markers) are automatically distributed over the pixels. For computing the hierarchy of partition, we follow [8,19] in order to compute a QFZ hierarchy and watershed hierarchies based on some attributes: (i) area; and (ii) and volume. The underlying graph corresponds to a 4-connected adjacency graph in which each edge is weighted by the dissimilarity measure between two pixels.

Finally, a label propagation is done following the procedure described in the Algorithm 1. The propagation is divided into two main steps: (i) from leaves to root (lines 3–9) to assign labels to the regions; and (ii) from root to leaves

---

Algorithm 1. Label propagation guided by a hierarchy of partitions.

Data: A hierarchy of partition $\mathcal{H}$ on the graph $\mathcal{G}$. The attribute $\mathcal{A}$ to be used by the criterion $\mathcal{C}$. A set of k seeds $S = \{s_1, s_2, \ldots, s_k\}$, which are also the labels to be propagated.

Result: The labelling ℓ on the leaves of $\mathcal{H}$ s.t. $\ell(\{x\}) \in \{s_1, s_2, \ldots, s_k, Undefined\}$, $\forall x \in V$. Leaves with the same label belong to the same superpixel.

1 **foreach** $x \in V$ **do** $\ell(\{x\}) \leftarrow Undefined$;
2 **foreach** $s_k \in S$ **do** $\ell(\{s_k\}) \leftarrow s_k$;
   `// For all nodes from leaves to root`
3 **for** all regions R in $\mathbf{R}_{\mathcal{H}}$ in increasing order **do**
4   **if** R is not a leaf **then**
5       $S \leftarrow sons(R)$;
6   **if** at least one son s of R in $S \neq Undefined$ **then**
         $\ell(R) \leftarrow$ **selectBestLabel**$(S, \mathcal{A}, \mathcal{C})$;
7   **else** $\ell(R) \leftarrow Undefined$;
8   **end**
9 **end**
   `// For all nodes from root to leaves`
10 **for** all regions R in $\mathbf{R}_{\mathcal{H}}$ in decreasing order **do**
11   **if** $R \neq V$ and $\ell(R) = Undefined$ **then**
12       $\ell(R) \leftarrow \ell(Parent(R))$
13   **end**
14 **end**

(lines 10–14) to assign labels to the pixels. In the first part, from leaves to root on the hierarchy, labels are propagated considering a competition strategy. In order to decide about which label must be propagated to a neighbor region in the case of conflict (line 4), we have used two different strategies (**selectBestLabel**(S, A, C)): (i) the label that is related to a region with highest attribute value is propagated; or (ii) the label that is related to a region with smallest attribute value is propagated. In the second part, from root to leaves, the pixels of the regions receive the labels which were assigned to it during the bottow-up procedure.

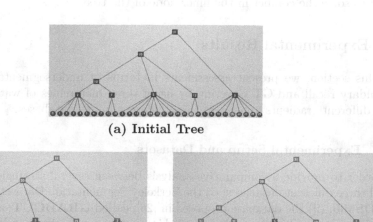

(a) Initial Tree

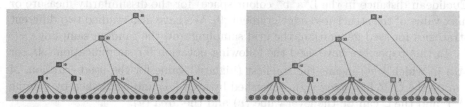

(b) **Propagation using the highest value attribute computed from each region: (left) bottom-up and (right) top-down**

(c) **Propagation using the highest area attribute computed from each region: (left) bottom-up and (right) top-down**

Fig. 1. Toy example for illustrating the label propagation taking into account two different criteria for solving the seed competition, the higher value and higher area.

It is worth to mention that some attributes may be directly extracted from the hierachy, that could be represented as a tree, such as the value of the hierarchy level, but other measures must dynamically be computed over the tree, *i.e.* area of the regions. In Fig. 1, we present a toy example for illustrating the label propagation procedure. In this example, we have used a QFZ hierarchy and we put three different seeds on the leaves Fig. 1(a). First, a bottom-up app-roach is made in which the labels are propagated from the leaves to the root. If there are label conflicts like in Figs. 1(b-left) and (c-left), the attributes com-puted from the hierarchy are taken into consideration for deciding which label must be propagated. For instance, in Figs. 1(b), the propagation is based on the smallest value of the hierarchy level, while in Figs. 1(b) it is based on the largest region area. As illustrated in Fig. 1(b-right) and (c-right), the obtained results are quite different. As can be observed, the leftmost part of the hierarchy are either assigned to yellow label or blue label. This occurs due to the criterion used to solve the conflict in the inner node of the tree.

4   Experimental Results

In this section, we present assessments in terms of undersegmentation error, boundary recall and GT Covering by using three hierarchies of watershed and two different gradients applied to three different image databases.

4.1   Experimental Setup and Datasets

In order to provide a comparative analysis between several strategies, we have used three different databases: (i) the Berkeley Segmentation Dataset [13], called **BSDS500**; (ii) the database proposed in [26], called **GRABCUT**; and (iii) the database proposed in [2] which is divided into two groups – single and two objects – called **WI1OBJ** and **WI2OBJ**, respectively. Here, we compare our method with several criteria to SLIC, which is the baseline of this work.

We considered a 4-adjacency relation with a Lab gradient (that is the Euclidean distance in the L*a*b* colour space) for the dissimilarity measure or max value of the structured edge gradient [9]. We have also studied two different strategies for seed generation, the grid sampling and the random sampling.

In this paper, we have used the following notation for simplification: $\mathcal{A}_\mathcal{C}^\downarrow$ (or $\mathcal{A}_\mathcal{C}^\uparrow$) in which $\downarrow$ ($\uparrow$) means the smallest (highest) value for the used criterion, $\mathcal{A}$ can be the QFZ hierarchy (Q), watershed by area (A) and watershed by volume (V), and the $\mathcal{C}$ can be the level value (v) and the area (a).

4.2   Quantitative and Qualitative Analysis

For a quantitative assessment, we illustrate in Figs. 2 and 3 several results com-puted over **BSDS500**, **GRABCUT**, **WI1OBJ** and **WI2OBJ** in terms of undersegmentation errors, boundary recall and GT covering. Due to lack of space, we present the results for structured edges as gradient since they outper-form in all measures the Lab gradient.

In a general way, the strategies with the highest value for solving the conflict have better GT Covering than the smallest value, but worse undersegmenta-tion error and boundary recall. In our opinion, the label propagation guided by

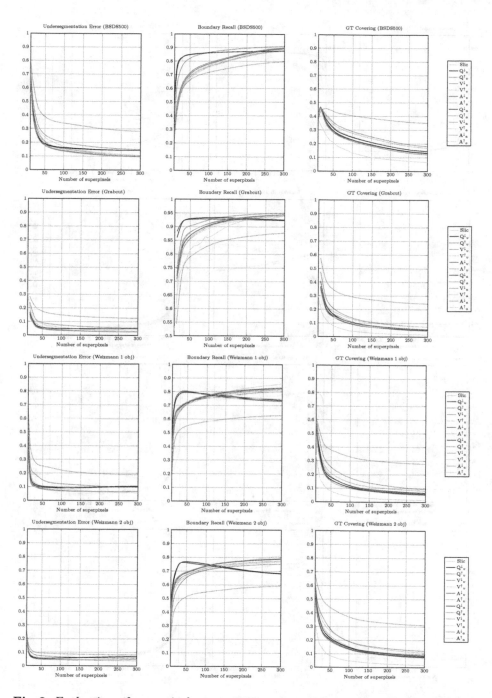

Fig. 2. Evaluation of superpixel computation using grid sampling. For hierarchical watersheds, we have used SE and Euclidean Distance as gradient. From top to bottom: (i) BSDS500; (ii) Grabcut; (iii) Weizmann 1 object; and (iv) Weizmann 2 objects.

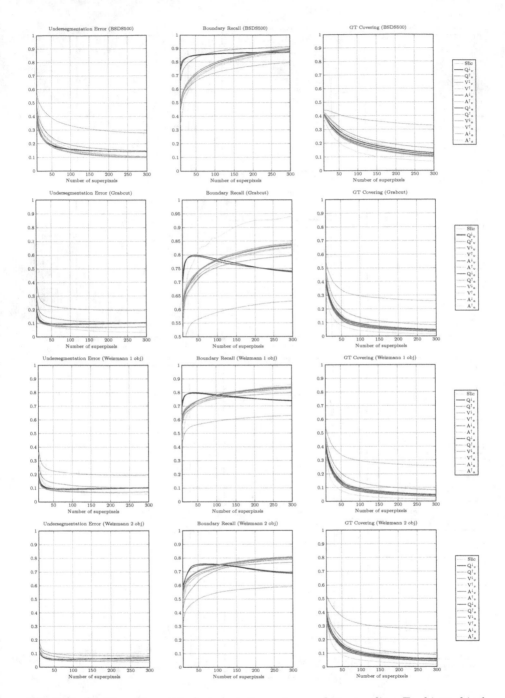

Fig. 3. Evaluation of superpixel computation using random sampling. For hierarchical watersheds, we have used SE and Euclidean Distance as gradient. From top to bottom: (i) BSDS500; (ii) Grabcut; (iii) Weizmann 1 object; and (iv) Weizmann 2 objects.

watershed by volume using the value of the level for solving the conflict outperforms other strategies in all databases. In particular, our strategies always outperform the SLIC for GT Covering. Regarding the seed sampling, there is no relevant difference in terms of the used measures between grid sampling and random sampling.

In Fig. 4, we illustrate some results obtained by our label propagation strategy. For computing the superpixels, we have used QFZ hierarchy Fig. 4(a) and Watershed by area Fig. 4(b). As we can see in these results, the superpixels computed from QFZ hierarchy are quite small. Considering that our strategy may produce disconnected regions, we can observe that despite that the number of seeds is defined, for example, in 8, the result presents more superpixels. Regarding the results for the watershed by area, we results are interesting since they better preserve the borders.

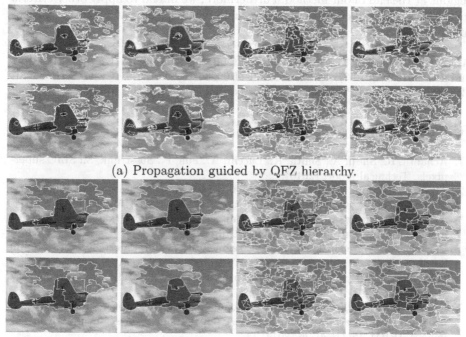

(a) Propagation guided by QFZ hierarchy.

(b) Propagation guided by watershed by area.

Fig. 4. Examples of label propagation. For computing the superpixels, we have used QFZ hierarchy (a) and Watershed by area (b). In order to devise about the conflict, we have used smallest level value of the hierarchy among the sons of a node (first row of each subfigure), and we have used smallest area related to the sons of a node (second row of each subfigure). Moreover, from left to right the used gradient and the number of superpixels are the following: L*a*b* with 8 seeds; SE with 8 seeds; L*a*b* with 128 seeds; and SE with 128 seeds.

5   Conclusions

In this paper, we have proposed a label propagation method guided by hierarchy of partitions for superpixel computation. The proposed strategy may be divided into three main steps: (i) seed generation; (ii) computation of the hierarchy of partitions; and (iii) label propagation. The main novelty of this work is related to the use of different criteria to decide about which of competing label should be propagated to neighbor region. According to our experiments, the proposed method outperforms the SLIC method, which is the baseline. Moreover, the propagation based on watershed by volume using the smallest hierarchy level as criterion to solve the conflict outperform the other tested criteria and hierarchy. At the end of our procedure, the same label could be assigned to disconnected regions. We have solved this problem by creating labels to be assigned to each disconnected region. As future works, we will study how to produce connected regions at the end of our method. Furthermore, we intend to apply other criteria for solving the conflict and other hierarchies such as the watershed by number of nodes.

Acknowledgments. The authors are grateful to CNPq (Universal 421521/2016-3 and PQ 307062/2016-3), FAPEMIG (PPM-00006-16), CAPES (Grant PVE 88887. 125000/2014-00) and PUC Minas for the financial support to this work.

References

1. Achanta, R., Shaji, A., Smith, K., Lucchi, A., Fua, P., Süsstrunk, S.: SLIC super-pixels. Technical report (2010)
2. Alpert, S., Galun, M., Brandt, A., Basri, R.: Image segmentation by probabilistic bottom-up aggregation and cue integration. PAMI **34**(2), 315–327 (2012)
3. Arbelaez, P., Maire, M., Fowlkes, C., Malik, J.: Contour detection and hierarchical image segmentation. PAMI **33**(5), 898–916 (2011)
4. Beucher, S.: Watershed, hierarchical segmentation and waterfall algorithm. In: Serra, J., Soille, P. (eds.) Mathematical Morphology and Its Applications to Image Processing. CIVI, vol. 2, pp. 69–76. Springer, Dordrecht (1994). https://doi.org/10.1007/978-94-011-1040-2_10
5. Buyssens, P., Gardin, I., Ruan, S.: Eikonal based region growing for superpixels generation: application to semi-supervised real time organ segmentation in CT images. IRBM **35**(1), 20–26 (2014)
6. Cousty, J., Najman, L.: Incremental algorithm for hierarchical minimum spanning forests and saliency of watershed cuts. In: Soille, P., Pesaresi, M., Ouzounis, G.K. (eds.) ISMM 2011. LNCS, vol. 6671, pp. 272–283. Springer, Heidelberg (2011). https://doi.org/10.1007/978-3-642-21569-8_24
7. Cousty, J., Najman, L., Kenmochi, Y., Guimarães, S.: Hierarchical segmentations with graphs: quasi-flat zones, minimum spanning trees, and saliency maps. J. Math. Imaging Vis. **60**(4), 479–502 (2018)
8. Cousty, J., Najman, L., Perret, B.: Constructive links between some morphological hierarchies on edge-weighted graphs. In: Hendriks, C.L.L., Borgefors, G., Strand, R. (eds.) ISMM 2013. LNCS, vol. 7883, pp. 86–97. Springer, Heidelberg (2013). https://doi.org/10.1007/978-3-642-38294-9_8

9. Dollár, P., Zitnick, C.L.: Fast edge detection using structured forests. PAMI **37**(8), 1558–1570 (2015)
10. Guigues, L., Cocquerez, J.P., Le Men, H.: Scale-sets image analysis. Int. J. Comput. Vis. **68**(3), 289–317 (2006)
11. Machairas, V., Faessel, M., Cárdenas-Peña, D., Chabardes, T., Walter, T., Decencière, E.: Waterpixels. IEEE Trans. Image Process. **24**(11), 3707–3716 (2015)
12. Maninis, K., Pont-Tuset, J., Arbeláez, P., Van Gool, L.: Convolutional oriented boundaries: from image segmentation to high-level tasks. IEEE PAMI **40**(4), 819–833 (2018)
13. Martin, D.R., Fowlkes, C.C., Malik, J.: Learning to detect natural image boundaries using local brightness, color, and texture cues. PAMI **26**(5), 530–549 (2004)
14. Meyer, F.: Color image segmentation. In: ISMM, pp. 303–306. IET (1992)
15. Meyer, F.: The dynamics of minima and contours. In: Maragos, P., Schafer, R.W., Butt, M.A. (eds.) Mathematical Morphology and its Applications to Image and Signal Processing. CIVI, vol. 5, pp. 329–336. Springer, Boston (1996). https://doi.org/10.1007/978-1-4613-0469-2_38
16. Meyer, F., Maragos, P.: Morphological scale-space representation with levelings. In: Nielsen, M., Johansen, P., Olsen, O.F., Weickert, J. (eds.) Scale-Space 1999. LNCS, vol. 1682, pp. 187–198. Springer, Heidelberg (1999). https://doi.org/10.1007/3-540-48236-9_17
17. Nagao, M., Matsuyama, T., Ikeda, Y.: Region extraction and shape analysis in aerial photographs. Comput. Graph. Image Process. **10**(3), 195–223 (1979)
18. Najman, L., Schmitt, M.: Geodesic saliency of watershed contours and hierarchical segmentation. PAMI **18**(12), 1163–1173 (1996)
19. Najman, L., Cousty, J., Perret, B.: Playing with kruskal: algorithms for morphological trees in edge-weighted graphs. In: Hendriks, C.L.L., Borgefors, G., Strand, R. (eds.) ISMM 2013. LNCS, vol. 7883, pp. 135–146. Springer, Heidelberg (2013). https://doi.org/10.1007/978-3-642-38294-9_12
20. Nhimi, F.T.L., Patrocínio Jr., Z., Perret, B., Cousty, J., Guimarães, S.J.F.: Evaluation of morphological hierarchies for supervised video segmentation. In: SAC, pp. 252–259. ACM (2018)
21. Perret, B., Cousty, J., Guimaraes, S.J.F., Maia, D.S.: Evaluation of hierarchical watersheds. TIP **27**(4), 1676–1688 (2018)
22. Perret, B., Cousty, J., Ura, J.C.R., Guimarães, S.J.F.: Evaluation of morphological hierarchies for supervised segmentation. In: Benediktsson, J.A., Chanussot, J., Najman, L., Talbot, H. (eds.) ISMM 2015. LNCS, vol. 9082, pp. 39–50. Springer, Cham (2015). https://doi.org/10.1007/978-3-319-18720-4_4
23. Pont-Tuset, J., Arbeláez, P., Barron, J.T., Marques, F., Malik, J.: Multiscale combinatorial grouping for image segmentation and object proposal generation. IEEE PAMI **39**(1), 128–140 (2017)
24. Ren, X., Malik, J.: Learning a classification model for segmentation. In: ICCV, p. 10. IEEE (2003)
25. Ren, Z., Shakhnarovich, G.: Image segmentation by cascaded region agglomeration. In: IEEE CVPR, pp. 2011–2018 (2013)
26. Rother, C., Kolmogorov, V., Blake, A.: "GrabCut": interactive foreground extraction using iterated graph cuts. ACM Trans. Graph. **23**(3), 309–314 (2004)
27. Salembier, P., Garrido, L.: Binary partition tree as an efficient representation for image processing, segmentation, and information retrieval. TIP **9**(4), 561–576 (2000)
28. Stutz, D., Hermans, A., Leibe, B.: Superpixels: an evaluation of the state-of-the-art. CVIU **166**, 1–27 (2018)

Disparity Image Analysis for 3D Characterization of Surface Anomalies

R. Marani, A. Petitti, M. Attolico, G. Cicirelli, A. Milella, and T. D'Orazio[✉]

STIIMA, CNR, via Amendola 122/D, Bari, Italy
{roberto.marani,tiziana.dorazio}@stiima.cnr.it

Abstract. The detection of internal defects in composite materials, due to anomalies during the production processes, is a big issue especially for the production of large structures in aeronautic contexts. The costs of the repair processes can weigh upon the total costs, and sometimes the repair itself can be unfeasible and cause the material to be rejected. The early detection of anomalies during the production phase can interrupt the production chain and the solution to the detected problems can be soon found. In this paper we propose the use of an appropriate sensorial setup, based on vision and laser, to monitor the production line and of a pipeline of signal processing methodologies to detect anomalies in the stratification of composite materials. Gaps and overlaps between adjacent stripes that are beyond or below the allowed ranges are soon detected and automatically highlighted to the human operators.

Keywords: 3D reconstruction · Anomalies detection ·
Model construction · Defect geometric characterization

1 Introduction

In the recent years, composite laminates have become the preferred materials for building large components in transportation industry because of their properties of lightweight, fatigue and corrosion resistance, capability to mold large complex shapes, high stability in space environment and so on. The possibility to have internal defects as a consequence of anomalies during the production process imposes rigid controls to the final structures by Non-Destructive Tests and Evaluations. Recently, in order to detect internal defects many signal processing algorithms [1–5] have been applied to temperature signals obtained by both lock-in (LT) and pulsed thermography (PT), and to ultrasound signals. However, the costs of repair processes can be excessive and in some cases the repair itself can be not applicable and lead to the rejection of the whole structure. For this reason the introduction of a visual system able to monitor the production process and support human operators in their checking tasks can greatly reduce the risks of internal defects, and increase the quality standard of the final components.

© Springer Nature Switzerland AG 2019
E. Ricci et al. (Eds.): ICIAP 2019, LNCS 11752, pp. 14–23, 2019.
https://doi.org/10.1007/978-3-030-30645-8_2

The reconstruction of three-dimensional surfaces of observed objects has been already used to highlight defects. In [6] a phase measuring profilometry has been applied to reconstruct the surface shape of wheels and detect wheel abrasions. An on-line quality detection system has been proposed in [7] to detect thick defect blocks found on the surface of rectangular steels observed by smart sensors based on red laser optics technologies. Fringe projection profilometry is one of the methods used to reconstruct surfaces, models, and inspect the integrity of structures. In [8] a digital fringe projection technique along with a look up table based gamma correction method has been used to detect surface damages such as dents, cracks and corrosion of aircraft structures. A photometric stereo 3D measurement system in [9] scans steel plate/strip and identify and locate 3D defects such as roll marks, cracks, and indentations. The authors of [10] propose the use of a combination of laser slice panoramic images and texture panoramic images to analyze simultaneously texture information and surface deformation and solve the problem of the pipeline defect detection. A triangulation-based laser scanner is used in [11–13] to extract a three-dimensional model of drilling tools and allow the fast detection and characterization of surface defects. The system, by using an innovative acquisition procedure, overcomes the occlusion problems due to the presence of grooves on the object surface and provides at the same time high precisions and fast measurements.

In this paper we propose the use of a non invasive and accurate experimental setup: a combination of camera and a laser light that models the 3D surface as the appearance of the laser spot changes according to the distance between the light source and the object surface. Quality controls are performed during the production of composite materials. After the stratification of every layer of the stratification, point clouds are acquired and thus used to build the 3D model of the surface. Then, by using a pipeline of signal processing methodologies, the differences between the expected model and the actual one are processed to detect the anomalies that could be occurred during the stratification, i.e. the presence of gap out of ranges or overlap between adjacent plies. The main novelty of the proposed methodology lies in the extraction of the reference model, which performed directly from the acquired surfaces and, consequently, is independent of the shape (e.g. curvature) of the laminate to be tested. The paper is organized as follows: Sect. 2 describes the experimental setup for laser triangulation and the proposed pipeline for signal processing; Sect. 3 reports the experimental results and the relative comments; final remarks and conclusions are in Sect. 4.

2   The Proposed Approach

The detection of anomalies during the stratification process of composite materials can be early done by analyzing, after each layer, the position of stripes and measuring the relative orientations and distances between adjacent ones. In Fig. 1 the experimental setup devised to solve this problem is shown. It is a laser profilometer placed on a motorized and encoded linear axis which scans all the production area (800 × 150 mm) and generates a point cloud of the surface.

The camera is the Dalsa Falcon 4m60, which is able to produce frames having resolution of 2352×1728 pixels at a frame rate (fullframe) of 60 fps. The camera-lens set is able to produce an out-of-plane resolution of the final 3D model, i.e. the minimum detectable alteration of laminate thickness, is equal to 0.07 mm. On the other hand, the in-plane spatial resolution, which is only ascribable to the resolution of the movement of the linear axis, is equal to 0.1 mm at a scan speed of 8 mm/s. Under these conditions, the whole scan of the production area is performed in 100 s.

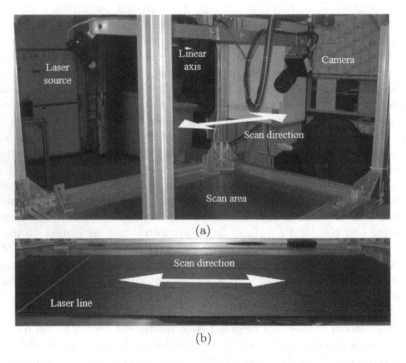

(a)

(b)

Fig. 1. (a) Laser profilometer for 3D modeling of the plies of composite taper; (b) example of a layer of composite to be tested. The arrows indicate the direction of the laser scan.

The production process of composite laminates is subjected to strict geometrical rules. Specifically, the positioning of each layer has to be done by respecting both some orientation constraints and distance values between adjacent plies (no overlaps and gaps in a fixed range). For instance, in the challenging field of aeronautics, the geometrical tolerance for gaps between adjacent plies is equal to 2.5 mm, whereas overlaps are always forbidden. In Fig. 2 examples of the 3D point clouds resulting from the proposed inspection setup are reported. In Fig. 2(a) an "in tolerance gap" is highlighted on the left and an "out of tolerance gap" on the right. In Fig. 2(b) an overlap between adjacent plies is reported.

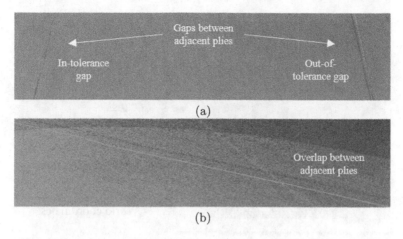

Fig. 2. 3D point clouds resulting from the proposed inspection. (a) Examples of in- and out-of-tolerance gaps and (b) overlap between adjacent plies.

As stated in the previous lines, the aim of this paper is the definition of a complete methodology for the in-line detection and characterization of this kind of anomalies. In Fig. 3 the whole processing pipeline is described. The input disparity image, representing the variations of the laser line with respect a fixed reference system, is processed in three steps:

- a model of the expected surface, obtained from the acquired data, is generated and the differences between the model and the input disparity are used to generate a corrected disparity map (the idea is quite similar to an unsharp masking procedure, ie. fine details are highlighted and noise is reduced);
- a binarization via image statistics is performed;
- a dedicated morphological processing is applied to filter binary images according to the domain, in order to generate images containing only significant information.

Final disparity images are then converted in 3D models in world coordinates through the application of the results of a preliminary calibration phase. Edge analysis on 3D models is thus able to give quantitative measures of the orientation and of the distance parameters of the inspected plies.

The input disparity image (see Fig. 4(a)) contains many information (the darker are the higher region, the brighter are the deeper). First, the overall surface appearance has some dark regions corresponding to not planar areas, which are due, for example, to the presence of air under the plies. In addition, the signs of previous stratifications generates further textures to the surface appearance (see the horizontal directions of the plies). Finally, the separations between adjacent plies during the last stratification produce the alteration of interest for the current analysis (see the extended oblique dark stripes of Fig. 4(a)). In order to extract only the valuable information for the overlap/gap detection, the following steps are carried out: after an initial smoothing, each point of the disparity

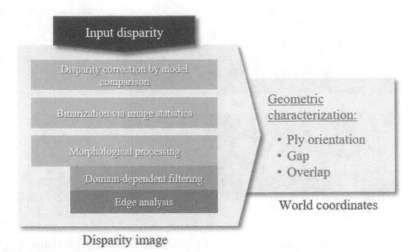

Fig. 3. Representation of the processing pipeline. Image processing (blue blocks) is performed on input disparity, whereas the final geometric characterization is completed in actual world coordinates. (Color figure online)

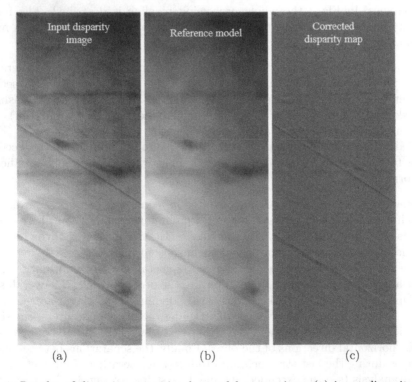

Fig. 4. Results of disparity correction by model comparison: (a) input disparity, (b) reference model due to median filtering and (c) final corrected disparity

image is treated by a median filter with an extended kernel, whose in-plane size, projected to the surface, is higher than 20×20 mm. In this way, a surface model, taking into account the global shape of the laminate, can be defined from the acquisition itself. The resulting reference model is shown in Fig. 4(b). Then a corrected disparity map is thus obtained by a differential analysis between the reference model and the initial disparity map (Fig. 4(c)). It is worth noticing that this processing is mandatory to correct the input disparity to rectify the scan plane to the shape of the laminate. In this way, relative alterations of depth detected by the laser profilometer due to the intrinsic shape of the laminate under testing, or to the misalignement of the scan plane with respect to the laminate surface, are automatically compensated and do not produce false positives in the analysis of 3D model.

The histogram of the resulting corrected disparity is thus centered on a specific value, directly linked to the distance between the laser profilomenter and the specimen surface. Its shape resembles on a Gaussian-shaped function, whose mean and standard deviation values, (μ, σ), can be estimated by the application of a curve fitting in the least square sense. All disparity values which fall in the range $(\mu - \sigma, \mu + \sigma)$ correspond to surface points, whose depth is within a range defined by σ, which takes into account for surface roughness and measurement uncertainty. The remaining disparity values under or above this range are informative, since they represent dips and peaks over the laminate. Gaps and overlaps belong to these two regions, respectively. The binarized images reported in Fig. 5(a) and (b) represents the low disparity regions (under the threshold $(\mu - \sigma)$) and the high disparity regions (above the $(\mu - \sigma)$).

The morphological filtering applies the domain knowledge: the areas between adjacent plies produce long connected regions crossing the image from one side to another. Connected regions which do not fulfill this simple hypothesis are rejected from the analysis. It is applied to both low disparity (LD) and high disparity (HD) images as the ones in Fig. 5(a) and (b) to detect gaps or overlaps, respectively. In Fig. 5(c) the results of the morphological filtering of the binarized HD image is reported. On the contrary, the results of morphological analysis on LD image is not shown as it has not produces any significant result, sing gaps are not present on the inspected surface.

Although this image contains a clear evidence of the presence of overlaps, it is not ready to allow the estimation of the values of the overlap (or gap) parameters. A transformation of the disparity values in world coordinates is applied by using the calibration parameters of the profilometry setup. Each point (i, j, d) is transformed in a world reference system having coordinates (x, y, z). At this point, with simple geometrical consideration the ply orientation, the gap measures, and the presence of overlaps can be estimated.

3   Experimental Results

The proposed setup and processing approach have been tested during a real experiment of stratification of a composite material carried out by a human

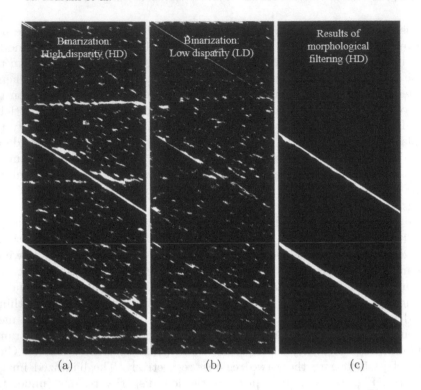

Fig. 5. Binarization of corrected disparity, according to image statistics. Binary images of (a) high and (b) low disparity values (HD and LD, respectively), and (c) results of morphological filtering on the HD binary image. Morphological filtering on the LD binary image produces no results, since there are no gaps on the laminate surface.

operator. During this production process 8 layers were placed on the working area. The plies were positioned under different orientations and present some anomalies voluntarily produced at specific layers in order to test the reliability of the proposed detection systems. These anomalies were certified by the human expert operators, who annotated their sizes and orientations. After each stratification the laser profilometer scanned the surface and all the 3D point clouds were processed to highlight anomalies.

In Fig. 6 the results obtained by application of the proposed approach to the inspection of defective laminate surfaces having overlaps and out-of-tolerance gaps are reported. In Fig. 6(a) an input disparity map containing two overlaps is shown; in Figs. 6(b) and (c) the disparity maps of in-tolerance gaps (spacing below 2.5 mm) and out-of-tolerance gaps are respectively displayed. The corresponding results of the geometric characterization in terms of edge orientation are displayed in Fig. 6(d), (e) and (f). These values are in good agreement with those measured by the human operator who performed the manual stratification, i.e. $-45°$, $90°$ and $45°$ for Fig. 6(a), (b) and (c), respectively.

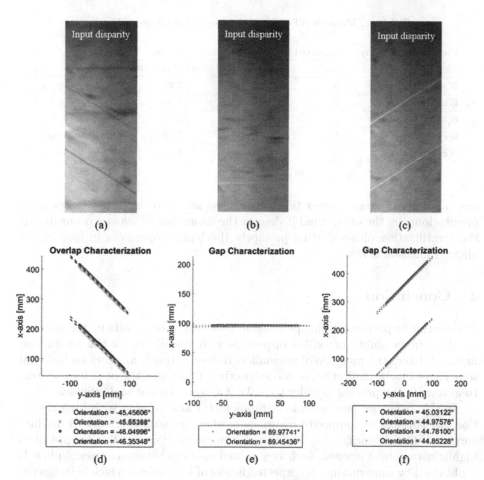

Fig. 6. Input disparity images of three layers having (a) two overlaps, (b) an intolerance gap and (c) two out-of-tolerance gaps between adjacent plies. (d), (e) and (f) show the corresponding outcomes of the geometrical characterization, including the computation of edge orientations.

In Table 1, in fact, all these measures are listed and compared. In particular, the first column reports the reference to the corresponding figure. Then the anomaly type is described in the second column, whereas the expected measurements, as evaluated by the human operator, are reported in the third column. The estimated measurements of both min and max values of the thickness of the detected overlaps/gaps, and the final decision of acceptance are reported in the last three columns.

As can be observed, all the measurements were correctly estimated, with improved resolution with respect to the one given by the human operatos. As a consequence, the real experiments confirm the accuracy and the effectiveness of the proposed system which provide the operators a twofold contribution: by

Table 1. Measures of estimated gaps and overlaps of Fig. 6.

Figure	Anomaly type	Expected measure (mm)	Estimated spacing		Result
			Min (mm)	Max (mm)	
6(a)	Overlap	3	3.1	3.81	NA
6(a)	Overlap	5	5.02	6.36	NA
6(b)	Gap	2	1.48	2.47	In tolerance
6(c)	Gap	5	5.04	5.19	Out of tolerance
6(c)	Gap	3	3.02	3.14	Out of tolerance

one hand the system verifies the correct positioning of the plies in terms of orientations; by the other hand it detects the anomalies which can occur during the stratification phase alerting promptly the human operators in case of not allowed measurements.

4   Conclusion

The routine inspections during production processes of composite materials relies on the human ability of skilled inspectors who visually check the production line and detect the presence of anomalies. However, this is a laborious task and sometimes maybe ineffective, or too subjective. This raises the need for a system to automate the process in order to make it faster, efficient and reliable.

In this paper we propose a laser profilometer able to scan with high resolution the surfaces of composite materials as they are stratified, and to produce corresponding disparity images. Then, an image analysis pipeline is applied to highlight targets of interest, such as gaps and overlaps between adjacent plies. It is obtained by constructing the expected model of the surface, which becomes the reference for a differential analysis. Finally, the dimensions of gaps and overlaps occurred during each stratification are determined in world coordinates, in order to state a final decision of acceptance. Experimental results obtained during a real stratification session demonstrate the reliability of the proposed system to support human inspectors in their tasks of quality control during production processes.

Future work will be addressed to test the system and the processing methodology on more complex surfaces and on different anomalies that could be found in industrial contexts.

Acknowledgments. The authors would like to thank Mr. Giuseppe Bono for his fundamental contribution during the experimental phase. This work is part of the Italian MIUR Project DITECO (Ref. PACPON03PE_00067_2).

References

1. Marani, R., Palumbo, D., Galietti, U., Stella, E., D'Orazio, T.: Automatic detection of subsurface defects in composite materials using thermography and unsupervised machine learning. In: IEEE 8th International Conference on Intelligent Systems (IS), pp. 516–521 (2016)
2. Marani, R., Palumbo, D., Galietti, U., Stella, E., D'Orazio, T.: Two-dimensional cross-correlation for defect detection in composite materials inspected by lock-in thermography. In: 22nd International Conference on Digital Signal Processing (DSP) (2017)
3. Marani, R., Palumbo, D., Reno, V., Galietti, U., Stella, E., D'Orazio, T.: Modeling and classification of defects in CFRP laminates by thermal non-destructive testing. Compos. Part B: Eng. **135**, 129–141 (2018)
4. Marani, R., Palumbo, D., Galietti, U., Stella, E., D'Orazio, T.: Enhancing defects characterization in pulsed thermography by noise reduction. NDT & E Int. **102**, 226–233 (2019)
5. Leo, M., Looney, D., D'Orazio, T., Mandic, D.: Identification of defective areas in composite materials by bivariate EMD analysis of ultrasound. IEEE Trans. Instrum. Meas. **61**(1), 221–232 (2011)
6. Li, J., Duan, F., Luo, L., Gao, X.: Wheel profile and tread surface defect detection based on phase measuring profilometry. In: IEEE 18th International Wheelset Congress (IWC), pp. 71–76 (2016)
7. Li, D., Wang, S., Yu, X.: Research and application of online quality detection system based on 3D vision in rectangular steel production line. In: Proceedings of 2018 IEEE International Conference on Mechatronics and Automation, pp. 843–848 (2018)
8. Vinayan, S., Ganesan, M., Joy, N., Augustin, M.J., Gupta, N.: Gamma corrected three-step fringe proefilometry for the detection of surface defects on aircraft surfaces. In: International Conference on Signal Processing and Communication (ICSPC 2017), pp. 221–226 (2017)
9. Wang, L., Xu, K., Zhou, P.: Online detection technique of 3D defects for steel strips based on photometric stereo. In: Eighth International Conference on Measuring Technology and Mechatronics Automation, pp. 428–432 (2016)
10. Yang, Z., Lu, S., Wu, T., Yuan, G., Tang, Y.: Detection of morphology defects in pipeline based on 3D active stereo omnidirectional vision sensor. IET Image Process. **12**(4), 588–595 (2018)
11. Marani, R., Nitti, M., Cicirelli, G., D'Orazio, T., Stella, E.: High-resolution laser scanning for three-dimensional inspection of drilling tools. In: Advances in Mechanical Engineering, vol. 5 (2013)
12. Marani, R., Nitti, M., Cicirelli, G., D'Orazio, T., Stella, E.: Design of high-resolution optical systems for fast and accurate surface reconstruction. In: Mason, A., Mukhopadhyay, S.C., Jayasundera, K.P. (eds.) Sensing Technology: Current Status and Future Trends III. SSMI, vol. 11, pp. 47–65. Springer, Cham (2015). https://doi.org/10.1007/978-3-319-10948-0_3
13. Marani, R., Roselli, G., Nitti, M., Cicirelli, G., D'Orazio, T., Stella, E.: HA 3D vision system for high resolution surface reconstruction. In: IEEE Seventh International Conference on Sensing Technology (ICST) (2013)

Personalized Expression Synthesis Using a Hybrid Geometric-Machine Learning Method

Sarra Zaied$^{(\boxtimes)}$, Catherine Soladie$^{(\boxtimes)}$, and Pierre-Yves Richard$^{(\boxtimes)}$

Institute of Electronics and Telecommunications of Rennes UMR CNRS 6164,
Research Team FAST CentraleSupelec, Rennes, France
{sarra.zaied,catherine.soladie,pierre-yves.richard}@centralesupelec.fr

Abstract. Actually, various Geometric and Machine Learning methods are employed to synthesize expressions. The geometric techniques offer high-performance shape deformation but lead to images which are lacking in texture details such as wrinkles and teeth. On the other hand, the machine learning methods (e.g. Generative Adversarial Network GAN) generate photo-realistic expressions and add texture details to the images but the synthesized expressions are not those of the person. In this paper, we propose a hybrid geometric-machine learning approach to synthesize photo-realistic and personalized joy expressions while keeping the identity of the emotion. Our approach combines a geometric technique based on 2D warping method and a generative adversarial network. It aims at benefiting from the advantages of both paradigms and overcoming their own limitations. Moreover, by adding a previous knowledge of the way of smiling of the subject, we personalize the synthesized expressions. Qualitative and quantitative results demonstrate that our person-specific hybrid method can generate personalized joy expressions closer to the ground truth than two generic state-of-the-art approaches.

Keywords: Expression synthesis · Person-specific model ·
Hybrid method MLS-GAN

1 Introduction

The theory of peripheral emotional feedback states that our emotional experiences are under the retroactive influence of our own expressions [13]. It has been an ongoing subject of debate in psychology since James [9]. Actually, facial expressions become a tool for psychological analysis [11]. The fact that putting on a smile or frown may have an implicit, automatic effect in one's emotional experience holds tremendous potential for clinical remediation in psychiatric disorders. We address this situation head-on, proposing a framework able to channel the psychological mechanism of facial feedback for clinical application

---

Work funded by ANR REFLETS project.

E. Ricci et al. (Eds.): ICIAP 2019, LNCS 11752, pp. 24–34, 2019.
https://doi.org/10.1007/978-3-030-30645-8_3

to post-traumatic stress disorders (PTSD). Via our framework implemented in a mirror-like device, the observers can see themselves in a gradually more positive way: without their knowing, their reflected face is algorithmically transformed to appear more positive. Using this system, we expect that observers believe the emotional tone of their transformed facial reflection as their own, and align their feelings with the transformation. One more thing, the expressions are highly personal and each person smiles differently. To act positively on the emotional state of a subject while keeping the credibility, we generate a person-specific joy expression basing on previous knowledge of her own way of smiling.

Our model leads to preserve the morphology shape and the identity of the emotion by reproducing the specific way of smiling of each subject. The first contribution is that we personalize the generated expression. As we cannot guess the specific way of smiling of a subject, we need previous knowledge of her way of smiling. The originality is that we first learn a Person-Specific model using one neutral and one smiling face of the person whose expression we want to change. The model is composed of several parameters which are specific to each subject and is used to perform a 2D warping on the neutral face to synthesize a specific and personalize joy expression. The second contribution of our method is that we use a GAN to refine the details in the synthesized images. The originality is that we introduce a hybrid method combining geometric and machine learning tools. The geometric part aims at preserving the identity shape and optimize the distortion made on the image. The GAN offers a realistic facial texture and allows to naturally refine the local-texture details of the synthesized images such as wrinkles and teeth. The last contribution is that our approach can synthesize smile expression with different intensities from a single image.

2 Related Work

Research work on synthesizing photo-realistic facial expressions on real subjects can be divided into two categories: Geometric techniques and machine learning methods. The first category mainly resorts to computer graphic techniques and is based on shape distortion. These methods directly deform the detected landmarks to generate an expressive face [2,12,18,24]. Most of the time, the shape distortion is based on a predefined translation of the landmarks [12,18,24]. The main limitation is that the participants must keep the neutral facial expression and they should not speak or change their head position during the expression generation. These constraints was tackled in the framework of Pablo et al. [2]. The proposed system adapts to the position of the user's face. Yet, the deformations in these works are still based on the same model for all the subjects. Then, these methods generate non-personalized expressions. However, the expressions (e.g. smile) are personal and it occurs in a different way for each person, it may be: straight, curved or elliptical. Finally, the texture refinement in these works are obtained by the moving least squares method [16] (MLS). This method provides a deformation that minimizes the amount of local scaling and optimizes the distortion made on the image in real time. However, it leads to generate images that miss fine details such as wrinkles and teeth.

The second category aims at building generative models [6] to synthesize facial expressions with predefined attributes [3,7,14,21,22]. These models are based on texture refinement. The GANs allow to synthesize different photo-realistic facial expressions [7,21] or to animate a single RGB image [3,14]. These models enable to generate natural and reasonable face expressions (e.g. different smiles) and generate images with fine local details. The deformations are based on a model which is learned on several subjects. So that the synthesized expressions are not the subject's own. Yet, each person has her own way to make expressions. Finally, images generated by such methods sometimes tend to be blurry and of low resolution.

The geometric methods provide a relevant shape deformation but it lacks local details in the generated images. The generative models succeed in adding texture details (wrinkles and teeth) but the generated smiles are not those of the person. To this aim, we propose a hybrid geometric-machine learning method that combines the benefits of the geometric and machine learning methods to synthesize person-specific joy expression. We use a geometric technique to deform the shape of a detected face to appear more positive. For each person, we learn a parametric model according to her own way of smiling using her neutral expression and her smile one. Then we use this model as previous knowledge of the way of smiling to synthesize a personalized joyful expression. As the synthesized images are lacking in details such as teeth and wrinkles, we employ a GAN to refine the texture and to add local fine details to these images. Our framework is able to synthesize person-specific joy expressions with different intensities while preserving the emotion user's identity.

3   Our Hybrid Approach

Our framework aims at generating personalized joy expression as illustrated in Fig. 1. Our algorithm starts with a learning step to build a person-specific model (Sect. 3.1). The model is learned using a neutral and a smile expression of the subject. We use the predefined model and a coefficient d to manipulate the intensity of the generated expression (Sect. 3.2). Finally, we use a GAN to refine the local-texture details on the synthesized images such as wrinkles and teeth (Sect. 3.3).

3.1   Learning a Person-Specific Shape Model

To preserve the identity of the emotion and to generate person-specific expressions, we need previous knowledge of the way of smiling of the subject. To this aim, we lean a person-specific model for each subject using her neutral frame X_n and her smiling frame X_s (Fig. 1: part 1). For the tracking, we use GenFace-Tracker of Dynamixyz [4]. This tracker detects the face and determines precisely the coordinates of 84 landmarks as well as the orientation, scale, and position of the face. A smile is expressed with the rise of the corners of the mouth and cheeks, as well as the lifting of the lower eyelids [5], we selected 10 landmarks

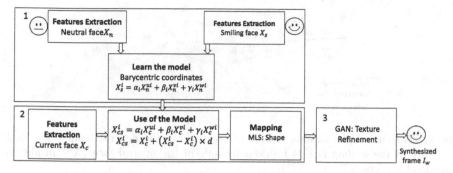

Fig. 1. Our framework is composed of 3 parts. In the first part, we track one neutral X_n and one smiling X_s face of the subject to extract the features which are the landmarks positions. Then, we learn a person-specific model from the detected landmarks of the two faces. In the second part, the learned model is used with each current frame X_c of the subject to generate a current smiling frame X_{cs}. We use the predefined model of the subject and a coefficient d to manipulate the intensity of the generated joy expressions. We employed a 2D warping method MLS [16] to deform the current face. In the third part, we use a generative adversarial network to refine local details on the synthesized frames.

which corresponds to the corners of the mouth and the lower points of the eyes to learn the deformations of the face ($i = \{64, 65, 69, 70, 71, 75, 45, 46, 51, 52\}$). Once the landmarks of the two faces X_n and X_s are aligned by homography, we perform a Delaunay triangulation on the neutral face. Each of the 10 selected landmarks X_s^i is located inside a neutral face triangle ($X_n^{u_i}$, $X_n^{v_i}$, $X_n^{w_i}$). Figure 2 gives an example for the landmark 64. We calculate the barycentric coordinates (α_i, β_i, γ_i) for each of the 10 points X_s^i. These coordinates are the parameters of our person-specific model. The model is composed of 10 vectors with 6 components. These components are the 3 vertices indexes of the triangle in which the landmark is located (u_i, v_i, w_i) and the 3 corresponding barycentric coordinates (α_i, β_i, γ_i). The calculation of X_s^i is formulated as follows:

$$X_s^i = \alpha_i X_n^{u_i} + \beta_i X_n^{v_i} + \gamma_i X_n^{w_i} \tag{1}$$

3.2 Expressions Shape Synthesis with Different Intensities

To generate a joy expression from a current detected image X_c of a subject, We use the learned specific model of this subject as previous knowledge of her way of smiling. We detect the landmarks X_c^i of the current detected face with GenFaceTracker [4]. Having the different coefficients α_i, β_i and γ_i of each of the 10 points of the smiling face, and knowing the coordinates of the triangles (u_i, v_i, w_i) in which are located these points, we determine the positions of the new 10 points of the current smiling face X_{cs}^i (the transformed current face with a smile) using Eq. (2).

$$X_{cs}^i = \alpha_i X_c^{u_i} + \beta_i X_c^{v_i} + \gamma_i X_c^{w_i} \tag{2}$$

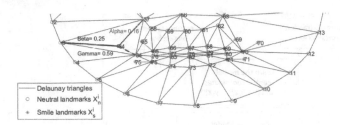

Fig. 2. Positions of the smiling landmarks relative to the neutral landmarks. Each landmark of the smiling face is inside a triangle of the neutral face (X_s^{64} inside the triangle of vertices X_n^{57}, X_n^3, X_n^{64}).

One of the originality's method is that we can generate this expression with different intensities according to a linear model.

$$X_{cs}^i = X_c^i + (X_{cs}^i - X_c^i) \times d \qquad (3)$$

Where d is the deformation coefficient. Increasing this coefficient increases the smile intensity and vice versa.

- If $d = 0$, the result is an unchanged face $X_{cs} = X_c$.
- If $d = 1$, the result is an expression of joy X_{cs} that matches the intensity of the one that was learned.

Figure 3 shows an example of the generated joy expressions with different intensities for one subject.

To generate a deformation, that minimizes the amount of local scaling, we applied the Moving Least Squares method MLS [2,16]. The rigid MLS is very effective for image deformation and optimizes the distortion made on the image in real-time. Given the time needed to perform the deformations and apply them, we make a time/esthetic's compromise as in [2]; we apply the algorithm on grids around each eye and around the mouth, not on each pixel of the image.

In this way, for each subject we built a geometric model that is used as a previous knowledge to generate personal joy expressions with different intensities. As shows Fig. 3 the generated joy expression is photo-realistic. However, it misses some details such as teeth and wrinkles.

Fig. 3. Generation of 6 joy expressions intensities with coefficient variation from 0 to 1 with step of 0.2.

3.3 Texture Refinement with GAN

To refine the texture details on the synthesized frames (add wrinkles, dimples, and teeth), we use a generative adversarial network [6]. The GAN in [8] achieved impressive results thanks to the used skip connections. It was employed in several researches of facial expressions [14,20,21]. These skip connections between G_{enc} and D_{enc} aims at increasing the resolution of the output. The encoder features are transmitted along these connections with the conditioned information to the decoder. In our framework, we use the same architecture, but we changed the data. Our first originality is that we use the synthesized (warped) images I_{wj} generated with the MLS and the real smiling expressions I_{sj} to train a conditional GAN as Fig. 4 shows. Our second originality is the use of a label vector L_{sj} that is composed of the normalized distance of the lips opening O_j concatenated with one hot vector V_j of 10 values which characterizes the intensity level. This label helps the GAN to correctly add the expression details such as the opening of the mouth, which indicate that it should add teeth. Furthermore, to capture the structural information of the images and achieve more realistic joy expressions, we adopt the feature matching loss term F_m of [15,23]. This function forces the generated image and the real smile image to share the same features. Thus, the generated expression will be closest to the real expression.

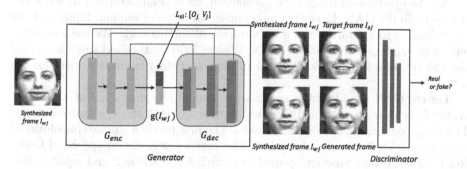

Fig. 4. The GAN is used to refine details on the synthesized geometric images I_{wj}. The synthesized images I_{wj} generated by the geometric step, are fed to the Generator. The encoding representation of the image $g(I_{wj})$ is concatenated with a label vector L_{sj} which is composed of the normalized distance of the lips opening O_j and one hot vector V_j to characterize the intensity. The decoder generates the expressive frame with more details. The discriminator D takes two couple of images; the synthesized frame I_{wj} with the real frame I_{sj} and the synthesized frame I_{wj} with the generated frame to determine if the latter is a real or a fake expression.

4 Experiments and Results

In this section, we present the implementation details on 3 datasets and our qualitative and quantitative results.

Database CK: This database [10] includes 486 sequences from 97 subjects. Each sequence begins with a neutral expression and proceeds to a peak expression. We select the 88 subjects who have smile sequences. Since almost all the sequences are grayscale, we use gray scale images in our experiments.

Database MMI: The database MMI [19] consists of over 2900 videos and high-resolution still images of 75 subjects. It is fully annotated for the presence of AUs in videos. We select the 56 smile videos of 28 subjects which are annotated with AU6 and AU12 (corresponding to smile). Each subject has 2 smiling videos so, we have the opportunity to learn the person-specific model on one video (using a neutral and a smiling face) and test it on another one. Those tests are referred to MMI* in Sect. 4.1.

Database Oulu-CASIA: The database contains 80 subjects [25] with the 6 basic expressions for each subject. We use smile sequences to carry out our experiments. The videos are captured with VIS camera with strong illumination.

The Protocol: With the 3 datasets, we obtain 196 subjects, so we built 196 geometric models. According to the results found in [1, 17] concerning the Onset-Apex duration, we choose to synthesize for each subject 10 frames with different intensities. So that we have a total of 1960 synthesized images with the geometric step.

All the synthesized images are normalized, aligned and cropped to 256×256 size to train the GAN. In the training phase, we perform random flipping of the input images to encourage the generalization of the network. We use leave-one-out cross-validation to train the GAN. We use 1950 synthesized smile images of the 195 subjects for the training and 10 images of the remained subject for the test.

For the GAN, we adopt the architecture from [8]. As shown in Fig. 4, the generator G is an auto-encoder U-Net which take as input the synthesized image. The G_{enc} contains 8 convolutional layers. The first one is a simple convolutional layer with a 5×5 kernel and stride 2. The others layers are composed of Leaky ReLU as activation function, convolution with 5×5 stride 2 and a batch normalization. G_{dec} is composed of 8 deconvolutional layers with 5×5 stride 2 and Leaky ReLU. To share the information between the input and the output features, the decoder layers have skip connections with their corresponding layers of G_{enc} (see Fig. 4). Adaptive Moment Estimation optimizer (ADAM) is used to train our model with $\beta = 0.5$, 0.0002 as learning rate and $\lambda = 100$.

In the test phase, we use a new neutral frame of the subject, his learned geometric model and a chosen intensity to synthesize a joyful frame. The frame result is fed to the trained GAN to add the missing details. For the MMI*, as each subject have 2 videos we use one video frames (neutral frame and smile frame) for learning the person-specific model and the second video for the test.

4.1   Quantitative Results

The metric we use to check the performances of our method is the angles between the ground truth smile trajectory and the trajectories of the generated smile with the method. This allows us to evaluate if the generated smile is that of the person or not and it permits to compare the slope of the real smile and the generated one. As shows Fig. 5, we define the trajectory as the 2D displacement of the mouth landmarks during the smile across the frames. To determine the angles, we use the linear regression $Y = a_{GT}X + b_{GT}$ of the ground truth trajectory. We assume that $Y = aX + b$ is the defined trajectory of the landmarks generated with one method. The angle is determined by:

$$\theta = \tan^{-1}\left|\frac{a_{GT} - a}{1 + a_{GT}a}\right| \tag{4}$$

Table 1 shows the statistical results for the landmark located on the left corner of the mouth. The same study was performed for the 10 landmarks involved in the joy expression. The results show that our method generates trajectories which are closer to the ground truth than the generic methods [2] and [21] ($\bar{\theta}$ closer to 0). In addition, we can consider that our method is more stable than the other two methods because of the low value of σ_θ. We observe that the results with MMI* are less good than the results with MMI because we use a second video of the person to test the model learned with another video of that person. But, we always stay better than the other two methods [2] and [21].

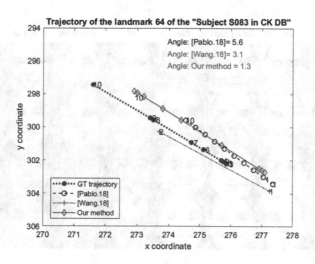

Fig. 5. The ground truth and the generated trajectories of the landmark located at the left corner of the mouth. We can notice that the angle between the GT trajectory and our method trajectory is smaller than the angle calculated with the two generic methods [2] and [21].

We measured the latency of the overall algorithm. Our tests performed on an Intel processor Core i7 at 3.30 GHz with an NVIDIA geforce GTX 1070. The mean time to process a single frame is of 65 ms. It is suitable for real time applications (15 fps) such as the mirror in our use case.

Table 1. Mean and standard deviation of angles calculated with the 3 methods on the 3 databases for the landmark of the left corner of the mouth for all the subjects. With MMI*, we learn a person-specific model with one video of the person and we test it with a second video.

Method	Database			
	CK	Oulu-CASIA	MMI	MMI*
[Pablo.18]	$\bar{\theta} = 12.10$	$\bar{\theta} = 17.81$	$\bar{\theta} = 12$	$\bar{\theta} = 12$
	$\sigma_\theta = 9.73$	$\sigma_\theta = 15.94$	$\sigma_\theta = 13.70$	$\sigma_\theta = 13.70$
[Wang.18]	$\bar{\theta} = 16.16$	$\bar{\theta} = 26$	$\bar{\theta} = 15.26$	$\bar{\theta} = 15.26$
	$\sigma_\theta = 12.24$	$\sigma_\theta = 18.21$	$\sigma_\theta = 12.66$	$\sigma_\theta = 12.66$
Our	$\bar{\theta} = \mathbf{7.65}$	$\bar{\theta} = \mathbf{6.85}$	$\bar{\theta} = \mathbf{5.83}$	$\bar{\theta} = \mathbf{9.20}$
	$\sigma_\theta = \mathbf{8.25}$	$\sigma_\theta = \mathbf{7.26}$	$\sigma_\theta = \mathbf{7.01}$	$\sigma_\theta = \mathbf{10.78}$

4.2   Qualitative Results

Qualitative results confirm that our method gives better results than [2] and [21]. Figure 6 illustrates the results[1] obtained for 2 intensities for 4 subjects with the 3 methods.

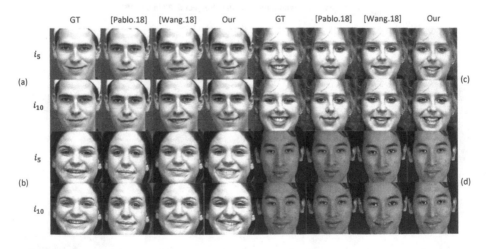

Fig. 6. The Ground Truth smile (GT) and the result frames of 4 subjects from the 2 databases (MMI and CK) with two intensities for each subject.

Concerning the shape, we observe that with the geometric method of Pablo et al. [2], the corner of the lips is systematically raised (steep slope) for all the subjects. We notice that the subjects (a) and (b) have a flat smile (low slope)

---

[1] More results are available on https://drive.google.com/file/d/1hY15DNrrYNjxnf9J mVFJhWUYhteTYnQa/view?usp=sharing.

in reality while the smiles generated with [2] is growing and not realistic. The GAN [21] generate different smiles but we can perceive that are not those of the subjects. For the subject(c), the real smile is opened but the GAN generate a tight smile for all the subjects.

Concerning the texture, We notice that with Pablo et al. all the generated smiles are without teeth whatever the texture shape of the smile. For the subjects (a) and (d), the real smile is without teeth but the GAN of [21] generate the teeth for these subjects. On the contrary, for the subject (b) the real smile has occurred with teeth but the GAN generate it without. Then, the GAN generate realistic joy expression but not those of the person.

The visual fidelity shows that our method generates the closest smile shape to the ground truth and maintain the same texture of the real smile for all the subjects.

5   Conclusion

In this paper, we proposed a hybrid approach aiming at learning a person-specific model for each person and transforming a captured face to appear more joyful. Our method generate for each subject a photo-realistic joy expression according to her own expression. Qualitative and quantitative results show that the synthesized joy expression with our method is closer to the ground truth than the expression generated with two generic methods. One of our research directions is make psychiatric experiments with our tool to see if we can act on the PTSD patients emotions.

References

1. Ambadar, Z., Cohn, J.F., Reed, L.I.: All smiles are not created equal: morphology and timing of smiles perceived as amused, polite, and embarrassed/nervous. J. Nonverbal Behav. **33**(1), 17–34 (2009)
2. Arias, P., Soladie, C., Bouafif, O., Robel, A., Seguier, R., Aucouturier, J.J.: Realistic transformation of facial and vocal smiles in real-time audiovisual streams. IEEE Trans. Affect. Comput. (2018)
3. Ding, H., Sricharan, K., Chellappa, R.: ExprGAN: facial expression editing with controllable expression intensity. In: AAAI (2018)
4. Dynamixyz: Genfacetracker: person-independent real-time face tracker (2017). http://www.dynamixyz.com
5. Ekman, P., Friesen, W.V.: Facial Action Coding System: Investigatoris Guide. Consulting Psychologists Press (1978)
6. Goodfellow, I., et al.: Generative adversarial nets. In: Advances in Neural Information Processing Systems, pp. 2672–2680 (2014)
7. Huang, Y., Khan, S.: A generative approach for dynamically varying photorealistic facial expressions in human-agent interactions. In: Proceedings of the 2018 on International Conference on Multimodal Interaction, pp. 437–445. ACM (2018)
8. Isola, P., Zhu, J.Y., Zhou, T., Efros, A.A.: Image-to-image translation with conditional adversarial networks. In: The IEEE Conference on Computer Vision and Pattern Recognition (CVPR), July 2017

9. James, W.: What is an emotion? Mind **9**(34), 188–205 (1884)
10. Kanade, T., Cohn, J.F., Tian, Y.: Comprehensive database for facial expression analysis. In: Proceedings of the Fourth IEEE International Conference on Automatic Face and Gesture Recognition, pp. 46–53. IEEE (2000)
11. Leo, M., et al.: Computational assessment of facial expression production in ASD children. Sensors **18**(11), 3993 (2018)
12. Nakazato, N., Yoshida, S., Sakurai, S., Narumi, T., Tanikawa, T., Hirose, M.: Smart face: enhancing creativity during video conferences using real-time facial deformation. In: Proceedings of the 17th ACM Conference on Computer Supported Cooperative Work & Social Computing, pp. 75–83. ACM (2014)
13. Niedenthal, P.M., Mermillod, M., Maringer, M., Hess, U.: The simulation of smiles (SIMS) model: embodied simulation and the meaning of facial expression. Behav. Brain Sci. **33**(6), 417–433 (2010)
14. Olszewski, K., et al.: Realistic dynamic facial textures from a single image using GANs. In: IEEE International Conference on Computer Vision (ICCV), pp. 5429–5438 (2017)
15. Salimans, T., Goodfellow, I.J., Zaremba, W., Cheung, V., Radford, A., Chen, X.: Improved techniques for training GANs. CoRR abs/1606.03498 (2016). http://arxiv.org/abs/1606.03498
16. Schaefer, S., McPhail, T., Warren, J.: Image deformation using moving least squares. In: ACM Transactions on Graphics (TOG), vol. 25, pp. 533–540. ACM (2006)
17. Schmidt, K.L., Bhattacharya, S., Denlinger, R.: Comparison of deliberate and spontaneous facial movement in smiles and eyebrow raises. J. Nonverbal Behav. **33**(1), 35–45 (2009)
18. Suzuki, K., et al.: FaceShare: mirroring with pseudo-smile enriches video chat communications. In: Proceedings of the 2017 CHI Conference on Human Factors in Computing Systems, pp. 5313–5317. ACM (2017)
19. Valstar, M., Pantic, M.: Induced disgust, happiness and surprise: an addition to the MMI facial expression database. In: Proceedings of the 3rd International Workshop on EMOTION (satellite of LREC): Corpora for Research on Emotion and Affect, p. 65 (2010)
20. Wang, T., Liu, M., Zhu, J., Tao, A., Kautz, J., Catanzaro, B.: High-resolution image synthesis and semantic manipulation with conditional GANs. CoRR abs/1711.11585 (2017). http://arxiv.org/abs/1711.11585
21. Wang, X., Li, W., Mu, G., Huang, D., Wang, Y.: Facial expression synthesis by u-net conditional generative adversarial networks. In: Proceedings of the 2018 ACM on International Conference on Multimedia Retrieval, pp. 283–290. ACM (2018)
22. Wu, X., Xu, K., Hall, P.: A survey of image synthesis and editing with generative adversarial networks. Tsinghua Sci. Technol. **22**(6), 660–674 (2017)
23. Xu, X., Sun, D., Pan, J., Zhang, Y., Pfister, H., Yang, M.H.: Learning to super-resolve blurry face and text images. In: Proceedings of the IEEE Conference on Computer Vision and Pattern Recognition CVPR, pp. 251–260 (2017)
24. Yoshida, S., Tanikawa, T., Sakurai, S., Hirose, M., Narumi, T.: Manipulation of an emotional experience by real-time deformed facial feedback. In: Proceedings of the 4th Augmented Human International Conference, pp. 35–42. ACM (2013)
25. Zhao, G., Huang, X., Taini, M., Li, S.Z., Pietikälnen, M.: Facial expression recognition from near-infrared videos. Image Vis. Comput. **29**(9), 607–619 (2011)

Problems with Saliency Maps

Giuseppe Boccignone(ID), Vittorio Cuculo(✉)(ID), and Alessandro D'Amelio(ID)

PHuSe Lab - Dipartimento di Informatica, University of Milan,
via Celoria 18, 20133 Milan, Italy
{giuseppe.boccignone,vittorio.cuculo,alessandro.damelio}@unimi.it,
http://phuselab.di.unimi.it

Abstract. Despite the popularity that saliency models have gained in the computer vision community, they are most often conceived, exploited and benchmarked without taking heed of a number of problems and subtle issues they bring about. When saliency maps are used as proxies for the likelihood of fixating a location in a viewed scene, one such issue is the temporal dimension of visual attention deployment. Through a simple simulation it is shown how neglecting this dimension leads to results that at best cast shadows on the predictive performance of a model and its assessment via benchmarking procedures.

Keywords: Saliency model · Visual attention · Gaze deployment

1 Introduction

Many efforts have been devoted in the past decade to the computational modelling of visual salience [6–10,38], and recently large breakthroughs have been achieved on benchmarks by resorting to deep neural network models [10].

Saliency models are appealing since, apparently, they represent a straightforward operational definition of visual attention - the allocation of visual resources to the viewed scene [8]: they take an image $\mathbf{I}(\mathbf{r})$ as input, and return topographic maps $\mathcal{S}(\mathbf{r})$ indicating the salience at each location $\mathbf{r} = (x, y)$ in the image, namely the likelihood of fixating at $\mathbf{r}$. Thus, saliency models to predict *where* we look have gained currency for a variety of applications in computer vision, image and video processing and compression, quality assessment [29].

Yet, salience modelling and benchmarking are most often handled in an elusive way, which casts doubts on a straightforward interpretation of results so far achieved [8,22,24,30,33]. Beyond the long debated controversy concerning the bottom-up vs. top-down nature of eye guidance control [17,33], factors such as context [36], spatial biases [34], affect and personality [16], dynamics of attention deployment [30,31] are likely to play a key role and might contribute in subtle ways to effectiveness and performance of saliency models [22,24,30,33]. Some controversial aspects related to salience definition and modelling are discussed in Sect. 2. In particular, the temporal unfolding of factors [30] involved in salience making has been overlooked, with some exceptions in video processing (e.g. [5,13]) but largely neglected in static images.

© Springer Nature Switzerland AG 2019
E. Ricci et al. (Eds.): ICIAP 2019, LNCS 11752, pp. 35–46, 2019.
https://doi.org/10.1007/978-3-030-30645-8_4

The hitherto underestimated point we are making in this note is that by explicitly taking into account temporal unfolding provides useful conceptual insights on the actual predictive capability of saliency models, with practical consequences on their use and benchmarking.

By and large, saliency models are learned and/or evaluated by simply exploiting the fixation map on an image as "freezed" at the end of the viewing process (i.e, after having collected all fixations on stimulus along an eye-tracking session). In a different vein, here we operationally take into account temporal aspects of attention deployment captured by a time-varying fixation map (Sect. 3). Through a simple experiment, we show (Sect. 4) that in such way the actual sampling of gaze shifts, namely *how* we actually allocate visual resources onto the scene (i.e., the scanpath), can depart from that achieved by classic analyses.

2   The Salience Conundrum: Background and Motivation

Saliency Models. The notion of salience originates in visual attention research (e.g., [21]). In the case of overt visual attention, actual eye movements are involved. Eye movements obviously occur according to a continuous dynamics but their spatial and velocity characteristics allow to classify them as fixations, saccades and smooth pursuit of moving objects. Fixations and pursuit aim to bring or keep objects of interest onto the fovea where the visual acuity is maximum, whilst saccades are ballistic shifts in eye position, allowing to jump from one location of the viewed scene to another. When considering overt attention involving gaze, then the aim of a computational model of attentive eye guidance is to answer the question *Where to Look Next?* by providing an account of the mapping from visual data of a natural scene, say $\mathbf{I}$ (the raw data representing either a static picture or a stream of images), to a sequence of time-stamped gaze locations $(\mathbf{r}_{F_1}, t_1), (\mathbf{r}_{F_2}, t_2), \cdots$, namely $\mathbf{I} \mapsto \{\mathbf{r}_{F_1}, t_1; \mathbf{r}_{F_2}, t_2; \cdots\}$. The common practice to derive such mapping is to conceive it as a two stage procedure: (i) Compute a suitable perceptual representation $\mathcal{W}$, i.e., $\mathbf{I} \mapsto \mathcal{W}$; (ii) Use $\mathcal{W}$ to generate the scanpath, $\mathcal{W} \mapsto \{\tilde{\mathbf{r}}_F(1), \tilde{\mathbf{r}}_F(2), \cdots\}$ (where we have adopted the compact notation $(\tilde{\mathbf{r}}_{F_n}, t_n) = \tilde{\mathbf{r}}_F(n)$).

Stimulus salience is one such perceptual representation $\mathcal{W}$. It is the driving force behind bottom-up or "exogenous" attention control, driven by low-level scene properties (brightness, colour, oriented edges, motion contrasts [19]) and independently of the internal mental state of the observer. Indeed, for the most part, the first computable models for the prediction of eye fixation locations in images relied on a "saliency map", $\mathcal{S}$ a topographic representation indicating *where* one is likely to look within the viewed scene [19], that is $\mathcal{S}(\mathbf{r}) \approx P(\mathbf{r} \mid \mathbf{F}(\mathbf{I}))$, where $\mathbf{F}(\mathbf{I})$ are low-level features computed from image $\mathbf{I}$.

By overviewing the field [6–8,33], it is easily recognised that computational modelling of visual attention has been mainly concerned with stage (i), that is calculating $\mathcal{W} = \mathcal{S}$. As to stage (ii), namely $\mathcal{S} \mapsto \{\mathbf{r}_F(1), \mathbf{r}_F(2), \cdots\}$, which actually brings in the question of *how* we look rather than *where*, it is seldom taken into account.

Model Performance. An issue that straightforwardly raises is how to measure and benchmark the performance of a saliency model accounting for the map $\mathbf{I} \mapsto \mathcal{S}$. The general idea is to measure the capability of the model output, namely the saliency map $\mathcal{S}$, to predict fixations (notice: *as if* they were performed). To such end, eye fixations $\{\mathbf{r}_F^{(s,i)}(1), \mathbf{r}_F^{(s,i)}(2), \cdots\}$ are typically used as to derive the ground-truth. These are collected in an eye-tracking experiment involving $s = 1 \cdots N_S$ subjects on a chosen data set $\{\mathbf{I}^i\}$ of $i = 1 \cdots N_I$ images (or videos). Some metrics use the original binary location map of fixations, say $\mathcal{M}^B$. Alternatively, the discrete fixations can be converted into a continuous distribution, a fixation map (a.k.a *heat map* or *attention map* when fixations are weighted by fixation time), $\mathcal{M}^D$ [9]. Precisely, for each stimulus $\mathbf{I}^i$ the map

$$\{\mathbf{r}_F^{(s,i)}(1), \mathbf{r}_F^{(s,i)}(2), \cdots\}_{s=1}^{N_S} \mapsto \mathcal{M}^{D(i)}, \tag{1}$$

is computed as an empirical fixation density (e.g., [23,25]); see Fig. 1 below. Eventually, a metric is evaluated either in the form $\mu(\mathcal{S}, \mathcal{M}^B)$ or $\mu(\mathcal{S}, \mathcal{M}^D)$, the result being a number assessing the similarity or dissimilarity between $\mathcal{S}$, and $\mathcal{M}$ (for an in-depth presentation, see Bylinskii *et al.* [9]).

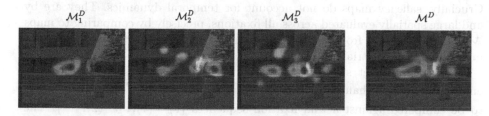

$\qquad\mathcal{M}_1^D \qquad\qquad\qquad \mathcal{M}_2^D \qquad\qquad\qquad \mathcal{M}_3^D \qquad\qquad\qquad \mathcal{M}^D$

Fig. 1. Example of different fixation density maps for a specific image. From left to right: the three temporal distribution maps obtained from fixations collected at seconds 1, 2 and 3, respectively, overlapped on the original stimulus; the standard fixation map resulting from the aggregation of all fixations available at the end of the eye-tracking procedure. The latter map is the one typically exploited in saliency modelling and benchmarking.

The Many Facets of Salience (and Benchmarking). Despite the considerable successes that salience has had in predicting fixations at above-chance levels, it has become increasingly clear that prediction requires high-level, semantically-meaningful elements (e.g. faces, objects and text [11,12]). Thus, prominent models of attention control posit a dichotomy between bottom-up and top-down, "endogenous" control, the latter being determined by current selection goals; in this case spotted items are selected in terms of their goal relevance, rather than physical salience. In the visual attention realm when top-down (relevance) and bottom-up (saliency) mechanisms are combined for eye guidance, the resulting map is termed priority map [17].

In a different vein, computer vision efforts to achieve benchmarking performance have resulted in the heuristic addition of high-level processing capabilities to attention models, which are still referred to as saliency models [6–10,18]. As a matter of fact, the term "saliency" now stands for any image-based prediction of which locations are likely to be fixated by subject guided by either low- or high-level cues [29]. Indeed, the success of deep networks exploiting convolutional filters that have been learned on other tasks, for instance object recognition in the ImageNet dataset, provides practical evidence of the usefulness of high-level image features for prediction purposes [10,24]. In recent evaluations on what should be the next steps in salience modelling and assessment [8,10], it has been shown that a large improvement in predictive performance could be gained by specifically addressing semantic issues such as actions in a scene, relative importance to different faces, informativeness of text, targets of gaze.

Meanwhile, such practice somehow limits a straightforward interpretation of benchmarking results so far achieved; thus, disentangling the different levels of control to understand to what extent fixations in free viewing are driven by low-level features or by high-level features is recently growing up as a research line *per se* [22,24,30]

3   Temporal Unfolding of Fixation Allocation

Crucially, saliency maps do not account for temporal dynamics. They are by and large spatially evaluated across all fixations, precisely by comparing to maps $\mathcal{M}^B$, or $\mathcal{M}^D$ derived from fixations accumulated in time after the stimulus onset until the end of the trial (Eq. 1).

As a matter of fact, surmising that S is predictive of human fixations does not entail an actual mechanism of fixation generation, $S_i \mapsto \{\widetilde{\mathbf{r}}_F^{(s,i)}(1), \widetilde{\mathbf{r}}_F^{(s,i)}(2), \cdots\}$ to be compared against actual fixation sequences $\{\mathbf{r}_F^{(s,i)}(1), \mathbf{r}_F^{(s,i)}(2), \cdots\}$. The assessment of the predictive capability of a model is just to be understood as the indirect measurement of any metric μ as introduced above. When using the mapping of Eq. 1, it is implicitly assumed that fixations, once collected, are exchangeable with respect to time ordering $\{1, \cdots, n\}$, namely

$$\{\mathbf{r}_F^{(s,i)}(1), \mathbf{r}_F^{(s,i)}(2), \cdots \mathbf{r}_F^{(s,i)}(n)\} = \{\mathbf{r}_F^{(s,i)}(\pi(1)), \mathbf{r}_F^{(s,i)}(\pi(2)), \cdots, \mathbf{r}_F^{(s,i)}(\pi(n))\}, \tag{2}$$

$\forall \pi \in \Pi(n)$ where $\Pi(n)$ is the group of permutations of $\{1, \cdots, n\}$. This assumption implies that any dynamical law $\widetilde{\mathbf{r}}_F^{(s,i)}(t) = f(\widetilde{\mathbf{r}}_F^{(s,i)}(t-1), \mathcal{W}_i)$ that takes as input the perceptual representation of the i-th image and the previous fixation location (as a system state) and returns the next location of fixation as its output is dismissed. However, dynamics is important in many respects. For instance, there is evidence for the existence of systematic tendencies in oculomotor control [34]: eyes are not equally likely to move in any direction. Yet, apart from the well known center bias [32], motor biases can be actually taken into account only when scanpath generation is performed.

In such perspective, Le Meur and colleagues [26] have proposed saccadic models as a new framework to predict visual scanpaths of observers while they freely watch static images. In such models the visual fixations are inferred from bottom-up saliency and oculomotor biases (captured as saccade amplitudes and saccade orientations) that are modeled using eye tracking data. Performance of these models can be evaluated either by directly comparing the generated scanpaths to human scanpaths or by computing new saliency maps, in the shape of densities from model generated fixations. There is a limited number of saccadic models available, see [26] for a comprehensive review; generalisation to dynamic scenes have been presented for instance in [4,28]. A remarkable result obtained by saccadic models is that by using simulated fixations $\{\widetilde{\mathbf{r}}_F^{(s,i)}(1), \widetilde{\mathbf{r}}_F^{(s,i)}(2), \cdots\}$ to generate a model-based fixation map, the latter has higher predictive performance than the raw salience map $\mathcal{S}$, in terms of similarity/dissimilarity μ with respect to human fixation maps. Beyond the improvement, it is worth noting that even in this case the model-generated attention map is eventually obtained *a posteriori*, as a 2-D spatial map of accumulated fixations. Such problem is somehow attenuated when dynamic stimuli (videos) are taken into account, though, the temporal unfolding as learned in a data-driven way presents complex albeit structured temporal patterns [5,14], that deserve being taken into consideration.

In a different vein, recent work by Schutt *et al.* [30] has for the first time considered the temporal evolution of the fixation density in the free viewing of static scenes. They provide evidence for a fixation dynamics which unfolds into three phases:

1. An initial orienting response towards the image center;
2. A brief exploration, which is characterized by a gradual broadening of the fixation density, the observers looking at all parts of the image they are interested in;
3. A final equilibrium state, in which the fixation density has converged, and subjects preferentially return to the same fixation locations they visited during the main exploration.

Beyond the theoretical insights offered by their analyses, by monitoring the performance of the empirical fixation density over time, they also pave the way to a more subtle and principled approach to unveil the actual predictive performance of saliency models [30].

Based on their approach, we propose a complementary analysis that relies on model-generated scanpaths, i.e. actual prediction. More precisely, we ask the following: do model-generated scanpaths differ from human scanpaths in the free viewing of static scenes when (1) the scanpath is generated by taking into account the three phases described above as opposed to when (2) the scanpath is generated by only taking into account the final fixation density?

In the work presented here, we use the time-varying fixation density as the attention map that moment-to-moment feeds the gaze shift dynamics. The main motivation is in the very fact that we want to assess differences rising at the oculomotor behavior while being free from any saliency model specific assumption. In brief we do the following:

Step 1. Compute three different empirical fixation density maps $\mathcal{M}_k^{D(i)}$ accounting for phases $k = 1, 2, 3$ above, by aggregating all the human fixations performed in the corresponding time window:

$$\{\mathbf{r}_F^{(s,i)}(m_{k-1}+1), \cdots, \mathbf{r}_F^{(s,i)}(m_k)\}_{s=1}^{N_S} \mapsto \mathcal{M}_k^{D(i)}, \quad k = 1, 2, 3. \qquad (3)$$

Step 2. Generate "subject" fixations depending on the three-phase unfolding defined above, by relying on a saccadic model $\mathbf{r}_F^{(s,i)}(n) = f(\mathbf{r}_F^{(s,i)}(n-1), \mathcal{W}(k)_i)$:

$$\mathcal{M}_k^{D(i)} \mapsto \{\widetilde{\mathbf{r}}_F^{(s,i)}(m_{k-1}+1), \cdots, \widetilde{\mathbf{r}}_F^{(s,i)}(m_k)\} = \mathcal{R}t_k^{(s,i)}, \quad k = 1, 2, 3 \qquad (4)$$

with $\mathcal{W}(k)_i = \mathcal{M}_k^{D(i)}$ being the phase-dependent perceptual representation of image i, so to obtain the "time-aware" scanpath $\mathcal{R}t^{(s,i)} = \{\mathcal{R}t_1^{(s,i)}, \mathcal{R}t_2^{(s,i)}, \mathcal{R}t_3^{(s,i)}\}$.

For comparison purposes, in the same way, but only by relying on the overall final fixation map $\mathcal{M}^{D(i)}$, we perform the mapping $\mathcal{M}^{D(i)} \mapsto \mathcal{R}s^{(s,i)}$, which represents the typical output of a saccadic model.

4 Simulation

Dataset. The adopted dataset is a publicly available one [20], that consists of eye tracking data (240 Hz) recorded from $N_S = 15$ viewers during a free-viewing experiment involving 1003 natural images. The stimuli were presented at full resolution for 3 s. The raw eye tracking data were classified in fixations and saccades by adopting an acceleration threshold algorithm [20].

Evaluation. As described in the Method section, we generated four different attention maps for each image $\mathbf{I}^i$ of the dataset. Three of these are the temporal density fixation maps $\mathcal{M}_1^{D(i)}, \mathcal{M}_2^{D(i)}, \mathcal{M}_3^{D(i)}$, with $t_{m_1} = 1, t_{m_2} = 2$ and $t_{m_3} = 3$ s (Eq. 3); the fourth is the classic, cumulative $\mathcal{M}^{D(i)}$ map. Figure 1 shows one example. These were used to support the generation of $N_S = 15$ scanpaths for both the temporal (Eq. 4) and the classic approach, collected into the sets $\mathcal{R}t^{(i)}$ and $\mathcal{R}s^{(i)}$, respectively. To such end we exploit the Constrained Levy Exploration (CLE [3])[1] saccadic model that has been widely used for evaluation purposes, e.g., [26,37]. Briefly, the CLE considers the gaze motion as given by the stochastic dynamics of a Lévy forager moving under the influence of an external force (which, in turn, depends on a salience or attention potential field). Namely, at time t the transition from the current position $\mathbf{r}(t)$ to a new position $\mathbf{r}_{new}(t)$, $\mathbf{r}(t) \rightarrow \mathbf{r}_{new}(t)$, is given by

$$\mathbf{r}_{new}(t) = \mathbf{r}(t) + \mathbf{g}(\mathcal{W}(\mathbf{r}(t))) + \boldsymbol{\eta}. \qquad (5)$$

The trajectory of the variable $\mathbf{r}$ is determined by a deterministic part $\mathbf{g}$, the drift - relying upon salience or fixation density -, and a stochastic part $\boldsymbol{\eta}$, where $\boldsymbol{\eta}$ is

---

[1] Code available at https://github.com/phuselab/CLE.

a random vector sampled from a heavy-tailed distribution, accounting for motor biases (cfr., the Appendix for a quick recap and [3] for theoretical details).

Figure 2 shows CLE generated scanpaths, compared against the actual set of human scanpaths $\mathcal{R}^{(i)} = \{\mathbf{r}_F^{(i)}(1), \cdots, \mathbf{r}_F^{(i)}(m_3)\}$. The example shows at a glance that when attention deployment is unfolded in time, the predicted scanpaths more faithfully capture the dynamics of actual scanpaths than the dynamics of those generated via the "freezed" map. To quantitatively support such insight, the quality of $\mathcal{R}t^{(i)}$ and $\mathcal{R}s^{(i)}$ has been evaluated on each image i of the dataset by adopting metrics based on the ScanMatch [15] and the recurrence quantification analysis (RQA, [2])[2].

$\mathcal{R}t$ $\mathcal{R}s$ $\mathcal{R}$

Fig. 2. Scanpaths for the image in Fig. 1. Left to right: 15 model-generated scanpaths, via Eq. 5 from the temporally unfolded fixation maps, 15 model-generated scanpaths from the standard fixation map, 15 scanpaths from actual human fixation sequences (ground-truth). Different colours encode different "observers" (artificial or human).

ScanMatch is a generalised scanpath comparison method that overcomes the lack of flexibility of the well-known Levenshtein distance (or string edit method) [27]. It consists of a preliminary step, where two scanpaths are spatially and temporally binned and then re-coded to create sequences of letters that preserve fixation location, time and order. These are then compared adopting the Needleman-Wunsch sequence alignment algorithm, widely used to compare DNA sequences. The similarity score is given by the optimal route throughout a matrix that provides the score for all letter pair substitutions and a penalty gap. A similarity score of 1 indicates that the sequences are identical; a score of 0 indicates no similarity. One of the strengths of this method is the ability to take into account spatial, temporal, and sequential similarity between scanpaths; however, as any measure that relies on regions of interest or on a grid, it suffers from quantisation issues.

RQA is typically exploited to describe complex dynamical systems. Recently [2] it has been adopted to quantify the similarity of a pair of fixation sequences by relying on a series of measures that are found to be useful for characterizing cross-recurrent patterns [1]. RQA calculates the cross-recurrence for each fixation of

---

[2] An implementation is provided at https://github.com/phuselab/RQAscanpath.

two scanpaths, resulting in the construction of the so-called recurrence plot: two fixations are cross-recurrent if they are close together in terms of their Euclidean distance. Since we are interested in whether two scanpaths are similar in terms of their fixations sequence, we adopted the determinism and center of recurrence mass (CORM) measures. The determinism represents the percentage of cross-recurrent points that form diagonal lines in a recurrence plot; it provides a measure of the overlap for a sequence of fixations considering the sequential information. The CORM is defined as the distance of the center of gravity of recurrences from the main diagonal in a recurrence plot; small values indicate that the same fixations from both scanpaths tend to occur close in time.

Results. All the generated scanpaths belonging to $\mathcal{R}t$ and $\mathcal{R}s$ have been evaluated against the human ones $\mathcal{R}$ for each image. Table 1 reports the average values over all the "observers" related to the same images in the dataset. To quantify the intra-human similarity, an additional measure resulting from the comparison of $\mathcal{R}$ with itself is provided. It can be noticed that the temporal approach outperforms the static one in all the three adopted metrics. Remarkably, as regards the determinism, the percentage of overlapping sequences when adopting the temporal approach is higher than that resulting from the comparison among human scanpaths. This would suggest that a high inter-subject variability occurs when looking at the same stimulus, and that the adoption of temporal maps does extract common behaviour among the observers, resulting in a lower spread of fixation locations.

Table 1. Average values (standard deviations) of the considered metrics evaluated over all the artificial and human "observers" related to the same images in the dataset.

	ScanMatch	Determinism	CORM
$\mathcal{R}s$ vs. $\mathcal{R}$	0.39 (0.08)	58.08 (11.18)	19.95 (5.90)
$\mathcal{R}t$ vs. $\mathcal{R}$	**0.43** (0.05)	**61.65** (8.51)	**15.26** (3.58)
$\mathcal{R}$ vs. $\mathcal{R}$	0.49 (0.05)	59.61 (7.71)	10.0 (2.09)

5   Conclusive Remarks

In this note by resorting to a straightforward simulation of scanpath generation, evidence has been given that: (i) the scanpaths sampled by taking into account the underlying process of visual attention unfolding in time (dynamic attention map) considerably differ from those generated by a static attention map; (ii) "time-aware" model-based scanpaths exhibit a dynamics akin to that of scanpaths recorded from human observers.

It should be intuitively apparent that the evolution of the empirical fixation density $\mathcal{M}_t^{D(i)}$ within the time interval $[t_0, T]$ from the onset of the stimulus i

up to time T, provides a source of information which is richer than that derived by simply considering its cumulative distribution function $\int_{t_0}^{T} \mathcal{M}_t^{D(i)} dt$. Yet, this very fact is by and large neglected in the saliency modelling practice. It has to be said that this pitfall is somehow mitigated when dynamic stimuli (videos) are taken into account. Though, a large body of research is still flourishing in pursuit of adequate computational models of salience in static images.

The analysis reported here bear some consequences.

On the one hand, it may suggest a more principled design of visual attention models specially when time dimension is crucial for the analysis. Here to keep the discussion simple, we have straightforwardly used empirical fixation density maps $\mathcal{M}_t^{D(i)}$ derived via the mapping (3). However, nothing prevents from building models based on a chain of sub-models, each contributing to the final scanpath, thus following the same route we have outlined above. For example, the three-stage processing suggested in [30], could be accounted for by (1) a center-bias model, (2) a context/layout model, and (3) an object-based model, respectively. A similar perspective has been taken, for instance, in video salience modelling; nevertheless, static image processing and recognition task could benefit from resorting to dynamics [35].

On the other hand, the approach could be used for fine-grained assessment of models as surmised in [30]; hence, being aware that a static saliency map might not be as predictive of overt attention as it is deemed to be.

Appendix: The Lévy Forager

The Lévy forager's dynamics formalised in Eq. 5 can be written

$$\mathbf{r}_{new}(t) = \mathbf{r}(t) - \nabla V + \boldsymbol{\eta}, \tag{6}$$

so that the new gaze position is determined by: (a) the gradient of V, the external force field shaped by the perceptual landscape, $V(\cdot, t)$ being defined as the time varying scalar field

$$V(x, y, t) = \exp(-\tau_V \mathcal{W}(x, y, t)), \tag{7}$$

(b) the stochastic vector $\boldsymbol{\eta}$ with components

$$\eta_x = l \cos(\theta), \qquad \eta_y = l \sin(\theta), \tag{8}$$

where the angle θ represents the flight direction and l is the jump length. Direction and length are sampled from the uniform and α-stable distribution, respectively:

$$\theta \sim Unif(0, 2\pi), \tag{9}$$

$$l \sim \varphi(\mathcal{W}) f(l; \alpha, \beta, \gamma, \delta). \tag{10}$$

Along the extensive stage, θ and l summarise the internal action choice of the forager and the function $\varphi(\mathcal{W})$ modifies the pure Levy flight, since the probability to move from one site to the next site depends on the "strength" of a bond

$$\varphi(\mathcal{W}) = \frac{\exp(-\beta_P(\mathcal{W}(\mathbf{r}(t)) - \mathcal{W}(\mathbf{r}_{new}(t))))}{\sum_{\mathbf{r}'_{new}} \exp(-\beta_P(s(\mathbf{r}(t)) - \mathcal{W}(\mathbf{r}'_{new}(t))))} \tag{11}$$

that exists between them. The shift proposal is weighed up according to an accept/reject Metropolis rule that depends on the perceptual gain $\Delta\mathcal{W}$ and on "temperature" T [3]. The values of T determine the amount of randomness in scanpath generation. If no suitable shift $\mathbf{r}(t)_{new}$ has been selected, the current fixation point $\mathbf{r}(t)$ is retained.

References

1. Anderson, N.C., Anderson, F., Kingstone, A., Bischof, W.F.: A comparison of scanpath comparison methods. Behav. Res. Methods **47**(4), 1377–1392 (2015)
2. Anderson, N.C., Bischof, W.F., Laidlaw, K.E., Risko, E.F., Kingstone, A.: Recurrence quantification analysis of eye movements. Behav. Res. Methods **45**(3), 842–856 (2013)
3. Boccignone, G., Ferraro, M.: Modelling gaze shift as a constrained random walk. Phys. A: Stat. Mech. Appl. **331**(1–2), 207–218 (2004)
4. Boccignone, G., Ferraro, M.: Ecological sampling of gaze shifts. IEEE Trans. Cybern. **44**(2), 266–279 (2014)
5. Boccignone, G., Cuculo, V., D'Amelio, A., Grossi, G., Lanzarotti, R.: Give ear to my face: modelling multimodal attention to social interactions. In: Leal-Taixé, L., Roth, S. (eds.) ECCV 2018. LNCS, vol. 11130, pp. 331–345. Springer, Cham (2019). https://doi.org/10.1007/978-3-030-11012-3_27
6. Borji, A., Itti, L.: State-of-the-art in visual attention modeling. IEEE Trans. Pattern Anal. Mach. Intell. **35**(1), 185–207 (2013)
7. Bruce, N.D., Wloka, C., Frosst, N., Rahman, S., Tsotsos, J.K.: On computational modeling of visual saliency: examining what's right, and what's left. Vis. Res. **116**, 95–112 (2015)
8. Bylinskii, Z., DeGennaro, E., Rajalingham, R., Ruda, H., Zhang, J., Tsotsos, J.: Towards the quantitative evaluation of visual attention models. Vis. Res. **116**, 258–268 (2015)
9. Bylinskii, Z., Judd, T., Oliva, A., Torralba, A., Durand, F.: What do different evaluation metrics tell us about saliency models? IEEE Trans. Pattern Anal. Mach. Intell. **41**(3), 740–757 (2019)
10. Bylinskii, Z., Recasens, A., Borji, A., Oliva, A., Torralba, A., Durand, F.: Where should saliency models look next? In: Leibe, B., Matas, J., Sebe, N., Welling, M. (eds.) ECCV 2016. LNCS, vol. 9909, pp. 809–824. Springer, Cham (2016). https://doi.org/10.1007/978-3-319-46454-1_49
11. Cerf, M., Frady, E., Koch, C.: Faces and text attract gaze independent of thetask: experimental data and computer model. J. Vis. **9**(12), 10 (2009)
12. Clavelli, A., Karatzas, D., Lladós, J., Ferraro, M., Boccignone, G.: Modelling task-dependent eye guidance to objects in pictures. Cogn. Comput. **6**(3), 558–584 (2014)
13. Coutrot, A., Guyader, N.: An efficient audiovisual saliency model to predict eye positions when looking at conversations. In: 23rd European Signal Processing Conference, pp. 1531–1535, August 2015
14. Coutrot, A., Guyader, N.: How saliency, faces, and sound influence gaze in dynamic social scenes. J. Vis. **14**(8), 5 (2014)

15. Cristino, F., Mathôt, S., Theeuwes, J., Gilchrist, I.D.: Scanmatch: a novel method for comparing fixation sequences. Behav. Res. Methods **42**(3), 692–700 (2010)

16. Cuculo, V., D'Amelio, A., Lanzarotti, R., Boccignone, G.: Personality gaze patterns unveiled via automatic relevance determination. In: Mazzara, M., Ober, I., Salaün, G. (eds.) STAF 2018. LNCS, vol. 11176, pp. 171–184. Springer, Cham (2018). https://doi.org/10.1007/978-3-030-04771-9_14

17. Egeth, H.E., Yantis, S.: Visual attention: control, representation, and time course. Annu. Rev. Psychol. **48**(1), 269–297 (1997)

18. Furnari, A., Farinella, G.M., Battiato, S.: An experimental analysis of saliency detection with respect to three saliency levels. In: Agapito, L., Bronstein, M.M., Rother, C. (eds.) ECCV 2014. LNCS, vol. 8927, pp. 806–821. Springer, Cham (2015). https://doi.org/10.1007/978-3-319-16199-0_56

19. Itti, L., Koch, C., Niebur, E.: A model of saliency-based visual attention for rapid scene analysis. IEEE Trans. Pattern Anal. Mach. Intell. **20**, 1254–1259 (1998)

20. Judd, T., Ehinger, K., Durand, F., Torralba, A.: Learning to predict where humans look. In: IEEE 12th International conference on Computer Vision, pp. 2106–2113. IEEE (2009)

21. Koch, C., Ullman, S.: Shifts in selective visual attention: towards the underlying neural circuitry. Hum. Neurobiol. **4**(4), 219–27 (1985)

22. Kong, P., Mancas, M., Thuon, N., Kheang, S., Gosselin, B.: Do deep-learning saliency models really model saliency? In: 2018 25th IEEE International Conference on Image Processing (ICIP), pp. 2331–2335. IEEE (2018)

23. Kümmerer, M., Wallis, T.S., Bethge, M.: Information-theoretic model comparison unifies saliency metrics. Proc. Natl. Acad. Sci. **112**(52), 16054–16059 (2015)

24. Kummerer, M., Wallis, T.S., Gatys, L.A., Bethge, M.: Understanding low-and high-level contributions to fixation prediction. In: Proceedings of the IEEE International Conference on Computer Vision, pp. 4789–4798 (2017)

25. Le Meur, O., Baccino, T.: Methods for comparing scanpaths and saliency maps: strengths and weaknesses. Behav. Res. Methods **45**(1), 251–266 (2013)

26. Le Meur, O., Coutrot, A.: Introducing context-dependent and spatially-variant viewing biases in saccadic models. Vis. Res. **121**, 72–84 (2016)

27. Levenshtein, V.I.: Binary codes capable of correcting deletions, insertions, and reversals. In: Soviet Physics Doklady, vol. 10, pp. 707–710 (1966)

28. Napoletano, P., Boccignone, G., Tisato, F.: Attentive monitoring of multiple video streams driven by a Bayesian foraging strategy. IEEE Trans. Image Process. **24**(11), 3266–3281 (2015)

29. Nguyen, T.V., Zhao, Q., Yan, S.: Attentive systems: a survey. Int. J. Comput. Vis. **126**(1), 86–110 (2018)

30. Schütt, H.H., Rothkegel, L.O., Trukenbrod, H.A., Engbert, R., Wichmann, F.A.: Disentangling bottom-up versus top-down and low-level versus high-level influences on eye movements over time. J. Vis. **19**(3), 1 (2019)

31. Tatler, B.W., Baddeley, R.J., Gilchrist, I.D.: Visual correlates of fixation selection: effects of scale and time. Vis. Res. **45**(5), 643–659 (2005)

32. Tatler, B.: The central fixation bias in scene viewing: selecting an optimal viewing position independently of motor biases and image feature distributions. J. Vis. **7**(14), 4 (2007)

33. Tatler, B., Hayhoe, M., Land, M., Ballard, D.: Eye guidance in natural vision: reinterpreting salience. J. Vis. **11**(5), 5 (2011)

34. Tatler, B., Vincent, B.: The prominence of behavioural biases in eye guidance. Vis. Cogn. **17**(6–7), 1029–1054 (2009)

35. Tavakoli, H.R., Borji, A., Anwer, R.M., Rahtu, E., Kannala, J.: Bottom-up attention guidance for recurrent image recognition. In: 2018 25th IEEE International Conference on Image Processing (ICIP), pp. 3004–3008. IEEE (2018)
36. Torralba, A., Oliva, A., Castelhano, M., Henderson, J.: Contextual guidance of eye movements and attention in real-world scenes: the role of global features in object search. Psychol. Rev. **113**(4), 766 (2006)
37. Xia, C., Han, J., Qi, F., Shi, G.: Predicting human saccadic scanpaths based on iterative representation learning. IEEE Trans. Image Process. 1 (2019)
38. Zhang, J., Malmberg, F., Sclaroff, S.: Visual Saliency: From Pixel-Level to Object-Level Analysis. Springer, Cham (2019). https://doi.org/10.1007/978-3-030-04831-0

A Region Proposal Approach for Cells Detection and Counting from Microscopic Blood Images

Cecilia Di Ruberto[1](✉), Andrea Loddo[1](✉), and Lorenzo Putzu[2](✉)

[1] Department of Mathematics and Computer Science, University of Cagliari,
via Ospedale 72, 09124 Cagliari, Italy
{dirubert,andrea.loddo}@unica.it
[2] Department of Electrical and Electronic Engineering, University of Cagliari,
Piazza d'Armi, 09123 Cagliari, Italy
lorenzo.putzu@unica.it

Abstract. In this paper, we propose a novel and efficient method for detecting and quantifying red cells from a microscopic blood image. The proposed system is based on a region proposal approach, namely the Edge Boxes, considered as the state-of-art region proposal method. Incorporating knowledge-based constraints into the detection process by Edge Boxes we can find cells proposals rapidly and efficiently. Experimental results on a well-known public dataset show both improved accuracy and increased over the state-of-art.

Keywords: Peripheral blood cell images · Cell counting · Region proposal · Edge Boxes

1 Introduction

Haematology is the branch of medicine involved in the diagnosis and treatment of patients who have disorders of the blood and bone marrow. Haematologists provide direct clinical care to patients with diagnostic work in the laboratory. Their tasks are the study, diagnosis, monitoring, treatment and prevention of diseases related to the blood and the bone marrow. In some cases, predicting how the bone marrow may have contributed to a clinical condition may be more important than identifying the patient's haematologic condition. Haematologists perform a wide range of laboratory tests to produce and interpret results assisting clinicians in their diagnosis and treatment of disease. For example, haematologists receive blood samples and check them for abnormalities. They look at blood film and if they suspect leukaemia or related pathologies, perform a bone marrow biopsy and examine and interpret the samples. The diagnosis must be made within a few hours since in some cases treatment must start immediately. Several diseases, disorders and deficiencies indeed affect the number and type of blood cells produced, their functions and their lifespan. Under

© Springer Nature Switzerland AG 2019
E. Ricci et al. (Eds.): ICIAP 2019, LNCS 11752, pp. 47–58, 2019.
https://doi.org/10.1007/978-3-030-30645-8_5

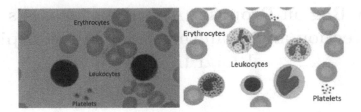

Fig. 1. Blood smear components: a real image and a schematic representation depicting all the leukocyte lineage

normal health conditions, bone marrow releases only mature and nearly mature cells into the bloodstream. However certain circumstances can induce the bone marrow to release immature or abnormal cells into the circulation. Among the several tests to monitor the cells' components proportions, the Complete Blood Count (CBC) indicates the numbers and types of cells in the peripheral circulation. The percentages of cells are compared with the reference ranges to determine if they are present in reasonable proportion to another, if a cell type is increased or decreased, or if immature cells are present. Reference ranges for blood tests are usually defined as the set of values in which 95% of the healthy population falls within. They are determined by collecting data from laboratory tests results performed over a representative set of the population. Quicker ways to perform an automatic CBC are the automatic cell counter or the flow cytometry, however, if the results from an automated cell count indicate the definite or possible presence of abnormal cells, a blood smear is realised and then analysed. Its analysis is particularly useful to categorise and identify pathological conditions that affect one or more types of blood cells or to monitor patients under treatment. It typically offers a description of the appearance of the cells as well as any cells abnormalities. The manual analysis of blood smears depends on the operator's skills and opinion. It is lengthy and repetitive, suffers from the absence of standard procedure, and it is subjective because the same scene can produce different results if analysed by several operators. Image processing techniques help to automatise the blood cells counting procedure as well as to provide information about their morphology. In this work we investigate a technique to provide an automatic counting of the red blood cells. The rest of the paper is organised as follows. Section 2 gives a background about peripheral blood analysis. Section 3 illustrates some related works. Section 4 presents the proposed method for cell detection and counting. Section 5 shows experimental results. Finally, Sect. 6 gives discussions, conclusions and future aspects.

2 Background

Under normal conditions, a blood image consists of three components: platelets, red blood cells (RBCs) and white blood cells (WBCs), as shown in Fig. 1. Platelets (or thrombocytes) are small non-nucleated disc-shaped cells. In

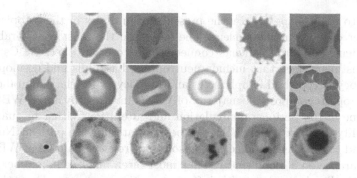

Fig. 2. Variations in RBCs appearance. (Top and middle) Shape and colour abnormalities: spherocyte, elliptocyte, tear, sickle, acanthocyte, echinocyte, keratocyte, byte, stomatocyte, target, schistocyte and rouleaux formation. (Bottom) Inclusions: Howelljolly bodies, siderotic granules, basophilic stippling, Heinz bodies, malaria and nucleated RBC. (Color figure online)

homoeostasis, they lead to the formation of blood clots. A sufficient number of platelets is necessary to control bleeding, even though this problem could cause bleeding, because many of the extra platelets may be dysfunctional also though they appear normal. A platelet count is usually evaluated by preparing a blood smear to visualise any anomalies in shape or size directly. RBCs (or erythrocytes) are uniform in size with a diameter of 7–8 μm. They are round and flattened like a doughnut, due to the presence of haemoglobin that is peripherally located. It gives an area with a central pallor equal to 1–3 μm, approximately 30–45% of the diameter of the cells. Considering that RBCs have not the same shape in their different types, any significant number of cells different in shape or size may indicate the presence of a disease [9]. Identifying normal and abnormal erythrocytes is essential because automated cell counters have not replaced the well-trained eye yet. Erythrocytes' colour is representative of haemoglobin concentration in the cell, while an abnormal shape may indicate the possible presence of a specific disease or disorder. The cytoplasm of all healthy RBCs is free of debris, granules, or other structures. Inclusions are the result of unique conditions, and their identification can be clinically helpful. Some examples of shape and colour abnormalities and inclusion bodies are shown in Fig. 2. WBCs or leukocytes are the biggest cells in the peripheral circulation, ranging in size from 10 to 20 μm. They have a nucleus surrounded by cytoplasm which permits to identify them more efficiently than the other regions, as their nucleus appear darker than the background. Nevertheless, the analysis and the processing of data related to the WBCs are problematic due to the wide cells variations in shape, dimensions and edges. The generic term leukocyte refers to a set of cells that are very different from each other. Indeed, although they are all derived from bone marrow stem cells, they differentiate into two main groups: cells containing granules, called granulocytic or myelocytic, and cells without granules called mononuclear or lymphoid. Thus, we can distinguish between these cells according to their shape or size, the presence of granules in the cytoplasm and the number of lobes in the nucleus. The lobes are the most considerable part of the nucleus, and thin filaments connect them to each other. WBCs mature into five distinct types, that include neutrophils, basophils and eosinophils for the granulocytic type and lymphocytes and monocytes for the non-granulocytic ones. Neutrophils compose the majority of WBCs in a healthy adult. WBCs have a short time in the peripheral circulation and alterations either in quantity or in the quality of a particular WBC can be dramatic for the patient. Numerous diseases and conditions can affect the absolute or relative number of WBCs and their appearance on a blood smear. They most often increase in number in individuals with allergies and parasitic infections, while more severe cases that need to be diagnosed are leukaemias. When the WBCs number rises, the peripheral smear usually shows more immature or abnormal cells. As previously said, the automated cells counters are not able to distinguish normal from abnormal cells and, even worse, they could fail due to the presence of abnormal cells. This is why many computer-aided systems from digitised images have been proposed in the last years.

3   Related Works

Among the proposed systems, few of them work on the whole analysis process, but they are mostly devoted to perform a single step or to analyse a single cell type. In particular, a considerable amount of work has been conducted to achieve leukocytes segmentation. For example, Madhloom [16] developed an automated system to localise and segment WBC nuclei based on arithmetical image operations and threshold operations. Sinha [21] attempted to differentiate the five types of leukocytes in cell images using a k-means clustering on the HSV colour space for WBCs segmentation and different classification models for cells differentiation. Often, images acquired from digital microscope are affected by uneven lighting and a very bright central area region, actually caused by the lens, lamp light and the presence of more marked shading area towards the corners. In this case, the use of a local approach for segmentation is more appropriate. In [7] a local fuzzy threshold has been proposed, to manage the local variations and the presence of noise or imprecision. Khan [12] proposed a method to count the cells. It uses an iterative threshold, determined from the histogram, to binarise the image. The count is performed by extracting the connected components, but neglecting overlapping or adjacent cells. Nguyen [19] also proposed a method to count all the cells types but adding a step to solve the overlapping cells problem that uses the distance transform. Unfortunately, this method produced good results only with the presence of almost round cells. The distance transform, in combination with the watershed algorithm, has also been used in [20] to separate cells agglomerates. The separation is less influenced by the shape of the cells, but it works only for small or simple cells agglomerates. Mahmood and Alomari instead [3,17] proposed two methods to count the WBCs and RBCs that use the Circular Hough transform (CHT). Mahmood applied the CHT on binary images obtained from the Lab colour space, while Alomari modified the CHT to reduce the number of cells candidate by selecting the one with the higher probability. Also in [4,23] the CHT has been used to count the RBCs starting from a binary image, instead the WBCs are in both cases counted by merely extracting the connected image component; thus they do not take into account the presence of touching leukocytes. The only difference between these two approaches is the segmentation phase, in the first case performed using k-means and in the second case using thresholds. Alilou has proposed a completely different approach in [2], where a detection phase using grey level co-occurrence matrix has been applied directly on the original images without a previous segmentation. As can be guessed, it produces a significant amount of false positives since it works without any restriction on the area of interest.

4   Our Approach for Cells Detection

Image region proposals are now considered as valid alternatives to objects detection algorithms as they can locate objects regions efficiently [18]. The computational efficiency was firstly shown with R-CNN [10]. After then, many other similar systems have been proposed. The most common region proposal algorithms include Selective Search [22] and Edge Boxes [24]. Edge Boxes is a novel approach for generating object bounding box proposals directly from edges. Built on the Structured Edge Detector [8], Edge Boxes uses the number of enclosed edges to find proposals and the number of edges at the border of boxes to rank them. In [11] the authors demonstrated experimentally that Edge Boxes is now the state-of-the-art region proposal system. For this reason, we have utilised this approach to address our problem too. R-CNN procedure is not needed in our approach since our interest is only devoted to cells location and it is unnecessary complex for the task we faced.

4.1   Edge Boxes

Edges provide a sparse but informative representation of an image. Also, the number of contours that are wholly contained in a bounding box is indicative of the likelihood of the box containing an object. By scoring a box based on the number of contours it wholly encloses generates a particularly useful proposal measure. On the contrary, merely counting the number of edge pixels within the box is not as informative. In the Edge Boxes system, a simple box objectness score is proposed. This score measures the number of edges that occur in the box minus those that are members of contours that overlap the box's boundary. An object is not searched at every image location and scale. Alternately, a set of object bounding box proposals is first generated to reduce the set of positions that need to be further analysed and consequently decreasing spurious false positives too. The approach is quite similar to superpixels straddling measure introduced by [1]; however, rather than measuring the number of straddling contours, such contours are removed from consideration. To obtain the initial edge map the fast and publicly available Structured Edge detector proposed in [8] is utilised. Given the dense edge responses, a procedure of Non-Maximal Suppression orthogonal to the edge response to finding edge peaks is then performed. Candidate boxes by using a sliding window approach are evaluated, in the same way as in traditional object detection. At every possible object position, scale and aspect ratio, a score indicating the likelihood of an object being present is generated. Promising candidate boxes are further refined using a simple coarse-to-fine search. By using efficient data structures, the approach is capable of rapidly finding the top object proposals from among millions of potential candidates.

4.2   Cells Detection Strategy

Since the Edge Boxes approach has been proposed for more general tasks, we added some useful steps to address our specific task, that is cells detection, by incorporating knowledge-based constraints in the detection strategy. Initially, to enhance the edges, both on the border of the cells and between overlapped cells, we perform a morphological gradient to the original image using a disk-shaped structuring element and size related to the expected cell size. The gradient image is the input image for the Edge Boxes algorithm which returns a ranked set of objects proposals containing cells. However, the number of top-scoring proposals are still high; also only some of them include single cells, that are our objects of interest.

To reduce the candidate bounding boxes to those consistent to single cells regions, we incorporate knowledge-based constraints to refine the edge boxes proposals and so remove false positive bounding boxes from consideration. The first observation is related to the bounding box size. We are interested only to proposals whose size is well matched to expected cell size. As a consequence, a larger (or smaller) box than the expected one can be immediately removed from consideration. Another important feature related to a red blood cell is its medium grey tone that is always greater than the grey tone of a white blood cell. So a candidate box contains a red cell if its medium grey tone is higher than the grey tone typically related to a white cell (in all our experiment the thresholding value has been chosen equal to 110). Finally, a box is of interest if it contains a circular object with a radius consistent with the expected cell size. Otherwise, if it does not contain any circle, or it contains more then one, the candidate box has to be discarded. Indeed, we are considering significant only boxes containing a single cell. Since we are analysing bounding boxes whose size is compatible with cell sizes, a box could contain at most two agglomerated cells. But before discarding such a box, we perform a further check, considering that, sometimes, even a single cell with an abnormal shape (see Fig. 2) could produce more circles. Thus, we consider as significant, a box containing circles whose area of union less intersection is less than half of the bounding box size, meaning that they belong to the same cell. All the candidate proposals returned by Edge Boxes algorithm satisfying the described constraints are selected as cells bounding boxes.

Promising selected cells boxes are further refined using a Non-Maximal Suppression procedure to eliminate overlapping bounding boxes. The confidence score used in all the experiments has been chosen equal to 0.1, and the bounding box overlap ratio is the area of intersection divided by the area of the union of two boxes.

The resulting strongest bounding boxes are detected as the most representative red blood cells in the analysed image and can be then quantified by annotating each cell centroid with a blue dot. A pipeline of the proposed cells detection strategy is shown in Fig. 3.

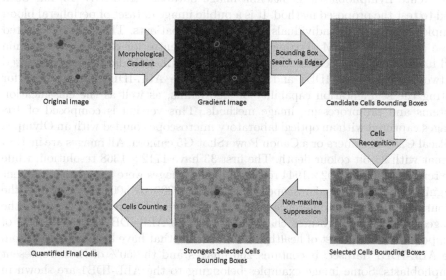

Fig. 3. A pipeline of the cells detection strategy. (Color figure online)

5   Experimental Results

For our experimentation, we used the open source MATLAB implementation of Edge Boxes made available by the authors [8]. The algorithm proposes a set of default parameters, tuned for generic datasets such as PASCAL, CalTech and ImageNet. For our dataset, we had to refine some of them to improve the quality of region proposals. The parameters modified were Alpha and Beta. Alpha indicates the Intersection over Union (IoU) for neighbouring candidate boxes; step sizes of the sliding windows are determined such that one step results in an IoU of Alpha. Beta is the Non-Maximal Suppression threshold of an object proposal, that is, if a neighbouring box is with an IoU greater than Beta, the lower ranked box is removed. We found that these two variables are the most influential at changing Edge Boxes' proposals. So, in our experiment Alpha and Beta have been chosen equal to 0.9 and 0.5, respectively. Another parameter modified was the max aspect ratio of boxes, chosen equal to 1.5. Other parameters such as the minimum score, Gamma and Kappa, did not affect the proposals significantly enough, so they were set as the defaults. Every other modules of the cells detection's proposed system have been implemented in MATLAB too. Average time to complete the entire procedure has been measured over the whole dataset images, reaching on average 35.24 s per image.

5.1 Dataset Description

The Acute Lymphoblastic Leukaemia image database ALL-IDB [13] has been used to test the proposed method. It is a public image dataset of peripheral blood samples from healthy individuals and leukaemia patients. The experts collected these samples at the M. Tettamanti Research Centre for childhood leukaemia and haematological diseases, Monza, Italy. The ALL-IDB database is composed of two versions: ALL-IDB1 and ALL-IDB2. The ALL-IDB1 can be used for testing the segmentation capability of algorithms, as well as the classification systems and pre-processing image methods. This version is composed of 108 images captured with an optical laboratory microscope coupled with an Olympus Optical C2500L camera or a Canon PowerShot G5 camera. All images are in JPG format with 24-bit colour depth. The first 33 have 1712 × 1368 resolution, while the remaining have 2592 × 1944 resolution. The images were taken with different magnifications of the microscope, ranging from 300 to 500, which brings the colour and brightness differences, that we managed by grouping together the images with same brightness characteristics. The ALL-IDB2 is a collection of cropped areas of interest of healthy and blast cells that have been extracted from the ALL-IDB1 dataset. It contains 260 images and the 50% of these represent lymphoblasts. Some image examples belonging to the ALL-IDB1 are shown in Fig. 4.

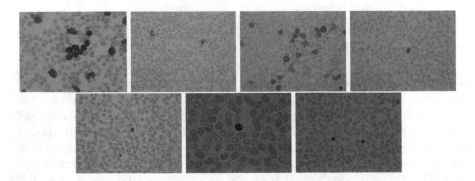

Fig. 4. Sample images from ALL-IDB1. They present different colouration and illumination conditions, therefore we identified 7 separate image sets. From top-left to bottom-right: examples representing each of the 7 identified subsets.

5.2   Results and Comparison with State-of-Art

As proposed in literature we evaluated the counting performances using *accuracy, precision, recall, F-measure*. The dataset has been divided into 7 different image subsets by grouping the images according to their magnification, brightness and colour conditions. In particular, Set1 contains images ranging from 1 to 33; Set2 goes from 34 to 47; Set3 from 48 to 63; Set4 from 64 to 77; Set5 from 78 to 93; Set6 from 94 to 95 and, finally, Set7 from 96 to 108. Table 1 presents the statistical measures regarding both all the dataset and the different image subsets. The ground truth for all the images has been determined by an expert and used to validate the proposed method. The counting results on the whole ALL-IDB are reported in Table 2, where they have been directly compared with the results obtained by other authors on the same dataset. In particular, the method proposed in [17] uses the CHT applied to different colour spaces without any restriction on the area of interest. This method was tested over 10 images and produced an accuracy of 64%. In both [4,23] the CHT has been applied after a segmentation phase, introducing some restriction on the area of interest to count the RBCs. In [4] the segmentation process has been performed using a fixed threshold over the G channel of the RGB colour space. They completed the counting just on 14 random images, obtaining an accuracy of 92.6%. In [23] they used K-means clustering for segmentation that brought to an accuracy of 90.9%, but the number of tested images is unknown. Also in [3], the circular Hough transform has been used, but in that case, the number of candidate circles has been reduced by selecting the one with the higher probability. This operation reduced the number of false positives but also increased the number of true positives, reaching an overall accuracy of 95% on 100 images. The method

Table 1. Detection performances of our approach on ALL-IDB: all dataset images and each identified image subset.

	All	Set1	Set2	Set3	Set4	Set5	Set6	Set7
Accuracy	95.6%	93.9%	96.6%	93.7%	97.0%	97.9%	95.7%	97.1%
Precision	98.4%	99.2%	98.2%	97.2%	98.5%	97.9%	97.7%	98.9%
Recall	96.6%	96.4%	96.8%	94.3%	97.8%	97.6%	95.7%	97.5%
F-measure	95.6%	93.9%	96.6%	93.7%	97.0%	97.9%	95.7%	97.1%

Table 2. RBCs counting performances compared with the state-of-the-art.

	Mahmood [17]	Loddo [15]	Alomari [3]	Yeldhos [23]	Bhavnani [4]	Our appr.
N° images	10	33	100	Unknown	14	108
Accuracy	64%	–	95%	90.9%	92.6%	95.6%
Precision	–	89%	95%	–	–	98.4%
Recall	–	98%	98%	–	–	95.0%
F-measure	–	93%	96%	–	–	96.6%

in [6] is based on a machine learning approach for segmentation by combining Nearest Neighbour and Support Vector Machine. It obtained an F-measure, a recall and a precision of 93%, 98% and 89%, respectively, yet limited to the first 33 dataset images. As it can be observed, the proposed approach improves the RBCs counting performances; in particular, it significantly enhances precision, reducing the number of false positives. To highlight the performances obtained with the proposed method, in Table 2 we also report the number of images used by the various authors to test their approach. Indeed none of the state-of-the-art techniques has been tested on the whole dataset. For this reason, we have also tested our method on different image subsets, demonstrating that some of them are easier than the others and at the same time to show how the performances can be affected by the number and kind of test set images.

6   Conclusions

In this paper, we proposed a novel and efficient method for detecting and quantifying red cells from a microscopic blood image. The proposed system is based on a region proposal approach, namely the Edge Boxes, considered as the state-of-art region proposal method that can evaluate millions of candidate boxes in a fraction of a second, returning a ranked set of a few thousand top-scoring proposals. Incorporating knowledge-based constraints, that can be extracted easily from some cell samples, we can find cells proposals rapidly and efficiently, also in case of overlapping or adjacent cells. Results show both improved accuracy and increased over the state-of-art. We are now working on an extension of the proposed system to create a fully complete blood cells detector, able to detect and count both red and white cells from a microscopic peripheral blood image, including morphological [5] and textural constraints [6]. Next future work will also include an evaluation of the framework on a new blood image dataset [14], containing images of malarial blood smears to detect and quantify the level of parasitaemia.

Acknowledgement. The research in this paper was partially supported by the Regione Autonoma della Sardegna research project "Algorithms and Models for Imaging Science [AMIS]" (RASSR57257, intervento finanziato con risorse FSC 2014-2020 - Patto per lo Sviluppo della Regione Sardegna).

References

1. Alexe, B., Deselaers, T., Ferrari, V.: Measuring the objectness of image windows. IEEE Trans. PAMI **34**(11), 2189–2202 (2012)
2. Alilou, M., Kovalev, V.: Automatic object detection and segmentation of the histocytology images using reshapable agents. Image Anal. Stereol. **32**(2), 89–99 (2013)
3. Alomari, Y.M., Sheikh Abdullah, S.N.H., Zaharatul Azma, R., Omar, K.: Automatic detection and quantification of WBCs and RBCs using iterative structured circle detection algorithm. Comput. Math. Methods Med. **2014**, 17 (2014)

4. Bhavnani, L.A., Jaliya, U.K., Joshi, M.J.: Segmentation and counting of WBCs and RBCs from microscopic blood sample images. Int. J. Image Graph. Sig. Process. **8**(11), 32–40 (2016)
5. Di Ruberto, C., Cinque, L.: Decomposition of two-dimensional shapes for efficient retrieval. Image Vis. Comput. **27**(8), 1097–1107 (2009)
6. Di Ruberto, C., Fodde, G., Putzu, L.: Comparison of statistical features for medical colour image classification. In: Nalpantidis, L., Krüger, V., Eklundh, J.-O., Gasteratos, A. (eds.) ICVS 2015. LNCS, vol. 9163, pp. 3–13. Springer, Cham (2015). https://doi.org/10.1007/978-3-319-20904-3_1
7. Di Ruberto, C., Putzu, L.: Accurate blood cells segmentation through intuitionistic fuzzy set threshold. In: International Conference SITIS on Signal-Image Technology and Internet-Based Systems, pp. 57–64, November 2014
8. Dollár, P., Zitnick, C.L.: Structured forests for fast edge detection. In: 2013 IEEE International Conference on Computer Vision, pp. 1841–1848, December 2013
9. Erhabor, O., Adias, T.C.: Hematology made easy. AuthorHouse (2013)
10. Girshick, R., Donahue, J., Darrell, T., Malik, J.: Rich feature hierarchies for accurate object detection and semantic segmentation. In: IEEE Conference on CVPR, pp. 580–587. IEEE Computer Society (2014)
11. Hosang, J., Benenson, R., Schiele, B.: How good are detection proposals, really? In: Proceedings of the British Machine Vision Conference. BMVA Press (2014)
12. Khan, S., Khan, A., Khattak, F.S., Naseem, A.: An accurate and cost effective approach to blood cell count. Int. J. Comput. Appl. **50**(1) (2012)
13. Labati, R.D., Piuri, V., Scotti, F.: All-IDB: the acute lymphoblastic leukemia image database for image processing. In: IEEE ICIP, pp. 2045–2048, September 2011
14. Loddo, A., Di Ruberto, C., Kocher, M., Prod'Hom, G.: MP-IDB: the malaria parasite image database for image processing and analysis. In: Lepore, N., Brieva, J., Romero, E., Racoceanu, D., Joskowicz, L. (eds.) SaMBa 2018. LNCS, vol. 11379, pp. 57–65. Springer, Cham (2019). https://doi.org/10.1007/978-3-030-13835-6_7
15. Loddo, A., Putzu, L., Di Ruberto, C., Fenu, G.: A computer-aided system for differential count from peripheral blood cell images. In: International Conference on Signal-Image Technology Internet-Based Systems (SITIS), pp. 112–118 (2016)
16. Madhloom, H.T., Kareem, S.A., Ariffin, H., Zaidan, A.A., Alanazi, H.O., Zaidan, B.B.: An automated white blood cell nucleus localization and segmentation using image arithmetic and automatic threshold. J. Appl. Sci. **10**(11), 959–966 (2010)
17. Mahmood, N.H., Lim, P.C., Mazalan, S.M., Razak, M.A.A.: Blood cells extractionusing color based segmentation technique. Int. J. LifeSci. Biotechnol. Pharma Res. **2**(2), 233–240 (2013)
18. McMahon, S., Sünderhauf, N., Upcroft, B., Milfordand, M.: How good are edge boxes, really? In: Workshop on Scene Understanding, IEEE CVPR, pp. 1–2 (2015)
19. Nguyen, N.T., Duong, A.D., Vu, H.Q.: Cell splitting with high degree of overlapping in peripheral blood smear. Int. J. Comput. Theory Eng. **3**(3), 473 (2011)
20. Putzu, L., Caocci, G., Di Ruberto, C.: Leucocyte classification for leukaemia detection using image processing techniques. AIM **62**(3), 179–191 (2014)
21. Sinha, N., Ramakrishnan, A.G.: Automation of differential blood count. In: TENCON Conference on Convergent Technologies for the Asia-Pacific Region, vol. 2, pp. 547–551 (2003)
22. Van de Sande, K.E.A., Uijlings, J.R.R., Gevers, T., Smeulders, A.W.M.: Segmentation as selective search for object recognition. In: ICCV, pp. 1879–1886, November 2011

23. Yeldhos, M., Peeyush, K.P.: Red blood cell counter using embedded image processing techniques. Res. Rep. **2** (2018)
24. Zitnick, C.L., Dollár, P.: Edge boxes: locating object proposals from edges. In: Fleet, D., Pajdla, T., Schiele, B., Tuytelaars, T. (eds.) ECCV 2014. LNCS, vol. 8693, pp. 391–405. Springer, Cham (2014). https://doi.org/10.1007/978-3-319-10602-1_26

A Single-Resolution Fully Convolutional Network for Retinal Vessel Segmentation in Raw Fundus Images

Ricardo J. Araújo[1,2(✉)] [iD], Jaime S. Cardoso[1,3] [iD], and Hélder P. Oliveira[1,2] [iD]

[1] INESC TEC, Porto, Portugal
ricardo.j.araujo@inesctec.pt
[2] Faculdade de Ciências da Universidade do Porto, Porto, Portugal
[3] Faculdade de Engenharia da Universidade do Porto, Porto, Portugal

Abstract. The segmentation of retinal vessels in fundus images has been heavily focused in the past years, given their relevance in the diagnosis of several health conditions. Even though the recent advent of deep learning allowed to foster the performance of computer-based algorithms in this task, further improvement concerning the detection of vessels while suppressing background noise has clinical significance. Moreover, the best performing state-of-the-art methodologies conduct patch-based predictions. This, put together with the preprocessing techniques used in those methodologies, may hinder their use in screening scenarios. Thus, in this paper, we explore a fully convolutional setting that takes raw fundus images and allows to combine patch-based training with global image prediction. Our experiments on the DRIVE, STARE and CHASEDB1 databases show that the proposed methodology achieves state-of-the-art performance in the first and the last, allowing at the same time much faster segmentation of new images.

Keywords: Retina · Vessel segmentation · Deep learning

1 Introduction

The retina is a tissue layer in the eye of vertebrates that participates in the production of nerve impulses that go to the visual cortex of the brain. Its vascularization is easily assessed in a non-intrusive manner by photography-based mechanisms, such that fundus imaging is often used as a diagnostic means of medical conditions affecting the morphology of vessels, such as hypertension, diabetes, arteriosclerosis, and cardiovascular disease [6]. It has been reported that 10% of all the diabetic patients have diabetic retinopathy, the main cause of blindness among people in the Western civilizations. Therefore, an early treatment is essential, and given that manual analysis by experts is very time consuming, automated vessel analysis is crucial for inclusion in screening programs [8].

This clinical relevance lead to the emergence of a large number of both unsupervised and supervised methodologies. Unsupervised approaches started

© Springer Nature Switzerland AG 2019
E. Ricci et al. (Eds.): ICIAP 2019, LNCS 11752, pp. 59–69, 2019.
https://doi.org/10.1007/978-3-030-30645-8_6

to appear before the advent of public databases and use theory from, one or a combination of, matched filters, vessel tracing, mathematical morphology, and scale-space representation [1,15,16]. Works resorting to supervised learning use manual annotations and different learning algorithms to find proper mapping functions between hand-crafted features and target segmentation [3,12]. The advent of deep learning further improved the performance of retinal vessel segmentation. Even though this approach is heavily dependent on labeled data and available databases contain at most dozens of images, researchers resort to dividing retinal images into small patches and transform the problem into a patch classification one [11]. However, this has implications at prediction time, as a patch has to be extracted for each pixel, leading to increased computational costs. This, associated with image preprocessing, which is also commonly conducted, may hinder the use of such systems in scenarios where a large number of images needs to be analyzed on the spot, as is the case of screening programs.

In this paper, we propose a Fully Convolutional Network (FCN) design that is able to segment an unseen image at a single step, even if it is trained in a patch-wise fashion (see Fig. 1).

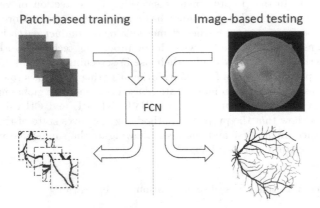

Fig. 1. Fully convolutional networks take images of arbitrary size, allowing to combine patch-based training and image-based prediction.

In practice, an adequate preprocessing facilitates the learning process, even though theory supports that a high number of non-linearities is able to adapt to the structure of data. Thus, in our experiments, we use raw color fundus images, to understand if this network is able to improve the state-of-the-art concerning vessel detection and background noise suppression, and simultaneously keep the prediction process as simple as possible. A FCN was proposed in the past [2], however its performance is significantly inferior to the best performing methods, indicating that other specific network design options may not have been ideal for retinal vessel segmentation.

1.1   Main Contributions

The main contributions of this work are:

- A neural network design allowing fast predictions on new data, which is crucial in all applications with high throughput of data, as is the case of screening programs;
- A methodology achieving high performance even being applied to raw fundus images, thus avoiding the need of using expensive preprocessing methods for image normalization.

1.2   Document Structure

This Section summarized the relevance and previous work regarding the topic of vessel segmentation in retinal fundus images, and the main contributions of our work; in Sect. 2, we discuss in detail the different options we took for designing the proposed model; in Sect. 3 we briefly describe the datasets used to assess the performance of our methodology, we introduce the conducted experiments and discuss the results; finally, Sect. 4 concludes the work and discusses possible directions for future research.

2   Methodology

Here, we discuss the motivations and preliminary empiric findings that led us into designing a fully convolutional network adapted to the specific task of vessel segmentation in raw color fundus images.

2.1   Fully Convolutional Network for Vessel Segmentation

Convolutional neural networks (CNNs) have revolutionized the field of computer vision, given their combination of deep hierarchical feature extraction (sequence of convolutional layers) and classification (fully connected layers) blocks. This was the type of deep neural network used in [11], where very small patches of the retina were fed into the model and it outputted the probability of the center pixel being a vessel. This highlights one of the problems of using typical CNNs for segmenting vessels, which is the need to divide a given image into a very large number of small patches and classify each of them, yielding a tremendous computational cost. A second problem is that fully connected layers force all the input images to have the same size.

A FCN design is a more adequate choice for segmentation problems, since it does not use fully connected layers. Thus, it is not mandatory to divide an image in order to obtain a complete segmentation map, which is crucial whenever we require fast predictions, as is the case of retinal screening programs, where a high volume of data is quickly generated. The inputs may also have varying size, making this design much more adaptable to different imaging conditions.

It allows us to train on smaller patches of the images and later still be able to obtain single-pass predictions of the entire images, as is represented in Fig. 1. Note that performing patch-wise training is an engineering option which facilitates avoiding wasting computational effort with portions of the images that do not contain information of the retina fundus.

2.2   Specific Design Considerations

After motivating the use of a FCN design for the segmentation of retinal vessels, now we delve into more specific aspects of the proposed network architecture, discussing some options we took based in previous works and empirical findings.

Spatial Resolution. Pooling or strided convolutions are commonly used to induce higher-level features to encode more neighborhood information. Recent results [11] suggest that pooling operations seem to not improve the performance of networks that are trained in small images. In preliminary experiments, we found that indeed a single-resolution deep network was more capable than a Unet-like model when extracting small capillaries. Even though the latter is able to combine low- and high-scale features, it seems that a deeper network at a fine scale is able to obtain better representations of small structures of interest, as is the case of very small vessels. Thus, in this work, the image resolution was kept across the entire network, contrarily to the previously proposed FCN [2].

Activation Units. All intermediate non-linearities were given by a Leaky Rectified Linear Unit (Leaky ReLU):

$$f(x) = \begin{cases} x & \text{if } x > 0, \\ ax & \text{otherwise} \end{cases} \tag{1}$$

where x represents the outcome of the previous convolution and a was set to 0.2. It was used over a ReLU just to allow the network to learn even for negative inputs. In the last layer, we used a Sigmoid activation unit, since we are dealing with a pixel-wise binary problem.

Batch Normalization. Whenever the statistics at test time differ from the ones found during training, batch normalization becomes problematic. In fact, this is the case when a model is trained in small retinal patches and at test time is applied to entire retinal images, whose statistics will be inevitably different. In preliminary experiments, we found that using batch normalization was indeed hurting the performance of the models, thus it was not considered in the final design.

Dropout. Turning off some computational connections along the network was useful to create more redundancies and thus obtain more robust models. We found it was also useful to apply dropout at the initial levels of the model, in order to add some noise to the initial representations.

Loss Function. Neural networks targeting binary segmentation problems usually minimize the Binary Cross Entropy (BCE) loss, a pixel-wise criterium that exponentially increases as the network becomes more confident when committing a mistake. Note however, that this loss is agnostic to class imbalance, thus it naturally biases models to be more confident identifying the most common class, which in our case, is the background. We are interested in alleviating this effect, in order to obtain models with good sensitivity and that do not simply ignore narrow vessels. Weighting differently each class is an option we consider for reaching fairer models. Furthermore, we used the recently proposed focal loss [10], an extension to the BCE loss that puts more focus in the misclassified examples:

$$FL(p) = -\Big(y \cdot \alpha (1-p)^\gamma \cdot \log(p) + (1-y) \cdot (1-\alpha) \cdot p^\gamma \cdot \log(1-p) \Big) \quad (2)$$

where $p \in [0,1]$ is the probability of class 1 (vessel) outputted by the network, $y \in \{0,1\}$ is the binary target variable, $\gamma \geq 0$ is a focusing parameter, and $\alpha \in [0,1]$ allows to give more weight to samples of a certain class. γ was set to 2 in this work. Even though the focal loss by itself is also agnostic to class imbalance, by performing hard training, it helps inducing the model to not ignore the potential hardest cases, such as small capillaries.

After all these considerations, architecture and hyper-parameter tuning was conducted (see Sect. 3.3). The final design we considered for segmenting vessels from raw color fundus images is represented in Fig. 2.

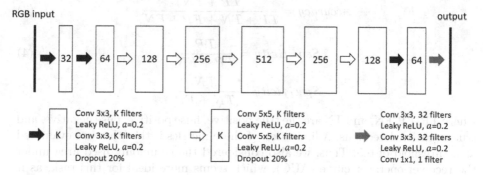

Fig. 2. Single-resolution fully convolutional network used in this work for segmenting vessels in raw fundus images.

3 Experiments and Results

The datasets and metrics used to assess the performance of our model will be briefly described here, then we provide details regarding how hyper-parameter tuning was conducted to obtain the final neural network design, and finally, we present and discuss the achieved results.

3.1   Datasets

Several public benchmarks of retinal vessel segmentation are available. In this paper, we conducted experiments in three of the most commonly used datasets among the literature works, which are the DRIVE [14], STARE [5], and CHASEDB1 [13] datasets.

The DRIVE database results from a diabetic retinopathy screening program in The Netherlands. Among the collected images, 40 photographs have been randomly selected, 7 of which showing signs of early diabetic retinopathy. The images were acquired using a Canon CR5 non-mydriatic 3CCD camera with a 45 degree field of view and later digitized to 584×565 pixels.

The STARE database comprises 20 retinal images captured by a TopCon TRV-50 fundus camera and digitized to 605×700 pixels. Half of the images are pathological.

Finally, the CHASEDB1 dataset includes retinal images of children from the Child Heart and Health Study in England. 28 fundus images of size 960×999 are available, with the particularity that central vessel reflex is abundant.

3.2   Model Evaluation

To evaluate how well a map of vessel probabilities fits the ground truth, we calculated the metrics that are commonly used in this task, which are accuracy, sensitivity, and specificity:

$$Accuracy = \frac{TP + TN}{TP + TN + FP + FN} \tag{3}$$

$$Sensitivity = \frac{TP}{TP + FN} \tag{4}$$

$$Specificity = \frac{TN}{TN + FP} \tag{5}$$

where TP, FP, FN, and TN are the true positive, false positive, false negative, and true negative detections. A limitation of these metrics is that they are evaluated at a threshold of 0.5. Thus, we also considered the commonly used area under the receiver-operator curve (AUC), which seems more ideal for this task, as it better depicts how well a method separates both classes.

3.3   Implementation Details

The architecture and hyper-parameters were tuned by randomly picking three images from DRIVE's training set for validation purposes and using the remaining ones to train varying model configurations, according to the considerations detailed in Sect. 2. Color images were solely normalized to the range $[0, 1]$. At each training epoch, 500 batches of N patches of size $M \times M$ were fed to the network. Patches were randomly extracted from images at valid positions, where valid means the center pixel belongs to the retinal fundus. Data augmentation was conducted via random transformations including vertical or horizontal flipping, and rotations in the range $[-\pi/2, \pi/2]$. We used the Adam optimizer with the parameters as provided in the original work [7], with the exception of the learning rate, which was initialized to 1e$-$4 and decreased to half every time the validation loss did not decrease for 10 epochs. A loss decrease was only considered if it surpassed the threshold of 1e$-$4. Early stopping occurred if there were 30 epochs without improvement. Our preliminary experiments achieved best performance in the validation set using the network design present in Fig. 2, and for $N = 16$ and $M = 64$, even though these hyper-parameters did not have a significant impact in the performance of the model.

We trained our final FCN design for 30 epochs. Starting from epoch 10, we performed linear learning rate decay by multiplying it by a constant of 0.75, and after epoch 20 the constant was changed to 0.5. Concerning DRIVE, we trained the network in the 20 images of the training set and evaluated it in the 20 images comprising the test set. Regarding STARE and CHASEDB1, datasets with few images and where a prior division does not exist, we followed the same approach of other researchers [11], which resorted to the *leave-one-out* validation.

3.4   Results and Discussion

The results obtained by conducting the described methodology in the referred databases are present in Table 1, along with the performance of state-of-the-art approaches. It is important to notice that the method of Azzopardi et al. [1], where a Combination of Shifted Filter Responses is used to enhance bar-like structures, belongs to the unsupervised category. Additionally, the work of Fraz et al. [3] uses traditional machine learning, where decision trees are ensembled to predict vessel probability from hand-designed features related with orientation and contrast. The rest of the methods included use deep learning techniques. Dasgupta and Singh [2] introduce a FCN design that takes preprocessed images, Fu et al. [4] couple a CNN with a Conditional Random Field to better model long-range interactions, Li et al. [9] perform patch-based segmentation using 3 fully connected layers having 400 neurons each and conduct pre-training by means of an autoencoder, and, finally, Liskowski and Krawiec [11] propose different variants of CNNs for conducting patch-based classification.

The analysis of the results shows that our FCN design is able to combine efficiency and strong predictive capabilities, even when using raw fundus images. By comparing the AUC of the methodologies, it is possible to conclude that the proposed methodology achieved superior performance in the DRIVE and CHASEDB1 databases. We believe that the performance in the STARE database was hindered due to the high variability of the raw color information among the images. This may indicate that preprocessing techniques leading to more uniform images are relevant in this dataset. Regarding DRIVE, we also tested $\alpha = 0.6$ (give more weight to the vessel class) to better show the compromises we can get between sensitivity and specificity. The results show that we were capable of reaching better compromises in terms of vessel detection and noise suppression in this dataset, as for similar specificity we achieved higher sensitivity than the

Table 1. Performance of the proposed methodology and state-of-the-art approaches in the DRIVE, STARE, and CHASEDB1 databases. Accuracy, sensitivity and specificity are abbreviated as acc, sen, and spe, respectively.

Method	DRIVE				STARE				CHASEDB1			
	AUC	acc	sen	spe	AUC	acc	sen	spe	AUC	acc	sen	spe
Azzopardi et al. [1]	96.1	94.4	76.6	98.1	95.6	95.0	77.2	97.0	94.9	93.9	75.8	95.9
Dasgupta and Singh [2]	97.4	95.3	76.9	98.0	–	–	–	–	–	–	–	–
Fraz et al. [3]	97.5	94.8	74.1	98.1	97.7	95.3	75.5	97.6	97.1	94.7	72.2	97.1
Fu et al. [4]	–	95.2	76.0	–	–	95.8	74.1	–	–	94.9	71.3	–
Li et al. [9]	97.4	95.3	75.7	98.2	98.8	96.3	77.3	98.4	97.2	95.8	75.1	97.9
Liskowski and Krawiec [11]												
balanc.-SP, $s = 3$	97.9	95.1	84.6	96.7	**99.3**	96.7	92.9	97.1	98.2	94.4	91.6	94.7
balanc.-SP, $s = 5$	97.9	95.3	81.5	97.5	**99.3**	97.0	90.8	97.7	98.4	95.8	87.9	96.7
no-pool-SP, $s = 5$	97.9	95.4	78.1	98.1	**99.3**	**97.3**	85.5	98.6	98.2	96.3	78.2	98.4
Proposed												
$\alpha = 0.5$	**98.2**	**95.6**	80.3	97.9	98.7	96.5	82.9	98.0	**98.6**	**96.5**	82.1	98.1
$\alpha = 0.6$	**98.2**	95.4	85.0	96.9	–	–	–	–	–	–	–	–

other methods. Note that by varying α, we could easily achieve models with very high sensitivity or specificity, thus we stress that it is the compromise that is relevant. Besides, this shows that the AUC metric is the most adequate to inspect the true model's capacity to distinguish both classes. We did not conduct this experiment in the other databases, since the number of models that are trained in a *leave-one-out* validation setting is very high. The use of focal loss over cross entropy lead to an improvement of 0.2% points regarding the AUC metric, when evaluating the system in the DRIVE database for $\alpha = 0.5$. The other metrics did not significantly change with this loss, meaning that it mostly induced the system to become slightly more confident on its predictions. Then, this seems to support that the single-resolution deep architecture was the main reason for our system to significantly outperform the FCN proposed in [2]. Figure 3 shows the best and worst predictions outputted by the proposed methodology for the considered databases, regarding AUC. It is possible to visualize that the model is able to cope with challenging imaging conditions, and even with the presence of severe pathology (4th row of Fig. 3).

Using a Nvidia GeForce GTX 1080 Ti GPU, it took us 2.1, 2.7, and 6.5 s to make a prediction for an image in DRIVE, STARE, and CHASEDB1 databases, respectively. The method of Liskowski and Krawiec [11] takes on average 92 s using the Nvidia GTX Titan GPU. Even though the GPUs are not identical, this strongly suggests that our method is significantly faster, thus being more adequate for real-time applications.

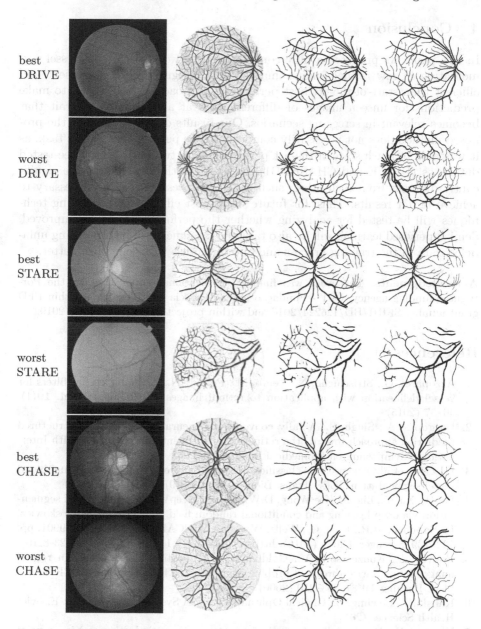

Fig. 3. Best and worst results for each database, concerning the AUC metric. From left to right: raw color fundus image, probability map outputted by the proposed methodology, segmentation obtained by thresholding probabilities at 0.5, and ground truth. (Color figure online)

4   Conclusion

In this paper we proposed a fully convolutional network to perform vessel segmentation in raw retinal fundus images. This design is more convenient and efficient than state-of-the-art best performing approaches, as it allows to make predictions for unseen images of different sizes at a single step, a trait that becomes relevant in screening scenarios. Our results demonstrate that the proposed method does not necessarily compromise the performance in this task, as it was able to reach state-of-the-art performance in two out of the three tested databases (DRIVE and CHASEDB1). In STARE, the raw images are significantly different from each other, such that preprocessing may be necessary to achieve better results. Thus, for future work, cost efficient preprocessing techniques will be tested for analyzing whether the performance can be improved. Semi-supervised learning will be also targeted, as a means of incorporating unlabeled data in the training process and obtain models that generalize better.

Acnowledgments. This work was financed by National Funds through the Portuguese funding agency, FCT - Fundação para a Ciência e a Tecnologia within PhD grant number SFRH/BD/126224/2016 and within project UID/EEA/50014/2019.

References

1. Azzopardi, G., Strisciuglio, N., Vento, M., Petkov, N.: Trainable cosfire filters for vessel delineation with application to retinal images. Med. Image Anal. **19**(1), 46–57 (2015)
2. Dasgupta, A., Singh, S.: A fully convolutional neural network based structured prediction approach towards the retinal vessel segmentation. In: IEEE 14th International Symposium on Biomedical Imaging, pp. 248–251. IEEE (2017)
3. Fraz, M., et al.: An ensemble classification-based approach applied to retinal blood vessel segmentation. IEEE Trans. Biomed. Eng. **59**(9), 2538–2548 (2012)
4. Fu, H., Xu, Y., Lin, S., Kee Wong, D.W., Liu, J.: DeepVessel: retinal vessel segmentation via deep learning and conditional random field. In: Ourselin, S., Joskowicz, L., Sabuncu, M.R., Unal, G., Wells, W. (eds.) MICCAI 2016. LNCS, vol. 9901, pp. 132–139. Springer, Cham (2016). https://doi.org/10.1007/978-3-319-46723-8_16
5. Hoover, A., Kouznetsova, V., Goldbaum, M.: Locating blood vessels in retinal images by piecewise threshold probing of a matched filter response. IEEE Trans. Med. Imaging **19**(3), 203–210 (2000)
6. Kanski, J., Bowling, B.: Clinical Ophthalmology: A Systematic Approach. Elsevier Health Sciences (2011)
7. Kingma, D., Ba, J.: Adam: a method for stochastic optimization. arXiv preprint arXiv:1412.6980 (2014)
8. Klonoff, D., Schwartz, D.: An economic analysis of interventions for diabetes. Diabetes Care **23**(3), 390–404 (2000)
9. Li, Q., Feng, B., Xie, L., Liang, P., Zhang, H., Wang, T.: A cross-modality learning approach for vessel segmentation in retinal images. IEEE Trans. Med. Imaging **35**(1), 109–118 (2016)
10. Lin, T., Goyal, P., Girshick, R., He, K., Dollár, P.: Focal loss for dense object detection. IEEE Trans. Pattern Anal. Mach. Intell. (2018)

11. Liskowski, P., Krawiec, K.: Segmenting retinal blood vessels with deep neural networks. IEEE Trans. Med. Imaging **35**(11), 2369–2380 (2016)
12. Marin, D., Aquino, A., Gegúndez-Arias, M., Bravo, J.: A new supervised method for blood vessel segmentation in retinal images by using gray-level and moment invariants-based features. IEEE Trans. Med. Imaging **30**(1), 146–158 (2011)
13. Owen, C., et al.: Measuring retinal vessel tortuosity in 10-year-old children: validation of the computer-assisted image analysis of the retina (CAIAR) program. Invest. Ophthalmol. Vis. Sci. **50**(5), 2004–2010 (2009)
14. Staal, J., Abràmoff, M., Niemeijer, M., Viergever, M., van Ginneken, B.: Ridge-based vessel segmentation in color images of the retina. IEEE Trans. Med. Imaging **23**(4), 501–509 (2004)
15. Yin, Y., Adel, M., Bourennane, S.: Retinal vessel segmentation using a probabilistic tracking method. Pattern Recogn. **45**(4), 1235–1244 (2012)
16. Zhang, B., Zhang, L., Zhang, L., Karray, F.: Retinal vessel extraction by matched filter with first-order derivative of Gaussian. Comput. Biol. Med. **40**(4), 438–445 (2010)

Tackling Partial Domain Adaptation
with Self-supervision

Silvia Bucci[1,2], Antonio D'Innocente[2,3], and Tatiana Tommasi[1(✉)]

[1] Politecnico di Torino, Turin, Italy
tatiana.tommasi@polito.it
[2] Istituto Italiano di Tecnologia, Genoa, Italy
{silvia.bucci,antonio.dinnocente}@iit.it
[3] Sapienza Università di Roma, Rome, Italy

Abstract. Domain adaptation approaches have shown promising results in reducing the marginal distribution difference among visual domains. They allow to train reliable models that work over datasets of different nature (photos, paintings *etc.*), but they still struggle when the domains do not share an identical label space. In the partial domain adaptation setting, where the target covers only a subset of the source classes, it is challenging to reduce the domain gap without incurring in negative transfer. Many solutions just keep the standard domain adaptation techniques by adding heuristic sample weighting strategies. In this work we show how the self-supervisory signal obtained from the spatial co-location of patches can be used to define a side task that supports adaptation regardless of the exact label sharing condition across domains. We build over a recent work that introduced a jigsaw puzzle task for domain generalization: we describe how to reformulate this approach for partial domain adaptation and we show how it boosts existing adaptive solutions when combined with them. The obtained experimental results on three datasets supports the effectiveness of our approach.

Keywords: Domain adaptation · Self-supervision · Multi-task learning

1 Introduction

Today the most popular synonym of *Artificial Intelligence* is *Deep Learning*: new convolutional neural network architectures constantly hit the headlines by improving the state of the art for a wide variety of machine learning problems and applications with impressive results. The large availability of annotated data, as well as the assumption of training and testing on the same domain and label set, are important ingredients of this success. However this closed set condition is not realistic and the learned models cannot be said fully *intelligent*. Indeed, when trying to summarize several definitions of intelligence from dictionaries, psychologists and computer scientists of the last fifty years, it turns out that all of them highlight as fundamental the ability to adapt and achieve goals in

© Springer Nature Switzerland AG 2019
E. Ricci et al. (Eds.): ICIAP 2019, LNCS 11752, pp. 70–81, 2019.
https://doi.org/10.1007/978-3-030-30645-8_7

a wide range of environments and conditions [13]. *Domain Adaptation* (DA) and *Domain Generalization* (DG) methods are trying to go over this issue and allow the application of deep learning models in the wild. Many DA and DG approaches have been developed for the object classification task to reduce the domain gap across samples obtained from different acquisition systems, different illumination conditions and visual styles, but most of them keep a strong control on the class set, supposing that the trained model will be deployed exactly on the same categories observed during training. When part of the source classes are missing at test time, those models show a drop in performance which indicates the effect of negative transfer in this *Partial Domain Adaptation* (PDA) setting. The culprit must be searched in the need of solving two challenging tasks at the same time: one that exploits all the available source labeled data to train a reliable classification model in the source domain and another that estimates and minimizes the marginal distribution difference between source and target, but disregards the potential presence of a conditional distribution shift. Very recently it has been shown that this second task may be substituted with self-supervised objectives which are agnostic with respect to the domain identity of each sample. In particular, [5] exploits image patch shuffling and reordering as a side task over multiple sources: it leverages the intrinsic regularity of the spatial co-location of patches and generalizes to new domains. This information appears also independent from the specific class label of each image, which makes it an interesting reference knowledge also when the class set of source and target are only partially overlapping. We dedicate this work to investigate how the jigsaw puzzle task of [5] performs in the PDA setting and how it can be reformulated to reduce the number of needed learning parameters. The results on three different datasets indicate that our approach outperforms several competitors whose adaptive solutions include specific strategies to down-weight the samples belonging to classes supposedly absent from the target. We also discuss how such a re-scaling process can be combined with the jigsaw puzzle obtaining further gains in performance.

2 Related Work

Closed Set Domain Adaptation. When the source and target data belongs to two different marginal distributions but the two domains share the same label set, it is relatively easy to train a source classifier that adapts to the target domain by adding extra conditions on the learned features. Several recent approaches minimize domain shift measures like the Maximum Mean Discrepancy [14–16,27], and the Wasserstein distance [8,12], or exploit other statistical moment matching constraints [20,30] or even introduce dedicated batch normalization layers in deep learning networks [6,18]. Another family of methods use adversarial losses that force the data to be indistinguishable in terms of their domain label [10,26]. Those solutions borrow the idea at the basis of Generative Adversarial Network (GAN, [11]) that can be also directly applied to match domains at pixel level [2,23,25]. All these methods exploit the availability of unsupervised target data at training time by leveraging on the domain identity of the samples. However, several other unsupervised models could be learned from those samples and used as extra regularization tools for the source model. A very common solution is that of measuring the source prediction uncertainty on the target data with an entropy loss which is minimized during training [15,17]. A recent stream of works has introduced techniques to extract self-supervisory signals from unlabeled data as the patch relative position [9,21], counting primitives [22], or image coloring [32]. They capture invariances and regularities that allow to train models useful as fine-tuning priors, and those information appear also independent from the specific visual domain of the data from which they are obtained. Indeed, [5] showed how shuffling and reordering image patches can be used as a side task to learn a robust model over multiple sources that generalizes even to unseen target samples.

Partial Domain Adaptation. The PDA setting relaxes the fully shared label space assumption among the domains and allows the target to cover only a subset of the source class set. Here it becomes important to adjust the adaptation process so that the samples with not shared labels would not influence the learning process. The first work which considered this setting focused on *localizing domain specific and generic image regions* [1]. The attention maps produced by this initial procedure are less sensitive to the difference in class set with respect to the standard domain classification procedure and allow to guide the training of a robust source classification model. Although suitable for robotics applications, this solution is insufficient when each domain has spatially diffused characteristics. In those cases the more commonly used PDA technique consists in adding a *re-weight source sample strategy* to a standard domain adaptation learning process. Both the Selective Adversarial Network (SAN, [3]) and the Partial Adversarial Domain Adaptation (PADA, [4]) approaches build over the domain-adversarial neural network architecture [10] and exploit the source classification model predictions on the target samples to evaluate a statistics on the class distribution. The estimated contribution of each source class either weights the class-specific domain classifiers [3], or re-scales the respective classification loss and a single overall domain classifier [4]. A different solution is proposed in [31], where each domain has its own feature extractor and the source sample weight is obtained from the domain recognition model rather than from the source classifier. An alternative view on the PDA problem is presented in two recent preprints [19,29]. The first work uses two separate deep classifiers to reduce the domain shift by enforcing a minimal inconsistency between their predictions on the target. Moreover the class-importance weight is formulated analogously to PADA, but averaging over the output of both the source classifiers. The second work does not attempt to aligning the whole domain distributions and focuses instead on matching the feature norm of source and target. This choice makes the proposed approach robust to negative transfer with good results in the PDA setting without any heuristic weighting mechanism.

Our work follow this research direction seeking a different solution with respect to the usual adversarial and sample weighting technique. We propose to leverage the self-supervised signal captured by a jigsaw puzzle task on the image patches as side objective to the classification model and show its effectiveness both alone and in combination with other more standard strategies.

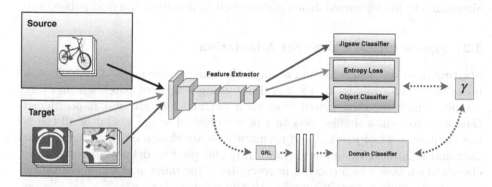

Fig. 1. Schematic representation of our SSPDA approach. All the parts in gray describe the main blocks of the network with the solid line arrows indicating the contribution of each group of training samples to the corresponding final tasks and related optimization objectives according to the assigned blue/green/black colors. The blocks in red illustrate the domain adversarial classifier with the gradient reversal layer (GRL) and source sample weighting procedure (weight γ) that can be added to SSPDA (refer to Sect. 3.4). (Color figure online)

3 Solving Jigsaw Puzzles for Partial Domain Adaptation

3.1 Problem Setting

Let us introduce the technical terminology for the PDA scenario. We have n^s annotated samples from a source domain $\mathcal{D}_s = \{(\mathbf{x}_i^s, \mathbf{y}_i^s)\}_{i=1}^{n^s}$, drawn from the distribution S, and n^t unlabeled examples of the target domain $\mathcal{D}_t = \{\mathbf{x}_j^t\}_{j=1}^{n^t}$ drawn from a different distribution T. The label space of the target domain is contained in that of the source domain $\mathcal{Y}_t \subseteq \mathcal{Y}_s$. Thus, besides dealing with the marginal shift $S \neq T$ as in standard unsupervised domain adaptation, it is necessary to take care of the difference in the label space which makes the problem even more challenging. If this information is neglected and the matching between the whole source and target data is forced, any adaptive method may incur in a degenerate case producing worse performance than its plain non-adaptive version. Still the objective remains that of learning both class discriminative and domain invariant feature models which can be formulated as a multi-task learning problem [7]. Instead of just focusing on the explicit reduction of the feature domain discrepancy, one could consider some inherent characteristics shared by any visual domain regardless of the assigned label and derive a learning problem to solve together with the main classification task. By leveraging the inductive bias of related objectives, multi-task learning regularizes the overall model and improves generalization having as an implicit consequence the reduction of the domain bias. This reasoning is at the basis of the recent work [5], which proposed to use jigsaw puzzle as a side task for closed set domain adaptation and generalization: the model named JiGen is described in details in the next subsection.

3.2   Jigsaw Puzzle Closed Set Adaptation

Starting from the n^s labeled and n^t unlabeled images, the method in [5] decomposes them according to an 3×3 grid obtaining 9 squared patches from every sample, which are then moved from their original location and re-positioned randomly to form a shuffled version $\mathbf{z}$ of the original image $\mathbf{x}$. Out of all the 9! possibilities, a set of $p = 1, \dots, P$ permutations are chosen on the basis of their maximal reciprocal Hamming distance [21] and used to define a jigsaw puzzle classification task which consists in recognizing the index p of the permutation used to scramble a certain sample. All the original $\{(\mathbf{x}_i^s, \mathbf{y}_i^s)\}_{i=1}^{n^s}$, $\{\mathbf{x}_j^t\}_{j=1}^{n^t}$ as well as the shuffled versions of the images $\{(\mathbf{z}_k^s, \mathbf{p}_k^s)\}_{k=1}^{K^s}$, $\{(\mathbf{z}_k^t, \mathbf{p}_k^t)\}_{k=1}^{K^t}$ are given as input to a multi-task deep network where the convolutional feature extraction backbone is indicated by G_f and is parametrized by θ_f, while the classifier G_c of the object labels and G_p of the permutation indices, are parametrized respectively by θ_c and θ_p. The source samples are involved both in the object classification and in the jigsaw puzzle classification task, while the unlabeled target samples deal only with the puzzle task. To further exploit the available target data, the uncertainty of the estimated prediction $\hat{\mathbf{y}}^t = G_c(G_f(\mathbf{x}^t))$ is evaluated through the entropy $H = -\sum_{l=1}^{|\mathcal{Y}_s|} \hat{y}_l^t \log \hat{y}_l^t$ and minimized to enforce the decision boundary to pass through low-density areas. Overall the end-to-end JiGen multi-task network is trained by optimizing the following objective

$$\arg \min_{\theta_f, \theta_c, \theta_p} \frac{1}{n^s} \sum_{i=1}^{n^s} \mathcal{L}_c(G_c(G_f(\mathbf{x}_i^s), y_i^s)) + \alpha_s \frac{1}{K^s} \sum_{k=1}^{K^s} \mathcal{L}_p(G_p(G_f(\mathbf{z}_k^s), p_k^s)) +$$

$$\eta \frac{1}{n^t} \sum_{j=1}^{n^t} H(G_c(G_f(\mathbf{x}_j^t))) + \alpha_t \frac{1}{K^t} \sum_{k=1}^{K^t} \mathcal{L}_p(G_p(G_f(\mathbf{z}_k^t), p_k^t)), \quad (1)$$

where $\mathcal{L}_c$ and $\mathcal{L}_p$ are cross entropy losses for both the object and puzzle classifiers. In the closed set scenario, the experimental evaluation of [5] showed that tuning two different hyperparameters α_s and α_t respectively for the source and target puzzle classification loss is beneficial with respect to just using a single value $\alpha = \alpha_s = \alpha_t$, while it is enough to assign a small value to η ($\sim 10^{-1}$).

3.3   Jigsaw Puzzle for Partial Domain Adaptation

The two $\mathcal{L}_p$ terms in (1) provide a domain shift reduction effect on the learned feature representation, however their co-presence seem redundant: indeed the features are already chosen to minimize the source classification loss and the self-supervised jigsaw puzzle task on the target back-propagates its effect directly on the learned features inducing a cross-domain adjustment. By following this logic, we decided to drop the source jigsaw puzzle term, which corresponds to setting $\alpha_s = 0$. This choice has a double positive effect: on one side it allows to reduce the number of hyper-parameters in the learning process leaving space for the introduction of other complementary learning conditions, on the other we let the self-supervised module focus only on the samples from the target without involving the extra classes of the source. In the following we indicate this approach as SSPDA: *Self-Supervised Partial Domain Adaptation*. A schematic illustration of the method is presented in Fig. 1.

3.4   Combining Self-Supervision with Other PDA Strategies

To further enforce the focus on the shared classes, SSPDA can be extended to integrate a weighting mechanism analogous to that presented in [4]. The source classification output on the target data are accumulated as follow $\gamma = \frac{1}{n^t} \sum_{j=1}^{n^t} \hat{\mathbf{y}}_j^t$ and normalized $\gamma \leftarrow \gamma / \max(\gamma)$, obtaining a $|\mathcal{Y}_t|$-dimensional vector that quantifies the contribution of each source class. Moreover, we can easily integrate a domain discriminator G_d with a gradient reversal layers as in [10], and adversarially maximize the related binary cross-entropy to increase the domain confusion, taking also into consideration the defined class weighting procedure for the source samples. In more formal terms, the final objective of our multi-task problem is

$$\arg\min_{\theta_f,\theta_c,\theta_p} \max_{\theta_d} \frac{1}{n^s} \sum_{i=1}^{n^s} \gamma_y \Big(\mathcal{L}_c(G_c(G_f(\mathbf{x}_i^s), y_i^s)) + \lambda \log(G_d(G_f(\mathbf{x}_i^s))) \Big) +$$

$$\frac{1}{n^t} \sum_{j=1}^{n^t} \gamma_y \Big(\eta H(G_c(G_f(\mathbf{x}_j^t))) + \lambda \log(1 - G_d(G_f(\mathbf{x}_j^t))) \Big) +$$

$$\alpha_t \frac{1}{K^t} \sum_{k=1}^{K^t} \mathcal{L}_p(G_p(G_f(\mathbf{z}_k^t), p_k^t)), \quad (2)$$

where λ is a hyper-parameter that adjusts the importance of the introduced domain discriminator. We adopted the same scheduling of [10] to update the value of λ, so that the importance of the domain discriminator increases with the training epochs, avoiding the noisy signal at the early stages of the learning procedure. When $\lambda = 0$ and $\gamma_y = 1/|\mathcal{Y}_s|$ we fall back to SSPDA.

4   Experiments

4.1   Datasets

We test our algorithm on three different Partial Domain Adaptation benchmarks following the setting previously used in [4].

Office-31 [24] is widely used in domain adaptation, it contains 4.652 images of 31 object categories common in office environments. Samples are drawn from three annotated distributions: Amazon (A), Webcam (W) and DSLR (D): we considered six different conditions by alternatively selecting one source domain and one target domain from AWD, and testing only 10 categories of the target which are those shared by Office-31 and Caltech-256.

Office-Home [28] is a domain adaptation dataset containing around 15,500 images organized in 65 categories of common home and office objects. It has four domains: Art (Ar), Clipart (Cl), Product(Pr) and Real world (Rw), and is more challenging compared to Office-31 due to strong domain shifts in distributions, class imbalances within the data and size variations of images. We considered 12 different settings by choosing source and target domain from the available domains, and removed from the target the last 40 classes in alphabetic order.

VisDA2017 is the dataset used in the 2017 Visual Domain Adaptation challenge (classification track). It has two domains, synthetic 2D object renderings and real images with a total of 208k images organized in 12 categories. In our experiments we focused on the synthetic-to-real shift, the same considered in the original challenge, but keeping only the first 6 categories of the target in alphabetic order. With respect to the other considered testbeds, VisDA2017 allow us to investigate our approach on a very large-scale sample size scenario.

4.2   Implementation Details

We implemented all our deep methods in PyTorch. Specifically the main backbone of our SSPDA network is a ResNet-50 pre-trained on ImageNet and corresponds to the feature extractor defined as G_f, while the specific object and puzzle classifiers G_c, G_p are implemented each by an ending fully connected layer. The domain classifier G_d is introduced by adding three fully connected layers after the last pooling layer of the main backbone, and using a sigmoid function for the last activation as in [10]. By training the network end-to-end we fine-tune all the feature layers, while G_c, G_p and G_d are learned from scratch. We train the model with backpropagation using SGD with momentum set at 0.9, weight decay 0.0005 and initial learning rate 0.0005. We use a batch size of 64 (32 source samples + 32 target samples) and, following [5], we shuffle the tiles of each input image with probability $1 - \beta$, with $\beta = 0.7$. Shuffled samples are only used for the auxiliary jigsaw task, therefore only unshuffled (original) samples are passed to G_d and G_c for domain and label predictions. The entropy weight η and jigsaw task weight α_t are set respectively to 0.2 and 1. Our data augmentation protocol is the same of [5].

Model Selection. As standard practice, we used 10% of the source training domain to define a validation set on which the model is evaluated after each epoch e. The obtained accuracy A_e is dynamically averaged with the value obtained at the previous epoch with $A_e \leftarrow wA_{e-1} + (1 - w)A_e$. The final model to apply on the target is chosen as the one producing the top accuracy over all the epochs $e = 1, \ldots, E$. We noticed that this procedure leads to a more reliable selection of the best trained model, preventing to choose one that might have overfitted on the validation set. For all our experiments we kept $w = 0.6$. We underline that this smoothing procedure was applied uniformly on all our experiments. Moreover the hyper-parameters of our model are the same for **all** the domain pairs within each dataset and also across all the datasets. In other words we did **not** select a tailored set of parameters for each sub-task of a certain dataset which could lead to further performance gains, a procedure used in previous works [3,4].

Table 1. Classification accuracy in the PDA setting defined on the Office-31 dataset with all the 31 classes used for each source domain, and a fixed set of 10 classes used for each target domain. The results are obtained using 10 random crop predictions on each target image and are averaged over three repetitions of each run.

	Office-31						Avg.
	A→W	D→W	W→D	A →D	D→A	W→A	
Resnet-50	75.37	94.13	98.84	79.19	81.28	85.49	85.73
DAN [14]	59.32	73.90	90.45	61.78	74.95	67.64	71.34
DANN [10]	75.56	96.27	98.73	81.53	82.78	86.12	86.50
ADDA [26]	75.67	95.38	99.85	83.41	83.62	84.25	87.03
RTN [15]	78.98	93.22	85.35	77.07	89.25	89.46	85.56
IWAN [31]	89.15	99.32	99.36	90.45	**95.62**	94.26	94.69
SAN [3]	93.90	99.32	99.36	94.27	94.15	88.73	94.96
PADA [4]	86.54	**99.32**	**100**	82.17	92.69	**95.41**	92.69
TWIN [19]	86.00	99.30	**100**	86.80	94.70	94.50	93.60
JiGen [5]	92.88	92.43	98.94	89.6	84.06	92.94	91.81
SSPDA	91.52	92.88	98.94	90.87	90.61	94.36	93.20
SSPDA-γ	99.32	94.69	99.36	96.39	86.36	94.22	95.06
SSPDA-PADA	**99.66**	94.46	99.57	**97.67**	87.33	94.26	**95.49**

4.3   Results of SSPDA

Here we present and discuss the obtained classification accuracy results on the three considered datasets: Office-31 in Table 1, Office-Home in Table 2 and VisDA in Table 3. Each table is organized in three horizontal blocks: the first one shows the results obtained with standard DA methods, the second block illustrates the performance with algorithms designed to deal with PDA and the third one includes the scores of JiGen and SSPDA. Only Table 1 has an extra fourth block that we will discuss in details in the following section.

Both JiGen and SSPDA exceed all plain DA methods and present accuracy value comparable to those of the PDA methods. In particular SSPDA is always

Table 2. Classification accuracy in the PDA setting defined on the Office-Home dataset with all the 65 classes used for each source domain, and a fixed set of 25 classes used for each target domain. The results are obtained by averaging over three repetitions of each run.

	Ar→Cl	Ar→Pr	Ar→Rw	Cl→Ar	Cl→Pr	Cl→Rw	Pr→Ar	Pr→Cl	Pr→Rw	Rw→Ar	Rw→Cl	Rw→Pr	Avg.
Resnet-50	38.57	60.78	75.21	39.94	48.12	52.90	49.68	30.91	70.79	65.38	41.79	70.42	53.71
DAN [14]	44.36	61.79	74.49	41.78	45.21	54.11	46.92	38.14	68.42	64.37	45.37	68.85	54.48
DANN [10]	44.89	54.06	68.97	36.27	34.34	45.22	44.08	38.03	68.69	52.98	34.68	46.50	47.39
RTN [15]	49.37	64.33	76.19	47.56	51.74	57.67	50.38	41.45	75.53	70.17	51.82	74.78	59.25
IWAN [31]	53.94	54.45	78.12	61.31	47.95	63.32	54.17	52.02	81.28	**76.46**	56.75	**82.90**	63.56
SAN [3]	44.42	68.68	74.60	67.49	64.99	**77.80**	59.78	44.72	80.07	72.18	50.21	78.66	65.30
PADA [4]	51.95	67.00	78.74	52.16	53.78	59.03	52.61	43.22	78.79	73.73	56.60	77.09	62.06
HAFN [29]	53.35	72.66	80.84	64.16	65.34	71.07	66.08	51.64	78.26	72.45	55.28	79.02	67.51
IAFN [29]	**58.93**	**76.25**	**81.42**	**70.43**	**72.97**	77.78	**72.36**	**55.34**	80.40	75.81	60.42	79.92	**71.83**
JiGen [5]	53.19	65.45	81.30	68.84	58.95	74.34	69.94	50.95	**85.38**	75.60	60.02	81.96	68.83
SSPDA	52.02	63.64	77.95	65.66	59.31	73.48	70.49	51.54	84.89	76.25	**60.74**	80.86	68.07

Table 3. Classification accuracy in the PDA setting defined on VisDA2017 dataset with all the 12 classes used for each source domain, and a fixed set of 6 classes used for each target domain. The results are obtained using 10 random crop predictions on each target image and are averaged over three repetitions of each run.

VisDA2017	
	Syn.→Real
Resnet-50	45.26
DAN [14]	47.60
DANN [10]	51.01
RTN [15]	50.04
PADA [4]	53.53
HAFN [29]	65.06
IAFN [29]	67.65
JiGen [5]	68.33
SSPDA	**68.89**

better than PADA [4] on average, and for both Office-Home and VisDA it also outperforms all the other competing PDA methods with the only exception of IAFN [29]. We highlight that this approach uses a competitive version of ResNet-50 as backbone, with extra bottleneck fully connected layers which add about 2 million parameters to the standard version of ResNet-50 that we adopted.

4.4   Results of SSPDA Combined with Other PDA Strategies

To analyze the combination of SSPDA with the standard PDA source re-weighting technique and the adversarial domain classifier, we extended the experiments on the Office-31 dataset. The bottom part of Table 1 reports the obtained results when we add the estimate of the target class statistics through the weight γ (SSPDA-γ) and when also the domain classifier is included in the network as in [4] (SSPDA-PADA). In the first case, estimating the target statistics helps

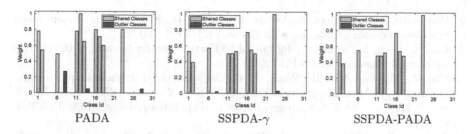

Fig. 2. Histogram showing the elements of the γ vector, corresponding to the class weight learned by PADA, SSPDA-γ and SSPDA-PADA for the A→W experiment.

the network to focus only on the shared categories, with an average accuracy improvement of two percentage points over the plain SSPDA. Moreover, since the technique to evaluate γ is the same used in [4], we can state that the advantage comes from a better alignment of the domain features, thus from the introduction of the self-supervised jigsaw task. Indeed, by comparing the γ values on the A→W domain shift we observe that SSPDA-γ is more precise in identifying the missing classes of the target (see Fig. 2). In the second case, since the produced features are already well aligned across domains, we fixed λ-max to 0.1 and observed a further small average improvement, with the largest advantage when the A domain is used as source. From the last bar plot on the right of Fig. 2 we also observe a further improvement in the identification of the missing target classes.

5   Conclusions

In this paper we discussed how the self-supervised jigsaw puzzle task can be used for domain adaptation in the challenging partial setting with some of the source classes missing in the target. Since the high-level knowledge captured by the spatial co-location of patches is unsupervised with respect to the image object content, this task can be applied on the unlabeled target samples and help to close the domain gap without suffering from negative transfer. Moreover we showed that the proposed solution can be seamlessly integrated with other existing partial domain adaptation methods and it contributes to a reliable identification of the categories absent in the target with a consequent further improvement in the recognition results. In the future we plan to further explore the jigsaw puzzle task also in the open-set scenario where the target contains new unknown classes with respect to the source.

References

1. Angeletti, G., Caputo, B., Tommasi, T.: Adaptive deep learning through visual domain localization. In: ICRA (2018)

2. Bousmalis, K., Silberman, N., Dohan, D., Erhan, D., Krishnan, D.: Unsupervised pixel-level domain adaptation with GANs. In: CVPR (2017)
3. Cao, Z., Long, M., Wang, J., Jordan, M.I.: Partial transfer learning with selective adversarial networks. In: CVPR (2018)
4. Cao, Z., Ma, L., Long, M., Wang, J.: Partial adversarial domain adaptation. In: Ferrari, V., Hebert, M., Sminchisescu, C., Weiss, Y. (eds.) ECCV 2018. LNCS, vol. 11212, pp. 139–155. Springer, Cham (2018). https://doi.org/10.1007/978-3-030-01237-3_9
5. Carlucci, F.M., D'Innocente, A., Bucci, S., Caputo, B., Tommasi, T.: Domain generalization by solving Jigsaw puzzles. In: CVPR (2019)
6. Carlucci, F.M., Porzi, L., Caputo, B., Ricci, E., Rota Bulò, S.: Autodial: automatic domain alignment layers. In: ICCV (2017)
7. Caruana, R.: Multitask learning. Mach. Learn. **28**(1), 41–75 (1997)
8. Damodaran, B.B., Kellenberger, B., Flamary, R., Tuia, D., Courty, N.: DeepJDOT: deep joint distribution optimal transport for unsupervised domain adaptation. In: Ferrari, V., Hebert, M., Sminchisescu, C., Weiss, Y. (eds.) ECCV 2018. LNCS, vol. 11208, pp. 467–483. Springer, Cham (2018). https://doi.org/10.1007/978-3-030-01225-0_28
9. Doersch, C., Gupta, A., Efros, A.A.: Unsupervised visual representation learning by context prediction. In: ICCV (2015)
10. Ganin, Y., et al.: Domain-adversarial training of neural networks. J. Mach. Learn. Res. **17**(1), 2096–2030 (2016)
11. Goodfellow, I., et al.: Generative adversarial nets. In: NIPS (2014)
12. Lee, C.Y., Batra, T., Baig, M.H., Ulbricht, D.: Sliced Wasserstein discrepancy for unsupervised domain adaptation. In: CVPR (2019)
13. Legg, S., Hutter, M.: A collection of definitions of intelligence. Preprint arXiv:0706.3639 (2007)
14. Long, M., Cao, Y., Wang, J., Jordan, M.I.: Learning transferable features with deep adaptation networks. In: ICML (2015)
15. Long, M., Zhu, H., Wang, J., Jordan, M.I.: Unsupervised domain adaptation with residual transfer networks. In: NIPS, pp. 136–144 (2016)
16. Long, M., Zhu, H., Wang, J., Jordan, M.I.: Deep transfer learning with joint adaptation networks. In: ICML (2017)
17. Luo, Z., Zou, Y., Hoffman, J., Fei-Fei, L.F.: Label efficient learning of transferable representations across domains and tasks. In: NIPS, pp. 165–177 (2017)
18. Mancini, M., Porzi, L., Rota Bulò, S., Caputo, B., Ricci, E.: Boosting domain adaptation by discovering latent domains. In: CVPR (2018)
19. Matsuura, T., Saito, K., Harada, T.: Twins: two weighted inconsistency-reduced networks for partial domain adaptation. Preprint arXiv:1812.07405 (2018)
20. Morerio, P., Cavazza, J., Murino, V.: Minimal-entropy correlation alignment for unsupervised deep domain adaptation. In: ICLR (2018)
21. Noroozi, M., Favaro, P.: Unsupervised learning of visual representations by solving Jigsaw puzzles. In: Leibe, B., Matas, J., Sebe, N., Welling, M. (eds.) ECCV 2016. LNCS, vol. 9910, pp. 69–84. Springer, Cham (2016). https://doi.org/10.1007/978-3-319-46466-4_5
22. Noroozi, M., Pirsiavash, H., Favaro, P.: Representation learning by learning to count. In: ICCV (2017)
23. Russo, P., Carlucci, F.M., Tommasi, T., Caputo, B.: From source to target and back: symmetric bi-directional adaptive GAN. In: CVPR (2018)

24. Saenko, K., Kulis, B., Fritz, M., Darrell, T.: Adapting visual category models to new domains. In: Daniilidis, K., Maragos, P., Paragios, N. (eds.) ECCV 2010. LNCS, vol. 6314, pp. 213–226. Springer, Heidelberg (2010). https://doi.org/10. 1007/978-3-642-15561-1_16
25. Sankaranarayanan, S., Balaji, Y., Castillo, C.D., Chellappa, R.: Generate to adapt: aligning domains using generative adversarial networks. In: CVPR (2018)
26. Tzeng, E., Hoffman, J., Darrell, T., Saenko, K.: Adversarial discriminative domain adaptation. In: CVPR (2017)
27. Tzeng, E., Hoffman, J., Zhang, N., Saenko, K., Darrell, T.: Deep domain confusion: maximizing for domain invariance. Preprint arXiv:1412.3474 (2014)
28. Venkateswara, H., Eusebio, J., Chakraborty, S., Panchanathan, S.: Deep hashing network for unsupervised domain adaptation. In: CVPR (2017)
29. Xu, R., Li, G., Yang, J., Lin, L.: Unsupervised domain adaptation: an adaptive feature norm approach. Preprint arXiv:1811.07456 (2018)
30. Zellinger, W., Grubinger, T., Lughofer, E., Natschläger, T., Saminger-Platz, S.: Central moment discrepancy (CMD) for domain-invariant representation learning. In: ICLR (2017)
31. Zhang, J., Ding, Z., Li, W., Ogunbona, P.: Importance weighted adversarial nets for partial domain adaptation. In: CVPR (2018)
32. Zhang, R., Isola, P., Efros, A.A.: Colorful image colorization. In: Leibe, B., Matas, J., Sebe, N., Welling, M. (eds.) ECCV 2016. LNCS, vol. 9907, pp. 649–666. Springer, Cham (2016). https://doi.org/10.1007/978-3-319-46487-9_40

On Image Enhancement for Unsupervised Image Description and Matching

Michela Lecca[1] , Alessandro Torresani[1,2](✉) , and Fabio Remondino[1]

[1] Fondazione Bruno Kessler - ICT, 38123 Trento, Italy
{lecca,atorresani,remondino}@fbk.eu
[2] Department of Computer Science, Università degli Studi di Trento,
38123 Trento, Italy

Abstract. An image enhancer improves the visibility and readability of the content of any input image by modifying one or more features related to vision perception. Its performance is usually assessed by quantifying and comparing the level of these features in the input and output images and/or with respect to a gold standard, often regardless of the application in which the enhancer is invoked. Here we provide an empirical evaluation of six image enhancers in the specific context of unsupervised image description and matching. To this purpose, we use each enhancer as pre-processing step of the well known algorithms SIFT and ORB, and we analyze on a public image dataset how the enhancement influence image retrieval. Our analysis shows that improving perceptual features like image brightness, contrast and regularity increases the accuracy of SIFT and ORB. More generally, our study provides a scheme to evaluate image enhancement from an application viewpoint, promoting an aware usage of the evaluated enhancers in a specific computer vision framework.

1 Introduction

An image enhancer is an algorithm that takes as input an image and processes one or more of its features in order to improve the visibility and readability of the visual content. These features usually reflect *perceptual* quality properties, i.e. visual characteristics that are highly significant for the human vision system, like image brightness and contrast, entropy of the color/intensity distribution, level of noise. The performance of an image enhancer is in general assessed by measuring the level of the modified perceptual properties and/or their variations between the input and output images or with respect to an *ideal* image, taken as gold-standard. Many measures have been designed so far to characterize perceptually image enhancement (see e.g. [9,11,19]), while to the best of our knowledge, few work has been done to investigate the impact of the perceptual changes in machine vision applications.

In this work we present an empirical evaluation of the image enhancement in the specific context of unsupervised image retrieval. In this framework, image enhancement is often needed to provide a rich and reliable description of the

© Springer Nature Switzerland AG 2019
E. Ricci et al. (Eds.): ICIAP 2019, LNCS 11752, pp. 82–92, 2019.
https://doi.org/10.1007/978-3-030-30645-8_8

visual content to be matched under many different circumstances, including difficult conditions due for instance to a wrong set-up of the camera parameters (e.g. low resolution or low exposure time) or to bad illumination (e.g low-light or back-light) that may adversely affect the detail visibility. In our study, we consider six image enhancers and two image retrieval algorithms. We use each enhancer as pre-processing step of each retrieval routine and we study how the enhancement affects the retrieval performance on a set of images with and without enhancement. To this purpose, we analyze how improving a set of perceptual features (i.e. image brightness, contrast, regularity and color distribution entropy) may influence the retrieval performance that is here measured in terms of number of image descriptors, correct matches and their spatial distribution, and retrieval dissimilarity score.

The enhancers considered here have been chosen among many others available in the literature since they are representative of three different methodologies: statistical local or global analysis (histogram equalization (HE) and contrast-limited adaptive histogram equalization (CLAHE)), spatial color processing with random or deterministic feature sampling (the Milano Retinex algorithms Light-RSR [4] and STAR [13]), and reflectance/illuminance image decomposition in constrained domains (LIME [8] and NPEA [20]).

The image description and matching algorithms used here are SIFT [14] and ORB [5], two well known and widely employed methods that, just because based on key-point extraction, require a good visibility of the image details.

We conducted our empirical analysis on the dataset MEXICO recently published on the net [3]. This dataset consists of 40 scenes of real-world indoor and outdoor environments characterized by issues challenging for both the enhancement and retrieval tasks, like the co-existence of dark and bright regions at different proportions, back-light, shadows, chromatic dominants of the illuminant, presence regions with different granularity, from uniform to highly textured.

Our study entails the following contributions: (1) it shows that image retrieval benefits from image enhancement, that enables a richer and more uniform description and matching; (2) it provides a general scheme to evaluate and characterize any image enhancer from an application viewpoint; (3) it promotes an aware use of enhancement techniques in the important field of image description and comparison; (4) finally, since carried out on a public image dataset, it enables further comparison with other methods.

2   Evaluated Algorithms for Image Enhancement

In this Section we briefly describe the six image enhancers considered in our empirical analysis. In the following, we grouped them in three classes upon the methodology and the assumptions they use.

Statistic-Based Image Enhancers - The histogram equalization (HE) and the contrast-limited adaptive histogram equalization (CLAHE) enhance any input image by stretching the probability density functions of one or more image components in a given color space. In the RGB space, considered here, HE processes the R, G, B channels separately and adjusts the channel intensities to flatten as much as possible the intensity histogram. To this purpose, HE maps any intensity value k of the channel I to the value $T(k)$ given by:

$$T(k) = floor\left(255\sum_{i=0}^{k} h(i)\right),\qquad(1)$$

where function $floor$ rounds its argument to the nearest greatest integer value and h is the histogram of I normalized tp sum up to 1. CLAHE is similar to HE, but works on a set of image patches by redistributing their pixel intensities so that their histogram bins do not exceed a pre-defined threshold (called *clip limit*) that prevents the over-enhancement of uniform image areas.

Retinex Inspired Image Enhancers - Milano Retinexes [17] are spatial color algorithms derived by Retinex theory [12] and thus related to human color vision. They enhance any real-world image by processing spatial and visual features extracted independently from each color channel, according to this equation:

$$L(x) = \frac{I(x)}{w(x)},\qquad(2)$$

where L is the so-called *lightness*, i.e. the enhanced version of the channel I, x is an image pixel and $w(x) \in (0, +\infty)$ is an intensity level named *local reference white at* x. The value of $w(x)$ is computed by processing a set of intensities (in some implementations along with other features) sampled from a neighborhood $N(x)$ of x. Milano Retinexes provide different levels of image enhancement, since the value of $L(x)$ depends on the spatial sampling of $N(x)$, on the features selected from $N(x)$ and on the mathematical expression of $w(x)$. Here we consider Light-RSR [4] and STAR [13] for their computational efficiency.

For each pixel x, Light-RSR samples $N(x)$ by a random spray, i.e. by a set of m pixels randomly selected with radial density around x. The value $L(x)$ is obtained by dividing the intensity $I(x)$ by the maximum intensity over the spray and by smoothing and blurring the result in order to reduce the chromatic noise due to the random sampling.

STAR extracts the features contributing to $w(x)$ from M regions $R_1,\ldots,R_M$ obtained by segmenting I with [7]. Precisely, from each segment R_i, STAR selects the maximum intensity $I(R_i)$ and the set $S(R_i)$ of pixels which are most internal to R_i. For any $x \in R_i$, STAR computes the mean value $u(x)$ of the intensities $I(R_j) > I(x)$, each of them weighted by a function inversely proportional to the minimum Euclidean distance between $S(R_i)$ and $S(R_j)$. The value $w(x)$ is obtained by dividing $u(x)$ by the sum of the weights contributing to $w(x)$.

Image Enhancers Based on Illuminant Estimation - Both the algorithms NPEA [20] and LIME [8] rely on the image formation model that represents the color image I as the product of the reflectance $\mathcal{R}$ of the materials depicted in the scene and the illumination $\mathcal{I}$. Precisely, for any pixel x of I,

$$I(x) = \mathcal{R}(x)\mathcal{I}(x).\qquad(3)$$

In this model, $\mathcal{I}$ and $\mathcal{R}$ express respectively the low- and the high- frequencies of the image. Discounting $\mathcal{I}$ from I allows to retain significant image details while smoothing unessential details, therefore it is a way to enhance the image. NPEA and LIME are grounded on this principle. They estimate $\mathcal{I}$ in a *constrained* domain, since in general the computation of $\mathcal{I}$ and $\mathcal{R}$ from I is an ill-posed problem. Both NPEA and LIME start from a coarse estimate of $\mathcal{I}$ as the maximum intensity over the color channels, then they refine this estimation according to different assumptions. Precisely, NPEA hypotheses that the reflectance is limited to a specific range and that the local relative order of the image intensities (i.e. the *image naturalness*) slightly changes over adjacent regions. LIME assumes the dark prior channel hypothesis [10] along with slight variations of the illuminant over the image. In addition, LIME imposes the fidelity between the coarse and the final estimation of $\mathcal{I}$. In NPEA, the enhanced image E is obtained as the product $E(x) = \mathcal{R}_e(x)\sigma(\mathcal{I}_e)$ where $\mathcal{R}_e$ is an estimate of $\mathcal{R}$ obtained by dividing I by the estimate $\mathcal{I}_e$ of $\mathcal{I}$ and σ is a smoothing function introduced to preserve image naturalness. In LIME, no reflectance is estimated, and E is computed from Eq. (3) by as the pixel-wise ratio between I by the estimated illumination $\mathcal{I}$. Of course, division by zero is always prevented.

3   Evaluated Methods for Unsupervised Image Description and Matching

This section describes the main principles and characteristics of SIFT [14] and ORB [5]. The goal of these algorithms is to match the content of a set of images to identify the common image regions. This is achieved in two phases: (a) *feature extraction*, i.e. identification of salient and locally distinguishable regions of the image, called key-points; (b) *feature description*, i.e. the computation and matching of the descriptors, which are discrete representations summarising the local structure around the detected key-points. The descriptors, in order to be effective, should be invariant to variations such as rotating, scaling and re-lighting.

Scale Invariant Feature Transform (SIFT) - Given an image I, SIFT builds up a pyramid structure whose base level contains the image I at full resolution, while the higher levels contain versions of I sequentially down-sampled. SIFT smooths each down-sampled version I_l of I by n Gaussian filters with increasing variance and computes the so-called *differences of Gaussians*, which encode the pixel-wise differences between the $n-1$ pairs of subsequent Gaussian smoothed versions of I_l. The key-points are defined as the corners corresponding to local maxima of the differences of the Gaussians within the pyramid. Every key-point is then identified by the quadruple $<p, s, r, f>$, where p is the key-point position in I, s is the scale (pyramid level), r is the orientation and f is the descriptor, which is a vector of 128 elements encoding the distribution of the orientation of the image gradients in the 16×16 window $W(x)$ centered at p. To make f invariant to rotations, the dominant orientation of the gradients in $W(x)$ is computed and used to rotate the image before computing f.

In SIFT, the dissimilarity measure between two key-points is defined as the L^2-distance between their descriptors.

Oriented FAST and Rotated BRIEF (ORB) - ORB is a combination of the feature extractor FAST [18] and the feature descriptor BRIEF [6] with some modifications which enable multi-scale matching and guarantee rotation invariance. In FAST, a pixel x is a key-point if its intensity exceeds by a pre-defined threshold the intensities of a set of pixels $y_1, \ldots, y_n$ equi-spaced on a circumference $\Gamma(x)$ centered at x. BRIEF associates to each FAST key-point x the n- dimensional vector whose i-th entry is zero if $I(x) < I(y_i)$ and one otherwise. To achieve invariance against re-scaling, ORB detects the FAST key-points (that are corners) at multiple scales. Moreover, for each key-point x, ORB defines the orientation $\theta(x)$ of x as the angle between x and the intensity weighted centroid of a circular region $C(x)$ around x. Finally, to grant robustness to rotation and noise, ORB computes the BRIEF descriptors of x on the patch $C(x)$ steered by $\theta(x)$ and smoothed by a Gaussian filter.

In ORB, the dissimilarity measure between two key-points is defined as the Hamming distance between their binary descriptors.

4   Evaluation

We assess the performance of each image enhancer by accounting for the variations of both the perceptual features and the retrieval accuracy.

Evaluation in Terms of Perceptual Changes - We quantify numerically the perceptual changes by four features, which reflect perceptual properties usually modified by an image enhancer: mean brightness, multi-resolution contrast [16], histogram flatness and NIQE [15].

Given a color image J, the mean brightness B of J is the mean value of the intensities of the mono-chromatic image $\mathcal{B}$, obtained by averaging pixel by pixel the channel intensities of J. The multi-resolution contrast $\mathcal{C}$ is the average of the mean contrasts of Z images $\mathcal{B}_1, \ldots, \mathcal{B}_Z$ obtained by half-scaling $\mathcal{B}$ sequentially. Here, the mean contrast of $\mathcal{B}_s$ $(s \in 1, \ldots, Z)$ is the average value of the pixel contrasts $C(\mathcal{B}_s(x))$ with $x \in \mathcal{B}_s$, where $C(\mathcal{B}_s(x))$ is the mean value of the differences $|\mathcal{B}_s(x) - \mathcal{B}_s(y)|$ with y belonging to a 3×3 window centered at x. The histogram flatness F measures the entropy of the probability density function h of $\mathcal{B}$ as the L^1 difference between h and an uniform probability density function. Finally, NIQE [15], here denoted by N, is a measure of *image naturalness*: it quantifies departures of J from image regularity, which is defined in terms of local second-order statistics.

Usually, an image enhancer increases the values of B and C, while decreases those of F and N, namely it makes the input image brighter and more contrasted, while it flattens its color distribution and smooths local irregularities. We observe that the exact amount of B, C, F and N and their variation after enhancement depend on the image at hand. In particular, for already clear images, the variation of B, C, F and N are negligible, while they are remarkable for unreadable images.

Evaluation in Terms of Image Description and Matching - We consider a dataset $\mathcal{D}$ with n indoor and outdoor scenes, each of them represented by m images differing to each other only for the exposure time under which they have been captured. We define the reference of each scene as the image with the lowest value of F: this criterion guarantees that the reference has a good detail visibility, being its brightness distribution the most uniform among those of that scene. We describe the references and the queries by SIFT and ORB with and without enhancement, then we match each input (enhanced, resp.) query Q against the corresponding input (enhanced, resp.) reference R. We evaluate the description and matching performance of SIFT and ORB by the following measures:

- the percentage N_d of images of $\mathcal{D}$ described by at least one key-point: if $N_d < 100\%$, then some images have no key-points;
- the numbers K_R and K_Q of key-points detected respectively on R and Q: in general, when $K_Q \ll K_R$, Q is poorly described with respect to R; when $K_R \ll K_Q$, the query is over-described and this is often due to a high percentage of noisy pixels that are wrongly detected as key-points; when $K_Q \simeq K_R$, R and Q are likely described similarly, but of course this does not grant that the key-points of R and Q are effectively similar;
- the number M_g of key-points of Q matching key-points of R with the same position on the image (*correct matches*);
- the number M_b of key-points of Q matching key-points of R with different position on the image (*wrong matches*);
- the *mean dissimilarity ratio* σ of Q, computed as follows: we match each key-point x of Q to the key-points of R, we order the key-points of R by their dissimilarity with x (from low to high) and we compute the ratio $\sigma(x)$ between the first and second dissimilarity scores in the ranked list of key-points of R; σ is the average of the ratios $\sigma(x)$ where x is a key-point of Q correctly matched; the lower σ, the higher the discrimination capability of the algorithm is;
- the flatness S of the spatial distribution of M_g over the image: to this purpose, we partition each query Q in four rectangular, non overlapping blocks Q_1, Q_2, Q_3, Q_4 whose top left corners are defined respectively by $(0, 0)$, $(0, W/2)$, $(H/2, 0)$, $(H/2, W/2)$, where H and W denote the height and width of Q; the flatter the distribution of the correct matches over these blocks, the more uniform the image description and matching and the higher the robustness of the retrieval algorithm to occlusions are.

The exact values of N_d, K_R, K_Q, M_g, M_b, σ depend on the image at hand: for instance, almost uniform images have a low number of key-points that do not vary by enhancement. Nevertheless, we expect that the use of an enhancer as pre-processing step of description and matching procedures increases the values of N_d, K_R, K_Q, M_g and σ, while decreases the value of S. As a drawback, in some cases, the enhancement may increase M_b since it may highlight noisy pixels.

Finally, we also report the retrieval performance of SIFT and ORB obtained by comparing the input (enhanced, resp.) queries versus the input (enhanced, resp.) references without the constraint on the spatial correspondence between query and reference key-points.

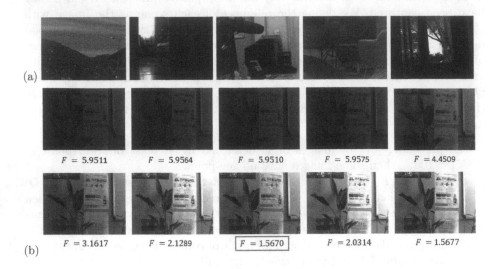

(a)

$F = 5.9511$ $F = 5.9564$ $F = 5.9510$ $F = 5.9575$ $F = 4.4509$

$F = 3.1617$ $F = 2.1289$ $\boxed{F = 1.5670}$ $F = 2.0314$ $F = 1.5677$

(b)

Fig. 1. (a) Some scenes from MEXICO. (b) A scene from MEXICO taken with increasing exposure times and the corresponding values of F. The lowest value of F (in the red box) identifies the reference image of this scene. (Color figure online)

5   Experiments, Results and Conclusions

In our test we employed the dataset MEXICO (Multi-Exposure Image COllection) [3], which consists of 40 scenes of indoor and outdoor environments captured by the FLIR camera [1] and each represented by 10 images acquired with increasing exposure time, ranging from 3 to 30 ms with regular steps of 3 ms (see Fig. 1). In all these images, the blocks Q_i's are not uniform. As already mentioned in Sect. 1, these scenes present challenging issues for image enhancement, description and matching, like dark and bright regions at different proportions, surfaces differently textured, several light conditions, including shadows, color cast, back-light. The parameters of STAR, LIME and NPEA are set as in their original paper, the clip limit of CLAHE is 8, and the number of spray pixels of Light-RSR is 250. We exploit the ORB and SIFT C++ routines included in OpenCV library [2]. We notify that the implementation of ORB sets to 500 the maximum number of key-points to be extracted from any image.

Figure 2 reports the distributions of the perceptual features B, C, F, N for the MEXICO images. By analyzing their joint distributions, we observed that too low and too high values of B, reported on very dark and saturated image regions, correspond to low values of C (i.e. low visibility of the details) and high values of F and N (i.e. poorly readable image content and noise). Table 1(a)

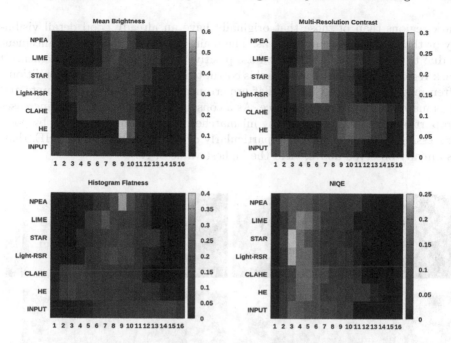

Fig. 2. Distributions (with 16 bins on the x-axis) of the perceptual features of MEX-ICO.

shows the mean values of B, C, F, N broken down by enhancers. On average, all the enhancers we considered increase the values of B and C, while decrease those of F. The mean value of N obtained on the MEXICO pictures without enhancement (case 'INPUT') is smaller than that output by all the enhancers, except for HE and CLAHE that generally tend to over-enhance the images and in this way introduce irregularities and emphasize noise.

For all the cases considered here, both SIFT and ORB described the references of MEXICO by at least one key-point, i.e. for the references $N_d = 100\%$. When no enhancement is used, both ORB and SIFT return a value of N_d smaller than 100%, meaning that no key-points have been detected on some queries (see Fig. 3, left for an example). Precisely, ORB and SIFT cannot describe the 13.89% and the 14.17% of the queries. On the contrary, all the enhanced queries are described by at least one key-point (i.e. $N_d = 100\%$), with K_Q ranging over [183, 500] for ORB and over [28, 7142] for SIFT.

Increasing the contrast is the key-point to improve the performance of ORB and SIFT, since these algorithms are based on the detection of key-points defined in terms of local intensity variations.

We observe that both too dark and saturated image areas present a low contrast value: while enhancers can improve the detail visibility in the dark regions, they cannot recover the visual signal in the saturated portions. Therefore, the values of K_R, K_Q, M_g and σ are higher on the enhanced versions of the queries that originally have been acquired with low exposure time or display dark regions than of those that originally have an already good detail visibility or that contains saturated areas. The main drawback of image enhancement is due to the generation of many false positive key-points: the enhancement of dark regions where the visual signal is corrupted due to difficult light conditions, often magnify also noisy pixels that are erroneously detected as key-points and thus matched against the reference. As a consequence, the value of M_b increases proportionally to K_Q, determining mismatches that should be removed by post-processing. This phenomenon is particularly evident for HE and CLAHE, that, as already observed above, yield the highest value of N.

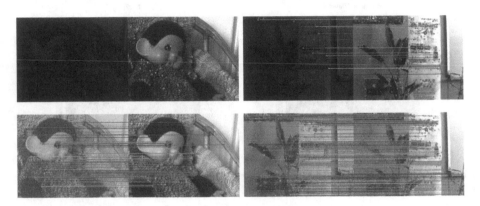

Fig. 3. On top: examples of key-point matching between a query and its reference by ORB (left) and SIFT (right) without enhancement. No key-points are detected on left, while the key-points detected on right are not uniformly distributed over the images. On bottom: key-point matching by ORB (left) and SIFT (right) on the images on top enhanced by STAR: the key-points have been uniformly detected over the images.

The spatial analysis of the distribution of M_g shows that the enhancement enables a more uniform image description, making the matching process more robust to occlusions with respect to the case 'INPUT' (see Fig. 3, right). In fact, as displayed in Tables 1(b) and (c), for all the enhancers, the values of S reported by ORB and SIFT are smaller than the case 'INPUT'. Finally, Tables 1(d) and (e) show that the description of the image is remarkably more uniform when an enhancer is applied. The best results are in general obtained by SIFT.

Additional tests were performed to measure the accuracy of the key-point matching when the queries are matched against all the references. To this purpose, for each image group e ('INPUT', 'HE', ..., 'NPEA') let Q_e and R_e be the sets of the queries and the references of e. We match each query $q_e \in Q_e$ against each reference $r_e \in R_e$, and we compute the dissimilarity between q_e and r_e as the mean value of the dissimilarities between the key-points of q_e matched with those of r_e, without the check on their spatial location. Table 1(f) shows the rate ρ of image retrieval on the different image groups, i.e. the number of queries assigned to the correct reference divided by the number of queries. The value of

ρ obtained on 'INPUT' is smaller than that achieved by enhancing the images, apart from 'NPEA' where noisy pixel adversely affect the SIFT performance. The bad results on 'INPUT' depend partly on the existence of dark images in which neither SIFT or ORB did not extract and match any feature.

We conclude that our experiments proved that modifying perceptual features like brightness, contrast, color distribution entropy and image regularity generally increases the description and matching performance since the enhancers allow to highlight the relevant details over the whole image. Future work will address the analysis of image enhancement in other machine vision applications.

Table 1. Evaluation summary

(a) Dataset Characterization

Algorithm	$\mathcal{B}$	$\mathcal{C}$	$F[\times 10^{-3}]$	$\mathcal{N}$
INPUT	51.97	9.08	5.36	4.20
HE	132.62	27.33	2.95	4.26
CLAHE	93.86	23.90	2.88	4.23
Light-RSR	102.65	15.92	3.80	3.94
STAR	121.56	14.97	4.11	3.81
LIME	128.07	17.62	3.68	4.02
NPEA	121.37	15.95	4.15	3.96

(b) Results of ORB

Algorithm	N_d	K_R	K_Q	M_g	M_b	σ	S
INPUT	86.11	469	272	133	37	0.51	0.78
HE	100	500	500	232	73	0.50	0.59
CLAHE	100	500	499	194	89	0.58	0.73
Light-RSR	100	456	487	237	79	0.52	0.71
STAR	100	499	481	233	75	0.52	0.65
LIME	100	499	493	204	93	0.58	0.66
NPEA	100	488	493	161	103	0.66	0.76

(c) Results of SIFT

Algorithm	N_d	K_R	K_Q	M_g	M_b	σ	S
INPUT	85.83	747	304	150	21	0.40	0.73
HE	100	2240	3741	545	333	0.54	0.45
CLAHE	100	3705	3259	657	402	0.59	0.48
Light-RSR	100	961	1169	349	82	0.46	0.54
STAR	100	1016	1123	365	88	0.47	0.51
LIME	100	1629	1415	483	145	0.54	0.49
NPEA	100	1625	2442	357	175	0.60	0.54

(d) Missed Block Matching [ORB]

Algorithm	Q_1	Q_2	Q_3	Q_4
INPUT	133	117	129	114
HE	10	23	6	31
CLAHE	28	34	26	56
Light-RSR	41	38	43	44
STAR	20	27	29	25
LIME	26	27	21	33
NPEA	42	36	47	70

(e) Missed Block Matching [SIFT]

Algorithm	Q_1	Q_2	Q_3	Q_4
INPUT	121	115	124	119
HE	1	9	0	3
CLAHE	1	13	4	7
Light-RSR	11	20	1	9
STAR	4	16	7	12
LIME	0	14	5	12
NPEA	2	12	9	11

(f) Retrieval Results

Algorithm	ρ_{ORB}	ρ_{SIFT}
INPUT	0.769	0.731
HE	0.992	0.767
CLAHE	0.986	0.983
Light-RSR	0.925	0.853
STAR	0.969	0.881
LIME	1.000	0.917
NPEA	0.856	0.639

Acknowledgements. The authors would like to thank Alessio Xompero (with Fondazione Bruno Kessler, IT) and (Queen Mary University, UK), for the fruitful discussions about this topic.

References

1. FLIR camera, datasheet. https://www.ptgrey.com/firefly-mv-03mp-color-usb-20-micron-mt9v022
2. OpenCV library. https://opencv.org/
3. MEXICO: Multi-exposure image collection (2019). https://tev.fbk.eu/technologies/image-enhancement-datasets-and-software
4. Banić, N., Lončarić, S.: Light random sprays Retinex: exploiting the noisy illumination estimation. IEEE Signal Process. Lett. **20**(12), 1240–1243 (2013)
5. Bradski, G., Konolige, K., Rabaud, V., Rublee, E.: ORB: an efficient alternative to SIFT or SURF. In: 2011 IEEE International Conference on Computer Vision (ICCV 2011) (ICCV), pp. 2564–2571, November 2011
6. Calonder, M., Lepetit, V., Ozuysal, M., Trzcinski, T., Strecha, C., Fua, P.: BRIEF: computing a local binary descriptor very fast. IEEE Trans. Pattern Anal. Mach. Intell. **34**(7), 1281–1298 (2012)
7. Felzenszwalb, P.F., Huttenlocher, D.P.: Efficient graph-based image segmentation. Int. J. Comput. Vis. **59**(2), 167–181 (2004)
8. Guo, X., Li, Y., Ling, H.: LIME: low-light image enhancement via illumination map estimation. IEEE Trans. Image Process. **26**(2), 982–993 (2017)
9. Lihuo, H., Fei, G., Weilong, H., Lei, H.: Objective image quality assessment: a survey. Int. J. Comput. Math. **91**(11), 2374–2388 (2014)
10. He, K., Sun, J., Tang, X.: Single image haze removal using dark channel prior. IEEE Trans. Pattern Anal. Mach. Intell. **33**(12), 2341–2353 (2011)
11. Kamble, V., Bhurchandi, K.M.: No-reference image quality assessment algorithms: a survey. Optik **126**(11), 1090–1097 (2015)
12. Land, E.H., McCann, J.J.: Lightness and Retinex theory. J. Opt. Soc. Am. **1**, 1–11 (1971)
13. Lecca, M.: STAR: a segmentation-based approximation of point-based sampling Milano Retinex for color image enhancement. IEEE Trans. Image Process. **27**(12), 5802–5812 (2018)
14. Lowe, D.G.: Distinctive image features from scale-invariant keypoints. Int. J. Comput. Vis. **60**(2), 91–110 (2004)
15. Mittal, A., Soundararajan, R., Bovik, A.C.: Making a completely blind image quality analyzer. IEEE Signal Process. Lett. **20**(3), 209–212 (2013)
16. Rizzi, A., Algeri, T., Medeghini, G., Marini, D.: A proposal for contrast measure in digital images. In: 2nd European Conference on Color in Graphics, Imaging, and Vision and Sixth International Symposium on Multispectral Color Science, CGIV 2004, Aachen, pp. 187–192 (2004)
17. Rizzi, A., Bonanomi, C.: Milano Retinex family. J. Electron. Imaging **26**(3), 031207 (2017)
18. Rosten, E., Drummond, T.: Machine learning for high-speed corner detection. In: Leonardis, A., Bischof, H., Pinz, A. (eds.) ECCV 2006. LNCS, vol. 3951, pp. 430–443. Springer, Heidelberg (2006). https://doi.org/10.1007/11744023_34
19. Phadikar, B.S., Maity, G.K., Phadikar, A.: Full reference image quality assessment: a survey. In: Bhattacharyya, S., Sen, S., Dutta, M., Biswas, P., Chattopadhyay, H. (eds.) Industry Interactive Innovations in Science, Engineering and Technology. LNNS, vol. 11, pp. 197–208. Springer, Singapore (2018). https://doi.org/10.1007/978-981-10-3953-9_19
20. Wang, S., Zheng, J., Hu, H.-M., Li, B.: Naturalness preserved enhancement algorithm for non-uniform illumination images. IEEE Trans. Image Process. **22**(9), 3538–3548 (2013)

A Gradient-Based Spatial Color Algorithm for Image Contrast Enhancement

Michela Lecca(✉)

Fondazione Bruno Kessler - ICT, 38123 Trento, Italy
lecca@fbk.eu

Abstract. This work presents GREAT-Mix, a novel contrast enhancer derived from the combination of the Retinex-inspired spatial color algorithms STRESS and GREAT. These algorithms improves the visibility of the details and content of any input image by adjusting its colors on the basis of local spatial and visual features processed channel by channel. Precisely, STRESS stretches the intensity $I(x)$ of each pixel x between two bounding values corresponding to the minimum and maximum intensities of sets of pixels randomly sampled with radial density around x, while GREAT re-scales $I(x)$ by a factor obtained by processing a set of edges deterministically selected over the image. GREAT-Mix implements the stretching function of STRESS but determines its bounding values from the edges sampled by GREAT. The result is a new spatial color algorithm that performs contrast enhancement similarly to STRESS, but that, thanks to the deterministic sampling of GREAT, grants robustness to noise and repeatability of the outcomes.

1 Introduction

A contrast enhancer is an algorithm that takes as input an image and increases the visibility of its details, making the image content more understandable for human observers while highlights visual cues relevant to machine vision tasks.

Among the many contrast enhancement techniques proposed in the literature (e.g. [2,3,5,22]), here we focus on the algorithms GREAT [15] and STRESS [6], that belong to the Milano Retinex (Mi-Retinex for short) family [24]. This latter is a set of spatial color algorithms grounded on the famous Retinex theory [8] and widely employed to enhance real-world images. Mi-Retinexes are of interest because the enhancement techniques they propose implement two important characteristics of the human color vision system, which are also at the basis of Retinex: (i) the independent analysis of the color components of the visual signal; (ii) the color adjustment based on local spatial and visual information. According to (i) and (ii), Mi-Retinexes process the R, G, B channel of any input image separately and they map the intensity $I(x)$ of each pixel x of the channel $I = R, G, B$ to a new value obtained by processing the visual features extracted from a set of pixels sampled around x. The result is a new image, named *lightness*,

© Springer Nature Switzerland AG 2019
E. Ricci et al. (Eds.): ICIAP 2019, LNCS 11752, pp. 93–103, 2019.
https://doi.org/10.1007/978-3-030-30645-8_9

which is an enhanced version of the input one: the lightness is usually brighter and more contrasted than the input one, while possible shadows and dominant cast due to the light are lowered. In case of real-world images, the Mi-Retinex lightness at any pixel x is usually obtained by dividing the channel intensity $I(x)$ by a strictly positive value $w_+(x) \geq I(x)$ called *local reference white* (LRW). Mi-Retinexes propose different spatial sampling procedures and equations for the LRW. For instance, the spatial sampling is performed by exploring the region around each pixel by Brownian paths in [19], by random paths proximate to edges in [13,20,25,26], by sets of unconnected pixels [16] chosen randomly in [12,14,21] while deterministically in [9,11,15]. Such paths and sets are the geometric support from which to extract the features that contribute to the LRW equation and that may include, in addition to the intensity, gradient and/or spatial information as e.g. in [9,11–15,25,26]. The different sampling schemes and the different equations of LRW yield to different enhancement levels and, in general, the use of one algorithm instead of another is driven by the tasks at the hand.

In this work, we present GREAT-Mix, a novel contrast enhancer derived from the combination of the Mi-Retinex algorithm GREAT [15] and the Mi-Retinex inspired algorithm STRESS [6]. GREAT proposes an interesting spatial sampling scheme that cuts down the complexity of the pixel-wise sampling process of many previous Mi-Retinexes. GREAT selects from each image channel I a set of edges with high gradient magnitude and uses them to compute pixel by pixel the LRW. The LRW at a pixel x is the average of the intensities exceeding $I(x)$ and belonging to the set of selected edges. To model the locality of the color adjustment and to account for the edge strength, in the LRW equation, each intensity is weighted by a term inversely proportional to the distance of the corresponding edge from x and directly proportional to its gradient magnitude. STRESS replaces the Mi-Retinex scaling function with a new operation: this stretches the intensity $I(x)$ between two bounding values computed by reworking the minimum and maximum intensities of random sets of pixels radially distributed around x [21]. The main disadvantage in using STRESS is due to the chromatic noise that random sampling may introduce in the enhanced image and that is particularly evident when few sprays are considered. The re-formulation of STRESS in to a population based model proposed in [4] (STRESS-P) avoids the random sampling and thus yields a noise-free lightness but at the prize of a much higher computational complexity and thus of a longer execution time.

The algorithm GREAT-Mix combines the sampling strategy of GREAT with the stretching function of STRESS, leading to a new contrast enhancer with a performance similar to that of STRESS but with the advantages of no chromatic noise generation, result repeatability and computational efficiency inherited from GREAT. The name 'GREAT-Mix' assembles the word 'GREAT' and the contraction of the words 'MInimum, maXimum' that refer to the bounding values of STRESS and at the same time it reminds that GREAT-Mix is obtained by 'mixing' the elements of other algorithms.

The paper outlines as follows: Sect. 2 describes GREAT, STRESS and STRESS-P; Sect. 3 explains GREAT-Mix; Sect. 4 reports the performance analysis of GREAT-Mix, while Sect. 5 draws conclusions and future work.

2 Related Works: GREAT and STRESS

The following notation will be used throughout the paper. Let $\overline{I}$, I and L be respectively a color image, a channel of $\overline{I}$ and the lightness of I. Here, I and L are represented as the functions $I, L : S \rightarrow (0, 1]$, where S is the support of I, i.e. the set of spatial coordinates of the pixels of I, and the intensity values of I and L are re-scaled to $(0, 1]$, with zero excluded to prevent division by zero.

2.1 GREAT

GREAT (from *Gradient RElevAnce for ReTinex*) enhances each image channel I by two steps:

1. **GREAT Global Processing:** GREAT extracts from I the set $\mathcal{R}$ of edges whose gradient magnitude exceed a pre-defined threshold $\tau \leq 1.0$, i.e.:

$$\mathcal{R} = \{y \in S : \| \nabla I(y) \| \geq \tau\}, \tag{1}$$

where ∇I indicates the gradient magnitude of I that here is normalized to range over $[0, 1]$.
Then, GREAT defines a function $M_+ : S \rightarrow (0, 1]$ that assigns to each pixel $y \in \mathcal{R}$ the maximum intensity value in a 3×3 window $N(y)$ centered at y, while sets to zero the values of $S \setminus \mathcal{R}$, i.e.:

$$M_+(y) = \begin{cases} \max\{I(u) : u \in N(y)\} & \forall\, y \in \mathcal{R} \\ 0 & \text{otherwise} \end{cases} \tag{2}$$

2. **GREAT Pixel-wise Processing:** for each $x \in S$, GREAT computes:
   - the set $P_+(x) = \{u \in S : M_+(u) > I(x)\}$.
   - the value $w_+(x) \in (0, +\infty)$ given by:

$$w_+(x) = \begin{cases} \dfrac{\sum_{u \in P_+(x)} (1-d(u,x))\|\nabla I(u)\| I(u)}{\sum_{u \in P_+(x)} (1-d(u,x))\|\nabla I(u)\|} & \text{if } P_+(x) \neq \emptyset \\ I(x) & \text{otherwise} \end{cases} \tag{3}$$

   where $d(u, x)$ indicates the Euclidean distance between u and x, divided by the length of the diagonal of the image support.
   - The value $L(x)$ is given by the ratio $L_{\text{GREAT}}(x) = \frac{I(x)}{w_+(x)}$.

The choice of strong edges (i.e. pixels with high gradient magnitude) as features relevant to the LRW is justified by the importance that strong contrasts play in human color vision [7]. The threshold τ determines the cardinality of $\mathcal{R}$, and thus the complexity of GREAT, which is $\mathcal{O}(|\mathcal{R}||I|)$. The work in [15] suggests to set τ unsupervisely as the mean value of the image gradient magnitude, i.e.:

$$\tau = \frac{1}{|S|} \sum_{y \in S} \| \nabla I(y) \| \tag{4}$$

An executable file of GREAT, running on Windows 10 × 64, is available at [10].

2.2 STRESS

For each channel I, STRESS (from *Spatio-Temporal Retinex-Inspired Envelopes with Stochastic Sampling*) defines two functions $E_m, E_M : S \to \mathbf{R}$ bounding I, i.e. for every $x \in S$, $E_m(x) \leq I(x) \leq E_M(x)$. The functions E_m and E_M are called respectively *the minimum and maximum envelopes* of I and they are computed pixel by pixel as follows. The neighborhood $N(x)$ of each pixel x. is sampled by n *random sprays* $S_1(x), \ldots, S_n(x)$, where, for any $k = 1, \ldots, K$, $S_k(x)$ is a set of p pixels randomly selected with radial density around x (see Fig. 1(b) and the work [21] where random sprays have been first introduced). The values $E_m(x)$ and $E_M(x)$ are computed by the following equations:

$$E_m(x) = I(x) - R(x)v(x), \quad E_M(x) = E_m(x) + R(x)$$

where $R(x) = \frac{1}{N}\sum_{k=1}^{n} R_k(x)$ and $v(x) = \frac{1}{N}\sum_{k=1}^{n} v_k(x)$, with

$$R_k(x) = E_{\max}^k(x) - E_{\min}^k(x), \quad v_k(x) = \begin{cases} \frac{1}{2} & \text{if } R_k(x) = 0 \\ \frac{I(x) - E_{\min}^k(x)}{R_k(x)} & \text{otherwise} \end{cases}$$

and $E_{\min}^k(x)$ and $E_{\max}^k(x)$ are respectively the minimum and maximum intensities of the spray $S_k(x)$:

$$E_{\min}^k(x) = \min\{I(y) : y \in S_k(x)\}, \quad E_{\max}^k(x) = \max\{I(y) : y \in S_k(x)\} \quad (5)$$

Finally, the lightness at x is given by:

$$L_{\text{STRESS}}(x) = \begin{cases} \frac{1}{2} & \text{if } E_M(x) = E_m(x) \\ \frac{I(x) - E_m(x)}{E_M(x) - E_m(x)} & \text{otherwise} \end{cases}$$

Figure 2(a) shows an example of envelopes computed on the red channel of the color image displayed in Fig. 1(a, left) along its version enhanced by STRESS (a, middle).

The computational complexity of STRESS is $\mathcal{O}(np)$, where p tunes the locality of the spatial processing, and n controls the level of noise due to the random sampling. This noise is the more evident the lower the number of sprays is. The values of p abd n are input user, generally fixed by a trial-and-error procedure as a compromise between enhancement level and image quality. Noise generation is completely avoided by STRESS-P [4], which is the exact mapping of STRESS into a population based model. Basically, STRESS-P estimates the lower and upper bounds of $I(x)$ as the probability to pick up the minimum and the maximum intensities from p points sampled from the probability density function $pdf(x)$ of the variable $I_x : S \setminus \{x\} \to (0,1]$ such that for any $y \in S \setminus \{x\}$, $I_y(x) = I(y)D^2/ \parallel x - y \parallel^2$ and D is the diagonal of S. It is to note that I_x is a spatially weighted version of the intensity I.

While STRESS-P grants robustness to chromatic noise, it requires long computational time, mainly due to the pixel-wise computation of the function pdf (see Sect. 4). The computational complexity of STRESS-P is $\mathcal{O}(|I|^2)$, where $|I|$ is the cardinality of S.

Fig. 1. From left to right: (a) an image from SCA-30 and its versions enhanced by STRESS and GREAT-Mix; and pixels sampled by (b) STRESS around the barycenter of the support and by (c) GREAT on the red, green and blue image channels. (Color figure online)

3   GREAT-Mix

GREAT-Mix adopts the 2-step computational scheme of GREAT, while replaces its intensity re-scaling with the stretching operation of STRESS. Precisely:

1. **GREAT-Mix Global Processing:** GREAT-Mix computes the set $\mathcal{R}$ in Eq. (1) and the map $\mathcal{M}_+$ in Eq. (8). Additionally it computes the map $\mathcal{M}_- : S \to (0, 1]$ such that

$$\mathcal{M}_-(y) = \begin{cases} \min\{I(u) : u \in N(y)\} & \forall\, y \in \mathcal{R} \\ 0 & \text{otherwise} \end{cases} \tag{6}$$

   where $N(y)$ is defined as in GREAT.
2. **GREAT-Mix Pixel-wise Processing:** GREAT-Mix computes

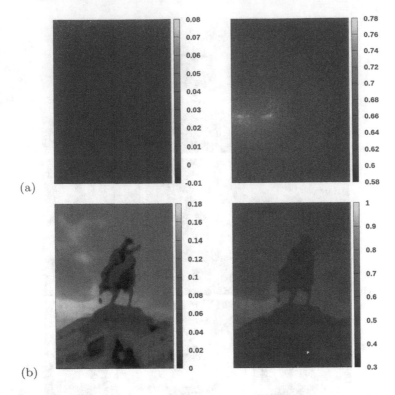

(a)

(b)

Fig. 2. Minimum and maximum envelopes of the red channel of Fig. 1 by (a) STRESS and (b) GREAT-Mix. (Color figure online)

- the set $P_+(x)$ and the value $w_+(x)$ as defined in the pixel-wise processing of GREAT;
- the set $P_-(x) = \{u \in S : \mathcal{M}_-(x) \le I(x)\}$;
- the value $w_-(x) \in (0, +\infty)$ such that

$$w_{\mathcal{M}-}(x) = \begin{cases} \frac{\sum_{u \in P_-(x)}(1-d(u,x))\|\nabla I(u)\|I(u)}{\sum_{u \in P_-(x)}(1-d(u,x))\|\nabla I(u)\|} & \text{if } P_-(x) \ne \emptyset \\ I(x) & \text{otherwise} \end{cases} \quad (7)$$

where $d(u, x)$ is the normalized Euclidean distance defined in GREAT.
- The value $L(x)$ output by GREAT-Mix is given by:

$$L_{\text{GREAT-Mix}}(x) = \begin{cases} \frac{I(x)-w_-(x)}{w_+(x)-w_-(x)} & \text{if } w_+(x) \ne w_-(x) \\ 1 & \text{otherwise} \end{cases} \quad (8)$$

The functions $w_+, w_- : S \to (0, 1]$ are the envelopes of GREAT-Mix: an example of w_+ and w_- is shown in Fig. 2(b) and refers to the red channel of the image in Fig. 1(a, left), whose GREAT enhancement is displayed in Fig. 1(a, right).

4   Experiments

The performance of GREAT-Mix has been evaluated on the public dataset SCA-30 [1]. SCA-30 includes 30 real-world images of indoor and outdoor environments captured with different devices and under different light conditions that make the images challenging to test spatial color algorithms. Some images of SCA-30 have been also employed to evaluate previous Mi-Retinexes, e.g. [9,11,16].

The evaluation reported here rely on the analysis of the following five features that are usually modified by enhancement:

1. Mean brightness B: the brightness $\mathcal{B}$ of a color image $\bar{I}$ is the gray-level image obtained by averaging pixel by pixel the color components of $\bar{I}$. B is the mean value of the intensities of $\mathcal{B}$. In general, an image with good detail visibility has a not too low nor too high value of B. In fact, very low (high, resp.) values of B correspond to dark (saturated, resp.) images, whose content is usually poorly understandable (lost, resp.);
2. Multi-resolution Contrast C [23] of $\mathcal{B}$: according to [23], the contrast $c(x)$ at a pixel x of $\mathcal{B}$ is the mean value of the L^1 distances between $\mathcal{B}(x)$ and the intensities values in a 3×3 window centered at x, while the contrast $C_\mathcal{B}$ of $\mathcal{B}$ is the average of the $c(x)$'s over the pixels of $\mathcal{B}$. The multi-resolution contrast C of $\mathcal{B}$ is the average of the contrasts of a set of images $\mathcal{B}_1 := \mathcal{B}, \ldots, \mathcal{B}_K$ ($K > 1$) where for each $1 = 2, \ldots, K$, $\mathcal{B}_i$ is the image $\mathcal{B}$ re-scaled by 2^{i-1}. The higher C, the higher visibility of the details of $\mathcal{B}$ and of $\bar{I}$ is;
3. Histogram Flatness F: this is a measure of the entropy of the distribution of the image brightness $\mathcal{B}$; precisely, F is the L^1 distance between the probability density function (pdf) of $\mathcal{B}$ and the uniform pdf defined over the variability range of $\mathcal{B}$ (that here is assumed to be $[0, 255]$). The pdf of $\mathcal{B}$ is computed by normalizing the histogram of to sum up to 1.0. Low (high, resp.) values of F are typical of images with a high (low, resp.) dynamic range and thus with good (poor, resp.) detail visibility;
4. Image Regularity Measures N_1 and N_2: NIQE (N_1) [18] and BRISQUE (N_2) [17] are perceptual metrics assessing the level of *naturalness* of a color image $\bar{I}$ (basically, its local smoothness) by comparing some second-order statistics of $\bar{I}$ against those of a training set. While the training set of NIQE contains also regular images, that of BRISQUE includes pictures classified by human observers as regular or irregular. The lower these metrics are, the higher the image naturalness is.

It is to note that the exact amount of B, C, F, N_1, N_2 depends on the visual characteristics of the image $\bar{I}$. In particular, for already clear (poor readable, resp.) images, the variations of these measures after enhancement will be negligible (remarkable, resp.). In general, a contrast enhancer is expected to increase the value of C and F and to maintain unchanged or to decrease those of N_1 and N_2.

Table 1 reports the mean value of B, C, F, N_1, N_2 for the original images of SCA-30 ('INPUT') and for their versions enhanced by GREAT-Mix, STRESS, STRESS-P and GREAT. In this experiments, the parameter τ of GREAT and

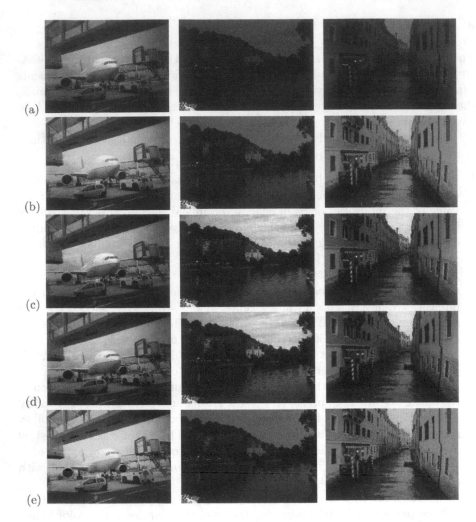

Fig. 3. Three images from SCA-30 (a) and their versions enhanced by GREAT-Mix (b), STRESS (c), STRESS-P (d) and GREAT (e).

GREAT-Mix has been set as in Eq. (4), while the parameters n and p of STRESS and STRESS-P are set respectively to 25 and 100. The lightness values, that in the previous Sections have been assumed to range over $(0, 1]$, are here re-scaled over $[0, 255]$.

On average, GREAT, STRESS, STRESS-P and GREAT-Mix report similar values of C, F, N_1 and N_2, while GREAT produces brighter images. This is mainly due to the stretching operation, that maps to zero the intensities equal to the lower bound and thus decreases B. It is also easy to prove that $L_{\text{GREAT}}(x) \geq L_i(x)$ for any $x \in S$ and $i = $ GREAT-Mix, STRESS. Both C and F are increased by enhancement, meaning that the algorithms considered

Table 1. Evaluation table

Algorithm	B	C	$F[\times 10^{-3}]$	N_1	N_2	T [sec]
INPUT	64.68	15.90	4.05	7.07	25.97	–
GREAT-Mix	79.13	19.49	3.53	7.16	25.62	31.47
STRESS $[(n,p)=(25, 100)]$	79.25	20.18	3.36	6.92	23.75	39.47
STRESS-P $[p=100]$	79.24	20.09	3.37	7.10	26.00	614.00
GREAT	95.60	20.13	3.24	7.23	25.24	31.40

here effectively improve the visibility of the image details while make the color distribution more uniform. The values of N_1 and N_2 after enhancement are on average slightly higher than those reported before enhancement: the distortions introduced by the enhancers are however exiguous and mainly due to an over-enhancement of noisy pixels located in low-light regions.

Table 1 also reports for each enhancer its average execution time per image (T). These data refer to a C++ implementation of the enhancers running on a standard PC with an Intel(R) Xeon(R) processor working at 3.70 GHz. Their comparison shows that the computational time of GREAT-Mix is very close to those of STRESS and GREAT, while it is remarkably smaller than that of STRESS-P: in this respect, GREAT-Mix bates STRESS-P since it provides similar, noise-free, repeatable results but with a much lower execution time. It is to note that no code optimization has been considered (e.g. Mi-Retinexes could be parallelized), thus the times reported in Table 1 may be further reduced. Nevertheless, such an optimization is out of the scope of this work.

Another advantage of GREAT-Mix versus STRESS and STRESS-P is the automatic estimation of its parameter τ, which is inherited from GREAT and that avoids the trial-and-error procedure used to set the values of n and p.

Figure 3 shows some examples of enhancement. While for the images on left and right, GREAT-Mix provides results close to those of STRESS and STRESS-P, for the image in the middle, the output of GREAT-Mix is more similar to that of GREAT than to those of STRESS and STRESS-P. This is due to the 'mix' of computational blocks of GREAT and STRESS performed by GREAT-Mix.

5   Conclusions

Originated from STRESS and GREAT, GREAT-Mix is a novel, noise-free, spatial color algorithm working as contrast enhancer. Future work will investigate possible applications of GREAT-Mix to cultural heritage. In this context, contrast enhancement is usually needed to study artworks that due to their location or structure cannot be captured by flash or cannot be well illuminated in all of their parts, making hard the work of archeologists and restorers (see Fig. 4). Contrast enhancement may contribute to cultural heritage studies and preservation by enabling the visual inspection and processing of digitalized artworks, that may help archeologists, restorers and scholars to plan their activities.

Fig. 4. Examples of contrast enhancement by GREAT-Mix applied to cultural heritage. (a) Three pictures showing from left to right: a particular of a paint in the cathedral of S. Vigilio in Trento, IT; a romanic arch and a mosaic in the Spazio Archeologico Sotterraneo del Sas (S.A.S.S.), Trento, IT; (b) Enhancement of the first two pictures in (a, left, middle) and of the particular of the mosaic highlighted in (a, right) by the red square. (Color figure online)

Acknowledgements. The author would like to thank Eleonora Grilli and Elisa Mariarosaria Farella from Fondazione Bruno Kessler, Trento (IT), for the discussion about contrast enhancement for cultural heritage and for the pictures of S.A.S.S. in Fig. 4.

References

1. SCA-30: Dataset for spatial color algorithms (2019). https://tev.fbk.eu/technologies/image-enhancement-datasets-and-software
2. Bedi, S.S., Khandelwal, R.: Various image enhancement techniques-a critical review. Int. J. Adv. Res. Comput. Commun. Eng. **2**(3) (2013)
3. Celebi, M.E., Lecca, M., Smolka, B.: Color Image and Video Enhancement, vol. 4. Springer, Cham (2015). https://doi.org/10.1007/978-3-319-09363-5
4. Gianini, G., Lecca, M., Rizzi, A.: A population based approach to point-sampling spatial color algorithms. J. Opt. Soc. Am. A **33**(12), 2396–2413 (2016)
5. Kaur, M., Kaur, J., Kaur, J.: Survey of contrast enhancement techniques based on histogram equalization. Int. J. Adv. Comput. Sci. Appl. **2**(7) (2011)
6. Kolas, O., Farup, I., Rizzi, A.: Spatio-temporal Retinex-inspired envelope with stochastic sampling: a framework for spatial color algorithms. J. Imaging Sci. Technol. **55** (2011)
7. Land, E.H.: The Retinex theory of color vision. Sci. Am. **237**(6), 108–128 (1977)
8. Land, E.H., McCann, J.J.: Lightness and Retinex theory. J. Opt. Soc. Am. **1**, 1–11 (1971)
9. Lecca, M.: STAR: a segmentation-based approximation of point-based sampling Milano Retinex for color image enhancement. IEEE Trans. Image Process. **27**(12), 5802–5812 (2018)

10. Lecca, M.: GREAT.exe (2019). https://drive.google.com/a/fbk.eu/file/d/1kmydflx00jse1sfyfnlqoam5puwnj6r2/view?usp=sharing
11. Lecca, M., Modena, C.M., Rizzi, A.: Using pixel intensity as a self-regulating threshold for deterministic image sampling in Milano Retinex: the T-Rex algorithm. J. Electron. Imaging **27**(1), 011005-1–011005-12 (2018)
12. Lecca, M., Rizzi, A.: Tuning the locality of filtering with a spatially weighted implementation of Random Spray Retinex. JOSA A **32**(10), 1876–1887 (2015)
13. Lecca, M., Rizzi, A., Gianini, G.: Energy-driven path search for Termite Retinex. JOSA A **33**(1), 31–39 (2016)
14. Lecca, M., Rizzi, A., Serapioni, R.P.: GRASS: a gradient-based random sampling scheme for Milano Retinex. IEEE Trans. Image Process. **26**(6), 2767–2780 (2017)
15. Lecca, M., Rizzi, A., Serapioni, R.P.: GREAT: a gradient-based color-sampling scheme for Retinex. JOSA A **34**(4), 513–522 (2017)
16. Lecca, M., Simone, G., Bonanomi, C., Rizzi, A.: Point-based spatial colour sampling in Milano-Retinex: a survey. IET Image Proc. **12**(6), 833–849 (2018)
17. Mittal, A., Moorthy, A.K., Bovik, A.C.: No-reference image quality assessment in the spatial domain. IEEE Trans. Image Process. **21**(12), 4695–4708 (2012)
18. Mittal, A., Soundararajan, R., Bovik, A.C.: Making a completely blind image quality analyzer. IEEE Signal Process. Lett. **20**(3), 209–212 (2013)
19. Montagna, R., Finlayson, G.D.: Constrained pseudo-Brownian motion and its application to image enhancement. J. Opt. Soc. Am. A **28**(8), 1677–1688 (2011)
20. Provenzi, E., De Carli, E., Rizzi, A., Marini, D.: Mathematical definition and analysis of the Retinex algorithm. J. Opt. Soc. Am. A: Opt. Image Sci. Vis. **22**(12), 2613–2621 (2005)
21. Provenzi, E., Fierro, M., Rizzi, A., De Carli, L., Gadia, D., Marini, D.: Random Spray Retinex: a new Retinex implementation to investigate the local properties of the model. Trans. Img. Proc. **16**(1), 162–171 (2007)
22. Rao, Y., Chen, L.: A survey of video enhancement techniques. J. Inf. Hiding Multimed. Signal Process. **3**(1), 71–99 (2012)
23. Rizzi, A., Algeri, T., Medeghini, G., Marini, D.: A proposal for contrast measure in digital images. In: Second European Conference on Color in Graphics, Imaging, and Vision and Sixth International Symposium on Multispectral Color Science, CGIV 2004, Aachen, pp. 187–192 (2004)
24. Rizzi, A., Bonanomi, C.: Milano Retinex family. J. Electron. Imaging **26**(3), 031207 (2017)
25. Simone, G., Audino, G., Farup, I., Albregtsen, F., Rizzi, A.: Termite Retinex: a new implementation based on a colony of intelligent agents. J. Electron. Imaging **23**(1) (2014)
26. Simone, G., Cordone, R., Serapioni, R.P., Lecca, M.: On edge-aware path-based color spatial sampling for Retinex: from Termite Retinex to Light Energy-driven Termite Retinex. J. Electron. Imaging **26**(3), 031203 (2017)

Sentiment Analysis from Images
of Natural Disasters

Syed Zohaib Hassan[1], Kashif Ahmad[2(✉)], Ala Al-Fuqaha[2], and Nicola Conci[1]

[1] University of Trento, Trento, Italy
syedzohaib.hassan@studenti.unitn.it, nicola.conci@unitn.it
[2] Hamad Bin Khalifa University, Doha, Qatar
{kahmad,aalfuqaha}@hbku.edu.qa

Abstract. Social media have been widely exploited to detect and gather relevant information about opinions and events. However, the relevance of the information is very subjective and rather depends on the application and the end-users. In this article, we tackle a specific facet of social media data processing, namely the sentiment analysis of disaster-related images by considering people's opinions, attitudes, feelings and emotions. We analyze how visual sentiment analysis can improve the results for the end-users/beneficiaries in terms of mining information from social media. We also identify the challenges and related applications, which could help defining a benchmark for future research efforts in visual sentiment analysis.

Keywords: Sentiment analysis · Natural disasters ·
Multi-label classification · CNNs · Social media

1 Introduction

Sudden and unexpected adverse events, such as floods and earthquakes, may not only damage the infrastructure but also have a significant impact on people's physical and mental health. In such events, an instant access to relevant information might help to identify and mitigate the damage. To this aim, information available on social networks can be utilized for the analysis of the potential impact of natural or man-made disasters on the environment and human lives [1].

Social media outlets along with other sources of information, such as satellite imagery and Geographic Information Systems (GIS), have been widely exploited to provide a better coverage of natural and man-made disasters [2,16]. The majority of the approaches rely on computer vision and machine learning techniques to automatically detect disasters, collect, classify, and summarize relevant information. However, the interpretation of *relevance* is very subjective and highly depends on the application framework and the end-users.

In this article, we analyze the problem from a different perspective and focus in particular on sentiment analysis of disaster-related images. Specifically, we

© Springer Nature Switzerland AG 2019
E. Ricci et al. (Eds.): ICIAP 2019, LNCS 11752, pp. 104–113, 2019.
https://doi.org/10.1007/978-3-030-30645-8_10

consider people's opinions, attitudes, feelings, and emotions toward the images related to the event by estimating the emotion/perceptual content evoked by a generic image [7,9,14]. We aim to explore and analyze how the visual sentiment analysis of such images can be utilized to provide more accurate description of adverse events, their evolution, and consequences. We believe that such analysis can serve as an effective tool to convey public sentiments around the world while reducing the bias of news organizations. This can lead to new beneficiaries beyond the general public (e.g., online news, humanitarian organizations, non-governmental organizations, etc.).

The concept of sentiment analysis has been utilized in Natural Language Processing (NLP) and in a wide range of application domains, such as education, entertainment, hosteling and other businesses [15]. On the other hand, Visual sentiment analysis is relatively new and less explored. A large portion of the literature on visual sentiment/emotion recognition relies on facial expressions [3], where face-close up images are analyzed to predict a person's emotions. More recently, the concept of emotion recognition has been extended to relatively more complex images having multiple objects and background details. Thanks to the recent advances in deep learning, encouraging results have been recently obtained [6,18].

In this article, we analyze the role of visual sentiment analysis in complex disaster-related images. To the best of our knowledge, no prior work analyzes disaster-related imagery from this prospective. We also identify the challenges and potential applications with the objective of setting a benchmark for future research on visual sentiment analysis.

The main contributions of this work can be summarized as follows:

- We extend the concept of visual sentiment analysis to disaster-related visual contents, and identify the associated challenges and potential applications.
- In order to analyze human's perception and sentiments about disasters, we conducted a crowd-sourcing study to obtain annotations for the experimental evaluation of the proposed visual sentiment analyzer.
- We propose a multi-label classification framework for sentiment analysis, which also helps in analyzing the correlation among sentiments/tags.
- Finally, we conduct experiments on a newly collected dataset to evaluate the performance of the proposed visual sentiment analyzer.

The rest of the paper is organized as follows: Sect. 2 provides detailed description of the related work; Sect. 3 describes the proposed methodology; Sect. 4 provides detailed description of the experimental setup, conducted experiments, and detailed analysis of the experimental results; Sect. 5 provides concluding remarks and identifies directions of future research.

2   Related Work

In contrast to other research domains, such as NLP, the concept of sentiment analysis is relatively new in visual content analysis. The research community has demonstrated an increasing interest in the topic and a variety of techniques have been proposed with particular focus on the feature extraction and classification strategies. The vast majority of the efforts in this regard aim to analyze and classify face-closeup images for different types of sentiments/emotions and expressions. Busso et al. [3] rely on facial expressions along with speech and other information in a multimodal framework. Several experiments have been conducted to analyze and compare the performance of different sources of information, individually and in different combination, in support of human emotions/sentiment recognition. A multimodal information based approach has also been proposed in [18], where facial expressions are jointly utilized with textual and audio features that are extracted from videos. Facial expressions are extracted through the Luxand FSDK 1.7[1] open source library along with GAVAM features [19]. Textual and audio features are extracted through the Sentic computing paradigm [4] and OpenEAR [8], respectively. Next, different feature and decision-level fusion methods are used to jointly exploit the visual, audio, and textual information for the task.

More recently, the concept of emotion/sentiment analysis has been extended to more complex images involving multiple objects and background details [6,7,12,22]. For instance, Wang et al. [23] rely on mid and low-level visual features along with textual information for sentiment analysis in social media images. Chen et al. [6] proposed DeepSentiBank, a deep convolutional neural network-based framework for sentiment analysis of social media images. To train the proposed deep model, around one million images with strong emotions have been collected from Flickr. In [22], Deep Coupled Adjective and Noun neural networks (DCAN), is proposed for sentiment analysis without the traditional Adjective Noun Pairs (ANP) labels. The framework is composed of three different networks, each aiming to solve a particular challenge associated with sentiment analysis. Some methods also utilized existing pre-trained models for sentiment analysis. For instance, Campose et al. [5] fine-tuned CaffeNet [11], on a newly collected dataset for sentiment analysis conducting experiments to analyze the relevance of the features extracted through different layers of the network. In [17] existing pre-trained CNN models are fine-tuned on a self-collected dataset. The dataset contains images from social media, which are annotated through a crowd-sourcing activity involving human annotators. Kim et al. [12] also rely on the transfer learning techniques for their proposed emotional machine. Object and scene-level information, extracted through deep models pre-trained on ImageNet and Places datasets, respectively, have been jointly utilized for this purpose. Color features have also been employed to perceive the underlying emotions.

3   Proposed Methodology

Figure 1 provides the block diagram of the framework implemented for visual sentiment analysis. As a first step, social media platforms are crawled for disaster-related images using different keywords (floods, hurricanes, wildfires, droughts,

---

[1] https://www.luxand.com/facesdk/.

landslides, earthquakes, etc.). The downloaded images are filtered manually and a selected subset of images are considered for the crowd-sourcing study in the second step where a large number of participants tagged the images. A CNN and a transfer learning method is used for multi-label classification to automatically assign sentiments/tags to images. In the next subsections, we provide a detailed description of the crowd-sourcing activity and the proposed visual deep sentiment analyzer.

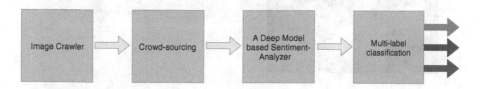

Fig. 1. Block diagram of the proposed framework for visual sentiment analysis.

3.1 The Crowd-Sourcing Study

In order to analyze human's perception and sentiments about disasters and how they perceive disaster-related images, we conducted a crowd-sourcing study. The study is carried out online through a web application specifically developed for the task, which was shared with participants including students from University of Trento (Italy), and UET Peshawar (Pakistan) as well as with other contacts with no scientific background. Figure 2 provides an illustration of the platform we used for the crowd-sourcing study. In the study, participants were provided with a disaster-related image, randomly selected from the pool of images, along with a set of associated tags. The participants were then asked to assign a number of suitable tags, which they felt relevant to the image. The participants were also encouraged to associate additional tags to the images, in case they felt that the provided tags were not relevant to the image.

One of the main challenges in the crowd-sourcing study was the selection of the tags/sentiments to be provided to the users. In the literature, sentiments are generally represented as *Positive, Negative* and *Neutral* [15]. However, considering the specific domain we are addressing (natural and man-made disasters) and the potential applications of the proposed system, we are also interested in tags/sentiments that are more specific to adverse events, such as pain, shock, and destruction, in addition to the three common tags. Consequently, we opted for a data-driven approach, by analyzing users' tags associated with disaster images crawled form social media outlets. Apart from the sentimental tags, such as *pain, shock* and *hope*, we also included some additional tags, such as *rescue* and *destruction*, which are closely associated with disasters and can be useful in different applications utilized by online news agencies, humanitarian, and non-governmental organizations (NGOs). The option for adding additional tags also helps to take the participants' viewpoints into account.

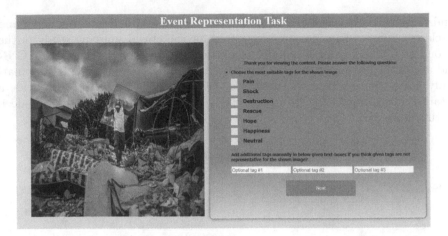

Fig. 2. Illustration of the platform used for the crowd-sourcing study. A disaster-related image and several tags are presented to the users for association. The users' are also encouraged to provide additional tags.

Table 1. Statistics of the crowd-sourcing study in terms of the total number of times each tags has been associated with images by the participants.

Sentiments/tags	Count
Destruction	871
Happiness	145
Hope	353
Neutral	214
Pain	454
Rescue	694
Shock	354

The crowd-sourcing activity was carried out on 400 images related to 6 different types of disasters: earthquakes, floods, droughts, landslides, thunderstorms, and wildfires. In total, we obtained 2,587 responses from the users, with an average of 6 users per image. We made sure to have at least 5 different users for each image. Table 1 provides the statistics of the crowd-sourcing study in terms of the total number of times each tag has been associated with images by the participants. As can be seen in Table 1, some tags, such as *destruction*, *rescue* and *pain*, are used more frequently compared to others.

During the analysis of the responses from the participants, we observed that certain tag pairs have been used to describe images. For instance, pain and destruction, hope and rescue, shock and pain, are used several times jointly. Similarly, shock, destruction and pain have been used jointly 59 times. The three tags: rescue, hope, and happiness, are also used often together. This correlation among the tag/sentiment pairs provides the foundation for our multi-label classification, as opposed to single-label multi-class classification, of the sentiments associated with disasters-related images. Figure 3 shows the number of times the sentiments/tags are used together by the participants in the crowd-sourcing activity. For final annotation, the decision is made on the basis of majority votes from the participants of the crowd-sourcing study.

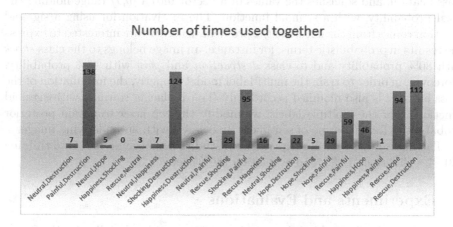

Fig. 3. Correlation of tag pairs: number of times different tag pairs used by the participants of the crowd-sourcing study to describe the same image.

3.2 The Visual Sentiment Analyzer

The proposed framework for visual sentiment analysis is inspired by the multi-label image classification framework[2] and is mainly based on a Convolutional Neural Network (CNN) and a transfer learning method, where the model pre-trained on ImageNet is fine-tuned for visual sentiment analysis. In this work, we analyze the performance of several deep models such as AlexNet [13], VggNet [20], ResNet [10] and Inception v-3 [21] as potential alternatives to be employed in the proposed visual sentiment analysis framework.

The multi-label classification strategy, which assigns multiple labels to an image, better suits our visual sentiment classification problem and is intended to show the correlation of different sentiments. In order for the network to fit the task of visual sentiment analysis, we introduced several changes to the model as will be described in the next paragraph.

---

[2] https://towardsdatascience.com/multi-label-image-classification-with-inception-net-cbb2ee538e30.

3.3 Experimental Setup

In order to fit the pre-trained model to multi-label classification, we create a ground truth vector containing all the labels associated with an image. We also made some modifications in the existing pre-trained Inception-v3 [21] model by extending the classification layer to support multi-label classification. To do so, we replaced the soft-max function, which is suitable for single-label multi-class classification, and squashes the values of a vector into a *[0,1]* range holding the total probability, with a sigmoid function. The motivation for using a sigmoid function comes from the nature of the problem, where we are interested to express the results in probabilistic terms; for instance, an image belongs to the class *shock* with 80% probability and to class *destruction* and *pain* with 40% probability. Moreover, in order to train the multi-label model properly, the formulation of the cross entropy is also modified accordingly (i.e., replacing softmax with sigmoid function). For the multiple labels, we modify the top layer to obtain posterior probabilities for each type of sentiment associated with an underlying image.

The dataset used for our experimental studies has been divided into training (60%), validation (10%), and evaluation (30%) sets.

4 Experiments and Evaluations

The basic motivation behind the experiments to provide a baseline for the future work in the domain. To this aim, we evaluate the proposed multi-label framework for visual sentiment analysis using several existing pre-trained state-of-the-art deep learning models including: AlexNet, VggNet, ResNet, and Inception v3. Table 2 provides the experimental results obtained using these deep models.

Table 2. Evaluation of the proposed visual sentiment analyzer with different deep learning models pre-trained on ImageNet.

Model	Accuracy (%)
AlexNet	79.69
VggNet	79.58
Inception-v3	80.70
ResNet	78.01

Considering the complexity of the task and the limited amount of training data, the obtained results are encouraging. Though there's no significant difference in the performance of the models, slightly better results are obtained with Inception-v3 models. Lowest accuracy has been observed for ResNet, but such reduction in the performance could be due to the size of the dataset used for the study.

In order to show the effectiveness of the proposed visual sentiment analyzer, we also provide some sample output images in Fig. 4, showing the output of the proposed visual sentiment analyzer in terms of the percentage/probabilities for each label. Table 3 provides the statistics for these samples in terms of the probability for each label and probabilities/percentages computed through human annotators. Due to space limitation, only four samples are provided in the paper to give an idea about the performance of the method. For this particular qualitative analysis, we converted the responses of the participants of the crowd sourcing study into percentages (i.e., the degree to which each image belongs to a particular label) for each label associated with each image. These percentages are different from the ground truth used during training and evaluation where images were assigned labels on a majority voting basis. For instance, the percentages based on the responses of the crowd sourcing study for the first image (leftmost in Fig. 4) are: *destruction* = 0.10, *happiness* = 0.0, *hope* = 0.10, *neutral* = 0.0, *pain* = 0.35, *rescue* = 0.30 and *shock* = 0.20 while the output of the proposed visual sentiment analyzer in terms of probabilities for each label/class are: *destruction* = 0.16, *happiness* = 0.04, *hope* = 0.06, *neutral* = 0.02, *pain* = 0.58, *rescue* = 0.28 and *shock* = 0.17. In most of the cases, the proposed model provides results that are similar to the percentages obtained from the users' responses, demonstrating the effectiveness of the proposed method.

Fig. 4. Some sample output of the proposed visual sentiment analyzer.

Table 3. Sample outputs in terms of ground truth obtained from users in terms of percentage in the crowd-sourcing study vis-a-vis predicted probabilities.

Image	Destruction		Happiness		Hope		Neutral		Pain		Rescue		Shock	
	GT	Pred.	GT	Pred.	GT	Pred.	GT	Pred.	GT	Pred.	GT	Pred.	GT	Pred.
1	0.10	0.16	0.0	0.04	0.1	0.06	0	0.027	0.35	0.58	0.30	0.28	0.20	0.17
2	0.24	0.24	0.0	0.05	0.0	0.08	0.34	0.36	0.429	0.44	0.514	0.59	0.20	0.33
3	0.167	0.23	0.0	0.05	0.10	0.13	0.16	0.17	0.46	0.59	0.33	0.26	0.0	0.13
4	0.10	0.18	0.0	0.03	0.09	0.05	0.20	0.26	0.0	0.33	0.72	0.72	0.0	0.20

5   Conclusions, Challenges and Future Work

In this paper, we addressed the challenging problem of visual sentiment analysis of disaster-related images obtained from social media. We analyzed how people respond to disasters and obtained their opinions, attitudes, feelings, and emotions toward the disaster-related images through a crowd-sourcing activity. We show that the visual sentiment analysis/emotions recognition, though a challenging task, can be carried out on more complex images using some deep learning techniques. We also identified the challenges and potential applications of this relatively new concept, which is intended to set a benchmark for future research in visual sentiment analysis.

Though the experimental results obtained during the initial experiments on the limited dataset are encouraging, the task is challenging and needs to be investigated in more details. Specifically, the reduced availability of suitable training and testing images is probably the biggest limitation. Since visual sentiment analysis aims to present human's perception of an entity, crowd-sourcing seems to be a valuable option to acquire training data for automatic analysis. In terms of visual features, we believe that object and scene-level features can play complementary roles in representing the images. Moreover, multi-modal analysis will further enhance the performances of the proposed sentiment analyzer. This suggests that within the domain of purely visual information, the conveyed information can differ, suggesting that the interpretation of the image is subject to change depending on the level of detail, the visual perspective, and the intensity of colors. We expect these elements to play a major role in the evolution of frameworks like the one we have presented, and when combined with additional media sources (e.g., audio, text, meta-data), can provide a well rounded perspective about the sentiments associated with a given event.

References

1. Ahmad, K., Pogorelov, K., Riegler, M., Conci, N., Halvorsen, P.: Social media and satellites. Multimed Tools Appl. **78**, 1–39 (2018)
2. Ahmad, K., et al.: Automatic detection of passable roads after floods in remote sensed and social media data. Signal Process.: Image Commun. **74**, 110–118 (2019)
3. Busso, C., et al.: Analysis of emotion recognition using facial expressions, speech and multimodal information. In: Proceedings of the 6th International Conference on Multimodal Interfaces, pp. 205–211. ACM (2004)
4. Cambria, E., Hussain, A., Havasi, C., Eckl, C.: Sentic computing: exploitation of common sense for the development of emotion-sensitive systems. In: Esposito, A., Campbell, N., Vogel, C., Hussain, A., Nijholt, A. (eds.) Development of Multimodal Interfaces: Active Listening and Synchrony. LNCS, vol. 5967, pp. 148–156. Springer, Heidelberg (2010). https://doi.org/10.1007/978-3-642-12397-9_12
5. Campos, V., Salvador, A., Giro-i Nieto, X., Jou, B.: Diving deep into sentiment: understanding fine-tuned CNNs for visual sentiment prediction. In: Proceedings of the 1st International Workshop on Affect & Sentiment in Multimedia, pp. 57–62. ACM (2015)
6. Chen, T., Borth, D., Darrell, T., Chang, S.F.: DeepSentiBank: visual sentiment concept classification with deep convolutional neural networks. arXiv preprint arXiv:1410.8586 (2014)
7. Constantin, M.G., Redi, M., Zen, G., Ionescu, B.: Computational understanding of visual interestingness beyond semantics: literature survey and analysis of covariates. ACM Comput. Surv. (CSUR) **52**(2), 25 (2019)

8. Eyben, F., Wöllmer, M., Schuller, B.: OpenEAR–introducing the Munich open-source emotion and affect recognition toolkit. In: 2009 3rd International Conference on Affective Computing and Intelligent Interaction and Workshops, pp. 1–6. IEEE (2009)

9. Gygli, M., Grabner, H., Riemenschneider, H., Nater, F., Van Gool, L.: The interestingness of images. In: Proceedings of the IEEE International Conference on Computer Vision, pp. 1633–1640 (2013)

10. He, K., Zhang, X., Ren, S., Sun, J.: Deep residual learning for image recognition. In: Proceedings of the IEEE Conference on Computer Vision and Pattern Recognition, pp. 770–778 (2016)

11. Jia, Y., et al.: Caffe: convolutional architecture for fast feature embedding. In: Proceedings of the 22nd ACM International Conference on Multimedia, pp. 675–678. ACM (2014)

12. Kim, H.R., Kim, Y.S., Kim, S.J., Lee, I.K.: Building emotional machines: recognizing image emotions through deep neural networks. IEEE Trans. Multimed. **20**, 2980–2992 (2018)

13. Krizhevsky, A., Sutskever, I., Hinton, G.E.: ImageNet classification with deep convolutional neural networks. In: Advances in Neural Information Processing Systems, pp. 1097–1105 (2012)

14. Machajdik, J., Hanbury, A.: Affective image classification using features inspired by psychology and art theory. In: Proceedings of the 18th ACM International Conference on Multimedia, pp. 83–92. ACM (2010)

15. Medhat, W., Hassan, A., Korashy, H.: Sentiment analysis algorithms and applications: a survey. Ain Shams Eng. J. **5**(4), 1093–1113 (2014)

16. Nogueira, K., et al.: Exploiting convnet diversity for flooding identification. IEEE Geosci. Remote Sens. Lett. **15**(9), 1446–1450 (2018)

17. Peng, K.C., Chen, T., Sadovnik, A., Gallagher, A.C.: A mixed bag of emotions: model, predict, and transfer emotion distributions. In: Proceedings of the IEEE Conference on Computer Vision and Pattern Recognition, pp. 860–868 (2015)

18. Poria, S., Majumder, N., Hazarika, D., Cambria, E., Gelbukh, A., Hussain, A.: Multimodal sentiment analysis: addressing key issues and setting up the baselines. IEEE Intell. Syst. **33**(6), 17–25 (2018)

19. Saragih, J.M., Lucey, S., Cohn, J.F.: Face alignment through subspace constrained mean-shifts. In: 2009 IEEE 12th International Conference on Computer Vision, pp. 1034–1041. IEEE (2009)

20. Simonyan, K., Zisserman, A.: Very deep convolutional networks for large-scale image recognition. arXiv preprint arXiv:1409.1556 (2014)

21. Szegedy, C., Vanhoucke, V., Ioffe, S., Shlens, J., Wojna, Z.: Rethinking the inception architecture for computer vision. In: Proceedings of the IEEE Conference on Computer Vision and Pattern Recognition, pp. 2818–2826 (2016)

22. Wang, J., Fu, J., Xu, Y., Mei, T.: Beyond object recognition: visual sentiment analysis with deep coupled adjective and noun neural networks. In: IJCAI, pp. 3484–3490 (2016)

23. Wang, Y., Wang, S., Tang, J., Liu, H., Li, B.: Unsupervised sentiment analysis for social media images. In: Twenty-Fourth International Joint Conference on Artificial Intelligence (2015)

Hand Detection Using Zoomed Neural Networks

Sergio R. Cruz$^{(\boxtimes)}$ and Antoni B. Chan

Department of Computer Science, City University of Hong Kong,
Kowloon, Hong Kong
scruzgome2-c@my.cityu.edu.hk, abchan@cityu.edu.hk

Abstract. The object detection problem has been widely focused due to the development of personal cameras allowing the general population to have access to high end cameras. This has resulted in cameras with various perspectives, one of which is the Egocentric Perspective, like the GoPro cameras. This new perspective opens the possibility of having hand detection as a special problem, due to the hands containing enough information to be detected and even for hand recognition and users's activity recognition. However, due to the perspective being new the databases are scarce, and most of them focus on generic object detection rather than hand detection. In this paper we address hand detection and hand disambiguation which focuses on detecting left and right hands as different objects.

This paper addresses these challenges by using the information of a left hand being the mirror image of the right hand for the hand disambiguation, and we also train a Neural Network to focus on the hand over all the image and another Neural Network to focus on the bottom area of the image, increasing the resolution as the hands go out of image, which is a characteristic of the hands in the Egocentric Perspective. In addition, we propose three Neural Network architectures using the hand and increase resolution bottom image information, and we compare them with current object/hand detection approaches.

Keywords: Neural Network · Hand detection · Hand disambiguation

1 Introduction

As technologies in cameras advance, they become more accessible and they present new technological features. One of the new features is wearable cameras, where they can be placed on the person to record the person's perspective, or Egocentric Perspective. These cameras, like the GoPro cameras, have the ability to record videos with high resolution and high frame rate, which is needed as the person can move rapidly. This allows people to record activities that have fast movements like outdoor sports, e.g., hiking, surfing and biking in various scenarios, and daily activities, e.g., handling objects at home or washing the dishes.

© Springer Nature Switzerland AG 2019
E. Ricci et al. (Eds.): ICIAP 2019, LNCS 11752, pp. 114–124, 2019.
https://doi.org/10.1007/978-3-030-30645-8_11

This creates videos with swift movements and blurry nature. The first approaches on the egocentric perspective were in controlled environments by staying indoors walking through different rooms [5], or outdoors staying in the same place [1], but they neglect doing daily activities.

Due to the nature of this perspective, the camera wearer's hands appear in the image in reasonable size for information retrieval, and are the most consistent objects in the view since the person interacts with the world using their hands. However, the hand's characteristics make hand detection more challenging than generic objects as the hand's shape can change dramatically because the fingers and wrist have high degrees of freedom. Hand detection can be a first step for more complex analysis like activity recognition [5,17], or hand pose estimation [15,25], making it an essential step in the computer vision pipeline.

The first works to address the challenges in the egocentric perspective have used hand properties rather than the hands themselves to simplify the problem [10,20]; however they do not detect the hand. For hand detection in the egocentric perspective, previous works have used segmentation [2,11] by using a combination of low level features like color to detect skin-like features. However, such approaches also detect any skin-like regions, such as the arms.

In this work we approach hand detection from the egocentric perspective as an object disambiguation problem, by having the left and right hand as different objects, rather than treating them as a single type of object. We use Neural Networks for feature extraction and classification to detect the hands, as they have shown to have good performance for obtaining object information from images, and they are robust to illumination changes and blurriness, which is needed in this perspective.

We notice that current methods can detect other people's hands well, but often fails on the wearer's hands. This is because the wearer's hands often change shape drastically and are partially occluded (due to grasping of objects), or are only partially visible (due to the hands' proximity to the bottom of the camera's field of view).

Hence we devise an architecture with two parts: we train a Neural Network that focuses on the whole image for generic object detection, and another Neural Network that focuses on the bottom area of the image, where the wearer's hands have different properties (often appearing smaller due to exiting the image). We then fuse the results of both Neural Networks at different levels to show their behavior and performance. While it is possible to augment the training dataset by flipping left hands to look like right hands, here we do not flip them during training so as to allow context information to help improve the detection of both hands. Finally, we provide an ablation analysis to see how each of the changes contribute to the final performance.

2 Related Work

Due to cameras being more available to the public more data has been gathered using the egocentric perspective, resulting in various research works. Activity recognition [3,5,16,17,21–23] recognizes the activity the wearer is doing by using the generic objects found in the image. However, because the wearer's hands often handle the those objects, they sometimes move rapidly and appear blurry.

After object detection, object recognition and tracking [4,7,8,10,20] focus on using the detections to recognize the different appearances the object can take. This requires a more fine-grained feature usage which makes it more challenging.

Following this, research has been done on Summarization and Video Retrieval [9,13,14,24], where the most representative parts of video sequences are extracted. This is usually achieved by focusing on the objects that contain the most information from the videos over time, in order to create a series of stories describing the videos sequences.

Combining hand detection and the egocentric perspective has been a recent problem, and only a few approaches have been developed. Early developments use hand characteristics like optical flow patterns to segment the image [20]. This takes advantage of the fact of the hands move noticeable differently than the background, as the hands follow the camera movement. However, this also makes any object that moves like a hand to be detected as well. In this pape, however we approach the problem using the shape to detect the hands.

Other approaches focus on color features to identify the skin using various approaches like scene-level feature probes [11] and random forests [10]. They provide a database that focuses on illumination change with drastic changes in the background by going indoors and outdoors, and changing rooms such as going into the kitchen and grabbing various objects. They approach the hand detection problem using segmentation, and select the best features that discriminate the hand pixels from the background. However this also identifies other pixels that resemble skin, such as the arms.

More recent work focuses on distinguishing the shape of the hands using Convolutional Neural Networks (CNN), which have had high performance on generic object detection. Bambach *et al.* [1] uses CNNs to recognize hands in various egocentric videos while multiple people interact with each other. They generate bounding box proposals using the probability of the location, bounding box size and color-like features, and apply a CNN to score them. Then they combine the obtained bounding boxes and the segmentation of the image using previous works to provide a more refined segmentation.

They focus on the hands of two people interacting as they play board games. They collect a database with various pairs of people interacting in indoor/outdoor places, and add illumination changes and background variability. Our approach addresses improving the detection of the wearer's hands, which can change shape drastically and be partially occluded (due to grasping of objects), or only partially visible (due to the proximity to the edge of the camera's field of view).

Finally, much research has focused on generic object detection based on CNNs using an end-to-end approach [12,18,19], where the CNN extracts the features, proposes object regions, and classifies the regions within the same network. In this paper we extend these approaches to egocentric hand detection.

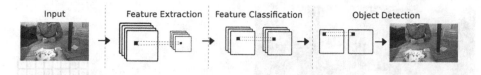

Fig. 1. Sections of the YOLO [18] neural network.

3 YOLO Detector

Due to the many variations of the hand shape caused by the egocentric perspective, hand detection and disambiguation is still a challenging problem even for approaches based on CNNs. The wearer's hands in this perspective move in and out of the image, sometimes only occupying a small area or even completely disappearing, which causes problems for standard CNN approaches. To address this issue, we devise an architecture using a backbone object detector that can specifically detect the wearer's hands.

We use YOLOv2 [18] as the backbone object detector due to its high performance and speed (we denote it as simply YOLO here). For YOLO, there is a limit on how large the input image resolution can be, as higher resolutions would only lead to an increase of false positives and decrease of overall performance. The YOLO architecture contains 3 sections (see Fig. 1): (1) feature extraction consisting of 18 convolutional layers and 5 max-pooling layers, resulting in a decrease in feature map resolution; (2) feature classification consisting of 8 convolutional layers; (3) object detection consisting of a final convolutional layer for bounding box regression and object classification.

The YOLO network has 5 outputs representing the bounding box and confidence, and the classification outputs. The bounding box outputs are the x coordinate (t_x), y coordinate (t_y), width (t_w) and height (t_h). Since this paper focuses on hand disambiguation we set the classification outputs as $C = 4$, as for hand disambiguation we detect left and right hands for wearer and other people as all different objects.

3.1 Detection Using Zoom Information

YOLO has a fixed resolution which has a limit on the size of the objects it is able to detect. If the object is too small it cannot extract enough information, which is a characteristic of some hand regions in the egocentric perspective. We address this using a second YOLO that focuses on the bottom of the image where the hands appear the smallest due to partial occlusion. We name it as ZOOM to distinguish from YOLO. We construct ZOOM to be able to see the small objects a standard YOLO cannot see, as seen in Fig. 2 where we highlight in green the area the ZOOM focuses on. We train ZOOM using only the ground truth bounding boxes that completely are contained in the bottom area of the image, creating a second smaller dataset with only small size hand regions.

Fig. 2. ZOOM takes as input one fourth of the image (green), and the bounding boxes that entirely fall into that area (red box) as ground truth. (Color figure online)

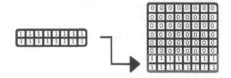

Fig. 3. Grid expansion from the ZOOM output grid cell by adding the upper grid cells and setting them to 0.

3.2   Fusion Architectures

We propose to combine YOLO and ZOOM as follows. First, we train YOLO separately as the standard framework, with full images and all the ground truth bounding boxes. Second, we train ZOOM separately using the hand bounding boxes in the bottom area of the image. The two trained networks form a two-stream architecture: the 1st stream is the standard YOLO networks for detecting hands, and the 2nd stream is the ZOOM network.

We fuse the two streams by concatenating the features at a given level into one big feature map, and then fine-tuning the rest of the layers. Since the second stream represents the bottom quarter of the first stream, we need to expand it and fill in the missing grid cells before the concatenation. First we apply the CNNs to obtain the grid from YOLO and ZOOM, then we expand the ZOOM grid by four times and put the new cells to 0, as seen in Fig. 3.

Specifically, we set the YOLO input resolution for the stream to be 384 so that the output grid size is 12×12. We then set the ZOOM input resolution so that the ZOOM output grid after the expansion is a multiple of the YOLO output grid in the width and height (up to twice the size of the YOLO grid). We set different widths to be of 384 and 768 pixels denoted as W384 and W768 respectively, and we set different heights to be of 96 and 192 pixels denoted as H96 and H192 respectively, resulting in 4 different resolutions for the ZOOM network. We found increasing the resolution even more decreases the performance.

We then concatenate the YOLO grid cells with the corresponding ZOOM grid cells of higher resolution, as seen in Fig. 4. These YOLO and ZOOM resolutions ensure that grid cells from both networks can be matched without any spatial displacement, as the ZOOM output grid sizes for W384 and W768 are 12 and 24 respectively, and the output grid sizes of H96 and H192 are 3 and 6 respectively.

To combine the two streams we propose three levels of fusion, as seen in Fig. 5. The first method concatenates both streams after the Feature Extraction section, and then fine-tunes the rest of the convolutions on the feature

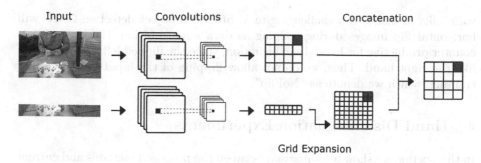

Fig. 4. Feature grid output from convolutions. ZOOM grid (red box) is expanded setting all the extra grid cells with 0 and then concatenates (blue squares) with the YOLO stream. (Color figure online)

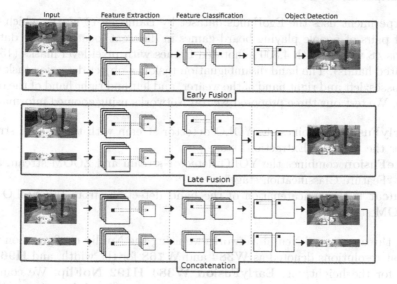

Fig. 5. Proposed network architectures combining the already trained YOLO and ZOOM streams.

combination on the Feature Classification and Object Detection sections, which we denote as "Early Fusion". The second method concatenates both streams after the Feature Classification section, and fine-tunes the final convolution on the Object Detection section, which we denote as "Late Fusion". Finally, the last combination concatenates the detection bounding boxes from the YOLO and ZOOM networks, and we denote it as "Concat".

3.3 Detection Using Non Flipped Information (NoFlip)

A subsequent step after hand detection is hand disambiguation, where the left and right hands are classified as different objects, but due to the hand shape variability it makes it a challenging task. Standard object detection CNNs will horizontal flip images during training as data augmentation. However, this is counter productive for hand disambiguation, since the flipped left-hand will look like the right hand. Thus, we do not allow flipping of the input images during training, which we denote as "NoFlip".

4   Hand Disambiguation Experiments

In this section we show a comparison between the proposed methods and current egocentric hand/object detection approaches, as well as an ablation study.

4.1   Experiment Setup

Our experiment uses the EgoHands dataset by Bambach *et al.* [1], which consists of pairs of people playing board games in different locations. The dataset contains 48 videos, with 4,800 annotated frames with pixel-level masks (15,053 annotated hands). The hand disambiguation task is a object detection task with four classes: left and right hand of the wearer, and left and right hand of the other person. We test our three proposed Neural Networks using zoomed information:

– **EarlyFusion** combines the YOLO detector stream with the ZOOM stream after the "Feature Extraction" stage.
– **LateFusion** combines the YOLO detector stream and ZOOM stream after the "Feature Classification stage".
– **Concat** is the concatenation of the hand detections from the YOLO and ZOOM streams.

For all three proposed Neural Networks we using the NoFlip configuration with different resolutions denoted as **W384** and **W768** for the width, and **H96** and **H192** for the height, e.g. **EarlyFusion W384 H192 NoFlip**. We compare against 4 baseline methods consisting of generic object/hand detection methods based on neural networks:

– **Bambach *et al.*** [1] generates object proposals using probability distributions of hand properties, and then uses a neural network to classify the proposals.
– **Faster R-CNN** [19] is a deep CNN that uses the region proposal network (RPN) to extract features from the image and then the Fast R-CNN Neural Network [6] on a fully convolutional network trained end-to-end. For the feature extraction CNN we use the VGG-16 version.
– **SSD** [12] uses a deep Neural Network for feature extraction and classification, and is trained end-to-end. It uses predefined bounding boxes with different aspect ratios and scales to predict the ground truth. We use the author's code and set the input resolution as 300×300 and keep the other settings as their defaults. During training we set the base learning rate to 0.0001.

- **YOLO** [18] uses a single Neural Network to predict bounding boxes and class probabilities, and is trained end-to-end. We use the code provided by the author with a 416 × 416 input resolution and keep the other settings as their defaults.

After running the detection algorithms, we use non-maximum suppression with overlap of 0.5 as post-processing.

4.2 Hand Disambiguation Results

Table 1 shows the breakdown of hand disambiguation performance using average precision (AP) and recall on all the hands. We first examine the baseline methods. Bambach *et al.* [1] has similar performance across all hands, showing their features are not affected by the number of instances and the hand sizes in the dataset. However the average precision is low while the recall is high, showing that the Neural Network classifier has problems telling apart hands.

Table 1. Experiment results for hand disambiguation. OL/OR are other's left/right hand, and WL/WR are wearer's left/right hand.

Method	Average precision					Recall
	OL	OR	WL	WR	All	
Bambach *et al.* [1]	0.556	0.698	0.596	0.553	0.587	0.771
Faster [19]	0.754	0.809	0.681	0.582	0.745	0.838
SSD [12]	0.839	0.870	0.847	0.700	0.834	0.930
YOLO [18]	0.869	0.894	0.771	0.694	0.790	0.890
EarlyFusion H96 W384 NoFlip	0.905	0.906	0.899	0.810	0.902	0.929
LateFusion H96 W768 NoFlip	0.905	0.907	0.899	0.806	0.903	0.929
Concat H192 W384 NoFlip	0.906	0.907	0.905	0.896	0.904	0.939

Faster R-CNN has a considerable decrease in performance on the wearer's hands (WL/WR), with the lowest being the right hand. This demonstrates that the baseline object detectors cannot handle small objects well, as well as they may be affected by the low number of training samples.

SSD [12] has similar performance across hands except on the wearer's right hand (WR), and outperforms Faster R-CNN, showing that the fine-grained features can increase performance. Finally, YOLO has lower recall and overall average precision than SSD. However the average precision on the Other person's hands is higher, which shows that YOLO does well on bigger objects, but encounters difficulties with small objects, more specifically on the wearer's left hand (WL).

Compared to the previous methods, our proposed methods have higher average precision (AP) on all hands, while maintaining similar or better recall. The biggest increase in AP is with the wearer's hands (more than 0.1), which demonstrates the impact of our proposed fusion method. The main difference in the performance among our fusions method is on the wearer's hands, as the wearer's hands go in and out of the camera view more often than the Other's hands, which are mainly completely in the view.

The "Concat" fusion has the best performance with a noticeable AP increase on the wearer's right hand. In contrast, Late and Early fusion have lower PA on the wearer's right hand. This suggests the combination of ZOOM and YOLO can obtain better performance if they are learned separately and making them more specialized, rather than having layers on the Neural Network to learn.

5   Ablation Study

Table 2 presents the breakdown of the impact of our proposed fusions for various configurations. The YOLO W384 NoFlip configuration increases the AP of all hands, showing the main difference between left and right hand shapes is its flipped characteristics. However the lowest AP are found in the wearer's hands, especially on the right hand, which shows the difficulty YOLO still has on these instances. The increase of the regular YOLO W416 over W384 shows the increase resolution is able help on distinguishing more hand shapes, as the main increase occurs on the Other's hands.

Table 2. Ablation study on variants of our proposed method. The right block of results uses NoFlip setting, while the left-block uses image flipping during training. OL/OR are other's left/right hand, and WL/WR are wearer's left/right hand.

Method	Flip						NoFlip					
	Average precision					Recall	Average precision					Recall
	OL	OR	WL	WR	All		OL	OR	WL	WR	All	
YOLO W384	0.796	0.833	0.773	0.675	0.784	0.873	0.902	0.907	0.898	0.806	0.899	0.919
YOLO W416	0.869	0.894	0.771	0.694	0.790	0.890	0.901	0.904	0.899	0.812	0.900	0.927
EarlyFusion H96 W384	0.892	0.904	0.897	0.809	0.890	0.915	0.905	0.906	0.899	0.810	0.902	0.929
EarlyFusion H96 W768	0.898	0.905	0.884	0.803	0.888	0.912	0.905	0.906	0.899	0.810	0.902	0.928
EarlyFusion H192 W384	0.901	0.903	0.882	0.801	0.895	0.918	0.905	0.906	0.897	0.807	0.901	0.928
EarlyFusion H192 W768	0.900	0.902	0.880	0.744	0.893	0.916	0.905	0.906	0.897	0.809	0.901	0.926
LateFusion H96 W384	0.803	0.883	0.833	0.694	0.788	0.890	0.906	0.907	0.896	0.803	0.902	0.926
LateFusion H96 W768	0.795	0.882	0.827	0.693	0.793	0.884	0.905	0.907	0.899	0.806	0.903	0.929
LateFusion H192 W384	0.798	0.885	0.848	0.701	0.795	0.891	0.906	0.907	0.897	0.806	0.902	0.926
LateFusion H192 W768	0.792	0.883	0.837	0.698	0.792	0.890	0.906	0.907	0.896	0.802	0.902	0.928
Concat H96 W384	0.798	0.879	0.816	0.683	0.770	0.898	0.906	0.907	0.904	0.893	0.903	0.938
Concat H96 W768	0.798	0.879	0.796	0.680	0.766	0.899	0.906	0.907	0.904	0.889	0.903	0.937
Concat H192 W384	0.798	0.879	0.817	0.681	0.773	0.895	0.906	0.907	0.905	0.896	0.904	0.939
Concat H192 W768	0.798	0.879	0.793	0.684	0.769	0.900	0.906	0.907	0.905	0.887	0.904	0.938

The proposed fusion networks have increased recall and overall performance, compared to standard YOLO, which shows that the ZOOM network is able to find more of the Wearer's hands, as they focus on the hands which go in and out of the bottom of the image. Among the different resolutions, using twice the resolution for the height (H192) the ZOOM Networks are able to find the most hands, showing the main struggle of the feature extraction as the hands leave the image is the decrease of the hand's height.

Using the Flip configuration for training, the performance increases with earlier fusion of the two streams. This suggests that solving the hand disambiguation task using the Flip configuration requires complex patterns extracted between the two streams.

This Flip configuration is also affected by the small number of instances on the training dataset, since there are not enough instances to learn such complex patterns.

Using the NoFlip configuration yields the opposite behavior compared to the Flip configuration – better performance is achieved with later fusion of the streams. This implies that the two streams can work well independently, and detection of Other's hands and wearer's hands do not affect each other significantly.

This shows the main challenge of the hands on the egocentric perspective is the different shapes between the left and right hands (they are flipped versions of each other), which is addressed by the NoFlip configuration, showing the highest performance compared to the Flip configuration of the different fusions. The addition of the fusions to the NoFlip configuration is able to find the most challenging hands, the Wearer's hands as they leave the image, especially the right hand.

6 Conclusions

We have proposed a variation of the YOLO Neural Network focusing on a zoomed area of the image, denoted as ZOOM, using the unique characteristics found on the hands in the egocentric perspective. We have proposed three different joint Neural Network architectures combining YOLO and ZOOM to improve on the disambiguation performance and we present a comparison with object/hand baseline detection methods. We showed how the extracted zoomed information and training without the flipped setting on the Neural Network can help finding small hand regions and disambiguating them.

References

1. Bambach, S., Lee, S., Crandall, D., Yu, C.: Lending a hand: detecting hands and recognizing activities in complex egocentric interactions. In: ICCV (2015)
2. Betancourt, A.: A sequential classifier for hand detection in the framework of egocentric vision. In: CVPRW 2014, pp. 600–605 (2014)
3. Fathi, A., Hodgins, J.K., Rehg, J.M.: Social interactions: a first-person perspective. In: CVPR, pp. 1226–1233 (2012)
4. Fathi, A., Ren, X., Rehg, J.M.: Learning to recognize objects in egocentric activities. In: CVPR 2011, pp. 3281–3288 (2011)
5. Fathi, A., Farhadi, A.: Understanding egocentric activities. In: ICCV 2011, pp. 407–414 (2011)
6. Girshick, R.: Fast R-CNN. In: International Conference on Computer Vision (ICCV) (2015)

7. Kolsch, M., Turk, M.: Robust hand detection. In: Proceedings of the Sixth IEEE International Conference on Automatic Face and Gesture Recognition, pp. 614–619 (2004)
8. Lee, S., Bambach, S., Crandall, D.J., Franchak, J.M., Yu, C.: This hand is my hand: a probabilistic approach to hand disambiguation in egocentric video. In: CVPRW, pp. 557–564 (2014)
9. Lee, Y.J., Ghosh, J., Grauman, K.: Discovering important people and objects for egocentric video summarization. In: CVPR, pp. 1346–1353 (2012)
10. Li, C., Kitani, K.M.: Pixel-level hand detection in ego-centric videos. In: 2013 IEEE Conference on Computer Vision and Pattern Recognition (CVPR), pp. 3570–3577, June 2013. https://doi.org/10.1109/CVPR.2013.458
11. Li, C., Kitani, K.M.: Model recommendation with virtual probes for egocentric hand detection. In: ICCV 2013, pp. 2624–2631 (2013)
12. Liu, W., et al.: SSD: single shot multibox detector. In: Leibe, B., Matas, J., Sebe, N., Welling, M. (eds.) ECCV 2016. LNCS, vol. 9905, pp. 21–37. Springer, Cham (2016). https://doi.org/10.1007/978-3-319-46448-0_2
13. Lu, Z., Grauman, K.: Story-driven summarization for egocentric video. In: CVPR 2013, pp. 2714–2721 (2013)
14. Min, W., Li, X., Tan, C., Mandal, B., Li, L., Lim, J.H.: Efficient retrieval from large-scale egocentric visual data using a sparse graph representation. In: CVPRW 2014, pp. 541–548 (2014)
15. Mueller, F., et al.: GANerated hands for real-time 3D hand tracking from monocular RGB. In: CVPR (2018)
16. Pirsiavash, H., Ramanan, D.: Detecting activities of daily living in first-person camera views. In: 2012 IEEE Conference on Computer Vision and Pattern Recognition (CVPR). IEEE (2012)
17. Poleg, Y., Arora, C., Peleg, S.: Temporal segmentation of egocentric videos. In: CVPR (2014)
18. Redmon, J., Farhadi, A.: Yolo9000: better, faster, stronger. arXiv preprint arXiv:1612.08242 (2016)
19. Ren, S., He, K., Girshick, R.B., Sun, J.: Faster R-CNN: towards real-time object detection with region proposal networks. CoRR (2015)
20. Ren, X., Gu, C.: Figure-ground segmentation improves handled object recognition in egocentric video. In: 2010 IEEE Conference on Computer Vision and Pattern Recognition (CVPR), pp. 3137–3144, June 2010
21. Ryoo, M.S., Matthies, L.: First-person activity recognition: what are they doing to me? In: 2013 IEEE Conference on Computer Vision and Pattern Recognition (CVPR) (2013)
22. Ryoo, M.S., Matthies, L.: First-person activity recognition: feature, temporal structure, and prediction. Int. J. Comput. Vis. 119, 307–328 (2016)
23. Song, S., et al.: Multimodal multi-stream deep learning for egocentric activity recognition. In: The IEEE Conference on Computer Vision and Pattern Recognition (CVPR) Workshops, June 2016
24. Spriggs, E.H., De la Torre Frade, F., Hebert, M.: Temporal segmentation and activity classification from first-person sensing. In: IEEE Workshop on Egocentric Vision, CVPR 2009, June 2009
25. Spurr, A., Song, J., Park, S., Hilliges, O.: Cross-modal deep variational hand pose estimation. In: CVPR (2018)

Wafer Defect Map Classification Using Sparse Convolutional Networks

Roberto di Bella[1], Diego Carrera[2], Beatrice Rossi[2], Pasqualina Fragneto[2], and Giacomo Boracchi[1(✉)]

[1] Politecnico di Milano, Milan, Italy
giacomo.boracchi@polimi.it
[2] STMicroelectronics, Agrate Brianza, Italy

Abstract. Chips in semiconductor manufacturing are produced in circular wafers that are constantly monitored by inspection machines. These machines produce a wafer defect map, namely a list of defect locations which corresponds to a very large, sparse and binary image. While in these production processes it is normal to see defects that are randomly spread through the wafer, specific defect patterns might indicate problems in the production that have to be promptly identified.

We cast wafer monitoring in a challenging image classification problem where traditional convolutional neural networks, that represent state-of-the-art solutions, cannot be straightforwardly employed due to the very large image size (say 20,000 × 20,000 pixels) and the extreme class imbalance. We successfully address these challenges by means of Submanifold Sparse Convolutional Networks, deep architectures that are specifically designed to handle sparse data, and through an ad-hoc data augmentation procedure designed for wafer defect maps. Our experiments show that the proposed solution is very successful over a dataset of almost 30,000 maps acquired and annotated by our industrial partner. In particular, the proposed solution achieves significantly high recall on normal wafer defect maps, that represent the large majority of the production. Moreover, our data augmentation procedure turns out to be beneficial also in smaller images, as it allows to outperform the state-of-the-art classifier on a public datasets of wafer defect maps.

Keywords: Sparse Convolutional Networks · Wafer Defect Map · Industrial monitoring · Pattern classification · Quality control

1 Introduction

Semiconductor manufacturing is a long and expensive process, which involves many specialized steps to yield wafers containing hundreds of chips, see Fig. 1(a). Multiple sophisticated *inspection tools* are employed along the production line, which locate defective regions inside each chip and assemble a Wafer Defect Map (WDM), namely a list of coordinates where all defects within a wafer lie. In normal production conditions, defects appear randomly distributed over WDMs,

E. Ricci et al. (Eds.): ICIAP 2019, LNCS 11752, pp. 125–136, 2019.
https://doi.org/10.1007/978-3-030-30645-8_12

without any specific spatial arrangement. In contrast, WDMs portraying *patterns* like those in Fig. 1 might indicate problems occurred during the production. In fact, some of these patterns can be traced to a particular problem in a manufacturing step and their prompt detection allows timely alerts to prevent huge production waste, thus substantially improving production efficiency. Therefore, automatic tools that identify patterns in WDMs are of paramount importance for semiconductor industries, which have to guarantee high-quality standards and high-throughput production to satisfy the growing demand of chips, lately further pushed by automotive/mobile/wearable/IoT sectors.

Algorithms for identifying defect patterns on wafers have been quite extensively investigated in the literature [1, 7], and the most effective solutions rely on classifiers [3, 4, 14, 15]. However, none of these classifiers handles WDMs directly, since each WDM corresponds to a very large binary image, whose size is limited only by the resolution of the inspection tool (in our case each WDM has resolution $20,000 \times 20,000$). This representation is impossible to handle by standard classifiers as they would require many computational resources (both in term of operations and memory) to process images of this size. Therefore, most of the existing solutions [3, 4, 10, 15] reduce the image size by a preliminary preprocessing step, which corresponds to a lossy conversion of the information contained in the original WDM that might prevent capturing the full diversity of defect patterns.

Our intuition is that, to successfully employ a classifier, and in particular a convolutional neural network (CNN) [8], two major challenges have to be addressed. First, the network should be designed to efficiently process very large inputs, to provide the classifier with the entirety of the WDM information content. Second, the training procedure should cope with severe class imbalance, since in real-world monitoring conditions some defect classes occur very rarely.

Here we adopt Submanifold Sparse Convolutional Networks (SSCN) [5] to handle our WDMs that are very large and at the same time sparse. Convolutional layers in a SSCN implement a convolution operator that modifies only the nonzero values in the feature maps. As a result, very deep SSCNs preserve the sparsity of the input data (which is reduced only by max pooling operations) and this property allows the network to better capture those peculiar patterns in the input. Moreover, the submanifold convolution operator is computationally more efficient than its traditional counterpart, both in terms of number of operations performed and memory required, since only the nonzero coefficients in each feature maps are stored and processed.

Our contribution is twofold: we are the first to adopt SSCN to classify images that are as large as WDMs by means of a very deep architecture. Moreover, to cope with class imbalance, we design an ad-hoc data-augmentation procedure to map each WDM in a set of realistic WDMs. In particular, we extend the set of standard geometric transformations performed in data augmentation routines, and introduce cropping and mixing with synthetically generated WDMs. To this purpose, we learn from our training set a statistical model of the distribution of random defects in normal WDMs, and perform data augmentation in a class-specific procedure that provides very rich information to the network and at the same time mitigates class imbalance.

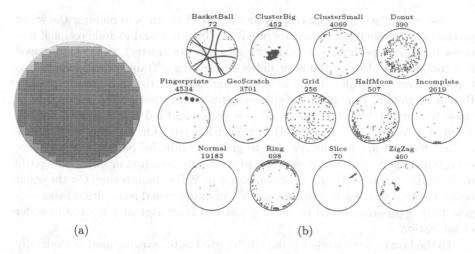

(a)   (b)

Fig. 1. (a) An example of wafer containing few hundreds of chips (the small cells). (b) An example of WDM for each of the class in ST Dataset. We also report the number of instances of each class in our dataset to emphasize the severe class imbalance.

Our experiments, performed on a large dataset of WDMs collected and annotated by our industrial partner, show that the proposed approach is a better option than a state-of-the-art pre-trained network (VGG-16 [13]) fine-tuned on low-resolution images obtained by preprocessing the WDMs. In particular, our SSCN achieves a significantly higher recall on normal WDMs, which represent the vast majority of the industrial production. Moreover, we show that, on the large WM811K dataset [14], CNNs trained by employing our class-specific image-augmentation procedure can outperform the solution in [14] based on hand-crafted features.

Related Works. All the solutions in the literature preprocess WDMs to reduce their size. Most often, WDMs are pre-processed to create a wafer bin map, namely a binary image where each pixel corresponds to a chip and indicates whether that chip contains defects or not. Since the number of chips in the wafer is relatively small (typically a few hundreds), wafer bin maps are much easier to handle. Wafer bin maps have been analyzed using either unsupervised or supervised methods. Unsupervised methods [1,7] create clusters of similar wafers by clustering algorithms such as Adaptive Resonance Theory, k-means and Particle Swarm Optimization. The solution in [1] combines the clustering with a statistical test based on Log Odd Ratio, that preliminary screens the wafer bin maps to determine which ones do not present any specific pattern (such as the WDMs in *Normal* class, see Fig. 1). Although unsupervised methods have the great advantage of not requiring annotated datasets, they are meant to group together similar wafers rather than associating each wafer to a class of a predefined set, which is instead the problem we address here.

Most supervised methods employ hand-crafted features to monitor the wafer production. Geometric features are often very intuitive and include regional features (e.g. area, perimeter, eccentricity of a defects cluster) and density-based features (e.g. location of the most defect-dense area). Transformed domain features analyze the wafer image in a different domain through transforms like Radon or Hough, that make specific patterns clearly noticeable. A mixture of these features [3,4,15] are assembled in a vector and fed to a classifier, usually a Support Vector Machine (SVM) or a decision tree. On the one hand, hand-crafted features are not always able to grasp meaningful patterns in whatever conditions might appear, e.g. when these are rotated, shifted or affect only parts of the wafer surface, to name common issues in WDM monitoring. On the other hand, the impressive achievements of CNN in many visual recognition tasks suggest that approaches based on learned features have a great potential in wafer classification.

To the best of our knowledge, only [9,10] use Deep Learning models to classify specific patterns in WDMs. However, as opposed to the approach we propose here, [9] operates on wafer bin maps and address a simpler classification problem that consists in distinguishing radial map patterns from non radial ones. The solution presented in [10] adopts a different preprocessing yielding low-resolution grayscale images (instead of wafer bin maps that are binary) where each pixel corresponds to a chip and its intensity value indicates the number of defects found in that chip. This solution has been trained exclusively on a synthetically generated dataset and tested on a small batch of real data, which does not cover all the classes considered during training. In [14] it is shown that performing transfer learning of a pretrained model (the Alexnet [8]) does not outperform the proposed solution based on hand-crafted features.

2   Problem Formulation

A WDM is a list of 2D coordinates indicating the locations of the defects inside the wafer. Obviously, a WDM can be represented as a binary image $w \in \{0,1\}^{K \times K}$ where each pixel (i,j) corresponds to a location on the wafer checked by the inspection machine and $w(i,j) = 1$ when a defect is found at (i,j). Each WDM w corresponds to a label $\ell \in \mathcal{L}$, depending on the spatial arrangements of defects in w. Our goal is to define a classifier $\mathcal{K}$ that associates to each WDM w a label $\widehat{\ell} = \mathcal{K}(w)$. To this purpose, we assume a training set of n labeled WDMs $\mathcal{W} = \{(w_1, \ell_1), \ldots, (w_n, \ell_n)\}$ is provided.

While these are rather customary settings, WDMs classification requires to address two major challenges. At first, the resolution of a WDM w is huge – in our case $K = 20,000$ – and a grayscale image of such resolution would require almost 3 GB to be loaded in memory in single precision. The second challenge is the severe class imbalance: while it is very easy to collect WDMs from *Normal* class, some patterns, such as *BasketBall*, occur very rarely during the production, thus are also very under-represented in the training set. Figure 1(b) illustrates the 13 classes of WDM patterns, as identified in our dataset by domain experts, and show that a few classes are heavily under represented in out training set.

3   Proposed Solution

In this section we present our solution to WDM classification. First, we introduce the network architecture we design to handle very large WDMs, then we describe the specific data-augmentation procedures we use both during training and test phases.

Network Architecture. As described in Sect. 2, our problem can be easily cast in the image classification framework, but traditional convolutional neural networks cannot be straightforwardly used for WDMs classification since they handle images at relatively low resolution (e.g., the VGG16 in [13] takes as input 224×224 RGB images). In fact, input of such dimension would require huge training and testing time and memory, to store all the feature maps of the CNN. To overcome this issue, we built a very deep network stacking Submanifold Sparse Convolutional (SSC) layers [5]. A SSC layer implements a modified convolution operator that is designed to process sparse data. The main advantage of the SSC w.r.t. its traditional counterpart is that it efficiently handles sparse data as a list of the coordinates of nonzero locations. Moreover, this layer preserves the sparsity of the input, since it does not increase the number of nonzero values in the feature maps. This property better preserves defect patterns through the layers of the network.

Our SSCN recalls for the VGG16 architecture, and the basic building block is composed by a SSC layer with ReLu activations followed by a max pooling layer with stride 2, thus the resolution of the feature maps is reduced by a factor 4 after each block. We stack 13 of these building blocks, followed by a convolutional layer and finally a fully connected one. The output of the last layer is a vector of #$\mathcal{L}$ scores, whose maximum value determines the class of the processed WDM. To the best of our knowledge, this is the first architecture trained to process very large binary images as the WDMs we consider.

We remark that our very deep architecture replaces preliminary binning that is typically employed to reduce the WDMs dimension [10]. As we will show in Sect. 4, our entirely data-driven solution outperforms CNN trained over low-resolution images of the wafer as this preprocessing is a-priori defined and not optimized over training data.

Data Augmentation. As shown in Fig. 1, our dataset is highly imbalanced and contains a relatively small number of WDMs compared to the datasets typically used in image classification. To increase the dataset size and avoid overfitting during training, we design a data augmentation procedure that implements a set $\mathcal{T}^{\ell}$ of label-preserving transformations on our WDMs:

$$\mathcal{T}^{\ell} = \left\{ T_{\theta}^{\ell} \colon \{0,1\}^{K \times K} \to \{0,1\}^{K \times K}, \; \theta \in \Theta_{\ell} \right\}, \tag{1}$$

where θ denotes the parameters defining each transformations, and Θ_{ℓ} is the set of transformations parameter which also depends on the label ℓ. In practice, each T_{θ}^{ℓ} is a composition of transformations commonly used for data augmentation, such as rotations around the center of the wafer, horizontal flip, and small translations of the defective coordinates. Moreover, we perform two transformations that were specifically designed for WDMs, namely noise injection and random mixing. Noise injection adds a small number of defects to each WDM to increase network robustness and reduce the risk of overfitting. In particular, WDMs in the *Normal* class can be seen as pure noise, since the defects in the wafer are not due to any specific problem during the production. Therefore, we estimate the distribution of the number of defects in *Normal* WDMs from the training set and use this distribution to draw the number N of defects that has to be added to each WDM. Our study and production engineers confirm that there is no particular arrangement of defects in normal WDMs, thus we uniformly sample defect coordinates within the WDM. This part of data augmentation is conveniently performed in polar coordinates since WDMs are circular. Adding noise does not change the class a WDM belongs to, because a few defects randomly spread in the WDM are present in every wafer. Random mixing consists in cropping portions of WDMs from samples of those classes that are very peculiar and are less represented in the training set, such as the *BasketBall* and *Donut*, and superimposing them to obtain novel WDMs that are used as additional training examples. In these cases, production engineers were not able to distinguish these mixed WDMs from the real ones. This data augmentation procedure is constantly invoked during training, generating new batches by transforming the original WDMs using T_θ^ℓ where the parameters θ are randomly sampled by Θ_ℓ.

In principle the network trained on augmented WDMs should extract a high-level representations [2] of a WDM that are invariant to the transformations in T^ℓ. However, invariance is hardly achieved in practice, thus we enforce data augmentation also when classifying WDMs by our SSCN. To this purpose, we define the set of transformations

$$T = \{T_\theta : \theta \in \Theta\}, \tag{2}$$

where $\Theta = \cap_{\ell \in \mathcal{L}} \Theta_\ell$ is the set of transformations common to all classes, thus preserving all the labels in $\mathcal{L}$. For each WDM w to be tested, we compute a set $\mathcal{A}(w)$ of N augmented WDMs:

$$\mathcal{A}(w) = \{T_{\theta_i}(w), \ i = 1, \ldots, N\}, \tag{3}$$

where each θ_i is randomly sampled from Θ. Then, the whole set $A(w)$ is fed to the network and the classifier output $\widehat{\ell} = \mathcal{K}(w)$ is the class achieving the maximum average score over $\mathcal{A}(w)$.

4   Experiments

Our experiments aim at showing that (i) our solution based on SSCN can successfully handle WDMs and outperforms traditional CNNs trained to classify images having lower resolution than WDMs, and (ii) a properly designed and trained deep architecture can outperform traditional classifiers based on hand crafted features also in WDMs classification.

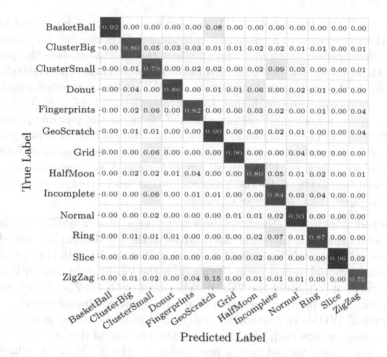

Fig. 2. Confusion matrix obtained by our SCNN on the ST dataset. Our network achieves very high accuracy on all the classes, and most misclassified samples belong to classes that are very similar, such as Incomplete and Cluster Small.

Datasets. We test our architectures on two different datasets. The first one is the ST dataset, which comprises 29,746 WDMs acquired in the production site of STMicroelectronics in Agrate Brianza, Italy. Beside the *Normal* class (which does not present any defect pattern), engineers have identified 12 classes illustrated in Fig. 1. The second one is the WM-811K, which is a public dataset [14] composed of 172,951 images provided by Taiwan Semiconductor Manufacturing Company. The dataset includes nine classes and is highly unbalanced: as in the ST dataset, the *Normal* class (called *None* in [14]) covers almost the 70% of the dataset. Differently from ST dataset, the WM-811K dataset contains wafer bin maps, which are very small resolution images ranging from 15×15 pixels to 200×200 pixels. We resize all this images to 64×64 using nearest neighbor interpolation, as this is by far the most common resolution in the dataset.

Figures of Merit. The traditional figure of merit used in multiclass classification problems is the *confusion matrix*, which assesses the classifier performance on each class separately, but it does not provide an overall measure of classification performance. The Area Under the ROC Curve (AUC) is probably the best option in binary classification, as it is independent from the class proportions and from the threshold employed, but it does not admit a straightforward extension to multiclass problems, thus we consider two versions of multiclass AUC.

The first one is the *1vsRest-AUC* [11] and corresponds to the average of all the binary AUCs computed in a one-versus-rest fashion. In particular, for each class, a binary classification problem is tested, where the selected class is the positive one and the remaining ones are merged in the negative class. The 1vsRest-AUC is then obtained as a weighted average of the AUC values computed for each of these binary classification problems. In contrast, the *1vs1-AUC* in [6] employs a one-versus-one scheme and average the AUC from all the possible pairs. The main difference between the two measures is that the *1vs1*-AUC is independent from the class proportions, while *1vsRest*-AUC is not. Since our model are relatively fast to train on a GPU, in all our experiments we assess classification performance by means of 10-fold cross validation, and average our results to reduce the variance in the figures of merit.

Considered Methods. To show the effectiveness of our SSCN on the ST dataset we consider the following alternatives in the ST dataset we consider as alternative solution a CNN obtained by training over the *VGG16* [13], a state-of-the-art convolutional neural network that won the localization task in ILSVRC 2014 competition [12]. Since the VGG16 takes as input 224×224 images, we perform a preliminary binning operation to obtain a low-resolution representation of the original WDM. In particular, each WDM is transformed in a 224×224 grayscale image where each pixel indicates the number of defects in the corresponding bin. Then, we perform a fine tuning on the ST dataset, which is a customary procedure in transfer learning. The VGG16 is trained and tested in the same conditions as our SSCN, i.e. we perform the same data augmentation on WDMs before binning. To assess the importance of data augmentation, we test the proposed SSCN both with data-augmentation and without (*SSCN w/o Aug*).

On the WM-811K dataset we adopt a traditional CNN rather than a sparse CNN, since the input images are rather small and not very sparse. Therefore, we consider a comparable architecture, though less deep, obtained by stacking traditional convolutional and max pooling layers. As alternative method, we consider the solution in [14] (denoted here as *SVM*), that extracts hand-crafted features and classify the feature vectors using a Support Vector Machine.

Advantages of Directly Handling WDMs Instead of Images. We train our SSCN network over the ST dataset using the Adadelta optimizer [16] with parameters $\rho = 0.9$ and $\epsilon = 10^{-6}$. Training requires about 8 h (for 100 epochs) and was performed using two GPUs (a Titan Xp and a Titan V), while the averaged time required to classify a WDM is 0.061 ± 0.055 s (we compute $N = 250$ augmented WDMs in (3)). The high variance is due to the fact that the number of operations performed by SSCNs highly depends on WDM sparsity, which varies a lot in our dataset.

Figure 2 shows the confusion matrix of the classification performance over the ST dataset. The accuracy over different classes indicate that our SSCN achieves very good classification performance and that most of classification errors are among very similar classes (e.g., *Incomplete* and *ClusterSmall*, see Fig. 1(b)). Due to space limitation, Table 1 reports only a comparison in terms of class

Table 1. Results on the STdataset.

Class	SSCN w/0 Aug.	SSCN	VGG16
Normal	94%	93%	89%
BasketBall	69%	92%	100%
ClusterBig	66%	80%	79%
ClusterSmall	71%	80%	82%
Donut	70 %	89%	91%
Fingerprints	55 %	85%	86%
GeoScratch	49 %	87%	89%
Grid	69%	91%	88%
HalfMoon	41%	77%	80%
Incomplete	75%	86%	92%
Ring	77 %	87%	86%
Slice	49%	96%	92%
ZigZag	44%	77%	75%
1vsRest-AUC	0.9824	**0.9902**	0.9887
1vs1-AUC	0.9430	**0.9860**	0.9858

accuracy for the proposed SSCN against *VGG16* and *SSCN w/o Aug*. These values correspond to the diagonals of the confusion matrices, and show that data augmentation is key to improve classification performance. When augmentation is omitted during training and testing, the classification accuracy drops below 50% in many classes.

The performance of SSCN and VGG16 are very similar in a few classes in terms of accuracy, and also the AUC values, shown in the last rows of Table 1, are rather close. However, when the AUC is close to 1, small improvements can be very significant. In fact, the first column indicates that the SSCN w/o Aug. is significantly worst than both SSCN and VGG16, although it achieves only slightly smaller 1vsRest-AUC values. Most importantly, our SSCN achieves 93% accuracy on the *Normal* class, while VGG does not exceed 89% accuracy. High accuracy on normal data is certainly important in an industrial monitoring scenario, since the vast majority of manufactured wafers belongs to the *Normal* class. Low accuracy on the *Normal* class results in a large number of false alarms. Therefore, directly handling the huge and sparse WDM (using our SSCN) greatly reduces the false alarms w.r.t. to a traditional CNN that operated on low-resolution images.

Finally, the difference between the two AUC measures indicates the effect of class imbalance: the 1vsRest-AUC is always higher than the 1vs1-AUC, since the latter is independent from the class proportion. This effect is more evident for *SSCN w/o Aug*, which achieves lower accuracy on the other classes.

Table 2. Class accuracy on the WM-811K dataset. The values of the 1vs1-AUC and 1vsRest-AUC of our CNN are 0.9989 and 0.9955, respectively. We cannot compute them for the classifier in [14], since no posterior probabilities were provided.

Class	SMV	CNN
Normal	95.7%	97.9%
Center	84.9%	94.0%
Donut	74.0%	97.1%
Edge-Loc	85.1%	85.2%
Edge-Ring	79.7%	96.8%
Loc	68.5%	72.7%
Near-Full	97.9%	99.3%
Random	79.8%	94.9%
Scratch	82.4%	87.6%

Comparison with Classification over Hand-Crafted Features. Table 2 reports the diagonals of the confusion matrices for both our CNN and the SVM in [14] over the WM-811K dataset. As in the experiments on the ST dataset, the proposed solution is evaluated using 10-fold cross validation, while the performance of [14] are reported from the paper, and have been computed on a specific training and test split.[1] Our CNN significantly outperforms SVM [14], achieving an accuracy gap ranging from a minimum of 0.1% for the *Edge-Loc*, up to a maximum of 23.1% for the *Donut*. Moreover, both the multiclass AUC values are above 0.99, indicating very good classification performance.

5   Conclusions

Accurate and automatic monitoring solutions are crucial for improving efficiency in semiconductor manufacturing. Here, we address the problem of classifying defect patterns on Wafer Defect Maps generated by inspection machines during the production. Our solution employs Submanifold Convolutional Neural Networks, which are perfectly suited for WDMs as they appear as huge and sparse binary images. As a result, our SCNN efficiently handles WDMs without any pre-processing procedure that alternative solutions typically require. Moreover, we propose a specific data-augmentation procedure for WDMs that turns out to be crucial to effectively train both SSCN and CNN. Our experiments, performed on a dataset of WDMs acquired in the production sites of our industrial partner, show that our SCNN achieves high accuracy on all the classes, and that outperforms all the alternatives on the *Normal*. Since *Normal* WDMs represent the vast majority of the production, this performance gap is very relevant as

---

[1] Unfortunately, the implementation of [14] has not been provided for a comparison over a 10-fold cross validation.

it yields few false alarms during monitoring. Future works address the problem of detecting unknown patterns appearing on WDMs, as this would enable to promptly react to problems that have never been observed before or that are too rare to collect enough training samples.

Acknowledgements. We gratefully acknowledge the support of NVIDIA Corporation with the donation of the Titan Xp and Titan V GPUs that researchers from Politecnico di Milano have used in this research.

References

1. Liu, C.W., Chien, C.F.: An intelligent system for wafer bin map defect diagnosis: an empirical study for semiconductor manufacturing. Eng. Appl. Artif. Intell. **26**(5), 1479–1486 (2013)
2. Bengio, Y., Courville, A., Vincent, P.: Representation learning: a review and new perspectives. IEEE Trans. Pattern Anal. Mach. Intell. **35**(8), 1798–1828 (2013)
3. Chang, C.W., Chao, T.M., Horng, J.T., Lu, C.F., Yeh, R.H.: Development pattern recognition model for the classification of circuit probe wafer maps on semiconductors. IEEE Trans. Compon. Packag. Manuf. Technol. **2**(12), 2089–2097 (2012)
4. Fan, M., Wang, Q., van der Waal, B.: Wafer defect patterns recognition based on OPTICS and multi-label classification. In: Proceedings of the IEEE Advanced Information Management, Communicates, Electronic and Automation Control Conference (IMCEC), pp. 912–915 (2016)
5. Graham, B., Engelcke, M., van der Maaten, L.: 3D semantic segmentation with submanifold sparse convolutional networks. In: Proceedings of the IEEE Conference on Computer Vision and Pattern Recognition (CVPR), pp. 9224–9232 (2018)
6. Hand, D.J., Till, R.J.: A simple generalisation of the area under the ROC curve for multiple class classification problems. Mach. Learn. **45**(2), 171–186 (2001)
7. Hsu, C.Y.: Clustering ensemble for identifying defective wafer bin map in semiconductor manufacturing. Math. Probl. Eng. **2015**, 11 (2015)
8. Krizhevsky, A., Sutskever, I., Hinton, G.E.: ImageNet classification with deep convolutional neural networks. In: Advances in Neural Information Processing Systems (NIPS), pp. 1097–1105 (2012)
9. Nakata, K., Orihara, R., Mizuoka, Y., Takagi, K.: A comprehensive big-data-based monitoring system for yield enhancement in semiconductor manufacturing. IEEE Trans. Semicond. Manuf. **30**(4), 339–344 (2017)
10. Nakazawa, T., Kulkarni, D.V.: Wafer map defect pattern classification and image retrieval using convolutional neural network. IEEE Trans. Semicond. Manuf. **31**(2), 309–314 (2018)
11. Provost, F., Domingos, P.: Tree induction for probability-based ranking. Mach. Learn. **52**(3), 199–215 (2003)
12. Russakovsky, O., Deng, J., Su, H., Krause, J., Satheesh, S., Ma, S., Huang, Z., Karpathy, A., Khosla, A., Bernstein, M., et al.: Imagenet large scale visual recognition challenge. Int. J. Comput. Vision **115**(3), 211–252 (2015)
13. Simonyan, K., Zisserman, A.: Very deep convolutional networks for large-scale image recognition. arXiv preprint arXiv:1409.1556 (2014)

14. Wu, M.J., Jang, J.S.R., Chen, J.L.: Wafer map failure pattern recognition and similarity ranking for large-scale data sets. IEEE Trans. Semicond. Manuf. **28**(1), 1–12 (2015)
15. Yu, J., Lu, X.: Wafer map defect detection and recognition using joint local and nonlocal linear discriminant analysis. IEEE Trans. Semicond. Manuf. **29**(1), 33–43 (2016)
16. Zeiler, M.D.: Adadelta: an adaptive learning rate method. arXiv preprint arXiv:1212.5701 (2012)

Blind Image Quality Assessment Based on the Use of Saliency Maps and a Multivariate Gaussian Distribution

Christophe Charrier[1]([⊠]), Abdelhakim Saadane[2],
and Christine Fernandez-Maloigne[3]

[1] Normandie Univ., UNICAEN, ENSICAEN, CNRS, GREYC,
14000 Caen, France
`christophe.charrier@unicaen.fr`
[2] Université de Nantes, XLIM, Nantes, France
`abdelhakim.saadane@univ-nantes.fr`
[3] Université de Poitiers, XLIM, Poitiers, France
`christine.fernandez@univ-poitiers.fr`

Abstract. With the widespread use of image processing technologies, objective image quality metrics are a fundamental and challenging problem. In this paper, we present a new No-Reference Image Quality Assessment (NR-IQA) algorithm based on visual attention modeling and a multivariate Gaussian distribution to predict the final quality score from the extracted features. Computational modeling of visual attention is performed to compute saliency maps at three resolution levels. At each level, distortions of the input image are extracted and weighted by the saliency maps in order to highlight degradations of visually attracting regions. The generated features are used by a probabilistic model to predict the final quality score. Experimental results demonstrate the effectiveness of the metric and show better performance when compared to well known NR-IQA algorithms.

Keywords: NR-IQA · Saliency maps · MVGD

1 Introduction

The development of image and video processing technologies and the exponential increase of new multimedia services raise the critical issue of assessing the visual quality. From several years, a number of investigations have been conducted to design robust Image Quality Assessment (IQA) metrics. Such metrics aim at predicting image quality that well correlates with Mean Opinion Scores (MOS). No-Reference IQA (NR-IQA) are interesting as they assume no knowledge of the reference image and can be embedded in practical and real-time applications. Three approaches may be used in the design of IQA algorithms.

This research is supported by the ANR project #ANR-16-CE39-0013.

© Springer Nature Switzerland AG 2019
E. Ricci et al. (Eds.): ICIAP 2019, LNCS 11752, pp. 137–147, 2019.
https://doi.org/10.1007/978-3-030-30645-8_13

The first one looks to mimic the behavior of the Human Visual System (HVS). The HVS models used in this context, include relevant properties such as the contrast sensitivity function, masking effects and detection mechanisms. A number of investigations [1] have shown that these models when included in IQA algorithms, improve their performance. The second approach is well suited for assessing the quality of images distorted by known distortions. The algorithms of this approach quantify one or more distortions such as blockiness [20,27], blur [2,22] or ringing [9,10] and score the image accordingly. The third and last approach is a general-purpose method. It considers that the HVS is very sensitive to structural information in the image and any loss of this structural information results in a perceptual loss of quality. To quantify loss of information, this approach uses Natural Scene Statistics (NSS). Generally, NSS-based algorithms apply a combination of learning-based approach with NSS-based extracted features. When a large ground truth is available, statistical modeling algorithms can achieve good performance. However, there is still an effort to provide to reach the subjective consistency of the HVS.

The work proposed in this paper is motivated by the interesting results of IQA when visual attention models are used. Computational visual saliency models extract regions that can attract human gaze. These regions are of a great interest in IQA. This paper presents a new NR-IQA based on the use of saliency maps to better weight the extracted distortions and combines these weighted distortions using a MultiVariate Gaussian distribution (MVGD).

2   The Proposed Approach

Figure 1 presents the overall synopsis of the multi-scale proposed approach, namely SABIQ (SAliency-based Blind Image Quality) index. First, a multi-scale

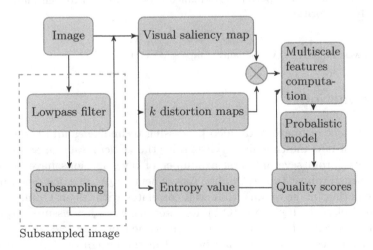

Fig. 1. Overall synopsis of the multi-scale proposed approach

decomposition is performed on the input image and a saliency map is computed at each level. The base level corresponds to the first image while the remaining ones are obtained by a low-pass filtering followed by a sub-sampling. Secondly, different distortion maps are generated at same scale levels. At each level, the Renyi entropy of the subsampled image is also computed. Thirdly, for each level, a weighting of each computed distortion map with the corresponding saliency map is performed in order to increase the strength of degradation in visually attracting areas. Finally, the combination at each level of the weighted distortion map with the computed Renyi entropy is performed to design a multiresolution distortion map. The final stage of the pipeline is a simple Bayesian model that predicts the quality score of the input image. The Bayesian approach maximizes the probability that the image has a certain quality score given the features extracted from the image. The associate posterior probability is modeled as a MultiVariate Gaussian Distribution (MVGD).

2.1 Visual Saliency Map

Visual attention is the ability of the HVS to rapidly direct our gaze towards regions of interest in our visual environment. Two attentional mechanisms are involved in such selection; bottom-up and top-down. Main features known to influence bottom-up attention include color, orientation, motion. Top-down attention is rather driven by the observer's experience, task and expectation. Many conducted investigations have helped in understanding visual attention and many computational saliency models have been proposed in the literature [12,13]. A recent state-of-the-art in visual attention is given in [5]. Most of these models use bottom-up approach and are based on the Feature Integration Theory of Treisman and Gelade [28]. They compute a 2D map that highlights locations where fixations are likely to occur. These image-based (stimulus-driven) models use the same architecture but vary in the selection of characteristics used to calculate the global saliency map.

The saliency models have addressed various applications, including computer vision [21], robotics [6] and visual signal processing [7,29]. In the context of IQA algorithms, the saliency models are intended to extract the most relevant visual features that when combined, produce a quality score highly correlated with human judgment [3].

Many research have been investigated to model the phenomenon that any human viewer can focus on attractive points at a first glance, and many saliency models have been proposed in the literature.

Saliency models can be categorized into (1) pixel-based models and (2) object-based models. The pixel-based models aim to highlight pixel locations where fixations are likely to occur. The object-based models focus on detecting salient objects in a visual scene. The majority of saliency models in the literature are pixel-based saliency models, such as ITTI [11], STB [30], PQFT [8], etc.

In this paper, the ITTI model [12] has been employed. This model combines multiscale image features into a single topographical saliency map. Three channels (Intensity, Color and Orientation) are used as low level features. First, feature maps are calculated for each channel via center-surround differences operation. Three kinds of conspicuity maps are then obtained by across-scale combination. The final saliency map is built through combining all of the conspicuity maps.

2.2 Distortion Maps

Many studies have shown that image quality degradations are well measured by features of local structure [31], contrast [31,32], multi-scale and multi-orientation decomposition [34].

Contrast Distortion Map. The image gradient is an interesting descriptor to capture both local image structure and local contrast [33]. Also according to this study, the partial derivatives and gradient magnitudes change with the strength of applied distortions.

Following this strategy and in order to generate the contrast distortion map, we compute both horizontal and vertical gradient component images $\partial I/\partial x$ and $\partial I/\partial y$ from the image I. From those two gradient images, the gradient magnitude image is computed as $\sqrt{(\partial I/\partial x)^2 + (\partial I/\partial y)^2}$ and then modelled by a Weibull distribution. This distribution fits well the gradient magnitude of natural images [25] and its 2 parameters (the scale parameter and the shape parameter) roughly approximate the local contrast and the texture activity in the gradient magnitude map, respectively. Larger values of the scale parameter imply greater local contrast.

Yet, instead of computing the contrast on the entire image, the image is first partitioned into equally sized $n \times n$ blocks (referred to as local image patches), then the local contrast is computed for each block yielding in final to a local contrast map $\mathcal{M}_C$.

Structural Distortion Map. The structural distortion map considered here uses structural distortion features that are extracted from both spatial and frequency information. To extract image structure information from frequency domain, the image is partitioned into equally sized $n \times n$ local image patches and then a 2D-DCT (Discrete Cosine Transform) is applied on each patch. The feature extraction is thus locally performed in the spatio-frequency domain according to local spatial visual processing property of the HVS [4]. To capture degradation depending on directional information in the image, block DCT coefficients are modeled along three orientations (0, 45 and 90°). For each orientation, a Generalized Gaussian is fitted to the associated coefficients, and the coefficient ζ is computed from the histogram model as $\zeta = \sigma(X)/\mu(X)$ where $\sigma(X)$ and $\mu(X)$ are the standard deviation and the mean of the DCT coefficient magnitudes, respectively. In order to select the most significant map from the three generated distortion maps, the variance of ζ is then computed for each orientation. The distortion map associated to the highest value of the variance of ζ is finally chosen and serve as structural distortion map, namely $\mathcal{M}_S$.

Since the DC (Direct Coefficient) does not convey any structural information, it is removed from all computations.

Multi-orientation Image Property Map. It is widely admitted that the HVS is sensitive to spatial frequency and orientation. In order to capture this sensitivity, the steerable pyramid transform [26] is used.

Let $a(i, j, f, \theta)$ be an original coefficient issued from the decomposition process located at the position (i, j) in the frequency band f and orientation band θ. The associated squared and normalized coefficient $r(i, j, f, \theta)$ is defined as:

$$r(i, j, f, \theta) = k \frac{a(i, j, f, \theta)^2}{\sum_{\phi \in [0,45,90,135]} a(i, j, f, \phi)^2 + \sigma^2} \tag{1}$$

In this paper, four orientation bands with bandwidths of 45° 0, 45, 90, 135 plus one isotropic lowpass filter are used yielding in five response maps $\{R_\theta, R_{iso}\}, \theta \in [0, 45, 90, 135]$. The distortion map associated to the highest value of the variance is finally selected and will serve as frequency variation distortion map, namely $\mathcal{M}_F$.

From the four orientation bands, we compute the energy ratio in order to take account the modification of local spectral signatures of an image. This approach is inspired from the quality BLIINDS2 index [24]. Each map associated to θ $\{R_\theta\}, \theta \in [0, 45, 90, 135]$ is decomposed into equally sized $n \times n$ blocks. For each obtained patch, the average energy in frequency band θ models the variance corresponding to band θ as $e_\theta = \sigma_\theta^2$.

For each $\theta \in [45, 90, 135]$, the relative distribution of energies in lower and higher bands is then computed as:

$$E_\theta = \frac{|e_\theta - 1/n \sum_{t<\theta} e_t|}{|e_\theta + 1/n \sum_{t<\theta} e_t|} \tag{2}$$

where $1/n \sum_{t<\theta} e_t$ represents the average energy up to frequency band θ. Three distortion maps are then generated.

The distortion map associated to the highest value of the variance of E_θ is finally selected and serves as energy ratio distortion map, namely $\mathcal{M}_E$.

2.3   Multiscale Features Computation

In this block, each distortion map is combined with the saliency map in order to obtain a saliency-based distortion map. From each saliency-based distortion map, a pooling strategy is applied by averaging over the highest 10th percentile coefficients across the distortion map. This pooling strategy is motivated by the fact that the "worst" distortions in an image heavily influence subjective impressions and that they are concentrated in few coefficients having higher values [18]. All the obtained values are referred to as $df^{10}(\cdot)$, where $(\cdot)$ represents one of the computed distortion maps $\{\mathcal{M}_C, \mathcal{M}_S, \mathcal{M}_F, \mathcal{M}_E\}$. In order to get information about the distribution of the distortions (over space or isolated distortions), the 100th percentile average of the local scores is also computed. The obtained values are referred to as $df^{100}(\cdot)$, where $(\cdot)$ represents one of the computed distortion maps $\{\mathcal{M}_C, \mathcal{M}_S, \mathcal{M}_F, \mathcal{M}_E\}$. The whole computation leads, in total, to 8 distortion features $\{df^{10}(k), df^{100}(k)\}$, $\forall k \in \{\mathcal{M}_C, \mathcal{M}_S, \mathcal{M}_F, \mathcal{M}_E\}$.

The final feature is computed at each scale level l as

$$\text{final-feature}_l^p(k) = df_l^p(k) * \text{entropy}_l \tag{3}$$

where $p \in \{10, 100\}$, $k \in \{\mathcal{M}_C, \mathcal{M}_S, \mathcal{M}_F, \mathcal{M}_E\}$, $df_l^p(k)$ represents the value of the distortion value $df^p(k)$ at level l, and entropy$_l$ is the Renyi entropy of the associated saliency-based distortion map. This strategy yields us to include information about the anisotropy property of distortion maps. In this paper, the number of scales l is set to 3 as this value achieves the best performance.

2.4   Probabilistic Model and Quality Score Prediction

The computed features and the DMOS (Difference of Mean Opinion Scores) values of training images are then used by the learning block to fit a MVGD. The resulting model SABIQ is given by:

$$\text{SABIQ}(x) = \frac{1}{(2\pi)^{k/2} |\Sigma|^{1/2}} \exp\left(-\frac{1}{2}(x-\beta)^T \Sigma^{-1} (x-\beta)\right) \tag{4}$$

where $x = (\{\text{final-feature}_l^p(k)\}, DMOS)$ corresponds to the extracted features (Eq. 3) to which is added DMOS. β and Σ denote the mean and covariance matrix of the MVGD model and are estimated using the maximum likelihood method. The features extracted from testing images with DMOS values lying between 0 and 100 with a step of 0.5, are fed into the learned SABIQ to assess quality of image under test.

3   Performance Evaluation

3.1   Apparatus

To provide comparison of NR-IQA algorithms, two publicly available databases are used: (1) TID2013 database [23] and (2) CSIQ database [15]. Since LIVE database [14] has been used to train both the proposed metric and most of the trail NR-IQA schemes, it has not been used to evaluate performances. To train our model, we used LIVE database running multiple train-test sequences. For each sequence, the image database is divided into distinct training and test sets. In each train-test sequence, 80% of the LIVE IQA Database content was chosen to design the training set, and the remaining 20% were dedicated to the test set. This means each training set contains 23 reference images and their associated distorted images. The quality scores are computed using a bootstrap process with 999 replicates.

Table 1. SROCC values of NR-IQA models on each distortion types for the TID2013 database.

TID2013 subset		BRISQUE	BLIINDS2	DIIVINE	SSEQ	ILNIQE	CORNIA	SABIQ
Single distortion	Additive Gaussian noise	0.852	0.722	0.855	0.807	0.876	0.756	**0.881**
	Add noise in color components	0.709	0.649	0.712	0.681	0.815	0.749	**0.817**
	Spatially correlated noise	0.491	0.767	0.463	0.635	0.923	0.727	**0.933**
	Masked noise	0.575	0.512	0.675	0.565	0.512	**0.726**	**0.726**
	High frequency noise	0.753	0.824	0.878	0.860	0.868	0.796	**0.910**
	Impulse noise	0.630	0.650	**0.806**	0.749	0.755	0.767	0.805
	Quantization noise	0.798	0.781	0.165	0.468	**0.873**	0.016	0.851
	Gaussian blur	0.813	0.855	0.834	0.858	0.814	**0.921**	0.861
	Image denoising	0.586	0.711	0.723	0.783	0.750	**0.832**	0.793
	JPEG compression	0.852	0.864	0.629	0.825	0.834	0.874	**0.902**
	JPEG2000 compression	0.893	0.898	0.853	0.885	0.857	**0.901**	**0.901**
	JPEG transmission errors	0.315	0.117	0.239	0.354	0.282	**0.686**	0.351
	JPEG2000 transmission errors	0.360	0.620	0.060	0.561	0.524	**0.678**	0.622
	Non eccentricity pattern noise	0.145	0.096	0.060	0.011	0.080	**0.286**	0.102
	Local block-wise distortions	**0.224**	0.209	0.093	0.016	0.135	0.218	0.220
	Mean shift	0.124	0.128	0.010	0.108	**0.184**	0.065	0.179
	Contrast change	0.040	0.150	0.460	0.204	0.014	0.182	**0.508**
	Change of color saturation	0.109	0.017	0.068	0.074	0.162	0.081	**0.182**
Multiple dist.	Multiplicative Gaussian noise	0.724	0.716	**0.787**	0.679	0.693	0.644	0.765
	Comfort noise	0.008	0.017	0.116	0.033	0.359	**0.534**	0.379
	Lossy comp. of noisy images	0.685	0.719	0.633	0.610	0.828	**0.862**	0.838
	Color quant. with dither	0.764	0.736	0.436	0.528	0.748	0.272	**0.810**
	Chromatic aberrations	0.616	0.539	0.661	0.688	0.679	**0.792**	0.762
	Sparse sampling and reconst.	0.784	0.816	0.834	0.895	0.865	0.862	**0.920**
Cumulative subsets		0.367	0.393	0.355	0.332	0.494	0.429	**0.567**

To assess the performance of SABIQ, the Spearman Rank Order Correlation Coefficient (SROCC) is computed between DMOS values and predicted scores from six state-of-the-art opinion-aware NR-IQA methods, including BRISQUE [17], BLIINDS2 [24], DIIVINE [19], CORNIA [17], ILNIQE [33] and SSEQ [16] which are all so far widely accepted in the research community.

3.2   Performance Evaluation

The SROCC between predicted DMOS and subjective DMOS is reported in Table 1 for the TID2013 database. From Table 1, one observes that SABIQ performs much better than the six other NR-IQA methods when the SROCC values for the whole database is considered. This significant gain in performance is likely induced by the visual attention that is used in the weighting of distortions. When single distortions are considered, SABIQ achieves performance comparable with CORNIA and performs better than the five remaining trail quality schemes. For multiple distortions, SABIQ performs better than BRISQUE, BLIINDS2, DIIVINE and SSEQ and competes very well with CORNIA and ILNIQE.

Similar results are shown in Table 2 for CSIQ Images database. SABIQ achieves better results for 4 out of 6 distortions and outperforms all trail NR-IQA algorithms when the entire database is considered. In this case, the gain in

Table 2. SROCC values of NR-IQA models on each distortion types for the CSIQ Images database.

CSIQ subset	BRISQUE	BLIINDS2	DIIVINE	SSEQ	ILNIQE	CORNIA	SABIQ
JP2K	0.866	0.895	0.830	0.848	0.906	0.746	**0.920**
JPEG	0.903	0.901	0.799	0.865	0.899	0.908	**0.941**
Gaussian noise	0.252	0.379	0.176	**0.872**	0.850	0.914	0.870
Add. Gaussian pink noise	**0.925**	0.801	0.866	0.046	0.874	0.420	0.895
Gaussian blur	0.903	0.891	0.871	0.873	0.858	0.917	**0.920**
Global contrast decrement	0.029	0.012	0.396	0.200	0.501	0.302	**0.509**
Cumulative subsets	0.566	0.577	0.596	0.528	0.815	0.663	**0.877**

performance is about 7% compared to ILNIQE and is at least 32% compared to other metrics.

We also trained the methods on TID2013 excluding multi-distorted subscts (MD), then tested them on the two other datasets and the remaining MD subsets of TID2013. The results are shown in Table 3. The NR-IQA methods IL-NIQE and SABIQ clearly outperform the other trial method when trained on single distortion. When considering the LIVE database, IL-NIQE and SABIQ achieve almost the same results, which is not surprising since many existing recent NR-IQA schemes reach high correlations on that database. Furthermore, SABIQ presents the highest SROCC value with CSIQ database. All these results tend to highlight a high generalization capability of the proposed approach.

Table 3. SROCC values when trained on TID2013, excluding multi-distortion subsets (MD)

	LIVE	CSIQ	MD TID2013 subsets
BRISQUE	0.522	0.639	0.122
BLIINDS2	0.511	0.456	0.322
DIIVINE	0.410	0.701	0.409
SSEQ	0.230	0.630	0.098
ILNIQE	0.899	0.631	0.568
CORNIA	0.399	0.656	0.412
SABIQ	0.896	0.787	0.562

4   Conclusion

In this paper, we investigated how the visual attention property of the HVS can be embedded in the NR-IQA algorithm design and in which way it can improve the prediction of image quality. The proposed approach, namely SABIQ, is based on the use of computational modeling of visual attention to compute the saliency map. At each of the three levels of the multiresolution scheme, distortions of the input image are generated and weighted by the saliency maps in order to highlight degradations of visually attracting regions. The extracted features are used by a probabilistic model to predict the final quality score. The obtained results demonstrate the effectiveness of the approach.

References

1. Babu, R.V., Perkis, A.: An HVS-based no-reference perceptual quality assessment of JPEG coded images using neural networks. In: Proceedings of the 2005 International Conference on Image Processing, ICIP 2005, Genoa, Italy, 11–14 September 2005, pp. 433–436 (2005). https://doi.org/10.1109/ICIP.2005.1529780
2. Barland, R., Saadane, A.: Blind quality metric using a perceptual map for JPEG-2000 compressed images. In: International Conference on Image Processing (ICIP) (2006)
3. Ben Amor, M., Kammoun, F., Masmoudi, N.: Improved performance of quality metrics using saliency map and CSF filter for standard coding H264/AVC. Multimed. Tools Appl. **77**(15), 19377–19397 (2018). https://doi.org/10.1007/s11042-017-5393-3
4. Blake, R., Sekuler, R.: Perception, 5th edn. McGraw-Hill Higher Education, New York (2006)
5. Borji, A., Itti, L.: State-of-the-art in visual attention modeling. IEEE Trans. Pattern Anal. Mach. Intell. **35**(1), 185–207 (2013). https://doi.org/10.1109/TPAMI.2012.89
6. Breazeal, C., Scassellati, B.: A context-dependent attention system for a social robot. In: 16th International Joint Conference on Artificial Intelligence (IJCAI), San-Francisco, CA, USA, pp. 1146–1153 (1999)
7. Christopoulos, C., Skodras, A., Ebrahimi, T.: The jpeg2000 still image coding system: an overview. IEEE Trans. Consum. Electron. **46**, 1103–1127 (2000)
8. Guo, C., Zhang, L.: A novel multiresolution spatiotemporal saliency detection model and its applications in image and video compression. IEEE Trans. Image Process. **19**(1), 185–198 (2010). https://doi.org/10.1109/TIP.2009.2030969
9. Hantao, L., Klomp, N., Heynderickx, I.: A no-reference metric for perceived ringing artifacts in images. IEEE Trans. Circuits Syst. Video Technol. **20**(4), 529–539 (2010)
10. Hu, S., Pizlo, Z., Allebach, J.P.: JPEG ringing artifact visibility evaluation. In: Proceedings of SPIE 9016, Image Quality and System Perfromance XI (2014)
11. Itti, L., Koch, C., Niebur, E.: A model of saliency-based visual attention for rapid scene analysis. IEEE Trans. Pattern Anal. Mach. Intell. **20**(11), 1254–1259 (1998). http://link.aip.org/link/?JEI/19/011006/1
12. Itti, L., Koch, C., Niebuhr, E.: A model of saliency-based visual attention for rapid scene analysis. IEEE Trans. Pattern Anal. Mach. Intell. **20**(11), 1254–1259 (1998)
13. Koch, C., Ullman, S.: Shifts in selective visual attention: towards the underlying neural circuitry. Human Neurobiol. **4**(4), 219–227 (1985)

14. Laboratory for Image & Video Engineering, University of Texas (Austin): LIVE Image Quality Assessment Database (2002). http://live.ece.utexas.edu/research/Quality
15. Larson, E.C., Chandler, D.M.: Most apparent distortion: full-reference image quality assessment and the role of strategy. J. Electron. Imaging **19**(1), 011006 (2010). https://doi.org/10.1117/1.3267105. http://link.aip.org/link/?JEI/19/011006/1
16. Liu, L., Liu, B., Huang, H., Bovik, A.: No-reference image quality assessment based on spatial and spectral entropies. Signal Process.: Image Commun. **29**(8), 856–863 (2014). https://doi.org/10.1016/j.image.2014.06.006
17. Mittal, A., Moorthy, A.K., Bovik, A.C.: No-reference image quality assessment in the spatial domain. IEEE Trans. Image Process. **21**(12), 4695–4708 (2012)
18. Moorthy, A.K., Bovik, A.C.: Visual importance pooling for image quality assessment. IEEE J. Sel. Topics Signal Process. **3**(2), 193–201 (2009). https://doi.org/10.1109/JSTSP.2009.2015374
19. Moorthy, A.K., Bovik, A.C.: Blind image quality assessment: from natural scene statistics to perceptual quality. IEEE Trans. Image Process. **20**(12), 3350–3364 (2011)
20. Muijs, R., Kirenko, I.: A no-reference blocking artifact measure for adaptive video processing. In: European Signal Processing Conference (Eusipco) (2005)
21. Navalpakkam, V., Itti, L.: An integrated model of top-down and bottom-up attention for optimizing detection speed. In: IEEE Computer Society Conference on Computer Vision and Pattern Recognition, vol. 2, pp. 2049–2056 (2006)
22. ParvezSazzad, Z., Kawayoke, Y., Horita, Y.: No-reference image quality assessment for JPEG-2000 based on spatial features. Signal Process.: Image Commun. **23**(4), 257–268 (2008)
23. Ponomarenko, N., Carli, M., Lukin, V., Astola, J., Battisti, F.: Color image database for evaluation of image quality metrics. In: International Workshop on Multimedia Signal Processing, Australia, pp. 403–408, October 2008
24. Saad, M., Bovik, A.C., Charrier, C.: Blind image quality assessment: a natural scene statistics approach in the DCT domain. IEEE Trans. Image Process. **21**(8), 3339–3352 (2012)
25. Scholte, H.S., Ghebreab, S., Waldorp, L., Smeulders, A.W.M., Lamme, V.A.F.: Brain responses strongly correlate with weibull image statistics when processing natural images. J. Vis. **9**(4), 29 (2009). https://doi.org/10.1167/9.4.29
26. Simoncelli, E.P., Freeman, W.T.: The steerable pyramid: a flexible architecture for multi-scale derivative computation. In: Proceedings. In: International Conference on Image Processing (ICIP), vol. 3, pp. 444–447, October 1995. https://doi.org/10.1109/ICIP.1995.537667
27. Song, X., Yang, Y.: A new no-reference assessmet metric of blocking artefacts on HVS masking effect. In: International Congress on Image and Signal Processing, pp. 1–6 (2009)
28. Treisman, A.M., Gelade, G.: A feature-integration theory of attention. Cogn. Psychol. **12**, 97–136 (1980)
29. Walther, D., Rutishauser, U., Koch, C., Perona, P.: Selective visual attention enables learning and recognition of multiple objects in cluttered scenes. Comput. Vis. Image Underst. **100**, 42–63 (2005)
30. Walther, D., Koch, C.: Modeling attention to salient proto-objects. Neural Netw. **19**(9), 1395–1407 (2006). https://doi.org/10.1016/j.neunet.2006.10.001. http://www.sciencedirect.com/science/article/pii/S0893608006002152. Brain and Attention

31. Wang, Z., Bovik, A., Sheikh, H., Simoncelli, E.: Image quality assessment: from error visibility to structural similarity. IEEE Trans. Image Process. **13**(4), 600–612 (2004)
32. Xue, W., Mou, X., Zhang, L., Bovik, A., Feng, X.: Blind image quality assessment using joint statistics of gradient magnitude and Laplacian features. IEEE Trans. Image Process. **23**(11), 4850–4862 (2014)
33. Zhang, L., Zhang, L., Bovik, A.: A feature-enriched completely blind image quality evaluator. IEEE Trans. Image Process. **24**(8), 2579–2591 (2015)
34. Zhang, Y., Chandler, D.: No-reference image quality assessment based on log-derivative statistics of natural scenes. J. Electron. Imaging **22**(4), 1–23 (2013)

Improving the Performance of Thinning Algorithms with Directed Rooted Acyclic Graphs

Federico Bolelli[(✉)] and Costantino Grana

Dipartimento di Ingegneria "Enzo Ferrari",
Università degli Studi di Modena e Reggio Emilia,
Via Vivarelli 10, 41125 Modena, MO, Italy
{federico.bolelli,costantino.grana}@unimore.it

Abstract. In this paper we propose a strategy to optimize the performance of thinning algorithms. This solution is obtained by combining three proven strategies for binary images neighborhood exploration, namely modeling the problem with an optimal decision tree, reusing pixels from the previous step of the algorithm, and reducing the code footprint by means of Directed Rooted Acyclic Graphs. A complete and open-source benchmarking suite is also provided. Experimental results confirm that the proposed algorithms clearly outperform classical implementations.

Keywords: Thinning · Skeletonization · Optimization · Decision trees · Binary image processing

1 Introduction

Thinning is a fundamental algorithm used in many computer vision and image processing tasks, which aims at providing an approximate and compact representation of the elements (objects) inside images. It can be defined as the successive removal of outermost layers of an object until only a skeleton of unit width remains [10]. Firstly introduced in the 1950 as a data compression strategy [11], the thinning procedure is nowadays used as a pre- or post-processing step in many different applications, ranging from medical imaging [33,34] to handwritten text recognition [7,19] and fingerprint analysis [22]. Therefore, having an efficient and effective algorithm is extremely important.

In the literature, a lot of approaches to solve the problem have been detailed. The algorithm proposed by Zhang and Suen (ZS) in [35] is one of the most famous and used, given its efficiency and simplicity. This algorithm is based on the 8-neighbor connectivity and exploits two sub-iterations that are iteratively performed to remove pixels and obtain the final result. In [8], Chen and Hsu (CH) improved the output visual appearance of the Zhang-Suen approach, by fixing some corner cases, and proposed a lookup table (LUT) solution to speed up the process.

© Springer Nature Switzerland AG 2019
E. Ricci et al. (Eds.): ICIAP 2019, LNCS 11752, pp. 148–158, 2019.
https://doi.org/10.1007/978-3-030-30645-8_14

Holt *et al.* [20] tackled the problem by a different perspective and proposed an improvement on the Zangh-Suen technique which requires less iterations, at the expense of examining a larger neighborhood (from 3×3 to 4×4). Even though the algorithm solves some of the ZS drawbacks, the need to access more pixels makes it slower, especially when implemented on sequential machines [16].

The algorithm by Guo and Hall [15] allows to better cope with 2×2 squares and diagonal lines inside images using a set of rules that is very similar to the one proposed by Lü and Wang [25].

These solutions have been proposed some decades ago, but are still commonly used [22,33,34] and included in many image processing libraries, such as OpenCV [27].

Given its intrinsically iterative nature the thinning procedure is expensive and usually very slow, especially when applied on high resolution images. Anyway, a lot of approaches have been proposed to improve performances without affecting the output result. Besides the already mentioned LUT technique, an efficient neighborhood exploration technique based on decision trees has been applied on the ZS algorithm [13]. The authors experimentally proved that the use of an optimal Decision Tree (DTree) allows to dramatically reduce the number of memory accesses to be performed in order to explore the neighborhood, thus improving the overall performance of the algorithm, even when compared to implementations based on lookup table.

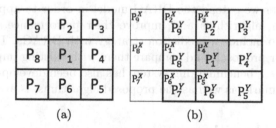

Fig. 1. Naming convention for the pixel in the neighborhood of P_1 (a) and their overlap when the mask is shifted for processing the next pixel (b).

Both of these approaches miss a classical optimization strategy used when working with local neighborhoods: when the scanning mask moves horizontally most of the pixels have already been read in the previous step (Fig. 1), so only the rightmost column needs to be read, and the others can be obtained by just shifting the positions of the previously inspected ones. This optimization approach is typically used with average/box filtering, running median [21], and Connected Components Labeling [18]. A solution for combining this *prediction* with DTrees was introduced in [12].

Moreover, in [3,6], a novel approach to model decision problems as Directed Rooted Acyclic Graphs (DRAGs) was introduced. Differently from DTrees, in which the same set of conditions required to reach the corresponding leaf may

---

Algorithm 1. Two subiteration thinning algorithm

1: **function** ITERATION(I, O, k)
2:     $O \leftarrow I$
3:     *changed* $\leftarrow$ **false**
4:     **for all** $p \in \mathcal{L}(I)$ **do**
5:       **if** $I(p) = 1$ **then**
6:         **if** SHOULD_REMOVE(I, p, k) **then**
7:           $O(p) \leftarrow 0$
8:           *changed* $\leftarrow$ **true**
9:     **return** *changed*

10: **procedure** THINNING(I, O)
11:     **repeat**
12:       $changed_0 \leftarrow$ ITERATION($I, O, 0$)
13:       $changed_1 \leftarrow$ ITERATION($O, I, 1$)
14:     **until** $\neg changed_0 \wedge \neg changed_1$

---

be checked in multiple subtrees, in a DRAG, being it a graph, these could be merged together. Even though this approach does not save any condition check with respect to the use of a DTree, it allows to sensibly reduce the number of machine instructions, and thus the impact on instruction cache. Indeed, the code generated from a DRAG will include the same checks only once.

With this paper we extend the DRAG model in order to apply it on state-of-the-art thinning algorithms and improve their performance. Moreover, we apply a solution to include a prediction strategy with DRAGs. To evaluate the effectiveness of our proposals and compare them with existing implementations, an open-source $C++$ benchmarking system has also been developed. The source code of the benchmark, as well as the proposed algorithms, is available in [31].

2   Thinning Algorithms

Many thinning algorithms belong to the class of parallel thinning algorithms [23]: every pixel is analyzed considering its neighborhood values in the current image, but the result is written into a different output mask, so that the procedure can be easily implemented on massively parallel architectures.

We consider three classical algorithms, which work with biased subiterations: at each iteration both subiterations must be performed and if neither of them modifies the image, the algorithm finishes. At each subiteration, the image is scanned and for each foreground pixel we check if the pixel should be removed (Algorithm 1).

The notation used in the algorithms is summarized here. Given I, an image defined over a two dimensional rectangular lattice $\mathcal{L}$, and $I(p)$ the value of pixel $p \in \mathcal{L}$, with $p = (p_x, p_y)$, we define the *neighborhood* of a pixel as follows:

$$\mathcal{N}(p) = \{q \in \mathcal{L} \mid \max(|p_x - q_x|, |p_y - q_y|) \leq 1\} \tag{1}$$

Algorithm 2. Removal logic functions for ZhangSuen and ChenHsu algorithms

1: **function** A(P)
2:      **return** $(\neg P_2 \wedge P_3) + (\neg P_3 \wedge P_4) + (\neg P_4 \wedge P_5) + (\neg P_5 \wedge P_6) +$
3:           $(\neg P_6 \wedge P_7) + (\neg P_7 \wedge P_8) + (\neg P_8 \wedge P_9) + (\neg P_9 \wedge P_2)$
4: **function** B(P)
5:      **return** $P_2 + P_3 + P_4 + P_5 + P_6 + P_7 + P_8 + P_9$

6: **function** ZS_SHOULD_REMOVE(I, p, k)
7:      $P \leftarrow I(\mathcal{N}(p))$
8:      **if** $k = 0$ **then**
9:           $c \leftarrow P_2 \wedge P_4 \wedge P_6$;
10:          $d \leftarrow P_4 \wedge P_6 \wedge P_8$;
11:     **else**
12:          $c \leftarrow P_2 \wedge P_4 \wedge P_8$;
13:          $d \leftarrow P_2 \wedge P_6 \wedge P_8$;
14:     **return** $(A(P) = 1) \wedge (2 \leq B(P) \leq 6) \wedge \neg c \wedge \neg d$

15: **function** CH_SHOULD_REMOVE(I, p, k)
16:     $P \leftarrow I(\mathcal{N}(p))$
17:     **if** $k = 0$ **then**
18:          $c \leftarrow P_2 \wedge P_4 \wedge P_6$;
19:          $d \leftarrow P_4 \wedge P_6 \wedge P_8$;
20:          $f \leftarrow P_2 \wedge P_4 \wedge \neg P_6 \neg P_7 \neg P_8$
21:          $g \leftarrow P_4 \wedge P_6 \wedge \neg P_2 \neg P_8 \neg P_9$
22:     **else**
23:          $c \leftarrow P_2 \wedge P_4 \wedge P_8$;
24:          $d \leftarrow P_2 \wedge P_6 \wedge P_8$;
25:          $f \leftarrow P_2 \wedge P_8 \wedge \neg P_4 \neg P_5 \neg P_6$
26:          $g \leftarrow P_6 \wedge P_8 \wedge \neg P_2 \neg P_3 \neg P_4$
27:     **return** $(2 \leq B(P) \leq 7) \wedge ((A(P) = 1) \wedge \neg c \wedge \neg d) \vee$
28:          $(A(P) = 2) \wedge (f \vee g))$

Two pixels, p and q, are said to be *neighbors* if $q \in \mathcal{N}(p)$, that implies $p \in \mathcal{N}(q)$. From a visual perspective, p and q are *neighbors* if they share an edge *or* a vertex. The set defined in Eq. 1 is called 8-neighborhood of p. In a binary image, meaningful regions are called *foreground* ($\mathcal{F}$), and the rest of the image is the *background* ($\mathcal{B}$). Following a common convention, we will assign value 1 to foreground pixels, and value 0 to background. The conditions for foreground pixel removal depend on the neighborhood and the algorithm flavor. Following the original notation of Zhang and Suen, pixels are enumerated in clockwise order, with the current pixel being P_1.

Algorithms 2 and 3 provide a detailed summary of the algorithms proposed by Zhang and Suen, Chen and Hsu and Guo and Hall. In all of them, k represents the subiteration index: $k = 0$ during the first subiteration and $k = 1$ during the second one. Support logic functions are used such as $A(P)$, which is the number of 01 patterns in clockwise order, and $B(P)$, which is the number of non zero

Algorithm 3. Removal logic function for GuoHall algorithm

1:	**function** GH_SHOULD_REMOVE(I, p, k)
2:	$P \leftarrow I(\mathcal{N}(p))$
3:	$C \leftarrow ((\neg P_2) \wedge (P_3 \vee P_4)) + ((\neg P_4) \wedge (P_5 \vee P_6)) +$
4:	$\quad ((\neg P_6) \wedge (P_7 \vee P_8)) + ((\neg P_8) \wedge (P_9 \vee P_2))$
5:	$N1 \leftarrow (P_9 \vee P_2) + (P_3 \vee P_4) + (P_5 \vee P_6) + (P_7 \vee P_8)$
6:	$N2 \leftarrow (P_2 \vee P_3) + (P_4 \vee P_5) + (P_6 \vee P_7) + (P_8 \vee P_9)$
7:	$N \leftarrow min(N1, N2)$
8:	**if** $k = 0$ **then**
9:	$\quad m \leftarrow (P_6 \vee P_7 \vee \neg P_9) \wedge P_8$
10:	**else**
11:	$\quad m \leftarrow (P_2 \vee P_3 \vee \neg P_5) \wedge P_4$
12:	**return** $(C = 1) \wedge (2 \leq N \leq 3) \wedge \neg m$

neighbors of P_1. The basic idea is to remove pixels at foreground connected components edges (*i.e.*, the block should not be totally foreground), without splitting that component.

Chen and Hsu [9] observed that given the eight neighbors of P_1 the outcome of the conditions is known, thus they built two lookup tables (LUT) for the two subiterations and used the pixel values as bits for the index of the LUT. This allows to save all the operations required to compute $A(P)$, $B(P)$ and the other two conditions, adding only one memory access. The same approach can obviously be applied to the GuoHall rules.

3   Techniques for Performance Optimization

The LUT approach suggests that thinning techniques can be modeled as decision tables [29]. A decision table is a tabular form that presents a set of conditions and their corresponding actions. A statement section reports a set of conditions which must be tested and a list of actions to perform. Each combination of condition entries (*condition outcomes*) is paired to an *action entry*. In the action entries, a column is marked to specify whether the corresponding action is to be performed or not. The aforementioned thinning algorithms can thus be modeled as a decision table in which the conditions are given by the current pixel and its neighborhood, and the only two possible actions are removing the current pixel or not. By plugging the subiteration index k as another condition, this results in a 10 conditions decision table (1024 rules).

The definition of decision tables requires all conditions to be tested in order to select the corresponding actions to be executed. Testing the conditions requires to access the corresponding pixel in the image, so solutions to avoid checking conditions allow to improve the algorithm computational requirements.

With a dynamic programming technique, Grana *et al.* [14] showed how to build an optimal decision tree that, by saving many memory accesses, resulted in a considerable improvement in execution times.

Following [12], we observe that it is possible to include *prediction* in the DTree, by keeping track of the examined pixels on the path to reach a leaf, and there selecting a different tree which employs only the unknown pixels. While this requires a pretty tedious work, the number of possible combinations is quite limited and it is doable. For instance, for the ZS algorithm, we obtain 18 different reduced trees. Its possible to note that P_8 disappears from all trees, because it is always known from the previous step (it was P_1). Moreover a degenerate case happens, because if P_4 was a background pixel, the next trees will have a root which directly contains the action "do nothing".

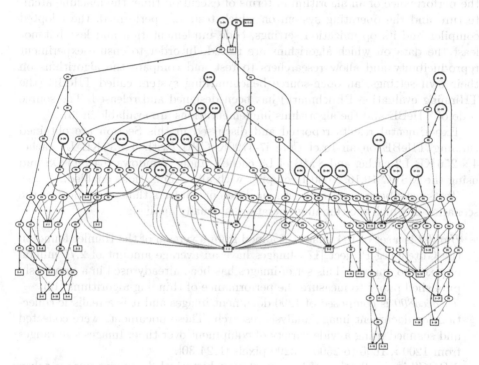

Fig. 2. Final DRAG for Zhang and Suen thinning algorithm. The octagonal shaped root is the starting node for the first pixel in a line, double circles are roots from which the algorithm will restart after reaching a leaf (the first number is their id), ellipses are decisions and rectangles are leaves. The first number in leaves is the action to be performed (1 = do nothing, 2 = don't remove, 3 = remove), while the second number is the next tree to be used. The special case (root 2) is marked as a double rectangle to stress that this root is also a leaf. Best viewed on the online version.

Additionally, as introduced in [3], a transformation from a DTree to a DRAG can be performed by substituting all equal subtrees with a single instance by making every parent node point to that unique exemplar. We can traverse the tree and, for every subtree, search an equal one and immediately perform the substitution. This transformation does not depend on the order in which the original tree is traversed. As already said, getting to a leaf still requires all the original checks, so the benefit of implementing decisions with DRAGs is that of reducing the code footprint. A visualization of the resulting graph for the Zhang and Suen algorithm is shown in Fig. 2.

4   Comparative Evaluation

The proposed algorithms are evaluated by comparing their performance with state-of-the-art implementations. There are many variables that could influence the performance of an algorithm in terms of execution time: the machine architecture and the operating system on which tests are performed, the adopted compiler and its optimization settings, code implementation and last but not least the data on which algorithms are tested. In order to ensure experiment reproducibility and allow researchers to test and compare the algorithms on their own settings, an open-source benchmarking system called THeBE (the THinning evaluation BEnchmark) has been designed and released. The source code of THeBE and the algorithms implementations are available in [31].

Experimental results reported and discussed in this Section are obtained running THeBE on an Intel Core i7-4790K CPU (with 4×32 KB L1 cache, 4×256 KB L2 cache, and 8 MB of L3 cache), under Windows (64 bit) OS and using the MSVC 19.16.27030.1 compiler with all optimizations enabled.

Tests have been performed on four different datasets that cover most of the scenarios in which the thinning operation is usually applied:

- *Hamlet* is a set of 104 images, scanned from a version of the Hamlet found on the Gutenberg Project [17]. Images have an average amount of 2.71 million of pixels to analyze. This set of images has been already used in a previously published paper to measure the performance of thinning algorithms [14].
- *Tobacco800* is composed of 1290 document images and it is a realistic collection for document image analysis research. These documents were collected and scanned using a wide variety of equipment over time. Images size ranges from 1200×1600 to 2500×3200 pixels [1, 24, 30].
- *XDOCS* is a collection of high resolution historical document images taken from the large number of civil registries available since the constitution of the Italian state [2, 4, 5]. XDOCS is composed of 1677 images with an average size of 4853×3387.
- *Fingerprints* counts 960 fingerprint images taken from three fingerprint verification competitions (FCV2000, FCV2002 and FCV2004) [26]. Images were collected by using low-cost optical sensors or synthetically generated. In order to fit them for a thinning application, fingerprints have been binarized using an adaptive threshold [28] and then negated. Resulting images have a size varying from 240×320 up to 640×480 pixels.

All images are provided in 1 bit per pixel PNG format, with 0 being background and 1 being foreground. The aforementioned datasets can be automatically downloaded during the installation of THeBE or they can be found in [32].

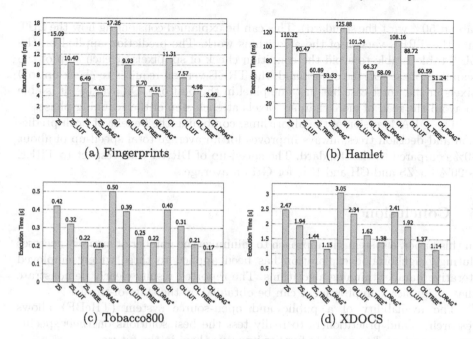

Fig. 3. Average run-time test on different datasets. Results are obtained under Windows (64 bit) OS with MSVC 19.16.27030.1 using an Intel Core i7-4790K CPU. For the sake of readability numbers are given in ms in (a) and (b), while they are give in s in (c) and (d). Our proposals are identified with *. Lower is better.

The results of the comparison are reported in Fig. 3. For convenience, all the acronyms used in this section are summarized in the following. ZS identifies the Zang and Suen algorithm originally presented in [35], GS is the algorithm by Guo and Hall [15], and CH is the algorithm proposed by Chen and Hsu in [8]. Moreover, the acronym LUT identifies the lookup table implementation of a given algorithm, TREE represents the version of the algorithm based on optimal decision trees (thus without prediction), and DRAG identifies the application of the complete pipeline proposed. It is important to note that both the "standard" and LUT versions of the algorithms also use prediction, avoiding to read pixels that have already been read in the previous step.

All the variations of a given algorithm (standard, LUT, TREE, and DRAG) differ only in execution time, and always produce the same output on the same input image. This is directly verified by THeBE.

Keeping in mind that the three thinning algorithms (ZS, GH, and CH) produce different results, and should be selected based on the task needs, we can observe that CH always shows the best performance. As reported in literature, the use of LUT always improves performance of about 25% with respect to the standard.

Even thought the LUT version of the algorithms employs prediction, the implementation based on optimal decision trees, which does not, performs better (about 50% w.r.t the standard). This can be explained considering how the LUT and the TREE version of the algorithms work. The prediction applied on the LUT table is able to avoid the condition check of six pixels at each step of the scanning phase. On the other hand, the TREE version requires to check up to 9 pixels in the worst case but just one pixel in the best one. On average, it is able to avoid the read of more than six pixels at each step of the scanning phase.

The DRAG version of the algorithms, combining the benefit of both prediction and decision trees, always improves for an average total speed-up of about 60% compared to the standard. The speed-up of DRAG with respect to TREE is 20% for ZS and CH and 15% for GH on average.

5   Conclusion

In this paper, a systematic approach to minimize the number of memory accesses during neighborhood exploration has been applied to three widely employed iterative parallel thinning algorithms. The reported results clearly demonstrate that a significant improvement can be obtained on the state-of-the-art.

The availability of a public and open-source system (THeBE) allows researchers and practitioners to really test the best solutions on their specific environment, and to possibly further improve them in the future.

References

1. Agam, G., Argamon, S., Frieder, O., Grossman, D., Lewis, D.: The complex document image processing (CDIP) test collection project. Illinois Institute of Technology (2006)
2. Bolelli, F.: Indexing of historical document images: ad hoc dewarping technique for handwritten text. In: Grana, C., Baraldi, L. (eds.) IRCDL 2017. CCIS, vol. 733, pp. 45–55. Springer, Cham (2017). https://doi.org/10.1007/978-3-319-68130-6_4
3. Bolelli, F., Baraldi, L., Cancilla, M., Grana, C.: Connected Components Labeling on DRAGs. In: International Conference on Pattern Recognition (ICPR), pp. 121–126. IEEE (2018)
4. Bolelli, F., Borghi, G., Grana, C.: Historical handwritten text images word spotting through sliding window hog features. In: Battiato, S., Gallo, G., Schettini, R., Stanco, F. (eds.) ICIAP 2017. LNCS, vol. 10484, pp. 729–738. Springer, Cham (2017). https://doi.org/10.1007/978-3-319-68560-1_65
5. Bolelli, F., Borghi, G., Grana, C.: XDOCS: an application to index historical documents. In: Serra, G., Tasso, C. (eds.) IRCDL 2018. CCIS, vol. 806, pp. 151–162. Springer, Cham (2018). https://doi.org/10.1007/978-3-319-73165-0_15
6. Bolelli, F., Cancilla, M., Baraldi, L., Grana, C.: Connected components labeling on DRAGs: implementation and reproducibility notes. In: Kerautret, B., Colom, M., Lopresti, D., Monasse, P., Talbot, H. (eds.) RRPR 2018. LNCS, vol. 11455, pp. 89–93. Springer, Cham (2019). https://doi.org/10.1007/978-3-030-23987-9_7
7. Chaudhuri, B.B., Adak, C.: An approach for detecting and cleaning of struck-out handwritten text. Pattern Recogn. **61**, 282–294 (2017)
8. Chen, Y.S., Hsu, W.H.: A modified fast parallel algorithm for thinning digital patterns. Pattern Recogn. Lett. **7**(2), 99–106 (1988)

9. Chen, Y.S., Hsu, W.H.: A modified fast parallel algorithm for thinning digital patterns. Pattern Recogn. Lett. **7**(2), 99–106 (1988). https://doi.org/10.1016/0167-8655(88)90124-9
10. Deutsch, E.S.: Thinning algorithms on rectangular, hexagonal, and triangular arrays. Commun. ACM **15**(9), 827–837 (1972)
11. Dinneen, G.: Programming pattern recognition. In: Proceedings of the Western Joint Computer Conference, pp. 94–100. ACM (1955)
12. Grana, C., Baraldi, L., Bolelli, F.: Optimized connected components labeling with pixel prediction. In: Blanc-Talon, J., Distante, C., Philips, W., Popescu, D., Scheunders, P. (eds.) ACIVS 2016. LNCS, vol. 10016, pp. 431–440. Springer, Cham (2016). https://doi.org/10.1007/978-3-319-48680-2_38
13. Grana, C., Borghesani, D.: Optimal decision tree synthesis for efficient neighborhood computation. In: Serra, R., Cucchiara, R. (eds.) AI*IA 2009. LNCS (LNAI), vol. 5883, pp. 92–101. Springer, Heidelberg (2009). https://doi.org/10.1007/978-3-642-10291-2_10
14. Grana, C., Borghesani, D., Cucchiara, R.: Decision trees for fast thinning algorithms. In: 20th International Conference on Pattern Recognition (ICPR), pp. 2836–2839 (2010)
15. Guo, Z., Hall, R.W.: Parallel thinning with two-subiteration algorithms. Commun. ACM **32**(3), 359–373 (1989)
16. Hall, R.W.: Fast parallel thinning algorithms: parallel speed and connectivity preservation. Commun. ACM **32**(1), 124–131 (1989)
17. The Hamlet Dataset. http://www.gutenberg.org. Accessed 02 May 2019
18. He, L., Zhao, X., Chao, Y., Suzuki, K.: Configuration-transition-based connected-component labeling. IEEE Trans. Image Process. **23**(2), 943–951 (2014)
19. He, S., Schomaker, L.: DeepOtsu: document enhancement and binarization using iterative deep learning. Pattern Recogn. **91**, 379–390 (2019)
20. Holt, C.M., Stewart, A., Clint, M., Perrott, R.H.: An improved parallel thinning algorithm. Commun. ACM **30**(2), 156–160 (1987)
21. Huang, T., Yang, G., Tang, G.: A fast two-dimensional median filtering algorithm. IEEE Trans. Acoust. Speech Signal Process. **27**(1), 13–18 (1979)
22. Khodadoust, J., Khodadoust, A.M.: Fingerprint indexing based on minutiae pairs and convex core point. Pattern Recogn. **67**, 110–126 (2017)
23. Lam, L., Lee, S.W., Suen, C.Y.: Thinning methodologies–a comprehensive survey. IEEE Trans. Pattern Anal. **14**(9), 869–885 (1992). https://doi.org/10.1109/34.161346
24. Lewis, D., Agam, G., Argamon, S., Frieder, O., Grossman, D., Heard, J.: Building a test collection for complex document information processing. In: Proceedings of the 29th Annual International ACM SIGIR Conference on Research and Development in Information Retrieval, pp. 665–666. ACM (2006)
25. Lü, H., Wang, P.S.P.: A comment on "a fast parallel algorithm for thinning digital patterns". Commun. ACM **29**(3), 239–242 (1986)
26. Maltoni, D., Maio, D., Jain, A.K., Prabhakar, S.: Handbook of Fingerprint Recognition. Springer, London (2009). https://doi.org/10.1007/978-1-84882-254-2
27. Documentation of the thinning function in OpenCV. https://docs.opencv.org/4.0.0/df/d2d/group__ximgproc.html#ga37002c6ca80c978edb6ead5d6b39740c. Accessed 02 May 2019
28. Sauvola, J., Pietikäinen, M.: Adaptive document image binarization. Pattern Recogn. **33**(2), 225–236 (2000)
29. Schutte, L.J.: Survey of decision tables as a problem statement technique. CSD-TR 80, Computer Science Department, Purdue University (1973)

30. The legacy tobacco document library (LTDL). University of California, San Francisco (2007)
31. Source code of the THeBE benchmarking system. https://github.com/prittt/THeBE. Accessed 02 May 2019
32. The THeBE dataset. http://aimagelab.ing.unimore.it/files/THeBE_dataset.zip. Accessed 02 May 2019
33. Uslu, F., Bharath, A.A.: A recursive Bayesian approach to describe retinal vasculature geometry. Pattern Recogn. **87**, 157–169 (2019)
34. Wang, X., Jiang, X., Ren, J.: Blood vessel segmentation from fundus image by a cascade classification framework. Pattern Recogn. **88**, 331–341 (2019)
35. Zhang, T., Suen, C.Y.: A fast parallel algorithm for thinning digital patterns. Commun. ACM **27**(3), 236–239 (1984)

Thick Line Segment Detection with Fast Directional Tracking

Philippe Even[1]([✉]), Phuc Ngo[1], and Bertrand Kerautret[2]

[1] Université de Lorraine, LORIA (UMR 7503), Nancy, France
{philippe.even,hoai-diem-phuc.ngo}@loria.fr
[2] Université Lyon 2, LIRIS (UMR 5205), Lyon, France
bertrand.kerautret@univ-lyon2.fr

Abstract. This paper introduces a fully discrete framework for a new straight line detector in gray-level images, where line segments are enriched with a thickness parameter intended to provide a quality criterion on the extracted feature. This study is based on a previous work on interactive line detection in gray-level images. At first, a better estimation of the segment thickness and orientation is achieved through two main improvements: adaptive directional scans and control of assigned thickness. Then, these advances are exploited for a complete unsupervised detection of all the line segments in an image. The new thick line detector is left available in an online demonstration.

Keywords: Line/segment detection · Discrete objects · Digital geometry

1 Introduction

Straight lines are commonly used as visual features for many image analysis processes. In particular in man-made environments, they are a suitable alternative to points for camera orientation [7,18], 3D reconstruction [16] or also simultaneous localization and mapping [10,17].

Therefore, straight line detection is always an active research topic centered on the quest of still faster, more accurate or more robust-to-noise methods [1,2,9,14,15]. Most of the times, they rely on the extraction of an edge map based on gradient magnitude. Gradient orientation is often used to discriminate candidates and thus provide better efficiency. However, they seldom provide an exploitable measure of the output line quality, based on intrinsic properties such as sharpness, connectivity or scattering. This information could be useful to get some confidence level and help to classify these features for further exploitation. It could also be a base for uncertainty propagation within 3D interpretation tools, in order to dispose of complementary measures to reprojection errors for local accuracy evaluation.

In digital geometry, new mathematical definitions of classical geometric objects, such as lines or circles, have been developed to better fit to the discrete

© Springer Nature Switzerland AG 2019
E. Ricci et al. (Eds.): ICIAP 2019, LNCS 11752, pp. 159–170, 2019.
https://doi.org/10.1007/978-3-030-30645-8_15

nature of most of today's data to process. In particular, the notion of blurred segment [4,6] was introduced to cope with the image noise or other sources of imperfections from the real world using a thickness parameter. Efficient algorithms have already been designed to recognize these digital objects in binary images [5]. Blurred segments seem well suited to reflect the required line quality information.

The present work aims at designing a flexible tool to detect blurred segments with optimal thickness and orientation in gray-level images for as well supervised as unsupervised contexts. User-friendly solutions are sought, with ideally no parameter to set, or at least quite few values with intuitive meaning. An interactive tool was already designed for live line extractions in gray-level images [12]. But the segment thickness was initially fixed by the user and not estimated, leading to erroneous orientations of the detected lines. Here, the limitations of this first detector are solved by the introduction of two new concepts: (i) adaptive directional scans designed to better track the detected line; (ii) control of assigned thickness to bound its scattering. As a side effect, these two major evolutions also led to a noticeable improvement of the time performance of the detector. They are also put forward within a global line extraction algorithm which can be evaluated through an online demonstration at: http://ipol-geometry.loria.fr/~kerautre/ipol_demo/FBSD_IPOLDemo.

In the next section, the main theoretical notions used in this work are introduced. The new detector workflow, the adaptive directional scan, the control of assigned thickness and their integration into both supervised and unsupervised contexts are then presented in Sect. 3. Experiments led to assess the achieved performance of this new detector are described in Sect. 4. Finally, Sect. 5 gives a short conclusion followed by some open perspectives for future works.

2   Theoretical Background

2.1   Blurred Segment

This work relies on the notion of digital straight line as classically defined in the digital geometry literature [13]. Only the 2D case is considered here.

Definition 1. *A **digital straight line** $\mathcal{L}(a,b,c,\nu)$, with $(a,b,c,\nu) \in \mathbb{Z}^4$, is the set of points $P(x,y)$ of $\mathbb{Z}^2$ that satisfy: $0 \leq ax + by - c < \nu$.*

In the following, we note $V(\mathcal{L}) = (a,b)$ the director vector of digital line $\mathcal{L}$, $w(\mathcal{L}) = \nu$ its arithmetical width, $h(\mathcal{L}) = c$ its shift to origin, and $p(\mathcal{L}) = max(|a|,|b|)$ its period (i.e. the length of its periodic pattern). When $\nu = p(\mathcal{L})$, then $\mathcal{L}$ is the narrowest 8-connected line and is called a *naive line*.

The *thickness* $\mu = \frac{\nu}{max(|a|,|b|)}$ of $\mathcal{L}(a,b,c,\nu)$ is the minimum of the vertical and horizontal distances between lines $ax + by = c$ and $ax + by = c + \nu$.

Definition 2. *A **blurred segment** $\mathcal{B}$ of assigned thickness ε is a set of points in $\mathbb{Z}^2$ that all belong to a covering digital straight line $\mathcal{L}$ of thickness $\mu = \varepsilon$. The **optimal line** of the blurred segment is the covering line with minimal thickness. The **thickness** of the blurred segment is the thickness of its optimal line.*

A linear-time algorithm to recognize a blurred segment of assigned thickness ε [6] is used in this work. It is based on an incremental growth of the convex hull of the blurred segment when adding each point P_i successively. As depicted on Fig. 1, the extension of the blurred segment $\mathcal{B}_{i-1}$ of assigned thickness ε and thickness μ_{i-1} at step $i-1$ with a new input point P_i is thus controlled by the recognition test $\mu_i < \varepsilon$.

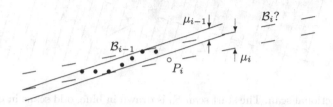

Fig. 1. A growing blurred segment $\mathcal{B}_i$: when adding the new point P_i, the blurred segment minimal thickness augments from μ_{i-1} to μ_i; if the new thickness μ_i exceeds the assigned thickness ε, then the new input point is rejected and $\mathcal{B}_i = \mathcal{B}_{i-1}$.

Associated to this primitive, the following definition of a directional scan is an important point in the proposed method.

2.2   Directional Scan

Definition 3. *A directional scan DS is an ordered partition restricted to the image domain $\mathcal{I}$ of a thick digital straight line $\mathcal{D}$, called the **scan strip**, into scans S_i, each of them being a segment of a naive line $\mathcal{N}_i$, called a **scan line**, orthogonal to $\mathcal{D}$.*

$$DS = \left\{ S_i = \mathcal{D} \cap \mathcal{N}_i \cap \mathcal{I} \,\middle|\, \begin{array}{l} V(\mathcal{N}_i) \cdot V(\mathcal{D}) = 0 \\ \wedge \ h(\mathcal{N}_i) = h(\mathcal{N}_{i-1}) + p(\mathcal{D}) \end{array} \right\} \tag{1}$$

In this definition, the clause $V(\mathcal{N}_i) \cdot V(\mathcal{D}) = 0$ expresses the orthogonality constraint between the scan lines $\mathcal{N}_i$ and the scan strip $\mathcal{D}$. Then the shift of the period $p(\mathcal{D})$ between successive scans guarantees that all points of the scan strip are traversed one and only one time.

The scans S_i are developed on each side of a start scan S_0, and ordered by their distance to the start line $\mathcal{N}_0$ with a positive (resp. negative) sign if they are on the left (resp. right) side of $\mathcal{N}_0$ (Fig. 2). The directional scan is iteratively parsed from the start scan to both ends. At each iteration i, the scans S_i and S_{-i} are successively processed.

A directional scan can be defined by its start scan S_0. If $A(x_A, y_A)$ and $B(x_B, y_B)$ are the end points of S_0, and if we note $\delta_x = x_B - x_A$, $\delta_y = y_B - y_A$, $c_1 = \delta_x \cdot x_A + \delta_y \cdot y_A$, $c_2 = \delta_x \cdot x_B + \delta_y \cdot y_B$ and $p_{AB} = max(|\delta_x|, |\delta_y|)$, it is then defined by the following scan strip $\mathcal{D}^{A,B}$ and scan lines $\mathcal{N}_i^{A,B}$:

$$\begin{cases} \mathcal{D}^{A,B} = \mathcal{L}(\delta_x, \ \delta_y, \ min(c1, c2), \ 1 + |c_1 - c_2|) \\ \mathcal{N}_i^{A,B} = \mathcal{L}(\delta_y, \ -\delta_x, \ \delta_y \cdot x_A - \delta_x \cdot y_A + i \cdot p_{AB}, \ p_{AB}) \end{cases} \tag{2}$$

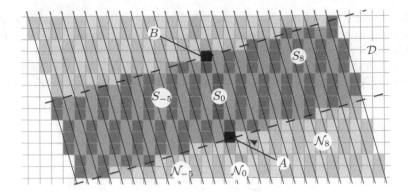

Fig. 2. A directional scan. The start scan S_0 is drawn in blue, odd scans in green, even scans in red, the bounds of scan lines $\mathcal{N}_i$ with plain lines and the bounds of scan strip $\mathcal{D}$ with dotted lines. (Color figure online)

A directional scan can also be defined by a central point $C(x_C, y_C)$, a direction $\boldsymbol{D}(X_D, Y_D)$ and a minimal thickness w. If we note $p_D = max(|X_D|, |Y_D|)$, $\nu_D = \lceil w \cdot p_D \rceil$, $c_3 = x_C \cdot Y_D - y_C \cdot X_D - \frac{\nu_D}{2}$, and $c_4 = x_C \cdot X_D + y_C \cdot Y_D - \frac{p_D}{2}$, it is then defined by the following scan strip $\mathcal{D}^{C,D,w}$ and scan lines $\mathcal{N}_i^{C,D,w}$:

$$\begin{cases} \mathcal{D}^{C,D,w} = \mathcal{L}(Y_D, \ -X_D, \ c_3, \ \nu_D) \\ \mathcal{N}_i^{C,D,w} = \mathcal{L}(X_D, \ Y_D, \ c_4 + i \cdot p_D, \ p_D) \end{cases} \tag{3}$$

3 The Detection Method

In this line detection method, only the gradient information is processed as it provides a good information on the image dynamics, and hence the presence of edges. Trials to use the intensity signal were also made through costly correlation techniques, but they were mostly successful for detecting shapes with a stable appearance such as metallic tubular objects [3]. Contrarily to most detectors, no edge map is built here, but gradient magnitude and orientation are examined in privileged directions to track edge traces. In particular, we use a Sobel operator with a 5×5 pixels mask to get high quality gradient information [11].

3.1 Previous Work

In a former paper [12], an efficient tool to detect blurred segments of fixed thickness in gray-level images was already introduced. It was based on a first rough detection in a local image area defined by the user. At that stage, the goal was to disclose the presence of a straight edge. Therefore as simple a test as the gradient maximal value was performed. In case of success, refinement steps were then run through an exploration of the image in the direction of the detected edge. In order to prevent local disturbances such as the presence of a sharper edge nearby, all the local gradient maxima were successively tested until a correct candidate with an acceptable gradient orientation was found.

Despite of a good behavior reported, several drawbacks remained. First, the blurred segment thickness was not measured but initially set by the user according to application requirements. The produced information on edge quality was rather poor, and especially when the edge is thin, the risk to incorporate outlier points was quite high, thus producing a biased estimation of the edge orientation. Then, two refinement steps were systematically performed. On the one hand, this is useless when the first detection is successful. On the other hand, there is no guarantee that this approach is able to process larger images. The search direction relies on the support vector of the blurred segment detected at former step. Because the numerization rounding fixes a limit on this estimated orientation accuracy, more steps are inevitably required to process larger images. In the following, we present the improvements in the new detector to overcome these limitations.

3.2   Workflow of the New Detection Process

The workflow of the detection process is summarized in the following figure (Fig. 3).

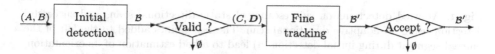

Fig. 3. The main workflow of the detection process.

The initial detection consists in building and extending a blurred segment B of assigned thickness ε_0, based on points with highest gradient magnitude found in each scan of a static directional scan defined by an input segment AB. The extension is stopped after five point addition failures on each side. Notice that the gradient direction is not used in this step.

Validity tests are then applied to decide of the detection pursuit. They aim at rejecting too small segments (less than 4 points) or too sparse ones (more than 50% of point addition failures) or also those with a close orientation to AB (less than $\pi/6$).

In the fine tracking step, another blurred segment B' is built and extended with points that correspond to local maxima of the image gradient, ranked by magnitude order, and with gradient direction close to start point gradient direction (less than $\pi/6$). At this refinement step, a *control of assigned thickness* is applied and an *adaptive directional scan* based on found position C and direction D is used in order to extend the segment in appropriate direction. These two notions are described in following Sects. 3.3 and 3.4.

Output segment $\mathcal{B}'$ is finally accepted based on application criteria. Final length and sparsity thresholds can be set accordingly. They are the only parameters of this local detector, together with the input assigned thickness ε_0.

3.3 Adaptive Directional Scan

The blurred segment is searched within a directional scan with position and orientation approximately drawn by the user, or blindly defined in unsupervised mode. In most cases, the detection stops where the segment escapes sideways from the scan strip (Fig. 4a). A second search is then run using another directional scan aligned on the detected segment (Fig. 4b). In the given example, an outlier added to the initial segment leads to a wrong orientation value. But even in case of a correct detection, this estimated orientation is subject to the numerization rounding, and the longer the real segment is, the higher the probability gets to fail again on an escape from the scan strip.

Fig. 4. Aborted detections on side escapes of static directional scans and successful detection using an adaptive directional scan. The last points added to the left of the blurred segment during initial detection (a) lead to a bad estimation of its orientation, and thus to an incomplete fine tracking with a classical directional scan (b). An adaptive directional scan instead of the static one allows to continue the segment expansion as far as necessary (c). Input selection is drawn in red color, scan strip bounds in blue and detected blurred segments in green. (Color figure online)

To overcome this issue, in the former work, an additional refinement step was run in the direction estimated from this longer segment. It was enough to completely detect most of the tested edges, but certainly not all, especially if big size images with much longer edges were processed. As a solution, this operation could be iterated as long as the blurred segment escapes from the directional scan using as any fine detection steps as necessary. But at each iteration, already tested points are processed again, thus producing a useless computational cost.

Here the proposed solution is to dynamically align the scan direction on the blurred segment all along the expansion stage. At each iteration i of the expansion, the scan strip is aligned on the direction of the blurred segment $\mathcal{B}_{i-1}$ computed at previous iteration $i-1$. More formally, an *adaptive directional scan* ADS is defined by:

$$ADS = \left\{ S_i = \mathcal{D}_i \cap \mathcal{N}_i \cap \mathcal{I} \middle| \begin{array}{l} \boldsymbol{V}(\mathcal{N}_i) \cdot \boldsymbol{V}(\mathcal{D}_0) = 0 \\ \wedge\ h(\mathcal{N}_i) = h(\mathcal{N}_{i-1}) + p(\mathcal{D}_0) \\ \wedge\ \mathcal{D}_i = \mathcal{D}^{C_{i-1}, D_{i-1}, \mu_{i-1}}, i > \lambda \end{array} \right\} \tag{4}$$

where C_i, D_i and μ_i are respectively a position, a director vector and a thickness observed at iteration i, used to update the scan strip and lines in accordance to Eq. 3. The last clause expresses the update of the scan bounds at iteration i: C_{i-1}, D_{i-1} and μ_{i-1} are respectively the intersection of the input selection and the central line of $\mathcal{B}_{i-1}$, the director vector of the optimal line of $\mathcal{B}_{i-1}$, and the thickness of $\mathcal{B}_{i-1}$. λ is a delay which is set to 20 iterations to avoid direction instabilities when too few points are inserted. Compared to static directional scans where the scan strip remains fixed to the initial line $\mathcal{D}_0$, here the scan strip moves while scan lines remain fixed. This behavior ensures a complete detection of the blurred segment even when the orientation of $\mathcal{D}_0$ is wrongly estimated (Fig. 4c).

3.4   Control of Assigned Thickness

The assigned thickness ε to the blurred segment recognition algorithm is initially set to a large value ε_0 in order to allow the detection of thick blurred segments. Then, when no more augmentation of the blurred segment thickness is observed after τ iterations ($\mu_{i+\tau} = \mu_i$), it is set to the observed thickness augmented by a half pixel tolerance factor, in order to take into account all the possible discrete lines which digitization fits to the selected points:

$$\varepsilon = \mu_{i+\tau} + \frac{1}{2} \tag{5}$$

This strategy aims at preventing the incorporation of spurious outliers in further parts of the segment. Setting the observation distance to a constant value $\tau = 20$ seems appropriate in most experimented situations.

3.5   Supervised Blurred Segments Detection

In supervised context, the user draws an input stroke across the specific edge that he wants to extract from the image. The detection method previously described is continuously run during mouse dragging and the output blurred segment is displayed on-the-fly. Details about the supervised mode are discussed in [12].

An option, called *multi-detection* (Algorithm 1), allows the detection of all the segments crossed by the input stroke AB. In order to avoid multiple detections of the same edge, an occupancy mask, initially empty, collects the dilated points of all the blurred segments, so that these points can not be used any more.

First the positions M_j of the prominent local maxima of the gradient magnitude found under the stroke are sorted from the highest to the lowest. For each of them the main detection process is run with three modifications:

1. the initial detection takes M_j and the orthogonal direction $AB_\perp$ to the stroke as input to build a static scan of fixed thickness $2 \cdot \varepsilon_0$, and M_j is used as start point of the blurred segment;
2. the occupancy mask is filled in with the points of the dilated blurred segments $\mathcal{B}'_j$ at the end of each successful detection (a 5×5 octagonal neighborhood region of 21 pixels is used);

Algorithm 1. MultiDetect: finds all segments crossing the selection stroke.

---

input : Stroke points A, B, occupancy mask $\mathcal{M}$, initial thickness ε_0
output: ListOfBS $\rightarrow$ list of detected blurred segments

ListOfBS $\leftarrow \emptyset$;
LocMax $\leftarrow$ ComputeAndSortGradientLocalMax (A, B);

for $i \leftarrow 0$ **to** Size *(LocMax)* **do**
   | BlurredSegment $\leftarrow$ detect (LocMax [i], $\boldsymbol{AB}_\perp$, $2\,\varepsilon_0$, $\mathcal{M}$);
   | UpdateOccupancyMask ($\mathcal{M}$, BlurredSegment);
   | ListOfBS $\leftarrow$ ListOfBS + BlurredSegment;
end

---

3. points marked as occupied are rejected when selecting candidates for the blurred segment extension in the fine tracking step.

3.6 Automatic Blurred Segment Detection

An unsupervised mode is also proposed to automatically detect all the straight lines in the image. A stroke that crosses the whole image, is swept in both directions, vertical then horizontal, from the center to the borders. At each position, the multi-detection algorithm is run to collect all the segments found under the stroke. Then small blurred segments are rejected in order to avoid the formation of misaligned segments when the sweeping stroke crosses an image edge near one of its ends. In such situation, any nearby disturbing gradient is likely to deviate the blurred segment direction, and its expansion is quickly stopped. The stroke sweeping step is an additional parameter for automatic detections, that could be set in relation to the final length threshold parameter.

The automatic detection is available for testing from the online demonstration and from a *GitHub* source code repository: https://github.com/evenp/FBSD.

4 Experimental Validation

In the experimental stage, the proposed approach is validated through comparisons with other recent line detectors: LSD [9], ED-Lines [1] and CannyLines [14], written in C or C++ language and without any parameter settings. Only LSD provides a thickness value based on the width of regions with same gradient direction. This information does not match the line sharpness or scattering quality addressed in this work, so that it can not be actually compared to the thickness value output by the new detector. Moreover, we did not find any data base with ground truth including line thickness. Therefore, we proceed in two steps: (i) evaluation on synthetic images of the new concepts enhancement on line orientation and thickness estimation; (ii) evaluation of more global performance of the proposed approach compared to other detectors. For all these experiments in unsupervised mode, the stroke sweeping step is set to 15 pixels.

At first, the performance of both versions of the detector (with and without the concepts) is tested on a set of 1000 synthesized images containing 10 randomly placed input segments with random thickness between 2 and 5 pixels. The initial assigned thickness ε_0 is set to 7 pixels to detect all the lines in the defined thickness range in unsupervised mode. The absolute value of the difference of each found segment to its matched input segment is measured. Results in Table 1 show that the new concepts afford improved thickness and angle measurements, better precision with a smaller amount of false detections, and that they help to find most of input segments. More results can be found in a public report: https://doi.org/10.5281/zenodo.3277091.

Table 1. Measured performance of both versions of the detector on a set of synthesized images. Old refers to the previous version [12], whereas new is the proposed detector (with adaptive directional scans and control of assigned width). S is the set of all the input segments, D the set of all the detected blurred segments.

Detector	Old	New
Detected blurred segments per image	17.06 ± 3.22	16.83 ± 3.11
Undetected input segments per image	0.152 ± 0.43	$\mathbf{0.003 \pm 0.05}$
Precision (%): $P = \#(D \cap S)/\#D$	80.46 ± 7.22	$\mathbf{83.87 \pm 6.04}$
Recall (ratio of true detection, %): $R = \#(D \cap S)/\#S$	90.23 ± 3.30	$\mathbf{91.15 \pm 2.52}$
F-measure (harmonic mean, %): $F = 2 \times P \times R/(P + R)$	84.87 ± 4.42	$\mathbf{87.23 \pm 3.59}$
Thickness difference (pixels) to matched input segment	0.70 ± 0.24	$\mathbf{0.59 \pm 0.19}$
Angle difference (degrees) to matched input segment	0.61 ± 0.66	$\mathbf{0.57 \pm 0.62}$

Next experiments aim at comparing the new approach with recent line detectors. Tests are run on the York Urban database [7] composed of 102 images with their ground truth lines. As it was set in the scope of Manhattan-world environments, only lines in the three main directions are provided. For these experiments, initial assigned thickness ε_0 is set to 3 pixels, considering that the other detectors are designed to find thin lines, and final length threshold to 10 points to suit the stroke sweeping step value. Output lines smaller than 10 pixels are discarded for all the detectors. Compared measures are execution time T, covering ratio C, detected lines amount N, cumulated length of detected lines L and mean length ratio L/N. On each image of the database and for each line detector, the execution time of 100 repetitions of a complete detection, gradient extraction included, was measured using Intel Core i5 processor; T is the mean value found per image. Then, assuming that a pixel of a ground truth line is identified if there is a detected line in its 8-neighborhood, measure C is the mean ratio of the length of ground truth line pixels identified on the total amount of ground truth line pixels. Results are given in Table 2.

The example of Fig. 5 indicates that the new detector produces many small segments which could be considered as visually non-meaningful. The other detectors eliminates them by a validation test based on Helmholtz principle [8]. Such

Fig. 5. Comparison of line detectors on one of the 102 ground truth images of the York Urban database: (a) input image, (b) ground truth lines, (c) LSD output, (d) ED-Lines output, (e) CannyLines output, (f) thick lines of the new detector.

Table 2. Measured performance of recent line detectors (LSD [9], ED-Lines [1] and CannyLines [14]) and of our detector on the York Urban Database [7].

Measure	T (ms)	C (%)	N	L (pixels)	L/N
LSD	63.5 ± 13.6	60.9 ± 11.2	536 ± 193	17745 ± 5337	34.6 ± 7.9
ED-Lines	55.5 ± 9.9	64.0 ± 11.2	570 ± 210	19351 ± 5669	35.8 ± 8.9
CannyLines	69.6 ± 10.5	60.5 ± 10.6	467 ± 138	17679 ± 4398	39.5 ± 10.1
Our detector	66.9 ± 15.6	$\mathbf{67.9 \pm 9.6}$	478 ± 110	19472 ± 3914	$\mathbf{41.7 \pm 7.5}$

test is not yet integrated into the new detector. But even so, the mean length of output lines is greater. Except for execution time where ED-Lines performs best, global performance of the new detector is pretty similar and competitive to the other ones. Furthermore, it provides additional information on the detected line quality through the estimated thickness.

5   Conclusion and Perspectives

This paper introduced a new straight line detector based on a local analysis of the image gradient and on the use of blurred segments to embed an estimation of the line thickness. It relies on directional scans of the input image around maximal values of the gradient magnitude, and on the integration of two new concepts: adaptive directional scans and control of assigned thickness. Comparisons to other recent line detectors show competitive global performance in terms of execution time and mean length of output lines, while experiments on synthetic images indicate a better estimation of length and thickness measurements brought by the new concepts.

A residual weakness of the approach is the sensitivity to the initial conditions. In supervised context, the user can select a favourable area where the awaited edge is dominant. But in unsupervised context, gradient perturbations in the early stage of the line expansion, mostly due to the presence of close edges, can affect the result. In future works, we intend to provide solutions by scoring the detection result on the basis of a characterization of the local context.

References

1. Akinlar, C., Topal, C.: EDPF: a real-time parameter-free edge segment detector with a false detection control. Int. J. Pattern Recogn. Artif. Intell. **26**(01), 1255002 (2012)
2. Almazàn, E.J., Tal, R., Qian, Y., Elder, J.H.: MCMLSD: a dynamic programming approach to line segment detection. In: IEEE International Conference on Computer Vision and Pattern Recognition, pp. 2031–2039 (2017)
3. Aubry, N., Kerautret, B., Even, P., Debled-Rennesson, I.: Photometric intensity profiles analysis for thick segment recognition and geometric measures. Math. Morphol. Theory Appl. **2**, 35–54 (2017)
4. Buzer, L.: A simple algorithm for digital line recognition in the general case. Pattern Recogn. **40**(6), 1675–1684 (2007)
5. Debled-Rennesson, I., Feschet, F., Rouyer-Degli, J.: Optimal blurred segments decomposition of noisy shapes in linear times. Comput. Graph. **30**, 30–36 (2006)
6. Debled-Rennesson, I., Feschet, F., Rouyer-Degli, J.: Optimal blurred segments decomposition in linear time. In: Andres, E., Damiand, G., Lienhardt, P. (eds.) DGCI 2005. LNCS, vol. 3429, pp. 371–382. Springer, Heidelberg (2005). https://doi.org/10.1007/978-3-540-31965-8_34
7. Denis, P., Elder, J.H., Estrada, F.J.: Efficient edge-based methods for estimating Manhattan frames in urban imagery. In: Forsyth, D., Torr, P., Zisserman, A. (eds.) ECCV 2008. LNCS, vol. 5303, pp. 197–210. Springer, Heidelberg (2008). https://doi.org/10.1007/978-3-540-88688-4_15
8. Desolneux, A., Moisan, L., Morel, J.M.: From Gestalt Theory to Image Analysis: A Probabilistic Approach. Interdisciplinary Applied Mathematics, vol. 34. Springer, New York (2008). https://doi.org/10.1007/978-0-387-74378-3
9. von Gioi, R.G., Jakubowicz, J., Morel, J.M., Randall, G.: LSD: a fast line segment detector with a false detection control. IEEE Trans. Pattern Anal. Mach. Intell. **32**(4), 722–732 (2010)
10. Hirose, K., Saito, H.: Fast line description for line-based SLAM. In: British Machine Vision Conference (2012)
11. Kekre, H., Gharge, S.: Image segmentation using extended edge operator for mammographic images. Int. J. Comput. Sci. Eng. **2**(4), 1086–1091 (2010)
12. Kerautret, B., Even, P.: Blurred segments in gray level images for interactive line extraction. In: Wiederhold, P., Barneva, R.P. (eds.) IWCIA 2009. LNCS, vol. 5852, pp. 176–186. Springer, Heidelberg (2009). https://doi.org/10.1007/978-3-642-10210-3_14
13. Klette, R., Rosenfeld, A.: Digital Geometry – Geometric Methods for Digital Picture Analysis. Morgan Kaufmann, Burlington (2004)

14. Lu, X., Yao, J., Li, K., Li, L.: CannyLines: a parameter-free line segment detector. In: International Conference on Image Processing, pp. 507–511. IEEE (2015)
15. Matas, J., Galambos, C., Kittler, J.: Robust detection of lines using the progressive probabilistic Hough transform. Comput. Vis. Image Underst. **78**(1), 119–137 (2000)
16. Park, S., Lee, H., Lee, S., Yang, H.S.: Line-based single view 3D reconstruction in Manhattan world for augmented reality. In: Proceedings of the 14th ACM SIGGRAPH International Conference on Virtual Reality Continuum and Its Applications in Industry, VRCAI 2015, pp. 89–92. ACM (2015)
17. Ruifang, D., Fremont, V., Lacroix, S., Fantoni, I., Changan, L.: Line-based monocular graph SLAM. In: IEEE International Conference on Multisensor Fusion and Integration for Intelligent Systems, pp. 494–500 (2017)
18. Xu, C., Zhang, L., Cheng, L., Koch, R.: Pose estimation from line correspondences: a complete analysis and a series of solutions. IEEE Trans. Pattern Anal. Mach. Intell. **39**(6), 1209–1222 (2017)

Image Memorability Using Diverse Visual Features and Soft Attention

Marco Leonardi[1], Luigi Celona[1(✉)], Paolo Napoletano[1], Simone Bianco[1],
Raimondo Schettini[1], Franco Manessi[2], and Alessandro Rozza[2]

[1] University of Milano - Bicocca, Milan, Italy
m.leonardi6@campus.unimib.it,
{luigi.celona,paolo.napoletano,simone.bianco,schettini}@unimib.it
[2] lastminute.com, Chiasso, Switzerland
{franco.manessi,alessandro.rozza}@lastminute.com

Abstract. In this paper we present a method for still image memorability estimation. The proposed solution exploits feature maps extracted from two Convolutional Neural Networks pre-trained for object recognition and memorability estimation respectively. The feature maps are then enhanced using a soft attention mechanism in order to let the model focus on highly informative image regions for memorability estimation. Results achieved on a benchmark dataset demonstrate the effectiveness of the proposed method.

Keywords: Memorability · Residual Neural Network · Convolutional Neural Network · Deep learning

1 Introduction

A remarkable feature of human cognition is the ability to remember different images that have been seen only once [14]. Furthermore, different people tend to remember or forget same pictures. This result suggests that people encode and discard very similar types of information. Precisely, images that are usually forgotten seem to lack distinctiveness and a fine-grained representation in human memory [14]. Taking into account the aforementioned considerations, it seems that memorable images have some kind of intrinsic visual features, making them easier to remember. Indeed, past studies have shown that memorability is a measurable stationary property of an image shared across different viewers [9] and that it is possible to determine a compact set of attributes characterizing the memorability of any individual image [8]. These results led researchers wondering how to predict accurately which images will be remembered and which will be not, resulting in the first large scale visual memorability estimation with near-human performance [11].

Nowadays, we are continuously being exposed to photographs when browsing the Internet or leafing through a magazine. Exploiting memorable pictures can have a huge impact in many applications, also thanks to the relationship

© Springer Nature Switzerland AG 2019
E. Ricci et al. (Eds.): ICIAP 2019, LNCS 11752, pp. 171–180, 2019.
https://doi.org/10.1007/978-3-030-30645-8_16

between emotions and memorability [3]. Just to give some examples, estimating the memorability can help to automatically select the images that can have a key role in optimizing the conversion rate for media advertisement and online shopping, or in improving the communication of a specific concept. More recently, researchers started to show interest in how to make an image more memorable, by exploiting deep architectures for generating memorable pictures by exploiting style-transfer techniques [24].

In this work, we propose a novel approach to compute memorability that exploits the combination of feature computed by different Convolutional Neural Networks (CNNs) and an attention map extracted from a caption generation model with visual attention. In details, the main contributions of the approach presented in this paper are:

- it achieves comparable or better results with respect to state-of-the-art approaches, respectively in terms of Spearman's rank correlation and Mean Squared Error (MSE);
- it reduces the amount of parameters with respect to the best performing technique in terms of Spearman's rank correlation.

The paper is organized as follows: in Sect. 2 the related works are summarized; in Sect. 3 the proposed method is described; in Sect. 4 the experimental results are presented; finally, conclusions and future works are summarized in Sect. 5.

2   Related Works

In the first works on image memorability, Isola et al. [8,9] showed the ability of our mind to remember certain images better than others and also that memorability is a stable property of an image shared across different viewers. They introduced a database for which they collected the probability that each image will be remembered after a single view as well as image attribute annotations (such as spatial layout, content and aesthetic properties) in order to:

- understand which features are highly informative about memorability;
- demonstrate that memorability is not influenced by content frequency or familiarity, namely the presence of particular objects, scene categories, relatives or famous monuments. However, some contents like faces are memorable, while vistas and peaceful settings are not;
- prove that memorability is not correlated with aesthetics, interestingness, and simple image features.

Furthermore, they developed a method to predict the memorability of an image involving the use of Support Vector Regressor machines on the combination of global image features – GIST [19], SIFT [15], HOG [4], SSIM [23], and color histogram. Following the intuition of Isola et al. [8] that memorability and visual attention are correlated, Mancas and Le Meur [17] demonstrated that attention-related features can effectively replace some of the low-level features used by Isola et al. [9] and thus reducing the dimensionality of the feature set. Afterwards,

Bylinskii *et al.* [2] proved that the interplay between intrinsic image properties (the fact that some scene categories are more memorable than others) and extrinsic factors, such as image context and observer behavior, are necessary to build an improved image memorability model. The effectiveness of the proposed solution has been assessed on FIne-GRained Image Memorability (FIGRIM) dataset that is composed by more than 9K images.

Khosla *et al.* [11] released LaMem, the first large scale dataset for image memorability containing 60K images. Alongside the dataset, they proposed MemNet, a CNN for memorability score estimation. The model is based on the fine-tuning of Hybrid-CNN [28], a CNN trained using 3.5 million images from 1,183 categories, obtained by merging the scene categories from Places database [28] and the object categories from ImageNet [22]. They achieved near human consistency rank correlation (0.68) for memorability. Fajtl *et al.* [5] proposed AMNet, a model consisting of a ResNet50 [7] pre-trained on ImageNet, a soft attention mechanism, and a Long Short-Term Memory [6] for memorability score regression. The AMNet model achieved a performance of 0.677 in terms of Spearman's rank correlation on LaMem dataset. Recently, Squalli-Houssaini *et al.* [26] approached the task of image memorability estimation as a classification problem instead of a regression one. They developed a model combining features extracted from both a VGG16 [25] pre-trained on ImageNet and an image captioning system [13] and outperformed both state-of-the-art and human consistency correlation (0.72) on LaMem dataset.

3   Proposed Method

Image memorability is influenced by some intrinsic image properties, namely *what* kind of objects and scenes are present and *what* are their characteristics, but also by extrinsic factors such as the image locations *where* humans focus their attention. Our approach tries to model memorability according to the aforementioned aspects by using a CNN for encoding intrinsic characteristics of objects, and a soft attention mechanism for estimating attention maps that highlight salient regions. Furthermore, we include in the proposed model a CNN pre-trained on image memorability for mapping *how* features encode memorability.

3.1   Architecture

The proposed model, depicted in Fig. 1, estimates a memorability score given as input an RGB image of size 256×256 pixels. It consists of two CNNs trained on two different tasks, and a soft attention mechanism based on a system originally designed for caption generation [27]. The aforementioned blocks (i.e. soft attention and memorability) are followed by two convolution layers preceding the last regressor module, which estimates the memorability score.

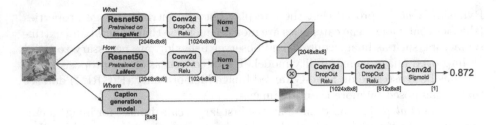

Fig. 1. Overview of the proposed model for image memorability estimation. The attention map produced by the caption generation model is combined channel-wise with the feature volume.

Feature Extraction. The two considered CNNs are two ResNet50 architectures pre-trained respectively for: image memorability estimation on LaMem dataset [11] and object recognition on Imagenet [22] dataset. We consider these two CNNs to provide the model prior information over the memorability of the image as well as knowledge of the image context. Both the architectures are truncated before their last average pooling layer in order to obtain two feature maps of size $2048 \times 8 \times 8$. These feature maps are first passed through a convolution layer which halves their channel dimension, then they are L2-normalized by dividing the feature map by its L2-norm, and finally stacked together obtaining a new feature map having a dimension equal to $2048 \times 8 \times 8$.

Soft Attention Mechanism. To focus the model attention on salient regions that are highly informative for memorability estimation, we include a state-of-the-art captioning generation approach [27] for extracting attention maps. This model is trained on the MS COCO dataset [16] and produces at most 50 attention maps with spatial size 8×8 pixels, each one focusing on a particular detail of the image. We exploit these maps by averaging them in order to get a single and global attention map.

Memorability Estimation. The feature map extracted from the two CNNs is weighted with the attention map generated from the captioning model replicated channel-wise. Finally, the resulted weighted feature map is given as input to a three-layer CNN to predict the memorability score.

3.2   Training Procedure

In order to improve the generalization of the model and minimize the risk of overfitting, we use data augmentation techniques during the training phase. Specifically, random scaling in the range $[0.8, 1.2]$ is first applied to the image, which then is randomly flipped along the vertical axis. Subsequently, random crop (0.8 to 1.0) of the image is applied before sub-sampling it to a size of 256×256 pixels. Finally, the image is normalized by subtracting and dividing each image by the mean and standard deviation estimated on the ImageNet training set [22] in order to limit the variability of the input range.

The training procedure consists of two phases. We first train one ResNet50 from scratch on LaMem [11] dataset for image memorability. Then we fine-tune the whole model on the same dataset freezing the weights of the two ResNet50 and the weights of the caption generation model with visual attention [27]. Both of the training processes are trained to minimize the mean squared error between the ground-truth and the predicted image memorability scores. For the first stage, we train the model for 150 epochs due to a larger number of parameters to learn, with a batch size of 10 images. For the second phase, the model is trained for only 50 epochs with a bigger batch size of 16 images.

During both the training processes, we use the technique of early stopping analyzing the Spearman's rank correlation see Sect. 4.2 for the definition) on the validation set. For both stages we use the ADAM optimizer [12] with starting learning rates respectively of 5×10^{-7} and 5×10^{-5} for the first and the second stage. Both the learning rates are decreased every epoch as follows:

$$LR(epoch) = \left[1 - \left(\frac{epoch}{total\ epochs} \right)^{0.9} \right] * LR_0, \qquad (1)$$

where *epoch* is the 0-based index of the actual epoch, LR_0 is the initial learning rate, and *total epochs* is the total number of epochs for the training process.

4   Experiments

In the following sections, the dataset and metrics adopted for evaluating the proposed method are described. Experimental results are then reported. We develop the proposed approach using the PyTorch framework [20], and we run experiments on a NVIDIA GTX 1070 GPU.

4.1   Dataset

We evaluate our model on the LaMem dataset [11], a massive collection of 58,741 images annotated with a memorability score. The images were sampled from different existing datasets and cover various indoor and outdoor scenes. Figure 2 shows some samples from the dataset. The provided memorability score were collected on Amazon Mechanical Turk using an improved version of the memorability game introduced in [9]. The data are divided into five random training, validation and test set splits. Each of these splits has respectively 45k images as training set, 3741 as validation and 10k as test set. For each split, training and validation sets are labeled from the same group of people while the test is labeled from a different group.

4.2   Evaluation Metrics

Following the previous work [11], we evaluate the performance of our method using the Spearman's rank correlation coefficient, ρ, [21] and the Mean Squared

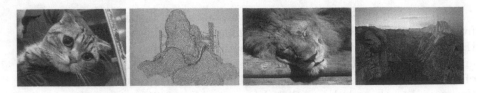

Fig. 2. Sample images from the LaMem dataset [11].

Error (MSE). The Spearman's rank correlation coefficient is a value, ranging from −1 to +1, which measures the monotonic relationships between the predicted and ground-truth ranking. A value of ρ equal to zero indicates no correlation between the two variable while values close to ±1 indicate relatively a strong positive (+1) or strong negative (−1) correlation. Spearman's rank correlation coefficient is defined as follows:

$$\rho = 1 - \frac{6 \sum d_i^2}{N(N^2 - 1)}, \tag{2}$$

where d_i is the difference between the two ranks of each variable and N is the number of samples.

The MSE measures the goodness of fit between reference and observations in terms of absolute numerical errors as shown in the following equation:

$$MSE(\hat{y}, y) = \frac{1}{N} \sum_{i=1}^{N} (\hat{y}_i - y_i)^2, \tag{3}$$

where $\hat{y}_i$ are the ground-truth values for the memorability, y_i the predicted memorability score and N is the number of samples.

4.3   Results

In this subsection we evaluate the performance of the proposed model by averaging both the Spearman's rank correlation and MSE over the five splits of LaMem dataset. The proposed model reaches an average rank correlation of 0.687 and a MSE of 0.0079 over the five splits of LaMem.

Table 1. Results of the ablation study on the LaMem dataset reported in terms of Spearman's rank correlation (ρ) and Mean Squared Error (MSE).

Method	$\rho \uparrow$	MSE $\downarrow$
ResNet50-LaMem	0.680	0.0083
ResNet50-LaMem + ResNet50-ImageNet	0.686	0.0080
Whole model	0.687	0.0079

In Table 1, we report the results of an ablation study investigating how each module of the proposed model affects the overall performance. In particular, a single ResNet50 [7] trained on the task of image memorability achieves a Spearman's rank correlation of 0.680 and a MSE of 0.0083. The model involving the combination of the feature maps extracted from the two ResNet50 without the use of the attention map increases the correlation by 0.006 and lowers the MSE by 0.0003. Finally, we can see that the whole model, i.e. the addition of the soft attention mechanism, increases performance by 0.001 for the Spearman's rank correlation and decreases the MSE by 0.0001.

In Table 2 we compare the proposed method with respect to the state-of-the-art on LaMem [11] dataset. We report the performance provided in terms of correlation and MSE as the average results over the five dataset splits. From the results reported in Table 2 we can observe that in terms of Spearman's rank correlation, our model performs slightly worse with respect to the best state-of-the-art model [26]. Given that Squalli *et al.* [26] do not provide the MSE, we have implemented their solution and obtained an error of 0.00923. Based on this result, our approach reduces the MSE by 0.0013 using a number of parameters equal to less than half of those used by [26]. We conduct an analysis of the efficiency of proposed solution respect to previous methods. To this end, in Fig. 3a we compare the Spearman's rank correlation and the number of parameters, while in Fig. 3b we plot the MSE and the number of parameters. Among the methods that outperform the human consistency correlation (0.68), our model achieves lower performance by using a reduced amount of parameters. Instead in terms of MSE, the proposed method is the solution exploiting more efficiently its parameters by obtaining the smallest MSE with the fewest parameters. In Fig. 4 we show samples from LaMem dataset with memorability scores estimated by the proposed solution as well as ground-truth memorability scores. Furthermore, we provide the corresponding attention maps for each image to highlight how these maps in most cases focus on the relevant subjects in the scenes.

Table 2. Comparison with state-of-the-art methods in terms of Spearman's rank correlation and MSE on the LaMem dataset. For each model the number of its parameters (in millions) is also reported.

Method	$\rho \uparrow$	MSE $\downarrow$	# parameters
AMNet [5]	0.677	0.0082	**39M**
MemNet [11]	0.640	N/A	62M
Squalli *et al.* [26]	**0.720**	0.0092*	280M
Ours	0.687	**0.0079**	130M

*Estimated by the authors.

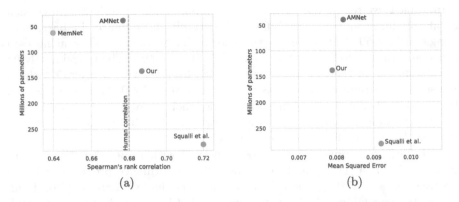

(a)   (b)

Fig. 3. Spearman's rank correlation vs. model parameters (the dashed line depicts the human consistency rank correlation [10]) (a). MSE vs. model parameters (b).

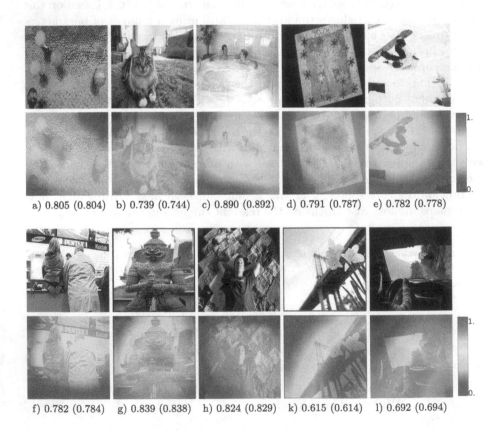

Fig. 4. Sample images from LaMem dataset with estimated and ground-truth (in brackets) memorability scores. Below each image its depicted the related visual attention map produced by the caption generation model.

5   Conclusion

This work presents a deep learning-based model for image memorability estimation. The proposed approach involves the use of two CNNs trained respectively on image recognition and image memorability. We use the features extracted from these two CNNs in order to exploit the knowledge of the context as well as the information about the memorability of the image. Moreover, we use a soft attention mechanism to focus the model attention on highly informative regions for memorability estimation. Results obtained on the LaMem benchmark dataset are comparable with respect to state-of-the-art approaches demonstrating the effectiveness of the proposed method. Moreover, our solution achieves the smallest MSE with the fewest parameters among the methods that outperform the human consistency correlation (0.68).

As a possible future work, we would like to experiment the approach proposed in [18] to learn combinations of base activation functions (such as the identity function, ReLU, and TanH), thus to improve the overall performance. Furthermore, we would investigate alternative attention mechanisms based on other saliency methods such as [1].

References

1. Bianco, S., Buzzelli, M., Schettini, R.: Multiscale fully convolutional network for image saliency. J. Electron. Imaging **27**, 27 (2018)
2. Bylinskii, Z., Isola, P., Bainbridge, C., Torralba, A., Oliva, A.: Intrinsic and extrinsic effects on image memorability. Vis. Res. **116**, 165–178 (2015)
3. Cahill, L., McGaugh, J.L.: A novel demonstration of enhanced memory associated with emotional arousal. Conscious. Cogn. **4**(4), 410–421 (1995)
4. Dalal, N., Triggs, B.: Histograms of oriented gradients for human detection. In: Conference on Computer Vision and Pattern Recognition (CVPR), vol. 1, pp. 886–893. IEEE (2005)
5. Fajtl, J., Argyriou, V., Monekosso, D., Remagnino, P.: AMNet: memorability estimation with attention. In: Conference on Computer Vision and Pattern Recognition (CVPR), pp. 6363–6372. IEEE (2018)
6. Greff, K., Srivastava, R.K., Koutník, J., Steunebrink, B.R., Schmidhuber, J.: LSTM: a search space odyssey. IEEE Trans. Neural Netw. Learn. Syst. **28**(10), 2222–2232 (2017)
7. He, K., Zhang, X., Ren, S., Sun, J.: Deep residual learning for image recognition. In: Conference on Computer Vision and Pattern Recognition (CVPR), pp. 770–778. IEEE (2016)
8. Isola, P., Parikh, D., Torralba, A., Oliva, A.: Understanding the intrinsic memorability of images. In: Advances in Neural Information Processing Systems, pp. 2429–2437 (2011)
9. Isola, P., Xiao, J., Torralba, A., Oliva, A.: What makes an image memorable? In: Conference on Computer Vision and Pattern Recognition (CVPR), pp. 145–152. IEEE (2011)
10. Khosla, A., Das Sarma, A., Hamid, R.: What makes an image popular? In: International Conference on World Wide Web, pp. 867–876. ACM (2014)

11. Khosla, A., Raju, A.S., Torralba, A., Oliva, A.: Understanding and predicting image memorability at a large scale. In: International Conference on Computer Vision (ICCV), pp. 2390–2398. IEEE (2015)
12. Kingma, D.P., Ba, J.: Adam: a method for stochastic optimization. CoRR abs/1412.6980 (2015)
13. Kiros, R., Salakhutdinov, R., Zemel, R.S.: Unifying visual-semantic embeddings with multimodal neural language models. arXiv preprint arXiv:1411.2539 (2014)
14. Konkle, T., Brady, T.F., Alvarez, G.A., Oliva, A.: Scene memory is more detailed than you think: the role of categories in visual long-term memory. Psychol. Sci. **21**(11), 1551–1556 (2010)
15. Lazebnik, S., Schmid, C., Ponce, J.: Beyond bags of features: spatial pyramid matching for recognizing natural scene categories. In: Conference on Computer Vision and Pattern Recognition (CVPR), vol. 2, pp. 2169–2178. IEEE (2006)
16. Lin, T.-Y., et al.: Microsoft COCO: common objects in context. In: Fleet, D., Pajdla, T., Schiele, B., Tuytelaars, T. (eds.) ECCV 2014. LNCS, vol. 8693, pp. 740–755. Springer, Cham (2014). https://doi.org/10.1007/978-3-319-10602-1_48
17. Mancas, M., Le Meur, O.: Memorability of natural scenes: the role of attention. In: International Conference on Image Processing (ICIP), pp. 196–200. IEEE (2013)
18. Manessi, F., Rozza, A.: Learning combinations of activation functions. In: International Conference on Pattern Recognition (ICPR), pp. 61–66 (2018)
19. Oliva, A., Torralba, A.: Modeling the shape of the scene: a holistic representation of the spatial envelope. Int. J. Comput. Vis. **42**(3), 145–175 (2001)
20. Paszke, A., et al.: Automatic differentiation in PyTorch (2017)
21. Pirie, W.: Spearman rank correlation coefficient, vol. 8, August 2006
22. Russakovsky, O., et al.: ImageNet large scale visual recognition challenge. Int. J. Comput. Vis. **115**(3), 211–252 (2015)
23. Shechtman, E., Irani, M.: Matching local self-similarities across images and videos. In: Conference on Computer Vision and Pattern Recognition (CVPR), Minneapolis, MN, vol. 2, p. 3 (2007)
24. Siarohin, A., Zen, G., Majtanovic, C., Alameda-Pineda, X., Ricci, E., Sebe, N.: How to make an image more memorable?: A deep style transfer approach. In: International Conference on Multimedia Retrieval (ICMR), pp. 322–329. ACM (2017)
25. Simonyan, K., Zisserman, A.: Very deep convolutional networks for large-scale image recognition. arXiv preprint arXiv:1409.1556 (2014)
26. Squalli-Houssaini, H., Duong, N.Q., Gwenaëlle, M., Demarty, C.H.: Deep learning for predicting image memorability. In: International Conference on Acoustics, Speech and Signal Processing (ICASSP), pp. 2371–2375. IEEE (2018)
27. Xu, K., et al.: Show, attend and tell: neural image caption generation with visual attention. In: International Conference on Machine Learning (ICML), pp. 2048–2057 (2015)
28. Zhou, B., Lapedriza, A., Xiao, J., Torralba, A., Oliva, A.: Learning deep features for scene recognition using places database. In: Advances in Neural Information Processing Systems, pp. 487–495 (2014)

A Graph-Based Color Lines Model
for Image Analysis

D. Duque-Arias[1]([⊠]), S. Velasco-Forero[1], J.-E. Deschaud[2], F. Goulette[2],
and B. Marcotegui[1]

[1] MINES ParisTech, CMM-Center of Mathematical Morphology,
PSL Research University, Paris, France
david.duque@mines-paristech.fr
[2] MINES ParisTech, CAOR-Centre de Robotique, PSL Research University,
Paris, France

Abstract. This paper addresses the problem of obtaining a concise
description of spectral representation for color images. The proposed
method is a graph-based formulation of the well-known Color Lines
model. It generalizes the lines to piece-wise lines, been able to fit more
complex structures. We illustrate the goodness of proposed method by
measuring the quality of the simplified representations in images and
videos. The quality of video sequences reconstructed by means of proposed color lines extracted from the first frame demonstrates the robustness of our representation. Our formalism allows to address applications
such as image segmentation, shadow correction among others.

Keywords: Color lines · Gaussian mixture model ·
Minimum Spanning Tree · Spectral representation ·
Graph-based modeling

1 Introduction

Color is an effective cue in computer vision for identifying objects/regions of
interest in images. On one hand, many efforts have been made to find an adequate
color representation via linear and non-linear color spaces as RGB, HSV, and
so on [1]. *Color modeling*, on the other hand, plays a different role to model the
color diversity as an information vector in a given representation space. These
techniques include statistical models [2], color versions of level sets [3,4], color
lines [5], color-unmixing [6], lattice structures on color spaces [7], among others.
In this work, we propose to model color information by piecewise linear functions,
computed from a simplified version of spectral representation in the same spirit of
color lines [5] which have demonstrated successful results in various applications
as video compression and segmentation [8], interactive shadows correction [9]
and image dehazing [10]. Our model considers non-straight lines by computing
successively longest path on a graph-based representation. Accordingly, we called
our model *Graph-based Color Lines* (GCL). The proposed method is mainly

© Springer Nature Switzerland AG 2019
E. Ricci et al. (Eds.): ICIAP 2019, LNCS 11752, pp. 181–191, 2019.
https://doi.org/10.1007/978-3-030-30645-8_17

divided in three steps: **(i)** Compute simplified spectral representation; **(ii)** Graph
modeling of the color representation; **(iii)** Build graph-based color lines. We note
that third step is a graph-based generalization of color lines method [5], based
of the spectral representation of images. Our GCL model, allows to identify
more complex geometrical structures in spectral representations than Straight
Color Lines (SCL) [8] but keeping at same time the potential to analyze the
image. Additionally, GCL are not constrained to have orientation in the positive
directions as it is the case of classical CL [5]. We highlight that motivation behind
our contribution is to obtain a reproducible model and preserving the versatility
of original color line model [5]. As a manner of example, we compare the results
obtained by the proposed method against SCL [8], in the example illustrated in
Fig. 1. For this case, four color lines were extracted for both representation and a
quantitative measure is reported (34.96 dB for GCL compared to 21.66 dB on the
SCL) by means of PSNR for a reconstructed image. Details of the computation
are presented in Sect. 3.

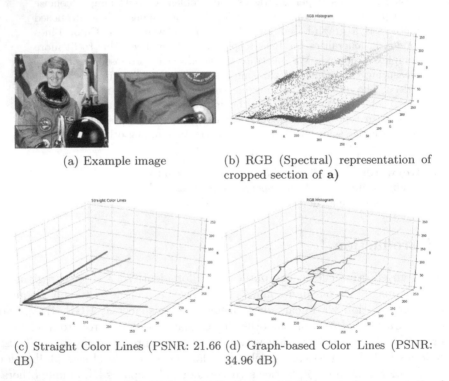

(a) Example image

(b) RGB (Spectral) representation of
cropped section of **a)**

(c) Straight Color Lines (PSNR: 21.66
dB)

(d) Graph-based Color Lines (PSNR:
34.96 dB)

Fig. 1. Comparison between SCL and GCL. Our model fits spectral representation by
piecewise lines. (Color figure online)

The rest of the paper is organized as follows: in Sect. 2, we describe the pro-
posed methodology and mathematical fundamentals for computing the proposed
GCL model. In Sect. 3, some experiments are presented to compare SCL and our
GCL for some images and videos. We conclude our findings in Sect. 4.

2   Graph-Based Color Lines Model

The proposed methodology for computing our Graph-based Color Lines (GCL) is divided in three stages. As descriptive example, the image in Fig. 1(a) was used to illustrate all required intermediate steps in Figs. 3, 4 and 6.

2.1   Simplified Color Representation

The aim of the first stage is to find a simplified spectral representation of the input image. We follow the same approach proposed by [5] and it is summarized in the workflow of Fig. 2.

Fig. 2. Steps for computing simplified spectral representation.

Firstly, the RGB histogram is computed and associated pixels to each color are stored. It is important to highlight that: **(i)** Each point of the spectral representation belongs to a different color in the image. In this work, we call it "color point"; **(ii)** A color point may be associated to more than one pixel from the image; **(iii)** Color points located further from the origin have a greater luminance. Figure 1(b) shows spectral representation from the image (a). There are visually identifiable geometric structures representing related colors in the image. This kind of structures are common in real world images as stated in [11]. From obtained spectral representation, the RGB space is divided in equally separated hemispheres to group the color points according to its luminance, as proposed by [5], to preserve the spectral diversity. The criteria to verify if a color point x is contained in a slice between two consecutive hemispheres with radius r_i and r_j, is given by $r_i \leq \|x\| < r_j$. Following the original formulation of color lines model [5], we fit a Gaussian mixture model (GMM) by hemisphere where the number of components is given by the number of local maxima. It allows to consider color points associated to colors with high density in the image. Additionally, as proposed by [5], the center of each Gaussian distribution is initialized at each local maximum, removing the instability of random initialization in GMMs. Due to spatial split in hemispheres, GMMs describe local behavior of pixels on the slice and global spectral diversity of the image is preserved.

Image (a) of Fig. 1 contains 13.851 color points. After the calculation of the local maxima by slice, the number of Gaussian distributions that describes the spectral representation is $n = 313$ (see Fig. 3).

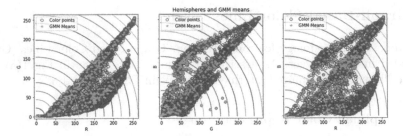

Fig. 3. Gaussian means of spectral representation of cropped section Fig. 1(a). (Color figure online)

2.2   Graph Modeling of Color Representation

In the second stage, the input is a simplified representation of the image given by the matrix $\mathbf{M}$, defined as $\mathbf{M} = [\mu_0, \mu_1, \ldots, \mu_n, \mathbf{0}]$, where μ_i is the mean vector of the $i\text{-}th$ Gaussian distribution, n is the number of distributions and $\mathbf{0}$ is the origin point vector of the color space. The expected output is a tree describing the geometric structures of color points. An approach to generate the color lines from $\mathbf{M}$ is to assume a linear behavior in geometric structures of color points as in [8]. In doing so, each color line may be built as a SCL intersecting the origin. Figure 4 shows (calculated) SCL from Fig. 1. It is seen that obtained color lines do not fit geometric structures of the spectral representation.

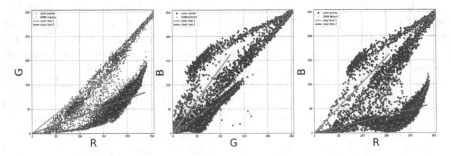

Fig. 4. First two SCLs of cropped section Fig. 1(a). (Color figure online)

We propose to generalize the method proposed by [5] to piecewise lines, able to represent more complex geometric structures of spectral representation. In detail, the first step is to calculate the complete graph $\mathcal{G}(\mathbf{M}, \mathbf{E})$ given by: $\mathbf{M}$ each node is a vector mean of the Gaussian distributions, and $\mathbf{E}$ as the matrix of Euclidean distances between the vectors in $\mathbf{M}$. Accordingly, we proposed a graph-based approach by linking Gaussian distributions in an economic way via a Minimum Spanning Tree (MST). A MST is a subgraph of $\mathcal{G}$ that satisfies following conditions: **(i)** It spans all the vertices; **(ii)** Is acyclic; **(iii)** Minimizes the sum of weights of its edges [12]. The use of MST at this point, is motivated for different links between density estimation and the MST from Euclidean distances [13,14].

2.3   Building Graph-Based Color Lines

In the third stage, we build a graph-based representation from color information. We note that the MST represents the spectral diversity of an image, in the spirit of color lines [5]. However, in our case, we define the color lines in the MST, as the path from the origin to each one of the leaves of the tree (nodes of degree one). We call each one of these path a *color line* induced by the MST. For some applications, one can be interested in the selection of most important *color lines*. Accordingly, we propose to rank obtained lines by their length, measured as sum of their edge weights (Euclidean distance between corresponding nodes). A simple algorithm to find the top-K lines by means of Dijkstra's algorithm [12] is given in Algorithm 1.

Input : M (Defined on Section 2.2)

Compute the MST of $\mathcal{G}(\mathbf{M}, \mathbf{E})$;
Add $\mathbf{0}$ to L_1;
for $k \leftarrow 1$ **to** K **do**

    Find longest path p from node $\mathbf{0}$ (Dijkstra algorithm);
    for *each edge (i,j) in p* **do**

        //If not visited yet
        if $\mathbf{E}(i, j) > 0$ **then**

            $\mathbf{E}(i, j) = 0$;
            Add (j) to L_k;
        end

    end

end
Output: $L_1, L_2, \ldots, L_K$ the top-K color lines
Algorithm 1. Compute top-K color lines

Figure 5 shows a simple example of the implementation of Algorithm 1 for computing top-3 GCL as follows: **(i)** In Fig. 5(a), the longest path from the origin is composed by $p = [0, 1, 4, 5]$ and so the first color line $L_1 = [0, 1, 4, 5]$; **(ii)** After updating weights in Fig. 5(b), the longest path from the origin is composed by $p = [0, 1, 2, 3]$ and so $L_2 = [2, 3]$; finally, **(iii)** After updating weights in Fig. 5(c), the longest path from the origin is composed by $p = [0, 1, 4, 6, 7]$ and so $L_3 = [6, 7]$; the assumption of assigning common nodes to longest line has some advantages: **(i)** Every color point is clustered; **(ii)** Darkest color points (close to the origin) are grouped on first nodes of the longest color line. According to the application where GCL is used, assigning common nodes to a particular line may affect performance. For example, as it is seen in Fig. 1(b), color points close to the origin represents dark colors or shadowed regions. This may mislead to identifying pixels as shadowed sections of the image instead of the actual colors.

Figure 6 shows the two longest GCL of the cropped section of Fig. 1(a) (it is seen how they adapt to spectrum geometry).

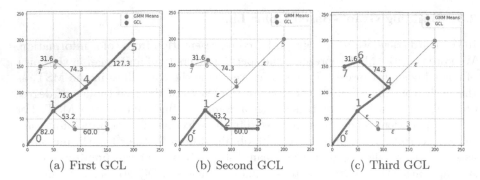

(a) First GCL   (b) Second GCL   (c) Third GCL

Fig. 5. Illustrative example of Algorithm 1 (Color figure online)

3   Experimental Results

The purpose of this section is to present the potential of our proposed GCL model. In order to evaluate the quality of image representation using GCL, we measured the error in the representation by mean of a projection into the model and then we are able to compare different methods *via* standard fidelity measures of representations as Peak Signal to Noise Ratio (PSNR) and Mean Squared Error (MSE).

3.1   Projection into GCL

In order to evaluate the quality of image simplification using our model, we propose to project the original image I_i into obtained GCL and measure the error of the reconstructed image. The procedure for projecting spectral representation is shown in Fig. 7:

1. *Interpolate GCL:* As presented in Sect. 2.3, each GCL is defined as a sequence of Gaussians of related colors. We calculated piecewise linear interpolation between means of the Gaussians belonging to the same GCL, to add soft color transitions over the line.
2. *Project original image I_i into GCL:* From Fig. 6, it can be seen that each GCL partially simplifies the color representation. In order to find the closest GCL for each color point, it is calculated Euclidean distance between each color point and every GCL. Then, it is re-assigned to each color point the value of the closest GCL. As a result, color diversity from original representation (I_i) is simplified (I_p) according to number of GCL.

For quantitative comparisons, Table 1 presents the results of PSNR and MSE using SCL and GCL. It is observed that: **(i)** PSNR is above 30 dB for images using GCL. The quality of our representation is greater than the one obtained using SCL; **(ii)** Images 1 and 3 have higher contrast and more different colors. Increasing the number of color lines allows a better fit to more complex geometrical structures. An example of fitting a complex structure is shown in Fig. 6,

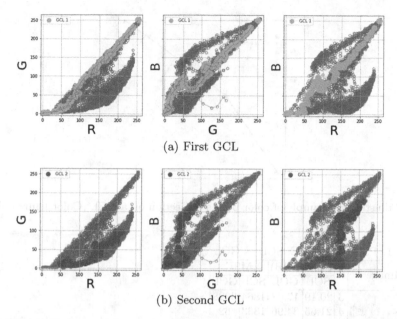

(a) First GCL

(b) Second GCL

Fig. 6. First two GCL of cropped section Fig. 1(a) (Color figure online)

specially in the second line; **(iii)** Images 2 and 4 do not present considerable variations on PSNR and MSE when the number of color lines increases. It occurs because the spectral representation of the image has few geometric structures so few color lines are required to represent the image. Table 2 shows percents of pixels grouped in each GCL. From obtained results, is found that in some images (1, 3 and 4), the percentage of pixels grouped in first four lines is over 85%.

Figure 8 displays the relationship between the number of hemispheres (varying from 1 to 40) against number of GCL (varying between 1 and 20), of full Astronaut image from Fig. 1(a). As it is seen on the top of Fig. 8, a reduced number of GCL and hemispheres represents the lowest image quality. Nevertheless, increasing both (lines and hemispheres) does not allow to indefinitely improve the quality of the simplification of the image.

To show the *capacity of generalization* [15] of our method, we performed an experiment measuring PNSR error for a set of images in a video, using GCL model computed uniquely from the first frame denoted by I_0. Note that an excellent model fitting does not guarantee good performance in predicting future frames, because of possible over-fitting on I_0. We have used two videos from [16] (*boxing-fisheye* and *mallard-fly*) and calculated the **top-5 GCLs** on the first frame (I_0). Figure 9 shows PSNR and MSE over the frames of each video.

We observe that PSNR and MSE were stable in the *boxing-fisheye* video. It occurs because the video corresponds to a sequence of frames without significant changes. In the video *mallard-fly*, the error increases for the last frames. It happens because there is camera panning and the last frames have nothing in

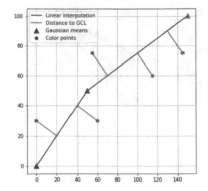

Fig. 7. Illustrative example of color points projection on a GCL (Color figure online)

Table 1. PSNR and MSE. SCL vs GCL

Id	Image	K	PSNR (dB)		MSE	
			SCL	GCL	SCL	GCL
1		3	20.19	17.68	1864	3328
		4	21.65	34.96	1333	62
		5	21.65	35.14	1333	59
2		3	21.44	33.54	1380	86
		4	21.56	34.10	1361	75
		5	21.57	34.11	1366	75
3		3	27.93	30.56	314	171
		4	28.56	35.96	271	49
		5	28.70	35.99	262	49
4		3	20.29	30.51	1822	173
		4	20.34	32.63	1800	106
		5	20.36	32.65	1794	105

Table 2. Percentage of pixels by GCL.

Id	% of pixels by line				
	L_1	L_2	L_3	L_4	Sum
1	8.21	17.75	1.6	57.86	85.41
2	69.45	1.96	0.01	1.79	73.2
3	76.58	0.19	7.81	3.5	88.07
4	86.71	5.27	0.82	1.03	93.83

common with I_0, for which GCL were calculated. More examples of our methods for different videos of [16] are available at http://www.cmm.mines-paristech.fr/~duque/gcl.

Figures 10 and 11 show the first frame from videos of Fig. 9. It is seen how the color diversity changes according to the number of GCL in the model. Even though, as is presented in Fig. 8, adding GCL to the model does not guarantee an indefinitely gain in PSNR.

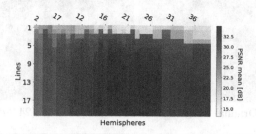

Fig. 8. PSNR varying the number of GCL and hemispheres from Table 1.

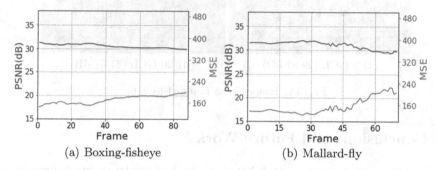

(a) Boxing-fisheye   (b) Mallard-fly

Fig. 9. PSNR and MSE in two videos from [16]. PSNR (blue) and MSE (red). (Color figure online)

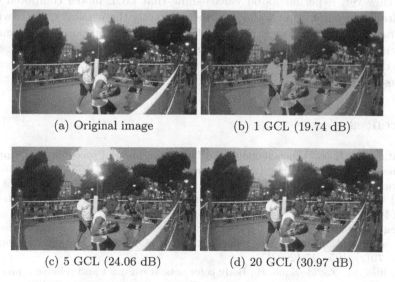

(a) Original image   (b) 1 GCL (19.74 dB)

(c) 5 GCL (24.06 dB)   (d) 20 GCL (30.97 dB)

Fig. 10. Images from boxing-fisheye [16].

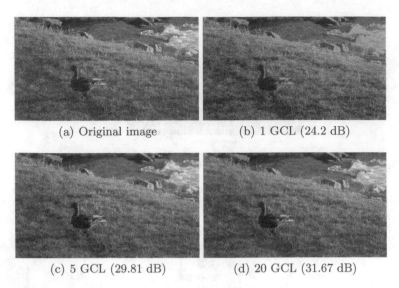

(a) Original image   (b) 1 GCL (24.2 dB)

(c) 5 GCL (29.81 dB)   (d) 20 GCL (31.67 dB)

Fig. 11. Images from mallard-fly [16].

4   Conclusions and Future Work

In this paper, we present a graph-based method to model spectral diversity of RGB images in the spirit of Color Lines [5]. The resulting GCL model performs better than [8] in most of the explored examples, which is natural due to the higher complexity of our model (piecewise linear function instead of straight lines). However, experiments on videos show that GCL model computed on a single frame does not over-fit and describes correctly the whole sequence, within the same scene. Finally, we noted that GCL is general-purpose model and we are planning to use it for image/video segmentation, image/video simplification, change detection, etc. In future research, we will also work on methods to correct shadows and dehazing images using GCL instead of CL as in [9,10].

References

1. Plataniotis, K.N., Venetsanopoulos, A.N.: Color Image Processing and Applications. Springer, Heidelberg (2013). https://doi.org/10.1007/978-3-662-04186-4
2. Permuter, H., Francos, J., Jermyn, I.: A study of Gaussian mixture models of color and texture features for image classification and segmentation. Pattern Recogn. **39**(4), 695–706 (2006)
3. Cremers, D., Rousson, M., Deriche, R.: A review of statistical approaches to level set segmentation: integrating color, texture, motion and shape. Int. J. Comput. Vis. **72**(2), 195–215 (2007)
4. Gouiffès, M., Zavidovique, B.: Body color sets: a compact and reliable representation of images. J. Vis. Commun. Image Represent. **22**(1), 48–60 (2011)

5. Omer, I., Werman, M.: Color lines: image specific color representation. In: Proceedings of the 2004 IEEE Computer Society Conference on Computer Vision and Pattern Recognition, CVPR 2004, vol. 2, p. II. IEEE (2004)
6. Aksoy, Y., Aydın, T.O., Smolić, A., Pollefeys, M.: Unmixing-based soft color segmentation for image manipulation. ACM Trans. Graph. **36**(2), 19:1–19:19 (2017)
7. Angulo, J.: Morphological colour operators in totally ordered lattices based on distances: application to image filtering, enhancement and analysis. Comput. Vis. Image Underst. **107**(1–2), 56–73 (2007)
8. Nishikawa, T., Tanaka, Y.: Dynamic color lines. In: 2018 25th IEEE International Conference on Image Processing (ICIP), pp. 2247–2251, October 2018
9. Yu, X., Li, G., Ying, Z., Guo, X.: A new shadow removal method using color-lines. In: Felsberg, M., Heyden, A., Krüger, N. (eds.) CAIP 2017. LNCS, vol. 10425, pp. 307–319. Springer, Cham (2017). https://doi.org/10.1007/978-3-319-64698-5_26
10. Fattal, R.: Dehazing using color-lines, vol. 34, pp. 1–14. ACM, New York (2014)
11. Buades, A., Lisani, J.L., Morel, J.-M.: On the distribution of colors in natural images (2010)
12. Cormen, T.H., Leiserson, C.E., Rivest, R.L., Stein, C.: Introduction to Algorithms. MIT Press, Cambridge (2009)
13. Sreevani, Murthy, C.A.: On bandwidth selection using minimal spanning tree for kernel density estimation. Comput. Stat. Data Anal. **102**, 67–84 (2016)
14. Yu, Z., Au, O.C., Tang, K., Xu, C.: Nonparametric density estimation on a graph: learning framework, fast approximation and application in image segmentation. In: 2011 IEEE Conference on Computer Vision and Pattern Recognition (CVPR), pp. 2201–2208. IEEE (2011)
15. Kawaguchi, K., Kaelbling, L.P., Bengio, Y.: Generalization in deep learning. arXiv preprint arXiv:1710.05468 (2017)
16. Perazzi, F., Pont-Tuset, J., McWilliams, B., Van Gool, L., Gross, M., Sorkine-Hornung, A.: A benchmark dataset and evaluation methodology for video object segmentation. In: Computer Vision and Pattern Recognition (2016)

Evaluating Deep Convolutional Neural Networks as Texture Feature Extractors

Leonardo F. S. Scabini[1(✉)], Rayner H. M. Condori[2], Lucas C. Ribas[2],
and Odemir M. Bruno[1]

[1] São Carlos Institute of Physics, University of São Paulo, São Carlos, SP, Brazil
{scabini,bruno}@ifsc.usp.br
[2] Institute of Mathematics and Computer Science, University of São Paulo,
São Carlos, SP, Brazil
{raynerhmc,lucasribas}@usp.br

Abstract. Texture is an important visual property which has been largely employed for image characterization. Recently, Convolutional Networks has been the predominant approach on Computer Vision, and their application on texture analysis shows interesting results. However, their popularity steers around object recognition, and several convolutional architectures have been proposed and trained for this task. Therefore, this works evaluates 17 of the most diffused Deep Convolutional Neural Networks when employed for texture analysis as feature extractors. Image descriptors are obtained through Global Average Pooling over the output of the last convolutional layer of networks with random weights or learned from the ImageNet dataset. The analysis is performed under 6 texture datasets and using 3 different supervised classifiers (KNN, LDA, and SVM). Results using networks with random weights indicates that the architecture alone plays an important role in texture characterization, and it can even provide useful features for classification for some datasets. On the other hand, we found that although ImageNet weights usually provide the best results it can also perform similar to random weights in some cases, indicating that transferring convolutional weights learned on ImageNet may not always be appropriate for texture analysis. When comparing the best models, our results corroborate that DenseNet presents the highest overall performance while keeping a significantly small number of hyperparameters, thus we recommend its use for texture characterization.

Keywords: Deep Convolutional Neural Networks · Texture analysis · Feature extraction

1 Introduction

Texture is a highly discriminating visual characteristic that has been widely studied since the 1960s. In Computer Vision (CV), texture analysis is an active field of research and there is a constant need for new methods for texture characterization in several areas that rely on image recognition systems. Many techniques have then been proposed in the past years [16] composing a wide and heterogeneous literature on texture analysis,

E. Ricci et al. (Eds.): ICIAP 2019, LNCS 11752, pp. 192–202, 2019.
https://doi.org/10.1007/978-3-030-30645-8_18

however, the recent advances on Deep Learning made Neural Networks the predominant approach on CV. This trend grew mainly after the success obtained by the AlexNet [11] Deep Convolutional Neural Network (DCNN) on the 2012 ImageNet [5] challenge. Several DCNN architectures have then been proposed for object recognition, with varying structural properties such as different convolutional blocks and their combinations. These models with pre-trained weights on ImageNet have then been employed as texture feature extractors [3,30], achieving promising results.

Although it has been shown that transferring the learning of some DCNN pre-trained on the ImageNet dataset into texture analysis usually provides good results, little is known on the impacts of different architectures on performance. Moreover, there are no obvious reasons to believe that the use of ImageNet weights, which have been trained for object recognition, is the best approach for texture characterization. Therefore, this works presents a broad evaluation of 17 DCNN models considering these aspects. Texture descriptors are obtained through the Global Average Pooling (GAP) over the output of the last convolutional layer, which is then fed to a supervised classifier. We analyze the importance of the architecture alone and the gain on using ImageNet weights for texture analysis by comparing the network performance with random weights. Moreover, our experiments include 6 texture datasets with varying properties and 3 classifiers (KNN, LDA, and SVM) in order to measure the capacity of each model. We also analyze the efficiency of the networks for texture analysis in terms of its size (number of hyperparameters) and average performance.

2   Theoretical Background

2.1   Texture Analysis

Texture is a key feature of many types of images and, over the decades, many methods for texture representation (i.e., extraction of features to describe the texture information) have been proposed. In the last century, the research in texture representation mainly focused on two-well established types of approaches: filtering-based and statistical-based [16]. In the filtering-based approaches, the image is convolved with a filter bank. In this category, some important techniques are Gabor filters, wavelet pyramids, and simple linear filters. The statistical-based approaches model the texture using kth order statistics and use probability distributions to characterize the images, such as the Markov Random Field, Fractal models and Gray Level Co-occurrence Matrix (GLCM).

At the end of the last century and in the 2000s, there was the propose of texton-based approaches such as Bag of Textons [13] and Bag of Words [4]. In these approaches, a dictionary of textons is obtained and the images are represented by statistics over the texton dictionary. Furthermore, the need for features invariant to scale, rotation, illumination and viewpoint stimulated the development of local invariant descriptors, such as SIFT [17] and LBP [19]. These local descriptors were extensively used in computer vision, however, more recently, there was a renaissance of deep neural networks approaches from the work of Krizhevsky et al. in 2012 [11]. In this way, actually, the research in textures and image analysis has focused on deep learning approaches. In texture analysis, important advances have been reported such as in [3,30].

2.2 Deep Convolutional Neural Networks

A convolutional network is a type of neural network that is mainly used for analyzing images, videos and any kind of spatially organized data, and it has been studied since the 1990's [12]. In a general fashion, we can split a convolutional neural network into two well-defined components: (i) the feature extraction part and (ii) the classification part. In most of the DCNN, the latter component is organized into one or more *fully-connected layers*, like a traditional multilayer neural network. On the other hand, the feature extraction part consists of convolutional layers which can vary greatly from one network to another, as various convolutional blocks have been proposed throughout the years. In early models [12] it consisted of a few convolutional and pooling layers, however, since the introduction of the *deep learning* concept new architectures are increasingly grouping layers. Moreover, different structures of convolutional blocks have been proposed such as the Inception modules [27] and Residual connections [8].

The input and output of layers in the feature extraction part of a DCNN consists of a set of $n_{\mathbf{A}^{(l)}}$ stacked 2-D matrices $\mathbf{A}^{(l)}$, that we refer here as "feature maps", where l indicates the layer's depth and $\mathbf{A}_j^{(l)}$ represents the j-th feature map ($1 \leq j \leq n_{\mathbf{A}^{(l)}}$). In the case of convolutional layers, the trainable weights are organized into a set of $n_{\mathbf{F}^{(l)}}$ filters of fixed size. This set, also known as the filter bank ($\mathbf{F}^{(l)}$), is in charge of computing a new set of feature maps $\mathbf{A}^{(l+1)}$ by convolving $\mathbf{A}^{(l)}$ with every filter in $\mathbf{F}^{(l)}$. In addition, there are vastly more types of layers in a DCNN that also yield a feature map, for example, the Dropout layer, the concatenation layer, and batch normalization.

The set of feature maps $\mathbf{A}^{(n)}$ represents the output of the last convolutional layer (n) of a DCNN, and it is usually flattened to fit into a fully-connected layer. Another approach is the use of Global Average Pooling (GAP) [14] to reduce the data before passing it to a classification layer

$$\varphi_j = \frac{\sum \mathbf{A_j}^{(n)}}{n_{\mathbf{A_j}^{(n)}}} \tag{1}$$

In other words, the GAP takes the mean value of every feature map $\mathbf{A}_j^{(n)}$ and concatenates into a vector φ. This vector acts as a final image descriptor, therefore pretrained DCNN can be used as feature extractors by obtaining φ.

3 Experiments

3.1 Considered Networks

For a broad analysis of DCNN architectures we considered 17 models with varying depth and modules proposed along the past years (between 2012 and 2018), details are given on Table 1. These are well-known models which have been extensively evaluated by the deep learning community recently, and its source code is open access[1]. All networks are applied as feature extractors by removing its last fully-connected layers and

---

[1] Keras models: https://keras.io/applications/
PyTorch models: https://github.com/Cadene/pretrained-models.pytorch.

taking the GAP from feature maps of the last convolutional layer, composing the feature vector φ. A more elaborated approach for feature map characterization is presented in [3], however, our goal here is to analyze the difference in performance between these architectures rather than maximizing the obtained results. Regarding the weight initialization policy, we considered the standard definition of the framework from which the model is imported, as this is the most common case when applying these networks. In the Keras 2.2.4 library, the 2D convolutional layers employ the Glorot uniform random weight initialization [6], and the bias terms are initialized with 0. In the case of AlexNet, PolyNet, PNASNet5 and all the Squeeze-and-Excitation networks, the PyTorch 1.0.0 default initialization policy is used, that is: the convolutional layer weights and bias are sampled from an uniform distribution $\mathcal{U}(-\sqrt{k}, \sqrt{k})$, where $k = 1/N_{w_c}$. The term N_{w_c} is the number of weights at the convolutional layer c. On the other hand, in the case of the ResNet and DenseNet models, the weights of the convolutional layers are initialized according to the Kaiming normal distribution [7], $\mathcal{N}$ (mean = 0 and std = $\sqrt{2/N_{w_c}}$), the batch normalization weights and bias are respectively initialized with 1s and 0s.

Table 1. Details on each DCNN considered for analysis. The network size is measured by the number of hyperparameters (full includes fully-connected layers and GAP refers to only the feature extraction part). $|\varphi|$ represents the size of the resulting feature vector.

Network	Weight initialization	Size (in millions)		$|\varphi|$	Framework
		Full	GAP		
AlexNet [11]	$\mathcal{U}(-\sqrt{k}, \sqrt{k}), k = 1/N_{w_c}$	61.1008	2.4697	256	Pytorch 1.0.0
VGG16 [25]	Glorot uniform	138.3575	14.7147	512	Keras 2.2.4
VGG19 [25]	Glorot uniform	143.6672	20.0244	512	Keras 2.2.4
InceptionV3 [27]	Glorot uniform	23.8518	21.8028	2048	Keras 2.2.4
ResNet18 [8]	Kaiming normal	11.6895	11.1765	512	Pytorch 1.0.0
ResNet50 [8]	Kaiming normal	25.5570	23.5080	2048	Pytorch 1.0.0
ResNet152 [8]	Kaiming normal	60.1928	58.1438	2048	Pytorch 1.0.0
InceptionResNetV2 [26]	Glorot uniform	55.8737	54.3367	1536	Keras 2.2.4
PolyNet [31]	$\mathcal{U}(-\sqrt{k}, \sqrt{k}), k = 1/N_{w_c}$	95.3666	93.3176	2048	Pytorch 1.0.0
DenseNet121 [10]	Kaiming normal	7.9789	6.9539	1024	Pytorch 1.0.0
DenseNet201 [10]	Kaiming normal	20.0139	18.0929	1920	Pytorch 1.0.0
PNASNet5 (large) [15]	$\mathcal{U}(-\sqrt{k}, \sqrt{k}), k = 1/N_{w_c}$	86.0577	81.7367	4320	Pytorch 1.0.0
SENet154 [9]	$\mathcal{U}(-\sqrt{k}, \sqrt{k}), k = 1/N_{w_c}$	115.0890	113.0400	2048	Pytorch 1.0.0
SEResNet50 [9]	$\mathcal{U}(-\sqrt{k}, \sqrt{k}), k = 1/N_{w_c}$	28.0880	26.0390	2048	Pytorch 1.0.0
SEResNet152 [9]	$\mathcal{U}(-\sqrt{k}, \sqrt{k}), k = 1/N_{w_c}$	66.8218	64.7728	2048	Pytorch 1.0.0
SEResNeXt50 [9,29]	$\mathcal{U}(-\sqrt{k}, \sqrt{k}), k = 1/N_{w_c}$	27.5599	25.5109	2048	Pytorch 1.0.0
SEResNeXt101 [9,29]	$\mathcal{U}(-\sqrt{k}, \sqrt{k}), k = 1/N_{w_c}$	48.9554	46.9064	2048	Pytorch 1.0.0

3.2 Experimental Protocol

Six color texture datasets with varying properties are used in our experiments. We considered well-known traditional datasets and also recent and more complicated ones:

(1) Vistex [20] (864 images, 54 classes); (2) USPtex [2] (2292 images, 191 classes); (3) Outex13 [18] (test suite Outex_TC_00013, 1360 images, 68 classes); (4) CUReT [28] (5612 images, 61 classes); (5) MBT [1] (2464 images, 154 classes, clipping of original images as in [22]); and (6) FMD [24] (1000 images, 10 classes). To process the datasets with the studied DCNN we resize the images to the corresponding network input, except for the FMD dataset where images are not square, thus we use the original images to preserve its proportions (the DCNN will produce valid feature maps for GAP). Regarding the gray-level images present in the FMD dataset, we transform them in RGB by replicating its values for all channels.

We considered different classifiers in our experiments: (1) a K-Nearest-Neighbors (KNN) approach with $k = 1$; (2) Linear Discriminant Analysis (LDA) using a least squares solution; (3) The Support Vector Machine (SVM) using a linear kernel and penalty parameter $C = 1$. The classification experiments are performed with 10 random splits into half for training and a half for the test in a stratified fashion. In the case of the network random weight initialization, 10 different networks are initialized and the classification is done using the same 10 random splits for each one, yielding a total of 100 train and test procedures. The performance is measured by the mean and standard deviation of the test accuracy over the iterations.

4 Results Analysis

4.1 Contribution of the Architecture Versus Learned Weights

Intriguing results [21] have shown that neural networks, convolutional or not, with completely random weights can achieve interesting performance. This is, in fact, similar to randomized neural networks [23], where a hidden layer with random weights has the purpose of projecting non-linearly the input data in another dimensional space where it is more likely that the feature vectors are linearly separable. Therefore, on these networks, the performance relies on the training of the output layer and the shape of the hidden layer rather than on its weights, as they are random. In the case of DCNN, the feature extraction part plays a similar role than the hidden layer of the randomized neural network, projecting the data. The discussion presented in [21] corroborates that the convolutional architecture alone is of high importance for object recognition, where they propose a fast method for architecture selection based on the performance on random weights. In this context, we verify the contribution of the architecture alone and the learned weights for texture analysis by analyzing the performance of DCNN using random weights or pre-trained on the ImageNet dataset. Figure 1 shows the results obtained with the simplest classifier, KNN, that we choose in this experiment in order to highlight the quality of the features itself so that the result does not rely mostly on the classification technique. We can verify the contribution of the learned weights over the random ones by the distance of the points to the dotted line, which represents $x = y$ (where random weight equals the accuracy of the ImageNet weights).

It is possible to notice different cases regarding random and ImageNet weights, where performance varies both according to the dataset or the DCNN model. First, the standard deviation on random weights indicates that different initialization has a relatively small impact in comparison to the architecture performance itself. Regarding the

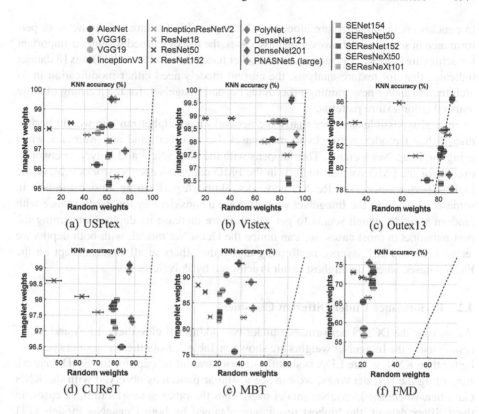

Fig. 1. Correlation between the accuracy using DCNN with random weights or pre-trained on ImageNet. The doted line represents the diagonal of the plan, i.e. $x = y$. The small black horizontal lines represents the standard deviation over 10 random networks.

variation between datasets, we observe in USPtex, Vistex, and CUReT a similar behavior, where the learned weights provide a small but relevant improvement. Nonetheless, in the Outex13 dataset, most of the networks have similar performance either with random or ImageNet weights, some of them, in fact, performs better with random weights. This raises questions concerning the applicability of the ImageNet weights for color texture characterization. On the other hand, in the MBT and FMD datasets, the gain from the learned weights is significantly higher for all networks. In terms of texture classification, these two datasets present different properties in comparison to the others. MBT, for instance, have complex intraband and interband spatial variations, forming unusual spectral texture patterns. It seems that these DCNN architectures alone are not capable of effectively capturing these spectral variations, while learned weights play a significant role in texture characterization. In the FMD dataset, the gain provided by the learned weights is the higher, where most networks with random weights perform poorly (around 20% and 30% of accuracy). FMD is a *in-the-wild* dataset, with texture images from various different objects in the same class, which explains why ImageNet weights are important here, as they are learned in a wide object recognition scenario.

In conclusion, the architecture alone may be responsible for most of the network performance in some cases, however, in most cases, the use of learned weights is important for achieving higher performance. On the other hand, the results on the Outex13 dataset indicates that, for texture analysis, the current models need either modification in its architecture and/or new training procedures beyond ImageNet, for the learning of more unusual color texture patterns.

It is also possible to notice that some networks have higher random weight performance than the other networks in most cases, but in other hand are overcome when using the ImageNet weights. This happens with the PNASNet5 and PolyNet networks, except for the FMD dataset. In fact, in the FMD dataset deeper networks achieve the highest performance. The ResNet networks, although performing among the best in some datasets using the ImageNet weights, have a considerably low performance with random weights, which seems to get worse as we increase its depth. Concerning the best networks in most cases, we can notice the DenseNet model, with both depths we tested (121 and 201 layers), performing above the others in all cases, except on the FMD dataset, where the highest result is achieved by PolyNet.

4.2 Performance Under Different Classifiers

We include the DCNN performance under two additional classifiers, LDA and SVM, results using the ImageNet weights are shown in Table 2. Both these classifiers perform better than KNN, where LDA is slightly superior overall (except for the FMD dataset). Regarding the best networks, we can see a similar pattern as observed with the KNN classifier, where the DenseNet model overcomes the other networks in most cases. In the USPtex dataset, the highest results are obtained by both DenseNet models (121 and 201 layers deep), with $99.8\% \pm 0.1$ of accuracy using either LDA or SVM. For the Vistex dataset, DenseNet201 achieves $100\% \pm 0.1$ with LDA and $99.9\% \pm 0.2$ with SVM, however various networks performs above 99.7% on this dataset, as ResNet50, PolyNet, PNASNET5, SENet154 and SEResNet152. For Outex13 results are significantly lower than for the former 2 datasets, and DenseNet201 present the higher performance ($91.8\% \pm 0.5$ with LDA and $90.8\% \pm 0.7$ with SVM). DenseNet201 also present the highest results for the CUReT ($99.4\% \pm 0.2$ with LDA and $99.8\% \pm 0.1$ with SVM) and MBT datasets ($97.6\% \pm 0.3$ with LDA and $97.2\% \pm 0.3$ with SVM). The results obtained on FMD vary if compared to the other datasets, where DenseNet is overcome by other networks such as PolyNet, SENet154, and SEResNet50. The highest results are obtained by PolyNet using LDA, with $87.3\% \pm 0.9$, and SENet154 using SVM, with $86.4\% \pm 0.8$. However, the standard deviation of their results on this dataset puts these networks in a similar performance range.

4.3 Efficiency Comparison

For a final comparison, we considered the efficiency of the network, defined here as the correlation between size (number of hyperparameters) and performance (mean accuracy for the six datasets). The number of hyperparameters of a network is directly related to the number of operations performed throughout its layers, which is a good measure for the cost of computing the image descriptor. Figure 2 shows this analysis with the three

Table 2. Results of each DCNN using the LDA and SVM classifiers, representing the mean accuracy and the standard deviation for 10 random data splits into half for train and half for test. Best results in each dataset are highlighted in bold type.

Network	USPtex	Vistex	Outex13	CUReT	MBT	FMD
LDA						
Alexnet	98.7 ± 0.2	99.4 ± 0.3	87.2 ± 1.0	90.5 ± 0.7	88.2 ± 0.9	70.0 ± 1.4
VGG16	98.7 ± 0.2	99.0 ± 0.4	86.6 ± 0.5	93.6 ± 0.5	93.4 ± 0.7	74.8 ± 1.3
VGG19	98.5 ± 0.3	98.8 ± 0.4	86.3 ± 0.9	93.2 ± 0.6	92.6 ± 0.7	72.5 ± 1.8
InceptionV3	98.4 ± 0.3	98.8 ± 0.5	86.1 ± 0.8	97.4 ± 0.2	92.2 ± 0.5	80.6 ± 1.2
InceptionResNetV2	97.7 ± 0.4	98.8 ± 0.3	88.2 ± 0.6	96.4 ± 0.5	91.2 ± 0.7	82.6 ± 2.2
ResNet18	98.8 ± 0.3	99.3 ± 0.3	86.9 ± 0.7	95.7 ± 0.4	91.3 ± 0.8	82.8 ± 0.4
ResNet50	99.4 ± 0.1	99.7 ± 0.3	90.5 ± 0.5	98.6 ± 0.2	94.1 ± 0.8	84.3 ± 1.5
ResNet152	99.6 ± 0.2	99.5 ± 0.3	89.4 ± 0.8	98.9 ± 0.2	94.8 ± 0.6	86.1 ± 0.7
PolyNet	99.3 ± 0.2	99.6 ± 0.4	88.5 ± 0.7	98.5 ± 0.2	95.4 ± 0.5	**87.3 ± 0.9**
DenseNet121	**99.8 ± 0.1**	99.9 ± 0.2	91.1 ± 0.8	98.9 ± 0.2	97.4 ± 0.3	85.9 ± 0.8
DenseNet201	**99.8 ± 0.1**	**100.0 ± 0.1**	**91.8 ± 0.5**	**99.4 ± 0.2**	**97.6 ± 0.3**	86.8 ± 1.1
PNASNet5(large)	98.7 ± 0.4	99.7 ± 0.3	86.9 ± 0.9	98.8 ± 0.3	93.5 ± 1.0	83.6 ± 1.6
SENet154	99.5 ± 0.2	99.7 ± 0.3	87.7 ± 0.7	98.1 ± 0.3	93.4 ± 0.4	87.1 ± 1.2
SEResNet50	99.5 ± 0.2	99.6 ± 0.3	88.7 ± 0.6	97.8 ± 0.2	93.2 ± 0.7	87.1 ± 0.7
SEResNet152	98.9 ± 0.2	99.8 ± 0.3	90.1 ± 0.9	96.9 ± 0.3	92.1 ± 0.4	86.0 ± 0.8
SEResNeXt50	99.2 ± 0.3	99.5 ± 0.3	86.2 ± 0.9	97.4 ± 0.3	92.0 ± 0.8	86.0 ± 0.9
SEResNeXt101	99.3 ± 0.3	99.5 ± 0.4	86.9 ± 0.7	96.9 ± 0.3	91.9 ± 0.5	86.2 ± 1.0
SVM						
Alexnet	98.9 ± 0.3	99.4 ± 0.4	86.8 ± 0.8	98.3 ± 0.2	86.6 ± 0.6	66.7 ± 2.3
VGG16	99.0 ± 0.2	99.4 ± 0.4	87.7 ± 0.7	98.6 ± 0.1	94.5 ± 0.7	72.5 ± 1.9
VGG19	98.5 ± 0.3	99.3 ± 0.3	87.5 ± 0.7	98.1 ± 0.3	93.3 ± 0.6	69.6 ± 2.4
InceptionV3	98.0 ± 0.3	99.0 ± 0.4	85.4 ± 1.3	99.0 ± 0.2	91.6 ± 0.4	80.7 ± 1.0
InceptionResNetV2	97.6 ± 0.2	98.7 ± 0.3	87.8 ± 1.0	98.6 ± 0.2	89.2 ± 0.5	81.5 ± 1.6
ResNet18	99.1 ± 0.2	98.9 ± 0.5	87.3 ± 0.6	98.9 ± 0.2	90.9 ± 0.8	80.7 ± 1.0
ResNet50	99.2 ± 0.4	99.5 ± 0.4	89.5 ± 0.8	99.3 ± 0.1	92.9 ± 0.6	82.8 ± 1.2
ResNet152	99.1 ± 0.3	99.5 ± 0.4	88.3 ± 0.8	99.4 ± 0.2	93.8 ± 0.6	84.6 ± 1.2
PolyNet	98.7 ± 0.3	99.7 ± 0.4	87.3 ± 0.6	99.2 ± 0.1	94.5 ± 0.6	86.1 ± 0.9
DenseNet121	**99.8 ± 0.1**	99.8 ± 0.2	90.3 ± 0.8	99.7 ± 0.1	96.9 ± 0.5	84.3 ± 1.2
DenseNet201	**99.8 ± 0.1**	**99.9 ± 0.2**	90.8 ± 0.7	**99.8 ± 0.1**	**97.2 ± 0.3**	85.2 ± 1.1
PNASNet5 (large)	98.0 ± 0.4	99.3 ± 0.4	85.0 ± 1.0	99.0 ± 0.2	91.5 ± 0.7	84.3 ± 1.1
SENet154	99.1 ± 0.2	99.6 ± 0.3	87.0 ± 0.6	99.3 ± 0.1	92.8 ± 0.7	**86.4 ± 0.8**
SEResNet50	99.0 ± 0.4	99.4 ± 0.5	87.5 ± 0.9	99.3 ± 0.1	92.3 ± 0.4	85.6 ± 1.0
SEResNet152	98.2 ± 0.3	99.4 ± 0.3	88.6 ± 0.7	99.1 ± 0.2	91.3 ± 0.6	84.8 ± 0.7
SEResNeXt50	98.7 ± 0.4	99.2 ± 0.5	85.6 ± 0.4	99.2 ± 0.2	91.5 ± 0.6	83.9 ± 0.9
SEResNeXt101	98.7 ± 0.4	99.1 ± 0.5	86.0 ± 0.9	99.0 ± 0.2	90.7 ± 0.7	84.7 ± 1.0

classifiers (KNN, LDA, and SVM), where network size refers to the feature extraction part only. The observed behavior for the three classifiers is similar where, overall, there is a positive correlation between the increase in size and performance. However, the DenseNet model seems to escape this rule, presenting the highest mean performance together with a relatively small size. It has a size around the smallest networks analyzed while performing significantly better. After DenseNet, the ResNet50 and SEResNet50 models present the highest efficiency, with performance similar to big networks while keeping a relatively small size.

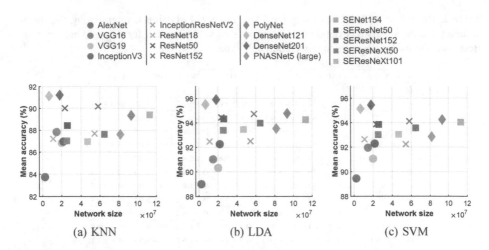

Fig. 2. The relation between the mean accuracy over the 6 datasets and the network size, i.e. the number of hyperparameters of the part used as feature extractor (no fully connected layers). Results are shown for 3 different classifiers (KNN, LDA and SVM).

5   Conclusion

On this work we performed a broad analysis of different DCNN models on texture analysis, specifically as texture feature extractors coupled with a supervised classifier. Our experiments include 17 DCNN, 6 texture datasets and 3 different classifiers (KNN, LDA, and SVM). The results indicate various interesting properties of these networks and datasets. First, we observed that the DCNN architecture alone is of great importance for texture characterization, as results with random weights point out, and learned weights make a complementary contribution for performance. However, weights learned on ImageNet may not be always appropriate for texture analysis, as results in the Outex13 dataset indicates, where random weights outperformed ImageNet weights for some networks. Regarding the performance of the models, our results indicate that the DenseNet architecture, both with 121 or 201 layers deep, is highly recommendable for texture analysis as it achieves the highest results in all datasets, except FMD. Moreover, our efficiency analysis indicates a positive correlation between the increase in network size and performance, but DenseNet escapes this rule as it has a significantly small size while keeping higher performance. The pattern of performance difference between networks is similar regardless of the chosen classifier. However, the LDA and SVM classifiers perform better than KNN, and LDA is slightly superior overall, except for the CUReT dataset where SVM is better. As future works for a better understanding of DCNN architectures, it is possible to explore the impact of different weight initialization techniques, as we considered here only the default from the frameworks. Moreover, it is possible to explore the use of more sophisticated feature map characterization techniques besides from GAP, in order to obtain better texture descriptors from each network.

Acknowledgements. L. F. S. Scabini acknowledges support from CNPq (grant #142438/2018-9) and the São Carlos Institute of Physics (CAPES funding). R. H. M. Condori acknowledges support from FONDECYT, an initiative of the National Council of Science, Technology and Technological Innovation-CONCYTEC (Peru). L. C. Ribas gratefully acknowledges the financial support grant #s 2016/23763-8 and 2019/03277-0, São Paulo Research Foundation (FAPESP). O. M. Bruno acknowledges support from CNPq (grants #307797/2014-7 and #484312/2013-8) and FAPESP (grants #14/08026-1 and #16/18809-9). The authors are also grateful to the NVIDIA GPU Grant Program for the donation of the Quadro P6000 and the Titan Xp GPUs used on this research.

References

1. Abdelmounaime, S., Dong-Chen, H.: New Brodatz-based image databases for grayscale color and multiband texture analysis. ISRN Mach. Vis. **2013**, 14 (2013)
2. Backes, A.R., Casanova, D., Bruno, O.M.: Color texture analysis based on fractal descriptors. Pattern Recogn. **45**(5), 1984–1992 (2012)
3. Cimpoi, M., Maji, S., Kokkinos, I., Vedaldi, A.: Deep filter banks for texture recognition, description, and segmentation. Int. J. Comput. Vis. **118**(1), 65–94 (2016)
4. Csurka, G., Dance, C., Fan, L., Willamowski, J., Bray, C.: Visual categorization with bags of keypoints. In: Workshop on Statistical Learning in Computer Vision, ECCV, Prague, vol. 1, pp. 1–2 (2004)
5. Deng, J., Dong, W., Socher, R., Li, L.J., Li, K., Fei-Fei, L.: ImageNet: a large-scale hierarchical image database. In: IEEE Conference on Computer Vision and Pattern Recognition, CVPR 2009, pp. 248–255. IEEE (2009)
6. Glorot, X., Bengio, Y.: Understanding the difficulty of training deep feedforward neural networks. In: Proceedings of the Thirteenth International Conference on Artificial Intelligence and Statistics, pp. 249–256 (2010)
7. He, K., Zhang, X., Ren, S., Sun, J.: Delving deep into rectifiers: surpassing human-level performance on ImageNet classification. In: Proceedings of the 2015 IEEE International Conference on Computer Vision (ICCV), ICCV 2015, pp. 1026–1034. IEEE Computer Society, Washington, DC (2015)
8. He, K., Zhang, X., Ren, S., Sun, J.: Deep residual learning for image recognition. In: Proceedings of the IEEE Conference on Computer Vision and Pattern Recognition, pp. 770–778 (2016)
9. Hu, J., Shen, L., Sun, G.: Squeeze-and-excitation networks. In: Proceedings of the IEEE Conference on Computer Vision and Pattern Recognition, pp. 7132–7141 (2018)
10. Huang, G., Liu, Z., van der Maaten, L., Weinberger, K.Q.: Densely connected convolutional networks. In: Proceedings of the IEEE Conference on Computer Vision and Pattern Recognition, pp. 4700–4708 (2017)
11. Krizhevsky, A., Sutskever, I., Hinton, G.E.: ImageNet classification with deep convolutional neural networks. In: Advances in Neural Information Processing Systems, pp. 1097–1105 (2012)
12. LeCun, Y., et al.: Handwritten digit recognition with a back-propagation network. In: Advances in Neural Information Processing Systems, pp. 396–404 (1990)
13. Leung, T., Malik, J.: Representing and recognizing the visual appearance of materials using three-dimensional textons. Int. J. Comput. Vis. **43**(1), 29–44 (2001)
14. Lin, M., Chen, Q., Yan, S.: Network in network. arXiv preprint arXiv:1312.4400 (2013)
15. Liu, C., et al.: Progressive neural architecture search. In: Ferrari, V., Hebert, M., Sminchisescu, C., Weiss, Y. (eds.) ECCV 2018. LNCS, vol. 11205, pp. 19–35. Springer, Cham (2018). https://doi.org/10.1007/978-3-030-01246-5_2

16. Liu, L., Chen, J., Fieguth, P., Zhao, G., Chellappa, R., Pietikäinen, M.: From BoW to CNN: two decades of texture representation for texture classification. Int. J. Comput. Vis. **127**(1), 74–109 (2019)

17. Lowe, D.G.: Distinctive image features from scale-invariant keypoints. Int. J. Comput. Vis. **60**(2), 91–110 (2004)

18. Ojala, T., Maenpaa, T., Pietikainen, M., Viertola, J., Kyllonen, J., Huovinen, S.: Outex-new framework for empirical evaluation of texture analysis algorithms. In: Proceedings of the 16th International Conference on Pattern Recognition, vol. 1, pp. 701–706. IEEE (2002)

19. Ojala, T., Pietikainen, M., Maenpaa, T.: Multiresolution gray-scale and rotation invariant texture classification with local binary patterns. IEEE Trans. Pattern Anal. Mach. Intell. **24**(7), 971–987 (2002)

20. Pickard, R., Graszyk, C., Mann, S., Wachman, J., Pickard, L., Campbell, L.: VisTex Database. MIT Media Lab, Cambridge (1995)

21. Saxe, A.M., Koh, P.W., Chen, Z., Bhand, M., Suresh, B., Ng, A.Y.: On random weights and unsupervised feature learning. In: ICML, vol. 2, p. 6 (2011)

22. Scabini, L.F., Condori, R.H., Gonçalves, W.N., Bruno, O.M.: Multilayer complex network descriptors for color-texture characterization. Inf. Sci. **491**, 30–47 (2019)

23. Schmidt, W.F., Kraaijveld, M.A., Duin, R.P.W.: Feedforward neural networks with random weights. In: Proceedings of the 11th IAPR International Conference on Pattern Recognition, Conference B: Pattern Recognition Methodology and Systems, vol. II, pp. 1–4 (1992)

24. Sharan, L., Rosenholtz, R., Adelson, E.: Material perception: what can you see in a brief glance? J. Vis. **9**, 784 (2009)

25. Simonyan, K., Zisserman, A.: Very deep convolutional networks for large-scale image recognition. arXiv preprint arXiv:1409.1556 (2014)

26. Szegedy, C., Ioffe, S., Vanhoucke, V., Alemi, A.A.: Inception-v4, Inception-ResNet and the impact of residual connections on learning. In: Thirty-First AAAI Conference on Artificial Intelligence (2017)

27. Szegedy, C., Vanhoucke, V., Ioffe, S., Shlens, J., Wojna, Z.: Rethinking the inception architecture for computer vision. In: The IEEE Conference on Computer Vision and Pattern Recognition (CVPR), June 2016

28. Varma, M., Zisserman, A.: A statistical approach to texture classification from single images. Int. J. Comput. Vis. **62**(1), 61–81 (2005)

29. Xie, S., Girshick, R., Dollár, P., Tu, Z., He, K.: Aggregated residual transformations for deep neural networks. In: Proceedings of the IEEE Conference on Computer Vision and Pattern Recognition, pp. 1492–1500 (2017)

30. Zhang, H., Xue, J., Dana, K.: Deep TEN: texture encoding network. In: Proceedings of the IEEE Conference on Computer Vision and Pattern Recognition, pp. 708–717 (2017)

31. Zhang, X., Li, Z., Change Loy, C., Lin, D.: PolyNet: a pursuit of structural diversity in very deep networks. In: Proceedings of the IEEE Conference on Computer Vision and Pattern Recognition, pp. 718–726 (2017)

Domain Adaptation for Privacy-Preserving Pedestrian Detection in Thermal Imagery

My Kieu, Andrew D. Bagdanov[⊠], Marco Bertini, and Alberto Del Bimbo

Media Integration and Communication Center, University of Florence,
50134 Florence, FI, Italy
{my.kieu,andrew.bagdanov,marco.bertini,alberto.delbimbo}@unifi.it

Abstract. Pedestrian detection is a core problem in computer vision, and is a problem that is gaining prominence due to its importance in assisted and autonomous driving applications. Many state-of-the-art approaches, especially those used for autonomous driving, combine thermal and visible spectrum imagery in order to robustly detect persons independent of time of day or weather conditions. In this paper we investigate two domain adaptation techniques for fine-tuning a YOLOv3 detector to perform accurate and robust pedestrian detection using *thermal* images. Our approaches are motivated by the fact that thermal imagery is *privacy-preserving* in the sense that person identification is difficult or impossible. Results on the KAIST dataset show that our approaches perform comparably to state-of-the-art approaches and outperform the state-of-the-art on nighttime pedestrian detection, even outperforming multimodal techniques that use both thermal and visible spectrum imagery at test time.

Keywords: Pedestrian detection · Thermal imaging ·
Domain adaptation · Privacy-preservation

1 Introduction

Object detection is a classical problem in computer vision, and person and pedestrian detection is one of the most important topics for safety and security applications such as video surveillance, autonomous driving, person re-identification, and numerous others. The estimate of the total number of installed video surveillance cameras range was already at 240 million worldwide in 2014 [16]. The advent of autonomous driving promises to add many more cameras, all detecting and observing humans in public spaces.

Recent works on pedestrian detection have investigated the use of thermal imaging sensors as a complementary technology for visible spectrum images [21]. Approaches such as these aim to combine thermal and RGB image information in order to obtain the most robust possible pedestrian and person detection and

© Springer Nature Switzerland AG 2019
E. Ricci et al. (Eds.): ICIAP 2019, LNCS 11752, pp. 203–213, 2019.
https://doi.org/10.1007/978-3-030-30645-8_19

Fig. 1. Thermal imaging and privacy preservation. Shown are three cropped images from the KAIST dataset. On the left of each is the RGB image, to the right the crop from the corresponding thermal image. Note how persons are readily identifiable in visible spectrum images, but not in corresponding thermal images. Although identity is concealed, there is still enough information in thermal imagery for detection. (Color figure online)

any time of the day or night. Such detectors require both visible spectrum and thermal images to function.

Citizens are naturally concerned that being observed violates their right to privacy. In this paper we are interested in investigating the limits of pedestrian detection using thermal imagery alone. Figure 1 gives an example of four matched pairs of color and thermal images from the KAIST dataset [10]. From these examples we see that, even in relatively low resolution color images, persons can be readily identified. Meanwhile, thermal images retain distinctive image features for detection while *preserving privacy*. Our hypothesis is that thermal images can guarantee the balance between security and privacy concerns.

The rest of this paper is organized as follows. In the next section, we briefly review related work from the computer vision literature on domain adaptation, thermal imaging, and pedestrian detection. In Sect. 3 we describe several approaches to domain adaptation that we apply to the problem of privacy-preserving person detection. We report on a range of experiments conducted in Sect. 4, and conclude in Sect. 5 with a discussion of our contribution and future research directions.

2   Related Work

In this section we review some recent work related to pedestrian detection, domain adaptation, and computer vision for thermal imagery.

Person and Pedestrian Detection. The literature, both classical and contemporary, on pedestrian detection is vast [3]. With the advent of deep neural networks in recent years, pedestrian detection is achieving higher and higher accuracy! [1]. However, pedestrian detection remains a challenging task due to occlusion, changing illumination and variation of viewpoint and background [17].

Several CNN-based pedestrian detection methods compete for the state-of-the-art on standard benchmark datasets for pedestrian detection. Examples include Pedestrian Detection aided by Deep Learning Semantic Tasks [24], Scale-Aware Fast RCNN [14], Learning Mutual Visibility Relationship [17]. These state-of-the-art techniques use RGB images as input, while our goal is to investigate the potential of detection in thermal imagery alone.

Domain Adaptation. Domain adaptation has played a main role in both supervised and unsupervised recognition in computer vision. Domain adaptation attempts to exploit learned knowledge from the source domain in the target domain. One of our approaches was inspired by the AdapterNet [8], which proposed adding a new shallow Convolutional Neural Network (CNN) before the original model that transforms the input image the target domain before passing through an unmodified network trained in the source domain. Several works have tried to mitigate the distance between the two domains by applying transformation techniques. For example, the idea from [9] was to transform infrared data (thermal domain) as close as possible to the color domain by using feature transformations: inversion, equalization and histogram stretching. A deep architecture, called Invertible Autoencoder (InvAuto), introduced a method to treat an encoder as an inverted version of a decoder in order to decrease the trainable parameters of image translation processing [20].

Pedestrian Detection Exploiting Thermal Imagery. Several works demonstrate that using thermal images in combination with RGB images can improve object detection results. An example is the work in [23], which suggests a method based on a cross-modality learning framework focusing only on visible images at test time. During training time, they use thermal image features to boost visible detection results. Their method has two main phases: Region Reconstruction Network (RRN), for learning a non-linear feature mapping between visible and thermal image pairs, and a Multi-Scale Detection Network (MDN) which performs pedestrian detection from visible images by exploiting the cross-modal representations learned with RRN.

A variety of recent works leverage two-stage network architectures to investigate the combination of visible and thermal features. In [22] the authors investigated two types of fusion networks. Another approach is the ACF+T+HOG technique [15] which considers four different network fusion approaches (early, halfway, late, and score fusion). The authors of [11] introduced a combination Fully Convolutional Region Proposal Networks (RPN) and Boosted Decision Trees Classifier (BDT) for person detection in multispectral video. Illumination-aware Faster R-CNN (IAF RCNN) [13] and Illuminating Pedestrians via Simultaneous Detection and Segmentation [4] used the Faster R-CNN detector to perform pedestrian detection on paired RGB and thermal imagery. A Fusion architecture network (MSDS-RCNN) including a multispectral proposal network (MPN) and a multispectral classification network (MCN) was proposed by [5]. This fusion network currently yields the best results on both visible and thermal image pairs on the KAIST dataset.

In a slightly different direction, the combination of HOG and SVM in [2] focused on only nighttime detection. Their method uses a Thermal Position Intensity Histogram of oriented gradient (TPIHOG) and the additive kernel SVM (AKSVM) for training and testing.

Differing from most of the above works which used two-stage detectors, some the papers utilize a one-stage detector [12,21]. The authors of [12] used a deconvolutional single shot multi-box detector (DSSD) to exploit correlation between visible and thermal features for person detection. A fast RGB single-pass network architecture (YOLOv2 [18]) was adopted by [21] for fine-tuning for person detection.

3   Domain Adaptation Approaches

In this section we describe the approaches to domain adaptation that we will later evaluate in Sect. 4. All of our approaches use the YOLOv3 detector which is adapted to a target domain through a sequence of domain adaptation steps. We use YOLOv3 pretrained on the ImageNet and subsequently fine-tuned on the MS COCO Person class 3.

3.1   Top-Down Domain Adaptation

We use the term *top-down domain adaptation* to refer to the fine-tuning approach to domain adaptation in which the network is fine-tuned in the new domain to adapt weights to the new input distribution. Thus it is top-down in the sense that adaptation happens only via backpropagation from the detection loss at the end of the network. We investigate three different top-down approaches. In the descriptions below we use a notational convention to refer to each technique that indicates which image modalities are used for training and testing. For example, the technique indicated as TD(VT, T) is Top-Down domain adaptation, with adaptation on Visible spectrum images, followed by adaptation on Thermal images, and finally tested on Thermal images.

Top-Down Visible: TD(V, V). This domain adaptation approach directly fine-tunes YOLOv3 on visible images in the target domain (pedestrians in the KAIST dataset for all experiments). Testing is performed on visible spectrum images. This baseline adaptation approach serves as a sort of upper bound for performance achievable during daytime (since visible spectrum images should contain most information).

Top-Down Thermal: TD(T, T). This approach directly fine-tunes YOLOv3 on thermal images by duplicating the thermal image three times, once for each input channel of the RGB-trained detector. Testing is performed only on thermal imagery. This baseline adaptation method serves as a sort of upper bound for the performance achievable at nighttime (since thermal images should convey most information).

Top-Down Visible/Thermal: TD(VT, T). This approach is a variant of the two top-down approaches described above. First we adapt YOLOv3 to the visible spectrum pedestrian detection domain, then we fine-tune that detector on thermal imagery. Testing is performed on thermal images. The idea here is to determine if knowledge from the visible spectrum can be retained and exploited after final adaptation to the thermal domain.

3.2   Bottom-Up Domain Adaptation: BU(VAT, T)

A hypothesis of ours is that in top-down domain adaptation, as described in the previous section, early convolutional layers are difficult and slow to adapt to the new input distribution due to their distance from the backpropagated loss. Here we propose a type of *bottom-up* domain adaptation which first trains a bottom-up adapter segment and then proceeds to fine-tune the detector using a top-down loss. A conceptual schema of this approach is given in Fig. 2. The main components of our bottom-up domain adaptation approach are as follows.

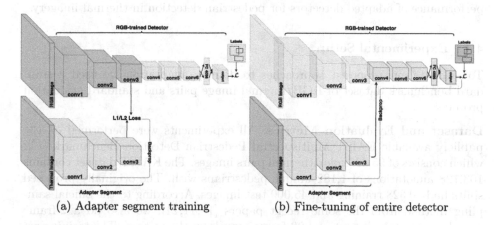

(a) Adapter segment training   (b) Fine-tuning of entire detector

Fig. 2. Bottom-up domain adaptation. (a) An *adapter segment* is first trained to take thermal images as input, then matches the feature activations of a RGB-pretrained detector on the corresponding RGB image. (b) After training the adapter segment, the RGB input branch is discarded and the entire detector pipeline is fine-tuned on thermal images.

Adapter Segment Training. As illustrated in Fig. 2(a), the main idea of the Adapter Segment is to intervene at some early stage of the RGB-trained detector network and to train a parallel branch that takes only thermal imagery as input and *matches* as best as possible the RGB feature maps at the point of intervention. In our implementation, we decapitate the YOLOv3 network after the first ten convolutional layers and train a ten-layer adapter segment to match the RGB-network using only thermal images as input. We use a simple L2 loss function on the output feature maps from the truncated network and adapter segment.

The starting point for this approach is the TD(V, V) network described above. That is, the detector weights we start from are already adapted to the KAIST domain on visible images. We then train the adapter segment using RGB/thermal image pairs from the KAIST training set. This is the "A" in the "VAT" for training in the mnemonic for this approach: BU(VAT, T).

Final Adaptation. After adapter segment training has converged, we reconnect the newly trained adapter segment to the original network for final fine-tuning of the entire detector on thermal images Fig. 2(b).

4   Experimental Results

In this section we report results of experiments we performed to evaluate the performance of adapted detectors for pedestrian detection in thermal imagery.

4.1   Experimental Setup

To evaluate our proposed approaches to domain adaptation we used a standard benchmark dataset of RGB/thermal image pairs and standard evaluation protocols.

Dataset and Evaluation Metrics. All experiments were performed on the publicly available KAIST Multispectral Pedestrian Detection Benchmark [10], which consists of 95,328 color-thermal pairs images. The KAIST dataset contains 103,128 annotations of 1,182 unique pedestrians with. The originally proposed splits had 50,328 training and 45,000 test images. According to the official sampling method from the some recent papers [10,11,21], we also do a 2-frame sample on the training set and 20-frame sample on the test set. The training set used contains 19,058 RGB/thermal pairs after sampling filtering (e.g occlusion, the bounding box under 50 pixels), and the test set consists of 2,252 images (after 20-frame sample).

To evaluate the performance of our detection results, we use log-average miss rate (miss rate) and precision/recall metrics, which almost all pedestrian detectors use and is described in [6]. The evaluation protocol we followed is the same as reported in [21], which is an updated version of the Matlab code from [6].

Implementation Details. We used the YOLOv3 [19] detector to evaluate our approach on KAIST. Our detectors were implemented using PyTorch, and we trained every domain adaptation strategy for 50 epochs with a learning rate 0.0001 and the Adam optimizer.

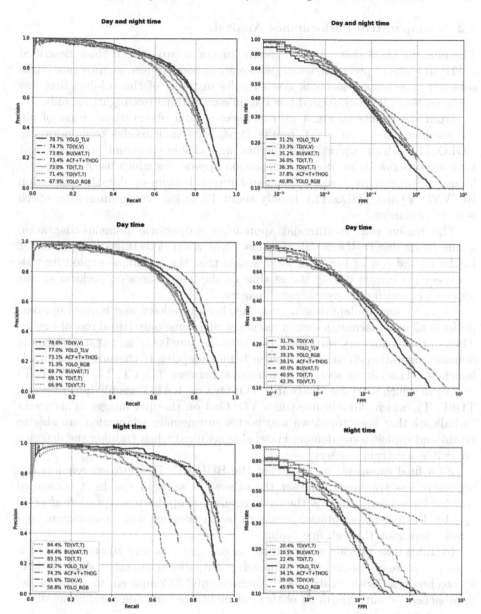

Fig. 3. Comparative performance analysis. Precision/Recall (left, higher is better) and Log-average Miss Rate (right, lower is better) of our method and other state-of-the-art papers are given. See text for detailed analysis.

4.2   Comparative Performance Analysis

The plots in Fig. 3 show detailed results for our approach and those described in [21] in terms of precision/recall (left column) and log-average miss rate (right column). The plots also break down results in terms of time-of-day: first row averaged over all times, second row daytime only, third row nighttime only.

From the results in Fig. 3 we can make several observations. First of all, for combined day and night results (first row) multimodal techniques like YOLO_TLV which exploit both thermal and visible spectrum images at test time are superior to our domain adaptation approaches which use only thermal imagery. Surprisingly, however, the gap between bottom-up domain adaptation BU(VAT, V) and YOLO_TLV is only about 4% in log-average miss rate, which is quite promising.

The reason that multimodal approaches outperform domain adaptation seems to be due to the advantage they have when detecting during the day. In the second row of Fig. 3, in fact, we see that the technique exploiting visible spectrum images during at test time on daytime images outperform all our approaches which only use thermal imagery.

Or two domain adaptation approaches, both top-down and bottom-up, outperform all other techniques when testing at nighttime only (third row of Fig. 3). Though this is not very surprising, of particular note is the fact that performing domain adaptation on to *visible* images before adapting to thermal input only is beneficial. This can be seen in the difference between TD(VT, T), BU(VAT, T) – both of which start by fine-tuning YOLOv3 on KAIST visible images – and TD(T, T), which directly fine-tunes YOLOv3 on thermal images. This seems to indicate that both top-down and bottom-up domain adaptation are able to retain and exploit some domain knowledge acquired when training the detector on visible spectrum imagery.

As a final comment, we note that the BU(VAT, T) approach requires significantly less training time that the others. In only 15 epochs it converged to 84.4% precision, which is the same result for top-down adaptation after 50 epochs. Bottom-up adaptation seems to be an effective way to accelerate top-down adaptation through fine-tuning.

In Table 1 we provide a comparison of our methods and 10 others methods from the state-of-the-art. Our approaches outperform all other single modality techniques (both visible- and thermal-only). Compared to multi-model approaches, we outperform all of them at nighttime, and comparably on all.

Table 1. Log-average miss rate on KAIST dataset (lower is better). The final two columns indicate which image modality is used at *test time*. Our approaches outperform all single-modality techniques from the literature, and outperform all methods at night.

Method	MR all (%)	MR day (%)	MR night (%)	Visible	Thermal
KAIST baseline [10]	64.76	64.17	63.99	✓	✓
Late fusion [22]	43.80	46.15	37.00	✓	✓
Halfway fusion [15]	36.99	36.84	35.49	✓	✓
RPN+BDT [11]	29.83	30.51	27.62	✓	✓
IATDNN+IAMSS [7]	**26.37**	**27.29**	24.41	✓	✓
YOLO_TLV [21]	31.20	35.10	22.70	✓	✓
DSSD-HC [12]	34.32	–	–	✓	✓
RRN+MDN [23]	49.55	47.3	54.78	✓	
TPIHOG [2]	–	–	57.38	✓	
SSD300 [9]	69.81	–	–		✓
Ours: TD(V, V)	33.30	31.70	39.00	✓	
Ours: TD(T, T)	36.00	40.90	22.40		✓
Ours: TD(VT, T)	36.30	42.30	**20.40**		✓
Ours: BU(VAT, T)	35.20	40.00	20.50		✓

4.3 Qualitative Evaluation

In Fig. 4 we show some example detection results on the KAIST dataset for our BU(VAT, T) domain adaptation approach in daytime (first row) and nighttime (second row). Note how, even though person identification is impossible in all of the example images, the detector adapted using bottom-up domain adaptation is able to detect pedestrians even in the presence of occlusion, scale variation, and changing illumination conditions.

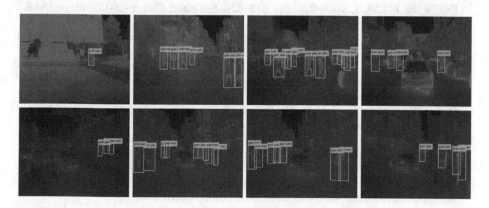

Fig. 4. Qualitative results on the KAIST test set. The first row gives example detections on daytime images from KAIST, and second row on nighttime images. Even in the presence of occlusions and scale variations, thermal imagery retains enough information to effectively perform pedestrian detection – day or night – in a privacy-preserving way without using any visible spectrum imagery at detection time.

5   Conclusions and Future Work

In this paper we investigated the potential of two domain adaptation strategies for adapting pedestrian detectors to work in the thermal domain. The goal of this work is to achieve the best possible person detection performance while relying *solely* on thermal spectrum imagery. This is motivated by the *privacy-preserving* aspects of thermal images, since persons are difficult, if not impossible, to reliably identify in thermal images.

Our results indicate that relatively simple domain adaptation schemes can be effective, and that the resulting detectors can outperform multimodal approaches (i.e. those that use thermal *and* visible images at test time) at nighttime, and can perform comparably when testing on day night images combined. Moreover, results seem to indicate that a first adaptation to visible imagery can be useful to acquire domain knowledge that can then be exploited after final adaptation to thermal spectrum images.

Ongoing work is concentrated on improving daytime and overall performance of adapted detectors. We are investigating techniques to retain more information from visible spectrum adaptation in order to close the gap between privacy-preserving detection in thermal imagery and multimodal techniques which require visible spectrum images.

References

1. Angelova, A., Krizhevsky, A., Vanhoucke, V., Ogale, A., Ferguson, D.: Real-time pedestrian detection with deep network cascades. In: BMVC (2015)
2. Baek, J., Hong, S., Kim, J., Kim, E.: Efficient pedestrian detection at nighttime using a thermal camera. Sensors **17**, 1850 (2017)
3. Benenson, R., Omran, M., Hosang, J., Schiele, B.: Ten years of pedestrian detection, what have we learned? In: Agapito, L., Bronstein, M.M., Rother, C. (eds.) ECCV 2014. LNCS, vol. 8926, pp. 613–627. Springer, Cham (2015). https://doi.org/10.1007/978-3-319-16181-5_47
4. Brazil, G., Yin, X., Liu, X.: Illuminating pedestrians via simultaneous detection and segmentation. In: ICCV, pp. 4960–4969 (2017)
5. Li, C., Song, D., Tong, R., Tang, M.: Multispectral pedestrian detection via simultaneous detection and segmentation. In: British Machine Vision Conference (BMVC), September 2018
6. Dollar, P., Wojek, C., Schiele, B., Perona, P.: Pedestrian detection: an evaluation of the state of the art. IEEE Trans. Pattern Anal. Mach. Intell. **34**, 743–761 (2012)
7. Guan, D., Cao, Y., Yang, J., Cao, Y., Yang, M.: Fusion of multispectral data through illumination-aware deep neural networks for pedestrian detection. Inf. Fusion **50**, 148–157 (2018)
8. Hazan, A., Shoshan, Y., Khapun, D., Aladjem, R., Ratner, V.: AdapterNet - learning input transformation for domain adaptation. CoRR (2018)
9. Herrmann, C., Ruf, M., Beyerer, J.: CNN-based thermal infrared person detection by domain adaptation. In: Autonomous Systems: Sensors, Vehicles, Security, and the Internet of Everything (2018)
10. Hwang, S., Park, J., Kim, N., Choi, Y., Kweon, I.S.: Multispectral pedestrian detection: Benchmark dataset and baselines. In: CVPR (2015)

11. Konig, D., Adam, M., Jarvers, C., Layher, G., Neumann, H., Teutsch, M.: Fully convolutional region proposal networks for multispectral person detection. In: 2017 IEEE Conference on Computer Vision and Pattern Recognition Workshops (2017)

12. Lee, Y., Bui, T.D., Shin, J.: Pedestrian detection based on deep fusion network using feature correlation. In: 2018 Asia-Pacific Signal and Information Processing Association Annual Summit and Conference (APSIPA ASC), pp. 694–699 (2018)

13. Li, C., Song, D., Tong, R., Tang, M.: Illumination-aware faster R-CNN for robust multispectral pedestrian detection. CoRR (2018)

14. Li, J., Liang, X., Shen, S., Xu, T., Yan, S.: Scale-aware fast R-CNN for pedestrian detection. CoRR (2015). http://arxiv.org/abs/1510.08160

15. Liu, J., Zhang, S., Wang, S., Metaxas, D.N.: Multispectral deep neural networks for pedestrian detection. CoRR (2016)

16. Markit, I.: 245 million video surveillance cameras installed globally in 2014. Web page (2019). https://technology.ihs.com/532501/245-million-video-surveillance-cameras-installed-globally-in-2014. Accessed 5 May 2019

17. Ouyang, W., Zeng, X., Wang, X.: Learning mutual visibility relationship for pedestrian detection with a deep model. Int. J. Comput. Vis. **120**, 14–27 (2016)

18. Redmon, J., Farhadi, A.: YOLO9000: better, faster, stronger. In: Proceedings of the IEEE Conference on Computer Vision and Pattern Recognition, pp. 7263–7271 (2017)

19. Redmon, J., Farhadi, A.: YOLOv3: an incremental improvement. CoRR (2018). http://arxiv.org/abs/1804.02767

20. Teng, Y., Choromanska, A., Bojarski, M.: Invertible autoencoder for domain adaptation. CoRR (2018)

21. Vandersteegen, M., Van Beeck, K., Goedemé, T.: Real-time multispectral pedestrian detection with a single-pass deep neural network. In: Campilho, A., Karray, F., ter Haar Romeny, B. (eds.) ICIAR 2018. LNCS, vol. 10882, pp. 419–426. Springer, Cham (2018). https://doi.org/10.1007/978-3-319-93000-8_47

22. Wagner, J., Fischer, V., Herman, M., Behnke, S.: Multispectral pedestrian detection using deep fusion convolutional neural networks. In: 24th European Symposium on Artificial Neural Networks, Computational Intelligence and Machine Learning (ESANN), pp. 509–514 (2016)

23. Xu, D., Ouyang, W., Ricci, E., Wang, X., Sebe, N.: Learning cross-modal deep representations for robust pedestrian detection. In: Proceedings of the IEEE Conference on Computer Vision and Pattern Recognition, pp. 5363–5371 (2017)

24. Tian, Y., Luo, P., Wang, X., Tang, X.: Pedestrian detection aided by deep learning semantic tasks. In: Proceedings of the IEEE Conference on Computer Vision and Pattern Recognition, pp. 5079–5087 (2015)

GADA: Generative Adversarial Data Augmentation for Image Quality Assessment

Pietro Bongini[✉], Riccardo Del Chiaro, Andrew D. Bagdanov,
and Alberto Del Bimbo

Media Integration and Communication Center, University of Florence,
50134 Florence, FI, Italy
{p.bongini,riccardo.delchiaro,andrew.bagdanov,alberto.delbimbo}@unifi.it

Abstract. We propose a No-reference Image Quality Assessment (NR-IQA) approach based on the use of generative adversarial networks. To address the problem of lack of adequate amounts of labeled training data for NR-IQA, we train an Auxiliary Classifier Generative Adversarial Network (AC-GAN) to generate distorted images with various distortion types and levels of image quality at training time. The trained generative model allow us to augment the size of the training dataset by introducing distorted images for which no ground truth is available. We call our approach Generative Adversarial Data Augmentation (GADA) and experimental results on the LIVE and TID2013 datasets show that our approach – using a modestly sized and very shallow network – performs comparably to state-of-the-art methods for NR-IQA which use significantly more complex models. Moreover, our network can process images in real time at 120 image per second unlike other state-of-the-art techniques.

Keywords: Image Quality Assessment ·
Generative Adversarial Networks · Data augmentation

1 Introduction

In the last few decades images are increasingly a part of everyday life and are used for many purposes. However, images are often not of the best possible quality. This can be caused by many factors, such as the device used for acquisition, the lossy compression algorithm used to store the information (e.g. JPEG), and the entire image acquisition, storage, and transmission process.

Image Quality Assessment (IQA) [21] refers to a range of techniques developed to automatically estimate the perceptual quality of images. IQA estimates should be highly correlated with quality assessments made by multiple human evaluators (commonly referred to as the Mean Opinion Score (MOS) [15,19]). IQA has been widely applied by the computer vision community for applications like image restoration [8], image super-resolution [20], and image retrieval [24].

© Springer Nature Switzerland AG 2019
E. Ricci et al. (Eds.): ICIAP 2019, LNCS 11752, pp. 214–224, 2019.
https://doi.org/10.1007/978-3-030-30645-8_20

IQA techniques can be divided into three different categories based on the available information on the image to be evaluated: full-reference IQA (FR-IQA), reduced-reference IQA (RR-IQA), and no-reference IQA (NR-IQA). Although FR-IQA and RR-IQA methods have obtained impressive results, the fact that they must have knowledge of the undistorted version of the image (called the *reference image*) for quality evaluation, makes these approaches hard to use in real scenarios. On the contrary, NR-IQA only requires the knowledge of the image whose quality is to be estimated, and for this reason is more realistic (and also more challenging).

In the last few years Convolutional Neural Networks (CNNs) have obtained great results on many computer vision tasks, and their success is partially due to the possibility of creating very deep architectures with millions of parameters, thanks to the computational capabilities of modern GPUs. Massive amounts of data are needed for training such models, and this is a big problem for IQA since the annotation process is expensive and time consuming. In fact, each image must be annotated by multiple human experts, and consequently most available IQA datasets are too small to effectively train CNNs from scratch.

In this paper, we propose an approach to address this lack of large, labeled datasets for IQA. Since obtaining annotated data to train the network is difficult, we propose a technique to generate new images with a specific image quality and distortion type. We learn how to generate distorted images using Auxiliary Classifier Generative Adversarial Networks (AC-GANs), and then use these generated images in order to improve the accuracy of a simple CNN regressor trained for IQA. In Fig. 1 we show patches of images generated with our approach alongside their corresponding patches with real distortions.

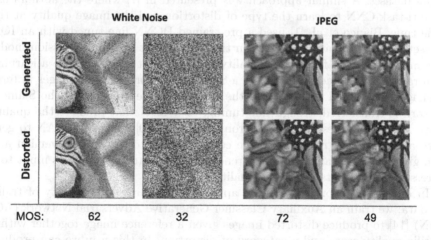

Fig. 1. Patches extracted from images generated by the proposed method compared with the same patches from true distorted images with the same image quality and distortion type.

2   Related Works

In this section we briefly review the literature related to No-Reference Image Quality Assessment (NR-IQA) and Generative Adversarial Networks (GANs).

No-Reference Image Quality Assessment. Most traditional NR-IQA can be classified into Natural Scene Statistics (NSS) methods and learning-based methods. In NSS methods, the assumption is that images of different quality vary in the statistics of responses to specific filters. Wavelets, DCT and Curvelets are commonly used to extract the features in different sub-bands. These feature distributions are parametrized, for example with the Generalized Gaussian Distribution. The aim of these methods is to estimate the distributional parameters, from which a quality assessment can be inferred. The authors of [12] propose to extract NSS features in the spatial domain to obtain significant speed-ups. In learning-based methods, local features are extracted and mapped to the MOS using, for example, Support Machine Regression or Neural Networks [3]. Codebook Methods combines different features instead of using local features directly. Datasets without MOS can be exploited to construct the codebook [25,26] by means of unsupervised learning, which is particularly important due to of the small size of existing datasets. Saliency maps can be used to model human vision system and improve precision in these methods.

Deep Learning for NR-IQA. In recent years several works have used deep learning for NR-IQA. These techniques requires large amounts of data for training and IQA datasets are especially lacking in this regard. Therefore, to address this problem different approaches have been proposed. Kang et al. [6] use small patches of the original images to train a shallow network and thus enlarging the initial dataset. A similar approach was presented in [7] where the authors use a multi-task CNN to learn the type of distortion and the image quality at the same time. Bianco et al. [1] used a pre-trained DCNN fine tuned with an IQA dataset to extract features, and then train a Support Vector Regression model that maps extracted features to quality scores. Liu et al. in [11] use a learning from rankings approach. They train a Siamese Network to rank images in term of image quality and subsequently the information represented in the Siamese network is transferred, trough fine-tuning, to a CNN that predicts the quality score. Another interesting work is from Lin et al. [10] who use a GAN to generate a hallucinated reference image corresponding to a distorted version and then give both the hallucinated reference and the distorted image as input to a regressor that predicts the image quality.

In our work we present a novel approach to address the scarcity of training data: we train an Auxiliary Classifier Generative Adversarial Network (AC-GAN) [14] to produce distorted images given a reference image together with a specific quality score and a category of distortion. In this way we can produce new labeled examples that we can use to train a regressor.

Auxiliary Classifier GANs. In the last few years GANs have been widely used in different areas of computer vision. The Auxiliary Classifier GAN (AC-GAN) [14] is a variant of the Generative Adversarial Network (GAN) [4] which uses label conditioning. This kind of network produces convincing results. Our aim is to use this architecture to generate distorted images conditioned to a distortion category and image quality value. Since the main objective of the work is NR-IQA and the performance of the quality regressor is highly related to the generated image, it is crucial that the generator produce convincing distortions.

3 Generative Adversarial Data Augmentation for NR-IQA

In this section we describe our approach to perform data augmentation for NR-IQA datasets. We first show the general steps that characterize our technique, and then describe the use of AC-GAN in this context.

3.1 Overview of Proposed Approach

The main idea of this work is to generate new distorted images with a specific image quality level and distortion type to partially solve the problem of the poverty of annotated data for IQA. We use an AC-GAN to generate new distorted images. Once the generator has learned to produce distorted images convincingly we use it to generate new examples to augment the training set as we train a deep convolutional regressor to estimate IQA. The pipeline of our technique is as follows:

1. **Training the AC-GAN.** Using patches of the training images we train an AC-GAN. The generator learns to generate distorted images with a given distortion class and quality level starting from reference images. The regressor, which aims is to predict the image quality, is trained with both generated and real distorted images using the adversarial GAN loss.
2. **Generative data augmentation.** Once the training of the AC-GAN converges, the generator is able to produce convincing distortions and we can stop its training. We continue training the discriminator branch, augmenting the training data via the trained generator. The regressor is trained with both real distorted images from the training set and images artificially distorted using the generator.
3. **Fine-Tuning of the regressor.** Once convergence is reached in step 2 we perform a final phase of fine-tuning: the regressor is trained with only real distorted images from the IQA training set.

3.2 Auxiliary Classifier GANs for NR-IQA

An Auxiliary Classifier Generative Adversarial Network is a GAN variant in which it is possible to condition the output on some input information. In the AC-GAN every generated sample has a corresponding class label, $c \sim p_c$, in addition to the noise z. This information is given in input to the generator which produces fake images $X_{\text{fake}} = G(c, z)$. The discriminator not only distinguishes between real and generated examples but predicts also the class label of the examples. The sub-network that classifies the input is called the *classifier*. The objective function is characterized by two components: a log-likelihood on the correct discrimination L_S and a log-likelihood on the correct class L_C:

$$L_S = E[\log P(S = \text{real} \mid X_{\text{real}})] + E[\log P(S = fake \mid X_{\text{fake}})] \tag{1}$$

$$L_C = E[\log P(C = c \mid X_{\text{real}})] + E[\log P(C = c \mid X_{\text{fake}})] \tag{2}$$

The discriminator is trained to maximize $L_S + L_C$ and the generator is trained to minimize $L_C - L_S$.

Our approach is slightly different from a standard AC-GAN: the latter expects only noise and class label as input, but in our case we want to generate an output image that is a *distorted* version of a reference one, so we also need to feed the reference image and force a reconstruction with an $L1$ loss. Moreover, we want to distort the reference image so that the output matches a target *image quality*, so we feed also this value as input. Because we would like to reconstruct a distorted version of the reference image given in input, we can write the additional $L1$ loss as it follows:

$$\mathcal{L}_{L1} = E[\|y - G(z, x, c, q)\|_1]$$

where y is the distorted ground truth image, z is a random Gaussian noise vector, x is the reference image, c is the distortion class and v is the image quality.

The goal of this work is to predict the quality score of images, so we introduce a regressor network whose aim is to predict the quality score of input images. The loss used to train this component is a mean squared error (MSE) between the predicted quality score and the ground truth:

$$L_E = E[(q - \hat{q})^2] \tag{3}$$

where q and $\hat{q}$ are the ground truth and the prediction of the image quality score, respectively.

The expectations for all losses defined here are taken over minibatches of either generated or labeled training samples.

3.3   The GADA Architecture

In Fig. 2 we give a schematic representation of the proposed model. The components of the GADA network are as follows.

Generator. The Generator follows the general auto-encoder architecture. It takes as input a high quality reference image, a distortion class, and a target image quality. The input information is encoded through three convolutional layers (one with 64 feature maps and two with 128). Before up-sampling we concatenate a noise vector z to the latent representation, together with an embedding of the distortion category and image quality. We use skip connections [5, 16] in the generator, which allows the network to generate qualitatively better results.

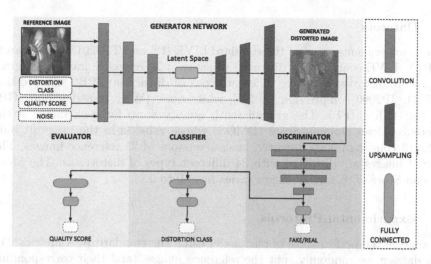

Fig. 2. A schematic representation of the proposed network.

Discriminator. The Discriminator takes as input a distorted image and through three convolutional layers (one with 64 feature maps, and two with 128 to mimic the encoder) followed by a 1×1 convolution extracts 1024 feature maps (that are also fed to the classifier and the regressor). A single fully-connected layer reduces these feature maps to a single value and a sigmoid activation outputs the prediction of the provenance of the input image (i.e. real or fake). This output is used to compute the loss defined in Eq. 1.

Classifier. The Classifier takes as input the feature maps described for the Discriminator. This network consists of two fully-connected layers. The first layer has 128 units and the second has a number of units equal to the number of distortion categories and is followed by a softmax activation function. The output of this module is used in the classifier loss for the AC-GAN as defined in Eq. 2.

Evaluator. The Evaluator takes as input the feature maps described for the Discriminator and should accurately estimate the image quality of the input image. This module consists of two fully-connected layers, the first with 128 and the second with a single unit. The MSE loss defined in Eq. 3 is computed using the output of this module.

4   Experimental Results

In this section we describe experiments conducted to evaluate the performance of our approach. We first introduce the datasets used for training and testing our network, then we describe the protocols adopted for the experiments.

4.1   Datasets

For our experiments we used the standard LIVE [18] and TID2013 [15] datasets for IQA. LIVE contains 982 distorted versions of 29 reference images. Original images are distorted with five different types of distortion: JPEG compression (JPEG), JP2000 compression (JP2K), white noise (WN), gaussian blur (GB) and fast fading (FF). The ground truth quality score for each image is the Difference Mean Opinion Score (DMOS) whose value is in the range $[0, 100]$. TID2013 consist of 3000 distorted images versions of 25 reference images. The original images are distorted with 24 different types of distortions. The Mean Opinion Score of distorted images varies from 0 to 9.

4.2   Experimental Protocols

We analyze the performance of our model using the standard IQA metrics. For each dataset we randomly split the reference images (and their corresponding distorted versions) in 80% used for training and 20% used for testing, as described in [6,28]. This process is repeated ten times. For each split we train from scratch and compute the final scores on the test set.

Training Strategy. At each training epoch, we randomly crop each image in the training-set using patches of 128×128 pixels and feed it to the model. For all the three phases we train using these crops with a batch size of 64. During the first one we use Adam optimizer with a learning rate of $1e^{-4}$ for the discriminator and $5e^{-4}$ for the generator, classifier and evaluator. During the second and third phases we divide the learning rate by 10.

Testing Protocol. At test time We randomly crop 30 patches from each test image as suggested in [1]. We then pass all 30 crops through the discriminator network (with only the evaluator branch) to estimate IQA. The average of the predictions for the 30 crops gives the final estimated quality score.

Evaluation Metrics. We use two evaluation metrics commonly used in IQA context: the Linear Correlation Coefficient (LCC) and Spearman Correlation Coefficient (SROCC). LCC is a measure of the linear correlation between the ground truth and the predicted quality scores. Given N distorted images, the ground truth of i-th image is denoted by y_i, and the predicted score from the network is $\hat{y}_i$. The LCC is computed as:

$$LCC = \frac{\sum_{i=1}^{N}(y_i - \overline{y})(\hat{y}_i - \overline{\hat{y}})}{\sqrt{\sum_i^N (y_i - \overline{y})^2}\sqrt{\sum_i^N(\hat{y}_i - \overline{\hat{y}})^2}} \tag{4}$$

where $\overline{y}$ and $\overline{\hat{y}}$ are the means of the ground truth and predicted quality scores, respectively.

Given N distorted images, the SROCC is:

$$SROCC = 1 - \frac{6\sum_{i=1}^{N}(v_i - p_i)^2}{N(N^2 - 1)}, \tag{5}$$

where v_i is the *rank* of the ground-truth IQA score y_i in the ground-truth scores, and p_i is the *rank* of $\hat{y}_i$ in the output scores for all N images. The SROCC measures the monotonic relationship between ground-truth and estimated IQA.

4.3 Generative Data Augmentation with AC-GAN

As described in Sect. 3.1 our approach consists of three phases: a first one where we train the generator, a second phase where we perform data augmentation, and the final fine-tuning phase of the evaluator over the original training-set. As a first experiment, we calculated the performance obtained after each of the three different phases and compared with the performance of a direct method which consists of training *only* the evaluator and classifier branches of the discriminator directly on labeled training data (e.g. no adversarial data augmentation). We trained and tested the proposed method and the direct baseline on the LIVE dataset as described in Sect. 4.2, but for this preliminary experiment we used crops of 64 × 64 pixels and a shallower regression network.

In Table 1 we give the LCC and SROCC values computed for the baseline and after each of the three phase of our approach. We note first that each phase of our training procedure results in improved LCC and SROCC, which indicates that generative data augmentation and fine-tuning both add to performance. At the end of phase 3 the LCC and SROCC results surpass the direct approach by ~2%, confirming the effectiveness of GADA with respect to direct training.

Table 1. Comparison of baseline and each phase of the GADA approach in LCC and SROCC. In the first block results for the direct baseline method (directly training the evaluator with only labeled IQA data) are shown. In the second block results for our method are shown after each of the three phases: training of the AC-GAN (Phase 1), generator data augmentation (Phase 2), and evaluator fine-tuning (Phase 3).

		JP2K	JPEG	WN	GBLUR	FF	ALL
Baseline	LCC	0.950	0.964	0.973	0.938	0.933	0.943
	SROCC	0.938	0.931	0.977	0.939	0.898	0.935
Phase 1	LCC	0.944	0.952	0.967	0.920	0.912	0.933
	SROCC	0.933	0.930	0.980	0.926	0.889	0.930
Phase 2	LCC	0.958	0.958	0.974	0.939	0.924	0.942
	SROCC	0.941	0.933	0.988	0.945	0.891	0.939
Phase 3	LCC	0.959	0.973	0.993	0.953	0.935	0.962
	SROCC	0.955	0.941	0.990	0.953	0.912	0.955

4.4 Comparison with the State-of-the-Art

Here we compare GADA with state-of-the-art results from the literature.

Results on LIVE. We trained on LIVE dataset following the protocol described in Sect. 4.2. The results are shown in Table 2. Each column of the table represents the partial scores for a specific distortion category of LIVE dataset. Our method seems to be very effective on this dataset despite the fact that many other approaches process larger patches (e.g. 224 × 224, the input size of the VGG16 network) and capture more context information. We observe from the table that our model performs very well on Gaussian noise (GN) and JPEG2000 (JP2K). We obtain worse results for Fast Fading (FF), which is probably due to the fact that FF is a local distortion and we process patches of small dimension, so for each crop the probability of picking a distorted region is not 1.

Table 2. Comparison between GADA and the state-of-the-art on LIVE.

	LCC						SROCC					
	JP2K	JPEG	GN	GB	FF	ALL	JP2K	JPEG	GN	GB	FF	ALL
DIVINE [13]	.922	.921	.988	.923	.888	.917	.913	.91	.984	.921	.863	.916
BLIINDS-II [17]	.935	.968	.980	.938	.896	.930	.929	.942	.969	.923	.889	.931
BRISQUE [12]	.923	.973	.985	.951	.903	.942	.914	.965	.979	.951	.887	.940
CORNIA [26]	.951	.965	.987	.968	.917	.935	.943	.955	.976	.969	.906	.942
CNN [6]	.953	.981	.984	.953	.933	.953	.952	.977	.978	.962	.908	.956
SOM [28]	.952	.961	.991	.974	.954	.962	.947	.952	.984	.976	.937	.964
BIECON [9]	.965	.987	.970	.945	.931	.962	.952	.974	.980	.956	.923	.961
PQR [27]	–	–	–	–	–	.971	–	–	–	–	–	.965
DNN [2]	–	–	–	–	–	.972	–	–	–	–	–	.960
RankIQA+FT [11]	.975	.986	.994	.988	.960	.982	.970	.978	.991	.988	.954	.981
Hall.-IQA [10]	.977	.984	.993	.990	.960	.982	.983	.961	.984	.983	.989	.982
NSSADNN [23]	–	–	–	–	–	**.984**	–	–	–	–	–	**.986**
GADA (ours)	**.977**	.978	**.994**	.968	.943	.973	.963	.948	**.991**	.958	.917	.964

Table 3. Comparison between GADA and the state-of-the-art on TID2013 (SROCC).

Method		#01	#02	#03	#04	#05	#06	#07	#08	#09	#10	#11	#12	#13
BLIINDS-II	[17]	0.714	0.728	0.825	0.358	0.852	0.664	0.780	0.852	0.754	0.808	0.862	0.251	0.755
BRISQUE	[12]	0.630	0.424	0.727	0.321	0.775	0.669	0.592	0.845	0.553	0.742	0.799	0.301	0.672
CORNIA-10K	[26]	0.341	-0.196	0.689	0.184	0.607	-0.014	0.673	**0.896**	0.787	0.875	0.911	0.310	0.625
HOSA	[22]	0.853	0.625	0.782	0.368	0.905	0.775	0.810	0.892	0.870	0.893	**0.932**	**0.747**	0.701
RankIQA+FT	[11]	0.667	0.620	0.821	0.365	0.760	0.736	0.783	0.809	0.767	0.866	0.878	0.704	**0.810**
NSSADNN	[23]	–	–	–	–	–	–	–	–	–	–	–	–	–
HALLUCINATED IQA	[10]	0.923	0.880	**0.945**	0.673	**0.955**	0.810	0.855	0.832	**0.957**	**0.914**	0.624	0.460	0.782
GADA (ours)		**0.932**	**0.897**	0.943	**0.825**	0.949	**0.920**	**0.919**	0.790	0.881	0.775	0.886	0.435	0.702

Method		#14	#15	#16	#17	#18	#19	#20	#21	#22	#23	#24	ALL
BLIINDS-II	[17]	0.081	0.371	0.159	-0.082	0.109	0.699	0.222	0.451	0.815	0.568	0.856	0.550
BRISQUE	[12]	0.175	0.184	0.155	0.125	0.032	0.560	0.282	0.680	0.804	0.715	0.800	0.562
CORNIA-10K	[26]	0.161	0.096	0.008	0.423	-0.055	0.259	0.606	0.555	0.592	0.759	0.903	0.651
HOSA	[22]	0.199	0.327	0.233	0.294	0.119	0.782	0.532	0.835	0.855	0.801	**0.905**	0.728
RankIQA+FT	[11]	0.512	**0.622**	**0.268**	0.613	0.662	0.619	0.644	0.800	0.779	0.629	0.859	0.780
NSSADNN	[23]	–	–	–	–	–	–	–	–	–	–	–	0.844
HALLUCINATED IQA	[10]	**0.664**	0.122	0.182	0.376	0.156	0.850	0.614	0.852	**0.911**	0.381	0.616	**0.879**
GADA (ours)		0.206	0.200	0.196	**0.739**	**0.688**	**0.950**	0.679	**0.937**	0.895	**0.843**	0.889	0.790

TID2013. We follow the same test procedure for TID2013 and report our SROCC results in Table 3. We see that for 11 of the 24 types of distortion we obtain the best results. For local and challenging distortions like #14, #15 and #16 the performance of our model is low, and again we hypothesize that the small size and uniform sampling of patches could be a limitation especially for extremely local distortions.

5 Conclusions

In this paper we proposed a new approach called GADA to resolve the problem of lack of training data for No-reference Image Quality Assessment. Our approach uses a modified Auxiliary Classifier GAN. This technique allows us to use the generator to generate new training examples and to train a regressor which estimates the image quality score. The results obtained on LIVE and TID2013 datasets show that our performance is comparable with the best methods of the state-of-the-art. Moreover, the very shallow network used for the regressor can process images with an high frame rate (about 120 image per second). This is in stark contrast to state-of-the-art approaches which typically use very deep models like VGG16 pre-trained on ImageNet.

We feel that the GADA approach offers a promising alternative to laboriously annotating images for IQA. Significant improvements can likely be made, especially for highly local distortions, through saliency-based sampling of image patches during training.

References

1. Bianco, S., Celona, L., Napoletano, P., Schettini, R.: On the use of deep learning for blind image quality assessment. arXiv preprint arXiv:1602.05531 (2016)
2. Bosse, S., Maniry, D., Wiegand, T., Samek, W.: A deep neural network for image quality assessment. In: Proceedings of ICIP, pp. 3773–3777. IEEE (2016)
3. Chetouani, A., Beghdadi, A., Chen, S., Mostafaoui, G.: A novel free reference image quality metric using neural network approach. In: Proceedings of the International Workshop on Video Processing and Quality Metrics for Consumer Electronics, pp. 1–4 (2010)
4. Goodfellow, I., et al.: Generative adversarial nets. In: Advances in Neural Information Processing Systems, pp. 2672–2680 (2014)
5. Isola, P., Zhu, J.Y., Zhou, T., Efros, A.A.: Image-to-image translation with conditional adversarial networks. In: 2017 IEEE Conference on Computer Vision and Pattern Recognition (CVPR), July 2017
6. Kang, L., Ye, P., Li, Y., Doermann, D.: Convolutional neural networks for no-reference image quality assessment. In: Proceedings of the IEEE Conference on Computer Vision and Pattern Recognition, pp. 1733–1740 (2014)
7. Kang, L., Ye, P., Li, Y., Doermann, D.: Simultaneous estimation of image quality and distortion via multi-task convolutional neural networks. In: 2015 IEEE International Conference on Image Processing (ICIP), pp. 2791–2795. IEEE (2015)
8. Katsaggelos, A.K.: Digital Image Restoration. Springer, Heidelberg (2012)
9. Kim, J., Lee, S.: Fully deep blind image quality predictor. IEEE J. Sel. Top. Signal Process. 11(1), 206–220 (2017)

10. Lin, K.Y., Wang, G.: Hallucinated-IQA: no-reference image quality assessment via adversarial learning. In: Proceedings of the IEEE Conference on Computer Vision and Pattern Recognition, pp. 732–741 (2018)
11. Liu, X., van de Weijer, J., Bagdanov, A.D.: RankIQA: learning from rankings for no-reference image quality assessment. In: Proceedings of the IEEE International Conference on Computer Vision, pp. 1040–1049 (2017)
12. Mittal, A., Moorthy, A.K., Bovik, A.C.: No-reference image quality assessment in the spatial domain. IEEE Trans. Image Process. **21**(12), 4695–4708 (2012)
13. Moorthy, A.K., Bovik, A.C.: Blind image quality assessment: from natural scene statistics to perceptual quality. IEEE Trans. Image Process. **20**(12), 3350–3364 (2011)
14. Odena, A., Olah, C., Shlens, J.: Conditional image synthesis with auxiliary classifier GANs. In: Proceedings of the 34th International Conference on Machine Learning, vol. 70. pp. 2642–2651 (2017). JMLR.org
15. Ponomarenko, N., et al.: Color image database TID2013: peculiarities and preliminary results. In: 2013 4th European Workshop on Visual Information Processing (EUVIP), pp. 106–111. IEEE (2013)
16. Ronneberger, O., Fischer, P., Brox, T.: U-Net: convolutional networks for biomedical image segmentation. In: Navab, N., Hornegger, J., Wells, W.M., Frangi, A.F. (eds.) MICCAI 2015. LNCS, vol. 9351, pp. 234–241. Springer, Cham (2015). https://doi.org/10.1007/978-3-319-24574-4_28
17. Saad, M.A., Bovik, A.C., Charrier, C.: Blind image quality assessment: a natural scene statistics approach in the DCT domain. IEEE Trans. Image Process. **21**(8), 3339–3352 (2012)
18. Sheikh, H.R., Wang, Z., Cormack, L., Bovik, A.C.: Live image quality assessment database. http://live.ece.utexas.edu/research/quality
19. Sheikh, H.R., Sabir, M.F., Bovik, A.C.: A statistical evaluation of recent full reference image quality assessment algorithms. IEEE Trans. Image Process. **15**(11), 3440–3451 (2006)
20. Van Ouwerkerk, J.: Image super-resolution survey. Image Vis. Comput. **24**(10), 1039–1052 (2006)
21. Wang, Z., Bovik, A.C., Lu, L.: Why is image quality assessment so difficult? In: 2002 IEEE International Conference on Acoustics, Speech, and Signal Processing (ICASSP), vol. 4, p. IV–3313. IEEE (2002)
22. Xu, J., Ye, P., Li, Q., Du, H., Liu, Y., Doermann, D.: Blind image quality assessment based on high order statistics aggregation. IEEE Trans. Image Process. **25**(9), 4444–4457 (2016)
23. Yan, B., Bare, B., Tan, W.: Naturalness-aware deep no-reference image quality assessment. IEEE Trans. Multimedia **PP**, 1 (2019)
24. Yan, J., Lin, S., Kang, S.B., Tang, X.: A learning-to-rank approach for image color enhancement. In: 2014 IEEE Conference on Computer Vision and Pattern Recognition (CVPR), pp. 2987–2994. IEEE (2014)
25. Ye, P., Doermann, D.: No-reference image quality assessment using visual codebooks. IEEE Trans. Image Process. **21**(7), 3129–3138 (2012)
26. Ye, P., Kumar, J., Kang, L., Doermann, D.: Unsupervised feature learning framework for no-reference image quality assessment. In: 2012 IEEE Conference on Computer Vision and Pattern Recognition (CVPR), pp. 1098–1105. IEEE (2012)
27. Zeng, H., Zhang, L., Bovik, A.C.: A probabilistic quality representation approach to deep blind image quality prediction (2017)
28. Zhang, P., Zhou, W., Wu, L., Li, H.: SOM: semantic obviousness metric for image quality assessment. In: Proceedings of the IEEE Conference on Computer Vision and Pattern Recognition, pp. 2394–2402 (2015)

Unsupervised Domain Adaptation Using Full-Feature Whitening and Colouring

Subhankar Roy[1,2], Aliaksandr Siarohin[1(✉)], and Nicu Sebe[1]

[1] Department of Information Engineering and Computer Science,
University of Trento, Trento, Italy
{subhankar.roy,aliaksandr.siarohin,niculae.sebe}@unitn.it
[2] Fondazione Bruno Kessler (FBK), Trento, Italy

Abstract. It is a very well known fact in computer vision that classifiers trained on source datasets do not perform well when tested on other datasets acquired under different conditions. To this end, Unsupervised Domain adaptation (UDA) methods address the shift between the source and target domain by adapting the classifier to work well in the target domain despite having no access to the target labels. A handful of UDA methods bridge domain shift by aligning the source and target feature distributions through embedded domain alignment layers that are based on batch normalization (BN) or grouped whitening. Contrarily, in this work we propose to align feature distributions with domain specific full-feature whitening and domain agnostic colouring transforms, abbreviated as F^2WCT. The proposed F^2WCT optimally aligns the feature distributions by ensuring that the source and target features have identical covariance matrices. Our claim is also substantiated by the experimental results on Digits datasets for both single source and multi source unsupervised adaptation settings.

Keywords: Feature whitening · Colouring ·
Unsupervised Domain Adaptation · Multi source domain adaptation

1 Introduction

In the recent years deep learning has been exceptionally successful in supervised object recognition tasks [1,2]. Despite its effectiveness in *supervised* regime, object recognition in *unsupervised* regime is still an open ended problem because the lack of labels makes the training complicated. Off-the-shelf networks pretrained on some domain do not work well when transferred to a novel but related domain due to a problem called *domain-shift* [3]. To mitigate domain shift among datasets numerous Unsupervised Domain Adaptation (UDA) methods [4–10] have been proposed which leverage *unlabeled* target data together with *labeled* source data to learn a predictor for the target samples.

UDA methods can be roughly categorized under two broad categories. The first category includes Generative Adversarial Network (GAN) based methods [10–12] that learn a cross-domain mapping to emulate *target*-like source

© Springer Nature Switzerland AG 2019
E. Ricci et al. (Eds.): ICIAP 2019, LNCS 11752, pp. 225–236, 2019.
https://doi.org/10.1007/978-3-030-30645-8_21

images, which are then leveraged for training a target classifier. The second category of methods aims to reduce the discrepancy between source and target domains by leveraging the first order statistics [13,14] or second order statistics [15,25]. Some of the methods from this category achieve alignment of feature distributions by directly embedding batch normalization (BN) based [9,16,17] *domain alignment* (DA) layers into the network.

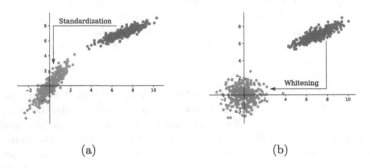

Fig. 1. Visualization of 2D features with different normalization transformations: (a) Feature standardisation; and (b) Feature whitening.

While BN based methods align feature distributions by setting variance of features to 1 and mean to 0, yet they leave the feature correlations intact (see Fig. 1a), leading to sub-optimal alignment. Conversely, we argue that to completely eliminate discrepancy between domains the source and target features should have the same covariance matrix. This can be ensured by projecting the feature distributions onto a canonical unit hyper-sphere through *full-feature whitening* (see Fig. 1b), such that both source and target domain features have identity covariance matrix. While Roy *et al.* [8] proposed to align feature distributions with domain-specific *grouped*-feature whitening (DWT), it suffers from imperfect alignment due to partial feature whitening (see Sect. 2).

To overcome the drawbacks of previous DA layers we propose to first *whiten* the feature representations and then apply *colouring*. Our *whiten* operation use domain specific whitening, while *colouring* operation is domain agnostic and is used to re-project the whitened features to a distribution having an arbitrary covariance matrix. Inspired by [18], we realize these transformations through **F**ull-**F**eature **W**hitening and **C**olouring **T**ransform (**F²WCT**) blocks, embedded inside the network, replacing the BN-based and DWT-based DA layers. However, different from [18], which uses these operations for conditional image generation, we propose this technique for UDA. We also extend this to multi-source unsupervised DA (MSDA) setting where multiple source domains are available during training. Finally, we evaluate our proposed method on the *digits* datasets for both single source UDA and MSDA settings and set new state-of-the-art results.

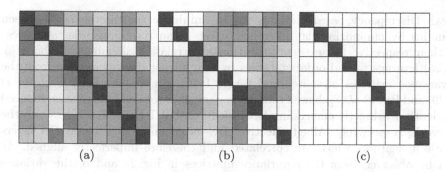

Fig. 2. Covariance matrices of features undergoing different normalization transformations: (a) BN [9]; (b) DWT [8]; and (c) Full-Feature Whitening. Black pixels denote value 1, white pixels denote value 0 and gray denotes intermediate values.

2   Related Works

Single Source UDA. Several UDA methods have been proposed in the recent years that operate under the assumption that there is only a single source domain. A multitude of UDA methods have utilized GAN [10–12] to learn a mapping between the source and target domains in order to generate synthetic data in the target domain. SBADA-GAN [10] and CyCADA [11] are trained with adversarial and cycle-consistent losses to generate labeled target-like source samples which are used for training a classifier for the target domain. Although very effective, GAN based methods require large amount of data from each domain to capture the inherent data distributions.

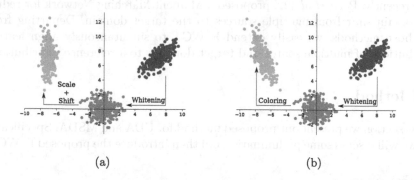

Fig. 3. Visualization of 2D features after whitening and different feature re-projection techniques: (a) whitening with scale and shift as in DWT [8]; and (b) proposed whitening with colouring for aligning feature distributions. (Color figure online)

Another genre of UDA methods aim to reduce the discrepancy between source and target domains by leveraging the first and second order statistics. Minimum

Mean Discrepancy based methods [13,14] minimize the discrepancy between domains by minimizing the difference of the mean (i.e., first order statistics) of their respective feature representations. Correlation alignment methods [5, 15,25] leverage second order statistics by minimizing the loss derived from the covariance matrices of source and target feature representations. Carlucci *et al.* [9] and Roy *et al.* [8] showed that discrepancy between domains can be reduced efficiently by directly embedding BN-based and DWT based DA layers into the network, respectively. Albeit effective, BN-based and DWT based DA layers result in features which are correlated and therefore imperfectly aligned. As can be observed from the covariance matrices in Fig. 2a and b, the variance of the features are 1 but the features are still correlated due to non-zero off-diagonal elements. Ideally, we would like to have *identity* covariance matrix, $\Sigma = I$, (see Fig. 2c) to achieve complete alignment of features. This is achieved with our proposed F^2WCT. Moreover, DWT [8] re-projects partially whitened features with scale and shift transforms of [9] which is sub-optimal because it reduces the capacity of the network [18]. Hence, we propose to re-project whitened features with colouring operation as shown in Fig. 3b. Different from scale and shift operation of DWT (see Fig. 3a), which can only have axis-aligned re-projection of features, our colouring operation can re-project the whitened features to any arbitrary orientation and the network is flexible to choose through training.

Multi Source UDA. In practical scenarios source data can possess different underlying marginal distributions and therefore multiple domain shifts need to be addressed coherently while adapting to the target domain. MSDA was first addressed in [19] which showed the necessity to borrow knowledge from nearest source domains to avoid *negative transfer*. Xu *et al.* [20] adapted to the *distribution-weighted* combining rule in [21] with an adversarial framework. More recently, Peng *et al.* [22] proposed a Moment Matching Network for reducing domain shift from multiple sources to the target domain. Departing from the above methods, we easily extend F^2WCT to simultaneously align feature distributions of multiple source and target domains to a reference distribution.

3   Method

In this section we present our proposed method for UDA and MSDA. Specifically, first we will discuss some preliminaries and then introduce the proposed F^2WCT.

3.1   Preliminaries

Let us assume that $\mathcal{S} = \{(I_j^s, y_j^s)\}_{j=1}^{N_s}$ be the labeled source dataset, where I_j^s is the jth source image and $y_j^s \in \mathcal{Y} = \{1, 2 \ldots, C\}$ be its associated label. Also, let $\mathcal{T} = \{I_i^t\}_{i=1}^{N_t}$ be the unlabeled target dataset where I_i^t is the ith target image *without* any associated label. The aim of UDA is to train a target domain predictor by jointly utilizing samples from $\mathcal{S}$ and $\mathcal{T}$.

A fairly common technique to bridge domain shift is to use DA layers, which can either be BN-based [9] or DWT-based [8], that project source and target feature distributions onto a canonical distribution through per feature standardisation and grouped feature whitening, respectively. As mentioned in Sect. 1, we propose to replace these feature alignment techniques with domain specific full-feature whitening and domain agnostic colouring. Before introducing the proposed F^2WCT we will briefly recap BN [23] below.

A BN layer takes as input a mini-batch $B = \{\mathbf{x}_1, \ldots, \mathbf{x}_m\}$ of m samples, where $\mathbf{x}_i$ is the ith element in the batch B and $\mathbf{x}_i \in \mathbb{R}^d$. As the name suggests, given a batch B the BN layer transforms each $\mathbf{x}_i \in B$ in the following way:

$$BN(x_{i,k}) = \gamma_k \frac{x_{i,k} - \mu_{B,k}}{\sqrt{\sigma_{B,k}^2 + \epsilon}} + \beta_k, \tag{1}$$

where k $(1 \leq k \leq d)$ signifies the k-th dimension of input data, $\mu_{B,k}$ and $\sigma_{B,k}$ are, respectively, the mean and the standard deviation corresponding to the k-th dimension of the samples in B and ϵ is used to prevent division by zero. Finally, γ_k and β_k are learnable scaling and shifting parameters. In essence, BN transforms a batch of features into having zero mean and unit variance and then re-projects the features with γ and β.

In Sect. 3.2 we present our proposed F^2WCT for UDA, while in Sect. 3.3 we extend the proposed F^2WCT for MSDA.

3.2   Full-Feature Whitening and Colouring Transform for UDA

As stated in Sect. 2 that BN based per-dimension feature *standardization* and DWT based *grouped feature whitening* is sub-optimal for marginal source and target distribution alignment due to the presence of correlated features. To alleviate domain shift we argue to replace BN and DWT with F^2WCT, derived from [18], and is defined as follows:

$$F^2 WCT(\mathbf{x}_i; \Omega) = \mathbf{\Gamma}\hat{\mathbf{x}}_i + \boldsymbol{\beta}, \tag{2}$$

$$\hat{\mathbf{x}}_i = W_B(\mathbf{x}_i - \boldsymbol{\mu}_B). \tag{3}$$

In Eq. (3), $\boldsymbol{\mu}_B$ is the mean of B while W_B is the whitening matrix such that: $W_B^\top W_B = \Sigma_B^{-1}$, where Σ_B is the covariance matrix derived from B. $\Omega = (\boldsymbol{\mu}_B, \Sigma_B)$ indicates the batch-specific first and second-order statistics. Equation (3) performs the *whitening* of $\mathbf{x}_i \in B$ and the resulting elements of $\hat{B} = \{\hat{\mathbf{x}}_1, \ldots, \hat{\mathbf{x}}_m\}$ lie in a hyper-spherical distribution, i.e., with a covariance matrix equal to the identity matrix (see Fig. 2c). Additionally, and differently from [8], in Eq. (2), with the help of learnable d dimensional vector $\boldsymbol{\beta}$ and $d \times d$ dimensional matrix $\mathbf{\Gamma}$ the *whitened* $\hat{B}$ is projected back to a multivariate Gaussian distribution having an arbitrary covariance matrix through the *colouring* operation. Implementation wise Eq. (2) can be realized with a convolutional layer having kernel size 1×1.

Our network, at any intermediate layer, takes as input two batches of input samples, $B^s = \{\mathbf{x}_1^s, \ldots, \mathbf{x}_m^s\}$ and $B^t = \{\mathbf{x}_1^t, \ldots, \mathbf{x}_m^t\}$ from the source and target domain, respectively. Every $\mathbf{x}_i^s \in B^s$ and $\mathbf{x}_i^t \in B^t$ is transformed through the F²WCT block, where the whitening operation is domain specific but the colouring operation is domain agnostic. In details, using Eqs. (2)–(3) the output of F²WCT blocks for the source and target samples are given respectively by:

$$F^2WCT(\mathbf{x}_i^s; \Omega^s) = \mathbf{\Gamma} W_{B^s}(\mathbf{x}_i^s - \boldsymbol{\mu}_{B^s}) + \boldsymbol{\beta}, \tag{4}$$

$$F^2WCT(\mathbf{x}_i^t; \Omega^t) = \mathbf{\Gamma} W_{B^t}(\mathbf{x}_i^t - \boldsymbol{\mu}_{B^t}) + \boldsymbol{\beta}. \tag{5}$$

Separate statistics $(\Omega^s = (\boldsymbol{\mu}_B^s, \Sigma_B^s)$ and $\Omega^t = (\boldsymbol{\mu}_B^t, \Sigma_B^t))$ are estimated for B^s and B^t which are then used for whitening the corresponding activations and then followed by colouring the spherical distribution to an arbitrary one (see Fig. 3b). Details about the computation of W_B can be found in [18]. In addition, the F²WCT blocks maintain a moving average of the statistics Ω_{avg}^t of the target domain which is used during inference.

3.3 Full-Feature Whitening and Colouring Transform for MSDA

In the MSDA scenario we have access to P labeled source datasets $\{\mathcal{S}_j\}_{j=1}^P$, where $\mathcal{S}_j = \{(I_i, y_i)\}_{i=1}^{N_j}$, and a target unlabeled dataset $\mathcal{T} = \{I_i\}_{i=1}^{N_t}$. Since, we are addressing closed-set DA all the datasets share the same categories and each of them is associated to a domain $\mathbf{D}_1^s, \ldots, \mathbf{D}_P^s, \mathbf{D}^t$, respectively. Our end goal is to learn a predictor for the target domain $\mathbf{D}_t$ exploiting the data in $\{\mathcal{S}_j\}_{j=1}^P \cup \mathcal{T}$.

Unlike many UDA methods [10,11], the proposed F²WCT can be extended to the MSDA setting in a very straightforward way by having dedicated F²WCT blocks for every domain $\mathbf{D}$, where the colouring parameters are shared amongst $P + 1$ domains. In details:

$$F^2WCT(\mathbf{x}_i^{\mathbf{D}_1^s}; \Omega^{\mathbf{D}_1^s}) = \mathbf{\Gamma} W_{B^{\mathbf{D}_1^s}}(\mathbf{x}_i^{\mathbf{D}_1^s} - \boldsymbol{\mu}_{B^{\mathbf{D}_1^s}}) + \boldsymbol{\beta}, \tag{6}$$

$$\vdots$$

$$F^2WCT(\mathbf{x}_i^{\mathbf{D}_P^s}; \Omega^{\mathbf{D}_P^s}) = \mathbf{\Gamma} W_{B^{\mathbf{D}_P^s}}(\mathbf{x}_i^{\mathbf{D}_P^s} - \boldsymbol{\mu}_{B^{\mathbf{D}_P^s}}) + \boldsymbol{\beta}, \tag{7}$$

$$F^2WCT(\mathbf{x}_i^{\mathbf{D}^t}; \Omega^{\mathbf{D}^t}) = \mathbf{\Gamma} W_{B^{\mathbf{D}^t}}(\mathbf{x}_i^{\mathbf{D}^t} - \boldsymbol{\mu}_{B^{\mathbf{D}^t}}) + \boldsymbol{\beta}. \tag{8}$$

The whitening operation of F²WCT projects the marginal feature distributions of all $P + 1$ domains onto a hyper-spherical reference distribution, thereby minimizing the multiple domain discrepancies in a coherent fashion. As in Sect. 3.2, the moving average of target statistics $\Omega_{avg}^{\mathbf{D}^t}$ is maintained during training and is used during inference.

3.4 Training

Let $B^s = \{\mathbf{x}_1^s, \ldots, \mathbf{x}_m^s\}$ and $B^t = \{\mathbf{x}_1^t, \ldots, \mathbf{x}_m^t\}$ be two batches of the network's last-layer activations, from the source and target domain, respectively. Since, the source samples are associated with labels, the standard cross-entropy loss (L^s) can be used for B^s:

$$L^s(B^s) = -\frac{1}{m}\sum_{i=1}^{m}\log p(y_i^s|\mathbf{x}_i^s), \tag{9}$$

However, for the target samples entropy loss is calculated as in [9], which acts as a regularizer. The entropy loss forces the network to be more confident in its predictions by producing peaked probability distribution at the output.

$$L^t(B^t) = -\frac{1}{m}\sum_{i=1}^{m} p(\mathbf{x}_i^t)\log p(\mathbf{x}_i^t), \tag{10}$$

Finally, the network is trained with a weighted sum of L^s and L^t:

$$L(B^s, B^t) = L^s(B^s) + \lambda L^t(B^t) \tag{11}$$

4   Experimental Results

In this section we describe the datasets and provide details about the experimental protocols adopted. We also report our experimental evaluation on the considered datasets and compare our proposed method with the state-of-the-art methods in UDA and MSDA, respectively.

4.1   Datasets

We conduct all our experiments on the *Digits-Five* dataset, built for recognizing digits, consists of five unique domains having numerical digits ranging between 0 and 9. It includes the USPS, MNIST, MNIST-M, SVHN and *Synthetic numbers* (SYN) datasets. SVHN contains images of real-world house numbers acquired from Google Street View. SYN includes about 500K computer generated digits having varying orientation, position, color, etc. USPS and MNIST are datasets of digits scanned from U.S. envelopes but having different resolutions. Finally, MNIST-M is the colored counterpart of MNIST.

4.2   Experimental Setup

To ensure fair comparison with other UDA and MSDA methods we adopt base networks from [8] and [22] for UDA and MSDA experiments, respectively. In the network we have plugged F^{2}WCT blocks right after each of the first two convolutional layers. We reason that strong alignment of low level features (e.g., colour and texture) is very important to bridge the domain gap. As a consequence, we act in the early convolutional layers of the network, which deal with low level features, by fully aligning intermediate feature distributions with F^{2}WCT blocks. A typical block in the network is given by (Conv Layer $\rightarrow$ F^{2}WCT $\rightarrow$ ReLU). For the remainder layers we have used BN based DA layers as in [9].

We trained the networks with Adam for 150 epochs with an initial learning rate of 1e−3 and we dropped the learning rate by a factor of 10 after 50 and 90 epochs. To ensure well-conditioned covariance matrices we have used a mini-batch size of 128 and 512 for the UDA and MSDA settings, respectively. The source and target samples are drawn randomly such that each domain is well represented in a mini-batch. The value of λ in Eq. 11 is set to 0.1 as in [9].

4.3   Results and Discussion

In this section we analyze the impact of the proposed components on the final classification accuracy and compare F^2WCT with the state-of-the-art methods.

Ablation Study. We conduct ablation studies on the digits dataset for single source UDA to demonstrate the benefits of performing full-whitening followed by a *colouring* transformation. We consider the following models: (i) F^2WCT, our full model, is composed of full-feature whitening and colouring; (ii) F^2WT where the colouring operation is replaced by *scale-shift* operation. This will validate the importance of *colouring* transform over scaling and shifting; and (iii) DWT [8] which considers *grouped* whitening. This comparison allows us to determine the necessity of full-feature whitening as opposed to grouped whitening.

Table 1. Ablation study of full-feature whitening and colouring transform versus relevant normalization techniques on Digits-Five. The target domain is shown in *italics*. The best numbers are highlighted in bold and the second best numbers are underlined.

Methods	MNIST → *USPS*	USPS → *MNIST*	SVHN → *MNIST*	MNIST → *MNIST-M*	Avg
Source only	78.9	57.1	60.1	63.6	64.92
F²WCT (Ours)	**99.13** ± 0.05	**98.81** ± 0.07	<u>97.37</u> ± 0.10	**96.33** ± 0.09	**97.91**
F²WT	99.03 ± 0.04	98.30 ± 0.07	78.96 ± 0.64	<u>81.41</u> ± 0.98	<u>89.42</u>
DWT [8]	<u>99.09</u> ± 0.09	<u>98.79</u> ± 0.05	**97.75** ± 0.10	45.46 ± 0.05	85.27
Target only	96.5	99.2	99.5	96.4	97.9

As can be observed from Table 1 our proposed F^2WCT outperforms all other baselines. F^2WT demonstrates that the need of colouring is particularly evident for more complicated adaptation settings as in SVHN → MNIST and MNIST → MNIST-M. While in simpler MNIST ↔ USPS settings the network has enough capacity already. DWT [8] is especially worse than F^2WCT in the MNIST → MNIST-M setting because grouped feature whitening can not align the source and target feature distributions optimally (see Sect. 2). Conversely, F^2WCT enables strong alignment of low level features through full whitening.

Comparison with State-of-the-Art Results. We compare our proposed F^2WCT with state-of-the-art methods, in both single source UDA and MSDA settings.

Table 2. Classification accuracy (%) on the Digits-Five for single source UDA settings in comparison with the state-of-the-art methods. The target domain is shown in *italics*. The best numbers are highlighted in bold and the second best numbers are underlined.

Methods	MNIST → *USPS*	USPS → *MNIST*	SVHN → *MNIST*	MNIST → *MNIST-M*	Avg
Source only	78.9	57.1	60.1	63.6	64.9
CORAL [5]	81.7	–	63.1	57.7	–
DANN [30]	85.1	73.0 ± 2.0	73.9	77.4	77.3
DSN [29]	91.3	–	82.7	83.2	–
CoGAN [12]	91.2	89.1 ± 0.8	–	62.0	–
ADDA [7]	89.4 ± 0.2	90.1 ± 0.8	76.0 ± 1.8	–	–
DRCN [28]	91.8 ± 0.1	73.7 ± 0.1	82.0 ± 0.2	–	–
ATT [27]	–	–	86.20	94.2	–
AutoDIAL [9]	97.96	97.51	89.12	36.86	80.36
SBADA-GAN [10]	97.6	95.0	76.1	**99.4**	<u>92.02</u>
GAM [26]	95.7 ± 0.5	98.0 ± 0.5	74.6 ± 1.1	–	–
MECA [25]	–	–	95.2	–	–
SE [24]	88.14 ± 0.34	92.35 ± 8.61	93.33 ± 5.88	–	–
DWT [8]	99.09 ± 0.09	98.79 ± 0.05	$\mathbf{97.75 \pm 0.10}$	45.46 ± 0.05	85.27
F^{2}WCT (Ours)	$\mathbf{99.13 \pm 0.05}$	$\mathbf{98.81 \pm 0.07}$	<u>97.37 ± 0.10</u>	<u>96.33 ± 0.09</u>	**97.91**
Target only	96.5	99.2	99.5	96.4	97.9

Single-Source Unsupervised Domain Adaptation. In Table 2 we consider single-source adaptation settings where we adapt from a single source domain to a target domain. We consider four adaptation settings: MNIST → USPS, USPS → MNIST, SVHN → MNIST and MNIST → MNIST-M. The entire *labeled* train set of the source domain and *unlabeled* train set of the target domain is used for training a network whereas the dedicated test set of the target domain is used for evaluating the performance. We have considered the baselines reported in [8]. It is to be noted that we have chosen the baselines that do not utilize data augmentation. The variant of SE [24] which does not make use of data augmentation is therefore reported for fair comparison with other methods. However, for some baselines we could not report all the numbers due to the lack of availability in the corresponding adaptation settings.

From Table 2 we observe that on average our proposed F^{2}WCT outperforms all considered state-of-the-art methods by a considerable margin. Individually, our F^{2}WCT has the best accuracy in MNIST ↔ USPS settings and is the second best in SVHN → MNIST and MNIST → MNIST-M settings. Particularly, SBADA-GAN performs the best in the MNIST → MNIST-M setting due to the implicit data-augmentation through generation of synthetic data. Surprisingly, in overall F^{2}WCT achieves at par performance with the *target only* setting

Table 3. Classification accuracy (%) on Digits-Five for multi-source domain adaptation settings. The target domain is shown in *italics*. Best number is in bold and second best is underlined.

Models	MNIST, USPS, SVHN, SYN → *MNIST-M*	MNIST-M, USPS, SVHN, SYN → *MNIST*	MNIST, MNIST-M, SVHN, SYN → *USPS*	MNIST, USPS, MNIST-M, SYN → *SVHN*	MNIST, USPS, SVHN, MNIST-M → *SYN*	Avg
Source combine						
Source only	63.70 ± 0.83	92.30 ± 0.91	90.71 ± 0.54	71.51 ± 0.75	83.44 ± 0.79	80.33
DAN [13]	67.87 ± 0.75	97.50 ± 0.62	93.49 ± 0.85	67.80 ± 0.84	86.93 ± 0.93	82.72
DANN [30]	70.81 ± 0.94	97.90 ± 0.83	93.47 ± 0.79	68.50 ± 0.85	87.37 ± 0.68	83.61
Multi-source						
Source only	63.37 ± 0.74	90.50 ± 0.83	88.71 ± 0.89	63.54 ± 0.93	82.44 ± 0.65	77.71
DAN [13]	63.78 ± 0.71	96.31 ± 0.54	94.24 ± 0.87	62.45 ± 0.72	85.43 ± 0.77	80.44
CORAL [5]	62.53 ± 0.69	97.21 ± 0.83	93.45 ± 0.82	64.40 ± 0.72	82.77 ± 0.69	80.07
DANN [30]	71.30 ± 0.56	97.60 ± 0.75	92.33 ± 0.85	63.48 ± 0.79	85.34 ± 0.84	82.01
ADDA [7]	71.57 ± 0.52	97.89 ± 0.84	92.83 ± 0.74	75.48 ± 0.48	86.45 ± 0.62	84.84
DCTN [20]	70.53 ± 1.24	96.23 ± 0.82	92.81 ± 0.27	77.61 ± 0.41	86.77 ± 0.78	84.79
M^{3}SDA [22]	72.82 ± 1.13	98.43 ± 0.68	96.14 ± 0.81	81.32 ± 0.86	89.58 ± 0.56	87.65
AutoDIAL [9]	80.15 ± 1.32	$\underline{99.30} \pm 0.04$	98.60 ± 0.09	80.87 ± 0.68	95.28 ± 0.13	90.84
DWT [8]	80.68 ± 1.35	99.26 ± 0.05	$\underline{98.81} \pm 0.08$	$\mathbf{86.11} \pm 0.25$	$\mathbf{95.94} \pm 0.10$	$\underline{92.16}$
F^{2}WCT (Ours)	$\mathbf{93.47} \pm 0.41$	$\mathbf{99.41} \pm 0.04$	$\mathbf{98.97} \pm 0.06$	$\underline{82.46} \pm 0.81$	$\underline{95.92} \pm 0.12$	**94.04**

without having access to any target label, demonstrating the effectiveness of our method.

Multi-source Unsupervised Domain Adaptation. In Table 3 we report results for MSDA setting where we adapt from multiple source domains to a single target domain. We consider all possible combinations of the 5 domains in Digits-Five for the experiments. For fairness in comparison with the baseline methods we follow the training protocol used in [22]. According to this protocol we randomly sample 25000 training images from each domain and 9000 images for evaluation. For the USPS, entire train and test set is used instead. We compare our method with DWT [8], Autodial: Automatic domain alignment layers [9] (AutoDIAL) and other baselines taken from [22]. We observe similar behaviour in the MSDA setting as our proposed F^{2}WCT also out-performs all the baselines on average accuracy, thereby obtaining state-of-the-art results. Notably, for the adaptation setting where MNIST-M is the target domain, the proposed full-feature whitening and colouring provides a boost of 12.79% over grouped whitening and scale-shifting in [8]. This validates our hypothesis that complete alignment of source and target feature distributions with full-feature whitening followed by colouring of the whitened features is more beneficial for tackling domain shift.

5   Conclusions

In this work we address UDA and MSDA by proposing domain alignment layers based on domain specific full-feature whitening and domain agnostic colouring with F^2WCT blocks. On the one hand, full-feature whitening of intermediate features allows optimal alignment of source and target feature distributions by guaranteeing same covariance matrices for both source and target features. On the other, the colouring transform helps in restoring the capacity of the network. The proposed F^2WCT blocks can be easily incorporated in any standard CNN. Our experiments on digits dataset show consistent improved performances over other state-of-the-art methods in both UDA and MSDA settings. As future work, we plan to adapt the proposed feature alignment technique for large scale benchmarks with deeper networks.

References

1. Krizhevsky, A., Sutskever, I., Hinton, G.E.: ImageNet classification with deep convolutional neural networks. In: NIPS (2012)
2. He, K., Zhang, X., Ren, S., Sun, J.: Deep residual learning for image recognition. In: CVPR (2016)
3. Torralba, A., Efros, A.A.: Unbiased look at dataset bias. In: CVPR (2011)
4. Zen, G., Sangineto, E., Ricci, E., Sebe, N.: Unsupervised domain adaptation for personalized facial emotion recognition. In: ICMI (2014)
5. Sun, B., Feng, J., Saenko, K.: Return of frustratingly easy domain adaptation. In: AAAI (2016)
6. Saha, S., Banerjee, B., Merchant, S.N.: Unsupervised domain adaptation without source domain training samples: a maximum margin clustering based approach. In: ICVGIP (2016)
7. Tzeng, E., Hoffman, J., Saenko, K., Darrell, T.: Adversarial discriminative domain adaptation. In: CVPR (2017)
8. Roy, S., Siarohin, A., Sangineto, E., Bulò, S.R., Sebe, N., Ricci, E.: Unsupervised domain adaptation using feature-whitening and consensus loss. In: CVPR (2019)
9. Cariucci, F.M., Porzi, L., Caputo, B., Ricci, E., Bulò, S.R.: AutoDIAL: automatic domain alignment layers. In: ICCV (2017)
10. Russo, P., Carlucci, F.M., Tommasi, T., Caputo, B.: From source to target and back: symmetric bi-directional adaptive GAN. In: CVPR (2018)
11. Hoffman, J., et al.: CyCADA: cycle-consistent adversarial domain adaptation. In: ICML (2018)
12. Liu, M.Y., Tuzel, O.: Coupled generative adversarial networks. In: NIPS (2016)
13. Long, M., Cao, Y., Wang, J., Jordan, M.I.: Learning transferable features with deep adaptation networks. In: ICML (2015)
14. Tzeng, E., Hoffman, J., Zhang, N., Saenko, K., Darrell, T.: Deep domain confusion: maximizing for domain invariance. arXiv preprint arXiv:1412.3474 (2014)
15. Sun, B., Saenko, K.: Deep CORAL: correlation alignment for deep domain adaptation. In: Hua, G., Jégou, H. (eds.) ECCV 2016. LNCS, vol. 9915, pp. 443–450. Springer, Cham (2016). https://doi.org/10.1007/978-3-319-49409-8_35
16. Mancini, M., Bulò, S.R., Caputo, B., Ricci, E.: AdaGraph: unifying predictive and continuous domain adaptation through graphs. In: CVPR (2019)
17. Mancini, M., Porzi, L., Rota Bulò, S., Caputo, B., Ricci, E.: Boosting domain adaptation by discovering latent domains. In: CVPR (2018)
18. Siarohin, A., Sangineto, E., Sebe, N.: Whitening and coloring batch transform for GANs. In: ICLR (2019)

19. Yao, Y., Doretto, G.: Boosting for transfer learning with multiple sources. In: CVPR (2010)
20. Xu, R., Chen, Z., Zuo, W., Yan, J., Lin, L.: Deep cocktail network: Multi-source unsupervised domain adaptation with category shift. In: CVPR (2018)
21. Mansour, Y., Mohri, M., Rostamizadeh, A.: Domain adaptation with multiple sources. In: NIPS (2009)
22. Peng, X., Bai, Q., Xia, X., Huang, Z., Saenko, K., Wang, B.: Moment matching for multi-source domain adaptation. arXiv preprint arXiv:1812.01754 (2018)
23. Ioffe, S., Szegedy, C.: Batch normalization: accelerating deep network training by reducing internal covariate shift. In: ICML (2015)
24. French, G., Mackiewicz, M., Fisher, M.: Self-ensembling for visual domain adaptation. In: ICLR (2018)
25. Morerio, P., Cavazza, J., Murino, V.: Minimal-entropy correlation alignment for unsupervised deep domain adaptation. In: ICLR (2017, 2018)
26. Huang, H., Huang, Q., Krähenbühl, P.: Domain transfer through deep activation matching. In: Ferrari, V., Hebert, M., Sminchisescu, C., Weiss, Y. (eds.) ECCV 2018. LNCS, vol. 11220, pp. 611–626. Springer, Cham (2018). https://doi.org/10.1007/978-3-030-01270-0_36
27. Saito, K., Ushiku, Y., Harada, T.: Asymmetric tri-training for unsupervised domain adaptation. In: ICML (2017)
28. Ghifary, M., Kleijn, W.B., Zhang, M., Balduzzi, D., Li, W.: Deep reconstruction-classification networks for unsupervised domain adaptation. In: Leibe, B., Matas, J., Sebe, N., Welling, M. (eds.) ECCV 2016. LNCS, vol. 9908, pp. 597–613. Springer, Cham (2016). https://doi.org/10.1007/978-3-319-46493-0_36
29. Bousmalis, K., Trigeorgis, G., Silberman, N., Krishnan, D., Erhan, D.: Domain separation networks. In: NIPS (2016)
30. Ganin, Y., et al.: Domain-adversarial training of neural networks. J. Mach. Learn. Res. **17**(1), 1–35 (2016). 2096-2030

View-Invariant Pose Analysis for Human Movement Assessment from RGB Data

Faegheh Sardari[1] , Adeline Paiement[2] , and Majid Mirmehdi[1](✉)

[1] Department of Computer Science, University of Bristol, Bristol, UK
{faegheh.sardari,m.mirmehdi}@bristol.ac.uk
[2] Laboratoire d'Informatique et des Systèmes, University of Toulon, Toulon, France
adeline.paiement@univ-tln.fr

Abstract. We propose a CNN regression method to generate high-level, view-invariant features from RGB images which are suitable for human pose estimation and movement quality analysis. The inputs to our network are body joint heatmaps and limb-maps to help our network exploit geometric relationships between different body parts to estimate the features more accurately. A new multiview and multimodal human movement dataset is also introduced part of which is used to evaluate the results of the proposed method. We present comparative experimental results on pose estimation using a manifold-based pose representation built from motion-captured data. We show that the new RGB derived features provide pose estimates of similar or better accuracy than those produced from depth data, even from single views only.

Keywords: Pose analysis · View-invariant CNN · Health monitoring

1 Introduction

Assessing the quality of human movement is of paramount importance in many areas of human activity, such as sports, health, and surveillance, exemplified by recent works such as [7,11–15]. For example, amongst many clinic and home-based tests for patient monitoring in Parkinsons disease [19], a patient's quality of walking or steadiness while standing must be observed, e.g. both soon after prescribing medication and longitudinally across weeks and months as the progression of the disease is assessed. Using computer vision to automate such rehabilitation assessments would eliminate the costs and subjective variability associated with clinicians, and allow the generation of clinical scores that are more consistently and autonomously applied, e.g. [9].

Our motivation is therefore to design a system that allows us to measure both *frame-by-frame and the overall abnormality* in human movement when performing certain actions – with the aim of eventual development of corresponding scores to reflect a measure of (ab)normality. These requirements call for the design of a robust pose estimation method that provides accurate *frame-by-frame* estimates. Our specific application area is for patient rehabilitation

© Springer Nature Switzerland AG 2019
E. Ricci et al. (Eds.): ICIAP 2019, LNCS 11752, pp. 237–248, 2019.
https://doi.org/10.1007/978-3-030-30645-8_22

actions, such as walking, sitting-to-standing, and so on [2,6,8]. Thus, the pose estimation must be based on robust features obtained from realistic sensor settings for home environments, such as affordable single, or just a small few, RGB cameras.

There is a significant body of work on vision-based human body motion analysis, which for our purposes may be categorised into: (i) traditional methods using high level human pose features [1,12,15,18], and (ii) deep learning approaches [10,13,14,20] that extract features directly from images using CNN networks. The latter may then score a movement's quality directly from such features, or they may use them to provide a body pose estimate, to be used for movement analysis in a later stage. We consider works that rely on wearable technology, such as [8,16], as out of scope, since we wish to focus on both remote sensing for patient comfort and design methods that may have potential use in other applications, such as sports and surveillance.

Pirsiavash et al. [15] proposed a regression-based method to score sport actions in an Olympic sports dataset, that they also released. They trained an SVM classifier on both low-level edge and velocity features and high-level pose features represented in the frequency domain by the discrete cosine transform. While their method was able to narrow down which segments included higher scoring movements, the performance of their features dropped particularly when encountering self-occlusions. Their method predicts action scores better than human non-experts, but it is far from human expert judgment.

Using 3D joints data to analyse human movements, often generated by RGBD cameras and VICON systems, has picked up pace in recent years, for example in [4,12,17,18]. Not surprisingly, the pose features derived from 3D data are richer and can be leveraged to assess a wider range of movements. However, then the curse of dimensionailty can strike and the application of dimensionality reduction methods, such as PCA or manifold learning, becomes necessary to reduce the redundancy presented in the 3D joints space. In [12], Paiement et al. used skeleton data to model pose information in a reduced dimension manifold for a stairs-climbing rehabilitation analysis application. They then trained a custom-designed statistical model on the pose information gathered from the action video to score the movement's quality on a frame-by-frame basis. Chaaraoui et al. [4] generated a body-joints motion history volume from 3D spatio-temporal skeleton joint features, and reduced the dimension of their volume based on axis projections. They then classified abnormal gait in their own frontal-view dataset using BagOfKeyPoses on their skeletal joints volume.

Deep learning based methods have also been increasingly applied to assess the quality of movement, for example [7,10,13,14]. Crabbe et al. [7] modified the work by Paiement et al. [12] by proposing a CNN regression approach to estimate the high dimensional body pose from depth silhouettes in the same low-dimensional manifold space that was developed for their SPHERE Stairs dataset [12]. AlexNet was applied to perform their pose estimation by mapping depth silhouettes onto the manifold space. The authors discussed that the use of depth silhouettes allowed simplifying the learning task for their deep CNN in the absence of a large training dataset. However, the extraction of good, accurate-enough silhouettes for movement quality assessment can be a difficult process. Parmar et al. [13] divided a video into 16-frame video clips and averaged the spatiotemporal features from all clips, obtained by applying 3D CNNs [20], to classify sports actions and estimate their score. Li et al. [10] also divided each video into several parts, and extracted their features using 3D CNNs [20]. Then, all features were concatenated and fed into a two-layer convolutional network to predict the action scores. Since such methods extract spatiotemporal features for a whole video, they are better suited to providing a global score rather than analysing human movement in each frame.

In a similar fashion to Paiement et al. [12], Liao et al. [11] verified that dimensionality reduction, implemented through an autoencoder in their case, combined with statistical modelling of a movement's kinematics may provide discriminating pose estimates and movement quality scores for an instance of a movement. They then trained three different types of NNs (CNN, RNN, and HNN) to perform a (whole) movement quality score prediction from sequences of raw VICON skeleton data. Although they effectively used multiview data to generate their model, the data for their testing must also be obtained by their mocap system which makes their method somewhat impractical for participants, especially in more everyday applications, and requires the presence of experts to set up the system. In addition, their fully integrated NN approach extracts spatiotemporal features that do not allow disentangling the pose from the kinematic problems and cannot finely analyze movement on a frame-by-frame basis.

In this paper, we propose a ResNet-based regression method that extracts high-level pose features from body joint heatmaps and body limb-maps from single RGB images of arbitrary viewpoint. A view-invariant manifold obtained from motion-captured 3D joint positions serves as the target pose estimate space for our CNN. A customised statistical model, from [12,18] is then used to detect and score movement abnormalities on a frame-by-frame basis using our pose

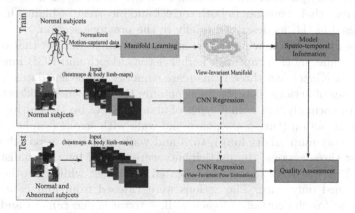

Fig. 1. The overall schema of the proposed approach (including training and testing phases) for normal/abnormal pose estimation.

estimate. The overall approach is illustrated in Fig. 1. The major contributions of our method are its ability to determine and score movement abnormality (in a healthcare setting) from any reasonable viewpoint given an RGB video and without relying on explicit 3D (skeleton or depth) information. Further, we introduce a new fully annotated multiview and multimodal dataset that will be available to the community for the development of health-related or rehabilitation methods. To the best of our knowledge, it is the first time that features extracted from single RGB images are demonstrated to be suitable for movement quality analysis in a healthcare application.

Next, in Sect. 2, a new multiview and multimodal dataset is introduced, followed by our proposed method in Sect. 3. Experiments and comparative results are presented in Sect. 4. Conclusions are in Sect. 5.

2   SMAD: Sphere Multiview and Multimodal Movement Assessment Dataset

There is increasingly more datasets becoming available for human movement analysis, but there is simply no 'one size fits all' that would be of use across different applications and outcomes. For example, the Olympics sports dataset introduced by Pirsiavash et al. [15], which includes diving and skating actions extracted from Youtube videos, is useful for assessment of overall human movement performance, but would not be of use in rehabilitation movement analysis. Parmar et. al [13] also collected a multiview dataset for the diving action. Paiement et al. [12,18] captured three single (frontal) view datasets of walking, walking up stairs, and sitting to standing movements, to evaluate their movement quality assessment method for health-related applications. The skeleton, depth, and colour data was captured by a Primesense camera [18], and a physiotherapist manually annotated all frames into normal and abnormal. Vakanski et al. [21] developed a skeletal movement dataset using a VICON system and a Kinect camera for physical rehabilitation exercises involving 10 healthy subjects who performed their exercises in both correct and incorrect fashion. This dataset was then used in [11] as described briefly in the previous section.

We have captured a new multiview human movement dataset that combines, for the first time, motion capture[1], and skeletons, depth and RGB images from one Microsoft Kinect and three Primesense cameras. While the dataset includes different types of actions, here we focus on only the 'turn and walk' action, performed both normally and with 3 types of abnormalities by 19 healthy subjects: turn and walk action (turn-walk), turn and walk with stroke (stroke), turn and walk with short limp (short limp), turn and walk with Parkinson (Parkinson). For the last three actions, the participants were trained by a specialist Physiotherapist. The turn-walk action was repeated five times, while the other actions were performed only once. The actions were videoed from four camera viewing directions for the entirety of each walk – towards one camera and back to

---

[1] We used the Optitrack Flex 3 acquisition system and VICON's NEXUS skeleton building software.

Fig. 2. Sample frames from the proposed dataset from four different viewing directions for turn-walk (top row), and limp action (bottom row).

the opposite camera, one side view, and one downward view of the scene. Two samples from the dataset are displayed in Fig. 2.

3 Proposed Method

To use 3D human body joints to generate a pose space and assess the quality of human movement, dimensionality reduction becomes inevitable to discard the redundant or correlated dimensions. Here, we follow the approach adopted by other works, such as [7,12,18], to generate a reduced dimensionality manifold to capture the pose variation in our dataset. However, while these previous works produced a pose manifold from PrimeSense or Kinect skeletons, we use the less noisy VICON skeletons derived from motion capture measurements.

A simple approach to view-invariant manifold learning would be to generate one manifold per view and operate on each independently to exhaustively seek a solution. In [22], Zhao et al. learnt a latent space multiview manifold from several images at once, which may be from different modalities, e.g. RGB or RGB-D, with locality alignment using both a supervised and an unsupervised algorithm. This effectively integrated several individual views of a scene into a single manifold. Motion-capture 3D skeletons combine information from multiple cameras and as such are view-independent. Therefore, we generate a view-invariant manifold by applying Diffusion Maps [5] on our motion capture skeletons, which as a result will allow a reduced dimensionality, view-independent model of an action.

We propose a CNN regression-based method to estimate human pose from single RGB images. The view-invariant pose manifold serves as a target space to our pose estimation method, which is trained from groundtruth poses obtained by projection of motion capture skeletons onto the manifold space. Our CNN is made view-invariant through the combined uses of a view-independent manifold and multiple RGB views in its training set.

Skeleton Data Normalization and Manifold Learning. As in [7,12,18], before applying Diffusion Maps, we must normalise our data since different subjects come in various shapes and sizes and they also do not perform actions at the same world coordinates. To normalise for translation, we considered the centre of the hip $(p^{(hip\ center)})$ as our coordinate centre and normalised the other joint positions relative to it as:

$$p_t^j = p_t^j - p_t^{(hip\ center)},\tag{1}$$

where t is the frame number, p is the joint position, and $j = \{1, 2, \ldots, J\}$ is the joint number for the $J = 39$ joint positions supplied by our motion capture system. To normalise for scaling, we defined a model skeleton as a template and then used its torso, hand and leg sizes for normalising the data as follows:

$$torso_{ratio} = torso\ size_{template}/torso\ size_{pose},$$
$$p_t^j = p_t^j * torso_{ratio},\ \text{where } j \in torso,\tag{2}$$

$$hand_{ratio} = hand\ size_{template}/hand\ size_{pose},$$
$$p_t^j = p_t^j * hand_{ratio},\ \text{where } j \in hand,\tag{3}$$

$$leg_{ratio} = leg\ size_{template}/leg\ size_{pose},$$
$$p_t^j = p_t^j * leg_{ratio},\ \text{where } j \in leg.\tag{4}$$

To normalise for rotation, we applied Procrustes analysis. This approach was not used for translation and scaling since the center of human body shape is different with the center computed by Procrustes, e.g. different body parts have different scale ratios while the Procrustes analysis method scales the whole shape at once.

Finally, we applied Diffusion Maps [5] to reduce the dimensionality of our data by selecting the manifold's first $N = 5$ dimensions to represent 95% of the total variance of our original data. This exceeds the 3 dimensions used in [7], but our more complex movement requires more dimensions to describe it. While in previous works a Robust Diffusion Map algorithm was used [7,12,18], the robust extension was not required in our case because we work with skeletons extracted from motion capture data, which do not suffer from the same level of noise as the Kinect or PrimeSense skeletons used in these previous works.

Proposed Network Architecture. The overall structure of the network is shown in Fig. 3. We propose a regression CNN that can exploit the geometric relationship between different body parts to allow the estimation of 3D pose in a reduced-dimensionality manifold space. To this end, and to prevent overfitting on subject appearance during the training of our CNN, we propose to explore body joint heatmaps and a set of 2D vectors which encode the orientation and location of body limbs (as limb-maps) as input, instead of RGB images. This has the added benefit of reducing our data input size. We apply OpenPose [3] to all our images, delimited by the bounding box containing the subject, to generate 26 body joint heatmaps and 52 body limb-maps. All the images are at first zero-padded and resized into 244 × 244 pixels to remove scale variations.

By injecting priors on position and structure of body parts to the CNN, we are able to estimate the 3D reduced pose of each person in manifold space accurately since we force the CNN to extract the features from our desired regions.

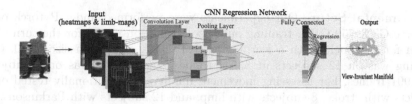

Fig. 3. The overall structure of the network to estimate high-level view-invariant human pose in our view-invariant manifold.

Our input contains $J + L$ channels, (J is the number of body joints, and L is the number of limbs) where each channel describes one body joint or limb, which leads to the size of the kernels in the first convolution layer to be $J + L$.

After [3], for each joint $j \in \{1, \ldots, J\}$, we produce a heatmap $\mathbf{H}_j$ whose value at pixel position p is

$$\mathbf{H}_j(p) = exp(-\frac{\|p - P_j\|_2^2}{\sigma^2}),\tag{5}$$

where P_j is position of joint j and σ determines the spread of the peak.

For each body limb $l \in \{1 \ldots L\}$, we generate a body limb-map $\mathbf{B}_l$, such that, if j_1 and j_2 are body joints defining a limb, then

$$\mathbf{B}_l(p) = \begin{cases} v & \text{if } p \text{ on limb } l \\ 0 & \text{otherwise} \end{cases} \quad \text{where} \quad v = \frac{p_{j1} - p_{j2}}{\|p_{j1} - p_{j2}\|}.\tag{6}$$

To implement our network, we use ResNet and modify its first and last layers. We replace the first layer with a convolutional layer, with a depth of $J + L$, and the last layer with a regression layer with the size of the manifold dimension. Our mean square error (MSE) loss function computes the difference between the groundtruth X and the 3D reduced pose Y estimated by the proposed method,

$$Loss(X, Y) = \frac{1}{N} \sum_{i=1}^{N} \|x_i - y_i\|_2^2.\tag{7}$$

4 Experimental Results

We perform 3 experiments on the turn-walk action. First we show the importance of our heatmap and limb-map in estimating high-level view-invariant human pose on normal subjects. Then, we probe our method's performance, given single and combined of views at training time, to assess the ability of a CNN to attain view invariance for pose estimation. Finally, we perform movement quality classification (into normal and abnormal) using spatio-temporal modeling.

Experimental Setup. Our experiments were performed under Pytorch on a GeForce GTX 750 GPU, training our pose estimation model for the turn-walk action for 15 epochs with a learning rate of 0.001, and batch size of 10. Our training was on 12 subjects at 53544 frames, and testing was on 5 subjects at 21991 frames. For assessing movement quality, we additionally tested on 6 subjects with stroke, 8 subjects with limp, and 12 subjects with Parkinsons.

For evaluation against the closest possible approach, in our first experiment, we compare against Crabbe et al. [7]. Since their dataset does not contain RGB data, the only possible comparative analysis is for us to apply their method using depth silhouettes generated from our data. In addition, [7]'s simple depth silhouette extraction method is not robust to cluttered environments. Instead, we use OpenPose [3] to obtain better depth silhouettes and do region growing from seeds located at joint positions estimated by OpenPose. For robustness, we only use as seeds the non-occluded torso joints. The same depth and contrast normalisation as in [7] was then applied to the silhouette and its background. Also, [7] used Alexnet to train their model, but for a fairer comparison, we apply ResNet for all our experiments. In the following experiments, since it is not simple to extract a depth silhouette, we *also* use the depth bounding box (Depth BB) of the subject to compare against. For accuracy, we compute the MSE between groundtruth pose and estimated human pose in our manifold space.

Comparison of Input Features. We train our network with different types of inputs, i.e. RGB bounding box (RGB BB) of subject, depth BB of subject, depth silhouette similar to Crabbe et al. [7] but extracted using OpenPose [3], body joint heatmaps, body limb-maps, and combined heatmap and limb-maps, from all our views, to assess the performance of the proposed method. Table 1 shows that when trained by using combined heatmap and body limb-maps, the network has the least error in estimating high-level pose. As a result, for the rest of our experiments, we only train the network with heatmaps and body limb-maps. The result from Crabbe et al. [7] using depth silhouettes is poorer than when Depth BB is used potentially due to the general difficulty in accurate silhouette extraction. While in [7] the small size of the dataset required simplifying the learning task for the CNN by extracting the depth silhouette as a preprocessing stage, with our dataset and ResNet architecture this is not the case anymore and the depth BB obtains good results. For this reason, for the rest of the experiments, instead of depth silhouettes, we compare against Crabbe et al.'s work with the simpler Depth BB put through the network.

Assessing Single and Combinations of Views. The first four rows of Table 2 report the pose estimation MSE when we train our method each time using single individual views only. View 1 and View 4 are the opposite camera views, View 2 is the camera view from the side, and View 3 is around 45° above View 1. View 3 provides the best result and will hereafter be used as the basis of all other experiments. Furthermore, for all single views, the proposed method performs better than Depth BB.

Table 1. The MSE for pose estimation when training with different inputs

Error	RGB BB	Depth BB	Depth silhouette [7]	Heatmap	Limb-map	Heatmap & limb-map
MSE	0.72	0.70	0.72	0.67	0.67	**0.66**

Row 5 in Table 2 illustrates that training from a single view only, even if it is the best view, is not sufficient if the test data comes from others views. We only show the case for the best single training view, i.e. View 3, while the results for the other train/test combinations are similar or worse. The remaining rows in Table 2 show the MSE between the estimated pose and groundtruth for different combinations of views for Depth BB and the proposed method. Again, we only show sample combinations that are rooted in View 3, including the combination of all views, while other results remain quite similar. These results indicate that the proposed method can maintain a high accuracy when more views are provided and has learnt well to distinguish between views.

Quality of Movement Assessment. We need to examine if the high-level view-invariant poses extracted by the proposed method are suitable for assessing the quality of human movement. For spatio-temporal analysis of the movement, we apply the framework proposed in [12] which generates two statistical models of normal pose and dynamics. A frame is classified as normal or abnormal depending on how far away from these models it is, based on an empirically determined threshold on log-likelihood. We test on both normal and abnormal sequences which contain all normal (resp. abnormal) frames.

For sequences with abnormal movements, no motion capture skeleton data is available. It is therefore not possible to measure MSE error for pose estimation due to lack of groundtruth. However, we may still assess our method's performance indirectly through movement quality analysis, which depends directly on the quality of pose estimate, as highlighted in [7].

We note from Table 3 the overall poorer performance of the movement quality assessment method compared to previous uses of it in [7,12,18]. This may not necessarily indicate a poor performance of pose estimation, but rather be due in large part to the method being designed for modelling and assessing the quality of single movements, while in our case we consider a more complex action made up of two distinct basic movements (walk-turn). Since improving on this method is not the topic of the present study, we leave this to future works, and we focus on comparing pose estimates from the Depth BB and proposed methods.

Table 3 shows that the specificity for the proposed method to estimate pose of normal sequences is higher at 0.60 than for depth BBs at 0.48, which implies that the estimated poses are close to motion-captured data. Table 4 shows that the movement analysis modelling mostly finds pose to be normal, while the dynamics is particularly abnormal in all abnormal sequences. This is in line with our scenarios where all three abnormality types mostly imply abnormal dynamics with relatively normal poses. The depth BB approach tends to yield

Table 2. MSE between estimated pose and groundtruth on single and multiple views.

Train set	Test set	Depth BB	Proposed method
View 1	View 1	0.73	**0.67**
View 2	View 2	0.76	**0.71**
View 3	View 3	0.70	**0.63**
View 4	View 4	0.73	**0.65**
View 3	View 1	1.13	**1.02**
	View 2	1.42	**1.36**
	View 4	1.10	**1.04**
Average (inc View 3)		1.21	**1.14**
Views 3, 4	View 1	1.07	**0.95**
	View 2	1.42	**1.36**
	View 3	1.59	**0.64**
	View 4	0.70	**0.64**
Average		1.19	**0.89**
Views 1, 3, 4	View 1	0.68	**0.67**
	View 2	1.40	**1.20**
	View 3	1.66	**0.64**
	View 4	0.68	**0.65**
Average		1.10	**0.79**
Views 2, 3, 4	View 1	1.09	**0.95**
	View 2	**0.73**	0.75
	View 3	1.63	**0.62**
	View 4	0.69	**0.62**
Average		1.03	**0.73**
Views 1, 2, 3, 4	View 1	**0.69**	**0.69**
	View 2	0.75	**0.72**
	View 3	1.73	**0.64**
	View 4	0.69	**0.64**
Average		0.96	**0.67**

more abnormal pose outcomes than ours, in line with the results of previous experiments (Tables 1 and 2). This may contribute to explaining its poorer classification results on normal sequences in Table 3 and its better results on abnormal sequences.

Table 3. Frame classification performance for normal and abnormal sequences

	Normal			Stroke		Limp		Parkinson		All sequences	
	TN	FP	Specificity	TP	FN	TP	FN	TP	FN	Precision	Recall
Depth BB	3795	4095	0.48	**3793**	**1497**	**5665**	**2663**	**8939**	**3950**	0.81	**0.69**
Proposed	**4780**	**3110**	**0.60**	3540	1750	4592	3736	6699	6190	**0.82**	0.55

Table 4. Percentage of frames classified as normal by the pose/dynamics models

	Normal	Stroke	Limp	Parkinson
Depth BB	79%/55%	79%/30%	78%/34%	80%/32%
Proposed method	86%/65%	78%/35%	81%/48%	85%/51%

5 Conclusions

We proposed a CNN regression method to extract high-level view-invariant pose and applied it to asses the overall quality of human movement. We also introduced a new multiview, multimodal human movement dataset to evaluate the performance of the proposed method and which we hope will be of use to the rest of the community. The implication of our approach is that a CNN may learn to estimate high-level pose from arbitrary view points. We also demonstrated the superiority of RGB-derived heatmaps and limb-maps as input data for pose estimation, over depth data. For future work, we plan to build on our method to produce a multiview framework that may combine any number of arbitrary view points for a more robust pose estimation.

References

1. Baptista, R., Demisse, G., Aouada, D., Ottersten, B.: Deformation-based abnormal motion detection using 3D skeletons. In: IPTA, pp. 1–6 (2018)
2. Buckley, T., Pitsikoulis, C., Hass, C.: Dynamic postural stability during sit-to-walk transitions in parkinson disease patients. Mov. Disord. **23**(9), 1274–1280 (2008)
3. Cao, Z., Simon, T., Wei, S.E., Sheikh, Y.: Realtime multi-person 2D pose estimation using part affinity fields. In: CVPR, pp. 7291–7299 (2017)
4. Chaaraoui, A.A., Padilla-López, J.R., Flórez-Revuelta, F.: Abnormal gait detection with RGB-D devices using joint motion history features. In: FG, vol. 7, pp. 1–6 (2015)
5. Coifman, R.R., Lafon, S.: Diffusion maps. ACHA **21**(1), 5–30 (2006)
6. Comelia, C.L., Stebbins, G.T., Brown-Toms, N., Goetz, C.G.: Physical therapy and Parkinson's disease: a controlled clinical trial. Neurology **44**(3), 376–376 (1994)
7. Crabbe, B., Paiement, A., Hannuna, S., Mirmehdi, M.: Skeleton-free body pose estimation from depth images for movement analysis. In: ICCVW, pp. 70–78 (2015)
8. Culhane, K., O'cconnor, M., Lyons, D., Lyons, G.: Accelerometers in rehabilitation medicine for older adults. Age Ageing **34**(6), 556–560 (2005)

9. Li, M.H., Mestre, T.A., Fox, S.H., Taati, B.: Vision-based assessment of parkinsonism and levodopa-induced dyskinesia with pose estimation. J. Neuroeng. Rehabil. **15**(1), 97 (2018)

10. Li, Y., Chai, X., Chen, X.: End-to-end learning for action quality assessment. In: Hong, R., Cheng, W.-H., Yamasaki, T., Wang, M., Ngo, C.-W. (eds.) PCM 2018. LNCS, vol. 11165, pp. 125–134. Springer, Cham (2018). https://doi.org/10.1007/978-3-030-00767-6_12

11. Liao, Y., Vakanski, A., Xian, M.: A deep learning framework for assessment of quality of rehabilitation exercises. arXiv preprint arXiv:1901.10435 (2019)

12. Paiement, A., Tao, L., Hannuna, S., Camplani, M., Damen, D., Mirmehdi, M.: Online quality assessment of human movement from skeleton data. In: BMVC, pp. 153–166 (2014)

13. Parmar, P., Morris, B.T.: What and how well you performed? A multitask learning approach to action quality assessment. arXiv preprint arXiv:1904.04346 (2019)

14. Parmar, P., Tran Morris, B.: Learning to score Olympic events. In: CVPRW, pp. 20–28 (2017)

15. Pirsiavash, H., Vondrick, C., Torralba, A.: Assessing the quality of actions. In: Fleet, D., Pajdla, T., Schiele, B., Tuytelaars, T. (eds.) ECCV 2014. LNCS, vol. 8694, pp. 556–571. Springer, Cham (2014). https://doi.org/10.1007/978-3-319-10599-4_36

16. Raso, I., Hervás, R., Bravo, J.: M-Physio: personalized accelerometer-based physical rehabilitation platform. In: MUCSSST, pp. 416–421 (2010)

17. Som, A., Anirudh, R., Wang, Q., Turaga, P.: Riemannian geometric approaches for measuring movement quality. In: CVPRW, pp. 43–50 (2016)

18. Tao, L., et al.: A comparative study of pose representation and dynamics modelling for online motion quality assessment. CVIU **148**, 136–152 (2016)

19. Toosizadeh, N., Mohler, J., Parvaneh, S., Sherman, S., Najafi, B.: Motor performance assessment in Parkinson's disease: association between objective in-clinic, objective in-home, and subjective/semi-objective measures. PloS **10**(4), e0124763 (2015)

20. Tran, D., Bourdev, L., Fergus, R., Torresani, L., Paluri, M.: Learning spatiotemporal features with 3D convolutional networks. In: ICCV, pp. 4489–4497 (2015)

21. Vakanski, A., Jun, H.P., Paul, D., Baker, R.: A data set of human body movements for physical rehabilitation exercises. Data **3**(1), 2 (2018)

22. Zhao, Y., et al.: Multi-view manifold learning with locality alignment. PR **78**, 154–166 (2018)

Frame Interpolation Using Phase Information and Guided Image Filtering

Fahim Arif[1], Sundas Amin[1], Abdul Ghafoor[1(✉)], and M. Mohsin Riaz[2]

[1] National University of Sciences and Technology (NUST), Islamabad, Pakistan
fahim@mcs.edu.pk, sundusamin@yahoo.com, abdulghafoor-mcs@nust.edu.pk
[2] COMSATS University, Islamabad, Pakistan
mohsin.riaz@comsats.edu.pk

Abstract. Videos with low frame rate lacks the visual quality element and unable to meet the standards of new multimedia systems. In this paper, a technique for frame interpolation utilizing phase information is proposed. Phase information gives the intuition that the motion of signals can be depicted as a phase shift. The two consecutive input frames of video are passed through a guided filter to preserve edges of objects in frames. These frames then decompose into multi scale pyramid and the difference in each pixel is calculated to compute the phase difference which then used to interpolate the in-between frame. The proposed technique can be used to increase the frame rate of videos. Subjective and objective comparison is performed with the state of art existing technique to prove the significance of proposed technique.

1 Introduction

Frame interpolation becomes the significant part of video processing. Frame interpolation is the process of generating intermediate frame based on the existing frames from the video sequence. Video frame interpolation plays an important function in increasing the frame rate of video and presents the smoother video playback. Traditional approaches to frame interpolation used two steps to interpolate a frame; first step is to compute the correspondences using stereo methods or leveraging (optical flow), and perform image warping based on correspondences. Generally correspondences computation is called motion estimation and image warping and blending of input frame is frame interpolation. Intermediate frame generation is a very complex task because of moving objects, object occlusion and sudden light changing.

Kim et al. [1] proposed hierarchical motion estimation method to track the motion. Modified 3-D recursive search along with the motion vector refining process is performed to achieve the higher efficiency. *Gracewell et al.* [2] proposed fast forward motion estimation method for the frame rate up conversion. Overlapped blocked motion compensation approach is used to reduces the blocking artifacts. Motion vectors are refined using spatial correlation between the neighbouring blocks. *Philip et al.* [3] proposed a modification in block matching technique

© Springer Nature Switzerland AG 2019
E. Ricci et al. (Eds.): ICIAP 2019, LNCS 11752, pp. 249–259, 2019.
https://doi.org/10.1007/978-3-030-30645-8_23

to increase the quality of video playback. Dynamic looping refined the motion vectors acquired from block matching. *Dikbas et al.* [4] proposed a true motion estimation technique with the low computational complexity using predictive search. Blocking artifacts catered at the interpolation stage are minimized by extracting the dense motion field in backward and forward direction. *Liu et al.* [5] trained a deep network by combining the benefits of optical flow methods and neural network methods. Missed frames were calculated by flowing pixel values in the available frames. The blurring artifacts were removed in most of the cases but constructing frames by using RGB differences failed to interpolate the true frame when scenes are repetitive.

Li et al. [6] proposed optical flow based video interpolation technique and used Laplacian cotangent mesh to preserve the smoothness in interpolated frames by minimizing differentials in mesh. Creating accurate mesh for the image of interest is complex and takes more computation time. *Huang et al.* [7] used the predictive square search motion estimation technique to refine the motion vectors. Markov random field correction and block refinement were incorporate to enhance the interpolated frames quality. The algorithm maintains to achieve better quality but it expend extensive amount of resources. *Xiao et al.* [8] proposed an algorithm to lessen the ghost and blurring artifacts. The algorithm performed classification of the edge blocks and flat blocks based on depth map threshold value and then the motion estimation was performed distinctively on blocks. Hole filling based interpolation was effectuated to remove the holes artifact from the interpolated frame.

Zhao et al. [9] presented a motion vector refinement method to correct the false motion vectors for the problems of holes and overlap. Motion vectors of holes and overlapping regions were obtained by constructing label array. The algorithm achieved the better results by removing holes but the blurriness near edges still exist. *Ji et al.* [10] presented a hybrid motion estimation technique by using spatial and temporal information. The algorithm was blend of unidirectional and bidirectional sum of absolute differences performed on multi resolution frames. However, the technique has the blurring artifact when the scene changes quickly. *Matsuo et al.* [11] proposed contrast compensation based linear filtering interpolation to reduce motion blur. This technique utilized spatiotemporal contrast information to enhance the frame rate of video. The algorithm improved the quality of interpolated frames however, this method induced other artifacts. *Lim et al.* [12] proposed motion compensated method based on region segmentation. Motion estimation step was based on the shapes that created arbitrarily by using pixel intensity. This makes this method computationally complex. *Jim et al.* [13] proposed a technique to reduce block artifacts in interpolated frames by estimating the true motion vectors. Sum of absolute differences (SAD) were calculated using three consecutive frames. However, SAD alone does not give the reliable results.

Kovacevic et al. [14] presented a block matching correlation method for frame rate up conversion. True motion vectors were calculated using phase plane correlation. However, this approach does not consider occlusion handling feature.

Okade et al. [15] proposed a technique to remove outlier motion vectors by using weighted vector median filter. Motion vector field was smoothed by median filtering to remove false motion vectors. The algorithm improves motion estimation but because of computational complexity unable to use in real-time applications. *Qu et al.* [16] proposed a post processing technique to extract refined motion vectors. Combination of bilateral and unilateral motion estimation techniques was introduced and the outliers of both were removed using vector extrapolation and weighted summation. However, motion jerkiness is still the issue in videos in which scenes are swiftly changing. *Lu et al.* [17] proposed a frame rate up conversion (FRUC) method utilizing spatial and temporal information of missing frames and integrated with HEVC coding for the limited bandwidth communication channels. However, the quality of reconstructed frames depends on accuracy of spatial and temporal information. *Umnyashkin et al.* [18] proposed a motion compensation technique utilizing hexagonal blocks. Motion estimation process was performed using mesh search structure instead of full search to lessen the computational load but the motion regions still have jerkiness.

Qu et al. [19] presented a non-integer FRUC technique to reduce motion blurriness and jerkiness in fast motion regions. The algorithm based on decimal multiples interpolation which is computationally expensive. *Lu et al.* [20] proposed a motion vector processing technique using artifact information metric to extract true motion vectors. It performed processing on those motion vectors that were unreliable and resulted in artifacts in frame interpolation. However, the complexity of this method is high if large numbers of initial motion vectors are unreliable. *Lu et al.* [21] also proposed the multi-frame based FRUC method and estimates motion vectors using unidirectional approach in both forward and backward directions. The motion dubiety regions were also handled using occlusion handling process. The computational complexity of method increase with the increase in occluded regions. *Kim et al.* [22] used prediction method motion vector smoothing in motion estimation process. It uses bidirectional motion estimation as a base algorithm which lacks to estimate reliable motion trajectories. *Dong et al.* [23] presented an image interpolation method which is based on sparse representation and depends on data fidelity term that fails to restrain the image local structures that lead to the increase in missing pixels.

In this paper, a technique for frame interpolation utilizing phase information is proposed. Phase information gives the intuition that the motion of signals can be depicted as a phase shift. The two consecutive input frames of video are passed through a guided filter to preserve edges of objects in frames. These frames then decompose into multi scale pyramid and the difference in each pixel is calculated to compute the phase difference which then used to interpolate the in-between frame. The proposed technique can be used to increase the frame rate of videos. Subjective and objective comparison is performed with the state of art existing technique to prove the significance of proposed technique.

Algorithm 1. Frame interpolation algorithm using phase information

---

1: Input frames F_1, F_2
2: Interpolation parameter α
3: Decomposition using steerable pyramid: $(PD_1, PD_2) \leftarrow decompose(F1, F2)$
4: Phase computation: $(\phi_1, \phi_2) \leftarrow phase(PD_1, PD_2)$
5: Amplitude extraction: $(A_1, A_2) \leftarrow amplitude(F1, F2)$
6: Phase difference computation: $\phi_{diff} \leftarrow phase(\phi_1, \phi_2)$
7: $\phi_{diff} = attan2(sin(\phi_1 - \phi_2), cos(\phi_1 - \phi_2))$
8: $l=$ current level; $L=$ total levels of steerable pyramid
9: **for all** l = L-1:1 **do**
10:     $\tilde{\phi}^l_{diff} \leftarrow$ correction of shift $(\tilde{\phi}^{l+1}_{diff})$
11: **end for**
12: to achieve smooth interpolation between phase ϕ_1 and phase ϕ_2:
13: $\hat{\phi}_{diff} \leftarrow phaseadjustment(\phi_{diff}, \tilde{\phi}_{diff})$
14: Interpolation of phase: $\phi_\alpha \leftarrow phaseinterpolation(\phi_1, \hat{\phi}_{diff}, \alpha)$
15: Output frame F_{12}

---

2 Proposed Methodology

The algorithm takes two consecutive frames input and performed three major steps (guided filtering, phase based interpolation and restoration).

2.1 Guided Filtering

Edge preserving guided filtering [24] transmit the guidance image structure to the filtering image to preserve edges. The proposed algorithm takes input of two consecutive frames. The filter is applied on first frame F_1 and extract the base layer and then it is applied on second frame F_2 to extract base layer of second frame. After that respective input frames are used to extract the detail layers using base layers. The edge-preserving smoothing is performed by decomposition of an frame F_1 into two layers i.e. [24],

$$F1 = O_x + t \tag{1}$$

where O_x is filtered output image and t is texture image. O_x is known as a base layer and t is a detail layer. The concept of image guided filter is based on the assumption that filtering output image O is a linear transform of guidance image G in a window w_y which is centred by the pixel y,

$$O_x = a_y G_x + b_y \forall x \in w_y \tag{2}$$

where a_y and b_y are linear coefficients and are assumed to remain constant in w_y. The efficient frame interpolation algorithm used the guided filter to decompose input frames into base layers and detail layers. The base layer is obtained by

(a)   (b)

(c)   (d)

Fig. 1. Example 1: (a, b) input frames (c) *Meyer et al.* [25] (d) proposed

applying guided filter to the input frame. After this, base layer O_x is used to obtained the detail layer t as,

$$t = F1 - O_x \tag{3}$$

In the next step, extracted base layers and detail layers of input frames are forwarded to the phase information algorithm to interpolate the intermediate frame.

2.2 Frame Interpolation Using Phase

After separating base layer and detail layer of input frames using guided filtering next step is interpolation. The phase based algorithm [25] takes base layers of frames as an input and then performs decomposition of frames using steerable pyramids. The steps of phase based algorithm are summarized in the Algorithm 1.

2.3 Joint Image Restoration

After frame interpolation, post-processing step is performed to improve the visually appealing quality of frame. To cater the light issues gradient loss and vari-

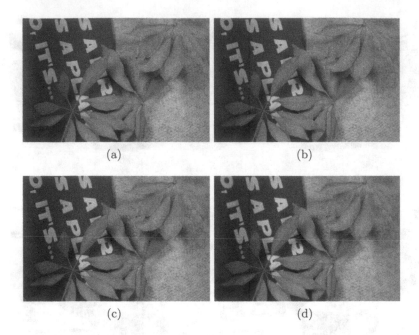

Fig. 2. Example 2: (a, b) input frames (c) *Meyer et al.* [25] (d) proposed

ation in gradient magnitude. The proposed efficient technique used joint image restoration algorithm [26]. The problems produced by intrinsic discrepancy in structure of images are called cross field problem [26]. Simple image filtering algorithm might create weak edges because of smoothing property of filter, even if gradients of reference image transferred to the noisy field outcome might appears artificial.

To solve this problem algorithm [26] construct a map. This map apprehend the structure discrepancy between both images. On the basis of this map an optimal scale map is derived to preserve edges and manipulate reference strength in the frames when sudden change in colors or brightness occur.

The algorithm takes input of interpolated frame F_{12} which might have noise and a reference frame R. In proposed algorithm $F2$ is considered as a reference frame. The algorithm recovered a frame from F_{12} with retained structure and removed noise. A map m is introduced with size of R. To estimate the map m and restore frame F, the main objective function is expressed as

$$DT(m, F) = DT_1(m, F) + \lambda DT_2(F) + \beta DT_3(\nabla m) \tag{4}$$

where DT_1, DT_2 and DT_3 are data terms used to remove various outliers. λ and β are parameters, λ is a confidence constraint and β controls smoothness of map m. DT_1 is used to remove outliers between map m and frame F using reference frame R. DT_2 is defined to control the wild difference between the noisy input frame F_{12} and restore frame F. DT_3 is used to produce the smooth

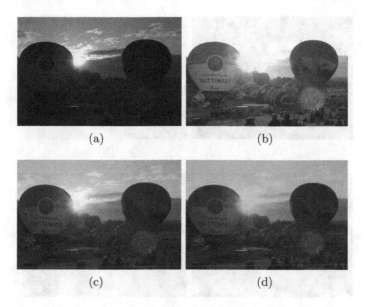

(a)   (b)

(c)   (d)

Fig. 3. Example 3: (a, b) input frames, (c) *Meyer et al.* [25], (d) proposed

map m with strong edges. The iterative method is proposed [26]. To solve function $DT(m, F)$, iterative re-weighted least squares (IRLS) [26] approach is used. After this step the proposed efficient frame interpolation algorithm is completed and the final interpolated frame having better edges is achieved especially the proposed approach handles the abrupt light changes more sophistically.

3 Experiment and Results

To test the abrupt change in brightness and light MEF datasets [27] is used which includes the images captured belong to the same scene but under different light condition. Quantitative analysis of the proposed and existing techniques are performed using Peak Signal to Noise Ratio (PSNR) and Structure Similarity Image Measure (SSIM).

Figure 1(a, b) shows the input frames of dump-truck sequence. Figure 1(a) is a frame in which the cars and truck are visible, the frame is challenging because it has brightness which is difficult to handle while interpolation because of not showing the correct pixels. Figure 1(b) is a frame in which cars and truck are move little forward with respect to their position. Both input frames have trees which shows the correct interpolation should also interpolate the trees movement in a natural way. Figure 1(c, d) shows the results of phase based approaches. Figure 1(c) shows the frame of existing technique *Meyer et al.* [25] interpolation result, which have blurriness around the edges of cars. Trees are also lacking the same colors of input frames. Figure 1(d) shows the proposed interpolation result in which the edges of cars and truck is more clear and blurriness is visibly reduced. The lines on roads are also more clear. Figure 2(a, b) show input

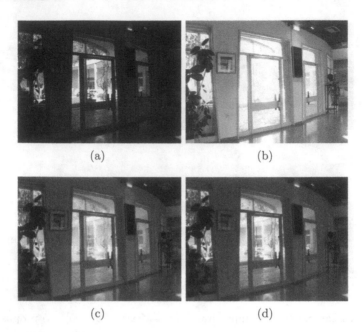

(a)   (b)

(c)   (d)

Fig. 4. Example 4: (a, b) input frames, (c) *Meyer et al.* [25], (d) proposed

frames of leaves which are placed on a two types of surface text and design of very short flowers, the frame have variety of different colors. Figure 2(b) is a frame in which leaves and the surface is moving clockwise, because the movement of text surface and the design surface it is a challenging frame sequence to interpolate. Figure 2(c, d) shows the interpolation results of phase based approaches. Figure 2(c) represents the frame of existing technique *Meyer et al.* [25] result, which shows blurry edges around the leaves. Surface also lacks the clarity of edges specially near text. Figure 2(d) represents the proposed interpolation result in which leaves edges are more sharp and blur factor is significantly reduced. The surface of text is also interpolated visually better result.

Figure 3(a) shows the frame which is underexposed and have very less information and Fig. 3(b) shows the frame which reveals the severe illumination change occur in scene. The first input frame is not able to show the writing on the balloons and colors of balloons because of very less lighting are also not visible in the first input frame. The second input frame shows the information better than the first frame but it has the effect of severe lighting and the edges of balloons exposed to sun are also not visible. Figure 4(c) shows the result of the *Meyer et al.* [25] and Fig. 3(d) shows the result of the proposed algorithm. It can be perceived that the frame created by proposed algorithm handles light change sophistically.

Figure 4(a) shows a frame which shows a frame from the inside of the building and some of the outside information is also visible. It has least information most of the scene is covered under darkness and the region around the door

Table 1. PSNR and SSIM comparison

Examples	Meyer et al. [25]		Proposed	
	PSNR	SSIM	PSNR	SSIM
Example 1	26.4819	0.9583	27.2222	0.9494
Example 2	31.4658	0.9749	32.0195	0.9868
Example 3	19.4597	0.8675	21.2116	0.8916
Example 4	22.6511	0.8714	22.4293	0.8500

is not showing proper edges. The inside plants are also not visible. It shows the region which is outside the building. Figure 4(b) shows the frame which has overexposure to light and most of the information is invisible because of light. The region outside the building is totally not visible because of the severe sun exposure. The region inside the building in clear in this frame and indoor plants are also clearly visible. This abrupt change in light becomes a challenge to interpolate in-between frame. Figure 4(c) *Meyer et al.* [25] represent the result of phase based approach which generate the better result and the Fig. 4(d) represents the proposed algorithm which represents the better edges, cater the sudden light exposed regions better as compared to existing phase based approach. The region around the door is more smooth and exhibiting sharp edges near light changing regions. The information shown outside the frame is also clearly visible in the proposed interpolated frame (Table 1).

4   Conclusion

A technique for frame interpolation utilizing phase information is proposed. Phase information gives the intuition that the motion of signals can be depicted as a phase shift. The two consecutive input frames of video are passed through a guided filter to preserve edges of objects in frames. These frames then decompose into multi scale pyramid and the difference in each pixel is calculated to compute the phase difference which then used to interpolate the in-between frame. The proposed technique can be used to increase the frame rate of videos. Subjective and objective comparison is performed with the state of art existing technique to prove the significance of proposed technique.

References

1. Kim, D., Park, H.: An efficient motion-compensated frame interpolation method using temporal information for high-resolution videos. J. Disp. Technol. **11**(7), 580–588 (2015)
2. Gracewell, J., John, M.: Motion compensation based multiple inter frame interpolation. In: International Conference on Signal Processing and Communication, pp. 261–265 (2016)

3. Philip, J.T., Samuvel, B.: Digital video frame rate up-conversion based on modified block matching technique. Int. J. Res. Comput. Commun. Technol. Adv. Technol. **5**(3), 135–140 (2016)
4. Dikbas, S., Altunbasak, Y.: A novel true-motion estimation algorithm and its application to motion-compensated temporal frame interpolation. IEEE Trans. Image Process. **22**(8), 2931–2945 (2013)
5. Liu, Z., Yeh, R., Tang, X., Liu, Y., Agarwala, A.: Video frame synthesis using deep voxel flow. In: International Conference on Computer Vision, pp. 4473–4481 (2017)
6. Li, W., Cosker, D.: Video interpolation using optical flow and laplacian smoothness. Neurocomputing **220**, 236–243 (2017)
7. Huang, Y., Chen, F., Chien, S.: Algorithm and architecture design of multi-rate frame rate up-conversion for ultra-HD LCD systems. IEEE Trans. Circ. Syst. Video Technol. **27**(12), 2739–2752 (2016)
8. Xiao, Y., Liu, J., Qu, A., Guo, Z.: Edge-consistency based adaptive interpolation method for stereoscopic video frame rate up conversion. In: IEEE International Conference on Multimedia and Expo Workshops, pp. 85–90 (2017)
9. Zhao, Y., Sun, G., Liu, J., Ge, J., Wan, W., Yang, X.: An improved FRUC scheme based on motion vector refinement. In: International Conference on Signal Processing, pp. 981–986 (2014)
10. Ji, B., Li, R., Wu, C.: Spatial-temporal correlation based multi-resolution hybrid motion estimation for frame rate up-conversion. In: Sun, X., Chao, H.-C., You, X., Bertino, E. (eds.) ICCCS 2017. LNCS, vol. 10603, pp. 408–417. Springer, Cham (2017). https://doi.org/10.1007/978-3-319-68542-7_34
11. Matsuo, Y., Sakaida, S.: Frame-rate conversion method by linear-filtering interpolation using spatio-temporal contrast compensation. In: IEEE International Conference on Consumer Electronics, pp. 243–244 (2017)
12. Lim, C., Park, H.: A region-based motion-compensated frame interpolation method using a variance-distortion. IEEE Trans. Circ. Syst. Video Technol. **25**(3), 518–524 (2015)
13. Kim, J., Kim, D., Choi, J., Kim, J., Han, D.: A novel frame-rate up conversion using pseudo-true motion vector. In: IEEE International Conference on Consumer Electronics, pp. 546–547 (2015)
14. Kovacevic, V., Pantic, Z., Beric, A., Jakovljevic, R.: Block-matching correlation motion estimation for frame-rate up-conversion. J. Sig. Process. Syst. **84**(2), 283–292 (2016)
15. Okade, M., Biswas, P.: A novel motion vector outlier removal technique based on adaptive weighted vector median filtering for global motion estimation. In: Annual IEEE India Conference, pp. 1–5 (2013)
16. Qu, A., Liu, J., Wan, W., Xiao, Y.: A frame rate up-conversion method with quadruple motion vector processing. In: IEEE International Conference on Acoustics, Speech and Signal Processing, pp. 1686–1690 (2016)
17. Lu, G., Zhang, X., Gao, Z.: A novel framework of frame rate up conversion integrated within HEVC coding. In: International Conference on Image Processing, pp. 4240–4244 (2016)
18. Umnyashkin, S., Sharonov, I.: Motion compensation in video compression using hexagonal blocks. SIViP **9**(1), 213–223 (2015)
19. Qu, A., Liu, J., Xiao, Y., Wan, W., Wang, Q.: Non-integer times frame rate up-conversion using reliable analysis of motion information. In: International Conference on Signal Processing, Communications and Computing, pp. 1–6 (2016)

20. Lu, Q., Wang, Y., Fang, X.: An artifact information based motion vector processing method for motion compensated frame interpolation. J. Disp. Technol. **10**(9), 775–784 (2014)
21. Lu, Q., Xu, N., Fang, X.: Motion-compensated frame interpolation with multiframe-based occlusion handling. J. Displ. Technol. **12**(1), 45–54 (2016)
22. Kim, U.S., Sunwoo, M.H.: New frame rate up-conversion algorithms with low computational complexity. IEEE Trans. Circ. Syst. Video Technol. **24**(3), 384–393 (2014)
23. Dong, W., Zhang, L., Lukac, R., Shi, G.: Sparse representation based image interpolation with non local autoregressive modelling. IEEE Trans. Image Process. **22**(4), 1382–1394 (2013)
24. He, K., Sun, J., Tang, X.: Guided image filtering. IEEE Trans. Pattern Anal. Mach. Intell. **35**(6), 1397–1409 (2013)
25. Meyer, S., Wang, O., Zimmer, H., Grosse, M., Hornung, A.S.: Phase-based frame interpolation for video. In: IEEE Conference on Computer Vision and Pattern Recognition, pp. 1410–1418 (2015)
26. Yan, Q., et al.: Cross-field joint image restoration via scale map. In: IEEE International Conference on Computer Vision, pp. 1537–1544 (2013)
27. Ma, K., Zeng, K., Wang, Z.: Perceptual quality assessment for multi-exposure image fusion. IEEE Trans. Image Process. **24**(11), 3345–3356 (2015)

Generalised Gradient Vector Flow
for Content-Aware Image Resizing

Tiziana Rotondo, Alessandro Ortis(✉), and Sebastiano Battiato

Department of Mathematics and Computer Science, University of Catania,
Catania, Italy
tiziana.rotondo@unict.it, {ortis,battiato}@dmi.unict.it

Abstract. Image retargeting is devoted to preserve the visual content
of images with a proper resizing, removing vertical and/or horizontal
paths of pixels which contain low semantic information. In this paper,
a method based on the Generalised Gradient Vector Flow (GGVF) is
presented. The GGVF formulation allows the balancing of the smoothing term and data term of the flow by proper parameter tuning. The
proposed approach has been tested by considering a data set of 1000
images and varying the percentage of resizing from 10% to 50% and for
different values of the aim involved parameter K. Results show that our
algorithm better preserves the important information compared to GVF
and Seam Carving approaches. Preliminary results show an underlying
relation between parameter K and the percentage of resizing has been
also exploited.

Keywords: Image resizing · Image retargeting · Seam carving · GGVF

1 Introduction

In the last years, with the improvement of technology, many display devices
are built with different resolution. This increases the request of image resizing
techniques aimed to guarantee the quality of salient visual information. The aim
of content-aware image resizing is the reduction of the overall number of pixel
of a given image, while preserving the content and aspect ratio of the depicted
objects. The problem of image retargeting is defined as follows. Given an image
I of size $H \times W$, the purpose is to map it in a new image I' of size $H \times W'$
($H' \times W$ in horizontal case), with $0 < W' < W$ ($0 < H' < H$), where W'
is defined as $W' = W - N$ ($H' = H - N$) and N is the number of paths to
be removed. The two simplest techniques to resize an image are cropping and
uniform scaling but they introduce deformation or distortion of the subjects.
Moreover, these methods do not take into account the content of the image (i.e.,
the semantic).

In 2007, Avidan et al. [1] proposed the seam carving technique, which consists
in finding proper pixel paths (called seams) which are related to background or
other parts not related to the semantic of the picture. In the last years, several

© Springer Nature Switzerland AG 2019
E. Ricci et al. (Eds.): ICIAP 2019, LNCS 11752, pp. 260–270, 2019.
https://doi.org/10.1007/978-3-030-30645-8_24

methods have been proposed. To establish the paths to be considered during the resizing, in [2], a method based on the Gradient Vector Flow (GVF) of the image is presented. The authors also proposed an approach which takes into account the visual saliency properties of the images, to find an optimal path in the resizing space. GVF, introduced in [14], is computed as a diffusion of the gradient vectors of a gray-level or binary edge map computed from the image. Xu et al. [15] proposed a method that generalises the GVF formulation, called Generalised Gradient Vector Flow (GGVF), to improve active contour (snake) convergence to long, thin boundary indentations, while maintaining other desirable properties of GVF. In particular, they add two weighting coefficients which can be dynamically changed in the image region. In [18] and [19] GGVF is improved in term of noise robustness, weak edge preserving and convergence, for the task of medical image segmentation. To solve the high computational cost of GVF, virtual electric field (VEF) [7] and its extension [16] have been proposed. The hypothesis of these methods is that each pixel of an image is an electron and all pixels generate a virtual electric filed.

Many approaches try to combine different techniques to resize images and define new metrics to measure the quality of proposed methods. In [5], an algorithm which iteratively applies seam carving, cropping, warping, and scaling is proposed. Structural Similarity Metric (i.e., SSIM) is adopted to measure the similarity between original and retargeted images. The work in [13] combines several resizing operators and defines a new image similarity measure which is used with a dynamic programming algorithm whereas in [12], the authors present a comprehensive perceptual study and analysis of image retargeting. The authors of [12] propose a metric that can predict human retargeting perception. A measure that simulates the human vision system is also proposed in [10]. In particular, global topological property is the core of the method and image scale space is considered to extract the global geometric structures from retargeted images. In [11], a real-time approach based on axis-aligned deformation space is introduced. It minimizes convex energy under feasible constraints with the aim to guarantee the convergence of the method and the quality of the results. In [6], a metric that measures the geometric distortion of a retargeted image based on the local variance of SIFT flow [9] vector fields of the image is presented. To measure the quality of retargeted image, the work in [8] proposes an objective quality assessment method which takes account the following factor: preservation of saliency regions, symmetry and global structure, influence od introduced artifacts and aesthetics.

In the last years, deep neural network models have been considered for image resizing. The work in [3] proposes a weakly- and self-supervised deep Convolutional Neural Network (CNN) that takes a source image and a target aspect ratio as input. In [17], it is presented a perceptually aware model that reduces the dimension of the original photo/video by deeply encoding human gaze shifting sequences. Even if CNN based methods show encouraging results, the end-to-end approach implemented by such encoder-decoder models creates a new image with a pre-defined aspect ratio, without any knowledge about the process that determined the pixels that have been removed.

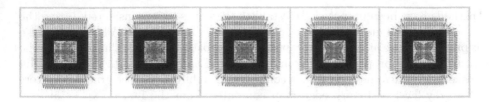

Fig. 1. GGVF of test image for different values of K. 1th column: K = 0.001, 2th column: K = 0.05, 3th column: K = 0.75, 4th column: K = 1, 5th column: K = 1.25.

In this paper, we present a new method for image retargeting which is based on GGVF. We assess and investigate the importance of one of the main involved parameter (K) of GGVF, which balances the smoothing term and data term. The proposed approach has been compared with respect to a method based on GVF [2] and a seam carving approach [1] for different values of percentage of resizing. Experimental results demonstrate the relation between K and the scale factor of retargeting. They also show that the proposed method is able to overcome some difficulties of method based on GVF.

The paper is organised as follows. In Sect. 2, the comparison between GVF and GGVF is introduced and our algorithm is detailed. Section 3 presents and discuss the results. Finally, conclusions and hints for future works are given in Sect. 4.

2   Proposed Method

Gradient Vector Flow [14] is a force field $\mathbf{F}$ of vector $\mathbf{v}(x, y) = [u(x, y), v(x, y)]$ that minimizes the following energy function:

$$E = \iint \mu(u_x^2 + u_y^2 + v_x^2 + v_y^2) + |\nabla f|^2 |\mathbf{v} - \nabla f| dx dy$$
$$= \iint \mu \nabla^2 \mathbf{v} + |\nabla f|^2 |\mathbf{v} - \nabla f| dx dy \tag{1}$$

where μ is a regularisation parameter that controls the trade-off between the first term, called smoothing term, and the second term, named data term, in the integrand. The terms u_x, v_x, u_y, v_y indicate the partial derivatives along x and y axes, f is an edge map of the input image, $|\nabla f|$ is the gradient of f and ∇^2 is the Laplacian operator. If $|\nabla f|$ is close to zero, the energy E in Eq. 1 is dominated by $\mu \nabla^2 \mathbf{v}$, hence GVF is a slowly varying field. On the other hand, when this quantity is large the values of GVF field are close to $|\nabla f|$ and presents slow variations in homogeneous regions.

To solve the difficulty of GVF in driving a path into long and thin indentations that could be due to the smoothing of the field near the boundaries, μ and $|\nabla f|^2$ are replaced by generic weighting coefficients. Therefore, GGVF field [15] is the equilibrium solution of the following partial differential equation:

$$\mathbf{v}_t = g(|\nabla f|)\nabla^2 \mathbf{v} - h(|\nabla f|)(\mathbf{v} - \nabla f). \tag{2}$$

To preserve the proprieties of GVF, the weighting function $g(\cdot)$ and $h(\cdot)$ should be monotonically non-increasing and non-decreasing functions of $|\nabla f|$, respectively. These coefficients are spatially varying, since they depend on the gradient of the edge map which is spatially dependent. In our experiments, the following function [15] are used:

$$g(|\nabla f|) = \exp -(|\nabla f|/K), \tag{3}$$

$$h(|\nabla f|) = 1 - g(|\nabla f|), \tag{4}$$

where the parameter K balances the smoothing term and data term. Hence, the deformation curve can converge rapidly in the flat field and protect weak borders. Figure 1 shows the output of GGVF applied on a test image for different values of K. As we can observe, the value of K affects the both the gradient distribution and intensity.

In this paper, the magnitude of GGVF is used to detect the seams to be removed. So, fixed K, the proposed algorithm computes GGVF and its normalisation from the input image I that was previously converted from RGB to grey scale. The seams are built starting from the top of the image and following the direction of the normalisation of GGVF, in order to preserve edges and propagates their contributions in the neighbouring pixels, by creating a repulsive field. A cost c_t is associated to each seam s_t by the following equation:

$$c_t = \sum_{(i,j) \in s_t} |GGVF(i,j)|. \tag{5}$$

The seam with the lower cost is hence removed from the image at each iteration. The GGVF map is then updated and a new iteration of the seam removal algorithm is performed for each seam to be removed. Such heuristic is partially inspired by the work in [2].

To drive the selection of seam to be removed and to maintain the strong edges of the images and propagates their contributions also in their neighbouring, the proposed method exploits the properties of the GGVF field without considering all the possible paths, as GVF approach present in [2]. GGVF comprises two weighting functions that are dependent on the gradient of the edge map, this guarantees the dynamic change of the field in each image region.

3   Results

In the experimental evaluation, we compared the proposed method with respect to the GVF scheme paired with seam carving approach [2] and only seam carving technique [1] on a dataset used in [2] and [4] which is composed by 1000 images, including several scenes and objects which appear in multiple instances and in different locations of the image. For each image I, the dataset provides the ground-truth map which denotes the pixels of the areas containing the main salient objects (i.e., the parts of the image that we want to preserve after the

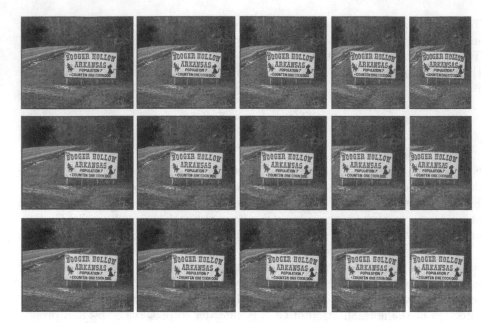

Fig. 2. Example of image reduction with resizing percentage from 10% to 50% with seam carving (1th row), GVF (2th row) and GGVF with $K = 0.75$ (3th row).

resizing). In our experiments, we evaluated the GGVF algorithm with several values of K, namely $0.001, 0.05, 0.75, 1, 1.25$ whereas the parameter μ of GVF is set to 0.1 as in [2]. The three retargeting approaches have been tested at varying the percentage of resizing from 10% to 50%. Figure 2 shows the progressive resizing of a sample image.

Figures 3 and 4 report some image examples obtained by resizing images with a scale factor of 30% and 50%, respectively, with respect the original resolution of the processed image. The three algorithms have different behaviours. In particular, comparing the seems generated by the proposed algorithm (3th column) and the ones generated by the GVF scheme (5th column) or by the seam carving approach (7th column), is possible to observe that the methods of the state of the art remove information from the object introducing deformations and distortions on the image, whereas the GGVF approach preserves the visual content of the scene by maintaining both size of the objects and the details related the visual stimuli of textures and edges.

To evaluate the performance of our algorithm for different values of K, the corresponding binary mask is used. Indeed, the same seams of the input image are removed from each mask and then the remaining pixels are counted. This number is compared with GVF results. More specifically, let N be the total number of images in the dataset (i.e., $N = 1000$). Let $T = \{x : n^{GGVF} \geq n^{GVF}\}$ be the set of images such that the number of pixels of the binary mask removed with our approach n^{GGVF} is greater or equal to the number of pixels removed

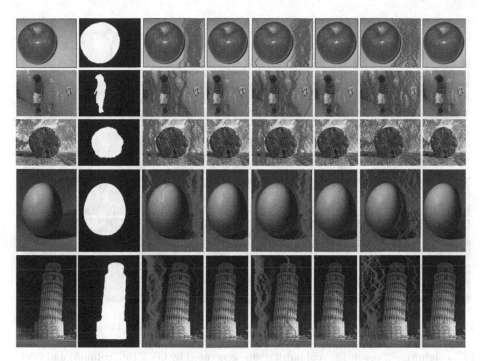

Fig. 3. Examples of image resizing at 70% of the original width. Original image (1th column), binary mask (2th column), seams generated by our approach with $K = 1$ (3th column), our result (4th column), seams generated by GVF (5th column), GVF result (6th column), seams generated by seam carving (7th column) and its result (8th column).

with approach based on GVF n^{GVF}. Based on these variables, the following evaluation score is computed:

$$Score_1 = \frac{|T|}{N} \tag{6}$$

where $|T|$ is the cardinality of set T, and N is the total number of images in the dataset.

Figures 7 and 8 show the obtained scores for each evaluation setting and the trend of this evaluation score by varying the value of K. The achieved results suggest that the best values of K are 0.75 and 1 if the percentages of resizing are in the range [10%–30%], whereas for larger scale factor (40% or 50%), the best values of parameter K are 0.05 and 0.001, respectively. Therefore, it seems that there is an inversely proportional relationship between K and the percentage of resizing.

Furthermore, for each i-th image, we considered the number of pixels in its binary mask p_i^{bm} and the number of successfully preserved pixels after the application of the Seam Carving (SC), the GVF and the GGVF methods, denoted as n_i^{SC}, n_i^{GVF} and n_i^{GGVF} respectively. The quality of a resized image is evaluated

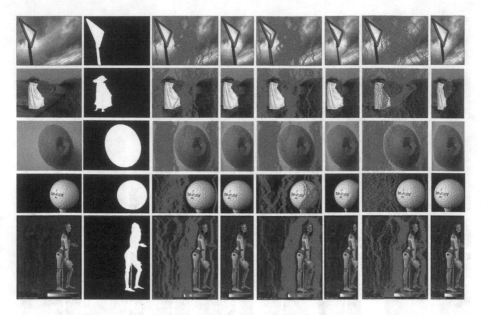

Fig. 4. Examples of image resizing at 50% of the original width. Original image (1th column), binary mask (2th column), seams generated by our approach with $K = 0.05$ (3th column), our result (4th column), seams generated by GVF (5th column) and GVF result (6th column), seams generated by seam carving (7th column) and its result (8th column).

by considering the ratio between n_i^m and p_i^{bm}:

$$q_i^m = \frac{n_i^m}{p_i^{bm}} \tag{7}$$

where $m \in \{SC, GVF, GGVF\}$ is the resizing method applied to the input image. Based on these definitions, the following evaluation score is computed:

$$Score_2 = \frac{1}{N} \sum_{i=1}^{|T|} q_i^m \tag{8}$$

Figure 9 shows the achieved experimental results in terms of average $Score_2$, by varying the resizing factor and the value of K. Figure 10 shows how the value of K affects the performances, depending on the resizing factor. The achieved results suggest that there is a relationship between K and the percentage of resizing. However, when the resizing factor is set to extreme values, the performances start to decrease after a certain value of K (see Fig. 10).

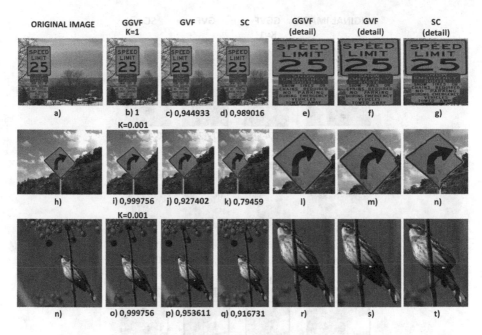

Fig. 5. Examples of image resizing at 40% of the original width. The original images are shown in the first column. The second column reports the resizing results obtained by applying GGVF and the related cost (i.e., Eq. 7). The third column shows the results obtained by GVF, whereas the fourth column reports the seam carving results. The last three columns show some details of the outputs obtained by GGVF, GVF and seam carving.

Figure 5 shows three examples with a scale factor of 40%. The 2th and 4th columns show the results obtained by GGVF (with the best choice for K), by GVF and by Seam Carving respectively. The values reported under each image are the cost obtained with Eq. 7. The 5th column highlights how our approach better preserves the main object of the input image with respect to other algorithms (6th and 7th column). Although the proposed method achieves interesting performances compared to the state of the art approaches, some challenging cases have been found, as shown in the Fig. 6. As we can observe, GGVF, GVF and seam carving methods do not preserve the main object introducing distortions with respect to the original image. However, the performances in terms of cost (i.e., Eq. 7) show that the proposed approach still achieves better performances compared to GVF.

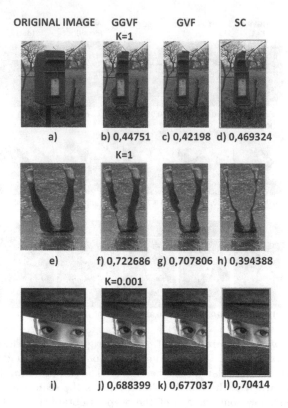

Fig. 6. Challenging cases by reducing image by 30%. The first column shows the original images, the second, third and fourth columns show the results obtained by applying the GGVF, GVF and seam carving approaches respectively. Each output image reports the results in terms of cost (i.e., Eq. 7). The best results are highlighted in green. (Color figure online)

	0.001	0.05	0.75	1	1.25
10%	74.1%	76.6%	79.7%	79.1%	79.3%
20%	67.7%	68.3%	70.3%	71.1%	70.2%
30%	60.6%	61.5%	62.3%	63.3%	61.7%
40%	57.7%	59.9%	56.1%	55.1%	53.9%
50%	52.6%	50.3%	41.9%	40.5%	39.8%

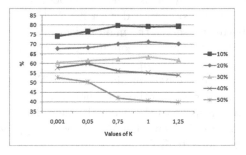

Fig. 7. Experimental results in terms of $Score_1$ (i.e., Eq. 6).

Fig. 8. Average GGVF performances in terms of $Score_1$ computed over 1000 images at varying of percentage of resizing and K.

	0.001	0.05	0.75	1	1.25
10%	72.7%	74.7%	78.2%	77.7%	77.9%
20%	65.!%	65.6%	67.7%	68.2%	67.6%
30%	56.4%	56.8%	57.6%	58.2%	57.1%
40%	50.3%	51.4%	48.4%	47.7%	46.7%
50%	44.1%	43.9%	38.9%	37.7%	37.7%

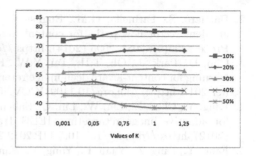

Fig. 9. $Score_2$ obtained with Eq. 8.

Fig. 10. Average $Score_2$ values achieved by the GGVF approach at varying of the resizing faction and the value of K.

4   Conclusions

This paper addresses the problem of content-aware image resizing. The proposed work evaluates the generalised version of the Gradient Vector Flow approach (i.e., GGVF) which allows the adaptation of the algorithm parameters. Indeed, the experiments shown that with a proper parametrization, the GVF and seam carving approaches are outperformed by its generalised version. According to our hypothesis, the GGVF can be controlled by varying the parameter K. Moreover, this parameter can be properly tuned based on the percentage of resizing. Our experiments demonstrated that a good choice of K can be a critical factor, and that there is a relationship between the percentage of resizing and the optimal K value. Moreover, our experiments considered extreme percentage values of resizing, with the aim to observe the behaviour of such relationship for extreme values. The results revealed that, for reasonable resizing factors (i.e., from 10% to 30%), the performances increase by augmenting the value of K. At a certain point, augmenting the value of K does not provide substantial improvements. However, when the resizing factor is set to extreme values (i.e., 40% to 50%), the algorithm is forced to remove a large amount of seams. As result, the algorithm removes some pixels related to the objects that we want to preserve.

In this paper, the best K has been obtained empirically for each considered percentage of resizing. In the future works, methods to automatically determine the best K will be investigated. Future experiments will include horizontal paths in the resizing process, in order to further improve the method performances. Furthermore, the exploitation of saliency maps in the algorithm will be also evaluated.

References

1. Avidan, S., Shamir, A.: Seam carving for content-aware image resizing. ACM Trans. Graph. **26**(3), 10 (2007)

2. Battiato, S., Farinella, G.M., Puglisi, G., Ravi, D.: Saliency-based selection of gradient vector flow paths for content aware image resizing. IEEE Trans. Image Process. **23**(5), 2081–2095 (2014). https://doi.org/10.1109/TIP.2014.2312649
3. Cho, D., Park, J., Oh, T.H., Tai, Y.W., Kweon, I.: Weakly- and self-supervised learning for content-aware deep image retargeting. In: ICCV, pp. 4568–4577, October 2017. https://doi.org/10.1109/ICCV.2017.488
4. Fang, Y., Chen, Z., Lin, W., Lin, C.: Saliency detection in the compressed domain for adaptive image retargeting. IEEE Trans. Image Process. **21**(9), 3888–3901 (2012). https://doi.org/10.1109/TIP.2012.2199126
5. Fang, Y., Fang, Z., Yuan, F., Yang, Y., Yang, S., Xiong, N.N.: Optimized multioperator image retargeting based on perceptual similarity measure. IEEE Trans. Syst. Man Cybern. Syst. **47**(11), 2956–2966 (2017). https://doi.org/10.1109/TSMC.2016.2557225
6. Hsu, C., Lin, C., Fang, Y., Lin, W.: Objective quality assessment for image retargeting based on perceptual geometric distortion and information loss. IEEE J. Sel. Top. Sig. Process. **8**(3), 377–389 (2014). https://doi.org/10.1109/JSTSP.2014.2311884
7. Park, H.K., Chung, M.J.: External force of snake: virtual electric field. Electron. Lett. **38**, 1500–1502 (2002). https://doi.org/10.1049/el:20021037
8. Liang, Y., Liu, Y.J., Gutierrez, D.: Objective quality prediction of image retargeting algorithms. IEEE Trans. Vis. Comput. Graph. **23**(2), 1099–1110 (2016)
9. Liu, C., Yuen, J., Torralba, A.: SIFT Flow: dense correspondence across scenes and its applications. IEEE Trans. Pattern Anal. Mach. Intell. **33**(5), 978–994 (2011). https://doi.org/10.1109/TPAMI.2010.147
10. Liu, Y., Luo, X., Xuan, Y., Chen, W., Fu, X.: Image retargeting quality assessment. Comput. Graph. Forum **30**(2), 583–592 (2011)
11. Panozzo, D., Weber, O., Sorkine, O.: Robust image retargeting via axis-aligned deformation. Comput. Graph. Forum **31**(2), 229–236 (2012)
12. Rubinstein, M., Gutierrez, D., Sorkine, O., Shamir, A.: A comparative study of image retargeting. ACM Trans. Graph. **29**(6), 160 (2010)
13. Rubinstein, M., Shamir, A., Avidan, S.: Multi-operator media retargeting. ACM Trans. Graph. **28**(3), 1–11 (2009). (Proceedings SIGGRAPH 2009)
14. Xu, C., Prince, J.: Snakes, shapes, and gradient vector flow. IEEE Trans. Image Process. **7**, 359–369 (1998). https://doi.org/10.1109/83.661186
15. Xu, C., Prince, J.: Generalized gradient vector flow external forces for active contours. Sig. Process. **71**, 131–139 (2000). https://doi.org/10.1016/S0165-1684(98)00140-6
16. Zhou, S., Lu, Y., Li, N., Wang, Y.: Extension of the virtual electric field model using bilateral-like filter for active contours. Sig. Image Video Process. (2019). https://doi.org/10.1007/s11760-019-01456-x
17. Zhou, Y., Zhang, L., Zhang, C., Li, P., Li, X.: Perceptually aware image retargeting for mobile devices. IEEE Trans. Image Process. **27**(5), 2301–2313 (2018). https://doi.org/10.1109/TIP.2017.2779272
18. Zhu, S., Gao, R.: A novel generalized gradient vector flow snake model using minimal surface and component-normalized method for medical image segmentation. Biomed. Sig. Process. Control **26**, 1–10 (2016). https://doi.org/10.1016/j.bspc.2015.12.004
19. Zhu, S., Zhou, Q., Gao, R.: A novel snake model using new multi-step decision model for complex image segmentation. Comput. Electr. Eng. **51**(C), 58–73 (2016). https://doi.org/10.1016/j.compeleceng.2016.02.023

A Block-Based Union-Find Algorithm
to Label Connected Components
on GPUs

Stefano Allegretti, Federico Bolelli($\boxtimes$), Michele Cancilla, and Costantino Grana

Dipartimento di Ingegneria "Enzo Ferrari",
Università degli Studi di Modena e Reggio Emilia,
Via Vivarelli 10, 41125 Modena, MO, Italy
{stefano.allegretti,federico.bolelli,
michele.cancilla,costantino.grana}@unimore.it

Abstract. In this paper, we introduce a novel GPU-based Connected Components Labeling algorithm: the Block-based Union Find. The proposed strategy significantly improves an existing GPU algorithm, taking advantage of a block-based approach. Experimental results on real cases and synthetically generated datasets demonstrate the superiority of the new proposal with respect to state-of-the-art.

Keywords: Connected Components Labeling · Image processing · GPU · CUDA

1 Introduction

In the last decades, the maturity of Graphic Processing Units (GPUs) encouraged the development of algorithms specifically designed to work in a data-parallel environment [4]. Indeed, applications characterized by irregular control flow and irregular memory access patterns usually break the parallel execution model when ported on GPU: they must be redesigned to take advantage of the GPU architecture [12]. Connected Components Labeling (CCL), an essential image processing algorithm that extracts objects inside binary images, is such a kind of algorithm. The labeling procedure transforms an input binary image into a symbolic one in which all pixels belonging to a connected component are given the same label. Even though labeling has an intrinsically sequential nature [7,19,24], many algorithms exploiting the parallelism of both CPUs and GPUs have been recently proposed [3,11,13,27,38].

CCL, originally introduced by Rosenfeld and Pfaltz in 1966 [35], has an exact solution, and the algorithms are mainly characterized by their execution time. Since labeling represents the base step of many image processing applications [14, 15,17,18,28,33,34], it is required to be as fast as possible. Unfortunately, CCL is not as easy to parallelize as other image processing tasks: CPU and GPU algorithms usually have comparable performance [32]. However, efficient data-parallel

© Springer Nature Switzerland AG 2019
E. Ricci et al. (Eds.): ICIAP 2019, LNCS 11752, pp. 271–281, 2019.
https://doi.org/10.1007/978-3-030-30645-8_25

algorithms are valuable for applications that totally run on GPU, allowing to remove the need for data transfers between CPU and GPU memory.

In this paper, we introduce a new 8-connectivity GPU-based connected components labeling algorithm, which improves previously proposed solutions by taking advantage of the 2 × 2 block-based approach originally presented in [21] for sequential algorithms. The proposed method reduces the amount of memory accesses, significantly improving state-of-the-art performance in terms of execution time over both real case and synthetically generated datasets. The source code of our proposal is available in [36].

The rest of this paper is organized as follows. In Sect. 2, the main contributions on parallel CCL are resumed. Section 3 analyzes the Union Find algorithm, which represents the basis of our work, then Sect. 4 details our proposal. Section 5 demonstrates the effectiveness of our approach in comparison with other state-of-the-art methods, providing an exhaustive evaluation. Finally, conclusions are drawn in Sect. 6.

2   Related Work

The first work on GPU CCL dates back in 2010, when Hawick *et al.* [22] proposed Label Equivalence (LE). LE is an iterative algorithm that propagates the minimum label through every connected component. The process is sped up by alternating the propagation phase with label equivalences resolution. In 2011, Kalentev *et al.* [26] proposed an optimization of Label Equivalence, which we will call OLE, obtained by removing overabundant operations and memory allocations. Komura Equivalence (KE) [27] was also created as an improvement over Label Equivalence, which removes the need for multiple iterations. The original algorithm employs 4-connectivity, and it has been extended to 8-connectivity in [2]. Zavalishin *et al.* [38] further improved OLE, applying a block-based strategy to reduce the number of temporary labels, and memory accesses. The result is known as Block Equivalence (BE). The benefit introduced by blocks was partially lessened by an increased allocation time, caused by the need for additional data structures to record block labels and connectivity information. Union Find (UF), by Oliveira and Lotufo [31], is a parallel algorithm that employs the *Union-*

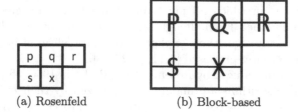

(a) Rosenfeld   (b) Block-based

Fig. 1. Neighborhood masks used by the algorithms described in the paper. UF employs the mask in (a), where the central pixel is x. The block-based mask (b) is used by BUF instead. Central block is X.

Find data structure, commonly used to solve labels equivalences by sequential algorithms [10, 21, 37].

3 Preliminaries

The proposal of this paper is an optimization of the Union Find algorithm (UF), by Oliveira and Lotufo, which is briefly introduced in this section. UF performs a partitioning of the output image L by creating subsets of connected pixels, and merging together those belonging to the same connected component. To perform this task, it takes advantage of the *Union-Find* paradigm, which represents subsets as directed rooted trees and provides convenient functions to deal with them: *Find* that returns the root of a tree and *Union* that joins together two different trees.

Trees are coded in the output image L, using temporary labels: for a pixel p, with raster index id_p, $L[id_p] = id_f$ is the father

Algorithm 1. Possible implementation of *Union-Find*. L is the *Union-Find* array, a and b are both array indexes and pixel identifiers.

```
1: function FIND(L, a)
2:     while L[a] ≠ a do
3:         a ← L[a]
4:     return a

5: procedure UNION(L, a, b)
6:     a ← Find(L, a)
7:     b ← Find(L, b)
8:     if a < b then
9:         L[b] ← a
10:    else if b < a then
11:        L[a] ← b
```

node of p. A possible implementation of the *Union-Find* functions is reported in Algorithm 1. A description follows:

- *Find(L, a)* consists of traversing the tree to which a belongs, starting from a up to the root node.
- *Union(L, a, b)* first calls *Find* twice to get the roots of the trees containing a and b, and then sets the smaller root as the father of the other one, thus joining the two trees into a single one. The procedure used in the source code is slightly more complicated, to avoid race hazards in a parallel environment.

An example of execution of the whole algorithm is depicted in Fig. 2. The algorithm consists of three kernels: *Initialization*, *Merge* and *Compression*. During *Initialization*, single-node trees are coded in the output image L, by assigning each foreground pixel its own raster index. All background pixels are set to 0.

The aim of the *Merge* kernel is to build a single tree for each connected component. To achieve this goal, each thread working on a foreground pixel x joins the tree of x to those of its foreground neighbors, by means of *Union* procedures. Since *Union* is symmetric, checking the whole neighborhood is not necessary. Instead, only half of it is considered, identified by the mask depicted in Fig. 1a. The effects of *Merge* on *Union-Find* trees are shown in Fig. 2c. In this example, the thread operating on pixel 15 performs a *Union* between 15 and 1, and then another *Union* between 15 and 5.

In the *Compression* kernel, every *Union-Find* tree is flattened, by linking every node directly to the root. This process ends the connected components

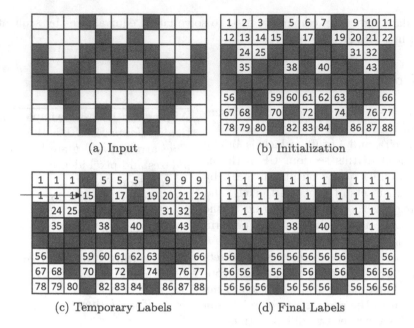

(a) Input

(b) Initialization

(c) Temporary Labels

(d) Final Labels

Fig. 2. Example of Union Find execution. (b) is the expected labels image after *Initialization*. (c) is a temporary result of *Merge* kernel, under the assumption that threads run in raster scan order, and the execution reached thread 15. (d) is the final labels image after the execution of the *Compression* kernel.

labeling task, because every pixel of the same connected component is given the same value.

4   Proposed Algorithm

Grana *et al.* noticed in [21] that, in the case of a two-dimensional image and 8-connectivity, all foreground pixels within 2×2 blocks always share the same label. Consequently, they designed a CCL algorithm that uses block labels instead of pixel labels throughout the process, to greatly reduce the total amount of memory accesses and speed up performance consequently.

We propose a new GPU CCL 8-connectivity algorithm, which is an optimized variation of UF obtained through the application of 2 × 2 blocks. Our proposal, named Block-based Union Find (BUF), inherits the base structure of Union Find (Sect. 3). The difference resides in the use of block labels. In fact, every thread works on a 2 × 2 block, which we will refer to as the X block. The algorithm implements the same kernels as UF, plus the additional *FinalLabeling*, which is needed to copy block labels into pixels. Differently from the work by Zavalishin *et al.* [38], we do not allocate memory for block labels. Instead, until the end of the algorithm, we store them directly in the output image: the label assigned to a block is stored in its top-left pixel, whose raster index is also used as the block *id*.

Algorithm 2. Block-based Union Find *Merge* kernel. I and L are input and output images, linearly stored in memory. A padding can be added at the end of rows for alignment purpose, so *step* stores their total size in memory. A thread is identified by $(t_x, t_y) \in \mathcal{N}^2$, with $t_x \in [0, \lceil cols/2 \rceil]$ and $t_y \in [0, \lceil rows/2 \rceil]$.

1: **kernel** MERGE($I, step_I, L, step_L$)
2:      $x_I \leftarrow 2 \times t_y \times step_I + t_x \times 2$
3:      $x_L \leftarrow 2 \times t_y \times step_L + t_x \times 2$

4:      $\mathcal{BS} \leftarrow 0$
5:      **if** $I[x_I] = 1$ **then** $\mathcal{BS} \mathrel{|}= $ 0x777
6:      **if** $I[x_I + 1] = 1$ **then** $\mathcal{BS} \mathrel{|}= $ (0x777 << 1)
7:      **if** $I[x_I + step_I] = 1$ **then** $\mathcal{BS} \mathrel{|}= $ (0x777 << 4)

8:      **if** $\mathcal{BS} > 0$ **then**
9:          **if** HasBit($\mathcal{BS}, 0$) **and** $I[x_I - step_I - 1]$ **then**
10:             Union($L, x_L, x_L - 2 \times step_L - 2$)

11:          **if** (HasBit($\mathcal{BS}, 1$) **and** $I[x_I - step_I]$) **or**
12:          (HasBit($\mathcal{BS}, 2$) **and** $I[x_I - step_I + 1]$) **then**
13:             Union($L, x_L, x_L - 2 \times step_L$)

14:          **if** HasBit($\mathcal{BS}, 3$) **and** $I[x_I - step_I + 2]$ **then**
15:             Union($L, x_L, x_L - 2 \times step_L + 2$)

16:          **if** (HasBit($\mathcal{BS}, 4$) **and** $I[x_I - 1]$) **or**
17:          (HasBit($\mathcal{BS}, 8$) **and** $I[x_I + step_I - 1]$) **then**
18:             Union($L, x_L, x_L - 2$)

The first kernel of the algorithm, *Initialization*, creates the starting *Union-Find* trees. At the beginning, one separate tree is built for each block X, by performing $L[id_X] \leftarrow id_X$. Then, the *Merge* kernel joins the trees of connected blocks, as illustrated in Algorithm 2. The block neighborhood mask, which contains half the neighborhood, is depicted in Fig. 1b. Since blocks connections are determined by lower level pixel connections, for every neighbor block of the mask we must check whether some of its pixels are connected to some internal pixels of block X. A naive approach, which just checks each adjacent block one by one, would require multiple readings of internal pixels. So, it is better to find a more efficient way. We adopted a strategy based on the work by Zavalishin *et al.* [38], which involves a preliminary scan of pixels inside the block: for each foreground one, its external neighbors are added to a set of pixels that will be checked subsequently. The aforementioned set of pixels is represented as a bitset that contains a bit for each pixel in a 4×4 square that encloses the X block, as reported in Fig. 4. Initially, every bit is set to 0. When an internal pixel a is read and recognized as foreground, each external pixel e neighbor to a must have its corresponding bit set to 1. To conveniently achieve this goal, the whole 3×3 square centered on a is set accordingly, by means of a bitmask (Fig. 4b). Bitmask 0x777 is required to set neighbors of the top-left pixel inside block X. The bitmasks of other pixels can be obtained in the following way: if the pixel is in the right column of the block, 0x777 is shifted one bit left. If the pixel is

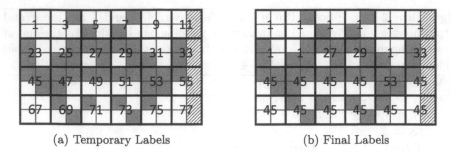

(a) Temporary Labels   (b) Final Labels

Fig. 3. Example of Block-based Union Find execution. (a) are the labels after *Initialization*. Every block has its own label, equal to the raster index of its top-left pixel. (b) are final block labels, after *Compression*. Blocks in the same connected component shares the same label, and the only remaining thing to do is to copy block labels into internal foreground pixels.

in the bottom row, the bitmask is shifted four bits left. The bottom-right pixel of X is never responsible for connections between blocks inside the mask, so it is never used. To find out which neighbor blocks are connected to X, the *Merge* kernel must then check which pixels of the bitset are set, and read their values. A *Union* is performed between X and connected blocks, as it happens for single pixels in UF.

The BUF *Compression* kernel then performs the flattening of *Union-Find* trees, by linking each block directly to the result of the *Find*. The effects of *Merge* and *Compression* on an input image are depicted in Fig. 3. Eventually, *FinalLabeling* copies the label of each block into its internal foreground pixels, thus producing the final output.

5   Comparative Evaluation

The proposed strategy is evaluated by comparing its performance with state-of-the-art algorithms. Experimental results reported and discussed in this Section are obtained running the YACCLAB benchmark [10,20] on an Intel Core i7-4770 CPU (with 4×32 KB L1 cache, 4×256 KB L2 cache, and 8 MB of L3

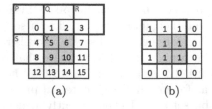

(a)   (b)

Fig. 4. (a) shows how pixels in a 4×4 square centered on the X block are numerated. These numbers correspond to the pixel position in the associated bitset. Bits 0, 1, 2, 3, 4, and 8 are used to record whether the corresponding pixel is to be checked for determining blocks connectivity or not. The other bits are stored for convenience. (b) depicts the 3×3 bitmask (`0x777`) corresponding to the neighbors of the top-left internal pixel.

Table 1. Average run-time results in ms obtained under Windows (64 bit) OS with MSVC 19.15.26730 and NVCC V10.0.130 compilers using a Quadro K2200 NVIDIA GPU. The bold values represent the best performing CCL algorithm on a given dataset. Our proposals are identified with *.

	3DPeS	*Fingerprints*	*Medical*	*MIRflickr*	*Tobacco800*	*XDOCS*
BUF*	**0.512**	**0.441**	**1.313**	**0.495**	**3.268**	**12.088**
BE [38]	1.517	1.164	2.730	1.165	5.966	20.278
UF [31]	0.594	0.529	2.040	0.659	4.304	17.316
OLE [26]	1.211	1.128	3.013	1.281	8.173	35.242
KE [2]	0.568	0.481	1.622	0.526	3.978	15.432

cache), and using a Quadro K2200 NVIDIA GPU with Maxwell architecture, 640 CUDA cores and 4 GB of memory. All the compared algorithms have been implemented using CUDA 10.0 and compiled for x64 architectures, employing MSVC 19.15.26730 and NVCC V10.0.130 compilers with optimizations enabled. The benchmark provides a set of datasets covering real case scenarios for CCL, among which we selected the most significant ones: *MIRflickr* [25], *Medical* [16], *Tobacco800* [1,29], *XDOCS* [6,8,9], *Fingerprints* [30], and *3DPeS* [5]. A complete description of these datasets can be found in [10]. The first experiment carried out is the comparison between algorithms in terms of average execution time over real datasets (Table 1). Our proposal outperforms state-of-the-art on all test collections. The speed-up between BUF and KE, the best among competitors, varies from 1.1 (*MIRflickr*) to 1.3 (*XDOCS*).

To better investigate the algorithms behavior, Fig. 5 is also reported, where bar charts report separately the time needed for allocating data structures and the time required by the labeling procedure. The allocation time is the same for each strategy, but for BE. Indeed, all the algorithms must only allocate memory for the output image. BE always requires a higher allocation time, since it relies on additional matrices to store equivalences between blocks and their labels. Obviously, this additional time is data dependent. We can notice that OLE always has the highest execution time. The main drawback of the algorithm is its iterative nature, which is inherited by its block-based variation, BE. In fact, the benefits introduced by blocks allow BE to only have comparable performance to UF, which employs a direct, non iterative approach. Moreover, BE is partially hindered by its increased allocation time.

With our approach, we greatly improve the performance of UF. In fact, the use of block labels allows to divide by four the initial number of *Union-Find* trees. Consequently, the amount of *Union* operations required to merge trees in the same connected component drastically decreases, and the lessened average depth of trees allows to simplify *Find* calls. Besides, BUF, while benefiting from the advantages of blocks, avoids the main flaw of BE, namely the allocation of additional memory.

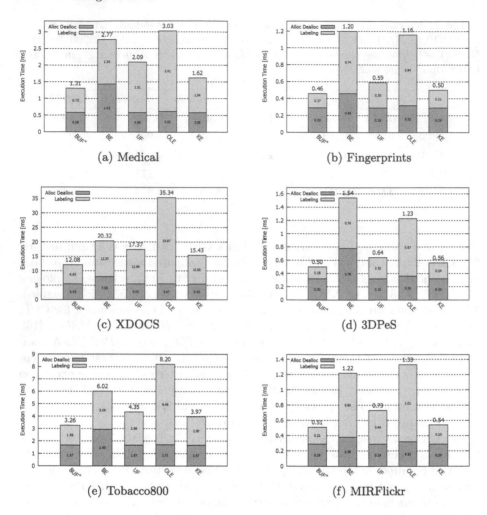

Fig. 5. Average run-time results with steps in ms. Lower is better.

Following a common approach in literature [21, 23, 37], additional tests have been performed on images with increasing foreground density, in order to highlight strengths and weaknesses of the algorithms (Fig. 6). OLE has an increasing trend in the execution time up to 40% of foreground density, and then a decreasing one after this value. Indeed, the number of iterations required by the labeling procedure reaches the highest value when foreground density is about 40%. BE has a similar behavior, albeit with better performance. The execution time of UF grows with foreground density. The reason is that each pixel thread has to perform one *Union* for each connected neighbor, and the number of those pixels depends on image density. BUF has a similar trend to UF, since it inherits its basic behavior. The adoption of a block-based approach, anyway, allows to decrease the amount of operations, drastically reducing the total execution time.

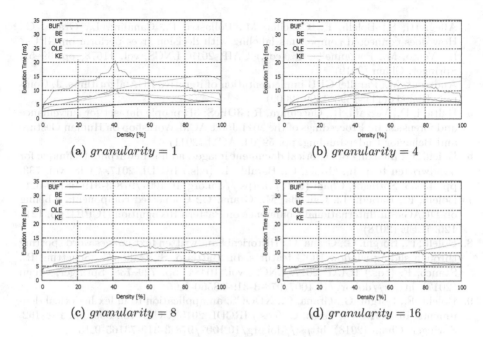

Fig. 6. Granularity results in ms on images at various densities. Lower is better.

At 80% density and above, the high number of *Union* operations makes BUF slower than BE. Anyway, such density values are rather uncommon in real cases.

6   Conclusion

In this paper, the problem of GPU-based Connected Components Labeling in binary images has been addressed. A new algorithm has been proposed, Block-based Union Find, which was obtained by combining an existing strategy with a block-based approach. This allows to considerably lessen the number of memory accesses and consequently reduce execution time. Experimental tests on a wide selection of real case datasets, covering most of the fields where CCL is commonly used, confirm that our proposal represents the state-of-the-art for GPU-based Connected Components Labeling.

References

1. Agam, G., Argamon, S., Frieder, O., Grossman, D., Lewis, D.: The complex document image processing (CDIP) test collection project. Illinois Institute of Technology (2006)
2. Allegretti, S., Bolelli, F., Cancilla, M., Grana, C.: Optimizing GPU-based connected components labeling algorithms. In: Third IEEE International Conference on Image Processing, Applications and Systems (IPAS), pp. 175–180. IEEE (2018)

3. Allegretti, S., Bolelli, F., Cancilla, M., Pollastri, F., Canalini, L., Grana, C.: How does connected components labeling with decision trees perform on GPUs? In: Vento, M., Percannella, G. (eds.) CAIP 2019. LNCS, vol. 11678, pp. 39–51. Springer, Cham (2019)
4. Andrecut, M.: Parallel GPU implementation of iterative PCA algorithms. J. Comput. Biol. **16**(11), 1593–1599 (2009)
5. Baltieri, D., Vezzani, R., Cucchiara, R.: 3DPeS: 3D people dataset for surveillance and forensics. In: Proceedings of the 2011 Joint ACM Workshop on Human Gesture and Behavior Understanding, pp. 59–64. ACM (2011)
6. Bolelli, F.: Indexing of historical document images: ad hoc dewarping technique for handwritten text. In: Grana, C., Baraldi, L. (eds.) IRCDL 2017. CCIS, vol. 733, pp. 45–55. Springer, Cham (2017). https://doi.org/10.1007/978-3-319-68130-6_4
7. Bolelli, F., Baraldi, L., Cancilla, M., Grana, C.: Connected components labeling on DRAGs. In: International Conference on Pattern Recognition (ICPR), pp. 121–126. IEEE (2018)
8. Bolelli, F., Borghi, G., Grana, C.: Historical handwritten text images word spotting through sliding window HOG features. In: Battiato, S., Gallo, G., Schettini, R., Stanco, F. (eds.) ICIAP 2017. LNCS, vol. 10484, pp. 729–738. Springer, Cham (2017). https://doi.org/10.1007/978-3-319-68560-1_65
9. Bolelli, F., Borghi, G., Grana, C.: XDOCS: an application to index historical documents. In: Serra, G., Tasso, C. (eds.) IRCDL 2018. CCIS, vol. 806, pp. 151–162. Springer, Cham (2018). https://doi.org/10.1007/978-3-319-73165-0_15
10. Bolelli, F., Cancilla, M., Baraldi, L., Grana, C.: Toward reliable experiments on the performance of connected components labeling algorithms. J. Real-Time Image Process. 1–16 (2018). https://doi.org/10.1007/s11554-018-0756-1
11. Bolelli, F., Cancilla, M., Grana, C.: Two more strategies to speed up connected components labeling algorithms. In: Battiato, S., Gallo, G., Schettini, R., Stanco, F. (eds.) ICIAP 2017. LNCS, vol. 10485, pp. 48–58. Springer, Cham (2017). https://doi.org/10.1007/978-3-319-68548-9_5
12. Brunie, N., Collange, S., Diamos, G.: Simultaneous branch and warp interweaving for sustained GPU performance. In: 39th Annual International Symposium on Computer Architecture (ISCA), pp. 49–60 (2012)
13. Cabaret, L., Lacassagne, L., Etiemble, D.: Distanceless label propagation: an efficient direct connected component labeling algorithm for GPUs. In: Seventh International Conference on Image Processing Theory, Tools and Applications (IPTA), pp. 1–6. IEEE (2017)
14. Canalini, L., Pollastri, F., Bolelli, F., Cancilla, M., Allegretti, S., Grana, C.: Skin lesion segmentation ensemble with diverse training strategies. In: Vento, M., Percannella, G. (eds.) CAIP 2019. LNCS, vol. 11678, pp. 89–101. Springer, Cham (2019)
15. Cucchiara, R., Grana, C., Prati, A., Vezzani, R.: Computer vision techniques for PDA accessibility of in-house video surveillance. In: First ACM SIGMM International Workshop on Video Surveillance, pp. 87–97. ACM (2003)
16. Dong, F., Irshad, H., Oh, E.Y., et al.: Computational pathology to discriminate benign from malignant intraductal proliferations of the breast. PLoS ONE **9**(12), e114885 (2014)
17. Dubois, A., Charpillet, F.: Tracking mobile objects with several kinects using HMMs and component labelling. In: Workshop Assistance and Service Robotics in a Human Environment, International Conference on Intelligent Robots and Systems, pp. 7–13 (2012)
18. Eklund, A., Dufort, P., Villani, M., LaConte, S.: BROCCOLI: software for fast fMRI analysis on many-core CPUs and GPUs. Front. Neuroinformatics **8**, 24 (2014)

19. Grana, C., Baraldi, L., Bolelli, F.: Optimized connected components labeling with pixel prediction. In: Blanc-Talon, J., Distante, C., Philips, W., Popescu, D., Scheunders, P. (eds.) ACIVS 2016. LNCS, vol. 10016, pp. 431–440. Springer, Cham (2016). https://doi.org/10.1007/978-3-319-48680-2_38

20. Grana, C., Bolelli, F., Baraldi, L., Vezzani, R.: YACCLAB - yet another connected components labeling benchmark. In: 23rd International Conference on Pattern Recognition (ICPR), pp. 3109–3114. IEEE (2016)

21. Grana, C., Borghesani, D., Cucchiara, R.: Optimized block-based connected components labeling with decision trees. IEEE Trans. Image Process. 19(6), 1596–1609 (2010)

22. Hawick, K.A., Leist, A., Playne, D.P.: Parallel graph component labelling with GPUs and CUDA. Parallel Comput. 36(12), 655–678 (2010)

23. He, L., Chao, Y., Suzuki, K.: A linear-time two-scan labeling algorithm. In: International Conference on Image Processing, vol. 5, pp. 241–244 (2007)

24. He, L., Zhao, X., Chao, Y., Suzuki, K.: Configuration-transition-based connected-component labeling. IEEE Trans. Image Process. 23(2), 943–951 (2014)

25. Huiskes, M.J., Lew, M.S.: The MIR flickr retrieval evaluation. In: Proceedings of the 2008 ACM International Conference on Multimedia Information Retrieval, MIR 2008. ACM, New York (2008)

26. Kalentev, O., Rai, A., Kemnitz, S., Schneider, R.: Connected component labeling on a 2D grid using CUDA. J. Parallel Distrib. Comput. 71(4), 615–620 (2011)

27. Komura, Y.: GPU-based cluster-labeling algorithm without the use of conventional iteration: application to the Swendsen-Wang multi-cluster spin flip algorithm. Comput. Phys. Commun. 194, 54–58 (2015)

28. Lelore, T., Bouchara, F.: FAIR: a fast algorithm for document image restoration. IEEE Trans. Pattern Anal. Mach. Intell. 35(8), 2039–2048 (2013)

29. Lewis, D., Agam, G., Argamon, S., Frieder, O., Grossman, D., Heard, J.: Building a test collection for complex document information processing. In: Proceedings of the 29th Annual International ACM SIGIR Conference, pp. 665–666 (2006)

30. Maltoni, D., Maio, D., Jain, A.K., Prabhakar, S.: Handbook of Fingerprint Recognition. Springer, London (2009). https://doi.org/10.1007/978-1-84882-254-2

31. Oliveira, V.M., Lotufo, R.A.: A study on connected components labeling algorithms using GPUs. In: SIBGRAPI, vol. 3, p. 4 (2010)

32. Playne, D.P., Hawick, K.: A new algorithm for parallel connected-component labelling on GPUs. IEEE Trans. Parallel Distrib. Syst. 29(6), 1217–1230 (2018)

33. Pollastri, F., Bolelli, F., Paredes, R., Grana, C.: Improving skin lesion segmentation with generative adversarial networks. In: 2018 IEEE 31st International Symposium on Computer-Based Medical Systems (CBMS), pp. 442–443. IEEE (2018)

34. Pollastri, F., Bolelli, F., Paredes, R., Grana, C.: Augmenting data with GANs to segment melanoma skin lesions. Multimed. Tools Appl. 1–18 (2019). https://doi.org/10.1007/s11042-019-7717-y

35. Rosenfeld, A., Pfaltz, J.L.: Sequential operations in digital picture processing. J. ACM 13(4), 471–494 (1966)

36. Source code of the proposed strategy. https://github.com/prittt/YACCLAB. Accessed 16 May 2019

37. Wu, K., Otoo, E., Suzuki, K.: Two strategies to speed up connected component labeling algorithms. Technical report, LBNL-59102, Lawrence Berkeley National Laboratory (2005)

38. Zavalishin, S., Safonov, I., Bekhtin, Y., Kurilin, I.: Block equivalence algorithm for labeling 2D and 3D images on GPU. Electron. Imaging 2016(2), 1–7 (2016)

Mask Guided Fusion for Group Activity Recognition in Images

Arif Akar[1]([envelope]) and Nazli Ikizler-Cinbis[2]

[1] Aselsan Inc., 06370 Ankara, Turkey
arifakar@gmail.com
[2] Department of Computer Science, Hacettepe University, 06800 Ankara, Turkey
nazli@cs.hacettepe.edu.tr
http://vision.cs.hacettepe.edu.tr/

Abstract. Recognizing group activities from still images is a challenging problem since images lack motion and temporal information that makes it easier to differentiate foreground from background. Nevertheless, images present rich spatial content that can be effectively leveraged for better feature representation and recognition. In this paper, we propose a two-stream convolutional neural network approach for group activity recognition. Our proposed approach is based on using person segment mask images to guide feature learning process. Our method is capable of inferring group relations without the need of bottom-up approaches and low-level annotations. To this end, we utilize three ways of fusing RGB and person segment mask feature maps. Experimental results demonstrate that person mask guidance provides a complementary learning process by outperforming previous methods with a large margin.

Keywords: Group activity recognition · Multi-stream fusion · Person segments

1 Introduction

Group activity recognition is a challenging task in various ways. It shares similar challenges with human activity recognition problem such as occlusions, background clutter and change of appearance over time. However, recognizing group activities needs a more refined semantic understanding of the group scene, inter-relations between members and their possible appearance features like view points. Although group activity recognition in videos is a considerably active topic of interest for computer vision community, group activity recognition in images is seldomly studied. It should be noted that recent successful methods [10,11,15] for group activity recognition in videos need complex hierarchical designs to explore semantic understanding of interactions with a bottom-up

This work was supported in part by the Scientific and Technological Research Council of Turkey (TUBITAK) Research Program (1001), Project No: 116E102.

E. Ricci et al. (Eds.): ICIAP 2019, LNCS 11752, pp. 282–291, 2019.
https://doi.org/10.1007/978-3-030-30645-8_26

Input Image

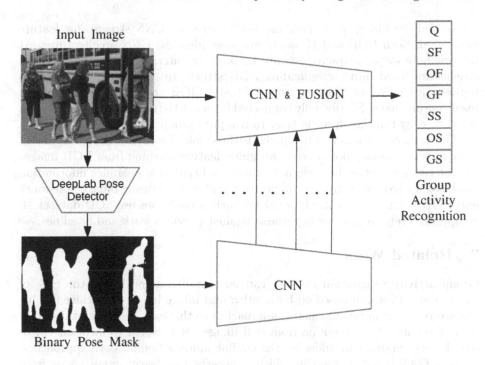

DeepLab Pose Detector

Binary Pose Mask

CNN & FUSION

CNN

Q
SF
OF
GF
SS
OS
GS

Group Activity Recognition

Fig. 1. The main framework of the proposed method.

approach. Although bottom-up approaches are effective to make use of such contextual information; they require intense annotation work and complex design of low level components. This is partly because there is an exponential possibility of interactions between individuals and group activities show high variance in appearance.

In this paper, we tackle with the problem of recognition of group activities in images and we demonstrate an effective and simple method to deal with the aforementioned challenges. Our method improves spatial feature learning that possibly includes rich interaction and orientation features fiercely needed for group activity recognition. We intend to use the guidance of binary pose mask stream onto RGB stream to achieve a better representation of group activities in still images. Group activities can be inferred as a product of the interaction between individuals, their orientation and appearance information. Therefore, we explore ways of utilizing mask information to lead feature representation process by localizing some potentially significant parts of the image. Namely, our goal is to emphasize rich potentials of the image more than the remaining parts to capture valuable information for representing interactions and appearances within a group.

A simple illustration summarizing the proposed method is given in Fig. 1. In our framework, for each input RGB image, a binary pose mask pair is generated using DeepLab [3] semantic image segmentation algorithm. Then, both RGB image and the binary pose mask are fed to separate CNN streams for feature extraction. Both RGB and Mask stream have identical CNN architectures. At intermediate steps, extracted feature maps from intermediate layers of Mask stream are fused into corresponding RGB stream to guide final feature map representation. We utilize three ways of fusing RGB and binary pose segment mask feature maps. Finally, fully connected layers at the end of the fused network is followed by the classification layer to compute group activity class scores.

The main contribution of this paper is three-fold. Firstly, we present a framework in which binary pose masks can guide feature learning from RGB images so that rich interaction between individuals and spatial appearance information can be extracted. Secondly, we evaluate different ways of fusing binary pose mask and RGB features in a convolutional network. Finally, we use SGD dataset [4] comprehensively to test our hypothesis against previous work and baselines.

2   Related Work

Group activity recognition research can be classified according to the type of source data. Research based on both video and image have been utilized in literature resulting in two distinctive approaches to this task. Although this paper focuses on activity recognition from still images, it is worth to mention video-based works in order to underline the similar motives behind both approaches. [8] is a GAN-based method in which generator can learn action codes from person level and group level features in a fusion scheme, while discriminator performs group activity recognition by validating the action codes as real or fake. In video-based research, RNNs are general preference to temporally reason over video frames. Authors in [2], propose a framework that is composed of fully-convolutional networks to extract a fixed-size representation and RNN to reason temporally for sequence of frames. In [11] and [10], LSTMs are utilized to capture temporal relations of the video and to represent and aggregate action dynamics. Another work using LSTMs is [15] in which authors designs a hierarchical LSTM network to model individual actions and interaction representations to reason on group activity. In [6], authors combine graphical models with RNN layers to leverage both rich spatial information and individual interactions. Inference algorithm reasons over individual estimates within a graphical model consisting of RNN nodes.

Group activity recognition using still images as the source of data has been limited by the availability of related datasets. One example is the work of Choi *et. al* [4], in which pose classifier, interaction classifier and group context classifier are learned using manually annotated RGB images. This bottom-up, hierarchical method makes a strong baseline for comparison. While this method uses rich low-level ground truth annotations including group, pose, orientation and interaction information during learning and detection (ground truth or poselet detector) information during test, we only use group information during the learning process.

Lack of crucial information in still images like temporal and motion components has been a natural force to find peculiar approaches for exploiting the most out of the spatial data. In [13], authors propose a method to compensate lack of temporal information. A Segnet based encoder-decoder framework is trained with segments of videos to learn temporal images hypothetically representing a sequence of frames. Then, these temporal representations are used to reason over still images for action recognition. Distinctively, [14] proposes a method to compensate for motion information missing in images. Unfortunately, both methods require manually annotated frames extracted from videos to recognize actions in images. Our method only relies on images during training without requiring extensive annotation burden.

3 Proposed Method

3.1 Problem Definition

Given a set of images I_N, the task of group activity recognition is defined as prediction of group activity classes for each image I_i. Let (I_i, Y_i) denotes the training set of RGB images and corresponding group activity class labels where Y_i takes labels from finite set, $L = \{1, 2, \ldots C\}$ for C classes. Then, we first obtain binary mask poses M_i for every image and form $(I_i^{H \times W \times 3}, M_i^{H \times W \times 1})$ input pairs. The final form of dataset can be denoted as $\{(I_i, M_i, Y_i) \mid I_i \in \mathbb{R}^{H \times W \times 3}, M_i \in \mathbb{R}^{H \times W \times 1}, Y_i \in \{1, 2, \ldots C\}$ for $i = 1, \ldots N\}$ where H and W denotes the resolution of the input. A pair of RGB and mask images is given in Fig. 2.

Fig. 2. A pair of RGB and mask inputs.

3.2 Approach

We propose a CNN-based two-stream framework to fuse RGB and binary pose masks as shown in Fig. 3. Streams of the network are fed with RGB images and its corresponding pose masks are extracted by a recently developed semantic image segmentation algorithm [3]. We use this segmentation tool for person class without any fine-tuning.

Our work is inspired by the encoder-decoder architecture proposed in [9] that uses depth images for semantic segmentation. Since we focus on classification task, our network streams consist of encoder architectures only. RGB and Mask streams include identical network architectures consisting of five sequential blocks of convolution, batch normalization and ReLU layers. Output of the encoder part is a combined feature map from two streams fused by one of the three fusion strategies. This is a high-level representation of a given image learnt from both RGB and binary pose masks. Finally, the combined feature map is fed to fully connected layers and a classification part to compute class scores.

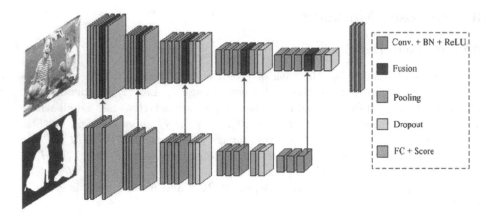

Fig. 3. Binary pose mask and RGB two-stream Convolutional Neural Network fusion architecture.

The network extracts feature maps in the guidance of masks through fusion operation. Then, classification scores for input image I is computed as $f_c(I, W)$ for each class c where W refers to parameter set of the network and C is number of classes. In order to transform scores to a class probability distribution, *Softmax* function is used:

$$p(c \mid x, W) = \frac{\exp(f_c(I; W))}{\sum_{j=1}^{C} \exp(f_j(I; W))}, \tag{1}$$

To learn network parameters, we follow the optimization process used in [9] and [1], and use cross-entropy loss that is very useful for multi-class classification problems. Cross-entropy loss measures the Kullback-Leibler (KL) divergence between an input probability distribution and a target distribution. Since number of samples per each class show an unbalanced nature, median frequency balancing [7] is applied. This method balances classes of large sample numbers with smaller weights to compensate the unbalance of class size during training.

3.3 Network Architecture

We use a VGG-16 based network with 13 convolutional and 3 fully connected layers as shown in Fig. 3. RGB and Mask streams are identical in terms of layer structure. We have 5 sequential blocks stacking convolutional, batch normalization and rectified linear unit layers (RELU). First two blocks have $2 \times (64, 128)$ weight layers respectively. Remaining 3 blocks have $3 \times (256, 512, 512)$ weight layers. We keep the original pooling layers from VGG-16 network at the end of each block. At the end of the network, 3 fully connected layers reside as in the original VGG-16 model. We think VGG-16 is a sufficient and well-purposed architecture for exploring fusion methods; nevertheless, more complex architectures can also be explored.

3.4 Fusion Methods

We fuse features from both streams to explore the effect of guidance. Here, we follow the approach from [9], in which fusion of maps is performed by addition operation. There could be multiple ways to fuse feature maps from two-stream networks. In fact, fusion by element-wise addition operation is simply shown to have a stronger signal than single channel activations [9].

We utilize two of proposed fusion methods in [9], sparse fusion (SF) and dense fusion (DF) and we explore one additional fusion strategy called late fusion (LF). In sparse fusion, fusion is applied at the end of each (Conv.+Batch N.+ReLU) block. In Fig. 4a, sparse fusion is shown for second and third (Conv.+Batch N.+ReLU) blocks. Feature map after second Convolution-BatchNorm-ReLU layer from Mask stream, referred as MASK2_2, is added to the corresponding feature map from RGB stream and fed to pooling layer of second (Conv.+Batch N.+ReLU) block. Therefore, there are five fusion connections for five (Conv.+Batch N.+ReLU) blocks in SF experiment. Dense fusion is a more dense one in which features are fused after each layer in every block. As can be seen in Fig. 4b, number of dense fusion connections are two for second (Conv.+Batch N.+ReLU) block. In other words, there will be 13 fusion connections in total for DF experiment as number of layers in each block are (2, 2, 3, 3, 3) for all five blocks. In late fusion (LF), we only fuse features for once at the end of fifth block, before FC layers. Illustration of these fusion types are given in Fig. 4.

4 Experiments

In this section, we present our results of the proposed approach for group activity recognition in still images.

4.1 Dataset

We use the Structured Group Dataset [4] that contains 600 images of groups of individuals generally encountered in daily life, such as at bus stop, cafeteria,

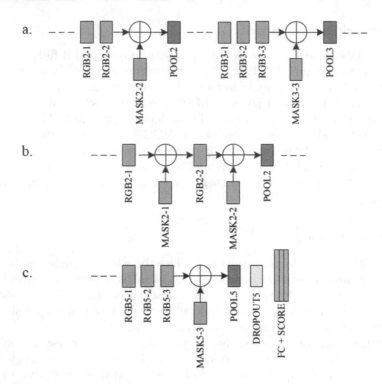

Fig. 4. Fusion methods for RGB and Mask streams of convolutional neural networks. a. Sparse fusion at 2nd and 3rd (Conv.+Batch N.+ReLU) block b. Dense fusion at 2nd (Conv.+Batch N.+ReLU) block c. Late fusion at 5th (Conv.+Batch N.+ReLU) block are shown.

classroom, conference, library and park. The dataset is rich in annotation-wise; group annotations, individual bounding boxes, 8 different viewpoints and individual poses (standing, sitting on an object, sitting on the floor) are provided for each image. There are 7 labeled group activities: queuing (Q), standing facing-each-other (SF), sitting on an object facing-each-other (OF), sitting on the ground facing-each-other (GF), standing side-by-side (SS), sitting on object side-by-side (OS) and sitting on the ground side-by-side (GS). Since there can be multiple groups in a single image, 600 images contain 1743 group bounding boxes in total. We exclude 19 erroneous ones that have no person or only one person with no collective activity. This results in 1724 group images. It is also stated in [4] that similar amount of group images are removed as being outliers but no information on these images was disclosed in detail.

We split 1724 images into 80%–20% train-test split. Training set is augmented by flipping all 1379 images horizontally, resulting in 2758 images in total. Test split contains 345 images. The original work [4] also performed augmentation by flipping operation on the whole dataset, of which we only did for training part.

4.2 Training

We train all models with a batch size of 8 for 250 epochs (86250 iterations in total) with random shuffling at each epoch. All models are trained end-to-end with stochastic gradient descent (SGD). Learning rates were initially assigned between [0.0003, 0.0005] and decayed 10% at every 20 epochs. All networks are initialized with the standard VGG-16 model [16] pretrained using ImageNet [12].

Pose masks were generated using a DeepLabV3 [3] pretrained on Inception [5] using MS-COCO and VOC2012. Next, we transform all mask images into binary masks by filtering out every detected segments except for human segments. Mask images were resized to the resolution of 240 × 320 and paired with RGB images.

4.3 Baselines

The closest previous work that we can compare our method is [4], where authors apply a bottom-up solution to recognize group activities by learning individual poses, interactions and group context classifiers. Throughout their learning process, they make use of ground truth information including individual poses, individual bounding boxes, view points and group annotations. Unlike their method, our method uses only group annotations.

Our interest is to find out whether pose masks provide strong signals in emphasizing group interaction inference by masking out irrelevant surrounding context. Therefore, we also train baselines using only RGB-stream or mask-stream to evaluate the effect of the fusion.

Table 1. Accuracy comparison with previous work for group activity recognition on Structured Group Dataset [4].

Method	Accuracy
Choi [4] (poselet det.)	52.7
Choi [4] (ground truth det.)	64.9
VGG-16 (RGB-only)	60.3
VGG-16 (mask-only)	64.6
Dense fusion	64.6
Late fusion	65.8
Sparse fusion	**70.4**

4.4 Results

We report experimental results for group activity recognition in Tables 1 and 2. Table 1 shows the overall accuracies of the baselines and related work, whereas Table 2 shows the classwise average precision, recall and F1 score comparisons between [4]'s best model and our best model.

Table 2. Class-wise average precision, recall and F1 scores over the Structured Group Dataset.

Method	P/R	Q	SF	OF	GF	SS	OS	GS	Avg
Choi [4] (ground truth det.)	Prec	41.86	55.78	62.48	60.19	39.08	53.85	37.65	50.13
	Recall	27.48	64.55	65.56	65.00	21.33	40.86	26.52	44.47
	F1	33.18	59.85	63.98	62.50	27.60	46.46	31.12	47.13
Our method (SF)	Prec	58.33	68.92	72.91	83.33	45.28	73.13	89.47	**70.19**
	Recall	38.89	66.23	87.50	71.42	58.53	72.06	58.62	**64.75**
	F1	46.67	67.55	79.54	76.92	51.06	72.59	70.83	**66.45**

As can be seen in Table 1, RGB-only model has the lowest accuracy amongst all of our models, whereas it still produces more accurate results than [4]'s model that operates on poselet detections. When using ground truth person detections, [4] method outperforms RGB-only CNN. Mask-only model is nearly on par with [4]-GT model; and this shows that person mask images can be a rich source for group activity recognition. It can be stated that dense fusion do not add much to learning more representative feature maps; probably due to the saturation in addition of similar inputs. This result also confirms findings in [9] where similar level of saturation observed for dense connections.

Late fusion of the RGB and pose mask streams seems to slightly increase the recognition performance; indicating that these two streams indeed carry complementary information, and pose masks extracted this way can be used as a guidance for focusing on the foreground and inferring collective group activity.

It is remarkable that sparse fusion of mask stream is able to improve group activity recognition accuracy with high margin. This result is interesting in two ways. Firstly, mask-guided fusion can lead network to learn high-level representative features within an end-to-end framework. This can help improvement of learning process for similar vision tasks even when a large-scale annotated data is not available. Secondly, the result implies that an optimum fusion method as in the case of sparse fusion is implicitly possible and can be searched in a finite architecture search space.

5   Conclusion

We have proposed a CNN-based two-stream fusion network to develop rich high-level representations of group activities. Our method does not require any low level annotations except for group activity label. In contrast to related work on the subject, our method directly infers interactions using binary person pose mask guidance. Experimental results show that mask guidance is complementary to learning feature maps from RGB stream, yielding superior recognition performance over bottom-up, annotation-heavy approaches for group activity recognition in images. Mask-based fusion can be applied to other tasks that need interaction inference for a better scene understanding.

References

1. Badrinarayanan, V., Kendall, A., Cipolla, R.: SegNet: a deep convolutional encoder-decoder architecture for image segmentation. arXiv preprint arXiv:1511.00561 (2015)
2. Bagautdinov, T., Alahi, A., Fleuret, F., Fua, P., Savarese, S.: Social scene understanding: end-to-end multi-person action localization and collective activity recognition. In: Conference on Computer Vision and Pattern Recognition (2017)
3. Chen, L.-C., Zhu, Y., Papandreou, G., Schroff, F., Adam, H.: Encoder-decoder with atrous separable convolution for semantic image segmentation. In: Ferrari, V., Hebert, M., Sminchisescu, C., Weiss, Y. (eds.) ECCV 2018. LNCS, vol. 11211, pp. 833–851. Springer, Cham (2018). https://doi.org/10.1007/978-3-030-01234-2_49
4. Choi, W., Chao, Y.-W., Pantofaru, C., Savarese, S.: Discovering groups of people in images. In: Fleet, D., Pajdla, T., Schiele, B., Tuytelaars, T. (eds.) ECCV 2014. LNCS, vol. 8692, pp. 417–433. Springer, Cham (2014). https://doi.org/10.1007/978-3-319-10593-2_28
5. Chollet, F.: Xception: deep learning with depthwise separable convolutions. arXiv preprint arXiv:1610.02357 (2017)
6. Deng, Z., Vahdat, A., Hu, H., Mori, G.: Structure inference machines: recurrent neural networks for analyzing relations in group activity recognition. In: CVPR (2016)
7. Eigen, D., Fergus, R.: Predicting depth, surface normals and semantic labels with a common multi-scale convolutional architecture. In: Proceedings of the IEEE International Conference on Computer Vision, pp. 2650–2658 (2015)
8. Gammulle, H., Denman, S., Sridharan, S., Fookes, C.: Multi-level sequence GAN for group activity recognition. arXiv preprint arXiv:1812.07124 (2018)
9. Hazirbas, C., Ma, L., Domokos, C., Cremers, D.: FuseNet: incorporating depth into semantic segmentation via fusion-based CNN architecture. In: ACCV (2016)
10. Ibrahim, M.S., Mori, G.: Hierarchical relational networks for group activity recognition and retrieval. In: Ferrari, V., Hebert, M., Sminchisescu, C., Weiss, Y. (eds.) ECCV 2018. LNCS, vol. 11207, pp. 742–758. Springer, Cham (2018). https://doi.org/10.1007/978-3-030-01219-9_44
11. Ibrahim, M.S., Muralidharan, S., Deng, Z., Vahdat, A., Mori, G.: A hierarchical deep temporal model for group activity recognition. In: CVPR (2016)
12. Russakovsky, O., et al.: Imagenet large scale visual recognition challenge. Int. J. Comput. Vis. **115**(3), 211–252 (2015)
13. Safaei, M., Balouchian, P., Foroosh, H.: TICNN: a hierarchical deep learning framework for still image action recognition using temporal image prediction. In: 2018 25th IEEE International Conference on Image Processing (ICIP), pp. 3463–3467. IEEE (2018)
14. Safaei, M., Foroosh, H.: A zero-shot architecture for action recognition in still images. In: 2018 25th IEEE International Conference on Image Processing (ICIP) (2018)
15. Shu, T., Todorovic, S., Zhu, S.C.: CERN: confidence-energy recurrent network for group activity recognition. In: IEEE Conference on Computer Vision and Pattern Recognition (2017)
16. Simonyan, K., Zisserman, A.: Very deep convolutional networks for large-scale image recognition. In: International Conference on Learning Representations (ICLR) (2015)

A Saliency-Based Convolutional Neural Network for Table and Chart Detection in Digitized Documents

I. Kavasidis[1]([✉]), C. Pino[1], S. Palazzo[1], F. Rundo[3], D. Giordano[1], P. Messina[2], and C. Spampinato[1]

[1] Department of Electrical, Electronic and Computer Engineering, University of Catania, Via S. Sofia 6, 95125 Catania, Italy
`kavasidis@dieei.unict.it`
[2] Tab2Ex, San Jose, USA
`http://www.tab2ex.com, https://www.snapchart.co/`
[3] STMicroelectronics - ADG Central R&D, Catania, Italy

Abstract. Within the realm of information extraction from documents, detection of tables and charts is particularly needed as they contain a visual summary of the most valuable information contained in a document. For a complete automation of the visual information extraction process from tables and charts, it is necessary to develop techniques that localize them and identify precisely their boundaries. In this paper we aim at solving the table/chart detection task through an approach that combines deep convolutional neural networks, graphical models and saliency concepts. In particular, we propose a saliency-based fully-convolutional neural network performing multi-scale reasoning on visual cues followed by a fully-connected conditional random field (CRF) for localizing tables and charts in digital/digitized documents. Performance analysis, carried out on an extended version of the ICDAR 2013 (with annotated charts as well as tables) dataset, shows that our approach yields promising results, outperforming existing models.

Keywords: Document analysis · Image classification · Object detection · Saliency detection

1 Introduction

Production and storage of digital documents have increased exponentially in the last two decades. Extracting and retrieving information from this massive amount of data have become inaccessible to human operators and a large amount of information captured in digital documents may go lost or never seen. As a consequence, a large body of research has focused on automated methods for document analysis. Most of these efforts are directed towards the development of Natural Language Processing (NLP) methods, that analyze both grammar and semantics of text with the goal of automatically extracting, understanding

© Springer Nature Switzerland AG 2019
E. Ricci et al. (Eds.): ICIAP 2019, LNCS 11752, pp. 292–302, 2019.
https://doi.org/10.1007/978-3-030-30645-8_27

and, eventually, summarizing key information from digital documents. However, while text is, inarguably, a fundamental way to convey information, there are contexts where graphical elements are much more powerful. For example, in scientific papers, many experiments, variables and numbers need to be reported in a concise way that fits better with tables/figures than text. *"A picture is worth a thousand words"* describes exhaustively the power that graphical elements possess in conveying information that would be otherwise cumbersome, both for the writer to express and the reader to understand. Thus, it is of primary importance for an effective automatic document processing approach to gather information from tables and charts. Several commercial software products that convert digitized and digital documents into processable text already exist. However, most of them either largely fail when dealing with graphical elements or require an exact localization of such elements to work properly. For this reason, a crucial pre-processing step in automated data extraction from tables and charts is to find their exact location. The problem of identifying objects in images traditionally falls in the object detection research area, where, nowadays, Deep Convolutional Neural Networks (DCNNs) play the leading role [14,18]. However, naively employing DCNN-based object detectors in digital documents, suitably transformed into images, leads to failures mainly because of the intrinsic appearance difference between digital documents and natural images (the data for which models are mainly thought for). Trying to train models from scratch may be unfeasible due to the large number of images required and to the lack of suitably annotated document datasets. Moreover, such approaches generally exploit the visual differences between object categories: while the visual characteristics of certain graphical elements (e.g., charts) significantly differ from text, the same cannot be said for tables, whose main differences from the surrounding content lie mostly in the layout. Finally, many of the existing object detectors are often prone to potential errors by upstream region proposal models and are not able to detect simultaneously all the objects of interest in an image [5,19].

In this paper we propose a general deep neural network model for pixelwise dense prediction, and consequently for detection of *arbitrary graphical elements*, rather than only for tables as existing methods, in digitized documents. The key intuition to make the whole model generalizable to arbitrary graphical elements is to pose the detection problem as a saliency detection one as those elements generally stand out in documents. Additionally, in order to provide a stronger supervision to the internal saliency detectors, we employ the approach introduced in [16], by adding a loss term related to the capability of the saliency maps to identify regions that are distinctive for visual classification in one of the four target categories. Finally, predictions of our network are enhanced with a fully connected Conditional Random Field (CRF) [12]. We demonstrate that our method generalizes well as demonstrated by the performance achieved on an extended version of ICDAR 2013 dataset (with annotated charts as well as tables and we also release).

2 Related Work

Given the large quantity of digital documents that are available today, it is mandatory to develop automatic approaches to extract, index and process information for long-term storage and availability. Consequently, there is a large body of research on document analysis methods attempting to extract different types of objects (e.g., tables, charts, pie charts, etc.) from various document types (text documents, source files, documents converted into images, etc.). Before the advent of deep learning, most works on document analysis for table detection were based on exploiting *a priori* knowledge on object properties by analyzing tokens extracted from source document files [2,3,21]. For example, [3] proposes a method for table detection in PDF documents, which uses tags of tabular separators to identify the table region. Of course, the main shortcoming of all methods that rely on detecting horizontal or vertical lines for table detection is that they fail to identify tables without borders. Alternatively, methods operating on image conversion of document files and exploiting only visual-cues for table detection have been proposed [9,15].

Similar computer vision–based methods have been proposed for detecting other types of graphical elements (e.g., charts, diagrams, etc.) than tables [8]. These methods basically employ simple computer vision techniques (e.g., connected components, fixed set of geometric constraints, edge detection, etc.) to extract chart images, but, as for the table detection case, they show scarce generalization capabilities. Low-level visual cues (e.g., intensity, contrast, homogeneity, etc.) in combination with shallow machine learning techniques have been used for specific object classification tasks [17] with fair performance, but these methods are mainly for classification as they tend to aggregate global features in compact representations which are less suitable for performing object detection. With the recent rediscovery of deep learning, in particular convolutional neural networks, and its superior representation capabilities for high-level vision tasks, the document analysis research community started to employ DCNNs for document processing, with a particular focus on document classification [1,7] or object (mainly chart) classification – after accurate manual detection [22]. One recent work presenting a DCNN exclusively targeted to table detection is [4], which employs Faster R-CNN for object detection. Nevertheless, this method suffers from the limitations mentioned in the previous section, i.e., its performance is negatively affected by the region proposal mistakes and it does not provide multiple detections for each image.

In this paper, we tackle the detection problem from a different perspective, i.e., we pose it as semantic image segmentation problem, by densely predicting—according to visual saliency principles—for each pixel of the input image the likelihood of being part of a salient object. This allows us to detect arbitrary graphical elements by only fine-tuning the classification stream as the salient objects have been already outlined by the saliency network of the proposed approach.

3 Deep Learning Models for Table and Chart Detection and Classification

The approach for table and chart extraction presented here works by receiving an image as input and generating a set of binary masks as output, from which bounding boxes are drawn. Each binary mask corresponds to the pixels that belong to objects of four specific classes: *tables, pie charts, line charts* and *bar charts*. The main processing engine driving our approach consists of a fully-convolutional deep learning model that performs table/chart detection and classification, followed by a conditional random field for enhancing and smoothing the binary masks (see Fig. 1).

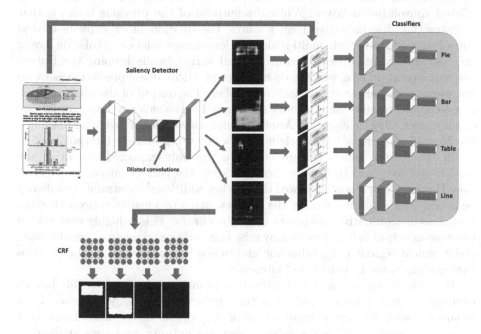

Fig. 1. The proposed system. An input document is fed to a convolutional neural network trained to extract class-specific saliency maps, which are then enhanced and smoothed by CRF models. Moreover, binary classifiers are trained to provide an additional loss signal to the saliency detector, based on how useful the computed saliency maps are for classification purposes.

Given an input document page transformed into an RGB image and resized to 300 × 300, the output of the system consists of four binary masks, one for each of the aforementioned classes. Pixels set to 1 in a binary mask identify document regions belonging to instances of the corresponding class, while 0 values are background regions (e.g., regular text).

We leverage visual saliency prediction to solve our object detection problem. As a result, the first processing block in our method is a fully-convolutional neural network (i.e., composed only by convolutional layer) that extracts four class-specific heatmaps from document images. Our saliency detection network is based on the feature extraction layers of the VGG-16 architecture. However, we applied a modification aimed at exploiting inherent properties of tables and charts: in particular, the first two convolutional layers do not employ traditional square convolution kernels, as in the original VGG-16 implementation, but use rectangular ones instead, of sizes 3×7 and 7×3. This set up gives our network the ability to extract table-related features (e.g., lines, spacings, columns and rows) even at the early stages. Padding was suitably added in order to keep the size of the output feature maps independent of the size of the kernels.

After the cascade of layers from the VGG-16 architecture, the resulting 75×75 feature maps are processed by a *dilation block*, consisting of a sequence of dilated convolutional layers. While the purpose of the previous layers is that of extracting discriminative local features, the dilation block exploits dilated convolutions to establish multi-scale and long-range relations. Dilation layers increase the receptive field of convolutional kernels while keeping the feature maps at a constant size, which is desirable for pixelwise dense prediction as we do not want to spatially compact features further. The output of the dilation block is a 4-channel feature map, where each channel is the saliency heatmap for one of the target object categories. After the final convolutional layer, we upsample the 75×75 maps back to the original 300×300 using bilinear interpolation.

In theory, the saliency maps could be the only expected output of the model, and we could train it by just providing the correct output as supervision. However, [16] recently showed that posing additional constraints to saliency detection—for example, forcing the saliency maps to identify regions that are also class-discriminative—improves output accuracy. This is highly desirable in our case as output saliency maps may miss non-salient regions (e.g., regular text) inside salient regions (e.g., table borders), while it is preferable to obtain maps that entirely cover the objects of interest.

For this reason, we add a classification branch to the model. This branch contains as many binary classifiers as the number of target object classes. Each binary classifier receives as input a crop of the original image around an object (connected component) in the saliency detector outputs, and aims at discriminating whether that crop contains an instance of target class. The classifiers are based on the Inception model and are architecturally identical, except for the final classification layer which is replaced by a linear layer with one neuron followed by a sigmoid nonlinearity.

To train the model we employ a multi-loss function that combines the error measured on the computed saliency maps with the classification error of the binary classifiers. The saliency loss function measured between the computed saliency maps $\mathbf{Y}$ (expressed as a $N \times 300 \times 300$ tensor, with N being the number of object classes, 4 in our case) and the corresponding ground-truth mask $\mathbf{T}$ (same size) is given by the mean squared error between the two:

$$\mathcal{L}_S(\mathbf{Y}, \mathbf{T}) = \frac{1}{N \cdot h \cdot w} \sum_{k=1}^{N} \sum_{i=1}^{h} \sum_{j=1}^{w} (Y_{kij} - T_{kij})^2 \tag{1}$$

where h and w are the image height and width (in our case, both are 300), and Y_{kij} and T_{kij} are the values of the respective tensors at location (i, j) of the k-th saliency map. The binary classifiers are first trained separately from the saliency network, so that they can be used to provide a reliable error signal to the saliency detector. Training is performed using original images cropped with ground-truth annotations. For example, for training the table classifier, we use table annotations (available in the ground truth) and crop input images so as to contain only tables: these are the "positive samples". "Negative samples" are, instead, obtained by cropping the original images with annotations from other classes (pie chart, bar chart and line chart) or with random background regions. This procedure is performed for each classifier to be trained. Since cropping may result in images of different sizes, all images are resized to 299×299 to fit the size required by the Inception network.

Each classifier is trained to minimize the negative log-likelihood loss function:

$$\mathcal{L}_{C_i}(\mathbf{I}, t_i) = -t_i \log C_i(\mathbf{I}) - (1 - t_i) \log (1 - C_i(\mathbf{I})) \tag{2}$$

where C_i $(1 \leq i \leq 4)$ is the classifier for the ith object class, and returns the likelihood that an object of the targeted class is present in image $\mathbf{I}$: t_i is the target label, and is 1 if i is the correct class, 0 otherwise. After training the classifiers, they are used to compute the classification loss for the saliency detector, as follows:

$$\mathcal{L}_C = \sum_{i=1}^{N} \mathcal{L}_{C_i}(\mathbf{I}, t_i) \tag{3}$$

The saliency detector, in this way, is pushed to provide accurate segmentation maps so that whole object regions are passed to the downstream classifiers. Indeed, if the saliency detector is not accurate enough in identifying tables, it will provide incomplete tables to the corresponding classifier, which may be then misclassified as non-table objects with a consequent increase in loss. Note that while training the saliency detector, the classifiers themselves are not re-trained, and are only used to compute the classification loss. This prevents the binary classifiers to learn to recognize objects from their parts, thus forcing the saliency network to keep improving its detection performance.

The multi-loss used for training the network in an end-to-end manner is, thus, given by the sum of the terms $\mathcal{L}_C$ and $\mathcal{L}_S$:

$$\mathcal{L} = \mathcal{L}_C + \mathcal{L}_S \tag{4}$$

The outputs of our fully convolution network, usually, show irregularities such as spatially-close objects fused in one object or one object oversegmented in multiple parts. In order to mitigate segmentation errors, we integrate in our system a downstream module based on the fully-connected CRFs employed in [13].

4   Performance Analysis

4.1   Dataset

Training Dataset. To train our method, we developed a web crawler that searched and gathered images from Google Images, using the following queries: *"tables in documents"*, *"pie charts"*, *"bar charts"*, *"line charts"*. Additionally, we manually collected a set of documents available online related to banking reports, using queries constructed by prefixing the name of a banking institute to "research report" and "financial report". All retrieved documents were then converted to images (one per page), resulting in a total of 50,466 images.

Training Annotations and Splits. Annotation was carried out on the web-crawled training dataset by paid annotators using an adapted version of the annotation tool in [10]. In particular, among the 50,442 retrieved images only 19,564 had at least one object of interest, while the remaining 30,878 images did not. The 19,564 images with positive instances had in total 22,544 annotations. From the set of retrieved images (and related annotations), 10% were used as a validation set for model selection, while the remaining 90% as training set. The distribution of instances of the four target classes between the training and validation sets were approximately equal.

Test Datasets. To test how well our approach generalizes we computed the performance on an extension of the ICDAR 2013 [6] benchmark. In particular we extended the ICDAR 2013 dataset (that contained table-only annotations) into a new version containing annotations of pie charts, line charts and bar charts. We refer to this new dataset as the "extended ICDAR 2013"; chart annotation was carried out as previously described for the training dataset. In terms of number of annotations, only 161 out of 238 images from ICDAR 2013 contained objects of interest. In these 161 images, there were 156 tables (with annotations already available) and 58 charts (of either "pie", "bar" and "line" types). We did not test on ICDAR 2017 as the test split is unavailable.

Saliency detector and binary classifiers were trained in an end-to-end fashion using an image as input and (a) the annotation masks as training targets for the saliency detector, and (b) presence/absence labels of target objects on image crops for the classifiers. The input image resolution was set to 300 × 300 pixels. The training phase ran for 45 epochs, which in our experiments was the point where the performance of the saliency network on the validation set stopped improving. All networks were trained using the Adam optimizer [11] (learning rate was initialized to 0.001, momentum to 0.9 and batch size to 32).

4.2   Performance Metrics

Our evaluation phase aimed at assessing the performance of our DCNN in localizing precisely tables and charts in digital documents, as well as in detecting and segmenting table/chart areas.

- **Table/chart localization performance.** To test localization performance we computed precision Pr, recall Re and F_1 score by calculating true positives, false positives and false negatives.
- **Segmentation accuracy** was measured by intersection over union (IOU). While the detection scores above provide information on the ability of the models to detect the tables and charts that overlap with the ground truth over a certain threshold, IOU measures per-pixel performance by comparing the exact number of the pixels that are detected as belonging to a table or chart. In other words, the IOU score reflects the accuracy in finding the correct boundaries of table and chart regions.

The proposed model consists of several functional blocks (saliency detection, binary classification) which are stacked together for final prediction. In order to assess how each block influenced performance, we computed the performance of the model when using only the saliency network (SAL); saliency detector followed by the binary classifiers (SAL-CL) and the whole system including all parts (saliency detection, fully connected CRF and binary classifiers) (ALL).

4.3   Results

The results obtained by the two configurations previously described are reported in Table 1. Our system performed very well in all object types, and this performance increased progressively from the baseline configuration (SAL) to the more complex architecture (i.e, ALL). In particular, the baseline configuration (SAL) achieved an average F_1 score of 69.0%, with the top performance achieved on the "Tables" category (76.3%) and the worst on the "Line charts" category (63.4%). By comparing with the results obtained by SAL-CL model, we can infer that the lower performance was due to the difficulty by the saliency detector alone in extracting discriminative features between these two types of charts. Indeed, this shortcoming was countered by introducing the classification loss in the model (SAL-CL configuration). The classifiers managed to aid the saliency detector network in recognizing the distinguishing features between line charts (increase of F_1 score of about 24%) and bar charts (increase of F_1 score of about 23%) w.r.t. the baseline, bringing the average F_1 score to 87%.

Finally, adding the fully-connected CRF to SAL-CL led to a further 6.4% increase to the system's performance, reaching a maximum average F_1 score of 93.4%. it appears evident that CRFs influence the number of false negatives and subsequently, the recall, more than they influence the number of false positives. In fact, w.r.t. the SAL-CL configuration, the CRF module increased more the recall (about 7.5%) than the precision (about 4.5%). This can be explained by the fact that the major contribution of CRF models consisted in filling gaps and holes resulting from the deep learning methods, especially for very large tables with extensive white areas. Figure 2 show examples of, respectively, good and bad detections obtained by our method.

Comparison against state of the art methods was done only in terms of table detection. In particular, we compared the performance of the four different

Table 1. Performance—in terms of precision, recall, F_1 and IOU—achieved by the two different configurations of our method on the extended ICDAR 2013 dataset. Values are in percentage.

Configuration	Class	Precision	Recall	F_1	IOU
SAL	Tables	78.4	74.4	76.3	65.3
	Pie charts	75.0	66.7	70.6	62.7
	Bar charts	62.5	69.0	65.6	63.5
	Line charts	61.9	65.0	63.4	62.1
	Average	69.5	68.8	69.0	63.4
SAL–CL	Tables	93.8	87.2	90.4	75.5
	Pie charts	87.5	77.8	82.4	72.2
	Bar charts	86.7	89.7	88.1	76.4
	Line charts	89.5	85.0	87.2	74.8
	Average	89.4	84.9	87.0	74.7
ALL	Tables	98.1	98.1	98.1	81.3
	Pie charts	100.0	88.9	94.1	78.1
	Bar charts	90.0	93.1	91.5	79.6
	Line charts	90.0	90.0	90.0	78.5
	Average	94.52	92.52	93.43	79.4

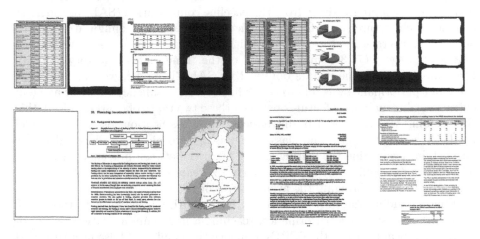

Fig. 2. Examples of good (top row) and bad (bottom row) detections.

configurations of our method to those achieved by both traditional and more recent approaches in detecting only tables on the ICDAR 2013. The comparison is reported in Table 2 and shows that our system achieved an F_1 score of 98.1%, outperforming all of the state-of-the-art methods.

Table 2. Comparison of state of the art methods in table detection accuracy on the standard ICDAR 2013 dataset (IoU = 0.5)

	Table detection		
	Precision	Recall	F_1
DeepDeSRT [20]	97.4	96.1	96.7
Tran [23]	95.2	96.4	95.8
Hao [7]	97.2	92.2	94.6
Silva [21]	92.9	98.3	95.5
Nurminen [6]	92.1	90.8	91.4
Our method	**98.1**	**98.1**	**98.1**

5 Conclusion

The identification of graphical elements such as tables and charts in documents is an essential processing block for any system that aims at extracting information automatically, and finds applicability to the analysis of financial documents, where numeric information is typically represented in tabular format. In this paper, we presented a method for automatic table and chart detection in document files converted to images, hence without exploiting format information (e.g., PDF tokens or HTML tags) that limit the general applicability of these approaches. The core of our model is a DCNN trained to detect salient regions from document images, with saliency based on the categories of objects that we aim to identify (tables, pie charts, bar charts, line charts). An additional loss signal based on the generated saliency maps' discriminative power in a classification task was provided during training, and a fully-connected CRF model was finally employed to smooth and enhance the final outputs. Performance evaluation, carried out on the standard UNLV dataset and ICDAR 2013 benchmark for table detection, and on an extended version of ICDAR 2013 with additional annotations for chart detection, showed that the proposed model achieves better performance than state-of-the-art methods in the localization of tables and charts. At Tab2ex, a technology based on the presented approach is employed at industrial level to extract tabular information from scanned images. Future directions of research in this complex task envision the detection of individual headers, rows and columns of tables, and the extraction of numeric data from charts based on axis values: such technologies would provide businesses with the means to process large amounts of documents (e.g. orders, invoices, financial trends) in an automated way.

References

1. Afzal, M.Z., et al.: DeepDocClassifier: document classification with deep convolutional neural network. In: IEEE ICDAR 2015 (2015)

2. Deivalakshmi, S., Chaitanya, K., Palanisamy, P.: Detection of table structure and content extraction from scanned documents. In: IEEE ICCSP 2014 (2014)
3. Fang, J., Gao, L., Bai, K., Qiu, R., Tao, X., Tang, Z.: A table detection method for multipage PDF documents via visual seperators and tabular structures. In: ICDAR 2011, pp. 779–783. IEEE (2011)
4. Gilani, A., Qasim, S.R., Malik, I., Abd Shafait, F.: Table detection using deep learning. In: ICDAR 2017. IEEE (2017)
5. Girshick, R.: Fast R-CNN. In: ICCV 2015 (2015)
6. Göbel, M., Hassan, T., Oro, E., Orsi, G.: ICDAR 2013 table competition. In: IEEE ICDAR 2013 (2013)
7. Hao, L., Gao, L., Yi, X., Tang, Z.: A table detection method for PDF documents based on convolutional neural networks. In: IEEE DAS 2016 (2016)
8. Huang, W., Liu, R., Tan, C.L.: Extraction of vectorized graphical information from scientific chart images. In: IEEE ICDAR 2007 (2007)
9. Jahan, M.A., Ragel, R.G.: Locating tables in scanned documents for reconstructing and republishing. In: IEEE ICIAfS 2014 (2014)
10. Kavasidis, I., Palazzo, S., Di Salvo, R., Giordano, D., Spampinato, C.: An innovative web-based collaborative platform for video annotation. Multimed. Tools Appl. 70(1), 413–432 (2014)
11. Kingma, D., Ba, J.: Adam: a method for stochastic optimization. arXiv preprint arXiv:1412.6980 (2014)
12. Krähenbühl, P., Koltun, V.: Efficient inference in fully connected CRFs with Gaussian edge potentials. In: NIPS 2011 (2011)
13. Krähenbühl, P., Koltun, V.: Efficient inference in fully connected CRFs with Gaussian edge potentials. In: Advances in Neural Information Processing Systems, pp. 109–117 (2011)
14. Li, J., et al.: Attentive contexts for object detection. IEEE Trans. Multimed. 19(5), 944–954 (2017)
15. Liu, Y., Mitra, P., Giles, C.L.: Identifying table boundaries in digital documents via sparse line detection. In: 2008 17th ACM Conference on Information and Knowledge Management (2008)
16. Murabito, F., Spampinato, C., Palazzo, S., Giordano, D., Pogorelov, K., Riegler, M.: Top-down saliency detection driven by visual classification. Comput. Vis. Image Underst. 172, 67–76 (2018)
17. Perez-Arriaga, M.O., Estrada, T., Abad-Mota, S.: TAO: system for table detection and extraction from PDF documents. In: FLAIRS Conference, pp. 591–596 (2016)
18. Redmon, J., Farhadi, A.: YOLO9000: better, faster, stronger. In: CVPR 2017 (2017)
19. Ren, S., He, K., Girshick, R., Sun, J.: Faster R-CNN: towards real-time object detection with region proposal networks. In: Advances in Neural Information Processing Systems, pp. 91–99 (2015)
20. Schreiber, S., Agne, S., Wolf, I., Dengel, A., Ahmed, S.: DeepDeSRT: deep learning for detection and structure recognition of tables in document images. In: IEEE ICDAR 2017 (2017)
21. Silva, A.C.: Learning rich hidden Markov models in document analysis: table location. In: IEEE ICDAR 2009 (2009)
22. Tang, B., et al.: DeepChart: combining deep convolutional networks and deep belief networks in chart classification. Sig. Process. 124, 156–161 (2016)
23. Tran, D.N., Tran, T.A., Oh, A., Kim, S.H., Na, I.S.: Table detection from document image using vertical arrangement of text blocks. Int. J. Contents 11(4), 77–85 (2015)

Training Efficient Semantic Segmentation CNNs on Multiple Datasets

Marco Leonardi, Davide Mazzini$^{(\boxtimes)}$, and Raimondo Schettini

University of Milano - Bicocca, Milano, Italy
m.leonardi6@campus.unimib.it, {davide.mazzini,schettini}@unimib.it

Abstract. In the past few years, various datasets for semantic segmentation have been presented. However, dense per-pixel groundtruths are difficult and expensive to obtain, therefore every single dataset contains only a subset of the semantic classes required to fully understand outdoor environments for real-world applications, e.g. autonomous or assisted driving. In this work, we investigate a simple approach to modify semantic segmentation CNNs in order to train them on multiple datasets with heterogeneous groundtruths. We trained and tested six efficient Deep CNN models on three datasets with different types of annotations such as generic objects, traffic signs and lane markings. Experiments show that the networks are trainable with the implemented method even though it highlights the limit of current efficient architectures when dealing with heterogeneous and large datasets.

Keywords: Deep Convolutional Neural Networks · Semantic segmentation · Scene understanding

1 Introduction

CNN architectures for semantic segmentation can be classified in two categories: accuracy-oriented and efficiency-oriented methods. Former methods achieve high accuracy with very high computational costs whereas latter methods attain very high inference speed and low memory footprint with evident loss in accuracy. Most efficiency-oriented methods are fast enough to run in real-time on recent embedded devices [7,9–11]. This enables novel applications in fields like autonomous or assisted driving where a complete scene understanding is of paramount importance. In such scenarios the perception model should be able to deal with a high number of heterogeneous classes in order to approach the real-world complexity. However, efficiency-oriented CNNs in literature are usually benchmarked on small datasets with a limited set of classes. In this work we modify six efficient Deep CNN models in order to enable them to deal with multiple datasets during training. We tested the networks on three datasets: Cityscapes, GTSDB and Vistas. GTSDB in particular has only bounding-box annotations, thus we investigate an approach, inspired by [12], to train semantic segmentation networks on dense per-pixel groundtruth along with bounding

© Springer Nature Switzerland AG 2019
E. Ricci et al. (Eds.): ICIAP 2019, LNCS 11752, pp. 303–314, 2019.
https://doi.org/10.1007/978-3-030-30645-8_28

boxes. We assess the performance of efficient CNN models focusing on three aspects: tracking model behavior when it deals with an increasing number of datasets; assessing the impact of decoder structure; and quantify the influence of pretraining.

2   Datasets

In the following sections we describe the datasets and metrics adopted to carry out our experiments (Fig. 1).

a) Cityscapes   b) GTSDB   c) Mapillary Vistas

Fig. 1. Sample images from *Cityscapes*, *GTSDB* and *Mapillary Vistas* together with their associated groundtruth maps. GTSDB annotations are very sparse and include traffic signs only. Mapillary Vistas exhibit a richer classes set compared to Cityscapes, e.g. including lane markings.

Cityscapes [2] is a dataset of urban scenes images with semantic pixelwise annotations. It consists of 5000 finely annotated high-resolution images (2048 × 1024) of which 2975, 500, and 1525 belong to train, validation and test sets respectively. Annotations include 30 different object classes but only 19 are used to train and evaluate models. With its basic classes hierarchy, Cityscapes it is not fully comprehensive of important annotations like lane markings or the different traffic signs. Such categories are instead annotated on other datasets presented in this Section.

German Traffic Sign Recognition Benchmark [5] (GTSDB) is a dataset for traffic sign localization and classification. It contains 900 images of street scenes acquired with different illumination and weather conditions. 43 classes of pole traffic signs are annotated with bounding-boxes. To our knowledge there is no publicly available dataset with per-pixel dense semantic segmentation annotations of traffic signs. GTSDB contains bounding-box annotations for traffic signs and no other annotations for different objects in the scene. In the next Section we introduce a technique, inspired by [12], to modify all the architectures in order to deal with bounding-box annotations.

Mapillary Vistas [13]. It is one of the biggest datasets for urban scene understanding publicly available to date. It is composed of 25000 images from different locations all over the world. It contains 18000, 2000 and 5000 images for training, validation and test respectively. Images have been acquired with a high variability of light and weather conditions. Annotations consist of 66 finely-annotated semantic classes. Since this dataset contains a large number of object categories, we employ it in two different settings: In the first setting we utilize only four classes relatives to lane markings (road, lane markings, crosswalk plain and crosswalk). In the following Sections, we will call it *Lane Markings* dataset, even though it is actually a subset of the Vistas dataset. In the second setting, we will make use of all the classes included in the dataset naming it *Vistas* in the next Sections.

2.1 Evaluation Metrics

Semantic segmentation quality has been evaluated by means of the *mean of class-wise Intersection over Union (mIoU)* which is computed, following [4], as the class-wise mean of the intersection over union measure. Models' speed is computed in *Frame Per Second (FPS)*, defined as the inverse of time needed for our network to perform a single forward pass on a single NVidia Titan Xp GPU.

3 Efficient Semantic Segmentation Networks

In this Section, we introduce and describe the efficient models for semantic segmentation considered in this work. We outline a brief overview of the peculiar characteristics of each architecture:

ENet [14] adopts an encoder-decoder design with 28 stacked bottleneck layers. Its efficiency is due to different factors, mainly the use of asymmetric convolutions. Different works investigated the use of asymmetric convolutions both from a theoretical point-of-view [1,17] and in a practical setting [18,19]. The main idea is to spatially decompose 3×3 convolutional filters into 3×1 followed by 1×3 filters. ENet introduced other design patterns that have become common in other efficient architectures: e.g. early downsampling and dilated convolutions [20].

GUNet [8] makes use of a multi-resolution encoder to exploit at the same time low-resolution structures and high-resolution details. The two resolutions are processed by different branches of the network which shares the same weights. Multi-resolution features are fused by means of a Fusion Module. The decoder part consists of a Guided Upsampling Module to efficiently output the prediction map improving the predictions near objects' boundaries.

ERFNet [15] employs an encoder-decoder structure inspired by ENet where the main building block is modified to increase model accuracy. It introduces a new block called Non-Bottleneck-1D and a fast downsampling strategy where the inner activations are spatially downsampled in the earlier part of the network to keep the majority of the computational burden for the deepest stages.

iGUM-Net [10] is an encoder-only architecture. In [10] is introduced an improved version of the GUM module, first presented in [8], that allows removing the decoder part of the network without any loss in segmentation quality. The encoder is inspired by ERFNet [15] with early downsampling and a modified Non-Bottleneck-1D Module.

Edanet [7] is heavily based on ERFNet. It makes use of asymmetric convolutions and dilated residual blocks. Subsampling is performed with ENet [14] downsampling blocks. The main difference with other architectures is the adoption of dense connectivity patterns between residual blocks. Like [10], Edanet is an encoder-only architecture but without any refinement module to improve high-resolution boundaries.

ESPNet [11] is an encoder-decoder architecture with concatenated skip connections similar to U-Net [16]. The peculiar trait of ESPNet is the introduction of the Efficient Spatial Pyramid (ESP) module. It consists in a *reduce-split-transform-merge* pattern. It is composed of point-wise convolutions to project features to a low-dimensional space, a pyramid of dilated convolutions to perform large receptive-field operations and point-wise convolutions to merge the computational paths (Fig. 2).

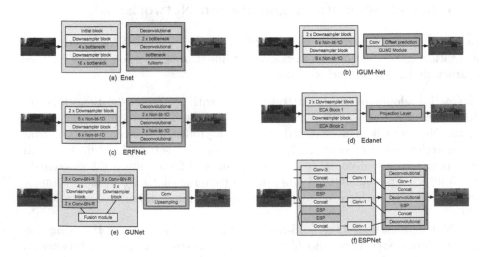

Fig. 2. Schematic view of the considered efficient CNN architectures. Light blue blocks represent encoders whereas darker blocks represents models' decoders. (Color figure online)

4 A Simple Method to Train on Heterogeneous Datasets

We modified each network in order to handle multiple heterogeneous datasets simultaneously during training. Our setup is inspired by [12] but presents some differences. We address the problem in a straightforward way, adopting one encoder and multiple decoders: one for each dataset. This is referred as *flat classification* in [12]. The main advantage of adopting such architectural choice is that we do not have to take care of the relations between the different dataset hierarchies. Each decoder is trained with an independent softmax on that specific dataset's classes, whereas the encoder is trained jointly. We made only one experiment towards modifying this general structure. We tested two different configurations modifying the network layers trained on the specific dataset: the whole decoder vs only a single final convolution. All the details of these experiments are described in Sect. 5.2.

Dealing with Bounding Boxes Annotations. All models considered in our evaluation have been conceived to produce a dense per-pixel prediction map of scene semantic segmentation. They are designed to be trained and tested with dense per-pixel annotations. However, the GTSDB dataset has only bounding boxes annotations. To overcome this issue we implemented a training setup, inspired by [12], that allows training semantic segmentation models with GTSDB annotations. A schematic view of the whole pipeline is depicted in Fig. 3. A per-pixel groundtruth is shaped in two steps: first, the GTSDB bounding-boxes are converted into pseudo per-pixel groundtruths, i.e. squared areas corresponding to the bounding box size and location. As a second step, they are merged with the prediction from the Cityscapes branch corresponding to the *generic* traffic sign class. The obtained groundtruth is then employed in the usual way to train the network branch with a per-pixel cross entropy loss.

Dealing with Heterogeneous Cardinalities. Each dataset adopted in our experiments has very different cardinality from each other. In order to balance the impact of each dataset when training CNNs, we replicate the datasets with lower dimension to the cardinality of the dataset with the maximum number of images, see Sect. 2 for details. We set the number of training iterations to a fixed number, corresponding to 150 Cityscapes epochs, to make the network see the same number of images independently of the dataset choice. Furthermore, to balance the information gain from each dataset, we weight the loss generated by each model branch with a learned variable parameter.

Architecture Alternatives. Many networks considered in this work have a complex decoder composed of multiple Conv-Batchnorm-Relu blocks followed by upsampling or transposed convolution operators. Duplicating the decoder part leads in computationally heavier models. For this reason, we also evaluate an alternative architectural choice in which only the last convolutional layer is repeated for each dataset instead of the whole decoder.

Training Recipe. We trained all models minimizing the cross entropy loss between the ground-truth and the predicted classes for each pixel. We employed

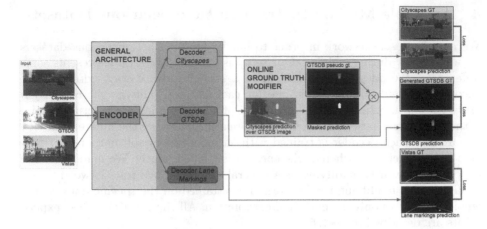

Fig. 3. Overview of the training setup to train models on multiple datasets simultaneously. Every model has been modified to follow this general architecture. The online ground truth modifier allows to train the GTSDB decoder with bounding box annotations.

ADAM as stochastic optimizer [6] with a base learning rate of 5×10^{-4}. We adopted a polynomial decay learning rate policy defined as follows: $LR(epoch) = \left(1 - (epoch/total\ epochs)^{0.9}\right) * LR_0$ where $epoch$ is the 0-based index of the actual epoch, LR_0 is the initial learning rate, and $total\ epochs$ is the total number of epochs for the training process. The batch size is set to six for all the experiments. Furthermore, we employed early stopping technique against overfitting, analyzing the mean intersection over union on the validation set for every epoch. The only preprocessing step consists in normalizing the input image by subtracting the mean and dividing by the standard deviation computed on Imagenet [3].

Data Augmentation. We adopted classical augmentation techniques during training. In particular, since images from different datasets have different sizes, we scale input images such as the longest axis is 1024 for the width or 512 for the height. We apply random scale augmentation sampling the scaling factor from a uniform distribution with interval $[0.5, 2]$.

5 Experiments

In order to assess the behaviour of the considered models on multiple heterogeneous datasets, we investigated three research directions that led to three related sets of experiments. In the first set, we benchmark CNN models and track their behaviour when dealing with an increasing number of datasets. In the second and third set of experiments, we evaluate respectively the impact of the decoder structure and the influence of pretraining.

5.1 Scaling up with Dataset Complexity

We evaluate each model in four experimental settings. In each set a dataset is added to the training set with new images and the set of object categories is extended:

1. **Baseline.** The baseline experiment consists of training on Cityscapes dataset: it comprises 19 semantic classes. CNN architectures have been evaluated on this dataset with no modification to the original structure. Unique images: 2975. We adopt this dataset as our baseline for two main reasons: first, Cityscapes is a well-known benchmark dataset for semantic segmentation methods and it is widely adopted in literature. The performance of all methods considered in this work has been evaluated on Cityscapes in the original papers. Second, it includes only the basic classes to perform a complete scene understanding on urban environments whereas the other datasets consist of a superset of Cityscapes i.e. Vistas, or they include only a specific subset of classes with finer annotations i.e. traffic signs or lane markings.
2. **Cityscapes + GTSDB.** In this experiment, models have to predict simultaneously Cityscapes and GTSDB classes for a total of 62 classes (i.e. 19 from Cityscapes + 43 from GTSDB). In this case, the architectures have been modified to include two decoders. Unique images: 3490. We included this dataset before Lane Markings or Vistas for reasons bound to the specific application. Traffic signs are a fundamental element when dealing with scene perception for autonomous driving.
3. **Cityscapes + GTSDB + Lane Markings.** In this setup CNN models predict 62 classes plus 4 classes form Lane Markings dataset. The number of decoders for each architecture in this setting is three. Unique images: 21490.
4. **Cityscapes + GTSDB + Vistas.** In this experiment, the models are required to predict all the 104 classes from all datasets. The number of decoders is three (since Vistas includes Lane Markings). Unique images: 21490.

In Fig. 4 is reported a plot of the mean Intersection over Union versus the number of datasets. With this visualization, we want to track the mean performance of each model when dealing with increasing images and/or classes cardinality. The general tendency is a degradation of the overall performance as the problem complexity increases. The considered models are not designed for highly complex problems, and since their limited number of parameters, their capacity is presumably close to saturation. Models behaviour with respect to the Lane Markings dataset seems a counter example to the general trend. This behaviour is plausible since the visual appearance of lane markings is very distinguishable from other semantic classes.

The same set of experiments can be visualized in Fig. 5 from a different point of view. It represents the mIoU computed on the Cityscapes validation set with Cityscapes classes only. By looking from this perspective we want to assess models behaviour on the original dataset when trained with additional images and extra classes. Interestingly the considered models exhibit better performance on

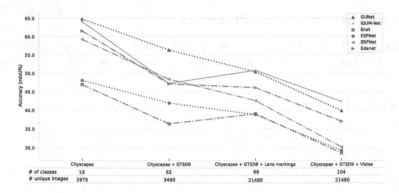

Fig. 4. Average mIoU measured on the joint datasets. On the x axis the datasets considered to train and test the models along with the resulting number of classes and unique images.

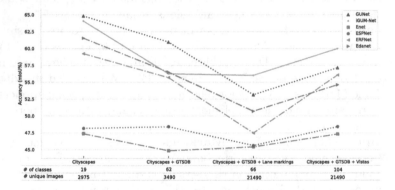

Fig. 5. mIoU on the Cityscape validation dataset versus the datasets employed in training along with the resulting number of classes and unique images.

Cityscapes + GTSDB + Vistas experiment than in previous experiments. Even if it is more complex with higher number of classes, this behaviour is plausible since the Vistas dataset includes a large superset of the Cityscapes class set.

In Table 1 we report the comprehensive set of results of the experiments introduced in this Section and shown in Figs. 4 and 5. We also included results from [12] which is the only work in the state of the art that experimented with a similar setup, main differences are: their network structure is specifically tailored to handle the classes hierarchy of the joint datasets; there is a difference in the cardinality of Cityscapes and Vistas classes. For Cityscapes they use more than 19 classes. For Vistas they report performance over all classes while our performance regards only the additional classes w.r.t Cityscapes.

Table 1. Benchmarks of different models trained and tested on different datasets (* number of classes is higher)

	mIoU								
Tested on	Cityscapes	Cityscapes	GTSDB	Cityscapes	GTSDB	Lane markings	Cityscapes	GTSDB	Vistas
# Classes	19	19	43	19	43	4	19	43	48
Meletis et al.	N/A	N/A	N/A	N/A	N/A	N/A	57.3*	41.5	**31.9***
GUNet	**64.8**	**61**	**51.7**	53.2	43.6	**54.7**	57.2	48.5	14.4
iGUM-Net	64.1	56.3	38.4	**56**	**49**	47.6	**60**	**50.6**	16.8
Enet	47.3	44.9	28.2	45.4	30.2	41.9	47.3	27.4	11.4
ESPNet	48.2	48.4	35.7	45.6	31.7	39.5	48.4	27.3	12.4
ERFNet	59.2	55.7	41.2	47.5	34.5	46.1	56.1	24.3	10.6
Edanet	61.5	56.5	37.9	50.7	43	44.9	54.6	41.7	15.2
Trained on	Cityscapes	Cityscapes + GTSDB		Cityscapes + GTSDB + Vistas			Cityscapes + GTSDB + Vistas		

5.2 Multiple vs Single Decoder

Figure 6 shows a comparison of mIoU versus model complexity, expressed in Parameters and FPS, tested on Cityscapes and GTSDB datasets. All models benefit in term of speed from the adoption of a single decoder whereas the number of parameters does not visibly decrease. Enet is the only model that take advantage even in terms of accuracy from this architectural design. Some models are represented by a single point in Fig. 6 i.e. GUNet, iGUM-Net and Edanet. They have been conceived, in their original structure, with a lightweight decoder design composed by only a convolutional layer.

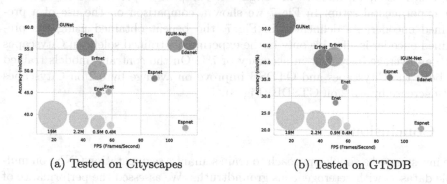

(a) Tested on Cityscapes   (b) Tested on GTSDB

Fig. 6. Multiple decoders (solid colors) vs single decoder (transparent colors): comparison between accuracy in terms of mean intersection over union and frame per second. Models have been trained jointly on Cityscapes and GTSDB and separately tested. Circle dimension reflects the number of model parameter.

5.3 Impact of Pretraining

It is well known from semantic segmentation literature that the overall model performance improves by adopting a pretrained encoder on Imagenet [8,10,15].

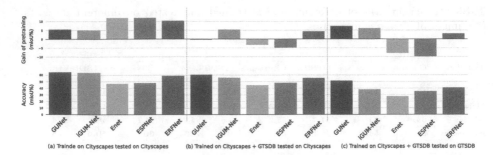

Fig. 7. mIoU on different combinations train and test datasets. Lower bars represent the non-pretrained baseline. Higher bars express the absolute gain when pretraining.

| Input | GUNet | iGUM-Net | Enet | ESPNet | ERFNet | Edanet | GT |

Fig. 8. Sample images from Cityscapes (first row), GTSDB (second row) and Mapillary Vistas (third row) datasets, together with their groundtruths.

For this reason, we want to investigate the impact of pretrained encoders on our experimental setup. In Fig. 7 we show a comparison on the use of a pretrained encoder. As delineated in Fig. 7, the benefit obtained using the pretrained encoder is effective only in the experiments trained solely on Cityscapes with an average increment in accuracy of 7%. On the contrary, models trained on both the Cityscapes and GTDSB improve on average by 0.2 on Cityscapes but decrease by −0.2 on GTSDB (Fig. 8).

6 Conclusions

We investigated a simple approach to train semantic segmentation CNNs on multiple datasets with heterogeneous groundtruths. We assessed the performance of six efficient semantic segmentation networks trained with such approach. We tracked the behavior of all models across different experiments with increased training datasets. Experimental results shows that, by training on increasingly large and diverse datasets, performance of all models decreases as a general trend. These results show that, actual efficient models, are probably not able to deal with more complex datasets and classes hierarchies. We also tested two different decoder variants to deal with multiple datasets and evaluated the impact of pretraining on models performance. Results of these experiments suggest that their influence on the overall pipeline is beneficial in terms of speed but not effective in terms of accuracy gain. As possible future work, it would be interesting to study the benefits and the drawbacks on the use of more complex architectures. Future experiments will also investigate the different elements involved in employing multiple heterogeneous datasets (e.g. diverse groundtruths, classes and images distributions) in order to disentangle the contribution of each factor.

Acknowledgments. This work was supported by TEINVEIN, CUP: E96D1700011 0009 - Call "Accordi per la Ricerca e l'Innovazione", cofunded by POR FESR 2014–2020. We gratefully acknowledge the support of NVIDIA Corporation with the donation of a Titan Xp GPU used for this research.

References

1. Alvarez, J., Petersson, L.: Decomposeme: simplifying convnets for end-to-end learning. arXiv:1606.05426 (2016)
2. Cordts, M., et al.: The cityscapes dataset for semantic urban scene understanding. In: Proceedings of the IEEE Conference on CVPR (2016)
3. Deng, J., Dong, W., Socher, R., Li, L.J., Li, K., Fei-Fei, L.: ImageNet: a large-scale hierarchical image database. In: 2009 IEEE Conference on Computer Vision and Pattern Recognition, pp. 248–255. IEEE (2009)
4. Everingham, M., Van Gool, L., Williams, C.K., Winn, J., Zisserman, A.: The pascal visual object classes (VOC) challenge. IJCV **88**(2), 303–338 (2010)
5. Houben, S., Stallkamp, J., Salmen, J., Schlipsing, M., Igel, C.: Detection of traffic signs in real-world images: the German traffic sign detection benchmark. In: International Joint Conference on Neural Networks, No. 1288 (2013)
6. Kinga, D., Adam, J.B.: A method for stochastic optimization. In: ICLR (2015)
7. Lo, S.Y., Hang, H.M., Chan, S.W., Lin, J.J.: Efficient dense modules of asymmetric convolution for real-time semantic segmentation. arXiv:1809.06323 (2018)
8. Mazzini, D.: Guided upsampling network for real-time semantic segmentation. In: British Machine Vision Conference (BMVC) (2018)
9. Mazzini, D., Buzzelli, M., Pau, D.P., Schettini, R.: A CNN architecture for efficient semantic segmentation of street scenes. In: 8th ICCE-Berlin, pp. 1–6. IEEE (2018)
10. Mazzini, D., Raimondo, S.: Spatial sampling network for fast scene understanding. In: Proceedings of the IEEE Conference on CVPR Workshops (2019)
11. Mehta, S., Rastegari, M., Caspi, A., Shapiro, L., Hajishirzi, H.: ESPNet: efficient spatial pyramid of dilated convolutions for semantic segmentation. arXiv:1803.06815 (2018)
12. Meletis, P., Dubbelman, G.: Training of convolutional networks on multiple heterogeneous datasets for street scene semantic segmentation. In: 2018 IEEE Intelligent Vehicles Symposium (IV), pp. 1045–1050. IEEE (2018)
13. Neuhold, G., Ollmann, T., Rota Bulo, S., Kontschieder, P.: The mapillary vistas dataset for semantic understanding of street scenes. In: Proceedings of the IEEE ICCV, pp. 4990–4999 (2017)
14. Paszke, A., Chaurasia, A., Kim, S., Culurciello, E.: ENet: a deep neural network architecture for real-time semantic segmentation. arXiv:1606.02147 (2016)
15. Romera, E., Alvarez, J.M., Bergasa, L.M., Arroyo, R.: ERFNet: efficient residual factorized convnet for real-time semantic segmentation. IEEE Trans. Intell. Transp. Syst. **19**(1), 263–272 (2018)

16. Ronneberger, O., Fischer, P., Brox, T.: U-Net: convolutional networks for biomedical image segmentation. In: Navab, N., Hornegger, J., Wells, W.M., Frangi, A.F. (eds.) MICCAI 2015. LNCS, vol. 9351, pp. 234–241. Springer, Cham (2015). https://doi.org/10.1007/978-3-319-24574-4_28
17. Sironi, A., Tekin, B., Rigamonti, R., Lepetit, V., Fua, P.: Learning separable filters. IEEE Trans. PAMI **37**(1), 94–106 (2015)
18. Szegedy, C., Ioffe, S., Vanhoucke, V., Alemi, A.A.: Inception-v4, inception-ResNet and the impact of residual connections on learning. In: AAAI, vol. 4, p. 12 (2017)
19. Szegedy, C., Vanhoucke, V., Ioffe, S., Shlens, J., Wojna, Z.: Rethinking the inception architecture for computer vision. In: Proceedings of the IEEE CVPR, pp. 2818–2826 (2016)
20. Yu, F., Koltun, V.: Multi-scale context aggregation by dilated convolutions. In: ICLR (2016)

Autocropping: A Closer Look at Benchmark Datasets

Luigi Celona⬦, Gianluigi Ciocca(✉)⬦, Paolo Napoletano⬦,
and Raimondo Schettini⬦

Department of Informatics, Systems and Communication,
University of Milano-Bicocca, Viale Sarca, 336, 20126 Milan, Italy
{luigi.celona,gianluigi.ciocca,paolo.napoletano,
raimondo.schettini}@unimib.it

Abstract. Image cropping is a common image editing task that aims
to improve the composition as well as the aesthetics of an image by
extracting well-composed sub-regions of the original image. For choosing
the "best" autocropping method it is therefore important to consider
on which datasets this method is validated and possibly trained. In this
work we conduct a detailed analysis of the main datasets in the state
of the art in terms of statistics, diversity and coverage of the selected
sub-regions, namely the ground-truth candidate views. An analysis of
how much semantics of ground-truth candidate views is preserved with
respect to original images and a comparison among dummy autocropping
solutions and state of the art methods is also presented and discussed.
Results show that each dataset models the cropping problem differently,
and in some cases very high performance can be reached by using a
dummy autocropping strategy.

Keywords: Autotagging · Dataset comparison · Evaluation

1 Introduction

Image cropping is an important step to improve the aesthetic quality of an
image. It can be used in many applications such as efficient image transmission,
image retargeting, or photo collages [1]. For choosing the "best" image cropping
method it is important to consider on which datasets this method is validated
and possibly trained. Computer Vision (CV) researchers benchmark algorithms
using public available datasets [11]. This practice allows to achieve quantitative
performance evaluation and comparison between algorithms as well as it helps
new researchers to get, in a short time, a clear view of the state of the art
performance. The availability of benchmark datasets is increasing in all the CV
domains ranging from object tracking [15] to object recognition [7]. Although
much effort has been made to enrich the number of available datasets, in contrast,
a little effort has been made to assess the quality of the available ones. Quality
is related to two aspects: (i) how much data are representative of the domain;
(ii) how much the ground-truth is consistent with the modeled problem.

© Springer Nature Switzerland AG 2019
E. Ricci et al. (Eds.): ICIAP 2019, LNCS 11752, pp. 315–325, 2019.
https://doi.org/10.1007/978-3-030-30645-8_29

In this paper we provide a thorough analysis of datasets that are commonly used for the benchmark of autocropping algorithms. In the last 10 years several benchmark datasets have been proposed by the scientific community as well as suitable measures to rank algorithms in terms of match between ground-truth sub-region or sub-regions with the one or ones selected by the algorithm [2, 6,21,22]. Each dataset usually consists in a set of images and corresponding cropped sub-region or sub-regions as selected by human subjects. In order to evaluate the characteristic and effectiveness of the datasets in the literature, in this paper, we analyze the most used datasets in terms of: (1) statistics of the ground-truth, namely position, size and aspect-ratio of the candidate views; (2) diversity and coverage of each candidate views with respect to the original image; (3) performance evaluation and comparison with the state of the art of a dummy solution that crops regions with area ranging from 100% to 10% of the image area; (4) semantic analysis in terms of number of times a semantic concept is preserved in ground-truth sub-regions with respect to original images.

2   Related Works

2.1   Datasets for Image Cropping Assessment

Many databases for the evaluation of image autocropping methods have been proposed in the literature. Table 1 summarizes the available datasets. For each dataset we report the number of images it contains, the number of views per image i.e. the number of crops available for each image, the source of the images, how the crops have been determined (either by human annotation, or by an automatic procedure), who validated the crops i.e. if the human subjects were experts in the field or not, whether the different views are ranked by preference, and finally the corresponding reference where the dataset has been presented for the first time. Briefly, the characteristics of the five datasets in Table 1 are the following.

Table 1. Comparison of publicly available image cropping databases.

Dataset	Images	Views	Source	Crops	Evaluation	Ranking	Ref
CPC	10,797	24	Misc[a]	Generated	AMT workers	Yes	[21]
CUHK-ICD	950	3	CUHKPQ	Human	Experts	No	[22]
FCDB	348	1	Flickr	Human	AMT workers	No	[2]
FLMS	500	10	Flickr	Human	Experts	No	[6]
XPView	992	≤ 23	Misc[b]	Generated	Experts	Yes	[21]

[a] AVA, MS-COCO, AADB, Places
[b] FCDB, CUHK-ICD, MS-COCO,...

Comparative Photo Composition Database. The Comparative Photo Composition (CPC) database contains 10,797 images [21]. For each image, 24 candidate views with 4 standard aspect-ratios have been pooled among candidates automatically generated by exploiting existing re-composition and cropping algorithms. Finally, the aforementioned candidate views have been ranked by 6 Amazon Mechanical Turk (AMT) workers. The source of the images is quite diverse. It consists of a combination of images taken from different benchmark datasets in the literature: AVA [16], MS-COCO [13], AADB [10] and the Places dataset [24]. Most of the images contain two or more principal objects.

CUHK Image Cropping Database. The CUHK Image Cropping Database (CUHK-ICD) is a collection of 950 images gathered from the CUHKPQ dataset [22]. It contains seven classes of images, i.e. *animal, architecture, human, landscape, night, plant* and *static*. A cropped region is respectively annotated for each image by three different professional photographers. The images are taken from an existing image quality assessment dataset, the CUHKPQ dataset [18]. The images are of varying aesthetic quality and are of different image categories.

Flickr Cropping Database. The Flickr Cropping database (FCDB) contains 1,743 non-iconic images gathered from Flickr [2]. The cropping annotation for each image derives from the choices of four AMT workers who evaluated several candidate views manually drawn. 348 out of the 1,743 images are adopted as test set and is the dataset's cardinality reported in Table 1. Also, since there are no multiple views for each image, and thus no ranking of different crops, in the table the "Ranking" attribute is set to "No" for this dataset.

FLMS Database. The FLMS database consists of 500 images crawled from Flickr [6]. These images have been selected for their imperfect composition and have different contents. Each image is cropped by 10 expert users on AMT who passed a strict qualification test. There is no ranking of the views. Each view is considered separately. No further details are provided in [6] about this dataset.

eXPert View Database. The eXPert View (XPView) database is a collection of 992 images with dense compositions [21]. This dataset has been created by the same authors of the CPC dataset in order to test their method on another, unrelated dataset. The origin of the XPView is mixed with the images taken from different sources. Specifically, the MS-COCO [13], the FCDB and CUHK-ICD datasets, and other, unspecified, sources. The candidate views have been generated as already described for the CPC dataset but with 8 diverse aspect-ratios. In this case, the candidate views are annotated by three experts, and a ranking of the views is provided. From the analysis of the dataset, each image has up to 23 views.

2.2 Image Cropping Algorithms

The problem of automatic image cropping has been traditionally tackled by designing ad-hoc algorithms based on different visual cues that are considered relevant. Many methods consider salient regions to guide the selection of the important portion of the images. For example, in [4], depending on the image contents, different cropping attributes are used such as faces, skin, saliency and the image category itself. Another example is [14]. Visual composition, boundary simplicity and content preservation are used in [6] as features to force a cropped image to contain a salient object. Yan et al. [22] propose a method for learning what features are important in a good crop among color, texture, foreground, shape complexity, sharpness, saliency maps, segmented regions, perspective ration, and prominent lines.

Recently, another category of cropping algorithms has emerged that incorporate aesthetic cues as a feature in order to select the best cropping region. For example, a Generative Adversarial Network is used in [5] with a discriminator that attempts to distinguish images of poor and good aesthetic quality. Aesthetic and gradient energy maps are used in [9] to learn a compositional model for the best crop. The View Finding Network (VFN) [3] tries to correctly rank candidate crops according to certain photographic guidelines learned on an aesthetically annotated database. In [19,20] candidate crops are firstly generated and then their aesthetic is assessed to generate the cropped image. A similar approach based on aesthetic quality classification is the CNN-based Cascaded Cropping Regression (CCR) method [8]. Li et al. [12] propose an Aesthetic Aware Reinforcement Learning (A2-RL) framework to sequentially search the best cropping windows automatically generated by applying a set of cropping actions. Finally, a fast View Proposal Net (VPN) is presented in [21], where a teacher network, is used to teach the VPN (i.e. the student) to output the correct score rankings for the crops.

3   Autocropping Ground-Truth: Candidate Views Analysis

Figure 1 shows some sample images generated from each dataset with the corresponding candidate views superimposed. For the CPC and the XPView datasets, the views are ranked so greenish colors represent the best ranked views while the reddish colors represent the worst ranked ones. As it can be seen, the views selected for both the CPC and XPView have a high degree of variability with the different views covering the most part of the original image. For the CUHK-ICD, we can see that the three views mostly overlap although in some cases they can be quite different (as in the case of the building and the cake). The single, favorite, candidate view of the FCDB dataset covers the relevant object in the image. Given the presence in the image of a single relevant subject, the images themselves seem quite simple to crop. Finally, for the FLMS dataset, again, the ten candidate views are quite diverse. For instance, the bounding boxes have small overlaps. This could indicate that the ten experts have different personal opinions about image aesthetics and composition. Following the above preliminary examination, we next analyze in details the five datasets, their annotations, and provide some observations on their use for the evaluation of automatic cropping algorithms.

Fig. 1. Sample images from the five cropping datasets. Superimposed are the crop regions. For the CPC and the XPView datasets, reddish to greenish colors represent ranked crops from worst to best. (Color figure online)

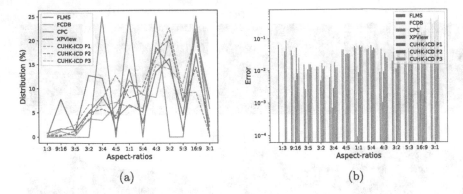

(a)   (b)

Fig. 2. *(Best viewed magnified.)* Distribution of candidate views for each considered dataset with respect to 13 aspect-ratios commonly used in digital photography (a). Average error between aspect-ratios of the candidate views and closest standard aspect-ratios for each database (b).

3.1   Diversity and Coverage

For each dataset, we quantitatively analyze several properties of candidate views. Firstly, we investigate the aspect-ratio of the candidate views to understand how much these differ from common aspect-ratios. We categorize candidate views aspect-ratios into 13 common classes in still camera photography, namely 1:1, 5:4, 4:3, 3:2, 5:3, 16:9, 3:1 and their complementary versions (4:5, 3:4, 2:3, 3:5, 9:16, and 1:3) [23]. Figure 2a shows the distribution of candidate views aspect-ratios for each database. As it can be seen, the majority of candidate views for all the datasets has a 16:9 aspect-ratio. CPC dataset candidate views equally distribute among 1:1, 4:3, 16:9, and 3:4 aspect-ratios. The other datasets (CUHK-ICD, FCDB, FLMS, and XPView) have a larger variety of candidate views aspect-ratios. Figure 2b reports the error resulting from the categorization step, that is the average distance between candidate views aspect-ratios and the closest standard aspect-ratios for each dataset. The small error for the CPC dataset is motivated by the fact that candidate views were also sampled from standard aspect-ratios as described in Sect. 2.1. Instead, the error for the other datasets is higher because candidate views have been freely chosen by humans.

Secondly, we consider the surface of all candidate windows for estimating their diversity and also their coverage with respect to the surface of the whole image. We scale the size of images as well as the corresponding candidate views to the same fixed dimension, then the value of the pixel o_{ij} of the heatmap, which represents the probability of being part of a candidate view, is obtained as follows:

$$o_{ij} = \frac{1}{N} \sum_{n=1}^{N} \alpha(x_{ij}) \qquad \alpha = \begin{cases} val, & \text{if } x_{ij} \in W_n \\ 0, & \text{otherwise} \end{cases} \qquad (1)$$

where N is the total number of candidate views for all dataset samples, W_n is the candidate n-th view and val corresponds to 1 for datasets that do not provide the rank of candidate views, namely CUHK-ICD, FCDB, and FLMS dataset. For CPC and XPView datasets, whose candidate views do not have all the same relevance, val is equal to w_n, where it represents the rank of the n-th candidate view, normalized in the interval [0,1]. In Fig. 3 we display the heatmaps for all the datasets. The heatmaps are normalized in the range [0,1], where pixel value close to 1 means that there is a high probability that the corresponding pixel belongs to a candidate view. The high energy in the center of the heatmaps for all the datasets shows that many candidate views crop the central region of the image. Moreover, we highlight that the energy is very high for almost the entire surface of CUHK-ICD images, while it is lower in the edges of the other datasets, in particular, those of the CPC and XPView. This means that most of the CUHK-ICD candidate views cover almost the total surface of the image, while the CPC and XPView candidate views are very different from each other and focus on image regions much smaller than the entire surface. The previous qualitative results are validated by quantitative analysis. Precisely, we estimate the average percentage of candidate views coverage respect to the whole image area. The values obtained for each photographer P of the CUHK-ICD dataset correspond respectively to: 82.07 ± 14.74 for P1, 82.69 ± 17.89 for P2, and 80.49 ± 16.76 for P3. For FCDB dataset, it is equal to 65.55 ± 16.64. The percentage coverage obtained for the candidate views of the FLMS dataset is 58.59 ± 17.41. Finally, CPC and XPView datasets have similar statistics equal respectively to 41.82 ± 16.95 and 43.68 ± 17.07.

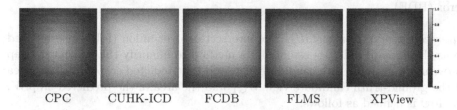

CPC   CUHK-ICD   FCDB   FLMS   XPView

Fig. 3. Heatmaps showing the spatial coverage of all candidate views for each dataset.

Finally, we analyze the semantic of images and how the crop of candidate view sub-regions alter it. To this end, we exploit the Hybrid-CNN [24], a CNN trained using 3.5 million images for 1,183 categories, obtained by merging the scenes categories from Places database [24] and the object categories from ImageNet [17]. The table in Fig. 4a reports the percentage of times that the semantic concept of an image is maintained in the crop obtained by applying the candidate views. Figure 4b presents the distribution of semantic concepts on the images of each dataset. We can see that the distributions are very spread across all the categories and some peaks are present in correspondence of landscape concepts like: promontory, lakeside, and valley.

Dataset		Same concept (%)
CPC		38.89
	P1	65.89
CUHK-ICD	P2	68.21
	P3	68.00
FCDB		50.87
FLMS		58.94
XPView		39.89

(a)

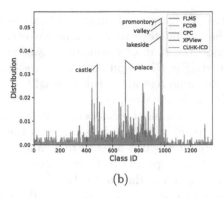

(b)

Fig. 4. Semantic analysis. Number of times semantic concept is preserved in candidate views for each dataset (a). Distribution on the 1,365 semantic concepts of the Hybrid-CNN for dataset images (b).

3.2 Performance Evaluation of Autocropping Algorithms

We measure the baseline by considering a dummy solution consisting of crops sampled in different ways with a surface that covers the image area with decreasing percentages from time to time. More in detail, we estimate the performance by cropping regions keeping from 100% to 10% of the image area, and by averaging the results of 100 iterations of random crops retaining from 100% to 10% of the image area. The evaluation metrics commonly used for cropping performance comparison are intersection-over-union (IoU) and boundary displacement error (BDE).

Intersection-over-Union (IoU). The intersection-over-union (IoU), also referred to as the Jaccard index, is essentially a method to quantify the percent overlap between the ground-truth candidate view and the predicted crop. Given the area of the ground-truth candidate view W_{GT} and the area of the predicted crop W, the IoU is defined as follows:

$$IoU = (W_{GT} \cap W)/(W_{GT} \cup W) \qquad (2)$$

Boundary Displacement Error (BDE). The boundary displacement error computes the distance between the four edges of the ground-truth candidate view and the corresponding edges of the predicted crop. By denoting the four edges of the ground-truth candidate view and of the predicted view respectively as $B_{GT}(l)$, $B_{GT}(r)$, $B_{GT}(t)$, $B_{GT}(b)$, and $B(l)$, $B(r)$, $B(t)$, $B(b)$. The BDE is estimated as follows:

$$BDE = \sum_{j=\{l,r,u,b\}} |B_{GT}(j) - B(j)|/4, \qquad (3)$$

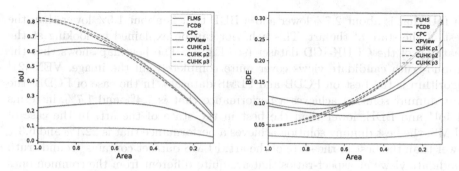

Fig. 5. IoU and BDE obtained by comparing ground-truth candidate views with dummy central crops covering image areas from 100% to 10%.

Table 2. Comparison in terms of IoU and BDE respectively for CUHK-ICD, FCDB and FLMS datasets. The *ΔBest* row reports the absolute error between the result (in blue) of the best method in the state of the art and the best value (in magenta) among the various scales of the dummy solution.

Method	CUHK-ICD						FCDB		FLMS	
	P1		P2		P3					
	IoU	BDE	IoU	BDE	IoU	BDE	IoU	BDE	IoU	BDE
VFN (2017) [3]	0.749	0.071	0.729	0.075	0.732	0.074	0.675	0.086	0.747	0.067
A2-RL (2018) [12]	0.802	0.052	0.796	0.053	0.790	0.053	0.663	0.089	0.820	–
ABP-AA (2017) [19]	0.813	0.030	0.806	0.032	0.816	0.032	–		0.810	0.057
AIC (2018) [20]	0.815	0.031	0.810	0.030	0.830	0.029	0.650	0.080	0.830	0.052
CCR (2018) [8]	0.850	0.032	0.837	0.033	0.828	0.035	–		–	
VPN (2018) [21]	–		–		–		0.711	0.073	0.835	0.044
VEN (2018) [21]	–		–		–		0.735	0.072	0.836	0.041
Dummy (100%)	0.823	0.046	0.830	0.046	0.808	0.050	0.636	0.100	0.586	0.116
Dummy (95%)	0.819	0.047	0.819	0.048	0.805	0.050	0.648	0.095	0.597	0.112
Dummy (85%)	0.798	0.052	0.778	0.058	0.778	0.058	0.661	0.089	0.615	0.104
ΔBest	0.027	0.015	0.007	0.016	0.022	0.021	0.074	0.017	0.221	0.063

Results. We collect performance for all the datasets at varying crop scales both for the center and random dummy solutions: the two dummy solutions achieved performance that is not significantly different. Figure 5 exhibits the IoU and the BDE at varying center crop scales for each database. As it is possible to see, the performance for the CUHK-ICD dataset is initially very high, both in terms of IoU and BDE, and declines in an almost linear fashion as the surface covered by the dummy crops decreases. Achieved results for FLMS and FCDB are linear until scale 0.5 where they go down. Finally, performance is stably low for CPC and XPView datasets. Table 2 shows comparison, in terms of IoU and BDE, between several algorithms in the state of the art with the dummy solution. We include CUHK-ICD, FCDB and FLMS because they are the datasets commonly used for benchmarking cropping algorithms. From the table is clear that CCR [8] and AIC [20] are the best methods in terms of IoU and BDE for the CUHK-ICD dataset. However, the best dummy solution achieves, on the same dataset, an IoU that is about 2.7% lower and a BDE that is about 1.5% lower than the best in the state of the art. This behavior can be explained by looking at the heatmap of the CUHK-ICD dataset (see Fig. 3). The heatmap shows that the ground-truth candidate views cover quite completely all the image. VEN [21] algorithm is the best on FCDB and FLMS datasets. In the case of FCDB, the best dummy solution achieves a performance that is 7.4% and 1.7%, in terms of IoU and BDE, lower than the best in the state of the art. In the case of FLMS, the best dummy solution achieves a performance that is 22.1% and 6.3% lower than the best in the state of the art. FLMS dataset contains ground-truth candidate views at aspect-ratios that are quite different from the common ones (see Fig. 2b). Moreover, Fig. 3 shows that candidate views do not cover the entire image.

4   Conclusions

In this work we conduct a detailed analysis of the main datasets in the state of the art for the evaluation of autocropping methods in terms of statistics, diversity and coverage of the ground-truth crops. Results show that each dataset models the cropping problem differently. Moreover, CPC and XPView datasets consist of very diverse candidate views, and most of the datasets do not consist of candidate views having standard aspect-ratios. Comparison between state of the art and dummy solutions show that, in case of the CUHK-ICD dataset, comparable results with the best solution in state of the art can be reached by using a dummy autocropping strategy that does not crop anything. Results obtained on the FCDB and FLMS show that these datasets are more challenging and diverse, with the dummy solutions performing worse than state of the art algorithms, and thus making them more suitable for the evaluation of autocropping algorithms.

References

1. Bianco, S., Ciocca, G.: User preferences modeling and learning for pleasing photo collage generation. ACM TOMM **12**(1), 6 (2015)
2. Chen, Y.L., Huang, T.W., Chang, K.H., Tsai, Y.C., Chen, H.T., Chen, B.Y.: Quantitative analysis of automatic image cropping algorithms: a dataset and comparative study. In: WACV, pp. 226–234. IEEE (2017)
3. Chen, Y.L., Klopp, J., Sun, M., Chien, S.Y., Ma, K.L.: Learning to compose with professional photographs on the web. In: ICM, pp. 37–45. ACM (2017)
4. Ciocca, G., Cusano, C., Gasparini, F., Schettini, R.: Self-adaptive image cropping for small displays. IEEE TCE **53**(4), 1622–1627 (2007)
5. Deng, Y., Loy, C.C., Tang, X.: Aesthetic-driven image enhancement by adversarial learning. In: ICM, pp. 870–878. ACM (2018)
6. Fang, C., Lin, Z., Mech, R., Shen, X.: Automatic image cropping using visual composition, boundary simplicity and content preservation models. In: ICM, pp. 1105–1108. ACM (2014)
7. Geiger, A., Lenz, P., Stiller, C., Urtasun, R.: The KITTI vision benchmark suite (2015). http://www.cvlibs.net/datasets/kitti

8. Guo, G., Wang, H., Shen, C., Yan, Y., Liao, H.Y.M.: Automatic image cropping for visual aesthetic enhancement using deep neural networks and cascaded regression. IEEE Trans. Multimed. **20**(8), 2073–2085 (2018)
9. Kao, Y., He, R., Huang, K.: Automatic image cropping with aesthetic map and gradient energy map. In: ICASSP, pp. 1982–1986. IEEE (2017)
10. Kong, S., Shen, X., Lin, Z., Mech, R., Fowlkes, C.: Photo aesthetics ranking network with attributes and content adaptation. In: Leibe, B., Matas, J., Sebe, N., Welling, M. (eds.) ECCV 2016. LNCS, vol. 9905, pp. 662–679. Springer, Cham (2016). https://doi.org/10.1007/978-3-319-46448-0_40
11. Kotsiantis, S., Kanellopoulos, D., Pintelas, P., et al.: Handling imbalanced datasets: a review. GESTS Int. Trans. Comput. Sci. Eng. **30**(1), 25–36 (2006)
12. Li, D., Wu, H., Zhang, J., Huang, K.: A2-RL: aesthetics aware reinforcement learning for image cropping. In: CVPR, pp. 8193–8201. IEEE (2018)
13. Lin, T.Y., et al.: Microsoft COCO: common objects in context. In: Fleet, D., Pajdla, T., Schiele, B., Tuytelaars, T. (eds.) ECCV 2014. LNCS, vol. 8693, pp. 740–755. Springer, Cham (2014). https://doi.org/10.1007/978-3-319-10602-1_48
14. Marchesotti, L., Cifarelli, C., Csurka, G.: A framework for visual saliency detection with applications to image thumbnailing. In: ICCV, pp. 2232–2239. IEEE (2009)
15. Milan, A., Leal-Taixé, L., Reid, I., Roth, S., Schindler, K.: MOT16: a benchmark for multi-object tracking. arXiv preprint arXiv:1603.00831 (2016)
16. Murray, N., Marchesotti, L., Perronnin, F.: AVA: a large-scale database for aesthetic visual analysis. In: CVPR, pp. 2408–2415. IEEE (2012)
17. Russakovsky, O., et al.: Imagenet large scale visual recognition challenge. IJCV **115**(3), 211–252 (2015)
18. Tang, X., Luo, W., Wang, X.: Content-based photo quality assessment. IEEE Trans. Multimed. **15**(8), 1930–1943 (2013)
19. Wang, W., Shen, J.: Deep cropping via attention box prediction and aesthetics assessment. In: CVPR, pp. 2186–2194. IEEE (2017)
20. Wang, W., Shen, J., Ling, H.: A deep network solution for attention and aesthetics aware photo cropping. IEEE TPAMI **41**, 1531–1544 (2018)
21. Wei, Z., et al.: Good view hunting: Learning photo composition from dense view pairs. In: CVPR, pp. 5437–5446. IEEE (2018)
22. Yan, J., Lin, S., Kang, S.B., Tang, X.: Learning the change for automatic image cropping. In: CVPR, pp. 971–978. IEEE (2013)
23. Zhang, M., Zhang, L., Sun, Y., Feng, L., Ma, W.: Auto cropping for digital photographs. In: ICME, pp. 4-pp. IEEE (2005)
24. Zhou, B., Lapedriza, A., Xiao, J., Torralba, A., Oliva, A.: Learning deep features for scene recognition using places database. In: Advances in Neural Information Processing Systems, pp. 487–495 (2014)

Combining Saliency Estimation Methods

Marco Buzzelli$^{(\boxtimes)}$, Simone Bianco, and Gianluigi Ciocca

University of Milano - Bicocca, Milan, Italy
{marco.buzzelli,simone.bianco,gianluigi.ciocca}@unimib.it

Abstract. We address the task of image saliency estimation through proper recombination of existing methods in the state of the art. We define a general scheme, which we then specialize to perform dataset-specific and image-specific recombination, based on either linear weight regression, or method selection. The advantage of this approach lies in the possibility of exploiting the different strengths of existing methods. Experiments are conducted with both deep learning and hand-crafted methods on a widely used dataset, using standard evaluation measures. The proposed recombination strategy allows us to improve upon the state of the art, by exploiting a linear combination of the saliency maps produced by existing methods. We also show that image-specific combination and selection of saliency maps is limited by the apparent lack of relevant information intrinsic in the image itself.

Keywords: Saliency estimation · Combining · Deep learning

1 Introduction

Saliency estimation refers to the localization of the areas in an image having particular clue for a human observer, while salient object detection refers to the detection and segmentation of the most salient objects in the scene. There is, however, no consensus about the definition of "what saliency is" in the community. Multiple observers may consider salient different elements in the scene, and some elements may be considered more salient than others depending on the scene context and/or on the observer's cultural background. This makes saliency estimation an ill-posed problem [1,29]. This is also reflected by the many saliency detection methods proposed in the literature. As demonstrated by the authors in [6] and [10], there is no best overall saliency detection algorithm that is able to achieve equally good results across different benchmark datasets. They analyze and benchmark many different saliency detection algorithms each based on different assumptions, heuristics and features that can be either hand-crafted, learned by Convolutional Neural Networks (CNN), or both.

Among the hand-crafted approaches is [17] that computes saliency from the perspective of image reconstruction error of background images generated at different level of details. A graph-based manifold ranking is used in [30] to classify superpixels into foreground and background regions. In [34] an image patch is

© Springer Nature Switzerland AG 2019
E. Ricci et al. (Eds.): ICIAP 2019, LNCS 11752, pp. 326–336, 2019.
https://doi.org/10.1007/978-3-030-30645-8_30

considered not salient if it is heavily connected to the image boundaries. Other graph-based approaches are the ones presented in [11], and [2]. In [32] is presented a graph-based approach that exploits a fast Minimum Barrier Distance to measure a pixel's connectivity to the image boundary. In [7] the saliency of each image region is carried out by simultaneously evaluating global contrast differences and spatial coherence with nearby regions. Color is used in [12] where the saliency is based on a linear combination of high-dimensional color spaces. In [22] global contrast, spatial sparsity, and object priors are integrated to estimate the saliency of image regions. Finally, an approach based on multiple features computed in a multi-level segmentation schema is presented in [26].

CNN-based approaches are able to process images extracting information at different levels of details, and can automatically learn what is the relevant information within an image given a specific task. For example, a multi-branch approach is proposed in [33] and [15], processing the image at a different level of details. In [16] the image is analyzed to produce pixel-level and super-pixel level segmentation maps that are then fused together, while a multi-task learning scheme based on saliency and segmentation is used in [18]. In [19] it is designed a novel network architecture that works in a global-to-local manner to improve saliency detection performance. In [14] both low level and high level features are exploited in a unified deep learning approach. A CNN is used in [31] as an embedding function to map pixels and their attributes to classify them as salient/background. Using different layers in the neural architecture provides multi-scale feature maps that can be exploited for an efficient salient object detection. Example of algorithms using this approach are [10], and [3]. Recurrent network architectures can effectively help reducing prediction errors by iteratively integrating contextual information which is important for saliency detection. To this end, recurrent convolutional networks are used to refine the saliency map by correcting errors during the learning process [20,27,28].

2   Proposed Approach to Saliency Estimation

Our approach to saliency estimation is based on the analysis, selection, and combination of existing saliency estimation methods.

Given an input image $i \in I$, and a set $S_i = \{s_{i,m} : m \in M\}$ of saliency predictions produced by $|M|$ existing saliency estimation methods, we construct a novel saliency map $\hat{s}_i$ by linear combination:

$$\hat{s}_i = \left(\sum_{m \in M} w_{i,m} \cdot s_{i,m} \right) \geq T \tag{1}$$

where $w_{i,m} \in \mathbb{R}$, and $T = 0.5$. Imposing a threshold T on the predictions eventually produces a binary estimation of image saliency, which has been shown to positively affect standard measures [3].

We introduce various additional constraints into Eq. 1, that allow us to frame the problem in terms of either combination of saliency methods, or selection of saliency methods.

2.1   Combination of Saliency Methods

Equation 1 is formulated in terms of linear combination of weights. A Convolutional Neural Network (CNN) is trained to generate the proper set of weights by processing either the RGB image itself, or the related existing saliency estimations. To this extent, preliminary investigation led to the adoption of a ResNet-18 [9], trained with the objective of reproducing the ground truth saliency maps. The hard threshold T cannot be directly applied during the training process, as its non-differentiability would compromise the gradient backpropagation. It has been instead replaced, at training-time only, with a soft threshold implemented through a steep sigmoid function. On top of this solution, we experiment with further constraints:

1. We impose a fixed set of weights for all images:

$$w_{i,m} = w_{j,m}, \ \ \forall i,j \in I \tag{2}$$

   In this case, the weights will be optimized globally on the defined training set, instead of learning to infer them from each RGB image.
2. We limit the linear combination to $M^{(N)}$, defined as the subset of the N best-performing methods. That is:

$$w_{i,m} = 0, \ \ \forall m \in M \setminus M^{(N)} \tag{3}$$

2.2   Selection of Saliency Methods

The weight-regression problem defined in the previous sections can be reformulated as a classification task:

$$\sum_{m \in M} w_{i,m} = 1, \ \ w_{i,m} \in \{0,1\} \tag{4}$$

To this extent, a CNN is trained with the objective of selecting, for each image, the best performing method. In this case, the model is trained with a softmax cross-entropy loss, comparing the performed selection with the defined best method. The ground truth best method can be determined as the one with the best performance evaluated with standard measures (see Sect. 3.1). The input to the neural model can either be the RGB image itself, or the related existing saliency maps.

Existing literature covers this classification-oriented view of the problem as an Ensamble Dictionary Learning task (EDL) [35]. Here we focus on whole-image selection of more-recently developed methods for saliency estimation.

3   Experimental Results

In this section we present the experimental setup, along with results obtained on saliency estimation with the proposed combination and selection of existing solutions.

3.1   Experimental Setup

State of the art methods for saliency estimation are often published along with the corresponding predictions on standard datasets. The most popular ones are the MSRAB dataset [21] and the related MSRA10K dataset [7]. In order to setup a common dataset among all algorithms exploited in this paper, we defined the MSRAB Validation Subset (366 images) and MSRAB Test Subset (1516 images), as the intersection between the original splits of MSRAB and the entire MSRA10K dataset. For the optimization of a fixed set of weights, we train on the MSRAB Validation Subset and evaluate on the MSRAB Test Subset. To learn the more complex image-specific models, instead, we train on a combination of existing datasets for saliency estimation from [3], and also evaluate on the MSRAB Test Subset. Following [10], evaluation is performed in terms of both MAE and F_β:

$$MAE = \frac{1}{|I|} \sum_{i \in I} \frac{1}{|C|} \sum_{c \in C} |PR_{i,c} - GT_{i,c}| \tag{5}$$

$$F_{\beta = \sqrt{0.3}} = \max_{t \in T} \frac{(1 + \beta^2) \frac{1}{|I|} \sum_{i \in I} Precision_i(t) \cdot \frac{1}{|I|} \sum_{i \in I} Recall_i(t)}{\beta^2 \cdot \frac{1}{|I|} \sum_{i \in I} Precision_i(t) + \frac{1}{|I|} \sum_{i \in I} Recall_i(t)} \tag{6}$$

where I is the set of images, C the set of coordinates for every given image, and T the set of possible thresholds. PR and GT are, respectively, the saliency prediction and ground truth. Expansion of $Precision$ and $Recall$ is here omitted for brevity reasons. A mixture measure can also be defined as the average of the complemented rescaled MAE, and the rescaled F_β:

$$mix_{i,m} = \left(1 - norm_{i,m}^{MAE}\right) + norm_{i,m}^{F_\beta} \tag{7}$$

where:

$$norm_{i,m}^x = \frac{x_{i,m} - \min_{m \in M}(x_{i,m})}{\max_{m \in M}(x_{i,m}) - \min_{m \in M}(x_{i,m})} \tag{8}$$

In this work we considered a total of 20 saliency estimation algorithms: ten hand-crafted, and ten deep-based. For the hand-crafted ones we analyzed SC [33], DHS [19], MDF [15], ELD [14], DS [18], DCL [16], RFCN [27], DRCN [20], DSS [10], and MFCN [3]. For the had-crafted algorithms, we considered GMR [30], DSR [17], MC [11], ST [22], RBD [34], EQC [2], MB+ [32], RC [7], HDCT [12], and RFI [26].

3.2   Dataset Content Analysis

Before evaluating the combination strategies, we investigated if there is any connection between image content and best performing algorithm. The first column in Table 1 shows a priori probabilities of each method (belonging to either the deep learning, or hand-crafted family) being the best one for the analyzed

Table 1. A priori and conditioned probabilities of different methods (M) given a certain type of content (belonging to either C_1 and C_2). Algorithms are sorted in descending order by the mixture measure defined in Eq. 7.

	Method	$P(M)$	$P(M|C_1)$			$P(M|C_2)$	
			Object	Scene/in	Scene/out	No-people	People
Deep learning (DL)	DHS [19]	0.553	0.517	0.709	0.593	0.553	0.553
	ELD [14]	0.193	0.249	0.109	0.117	0.206	0.142
	DSS [10]	0.144	0.118	0.073	0.190	0.130	0.198
	RFCN [27]	0.012	0.018	0.000	0.003	0.013	0.006
	DCL [16]	0.046	0.038	0.036	0.059	0.044	0.053
	DS [18]	0.003	0.002	0.018	0.002	0.003	0.003
	MFCN [3]	0.007	0.008	0.000	0.005	0.006	0.009
	SC [33]	0.001	0.002	0.000	0.000	0.002	0.000
	MDF [15]	0.033	0.041	0.055	0.019	0.037	0.019
	DRCN [20]	0.008	0.006	0.000	0.012	0.006	0.016
Hand-crafted (HC)	EQC [2]	0.201	0.193	0.200	0.214	0.216	0.145
	DRFI [26]	0.119	0.104	0.127	0.139	0.114	0.138
	ST [22]	0.171	0.159	0.200	0.185	0.169	0.179
	MB+ [32]	0.108	0.097	0.091	0.126	0.105	0.119
	RBD [34]	0.113	0.139	0.055	0.080	0.119	0.088
	GMR [30]	0.123	0.148	0.182	0.081	0.125	0.116
	DSR [17]	0.068	0.057	0.073	0.083	0.063	0.085
	RC [7]	0.030	0.026	0.000	0.039	0.028	0.041
	MC [11]	0.035	0.052	0.018	0.012	0.040	0.016
	HDCT [12]	0.032	0.024	0.055	0.041	0.021	0.072

dataset. We can see how these distributions change when conditioned on two types of image content: the first conditioning (C_1) partitions the possible subjects into "object", "scene (indoor)", and "scene (outdoor)". The second conditioning (C_2) considers the presence or absence of people in the image. We observe little impact on the probability distribution over M with or without different types of conditioning. This suggests little to no connection between the considered image content and best performing method.

3.3   Combination of Saliency Methods

The first experiment consists in determining a set of linear combination weights specific for each input image. This has been dealt with by defining a CNN that predicts the linear weights as a function of either the RGB image itself, or the saliency estimation maps produced by existing saliency estimation methods.

The second experiment consists in evaluating a dataset-specific weights combination instead of image-specific ones. In order to do this, we optimize a fixed set of weights in Eq. 1 to be applied for all the images. As shown in the third and fourth rows of Table 2, for this experiment the best results were obtained on deep learning methods using as input the RGB images, producing 0.0253 MAE and 0.9418 F_β. These values represent an improvement with respect to the reported baselines in the first and second rows of Table 2: best single method and combination with uniform weights. The best single method refers, respectively, to

Table 2. Performance obtained with method combination on the MSRAB Test Subset.

	Deep learning (DL)		Hand-crafted (HC)	
	MAE	F_β	MAE	F_β
Single best method (DHS [19] and EQC [2])	0.0275	0.9365	0.0927	0.8365
Uniform weights	0.0265	0.9407	0.0715	0.8803
Image-specific weights (from RGB)	0.0253	0.9418	0.0601	0.8928
Image-specific weights (from saliency)	0.0254	0.9426	0.0590	0.8953
Dataset-specific weights (fixed)	0.0242	0.9445	0.0528	0.8887

DHS for deep learning solutions and EQC for what concerns hand-crafted algorithms. The fixed weights optimization allowed reaching 0.242 MAE and 0.9445 F_β on deep learning methods, compared to the best single-method DHS (0.0275 MAE and 0.9365 F_β). Significant improvements are also observed on hand-crafted methods, although the obtained performance does not reach the level of deep learning solutions. As a general observation, the simpler fixed-weights setup appears to outperform the generation of image-specific weights. We hypothesize that the RGB images do not contain enough information to provide the necessary nuanced image-specific sets of weights.

To further explore the promising fixed-weights setup, we optimize on a varying subset of saliency estimation methods. Figure 1 shows the performance obtained, in terms of MAE and F_β, by imposing zero weights on all but the first N best performing methods, as ordered as in Table 1. As a comparison, uniform weights are also reported. It can be seen that introducing more than four best-performing methods in a uniform-weight linear combination, deteriorates the overall performance. This is especially evident for what concerns the deep learning methods (sub-figures (a) and (b)). Corroborating this observation, the improvement introduced by proper weight optimization on less performing methods appears to be negligible. Notice that the curve trend on the training set is not strictly decreasing due to the optimization being guided by a mixture of the two metrics, and due to the randomness of the mini-batch training process.

3.4 Selection of Saliency Methods

In this Section, we present an analysis on image-specific selection of saliency estimation methods. To this extent, Table 3 offers several baselines: uniform sampling is a purely random selection of the input saliency estimation method, while prior sampling takes into account the *a priori* probability of each method being the best solution on the MSRAB Test Subset. It should be noted that the prior sampling under-performs with respect to the best single method, due to the adopted metrics not being directly related to classification accuracy. An ideal oracle could be based on MAE, F_β, or a mix of the two measures, as shown in rows four to six in Table 3, reaching in the best scenario 0.0200 MAE and 0.9553 F_β for deep learning methods. These values can therefore be considered the upper-bound of any solution for automated selection of image-specific saliency estimation methods.

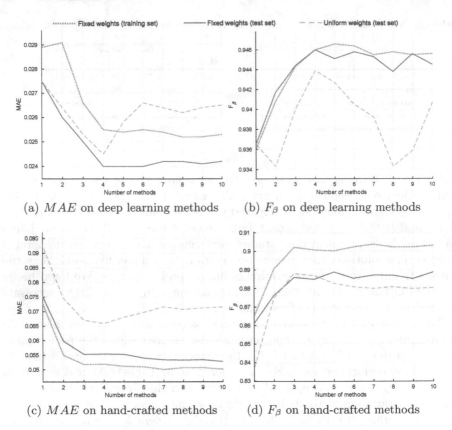

(a) MAE on deep learning methods   (b) F_β on deep learning methods

(c) MAE on hand-crafted methods   (d) F_β on hand-crafted methods

Fig. 1. Performance of fixed weights on the MSRAB Validation Subset and Test Subset, obtained by optimizing on only the first N best performing saliency estimation methods.

For this experiment, a CNN has been trained with the task of replicating the effect of each mix-based oracle, in selecting the best saliency estimation method for each specific image, based on a processing of the RGB image or the existing saliency estimation maps. The results reported in the last two rows of Table 3 show that, for deep learning solutions, only a small improvement over the best single method can be obtained by analyzing the available saliency maps, while the RGB images do not contain enough information to perform the task. This is in line with what has already been observed for methods combination. In the case of hand-crafted methods, the results obtained by the trained neural models outperform all reported baselines (Fig. 2).

3.5   Embedding Analysis

In this section we want to assess if indeed the RGB images contain enough information to capture the necessary nuanced for the optimization of image-specific weights (Sect. 3.3) or to predict the best method to apply (Sect. 3.4). To

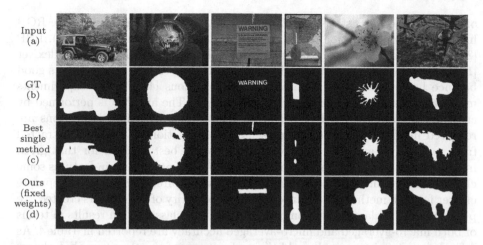

Fig. 2. Visual results of our approach to combination of saliency estimation maps. Rows (a) and (b) show, respectively, the starting image and the corresponding ground truth annotation. Row (c) is the best single method solution. Row (d) is our fixed-weight optimization.

Table 3. Performance obtained with method selection on the MSRAB Test Subset.

	Deep learning (DL)		Hand-crafted (HC)	
	MAE	F_β	MAE	F_β
Single best method (DHS [19] and EQC [2])	0.0275	0.9365	0.0927	0.8365
Uniform sampling	0.0734	0.8632	0.0889	0.8406
Prior sampling	0.0355	0.9213	0.0863	0.8444
Oracle (MAE)	0.0173	0.9538	0.0473	0.9105
Oracle (F_β)	0.0200	0.9521	0.0610	0.8997
Oracle (mix)	0.0175	0.9553	0.0465	0.9171
Image-specific selection (from RGB)	0.0298	0.9319	0.0795	0.8565
Image-specific selection (from saliency)	0.0270	0.9368	0.0835	0.8524

this end, we extract a set of features that describe images from different points

Table 4. 1-NN classification performance of the different features considered.

Features	Accuracy (macro)	Accuracy (micro)
Single best method (DHS [19])	0.4677	0.1000
RGB	0.2863	0.1066
RGB histogram	0.2850	0.1060
LBP	0.2876	0.1206
HOG	0.2559	0.0945
AlexNet	0.3008	0.1209
Inception-ResNet-v2	0.3047	0.1200

of view: simple RGB statistics (channel average and standard deviation), RGB histograms (concatenation of the channel histograms each with 16 bins), LBP [24], HOG [8], CNN features from two models trained on ImageNet: AlexNet [13], chosen for its popularity, and Inception-ResNet-v2 [25], chosen for its good balance between accuracy and number of operations [4]. Further experiments might also take into account local descriptors [5]. The analysis is performed by creating 2D projections of each feature with t-SNE [23]. The projections are reported in Fig. 3. Each point represents the projection of a feature extracted from one image, and its color corresponds to the best method for that given image. From the projections it is possible to notice that for certain features some clusters emerge. In the ideal case, an informative feature, would create a separate cluster for each method. In order to measure the purity of the clusters created, we perform a 1-NN classification on each feature. The classification results in terms of both macro-averaged and micro-averaged accuracy are reported in Table 4. As a further comparison, we also add the performance of the classifiers that always predicts to use the global best method (i.e. DHS). From the results reported it is possible to notice that the best results are obtained by the CNN features, but that the results are very low, suggesting a large impurity in the clusters thus enforcing the hypothesis that the RGB images do not contain enough information (or do not provide suitable information) to perform this task.

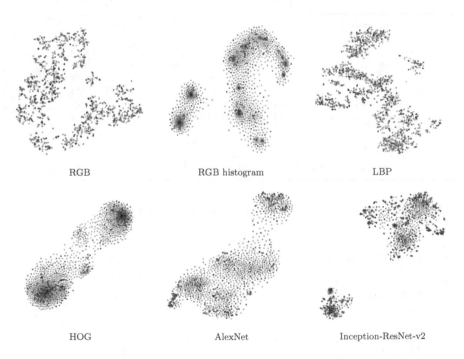

Fig. 3. 2D t-SNE [23] projections of each feature considered. (Color figure online)

4 Conclusions

By considering all the different rationales in existing saliency estimation algorithms, and their diverse levels of performance, we define a general scheme for saliency estimation through proper recombination of existing methods in the state of the art. The advantage of this approach lies in the possibility of exploiting the different strengths of existing methods. We treat the combination problem as either linear weight regression, or method selection. We are able to improve performance on the state of the art by optimizing a linear combination over a subset of saliency estimation method. Several attempts at producing image-specific combination resulted in sub-optimal results. Further analysis showed the apparent non-correlation between image content and best performing saliency estimation algorithm for both the combination and selection tasks.

Acknowledgments. The research leading to these results has received funding from TEINVEIN: CUP: E96D17000110009, cofunded by POR FESR 2014–2020.

References

1. Amirul Islam, M., Kalash, M., Bruce, N.D.: Revisiting salient object detection: simultaneous detection, ranking, and subitizing of multiple salient objects. In: IEEE CVPR, pp. 7142–7150 (2018)
2. Aytekin, Ç., Ozan, E.C., Kiranyaz, S., Gabbouj, M.: Visual saliency by extended quantum cuts. In: IEEE ICIP, pp. 1692–1696 (2015)
3. Bianco, S., Buzzelli, M., Schettini, R.: Multiscale fully convolutional network for image saliency. JEI **27**, 051221 (2018)
4. Bianco, S., Cadene, R., Celona, L., Napoletano, P.: Benchmark analysis of representative deep neural network architectures. IEEE Access **6**, 64270–64277 (2018)
5. Bianco, S., Schettini, R., Mazzini, D., Pau, D.P.: Quantitative review of local descriptors for visual search. In: IEEE Third ICCE-Berlin, pp. 98–102. IEEE (2013)
6. Borji, A., Cheng, M., Jiang, H., Li, J.: Salient object detection: a benchmark. IEEE TIP **24**(12), 5706–5722 (2015)
7. Cheng, M., Mitra, N.J., Huang, X., Torr, P.H.S., Hu, S.: Global contrast based salient region detection. IEEE TPAMI **37**(3), 569–582 (2015)
8. Dalal, N., Triggs, B.: Histograms of oriented gradients for human detection. In: IEEE CVPR, vol. 1, pp. 886–893. IEEE Computer Society (2005)
9. He, K., Zhang, X., Ren, S., Sun, J.: Deep residual learning for image recognition. In: Proceedings of the IEEE CVPR, pp. 770–778 (2016)
10. Hou, Q., Cheng, M., Hu, X., Borji, A., Tu, Z., Torr, P.H.S.: Deeply supervised salient object detection with short connections. IEEE TPAMI **41**, 815–828 (2018)
11. Jiang, B., Zhang, L., Lu, H., Yang, C., Yang, M.H.: Saliency detection via absorbing markov chain. In: IEEE ICCV, pp. 1665–1672 (2013)
12. Kim, J., Han, D., Tai, Y., Kim, J.: Salient region detection via high-dimensional color transform and local spatial support. IEEE TIP **25**(1), 9–23 (2016)
13. Krizhevsky, A., Sutskever, I., Hinton, G.E.: Imagenet classification with deep convolutional neural networks. In: NIPS, pp. 1097–1105 (2012)
14. Lee, G., Tai, Y.W., Kim, J.: Deep saliency with encoded low level distance map and high level features. In: IEEE CVPR, pp. 660–668 (2016)

15. Li, G., Yu, Y.: Visual saliency based on multiscale deep features. In: IEEE CVPR, pp. 5455–5463 (2015)
16. Li, G., Yu, Y.: Deep contrast learning for salient object detection. In: IEEE CVPR, pp. 478–487 (2016)
17. Li, X., Lu, H., Zhang, L., Ruan, X., Yang, M.: Saliency detection via dense and sparse reconstruction. In: ICCV, pp. 2976–2983 (2013)
18. Li, X., et al.: Deepsaliency: multi-task deep neural network model for salient object detection. IEEE TIP **25**(8), 3919–3930 (2016)
19. Liu, N., Han, J.: DHSNet: deep hierarchical saliency network for salient object detection. In: IEEE CVPR, pp. 678–686 (2016)
20. Liu, N., Han, J.: A deep spatial contextual long-term recurrent convolutional network for saliency detection. IEEE TIP **27**(7), 3264–3274 (2018)
21. Liu, T., et al.: Learning to detect a salient object. IEEE TPAMI **33**(2), 353–367 (2011)
22. Liu, Z., Zou, W., Meur, O.L.: Saliency tree: a novel saliency detection framework. IEEE TIP **23**(5), 1937–1952 (2014)
23. van der Maaten, L., Hinton, G.: Visualizing data using t-SNE. J. Mach. Learn. Res. **9**(1), 2579–2605 (2008)
24. Ojala, T., Pietikäinen, M., Mäenpää, T.: Multiresolution gray-scale and rotation invariant texture classification with local binary patterns. IEEE TPAMI **7**, 971–987 (2002)
25. Szegedy, C., Ioffe, S., Vanhoucke, V., Alemi, A.A.: Inception-v4, inception-resnet and the impact of residual connections on learning. In: AAAI Conference on AI (2017)
26. Wang, J., Jiang, H., Yuan, Z., Cheng, M.M., Hu, X., Zheng, N.: Salient object detection: a discriminative regional feature integration approach. IJCV **123**(2), 251–268 (2017)
27. Wang, L., Wang, L., Lu, H., Zhang, P., Ruan, X.: Salient object detection with recurrent fully convolutional networks. IEEE TPAMI **41**, 1734–1746 (2018)
28. Wang, T., et al.: Detect globally, refine locally: a novel approach to saliency detection. In: IEEE CVPR, pp. 3127–3135 (2018)
29. Wei, Y., Wen, F., Zhu, W., Sun, J.: Geodesic saliency using background priors. In: Fitzgibbon, A., Lazebnik, S., Perona, P., Sato, Y., Schmid, C. (eds.) ECCV 2012. LNCS, vol. 7574, pp. 29–42. Springer, Heidelberg (2012). https://doi.org/10.1007/978-3-642-33712-3_3
30. Yang, C., Zhang, L., Lu, H., Ruan, X., Yang, M.: Saliency detection via graph-based manifold ranking. In: IEEE CVPR, pp. 3166–3173 (2013)
31. Zeng, Y., Lu, H., Zhang, L., Feng, M., Borji, A.: Learning to promote saliency detectors. In: IEEE CVPR, pp. 1644–1653 (2018)
32. Zhang, J., Sclaroff, S., Lin, Z., Shen, X., Price, B., Mech, R.: Minimum barrier salient object detection at 80 FPS. In: IEEE ICCV, pp. 1404–1412 (2015)
33. Zhao, R., Ouyang, W., Li, H., Wang, X.: Saliency detection by multi-context deep learning. In: IEEE CVPR, pp. 1265–1274 (2015)
34. Zhu, W., Liang, S., Wei, Y., Sun, J.: Saliency optimization from robust background detection. In: IEEE CVPR, pp. 2814–2821 (2014)
35. Zhu, Z., Chen, Q., Zhao, Y.: Ensemble dictionary learning for saliency detection. Image Vis. Comput. **32**(3), 180–188 (2014)

The Impact of Padding on Image Classification by Using Pre-trained Convolutional Neural Networks

Hongxiang Tang, Alessandro Ortis$^{(\boxtimes)}$ (iD), and Sebastiano Battiato (iD)

Department of Mathematics and Computer Science,
University of Catania, Viale A. Doria, 6, 95125 Catania, Italy
hongxiang.tang@unict.it,{ortis,battiato}@dmi.unict.it

Abstract. The work presented in this paper aims to investigate the effect of pre-processing on image classification by using CNN pre-trained models. By considering how different quality factors of the input images affect the performances of a CNN based classifier, we propose a pre-processing pipeline (i.e., padding) that is able to improve the classification of the model on challenging images. The presented study allows to improve the performances by only acting on the input images, instead of re-training the model or augmenting the number of CNN's parameters. This finds very practical applications, since such model adaptation requires high amounts of labelled data and computational costs.

Keywords: Image preprocessing · Padding · Convolutional · Neural network

1 Introduction

In this paper, we investigated the impact of three different padding strategies in the usage of pre-trained Convolutional Neural Networks (CNNs) for the task of image classification. CNNs play a central role in Computer Vision since 2012, when AlexNet [5] dramatically decreased the state-of-the-art error rate in the ImageNet Large Scale Visual Recognition Challenge (ILSVRC) [9]. From that on, innovative and increasingly complex architectures have been proposed year by year with the aim to further improve the performances.

CNNs usually require a fixed size for the input images. Typical input sizes for a CNN are 224×224 [5] or 299×299 [10]. When training a CNN, the scale invariance is usually addressed by changing the input scale and presenting cropped version of the variable size image to the network. This is usually done by considering very high quality images containing only one subject related to the image class. However, in real-case scenarios, images are acquired in very low quality conditions depending on the device's settings and environment conditions such as distance and target's pose. Typical example tasks are licence plate recognition from street surveillance cameras and low-resolution target recognition [3].

© Springer Nature Switzerland AG 2019
E. Ricci et al. (Eds.): ICIAP 2019, LNCS 11752, pp. 337–344, 2019.
https://doi.org/10.1007/978-3-030-30645-8_31

In these contexts, a previously trained CNN on high quality images would not be able to adapt to real image domain [8]. Usually, when the input image has a resolution lower than the network input size, the image is padded with zero or an up-scaling of the image is performed (i.e., interpolation). Image resizing faces an amount of issues, indeed, downscaling causes loosing of information, whereas upscaling introduces a sort of "structured" noise to the input image. Saliency based seam carving [1] might be a effective approach to preserve the salient image information but it requires additional time and computational efforts. Moreover, is not possible to detect in a deterministic way regions of the background are not exploited by the CNN to perform the prediction (e.g., subject's context).

Only few works investigated image pre-processing approaches to improve the CNN classification results. The work in [7] evaluated different pre-processing strategies for CNN inputs, namely Mean Normalization, Standardization and Zero Component Analysis. The authors of [6] performed successful pre-processing studies on histopathological images. However, in both works, the model needs to be trained with the new pre-processed images to achieve performance improvements. The work in [4] evaluated several CNN models by degrading images with blurring, adding noise, reducing contrast and JEPG compression. Improvements can be further provided by data augmentation techniques [2]. Previous works on the evaluation of the effect of input image resolution in CNNs shown that the performances are stable for mid-resolution images, but there is a drop in performances when decreasing image resolution at 50×50 pixels [3] (i.e., critical resolution).

In the proposed work, we first show how input image quality factors affect CNN performances. Then, for very low resolution images, we evaluate the effect of three padding strategies. The achieved results show that is possible to improve the classification performances on low quality images by applying proper padding strategies, without editing the architecture structure nor performing fine-tuning on the new image domain.

2   Proposed Approach

Figure 1 shows the proposed evaluation pipeline. The input image is first transformed by applying the padding. Then, for each resulting image, three images with resolution 500×500, 100×100 and 70×70 are generated. In order to process such images by the pre-trained CNN, they need to be resized to the input resolution of the CNN (i.e., 299×299). Therefore, the images with resolution 500×500 are downscaled by sampling, whereas images with lower resolution (i.e., 100×100 and 70×70) are scaled-up by interpolation. In our experiments, we evaluated the classification accuracy on very low resolution images of the pre-trained CNN named InceptionV3 [10], which input resolution is 299×299 (see Fig. 1). A schema of the eight resulting padding patches, after the original image is centered in the padding area is shown in Fig. 2.

We evaluated the following padding strategies:

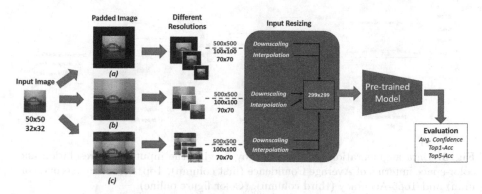

Fig. 1. Proposed pipeline: the low resolution input images are first padded by using one of the three proposed strategies, then different resolutions of the padded images are generated. The images with resolution higher than the input size of the employed CNN (i.e, 299 × 299) are downscaled, whereas the other images are resized by interpolating pixels. The resulting 299 × 299 images are then fed to the pre-trained CNN for evaluation.

P_1	P_2	P_3
P_4	Image	P_5
P_6	P_7	P_8

Fig. 2. Overall schema of the eight image patches that can be treated differently based on the padding strategy.

- **Constant Padding:** the image is surrounded by a constant value padding (see Fig. 1 (a)). In our experiments we filled the padding area with all 0;
- **Edge Padding:** in this case, the edge pixels (i.e., top/bottom rows and left/right columns) of the original image are repeated along the related direction (see Fig. 1(b)). The patch P_2 is filled by repeating the top pixel row of the image, patch P_7 with the bottom row, patch P_4 with the most left column and patch P_5 with the most right column. P_1, P_3, P_6 and P_8 are defined by repeating the value of the top-left, top-right, bottom-left and bottom-right corner pixel of the image respectively;
- **Mirror Padding:** in this case each row/column is padded with the wrap of the corresponding vector along the axis. The first values are used to pad the end, and the end values are used to pad the beginning (see Fig. 1(c)). Therefore, for instance, the left part of the image is mirrored in P_5, whereas the right part of the image is mirrored in P_4 (see Fig. 2).

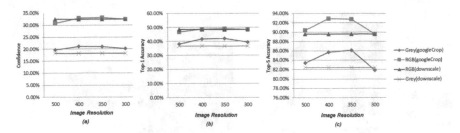

Fig. 3. Data augmentation performances by varying the input image resolution and color-space in terms of Average Confidence (first column), Top1-Accuracy (second column) and Top5-Accuracy (third column). (Color figure online)

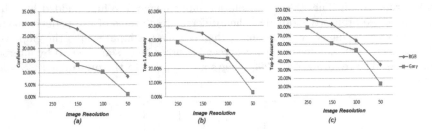

Fig. 4. Performances by varying the input image resolution and color-space in terms of Average Confidence (first column), Top1-Accuracy (second column) and Top5-Accuracy (third column). (Color figure online)

The images lose their information when resolution or color space reduced. In order to quantitatively analyze the information lost, we evaluate the CNN performance by image downscaling as well as changing color space from the RGB to grey scale. These two approaches along with the data augmentation method [10] compared in Fig. 3. In order to assess the improvements provided by the proposed pre-processing approaches, we also performed experiments without applying padding as our baseline, by just resizing the input low resolution image to the CNN input size (i.e., 299 × 299). In the following, we refer to this baseline experimental setting as "interpolation" for which bilinear method has been implemented.

The classification results have been evaluated considering the Top-1 and Top-5 accuracy, as well as the classifier average confidence. In particular, the average confidence is the mean probability assigned by the CNN classifier to the correct class label (i.e., class confidence). This measure is useful to assess the confidence of a model with respect to the correct class. Indeed, considering only the top$k$ highest probability outputs give an indication about the capability of the model to classify. With this metric we want to measure the confidence of the model in assigning the right class. In other words, we are interested in measuring what is the probability score by which the model would assign the input to the right class, beside the general classification capability.

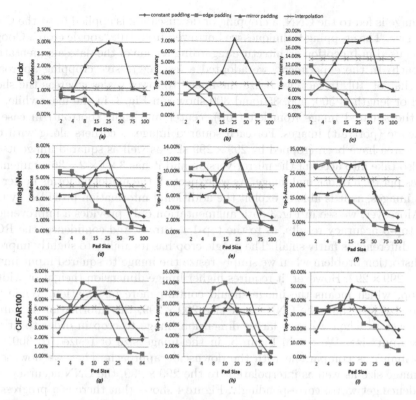

Fig. 5. Experimental results in terms of Average Confidence, Top1-Accuracy and Top5-Accuracy by varying the padding stride (i.e., step size). For each plot, the results obtained by the three evaluated padding approaches and the interpolation are compared.

3   Experiments and Results

In our experiments we considered three different image datasets and the InceptionV3 CNN model [10] previously trained on ImageNet.

3.1   Problem Exploration

We first performed some preliminary experiments aimed to assess how the quality of the input images, in terms of resolution and color-space (i.e., RGB or grayscale), affects the CNN classification results. To this aim, we tested the model performances on a dataset of Flickr images depicting the image of an "apple". Specifically, we downloaded 100 RGB images related to the category "granny smith" with resolution higher than 500 × 500. Figure 3 shows the results related to the top-5 considered resolutions, ranging from 500 × 500 to 300 × 300 pixels, whereas the Fig. 4 shows the results obtained with low resolution images (i.e., images with resolution lower than the CNN input size). Before the image is fed to the CNN, a cropping or downscaling is applied to fit the CNN input size. The cropping techniques we borrowed from [10] "google crop". Google crop is used in Inception architecture regarding as one of the data augmentation approach. In the experiment, we adopted a less aggressive cropping approach than that of [10]. In fact, we resize the image to lower scales whereas the short width or length is 500, 400, 350 and 300 shown in Fig. 3, in the meanwhile, we take the squared image from left (top), center and right (bottom) in case of landscape (portrait) images. For each squared image, 4 corners along with the center area have been cropped by 299×299 size as well as squared image itself. We also take into account the mirror version and it has $3 \times 6 \times 2 = 36$ augmented images per each of original image. As we expected, the model performs better on RGB images, as it is able to exploit the additional information provided by colors. Moreover, we see in Fig. 3 data augmentation only provides a improvement with top-5 accuracy results, as to the top-1 accuracy and confidence, the RGB space difference is fairly small. The google crop has its ability to slightly improve the distortion problem when we simply resize the image to squared input image size to 299×299. However, it requires higher image dimension (height or width) to crop, which means the image should contain more information. While the image size less than the CNN input size 299×299, the information is hardly to recover as when we have larger dimension image to crop in order to fit the CNN input size. We see in Figure 3, in the image size of resized to 300, the performance is comparable with the downscale approach. Then we downscale the image size as well as interpolate it to the 299×299, the CNN accuracy and confidence get worse correspondingly. Figure 4 shows that there is a progressive decrease in performances when the image resolution is reduced, with a drop at 50×50. The results obtained in the above described experiments show that the resolution of the original image is a crucial factor for the model performances, and that the most challenging scenario occurs with gray 50×50 images. The aim of the above exploratory experiments was to find the input image quality factor that are critical for CNNs. Our pipeline is hence aimed to stress the CNN classification by tuning the input quality in several ways.

3.2   Image Padding

The second part of evaluation is devoted to assess the effect of the proposed pre-processing pipeline (Fig. 1), based on several padding approaches, to the model performances. In addition to the above described Flickr images, we considered other two datasets: a subset of ImageNet including $\sim 10K$ images related to 5 classes (i.e., jelly fish, electric guitar, steel bridge, acoustic guitar, fish), and 500 images from CIFAR100 related to 5 classes (i.e., clock, keyboard, lamp, telephone, television). In particular, considering the results obtained in the preliminary exploration of the problem, we considered only gray images with resolution 50×50 (i.e., Flickr and ImageNet) or 32×32 (i.e., CIFAR100). Figure 5 shows the results obtained by the proposed pipeline considering different values of padding stride (i.e., step size) from a minimum of 2 to a maximum equal to the double of the original image dimension (i.e, 100 or 64 pixels). Each plot compares the three padding approaches and interpolation as the baseline. In the experiments on Flickr dataset, the mirror padding with a padding stride between 15 and 50 pixels allows an improvement in the CNN classification performances with respect to the classic approach (i.e., interpolation) considering either the Average Confidence, the Top-1 and the Top-5 accuracy. Intrinsically, the Flickr dataset are made of a swarm of apples that make sense on mirror padding better than others. We also observe on ImageNet the object duplicated has excellent performance by mirror padding such as jellyfish, while in the scenario of outdoor, small stride edge padding makes sense because it has ability to limit the prediction on outdoor images. Constant padding seems as the traditional method extracting image edge outperform the interpolation as well. However, the padding size also affect the performance which means the large padding stride conduct the saliency vanishing and small one will not be so helpfully effect the image. In particular, the best results have been obtained with padding stride equal to 25 in ImageNet, 16 in cifar-100 that the window approximately half of image size. In this setting, the proposed method is able to more than double the performances in terms of Top1-Accuracy, as well as to achieve an improvement of 4% for both Average Confidence and Top5-Accuracy. A possible reason is that the mirror padding produces a periodic redundancy that allows the neurons related to the correct classification to be activated even though the low quality of the input image (i.e., 50×50 gray image). The experimental results on larger datasets considering more classes (i.e., CIFAR100 and Imagenet) show that also the constant and edge padding outperform the baseline method for a range of padding stride values. In all the experiments we observed that when the padding stride is over the input dimension (i.e., 50 or 32) the performances have a sharp drop (see Fig. 5).

4   Conclusions and Future Works

In this study we have investigated various image pre-processing approaches with the aim of improving the classification performances using pre-trained CNN classifiers. First, we have experimentally studied the effects of several qualitative image factors on the classification performances, including image resolution and color-space. Then, we have evaluated three different padding strategies, for a specific challenging scenario. The experiment results show that a padding with a stride size set with a value close to the half of the image dimension improves the performance and, in some cases, allows to double the classification accuracy with respect to the standard pipeline. Results and insights achieved by the presented study have an impact on all the scientific works and applications aimed to employ CNNs on real-case input images characterized by very low quality, or when the adaptation of the model to a specific domain is not possible. If we evaluate the effects of this approach only on pre-trained models, the proposed method can be easily applied to improve the performances of CNNs trained classifiers from scratch. Further efforts will be employed toward this direction. In future works, we will extend the experiments to a larger number of pre-processing approaches, as well as several CNN models. We will continue to work understand how padding strategies produce proper redundancy patterns that are exploited by CNNs to accomplish the classification task. Furthermore, we will evaluate the proposed pipeline on a challenging scenario concerning real-case low quality images, such as license plate classification from surveillance images.

References

1. Battiato, S., Farinella, G.M., Puglisi, G., Ravi, D.: Saliency-based selection of gradient vector flow paths for content aware image resizing. IEEE Trans. Image Process. **23**(5), 2081–2095 (2014)
2. Buslaev, A., Parinov, A., Khvedchenya, E., Iglovikov, V.I., Kalinin, A.A.: Albumentations: fast and flexible image augmentations. arXiv preprint arXiv:1809.06839 (2018)
3. Chevalier, M., Thome, N., Cord, M., Fournier, J., Henaff, G., Dusch, E.: Low resolution convolutional neural network for automatic target recognition. In: 7th International Symposium on Optronics in Defence and Security (2016)
4. Dodge, S., Karam, L.: Understanding how image quality affects deep neural networks, pp. 1–6 (2016)
5. Krizhevsky, A., Sutskever, I., Hinton, G.E.: ImageNet classification with deep convolutional neural networks. In: Advances in Neural Information Processing Systems, pp. 1097–1105 (2012)
6. Öztürk, Ş., Akdemir, B.: Effects of histopathological image pre-processing on convolutional neural networks. Procedia Comput. Sci. **132**, 396–403 (2018)
7. Pal, K.K., Sudeep, K.: Preprocessing for image classification by convolutional neural networks. In: IEEE International Conference on Recent Trends in Electronics, Information & Communication Technology (RTEICT), pp. 1778–1781. IEEE (2016)
8. Peng, X., Hoffman, J., Yu, S.X., Saenko, K.: Fine-to-coarse knowledge transfer for low-res image classification. arXiv preprint arXiv:1605.06695 (2016)
9. Russakovsky, O., et al.: ImageNetLarge scale visual recognition challenge. Int. J. Comput. Vis. (IJCV) **115**(3), 211–252 (2015). https://doi.org/10.1007/s11263-015-0816-y
10. Szegedy, C., et al.: Going deeper with convolutions. In: Proceedings of the IEEE Conference on Computer Vision and Pattern Recognition, pp. 1–9 (2015)

On the Detection of GAN-Based Face Morphs Using Established Morph Detectors

Luca Debiasi[1(✉)], Naser Damer[2,3], Alexandra Moseguí Saladié[2],
Christian Rathgeb[4], Ulrich Scherhag[4], Christoph Busch[4],
Florian Kirchbuchner[2], and Andreas Uhl[1]

[1] University of Salzburg, Salzburg, Austria
{ldebiasi,uhl}@cs.sbg.ac.at
[2] Fraunhofer Institute for Computer Graphics Research IGD, Darmstadt, Germany
{naser.damer,florian.kirchbuchner}@igd.fraunhofer.de,
alexamosegui93@gmail.com
[3] TU Darmstadt, Darmstadt, Germany
[4] Hochschule Darmstadt, Darmstadt, Germany
{ulrich.scherhag,christian.rathgeb,christoph.busch}@h-da.de

Abstract. Face recognition systems (FRS) have been found to be highly vulnerable to face morphing attacks. Due to this severe security risk, morph detection systems do not only need to be robust against classical landmark-based face morphing approach (LMA), but also future attacks such as neural network based morph generation techniques. The focus of this paper lies on an experimental evaluation of the morph detection capabilities of various state-of-the-art morph detectors with respect to a recently presented novel face morphing approach, MorGAN, which is based on Generative Adversarial Networks (GANs).

In this work, existing detection algorithms are confronted with different attack scenarios: known and unknown attacks comprising different morph types (LMA and MorGAN). The detectors' performance results are highly dependent on the features used by the detection algorithms. In addition, the image quality of the morphed face images produced with the MorGAN approach is assessed using well-established no-reference image quality metrics and compared to LMA morphs. The results indicate that the image quality of MorGAN morphs is more similar to bona fide images compared to classical LMA morphs.

Keywords: Face morphing · Generative adversarial networks · Presentation attack detection

This work was supported by the European Union's Horizon 2020 Research and Innovation Program under Grant 690907 (IDENTITY) and by the German Federal Ministry of Education and Research (BMBF) as well as by the Hessen State Ministry for Higher Education, Research and the Arts (HMWK) within the National Research Center for Applied Cybersecurity CRISP.

© Springer Nature Switzerland AG 2019
E. Ricci et al. (Eds.): ICIAP 2019, LNCS 11752, pp. 345–356, 2019.
https://doi.org/10.1007/978-3-030-30645-8_32

1   Introduction

Recently, automated face recognition systems (FRSs) are increasingly being used in different application scenarios, such as mobile device authentication or Automated Border Control (ABC). This wide spread deployment makes them attractive for attacks. In particular, their expected robustness to different environmental and user-specific conditions, e.g. varying illumination and subject poses, and the widespread use of deep neural networks in FRS has been found to increase their vulnerability against presentation attacks [14]. In this context, face morphing attacks have attracted notable interest from the research community in the recent past.

Ferrara et al. [6] unleashed the vulnerability of FRSs against attacks based on morphed face images, which can be introduced in the issuance process of electronic travel documents due to security gaps. They compared morphed images with images of the original subjects using two commercial face recognition solutions, and concluded with the high vulnerability of face recognition to such attacks. Further studies considered the human expert vulnerability to morphed face images when comparing faces [7,20]. They found out that human experts fails most of the times in detecting morphing attacks.

Different solutions were developed to detect face morphing attacks. Ramachandra et al. [19] were first to propose the automated detection of morphed face images. They applied local image descriptors such as the Binarised Statistical Image Features (BSIF) that capture textural properties of the image, which are later classified using a Support Vector Machine (SVM). Later works looked into using convolutional neural network(CNN) based features [18], image quality measures [16], the effect of printing and re-scanning the images [23], and differences between triangulating and averaging the facial landmarks on the detection [17]. Recent works by Debiasi et al. [4] propose to exploit the Photo Response Non-Uniformity (PRNU) of an image sensor to detect morphed face images, which is a widely used tool in the field of Digital Image Forensics (e.g. image forgery detection).

A standardised manner to evaluate the vulnerability of biometric systems to morphing attacks was recently proposed by Scherhag et al. [22]. A recent work by Ferrara et al. [8] viewed the morphing attack detection problem from a different perspective by proposing an approach to revert the morphed face image (demorph) enough to reveal the identity of the legitimate document owner, given a bona fide capture.

Other works considered that it might be possible in practice to use a live probe image along with the investigated image to detect a morphing attacks. This was done either by looking at the differential vector between both images [24], analysing the absolute distances and angles of the landmarks in both images [21], analysing the directed distances between these landmarks [1], or using the live probe image for demorphing [8]. The mentioned works so far developed and evaluated their approaches based on morphing attacks databases that were created based on facial landmarks.

Recently, a work by Damer *et al.* [2] proposed a new possibility of morphing attacks. They built their solution on generative adversarial networks (MorGAN). They morphed the latent representation of the morphed images and generated the morphing attacks based on that morphed latent vector. These morphing attacks proved to be hard to detect in the cases where they were not considered in the training process of the morphing detector [2].

The work presented in this paper aims at evaluating the detectability of LMA- and GAN-based morphed face images in different attack scenarios (known and unknown attacks) using several state-of-the-art morph detectors based on different features. The experimental evaluation performed in this work gives a preliminary outlook on the detectability future face morphing attacks. These attacks might include novel morphing strategies such as GANs for face morph generation, where it is not clear how the morph detection performance is affected by the artefacts that they introduce. For example, it is not clear if the properties of the image's PRNU are preserved in morphed images generated using a GAN-based approach or if the properties are altered, which has a decisive impact on the detection performance of PRNU-based morph detection approaches. Furthermore, this work also includes an image quality assessment of morphed face images generated using the MorGAN approach compared to classical LMA morphs.

The paper is organised as follows: the MorGAN approach and data set are described in Sect. 2. The image quality assessment of the generated MorGAN images is reported in Sect. 3, while the experimental setup and investigated state-of-the-art morph detectors are described in Sect. 4. The experimental results are reported and discussed in Sect. 5 and the paper is concluded in Sect. 6.

Fig. 1. Examples of the used morphing attacks, both the MorGAN and LMA. Original reference images are on the right and left.

2   MorGAN Dataset

A database containing attacks created by the conventional landmark-based morphing technique, as well as the recently MorGAN-based approach, is used in this work. This allows the evaluation of detection performance of known and unknown attacks of the investigated morph detection approaches.

The database is based on recent work by Damer *et al.* [2] foreseeing using GANs to create morphing attacks and built on the CelebA [12] data set.

The MorGAN database contains a total of 1500 bona fide references, 1500 bona fide probes, 1000 LMA morphing attacks, and 1000 MorGAN morphing attacks. The database is split into disjoint (identity and image) and equal train and test sets, each including 750 bona fide references, 750 bona fide probes, and 500 attack images from each of both attack types (LMA and GAN). Because of computational and structural limitations of the MorGAN approach, the Mor-GAN attack images are of 64×64 pixels size (below the ICAO recommendations). Examples of the resulting image attacks and the original images creating these attacks are presented in Fig. 1.

3   Quality of Morphed Face Images

As shown in [2] by Damer *et al.*, the morphed face images contained in the MorGAN data set are capable of successfully attacking pre-trained FRS, i.e. OpenFace and VGG-Face. They conclude that MorGAN attacks are weaker than the LMA ones, however, still make successful attacks on both FRSs. It has to be noted that the MorGAN approach has only recently been presented and that images with higher quality and resolution are expected to be generated with future versions of the approach.

In this work, the insights on the vulnerability of FRSs against face morph presentation attacks are complemented by an image quality analysis of the Mor-GAN morphs, which is compared to the quality of bona fide images and LMA morphs. Ferrara *et al.* [6] demonstrated, that even human experts are not able to discriminate between bona fide and high quality morphed face images. Therefore, the image quality of morphed plays an important role, since common pattern recognition techniques and humans in particular can easily detect obvious artefacts within the images. For examples on such obvious artefacts, the reader is referred to [22]. In order to assess the image quality of the different images in the MorGAN data set (bona fide, MorGAN and LMA morphs), the following no-reference image quality metrics have been evaluated on all 1500 bona fide, 1000 MorGAN and 1000 LMA images: BIQI [15], BRISQUE [13], OG-IQA [10] and SSEQ [11]. To render a fair comparison with the MorGAN images possible, LMA and bona fide images have been downsized to the same resolution of 64×64 pixels. We did not consider any face-specific sample quality assessment metrics in this work due to the small resolution of the MorGAN images.

All image quality results are illustrated in Table 1, while only two selected quality metrics are presented in Fig. 2. Overall, the evaluation shows that the image quality of both morphed MorGAN and LMA images is very similar to the image quality of the bona fide images within the MorGAN data set. BIQI, OG-IQA and SSEQ show that the image quality score distributions of MorGAN images are more resemblant of the bona fide distribution compared to LMA

Table 1. Statistical properties of image quality metrics for bona fide images and LMA and MorGAN-based morphed images.

Metric	Property	Bona fide	MorGAN	LMA
BIQI	Mean	35.06	34.56	43.55
	Std	8.95	9.51	10.71
	Min	8.43	10.83	17.47
	Max	71.86	67.13	73.17
BRISQUE	Mean	25.22	17.23	28.30
	Std	9.13	9.45	8.50
	Min	−3.31	−12.71	2.28
	Max	59.76	90.29	59.29
OG-IQA	Mean	−0.82	−0.87	−0.74
	Std	0.09	0.07	0.10
	Min	−0.95	−0.95	−0.94
	Max	−0.25	−0.39	−0.39
SSEQ	Mean	30.25	29.51	37.80
	Std	9.30	7.82	7.70
	Min	−6.78	4.71	3.48
	Max	59.76	55.81	62.26

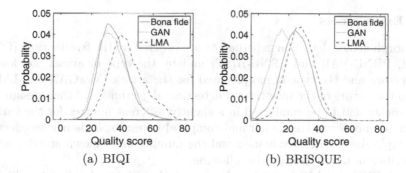

(a) BIQI   (b) BRISQUE

Fig. 2. Image quality score distributions of bona fide images compared to LMA and MorGAN-based morphs.

morphs. Only BRISQUE shows a different result, where the quality scores of LMA morphs are more alike the ones of bona fide images compared to MorGAN morphs. Due to time and space constraints, this deviation will be investigated more thoroughly in future work.

These results, using equally sized images of 64 × 64 pixels, reveal that morphed images generated with the MorGAN approach are more similar to bona fide images compared to the classical LMA approach in respect to their image quality, which is underlined by the distortion independence (BIQI), generalisability (OG-IQA) and closeness to human perception (SSEQ) of the image quality metrics supporting these results.

4   Experimental Setup

This study aims at investigating the detection performance of various morph detection approaches based on distinct features for MorGAN attacks. In particular, their ability of dealing with known and unknown attacks is of special interest, especially when future attacks based on unknown (neural network based) morphing techniques are considered.

4.1   Morph Detection Algorithms

Our morph attack detection methodology aims at enabling a wider range of conceptual evaluation and more diverse coverage of the state-of-the-art by considering image feature extraction methods of three different natures. One is the hand crafted classical image descriptors, the Local Binary Pattern Histogram (LBPH) [18], the second is based on transferable deep-CNN features [19] and the third type is based on the Photo Response Non-Uniformity (PRNU) [3,4]. All three types of features were previously utilised for the detection of face morphing attacks based on LMA approaches.

4.2   Experiments

The morph attack detection experiments are ordered by the feature type (CNN, LBPH, PRNU-VAR and PRNU-HIST) and by the type of attack, i.e. known or unknown and the type of morphs used for the attack (MorGAN and LMA). Due to the nature of the investigated detection algorithms and their design, the experiments had to be conducted in a slightly different manner for the various detectors, in order to ensure fair and comparable results. This has an effect on the sample size used for evaluation and the number of unknown attacks, which is described in more detail in the following.

Since CNN and LBPH are learning-based algorithms, the data is split into distinct train and test sets, both containing 750 bona fide images and 500 images for each attack type (LMA and MorGAN). A "known" attack (K) is given when the algorithm is evaluated with the same attack type as it is trained with, e.g. the algorithm was trained using LMA morphs and is evaluated on LMA morphs. An "unknown" attack (U), on the other hand, is given when different attack types are used to train and evaluate the algorithm, e.g. the algorithm is trained using LMA morphs and evaluated on MorGAN morphs. This leads to the following attack types for CNN and LBPH:

- K-LMA: Trained with LMA morphs, tested with LMA morphs.
- K-MorGAN: Trained with MorGAN morphs, tested with MorGAN morphs.
- U-LMA: Trained with MorGAN morphs, tested with LMA morphs.

– U-MorGAN: Trained with LMA morphs, tested with MorGAN morphs.

The two PRNU-based algorithms, PRNU-VAR and PRNU-HIST, do not rely on any training for classification, thus the whole data set, comprised of 1500 bona fide images and 1000 images for each attack type (LMA and MorGAN), is used for evaluation of the detectors. Therefore, all attacks with LMA or MorGAN morphs can be considered as "unknown" (U) for the PRNU-based algorithms. This leads to the following attack types for PRNU-VAR and PRNU-HIST:

– U-LMA: Tested with LMA morphs.
– U-MorGAN: Tested with MorGAN morphs.

4.3   Evaluation

The assessment of the morph detection performance is based on metrics defined in ISO/IEC 30107-3 [9]: Attack Presentation Classification Error Rate (APCER) and Bona Fide Presentation Classification Error Rate (BPCER), as suggested in literature [22]. APCER defines the proportion of morphed face presentations incorrectly classified as bona fide presentations, while BPCER is the proportion of bona fide presentations incorrectly classified as morphed face presentation attacks. The detection systems are evaluated at different operating points: The operation point of the system, where APCER = BPCER, is defined as detection equal error rate D-EER. Furthermore, two additional operation points, BPCER10 (where APCER = 10%) and BPCER20 (where APCER = 5%), are reported.

5   Morph Detection Results

The outcome of the morph detection experiments described in Sect. 4, are summarised in Table 2 and illustrated with DET plots in Fig. 3.

Table 2 shows the D-EER, BCPER10 and BCPER20 results for the various attack scenarios and morph detection algorithms described in Sect. 4. CNN shows the best performance at detecting LMA morphs, independent of the attacks being known or unknown. It achieves a perfect result for the K-LMA attack, and a D-EER of only 4% for U-LMA. However, it struggles in case of K-MorGAN or completely fails to detect U-MorGAN attacks. LBPH yields the overall lowest error rates among all morph detection algorithms and across all attack scenarios. It is able to detect both LMA and MorGAN morphs, but the performance gap between known and unknown attacks is very large. For known attacks, it is able to achieve low D-EERs of 9% for LMA and 1% for MorGAN attacks, while for unknown attacks the performance drops significantly to 23% and 19%, respectively. The results indicate that the CNN and LBPH detectors are not able to generalise well over different attack types, as it can be clearly seen in Fig. 3(a) and (b), which might be caused by the closed-set training design of both algorithms.

Table 2. Morph detection performance of investigated algorithms under different attack scenarios.

Algorithm	Attack type	D-EER	BCPER10	BCPER20
CNN	K-LMA	0.00	0.00	0.00
	K-MorGAN	0.34	0.67	0.78
	U-LMA	0.04	0.00	0.02
	U-MorGAN	0.50	0.90	0.95
LBPH	K-LMA	0.09	0.08	0.14
	K-MorGAN	0.01	0.00	0.00
	U-LMA	0.23	0.38	0.49
	U-MorGAN	0.19	0.29	0.39
PRNU-VAR	U-LMA	0.47	0.85	0.92
	U-MorGAN	0.43	0.85	0.92
PRNU-HIST	U-LMA	0.30	0.49	0.58
	U-MorGAN	0.33	0.69	0.81

The performance of the two PRNU-based algorithms is worse compared to the previously discussed CNN and LBPH algorithms, with D-EERs around 45% for PRNU-VAR and 30% for PRNU-HIST. Nonetheless, the results for these two algorithms show a very promising property: their stable performance across all attack types (known and unknown) and morph types (MorGAN and LMA). This consistency becomes evident when looking at Fig. 3(c) and (d). While they might not perform as well as CNN and LBPH in some cases, the results indicate a high potential for the generalisabilty of PRNU-based algorithms across different morph types, independently of the morph type being known or unknown. Furthermore, it can be observed that the PRNU of MorGAN morphs shows similar properties as the PRNU of LMA-based morphs, which leads to an almost equal detection performance for the PRNU-based detectors. Due to time and space constraints, a more thorough investigation of the PRNU signal resulting from the GAN operations is left for future research, in particular whether a PRNU-based identification of the source camera in images generated with GANs might still be possible. The D-EER performance of the two approaches is reported to be much better for larger images (320×320 pixels) in [4] and [3], thus we conclude that the overall poor performance for the PRNU-VAR and PRNU-HIST is a result of the small image size of 64×64 pixels in the MorGAN data set. It is commonly known in the field of Digital Image forensics, that the performance of PRNU-based approaches tends to degrade significantly with smaller image resolutions, as it is shown in [5].

Summarising the morph detection results, it can be observed that all investigated detection algorithms have their advantages and drawbacks. CNN works well for detecting LMA attacks, but fails at detecting MorGAN attacks. LBPH works quite well overall, but shows a high performance gap between known and

unknown attacks, leaving it vulnerable for unknown attacks. PRNU-HIST and
PRNU-VAR show an overall weak performance (presumably caused by the low
image resolution), but they have the big advantage of being very stable across all
evaluated attacks. If the general performance of the PRNU-based algorithms can
be improved, it can be expected that they will show a high robustness against
many unknown attack scenarios.

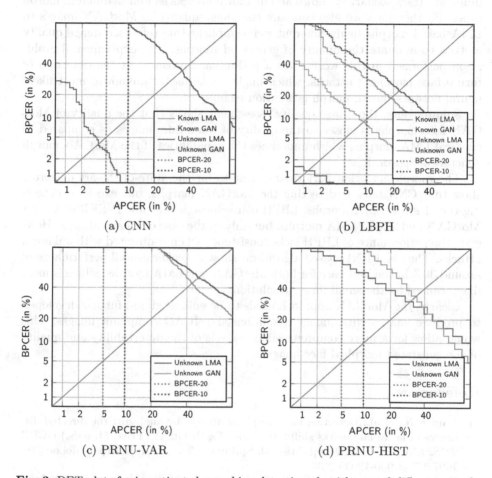

Fig. 3. DET plots for investigated morphing detection algorithms and different attack
scenarios.

6   Conclusion

The detection of morphed face images has become an important part of automated face recognition systems, due to their severe vulnerability to such attacks.

In this work, we investigate the performance of different state-of-the-art face morph detection algorithms on the recently proposed MorGAN data set. This data set, besides containing bona fide images and classical landmark-based morphs, also contains morphed images generated using the MorGAN approach. As the name implies, this novel type of morphed face images is created using Generative Adversarial Networks. The focus of this work lies on the evaluation of different attack scenarios: known and unknown attacks as well as different morph types. Furthermore, we also compare the image quality of MorGAN images to LMA based morphs using different well-established no-reference image quality metrics to evaluate the quality of generated morphs. The experimental evaluation performed in this work gives a preliminary prospect at the detection of future face morphing attacks, which might make use of unknown, most likely neural network based, morph generation techniques.

Summarising, the image quality assessment shows that the quality of MorGAN face morphs is closer to the quality of bona fide images as compared to classical LMA morphs, which underlines the capabilities of the MorGAN morph generation approach.

The morph detection performance results for the state-of-the-art detectors show that CNN fails at detecting the MorGAN morphs, but excels at detecting the classical LMA morphs. LBPH can achieve a very low D-EER of 1% for MorGAN and 9% for LMA morphs, but only in the case of known attacks. However, the performance of LBPH lacks consistency when confronted with unknown attacks. The two PRNU-based algorithms show a weaker overall performance of around 30% in the best case for both MorGAN and LMA morphs, which is most likely caused by the small image resolution.

Clearly, the MorGAN approach needs to be enhanced and further developed to produce images with higher resolutions, i.e. ICAO compliant images. This would allow for a more comprehensible analysis of the detectability and quality of the generated morphed face images.

References

1. Damer, N., et al.: Detecting face morphing attacks by analyzing the directed distances of facial landmarks shifts. In: Brox, T., Bruhn, A., Fritz, M. (eds.) GCPR 2018. LNCS, vol. 11269, pp. 518–534. Springer, Cham (2019). https://doi.org/10.1007/978-3-030-12939-2_36
2. Damer, N., Saladie, A.M., Braun, A., Kuijper, A.: MorGAN: recognition vulnerability and attack detectability of face morphing attacks created by generative adversarial network. In: 9th IEEE International Conference on Biometrics Theory, Applications and Systems (BTAS 2018). IEEE (2018)
3. Debiasi, L., Rathgeb, C., Scherhag, U., Uhl, A., Busch, C.: PRNU variance analysis for morphed face image detection. In: Proceedings of the IEEE 9th International Conference on Biometrics: Theory, Applications, and Systems (BTAS 2018), Los Angeles, California, USA, pp. 1–8, October 2018
4. Debiasi, L., Scherhag, U., Rathgeb, C., Uhl, A., Busch, C.: PRNU-based detection of morphed face images. In: 2018 International Workshop on Biometrics and Forensics (IWBF 2018), pp. 1–7, June 2018

5. Debiasi, L., Uhl, A.: PRNU enhancement effects on biometric source sensor attribution. IET Biometrics **6**(4), 256–265 (2017)
6. Ferrara, M., Franco, A., Maltoni, D.: The magic passport. In: IEEE International Joint Conference on Biometrics (IJCB 2014), pp. 1–7. IEEE (2014)
7. Ferrara, M., Franco, A., Maltoni, D.: On the effects of image alterations on face recognition accuracy. In: Bourlai, T. (ed.) Face Recognition Across the Imaging Spectrum, pp. 195–222. Springer, Cham (2016). https://doi.org/10.1007/978-3-319-28501-6_9
8. Ferrara, M., Franco, A., Maltoni, D.: Face demorphing. IEEE Trans. Inf. Forensics Secur. **13**(4), 1008–1017 (2018)
9. ISO/IEC JTC1 SC37 Biometrics: ISO/IEC IS 30107-3:2017, IT - Biometric presentation attack detection - Part 3: Testing and Reporting
10. Liu, L., Hua, Y., Zhao, Q., Huang, H., Bovik, A.C.: Blind image quality assessment by relative gradient statistics and adaboosting neural network. Sig. Process. Image Commun. **40**, 1–15 (2016)
11. Liu, L., Liu, B., Huang, H., Bovik, A.C.: No-reference image quality assessment based on spatial and spectral entropies. Sig. Process. Image Commun. **29**(8), 856–863 (2014)
12. Liu, Z., Luo, P., Wang, X., Tang, X.: Deep learning face attributes in the wild. In: Proceedings of International Conference on Computer Vision (ICCV 2015), December 2015
13. Mittal, A., Moorthy, A.K., Bovik, A.C.: No-reference image quality assessment in the spatial domain. IEEE Trans. Image Process. **21**(12), 4695–4708 (2012)
14. Mohammadi, A., Bhattacharjee, S., Marcel, S.: Deeply vulnerable: a study of the robustness of face recognition to presentation attacks. IET Biometrics **7**(1), 15–26 (2018)
15. Moorthy, A.K., Bovik, A.C.: A two-step framework for constructing blind image quality indices. IEEE Signal Process. Lett. **17**(5), 513–516 (2010)
16. Neubert, T.: Face morphing detection: an approach based on image degradation analysis. In: Kraetzer, C., Shi, Y.-Q., Dittmann, J., Kim, H.J. (eds.) IWDW 2017. LNCS, vol. 10431, pp. 93–106. Springer, Cham (2017). https://doi.org/10.1007/978-3-319-64185-0_8
17. Ramachandra, R., Raja, K.B., Venkatesh, S., Busch, C.: Face morphing versus face averaging: Vulnerability and detection. In: IEEE International Joint Conference on Biometrics (IJCB 2017), pp. 555–563. IEEE (2017)
18. Ramachandra, R., Raja, K.B., Venkatesh, S., Busch, C.: Transferable deep-CNN features for detecting digital and print-scanned morphed face images. In: 2017 IEEE Conference on Computer Vision and Pattern Recognition Workshops, CVPR, pp. 1822–1830. IEEE Computer Society (2017)
19. Ramachandra, R., Raja, K.B., Busch, C.: Detecting morphed face images. In: 8th IEEE International Conference on Biometrics Theory, Applications and Systems (BTAS 2016), pp. 1–7. IEEE (2016)
20. Robertson, D.J., Kramer, R.S.S., Burton, A.M.: Fraudulent id using face morphs: experiments on human and automatic recognition. PLoS ONE **12**(3), 1–12 (2017)
21. Scherhag, U., Budhrani, D., Gomez-Barrero, M., Busch, C.: Detecting morphed face images using facial landmarks. In: Mansouri, A., El Moataz, A., Nouboud, F., Mammass, D. (eds.) ICISP 2018. LNCS, vol. 10884, pp. 444–452. Springer, Cham (2018). https://doi.org/10.1007/978-3-319-94211-7_48
22. Scherhag, U., et al.: Biometric systems under morphing attacks: assessment of morphing techniques and vulnerability reporting. In: International Conference of the Biometrics Special Interest Group (BIOSIG 2017), pp. 1–12 (2017)

23. Scherhag, U., Ramachandra, R., Raja, K.B., Gomez-Barrero, M., Rathgeb, C., Busch, C.: On the vulnerability of face recognition systems towards morphed face attacks. In: 5th International Workshop on Biometrics and Forensics (IWBF 2017), pp. 1–6. IEEE (2017)
24. Scherhag, U., Rathgeb, C., Busch, C.: Towards detection of morphed face images in electronic travel documents. In: 13th IAPR International Workshop on Document Analysis Systems (DAS 2018), pp. 187–192. IEEE Computer Society (2018)

Recognition of Human Activities in Daubechies Complex Wavelet Domain

Manish Khare[✉]

Dhirubhai Ambani Institute of Information and Communication Technology
(DA-IICT), Gandhinagar, India
mkharejk@gmail.com

Abstract. Recognition of accurate human activities is a challenging research problem in video surveillance problem of computer vision research. The task of recognizing activities of human from video sequence exhibits more challenges because of real time processing of data. In this paper, we have proposed a method for recognition of human activities based on Daubechies complex wavelet transform (DCxWT). Better edge representation and approximate shift invariant properties of DCxWT over the other real valued wavelet transform motivates us to utilize properties of DCxWT in recognition of human activities. The multi-class SVM is used for classifying the recognized human activities. The proposed method is compared with other state-of-the-art method, on various standard publicly available dataset, in terms of different quantitative performance measures. We found that the proposed method has better recognition accuracy in comparison to other state-of-the-art methods.

Keywords: Human activity recognition · Daubechies complex wavelet transform · Multiclass support vector machine · Feature extraction

1 Introduction

Recognition of human activity is crucial and popular area in computer vision research, because it is the foundation of development of many applications [1, 2]. Human monitoring-based surveillance system has many industrial applications [3]. These types of system are also very useful in police investigation after a crime or any other illegal action has occurred. Hence, one can say that, human activity recognition-based system is very essential for effective video surveillance system. Clutter background, multi-view point, varying lighting condition, and other similar problems, make accurate and efficient human activity recognition a challenging task. The objective of human activity recognition is to automatically analyze ongoing activities from a video (sequence of frames), and classify an activity which is a member of a given set of abstract activities into one such abstract activity, for ex. Running, walking, jumping, etc.

Based on different detail studies [1, 2, 4, 5], human activity recognition approach can be classified in various categories. According to analysis done by Aggarwal and Ryoo [2], human activities can be conceptually categorized into four levels, depending on their complexities: gesture, actions, interaction, and group activities. Gesture are

E. Ricci et al. (Eds.): ICIAP 2019, LNCS 11752, pp. 357–366, 2019.
https://doi.org/10.1007/978-3-030-30645-8_33

elementary movements of body part of a person for ex. 'raising a leg' or 'stretching an arm'. Actions are single person activity that are results of multiple gestures temporally such as 'walking', running', 'jogging', etc. In Interaction type of human activity, two or more persons and/or objects are involved, for ex. 'two-person fighting' is an interaction between two humans. Group activities have more complexity is comparison to other three types. In group activities, activities are performed by a one group, which is composed of multiple persons and/or objects. For ex. 'A group of persons marching' is a typical example of group activities.

Now a day's machine learning based approach for human activity recognition is widely used because the amount of unannotated training data is readily available for the unsupervised training of these systems. In this type of approach, after learning from a collection of data, algorithm try to answer questions related to that data. The training used in this type of approach is either pixel-based or feature-based [6]. Feature-based approach is better than the pixel-based approach in terms of execution time and speed. For any good computer vision application, an activity recognition algorithm should hold two properties - (i). activity recognition algorithm should perform under real time constraint, and (ii). activity recognition algorithm should be able to solve multi-view as well as multiclass problem.

A lot of works have been proposed to solve activity recognition problem in last few decades. A method for activity recognition using Principal Component Analysis, and Hidden Markov Model was proposed by Uddin et al. [7]. Method based on background subtraction with shape and motion information features for activity recognition method was proposed by Qian et al. [8] for a smart surveillance system. Bobick and Davis [9] proposed an activity recognition method based on motion templates. Human recognition method based on constrained Delaunay triangulation technique, which divides the posture into different triangular meshes, was proposed by Hsieh et al. [10]. Holte et al. [11] proposed a machine learning-based approach to detect motion of the actors by computing the optical flow in video data.

While most existing human action recognition methods adopted feature(s) that works for single resolution of images, an image can be with complex structures and consists of varying levels of details. To remedy this issue, multi-resolution analysis (MRA) can be adopted. In MRA, images can be analyzed at more than one resolution, so that the features that are left undetected at one level can get a chance to consider in another level. Wavelet transform is the most popular tool of MRA. Wavelet transform can be categorized into real valued and complex valued wavelet transforms. Real valued wavelet transform uses real-valued filters to get real valued coefficients while complex wavelet transform uses complex valued filters to get complex valued coefficients.

Method proposed by Khare et al. [12] uses real valued wavelet transform for activity recognition, but real valued wavelet transform is not suitable in various computer vision application. Use of complex wavelet transform can avoid different shortcomings of real valued wavelet transform. Khare et al. [13] proposed dual tree complex wavelet transform based approach for human action recognition. Dual tree complex wavelet transform is not a true sense complex wavelet transform and its implementation is based on real valued wavelet transform.

Motivated by the work of Khare et al. [12, 13], in this paper, we have proposed Daubechies complex wavelet transform (DCxWT) based approach for recognition of human activities. DCxWT is a true sense complex wavelet transform and having advantages of approximate shift-invariance and better edge representation as compared to real valued wavelet transform. We have used multiclass support vector machine as a classifier for classifying different human activities in video frames. We have experimented the proposed method at multiple levels of DCxWT and shown that performance of the proposed method is becoming better as we move toward higher levels. We have conducted the experiments on different standard action datasets for evaluation of the proposed method. The proposed method is compared with some other state-of-the-art methods proposed by Qian et al. [8], Holte et al. [11], and Khare et al. [12, 13], for showing effectiveness of DCxWT.

The rest of paper is organized as follows: Sect. 2 describes DCxWT used as a feature for recognition of human activities. Section 3 describes the proposed method in detail. Experimental results of the proposed method and other state-of-the-art methods are given in Sect. 4. Finally, conclusions of the work are given in Sect. 5.

2 Daubechies Complex Wavelet Transform

In any recognition algorithm, selection of appropriate feature is very important. If correct feature is selected for recognition then performance of classifier will improve. In our proposed work for recognition of human activities, we have used DCxWT coefficients as feature set. A brief description of Daubechies complex wavelet transform and why this is useful for recognition of human activities is given in below –

For activity recognition, we require a feature which remains invariant by shift, translation and rotation of object, because object may be present in translated and rotated form among different scenes. Due to its approximate shift-invariance and better edge representation property, we have used DCxWT as a feature for recognition of human activity.

Any function $f(t)$ can be decomposed into complex scaling function and mother wavelet as:

$$f(t) = \sum_k c_k^{j_0} \phi_{j_0,k}(t) + \sum_{j=j_0}^{j_{max}-1} d_k^j \psi_{j,k}(t) \tag{1}$$

where j_0 is given low resolution level, $\{c_k^{j_0}\}$ and $\{d_k^j\}$ are approximation coefficients $\left[\phi(u) = 2\sum_i a_i \phi(2u - i) \right]$ and detail coefficients $\left[\psi(t) = 2\sum_n (-1)^n \overline{a_{1-n}} \phi(2t - n) \right]$. where $\phi(t)$ and $\psi(t)$ share same compact support $[-L, L + 1]$ and a_i's are coefficients. The a_i's can be real as well as complex valued and $\sum a_i = 1$.

Daubechies's wavelet bases $\{\psi_{j,k}(t)\}$ in one-dimension is defined through above scaling function $\phi(u)$ and multiresolution analysis of $L_2(\Re)$[14]. During the formulation of general solution if we relax the condition for a_i to be real [14], it leads to complex valued scaling function.

DCxWT holds various properties [14], in which reduced shift sensitivity and better edge representation properties of DCxWT are important one for classification

3   The Proposed Method

This section describes, new method for human activity recognition, in which we used Daubechies complex wavelet transform coefficients as a feature of objects. Block diagram of the proposed method is given in following Fig. 1.

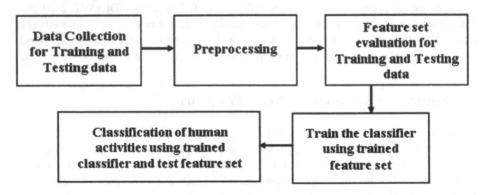

Fig. 1. Block diagram of the proposed method

Details of the proposed method are described in following steps –

Step 1: first step of the proposed method is to collect and represent data for training and testing. In our method, we have tested the proposed method with various publicly available standard datasets for ex. CASIA dataset [15] and KTH dataset [16]. Human activities are presented in form of video which is a sequence of frames. These videos can be used either for training or testing, depends on purpose. Each frame of video can be considered as an image.

Step 2: Videos in dataset, are may be of different size or having different color format. Therefore, normalization of these videos is required to reduce complexity and maintain uniformity between all dataset with respect to algorithm. In the present work, the collected data are scale normalized to 256×256-pixel dimension. After scale normalization, color format of normalized collected data was converted into gray-level format.

Step 3: Third step of the proposed method is feature set computation. For feature set computation in the proposed method, frames of video dataset are decomposed into complex wavelet coefficients using DCxWT. After applying DCxWT, coefficients are in form of four sub-bands namely – LL, HL, LH, HH, in which LL is approximately coefficients and rest other HL, LH, HH gives details coefficients. Each detail coefficient matrix (HL, LH, and HH) is used separately to construct feature vector. Values of LL sub-bands are dropped for construction of feature and this is used for further higher-level decomposition due to multi-resolution property of DCxWT. When we decompose wavelet transform for level 2, then in this level, we further decompose approximation coefficients (LL sub-band) of level 1. This again produces one approximation coefficients and three detail coefficients matrix. In case of level 2, the feature of level 1 are combined with the present level 2, which constitute level 2. Similar process is repeated for successive level of decomposition.

Step 4: Forth and last step of the proposed method is recognition of human activities. For this process, we have performed classification-based recognition of human activity. For this process, we compute feature set of test and trained video dataset using step 1–3 of the proposed method, then both trained and test feature sets are supplied into multi-class SVM classifier. Multi-class SVM classifier analyzes test feature set with trained feature set and gives result in form of recognized human activities. Same process will repeat for all other video datasets. In multi-class SVM classifier we have used radial basis function (RBF) as a kernel function.

4   Experimental Results

In this section, we demonstrate the experimental results of the proposed method, with those of the method proposed by Qian et al. [8], Holte et al. [11], and Kharc et al. [12, 13], in terms of Precision, Recall, F-Score, and Recognition Accuracy. The proposed method and other state-of-the-art methods, mentioned above for human activity recognition have been presented here for CASIA action datasets [15] and KTH dataset [16].

CASIA dataset is a collection of sequences of human activities captured by video cameras in outdoor environment from different angle of view. In CASIA dataset, video sequences have non-uniform background. In this dataset, a total of 1446 video sequences, containing fifteen types of different actions. All video sequences were taken simultaneously with three non-calibrated cameras from different view angles (horizontal view, angle view, and top-down view). Resolution of videos in dataset is 320×240 pixels with frame rate 25 frames per second. Figure 2, shows the different activities with different viewpoints of CASIA dataset, in which we have performed experiments. For the experiments, we have taken five different activities out of 15 activities, namely – walk, run, bend, fight, and rob. KTH dataset [16] is one of the largest dataset with 192 videos for training, 192 videos for validation, and 216 videos for testing, in which six types of human actions (Walking, Jogging, Running, Boxing, Hand waving, and Hand clapping), performed by 25 persons. Figure 3 shows the different activities of KTH dataset [16].

362 M. Khare

From the Figs. 2 and 3, one can see that, human activities are differently illuminated and objects are scaled in different camera positions as well as one can observe that both frontal as well as side view of objects are taken for experimentation of human action recognition.

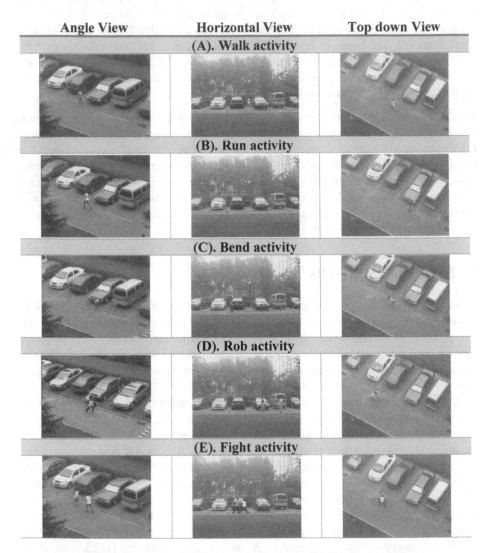

Fig. 2. Examples of different activities in the CASIA Dataset [15]

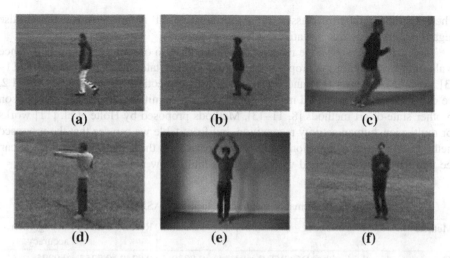

Fig. 3. Examples of KTH Dataset frames for different activities [16] [(a) Walking, (b) Jogging, (c) Running, (d) Boxing, (e) Hand waving, (f) Hand clapping]

Recognition results for CASIA dataset [15] and KTH dataset respectively are shown in Tables 1 and 2 for the proposed method and other state-of-the-art methods [8, 11–13]. For comparison we have used four different performance metrices [17] including Precision, Recall, F-score and Recognition accuracy.

Precision is an average per-class agreement of the data class labels with those of a classifier. Recall is an average per-class effectiveness of a classifier to identify class labels. F-Score is a relation between data positive labels and those given by a classifier based on a per-class average; it conveys the balance between the precision and recall. Recognition accuracy is an average per-class effectiveness of a classifier.

$$Precision = \frac{\sum_{i=1}^{L}\left(\frac{TP_i}{TP_i + FP_i}\right)}{L} \tag{2}$$

$$Recall = \frac{\sum_{i=1}^{L}\left(\frac{TP_i}{TP_i + FN_i}\right)}{L} \tag{3}$$

$$F-Score = 2.\left(\frac{Precision * Recall}{Precision + Recall}\right) \tag{4}$$

$$Accuracy = \frac{\sum_{i=1}^{L}\left(\frac{TP_i + TN_i}{TP_i + FN_i + FP_i + TN_i}\right)}{L} \tag{5}$$

where L is the number of classes, TP is true positive, FP is false positive, FN is false negative, and TN is true negative.

Tables 1 and 2, shows the recognition results in form of four different performance evaluation matrices for the proposed method and other state-of-the art methods [8, 11–13] for CASIA dataset [15] and KTH dataset [16] respectively. From Tables 1 and 2, we can see that, the proposed method gives better recognition accuracy in comparison to other state-of-art methods [8, 11–13]. Methods proposed by Holte et al. [11] works for multi-view human activity recognition, but from table we can see that the proposed method gives better recognition results in comparison to these methods, so that we can see that the proposed method works good for multi-view poses as well.

Table 1. Performance measures values for CASIA Dataset [15]

Method		Precision	Recall	F-score	Recognition accuracy
The proposed method with	DCxWT (Level - 1) as a feature	0.8339	0.8240	0.8257	0.9295
	DCxWT (Level - 3) as a feature	0.8606	0.8520	0.8534	0.9408
	DCxWT (Level - 5) as a feature	0.8852	0.8780	0.8789	0.9512
	DCxWT (Level - 7) as a feature	0.8981	0.8940	0.8938	0.9572
Method with DTCWT as feature (Khare et al. [13])	DTCWT (Level - 1) as a feature	0.8008	0.7980	0.7985	0.9192
	DTCWT (Level - 3) as a feature	0.8221	0.8200	0.8203	0.9280
	DTCWT (Level - 5) as a feature	0.8408	0.8380	0.8385	0.9352
	DTCWT (Level - 7) as a feature	0.8610	0.8580	0.8584	0.9430
Method with DWT as a feature (Khare et al. [12])	DWT (Level - 1) as a feature	0.7544	0.7440	0.7456	0.8976
	DWT (Level - 3) as a feature	0.7761	0.7660	0.7682	0.9068
	DWT (Level - 5) as a feature	0.7899	0.7820	0.7835	0.9128
	DWT (Level - 7) as a feature	0.8164	0.7791	0.7964	0.9181
Qian et al. [8]		0.7719	0.7640	0.7658	0.9056
Holte et al. [11]		0.8189	0.8180	0.8182	0.9272

Table 2. Performance measures values for KTH Dataset [16]

Method		Precision	Recall	F-score	Recognition accuracy
The proposed method with	DCxWT (Level - 1) as a feature	0.8210	0.8117	0.8148	0.9378
	DCxWT (Level - 3) as a feature	0.8277	0.8317	0.8333	0.9439
	DCxWT (Level - 5) as a feature	0.8632	0.8583	0.8598	0.9528
	DCxWT (Level - 7) as a feature	0.9013	0.8983	0.8993	0.9661
Method with DTCWT as feature (Khare et al. [13])	DTCWT (Level - 1) as a feature	0.8008	0.7933	0.7946	0.9311
	DTCWT (Level - 3) as a feature	0.8216	0.8283	0.8227	0.9400
	DTCWT (Level - 5) as a feature	0.8573	0.8517	0.8525	0.9506
	DTCWT (Level - 7) as a feature	0.8755	0.8716	0.8724	0.9572
Method with DWT as a feature (Khare et al. [12])	DWT (Level - 1) as a feature	0.7320	0.7284	0.7292	0.9094
	DWT (Level - 3) as a feature	0.7733	0.7567	0.7599	0.9189
	DWT (Level - 5) as a feature	0.7838	0.7700	0.7728	0.9233
	DWT (Level - 7) as a feature	0.7854	0.7717	0.7745	0.9239
Qian et al. [8]		0.8252	0.8183	0.8200	0.8394
Holte et al. [11]		0.9445	0.9350	0.9391	0.9297

5 Conclusion

In this paper, we demonstrated a new method for recognition of human activities. The proposed approach used DCxWT coefficients as a feature of activities of human objects. We evaluated results for multiple levels of DCxWT. we compared results of the proposed method with other state-of-the-art methods [8, 11–13] on CASIA dataset [15] and KTH dataset [16], in terms of four different performance measures: Precision, Recall, F-Score, and Recognition accuracy. From the results, we could conclude that the proposed method for human action recognition has better recognition accuracy at higher levels of DCxWT in comparison to DWT or DTCWT, and the proposed method outperforms the other methods. From the results, we can conclude that the complex wavelet transform is better than real wavelet transforms for action recognition in terms of the different performance measures.

References

1. Vrigkas, M., Nikou, C., Kakadiaris, I.A.: A review of human activity recognition methods. Frontiers Robot. AI **2**, 28 (2015)
2. Aggarwal, J.K., Ryoo, M.S.: Human activity analysis: a review. ACM Comput. Surv. **43**(3), 15 (2011)
3. Collins, R.T., Lipton, A.J., Kanade, T.: Introduction to the special section on video surveillance. IEEE Trans. Pattern Anal. Mach. Intell. **22**(8), 745–746 (2000)
4. Ziaeefard, M., Bergevin, R.: Semantic human activity recognition: a literature review. Pattern Recogn. **48**(8), 2329–2345 (2015)
5. Borges, P.V.K., Conci, N., Cavallaro, A.: Video-based human behavior understanding: a survey. IEEE Trans. Circuits Syst. Video Technol. **23**(11), 1993–2008 (2013)
6. Moeslund, T.B., Hilton, A., Kruger, V.: A survey of advances in vision-based human motion capture and analysis. Comput. Vis. Image Underst. **104**(2–3), 90–126 (2006)
7. Uddin, M.Z., Lee, J.J., Kim, T.S.: Independent shape component-based human activity recognition via hidden markov model. Appl. Intell. **33**(2), 193–206 (2010)
8. Qian, H., Mao, Y., Xiang, W., Wang, Z.: Recognition of human activities using SVM multi-class classifier. Pattern Recogn. Lett. **31**(2), 100–111 (2010)
9. Bobick, A.F., Davis, J.W.: The recognition of human movement using temporal templates. IEEE Trans. Pattern Anal. Mach. Intell. **23**(3), 257–267 (2001)
10. Hsieh, J.W., Hsu, Y.T., Liao, H.Y.M., Chen, C.C.: Video-based human movement analysis and its application to surveillance systems. IEEE Trans. Multimed. **10**(3), 372–384 (2008)
11. Holte, M.B., Moeslund, T.B., Nikolaidis, N., Pitas, I.: 3D human action recognition for multi-view camera systems. In: Proceeding of International Conference on 3D Imaging, Modeling, Processing, Visualization and Transmission, pp. 342–349 (2011)
12. Khare, M., Jeon, M.: Towards discrete wavelet transform based human activity recognition. In: Proceeding of 2nd International Workshop on Pattern Recognition (IWPR 2017), p. 1044308 (1-5), Singapore (2017)
13. Khare, M., Gwak, J., Jeon, M.: Complex wavelet transform-based approach for human action recognition in video. In: Proceeding of International Conference on Control, Automation and Information Sciences (ICCAIS 2017), pp. 157–162, Thailand (2017)
14. Clonda, D., Lina, J.M., Goulard, B.: Complex daubechies wavelets: properties and statistical image modeling. Sig. Process. **84**(1), 1–23 (2004)
15. Wang, Y., Huang, K., Tan, T.: Human activity recognition based on R transform. In: Proceedings of International Conference Computer Vision and Pattern Recognition (CVPR 2007), pp. 1–7 (2007). http://www.cbsr.ia.ac.cn/english/Action%20Databases%20EN.asp
16. Schuldt, C., Laptev, I., Caputo, B.: Recognizing human actions: a local SVM approach. In: Proceedings of 17th International Conference on Pattern Recognition, vol. 3, pp. 32–36 (2004). http://www.nada.kth.se/cvap/actions/
17. Sokolove, M., Lapalme, G.: A systematic analysis of performance measures for classification tasks. Inf. Process. Manage. **45**, 427–437 (2009)

Automatic Framework for Multiple Sclerosis Follow-up by Magnetic Resonance Imaging for Reducing Contrast Agents

Giuseppe Placidi[1([⊠])], Luigi Cinque[2], Matteo Polsinelli[1],
Alessandra Splendiani[3], and Emanuele Tommasino[3]

[1] A2VI-Laboratory, c/o Department of Life, Health and Environmental Sciences,
University of L'Aquila, Coppito 2, 67100 L'Aquila, AQ, Italy
giuseppe.placidi@univaq.it
[2] Department of Computer Science, Sapienza University of Rome,
Via Salaria 113, 00198 Rome, RM, Italy
[3] Department of Biotechnological and Applied Clinical Science,
University of L'Aquila AQ, Via Vetoio 1, 67100 L'Aquila, AQ, Italy

Abstract. An automatic framework for multiple sclerosis (MS) follow-up by Magnetic Resonance Imaging (MRI) is presented. It is based on the identification and segmentation of lesions by using convolutional neural network (CNN) architecture applied to the volumes collected by different imaging modalities and on the registration of the volumes obtained by two consecutive examinations. The resulting binary masks obtained from the identification/segmentation strategy on each examination are used to calculate the volume of each lesions, their status (chronic or active) and, hence, to estimate the progression of the disease. Preliminary results are reported demonstrating that the calculations performed by the proposed framework are capable, when the disease is stable, to gather the same information obtainable when the contrast agent (CA) is administered to the patient.

Keywords: Image registration · Image segmentation · Multiple sclerosis · MRI · Deep learning · Convolutional neural networks

1 Introduction

Multiple sclerosis (MS) is a chronic and degenerative disease of the brain and spinal cord with very heterogenous clinical presentation which can vary greatly between patients in severity and symptoms [1]. Also the clinical course of MS is unpredictable and most patients are initially diagnosed as having relapsing-remitting MS characterized by inflammatory attacks separated by variable periods of remission and recovery. After this first phase, the majority of patients transit into a progressive phase consisting in an unremitting and progressive accumulation of disability. Actually there is no cure for MS and existing therapies focus on symptomatic management and prevention of further damage, with variable effectiveness, though recent advancements are promising. MS origins are not well understood but characteristic signs of tissue damages are recognizable, such as white matter lesions and brain atrophy or shrinkage due to

© Springer Nature Switzerland AG 2019
E. Ricci et al. (Eds.): ICIAP 2019, LNCS 11752, pp. 367–378, 2019.
https://doi.org/10.1007/978-3-030-30645-8_34

degeneration. These signs can be observed by MRI which has become a special tool to follow-up MS patients with reduced invasiveness due to the usage of specific contrast agents. In fact, focal lesions in the brain and spinal cord are primarily visible in the white matter on structural MRI observable as hyperintensities on T2-weighted images, proton-density images (PD), or fluid-attenuated inversion recovery images (FLAIR), and as hypointensities, or "black holes", on T1-wheighted images [2]. These imaging procedures are all performed in a single MRI examination and the corresponding images (thousands), collected both in pre and post CA administration, are all used for MS monitoring and follow-up. Identification of the lesions affecting the white matter and their count and volume calculation by MRI have become well established protocols for assessing the progression of MS and treatment effect. For this reason, MRI is currently used routinely in clinical practice, though it is not well correlated with clinical disability progression due to the presence of different forms of disability (besides physical impairments, also cognitive impairments could occur), to neuroplasticity and to the effects of de-myelinization of nerves, a critical effect of MS, which is not observed by MRI (white matter could appear normal though it has reduced myelin). Moreover imaging markers are capable to capture volumetric changes but they are unable to indicate brain changes and spatial dispersion of the lesions. Besides that, MS patients routinely have MR imaging with CA every 6–12 months to assess response to medication but, recently [3], evidence has been provided of tissue deposition of contrast agents questioning the long-term safety of CA. Since in [3] it has been shown that there is no added benefit of CA over and above that of increased lesion burden, it could be argued that, since the proportion of individuals with worsening lesion load is a small proportion, there is no need for CA administration in those with stable disease.

In what follows, we present a framework to increase the precision and the objectiveness of MRI analysis in monitoring MS by improving lesion identification and comparison of the actual control with those collected previously in order to establish if new lesions have occurred and if old lesions have expanded or modified. Moreover, the framework is intended to optimize the use of CA, by eliminating it when the disease is stable. To the best of our knowledge, the proposal of a system which merges the advantages of an automatic MS lesion identification/segmentation strategy with those of registering data collected at different times to perform numerical comparisons of lesions is new.

The manuscript is structured as follows: Sect. 2 provides the related work, Sect. 3 details the proposed framework, Sect. 4 presents promising, though preliminary, results and Sect. 5 concludes the paper.

2   Related Work

MRI is considered the gold standard between imaging modality for identification and evaluation of MS lesions affecting white matter, thanks to its richness of imaging parameters, which allow to highlight the shape of these lesions with respect to the healthy tissue, to the usage of CA to establish the status of the lesions (active or chronic) and to new perspectives offered by MRI evolutions [4]. Thousands of MRI images composing a single examination are usually analyzed by expert radiologists: the operation is time consuming, subjective and difficult to be carried out without errors due to the huge number of evaluations required for each of the identified lesions. Moreover, additional evaluations and comparisons are required between the current examination and data collected previously, necessary to follow-up the disease. This has implied that both registration methods between data from different examinations and lesion identification process were automatized.

Regarding automatic segmentation of MS lesions by MRI images segmentation, several attempts have been done with success, though the huge variability of MS lesions in size, shape, intensity and location make automatic and accurate identification and segmentation really challenging [5–7]. Though classical segmentation techniques, based on shapes, could be effective [8], a particular attention to deep neural networks is necessary, due to their accuracy in solving computer-vision tasks with low manual intervention with respect to other approaches. The great advantage of deep learning is that the feature set would be no longer defined by the user but learned directly by the system from the training images. This is a useful property because it is often difficult for people to characterize features that best serve to separate healthy tissue from MS lesions. From the perspective of deep learning application, the high dimensionality of the MR images, the difficulty of obtaining reliable ground truth and the high accuracy required for clinical practice, all contribute to make white matter lesion segmentation a worthy test application. CNN have demonstrated breaking performance also in brain imaging segmentation [9–11]. In particular, Yoo et al. [9] were the first to propose an automated learning approach for MS lesion segmentation. Besides the architecture of the used system, the interesting innovations were that 3D patches of the MRI volume were used and that segmentation preferred combinations (co-registration) of T2-w and PD images because they were proven to carry more information than MRI images by other modalities and more information than T2-w or PD taken singularly. In 2015, Vaidya et al. [10] proposed a method that used 3D CNNs to learn features by different datasets of the same patient: T1-w, T2-w, PD and FLAIR MRIs. The method proposed in [11] has proven to use efficiently the information carried on by different MRI imaging modalities by reducing the number of parameters (and hence the training set) through the usage of two CNNs in cascade, trained separately. To date, the method presented in [11] represents for MS lesion segmentation one of the benchmark architectures.

Regarding registration techniques, the problem has been afforded since medical imaging moved its first steps [12] due to the necessity of matching images by different modalities. In the following years, the problem has been refined and effectively solved by using recently proposed learning-based deformable strategies and optimization, suitably studied for MRI of the brain [13, 14].

3   The Proposed Framework

The framework we propose is based on the utilization of both the data collected in the current examination and those collected in the previous examination, in turn composed by MRI data and by its corresponding lesion identification/segmentation. The framework sketch is reported in Fig. 1.

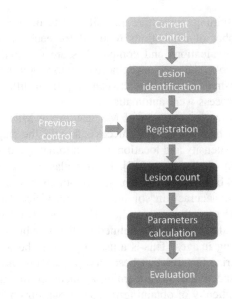

Fig. 1. Framework description. Two temporal controls (examinations) concur to evaluate the disease progression. The recent control is first classified for identifying lesions. Then its data are registered with those of the previous control (also previously classified) and logically compared with it in order to evaluate the status of the identified lesions.

After the acquisition of the current MRI data, lesions are identified and segmented by using the method described below. Following lesion segmentation, data from the current and the previous exams follow a 3D registration (also summarized below). After volume registration, the binary images containing ones where lesions are present and zeros elsewhere are used for binary operations to obtain resulting binary images indicating whether a lesion was present in both examinations (chronic lesion), if a lesion, though present in both examinations, has grown up with time (increased volume) or, finally, if a lesion is present in the actual examination and absent previously (new and, potentially, acute and active lesion). Moreover, a lot of objective numerical calculations are possible, such as: the number of lesions (calculated as the number of connected classified regions); single volume calculation; global volume occupied by lesions; calculation of the brain volume in the actual examination with respect to the previous exam or any other modification occurring in the brain that can be calculated numerically.

3.1 Lesion Segmentation

Being a benchmark method, we have used the supervised paradigm presented in [11] by extending its concept to contain, besides the parallel pipeline involving T1-w, T2-w, PD-w and FLAIR images also the linear combination T2-w + PD. The reason of using also T2-w + PD is because this modality has more information than the others regarding MS lesions [9]. Moreover, the linear combination contains more information than each of the singular modality (in particular, it increases the contrast of the lesions with respect to the background). In this way, we provided a simpler segmentation task to the system, thus increasing the segmentation accuracy while reducing the dimension of the training, labeled, dataset. This, in MS lesion segmentation, still remains a critical point because the number of available images with data is usually low [5]. A scheme of the used assembly is reported in Fig. 2.

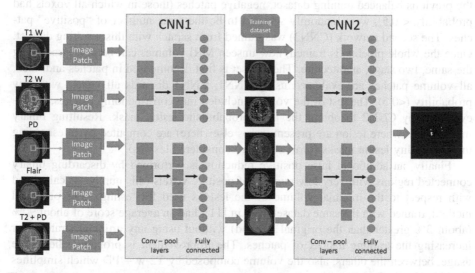

Fig. 2. Two stage CNNs architecture used for identifying and segmenting MS lesions. Input of the system are the volume collected by different imaging modalities and by a linear combination of some of them. Training of CNN2 is made with a separated dataset.

The method is based on a cascade of two CNNs. Though computer vision architectures used for object recognition in natural images usually require up to hundreds of layers [15], the low variations of contrast in MRI images allows the use of smaller networks, thus reducing the training set dimension. The used method consisted of a 7-layers architecture for each of the two CNNs. Each network consisted of two stacks of convolution and max-pooling layers with 32 and 64 filters, respectively. Convolutional layers were followed by a fully-connected layer of size 256 and a soft-max fully connected layer of size 2 whose output was the probability of each voxel to belong to a lesion. For a complete specification of the used parameters, please refer to [11]. In the proposed approach, MS lesions were calculated using 3D neighboring patch features from the different input modalities. The used 3D patches were cubic, $11 \times 11 \times 11$ voxels. The splitting in two different CNNs allowed to separate the training procedure in two and this allowed a reduction of the number of parameters without reducing accuracy. To reorder data balance for training, that is to equilibrate the number of "positive" patches (those containing lesions) with "negative" patches (those containing no lesions, much greater than the other), the dataset used for training consisted of the whole dataset of positive patches and of an equal number of randomly selected negative, healthy patches. In this way, the first network (CNN1) was trained by using the resulting balanced dataset and then tested on the whole dataset, thus obtaining a list of probabilities for each voxel of each patch to be "positive" (part of a lesion). After that, a balanced dataset was created by using the previous test results and by considering as positive all patches containing voxels whose probability was greater than 0.5. As for the previous balanced training dataset, negative patches (those in which all voxels had probability < 0.5), were randomly selected to be the same number of "positive" patches. The second network (CNN2) was trained from scratch with this resulting dataset. Once the whole pipeline is trained, new unseen MRI volumes can be processed using the same, two stage, architecture. The dataset is first decomposed in patches and, then, all volume patches are evaluated using CNN1. CNN1 discards all voxels with low probability (<0.5). The rest of the voxels, included into corresponding patches, are re-evaluated by CNN2 to obtain the final probabilistic lesion mask. Resulting binary masks (ones where lesion are present, zeros elsewhere) are computed by thresholding the probability lesion masks (prob > 0.5 are considered lesions).

Finally, an additional false positive reduction is performed by discarding binary connected regions with very low number of positive voxels (this number is calculated with respect to the minimal volume of the lesions used for testing). The proposed method, trained with the same dataset used in [11], had an average score of about 90% (about 3% greater than the original method) without using any artificial strategy for increasing the training dataset of patches. The improvement is probably due to the usage, between the others, also the volume composed by T2-w + PD which simplifies the identification/segmentation process.

4   Image Registration

Let assume that we want to compare and register two volumes composed by slices. We have the situation that some R(x, y, z) points (actual examination) are the reference points and some M(x, y, z) points (previous examination) are those to register with. Then the major goal of image registration is to find a geometric transformation T such that T(M(x, y, z)) is as close to R(x, y, z) as possible. Mathematically, the image registration problem can be formulated as a maximization problem:

$$T_{opt} = \arg\ max_{T \in \Omega_T} S(R, T(M)) \tag{1}$$

where T_{opt} denotes the optimal transformation, S is a selected similarity metric and Ω_T is the space of all possible transformations [16].

A conventional registration process is performed by applying the optimization (1) after having selected a similarity metric S. One way to solve the maximization (1) is not using the whole datasets to find the optimal T but to select a series of N fiducial corresponding points (landmarks, or control points) in both examinations and to search the optimal T to best match the two point sets in the two datasets. More specifically, let $(x_i, y_i, z_i), i = 1, 2, \ldots, N$ and $(X_i, Y_i, Z_i), i = 1, 2, \ldots, N$ be the two point sets in R(x, y, z) and in M(x, y, z), respectively. Then the task of mapping M to R becomes the problem of finding a transformation T such that T (X_i, Y_i, Z_i) are close to (x_i, y_i, z_i). This transformation can be regarded as a coordinate transformation which transform the coordinate of the N points in M to the N points in R. By applying T on all the points of M, we can also use it as an interpolation strategy, as used in [17, 18].

We can indicate the transformation T as its representation in homogeneous coordinates:

$$T = \begin{bmatrix} t_{1,1} & t_{1,2} & t_{1,3} & t_{1,4} \\ t_{2,1} & t_{2,2} & t_{2,3} & t_{2,4} \\ t_{3,1} & t_{3,2} & t_{3,3} & t_{3,4} \\ 0 & 0 & 0 & 1 \end{bmatrix} \tag{2}$$

The transformation T is considered to be affine because different MRI examinations could be performed by different equipment, different imaging parameters and different resonators that could produce, besides translations and rotations, also scale variations and shear (scaling is produced by setting different field of view or different resolution and shear can be produced by magnetic field inhomogeneities [19]). The optimization problem is to find the coefficients of T that best fit M into R. The N points can be selected manually or automatically by a computer (we used a manual selection).

The similarity metric S that we have used in our optimization (1) is the least-squares metric:

$$min_{T \in \Omega_T} \sum_{i=1}^{n} [R(x_i, y_i, z_i) - T(M(X_i, Y_i, Z_i))]^2 \tag{3}$$

We could choose between different metrics [20] but we decided for the least squares metric (LSM) for two reasons: the examinations we aimed at register were both MRI of the same subject, though at different times, and, for this reason, had a high degree of correlation; LSM is the classical, simple, and most widely employed metric.

5   Preliminary Results

The proposed framework has been tested on data collected at 4 different times (4 consecutive examinations: 2010, 2011, 2017 and 2018, compared in couples: 2010–2011 and 2017–2018) a 55 years old male patient with a GE Healthcare Signa 1.5T system (https://www.gehealthcare.com/en/products/magnetic-resonance-imaging/1-5t). Some representative results are reported in Figs. 3 and 4 (2010–2011) and Figs. 5 and 6 (2017–2018).

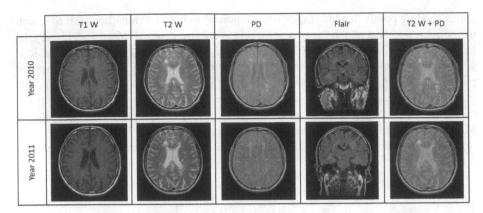

Fig. 3. Representation of one of the slices of the volume collected by each of the MRI imaging modalities (columns) for the examinations collected at consecutive times (2010, first row, and 2011, second row) for the same patient. Exception is represented by the FLAIR section representation which served to better individuate the lesions at the sagittal plane. Last column contain the image obtained by summing T2w image and PD image (not directly collected by the MRI equipment).

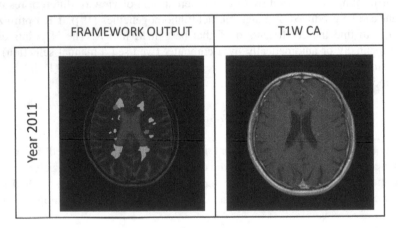

Fig. 4. The slice corresponding to Fig. 3 after the calculation with the proposed framework (left) and after the administration of the CA (right). Different colors (left) are used for indicating different information. Green is used for chronic lesions, red for new lesions and blue for lesions segmented in the previous examination but absent in the following (outliers or reabsorbed edema). Both images are referred to the situation at the time of the second control (2011, in this case). (Color figure online)

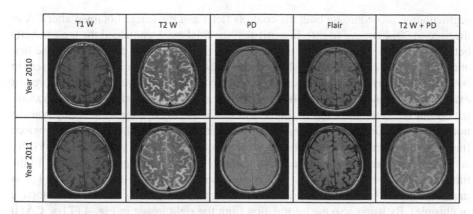

Fig. 5. Representation of one of the slices of the volume collected by each of the MRI imaging modalities (columns) for the examinations collected at consecutive times (2017, first row, and 2018, second row) for the same patient. The Figure has the same significance of Fig. 3. No exception has been made for FLAIR image because no relevance was found in the present lesions.

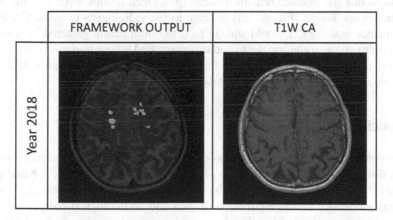

Fig. 6. The Figure has the same significance of Fig. 4. No red and blue regions are present, to indicate the absence of new lesions (red) and of old lesions (blue) appeared in the old control but not detected in the recent control by the classification strategy. Both images are referred to the situation at the time of the second control (2018, in this case). (Color figure online)

In particular, Fig. 3 shows one of the slices, after registration, for the two controls (2010 in the first row, 2011 in the second row), collected with different imaging modalities (columns). Exception is made for the FLAIR image to better highlight the extension of the lesions. The last column contains T2-w + PD. All the reported volumes were the input of the segmentation method. Figure 4 shows the mask of the lesions calculated by using the proposed framework from the masks obtained by the segmentation procedure on both the controls (left) and the image obtained after CA in the second 2011 control (right). In particular, the final mask contained the logical AND between: the two masks (green); the second and the negative of the first (red); the first and the negative of the second (blue). Green indicates old, chronic, lesions (present in both examinations); red indicates new, maybe acute, lesion (present in the most recent examination but not in the previous); blue indicates lesions present in the old examination but not in the most recent (outliers or old, reabsorbed, edema). It is important to note that in the last image relevant information are represented by the colored regions (the brain image was just reported for reference but it was not part of the mask). By analyzing left image of Fig. 4, it could be deduced that some lesions occurred in the time between the two controls. If CA was not used (right image of Fig. 4 was unavailable), the framework could not decide regarding the status of red lesions (active or chronic). By using also the information from the right image in Fig. 4 (T1-w CA) it could be better defined the status of the new lesions in the red regions: that in the right hemisphere was active, the other was not. CA was, in this case, useful to ascertain better the disease progression. However, since new lesions occurred in between controls, the framework results helped in deciding for the CA administration.

By considering the consecutive controls performed recently (Figs. 5 and 6), it could be deduced that the diseases remained stable (just green lesions were present). In this case, framework results (Fig. 6, left) indicate to the radiologists to avoid CA administration since nothing CA would add. In fact, the information gathered by using CA (Fig. 6, right) allow to confirm the hypothesis suggested by our framework (CA was, in that case, unnecessary). The usage of the proposed framework before CA administration would have avoid CA administration in the control of 2018.

6 Conclusion

We have presented an automatic framework to analyze and evaluate the progression of the MS disease by evaluating the status of the lesions. The framework is based on the separate classification of data collected by using MRI, in different modalities, from two consecutive controls, on the registration of data and on the logical comparison of the binary masks containing lesions. The framework is capable to identify the status of the lesions (chronic od new). Preliminary results have demonstrated that it could be possible to ascertain the relevance of the disease progression and, in case of irrelevant disease progression, the framework is capable to avoid CA administration. Future work will be dedicated to an extensive system evaluation and characterization to perform an accurate quantitative analysis, to calculate other important numerical parameters and to optimize the overall running time that could allow its usage during data acquisition for helping radiologists to take the correct decision regarding the CA administration. Moreover, it will be studied how to use the results of the framework to improve the performances of the segmentation algorithm, in particular for reducing outliers.

References

1. Steinman, L.: Multiple sclerosis: a coordinated immunological attack against myelin in the central nervous system. Cell **85**(3), 299–302 (1996)
2. Trip, S.A., Miller, D.H.: Imaging in multiple sclerosis. J. Neurol. Neurosurg. Psychiatry **76**, iii11–iii18 (2005)
3. Mattay, R.R., Davtyan, K., Bilello, M., Mamourian, A.C.: Do all patients with multiple sclerosis benefit from the use of contrast on serial follow-up MR imaging? A retrospective analysis. AJNR Am. J. Neuroradiol. **39**, 2001–2006 (2018)
4. Di Giuseppe, S., Placidi, G., Sotgiu, A.: New experimental apparatus for multimodal resonance imaging: initial EPRI and NMRI experimental results. Phys. Med. Biol. **46**(4), 1003–1016 (2001)
5. Lladó, X., et al.: Segmentation of multiple sclerosis lesions in brain MRI: a review of automated approaches. Inf. Sci. **186**(1), 164–185 (2012)
6. García-Lorenzo, D., Francis, S., Narayanan, S., Arnold, D.L., Collins, D.L.: Review of automatic segmentation methods of multiple sclerosis white matter lesions on conventional magnetic resonance imaging. Med. Image Anal. **17**(1), 1–18 (2013)
7. Danelakis, A., Theoharis, T., Verganelakis, D.A.: Survey of automated multiple sclerosis lesion segmentation techniques on magnetic resonance imaging. Comput. Med. Imaging Graph. **70**, 83–100 (2018)
8. Franchi, D., Gallo, P., Marsili, L., Placidi, G.: A shape-based segmentation algorithm for X-ray digital subtraction angiography images. Comput. Methods Programs Biomed. **94**(3), 267–278 (2009)
9. Yoo, Y., Brosch, T., Traboulsee, A., Li, D.K.B., Tam, R.: Deep learning of image features from unlabeled data for multiple sclerosis lesion segmentation. In: Wu, G., Zhang, D., Zhou, L. (eds.) MLMI 2014. LNCS, vol. 8679, pp. 117–124. Springer, Cham (2014). https://doi.org/10.1007/978-3-319-10581-9_15
10. Vaidya, S., Chunduru, A., Muthuganapathy, R., Krishnamurthi, G.: Longitudinal multiple sclerosis lesion segmentation using 3D convolutional neural networks. In: Proceedings of the IEEE International Symposium on Biomedical Imaging (ISBI) (2015)
11. Valverde, S., et al.: Improving automated multiple sclerosis lesion segmentation with a cascaded 3D convolutional neural network approach. NeuroImage **155**, 159–168 (2017)
12. Elsen, P.A., Pol, E.-J.D., Viergever, M.A.: Medical image matching - a review with classification. IEEE Eng. Med. Biol. **12**, 384–396 (1993)
13. Wu, G., Qi, F., Shen, D.: Learning-based deformable registration of MR brain images. IEEE Trans. Med. Imag. **25**, 1145–1157 (2006)
14. Qiu, P., Nguyen, T.: On image registration in magnetic resonance imaging. In: International Conference on BioMedical Engineering and Informatics, Sanya, pp. 753–757 (2008)
15. He, K., Zhang, X., Ren, S., Sun, J.: Deep residual learning for image recognition. In: IEEE CVPR, pp. 770–778 (2016)
16. Franchi, D., Maurizi, A., Placidi, G.: Characterization of a SimMechanics model for a virtual glove rehabilitation system. In: Barneva, R.P., Brimkov, V.E., Hauptman, H.A., Natal Jorge, R.M., Tavares, J.M.R.S. (eds.) CompIMAGE 2010. LNCS, vol. 6026, pp. 141–150. Springer, Heidelberg (2010). https://doi.org/10.1007/978-3-642-12712-0_13
17. Placidi, G.: Adaptive compression algorithm from projections: application on medical greyscale images. Comput. Biol. Med. **39**(11), 993–999 (2009)

18. Placidi, G., Alecci, M., Sotgiu, A.: Angular space-domain interpolation for filtered back projection applied to regular and adaptively measured projections. J. Magn. Reson. Ser. B **110**(1), 75–79 (1996)
19. Placidi, G.: MRI: Essentials for Innovative Technologies. CRC Press, Boca Raton (2012)
20. Freire, L., Roche, A., Mangin, J.-F.: What is the best similarity measure for motion correction in fMRI times series? IEEE Trans. Med. Imag. **21**, 470–484 (2002)

Learning an Optimisable Semantic Segmentation Map with Image Conditioned Variational Autoencoder

Pengcheng Zhuang[1(✉)], Yusuke Sekikawa[1,2], Kosuke Hara[1], and Hideo Saito[1]

[1] Graduate School of Science and Technology,
Keio University, Yokohama 223-8522, Japan
zpc0113@keio.jp
[2] Denso IT Laboratory, Tokyo 150-0002, Japan

Abstract. Recent semantic segmentation systems have achieved significant improvement by performing pixel-wise training with hierarchical features using deep convolutional neural network models. While the learning process usually requires pixel-level annotated images, it is difficult to get desirable amounts of fine-labeled data and thus the training set size is more likely to be limited, often in thousands. This means that top methods for a dataset can be fine-tuned for a specific situation, making the generalization ability unclear. In real-world applications like self-driving systems, ambiguous region or lack of context information can cause errors in the predicted results. Resolving such ambiguities is crucial for subsequent operations to be performed safely.

We are inspired by work from CodeSLAM where optimizable pixel-wise depth representation is learned. We modify the regression method to work on the pixel-wise classification problem. By training a variational auto-encoder network conditioned with a color image, the computed latent space works as a low-dimensional representation of semantic segmentation, which can be efficiently optimized. As a consequence, our model can correct the error or ambiguity of the prediction during the inference phase given useful scene information. We show how this approach works by giving partial scene truth and perform optimization on the latent variable.

Keywords: Semantic segmentation · Variational autoencoder · Optimization

1 Introduction

Semantic segmentation task aims to predict the categorical label for every pixel in the image, which has been one of the grand challenges in computer vision domain. It is a topic of broad interest because of potential applications like automatic driving. Most of the state-of-the-art semantic segmentation works [4,17,19] are based on FCN [10] liked networks, where performing end-to-end training is

© Springer Nature Switzerland AG 2019
E. Ricci et al. (Eds.): ICIAP 2019, LNCS 11752, pp. 379–389, 2019.
https://doi.org/10.1007/978-3-030-30645-8_35

possible along with useful hierarchical features to catch both context and localization information. However, the successful training of these networks usually requires large number of annotated training samples, which are usually beyond reach in many cases. That leads to a problem that for most of the current FCN based models, the generalization ability is questioned when applied to dynamic and complex scenes. Ambiguities and errors are common in the results, and in real-world applications, enhancing the prediction accuracy is important before further actions are made.

In this paper, we use image-conditioned variational auto-encoder to encode semantic segmentation map, making it possible to optimize predicted result with changeable latent space. While some models [2,3,16] adopt conditional random fields (CRFs) as a post-processing step to refine the prediction result, our proposed model maintains a trainable end-to-end system by incorporating the stochastic neurons inside the network architecture as in [9,12,15]. Besides, since our work models the conditional distributions of semantic segmentation output by using sampled latent variable, different modes of result can be inferred as the variants change. That is to say, unlike other deterministic models, our model can make diverse predictions and thus initial prediction can be optimized as long as additional scene information provided.

Our work is inspired by CodeSLAM from Bloesch et al. [1] where pixel-wise depth information is encoded with the latent space named code. The code is a compact representation of dense scene geometry, which can be jointly optimized with camera poses when multiple overlapping frames are available. While [1] is a regression model using encoded information to retrieve shape parameters that can't be predicted with a single image, our model is its counterpart in the classification task. Provided additional information of the scene, we can perform optimization on latent space using constraints like consistency of semantic context or geometry. In self-driving systems, depth data, ego-motion or methods like white line detection can serve to provide such additional information, making it able to resolve ambiguities in semantic segmentation results. In our current implementation, instead of combining with other methods or sensors to attain additional information, we manually provide partial scene truth by giving true label of one certain class and evaluate optimization result. This is practical in a similar way to active learning introduced in [11].

Two key contributions of our paper are:

- The extension of the architecture in CodeSLAM that makes it possible to optimize semantic segmentation result on learned models.
- The design of a unique cost function to attenuate error term in learning process using heteroscedatic uncertainty.

In the rest of this paper, we will explain our model and then we show how the learned multimodal distribution of semantic segmentation model can resolve ambiguities and errors of prediction.

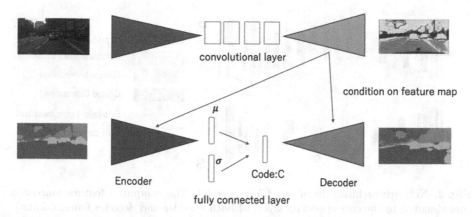

μ

σ

Code:C

convolutional layer

condition on feature map

Encoder   Decoder

fully connected layer

Fig. 1. Illustration of our learning framework. Top part: U-net [13]. Bottom part: VAE. Top left: input color image. Bottom left: input ground truth label. Top right: prediction uncertainty. Bottom right: reconstruction of semantic segmentation (Color figure online)

2 Color Image Conditioned VAE

Similar to CodeSLAM, our model uses an image conditioned variational auto-encoder (CVAE) to learn the semantic representation. The basic learning framework is shown in Fig. 1. The bottom part is a variational auto-encoder network that learns the conditional probability densities of semantic segmentation, with the conditioning feature maps provided by the U-Net [13] on the top part. As described in [1,14], a naive implementation of auto-encoder will be limited by the information bottleneck, making only major traits of input able to be retrieved. By conditioning with feature maps from color image, the auto-encoder part no longer need to encode full scene information. The semantic segmentation prediction SS thus becomes a function (decoder) of image I and c, where c(named code in CodeSLAM) is the latent space composed of a N-dimensional vector.

$$SS = f(I, c) \qquad (1)$$

We can say that common semantic segmentation architectures solve a none-code version of the above problem. Due to the introduction of the latent variants (code c), the model becomes able to efficiently produce unlimited number of hypotheses. Our model is a combination of common FCN based semantic segmentation and probabilistic generative model (VAE), where every random sample on the latent space can produce a corresponding segmentation map. Provided useful information about the scene, we can find the optimized code to resolve ambiguities during the inference phase.

2.1 Network Architecture

Our detailed network architecture is provided in Fig. 2. Ground truth segmentation labels are one-hot encoded before being inputted to the Conditional Varia-

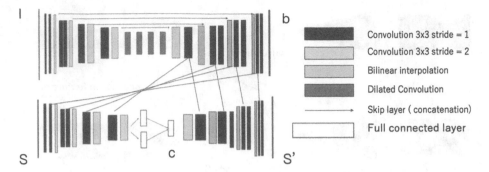

Fig. 2. Network architecture of our CVAE model. The computed feature maps are concatenated to the corresponding layers of both encoder and decoder (conditioning). The bottleneck of VAE is composed of two fully connected layer, each meaning mean and variance. Then latent space is sampled according to Gaussian distribution. We use stride length 2 to perform down-sampling, and bilinear interpolation to perform up-sampling. While the VAE part outputs S' as the reconstructed segmentation map, the U-Net part outputs b as uncertainty.

tional Auto-encoder. Then latent space is calculated through two fully connected layers in the bottleneck part, each with a dimension of N, computing mean and variance respectively. Then, we sample the latent space according to the Gaussian distribution. During the learning process, a KL-divergence cost is added to reconstruction loss as described in [8]. In the equation below 2, N stands for the length of latent vector (code size). μ and σ represent mean and variance respectively.

$$L_{kld} = \sum_{x=1}^{N}(-\log(\sigma^x) - 1 + \sigma^x + \mu^2) \qquad (2)$$

We perform condition on the VAE by concatenating feature maps calculated by the U-Net to corresponding layers (same resolution) in both encoder and decoder part. At each downsampling step we double the number of channels for the feature maps, and at every upsampling step we half the number of feature channels. Between every downsampling and upsampling pair, skip layer connection is used to take advantage of both coarse but discriminative features and fine, shallow features. Unlike the U-Net architecture in CodeSLAM [1] or original paper [13], we stop downsampling at ×16 times and replace the bottleneck part with recently popular dilated convolution [4, 17–19]. Dilated convolution enlarges the receptive field of the network while maintaining the resolution by inserting holes in the convolution kernels, which effectively prevents the information loss caused by repetitive downsampling operations.

Besides the prediction of segmentation map S', we predict a pixel-wise uncertainty b to attenuate the cost function. While [1] uses a cost term computing negative log-likelihood of the observed depth, we follow the classification model introduced in [7] to form our own loss function. For every pixel i, S'_i is the predicted logits before the final softmax layer. And b_i is the predicted uncertainty (variance). We sample from these logits T times following Gaussian distribution, each represented by $S_{i,t}$. With the ground truth label being c for pixel i, Eq. 4 gives the uncertainty aware loss function for our model.

$$S_{i,t} = P_i' + b_i \epsilon_t \qquad \epsilon_t \sim \mathcal{N}(0, I) \tag{3}$$

$$L_S = \sum_i \log \frac{1}{T} \sum_t \exp(\hat{S}_{i,t,c} - log \sum_{c'} \exp \hat{S}_{i,t,c'}) \tag{4}$$

The network will learn and adjust the pixl-wise uncertainty b so that loss attenuation can be achieved to get better segmentation result, in a similar way to its regression counterpart in CodeSLAM. We also use ReLu as activations for most of the layers, except for the computation of fully connected layer in latent space, the decoder part of VAE and final output where identity activations are used. Especially, the decoder part without nonlinear activations are regarded as linear decoder, allowing the pre-computation of the Jacobians.

2.2 Training

Our network is trained on the CityScapes Dataset [5]. The Cityscapes Dataset is a large dataset mainly focusing on semantic understanding of urban street scenes. The fine labeled dataset we use contains 5000 images, with the training, validation, and test set contains 2975, 500, and 152 images respectively.

We choose the ADAM optimiser with an initial learning rate of 10^{-4}. With a batch size of 8, we train the network for 80 epochs. We also adopt batch normalization [6] for smoother training process.

As is mentioned in Sect. 2.1, our model's loss function is composed of both a KL-divergence cost and an attenuated segmentation loss, given by Eqs. (3) and (5) respectively. We put a relative weight W_k on KL-divergence and found a code size of 128 and weight factor of 8 work fine in our current training model.

$$Loss = L_S + W_k L_{kld} \tag{5}$$

3 Inference and Refinement

During the inference phase, the encoder part of VAE is not used due to the absence of ground truth label. We assign the code with 0 value at first and thus the initial prediction is given in Eq. 6.

$$SS = f(I, 0) \tag{6}$$

This zero code prediction can be regarded as a model close to common single image semantic segmentation, where ambiguities and errors may remain. As we perform optimization on latent space with additional information of the scene, we can get a refined segmentation map. Although it's able to be combined with framework like CodeSLAM to have joint optimization by keeping both geometric and semantic consistency, we use a simpler refinement method to evaluate the optimization validity of our model. In our current work, we give partial truth information of a certain scene and perform optimization on that truth-aware region. Let c be the class that truth is given when M class exists. For every pixel j that belongs to the truth-aware area belong to c, T_i is the true one-hot label, and P_i gives the predicted probability vector.

$$T_i = [0, 0, ...1, ..0] \tag{7}$$

$$P_i = [p_0, p_1, ...p_c, ...p_{M-1}] \tag{8}$$

We use the Euclidean distance between two vectors to measure the semantic error. Especially, the probability vector is computed from code c and image I through the linear decoder according to Eq. 1, derivative of the probability w.r.t the code thus can be computed to allow optimization. The low-dimensional latent space learnt should also encode the semantic correlation among different classes, what we are expecting is that by performing optimization to reduce the semantic error on truth-aware area, prediction of both adjacent and non-adjacent area can also be refined.

4   Experiments

In this section, we first present how our model works by showing different output examples in Fig. 3. Although the zero-code segmentation results are close to those predicted from code encoded by ground truth label, errors and ambiguities appear. Especially in the left and middle columns of Fig. 3, we can observe that zero code prediction show errors in areas close to sidewalk and road, and get confused with bus and car. These errors are corrected in the output predicted from encoded information, i.e., the encoded information brought higher accuracy to the model. The output uncertainty is learned during training to attenuate cost in difficult regions as described in Sect. 2.1.

4.1   Optimization on Partial Region

Since the semantic error term is differentiable w.r.t to the latent space, additional semantic information can serve to optimize the code enhance the prediction. Due to the use of indentity activations in decoder part of VAE, the derivative of probability maps w.r.t to the code are effectively pre-computed, accelerating the evaluation of Jacobians when performing optimization. This may be helpful for faster runtime when realtime performance is required to perform joint optimization, especially in self-driving systems. As mentioned in Sect. 3, we use partial scene truth to perform optimization in our current simple experiment. In the following sections, we will first show the qualitative refined results when given road class truth. Then we compare the quantitative evaluation of class mIoU and pixel accuracy when optimizing using different class truth.

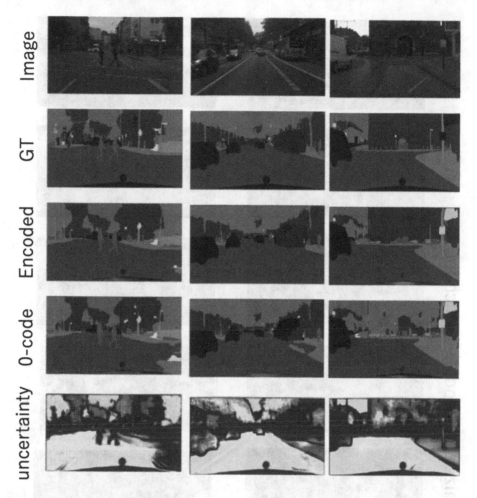

Fig. 3. The learnt output examples of our model on CityScapes Dataset. From top to bottom: color image, ground truth label, reconstructed segmentation map with encoded code, segmentation with zero code, learnt uncertainty. (Color figure online)

4.2 Qualitative Result

In Fig. 4 we compare segmentation results before and after optimization is performed. Although the prediction with zero-code captures scene objects correctly in general, we can see obvious errors occur near boundary regions. After providing road class truth to optimize the code, we can see how errors are corrected in the bottom line of optimized result. In the left example there are no other big changes except for the road and sidewalk class. However, in the left half result, not only road or adjacent regions, details of vegetation and cars' internal areas are also refined (high light with red squares). Although not as accurate as ground truth segmentation, we can observe how the optimized result get refined towards those decoded from ground truth label encoded information.

386   P. Zhuang et al.

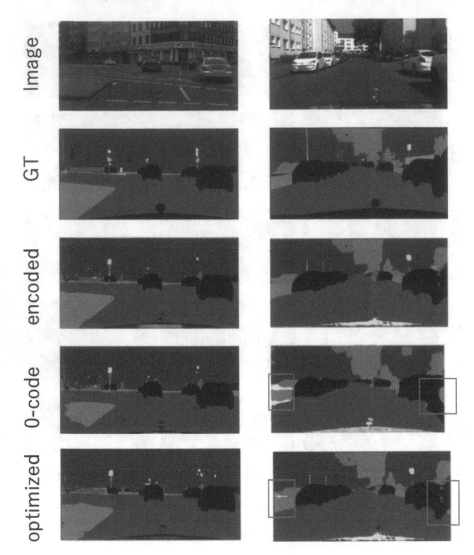

Fig. 4. The qualitative optimization examples on CityScapes Dataset. From top to bottom: color image, ground truth label, reconstructed segmentation map with encoded code, segmentation with zero code, optimized result given truth on road class. (Color figure online)

4.3   Quantitative Evaluation

To evaluate the effectiveness of optimization on partial region, we calculate IoU and pixel accuracy before and after the optimization, using 500 validation images on CityScapes Dataset. The results are shown in Fig. 5 and Table 1.

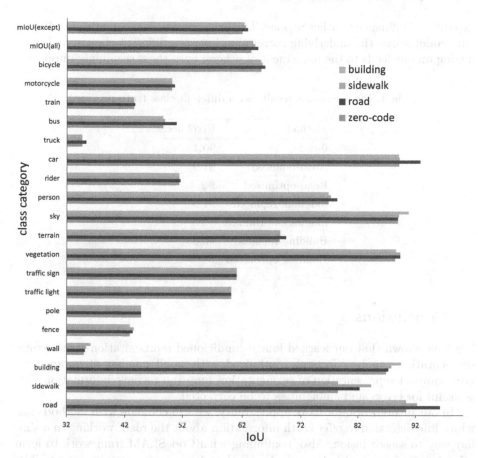

Fig. 5. IoU of our optimization result given different class truth. Besides class-wise IoU, we also calculate the mIoU for all classes (second row) and mIoU excluding truth-given class (first row)

We can see from the IoU result that, by giving one specific class truth as additional information, the refined result naturally improves impressively at both that specific class and adjacent class regions (e.g. road and sidewalk). What's more, in areas that may seem unrelated to hardly get any influence, we can still observe improvement with IoU. Comparing the mean IoU for classes excluding the optimized one (first row of the graph), we find that a general refinement of result is possible with our partial optimization method. On the other hand, we compare the pixel accuracy before and after the optimization, and also calculate the pixel accuracy when simply replacing partial prediction with true labels, without any optimization. Besides an obvious improvement when comparing with result from zero-code prediction, we also find that partial optimization in all the three cases (road, sidewalk and building) performs better than simply replacing data with true labels. That means that optimization on one class region expands its influence to other regions. The low dimensional semantic encoding in our model learns the underlying correlation between different classes, and optimizing on one leads to the refinement of others, even those seemingly unrelated.

Table 1. Pixel accuracy results with different class truth provided.

Method	Pixel acc.
0-code	90.1
Road-replaced	91.9
Road-optimized	92.4
Sidewalk-replaced	91.5
Sidewalk-optimized	92.1
Building-replaced	90.8
Building-optimized	91.6

5   Conclusions

We have shown that our learned image-conditioned representation for semantic segmentation can be effectively optimized with small number of parameters. Our compact representation of segmentation map can retrieve information that is useful for errors and ambiguities to be corrected.

In our future work, for more applicability, we will combine with methods like white line detection to offer truth information about the road, working in a similar way to sensor fusion. Also, combining with CodeSLAM framework to form a joint optimization of both semantic label and scene geometry is also possible. In our current implementation, we use U-Net to extract features, which may not be a good choice for complex urban scene segmentation. In the longer term, we would like to combine state-of-the-art semantic segmentation architecture with our probabilistic inference module. If we can refine the prediction result even on top of those high accuracy methods, our compact representation of segmentation may serve as an optional optimization technique for general models, similar to CRF but different in that our method being unified in an end-to-end inference framework, adjustable as scene and provided information change.

References

1. Bloesch, M., Czarnowski, J., Clark, R., Leutenegger, S., Davison, A.J.: CodeSLAM-learning a compact, optimisable representation for dense visual SLAM. In: CVPR, pp. 2560–2568 (2018)
2. Chandra, S., Kokkinos, I.: Fast, exact and multi-scale inference for semantic image segmentation with deep gaussian CRFs. In: Leibe, B., Matas, J., Sebe, N., Welling, M. (eds.) ECCV 2016. LNCS, vol. 9911, pp. 402–418. Springer, Cham (2016). https://doi.org/10.1007/978-3-319-46478-7_25

3. Chen, L.C., Papandreou, G., Kokkinos, I., Murphy, K., Yuille, A.L.: Semantic image segmentation with deep convolutional nets and fully connected CRFs. arXiv preprint arXiv:1412.7062 (2014)
4. Chen, L.-C., Zhu, Y., Papandreou, G., Schroff, F., Adam, H.: Encoder-decoder with atrous separable convolution for semantic image segmentation. In: Ferrari, V., Hebert, M., Sminchisescu, C., Weiss, Y. (eds.) ECCV 2018. LNCS, vol. 11211, pp. 833–851. Springer, Cham (2018). https://doi.org/10.1007/978-3-030-01234-2_49
5. Cordts, M., et al.: The cityscapes dataset for semantic urban scene understanding (2016)
6. Ioffe, S., Szegedy, C.: Batch normalization: accelerating deep network training by reducing internal covariate shift. arXiv preprint arXiv:1502.03167 (2015)
7. Kendall, A., Gal, Y.: What uncertainties do we need in bayesian deep learning for computer vision? In: NIPS, pp. 5574–5584 (2017)
8. Kingma, D.P., Welling, M.: Auto-encoding variational bayes. In: Proceedings of the International Conference on Learning Representations (ICLR) (2014)
9. Kohl, S., et al.: A probabilistic u-net for segmentation of ambiguous images. In: NIPS, pp. 6965–6975 (2018)
10. Long, J., Shelhamer, E., Darrell, T.: Fully convolutional networks for semantic segmentation. In: Proceedings of the IEEE Conference on Computer Vision and Pattern Recognition, pp. 3431–3440 (2015)
11. Mackowiak, R., Lenz, P., Ghori, O., Diego, F., Lange, O.: Cereals - cost-effective region-based active learning for semantic segmentation. In: BMVC (2018)
12. Rezende, D.J., Mohamed, S., Wierstra, D.: Stochastic backpropagation and approximate inference in deep generative models. In: Proceedings of the 31st International Conference on Machine Learning PMLR, vol. 32, pp. 1278–1286, 22–24 June 2014
13. Ronneberger, O., Fischer, P., Brox, T.: U-net: convolutional networks for biomedical image segmentation. In: Navab, N., Hornegger, J., Wells, W.M., Frangi, A.F. (eds.) MICCAI 2015. LNCS, vol. 9351, pp. 234–241. Springer, Cham (2015). https://doi.org/10.1007/978-3-319-24574-4_28
14. Rumelhart, D.E., Hinton, G.E., William, R.J.: Learning internal representations by error propagation. In: Parallel Distributed Processing: Explorations in the Microstructure of Cognition, vol. 1, pp. 318–362. MIT Press (1986)
15. Sohn, K., Lee, H., Yan, X.: Learning structured output representation using deep conditional generative models. In: NIPS, pp. 3483–3491 (2015)
16. Vemulapalli, R., Tuzel, O., Liu, M.Y., Chellappa, R.: Gaussian conditional random field network for semantic segmentation. In: CVPR (2016)
17. Wang, P., et al.: Understanding convolution for semantic segmentation (2018)
18. Yu, F., Koltun, V.: Multi-scale context aggregation by dilated convolutions. In: ICLR (2016)
19. Zhao, H., Shi, J., Qi, X., Wang, X., Jia, J.: Pyramid scene parsing network. In: CVPR, pp. 2881–2890 (2017)

Discovering Latent Domains for Unsupervised Domain Adaptation Through Consistency

Massimiliano Mancini[1,2,5(✉)], Lorenzo Porzi[3], Fabio Cermelli[4,5],
and Barbara Caputo[4,5]

[1] Sapienza University of Rome, Rome, Italy
[2] Fondazione Bruno Kessler, Trento, Italy
mancini@diag.uniroma1.it
[3] Mapillary Research, Graz, Austria
lorenzo@mapillary.com
[4] Politecnico di Torino, Turin, Italy
[5] Italian Institute of Technology, Turin, Italy
fabio.cermelli@iit.it, barbara.caputo@polito.it

Abstract. In recent years, great advances in Domain Adaptation (DA) have been possible through deep neural networks. While this is true even for multi-source scenarios, most of the methods are based on the assumption that the domain to which each sample belongs is known a priori. However, in practice, we might have a source domain composed by a mixture of multiple sub-domains, without any prior about the sub-domain to which each source sample belongs. In this case, while multi-source DA methods are not applicable, restoring to single-source ones may lead to sub-optimal results. In this work, we explore a recent direction in deep domain adaptation: automatically discovering latent domains in visual datasets. Previous works address this problem by using a domain prediction branch, trained with an entropy loss. Here we present a novel formulation for training the domain prediction branch which exploits (i) domain prediction output for various perturbations of the input features and (ii) the min-entropy consensus loss, which forces the predictions of the perturbation to be both consistent and with low entropy. We compare our approach to the previous state-of-the-art on publicly-available datasets, showing the effectiveness of our method both quantitatively and qualitatively.

Keywords: Domain Adaptation · Visual recognition · Deep learning

1   Introduction

Most learning based models rely on the assumption that training and test data are drawn from the same distribution. Unfortunately, this assumption does

E. Ricci et al. (Eds.): ICIAP 2019, LNCS 11752, pp. 390–401, 2019.
https://doi.org/10.1007/978-3-030-30645-8_36

not hold in many real-world computer vision applications due to unpredictable changes in the environment (*e.g.* weather, illumination, occlusions). Despite the progress brought in visual recognition by deep learning and the availability of large fully annotated dataset, models trained on a given distribution different from the test one still struggle to generalize, giving poor performance. This problem is commonly referred to as *domain shift* and it is especially relevant in computer vision due to the large appearance variability of the visual data. The domain shift problem has been widely studied in the last decade and many techniques have been proposed to limit its effect [29].

Domain Adaptation (DA) methods specifically focus on learning a given task in a *source* domain, then transferring the acquired knowledge in the domain of interest, *i.e.* the *target* domain. In past years, researchers studied the theoretical aspects of this problem [1,28] and proposed several shallow [14] and deep learning based [4,10,21,22] algorithms. However, recent studies [7] have shown that the domain shift problem can only be alleviated but not entirely solved even adopting deep architectures.

Often, DA methods consider a single-source, single-target scenario, but a setting in which multiple source domains are available is arguably more interesting and realistic. In fact, datasets could contain images taken with different cameras, from many viewpoints or with different lighting conditions. Approaching such cases with single-source DA algorithms will lead to poor results. For this reason, many DA methods have been proposed to learn from multiple sources [3,8,25,28,35]. However, these approaches assume to know the domain label of each sample. A more challenging scenario arises when the domain to which a sample belongs is not known in advance. This problem, also referred to as *latent domain discovery*, consider the presence of multiple but mixed sources and/or target domains, offering either partial or no information, about the ground-truth domain of each sample. In previous years, few works [11,13,27,36] focused on this setting, simultaneously performing the discovery of latent domains and using the information to learn a classification model for the target one.

In this paper, we propose a novel formulation for the domain discovery algorithm proposed in [27]. In particular, we enhance the domain classifier training by employing a different objective. This objective is based on (i) producing multiple domain predictions on perturbations of the features of a given sample and (ii) applying on those predictions the recently proposed Min-Entropy Consensus (MEC) Loss [30]. This loss enforces both consistency and low entropy for the perturbed domain predictions of a single sample. An overview of the method is reported in Fig. 1. Our empirical study demonstrates that we are able to extract meaningful latent domains from the source samples, achieving better performance than previous latent domain discovery DA methods on popular benchmarks, such as Office-31 [32] and PACS [18].

2   Related Works

Deep Domain Adaptation. In recent years, deep learning based DA approaches have show to be very effective in addressing this task. Usually, robust domain-invariant features are learned in deep architectures using either supervised neural networks [4,10,21,30] or deep autoencoders [39]. Some methods [21,22] rely on the idea of aligning source and target features by minimizing the Maximum Mean Discrepancy (MMD). A different approach is represented by methods that operates in a domain-adversarial setting [10], *i.e.* they focus on learning a domain-agnostic feature space by minimizing a domain confusion loss. Recent works have also explored the use of generative models [2,31]. Our work is close to recent trends exploring the use of domain-specific batch-normalization layers [4,5,25,26], since we use a variant of those layers [27] to adapt the model from the latent source domains to the target one. Our approach is also linked to consistency-based DA strategies [9,30,33]. Different from these works, we employ a consistency loss [30] for learning the domain prediction branch. Our work is also related to multi-source DA [8,35,37] and domain generalization [3,6,18,23,24]. Similarly to these scenarios, we assume the presence of multiple source domains. However, in our case these domains are mixed and we must discover them in order to exploit the advantages of multi-source DA approaches.

Latent Domain Discovery for DA. Very few works tried to address the latent domain discovery problem in the literature. While previous works on shallow features considered the use multiple Gaussian distributions [13], domain distinctiveness [11], exemplar SVMs [19,38] and manifold learning [36], only one work addressed this problem in the context of deep DA [27]. In [27] we proposed to exploit a domain prediction branch and domain alignment layers [4,5] to discover latent domains and improve the DA performances on the target domain. While in [27] the domain prediction branch was trained through an entropy loss, in this work we show how we can achieve similar or better results by employing a different loss, [30] which encourages both low entropy and consistency on the domain predictions for perturbations of the same input features.

3   Method

3.1   Problem Formulation and Notation

As in standard Unsupervised Domain Adaptation (UDA), we assume to have access to a source and a target domain. The source domain contains semantically labeled samples, while the target domain contains only unlabelled samples. However, different from standard UDA, we assume that the source domain is composed of a mixture of multiple domains and, contrary to multi-source DA, we do not assume to know to which domain each source sample belongs. Following previous works [27], we assume to have k *source* domains. Notice that this number might not be known a priori: in our current formulation we leave it has an hyperparameter. Source domains are characterized by unknown probability distributions $p_{xy}^{s_1}, \ldots, p_{xy}^{s_{k_s}}$ defined over $\mathcal{X} \times \mathcal{Y}$, where $\mathcal{X}$ is the input space (*e.g.* images in our case) and $\mathcal{Y}$ the output space (*e.g.* object categories). The source data are thus modelled as a set $\mathcal{S} = \{(x_1^s, y_1^s), \ldots, (x_n^s, y_n^s)\}$ with $x_{\mathcal{S}} = \{x_1^s, \ldots, x_n^s\}$ and $y_{\mathcal{S}} = \{y_1^s, \ldots, y_n^s\}$, the source data and label sets, respectively. The set $\mathcal{S}$

contains i.i.d. observations from a mixture distribution $p_{xy}^s = \sum_{i=1}^{k_s} \pi_{s_i} p_{xy}^{s_i}$, where π_{s_i} is the unknown probability of sampling from a source domain s_i. Similarly, we assume to have target domain data $\mathcal{T} = \{x_1^t, \ldots, x_m^t\}$ of i.i.d. observations drawn from p_x^t.

During training we receive semantically labeled source samples with unknown domain membership plus unlabeled target samples. Our goal is to learn a model able to address a given task (*i.e.* classification) in the target domain. Following [27], we address this task by using domain specific batch-normalization [15] (BN) layers to perform DA [4,5,20,26]. These layers are influenced by the latent domain discovery process, performed by a domain prediction branch. With respect to [27] we propose a new objective for the domain prediction branch. In the following we will review how BN can be used to address DA [4,5,26] and how a simple variant can be used in the case where we have multiple but unknown source domains [27]. We will then describe how the domain assignment branch can be trained by using the Min-Entropy Consensus loss [30] (Sect. 3.3), building the whole objective for the training procedure.

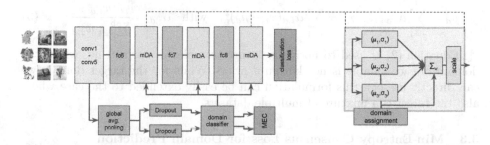

Fig. 1. Schematic representation of our method applied to the AlexNet architecture (left) and of an mDA-layer (right). The features in input to the domain classifier are perturbed through Dropout [34]. The Min-Entropy Consensus (MEC) loss is then applied to the output of the domain classifier, to enforce the same domain assignment for different perturbations of the same input.

3.2 Multi-domain DA-Layers

BN-based DA methods [4,5,20] are a simple yet effective way to tackle the DA problem. Since features extracted by a neural network tend to follow domain-dependent distributions [20], we can align them through domain specific normalization layers. Following [27], let us denote as q_x^d the distribution of activations for a given feature channel and domain d. *Domain Alignment Layers* [4,5] (DAL) normalize an input $x^d \sim q_x^d$ according to

$$\text{DAL}(x^d; \mu_d, \sigma_d) = \frac{x^d - \mu_d}{\sqrt{\sigma_d^2 + \epsilon}}, \tag{1}$$

where $\mu_d = \mathrm{E}_{x \sim q_x^d}[x]$, $\sigma_d^2 = \mathrm{Var}_{x \sim q_x^d}[x]$ are mean and variance of the input distribution, respectively, and $\epsilon > 0$ is a small constant to avoid numerical issues. During training the statistics $\{\mu_d, \sigma_d^2\}$ are computed over the current mini-batch, thus we apply standard BN but separately for each available d.

The previous formulation requires full domain knowledge (*i.e.* d) for each sample, something that we do not have in our setting for the source domain. In [27] a variant of the DAL layers called *Multi-Domain Alignmet Layers* (mDA) has been proposed to tackle this issue. mDA layers exploit the probabilities that a source sample belongs to one of the latent domains. Formally, denoting as $w_{i,d}$ the probability of x_i belonging to d and a source mini-batch $\mathcal{B} = \{x_i\}_{i=1}^b$, mDA layers normalize x_i as follows:

$$\mathrm{mDA}(x_i, \boldsymbol{w}_i; \hat{\boldsymbol{\mu}}, \hat{\boldsymbol{\sigma}}) = \sum_{d \in \mathcal{D}} w_{i,d} \frac{x_i - \hat{\mu}_d}{\sqrt{\hat{\sigma}_d^2 + \epsilon}}, \tag{2}$$

where $\boldsymbol{w}_i = \{w_{i,d}\}_{d \in \mathcal{D}}$, $\hat{\boldsymbol{\mu}} = \{\hat{\mu}_d\}_{d \in \mathcal{D}}$, $\hat{\boldsymbol{\sigma}} = \{\hat{\sigma}_d^2\}_{d \in \mathcal{D}}$ and $\mathcal{D}$ is the set of source latent domains. Notice that μ_d and σ_d^2 are computed in a weighted fashion:

$$\mu_d = \sum_{i=1}^b \alpha_{i,d} x_i, \quad \sigma_d^2 = \sum_{i=1}^b \alpha_{i,d}(x_i - \mu_d)^2, \quad \text{with} \quad \alpha_{i,d} = \frac{w_{i,d}}{\sum_{j=1}^b w_{j,d}} \tag{3}$$

Equation (2) is used to normalize source samples in our setting, where the domain of each sample is not known a priori. While for the target domain we can directly use (1), this formulation can be easily extended to the case where also the target is a mixture of multiple datasets.

3.3   Min-Entropy Consensus Loss for Domain Prediction

A crucial aspect of mDA layers is the domain assignment $\boldsymbol{w}_i$ that each sample receives. To this extent, as in [27] we employ a domain prediction branch. This branch is composed by a minimal set of layers followed by a softmax operation on k outputs. This branch is a different section of the network which shares with the classification part only the bottom-most layers, due to their higher domain specificity [27]. In [27] the domain prediction branch is trained by exploiting an entropy loss. In this work, we argue that we can train a more effective domain prediction branch if we enforce the entropy loss through consensus among domain assignments for perturbations of the same input.

Formally, let us define as g^θ the domain prediction branch, parametrized by θ. We split it into two parts: g_E^θ and g_D^θ, denoting the feature extractor and the domain classifier respectively. Given the low-level features x_i, in [27] the domain prediction branch produces the domain assignments $\boldsymbol{w}_i$ as follows:

$$\boldsymbol{w}_i = g^\theta(x_i) = g_D^\theta(g_E^\theta(x_i)) \tag{4}$$

In order to obtain multiple assignments of perturbed version of the input, we employ a non-parametric random transformation ϕ. The assignment of the perturbed sample is obtained by replacing the feature extraction function g_E^θ with $\phi \circ g_E^\theta$:

$$\hat{w}_i = g^\theta(x_i) = g_D^\theta(\phi(g_E^\theta(x_i))) \tag{5}$$

where $\hat{w}_i$ denotes the assignment given to the perturbed features. Since ϕ is random, applying this function multiple times on the same input will produce different outputs. With this in mind we can create a matrix $\hat{W}_i = [\hat{w}_i^1, \cdots, \hat{w}_i^r]$ where each element $\hat{w}_i^j$ is obtained by classifying with g_D^θ a different application of ϕ on the features extracted by g_E^θ.

Since $\hat{W}_i$ is a set of r predictions related to different perturbations of the same sample, we can enforce consistency within $\hat{W}_i$, obtaining an unsupervised objective for the domain prediction branch. However, as noted in [30], standard consistency loss [9,33] force only consistent predictions across perturbations of the same sample, without taking into account the actual confidence on the assignment. To this extent, we follow [30] and we employ the Min-Entropy Consensus (MEC) loss as an objective for the domain classifier. Given a set $\hat{W}_i = [\hat{w}_i^1, \cdots, \hat{w}_i^r]$, we minimize the following objective:

$$\mathrm{MEC}(x_i) = -\frac{1}{r} \max_{d \in D} \sum_{j=1}^{r} \log(w_{i,d}^j) \tag{6}$$

The domain loss on the full source set is:

$$L_{\mathrm{dom}} = \frac{1}{n} \sum_{x \in x_S} \mathrm{MEC}(x_i) \tag{7}$$

With (7) we have defined a loss which allows to obtain domain predictions that are both consistent and confident for a given sample. In the experiments we use Dropout [34] as ϕ with ratio 0.5, setting r = 2 as in [30].

To train the full architecture we need to define an objective for the semantic classification part. Following [4,5,27] we employ a cross-entropy loss on the labeled source samples and an entropy loss for the unlabeled target ones. Denoting as f_C^θ the classification branch we have:

$$L_{\mathrm{cls}}(\theta) = -\frac{1}{n} \sum_{i=1}^{n} \log f_C^\theta(y_i^s; x_i^s) + \frac{\lambda_C}{m} \sum_{i=1}^{m} H(f_C^\theta(\cdot; x_i^t)). \tag{8}$$

The first term on the right-hand-side is the average log-loss related to the supervised examples in $\mathcal{S}$, where $f_C^\theta(y_i^s; x_i^s)$ denotes the output of the *classification branch* of the network for a source sample, *i.e.* the predicted probability of x_i^s having class y_i^s. The second term on the right-hand-side of (8) is the entropy H of the classification distribution $f_C^\theta(\cdot; x_i^t)$, averaged over all unlabeled target examples x_i^t in $\mathcal{T}$, scaled by a positive hyperparameter λ_C. The full objective is:

$$L(\theta) = L_{\mathrm{cls}}(\theta) + \lambda_D L_{\mathrm{dom}}(\theta), \tag{9}$$

where L_{cls} is a loss term that penalizes based on the final classification task, while L_{dom} accounts for the domain classification task, with a hyperparameter λ_D balancing the two. We highlight that, due to dependency of the classification branch on the mDA layers, the network learns to predict domain assignment probabilities that also result in a low classification loss. A schematic representation of our architecture is depicted in Fig. 1. Since the semantic classification part needs a single domain assignment for each sample, we set $\boldsymbol{w}_i$ as the average of the domain predictions on perturbed inputs: $i.e.$ $\boldsymbol{w}_i = \frac{1}{r} \sum_j = 1^r \hat{w}_i^j$.

4   Experiments

4.1   Experimental Setup

In our evaluation we consider the following benchmarks: the PACS dataset [18] and the Office-31 [32] dataset.

Office-31 is a widely used DA benchmark which contains images of 31 object categories collected from 3 different sources: Webcam (W), DSLR camera (D) and the Amazon website (A). We test our model on the multi-source setting [36], where each domain is in turn considered as target, while the others as sources. We use this benchmark to compare with [27] as well as previous shallow algorithms [11,13,36]. In this setting we use as input to our algorithm the activations of the fc7 layer of an AlexNet [17] architecture, applying mDA layers to the features and after the domain classifier, as in [27]. The structure of the domain prediction branch is the same of [27], except for the addition of a BN layer (without scale and bias) to the domain logits, since we found that this addition stabilizes the training procedure. The hyperparameters used for training are the same of [27], with $\lambda_D = 0.5$ and $k = 2$.

PACS [18] is a recently proposed dataset which contains images of 7 categories extracted from 4 different representations, with significant domain shift: $i.e.$ Photo (P), Art paintings (A), Cartoon (C) and Sketch (S). Following [18], we train our model considering 3 domains as sources and the remaining as target, using all the images of each domain. Differently from [18] we consider a DA setting ($i.e.$ target data are available at training time). For the experiments on the PACS dataset we consider the ResNet-18 architecture [12]. As in [27], to apply our approach, we replace each BN layer in the network with an mDA-layer. As in the previous case, the structure of the domain prediction branch and the hyperparameters selected for training are the same of [27], with $\lambda_D = 0.5$ and $k = 3$ and with the insertion of a BN layer after the domain prediction logits.

We implement all the models with the Caffe [16] framework and our evaluation is performed using a NVIDIA GeForce 1080 GTX GPU. Both the architectures have been initialized with their weights pretrained on ImageNet: for AlexNet we take the pre-trained model available in Caffe, while for ResNet we use the converted version of the original model developed in Torch[1].

4.2   Results

Analysis of Our Method. In a first series of experiments we compare our model and [27] on the PACS dataset using the ResNet-18 architecture. As a

---

[1] https://github.com/HolmesShuan/ResNet-18-Caffemodel-on-ImageNet.

baseline we report the performances of the base architecture, the single source
DA model of [5] (DIAL) and the multi-source version of [5] which is our upper
bound since it assumes perfect domain separation (Multi-source DA). The results
are shown in Table 1. As the table shows our model achieves comparable performances with respect to [27] in average. By analyzing the results it is possible to see that our model performs comparably to the Multi-source DA upper
bound in the domains where the gap with the single source baseline is minimal
(*Photo* and *Art*). However our model largely outperforms [27] when Sketch is
used as target. We ascribe this behaviour to the fact that enforcing consistency
allows to regularize and strengthen the latent domain discovery process, providing favourable domain separation even when the difference among the domains
is less pronounced (as in this case, where *Photo*, *Art* and *Cartoon* are the source
domains). At the same time, this regularization could harm the confidence of
the domain prediction branch and the statistics estimated by Eq. 2 if the source
domains are close. This happens for instance when *Cartoon* is employed as target, where there two domains (*Photo* and *Art*) are close to each other and far
from the third domain (*Sketch*).

Table 1. PACS dataset: comparison of different methods using the ResNet architecture. The first row indicates the target domain, while all the others are considered as
sources.

Method	Sketch	Photo	Art	Cartoon	Mean
ResNet [12]	60.1	92.9	74.7	72.4	75.0
DIAL [5]	66.8	**97.0**	87.3	85.5	84.2
mDA [27]	69.6	**97.0**	**87.7**	**86.9**	85.3
Ours	**71.1**	96.8	87.3	86.4	**85.4**
Multi-source DA	71.6	96.6	87.5	87.0	85.7

To understand the outcome of the latent domain discovery process, we report
histograms analyzing how many samples of a domain receive a given probability
to belong to a latent domain. The analysis is shown in Fig. 2. As the figure
shows, every time *Sketch* is among the source domains (yellow bar) almost all
its samples are assigned to a single latent domain. Moreover, when *Sketch* is
present, since the difference among the other source domains is more subtle,
they tend to receive assignments spread among the other two latent domains,
even if with different distributions. This is clear in Fig. 2b where *Photo* samples
tend to be assigned to the first latent domain and *Cartoon* samples to the second
one. Similarly, in the case where *Sketch* is the target (Fig. 2d), *Cartoon* samples
are assigned to the first latent domains, with *Photo* samples mainly assigned to
the second, and *Art* samples spread among the three latent domains. This latter
outcome is reasonable due to the fact that *Art* is a domain which is visually
intermediate between *Photo* and *Cartoon*. A similar effect can be noted when
Cartoon and *Sketch* are both source domains: due to the fact that *Cartoon* is

the closest visual domain to *Sketch*, its samples may receive probabilities even in the latent domain to which *Sketch* samples are assigned.

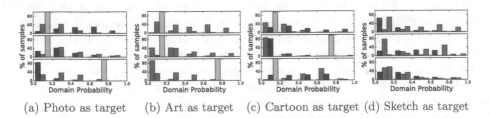

(a) Photo as target　　(b) Art as target　　(c) Cartoon as target (d) Sketch as target

Fig. 2. PACS dataset: analysis of the assignments of source samples to each latent domain. Each row is a different latent domain and each color a different source domain: red for *Photo*, blue for *Art*, green for *Cartoon* and yellow for *Sketch*. (Color figure online)

To further confirm this analysis, Fig. 3, reports the top images assigned to each of the latent domains. The figure highlights also how the appearance plays a crucial role in the domain discovery process, since the dominant color of an image highly influences its domain assignment. This can be an important aspects for exploring future applications in the real world, where the shift might be caused by changes in *e.g.* illumination and weather condition.

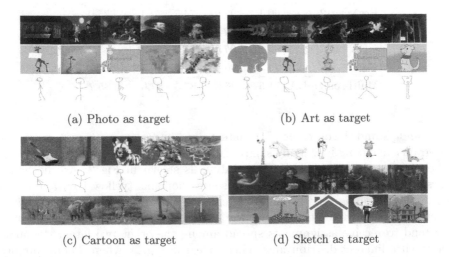

(a) Photo as target　　　　　　　(b) Art as target

(c) Cartoon as target　　　　　　(d) Sketch as target

Fig. 3. PACS dataset: analysis of the top-5 images assigned to each of the latent domains for each source-target scenario. Each row is a different latent domain.

Comparison with the State-of-the-Art. Finally, we compare the performances of our model against state of the art approaches on the Office-31 dataset, using as input fc7 features of the AlexNet architecture. We compare with deep approach of [27] and with the shallow ones [11,13,36], which are among the few approaches tackling the latent domain discovery problem. The results are shown in Table 2. Our model outperforms both shallow [11,13,36] and deep [27] methods. Our algorithm obtains a gain of almost 1% in average with respect to the baseline [27], confirming the effectiveness of the proposed training objective for the domain classification branch and the fact that our algorithm performs better than [27] when the difference among the source domains is less marked.

Table 2. Office-31: comparison with state-of-the-art algorithms. In the first row we indicate the source (top) and the target domains (bottom).

Method	Sources	A-D	A-W	W-D	Mean
	Target	W	D	A	
Hoffman et al. [13]		24.8	42.7	12.8	26.8
Xiong et al. [36]		29.3	43.6	13.3	28.7
Gong et al. (AlexNet) [11]		91.8	94.6	48.9	78.4
mDA [27]		93.1	94.3	64.2	83.9
Ours		**94.1**	**95.1**	**64.9**	**84.7**

5   Conclusions

In this work we have presented an algorithm for addressing the problem of latent domain DA, where the source domain is a mixture of multiple datasets and we do not know the domain membership of each sample. Our method is based on [27], where the latent DA task is solved by employing domain-specific alignment layers. These layers perform a normalization weighted on the probability of a sample to belong to a given domain, with the probability predicted by a domain classifier. While in [27] an entropy loss is employed to train the domain prediction branch, here we propose to use the Minimal-Entropy Consensus (MEC) loss [30] on perturbed version of the features that we provide to the domain classifier for a single sample. Due to the consistency, this loss is more stable with respect to standard entropy and regularizes the domain separation process. Results on the PACS and Office-31 datasets show that our model outperforms all the baselines in Office-31, while achieving similar or higher performances on PACS with respect to [27]. In future works we plan to expand the findings of this work by exploring the impact of using various perturbation and consensus strategies.

Acknowledgements. This work was partially supported by the ERC grant 637076 - RoboExNovo.

References

1. Ben-David, S., Blitzer, J., Crammer, K., Kulesza, A., Pereira, F., Vaughan, J.W.: A theory of learning from different domains. Mach. Learn. **79**(1), 151–175 (2010)
2. Bousmalis, K., Silberman, N., Dohan, D., Erhan, D., Krishnan, D.: Unsupervised pixel-level domain adaptation with generative adversarial networks. In: CVPR (2017)
3. Carlucci, F.M., D'Innocente, A., Bucci, S., Caputo, B., Tommasi, T.: Domain generalization by solving jigsaw puzzles. In: CVPR (2019)
4. Carlucci, F.M., Porzi, L., Caputo, B., Ricci, E., Rota Bulò, S.: Autodial: automatic domain alignment layers. In: ICCV (2017)
5. Carlucci, F.M., Porzi, L., Caputo, B., Ricci, E., Bulò, S.R.: Just DIAL: domain alignment layers for unsupervised domain adaptation. In: Battiato, S., Gallo, G., Schettini, R., Stanco, F. (eds.) ICIAP 2017. LNCS, vol. 10484, pp. 357–369. Springer, Cham (2017). https://doi.org/10.1007/978-3-319-68560-1_32
6. D'Innocente, A., Caputo, B.: Domain generalization with domain-specific aggregation modules. In: Brox, T., Bruhn, A., Fritz, M. (eds.) GCPR 2018. LNCS, vol. 11269, pp. 187–198. Springer, Cham (2019). https://doi.org/10.1007/978-3-030-12939-2_14
7. Donahue, J., et al.: Decaf: a deep convolutional activation feature for generic visual recognition. In: ICML (2014)
8. Duan, L., Tsang, I.W., Xu, D., Chua, T.S.: Domain adaptation from multiple sources via auxiliary classifiers. In: ICML (2009)
9. French, G., Mackiewicz, M., Fisher, M.: Self-ensembling for visual domain adaptation. In: ICLR (2018)
10. Ganin, Y., Lempitsky, V.: Unsupervised domain adaptation by backpropagation. In: ICML (2015)
11. Gong, B., Grauman, K., Sha, F.: Reshaping visual datasets for domain adaptation. In: NIPS (2013)
12. He, K., Zhang, X., Ren, S., Sun, J.: Deep residual learning for image recognition. In: CVPR, pp. 770–778 (2016)
13. Hoffman, J., Kulis, B., Darrell, T., Saenko, K.: Discovering latent domains for multisource domain adaptation. In: Fitzgibbon, A., Lazebnik, S., Perona, P., Sato, Y., Schmid, C. (eds.) ECCV 2012. LNCS, pp. 702–715. Springer, Heidelberg (2012). https://doi.org/10.1007/978-3-642-33709-3_50
14. Huang, J., Gretton, A., Borgwardt, K.M., Schölkopf, B., Smola, A.J.: Correcting sample selection bias by unlabeled data. In: NIPS (2006)
15. Ioffe, S., Szegedy, C.: Batch normalization: accelerating deep network training by reducing internal covariate shift. arXiv preprint arXiv:1502.03167 (2015)
16. Jia, Y., et al.: Caffe: convolutional architecture for fast feature embedding. In: ACM-Multimedia, pp. 675–678. ACM (2014)
17. Krizhevsky, A., Sutskever, I., Hinton, G.E.: ImageNet classification with deep convolutional neural networks. In: NIPS, pp. 1097–1105 (2012)
18. Li, D., Yang, Y., Song, Y.Z., Hospedales, T.M.: Deeper, broader and artier domain generalization. In: ICCV (2017)
19. Li, W., Xu, Z., Xu, D., Dai, D., Van Gool, L.: Domain generalization and adaptation using low rank exemplar SVMs. IEEE T-PAMI **40**(5), 1114–1127 (2018)
20. Li, Y., Wang, N., Shi, J., Liu, J., Hou, X.: Revisiting batch normalization for practical domain adaptation. arXiv preprint arXiv:1603.04779 (2016)

21. Long, M., Wang, J.: Learning transferable features with deep adaptation networks. In: ICML (2015)
22. Long, M., Wang, J., Jordan, M.I.: Unsupervised domain adaptation with residual transfer networks. In: NIPS (2016)
23. Mancini, M., Bulò, S.R., Caputo, B., Ricci, E.: Best sources forward: domain generalization through source-specific nets. In: ICIP (2018)
24. Mancini, M., Bulò, S.R., Caputo, B., Ricci, E.: Robust place categorization with deep domain generalization. IEEE RAL **3**(3), 2093–2100 (2018)
25. Mancini, M., Bulò, S.R., Caputo, B., Ricci, E.: Adagraph: Unifying predictive and continuous domain adaptation through graphs. In: CVPR (2019)
26. Mancini, M., Karaoguz, H., Ricci, E., Jensfelt, P., Caputo, B.: Kitting in the wild through online domain adaptation. In: IROS (2018)
27. Mancini, M., Porzi, L., Bulò, S.R., Caputo, B., Ricci, E.: Boosting domain adaptation by discovering latent domains. In: CVPR (2018)
28. Mansour, Y., Mohri, M., Rostamizadeh, A.: Domain adaptation: Learning bounds and algorithms. arXiv preprint arXiv:0902.3430 (2009)
29. Pan, S.J., Yang, Q.: A survey on transfer learning. IEEE Trans. Knowl. Data Eng. **22**(10), 1345–1359 (2010)
30. Roy, S., Siarohin, A., Sangineto, E., Bulo, S.R., Sebe, N., Ricci, E.: Unsupervised domain adaptation using feature-whitening and consensus loss. In: CVPR (2019)
31. Russo, P., Carlucci, F.M., Tommasi, T., Caputo, B.: From source to target and back: symmetric bi-directional adaptive GAN. In: CVPR (2018)
32. Saenko, K., Kulis, B., Fritz, M., Darrell, T.: Adapting visual category models to new domains. In: Daniilidis, K., Maragos, P., Paragios, N. (eds.) ECCV 2010. LNCS, vol. 6314, pp. 213–226. Springer, Heidelberg (2010). https://doi.org/10.1007/978-3-642-15561-1_16
33. Saito, K., Ushiku, Y., Harada, T.: Asymmetric tri-training for unsupervised domain adaptation. arXiv preprint arXiv:1702.08400 (2017)
34. Srivastava, N., Hinton, G.E., Krizhevsky, A., Sutskever, I., Salakhutdinov, R.: Dropout: a simple way to prevent neural networks from overfitting. J. Mach. Learn. Res. **15**(1), 1929–1958 (2014)
35. Sun, Q., Chattopadhyay, R., Panchanathan, S., Ye, J.: A two-stage weighting framework for multi-source domain adaptation. In: NIPS (2011)
36. Xiong, C., McCloskey, S., Hsieh, S.H., Corso, J.J.: Latent domains modeling for visual domain adaptation. In: AAAI (2014)
37. Xu, R., Chen, Z., Zuo, W., Yan, J., Lin, L.: Deep cocktail network: multi-source unsupervised domain adaptation with category shift. In: CVPR (2018)
38. Xu, Z., Li, W., Niu, L., Xu, D.: Exploiting low-rank structure from latent domains for domain generalization. In: Fleet, D., Pajdla, T., Schiele, B., Tuytelaars, T. (eds.) ECCV 2014. LNCS, vol. 8691, pp. 628–643. Springer, Cham (2014). https://doi.org/10.1007/978-3-319-10578-9_41
39. Zeng, X., Ouyang, W., Wang, M., Wang, X.: Deep learning of scene-specific classifier for pedestrian detection. In: Fleet, D., Pajdla, T., Schiele, B., Tuytelaars, T. (eds.) ECCV 2014. LNCS, vol. 8691, pp. 472–487. Springer, Cham (2014). https://doi.org/10.1007/978-3-319-10578-9_31

re-OBJ: Jointly Learning the Foreground and Background for Object Instance Re-identification

Vaibhav Bansal[1,3]([✉]), Stuart James[2], and Alessio Del Bue[1]

[1] Visual Geometry and Modelling (VGM),
Istituto Italiano di Tecnologia, Genoa, Italy
vaibhav.bansal@iit.it
[2] Center for Cultural Heritage Technology (CCHT),
Istituto Italiano di Tecnologia, Genoa, Italy
[3] Università degli studi di Genova, Genoa, Italy

Abstract. Conventional approaches to object instance re-identification rely on matching appearances of the target objects among a set of frames. However, learning appearances of the objects alone might fail when there are multiple objects with similar appearance or multiple instances of same object class present in the scene. This paper proposes that partial observations of the background can be utilized to aid in the object re-identification task for a rigid scene, especially a rigid environment with a lot of reoccurring identical models of objects. Using an extension to the Mask R-CNN architecture, we learn to encode the important and distinct information in the background jointly with the foreground relevant to rigid real-world scenarios such as an indoor environment where objects are static and the camera moves around the scene. We demonstrate the effectiveness of our joint visual feature in the re-identification of objects in the ScanNet dataset and show a relative improvement of around 28.25% in the rank-1 accuracy over the deepSort method.

Keywords: Re-identification · Object detection · Multi-view ·
Triplet loss

1 Introduction

Multiple object matching and association are classical problems in many important tasks such as video surveillance, semantic scene understanding and also, Simultaneous Localization And Mapping (SLAM). Given an indoor scene, where the environment is frequently cluttered with several near-identical objects, it is challenging to identify and track a particular instance of an object among a number of objects present in the scene, e.g. see Fig. 1. The problem is even more challenging when there is a wide baseline among multiple views (or temporally disjoint). It is complex to re-identify a vast variety of objects based on appearance only. There are many challenges for the association problem i.e. occlusions, motion blur, mis-detections, etc. Conventional methods use two major

© Springer Nature Switzerland AG 2019
E. Ricci et al. (Eds.): ICIAP 2019, LNCS 11752, pp. 402–413, 2019.
https://doi.org/10.1007/978-3-030-30645-8_37

approaches to build a re-ID system - appearance-based and motion-based. Most methods use an appearance-based approach because motion prediction based systems try to localize each object instance based on a motion model, however, due to the possibility of huge unpredictable trajectories across the frames, these methods tend to fail when the same object instance reappear after a long time.

Fig. 1. Similar looking objects in rigid, indoor scenes from ScanNet dataset. Multiple instances of the same object class, chair, in this case, are hard to differentiate with each other. In such cases, background can be highly useful to re-identify a particular instance in multiple views.

Many previous studies focus on *person* re-identification where the goal is to assign a correct ID of an instance of a specific class (i.e. a pedestrian) across multiple-views obtained from cameras with possibly non-overlapping views. In general, these methods try to learn discriminative features based on person's face [18], clothing [14] or symmetry-driven local features [9] to re-ID people. In contrast, the problem of associating an unique ID to instances of objects is often solved as the association of multiple unknown objects between views [16]. This problem is closely related to person re-ID and often evaluated in the pedestrian (person) scenario with early work on PET2009 [5].

However, the specific task of re-identifying multiple near-identical objects in a rigid scene presents a different challenge, we refer to as re-OBJ, a specific case of re-ID. In this paper, we consider a static indoor video dataset where large displacement in the camera motion is unlikely and so the background of an instance cannot undergo a sudden drastic change. Therefore, we propose to jointly learn the foreground and the background to build a robust object re-identification system at the instance level. We propose not only to learn the appearance of an object but also the background that can provide a lot of useful information regarding the surroundings of an instance which is unique to that instance at any given viewpoint. Consider a scene of an office room with multiple chairs and tables present. To re-identify a particular object instance across multiple images, it is important to be able to distinguish it from other instances of the same object class. Intuitively, if we can observe and encode the surroundings of that particular instance within a stream of images, we can be confident to an extent that the object instance in consideration has been seen before and it is different from other instances of the same class because the environment around it is unique at any given point of time even when other instances have similar appearance (see Fig. 1).

2   Related Work

There is a vast literature for object re-identification that is mostly focused on person re-identification. The ability to re-identify objects in the images heavily relies on finding a similar set of images for a given image of the target object, possibly with multiple instances, using visual search to retrieve similar images to the given query image. Some works in the literature like [2,9] exploit the knowledge that the same individual is been detected in consecutive frames and then learning an appearance-based transfer function for a robust re-identification system. Additionally, in [9], they extract features from three different complementary modalities: the chromatic content, spatial arrangement of colors and local motifs derived from different parts of the human body to accumulate local features. Other deep learning models learn the category-level similarity [20] that mainly involves semantic similarity. The study highlights the effect of significant visual variability within a category although the semantic and visual similarities are generally quite consistent across different categories. Thus, applications that involve the computation of image similarity like re-identification, image retrieval, search-by-example require learning a fine-grained image similarity that can also distinguish the differences between different images of the same category. Relative attribute [17] learns image attribute ranking among the images with the same attributes. OASIS [4] performs local distance learning [10] learn image similarity ranking models on top of the hand-crafted features. Such appearance-based approaches are good at distinguishing intra-class variation, in contrast, we focus on the objects' relationship to the background to jointly learn a foreground and background discriminative appearance feature.

Many image similarity models [3,4,20] simply extract features like Gabor filters, SIFT [15], HOG [7] features to learn similarity between images. However, the representation of the hand-crafted features limits the performance of these methods. Some deep learning-based models popular in image classification tasks [13] have shown great success in learning features from the images but these models cannot directly fit similar image ranking especially the fine-grained distinction between similar images. Thus, in order to learn the fine-grained image similarity deep ranking model has been proposed by [21]. Pairwise ranking model is a widely used learning-to-rank formulation. It is used to learn image ranking models in [4,10,17]. Generating good triplet samples is a crucial aspect of learning pairwise ranking model. FaceNet [18] showed that the triplet loss is a suitable loss function for the verification, recognition and clustering than the verification loss [19]. The difference is that the verification loss minimizes the $L2$-distance between objects of the same identity and enforces a margin between the distance of objects of different identities whereas the triplet loss also encourages a relative distance constraint and thus, enhancing the ability to discriminate between dissimilar identities. In [4] and [17], the triplet sampling algorithms assume that we can load the whole dataset into memory, which is impractical for a large dataset. Our work is built upon the deep ranking model proposed by [21] with an efficient triplet sampling algorithm that does not require loading the whole dataset into the memory.

3   Object Instance Separation Encoding

For a robust object re-identification system for a rigid scenario, we hypothesize that the background information is useful in order to discriminate between multiple instances of the same semantic class and also the objects that have a similar appearance as shown intuitively in Fig. 1. To include the background information, the first step in our approach is to use an off-the-shelf object detector, i.e. Mask-RCNN (Sect. 3.1), and obtain foreground masks of the objects with the bounding boxes that are expanded (see Sect. 4) in order to include a substantial background around the object within the bounding boxes. Encodings from the separated masked foregrounds and the masked backgrounds are extracted using ResNet50 (Sect. 3.2), which are concatenated to obtain joint embeddings. These embeddings then are sampled into triplets $\{positive, negative, anchor\}$ and fed to a triplet-based network architecture consisting of three identical ConvNets (see Figs. 3 and 4) with the pairwise ranking model to learn image similarity for a triple-based ranking loss function.

3.1   Object Detection

Our approach relies on previous work, Mask-RCNN [11] which uses region-based object detector like Faster R-CNN to detect objects. It does not only provide a bounding box around an object but also performs image segmentation and provides a mask representing a set of pixels belonging to the same object. A Region Proposal Network (RPN) is used to generate a number of region proposals followed by a position-sensitive RoI pooling layer to warp them into a fixed dimension. Finally, it is fed into fully-connected layers to produce class scores and the bounding box predictions. A parallel branch of two additional fully-connected layers provides the mask. Using the output from the Mask-RCNN, we extract each bounding box including masks as separate images and resize them into images of a fixed size in order to train our network to learn a visual encoding of the objects' mask and the background surrounding them within the bounding boxes (see first column, Fig. 2).

3.2   Object Visual Encoding

For each object of the input images, we create two sets of images $F = \{I_f, I_b\}$. Using the detections obtained from Mask-RCNN, one set is created by extract-

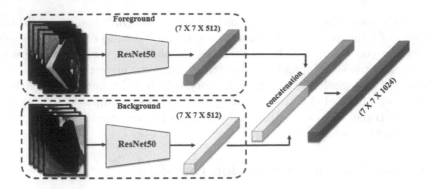

Fig. 2. As input, our network takes expanded bounding boxes (see Sect. 3.2) which construct a pair of images for masked foreground and masked background (seen on left of image). Each of the pair of images is passed through a ResNet50 where we take an intermediary representation $7 \times 7 \times 512$ providing spatial information, which is concatenated to provide a joint representation of $7 \times 7 \times 1024$.

ing masks representing objects in the foreground (I_f). The other set only contains the background with the subtracted foreground (I_b). As shown in Fig. 2, a pair of images is taken from each set to pass through two identical streams to learn an encoding between the masked foreground and the background. Each of the images, the masked background and the masked foreground is input to a ResNet50 [12] deep model pre-trained on ImageNet [8] dataset to extract the features. We take from an intermediary layer of the network providing $I_{(.)} \in \mathbb{R}^{7 \times 7 \times 512}$ representation of the two images retaining spatial context, the tensors are then concatenated to provide an embedding $F \in \mathbb{R}^{7 \times 7 \times 1024}$.

3.3   Triplet Loss

An effective algorithm for object instance re-identification should be able to distinguish not only between the images of different objects but also between different instances of the same object class. Especially, in the indoor scenes where multiple instances of the same object category are present, i.e. an office with multiple tables and chairs; it is highly challenging to re-identify a particular object instance amongst others.

A triplet of images has three kinds of images: an *anchor* which acts like a query template, a *positive* and a *negative* image. In order to ensure an effective re-identification at the instance level, it is important to also consider the intra-class variations and different instances of the same object as negative examples. For example, a backpack and a chair are definitely an example of *anchor-negative* pairs but two different instances of the same chair (with a different background) should also be considered an *anchor-negative* pair. We use a triplet-based network architecture with the pairwise ranking model to learn image similarity for the triple-based ranking loss function, inspired from [21]. If we have a set of $F = f_1, ...f_F$ images and $s_{i,j} = s(f_i, f_j)$ that gives the pairwise similarity score between the images f_i and f_j. The score s is higher for more similar images and is lower for more dissimilar images. If we have a triplet $t_i = (f_{iA}, f_{iP}, f_{iN})$ where f_{iA}, f_{iP} and f_{iN} are the anchor, positive and negative images, respectively. The goal of the training is to learn an embedding function such that:

$$D(f_{iA}, f_{iP}) < D(f_{iA}, f_{iN}), s(f_{iA}, f_{iP}) > s(f_{iA}, f_{iN}) \qquad (1)$$

where $D(.)$ is the squared Euclidean distance in the embeddings space. A triplet incorporates a relative ranking based on the similarity between the anchor, positive and the negative images.

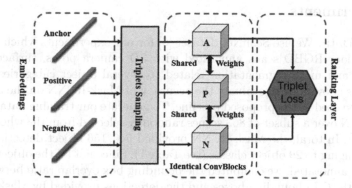

Fig. 3. Triplet of input tensors corresponding to images. Each tensor contains an embeddings of the anchor image A, positive image P and a negative Image N which are fed into three identical deep neural networks independently with shared weights where the triplet loss is optimized.

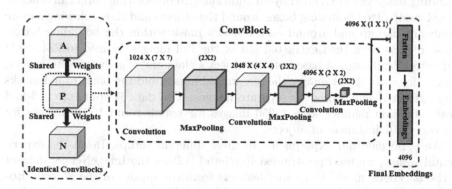

Fig. 4. Our ConvBlock takes in the encoding from Fig. 2. The ConvBlock consists of a network of convolutional and maxpooling layers, which pool the spatial information and merge the foreground and background encodings to obtain final embeddings.

The triplet ranking loss function is given as:

$$l(f_{iA}, f_{iP}, f_{iN}) = max\{0, M + D(f_{iA}, f_{iP}) - D(f_{iA}, f_{iN})\} \tag{2}$$

where M is a parameter called *margin* that regulates the gap between the pairwise distance: (f_{iA}, f_{iP}) and (f_{iA}, f_{iN}). The model learns to minimize the distance between more similar images and maximize the distance between the dissimilar ones. Our model is based on the work proposed in [21] with the difference that the input image triplets we use are the concatenated embeddings of the masked foregrounds and backgrounds.

4   Experiments

Training Data. We use ScanNet dataset [6] for our experiments which consists of 1500 indoor RGBD scans annotated with 3D camera poses, surface reconstructions, and mesh segmentation related to several object categories. These annotations allowed us to evaluate the accuracy of Mask-RCNN on the ScanNet images to be used in the proposed pipeline. To generate our training data, we ran Mask-RCNN over a subset of 863 scenes randomly selected from the whole ScanNet dataset. In total, the Mask-RCNN provided 646, 156 object detections with masks belonging to 29 object classes (see Table 1). Since not all the objects in the dataset are annotated, we computed the bounding box overlap ratio between the ground truth (GT) bounding boxes and the detections provided by Mask-RCNN to select only the *valid* detections. If the overlap ratio was higher than 60% and the label of the detected object matches with the GT label, it was considered a *valid* detection.

After mapping each detection obtained from the Mask-RCNN with the corresponding 2D ground truth (GT), we found 9.11% of the total, i.e. around 58876 detections to be considered fit for the experiments. The regions indicated by the bounding boxes were extended by an additional 10 pixels-wide border in order to allow loosely-fitted bounding boxes around the objects and thus, allowing a more significant background around each object's mask within the bounding boxes. These regions were then extracted out of the full images, resized to 224×224 and categorically stored based on the object's class and it's observed instances. Finally, for each object image, the foreground masks and the background masks were extracted and stored as separate images. The data is split into a 3-fold cross-validation manner with 39250 images for training and 19626 images for test over 1701 instances of objects.

We performed our experiments in three different setups. In all the experimental setups, we used pre-trained ResNet50 [12] on the ImageNet [8] dataset as the backbone model to extract features from the images of the objects. **notrain:** In this setup, the features extracted from full images were matched against each other by using an $L2$ distance-based metric, without any training. **full:** In another setup, our model is trained on the embeddings obtained using the full images without extracting separate foreground and background masks. **concat:** The third type of experimental setup is the approach proposed in this paper

Table 1. Number of views after mapping with GT for *valid* detections, selected based on object's label and the bounding box overlap ratio and the number of unique instances for each object category.

No. of views and unique instances per object class					
Class	No. of views	No. of instances	Class	No. of views	No. of instances
Bicycle	110	6	Toilet	1755	103
Bench	27	4	Tv	562	46
Backpack	1563	117	Laptop	600	41
Handbag	486	32	Mouse	59	6
Suitcase	377	30	Keyboard	1879	67
Sports ball	379	21	Microwave	667	61
Bottle	903	27	Oven	72	6
Cup	278	25	Toaster	11	4
Chair	38203	508	Sink	2694	157
Couch	1371	75	Refrigerator	60	11
Potted plant	1294	55	Book	3124	65
Bed	83	17	Clock	25	6
Bowl	121	8	Person	260	8
Dining table	1853	185	Teddy bear	47	8
Vase	13	2	-	–	–

where the model is trained on the embeddings obtained by concatenating the features from masked foregrounds and the backgrounds. In *concat* setup, the model learns to minimize the difference between the anchor f_{iA} and the positive f_{iP} images while also learning to maximize the difference between the anchor f_{iA} and the negative f_{iN} images by employing the triplet-loss based training.

Evaluation Metrics. Most re-ID algorithms use Cumulative Matching Characteristic (CMC) curve as a standard metric to measure their performance which compares the identification rate vs rank. The proportions of good matches of the probe image with the set of images in rank-1 would indicate a good or bad performance of the algorithm. A CMC curve is computed for all these individual ranks. In our evaluation procedure, however, we compare with the deepSort [22] tracking algorithm which is used here as a rank-1 re-ID method, which is why we cannot compare with a CMC curve. Also, it will not be fair to compare recall and precision values between the deepSort and our method. Thus, we compute the rank-1 accuracy by measuring the percentage of correctly identified objects.

Analysis. Evaluated using the aforementioned experimental setup, the proposed method achieves the best performance on the ScanNet dataset in regards to both the rank-1 accuracy as shown in Table 2. Figure 5 shows that the proposed method, *concat* was able to find the best match with the probe image. In the bottom row, *no-train* and *full* tried to match with an image which either had an object of the same color or the shape. However, the proposed method, *concat* could not always correctly identify the images and was performing occasionally poor as can be seen in Fig. 6. Overall, the results from Table 2 show that the *concat* method was able to improve the rank-1 accuracy by 22.19% and 17.1% against *no-train* and *full*, respectively.

Table 2. Scores on our ScanNet validation data split with Rank-1, -5, -20 and -50 accuracy values. The best performing type of setups is highlighted in bold.

Type	Rank-1 (%)	Rank-5 (%)	Rank-20 (%)	Rank-50 (%)
no-train	55.66	66.67	77.46	89.67
full	60.75	69.61	80.90	95.21
concat	**77.85**	**91.55**	**98.36**	**99.80**

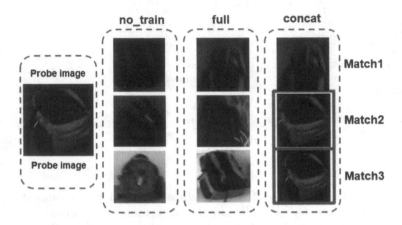

Fig. 5. The visualizations show some examples of the matches found in *no-train*, *full* and *concat* setups. The right matches with the probe image are highlighted in green color. (Color figure online)

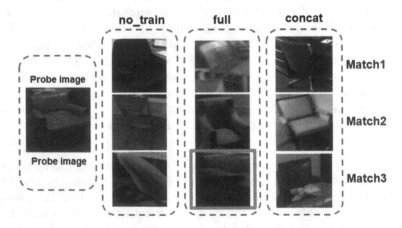

Fig. 6. Examples of the matches found in *no-train*, *full* and *concat* setups. The right matches with the probe image are highlighted in green color. (Color figure online)

Comparison with deepSort. deepSort [22] is an open-source implementation of the original SORT [1] algorithm which employs deep appearance descriptors to improve the performance in multiple object tracking. deepSort learns discriminative feature embeddings offline in order to obtain a deep association metric for a person re-identification dataset in the original work. For our experiments, we provided two random sets of image pairs obtained from the ScanNet scenes to the algorithm to identify multiple objects ensuring that an image pair is not consisting of images from two different scenes. We computed the performance by measuring the percentage of matched object instances across all the image pairs. Figure 7 shows the possible problems that standard object matching or tracking algorithms might face in re-identifying objects. The figure shows that the deepSort was able to match an object (in yellow bounding box) in multiple frames but lost an object (in red bounding box) when the camera revisits a similar view later. deepSort achieved a rank-1 accuracy of 49.60% against the rank-1 accuracy of 77.85% obtained with our method.

Fig. 7. An example object being matched by the deepSort algorithm inside the yellow bounding box and the lost object in the red bounding box. (Color figure online)

5   Conclusion

The contribution of this paper was to explore the intuition that the information obtained from the background surrounding the detected target objects in a rigid scene could be highly useful in discriminating two near-identical objects or two instances of the same object class. The discriminative features learned from the explicit concatenated foreground and background can be utilized to re-identify objects at the instance-level throughout the dataset. Our experiments have shown that the proposed method performs well even in the case of highly cluttered rigid environments like the indoor scenes obtained from Scan-Net dataset. In future, we plan to explore if the temporal information obtained from multiple views in a video dataset can be integrated with our object instance re-identification system for a robust multiple object tracking algorithm in case of rigid and static scenes.

References

1. Bewley, A., Ge, Z., Ott, L., Ramos, F., Upcroft, B.: Simple online and realtime tracking. In: Proceedings of IEEE International Conference on Image Processing, pp. 3464–3468, September 2016
2. Bhuiyan, A., Perina, A., Murino, V.: Exploiting multiple detections to learn robust brightness transfer functions in re-identification systems. In: Proceedings of IEEE International Conference on Image Processing, pp. 2329–2333, September 2015
3. Boureau, Y., Bach, F., LeCun, Y., Ponce, J.: Learning mid-level features for recognition. In: Proceedings of IEEE Conference on Computer Vision and Pattern Recognition, pp. 2559–2566, June 2010
4. Chechik, G., Sharma, V., Shalit, U., Bengio, S.: Large scale online learning of image similarity through ranking. J. Mach. Learn. Res. 11(Mar), 1109–1135 (2010)
5. Conte, D., Foggia, P., Percannella, G., Vento, M.: Performance evaluation of a people tracking system on pets2009 database. In: Proceedings of IEEE International Conference on Advanced Video and Signal Based Surveillance, pp. 119–126, August 2010
6. Dai, A., Chang, A.X., Savva, M., Halber, M., Funkhouser, T., Nießner, M.: Scannet: Richly-annotated 3D reconstructions of indoor scenes. In: Proceedings of IEEE Computer Vision and Pattern Recognition, pp. 5828–5839 (2017)
7. Dalal, N., Triggs, B.: Histograms of oriented gradients for human detection. In: Proceedings of IEEE Conference on Computer Vision and Pattern Recognition, vol. 1, pp. 886–893. IEEE (2005)
8. Deng, J., Dong, W., Socher, R., Li, L.J., Li, K., Fei-Fei, L.: ImageNet: a large-scale hierarchical image database. In: Proceedings of IEEE Conference on Computer Vision and Pattern Recognition, pp. 248–255. IEEE (2009)
9. Farenzena, M., Bazzani, L., Perina, A., Murino, V., Cristani, M.: Person re-identification by symmetry-driven accumulation of local features. In: Proceedings of IEEE Conference on Computer Vision and Pattern Recognition, pp. 2360–2367. IEEE (2010)
10. Frome, A., Singer, Y., Malik, J.: Image retrieval and classification using local distance functions. In: Advances in Neural Information Processing Systems, pp. 417–424 (2007)
11. He, K., Gkioxari, G., Dollár, P., Girshick, R.: Mask r-cnn. In: Proceedings of IEEE International Conference on Computer Vision, pp. 2961–2969 (2017)
12. He, K., Zhang, X., Ren, S., Sun, J.: Deep residual learning for image recognition. In: Proceedings of Ieee Conference on Computer Vision and Pattern Recognition, pp. 770–778 (2016)
13. Krizhevsky, A., Sutskever, I., Hinton, G.E.: Imagenet classification with deep convolutional neural networks. In: Advances in Neural Information Processing Systems, pp. 1097–1105 (2012)
14. Li, A., Liu, L., Wang, K., Liu, S., Yan, S.: Clothing attributes assisted person reidentification. IEEE Trans. Circuits Syst. Video Technol. 25(5), 869–878 (2015)
15. Lowe, D.G.: Object recognition from local scale-invariant features. In: Proceedings of IEEE International Conference on Computer vision, vol. 2, pp. 1150–1157. IEEE (1999)
16. Milan, A., Leal-Taixé, L., Reid, I., Roth, S., Schindler, K.: MOT16: a benchmark for multi-object tracking. arXiv preprint arXiv:1603.00831 (2016)
17. Parikh, D., Grauman, K.: Relative attributes. In: Proceedings of International Conference on Computer Vision, pp. 503–510. IEEE (2011)

18. Schroff, F., Kalenichenko, D., Philbin, J.: FaceNet: a unified embedding for face recognition and clustering. In: Proceedings of IEEE Conference on Computer Vision and Pattern Recognition, pp. 815–823 (2015)
19. Schultz, M., Joachims, T.: Learning a distance metric from relative comparisons. In: Advances in Neural Information Processing Systems, pp. 41–48 (2004)
20. Taylor, G.W., Spiro, I., Bregler, C., Fergus, R.: Learning invariance through imitation. In: Proceedings of IEEE Conference on Computer Vision and Pattern Recognition, pp. 2729–2736. IEEE (2011)
21. Wang, J., et al.: Learning fine-grained image similarity with deep ranking. In: Proceedings of IEEE Computer Vision and Pattern Recognitionm, pp. 1386–1393 (2014)
22. Wojke, N., Bewley, A., Paulus, D.: Simple online and realtime tracking with a deep association metric. In: Proceedings of IEEE International Conference on Image Processing, pp. 3645–3649. IEEE (2017)

Automatic Segmentation Based on Deep Learning Techniques for Diabetic Foot Monitoring Through Multimodal Images

Abián Hernández[1]([⊠]) [iD], Natalia Arteaga-Marrero[2] [iD],
Enrique Villa[2] [iD], Himar Fabelo[3] [iD], Gustavo M. Callicó[3] [iD],
and Juan Ruiz-Alzola[1] [iD]

[1] Research Institute in Biomedical and Health (iUIBS),
University of Las Palmas de Gran Canaria, Las Palmas de Gran Canaria, Spain
{abian.hernandez, juan.ruiz}@ulpgc.es
[2] Instituto de Astrofísica de Canarias (IAC), La Laguna, Tenerife, Spain
{narteaga, evilla}@iac.es
[3] Institute for Applied Microelectronics (IUMA),
University of Las Palmas de Gran Canaria, Las Palmas de Gran Canaria, Spain
{hfabelo, gustavo}@iuma.ulpgc.es

Abstract. Temperature data acquired by infrared sensors provide relevant information to assess different medical pathologies in early stages, when the symptoms of the diseases are not visible yet to the naked eye. Currently, a clinical system that exploits the use of multimodal images (visible, depth and thermal infrared) is being developed for diabetic foot monitoring. The workflow required to analyze these images starts with their acquisition and the automatic feet segmentation. A novel approach is presented for automatic feet segmentation using Deep Learning employing an architecture composed of an encoder and decoder (U-Net architecture) and applying a segmentation of planes in point cloud data, using the depth information of pixels labeled in the neural network prediction. The proposed automatic segmentation is a robust method for this case study, providing results in a short time and achieving better performance than other traditional segmentation methods as well as a basic U-Net segmentation system.

Keywords: RGB-D images · Multimodal images · Deep Learning · Automatic segmentation

1 Introduction

Healthy humans keep their inner temperature within a narrow range of 36.8 °C, thus the measurement of skin temperature is commonly used as a method for diagnosing several diseases, such as diabetes mellitus. Diabetes is a chronic disease caused by high levels of glucose due to the inability of the body to produce or use insulin effectively [1, 2]. This disease requires continuous medical care to prevent complications since, over time, diabetes can damage the heart, blood vessels, eyes, kidneys or nerves [2]. The International Diabetes Federation (IDF) estimated about 425 million people with diabetes in 2017 and 629 million are expected in 2045 [1]. Patients affected by diabetes

© Springer Nature Switzerland AG 2019
E. Ricci et al. (Eds.): ICIAP 2019, LNCS 11752, pp. 414–424, 2019.
https://doi.org/10.1007/978-3-030-30645-8_38

mellitus may experience a medical complication named foot ulcers [1]. Commonly known as diabetic foot, this condition is associated with neuropathy disorders and peripheral vascular disease in the lower limbs. An anomalous temperature measurement can be indicative of an ulcer formation in an early stage. Therefore, temperature monitoring can be used for the detection and assessment of the disease before other symptoms are perceived [2].

Traditionally, medical instrumentation has measured skin temperature using contact sensors but contactless thermal sensors are promising imaging technologies that offer a competitive and reliable alternative. Furthermore, reduced-cost infrared detectors demonstrate improved capabilities for ulceration risk monitoring in diabetic foot patients. For this application, a standard contralateral analysis is complemented by the analysis of the temperature pattern [2–4] to detect anomalies that may correspond to a possible ulceration.

In order to analyse the temperature, the segmentation of the soles of the patient's feet is required. The segmentation procedure can be performed manually by the final user but it is a time-consuming task that might offer inaccurate results since is affected by subjective considerations. For this reason, the development of an automatic segmentation, by using supervised learning, is one of the best options.

In recent years, the recognition of patterns through Machine Learning or Deep Learning techniques has become very popular, being a clear example of this fact the promising convolutional network U-Net [5]. One of the most successful state-of-the-art deep learning methods is based on the Fully Convolutional Networks (FCN) [6]. However, this architecture includes a fully-connected layer at the end [7–9] while U-Net just apply convolutional layers. U-Net is very useful in dense prediction tasks, in which each pixel must be labeled (so-called semantic segmentation), and it is able to converge with few training samples.

In this paper, the segmentation of the soles of the feet is performed automatically by employing a Deep Learning architecture based on visible images, which is then improved by using the spatial information (depth image) of the labeled pixel.

2   Materials and Methods

The segmentation is performed by using RGB-D (Red, Green and Blue color space and Depth information of a pixel) images of the soles of the feet and subsequently applied on thermal images. This process requires calibration and registration among different imaging modalities, for this extent, a custom acquisition system has been designed. The segmentation is not performed directly on thermal images due to the difficulty of identifying boundaries between two elements superimposed at the same temperature, e.g. the patient's foot and his hand in the background. Therefore, the gold reference was created from the RGB-D images.

2.1   Acquisition System

The acquisition system employed to generate the foot image database is composed by an Intel® RealSense™ D415 camera (Intel Corporation, Santa Clara, CA, USA) for visible as well as depth (RGB-D), and a Thermal Expert™ TE-Q1 Plus (i3system Inc, Korea) for the thermal infrared (IR) modality. In addition, a customized camera support was manufactured in a 3D printer to align both cameras (Fig. 1). Table 1 details the specifications of each camera employed in the acquisition system. The RGB-D images were acquired in VGA resolution (640 × 480 pixels) and the thermal infrared images were acquired with a resolution of 384 × 288 pixels, i.e. the maximum Thermal Expert™ TE-Q1 Plus resolution. The multimodal images were saved in DICOM (Digital Imaging and Communications On Medicine) format, which is the international standard format for medical images.

Fig. 1. The acquisition system using Intel RealSense RGB-D and Thermal Expert TE-Q1 Thermal cameras connected to a laptop with the 3D Slicer interface.

Table 1. Acquisition cameras specifications.

	Intel RealSense D415	Thermal Expert TE-Q1-Plus
Sensor maximum resolution (pixels)	(RGB) 1920 × 1080 (Depth) 1280 × 720	384 × 288
Frame rate (Hz)	>90	<9
Size (W × H×D) (mm³)	99 × 23 × 20	47 × 25 × 16

The 3D Slicer (Slicer) software [10] was employed for data management and processing. This software is an open source platform for medical image informatics, image processing, and 3D visualization. The cameras were connected to Slicer using the server provided in PlusToolkit [11], which allows camera integration. A customized module was developed for the acquisition, extending the Slicer software architecture.

2.2   Gold Reference Dataset

As described before, monitoring of foot ulcers in diabetic patients is intended by comparing the temperature of each foot, this is, performing a contralateral temperature symmetry analysis. This requires the segmentation of each sole, in which the image is focused, but this task is currently performed manually by the final user. The aim is to perform the segmentation process automatically, without end-user interaction, by using supervised learning methods. Hence, a gold reference dataset is required to generate a model for the supervised learning. This dataset was created by manual segmentation using a specific Slicer segmentation module which allows the implementation of image thresholding, growing from seed or watershed, among others.

The gold reference dataset consisted of 59 images, acquired from the Intel Real-Sense camera and manually labeled. These images were split into two non-overlapped groups, one group was used to train the supervised algorithm (30 images) and the other was employed in the testing procedure (29 images).

3 Automatic Segmentation

The supervised segmentation algorithm developed in this work is based on both RGB and depth image information obtained by the Intel® RealSense™ camera. Images are resized by bicubic interpolation to adjust the resolution images to the input size of the neural network which is used to perform the feet segmentation binarized by thresholding. The depth information is employed to improve the segmentation results provided by the neural network throughout a segmentation of planes in the depth image represented as a point cloud (see Fig. 2). The segmentation output is a region of interest (ROI) delimited and discriminated from the rest of the elements that have no interest in the image, the so-called *background*. The amount of background within the images could be reduced using a smaller field of view and acquiring images closer to the feet. Although this could simplify the segmentation process, our aim is to obtain an independent clinical system that performs well in any conditions, this is with no prior requirements regarding image acquisition.

The neural network used initially in the automatic segmentation procedure is based on U-Net architecture that is composed of convolution layers, without fully-connected layers. The output of each layer in the U-Net architecture is a 3D array of size $h \times w \times f$, where h and w are spatial-dimensions and f is the feature or channel dimension. Each layer operates some basic functions (convolutional, pooling and activation) on local regions of the input image. A great performance of this architecture using a training dataset of 30 images has been demonstrated earlier [5]. However, the number of samples is important and it is possible to increase it by applying data augmentation techniques.

3.1 U-Net Network Architecture and Training

An U-Net architecture contains a contracting path (encoder), which extracts features and reduces the spatial dimension, and an expanding path (decoder), which is able to use these features to make its decisions (the output). The encoder follows a typical architecture of convolutional network, applying convolutions and activation functions per layer and down-sampling by max-pooling, without overlapping windows. This max-pooling operation is superior to other methods for capturing invariances in image-like data. However, overlapping pooling windows do not improve recognition rates [12]. Hence, the decoder increases the resolution of the output by upsampling the feature map followed by a convolution. The result of this model is a semantic segmentation, i.e. a pixel-wise segmentation.

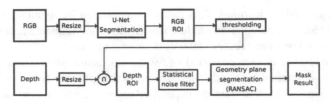

Fig. 2. Proposed workflow for feet segmentation where the images are represented as squares and the operations as rectangles. The network prediction is used to set the ROI on the depth image, the point cloud, and then a second segmentation was applied to extract geometry models, specifically planes. Resizing step is applied because encoder path of the U-Net was pre-trained using a large-scale database with a different resolution than ours.

Usually, U-Net is trained by using randomly initialized weights. However, the U-Net performance can be improved by using transfer-learning or fine-tuning techniques. These techniques are widely used when the training set is small to avoid overfitting during the training process. Vladimir Iglovikov *et al.* used a Visual Geometry Group (VGG) family network with pre-trained convolution layers as encoder in their U-Net architecture [13]. Similarly, the proposed U-Net architecture (Fig. 3) uses an encoder constructed by an VGG11, removing the fully connected layer and replacing it with a convolutional layer. The decoder is created following the encoder shape and the weights randomly initialized, so the transfer-learning is just applied in the encoder. The number of trainable parameters in our network is 21,158,977. However, 9,220,480 parameters (the encoder parameters) are pre-trained from ImageNet [14]. In addition, some U-Net architecture implementations reduce the number of parameters using an interpolation instead of the transposed convolution for the upsampling process.

Finally, the training dataset (30 images) was augmented by performing random scaling, rotations, elastic distortions and contrast gamma adjusting. Although these images are distorted, they still look similar to the original and could produce overfitting during the training process. Therefore, the number of augmented images must be limited since the images are related to our dataset. In total, the generated training dataset is composed of 47 images.

3.2 Point Cloud Plane Segmentation

The depth information is useful to discard elements that are limited by the neural network but out of the ROI, thus leading to improve the segmentation results.

The robotics and computer graphics communities have developed a set of approaches for segmenting a scene into geometric primitive shapes which includes the extraction of plane segments. This is particularly interesting for the current application since the sole of the feet are right in front of the camera and can be considered as a planes.

The RANdom SAmple Consensus (RANSAC) approach is a popular and simple robust estimator method for segmenting a point cloud (depth image) [15]. The principle of this algorithm consists of searching the best plane among a point cloud, being reliable even in the presence of a high proportion of outliers. In addition, RANSAC can be used to extract different shapes such as spheres, cylinders or cones in point clouds.

The mask resulting from the neural network operation was applied on the depth image. Subsequently, the result is filtered to discard the noise points generated by the Intel RealSense camera on the edges of the elements captured in the image. After that, the RANSAC estimator is implemented to extract planes in the filtered point cloud. As a result, the segmented feet are obtained, improving the neural network prediction. For this task, the Point Cloud library (PCL) [16] is used, adjusting the distance threshold parameter in the estimator, which is used to identify the outliers, allowing to segment both soles in case they are not exactly aligned in the same plane. This parameter is set as the mean value of the depth distance of the filtered point cloud.

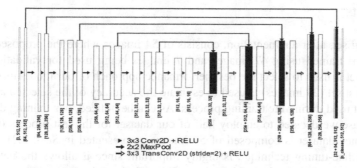

Fig. 3. U-Net architecture employed with the VGG11 neural network without fully connected layer as encoder. Each rectangle represents a convolution layer of dimensions $f \times h \times w$. The arrows on top, called skip connections, show transfer of information from each encoding layer and the black rectangles indicates information concatenated to the corresponding decoding layer.

3.3 Metrics

Three different metrics are employed to train and evaluate the proposed model. In the following equations, the target y and prediction x correspond to a batch of N flatten images, by row-major order, of size $h \times w$ represented as M.

For the neural network training, the Dice coefficient is used as a similarity measurement between two sets. This coefficient, adapted for discrete objects, is defined in Eq. 1, where ε is a regularization term introduced to handle the singularity that occurs when prediction and target are simultaneously background. The index n indicates the iteration among batches, and m indicates iteration among pixels. In addition, since the segmentation may be considered as a pixel classification problem, the binary cross-entropy (BCE) metric is used (Eq. 2). Finally, the loss function (L) is a linear combination of both expressions (see Eq. 3), where the weight of each function is obtained using the α parameter. This parameter directly affects the neural network during the training process. Based on our experience, emphasizing the BCE by setting α to a value greater than 0.5, during the training process makes the network more accurate at correctly detecting pixels labeled as feet, but it slightly reduces the number of pixels labeled. Thus, the feet are not entirely extracted. However, this reduction is minimal and a fixed α parameter was established to a value of 0.5.

$$Dice(x,y) = 1 - \frac{2\sum_{n=1}^{N}\sum_{m=1}^{M} x_{nm}y_{nm} + \varepsilon}{\sum_{n=1}^{N}\sum_{m=1}^{M} x_{nm} + \sum_{n=1}^{N}\sum_{m=1}^{M} y_{nm} + \varepsilon} \tag{1}$$

$$BCE(x,y) = -\frac{1}{N}\sum_{n=1}^{N}\sum_{m=1}^{M} (y_{nm}logx_{nm} + (1-y_{nm})\log(1-x_{nm})) \tag{2}$$

$$L(x,y) = \alpha BCE(x,y) + (1-\alpha)Dice(x,y) \tag{3}$$

4 Results

The training set, after augmentation, consists of 54 images where the proposed neural network was trained using 47 images and 7 images being used for validation. This validation set is used to select the best performance approach of our model using these data. The test set (29 images) is used to estimate the accuracy of the selected approach and it is not used during the training process. As can be noticed, our training dataset is small because we decided to employ half of our dataset for the test process (the total gold reference dataset is composed of 59 images as presented in Sect. 2.2). For this reason, the fine-tuning technique is highly important since it allows the network to converge in a smaller number of iterations. This effect can be appreciated in Fig. 4a, where the no-pre-trained results performs worse than the other solutions.

The linear behavior defined by the α parameter does not significantly affect the loss function result observed in Fig. 4a. However, it is reflected in the independent graphs (Fig. 4b and c) where Dice coefficient is lower at the end of the training process with a greater α value, while observing the opposite behavior in the BCE metric.

In addition, the training of the neural network was quite fast, as it can be seen in Fig. 4d. It required ~ 3.5 min to finish using the testing platform composed by an AMD Ryzen 1700 CPU (Central Processing Unit) and a NVIDIA GTX 1060 GPU (Graphics Processing Unit) specified in Table 2. For the training, we used the Adam optimizer for 45 epochs with a learning rate of 0.0001, decreasing 0.1 every 18 epochs. Due to the GPU global memory is 6 GB, the batch size was fixed to six samples.

Table 2. Main specifications of the testing platform.

	GPU				
	CUDA Capability	Global memory (Gb)	Stream Multiprocessors (SMX)	CUDA Cores	Max. Clock Speed (GHz)
NVIDIA GTX 1060	6.1	6	10	1280	1.85
	CPU				
	Cores		Threads		Clock speed (GHz)
AMD Ryzen 1700	8		16		3

After the neural network prediction, the workflow (Fig. 5) continues applying a threshold to discard pixels labeled as foot with low probability, having only binary pixel values (Fig. 5a). This threshold is set to a value of 0.5. This value was established using the validation dataset. Next, the depth image is masked with the result of the network, obtaining the depth information of the ROI generated by the proposed neural network (Fig. 5b). Subsequently, a statistical filter for noise removal (Fig. 5c) is applied as well as the point cloud segmentation described above (Fig. 5d). Finally, the final segmentation is shown in Fig. 5e.

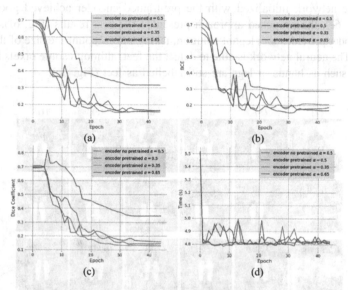

Fig. 4. (a) Progress of proposed loss function, (b) BCE and (c) Dice coefficient with the validation set and different α parameter values to networks with encoder pre-trained during the training process. (d) Training elapsed time per epoch.

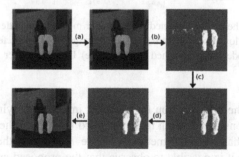

Fig. 5. Proposed workflow for feet segmentation. Each image represents a subsequent step from the neural network, a threshold is applied to the ROI from the RGB to have a binary image (a), then the point cloud is masked (b) and noise filter applied (c) previous to the RANSAC plane segmentation (d). Finally, the improved network prediction is displayed (e).

For comparison purposes, Fig. 6 displays the results obtained by using four different methods: a method based on Otsu thresholding [17], the U-Net no-pre-trained, U-Net pre-trained and our approach, which employed the U-Net pre-trained complemented by the point cloud plane segmentation from depth images. The Otsu-based method consists of using YC_bC_r (luma, blue-difference and red-difference) color space for calculating the difference between C_r and the inverse of C_b, C_b^{-1} in order to generate a bimodal histogram and calculate a threshold value by Otsu algorithm.

Figure 6d provides a clear example in which the U-Net is not initialized with the pre-trained encoder and it is able to detect the feet but not accurately. However, although the network initialized with the pre-trained encoder achieved good performance (Fig. 6e), the proposed approach presented the best results (Fig. 6f). The pre-trained encoder provides an elegant solution, taking into account the size of the dataset employed. The neural network is able to detect the feet, although some pixels located in other areas such as hands or legs are still labelled as feet (Fig. 6e).

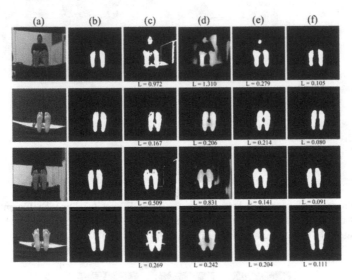

Fig. 6. Comparison of the results obtained with the four methods for different images of the test set with their respective loss function value. (a) RGB image. (b) Gold reference. (c) Otsu-based method. (d) U-Net encoder no-pre-trained ($\alpha = 0.5$). (e) U-Net encoder pre-trained ($\alpha = 0.5$). (f) Proposed method.

Figure 7a shows the loss function for each test image employing the four different methods previously considered. Both the pre-trained U-Net and the proposed approach perform much better than the other methods. Figure 7b displays the average results for the test dataset, where it is possible to observe that the proposed approach reduced the loss average from 0.150, in U-Net pre-trained, to 0.123. In the proposed approach, the worst case presented an error of 0.176 mainly due to the RANSAC method that generated a hole in the middle of the feet. However, this hole could be reduced using morphological operations and its use will be explored in future works. Nevertheless, it is clear that the use of RGB-D information provides improvement over a standard RGB segmentation.

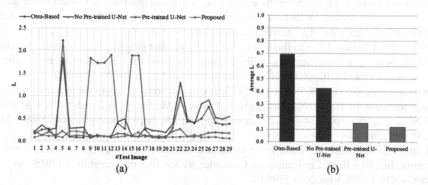

Fig. 7. Loss function (L, $\alpha = 0.5$) results. (a) Results obtained with each image in the test dataset for the four different methods. Values greater than 1 are due to the logarithmic behavior of the BCE equation. (b) Average results for each method.

5 Conclusions and Future Works

An automatic segmentation using multimodal images (RGB-D) is approached for feet identification and delineation using a small training dataset. In cases where a reduced number of samples is available, the use of the U-Net network has demonstrated a great performance complemented with a fine-tuning for the encoder path. Moreover, this result was improved by using the depth information of the labeled pixels, applying a segmentation of planes with the RANSAC method as robust estimator. The proposed approach resulted in an improved performance with two main advantages, a fast execution and the possibility to be implemented in the next smartphone device generation. Thus, home-care devices for monitoring the diabetic foot could be developed in the near future. In particular, such devices will have a two-fold objective providing early detection of ulcers and raising awareness about proper care for diabetic patients.

This approach is the first step to automatize our current research on diabetic foot monitoring workflow, which aims to obtain an automatic robust demonstrator to be used in clinical trials with diabetic foot patients for ulceration risk monitoring. The proposed approach will replace the standard time-consuming manual feet segmentation. Furthermore, segmentation of infrared images, after calibration and registration processes, could be performed in real-time aided by the automatization and fast execution of the proposed approach.

References

1. International Diabetes Federation (IDF): Eighth edition 2017 (2017)
2. Lavery, L.A., et al.: Preventing diabetic foot ulcer recurrence in high-risk patients. Diab. Care **30**, 14–20 (2007). https://doi.org/10.2337/DC06-1600
3. Hernandez-Contreras, D., Peregrina-Barreto, H., Rangel-Magdaleno, J., Gonzalez-Bernal, J.: Narrative review: diabetic foot and infrared thermography. Infrared Phys. Technol. **78**, 105–117 (2016). https://doi.org/10.1016/j.infrared.2016.07.013
4. Liu, C., van Netten, J.J., van Baal, J.G., Bus, S.A., van der Heijden, F.: Automatic detection of diabetic foot complications with infrared thermography by asymmetric analysis. J. Biomed. Opt. **20**, 026003 (2015). https://doi.org/10.1117/1.jbo.20.2.026003
5. Ronneberger, O., Fischer, P., Brox, T.: U-Net: convolutional networks for biomedical image segmentation. In: Navab, N., Hornegger, J., Wells, W.M., Frangi, A.F. (eds.) MICCAI 2015. LNCS, vol. 9351, pp. 234–241. Springer, Cham (2015). https://doi.org/10.1007/978-3-319-24574-4_28
6. Long, J., Shelhamer, E., Darrell, T.: Fully convolutional networks for semantic segmentation. In: 2015 IEEE Conference on Computer Vision Pattern Recognition (2015). https://doi.org/10.1109/CVPR.2015.7298965
7. Szegedy, C., et al.: Going deeper with convolutions. In: Proceedings of the IEEE Computer Society Conference Computer Vision Pattern Recognition, 07–12 June, pp. 1–9 (2015). https://doi.org/10.1109/CVPR.2015.7298594
8. He, K., Zhang, X., Ren, S., Sun, J.: Deep residual learning for image recognition. In: 2016 IEEE Conference on Computer Vision Pattern Recognition, pp. 770–778 (2015). https://doi.org/10.1109/CVPR.2016.90
9. Krizhevsky, A., Sutskever, I., Hinton, G.E.: 2012 AlexNet. Adv. Neural Inf. Process. Syst. 1–9 (2012). http://dx.doi.org/10.1016/j.protcy.2014.09.007
10. Fedorov, A., et al.: 3D slicers as an image computing platform for the quantitative imaging network. Magn. Reson. Imaging **30**, 1323–1341 (2012). https://doi.org/10.1016/j.mri.2012.05.001.3D
11. Lasso, A., Heffter, T., Rankin, A., Pinter, C., Ungi, T., Fichtinger, G.: PLUS: open-source toolkit for ultrasound-guided intervention systems. IEEE Trans. Biomed. Eng. **61**, 2527–2537 (2014). https://doi.org/10.1109/TBME.2014.2322864
12. Scherer, D., Müller, A., Behnke, S.: Evaluation of pooling operations in convolutional architectures for object recognition. In: Diamantaras, K., Duch, W., Iliadis, L.S. (eds.) ICANN 2010. LNCS, vol. 6354, pp. 92–101. Springer, Heidelberg (2010). https://doi.org/10.1007/978-3-642-15825-4_10
13. Iglovikov, V., Shvets, A.: TernausNet: U-Net with VGG11 encoder pre-trained on ImageNet for image segmentation (2018)
14. Russakovsky, O., et al.: ImageNet large scale visual recognition challenge. Int. J. Comput. Vis. **115**, 211–252 (2015). https://doi.org/10.1007/s11263-015-0816-y
15. Fischler, M.A., Fischler, M.A., Bolles, R.C., Bolles, R.C.: Random sample consensus. A paradigm for model fitting with applications to image analysis and automated cartography. Graph. Image Process. **24**, 381–395 (1981)
16. Aldoma, A., et al.: Tutorial: point cloud library: three-dimensional object recognition and 6 DOF pose estimation. IEEE Robot. Autom. Mag. **19**, 80–91 (2012). https://doi.org/10.1109/MRA.2012.2206675
17. Otsu, N.: A threshold selection method from gray-level histograms. IEEE Trans. Syst. Man. Cybern. **9**, 62–66 (1979). https://doi.org/10.1109/TSMC.1979.4310076

Weakly Supervised Semantic Segmentation Using Constrained Dominant Sets

Sinem Aslan[1,2,3(✉)] and Marcello Pelillo[1,2]

[1] DAIS, Ca' Foscari University of Venice, Venice, Italy
{sinem.aslan,pelillo}@unive.it
[2] ECLT, Ca' Foscari University of Venice, Venice, Italy
[3] International Computer Institute, Ege University, Izmir, Turkey

Abstract. The availability of large-scale data sets is an essential prerequisite for deep learning based semantic segmentation schemes. Since obtaining pixel-level labels is extremely expensive, supervising deep semantic segmentation networks using low-cost weak annotations has been an attractive research problem in recent years. In this work, we explore the potential of *Constrained Dominant Sets (CDS)* for generating multi-labeled full mask predictions to train a fully convolutional network (FCN) for semantic segmentation. Our experimental results show that using CDS's yields higher-quality mask predictions compared to methods that have been adopted in the literature for the same purpose.

Keywords: Semantic image segmentation ·
Weak training set annotations · Dominant sets ·
Constrained Dominant Sets · Weakly supervised semantic segmentation

1 Introduction

Semantic segmentation is one of the most well-studied research problems in computer vision. The goal is to achieve pixel-level classification, i.e., to label each pixel in a given input image with the class of the object or region that covers it. Predicting the class of each pixel yields to complete scene understanding which is the main problem of a wide range of computer vision applications, e.g. autonomous driving [7], human-computer interaction [15], earth observation [3], biomedical applications [27], dietary assessment systems [2], etc. Stunning performances of DCNNs (Deep Convolutional Neural Networks) at image classification tasks have encouraged researchers to employ them for pixel-level classification as well. Outstanding methods in well-known benchmarks, e.g. PASCAL VOC 2012, train some fully convolutional networks (FCN) with supervision

This work is supported by The Scientific and Technological Research Council of Turkey under TUBITAK BIDEB-2219 grant no 1059B191701102.

© Springer Nature Switzerland AG 2019
E. Ricci et al. (Eds.): ICIAP 2019, LNCS 11752, pp. 425–436, 2019.
https://doi.org/10.1007/978-3-030-30645-8_39

of fully-annotated ground-truth masks. However, obtaining such precise fully-annotated masks is extremely expensive and this limits the availability of large-scale annotated training sets for deep learning architectures. In order to address the aforementioned issue, recent works explored supervision of DCNN architectures for semantic segmentation using low-cost annotations like image-level labels [11], point tags [4], bounding box [8,12,16] and scribbles [13,21,23,26], that are weaker than the pixel-level labels.

Creating weak annotations is much easier than creating full annotations which helps to obtain large training sets for semantic segmentation. However, these annotations are not as precise as full annotations and their quality depends on the decisions made by the users, which degrades their reliability. Hence, literature works proposed different strategies for weakly-supervised semantic segmentation to deal with these issues. While a number of works [21,23] proposed to employ a genuine cost function to get into account only the initially given true weak annotations at the training stage, another and the most common approach [8,12,13,16,26] has been supervising DCNN architectures by *predicted full mask annotations* which are obtained by post-processing the weak-annotations.

Among these two strategies, we follow the second one and propose to generate full mask annotations from scribbles by an interactive segmentation technique which has proven to be extremely effective in a variety of computer vision problems including image and video segmentation [18,28]. For the same purpose, literature works have used a number of shallow interactive segmentation methods, e.g. variants of GrabCut [20] are used in [12,16] for propagating bounding box annotations to supervise a convolutional network. In order to propagate bounding box annotations, [8] proposed to perform iterative optimization between generating full mask approximations and training the network. Using a similar iterative scheme, [13] propagated scribble annotations by superpixels via optimizing a multi-label graph cuts model of [5]. [26] proposed a random-walk based label propagation mechanism to propagate scribble annotations.

In this paper, we aim to explore the potential of *Constrained Dominant Sets* (*CDS*) [28,29] for generating predicted full annotations to be used in supervision of a convolutional neural network for semantic segmentation. Representing images in an edge-weighted graph structure, main idea in constrained segmentation approach in [28] is finding the collection of dominant set clusters on the graph that are constrained to contain the components of a given annotation. CDS approach is applied for co-segmentation and interactive segmentation using modalities of bounding box or scribble and superiority of it over the state of the art segmentation techniques like Graph Cut, Lazy Snapping, Geodesic Segmentation, Random Walker, Transduction, Geodesic Graph Cut, Constrained Random Walker is proved in [28]. Motivated by the reported performance achievements for single cluster extraction (i.e. foreground extraction) in [28], we used CDS for multiple cluster extraction involving multi-label scribbles for the PASCAL VOC 2012 dataset. Since our goal is mainly exploring the performance of CDS in full mask prediction for weakly-supervised semantic segmentation, we trained a basic segmentation network, namely Fully Convolutional Network (FCN-8s) of

[14] based on VGG16 architecture, and compared our performance with other full mask prediction schemes in the literature that supervise the same type of deep learning architecture. Our experimental results on the standard dataset PASCAL VOC 2012 show the effectiveness of our approach compared to existing algorithms.

2 Constrained Dominant Sets

Dominant Set Framework. In the dominant-set clustering framework [17, 18], an input image is represented as an undirected edge-weighted graph with no self-loops $G = (V, E, w)$, where $V = \{1, ..., n\}$ is the set of vertices that correspond to image points (pixels or superpixels), $E \subseteq V \times V$ is the set of edges that represent the neighborhood relations between vertices, and $w = E \rightarrow R_+^*$ is the (positive) weight function that represent the similarity between linked node pairs. A symmetric affinity (or similarity) matrix is constructed to represent the graph G that is denoted by $A = (a_{ij})_{n \times n}$ where $a_{ij} = w(i, j)$, if $(i, j) \in E$ and $a_{ij} = 0$ otherwise.

Next, a weight $w_S(i)$, which is (recursively) defined as Eq. 1, is assigned to each vertex $i \in S$,

$$w_S(i) = \begin{cases} 1 & \text{if } |S| = 1, \\ \sum_{j \in S \setminus \{i\}} \phi_{S \setminus \{i\}}(j, i) w_{S \setminus \{i\}}(j), & \text{otherwise.} \end{cases} \tag{1}$$

where $\phi_S(i, j)$ denotes the (relative) similarity between nodes j ($j \notin S$) and i, with respect to the average similarity between node i and its neighbours in S (defined by $\phi_S(i, j) = a_{ij} - \frac{1}{|S|} \sum_{k \in S} a_{ik}$).

A positive $w_S(i)$ indicates that adding i into its neighbours in S will increase the internal coherence of the set, while when it is negative overall coherence gets decreased. Based on aforementioned definitions, a non-empty subset of vertices $S \subseteq V$ such that $\sum_{i \in T} w_T(i) > 0$ for any non-empty $T \subseteq S$, is said to be *dominant set* if it is a maximally coherent data set, i.e. satisfying two basic properties of a cluster that are *internal coherence* ($w_S(i) > 0$, for all $i \in S$) and *external incoherence* ($w_{S \cap \{i\}} < 0$, for all $i \notin S$).

Consider the following linearly-constrained quadratic optimization problem,

$$\begin{aligned} \text{maximize } & f(x) = x'Ax \\ \text{subject to } & x \in \Delta \end{aligned} \tag{2}$$

where x' is the transposition of the vector x and Δ is the standard simplex of R^n, defined as $\Delta = \{x \in R^n : \sum_{i=1}^n x_i = 1, \text{ and } x_i \geq 0 \text{ for all } i = 1...n\}$. With the assumption of affinity matrix A is symmetric, it is shown by [17] that if S is an dominant set, then its *weighted characteristic vector* $x^S \in \Delta$ defined as in Eq. 3 is the strict local solution of the Standard Quadratic Program in Eq. 2.

$$x_i^S = \begin{cases} \frac{w_S(i)}{\sum_{j \in S} w_S(j)}, & i \in S \\ 0, & \text{otherwise} \end{cases} \tag{3}$$

Conversely, if x^* is a strict local solution to Eq. 2, then its *support* $\sigma(x^*) = \{i \in V : x_i > 0\}$ is a dominant set of A. Thus, a dominant set can be found by localizing a solution of Eq. 2 by a continuous optimization technique and gathering the support set of the found solution. Notice that the value of a component in the found $x^S \in \Delta$ provides a measure of how strong that component contributes to the cohesiveness of the cluster.

Constrained Dominant Set Framework. In [28,29] the notion of a constrained dominant set is introduced, which aims at finding a dominant set constrained to contain vertices from a given seed set $S \subseteq V$. Based on the edge-weighted graph definition with affinity matrix A, a parameterized family of quadratic programs is defined as in Eq. 4 [28] for the set S and a parameter $\alpha > 0$,

$$
\begin{aligned}
\text{maximize } & f_S^\alpha(x) = x'(A - \alpha \hat{I}_S)x \\
\text{subject to } & x \in \Delta
\end{aligned}
\tag{4}
$$

where $\hat{I}_S$ is the $n \times n$ diagonal matrix whose elements are set to 1 if the corresponding vertices are in $V \setminus S$ and to 0 otherwise. It is theoretically proven, and empirically illustrated for interactive image segmentation [28], that if S is the set of vertices selected by the user, by setting $\alpha > \lambda_{\max}(A_{V \setminus S})$ it is guaranteed that all local solutions of (4) will have a support that necessarily contains at least one element of S. Here, $\lambda_{\max}$ is the largest eigenvalue of the principal submatrix of A indexed by elements of $V \setminus S$.

In order to find constrained dominant sets by solving the aforementioned quadratic optimization problem (4), [28] used Replicator Dynamics that is developed and studied in evolutionary game theory [17]. In this work we use Infection and Immunization Dynamics (InImDyn) [19] which proved to be a faster and as accurate alternative to it.

3 Proposed Approach

We propose to generate full mask predictions (to be used for supervising a semantic segmentation network) by post-processing weak annotations, i.e. scribble annotations, using CDS. Moreover, we propose to use CDS for multiclass clustering of pixels, i.e. semantic segmentation, while previously CDS has been used only for interactive foreground segmentation [28,29].

3.1 Preprocessing Step for CDS

Superpixel Generation. A common approach followed by image segmentation works has been using superpixels as input entities instead of image pixels. A superpixel is a group of pixels with similar colors and using superpixels not only provides reduced computational complexity, but also yields computing features on meaningful regions. Among a variety of techniques, i.e. SLIC, Oriented Watershed Transform (OWT), we have preferred to use the method developed by Felzenszwalb and Huttenlocher [9] similar to [24] which is a fast and publicly available algorithm. Method of Felzenszwalb and Huttenlocher [9] has also been used in another weakly-supervised semantic segmentation framework [13] experimenting on the same dataset with us. Proposed method in [9] is a graph-based segmentation scheme where a graph is constructed for an image such that each element to be segmented represents a vertex of the graph and dissimilarity, i.e. color differences, between two vertices constitutes a weighted edge. The vertices (or subgraphs) are started to be merged regarding to a merging criteria given in Eq. 5, where e_{ij} is the edge between two subgraphs C_i and C_j, $w(e)$ is the weight on edge e and MST(C_x) be the minimum spanning tree of C_x.

$$w(e_{ij}) \leq \min_{x \in \{i,j\}} \left(\max_{e \in \text{MST}(C_x)} w(e) + \frac{k}{|C_x|} \right) \tag{5}$$

Here, $\frac{k}{|C_x|}$ is a threshold function in which k is decided by the user, i.e. high values of k yield to lower number of (large) segments, and vice-versa. Another parameter given by the user is the smoothing factor (we denote by σ_{FH}) of the Gaussian kernel that is used to smooth the image at the preprocessing step.

Feature Extraction. Once the superpixels are generated on the image, a feature vector is computed for each superpixel. In the application of CDS model for interactive image segmentation in [28], median of the color of all pixels in RGB, HSV, and L*a*b* color spaces and Leung-Malik (LM) Filter Bank are concatenated in the feature extraction process. Differently from [28], we compute the same feature types with ScribbleSup [13], which has experimented on the same dataset with us, that are color and texture histograms denoted by $h_c(.)$ and $h_t(.)$ in Eq. 6. More specifically, $h_c(x_i)$ is a histogram computed on the color space using 25 bins and $h_t(x_i)$ is a histogram of gradients at the horizontal and vertical orientations where 10 bins are used for each orientation for the superpixel x_i.

3.2   Application of CDS for Full Mask Predictions

In order to generate full mask predictions using the CDS model, an input image is represented as a graph G where vertices depict the superpixels of the image and edge-weights between vertices reflect the similarity between corresponding superpixels. We use scribbles as the given weak annotations in this work which serve as constraints in the CDS implementation. Previously, CDS has been applied for interactive foreground segmentation [28] where dominant set clusters covering a set of given nodes S for a single object class were explored. In this work our problem demand for multiclass clustering of pixels. Hence, here S_c represents the manually selected pixels of the class c where $c \in \{1, ..., C\}$ and C is the number of classes in the dataset, e.g. $C = 21$ for PASCAL VOC 2012.

Accordingly, for each class of scribbles that exist in a given image, by ignoring the existence of the remaining classes in the image we perform foreground segmentation, i.e. 2-class clustering of image pixels, as in [28] by computing its CDS's. Thus, for the class c the union of the extracted dominant sets, i.e.

$UDS_c = D_1 \cup D_2 \cup ...D_L$ if L dominant sets are extracted which contain the set S_c, represents the segmented regions of object in class c. We then repeat this process for every class that exist in the image using the corresponding S_c information. If a node, i.e. superpixel, is found in more than one class of UDS_c, we assign it to the one having the highest value in its weighted characteristic vector $x^{S_c} \in \Delta$ which is found by solving the quadratic program in Eq. 4 by InImDyn (see Sect. 2).

Computation of the Affinity Matrix. Before computing the CDS clusters, the affinity (or similarity) between superpixels should be computed to construct the matrix A in Eq. 4. In [28], dissimilarity measurements are transformed to affinity space by using the Gaussian kernel $A_{ij}^\sigma = \mathbb{1}_{i \neq j} \exp\left(\frac{||f_i - f_j||^2}{2\sigma^2}\right)$, where f_i is the feature vector of the superpixel i, σ is the scale parameter for the Gaussian kernel and $\mathbb{1}_P = 1$ if P is true, 0 otherwise. Differently from [28], we use the Gaussian kernel in Eq. 6 where different σ values are used for different feature types. The kernel in Eq. 6 is also adopted in [13] which experiments on the same dataset and uses the same feature types with us.

$$A_{ij}^{\sigma_c, \sigma_t} = \mathbb{1}_{i \neq j} \exp\left(-\frac{||h_c(x_i) - h_c(x_j)||_2^2}{\sigma_c^2} - \frac{||h_t(x_i) - h_t(x_j)||_2^2}{\sigma_t^2}\right) \quad (6)$$

Using Different Color Spaces. Quality of generated superpixels effects the performance of the segmentation algorithm directly and a number of segmentation works (examples include but not limited to [1,24]) have emphasized that higher segmentation performances can be obtained by using different color transformations of the input image to deal with different scene and lighting conditions. Motivated by the related literature studies [1,24], we compute superpixels in a variety of color spaces with a range of invariance properties. Specifically, we use five color spaces, that were also used in [24] for determining high quality object locations by employing segmentation as a selective search strategy, that are *Intensity* (grey-scale image), *Lab*, *rgI* which denotes *rg* channels of normalized *RGB* plus intensity, *HSV*, *H* that denotes the Hue channel of *HSV*. We generate superpixels and compute mask predictions using CDS model for each color space of the input image, then we decide the final label for a pixel based on most frequently occurred class label, i.e. by using the scheme of majority voting. In addition to using different color spaces we also vary the threshold parameter k (in Eq. 5) to get benefit from a large set of diversification as recommended in [24].

4   Experiments

Dataset and Evaluation. We trained the models on the 10582 augmented PASCAL VOC training set [10] and evaluated them on the 1449 validation set. We used the scribble annotations published in [13]. In what follows accuracy is evaluated using *pixel accuracy* $(\sum_i n_{ii} / \sum_i t_i)$, *mean accuracy* $((1/n_{cl}) \sum_i n_{ii} / \sum_i t_i)$

and *mean Intersection over Union* $((1/n_{cl}) \sum_i n_{ii}/(t_i + \sum_j n_{ji} - n_{ii})$ as in [14], where n_{ij} is the number of pixels of class i predicted to belong to class j, n_{cl} is the number of different classes, and $t_i = \sum_j n_{ij}$ be the total number of pixels of class i.

Implementation Details. We used the VGG16-based FCN-8s network [14] of the MatConvNet-FCN toolbox [25] which we initialized by ImageNet pretrained model, i.e. VGG-VD-16 in [25]. We trained by SGD with momentum and, similar to [14], we used momentum 0.9, weight decay of 5^{-4}, mini batch size of 20 images and learning rate of 10^{-3}. With these selected hyperparameters we observed that the pixel accuracy is being converged on the validation set.

Performance of CDS is sensitive to the selection of the σ parameter of the Gaussian kernel (see Sect. 3.2) and in [28] three different results are reported for different selections of σ: (1) *CDSBestSigma*, where best σ is selected separately for every image; (2) *CDSSingleSigma*, by searching in a fixed range, i.e. 0.05 and 0.2; (3) *CDSSelfTuning*, where σ^2 is replaced by $\sigma_i \times \sigma_j$, where $\sigma_i = mean(KNN(f_i))$, i.e. the mean of the K-NearestNeighbor of the sample f_i, K is fixed to 7. To decide values of the σ_c and σ_t parameters (in Eq. 6) we followed *CDSBestSigma* strategy in [28]. Additionally, in the graph structure we cut the edges between vertices correspond to non-adjacent superpixels vertices by setting the corresponding items to zero in the affinity matrix A like has been done in [13], which has provided better segmentation maps. We then min-max normalized the matrix A to be scaled in the range of $[0,1]$ and symmetrized it.

Performance Evaluation. We first explored the performance using different color spaces on the predicted full annotations of 10582 images (denoted by *PredSet* to mention "Predicted Set" in Table 1), before training the network with them. Then, by training the network with the Predicted Sets we report performance on the Test Set, i.e. PASCAL VOC 2012 Val set. In the implementation of the superpixel generation of [9] we used smoothing factor of $\sigma_{FH} = 0.8$ (*FH* stands for Felzenszwalb and Huttenloche [9]) in the experiments of Table 1. For each color space we performed majority voting (denoted by *MV* both in Tables 1 and 2) over obtained maps with $k = \{225, 250, 300, 400\}$ (in Eq. 5).

We see at Table 1 that using different color spaces affects the quality of the predicted full annotations (*PredSet*) and highest quality mask predictions in terms of mIoU are obtained when we use the Intensity (66.51%). Performing majority voting over maps obtained in all color spaces provided highest quality mask predictions for both CDS (73.28%) and GraphCut (63.51%). We then trained the network with the predicted sets of *CDS-Intensity*, *CDS-MV*, *GraphCut-MV* and published full mask annotations and present their performance on the test set in Table 1. We see that by using CDS-MV in training we outperform GraphCut (which was employed in [13]) significantly and we are quiet approaching to the performance of fully-annotated mask training (59.2% vs. 61.6%).

Comparison with Other Full-Mask Prediction Methods. There is a large variety of interactive segmentation algorithms that can be used for full mask prediction

Table 1. Quality of obtained mask predictions (*PredSet*) and using them in network training performance on the PASCAL VOC 2012 Val set (*TestSet*) (MV: Majority Voting, [*] implementation of GraphCut in our framework.)

Color space	mean IoU	Pixel Acc.	mean Acc.
PredSet-CDS-*Intensity*	66.51	89.05	75.95
PredSet-CDS-*Lab*	65.47	88.36	76.15
PredSet-CDS-*rgI*	64.70	88.13	75.29
PredSet-CDS-*HSV*	66.49	89.27	74.60
PredSet-CDS-*H*	57.16	85.12	68.21
PredSet-CDS-*MV*	73.28	91.47	82.05
PredSet-GraphCut[*]-*MV*	63.51	86.48	81.83
TestSet-CDS-Intensity	57.41	89.01	70.56
TestSet-CDS-MV	59.20	89.59	73.05
TestSet-GraphCut[*]-*MV*	52.25	85.80	72.43
TestSet-With Full Masks	61.60	90.27	78.95

to train a semantic segmentation network. To be as fair as possible we make comparison with the reported performances of the methods that are carried on in similar conditions with us, e.g. the ones which employ scribbles as weak annotations, achieve network training using cross entropy loss computed over all pixel predictions but not only on given weak annotations, and do not iterate between the shallow segmentation method and network training with the obtained mask predictions as in ScribbleSup [13]. On the other hand, we performed the Graph Cut algorithm employed in ScribbleSup [13] in our framework by using the published code[1] referred in [13] and present its performance. In fact, our approach can be considered as the first iteration step of such an iterative scheme, and it can be extended to be used in further iterations by updating initial scribble annotations by considering network scores obtained with high confidence.

Considering the above issues we compare with the methods whose accuracy on the test set is reported when their mask predictions are used to train a segmentation network. Specifically, we refer to the performance results of the popular methods GrabCut [20], NormalizedCut [21], and KernelCut [22] reported in [21]. It is mentioned in [21,22] that for each image pixel, RGB (color) and XY (location) features are concatenated to be used in these algorithms. Then, segmentation proposals generated by them are used to train a VGG16-based DeepLab-Msc-largeFOV network [6]. It is reported in [6] that DeepLab-Msc-largeFOV, which employs atrous convolution and multiscale prediction, outperforms FCN-8s by around 9% (71.6% vs. 62.2%) at PASCAL VOC 2012 validation set when trained by full mask annotations, which provides an advantage at comparative works. On the other hand, we also present the performance gap between weak and full mask training to provide a more fair comparison in Table 2. In Table 2,

---

[1] mouse.cs.uwaterloo.ca/code/gco-v3.0.zip.

the performance results of full mask training (64.1 %), GrabCut [20], Normal-izedCut [21], and KernelCut [22] are acquired from [21].

Table 2. Performance comparison on PASCAL VOC 2012 val set.

Method	mIoU	Gap between full and weak supervision
With Full Masks [21]	64.1	
GrabCut [20]	55.5	8.6
NormalizedCut [21]	58.7	5.4
KernelCut [22]	59.8	4.3
With Full Masks	61.6	
GraphCut$^{(*)}$-MV$_{(\sigma_{FH}=0.8)}$	52.25	9.35
CDS-MV$_{(\sigma_{FH}=0.8)}$	59.20	2.40
CDS-MV$_{(\sigma_{FHBest})}$	60.22	1.38

For CDS, we train with mask predictions generated by two different selections of σ_{FH}: (i) $\sigma_{FH} = 0.8$ (corresponding to PredSet-CDS-MV in Table 1); and (ii) σ_{FHBest}, where we selected the best among $\sigma_{FH} = 0.7$ and $\sigma_{FH} = 0.8$ for each image. It can be seen at the segmentation performances on the val set given in Table 2 that we outperform the literature works at σ_{FHBest} (60.22%), and we are superior at both parameter selections in terms of performance gap between full and weak supervision, i.e. we approach to the performance of our full mask training (61.6%) by 2.4% and 1.38% at selection of $\sigma_{FH} = 0.8$ and σ_{FHBest}, respectively. Two example images from the generated set, i.e. PredSet, of σ_{FHBest} are presented in Fig. 1. Figure 2 shows examples from testing on the val set when it is trained by PredSet-CDS-MV $_{\sigma_{FHBest}}$. It can be seen in Figs. 1 and 2 that our results are the ones most closest to the ground truth of input images.

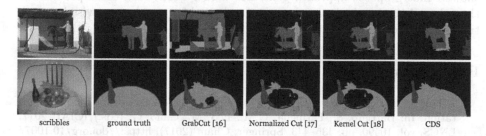

scribbles   ground truth   GrabCut [16]   Normalized Cut [17]   Kernel Cut [18]   CDS

Fig. 1. Generated mask predictions (Images for GrabCut [20], Normalized Cut [21], and KernelCut [22] are acquired from [21])

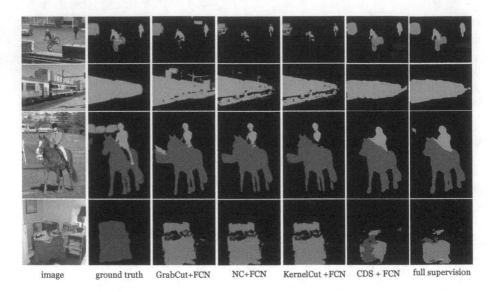

image   ground truth   GrabCut+FCN   NC+FCN   KernelCut +FCN   CDS + FCN   full supervision

Fig. 2. Testing on PASCAL VOC 2012 *val* set. (Images for GrabCut [20], Normalized Cut [21], and KernelCut [22] are acquired from [21])

5   Conclusions

In this paper we have proposed to apply Constrained Dominant Set (CDS) model, which is proved to be an effective method compared to state-of-the-art interactive segmentation algorithms, for propagating weak scribble annotations of a given set of images to obtain the multi-labeled full mask predictions of them. Achieved mask predictions are then used to train a Fully Convolutional Network for semantic segmentation. While CDS has been applied for pixelwise binary classification problem, it has not been explored for semantic segmentation before and this paper presents our work in this direction. Experimental results showed that proposed approach generates higher quality full mask predictions than the existing methods that have been adopted for weakly-supervised semantic segmentation in literature works.

References

1. Aslan, S., Ciocca, G., Schettini, R.: On comparing color spaces for food segmentation. In: Battiato, S., Farinella, G.M., Leo, M., Gallo, G. (eds.) ICIAP 2017. LNCS, vol. 10590, pp. 435–443. Springer, Cham (2017). https://doi.org/10.1007/978-3-319-70742-6_42
2. Aslan, S., Ciocca, G., Schettini, R.: Semantic food segmentation for automatic dietary monitoring. In: IEEE 8th International Conference on Consumer Electronics - Berlin (ICCE-Berlin) (2018)

3. Audebert, N., Le Saux, B., Lefèvre, S.: Semantic segmentation of earth observation data using multimodal and multi-scale deep networks. In: Lai, S.-H., Lepetit, V., Nishino, K., Sato, Y. (eds.) ACCV 2016. LNCS, vol. 10111, pp. 180–196. Springer, Cham (2017). https://doi.org/10.1007/978-3-319-54181-5_12

4. Bearman, A., Russakovsky, O., Ferrari, V., Fei-Fei, L.: What's the point: semantic segmentation with point supervision. In: Leibe, B., Matas, J., Sebe, N., Welling, M. (eds.) ECCV 2016. LNCS, vol. 9911, pp. 549–565. Springer, Cham (2016). https://doi.org/10.1007/978-3-319-46478-7_34

5. Boykov, Y., Kolmogorov, V.: An experimental comparison of min-cut/max-flow algorithms for energy minimization in vision. IEEE Trans. Pattern Anal. Mach. Intell. **9**, 1124–1137 (2004)

6. Chen, L.C., Papandreou, G., Kokkinos, I., Murphy, K., Yuille, A.: Semantic image segmentation with deep convolutional nets and fully connected CRFs. In: International Conference on Learning Representations (2015)

7. Cordts, M., et al.: The cityscapes dataset for semantic urban scene understanding. In: IEEE Conference on Computer Vision and Pattern Recognition, pp. 3213–3223 (2016)

8. Dai, J., He, K., Sun, J.: BoxSup: exploiting bounding boxes to supervise convolutional networks for semantic segmentation. In: IEEE International Conference on Computer Vision, pp. 1635–1643 (2015)

9. Felzenszwalb, P.F., Huttenlocher, D.P.: Efficient graph-based image segmentation. Int. J. Comput. Vis. **59**(2), 167–181 (2004)

10. Hariharan, B., Arbeláez, P., Bourdev, L., Maji, S., Malik, J.: Semantic contours from inverse detectors. In: IEEE International Conference on Computer Vision (ICCV), pp. 991–998 (2011)

11. Huang, Z., Wang, X., Wang, J., Liu, W., Wang, J.: Weakly-supervised semantic segmentation network with deep seeded region growing. In: Proceedings of the IEEE Conference on Computer Vision and Pattern Recognition, pp. 7014–7023 (2018)

12. Khoreva, A., Benenson, R., Hosang, J., Hein, M., Schiele, B.: Simple does it: weakly supervised instance and semantic segmentation. In: IEEE Conference on Computer Vision and Pattern Recognition, pp. 876–885 (2017)

13. Lin, D., Dai, J., Jia, J., He, K., Sun, J.: ScribbleSup: scribble-supervised convolutional networks for semantic segmentation. In: IEEE Conference on Computer Vision and Pattern Recognition, pp. 3159–3167 (2016)

14. Long, J., Shelhamer, E., Darrell, T.: Fully convolutional networks for semantic segmentation. In: IEEE Conference on Computer Vision and Pattern Recognition, pp. 3431–3440 (2015)

15. Oberweger, M., Wohlhart, P., Lepetit, V.: Hands deep in deep learning for hand pose estimation. arXiv preprint arXiv:1502.06807 (2015)

16. Papandreou, G., Chen, L.C., Murphy, K.P., Yuille, A.L.: Weakly- and semi-supervised learning of a deep convolutional network for semantic image segmentation. In: The IEEE International Conference on Computer Vision (ICCV) (2015)

17. Pavan, M., Pelillo, M.: Dominant sets and pairwise clustering. IEEE Trans. Pattern Anal. Mach. Intell. **29**(1), 167–172 (2007)

18. Rota Bulò, S., Pelillo, M.: Dominant-set clustering: a review. Eur. J. Oper. Res. **262**(1), 1–13 (2017)

19. Rota Bulò, S., Pelillo, M., Bomze, I.M.: Graph-based quadratic optimization: a fast evolutionary approach. Comput. Vis. Image Underst. **115**(7), 984–995 (2011)

20. Rother, C., Kolmogorov, V., Blake, A.: GrabCut: interactive foreground extraction using iterated graph cuts. In: ACM Transactions on Graphics (TOG), vol. 23, pp. 309–314 (2004)

21. Tang, M., Djelouah, A., Perazzi, F., Boykov, Y., Schroers, C.: Normalized cut loss for weakly-supervised CNN segmentation. In: IEEE conference on Computer Vision and Pattern Recognition (CVPR), Salt Lake City (2018)

22. Tang, M., Marin, D., Ayed, I.B., Boykov, Y.: Normalized cut meets MRF. In: Leibe, B., Matas, J., Sebe, N., Welling, M. (eds.) ECCV 2016. LNCS, vol. 9906, pp. 748–765. Springer, Cham (2016). https://doi.org/10.1007/978-3-319-46475-6_46

23. Tang, M., Perazzi, F., Djelouah, A., Ayed, I.B., Schroers, C., Boykov, Y.: On regularized losses for weakly-supervised CNN segmentation. In: Ferrari, V., Hebert, M., Sminchisescu, C., Weiss, Y. (eds.) ECCV 2018. LNCS, vol. 11220, pp. 524–540. Springer, Cham (2018). https://doi.org/10.1007/978-3-030-01270-0_31

24. Uijlings, J.R., Van De Sande, K.E., Gevers, T., Smeulders, A.W.: Selective search for object recognition. Int. J. Comput. Vis. **104**(2), 154–171 (2013)

25. Vedaldi, A., Lenc, K.: MatConvNet - convolutional neural networks for MATLAB. In: Proceeding of the ACM International Conference on Multimedia (2015)

26. Vernaza, P., Chandraker, M.: Learning random-walk label propagation for weakly-supervised semantic segmentation. In: IEEE Conference on Computer Vision and Pattern Recognition, pp. 7158–7166 (2017)

27. Wang, J., MacKenzie, J.D., Ramachandran, R., Chen, D.Z.: A deep learning approach for semantic segmentation in histology tissue images. In: Ourselin, S., Joskowicz, L., Sabuncu, M.R., Unal, G., Wells, W. (eds.) MICCAI 2016. LNCS, vol. 9901, pp. 176–184. Springer, Cham (2016). https://doi.org/10.1007/978-3-319-46723-8_21

28. Zemene, E., Alemu, L.T., Pelillo, M.: Dominant sets for "constrained" image segmentation. IEEE Trans. Pattern Anal. Mach. Intell. (2018)

29. Zemene, E., Pelillo, M.: Interactive image segmentation using constrained dominant sets. In: Leibe, B., Matas, J., Sebe, N., Welling, M. (eds.) ECCV 2016. LNCS, vol. 9912, pp. 278–294. Springer, Cham (2016). https://doi.org/10.1007/978-3-319-46484-8_17

Segmentation of Pigment Signs in Fundus Images for Retinitis Pigmentosa Analysis by Using Deep Learning

Nadia Brancati[1], Maria Frucci[1], Daniel Riccio[1,2(✉)], Luigi Di Perna[3], and Francesca Simonelli[3]

[1] Institute for High Performance Computing and Networking National Research Council of Italy (ICAR-CNR), Naples, Italy
{nadia.brancati,maria.frucci,daniel.riccio}@cnr.it
[2] University di Napoli Federico II, Naples, Italy
daniel.riccio@unina.it
[3] Eye Clinic, Multidisciplinary Department of Medical, Surgical and Dental Sciences, University of Campania "Luigi Vanvitelli", Naples, Italy
luigidiperna85@gmail.com,
francesca.simonelli@unicampania.it

Abstract. The adoption of Deep Learning (DL) algorithms into the practice of ophthalmology could play an important role in screening and diagnosis of eye diseases in the coming years. In particular, DL tools interpreting ocular data derived from low-cost devices, as a fundus camera, could support massive screening also in resource limited countries. This paper explores a fully automatic method supporting the diagnosis of the Retinitis Pigmentosa by means of the segmentation of pigment signs in retinal fundus images. The proposed approach relies on an U-Net based deep convolutional network. At the present, this is the first approach for pigment signs segmentation in retinal fundus images that is not dependent on hand-crafted features, but automatically learns a hierarchy of increasingly complex features directly from data.

We assess the performance by training the model on the public dataset RIPS and comparisons with the state of the art have been considered in accordance with approaches working on the same dataset. The experimental results show an improvement of 15% in F-measure score.

Keywords: Retinitis Pigmentosa · Pigment signs · Medical image analysis · Segmentation · Deep Learning

1 Introduction

Recent studies have shown that DL models are able to detect and diagnosing various retinal diseases interpreting ocular data derived from different diagnostic modalities including digital photographs, optical coherence tomography (OCT), and visual fields [1]. DL systems can already be applied to teleophthalmology programs to identify abnormal retinal images reducing the clinic workload for disease screening. Furthermore, DL tools could enable ophthalmic self-monitoring by patients via smartphone

© Springer Nature Switzerland AG 2019
E. Ricci et al. (Eds.): ICIAP 2019, LNCS 11752, pp. 437–445, 2019.
https://doi.org/10.1007/978-3-030-30645-8_40

retinal photography. Most of the initial studies have centered around automatic detection of diabetic retinopathy, age-related macular degeneration, and glaucoma [2–4, 14], while only a few methods have been developed for the automatic diagnosis of genetically heterogeneous retinal disorders. Many of these genetic eye disorders lead to blindness and an early diagnosis, even by means of a simple ophthalmoscopy, can reduce preventable vision loss. Automatic diagnostic systems are able to analyze ocular data and could be also used by non-ophthalmologists to screen patients who do not yet show signs of weakness in visual acuity. The aim of this work is to investigate a DL system for segmenting pigment signs (PSs) that represent a symptom of the Retinitis Pigmentosa (RP). The RP is one of the most common disease caused by genetic eye disorders and leads to night blindness and a progressive constriction of the visual field from the periphery to the center. Progression leads to central acuity loss and legal blindness in most patients. At present, no cure exists to stop the progression of the disease but, if an early diagnosis of RP is available, the progressive degeneration of RP can be delayed through the intake of vitamin A and other nutritional interventions [5]. Clinical diagnosis is possible through fundus examination revealing the presence of PSs, arteriolar attenuation, and pallor of optic disc. In Fig. 1, a healthy and a severely degenerated retina are shown.

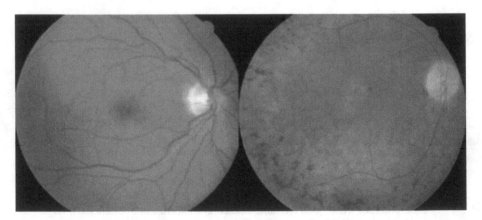

Fig. 1. Fundus images of a healthy retina (left) and a retina with Retinitis Pigmentosa (right). In the image of the diseased eye, peripheral pigment signs, attenuated retinal arterioles and optic-disc pallor are evident.

PSs are a consequence of a degeneration of the photoreceptors and accumulate over years, so they could not be present in younger individuals. However, PSs are the most easily identifiable signs on a retinal fundus image by a non-ophthalmologist and should be prompt referred. Further detailed ophthalmic examinations (visual test, OCT, electroretinography and fundus autofluorescence) are adopted to determine the severity of the disease and to monitor the disease progression [6]. Many automatic methods to quantify RP and to track its progression are based on the analysis of OCT [3, 7, 8]. The diagnosis by fundus camera represents the best solution for RP screening by performing retinal image acquisition in resource-limited setting, since fundus images can be acquired with inexpensive devices.

Though many approaches to automatically analyze the retinal vessel structure and the pallor of the optic disk were developed [9–13], the literature about the automatic detection of PSs in fundus images is extremely limited [14–16]. In our previous work [16], we have proposed a supervised method to segment PSs in fundus images, which extract pixel-wise/region-wise hand-crafted features that are fed to machine learning techniques (i.e. Random Forests and AdaBoost.M1) to discriminate between PSs and normal fundus. Furthermore, we made publicly available a dataset of Retinal Images for Pigment Signs (RIPS) [17] for the evaluation of the performance of PSs segmentation algorithms.

DL based segmentation is a hot topic and has gained increasing attention, as deep neural networks learn a hierarchy of feature maps directly from data without requiring any hand-crafted features. Most of the early DL approaches for segmentation translate the segmentation task into a pixel-wise classification problem. However, in order to solve the image classification problems, DL models require a large number of images to be trained. Moreover, the classification of all the pixels in a test image is carried out by sliding a window on the image and classifying the current central pixel, that entails a slow prediction time. Other DL architectures specifically devoted to segmentation are based on an encoder-decoder scheme that learns to decode low-resolution images on pixel-wise predictions. In this work, the adopted DL model to segment PSs is a U-Net based convolutional neural network, that is an encoder-decoder network for pixel-wise prediction [18].

2 The Proposed Model

The proposed deep model is based on U-Net, which has been successfully used for segmenting medical images in several contests [9, 14]. This model is an encoder-decoder network implementing a contracting/expanding path consisting of convolutional, downsampling and upsampling layers.

In this work, the network has been modified with respect to its original architecture. Indeed, two of the five blocks have been dropped out (i.e. convolutions, pooling/upsampling) and the number of filters was halved. The architecture of the network is shown in Fig. 2.

In the encoding part of the network each feature map is downsampled by applying a pooling operation in order to spatially reduce the input as well as the number of parameters to be learned in the following layer. In our case, max-pooling has been adopted for all downsampling layers. Upsampling layers increase the dimension of feature maps by learning to deconvolve them. The decoder feature maps and the corresponding encoder feature maps are concatenated to produce the output. In order to stabilize the learning process and to reduce the number of training epochs, we also introduce batch normalization, while dropout (0.2) is introduced to prevent over-fitting.

In more details, both the encoder and decoder include five convolutional layers, whose filters have size 3×3, a stride of 1 and adopt the rectification non linearity (ReLU) and Batch Normalization. Moreover, dropout of 0.2 is applied alternately to odd convolutional layers. In the contracting path, the second convolution of the first two blocks feeds a max-pooling layer that is computed on a window of size 2×2 with a stride equal to 2. In the expanding path, the first convolution of the last two blocks is preceded by an upsampling layer, which doubles the size of the feature map and concatenates it with the corresponding feature map coming from the contracting path.

At the end, a soft-max classifier computes the probability of each pixels of being a PS (foreground) or background.

Given the nature of PSs, choosing the right metric to be optimized represents a crucial aspect. Indeed, PSs represent a small percentage of the pixels of the image, that translates in very few positive pixels and a high number of true negatives in the segmented image. The most of works in literature consider the accuracy as the metric to be optimized during training. However, accuracy can be heavily contributed by a large number of true negatives, thus F1-score might be a better measure to use if one need to seek a balance between precision and recall and there is an uneven class distribution. For this reason, the F1-measure has been considered in our model. Furthermore, to increase the robustness of the training process, the Adadelta [19] optimizer has been selected, as it does not require manual tuning of the learning rate and has been shown to be robust to noisy gradient information and different model architectures.

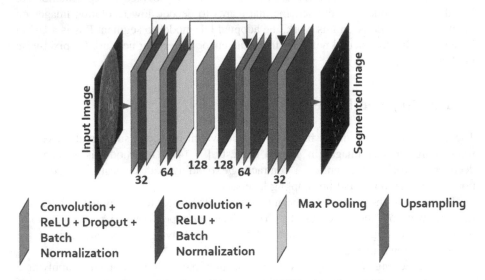

Fig. 2. Architecture of the proposed U-Net based network.

3   Experiments

3.1   Materials and Methods

The experiments have been performed on the Retinal Images for Pigment Signs dataset, namely RIPS. This dataset consists of 120 retinal fundus images with a resolution of 1440×2160 pixels captured from four patients, who underwent three different acquisition sessions. During each session, five images per eye were acquired covering different regions of the fundus. The time lapse between two consecutive sessions is at least six months, while time interval between the first and last session always exceeds one year. Images were acquired using the digital retinal camera Canon CR4-45NM (Canon UK, Reigate, UK) and show a high variability in terms of color balancing, contrast and sharpness/focus, also for the same patient. Two binary masks are associated to each image, where the foreground representing PSs has been marked by two experts in the field of ophthalmology. Moreover, for each image, a mask image is provided to delineate the FOV.

3.2 Training Strategy and Image Prediction

The resolution of retinal images makes it unfeasible to train the existing DL architectures on the whole image. Most commonly used approaches to cope with this problem are either to reduce the image resolution or to partition the image in patches. The main drawback of a severe image downsampling is that small PSs could disappear. On the other hand, image partitioning produces a high number of patches with large size when working on high resolution images. For this reason, we adopted a compromise by reducing the image size of a factor equal to 0.5 that allows to extract patches with small size, but still representative enough. Only a subset of patches randomly extracted from each image is included in the training set. Indeed, PSs appears only in some regions of the image and could have a very small size, so considering only patches including at least one pixel marked as PS in the corresponding mask yield a training set sufficiently representative also for the background.

In the testing process, the input image is downsampled of a factor 0.5. The image prediction is performed by extracting patches according to a window sliding with a stride $s > 0$. Patches are fed to the network and pixels are assigned a probability of being PS. For values of s smaller than the window size, patch overlapping occurs, so that each pixel receives multiple predictions as belonging to several patches. The global score of a pixel is computed by summing up all predictions. Scores are normalized in the range [0, 1] and the foreground image is obtained by applying a threshold of 0.5.

3.3 Experimental Setup and Results

In the experiments, a per patient cross-validation protocol was applied considering samples from three out of the four patients for the training and the data of the fourth patient for the validation. The number of training epochs has been set to 30, while the batch size is equal to 32. To train our network, we used a NVIDIA GeForce GTX 1050 with 4 Gb of RAM.

The first experiment aims to verify that F-measure provides better performance than accuracy when used as loss function to train the network. In this experiment, the patch size is fixed to 48 × 48 pixels and the stride of the sliding window is set to 6 in the prediction process. Results are reported in Table 1.

Table 1. Performance measures of the proposed U-Net based network when F-measure or accuracy is used as loss function.

Loss function	Sensitivity		Specificity		Precision		Accuracy		F-measure	
	Avg.	Std.	Avg.	Std.	Avg.	Std.	Avg.	Std.	Avg.	Std.
Accuracy	0.568	0.077	0.994	0.005	0.450	0.084	0.990	0.006	0.496	0.048
F-measure	0.557	0.035	0.994	0.005	0.480	0.086	0.990	0.006	0.506	0.035

The values in Table 1 show that the accuracy is very high in both cases, while the precision increases considerably when the F-measure is used as a loss function. This is because accuracy is heavily influenced by the number of true negatives, so it approaches to 1.0 even when the precision is very low. The experimental results confirm that the F-measure outperforms the accuracy for the PSs segmentation task.

In the second experiment we have analyzed the improvements obtained in terms of f-measure when the patch size increases. The proposed U-Net based architecture has been tested for three different patch sizes, namely 48 × 48, 72 × 72, and 96 × 96 and numerical results are reported in Table 2.

Table 2. Performance measures of the proposed model for different patch sizes.

Patch size	Sensitivity		Specificity		Precision		Accuracy		F-measure	
	Avg.	Std.	Avg.	Std.	Avg.	Std.	Avg.	Std.	Avg.	Std.
48 × 48	0.557	0.035	0.994	0.005	0.480	0.086	0.990	0.006	0.506	0.035
72 × 72	0.626	0.067	0.993	0.005	0.465	0.081	0.990	0.006	0.528	0.049
96 × 96	0.552	0.070	0.996	0.003	0.561	0.076	0.992	0.005	0.551	0.033

Results in Table 2 mainly highlight that F-measure proportionally increases with respect to the patch size. In particular, we have observed that the larger the size of the patch is, the better the model performs in discriminating PSs from blood vessels.

Figure 3 shows the segmented images produced by the proposed model when it is trained with patches of size 48 × 48, 72 × 72, and 96 × 96 pixels, respectively. In Fig. 4, one image for each of the four patient is shown together with the corresponding ground truth and the segmented image produced by our model when patches of 96 × 96 pixels are considered.

The performance of the proposed U-Net based model has been compared with state of the art approaches. In particular, the machine learning based approach proposed in [16] was considered. Numerical results are reported in Table 3.

Table 3. Performance measures of different methods.

Method	Sensitivity	Specificity	Precision	Accuracy	F-measure
RF-PB [16]	0.582	0.994	0.461	0.991	0.479
AB-PB [16]	0.642	0.993	0.424	0.990	0.467
Proposed model	0.552	0.996	0.561	0.992	0.551

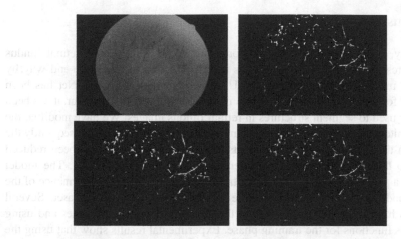

Fig. 3. Segmented images obtained for different patch sizes: input image (top-left), 48 × 48 pixels (top-right), 72 × 72 pixels (bottom-left), and 96 × 96 pixels (bottom-right).

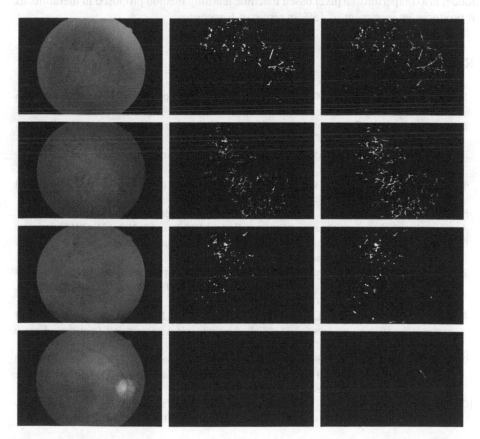

Fig. 4. Results from the RIPS dataset. Top to bottom: patients from 1 to 4. Left to right: the original image, the ground truth, the result of the proposed model.

4   Conclusions

In this study, a deep-learning based approach for segmenting PSs in retinal fundus images is presented. The segmentation has been performed in an end-to-end way by using a DL model. We have proposed a U-Net based model, since U-Net has been largely used for segmenting medical images in several contests. In particular, it has been successfully used to segment structures in retinal fundus images. We have modified the original architecture of U-Net to reduce the number of parameters, and consequently the computation time and memory requirements. The number of blocks has been reduced from five to three and the number of filters per block has been halved. The model implements a patch based strategy both for training and testing. The performance of the proposed model has been assessed on the publicly available RIPS dataset. Several experiments have been performed varying the size of the extracted patches and using different loss functions for the training phase. Experimental results show that using the F-measure in place of the accuracy improves the quality of segmentation. Moreover, the quality of the segmentation increases proportionally with the patch size. The proposed model also outperforms a pixel based machine learning method proposed in literature, as it produces an increment of 15% in terms of F-measure.

References

1. Grewal, P.S., Oloumi, F., Rubin, U., Tennant, M.T.: Deep learning in ophthalmology: a review. Can. J. Ophthalmol. **53**(4), 309–313 (2018)
2. Gargeya, R., Leng, T.: Automated identification of diabetic retinopathy using deep learning. Ophthalmology **124**(7), 962–969 (2017)
3. Meriaudeau, F.: Machine learning and deep learning approaches for retinal disease diagnosis. Procedia Comput. Sci. **135**, 2 (2018)
4. Tan, J.H., et al.: Age-related macular degeneration detection using deep convolutional neural network. Future Gener. Comput. Syst. **87**, 127–135 (2018)
5. Dias, M.F., et al.: Molecular genetics and emerging therapies for retinitis pigmentosa: basic research and clinical perspectives. Progress Retinal Eye Res. **63**, 107–131 (2018)
6. Fahim, A.: Retinitis pigmentosa recent advances and future directions in diagnosis and management. Curr. Opin. Pediatr. **30**(6), 725–733 (2018)
7. Cunefare, D., et al.: Deep learning based detection of cone photoreceptors with multimodal adaptive optics scanning light ophthalmoscope images of achromatopsia. Biomed. Opt. Express **9**(8), 3740–3756 (2018)
8. Ramachandran, R., Zhou, L., Locke, K.G., Birch, D.G., Hood, D.C.: A comparison of methods for tracking progression in x-linked retinitis pigmentosa using frequency domain oct. Translational Vis. Sci. Technol. **2**(7), 5 (2013)
9. Xiancheng, W., et al.: Retina blood vessel segmentation using a U-net based Convolutional neural network. In: Procedia Computer Science: International Conference on Data Science (ICDS 2018), Beijing, China, 8–9 June (2018)
10. Oliveira, A., Pereira, S., Silva, C.A.: Retinal vessel segmentation based on fully convolutional neural networks. Expert Syst. Appl. **112**, 229–242 (2018)

11. Brancati, N., Frucci, M., Gragnaniello, D., Riccio, D.: Retinal vessels segmentation based on a convolutional neural network. In: Mendoza, M., Velastín, S. (eds.) CIARP 2017. LNCS, vol. 10657, pp. 119–126. Springer, Cham (2018). https://doi.org/10.1007/978-3-319-75193-1_15

12. Yang, H.K., Oh, J.E., Han, S.B., Kim, K.G., Hwang, J.M.: Automatic computer-aided analysis of optic disc pallor in fundus photographs. Acta Ophthalmologica **97**, e519–e525 (2018)

13. Das, H., Saha, A., Deb, S.: An expert system to distinguish a defective eye from a normal eye. In: 2014 International Conference on Issues and Challenges in Intelligent Computing Techniques (ICICT), pp. 155–158. IEEE, Ghaziabad (2014)

14. Sevastopolsky, A.: Optic disc and cup segmentation methods for glaucoma detection with modification of U-Net convolutional neural network. Pattern Recogn. Image Anal. **27**(3), 618–624 (2017)

15. Brancati, N., Frucci, M., Gragnaniello, D., Riccio, D., Di Iorio, V., Di Perna, L.: Automatic segmentation of pigment deposits in retinal fundus images of Retinitis Pigmentosa disease. Comput. Med. Imaging Graph. **66**, 73–81 (2018)

16. Brancati, N., et al.: Learning-based approach to segment pigment signs in fundus images for Retinitis Pigmentosa analysis. Neurocomputing **308**, 159–171 (2018)

17. RIPS (2018). https://www.icar.cnr.it/sites-rips-datasetrips/

18. Ronneberger, O., Fischer, P., Brox, T.: U-Net: convolutional networks for biomedical image segmentation. In: Navab, N., Hornegger, J., Wells, W.M., Frangi, A.F. (eds.) MICCAI 2015. LNCS, vol. 9351, pp. 234–241. Springer, Cham (2015). https://doi.org/10.1007/978-3-319-24574-4_28

19. Zeiler, M.D.: ADADELTA: an adaptive learning rate method. arXiv preprint arXiv:1212.5701 (2012)

SWIR Camera-Based Localization and Mapping in Challenging Environments

Viachaslau Kachurka$^{(\boxtimes)}$ ⃝, David Roussel ⃝, Hicham Hadj-Abdelkader ⃝,
Fabien Bonardi ⃝, Jean-Yves Didier ⃝, and Samia Bouchafa ⃝

IBISC, Univ Evry, Université Paris-Saclay, 91025 Evry, France
{viachaslau.kachurka,david.roussel,hicham.hadjabdelkader,
fabien.bonardi,jeanyves.didier,samia.bouchafa}@ibisc.univ-evry.fr
http://www.ibisc.univ-evry.fr

Abstract. This paper assesses a monocular localization system for complex scenes. The system is carried by a moving agent in a complex environment (smoke, darkness, indoor-outdoor transitions). We show how using a short-wave infrared camera (SWIR) with a potential lighting source is a good compromise that allows to make just a slight adaptation of classical simultaneous localization and mapping (SLAM) techniques. This choice made it possible to obtain relevant features from SWIR images and also to limit tracking failures due to the lack of key points in such challenging environments. In addition, we propose a tracking failure recovery strategy in order to allow tracking re-initialization with or without the use of other sensors. Our localization system is validated using real datasets generated from a moving SWIR-camera in indoor environment. Obtained results are promising, and lead us to consider the integration of our mono-SLAM in a complete localization chain including a data fusion process from several sensors.

Keywords: Visual SLAM · Visual odometry ·
Short-wave Infrared (SWIR) camera

1 Introduction

The problem of accurate localization of emergency response agents (civil security, firefighters, etc.), law enforcement or armed forces agents in a closed, unknown, non-cooperative environment remains an open problem nowadays since no sufficiently reliable system meeting all specific constraints currently exists. However, many military and civil applications would benefit from being equipped with such systems. Such localization task focuses on the idea that the command center should have the most accurate location of its agent in unknown conditions, while also receiving information about the environment (e.g. reckon missions in armed forces, or operative information on a fire).

While indoor positioning problem by itself already imposes additional difficulties, such as a need of high accuracy level and non-existence of GPS signal [12], the given problem formulates even a higher-level difficulty extension to it.

ⓒ Springer Nature Switzerland AG 2019
E. Ricci et al. (Eds.): ICIAP 2019, LNCS 11752, pp. 446–456, 2019.
https://doi.org/10.1007/978-3-030-30645-8_41

One can see such task as a use case for Simultaneous Localization and Mapping (SLAM) techniques; however, the main challenge for SLAM techniques in such context is the lack of suitable technologies that can take into account the technical limits (the equipment should be quite small and efficient), technological requirements (diversity of sensors to make the system more robust to ensure the mission) and environmental constraints (hazardous or non-cooperative environment), as shown in the article which defines a similar problem [18].

The multi-sensor solutions have been studied in the field of mobile robotics for several decades and usually consider a wheeled vehicle, moving in pretty homogeneous conditions: such as a mobile robot in [16] or, more recently, a flying drone [6]. In most cases data fusion from multiple sensors is required with special interest in combination of inertial measurement unit (IMU) with other sensors such as cameras [17] or LIDAR [11].

While during decades the imaging sensor appeared to be among the least appealing in the field of robust real-time indoor positioning due to high computational complexity and susceptibility to fail in non-cooperative environment, recent convergence of visual SLAM field (as observed in [21]) enabled more robust approaches and reopened this niche. Consequently, this last decade has seen a profusion of works in the field of localization and SLAM. However, there exists a certain lack of works offering hardware and software solutions specific to complex environments.

The aforementioned "non-cooperative environment", as described in [18], is an environment where the conditions tend to render the work of any type of localization approach as difficult as possible. In the context of a visual odometry approach, some relevant constraints that should be addressed, are: rapid and drastic change of light conditions such as outdoor/indoor transitions, presence of heavy smoke and human motion which implies a wide range of irregular translations and rotations speeds. In the frame of this work we solely focus on the aforementioned visual odometry problem under major limitations of the imaging sensor, trying to assess applicability of some existing approaches to this ambitious task, as a part of a larger multi-sensor system which is out of scope of this paper. Also, among the various constraints we have taken into account, the current localization should be available (and possibly transmitted to control center) in real-time, whereas complete localization trajectory and reconstructed map can be retrieved and processed later.

This paper is organized as follows: next section is devoted to the specific short-wave infrared imaging system that we propose in order to take into account some complex smoky environments. A study of the sensor spectral characteristics along with the most suitable features that we can extract from the resulting images is provided. Section 3 shows how a classical SLAM (here ORB-SLAM) algorithm is adapted to meet our specific requirements. In particular, we focus on the tracking re-initialization step. Section 4 presents experimental results on existing benchmarks and data obtained from our shortwave infrared camera, moving in an indoor and outdoor environment. Finally, the paper ends with a conclusion and some future works.

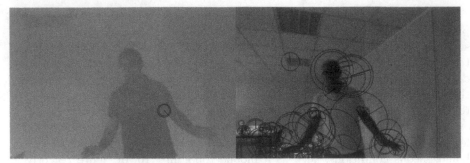

(a) Room viewed by standard RGB-camera   (b) Room viewed by SWIR camera

Fig. 1. A medium-sized room, filled with cold smoke with detected ORB [20] features

2   SWIR Camera Characteristics and Features

A conventional RGB-camera sensor does not see through heavy smoke. Figures 1a and b present a room, filled with common dry smoke. Nevertheless, most types of smoke (either artificial dry smoke [22] or several types of "natural" smoke [1]) are transparent to infra-red imaging sensors, most likely for the Short-Wave Infra-Red (SWIR) camera—in the spectral band 0.9–1.7 μm.

However, SWIR imaging is still subject to poor lighting conditions provided by dark places or cold lights such as fluorescent or LED lighting, since the latter ones do not emit enough light in the SWIR band [23]. An example of a SWIR image of the underground parking, lighted-up with neon tubes, is shown in Fig. 2(c), where the scene is clearly unseen by the SWIR camera. Otherwise, this visibility limitation does not appear when the scene is illuminated by light bulb or sun (see illuminated room beyond the doorway in Fig. 2(c) and the outdoor parking in Fig. 2(d)). Hence, cold lighting conditions would require an external SWIR-band emitting light source to illuminate the scene (e.g. the one described in [5]).

Non-cooperative environments can feature drastic and rapid changes in the global lighting conditions. Such changes can be described by transition from dark indoor to sunny outdoor (and vice-versa), moving elements (flashlights or personnel), or non-constant lighting produced by open fire.

Also, as there can be no information of the light conditions of the explored area *a priori*, we can not apply any photometric calibration or rely on the data about scene luminosity, used in most of direct visual SLAMs. A transition from underground to sunny outdoor parking lot presents such lighting condition differences, that the resulting histograms do not even intersect within the chosen camera sensitivity spectrum (encoded with 16 bits depth) as it can be seen on Figs. 2(a) and (b). This leads to usage of general histogram equalization approach, forbidding any direct visual SLAM such as DSO [4] (which requires an accurate photometric calibration and constant shutter time [3]). In our case we employed an automatic gain control-like algorithm (AGC), which deletes the

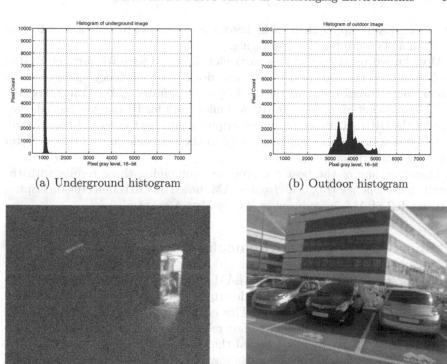

(a) Underground histogram

(b) Outdoor histogram

(c) Underground parking lot after histogram equalization

(d) Outdoor parking lot after histogram equalization

Fig. 2. Top row: Histograms for raw image data, extracted from SWIR camera with exposure time of 20 ms. **Bottom row:** the same images after histogram equalization treatment (automatic gain control-like algorithm, AGC)

points beyond 3σ-limits from both sides of histogram, and then spreads it across the whole 16-bit range.

Such an approach defies the problems of rapid luminosity changes, also avoiding the glare effect, and provides comparable images for comparable scenes in different luminosity conditions. However, it fails in the cases of very narrow histogram (as also can be seen in the left column of Fig. 2) and introduces noise. The only way to avoid very narrow histograms is to add a portable infrared light source as discussed previously. This line of consideration leads us to an idea of using an indirect visual SLAM, which relies on a feature detector algorithm.

2.1 Feature Detection in Infrared Imaging Sensors

While there has been a lot of research in recent years regarding feature points, few of them concern infra-red sensors. These sensors usually provide images with characteristics not equal to those of standard cameras. Therefore, one cannot automatically apply their most known *pros et cons* to the task of feature detection and description in IR-imaging.

Most known researches in this particular direction were Ricaurte et al. [19], which compared the feature detection and description efficiency against several typical image transformations on the long-wave infrared (LWIR) imaging sensors. Johannson et al. propose in [10] a similar work for IR-images. Indeed, they consider the ORB [20] detector and descriptor couple as the second-best regarding robustness and efficiency, losing only to the combination of ORB detector and BRISK descriptor.

Therefore, one of the best compromises, combining these results with the overall time efficiency [13], is a visual SLAM, based on ORB detector-descriptor, such as ORB-SLAM, introduced in [14] by Mur-Artal et al.

3   Shortwave Infrared Monocular ORB-SLAM

One of the strongest points of ORB-SLAM according to the comparative study in [9] is the usage of the same ORB descriptors for tracking, map point generation, and environment recognition. This enables a bag-of-words (BoW) based scene description [7], and therefore a fast relocalization. However, this approach also bases itself on the assumption that the movement between two consecutive frames is relatively small, which is not always the case in the context of a human agent in non-cooperative environment (rapid turns, pose changes, etc).

3.1   ORB-SLAM: Short Technical Description

ORB-SLAM bases itself on the idea of KeyFrames observing MapPoints (generated from matched features, observed during three consecutive KeyFrames). The consecutive KeyFrames are bound into an "essential graph", sub-graph of a "covisibility graph", where the KeyFrames are connected if they both observe a significant number of common MapPoints.

As most contemporary visual SLAMs, ORB-SLAM employs tracking, local mapping, loop closure, as well as bundle adjustments, both global (GBA) and local (LBA), in a multi-threaded framework. It also introduces a novel approach to monocular initialization, based on random sample consensus (RANSAC), which usually catches the movement within 10–15 frames and initializes the tracking and mapping with point and trajectory positioning up to a scale factor. In the context of our task, where the visual odometry is seen as a part of a bigger multi-sensor system, the problem of scale factor should be addressed on a higher level of a multi-sensor fusion.

GBA is employed only in the cases of LC and relocalization as it consumes a significant amount of resources. Both loop closure and relocalization work in a similar manner - comparison of the scene BoW signature with those "already seen", and relocation of current camera position to an already existing matched scene, with further propagation of error between these two positions along the whole trajectory via GBA. Relocalization allows to resume tracking when it fails.

Such tracking failures can be pretty numerous due to the assumption of small movement between frames: if current frame and the last KeyFrame have a decreasing number of mutual MapPoint observations, a new KeyFrame is created. However, if this decay is too fast, tracking might be lost. The next section addresses this specific issue.

3.2   Tracking Re-initialization

Most SLAM algorithms are designed to work on existing benchmark datasets such as KITTI VO [8] or EUROC MAV [2], and as such are tailored not to fail on such datasets. This is often not the case when we submit these algorithms to more difficult conditions in which visual tracking can fail. This type of tracking loss occurs, for example, during fast rotations or high acceleration motions which are likely to occur when the tracking system is worn by a human being.

The default behavior of the visual tracking when the tracking is lost leads to a relocation based on BoW-signatures. However, it is likely to succeed only when the camera returns to a location already registered in a KeyFrame, which might take a while to occur and therefore induce a gap in localization data. We have therefore modified the default behavior to initiate a nondestructive tracking reset (thus preserving the KeyFrames and MapPoints recorded in the current Map) in parallel with the relocalization procedure.

Figure 3 shows the scheme of tracking algorithm, divided into several states and procedures, where the relocalization was the only usable procedure by default when tracking was lost. We added a new state "REINITIALIZING" and a new procedure of re-initialization to restart the tracking based on the current motion, without having to wait for a possible relocalization, while preserving the current map. This procedure initializes new tracking with a new map (then merged with the old map) from a given initial pose. In standalone mode the re-initialization procedure uses the last motion, available before the loss of tracking, to provide such an initial pose.

However, multi-sensor-based SLAM can provide the most accurate possible initial pose when the re-initialization procedure succeeds, and fixes the scale factor problem of pure monocular tracking. We should also mention, that a visual-inertial extension of ORB-SLAM has already been presented in [15], however without an open-source implementation it can not yet be assessed and used *as is*.

4   Experimental Results

The task of visual odometry in last years has been very popular in the field of robotic navigation and even has grown to have a competition against several renown data benchmarks. One can cite the famous ones like the aforementioned EUROC MAV, KITTI VO, as well as TUM MVO [3].

EUROC MAV and KITTI VO datasets are based on camera motion, mounted on a vehicle, featuring less pitch and roll compared to human motion, and therefore do not meet all the criteria of our operating context.

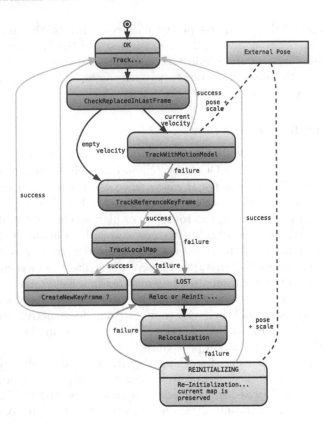

Fig. 3. Part of the general ORB-SLAM tracking scheme following a successful initialization, showing the tracking states "OK" and "LOST", as well as the tracking stages.

In this section, we first validate the proposed re-initialization approach using the TUM MVO dataset since it is produced by a handheld camera for tracking evaluation. Then, we validate the usage of the SWIR-camera based SLAM under several constraints.

4.1   TUM MVO Dataset

In order to be able to achieve stable initialization and tracking for the TUM MVO dataset sequences, we had to adjust several parameters of ORB-SLAM. Table 1 shows the adjusted parameters compared to the values used in origianl version for respectively Outdoor and Indoor tracking. Lowering various thresholds and increasing the RANSAC iteration count provides better grip on tracking in any situation. However, these modifications can diminish the quality of triangulation since the scale drift can increase. Therefore, low thresholds are suggested when other sensors can be used to correct the drift on the higher level of data fusion.

The TUM MVO dataset lacks full-trajectory ground truth (GT) data, providing only partial coverage. Therefore, in the view of re-initialization validation, we

Table 1. Parameters values, used in our experiments, for more stable tracking in human movement

Parameter name	Original	Outdoors	Indoors
Number of ORB extractor features	1000	2000	2000
Initial FAST threshold	20	15	20
Minimal FAST threshold	7	5	10
ORB matcher lower threshold count	50	40	40
Minimal projection matches number	20	15	15
Minimal inliers number after reloc	50	30	30
Motion model minimal matches number	20	15	15
Initializer RANSAC iterations count	200	300	300
Initializer min matched keypoint count	100	30	30

are not going to run the qualitative tests against this partial GT data (besides, the original TUM MVO paper already presents the results of such tests [3]); moreover, our target here is to test the algorithm stability against tracking failures with different configurations: "Original" (O), with original parameters values as provided by Mur-Artal and no re-initialization; "Original with Reinit" (OR), with original parameters values but re-initialization added; and "Modified with Reinit" (MR), with ajusted parameters values from Table 1 and re-initialization.

We made the system do 25 runs for each of these three sets of parameters against several chosen sequences in TUM MVO dataset, in order to count the percentage of lost data (due to tracking failures). Table 2 shows the results of such validation: for sequence 24 the original set of parameters with reinitialization works better, than ours; sequence 35 shows drastic difference, and other sequences show a small increase of efficiency. This shows a crucial need for a fine tuning (or even a strategy of on-the-fly adjustment) of the parameters in each case even for the same hardware combinations, and therefore, a necessity of an additional study.

4.2   IBISC SWIR Dataset

The dataset we used in the following experiments represents a capture of a handheld SWIR camera during an exploration scenario. It is composed of about 60 K images, captured at a frequency of 29 frames per second, for a duration of about half an hour. The AGC-like histogram equalization approach, mentioned in Sect. 2, is applied automatically to each image.

The exploration course presents multiple difficulties, which favor challenging tracking situations, such as: rapid changes of direction, indoor/outdoor transitions, doorways crossing. It also features regular "loop closing locations" (passing through the same place several times), which allow trajectory and map optimization through global bundle adjustment.

Table 2. Levels of tracking failures for "original" (O), "original with reinitialization" (OR) and "modified with reinit" (MR) configurations against several TUM MVO sequences. The percentage level shows, how much frames were lost during state "Tracking lost", as compared to total frame count of the sequence.

Sequence num	Data loss, % (O)	Data loss, % (OR)	Data loss, % (MR)
Seq. 24 (parking)	33.93	**5.14**	5.97
Seq. 25 (parking)	6.94	1.62	**1.34**
Seq. 29 (street)	2.24	0.53	**0.00**
Seq. 30 (backyard)	48.38	19.47	**18.47**
Seq. 35 (indoors)	58.74	56.69	**30.97**

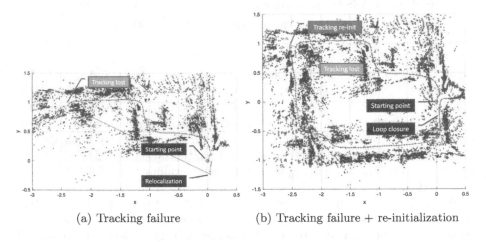

(a) Tracking failure   (b) Tracking failure + re-initialization

Fig. 4. Examples of tracking with and without re-initialization

Figure 4 shows two tracking scenarios using the same sub-sequence of the aforementioned dataset: Fig. 4(a) shows a tracking failure due to a fast rotation with a relocalization event at the end of the trajectory. Since ORB-SLAM uses a random sample consensus to choose points during tracking, it is quite common to see the tracking either succeed or fail on the same data. Figure 4(b) shows the same tracking failure followed by a tracking re-initialization, hence preserving previous trajectory and map with also a loop closure event at the end of the trajectory. Moreover, since we only used visual tracking without integrating any other sensor, the motion model used during re-initialization assumes a continuous motion estimated over the last frames before tracking failures, which can lead to inconsistent reinitialized location if the re-initialization takes too much time (more than 1 s). In our case the trajectory has been regularized by the loop closure event which triggers a global bundle adjustment along the whole trajectory. It would be appropriate during this re-initialization to use data from other sensors (inertial unit for instance) to obtain a more consistent re-initialization pose.

5   Conclusion and Future Work

This paper has presented a first step towards a complete localization system in challenging environments. We have shown how a specific camera (SWIR) with an adaptation of a SLAM technique (ORB-SLAM) is a promising solution. Our next step will be to integrate the proposed approach in a multi-sensor system including an inertial measurement unit in a local fusion scheme. Another perspective of our work is to couple the SWIR camera with a conventional one in order to benefit from a heterogeneous stereo image pair. The main advantage of this latter solution is to provide a complete visual SLAM that is able to fix the scale factor without any fusion with other sensor. The main fusion process in this case will remain global, by combining homogeneous poses estimations from different sensors/algorithms. Eventually, we would also like to release publicly a SWIR image dataset, dedicated to non-cooperative environment. Such task is not possible for us yet, as it lacks ground truth estimation.

Acknowledgements. This work takes part in the LOCA3D project in the framework of the challenge MALIN funded with the support of Directorate General of Armaments and French National Research Agency (https://challenge-malin.fr).

References

1. Bergstrom, R.W., et al.: Spectral absorption properties of atmospheric aerosols. Atmos. Chem. Phys. **7**(23), 5937–5943 (2007)
2. Burri, M., et al.: The EuRoC micro aerial vehicle datasets. Int. J. Robot. Res. **35**(10), 1157–1163 (2016)
3. Engel, J., Usenko, V., Cremers, D.: A photometrically calibrated benchmark for monocular visual odometry. In: arXiv:1607.02555, July 2016
4. Engel, J., Koltun, V., Cremers, D.: Direct sparse odometry. IEEE Transact. Pattern Anal. Mach. Intell. **40**(3), 611–625 (2018)
5. Ettenberg, M.H., Blessinger, M.A., O'Grady, M.T., Huang, S.C., Brubaker, R.M., Cohen, M.J.: High-resolution SWIR arrays for imaging at night. In: Infrared Technology and Applications XXX. vol. 5406, pp. 46–56. International Society for Optics and Photonics (2004)
6. Forster, C., Pizzoli, M., Scaramuzza, D.: SVO: fast semi-direct monocular visual odometry. In: 2014 IEEE International Conference on Robotics and Automation (ICRA), pp. 15–22. IEEE, June 2014
7. Gálvez-López, D., Tardós, J.D.: Bags of binary words for fast place recognition in image sequences. IEEE Transact. Robot. **28**(5), 1188–1197 (2012)
8. Geiger, A., Lenz, P., Stiller, C., Urtasun, R.: Vision meets robotics: The KITTI dataset. Int. J. Robot. Res. **32**(11), 1231–1237 (2013)
9. Huletski, A., Kartashov, D., Krinkin, K.: Evaluation of the modern visual SLAM methods. In: 2015 Artificial Intelligence and Natural Language and Information Extraction, Social Media and Web Search FRUCT Conference (AINL-ISMW FRUCT), pp. 19–25. IEEE, November 2015
10. Johansson, J., Solli, M., Maki, A.: An evaluation of local feature detectors and descriptors for infrared images. In: Hua, G., Jégou, H. (eds.) ECCV 2016. LNCS, vol. 9915, pp. 711–723. Springer, Cham (2016). https://doi.org/10.1007/978-3-319-49409-8_59

11. Levinson, J., Thrun, S.: Robust vehicle localization in urban environments using probabilistic maps. In: Proceedings of the IEEE International Conference on Robotics and Automation (ICRA), pp. 4372–4378. IEEE, May 2010
12. Mautz, R.: Overview of current indoor positioning systems. Geodezija ir kartografija **35**(1), 18–22 (2009)
13. Miksik, O., Mikolajczyk, K.: Evaluation of local detectors and descriptors for fast feature matching. In: Proceedings of the 21st International Conference on Pattern Recognition (ICPR2012), pp. 2681–2684. IEEE, November 2012
14. Mur-Artal, R., Montiel, J.M.M., Tardos, J.D.: ORB-SLAM: a versatile and accurate monocular SLAM system. IEEE Transact. Robot. **31**(5), 1147–1163 (2015)
15. Mur-Artal, R., Tardós, J.D.: Visual-inertial monocular SLAM with map reuse. IEEE Robot. Autom. Lett. **2**(2), 796–803 (2017)
16. Nistér, D., Naroditsky, O., Bergen, J.: Visual odometry. In: Proceedings of the 2004 IEEE Computer Society Conference on Computer Vision and Pattern Recognition 2004, CVPR 2004. vol. 1, pp. I-I. IEEE, July 2004
17. Nützi, G., Weiss, S., Scaramuzza, D., Siegwart, R.: Fusion of IMU and vision for absolute scale estimation in monocular SLAM. J. Intell. Robot. Syst. **61**(1), 287–299 (2011)
18. Rantakokko, J., et al.: Accurate and reliable soldier and first responder indoor positioning: multisensor systems and cooperative localization. IEEE Wirel. Commun. **18**(2), 10–18 (2011)
19. Ricaurte, P., Chilán, C., Aguilera-Carrasco, C., Vintimilla, B., Sappa, A.: Feature point descriptors: Infrared and visible spectra. Sensors **14**(2), 3690–3701 (2014)
20. Rublee, E., Rabaud, V., Konolige, K., Bradski, G.: ORB: an efficient alternative to SIFT or SURF. In: Proceedings of the 2011 International Conference on Computer Vision, ICCV 2011, pp. 2564–2571. IEEE Computer Society, Washington, DC, USA (2011)
21. Saputra, M.R.U., Markham, A., Trigoni, N.: Visual SLAM and structure from motion in dynamic environments: a survey. ACM Comput. Surv. (CSUR) **51**(2), 37 (2018)
22. Schneider, J., Koch, E.C., Dochnahl, A.: Method of producing a screening smoke with one-way transparency in the infrared spectrum, US Patent 6,484,640, 26 November 2002
23. Schubert, E.F.: White light sources based on wavelength converters. In: Light Emmitting Diodes, 2nd edn., chap. 21, pp. 346–366. Cambridge University Press (2006)

Feature-Based SLAM Algorithm for Small Scale UAV with Nadir View

Danilo Avola[1], Luigi Cinque[1], Alessio Fagioli[1], Gian Luca Foresti[2], Cristiano Massaroni[1], and Daniele Pannone[1(✉)]

[1] Department of Computer Science, Sapienza University,
Via Salaria 113, 00198 Rome, Italy
{avola,cinque,fagioli,massaroni,pannone}@di.uniroma1.it
[2] Department of Mathematics, Computer Science and Physics, University of Udine,
Via Delle Scienze 206, 33100 Udine, Italy
gianluca.foresti@uniud.it

Abstract. Small-scale Unmanned Aerial Vehicles (UAVs) have recently been used in several application areas, including search and rescue operations, precision agriculture, and environmental monitoring. Telemetry data, acquired by GPSs, plays a key role in supporting activities in areas like those just reported. In particular, this data is often used for the real-time computation of UAVs paths and heights, which are basic prerequisites for many tasks. In some cases, however, the GPS sensors can lose their satellite connection, thus making the telemetry data acquisition impossible. This paper presents a feature-based Simultaneous Localisation and Mapping (SLAM) algorithm for small-scale UAVs with nadir view. The proposed algorithm allows to know the travelled route as well as the flight height by using both a calibration step and visual features extracted from the acquired images. Due to the novelty of the proposed algorithm no comparisons with other methods are reported. Anyway, extensive experiments on the recently released UAV Mosaicking and Change Detection (UMCD) dataset have shown the effectiveness and robustness of the proposed algorithm. The latter and the dataset can be used as baseline for future research in this application area.

Keywords: UAVs · SLAM algorithm · Mosaicking · A-KAZE

1 Introduction

Nowadays, robots and small-scale UAVs are used in several fields, such as SAR [1,2], environment monitoring and inspection [3–6] and precision agriculture [7,8] due to their low cost and easiness of deployment. These devices are equipped with different sensors, such as gyroscope, accelerometer, compass, and GPS, thus allowing to know the state of the UAV (e.g., breakdown occurrences, travel speed, etc.) with a very high precision. During the execution of a task, it may happen that the UAV loses the connection with the satellites, thus making it

© Springer Nature Switzerland AG 2019
E. Ricci et al. (Eds.): ICIAP 2019, LNCS 11752, pp. 457–467, 2019.
https://doi.org/10.1007/978-3-030-30645-8_42

impossible to retrieve data such as the flight height, or to use the GPS coordinates to know the overflown route. In robotics and computer vision, the most common approaches to determine both position and orientation of the robot are Simultaneous Localization and Mapping (SLAM) [9] and Visual Odometry (VO) [10–12]. The simplest sensor that can be used in performing SLAM and VO is the RGB camera. There are two main categories of works using a RGB camera: methods using monoscopic cameras [13–18] or methods based on stereo camera [19–21]. The major difference between stereo and monoscopic cameras is that the former allows to feel the distance from objects within the scene, as if it had a third dimension. Human vision is stereoscopic by nature due to the binocular view and to our brain, which is capable of synthesizing an image with stereoscopic depth. It is important to notice that a stereoscopic camera must have at least two sensors to produce a stereoscopic image or video, while the monoscopic camera setup is typically composed by a single camera with a 360° mirror. Whenever the scene-to-stereo camera distance is much larger than the stereo baseline, stereo VO can be degraded to the monocular case, and stereo vision becomes ineffectual [22]. Authors in [11] present the first real-time large-scale VO with a monocular camera based on a feature tracking approach and random sample consensus (RANSAC) for outlier rejection. The new upcoming camera pose is computed through 3D to 2D camera-pose estimation. The work in [16] leverages a monocular VO algorithm for feature points tracking on the world ground plane surrounding the vehicle, rather than a traditional tracking approach applied on the perspective camera image coordinates. Two real-time methods for simultaneous localization and mapping with a freely-moving monocular camera, are proposed by the LSD-SLAM [17] and ORB-SLAM [18] algorithms. In [13], the FAST corners and optical flow are used to perform a motion estimation task and, subsequently, a mapping thread is executed through a depth filter formalized as a Bayesian estimation problem. Other works, such as [14,15], propose a robust framework which makes direct use of the pixel intensity, without exploiting a feature extraction step.

In this paper, a feature-based SLAM algorithm for small-scale UAVs with a nadir view is proposed. In detail, a first calibration step is performed to know the ratio between pixels/meters and flight height. Then, during flights, keypoints extracted from the video stream are exploited to know if the flight height changed, while the center of mass of the frames are used for route estimation. Exhaustive experiments performed on the recently released UMCD dataset highlight the robustness and the reliability of the proposed approach. To the best of our knowledge, there are no works in literature that estimates both the trajectory and the flight height of a UAV. Hence, no comparisons with other SLAM algorithm are provided, and the obtained results are meant to be considered as a baseline for future works.

The remainder of the paper is structured as follows. In Sect. 2, the proposed method is described in detail. In Sect. 3, the performed experiments and the obtained results are discussed. Finally, Sect. 4 concludes the paper.

2   Proposed Method

The proposed method main idea is to exploit keypoint matching between two consecutive video frames, received from the UAV, in order to determine the flight height, while the frames center of mass is used to determine the overflown route. A necessary condition for the algorithm correctness, is that features must always be matched between frames, otherwise it is not possible to estimate the correct flight height.

2.1   System Calibration

In order to find the relation between the spatial resolution of the RGB sensor and the flight height, a calibration step is required. To perform this calibration, a marker of known dimensions (e.g., 1×1 m) is placed on the ground and it is then acquired at a known height (e.g., 10 m), through the UAV sensors. During this process, the GPS sensor of the UAV is used to know the exact height. Markers have been chosen for this step due to their robustness and easiness of recognition within the observed environment [23,24]. With this procedure, it is possible to compute the pixels/meters ratio needed to initialize the system. In Fig. 1, the marker detected during the calibration step is depicted.

Fig. 1. System calibration step example. By knowing both the UAV height and the marker size, it is possible to estimate the pixels/meters ratio which is a requirement for the algorithm.

In case information about the camera focal length f is not available, this calibration step also allows its estimation. Let us consider the height h of the UAV during the calibration step, the marker to have a real size of w meters and a pixel size at height h of p pixels. Then, f can be computed as follows:

$$f = \frac{(h \times p)}{w} \tag{1}$$

By knowing how to compute the focal length, the height estimation step can be performed with any kind of sensor, as shown in the next Section.

2.2 Flight Height Estimation

For the flight height estimation, keypoints extracted from the video stream frames are used. The A-KAZE [25,26] feature extractor is adopted due to its performance, allowing for a faster feature extraction with respect to SIFT, SURF, and ORB [27]. In more details, features are extracted and matched between two consecutive frames f_{t-1} and f_t, creating two sets of keypoints K_{t-1}, K_t and a set of matches Θ_t. Subsequently, the affine transformation matrix is computed from these matches, and is used to determine the scale changes between keypoints. More thoroughly, if we have an incremental scale change it means that a zoom in operation is performed, so the UAV is lowering the flight height. On the contrary, if we have a decremental scale change it means that a zoom out operation is performed, so the UAV is increasing the flight height. In the flight height estimation, two goals are pursued:

- To filter the identified matches and exclude keypoints belonging to the foreground component (i.e., dynamic elements within the scene) during the drone movement estimation, in order to avoid moving objects negatively influencing the height estimation;
- To estimate all altitude variations.

The first goal is obtained using the set of matches Θ_t, and the homography matrix H_t that maps the coordinates of a keypoint $k \in K_{t-1}$ into the coordinates of a keypoint $\hat{k} \in K_t$. The matrix H_t is computed applying the RANdom SAmple Consensus (RANSAC) algorithm [28] on the matches contained in Θ_t. The reprojection error in H_t can be minimized through the use of the Levenberg-Marquardt optimization [29]. To find the keypoints belonging to the moving objects present in the scene, the following check is performed for each match $(k, \hat{k}) \in \Theta_t$:

$$\gamma = \begin{cases} 1 \text{ if } \sqrt{(k - \hat{k})^2} - \sqrt{(k - (Hk))^2} \geq \rho \\ 0 \text{ otherwise.} \end{cases} \quad (2)$$

where ρ is a tolerance applied on the difference between the estimated distance obtained by homography and the estimated distance obtained by Θ_t. If ρ has a low value, then a large number of keypoints found in the background result as static and, consequently, many false positives can occur for the background keypoint estimation. Instead, if ρ has a high value, the estimation of the keypoint movements is less restrictive, but a large number of false negatives can occur. According to [30], the value of ρ has been fixed to 2.0. In more details, if $\gamma = 0$, then the keypoint $\hat{k}$ is a background keypoint, otherwise $\hat{k}$ is a foreground keypoint. Finally, all background keypoint matches are used to compose a new filtered set of matches called $\hat{\Theta}_t$.

In order to achieve the second goal, an affine transformation matrix A is computed. Given three pairs of matches (k_a, k_b), (k_c, k_d), and $(k_e, k_f) \in \hat{\Theta}_t$ with $k_a, k_c, k_e \in K_{t-1}$ and $k_b, k_d, k_f \in K_t$, the A matrix can be calculated as follows:

$$A = \begin{bmatrix} \lambda_x & 0 & \tau_x \\ 0 & \lambda_y & \tau_y \\ 0 & 0 & 1 \end{bmatrix} = \begin{bmatrix} x_{k_b} & x_{k_d} & x_{k_f} \\ y_{k_b} & y_{k_d} & y_{k_f} \end{bmatrix} \begin{bmatrix} x_{k_a} & x_{k_c} & x_{k_e} \\ y_{k_a} & y_{k_c} & y_{k_e} \\ 1 & 1 & 1 \end{bmatrix}^{-1} \tag{3}$$

The translations on the x and y axes are indicated by the τ_x and τ_y, respectively. Drone altitude variations are estimated using the λ_x and λ_y, representing the scale variation on the x and y axes. Once λ_x, λ_y values are computed, we can multiply them by the original pixels/meters ratio to determine the UAV flight height variation. Notice that, altitude changes cause zoom-in (or zoom-out) operations in the frames acquired by the drone and, in those cases, we obtain $\lambda_x = \lambda_y$. Also recall that in order to know the altitude variation, there must always be a match between two consecutive frames, so that it is possible to estimate the transformation matrix and the λ_x, λ_y values. Otherwise, it is unfeasible to correctly estimate the variation.

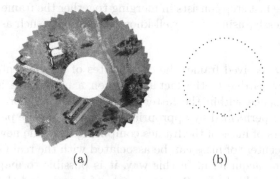

(a)   (b)

Fig. 2. Example of route estimated with the proposed method. In 2(a), the mosaic of the overflown area is shown, while in 2(b) the route estimates through frames center of mass is depicted.

By using Eq. 1, it is possible to estimate the flight height h' through the triangle similarity:

$$w' = \lambda \times w \tag{4}$$

$$h' = \frac{w' \times f}{p} \tag{5}$$

where λ can be either λ_x or λ_y.

2.3   Route Estimation

Concerning the UAV route estimation, centers of mass from the received video stream frames are used. In order to know where the new center of mass must be positioned with respect to the others, a reference coordinate system must be used. In the proposed method, we use the mosaic of the area overflown by the UAV as reference for the centers of mass. By following the steps shown in [31], a mosaic is built incrementally and in real-time in the following way:

1. Frame Correction: In this step, the radial and tangent distortions are removed (if needed) from the received frame. To perform this step, a matrix containing the calibration values of the camera is required, and it is computed by using well-known methods [32];
2. Feature Extraction and Matching: In this step, keypoints are extracted from the current video frame and the partial mosaic is built up to the previous algorithm iteration. Then, features are matched together and a similarity transformation matrix is generated;
3. Frame Transformation: The similarity transformation matrix generated at the previous step is used to scale, rotate, and translate the received frame in order to align it with the partial mosaic;
4. Stitching: The last step consists in merging together the frame and the partial mosaic seamlessly, using some well-known techniques such as the multiband blending [33].

For each new received frame, the coordinates of all the centers of mass are recomputed. This is due to the fact that when a new frame is added to the partial mosaic, space within the latter must be allocated for the new frame. This operation is performed by appropriately translating the partial mosaic, as well as the centers of mass of the frames composing it, in the new mosaic image. Notice that the centers of mass can be associated with the real GPS coordinates of the UAV frame acquisition. In this way, it is possible to map the estimated route to the real world. In Fig. 2, an example of mosaic and the corresponding estimated route is shown. To summarize, Algorithm 1 shows all the performed steps for both route and flight height estimation.

3   Experiments

In this section, the results obtained in the performed experiments are reported.

3.1   Dataset

In our experiments, the recently released UMCD dataset [34] is used. The latter provides 50 geo-referenced aerial videos that can be used for mosaicking and change detection tasks at very low altitudes. The authors provide, together with the videos and the GPS coordinates, a basic mosaicking algorithm that has been used in our experiments as ground truth. In addition to the dataset, we have acquired 12 new videos. The latter have been acquired by following the same protocol of the used dataset, in order to have homogeneous testing data. Moreover, the same drone used for building the UMCD dataset, i.e., the DJI Phantom 3, has been used. Since within the dataset there are no videos with a ground marker, the calibration step for those videos has been performed by using

Algorithm 1. Steps performed by the proposed algorithm to estimate UAV route and flight height.

Require: Video stream sent by UAV
Ensure: Estimated flight height and route overflown by the UAV
1: Estimate the pixels/meters ratio through calibration step
2: **while** UAV sends video data or it is impossible to match features **do**
3:     Extract features from two consecutive frames
4:     Match the features to create both the Θ_t set and A matrix
5:     Compare A matrix with the matrix generated at the previous iteration in order to determine the scale changes
6:     Compute the center of mass for the received frame.
7:     Use A matrix to align the new received frame with the mosaic generated up to the current iteration
8:     Translate the centers of mass of the frames in the correct position by using the A matrix
9:     Stitch the new frame to the mosaic generated up to the current iteration
10: **end while**

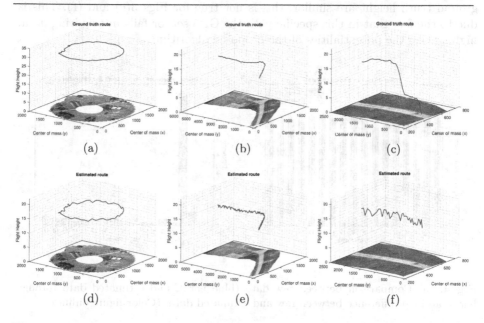

Fig. 3. Example of paths used for testing the proposed method. In 3(a), (b) and (c), the ground truth data is reported, while in 3(d), (e) and (f) the estimated data is shown. In the x and y axes the centers of mass coordinates are represented, while in the z axis the flight height is shown.

the change detection procedure. This is possible due to the fact that the authors also provide the real size of the objects, in conjunction with the videos. Finally, through the given GPS file, it is possible to know the UAV flight height when in proximity of an object, allowing to compute the pixels/meters ratio needed for the calibration.

3.2   Qualitative Results

For each test, a mosaic of the overflown area has been built to extract the center of mass of each frame, and to estimate the flight route. Since the proposed method relies on the mosaicking algorithm, whenever the mosaic generation failed only a partial route and flight height estimation was given as a result. In Fig. 3, some experimental results are shown. The Figs. 3(a), (b) and (c) show the ground truth for both flight height and route, while the Figs. 3(d), (e) and (f) present the results obtained with the proposed method. In detail, Figs. 3(a) and (d) depict the route of an area of our own acquisitions, while the other figures show two paths provided in the UMCD dataset. As presumed, the results obtained with the proposed algorithm reflect, approximately, the ground truth data. Despite the estimated route and the ground truth route being almost similar, we have more variations on the estimated flight height. This is due to the features matching problem being sensible to outliers, as well as features mismatches. While for Figs. 3(a), (d) and (b), (e) the estimated height and the ground truth height are similar, this is not true for Figs. 3(c) and (f). This is due to the fact that in this specific path the GPS sensor fails in acquiring data, highlighting the potentialities of the proposed algorithm.

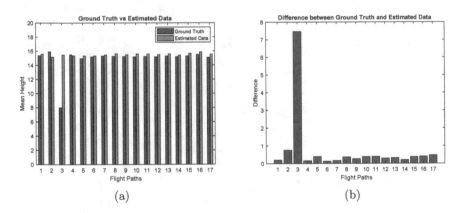

Fig. 4. (a) Comparison between raw data (blue bars), and estimated data (orange bars), and (b) difference between raw and estimated data. (Color figure online)

3.3   Quantitative Results

In Fig. 4, the ground truth and estimated data, together with their difference, is reported. As shown in both Figs. 4(a) and (b), the results obtained with the proposed method are very close to the raw data obtained through the sensors. From Fig. 4(a) it is possible to notice that, in average, the estimated data is slightly overestimated with respect to the ground truth. An exception regards the third flight path, which corresponds to the example shown in Fig. 3(c). In this case, we have a higher distance since the UAV lost the GPS signal during the experiments.

Concerning the execution time, the proposed method strongly depends on the mosaicking algorithm since both keypoints and centers of mass are computed during the process. This means that using new generation hardware and optimizing the algorithm for multicore CPUs or GPUs allows to reach real-time performances.

4   Conclusion

In this paper, a feature-based SLAM algorithm for small-scale UAV with a nadir view is presented. The proposed method exploits a state-of-the-art mosaicking algorithm to estimate the UAV flight route, while image features in conjunction with an affine transformation are used to estimate the flight height. Experimental results are performed on our aerial acquisitions and on the recently released UMCD dataset, showing the effectiveness of the proposed approach.

Acknowledgement. This work was supported in part by the MIUR under grant "Departments of Excellence 2018-2022" of the Department of Computer Science of Sapienza University.

References

1. Qi, J., et al.: Search and rescue rotary-wing uav and its application to the lushan ms 7.0 earthquake. J. Field Robot. **33**(3), 290–321 (2016)
2. Ho, Y.-H., Chen, Y.-R., Chen, L.-J.: Krypto: assisting search and rescue operations using wi-fi signal with UAV. In: Proceedings of the First Workshop on Micro Aerial Vehicle Networks, Systems, and Applications for Civilian Use, DroNet 2015, pp. 3–8. ACM, New York (2015)
3. Meng, X., Wang, W., Leong, B.: SkyStitch: a cooperative multi-UAV-based real-time video surveillance system with stitching. In: Proceedings of the 23rd ACM International Conference on Multimedia, MM 2015, pp. 261–270. ACM, New York (2015)
4. Avola, D., Foresti, G.L., Martinel, N., Micheloni, C., Pannone, D., Piciarelli, C.: Aerial video surveillance system for small-scale UAV environment monitoring. In: 2017 14th IEEE International Conference on Advanced Video and Signal Based Surveillance (AVSS), pp. 1–6 (2017)
5. Avola, D., Cinque, L., Foresti, G.L., Marini, M.R., Pannone, D.: A rover-based system for searching encrypted targets in unknown environments. In: Proceedings of the 7th International Conference on Pattern Recognition Applications and Methods - Volume 1: ICPRAM, INSTICC, pp. 254–261. SciTePress (2018)
6. Piciarelli, C., Avola, D., Pannone, D., Foresti, G.L.: A vision-based system for internal pipeline inspection. IEEE Transact. Industr. Inf. **15**(6), 3289–3299 (2019)
7. Faiçal, B.S., et al.: An adaptive approach for UAV-based pesticide spraying in dynamic environments. Comput. Electron. Agric. **138**, 210–223 (2017)
8. Tokekar, P., Hook, J.V., Mulla, D., Isler, V.: Sensor planning for a symbiotic uav and ugv system for precision agriculture. IEEE Trans. Rob. **32**(6), 1498–1511 (2016)

9. Davison, A.J., Murray, D.W.: Simultaneous localization and map-building using active vision. IEEE Transact. Pattern Anal. Mach. Intell. **24**(7), 865–880 (2002)
10. Aqel, M.O.A., Marhaban, M.H., Saripan, M.I., Ismail, N.B.: Review of visual odometry: types, approaches, challenges, and applications. SpringerPlus **5**(1), 1897 (2016)
11. Nister, D., Naroditsky, O., Bergen, J.: Visual odometry. In: Proceedings of the 2004 IEEE Computer Society Conference on Computer Vision and Pattern Recognition 2004, CVPR 2004, vol. 1, pp. I-652–I-659, June 2004
12. Shan, M., et al.: A brief survey of visual odometry for micro aerial vehicles. In: 42nd Annual Conference of the IEEE Industrial Electronics Society 2016, IECON 2016, pp. 6049–6054 (2016)
13. Faessler, M., Fontana, F., Forster, C., Mueggler, E., Pizzoli, M., Scaramuzza, D.: Autonomous, vision-based flight and live dense 3D mapping with a quadrotor micro aerial vehicle. J. Field Robot. **33**(4), 431–450 (2016)
14. Bloesch, M., Omari, S., Hutter, M., Siegwart, R.: Robust visual inertial odometry using a direct EKF-based approach. In: 2015 IEEE/RSJ International Conference on Intelligent Robots and Systems (IROS), pp. 298–304, September 2015
15. Forster, C., Pizzoli, M., Scaramuzza, D.: SVO: fast semi-direct monocular visual odometry. In: 2014 IEEE International Conference on Robotics and Automation (ICRA), pp. 15–22, May 2014
16. Hamme, D.V., Goeman, W., Veelaert, P., Philips, W.: Robust monocular visual odometry for road vehicles using uncertain perspective projection. EURASIP J. Image Video Process. **1**, 2015 (2015)
17. Engel, J., Schöps, T., Cremers, D.: LSD-SLAM: large-scale direct monocular SLAM. In: Fleet, D., Pajdla, T., Schiele, B., Tuytelaars, T. (eds.) ECCV 2014. LNCS, vol. 8690, pp. 834–849. Springer, Cham (2014). https://doi.org/10.1007/978-3-319-10605-2_54
18. Mur-Artal, R., Montiel, J.M.M., Tardós, J.D.: ORB-Slam: a versatile and accurate monocular slam system. IEEE Transact. Robot. **31**(5), 1147–1163 (2015)
19. Leutenegger, S., Lynen, S., Bosse, M., Siegwart, R., Furgale, P.: Keyframe-based visual-inertial odometry using nonlinear optimization. Int. J. Robot. Res. **34**(3), 314–334 (2015)
20. Witt, J., Weltin, U.: Robust stereo visual odometry using iterative closest multiple lines. In: 2013 IEEE/RSJ International Conference on Intelligent Robots and Systems, pp. 4164–4171, November 2013
21. Heng, L., Choi, B.: Semi-direct visual odometry for a fisheye-stereo camera. In: 2016 IEEE/RSJ International Conference on Intelligent Robots and Systems (IROS), pp. 4077–4084, October 2016
22. Scaramuzza, D., Fraundorfer, F.: Visual odometry [tutorial]. IEEE Robot. Autom. Mag. **18**(4), 80–92 (2011)
23. Avola, D., Cinque, L., Foresti, G.L., Mercuri, C., Pannone, D.: A practical framework for the development of augmented reality applications by using ArUco markers. In: Proceedings of the 5th International Conference on Pattern Recognition Applications and Methods, pp. 645–654 (2016)
24. Bergamasco, F., Albarelli, A., Cosmo, L., Rodolà, E., Torsello, A.: An accurate and robust artificial marker based on cyclic codes. IEEE Transact. Pattern Anal. Mach. Intell. **38**(12), 2359–2373 (2016)
25. Alcantarilla, P.F., Nuevo, J., Bartoli, A.: Fast explicit diffusion for accelerated features in nonlinear scale spaces. In: British Machine Vision Conference (BMVC) (2013)

26. Avola, D., Cinque, L., Foresti, G.L., Martinel, N., Pannone, D., Piciarelli, C.: Low-level feature detectors and descriptors for smart image and video analysis: a comparative study. In: Kwaśnicka, H., Jain, L.C. (eds.) Bridging the Semantic Gap in Image and Video Analysis. ISRL, vol. 145, pp. 7–29. Springer, Cham (2018). https://doi.org/10.1007/978-3-319-73891-8_2

27. Avola, D., Cinque, L., Foresti, G.L., Massaroni, C., Pannone, D.: A keypoint-based method for background modeling and foreground detection using a PTZ camera. Pattern Recogn. Lett. **96**, 96–105 (2017)

28. Fischler, M.A., Bolles, R.C.: Random sample consensus: a paradigm for model fitting with applications to image analysis and automated cartography. Commun. ACM **24**(6), 381–395 (1981)

29. Marquardt and Donald: An algorithm for least-squares estimation of nonlinear parameters. SIAM J. Appl. Math. **11**(2), 431–441 (1963)

30. Avola, D., Bernardi, M., Cinque, L., Foresti, G.L., Massaroni, C.: Combining keypoint clustering and neural background subtraction for real-time moving object detection by PTZ cameras. In: Proceedings of the 7th International Conference on Pattern Recognition Applications and Methods - Volume 1: ICPRAM, INSTICC, pp. 638–645. SciTePress (2018)

31. Avola, D., Foresti, G.L., Martinel, N., Micheloni, C., Pannone, D., Piciarelli, C.: Real-time incremental and geo-referenced mosaicking by small-scale UAVs. In: Battiato, S., Gallo, G., Schettini, R., Stanco, F. (eds.) ICIAP 2017. LNCS, vol. 10484, pp. 694–705. Springer, Cham (2017). https://doi.org/10.1007/978-3-319-68560-1_62

32. Zhang, Z.: A flexible new technique for camera calibration. IEEE Transact. Pattern Anal. Mach. Intell. **22**(11), 1330–1334 (2000)

33. Brown, M., Lowe, D.G.: Automatic panoramic image stitching using invariant features. Int. J. Comput. Vis. **74**(1), 59–73 (2007)

34. Avola, D., Cinque, L., Foresti, G.L., Martinel, N., Pannone, D., Piciarelli, C.: A UAV video dataset for mosaicking and change detection from low-altitude flights. IEEE Transact. Syst. Man Cybern. Syst. **PP**(99), 1–11 (2018)

Vision Based Driver Smoking Behavior Detection Using Surveillance Camera Images

Yusuf Artan[✉], Burak Balcı, Alperen Elihoş, and Bensu Alkan

Video Analysis Group, Havelsan Incorporation, Ankara, Turkey
{yartan,bbalci,aelihos,balkan}@havelsan.com.tr

Abstract. Intelligent traffic enforcement has gained immense traction in the computer vision community. Recently, automated violation enforcement methods have been proposed towards seat belt violation, cell phone violation and occupancy violation detection tasks. Smoking while driving is another common violation type that has been prohibited in many countries. Smoking inspections are typically performed manually by the road side officers. In this study, we propose an automated approach towards driver smoking behavior detection using near infrared (NIR) surveillance camera images. During the puff, cigarette tip reaches 800–900 °C creating a hot-spot on the NIR image. Proposed method aims to detect these hot-spots around the drivers' head region. First, we utilize a deep learning based object detection technique to localize the front windshield and driver head region, sequentially. Next, we perform a dual window (local) anomaly detector on the localized region to determine white hot-spot, hence, the driver smoking behavior. We have collected 1472 real world NIR images to evaluate the performance of the proposed approach. Proposed method achieved an overall accuracy rate of % 84 and sensitivity rate of % 70 on the test set.

Keywords: Traffic enforcement · Near infrared (NIR) image · Single shot multi-box detector (SSD) · Anomaly detection

1 Introduction

In recent years, we have seen a surge in the applications of computer vision and machine learning towards transportation industry including traffic enforcement, driving assistive systems and autonomous driving [1, 2]. Traffic enforcement on highways and roads is mostly performed manually by the road side police officer. However, this is known to be laborious and ineffective due to the lack of enough police personnel to perform the inspection. In recent years, various camera based automated enforcement solutions have been proposed by researchers [3–7]. Due to their robustness and high success rates in their analysis, these solutions have been gaining popularity in many countries. Typical camera based enforcement applications include red light violation, vehicle occupancy detection, seat belt violation detection, cell phone usage violation detection and speed violation detection to name a few [3–7]. As shown in an earlier study [8], drivers smoking habits exposes passengers including children to second hand smoke. Therefore, cigarette usage while driving has already been banned in several

© Springer Nature Switzerland AG 2019
E. Ricci et al. (Eds.): ICIAP 2019, LNCS 11752, pp. 468–476, 2019.
https://doi.org/10.1007/978-3-030-30645-8_43

countries such as Canada, Costa Rica. Considering these prohibitions and foresights, a novel automated driver smoke monitoring method is introduced in this study. Temperature distribution of a cigarette typically varies between 800–900 °C during a puff, and around 700–800 °C during the natural smolders between the puffs [9]. Tip of the cigarette can be considered as a hot-spot generator. As shown in an earlier study [10], NIR cameras offer an ideal solution for hot-spot detection in terms of the cost and response timings. Therefore, in this study, we propose an automated method for driver smoking detection in the vehicle using NIR camera images.

Earlier studies on this subject have presented several imaging/non-imaging based solutions toward cigarette usage detection [11–15] inside vehicles. In contrast to existing human-based systems or integrated systems within the vehicle, camera based monitoring systems allow authorities to obtain a visual evidence. Proposed method applies image processing and deep learning techniques on NIR images that are collected using cameras, placed on fixed camera carrier platforms. In recent years, deep learning algorithms have shown to be the most effective methods producing state-of-the-art results on many challenging application areas such as object detection, image recognition, and speech processing [16–18]. As shown in our experiments, proposed method achieves high detection rates on real world images independent of day-time/night-time imaging.

Figure 1 shows the overall outline of the approach proposed in this study. Upon the capture of a vehicle image, we detect the windshield and driver head region sequentially within the incoming vehicle image using a deep learning based object detector. Next, we check the existence of a small hot-spot region using a dual window (local) anomaly detection technique. High confidence anomaly blobs indicate the presence of a smoking behavior. In Sect. 2, we present the details of our methodology for driver smoke detection from camera images. In Sect. 3, we report our experiments in more details. Finally, Sect. 4 presents our conclusions and future research directions.

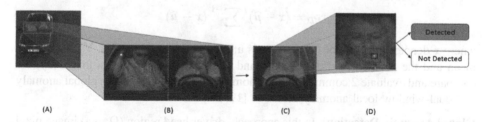

Fig. 1. Overview of the proposed method. Part (A) shows the original NIR camera surveillance image. Part (B) shows the output of windshield detector. Part (C) is the driver head localization on the right half of the windshield region. Part (D) presents the anomaly detector result (shown in red). (Color figure online)

2 Methodology

In this section, we describe the stages of the proposed methods in more detail.

2.1   Front Windshield Region Detection

The first step, in our analysis, is the localization of the windshield region of the vehicle. This would allow us to ignore the rest of the image since it is irrelevant to smoking behavior analysis. Similar to earlier studies [3, 7], we utilize a deep learning based object detection technique, namely Single Shot Detector (SSD) in detecting the front windshield of the vehicle [16]. We used a pre-trained SSD300 model that utilizes VGG16 in its base architecture [17]. We have fine-tuned this SSD model to detect windshields using an annotated training dataset. Manual annotation is performed by selecting the windshield region (blue rectangle) in the raw NIR image as shown in Fig. 1(A).

2.2   Driver Head Region Detection

After localizing the windshield region of a vehicle within the raw NIR image, we need to determine the drivers' head region on the right side of the windshield region, see Fig. 1(B). We followed a similar approach to windshield region detection and built an SSD based head detector model. So, we have again fine-tuned a pre-trained SSD model using an annotated training dataset. Annotation is performed by selecting the driver head region in the right half of the front windshield as shown in Fig. 1(C).

2.3   Anomaly Detection

Due to the high temperature of a burning cigarette, the tip of cigarette creates a hot-spot on the NIR image. Therefore, once the drivers' head region is localized, we search for an anomalous white blob that is significantly distinct from the background. In our analysis, we utilized mahalanobis distance (r_{MD}) as a metric to quantify this distinction [19]. The equation used for calculating r_{MD} is shown in Eq. (1).

$$r_{MD} = (x - \hat{\mu})^T \sum\nolimits^{-1} (x - \hat{\mu}) \tag{1}$$

where x denotes the pixel of interest that is under consideration, and μ, $\sum$ denotes the mean and the covariance of the background Gaussian distribution. In this study, we compare and evaluate 2 commonly used anomaly detection techniques; global anomaly and dual-window local anomaly detection [19, 20].

<u>Global Anomaly Detection:</u> In this approach, driver head region (Ω_{global}) image pixel intensities, Fig. 1(D), are assumed to form a unimodal Gaussian distribution with $\hat{\mu} = \mu_{global}$ and $\sum = \sum_{global}$, Eq. (2), as shown in Fig. 2,

$$\mu_{global} = \frac{1}{N_{global}} \sum_{i \in \Omega_{global}} x_i$$

$$\sum\nolimits_{global} = \frac{1}{N_{global} - 1} \sum\nolimits_{i \in \Omega_{global}} (x_i - \mu_{global}) (x_i - \mu_{global})^T \tag{2}$$

We compute r_{MD} value for each pixel, x, over the driver head region and perform thresholding (threshold level is learnt in the training stage as described in Sect. 3.2) operation on the anomaly map. Finally, we declare the highest anomaly score location as the cigarette location.

Dual Window (Local) Anomaly Detection: In this approach, we compute the distinctness of a target pixel locally using a local background region (Ω_{local}) while leaving a guard band in between as shown in Fig. 2. For a target pixel, x corresponds to the mean intensity value of the pixel group (black inner rectangle) whose center is the pixel under consideration, and $\widehat{\mu} = \mu_{local}$ represents the mean of the N_1 (local background) region, and $\sum = \sum_{local}$ is the variance of the pixel values of the N_1 region.

$$\mu_{local} = \frac{1}{N_{local}} \sum_{i \in \Omega_{local}} x_i$$

$$\sum_{local} = \frac{1}{N_{local} - 1} \sum_{i \in \Omega_{local}} (x_i - \mu_{local})(x_i - \mu_{local})^T \quad (3)$$

Similar to global anomaly case, we compute r_{MD} value for each pixel over the driver head region and perform thresholding on the anomaly map. Note that the threshold level is learnt in the training stage as explained in experiments. If there exists no blob (connected pixels) for the given threshold level, it indicates that there is no cigarette usage. Otherwise, we pick one location with the highest anomaly score as the cigarette location.

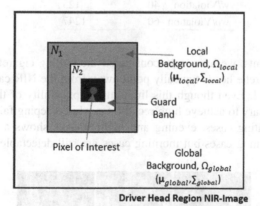

Driver Head Region NIR-Image

Fig. 2. Overview of the global anomaly and local dual-window anomaly detection methods, see [19] for details. In local anomaly detection, N_1 denotes local background region, N_2 denotes guard band and black rectangle is the pixel of interest.

3 Experiments

3.1 Image Acquisition

In this study, we utilized a 3MP (2048 × 1536) NIR camera that is placed on a gantry approximately 4.5 m above the ground. Video based triggering is used during the image acquisition. Figure 3 demonstrates several sample images acquired in our study. We collected and annotated 1472 images to be used in smoking behavior detection task. Note that, we used a separate dataset for windshield and driver head detection tasks. Table 1 presents our experimental data breakout in detail. Note that training data is only used to learn the scalar threshold level for anomaly detection algorithms.

Fig. 3. Raw sample NIR images from driver smoking behavior dataset.

Table 1. Table shows the number of images used in this study. Data breakout with (without) violation is given below.

No. images	Training data	Test data
w/Violation	40	125
wo/Violation	60	1247

In the experiments, we have only considered the puffing cigarette detection since the smoldering cigarette heads typically point away from the NIR camera as shown in the 1st row in Fig. 4. Even though this limits the applicability of the proposed algorithm, this is necessary to achieve high recall rates while keeping false alarm rate low. In terms of the puffing cases, evening and night images shows a stronger cigarette signal than the morning cases but morning cases are still detectable.

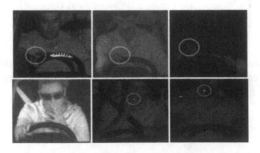

Fig. 4. First row shows the smoldering cigarette cases that are not considered in this study. 2nd row shows puffing cigarettes at morning (left), early evening (middle) and night cases (right).

3.2 Results

We have conducted our experiments using a 1372 NIR test image set, see Table 1, collected on a highway for a 24-hour period in Ankara, Turkey. Note that the class imbalance in the test set reflects the real world conditions. In terms of training the SSD models for windshield and driver head region, we utilized a separate training dataset consisting of 400 NIR images. We have fine-tuned a pre-trained SSD model using these 400 NIR images as mentioned in Sect. 2. In the front windshield detection and head detection tasks, we considered the detection as correct if the overlap between detector output and ground truth is greater than % 70. On the NIR test images, the windshield detection model is achieved an overall accuracy of % 98 on the test images. Similarly, driver head detection model generated an overall accuracy of % 99 on the windshield detector output images. If the driver cannot be detected in the windshield area then we ran the anomaly detector on the entire driver region which, however, increases run-time duration.

In the training stage, using 100 images listed in Table 1, we determined threshold levels for anomaly detection methods by counting the number of true positive versus the number false positives at various threshold levels. Figure 5 illustrates the mean value of the number of true positives (TPs) and false positives (FPs) achieved at different threshold levels. For both anomaly algorithms, we set the threshold level that achieves an average false positive rate of 0.05. This threshold level is selected to emulate the real world conditions.

During the testing stage, we evaluated the performance of the proposed methods using various quantitative metrics such as accuracy, sensitivity and specificity. Moreover, we compared the performance of the proposed approach to still image based action recognition methods based on locally aggregated descriptors (such as BoF (bag of features), VLAD (vector of locally aggregated descriptors)) and deep feature extraction techniques [6, 12, 17]. For locally aggregated descriptors, we extracted features from 16×16 pixel patches on regular grids (every 2 pixels) at 3 scales. We only extracted 128-D SIFT descriptors for these image patches. For all descriptors (i.e., BoF, VLAD), we used Gaussian mixture models (GMM) with K = 256 clusters to compute the descriptors. The GMM's are trained using the maximum likelihood (ML) criterion and a standard expectation maximization (EM) algorithm. For local descriptors, we have also applied the power and L_2 normalization to descriptors to improve the classification performance. In the case of deep feature extraction, we utilized a pre-trained VGG16 model to extract feature vectors, specifically we extracted the 1×4096 feature vector from 'fc2' layer output to represent the image. Once the features are extracted (for positive and negative training images) using one of the local aggregation methods presented above, we train a linear 2-class SVM classifier to perform the classification task.

Table 2 presents the performance comparison of various methods in cigarette usage detection task. As shown in Table 2, local anomaly detector significantly outperforms the global anomaly detector as well as other methods. To analyze the effect of the window size on the cigarette detection performance, we considered various dual window sizes in our analysis ($N_{inner} = 3 - 7$ pixels in diameter). In terms of local anomaly detection performances, we notice similar performance levels for accuracy and specificity but sensitivity levels.

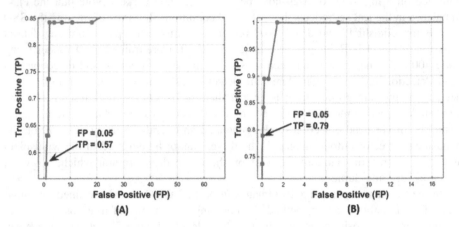

Fig. 5. Mean value of the number of True Positive and number of false positives for various threshold levels. Threshold levels that yield FP = 0.05 are selected for global anomaly (A) and local anomaly (B) method.

We notice high accuracy and specificity rates but relatively low sensitivity rates. This is due to cases with faint hot-spots in NIR image. Moreover, glowing objects such as glass, jewelry and watch in the drivers' head region and excessive amount of light and reflection on the drivers' face generate false alarms, hence, negatively impacting the performance of the proposed method. Local anomaly detector output for several detected head region images under various illumination conditions are presented in the Fig. 6.

Table 2. Performance comparison of anomaly detector on test data using sensitivity, specificity and accuracy metrics.

Method\Metric		Accuracy	Sensitivity	Specificity
BOF [12]		0.697	0.225	0.741
VLAD [6]		0.801	0.595	0.820
VGG-16 [17]		0.779	0.552	0.699
Global anomaly		0.697	0.719	0,695
Local anomaly	$N_{inner} = 3$ $N_{outer} = 11$ $N_{Guard} = 9$	**0.841**	**0.696**	**0,856**
	$N_{inner} = 5$ $N_{outer} = 13$ $N_{Guard} = 11$	0.860	0.466	0,897
	$N_{inner} = 7$ $N_{outer} = 15$ $N_{Guard} = 13$	0,871	0,305	0,926

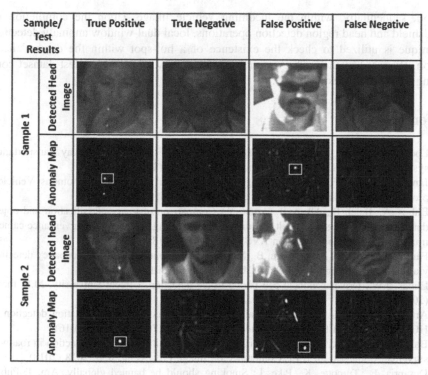

Sample/ Test Results		True Positive	True Negative	False Positive	False Negative
Sample 1	Detected Head Image				
	Anomaly Map				
Sample 2	Detected head Image				
	Anomaly Map				

Fig. 6. A visual illustration of anomaly detector output for 2 sample images for each result category. Points covered by rectangle shows the detected cigarette use in the anomaly map of driver head images.

The computation time of proposed methods are analyzed using a computer with Nvidia GeForce GTX 780 Ti GPU card, 16 GB RAM, Intel Core i7 processor. SSD based windshield and drivers' head region detection tasks are analyzed on GPU. Anomaly detection runs on the CPU. SSD-300 model performs windshield detection and driver head region detection at 60 ms. Global anomaly stages takes approximately 40 ms and local dual window anomaly detection takes approximately 500 ms on average as presented in Table 3.

Table 3. Run time analysis of proposed methods.

	Global anomaly	Local anomaly
Run time (sec)	0,04	0,50

4 Conclusion

In this study, we proposed a novel method for driver smoking behavior detection in roadways using NIR surveillance camera images. Proposed method utilized deep learning based SSD object detector to localize the front windshield and driver head region, sequentially, within the incoming vehicle image. Upon the completion of windshield and head region detection operations, local dual-window anomaly detection technique is utilized to check the existence of a hot-spot within the drivers' head region. Proposed method achieves an overall accuracy of 84% for a test dataset consisting of 1372 images (Table 2).

References

1. Loce, R.P., Bernal, E.A., Wu, W., Bala, R.: Computer vision in roadway transportation systems: a survey. J. Electron. Imaging 22(4), 041121 (2013)
2. Janai, J., Guney, F., Behl, A., Geiger, A.: Computer vision in Autonomous Vehicles: problems, datasets and state-of-the-art, arXiv: 1704.05519 (2017)
3. Elihos, A., Balci, B., Alkan, B., Artan, Y.: Comparison of image classification and object detection for passenger seat belt violation detection using NIR & RGB surveillance camera images. In: IEEE Conference on AVSS Workshop (2018)
4. Fan, Z., Islam, A.S., Paul, P., Xu, B., Mestha, L.K.: Front seat vehicle occupancy detection via seat pattern recognition, USPTO: US8611608B2 (2013)
5. Elings, J.W.: Driver handheld cell phone usage detection. Utrecht University, M.S. thesis (2018)
6. Artan, Y., Bulan, O., Loce, R.P., Paul, P.: Passenger compartment violation detection in HOV/HOT lanes. IEEE Transact. Intell. Transp. Syst. 17(2), 395–405 (2016)
7. Balci, B., Elihos, A., Alkan, B., Artan, Y.: Front seat child occupancy detection in roadway surveillance images. In: IEEE Conference on Image Processing, ICIP 2018 (2018)
8. Desapria, E., Turcotte, K., Pike, I.: Smoking should be banned globally. Am. J. Public Health 99(7), 1158–1159 (2009)
9. Baker, R.A.: Temperature Distribution inside a burning cigarette. Nature 247, 405–406 (1974)
10. Maoult, Y.L., Sentenac, T., Orteu, J.-J., Arcens, J.-P.: Fire detection-a new approach based on a low cost CD camera in the near infrared. Process Safety Environ. Prot. Elsevier 85(3), 193–206 (2007)
11. Yang, M., Ji, S., Xu, W., Wang, J., Lv, F., Yu, K.: Detecting human actions in surveillance videos. In: TREC Video Retrieval Evaluation Workshop (2009)
12. Delaitre, V., Laptev, I., Sivic, J.: Recognizing human actions in still images: a study of bag-of-features and part-based representations. In: Proceedings of the 21st British Machine Vision Conference (BMVC) (2010)
13. Jin, C.B., Li, S., Kim, H.: Real-time action detection in video surveillance using sub-action descriptor with multi-CNN, arXiv: 1710.03383 (2016)
14. Bin, L., Zhe, L., Zhenmin, Z., Peng, W.: Detection method suitable for smoking behavior of driver under multiple postures. Chinese Patent Office (CNPTO) No: 105260703 (A) (2015)
15. Zeping, T., Guochang, H., Boshi, T.: Smoking driving reminding device and car. Chinese Patent Office (CNPTO) No: 202806546 (U) (2012)
16. Liu, W., et al.: SSD: Single Shot MultiBox Detector, arXiv 1512.02325 (2015)
17. Simonyan, K., Zisserman, A.: Very deep convolutional networks for large scale image recognition. In: NIPS (2015)
18. Dai, J., Li, Y., He, K., Sun, J.: R-FCN: object detection via region based fully convolutional networks, in arXiv 1605.06409 (2016)
19. Eismann, M.T.: Hyperspectral Remote Sensing, SPIE Press, Ch. 14 (2012)
20. Reed, I.S., Yu, X.: Adaptive multiband CFAR detection of an optical pattern with unknown spectral distribution. IEEE Trans. Acous. Speech Sig. Proc. 38(10), 1760–1770 (1990)

Memory Efficient Deployment of an Optical Flow Algorithm on GPU Using OpenMP

Olfa Haggui[1,2]($\boxtimes$), Claude Tadonki[1], Fatma Sayadi[3], and Bouraoui Ouni[2]

[1] Centre de Recherche en Informatique (CRI), Mines ParisTech-PSL University,
60 boulevard Saint-Michel, 75006 Paris, France
{olfa.haggui,claude.tadonki}@mines-paristech.fr
[2] Networked Objects Control and Communications Systems (NOCCS),
Sousse National School of Engineering, University of Sousse,
BP 264, 4023 Sousse Erriadh, Tunisia
[3] Electronics and Microelectronics Laboratory, Faculty of Sciences,
University of Monastir, 5000 Monastir, Tunisia

Abstract. In this paper, we consider the recent set of OpenMP directives related to GPU deployment and seek an evaluation through the case of an optical flow algorithm. We start by investigating various agnostic transformations that attempt to improve memory efficiency. Our case study is the so-called *Lucas-Kanade* algorithm, which is typically composed of a series of convolution masks (approximation of the derivatives) followed by 2×2 linear systems for the optical flow vectors. Since, we are dealing with a stencil computation for each stage of the algorithm, the overhead of memory accesses together with the impact on parallel scalability are expected to be noticeable, especially with the complexity of the GPU memory system. We compare our OpenMP implementation with an OpenACC one from our previous work, both on a Quadro P5000.

Keywords: Optical flow · Lucas-Kanade · Optimization · GPU · OpenMP

1 Introduction

The use of hybride programming model has gained an increasing attention in recent years, with a special consideration on heterogeneous architectures. In order to take advantage of modern computing resources, scientific application developers need to make significant changes to their implementations. There are many benchmarks and applications in computer vision that are built with OpenMP 4.x and 5.x [1–3], which provide an excellent opportunity to get access to the noticeable computational power of the GPUs through a directive based deployment. However, this programming style generally yields some unnecessary overhead that is inherent to the paradigm, thus the programmer needs to consider this aspect beside its application driven optimizations. The main goal of

© Springer Nature Switzerland AG 2019
E. Ricci et al. (Eds.): ICIAP 2019, LNCS 11752, pp. 477–487, 2019.
https://doi.org/10.1007/978-3-030-30645-8_44

the current investigation is to study how to get a more efficient implementation from a code written by an experienced OpenMP programmer with no specific GPU programming skills. To address the challenges on improving the execution of high-level parallel code in GPU using OpenMP, we chose the Lucas-Kanade optical flow algorithm. So the aim is to derive and evaluate an optimized GPU implementation of the optical flow algorithm using OpenMP and to highlight the main programming techniques that we have considered. Implementation of the Lucas-Kanade algorithm [5] on the graphics processor Unit (GPU) is seriously considered. Regarding the multicore parallelization of the algorithm, the work by [10] for instance describes an updated method in order to speed up the objects movement between frames in a video sequence using OpenMP. Another multi-core parallelization is proposed in [11]. Pal, Biemann and Baumgartner [12] discuss how the velocity of vehicles can be estimated using optical flow implementation parallelized with OpenMP. Moreover, another hybrid model mitigate the bottleneck of motion estimation algorithms with a small percentage of source code modification. In [16], Nelson and Jorge proposed the first implementation of optical flow of Lucas-kanade algorithm based on directives of OpenACC programming paradigms on GPU. In the same context of hybride model, OpenMP provides an excellent opportunity to target hardware accelerators (GPUs) with the new version (4.0, 4.5) which is very similar to the OpenACC model. In order to take advantage, many research begun using OpenMP GPU offloading in different domain. However, the implementation of optical flow algorithm with the new version of OpenMP still limited until now. In this context, this research aims to accomplish an efficient application of Lucas-Kanade algorithm for intensive computation using OpenMP GPU offloading implementation which processes and analyzes the bottlenecks of the accesses memory. In this paper, there are a number of contributions presented: First, we propose a sequential optimization strategies to improve the performance. We also evaluate the different challenges of implementing several of them to overcome some memory problems. Then, we explore the feasibility of a high level directive based model OpenMP4.0 to port Lucas-Kanade algorithm to heterogeneous architecture (GPU) using offloading model. Finally, we compare the performance obtained from a new OpenMP version and the OpenACC implementation [4] described in our previous work.

The remainder of the paper is organized as follows. Section 2 provides a basic background of the optical flow method and describes the Lucas-kanade algorithm. Our sequential optimization strategies are explained in Sect. 3. In Sect. 4, we investigate the impact of GPU parallelization and optimization, we provide a commented report of our experimental results, and compare our results with the OpenACC results from our previous work. Section 5 concludes the paper and outlines some perspectives.

2   Optical Flow Algorithm

Optical flow is a family of algorithms which are used to calculate the apparent motion of features across two consecutive frames of a given video, thus estimating a global parametric transformation and local deformations. It is based mainly on local spatio-temporal convolutions that are applied consecutively. The optical flow is an important clue for motion estimation, tracking, surveillance, and recognition applications. To estimate optical flow in real time is a challenging task, it requires a lot of computation effort. So more than a hundred optical flow algorithm exist, Horn and Schunck algorithm [6] and Lucas-kanade algorithm [5] have became the most widely used techniques in computer vision. This article focuses on Lucas-kanade's approach because is the most adequate in terms of calculation complexity and requires less computing resources. Its computation method is suitable for CPU and GPU implementations. The main principle of the Lucas-Kanade optical flow estimation is to assume the brightness constancy to find the velocity vector between two successive frames (t and $t+1$) as shown in Fig. 1(a) and (b). The optical flow vectors are drawn in Fig. 1(c).

Fig. 1. Optical Flow computation   Fig. 2. Workflow of Lucas-Kanade

2.1   Lucas-Kanade Algorithm

The idea of Lucas-Kanade is to compute the spatiotemporal derivatives on a smoothed image to minimize the intensity variations over time. This requires a focus on a representative pixels which are then checked for motion across consecutive frames through intensity variations between the scene and the camera, followed by a construction of the least square matrix in a spatial neighborhood to calculate the optical velocity flow. Consider for a 2D image I, a small motion is approximated by a translation. We need to determine the motion flow vectors for the image pixel $I(x, y)$. Thus if the current frame is represented by its intensity function I, then the intensity function H of the next frame is such that where (u, v) is the displacement vector. Here, we briefly describe the correspondence of equations with different steps of the Lucas-Kanade algorithm.

$$H(x, y) = I(x + u, y + v), \tag{1}$$

Therefore, we have to solve for every pixel the following so-called *Lucas-Kanade equation*:

$$\begin{bmatrix} \sum I_x^2 & \sum I_x I_y \\ \sum I_x I_y & \sum I_y^2 \end{bmatrix} \begin{bmatrix} u \\ v \end{bmatrix} = - \begin{bmatrix} \sum I_x I_t \\ \sum I_y I_t \end{bmatrix} \tag{2}$$

where I_x, I_y and I_t are the derivatives of the intensity along x, y and t direction respectively. A least-square approach are implemented in Lucas-Kanade system to find the most likely displacement (u, v), since the original system is over determined. The summations within Eq. (2) are over the pixels inside the sampling window. If the condition number of the normal matrix is above a given threshold, then we compute the solution of the system (using Kramer method for instance) and thus obtain the components of the optical flow vector for the corresponding pixel. Figure 2 summarizes a sequence of computation stages of the Lucas-Kanade algorithm where the derivatives I_x, I_y, and I_t are computed through their Taylor approximations using the corresponding convolution 6 kernels. Then follows their point-wise products compute the products I_x^2, I_y^2, $I_x I_t$, $I_y I_t$, and $I_x I_y$. Computes for each pixel the normal matrix and the right hand side of the linear system as described in Eq. (2).

3   Sequential Optimization Strategies

For many algorithms, especially in computer vision and image processing field, a stencil computation are a common programming pattern. Usually, image processing algorithms combine the challenges of stencil computations and that of real-time processing. Therefore, an efficient implementation requires to focus on data locality and to consider a scalable parallelisation. More precisely, We should take care about redundant memory accesses, cache misses, and unalignement issues. We now describe some techniques that we have considered for the aforementioned concerns.

3.1   Operators Clustering

Operators clustering aims at merging two or more operators into a single one, in order to reduce the lifetime of the intermediate results in between and to improve data locality. In its *Nopipe* version, the Lucas-Kanade algorithm is composed of four computation stages: computation of the gradients, product of the gradients, computation of the matrix coefficients together with the corresponding right and sides, and solving the linear systems for the optical flow vectors. This computation chain requires accessing nine intermediate arrays. For our case, several combinations are possible [15]. For instance, we can choose to pipeline the Grad and Mul operators one hand, and the Matrix and solve operators on the other hand, this transformation is called *Halfpipe* and it reduces both the number of floating point operations and memory accesses. For our scenario, the most balanced one seems to fully pipeline the operators, thus removing all intermedi 6 ate memory accesses. This is called *full-pipe*, where we form the unique cluster GRAD+MUL+MATRICE+SOLVE. Figure 4 illustrates the full-pipe workflow.

3.2   Loop Optimization

Stencils represent a challenging computational pattern for Memory optimization, the resulting computation loop therefore needs to be optimized. Loops optimization plays an important role in high performance computing. Possible goals are:

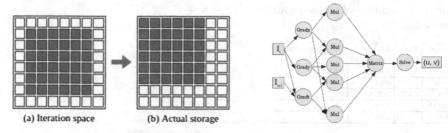

Fig. 3. Upper-left shift storage   **Fig. 4.** Full-pipe organization

improving data reuse and data locality, reducing the overheads associated with loops management, and maximizing parallelism. Loop transformations can be performed at different levels for our work. In this context, we present a loop shifting technique, which minimizes the memory needed to carry on the main arrays. In fact, we apply an upper-left shift for the output matrix, which means that (i, j) is stored at position $(i - 1, j - 1)$ [15]. Figure 3 illustrates our re-indexation and the corresponding storage strategy. After applying loop shifting, we apply a Loop fusion to improve the readability of the code and to make programs faster by replacing multiple loops with a single one. Furthermore, loop fusion can help to have a more coarse grained parallelism. For the next point, we study the effect of array contraction on data reuse and data locality.

3.3 Array Contraction

In this paper, we consider another optimization strategy to benefit from the cache. The so-called *array contraction*, which aims at reducing the memory footprint [14], is a program transformation which reduces the size of intermediate arrays by means of location reuses. We use the modulo to round up on i direction. This approach clearly reduce the number of loads. In order to improve the register use, we consider a special case of array contraction, namely *scalarization*, where each element of an array is defined and immediately used within the same iteration. To illustrate the potential benefit of these strategies, we include preliminary results showing the improvement that is achieved when collective loop transformations with a contraction array are applied. We run on a dual-socket intel broadwell. Table 1 shows the performance results of our strategy using different image sizes. We can see that with the optimized case we achieve better execution times compared to the basic one, and we can also process larger images (like 8000 × 8000 and 16000 × 16000), which was not possible with the basic implementation because of memory limitations. Figure 5 shows a noticeable improvement, which demonstrates the impact of our optimization and the potential of 6 more performance gain.

Table 1. Evaluation of the sequential optimization

Image size	T(s) Basic	T(s) optimized	% Improvement
2000^2	0.752	0.078	89.62
4000^2	1.058	0.315	70.22
8000^2	1.775	1.264	28.79
12000^2	–	2.846	–
16000^2	–	5.065	–

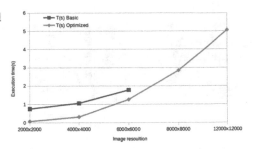

Fig. 5. Improvement of sequential implementation

4   Impact of GPU Parallelization and Optimization

4.1   Hardware Configuration

We use OpenMP4.0 and run on an NVIDIA Quadro P5000 GPU accelerator (Pascal architecture). It includes 2560 CUDA cores with 16 GB GDDR5 memory. The host is an Intel(R) Xeon(R) CPU E5-1620 v4 processors with 4 cores. We use GCC compiler version 7.3.

4.2   Results of the GPU Parallelization

Our performance analysis considers different stages, each focusing on the comparison between the results obtained with our OpenMP4.0 implementation and those of our previous OpenACC implementation. Some directive based optimization were performed to improve memory accesses and memory locality. In our experiments, we use different frame sizes and run our Lucas-Kanade implementation for the optical flow vectors. We start with a baseline sequential implementation in C, then we consider the derived OpenMP version without any data directives. OpenMP4.0 version introduces a number of features for targeting heterogeneous architectures [13]. The first step of the algorithm consists in loading the data from the CPU to the GPU's global memory. This step (typically) yields a significant overhead. Then, we define which part will be accelerated with the device (kernel) using the basic directives (`#pragma omp target`). The target directives provide a mechanism to move the execution of the thread from the CPU to another device and to relocate the data. We can see from Table 3 that the parallel CPU version outperforms the OpenMP code on the GPU. The reason of this is that OpenMP was originally designed for automatic multithreading on a shared memory processors, so the parallel directive only creates a single level of parallelism. Beside this one, the version at this stage does not contain any optimization directive, so there is a *potential* room for improvement. To evaluate this potential, we used the NVIDIA runtime profiler on our kernels to identify locations where memory access seems too important. We use `nvprof --print-gpu-trace` to print all the information about how to optimize the code. We can see from the results another clear difference between

OpenMP and OpenACC implementations, where the performance achieved by the OpenACC is quite higher compared to OpenMP and CPU versions. However, OpenACC is very similar to OpenMP but OpenACC was designed from the beginning to address both portability and productivity of GPU programming without too much effort, with OpenMP we must skillfully exploit these new features. Figure 7 demonstrates the performance of GPU implementation using OpenACC. To overcome theses issues, we consider several specific directives. We start with the teams directive to express a second level of scalable parallelism. In order to make better use of GPU resources, we have used many use many thread teams via the `teams` directive and the `directive` to distribute the iterations of the next loop to the master threads of the teams in order to spread parallelism across the entire GPU. In order to increase the parallelism, we start by increasing the number of teams using the `num-teams` clause and the `num-thread` clause to generate the number of threads per teams which might yield the best performance and achieves a good balance between teams and threads. In addition, we can further increase parallelism by using our distributed and work shared parallelism from the same loop. We can collapse them together and we split `teams distribute` from `Parallel For` by moving them to the inner loop. In our case we use the `COLLAPSE(N)` clause to have the next N loops collapsed into one loop with a larger iteration space. This will give us more parallelism to distribute.

Table 2. Evaluation of the OpenMP GPU deployment

	2000^2	4000^2	6000^2	8000^2	12000^2
(1)	0.046	0.184	0.416	0.741	1.666
(2)	0.142	0.343	0.662	0.910	2.556
(3)	0.103	0.240	0.428	0.690	1.356
(4)	0.079	0.123	0.355	0.502	1.008
(5)	0.075	0.115	0.330	0.488	0.984
(6)	0.062	0.094	0.275	0.428	0.882

Table 3. Evaluation of the GPU parallelization

Image size	CPU(s)	GPU(s) OpenMP	GPU(s) OpenACC
2000^2	0.046	0.142	0.018
4000^2	0.184	0.343	0.057
6000^2	0.416	0.628	0.131
8000^2	0.741	0.391	0.250
12000^2	1.666	2.556	0.640

- (1) : Basic CPU   (2): GPU threaded
- (3) : GPU teams/distribute   (4): (3) + GPU team/thread balance
- (5) : (4) + GPU collapse   (6): (5) + GPU SIMD

Table 2 lists the different stages of the results, which demonstrate that there is a significant improvement most of the time. We investigate the effects on the performances when combined parallelization and vectorization in GPU. In fact, vectorization using SIMD constructs is very efficient in exploring data level parallelism since it executes multiple data operations concurrently using a single instruction. Therefore, OpenMP4.0 provides the `pragma omp simd` directive, which execute multiple iterations of the loop using vector instructions when possible. As shown in Fig. 6, the highest performance we have achieved when combined all the directives used in parallelization with the vectorization, which make the results more fast but the time is still limited due to the heavy implicit access to memory.

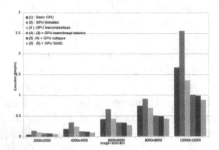

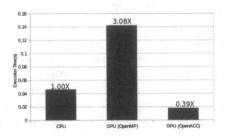

Fig. 6. Performance comparison between different OpenMP GPU offloading optimization

Fig. 7. The performance of GPU Offloading with OpenMP4 and OpenACC

4.3 Managing Memory and Data Optimization

One of the major bottleneck of a GPU is the data transfer latency, because it takes more than 400–600 cycles to access the global memory. If access to global memory is frequent, then with the cost of moving data between the CPU and GPU at every loop, the computation benefit of porting a parallel application to a GPU will be lost. We discuss now how we schedule memory accesses in order to reduce the overhead of data exchanges and get ride of intermediate data accesses whenever possible. We analyze the behavior of the major data movement with the OpenMP4.0 offloading target using the target data *directives* and *map clauses* to control and reduce data movement between CPU and GPU. OpenMP4.0 allows an explicit control of data allocation together with the corresponding transactions through appropriates clauses (`copyin, copyout, present, create`) with different map-type (`to,from, tofrom,alloc`) to optimize the mapping of buffers to the device data environment.

Basically, CPUs and GPUs have separate memories and 6 can not access each other's memory which must be handled explicitly by programmers. Instead of this, a new concept of *unified memory* provided by NVIDIA, which allows the GPU and the host CPU to share the same global address space. This permits the host to refer to memory locations on the attached devices, and the devices to access addresses on their host. The unified memory enables fast memory accesses with large data sets where the movement data is managed by the underlying system automatically [1]. There is no need for address translation, and both CPU and GPU can use the same pointer. Moreover, leveraging the unified memory features makes it feasible to run kernels with memory footprints larger than the GPU memory capacity. In current OpenMP GPU offloading, we illustrate how the function and data transfer work with the unified memory [1]. To do this, we use `omp-target-alloc` for data allocation and `is-device-ptr` clauses to pass them to target regions, in contrary to OpenACC compiler which provides the flag `-ta=tesla:managed` for the unified memory consideration. When this option is used at compile time, the PGI compilers will intercept and replace all user defined allocations with managed data allocations.

Table 4. Evaluation of our data GPU optimization

	2000^2	4000^2	6000^2	8000^2	12000^2
(1)	0.062	0.094	0.275	0.428	0.882
(2)	0.011	0.024	0.101	0.228	0.689
(3)	0.007	0.014	0.077	0.105	0.481
(4)	0.005	0.010	0.041	0.068	0.137

- (1): Basic GPU parallelization
- (2): (1) + Data movement performance
- (3): (1) + Unified memory
- (4): (2) + pinned

We also highlighted the benefits of using "pinned me 6 mory" on the memory copies which offers the best performances. Furthermore, if the memory is going to be used for many asynchronous transfers, then we request page-locked memory allocations (pinned memory). It is a memory allocated using the `cudaMallocHost` function, which prevents the memory from being swapped out and thereby provides improved transfer speeds, contrary to the non-pinned memory obtained with a plain `malloc`. The benefit of using pinned memory is that we can solve larger problems because the size of the pinned memory is much larger than that of the global memory. The pointer association between CPU-GPU is preserved, thus preventing the operating system from moving this memory to another location. Presently, none of the pragmas can allocate pinned memory and compiler flag. Hence, OpenMP GPU offloading use the `cudaMallocHost` function for pinned memory, which is not the case with OpenACC who considers the flag compiler `-ta=tesla:pinned`. The experimental results of our optimization investigation are summarized in Table 4. The Fig. 8 outlines the speedup ratio of the total execution time for each of the different versions compared to the baseline version. We can see a remarkable speedup with our incremental OpenMP GPU offloading data optimization, when using a simple data movement with unified memory and pinned memory directives. We have found that pinning the same amount of memory was more faster than the use of unified memory and the basic data movement directives. This technique is more efficient and it often reduces the overall amount of host-device data transfers. Overall, our work makes several important research contributions, we evaluate the effectiveness of OpenMP GPU offloading directives as a potential solution to the performance portability problem of modern architectures and we get decent speedups. Right now, OpenACC support is very selective and limited both for devices and compilers. Whereas, OpenMP GPU offloading is very widely supported and exhaustive. However, to better understand the computational costs of the different versions, Fig. 9 displays a comparison between the OpenMP 4.0 implementation and the OpenACC implementation for each version. As we can see, the management of the data using directives with OpenMP on the GPU is more costly than with OpenACC in this stage. However, with the use of the unified memory, we notice that the OpenMP version is better than the OpenACC version due to the use of a compiler flag. Moreover, the line labeled OpenMP Pinned Memory shows the timings of both OpenMP and OpenACC which are so close with pinned memory.

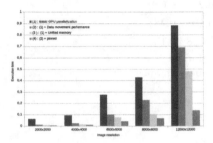
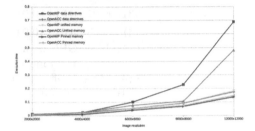

Fig. 8. Speedup of the three versions over the baseline version

Fig. 9. Basic CPU and fully optimized GPU

5   Conclusion

In this paper, we have carried out a detailed study of some of the most popular parallelization approaches and programming languages used to program GPUs. An OpenMP GPU offloading and OpenACC are used in this work, which are considered as the most flexible high level languages for GPU deployment. It makes possible to migrate standard CPU code in a straightforward way without making too many modifications, and obtain a decent performance compared to other complex programming models like CUDA and OpenCL. OpenMP 4.x directives provide an excellent opportunity to GPU deployment. We investigate an OpenMP deployment of the Lucas-Kanade optical flow algorithm with OpenMP and strive to obtain better performance than that of a parallel version on a manycore processor. The performances are very close to our previous OpenACC version. For the future works, we will investigate a combination of OpenMP and OpenACC both for GPU and manycore deployments.

References

1. Mishra, A., Li, L., Kong, M.: Benchmarking and evaluating unified memory for OpenMP GPU offloading. In: Proceedings of the Fourth Workshop on the LLVM Compiler Infrastructure in HPC. ACM, New York (2017)
2. Chikin, A., Gobran, T., Amaral, J.N.: OpenMP code offloading: splitting GPU kernels, pipelining communication and computation, and selecting better grid geometries. In: Chandrasekaran, S., Juckeland, G., Wienke, S. (eds.) WACCPD 2018. LNCS, vol. 11381, pp. 51–74. Springer, Cham (2019). https://doi.org/10.1007/978-3-030-12274-4_3
3. Martineau, M., et al.: Performance analysis and optimization of Clang's OpenMP 4.5 GPU support. In: 2016 IEEE 7th International Workshop on Performance Modeling, Benchmarking and Simulation of High Performance Computer Systems (2016)
4. Haggui, O., Tadonki, C., Sayadi, F., Bouraoui, O.: Efficient GPU implementation of Lucas-Kanade through OpenACC. In: Proceedings of the 14th International Joint Conference on Computer Vision, Imaging and Computer Graphics Theory and Applications, VISAPP, Prague, Czech Republic, vol. 5, 768–775 (2019)
5. Lucas, B.D., Kanade, T.: An image registration technique with an application to stereo vision. In: Proceedings of Image Understanding Workshop, pp. 121–130 (1981)
6. Horn, B.K.P., Schunck, B.G.: Determining optical flow. Artif. Intell. **17**(185), 185–203 (1981)
7. Gibson, J.: The Perception of the Visual World. Houghton Mifflin, Boston (1950)
8. Baker, S., Mattews, I.: Lucas Kanade 20 years on: a unifying framework. Int. J. Comput. Vis. **56**(3), 221–255 (2004)
9. Anguita, M., Diaz, J., Ros, E., Javier Fernandez-Baldomero, F.: Optimization strategies for high-performance computing of optical-flow in general-purpose processors. IEEE Trans. Circ. Syst. Video Technol. **19**(10), 1475–1488 (2009)
10. Kruglov, A.V., Kruglov, V.N.: Tracking of fast moving objects in real time. Pattern Recogn. Image Anal. **26**(3), 582–586 (2016). ISSN 1054-6618
11. Sánchez, J., Monzón López, N., Salgado de la Nuez, A.J.: Parallel implementation of a robust optical flow technique. Las Palmas de Gran Canaria, 16 March 2012
12. Pál, I., Biemann, R., Baumgartner, S.V.: A comparison and validation approach for traffic data, acquired by airborne radar and optical sensors using parallelized Lucas-Kanade algorithm. VDE VERLAG GMBH Berlin Offenbach (2014). ISBN 978-3-8007-3607-2. ISSN 2197-4403
13. https://www.openmp.org/wp-content/uploads/OpenMP4.0.0.pdf
14. Song, Y., Xu, R., Wang, C., Li, Z.: Improving data locality by array contraction. IEEE Trans. Comput. **53**(9), 1073–1084 (2004)
15. Haggui, O., Tadonki, C., Lacassagne, L., Sayadi, F., Ouni, B.: Harris corner detection on a NUMA manycore. Future Gener. Comput. Syst. (2018). https://doi.org/10.1016/j.future.2018.01.048
16. Martin, N., Collado, J., Botella, G., Garcia, C., Prieto, M.: Manuel: OpenACC-based GPU acceleration of an optical flow algorithm. In: ACM Digital Library, SAC 2015, Salamanca, Spain, 13–17 April (2015)

Automatic Creation of Large Scale Object Databases from Web Resources: A Case Study in Robot Vision

Dario Molinari[1], Giulia Pasquale[2], Lorenzo Natale[2], and Barbara Caputo[2,3(✉)]

[1] Sapienza Università di Roma, Rome, Italy
[2] Istituto Italiano di Tecnologia, Genoa, Italy
[3] Politecnico di Torino, Turin, Italy
barbara.caputo@polito.it

Abstract. A fundamental ingredient in the success of deep learning for computer and robot vision is the availability of very large-scale annotated databases. ImageNet, with its 1000 object classes and 1.2 million images, tends to be the dominant data collection for creating pre-trained deep architectures. A less investigated avenue is how the possibility to create task-specific data collections on demand, with limited or without manual effort, would affect the performance of convolutional architectures. This would be useful for all those cases where contextual information about the deployment of the deep net is available, and it would be particularly relevant for robot vision applications, where such knowledge is usually available. The goal of this work is to present a protocol for the automated creation of task specific datasets starting from a pre-defined list of object classes, exploiting the Web as a source of information in an automated fashion. Our pipeline consists of (a) an algorithm for automatic Web crawling that searches for "image class seeds", i.e., informative images of object classes of interest, (b) algorithms for figure-ground segmentation of the object of interest and pasting of the segmented item in contextual images close to where the agent is going to work, and (c) a tailored data augmentation routine for maximizing the informative content of the generated images. A thorough set of experiments on a public benchmark, as well as deployment to a robot platform, prove the value of the proposed approach.

Keywords: Object categorization · Robot vision · Web vision

1 Introduction

Robots need to have a visual understanding of their surroundings in order to have cognitive behaviors. From visually perceiving an object, to recognizing it, to understanding what it is, what its properties are and how it should be acted

---

D. Molinari and G. Pasquale—Equal contribution.

© Springer Nature Switzerland AG 2019
E. Ricci et al. (Eds.): ICIAP 2019, LNCS 11752, pp. 488–498, 2019.
https://doi.org/10.1007/978-3-030-30645-8_45

upon, all these are crucial components to have truly intelligent and autonomous systems. Since the seminal work of Krizhevsky et al [9], the overwhelming majority of state of the art approaches in computer and robot vision for object recognition are based on Convolutional Neural Networks (CNNs, [11]), which use end-to-end architectures achieving feature learning and classification at the same time. Compared to shallow learning approaches, where feature extraction and classification are two separate steps often laded with heuristics, CNNs offer several advantages: first, they have proved over countless benchmarks to be able to achieve much higher accuracies on basically any visual recognition problem; second, they offer a conceptual simplicity of use that has made them very quickly the dominant learning tool of the community. Despite these advantages, they also present some limitations, such as high computational cost, long training time and the demand for large datasets, to name a few. As CNNs are data-hungry algorithms, the possibility to train a given model on very large scale annotated data collections is crucial for their success. As a consequence, architectures trained over ImageNet [2] are the cornerstone of the vast majority of CNN-based object recognition methods; such architectures are then adapted to various classification needs through fine-tuning. This again, in turn, requires annotated data collection and non trivial manual effort, although not of the same scale needed for end-to-end training of CNNs.

This paper addresses this issue, following the recent trend of developing algorithms for the automatic creation of annotated data from the Web through smart downloading approaches [13]. As opposed to dealing with the automatic creation of a very large scale data collection, that inevitably brings with it issues related to the percentage of noisy images downloaded and of their effect on the training of the network, we propose a protocol for generating automatically task-specific databases for the fine tuning of pre-trained architectures. Given a list of object categories that the robot is expected to encounter while performing its assigned task, we first search the Web for a limited number of images representing the object of interest, in white/empty backgrounds. By taking only the first images resulting from the search, we strongly limit the amount of wrong/noisy images in our download. Once obtained the images, we figure ground segment them to remove any possible artifact in the background, and we paste them on generic backgrounds resembling the environment where the robot will be deployed. Further data augmentation contributes to bridge the perceptual gap between images found on the Web and images that might be acquired in the actual robot setting. Figure 1 gives an overview of the overall protocol. We evaluated the contribution of each step of the data generation pipeline by fine-tuning a deep network to address an object categorization task on a publicly available benchmark (Fig. 1, bottom left). We then deployed the pipeline on a robot platform (Fig. 1, bottom right), where we show that it can run "on-the-fly" to generate image sets for training standard SVM classifiers for fast object categorization learning.

The rest of the paper is organized as follows: after a review of relevant previous work (Sect. 2), we describe the protocol proposed for the automatic creation of databases (Sect. 3); Sect. 4 describes the experiments performed and our findings, while conclusions and future works are discussed in Sect. 5.

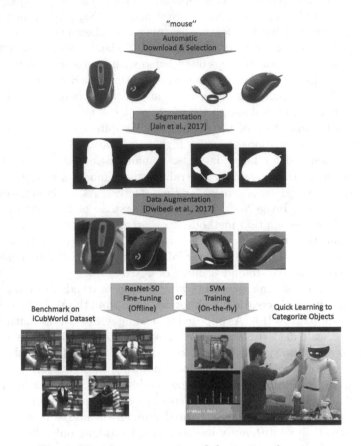

Fig. 1. Visual representation of the proposed system.

2 Related Works

Earlier work explored the possibility of mining the Web for semantic information to be used in robot systems, mostly to populate automatically on-board knowledge base representations [17–19]. Still, semantic information alone will not suffice: visual perceptual capabilities are crucial for robots to operate in unconstrained, task-oriented settings. As the leading deep learning paradigm for robot vision relies heavily on the availability of data collections, the ability to recognize large classes of objects is linked to the creation of such data corpora.

Database creation from the Web has been attempted in the past with the use of semantic query expansions [1,13], where the query expansion helps in reducing the amount of noisy and mislabeled images automatically downloaded, while at the same time helps in guaranteeing the visual richness of the collection. In spite of this, automatic data creation from the Web tends to include a non-trivial percentage of noise in the data, that might negatively affect the performance of convolutional networks trained on them. Several authors proposed strategies to deal with it [3]. Researchers have also started working on automatic data mining for robot vision applications with deep networks and the results are promising [13]. All the works revised above target explicitly the creation of general purpose databases, mimicking ImageNet.

We are not aware of previous work attempting to create task specific databases from the Web without manual annotation, nor attempting to use Web data as starting point for the creation of artificial, synthetic images.

3 Method

This section details the steps of our pipeline, as outlined in Fig. 1.

Images Download From the Web. This step requires dealing with noisy images (i.e., images found when searching the Web for a given object that instead show something else). We address this issue by noticing that, for the vast majority of publicly available search engines, the top-retrieved images tend to depict the object of interest on an uniform background. Thus, we developed a simple script that, given a label, downloads the first N images found in the Web (after duplicate removal), that we use as "seed images", to be augmented with synthetic transformations. While this does not guarantee the lack of noise in the seeds, we verified heuristically that, by keeping $N \sim 100$, its impact is largely reduced.

Object Mask Extraction. For creating the synthetic images, it is first necessary to "extract" the objects of interest from the downloaded image. To do this automatically, we applied the foreground/background segmentation method from [7]. The authors showed that a fully convolutional network with backbone weights pre-trained on a large-scale image classification dataset (like ImageNet [2]) can learn to produce dense binary segmentation masks by fine-tuning on a relatively small set of images with foreground/background pixel-level annotations. The idea is to leverage the notion of "pixel objectness" learned by the network on the large classification task, and fine-tune it to 'extend' its activation responses from fragments to entire objects. We used the model released by [7], which worked well off-the-shelf. We note that, being the pipeline fully automatic, it has to deal with the noise in the masks.

Synthetic Data Generation. At this stage, the segmented "seed" objects must be placed on suited background images. We opted for backgrounds from environments that are coherent with the categories of choice. As our case study considers mostly office objects, we tried using either (i) the backgrounds provided with the Washington RGB-D dataset [10] (the ones representing offices/desks), or (ii) a set of backgrounds acquired directly in the robot's operation setting.

To implement this step we exploited the work of [4], which provides methods (with code) to alleviate the artifacts that appear when an object is pasted onto a different background. To augment the size and variability of the final data collection, we applied also the provided set of transformations (2D rotations, scaling, occlusions, etc.) with the addition of illumination changes (brightness, contrast and saturation).

Training. In all our experiments we rely on a convolutional neural network pre-trained on the object categorization task of the ImageNet Large Scale Visual Recognition Challenge (ILSVRC) [2], specifically, the Caffe [8] implementation[1] of ResNet-50 [6].

We adopt two different transfer-learning methods in the two settings considered in this paper. When targeting object categorization on a benchmark dataset, we fine-tune the network on the generated synthetic training sets. This leads to adapt the image representation to the considered task, but also to the synthetic domain. Since we do not apply sophisticated computer graphics, in this setting we evaluate the trade-off between the benefit of gathering semantically rich images at no cost, and the domain shift possibly introduced in the network by the lack of realism. Differently, in the robotic application we opted to fix the image representation to the one learned on ImageNet and use the synthetic image sets to train linear SVMs on top. We call this on-the-fly learning, because fine-tuning the network takes several minutes/hours, while the training time of the linear SVMs is of the order of seconds and can be interactive.

When fine-tuning, we relied on standard Caffe protocols and just ensured that the learning rate policy was leading to convergence. We used a validation set to stop the training when we observed no accuracy gain and in any case no later than 30 epochs. For each experiment we performed three fine-tuning trials, averaging the results and observing around 1% of performance oscillation across trial. The code for training SVMs employs the *liblinear* [5] package. In this case, cross-validation for the regularization parameter was performed once on an example task.

4   Results

In this section we report on the experimental evaluation that we performed to asses the feasibility of the proposed pipeline for data generation. In all the experiments we use synthetic images generated with our pipeline for training and test on real images acquired by recording from the camera of humanoid robots. In Sect. 4.1, we present a quantitative evaluation of the performance benefit of each step of the pipeline. To this end, we fine-tune ResNet-50 from ImageNet to address an object categorization task on the iCubWorld dataset [15] which, being recorded from the camera of a robot (iCub[2]) while this is observing hand-held objects, provides a faithful benchmark for real robotic operation settings. In

---

[1] https://github.com/KaimingHe/deep-residual-networks.
[2] http://www.icub.org/.

Sect. 4.2, we show that the proposed data generation can also be performed on a robot on-the-fly, to quickly train linear SVMs on specific object categories asked by a user. To this end, we report qualitative results of the pipeline deployment within an interactive object learning application running on the R1 robot[3].

4.1 Benchmark on iCubWorld

In this section we assess if the difference between the synthetic and real domain is such to prevent the suggested approach to be effective for training deep networks. We first report the performance achieved by progressively introducing more processing steps in the proposed image generation pipeline. Then, we show how it is possible to achieve good performance on iCubWorld by injecting a limited amount of real images in a purely synthetic training set.

Real vs. Synthetic Datasets

Test on iCubWorld. We consider the "iCubWorld Transformations" dataset [15] as our test set (iCWT in the following). This dataset represents 20 object categories of daily use (10 objects per category), each recorded in five image sequences while undergoing isolated viewpoint transformations (e.g., SCALE, 2/3D ROT, BKG, etc.). Each sequence is acquired in two sessions with little setting variations and comprises around 150 frames. We refer the reader to [15] for details. In all experiments, we target a 20-class categorization task and consider, as test set, 5 object instances per category (out of the 10 available) in the BKG sequence. In this sequences the objects are moved by the operator around the robot, keeping their face fixed thus making only the background change. We randomly sampled 50 frames from each sequence, hence our test set is composed of 5K images.

Synthetic Training Sets. To address this task, we downloaded from the Web 80 images for each category in iCWT (see Sect. 3). We randomly selected 60 images per category for training, for a total of 1200 images. The remaining 20 images per category have been used as validation set. After passing the images through foreground segmentation, we remained with around 1150 training images (it is possible that the network used [7] is not able to detect the object, returning an empty mask that is discarded). We tried using two different image sets for the following background replacement step. The first one is from the background images publicly available in Washington RGB-D dataset [10]. Specifically, we selected around 350 background images in tabletop-like settings. The second one is a set of the same size, but recorded in the acquisition setting of the iCWT dataset. As explained in Sect. 3, since we relied on the data augmentation procedure from [4], we optionally applied scale, in-plane rotation and light augmentation while replacing the background. In this data augmentation step, for each source image we generated 4 synthetic images, producing a total of around 4600 training images.

---

[3] https://www.youtube.com/watch?v=TBphNGW6m4o.

Table 1. Classification accuracy achieved by performing diverse processing steps on the downloaded images.

Training set	Number of images	Accuracy [%]
Chance level	–	5
Web	1200	22
White	1150	18
RGBD	1150	32
iCWT	1150	35
RGBD₊	**4600**	**42**

Reducing The Domain Shift - Part I

Ablation Experiment. We evaluated the performance achieved after applying each step of the data generation pipeline and report results after fine-tuning the network on each of the following "intermediate" datasets:

- Images downloaded from the Web (Web).
- Web images segmented with background replacement. We tried a white background (White) or the background from either Washington RGB-D or the iCWT settings (RGBD or iCWT).
- Web images segmented with background replacement and data augmentation. In this case we opted for using the background from Washington RGB-D dataset, since the goal of this work is to build training sets fully automatically and without the need for the user to acquire any data in the operation setting ($RGBD_+$).

We report results in Table 1. We see that just by downloading 60 images per category from the Web we are able to achieve 22% accuracy (chance level is 5%). As expected, the white background replacement is detrimental for performance, while replacing backgrounds which are similar to the one of the test set, does improve results. In this case, the *exact* same background of the test set (iCWT) provides higher results (35%) than one which is similar (RGBD, 32%). However, it is interesting to observe that the performance difference is small, motivating our choice. A relatively high accuracy (42%) is achieved by applying the data augmentation from [4] to the RGBD training set. However, we note that we are still far from achieving perfect performance. This result establishes a baseline achieved with simple image processing steps. On the one hand, this proves the effectiveness and the potential of the approach. On the other hand, it shows that a better covering of the domain shift is critical to improve performance.

Reducing the Domain Shift - Part II

Injection of Real Images. Given the above results, two options can be considered in order to increase performance: (i) improving the realism of the synthetic images

Table 2. Classification accuracy achieved by performing diverse processing steps on the downloaded images (like in Table 1) and by adding real images from iCWT.

Training set	iCWT objects	Number of images	Accuracy [%]
Web	–	1200	22
Web	1	1200 + 120 (10%) real	46
RGBD$_+$	–	4600	42
RGBD$_+$	1	4600 + 600 (13%) real	**65**
RGBD	1	1150 + 600 (52%) real	63
iCWT	1	1150 + 600 (52%) real	62
Web	1	1200 + 600 (50%) real	62
White	1	1150 + 600 (52%) real	62
RGBD$_+$	5	4600 + 600 (13%) real	73
RGBD$_+$	5	4600 + 5K (109%) real	85
–	5	5K (100%) real	87

and/or (ii) considering the injection of a small set of real images. We opted to evaluate this second possibility, following the suggestion of the authors [4].

In this experiment, we evaluate the performance achieved by adding, to the synthetic training sets considered in the previous section, images of objects from iCWT. For the addition, we sample objects from the remaining 5 instances per category (excluding the test set). Results are reported in Table 2 for two sets of experiments.

We started considering the addition of a single object example per category. We hence sampled from iCWT a few images for each of 20 objects not in the test set (from BKG sequences) and added them to the Web and RGBD$_+$ training sets. We kept the real to synthetic ratio around 10% and used $6 \times 20 = 120$ real images for the Web and $30 \times 20 = 600$ real images for the RGBD$_+$. In rows 1–4 of Table 2, we observe around 23% performance increase in both cases, achieving 65% with the RGBD$_+$ training set.

To further investigate to which extent this result depends on the real or synthetic data, in rows 5–8 of Table 2 we increased the real to synthetic ratio up to around 50%, by considering the same 600 real images but adding them to the not augmented synthetic training sets. We observed that performance was almost the same, independently on the quality of synthetic images. It is interesting to note that the addition of as few as 30 frames of a single example instance per category provides a performance gain increase of 40% (from 22 to 62%) when using just Web images. A similar gain is achieved by combining data augmentation (from 22 to 42%) and injection of even less real images (from 42 to 65%).

We finally added all available 5 object examples per category in iCWT to the synthetic training sets (rows 9–11 in Table 2). In this case, with 6 real images per object (for a total of $6 \times 5 \times 20 = 600$ images) we achieve 73% accuracy.

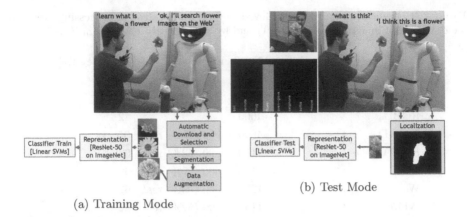

(a) Training Mode

(b) Test Mode

Fig. 2. Block diagram of the application running on the robot: (a) Training Mode, images are downloaded from the web and used to train the SVMs on the new category; (b) Test Mode, the robot localizes the closest object in the scene and classifies it.

Furthermore, adding to the training set as much real images as the synthetic ones (50 frames per object for a total of 5K images) leads to 85% accuracy. This error rate is probably dominated by the information available in the real object examples. This is confirmed by the 87% accuracy achieved by training only on the real images.

4.2 On-the-Fly Learning of Object Categories

In this section we briefly describe the deployment of the data generation pipeline to an application running on the R1 robot platform.

The current object recognition system on R1 is the same as the one on the iCub robot and is based on a deep neural network for feature extraction (ResNet-50 trained on ImageNet classification task) and shallow classifiers that are trained on-the-fly to learn the objects shown by a user [14]. Learning on images acquired during the robot's operation allows for flexibility. However, while this works well for object identification (the robot can observe objects from varied viewpoints) it is time consuming for object categorization [15].

Integrating this data generation pipeline offered an improvement in this direction. To teach a category (Fig. 2(a)), the user tells the label to the robot; the system produces a synthetic training set, that is used to train on-the-fly a classifier. It takes no more than one or two minutes to download and process around 100 images on a standard laptop and internet connection. Images are then encoded into ResNet-50's representation and used to train an SVM (linear Kernel). The feature extraction and classifier training are fast and part of the usual learning pipeline employed on the robot. As showed in the benchmark in Sect. 4.1, the synthetic dataset can also be integrated with real example images acquired by the robot autonomously (see, e.g., our previous work[4]). After training, the robot recognizes the category (Fig. 2(b)). A simple depth segmentation [16] localizes a region of interest as the closest object in the scene, which is then classified.

A video showing qualitatively the performance of the running system is available here[5]. The pipeline deployed on the robot applies data augmentation over background images from Washington RGB-D (the video shows also the kind of noise affecting the content or the foreground masks of the generated images).

The code of the application can run on a normal laptop and can be made publicly available upon request at the same GitHub repository of the original application[6].

While we do not have yet a quantitative benchmark for this data generation pipeline within the on-the-fly training strategy adopted on the robot, we plan to perform such evaluation. Specifically, it would be interesting to compare with prior work [15], where it was shown that, for object categorization in absence of enough object examples, classifier training on top of ImageNet features was more effective than fine-tuning.

5   Conclusions and Future Work

We have studied an automatic pipeline to create task-specific training sets for object categorization. We built the pipeline by downloading "image class seeds" from the Web and composing publicly available code blocks to apply standard image processing, i.e., figure-ground segmentation and blending onto contextual images. This approach is useful in those situation in which example objects are difficult to obtain, as in the case of a robotic system.

Our results showed that simple image processing and data augmentation remarkably improve the performance of the object recognition system (20%) and demonstrated that an additional performance gain (40%) can be obtained by integrating the synthetic dataset with a small set of real images of a similar object, taken from the robot. This is interesting, because such a set could also be used to disambiguate the web research, by providing a visual example together with the category label.

The approach presented in this paper can potentially be extended to other tasks in robotics, in which fast adaptation is hampered by the cost of acquiring training samples. For example, in future work we plan to address object detection tasks, by combining our recent work [12]. In this perspective, this line of research could be key to develop vision systems trainable on-the-fly on novel categories.

Acknowledgements. B. C. acknowledges the financial support of the Project ERC RoboExNovo.

---

[4] https://youtu.be/HdmDYIL48H4.
[5] https://youtu.be/eIb9GjIOYXo.
[6] https://github.com/robotology/onthefly-recognition.

References

1. Cheng, D.S., Setti, F., Zeni, N., Ferrario, R., Cristani, M.: Semantically-driven automatic creation of training sets for object recognition. Comput. Vis. Image Underst. **131**, 56–71 (2015)
2. Deng, J., Dong, W., Socher, R., Li, L.-J., Li, K., Fei-Fei, L.: ImageNet: a large-scale hierarchical image database. In: Proceedings of the CVPR (2009)
3. Divvala, S.K., Farhadi, A., Guestrin, C.: Learning everything about anything: webly-supervised visual concept learning. In: Proceedings of the CVPR (2014)
4. Dwibedi, D., Misra, I., Hebert, M.: Cut, paste and learn: surprisingly easy synthesis for instance detection. In: Proceedings of the ICCV (2017)
5. Fan, R.-E., Chang, K.-W., Hsieh, C.-J., Wang, X.-R., Lin, C.-J.: Liblinear: a library for large linear classification. J. Mach. Learn. Res. **9**, 1871–1874 (2008)
6. He, K., Zhang, X., Ren, S., Sun, J.: Deep residual learning for image recognition. In: Proceedings of the CVPR (2016)
7. Jain, S.D., Xiong, B., Grauman, K.: Pixel objectness. arXiv:1701.05349 (2017)
8. Jia, Y., et al.: Caffe: convolutional architecture for fast feature embedding. In: Proceedings of the ACM, pp. 675–678. ACM (2014)
9. Krizhevsky, A., Sutskever, I., Hinton, G.E.: ImageNet classification with deep convolutional neural networks. In: Proceedings of the NIPS (2012)
10. Lai, K., Bo, L., Ren, X., Fox, D.: A large-scale hierarchical multi-view RGB-D object dataset. In: Proceedings of the ICRA (2011)
11. LeCun, Y., et al.: Handwritten digit recognition with a back-propagation network. In: Proceedings of the NIPS (1990)
12. Maiettini, E., Pasquale, G., Rosasco, L., Natale, L.: Speeding-up object detection training for robotics with FALKON. In: Proceedings of the IROS (2018)
13. Massouh, N., Babiloni, F., Tommasi, T., Young, J., Hawes, N., Caputo, B.: Learning deep visual object models from noisy web data: how to make it work. In: Proceedings of the IROS (2017)
14. Pasquale, G., Ciliberto, C., Odone, F., Rosasco, L., Natale, L.: Teaching iCub to recognize objects using deep convolutional neural networks. In: Proceeding of the ICML Workshop on Machine Learning for Interactive Systems, vol. 43 (2015)
15. Pasquale, G., Ciliberto, C., Odone, F., Rosasco, L., Natale, L.: Are we done with object recognition? The iCub robot perspective. Robot. Auton. Syst. **112**, 260–281 (2019)
16. Pasquale, G., Mar, T., Ciliberto, C., Rosasco, L., Natale, L.: Enabling depth-driven visual attention on the icub humanoid robot: instructions for use and new perspectives. Front. Robot. AI **3**, 35 (2016)
17. Samadi, M., Kollar, T., Veloso, M.: Using the web to interactively learn to find objects. In: Proceedings of the AAAI (2012)
18. Waibel, M., et al.: RoboEarth - a world wide web for robots. Robot. Autom. Mag. **18**(2), 69–82 (2011)
19. Young, J., Basile, V., Kunze, L., Cabrio, E., Hawes, N.: Towards lifelong object learning by integrating situated robot perception and semantic web mining. In: Proceedings of the ECAI (2016)

Semantic Guided Deep Unsupervised Image Segmentation

Sudipan Saha[1,2]($\boxtimes$) (iD), Swathikiran Sudhakaran[1,2], Biplab Banerjee[3],
and Sumedh Pendurkar[4]

[1] Fondazione Bruno Kessler, Trento, Italy
{saha,sudhakaran}@fbk.eu
[2] University of Trento, Trento, Italy
[3] Indian Institute of Technology Bombay, Mumbai, India
bbanerjee@iitb.ac.in
[4] College of Engineering Pune, Pune, India
sumedh.pendurkar@gmail.com

Abstract. Image segmentation is an important step in many image processing tasks. Inspired by the success of deep learning techniques in image processing tasks, a number of deep supervised image segmentation algorithms have been proposed. However, availability of sufficient labeled training data is not plausible in many application domains. Some application domains are even constrained by the shortage of unlabeled data. Considering such scenarios, we propose a semantic guided unsupervised Convolutional Neural Network (CNN) based approach for image segmentation that does not need any labeled training data and can work on single image input. It uses a pre-trained network to extract mid-level deep features that capture the semantics of the input image. Extracted deep features are further fed to trainable convolutional layers. Segmentation labels are obtained using argmax classification of the final layer and further spatial refinement. Obtained segmentation labels and the weights of the trainable convolutional layers are jointly optimized in iterations in a mechanism that the deep network learns to assign spatially neighboring pixels and pixels of similar feature to the same label. After training, the input image is processed through the same network to obtain the labels that are further refined by a segment score based refinement mechanism. Experimental results show that our method obtains satisfactory results inspite of being unsupervised.

Keywords: Unsupervised image segmentation · Semantic guided ·
Deep learning

1 Introduction

Image segmentation refers to the process of extracting perceptually meaningful regions of the image and accordingly assigning unique labels to the image pixels [15]. Image segmentation is treated as a high level image analysis paradigm and

E. Ricci et al. (Eds.): ICIAP 2019, LNCS 11752, pp. 499–510, 2019.
https://doi.org/10.1007/978-3-030-30645-8_46

it acts as a precursor step for many visual inference tasks [19]. Image segmentation is a challenging problem given complex interaction between different objects present in the image. Traditionally, image segmentation problem has been dealt in unsupervised way in the literature [9]. The unsupervised segmentation methods generally exploit region based techniques [7] to obtain spatially coherent group of pixels that share the spectral characteristics. The contour based strategies have also been proposed in the literature that connect the points of interest (e.g., edge pixels or corner pixels) in the image to delineate the boundaries separating adjoining regions [1]. Unsupervised segmentation may sometimes involve complex segment threshold calculation [26]. Considering the fact that unsupervised segmentation into arbitrary number of labels is challenging, many unsupervised segmentation approaches restrict the number of labels to foreground and background [16].

In contrary to the unsupervised models, the supervised models exploit available training pixels to learn a classifier model that can be subsequently used to obtain segmentation labels. Usually, low-level shallow features are constructed exploiting the spectral properties and subsequently different feature encodings like bag of words, Vector of Locally Aggregated Descriptors (VLAD) are used for effective representation of the pixels in the feature space. Supervised algorithms, e.g., SVM, Naive Bayes, Neural Networks etc. are henceforth used to learn the classification model. However, sole application of the traditional classifiers in this respect may not preserve the image discontinuities and further may get affected by outliers. Additionally, most supervised methods impose spatial homogeneity constraints using structured learning approaches [3,4,12]. Supervised methods are preferred when grouping into many labels is required.

Recently, deep learning, especially, Convolutional Neural Network (CNN) based techniques have obtained state-of-the-art performance in most computer vision tasks. Inspired by this success, several approaches for image segmentation using deep learning have been proposed in the literature. These approaches belong to the category of the supervised approaches and require large training datasets with pixel-level labels. Obtaining abundant labeled data requires lot of effort and may not be available in many domains.

To circumnavigate the absence of labeled data, many image processing applications have recently successfully employed pre-trained deep networks as deep feature extractor in unsupervised [22] and semi-supervised settings [21]. Such features capture the image semantics in a more effective way than the low-level shallow features. Motivated by this, we approach the problem of deep unsupervised image segmentation by exploiting such features cascaded with a series of trainable convolutional layers. We assume a single image input and reference labels of pixels are not present. The input image is processed through a pre-trained VGG Net as deep feature extractor that are further fed to a series of trainable convolutional layers. The final convolutional layer is processed through a decision process to obtain the predicted labels. Predicted labels and the learnable parameters of the trainable convolutional layers are jointly optimized in iterations such that the deep network keeps evolving learning to identify the unique segments present in the image. More specifically, the network learns to assign pixels having similar features and neighboring pixels to the same label. After completion of training process, same network is used to obtain the labels from the input image. To further address over-segmentation problem, the labels are refined through a segment score based refinement mechanism.

The rest of this paper is organized as follows. A number of related methods are discussed briefly in Sect. 2. We describe the proposed algorithm in Sect. 3. We present the experimental results in Sect. 4. Finally, we conclude the paper and discuss scope of future works in Sect. 5.

2 Related Works

Considering the attention of the proposed work, we mainly discuss the deep learning based approaches on image segmentation. A significant number of deep learning based segmentation algorithms have been proposed in the recent past.

2.1 Supervised Deep Segmentation

The supervised approaches for the image segmentation is implicitly same as the pixel level classification task given a set of reliable training pixels. Generally, the segmentation methods employing deep neural network relies on bottom-up region proposals generation techniques to supervise the segmentation process. There has been a number of works involving deep neural networks for image segmentation [2,5,6,10,13,17,20,27]. Though not a deep learning based method, in [5] one of the first applications of pooling layer was proposed for semantic segmentation. Pooling forms indispensable part in most CNNs recently. In [10], region proposal is combined with CNN for object detection and semantic segmentation. Fully convolutional networks (FCNs) [13] that replace the fully connected layers with the convolutional layers is one of the simple yet effective model for supervised semantic segmentation problem. Such network has ability to take input of arbitrary spatial dimension and generate same size pixelwise segmentation map. [20] presents a variant of FCN that has a U-shaped architecture that supplements an usual contracting network by successive layers to capture context and a symmetric expanding path that improves the localization accuracy. Compared to FCN, U-Net has more upsampling layers and utilizes learnable weights instead of fixed interpolation strategies. SegNet [2] is another variation that uses a novel strategy to decode or upsample encoded features by storing the max-pooling indices used in pooling layer. Inspite of varying architectures, all these methods require substantial amount of training data and hence their use on every application domain is not possible. In case they are used in other application domains, they are trained with the images from that domains, e.g., semantic segmentation for remote sensing images [27].

2.2 Unsupervised Deep Segmentation

As deep learning techniques are maturing, there has been an increased interest in exploiting deep learning techniques in unsupervised way. There are two major trends in this direction, transfer learning based methods that effectively transfers a network trained for a task on other tasks [23] and Generative Adversarial Network based methods that still require a lot of unlabeled data [24]. Aligned with trend of increased interest in unsupervised deep learning, very recently we observe that few works have been proposed to address the image segmentation problem in an unsupervised way [11,28]. In [28], popular U-Net architecture is modified to a W-shaped network that is optimized to reconstruct the input images and simultaneously predicts a segmentation map without using any labeling information. However, the network is pretty complex consisting of 46 convolutional layers that are grouped into 18 modules that are further grouped into two groups of 9 modules each. The first one of these two forms the dense encoding an prediction part of the network and the second one forms the reconstruction decoder. In our opinion, such network complexity is not desired in unsupervised settings that involve zero to few training samples. Even though the method in [28] don't use label information for training, it still requires a substantially big dataset for training (trained on Pascal VOC 2012 dataset [8]). Our proposed method involves an architecture much simpler than this and still obtains reliable result. Inspired by unsupervised deep clustering [29], in [11] an unsupervised image segmentation method is proposed that uses few convolutional layers. The output label is obtained at the final layer using argmax classification that is further regulated by superpixel based refinement. Predicted pixel labels and network weights are jointly optimized in an iterative fashion by gradient descent method. Our method is related to this method in essence that we also build up on joint optimization of pixel labels along with weights of the learnable convolutional layers. However, instead of feeding the learnable layers with raw image inputs, our semantically guided method feeds the deep features extracted from an intermediate layer of a pre-trained network. Such features that carry much rich information than pixel values guides the subsequent learnable layers to optimize in more effective fashion. Moreover, we exploit mode statistics based spatial filtering along with argmax classification to obtain image labels that captures the spatial context in contrary to [11] that uses a superpixel based refinement. We also propose a segment score based refinement step to effectively reduce the over-segmented clusters.

3 Proposed Algorithm

3.1 Problem Definition

Let us assume that we have a RGB image X consisting of a set of N pixels x_n $(n = 1, \ldots, N)$. The label information related to any pixels in x_n $(n = 1, \ldots, N)$ is not known. Our goal is to assign meaningful segment labels c_n^{final} to all of the N pixels by learning a mapping function $f(x_n)$. The mapping function

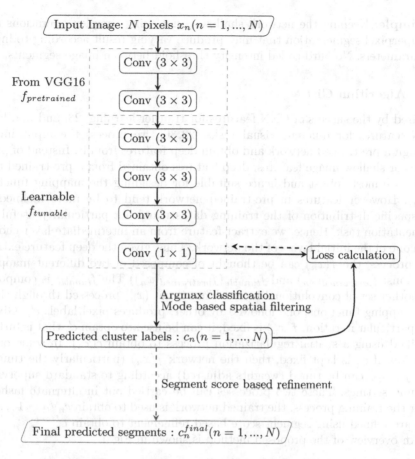

Fig. 1. Proposed unsupervised deep image segmentation framework. Input image are processed through a fixed pre-trained feature extractor $f_{pretrained}$ followed by learnable $f_{pretrained}$. Labels c_n corresponding to all input pixels x_n $(n = 1, \ldots, N)$ are shown obtained through a decision process consisting of argmax classification and spatial filtering. Training loss is computed using output of the final conv. (1×1) layer and the predicted labels. The segment score based refinement to obtain final predicted labels is not performed during training iterations. ReLu activation function and batch normalization layers are not shown here.

is learned using a series of convolutional layers, however in an unsupervised way, i.e., not using any label information about x_n. In designing the mapping function $f(x_n)$, we are guided by following notions:

1. **Knowledge from other:** Use of pre-trained network as a semantic guide to enhance the segmentation process, i.e., to harvest the knowledge that has been already learned by such a network for other tasks.

2. **Simple:** Keeping the network shallower, not using complex operations like superpixel segmentation that may produce varying result according to input parameters. No hard-coded intensity threshold between image segments.

3.2   Algorithm Gist

Inspired by the success of CNN features for transfer learning [23] and mid level CNN features for different visual tasks [22,30], we process the input image through a pre-trained network and obtain deep features from it. Instead of pixel values or shallow image features, deep features obtained from a pre-trained networks are most robust and hence suitable for designing the mapping function $f(x_n)$. However features in pre-trained network tend to be more inclined to the specific distribution of the training dataset and not particularly useful for segmentation task. Hence, we extract feature from an intermediate layer chosen from one of the initial layers of the network. Thus, given the deep feature extraction process, the $f(x_n)$ can be thought of composed of two different mapping functions: $f_{pretrained}(x_n)$ and $f_{tunable}(f_{pretrained}(x_n))$ The $f_{tunable}$ is composed of another set of convolutional layers. Thus input (x_n) processed through these two mapping functions, one followed by other, produces pixel labels c'_n. Given, at a particular iteration, $f(x_n)$ is fixed, it can be used to obtain c'_n that is further modified using a spatial regularization process to obtain $c(x_n)$. In some other iteration, if c_n is kept fixed, then the network $f(x_n)$ (particularly the tunable part $f_{tunable}$ can be tuned (weights adjusted) according to standard supervised learning settings. These two processes can be carried out in alternate fashion. After the training process, the trained network is used to obtain $c_n \forall n = 1 \ldots, N$ that are refined using segment score based refinement to obtain c_n^{final}.

An overview of the proposed method is shown in Fig. 1.

3.3   Algorithm Details

Pre-trained Deep Feature Extraction. Here we explain in details the process of deep feature extraction using pre-trained network (i.e., the mapping function $f_{pretrained}(x_n)$). Deep feature extraction process is based on the assumption that features captured by the convolutional filter banks of the pre-trained CNN are more effective in capturing spatial context and spectral information than the raw pixel values. In particular we chose VGG16 network [25] pretrained on ImageNet dataset. We use PyTorch [18] for implementation purposes and pre-trained network is provided by it. As discussed in Sect. 3.2, deep features required for segmentation is not required to be from very deeper layers. Hence, we extract deep features from the second convolutional layer of VGG16. Thus the part of the VGG16 used for feature extraction consists of a convolutional layer followed by a ReLU activation function and another convolutional layer. Since there is no pooling layer upto second convolutional layer, hence we can input image of any size to obtain the feature map of size 64 while retaining the same spatial dimension. The mapping function $f_{pretrained}(x_n)$ transforms 3-band input pixels x_n to 64 channel feature maps. These 64 filter maps provides semantic guidance to the subsequent steps. Note that this is a striking difference of our method from [11] that uses pixel values as input to the learnable layers.

Learnable Convolutional Layers. Here we describe the details of $f_{tunable}$. Though features extracted from pre-trained deep network is robust, they are not attuned for the given input image. Moreover, we need to obtain a response map y_n corresponding to each pixel x_n to classify the pixels into different labels. Hence, we use learnable convolutional layers designed for these purposes. More specifically, we use four convolutional layers, each followed by batch normalization. The first three convolutional layer consists of filters of size 3×3 and helps in further modulating the features obtained from the pre-trained network. The first one takes 64 dimensional input and converts it into 100 dimensions. The following two take 100 dimensional input and maintains same dimension. The last convolutional layer consists of filters of size 1×1 and is meant to obtain a response map y_n by applying a linear classifier on the features. It takes 100 dimension input and maintains the dimension. The response map is further processed using batch normalization to obtain y'_n. Such normalization helps in controlling number of clusters as described in [11]. All these four layers comprise of learnable weights.

Training Learnable Layers. Here we describe mechanism to adjust weights of $f_{tunable}$. The response map y'_n is processed to obtain the cluster label c_n for each pixel x_n. In details, c'_n for a specific pixel x_n is obtained by argmax classification, i.e., choosing the dimension in y'_n that has maximum value in y'_n [11]. Considering that spatial continuity is important in image segmentation, we use a simple sliding window mode (most common value in a window) based image filtering to further refine the prediction map and we obtain c_n. This also helps in eliminating spurious redundant cluster labels. In this way we force pixel labels to take spatial information into account, however using a very simple process instead of complicated superpixel segmentation. The training process is accomplished in iterations, where in one iteration the c_n is obtained by keeping the weights of the $f_{tunable}$ fixed. In another iteration the weights corresponding to the $f_{tunable}$ are adjusted by keeping the c_n fixed. Cross-entropy loss is calculated between c_n and y'_n and loss is propagated back to the network for weight adjustment. However, weights corresponding to first two convolutional layers (obtained from VGG16) are not modified.

Obtaining Cluster Labels. To accomplish a reasonable training process, the training is executed for 500 iterations. However, if total number of clusters prematurely (i.e., before 500 iteration) reach 3, then the training process is stopped prematurely. In each training iteration, the number of clusters reduces as smaller labels merge into bigger labels. After completion of training iterations, the same network is used to obtain cluster label map (i.e., c_n for each x_n). Note that the cluster labels obtained at this stage need not be spatially continuous and can

have same labels for two spatially disconnected region. They are further refined
through a segment based refinement process to obtain final segment map c_n^{final}
for each x_n.

Segment Score Based Refinement. We detect each unique label segments
from the predicted map consisting of N labels c_n $(n = 1, \ldots, N)$. This is accomplished by using following principle:

1. Two spatially disconnected regions having same label are considered different
   segments.
2. Two spatially connected regions having different labels are considered different segments.

Here, we use the concept of 8-neighbor connectivity. Once M segments are
detected from the from the cluster label map, we define a segment score $\alpha_{m_1 m_2}$
between each pair of segments m_1 and m_2 in M such that:

1. If segments m_1 and m_2 are not neighbor, $\alpha_{m_1 m_2} = 0$.
2. If segments m_1 and m_2 are neighbor, number of pixels in m_1 (denoted by
   $\mathcal{A}_{m_1}$) and in m_2 (denoted by $\mathcal{A}_{m_2}$) are calculated. We define $\alpha_{m_1 m_2} = \frac{\mathcal{A}_{m_1}}{\mathcal{A}_{m_2}}$.

If $\alpha_{m_1 m_2} =\geq 50$, then segment m_2 is merged with segment m_1. After this refinement process, we obtain the final segment map c_n^{final} $(n = 1, \ldots, N)$.

4   Result

4.1   Dataset

For experimental evaluation, we use the popular Berkeley Segmentation Dataset
and Benchmark (BSDS500). We test on the 200 test images from the BSDS500
dataset [1,14]. Since our method is unsupervised, we do not use the training
images from this dataset.

4.2   Method

For each image, the proposed model is trained for 500 iterations and subsequently
the trained model is used to predict segmentation map as described in Sect. 3.3.
The number of iterations is set as equal to the same used in [11].

4.3   Qualitative Result

Sample results from our method is shown in Fig. 2. We observe that the proposed
method is able to delineate meaningful object segments. We further observe that
the proposed method is able to handle cases where object has significant variation in texture (e.g., in case of giraffe, Fig. 2(c) and (g)). The stairs in complex
building scenario (Fig. 2(d) and (h)) are partially detected. This shows the effectiveness of the proposed method based on pre-trained deep feature extraction and
learnable convolutional layers. It is evident in Fig. 2 that the proposed method
is not prone to over-segmentation. This shows the efficacy of the segmentation
refinement process based on segment score.

4.4   Quantitative Result

For quantitative comparison, we follow the procedures used in [11]. We calculate Intersection over Union (IoU) of the detected segments and ground truth segments. The detected segment is considered correctly detected if maximum IoU is greater than a IoU threshold 0.5. By following this procedure, for IoU threshold 0.5, proposed method obtains an average precision score of 0.1640 in comparison to 0.1394 by [11], 0.049 by kMeans clustering, and 0.1161 by [9]. Thus the proposed method outperforms the deep learning based unsupervised method in [11] that does not use pre-trained weights. Proposed method is able to obtain significant gain of average precision score (0.0246 gain from [11]). This further demonstrates that the proposed method is able to obtain satisfactory quantitative result and the usage of pre-trained weights before the trainable layers is indeed useful to obtain better segmentation.

We do not perform a direct quantitative comparison to supervised methods or those unsupervised methods that are dependent on large unlabeled dataset. Since those methods are more data driven, it is expected that those methods will possibly outperform the proposed method and they are beyond the scope of this paper.

4.5   Comments on Timing Complexity

Though we did not investigate timing requirements in detail, the method takes approximately 90 s per image (images of 481×321 pixels [1,14]) on a computer having GPU NVidia Geforce GTX 1080 Ti, Intel I7 CPU (3.2 GHz), and 32 GB RAM.

(a)   (b)   (c)   (d)

(e)   (f)   (g)   (h)

Fig. 2. Illustrations of the obtained segmentation map, input images in top row (a, b, c, d) and respective segmented images in bottom row (e, f, g, h)

5   Conclusion

In this paper, we propose an unsupervised image segmentation method. The proposed method does not require any labeled training pixels or availability of many unlabeled images. The proposed method can work on single image input using intermediate deep feature extracted from a pre-trained network followed by a series of trainable convolutional layers. The weights for the trainable layers are learned on the input image itself while optimizing the segmentation prediction map. Finally the label map is further refined using a simple refinement process to obtain final segment map. The results obtained on the benchmark dataset confirm the effectiveness of the proposed framework. The proposed method can be easily extended for image foreground extraction. The network trained by the proposed method on a particular image may be potentially reused on other images of similar content. By exploiting this assumption, we plan to extend the method for image co-segmentation.

References

1. Arbelaez, P., Maire, M., Fowlkes, C., Malik, J.: Contour detection and hierarchical image segmentation. IEEE Trans. Pattern Anal. Mach. Intell. **33**(5), 898–916 (2011)
2. Badrinarayanan, V., Kendall, A., Cipolla, R.: SegNet: a deep convolutional encoder-decoder architecture for image segmentation. IEEE Trans. Pattern Anal. Mach. Intell. **39**(12), 2481–2495 (2017)
3. Banerjee, B., Saha, S., Merchant, S.N.: Image foreground extraction—a supervised framework based on region transfer. In: 2016 International Conference on Signal and Information Processing (IConSIP), pp. 1–5. IEEE (2016)
4. Besag, J.: Spatial interaction and the statistical analysis of lattice systems. J. Roy. Stat. Soc.: Ser. B (Methodol.) **36**, 192–236 (1974)
5. Carreira, J., Caseiro, R., Batista, J., Sminchisescu, C.: Semantic segmentation with second-order pooling. In: Fitzgibbon, A., Lazebnik, S., Perona, P., Sato, Y., Schmid, C. (eds.) ECCV 2012. LNCS, vol. 7578, pp. 430–443. Springer, Heidelberg (2012). https://doi.org/10.1007/978-3-642-33786-4_32
6. Chen, L.C., Papandreou, G., Kokkinos, I., Murphy, K., Yuille, A.L.: DeepLab: semantic image segmentation with deep convolutional nets, atrous convolution, and fully connected CRFs. IEEE Trans. Pattern Anal. Mach. Intell. **40**(4), 834–848 (2018)
7. Cooper, M.C.: The tractability of segmentation and scene analysis. Int. J. Comput. Vis. **30**(1), 27–42 (1998)
8. Everingham, M., Van Gool, L., Williams, C.K.I., Winn, J., Zisserman, A.: The PASCAL Visual Object Classes Challenge 2012 (VOC 2012) Results. http://www.pascal-network.org/challenges/VOC/voc2012/workshop/index.html
9. Felzenszwalb, P.F., Huttenlocher, D.P.: Efficient graph-based image segmentation. Int. J. Comput. Vis. **59**(2), 167–181 (2004)
10. Girshick, R., Donahue, J., Darrell, T., Malik, J.: Rich feature hierarchies for accurate object detection and semantic segmentation. In: 2014 IEEE Conference on Computer Vision and Pattern Recognition (CVPR), pp. 580–587. IEEE (2014)

11. Kanezaki, A.: Unsupervised image segmentation by backpropagation. In: 2018 IEEE International Conference on Acoustics, Speech and Signal Processing (ICASSP), pp. 1543–1547. IEEE (2018)
12. Li, S.Z.: Markov Random Field Modeling in Image Analysis. Springer, London (2009). https://doi.org/10.1007/978-1-84800-279-1
13. Long, J., Shelhamer, E., Darrell, T.: Fully convolutional networks for semantic segmentation. In: Proceedings of the IEEE Conference on Computer Vision and Pattern Recognition, pp. 3431–3440 (2015)
14. Martin, D., Fowlkes, C., Tal, D., Malik, J., et al.: A database of human segmented natural images and its application to evaluating segmentation algorithms and measuring ecological statistics. ICCV, Vancouver (2001)
15. Pal, N.R., Pal, S.K.: A review on image segmentation techniques. Pattern Recogn. **26**(9), 1277–1294 (1993)
16. Park, K., Lee, J., Moon, Y.: Unsupervised foreground segmentation using background elimination and graph cut techniques. Electron. Lett. **45**(20), 1025–1027 (2009)
17. Paszke, A., Chaurasia, A., Kim, S., Culurciello, E.: ENet: a deep neural network architecture for real-time semantic segmentation. arXiv preprint arXiv:1606.02147 (2016)
18. Paszke, A., et al.: Automatic differentiation in PyTorch (2017)
19. Ribbens, A., Hermans, J., Maes, F., Vandermeulen, D., Suetens, P.: Unsupervised segmentation, clustering, and groupwise registration of heterogeneous populations of brain MR images. IEEE Trans. Med. Imaging **33**(2), 201–224 (2014)
20. Ronneberger, O., Fischer, P., Brox, T.: U-Net: convolutional networks for biomedical image segmentation. In: Navab, N., Hornegger, J., Wells, W.M., Frangi, A.F. (eds.) MICCAI 2015. LNCS, vol. 9351, pp. 234–241. Springer, Cham (2015). https://doi.org/10.1007/978-3-319-24574-4_28
21. Roy, S., Sangineto, E., Sebe, N., Demir, B.: Semantic-fusion GANs for semi-supervised satellite image classification. In: 2018 25th IEEE International Conference on Image Processing (ICIP), pp. 684–688. IEEE (2018)
22. Saha, S., Bovolo, F., Bruzzone, L.: Unsupervised deep change vector analysis for multiple-change detection in VHR images. IEEE Trans. Geosci. Remote Sens. **57**, 3677–3693 (2019)
23. Sharif Razavian, A., Azizpour, H., Sullivan, J., Carlsson, S.: CNN features off-the-shelf: an astounding baseline for recognition. In: Proceedings of the IEEE Conference on Computer Vision and Pattern Recognition Workshops, pp. 806–813 (2014)
24. Shrivastava, A., Pfister, T., Tuzel, O., Susskind, J., Wang, W., Webb, R.: Learning from simulated and unsupervised images through adversarial training. In: Proceedings of the IEEE Conference on Computer Vision and Pattern Recognition, pp. 2107–2116 (2017)
25. Simonyan, K., Zisserman, A.: Very deep convolutional networks for large-scale image recognition. arXiv preprint arXiv:1409.1556 (2014)
26. Tang, Z., Wu, Y.: One image segmentation method based on Otsu and fuzzy theory seeking image segment threshold. In: 2011 International Conference on Electronics, Communications and Control (ICECC), pp. 2170–2173. IEEE (2011)
27. Volpi, M., Tuia, D.: Dense semantic labeling of subdecimeter resolution images with convolutional neural networks. IEEE Trans. Geosci. Remote Sens. **55**(2), 881–893 (2017)
28. Xia, X., Kulis, B.: W-Net: a deep model for fully unsupervised image segmentation. arXiv preprint arXiv:1711.08506 (2017)

29. Xie, J., Girshick, R., Farhadi, A.: Unsupervised deep embedding for clustering analysis. In: International Conference on Machine Learning, pp. 478–487 (2016)
30. Yang, B., Yan, J., Lei, Z., Li, S.Z.: Convolutional channel features. In: Proceedings of the IEEE International Conference on Computer Vision, pp. 82–90 (2015)

Gaze-Based Human-Robot Interaction by the Brunswick Model

Riccardo Berra[1]([✉]), Francesco Setti[1,3]([iD]), and Marco Cristani[1,2,3]([iD])

[1] Department of Computer Science, University of Verona,
Strada le Grazie 15, 37134 Verona, Italy
riccardo.berra@studenti.univr.it,
{francesco.setti,marco.cristani}@univr.it
[2] PAVIS - Pattern Analysis and Computer Vision, Istituto Italiano di Tecnologia,
via Enrico Melen 83, Edificio B, 16152 Genoa, Italy
[3] Institute for Cognitive Sciences and Technologies, National Research Council,
via alla Cascata 56C, 38123 Trento, Italy

Abstract. We present a new paradigm for human-robot interaction based on social signal processing, and in particular on the Brunswick model. Originally, the Brunswick model copes with face-to-face dyadic interaction, assuming that the interactants are communicating through a continuous exchange of non verbal social signals, in addition to the spoken messages. Social signals have to be interpreted, thanks to a proper recognition phase that considers visual and audio information. The Brunswick model allows to quantitatively evaluate the quality of the interaction using statistical tools which measure how effective is the recognition phase. In this paper we cast this theory when one of the interactants is a robot; in this case, the recognition phase performed by the robot and the human have to be revised w.r.t. the original model. The model is applied to *Berrick*, a recent open-source low-cost robotic head platform, where the gazing is the social signal to be considered.

Keywords: Human robot interaction · Machine learning · Social signal processing · Face detection

1 Introduction

There is an increasing interest, both from academic people and from robot manufacturers, in the design of robots that are able to work side by side with human operators for the execution of complex tasks. Human-Robots Collaboration (HRC) is gaining popularity in many environments, from home living to manufacturing, from education [32] to healthcare [22]. The execution of complex tasks, such as assembly multiple parts or cooking a meal, require both the precision and speed of autonomous agents as well as the dexterity and intelligence of human operators. HRC brings benefits to all these application scenarios in terms of speed, efficiency, better quality of the production and better quality of the workplace (ergonomic) [12].

© Springer Nature Switzerland AG 2019
E. Ricci et al. (Eds.): ICIAP 2019, LNCS 11752, pp. 511–521, 2019.
https://doi.org/10.1007/978-3-030-30645-8_47

It is the explicit design of anthropomorphic features, such as a head with eyes and a mouth, that may facilitate social interaction with a robot. This highlights the issue that social interaction is fundamentally observer-dependent, and exploring the mechanisms underlying anthropomorphism provides the key to the social features required for a machine to be socially engaging.

Many humanoid robots have been developed and are successfully used in the daily lives of humans, like the RIBA [22] and the Robovie-R [32]. Most of these robots have been designed with the aim of reproducing on the robot a natural human-like behaviour. On the contrary, we adopt an opposite approach, grounding on the Brunswick model. We start from the sociological observation that we (humans) implicitly agree that robots are artificial agents and thus we build an ad-hoc interaction model [1]. In this paper we use a robotic head platform (*Berrick*) provided with a coloured led system integrated into the ocular cavities to give feedbacks to the human counterpart. We will show that this system is suitable to instantiate an effective interaction with a human. We will demonstrate this claim by using the gaze of the robot as social signal.

2   The *Berrick* Platform

Berrick is a completely open-source, low-cost robotic head platform. *Berrick* takes from *InMoov* [17], we isolated the head and redesigned some components in order to improve the HRI capabilities of the platform. In particular, *Berrick* inherits the *InMoov* look, accompanied by the general mechanic motion system with 5 d.o.f., but offers a completely new design for what concerns the electronic architecture and the ocular structure. *Berrick* is thought as a way to encourage study and research on social HRI, since its optimal compromise between costs and benefits.

In this paper we will show how *Berrick* can be employed to study HRI paradigms with special emphasis on situated exchanges, that is, interactions where the robots do reason about their surroundings, and engage in fluid interaction with humans in certain physical settings [16]. Situated interactions imply the robot as fully understanding signals of engagement, attention, proximity, interruptability, turn-taking, group dynamics, social expectations, human memory and goals, going beyond the mere verbal language understanding [11]. In particular, here we will focus on the aspect of *gazing*.

2.1   Gazing with *Berrick*

Since humans are a profoundly social species, it is widely-accepted that people will generally apply a social model when observing and interacting with autonomous robots [7]. Therefore, a successful interaction may happen when the robot supports and validates this model [8], with the main benefit of making the interaction seamless, effective, and increasing the human trust [24]. The issue is that the human social model is not fully observable, but is based on implicit cognitive processes that *produce* and *evaluate* observable cues, *i.e. social signals* [30]. Social signals can be very explicit and communicative (like arm gestures), or subtle and of short duration (like gazing, sweating), making the social exchange very demanding in terms of attention [30].

In particular, we focus here on gazing, *i.e.* when the eyes appear to gaze directly at a participant during a social exchange [13]. Gazing is a fundamental social signal for situated interactions, which drives the communication by controlling the turn-taking, enacting deictic reference, triggering (shared) attention and engagement [1,3,23,30]. In particular, making eye contact (*i.e.* start gazing an interlocutor) is the primary *thin slice of behaviour* [2] to start an interaction [1,25,29]. In addition, keeping the eye contact is beneficial for the exchange quality, especially in scenarios with social groups to take the turn [27], or when the dialog activity between human and robot is interleaved with other activities (for example while cooking, with the human consulting the robot while preparing the food) [19].

In general, mutual gaze is important to reach a crucial state during the interaction, which is that of *joint attention* [27], that is a mutual awareness of the other's internal cognitive state. In a human-human conversational scenario, prior to start interacting and during the conversation, both the humans are aware that the partner is focusing on the exchange by mainly reciprocal gazing, with secondary optional additional cues (nodding, short confirmation utterances, positive facial expressions, etc.) [5,9]. When it comes to human-robot interaction, this type of bilateral awareness is harder to get. In facts, while the robot may understand that the human is focused by advanced pattern recognition algorithms working on the face expressiveness [21], the human has a harder recognition job since the robot is usually showing less expressivity due to its limited facial mobility [6].

In this work, we focus exactly on this last direction, exploring with *Berrick* a way to easily communicate to the human the internal cognitive state of the robot through a gazing cue. In particular, the goal is to communicate to the human that the robot is focusing at his face. In practice, *Berrick* is equipped with a standard yet sufficiently performing face detector [20] which gives, other than the detection bounding box, the detection confidence too. Once the confidence is higher than a given threshold, this has to be communicated through a gazing-related cue to the human.

To this sake, we build our proposed solution upon 2 facts:

1. Humans implicitly agree that the robot is not a human being while interacting [1] and has to be treated differently; this is especially true with gazing, with people spending significantly more time looking at a robot partner's face than at a human partner's face for example when naming an object, indicating the need to be sure that the robot is attending to the object into play [33].
2. Expressive lights are very effective in communicating the internal state of robots, complementing existing modalities of interaction that are naturally transient (*e.g.* speech) or that may have problem at a high distance (*e.g.* on-screen text) [4].

Fig. 1. *Berrick* without any detected face in its field of view (left) and detecting a face (right): the light signal is switched on. (Color figure online)

Our solution consists in the use of two coloured lights (yellow in our case) in the area around the *Berrick*'s pupils; the lights communicate that the human face has been captured with high confidence by the robot: they are switched on whenever the robot detects the human's face above a certain confidence θ_h, kept off otherwise. Figure 1 shows *Berrick* in these two states.

It is worth noting that the use of lights for non-verbal communication on robots is at its infancy, since lights so far did not have a direct functional role but rather they served as very basic indicators (*e.g.* battery level) or to express emotions [15]. The most similar idea is discussed in [4], where anyway robots are not anthropomorphic and different color codes are adopted, implying a certain cognitive load by the users. On the contrary, our eye-mounted lighting system may trigger *cognitive affordance*, simplifying the association of the light signal to a precise social signal related to gazing [14]. In particular, in this work we will explore how effective is this signal in communicating the state of the robot.

3 Brunswick

In this section we first present a HRI social interaction paradigm which consider social signals in a *computable* way, which originates from the Brunswick Lens [5, 9]. The Brunswick Lens comes with computable metrics to assess how much effort human and robot must contribute (independently and jointly) to effectively accomplish a task. These metrics are well-suited for HRI, and in particular can be used to evaluate the *operator performance* and the *robot performance*, following a widely-cited HRI metrics taxonomy [28].

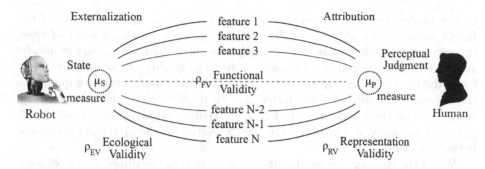

Fig. 2. The Brunswik Lens model for the HRI scenario. Ecological and representation validities are measured with the Spearman coefficient.

Subsequently, we cast the Brunswick Lens into a HRI scenario where *Berrick* has to perform a detection task on a given object and a human user has to understand when the object is docked, demonstrating from one side how *Berrick* can effectively perform detection (so showing the validity of its current hardware and software setup), and on the other side how the Brunswick Lens can be applied on *Berrick* to evaluate the quality of the HRI.

3.1 Brunswick Lens for HRI

This section provides an implementation of the *Brunswik's Lens* model which is compliant with an HRI scenario. The model was originally proposed in [9], and successively modified to investigate the influence of nonverbal behavior in face-to-face interactions [26] or the judgment of rapport [5].

Figure 2 sketches how the Brunswick model can analyze a single interaction instance occurring when the Robot emits a social signal and the Human codifies it. The other way around is symmetrical, with the Robot codifying the social signals emitted by the Human (the *Externalization* and *Attribution* labels flip, as so as the other lateral attributes). This latter direction will not analyzed for the sake of space and left for another communication.

The Robot is always assumed to be in a certain *state* that is assumed as *transient*[1] (see below for an example). In operational terms, the states are defined as quantitative measures (identified as μ_S in Fig. 2) to be obtained via objective processes depending on the particular case under observation. For example, in an object detection scenario, the state can be as "Searching for an object" or "Object i individuated", where i spans over C possible objects, and can be exactly measured by evaluating the internal state of the recognition algorithm (*i.e.* the last layer of a neural network) which is running in the robot. According

---

[1] The Brunswick model analyzes also *stable* states, *i.e.* social signals like personality traits, values, social status, etc. [30], which for simplicity are considered here as not characterizing a robot. In fact, a consistent body of research is focusing on these social signals and we suggest the reader to refer to [10, 18, 31] for a review.

to the model, visible cues emitted by the robot are an *externalization* of the Robot state, *i.e.* an observable effect of it. From an operational point of view, the cues are tangible *features* that should be acquired by the Human but also be automatically measured (by a sensor) to test the quality of the interaction. In facts, the empirical covariation of state measures and tangible features quantifies the *ecological validity* of these latter, *i.e.* their effectiveness in systematically accounting for the Robot state. In Fig. 2, the ecological validity is indicated with ρ_{EV} and, typically, it corresponds to the correlation or the Spearman coefficient between features and μ_S.

When the Human observe the Robot, he assigns to the Robot a state of measure μ_P. This process is called *attribution* and μ_P is referred to as *perceptual judgment*. For example, the Human can attribute that the Robot is in a particular (hidden) state based on the signals it is emitting, and this can be measured by asking the user to acknowledge when he think the robot has reached a particular state (*i.e.* when the Robot has detected/recognized an object of interest). We will see later in the experiments how all of these elements will have a clear association when considering the detection/classification task. In principle, μ_S and μ_P should have the same value (or at least similar values), but communication processes are always noisy, and this holds always when the communication has a human as interactant.

The empirical covariation between features and perceptual judgments accounts for the *representation validity* of the features (identified as ρ_{RV}), i.e. for the influence these latter have on the attribution process. In practice, ρ_{RV} measures how much the features emitted from the Robot are always interpreted in the same way by the Human. Like in the case of ρ_{EV}, the most common measurements of ρ_{RV} are correlation and Spearman coefficient.

As final mechanism to characterize an HRI instance, the empirical covariation of μ_S and μ_P (identified as ρ_{FV} in Fig. 2) accounts for measuring how much the communication from the Robot to the Human has worked properly, and the Human consistently knows what is the internal state of the Robot. This last measure is called *functional validity*.

4   Experiments

Experiments have been carried out for two purposes: (1) To show a scenario where the Brunswick model can be applied, illustrating all of its components and how they can be instantiated; (2) to investigate the effectiveness of the light-based gazing social signal sent by *Berrick* to communicate the internal state of the robot.

The experimental scenario is shown in Fig. 3. *Berrick* (in short, R) is placed on a rectangular table of height 0.75 m, with a 0° pan angle vector perpendicularly oriented w.r.t. the longer table side. The maximum pan angle of R is about 50° right and left. In front of the table, the human interactant (H) is located at a distance of approx 1.80 m. The goal of the experiment is to test how much the light-based gazing is useful in communicating the state of R, that is, that R has

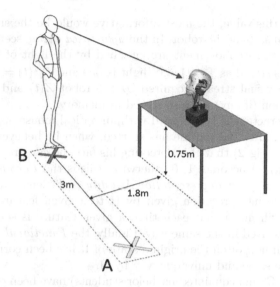

Fig. 3. Experimental scenario for the analysis of the light-based gazing social cue. (Color figure online)

detected the face of H. We compare two different *setups*: (1) *No-light*: R can pan its head, but the eye light is kept switched off; (2) *light-based gazing*: R can pan its head, and switches on the light whenever its face detector gives a hit with a confidence higher than $\theta_h = 0.8$.

H has to move right and left w.r.t. R, *looking at him as much as possible*, covering a straight line of 3 m in total, so that R has to rotate its head to have the face of H in its field of view[2]. In the detail, H is requested to *continuously move* from the extrema of the 3 m line (the yellow and blue crosses in Fig. 3) while looking at R, *at a fixed velocity*. The straight line is located 1.8 m w.r.t. the floor projection of the H's center of mass. This routine starts at $t = 0$ and holds for 180 s.

R starts with the detector and H starts moving from the center of the 3 m line. During the routine, R produces a boolean 1 Hz signal $\mu_S(t)$ representing its internal *State measure* (see Fig. 2), here enriched with the time index t: $\mu_S(t) = 0$ means no detection, $\mu_S(t) = 1$ means a face is detected with at least 0.8 of confidence. Following the Brunswick model, in the *No-light* scenario, the head orientation of R and its movement are the only *features* which may transmit its internal state, through the *Externalization* process (Fig. 2). In fact, R pans its head in order to put the detection at the center of its field of view. To gather this signal, we collect the head movement as $f_S^{(h)}(t) = 0$ (the head is not moving) and $f_S^{(h)}(t) = 1$ (the head is moving). To describe the effectiveness with which the internal state of R is sent, we will evaluate the *Ecological Validity* coefficient

---

[2] The robot moves the head until the detected object is at the center of its field of view.

ρ_{EV}. The higher this value, the most informative would be the signal sent to H about the internal state of the robot. In the *light-based gazing* scenario, the head orientation of R and its movement are enriched by the light of the eyes of R. The light signal is stored as $f_S^{(l)}(t) = 0$ (light is off) and $f_S^{(l)}(t) = 1$ (light is on). Additionally, the visual stream acquired by the robot $Z(t)$ and the bounding box of the detection (if any) are also stored in memory.

The other interactant H is equipped with an optical mouse opportunely programmed so that, after the routine has started, when he believes (through the *Attribution* phase, Fig. 2) that R is detecting his face, he can press a button and a related signal $\mu_P(t)$ becomes 1, 0 otherwise: this is the *Perceptual Judgment measure*. In this case, the *Representation Validity* coefficient ρ_{RV} will tell how much stable is the interpretation given by H to a given feature expressed by R. A high ρ_{RV} will mean that each time a given feature is sent to the user, this is always perceived in the same way. Finally, the *Functional Validity* coefficient ρ_{FV} will tell how often the original state of R has been correctly sent and interpreted in the same and univoque way by H.

Ten subjects (CS unacquainted bachelor students) have been enrolled to play the routine in both the light-based gazing and no-light regimes. Each routine has been repeated 3 times to deal with within human subject variability. Prior to compute classification figures, a quantitative manual analysis has been carried out to check whether the face detection is providing high precision results: in practice, a human operator was checking the labeled $Z(t)$. Due to the controlled environment, the number of false positives generated by the R detector is lower than the 1%. Concerning the detection recall performances, the robot was capable to detect the human in around 83% of times, making the experiment not trivial (it would have been trivial in the case the robot was capable of detecting H all of the time: in such a case it would have to communicate just a single state).

4.1   Results

In the *No-light* scenario, the average Ecological Validity (across the diverse test) is $\rho_{EV} = 0.1$, *i.e.* when correlating $f_S^{(h)}(t)$ and $\mu_S(t)$. This low value is due to the fact that R was detecting H even standing still, so that the pan movement was not the most reliable indicator of the internal state of R. Concerning the Representation Validity (that is, correlating $f_S^{(h)}(t)$ and $\mu_P(t)$), this was pretty high, $\rho_{RV} = 0.98$, since almost every tester was convinced that the head movement was a proxy for the detection performed by R. Finally, the average Functional Validity is $\rho_{FV} = 0.08$, as a consequence that the perceived state of R was based on a poor feature.

In the *Light-based gazing* scenario, the average Ecological Validity (across the diverse test) is high: $\rho_{EV} = 1$: in fact, the light based gazing was deterministically indicating when R was detecting H, by definition of light-based gazing. In a similar manner, the Representation Validity was pretty high, $\rho_{RV} = 0.74$, since all of the subjects reacted properly to the light of the eyes of R. The correlation is

Table 1. Accuracy measures on correctly inferring the internal robot cognitive state. In the first column, as reference, the mean (standard deviation) statistics of the detections carried out by *Berrick*. The last three columns report Ecological Validity (ρ_{EV}), Representation Validity (ρ_{RV}), and Functional Validity (ρ_{FV}).

Setup	# detections	Precision	Recall	ρ_{EV}	ρ_{RV}	ρ_{FV}
No-light	152.7 (*5.03*)	0.89	0.36	0.10	0.98	0.08
Light gazing	143.8 (*7.61*)	0.94	0.94	1.00	0.74	0.68

not higher since the detection done by R, driven by a detector working at a high frame rate, was producing in many times some flickering effects (due to the fact that in a single second the light could have been on and off in consequence to the rapid change of the detector response) leaving H a little confused on about what to press. Finally, the Functional Validity of the system is $\rho_{FV} = 0.68$ showing a correlation which is definitely higher than the one obtained with the No-light scenario (Table 1).

5   Conclusion

In this paper we presented a system to evaluate the quality of a face-to-face human-robot interaction, borrowed from the social signal processing literature. The system comes from the Brunswick model, and is particularly appealing since it is the first that explicitly deals with the internal state of the robot, which is the robotic counterpart of the cognitive processes that characterize humans.

Acknowledgements. This work has been partially supported by the project of the Italian Ministry of Education, Universities and Research (MIUR) "Dipartimenti di Eccellenza 2018–2022", and has been partially supported by the POR FESR 2014–2020 Work Program (Action 1.1.4, project No. 10066183).

References

1. Admoni, H., Scassellati, B.: Social eye gaze in human-robot interaction: a review. J. Hum.-Robot Interact. **6**(1), 25–63 (2017)
2. Ambady, N., Rosenthal, R.: Thin slices of expressive behavior as predictors of interpersonal consequences: a meta-analysis. Psychol. Bull. **111**(2), 256 (1992)
3. Argyle, M., Ingham, R., Alkema, F., McCallin, M.: The different functions of gaze. Semiotica **7**(1), 19–32 (1973)
4. Baraka, K., Rosenthal, S., Veloso, M.: Enhancing human understanding of a mobile robot's state and actions using expressive lights. In: International Symposium on Robot and Human Interactive Communication (RO-MAN). IEEE (2016)
5. Bernieri, F.J., Gillis, J.S.: Judging rapport: employing Brunswik's lens model to study interpersonal sensitivity. In: Interpersonal Sensitivity. Theory and Measurement. Lawrence Erlbaum (2001)

6. Breazeal, C.: Emotion and sociable humanoid robots. Int. J. Hum.-Comput. Stud. **59**(1–2), 119–155 (2003)
7. Breazeal, C.: Toward sociable robots. Robot. Auton. Syst. **42**(3–4), 167–175 (2003)
8. Breazeal, C.: Social interactions in HRI: the robot view. IEEE Trans. Syst. Man Cybern. Part C (Appl. Rev.) **34**(2), 181–186 (2004)
9. Brunswik, E.: Perception and the Representative Design of Psychological Experiments. University of California Press, Berkeley (1956)
10. Francis Jr., A.G., Lewis, T.: Methods and systems for robot personality development, US Patent 8,996,429, 31 March 2015
11. Goodwin, C.: Action and embodiment within situated human interaction. J. Pragmat. **32**(10), 1489–1522 (2000)
12. Gravot, F., Haneda, A., Okada, K., Inaba, M.: Cooking for humanoid robot, a task that needs symbolic and geometric reasonings. In: International Conference on Robotics and Automation (ICRA). IEEE (2006)
13. de C. Hamilton, A.F.: Gazing at me: the importance of social meaning in understanding direct-gaze cues. Philos. Trans. Roy. Soc. B: Biol. Sci. **371**(1686), 20150080 (2016)
14. Hartson, R.: Cognitive, physical, sensory, and functional affordances in interaction design. Behav. Inf. Technol. **22**(5), 315–338 (2003)
15. Kim, M.G., Lee, H.S., Park, J.W., Jo, S.H., Chung, M.J.: Determining color and blinking to support facial expression of a robot for conveying emotional intensity. In: International Symposium on Robot and Human Interactive Communication (RO-MAN). IEEE (2008)
16. Kruijff, G.J.M., et al.: Situated dialogue processing for human-robot interaction. In: Christensen, H.I., Kruijff, G.J.M., Wyatt, J.L. (eds.) Cognitive Systems. COSMOS, vol. 8, pp. 311–364. Springer, Heidelberg (2010). https://doi.org/10.1007/978-3-642-11694-0_8
17. Langevin, G.: InMoov-open source 3D printed life-size robot (2014). http://inmoov.fr, License http://creativecommons.org/licenses/by-nc/3.0/legalcode
18. Lee, K.M., Peng, W., Jin, S.A., Yan, C.: Can robots manifest personality?: An empirical test of personality recognition, social responses, and social presence in human-robot interaction. J. Commun. **56**(4), 754–772 (2006)
19. Lemaignan, S., Ros, R., Sisbot, E.A., Alami, R., Beetz, M.: Grounding the interaction: anchoring situated discourse in everyday human-robot interaction. Int. J. Soc. Robot. **4**(2), 181–199 (2012)
20. Lienhart, R., Maydt, J.: An extended set of Haar-like features for rapid object detection. In: International Conference on Image Processing (ICIP). IEEE (2002)
21. McColl, D., Hong, A., Hatakeyama, N., Nejat, G., Benhabib, B.: A survey of autonomous human affect detection methods for social robots engaged in natural HRI. J. Intell. Robot. Syst. **82**(1), 101–133 (2016)
22. Mukai, T., et al.: Development of a nursing-care assistant robot RIBA that can lift a human in its arms. In: IEEE/RSJ International Conference on Intelligent Robots and Systems (IROS) (2010)
23. Nakano, Y.I., Ishii, R.: Estimating user's engagement from eye-gaze behaviors in human-agent conversations. In: International Conference on Intelligent User Interfaces, pp. 139–148. ACM (2010)
24. Sadrfaridpour, B., Wang, Y.: Collaborative assembly in hybrid manufacturing cells: an integrated framework for human-robot interaction. IEEE Trans. Autom. Sci. Eng. **15**(3), 1178–1192 (2018)

25. Sato, R., Takeuchi, Y.: Coordinating turn-taking and talking in multi-party conversations by controlling robot's eye-gaze. In: International Symposium on Robot and Human Interactive Communication, pp. 280–285. IEEE (2014)
26. Scherer, K.: Personality markers in speech. In: Social Markers in Speech, pp. 147–209. Cambridge University Press, Cambridge (1979)
27. Skantze, G., Hjalmarsson, A., Oertel, C.: Turn-taking, feedback and joint attention in situated human-robot interaction. Speech Commun. **65**, 50–66 (2014)
28. Steinfeld, A., et al.: Common metrics for human-robot interaction. In: ACM SIGCHI/SIGART Conference on Human-Robot Interaction. ACM (2006)
29. Vertegaal, R., Slagter, R., Van der Veer, G., Nijholt, A.: Eye gaze patterns in conversations: there is more to conversational agents than meets the eyes. In: Conference on Human Factors in Computing Systems (SIGCHI), pp. 301–308. ACM (2001)
30. Vinciarelli, A., Pantic, M., Bourlard, H.: Social signal processing: survey of an emerging domain. Image Vis. Comput. **27**(12), 1743–1759 (2009)
31. Walters, M.L., Syrdal, D.S., Dautenhahn, K., Te Boekhorst, R., Koay, K.L.: Avoiding the uncanny valley: robot appearance, personality and consistency of behavior in an attention-seeking home scenario for a robot companion. Auton. Robots **24**(2), 159–178 (2008)
32. Yousuf, M.A., Kobayashi, Y., Kuno, Y., Yamazaki, A., Yamazaki, K.: Development of a mobile museum guide robot that can configure spatial formation with visitors. In: Huang, D.-S., Jiang, C., Bevilacqua, V., Figueroa, J.C. (eds.) ICIC 2012. LNCS, vol. 7389, pp. 423–432. Springer, Heidelberg (2012). https://doi.org/10.1007/978-3-642-31588-6_55
33. Yu, C., Schermerhorn, P., Scheutz, M.: Adaptive eye gaze patterns in interactions with human and artificial agents. ACM Trans. Interact. Intell. Syst. **1**(2), 13 (2012)

Texture Retrieval in the Wild Through Detection-Based Attributes

Christian Joppi[1]([⊠]), Marco Godi[1], Andrea Giachetti[1], Fabio Pellacini[2], and Marco Cristani[1]

[1] University of Verona, Verona, Italy
christian.joppi@univr.it
[2] Sapienza University of Rome, Rome, Italy

Abstract. Capturing the essence of a textile image in a robust way is important to retrieve it in a large repository, especially if it has been acquired in the wild (by taking a photo of the textile of interest). In this paper we show that a texel-based representation fits well with this task. In particular, we refer to Texel-Att, a recent texel-based descriptor which has shown to capture fine grained variations of a texture, for retrieval purposes. After a brief explanation of Texel-Att, we will show in our experiments that this descriptor is robust to distortions resulting from acquisitions in the wild by setting up an experiment in which textures from the *ElBa* (an Element-Based texture dataset) are artificially distorted and then used to retrieve the original image. We compare our approach with existing descriptors using a simple ranking framework based on distance functions. Results show that even under extreme conditions (such as a down-sampling with a factor of 10), we perform better than alternative approaches.

Keywords: Texture descriptor · Attribute-based descriptor · Content based image retrieval

1 Introduction

Texels [1] are nameable elements that, distributed according to statistical models (see Fig. 1a–b), form textures that can be defined as *Element-based* [11,18,20,21]. Textures of this kind are of interest in the textile, fashion and interior design industry, since websites or catalogues (containing many products) have to be browsed by users that want to buy or take inspiration from [14,15]. Two examples taken from the popular e-commerce website Zalando are shown in Fig. 1b. For each item multiple pictures are usually available, including close-up pictures of the fabric highlighting the texture. Not all textures can be defined as Element-based; some can only be characterized at a *micro* scale (*e.g.* in the case of material

---

C. Joppi, M. Godi—These authors contributed equally to this work.

© Springer Nature Switzerland AG 2019
E. Ricci et al. (Eds.): ICIAP 2019, LNCS 11752, pp. 522–533, 2019.
https://doi.org/10.1007/978-3-030-30645-8_48

textures in Fig. 1c), but usually the patterns that decorate textile materials are based on repeated elements.

In the fashion domain browsing for textures is a common task. A shopper that is in possession of an item (e.g. a shirt) with a specific pattern could wish to shop for another item (e.g. pants with a matching pattern) to combine with by taking a close-up picture to highlight the desired texture. A fashion designer could want to take inspiration from an existing garment with only a low resolution picture of the texture available. In these scenarios, it would be useful to be able to search in a database for the desired texture using only a low-quality picture (i.e. in diverse lighting conditions and resolution) as a query. Texture retrieval that is robust to these conditions is an important addition for a fashion e-shop [13, 30] or for fashion designer tools [19]. To be able to achieve this for textures, it is very important to describe them and their structural information in an intuitive and interpretable way, in order to achieve a precise description that enables an accurate retrieval [25] based on the image content.

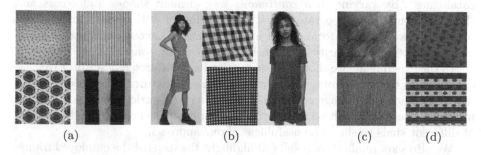

Fig. 1. (a) Examples of element-based textures in the DTD [5]: the *dotted* (left) and *banded* (right) classes are examples where texels are dots and bands, respectively; (b) Zalando shows for each clothing a particular on the texture; (c) examples of DTD [5] textures which are *not* element-based: (*marbled* on top and *porous* on bottom); here is hard to find clearly nameable local entities; (d) examples of *ElBa* textures: polygon on top, multi-class lined+circle texture on bottom.

For the purpose of achieving a discriminative and nameable description, attribute-based texture features [4,5,16,23] are explicitly suited. In the literature, the 47 perceptually-driven attributes such as *dotted, woven, lined,* etc. learned on the Describable Texture Dataset (DTD) [5] are the most known.

These 47 attributes are limited in the sense that they describe the properties of a texture image *as a single whole atomic entity*: in Fig. 1a, two different (element-based) attributes are considered: *dotted* (left) and *banded* (right) each one arranged in a column. Images in the same column, despite having the same attribute, are strongly different: for the dots, the difference is on the area; for the bands, the difference is on the thickness. In Fig. 1b (Zalando examples), both garments come with the same "checkered" attribute, despite the different sized squares.

It is evident that one needs to focus on the recognizable *texels* that form textures to achieve a finer expressivity.

In this paper, we employ *Texel-Att* [8], a fine-grained, attribute-based texture representation and classification framework for element-based textures.

The pipeline of Texel-Att first detects the single texels and describes them by using *individual attributes*. Then, depending on the individual attributes, they are grouped and these groups of texels are described by *layout attributes*.

The Texel-Att description of the texture is formed by joining the individual and layout attributes, so that they can be used for classification and retrieval. The dimensionality of the Texel-Att descriptor isn't pre-defined, it depends on which attributes are selected for the task. In this paper, we just give some examples to illustrate the general framework.

A Mask-RCNN [10] is used to detect texels; this shows that current state-of-the-art detection architectures can produce element-based descriptions (further improvements are foreseeable as we will discuss later). We design *ElBa*, the first *El*ement-*Ba*sed texture dataset, inspired by printing services and online catalogues[1]. By varying in a *continuous* way element shapes and colors and their distribution, we generate realistic renderings of 30K texture images in a procedural way using a total of 3M localized texels. Layout attributes such as local symmetry, stationarity and density are known by construction.

In the experiments we show that, using the attribute-based descriptor that we extract with our framework, we are able to retrieve textures in a more accurate way under simulated image conditions mimicking real-world scenarios. The performance of our approach is compared against state of the art texture descriptors of different kinds to show the usefulness of our approach.

We also show qualitative results to highlight the steps of the employed framework, such as the texel detection (detailed in Sect. 2.1).

2   Method

In this section we explain the Texel-Att framework step-by-step. Then we propose a simple method for texture retrieval that can be employed with this framework.

2.1   The Texel-Att Framework

Figure 2 shows a block diagram of the Texel-Att description creation pipeline.

The main concept is extracting texels using an object detection framework (trained for the task). Then, texels are described with *individual* attributes, *i.e.* labelled according to category, appearance and size. Texels are then grouped and filtered according to the individual labels. For each group, descriptions of the spatial layout of groups are estimated and aggregated into *layout* attributes. The

---

[1] https://www.spoonflower.com/, https://designyourfabric.ca/, https://patternizer.com/d0Wp and https://www.contrado.com/ respectively.

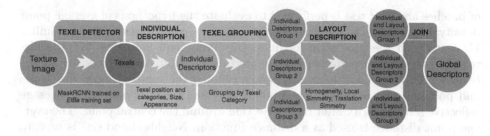

Fig. 2. Block diagram of the formation of the Texel-Att element-based texture descriptor. On the bottom of each plate, the specific choices made in this paper, which can be varied.

composite Texel-Att descriptor is formed by individual and layout attributes. In the following, each processing block is detailed.

Texel Detector. The Mask-RCNN [10] model handles the texel detection by localizing (with bounding boxes and segmentation masks) and classifying objects. The model is trained on the *ElBa* dataset's training set, learning to detect and classify texels such as *lines, circles, polygons* (see Sect. 3). Texels are easily handled in any displacement (while a few years ago it was a quite complicated task limited to specific scenarios *i.e.*, lattices [9,17]).

Individual Description of Texels. By using attributes related to shape and human perception it is possible to characterize each detected texel; in particulare we make use of: (i) the *label* indicating its shape, classified by the Mask-RCNN model; (ii) histogram of 11 *colors* using a color naming procedure [28]; (iii) *orientation* of texels; (iv) *size* of texels, represented by the area in pixels. By aggregating (e.g. through averages or histograms, see in the following sections) it is possible to characterize the whole texture. It is worth noting that in this work we are not showing "the best" set of features, but we are highlighting the portability and effectiveness of the framework; in fact, different attributes could be used instead.

Texel Grouping. Texels with the same appearance are clustered, so that spatial characteristics of similar elements can be captured using layout attributes. In this work we simply group texels by the assigned shape labels (*circle, line* or *polygon*). Groups with less than 10 texels are removed.

Layout Description of Texels. Spatial characteristics of each texel group, are described by measuring attributes using the spatial distribution of the centroids of the texels. We can refer to the literature on spatial points pattern analysis, where measures for symmetry, randomness, and regularity [2,7,29] are available; we select a simple and general set of measures. They are: (i) texel *density, e.g.* the average number of texels per unit of area (for circles and polygons) or line density (*e.g.* by projecting centroid on to the direction perpendicular to their principal orientation density is measured on one spatial dimension). (ii) Quadratic counts-based *homogeneity* evaluation [12]: the original image is divided into a number of patches and a χ^2 test is performed to evaluate the hypothesis of average point density in each patch. Similarly to the previous case, we estimated a similar 1D feature on the projection for lines. (iii) Point pair statistics [31]: the histogram of *vectors orientation* is estimated using point pair vectors for all the texel centers. (iv) *Local symmetry*: we considered the centroids' grid for circles and polygons and measured, for 4-points neighborhoods of points, the average reflective self-similarity after their reflection around the central point. The average point distance is used as a distance function. Neighborhood size is used to normalize it. *Translational symmetry* is estimated in a similar way by considering 4-point neighborhoods of the centroids translated by the vectors defined by point pairs in the neighborhood and measuring the average minimum distance of those points. For line texels, we compute on 1D projections.

We report the dimensionalities for each of these attributes in Table 1. Multidimensional attributes are histograms, while 1-dimensional ones are averages. By concatenating and Z-normalizing spatial pattern attributes, individual texel attributes statistics and the color attributes of the *background*, the final descriptor for the texture is built.

Table 1. Dimensionality of descriptor attributes. On the left, the attributes computed from the individual characterization of texels; on the right, attributes computed from statistics resulting from the spatial layout. The total dimensionality of the descriptor is 36.

Label Histogram	Color Histogram	Orientation	Size	**Total**
3	11	3	1	18

Density	Homogeneity	Vector Orientations	Local Symmetry	Traslational Symmetry	Background Color	**Total**
1	1	3	1	1	11	18

2.2   Element-Based Texture Retrieval

The descriptor detailed in the previous section can be used to compute distances between element-based textures using the corresponding attributes. We define *database set* the set of images that we want to search into using a *query image*. The idea is that database texture closest to the query image (in terms of descriptor distance) are also the most similar ones in the database set.

The pipeline is as follows: a query image (e.g. a picture of a textured captured by a user) is processed by the Texel detector, allowing for the computation of individual and layout attributes and thus obtaining a descriptor. A standard distance function (such as cosine distance) is computed between every database image and the query image. The database set is then sorted according to the distance and the resulting ranking can be shown to the user for browsing.

3   *ElBa*: Element-Based Texture Dataset

While available datasets such as the DTD [5] include some examples of element-based textures mixed with other texture types (Fig. 1(a)), there is no dataset focused on this particular domain. In this work, we present *ElBa*, the first element-based texture dataset. As shown in Fig. 1(d), photo-realistic images are included in the *ElBa* dataset. Training a model with synthetic data is a common practice [3,27] and annotations for texels are easily made available as an output of the image generation process. *Layout* attributes and *individual* ones (addressing the single texel) can be varied in our proposed parametric synthesis model. For example individual attributes such as texel shape, size and orientation and color can be varied. Available shapes are *polygons* (squares, triangles, rectangles), *lines* and *circles* (inspired by the 2D shape ontology of [24]). The idea is that these kind of shapes are common in geometric textiles and they approximate other more complex shapes. Orientation and size are varied within a range of values. We choose colors from color palettes to simulate a real-world use of colors.

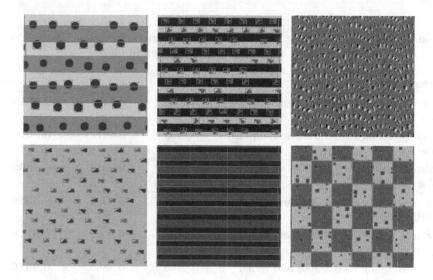

Fig. 3. Texel-Att detection qualitative results on *ElBa* datasets. In green the correct detections, in red the false positives and in blue the false negatives. (Color figure online)

As for Layout Attributes, we select different 2D layouts based on symmetries to place texels. Linear and grid-based layouts are considered; one or two non-orthonormal vectors define the translation between texels in the plane. With this parametrization, we can represent several tilings of the plane. As for randomized distributions, we jitter the regular grid, creating a continuous distribution between randomized and regular layouts.

We also consider multiple element shapes within a single image, creating for example dotted+striped patterns. Each group of elements of the same shape is distributed with its own spatial layout, creating arbitrary multi-class element textures as in Fig. 1(d).

We made use of Substance Designer for pattern generation (which gives high-quality output and pattern synthesis, and is easily controllable) and IRay (which is a physically-based renderer)[2]. Substance gives high-quality pattern synthesis, easy control and high-quality output including pattern antialiasing. Low-frequency distortions of the surface of the plane where the pattern is represented and high frequency patterns are added to simulate realistic materials.

A total of 30K texture images (for a total 3M annotated texels) rendered at a resolution of 1024×1024 has been generated by this procedure. For each image ground-truth data (such as texel masks, texel bounding boxes and attributes) is available. *ElBa* does not come with a partition into classes: differently from other datasets used in texture analysis semantic labels for classification tasks can be computed from ground truth attributes or by user studies.

The dataset is randomly partitioned with a 90/10 split for, respectively, training and testing set.

Table 2. *AUC (Area Under Curve)* for each distortion variant. Texel-Att performs better on every one of them. The related CMC are shown in Fig. 4.

Distortions	Tamura [26]	FV-CNN [6]	Texel-Att
Down-sampling (100 × 100) and impulsive noise (p = 0.2)	0.1380	0.3304	**0.6618**
Down-sampling (200 × 200) and impulsive noise (p = 0.2)	0.2103	0.4811	**0.8011**
Down-sampling (300 × 300) and impulsive noise (p = 0.2)	0.2284	0.5640	**0.8560**
Down-sampling (100 × 100) and radial lighting effect	0.1611	0.4394	**0.6356**
Down-sampling (200 × 200) and radial lighting effect	0.1728	0.8001	**0.8746**
Down-sampling (300 × 300) and radial lighting effect	0.2708	0.8855	**0.9376**

4   Experiments

Experiments show the potential of our framework for the description of element-based textures, with a focus on difficult environmental conditions (low resolution and diverse lighting) ensuring an accurate retrieval inside large catalogues of textures in real-world applications.

---

[2] https://www.allegorithmic.com/ and https://bit.ly/2Hz4ZVI respectively.

4.1 Qualitative Detection Results

We briefly show the detection results over our dataset, a fundamental step of our framework, through some qualitative results in Fig. 3. Texels are highlighted by bounding boxes which are then used to compute the attributes (described in Sect. 2.1) that we employ in the following experiment.

4.2 Texture Retrieval Results

In this experiment, we highlight the effectiveness of Texel-Att in a retrieval task under simulated real-world conditions following the procedure detailed in Sect. 2.2. We compare our approach with both state-of-the-art texture descriptor FV-CNN [5] and Tamura attribute-based descriptor [26]. The *database set* for this retrieval experiment is the whole test partition of the *ElBa* dataset (composed of ~3000 images). To simulate the real challenging conditions, we generated 6 variants of each image, down-sampling at one of 3 different resolutions (100×100, 200×200, 300×300) and up-sampling them back to the original image size (1024×1024). Then we apply one of the following distortions:

- impulsive noise with a pixel's probability of 0.2 over all the image;

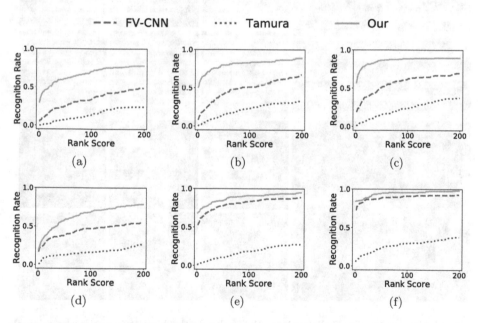

Fig. 4. *CMC curves* on the retrieval experiments. Different plot for different variants of distortion: (a) 100×100 down-sampling and impulsive noise (b) 200×200 down-sampling and impulsive noise (c) 300×300 down-sampling and impulsive noise (d) 100×100 down-sampling and radial lighting effect. (e) 200×200 down-sampling and radial lighting effect. (f) 300×300 down-sampling and radial lighting effect. On the x axis the rank score (first 200 positions). On the y axis the recognition rate.

– radial lighting effect, increasing the brightness on a random point on the
  image and gradually decreasing it more in each pixel the farther from the
  chosen point it is.

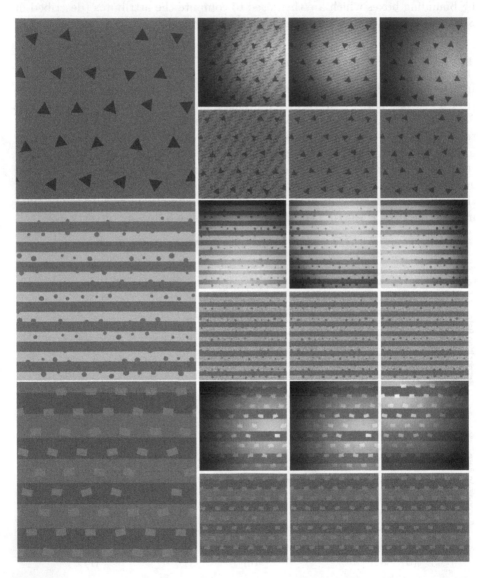

Fig. 5. Three examples of distortions. For each one the biggest image is the original
pattern. On the right, the first row depicts the radial lighting effect while the second
one the impulsive noise distortion. The column are organized from the 100×100 down-
sampling to 300×300 down-sampling.

Some examples of these images are shown in Fig. 5. It can be seen that distorted images simulate pictures that could be captured by users wishing to employ a retrieval application. The lighting effect simulates the flash of a camera while impulsive noise simulates general defects in the image acquisition process.

We consider each of the 6 variants as *query set* and we test each one separately. Given a distorted image from the query set, the task is to retrieve the corresponding original one from the database set. The position of the correct match in the computed ranking is recorded. This process is repeated for every image in a query set.

To distance functions used for ranking is chosen according to the descriptor; for each descriptor we selected the best performing distance function between all of the ones available in the MATLAB software [22]. More specifically, for the FV-CNN descriptor and our descriptor we employ the cosine distance while for the Tamura descriptor the cityblock distance function performs best.

Table 2 shows the results of this experiment in all of the 6 variants previously described. In each case Texel-Att reaches the best results in terms of *AUC: Area Under Curve* index related to CMC (Cumulative Matching Characteristics) curves shown in the plots in Fig. 4. We show only the first 200 positions for the CMC curve rank as we consider higher ranking positions less useful for a retrieval application (a user will rarely check results beyond 200 images).

5 Conclusion

This paper promotes to describe element-based textures by using attributes which focus on texels. Our framework, Texel-Att, can successfully describe and retrieve this type of patterns inside large databases even under simulated real-world factors such as poor resolution, noise and lighting conditions. The experiments show that we perform better in this task with our texel based attributes than by using state-of-the-art general texture descriptors, paving the way for retrieval applications in the fashion and textile domains where element-based textures are prominent.

Acknowledgements. This work has been partially supported by the project of the Italian Ministry of Education, Universities and Research (MIUR) "Dipartimenti di Eccellenza 2018–2022", and has been partially supported by the POR FESR 2014–2020 Work Program (Action 1.1.4, project No. 10066183). We also thank Nicolò Lanza for assistance with Substance Designer software.

References

1. Ahuja, N., Todorovic, S.: Extracting texels in 2.1 D natural textures. In: 2007 IEEE 11th International Conference on Computer Vision, pp. 1–8. IEEE (2007)
2. Baddeley, A., Rubak, E., Turner, R.: Spatial Point Patterns: Methodology and Applications with R. Chapman and Hall/CRC, New York (2015)

3. Barbosa, I.B., Cristani, M., Caputo, B., Rognhaugen, A., Theoharis, T.: Looking beyond appearances: synthetic training data for deep CNNs in re-identification. Comput. Vis. Image Underst. **167**, 50–62 (2018)
4. Bormann, R., Esslinger, D., Hundsdoerfer, D., Haegele, M., Vincze, M.: Robotics domain attributes database (RDAD) (2016)
5. Cimpoi, M., Maji, S., Kokkinos, I., Mohamed, S., Vedaldi, A.: Describing textures in the wild. In: Proceedings of the IEEE Conference on Computer Vision and Pattern Recognition, pp. 3606–3613 (2014)
6. Cimpoi, M., Maji, S., Kokkinos, I., Vedaldi, A.: Deep filter banks for texture recognition, description, and segmentation. Int. J. Comput. Vis. **118**(1), 65–94 (2016)
7. Diggle, P.J., et al.: Statistical Analysis of Spatial Point Patterns. Academic press, London (1983)
8. Godi, M., Joppi, C., Giachetti, A., Pellacini, F., Cristani, M.: Texel-Att: representing and classifying element-based textures by attributes (2019)
9. Gui, Y., Chen, M., Ma, L., Chen, Z.: Texel based regular and near-regular texture characterization. In: 2011 International Conference on Multimedia and Signal Processing, vol. 1, pp. 266–270. IEEE (2011)
10. He, K., Gkioxari, G., Dollár, P., Girshick, R.: Mask R-CNN. In: 2017 IEEE International Conference on Computer Vision (ICCV), pp. 2980–2988. IEEE (2017)
11. Ijiri, T., Mech, R., Igarashi, T., Miller, G.: An example-based procedural system for element arrangement. In: Computer Graphics Forum, vol. 27, pp. 429–436. Wiley Online Library (2008)
12. Illian, J., Penttinen, A., Stoyan, H., Stoyan, D.: Statistical Analysis and Modelling of Spatial Point Patterns, vol. 70. Wiley, Hoboken (2008)
13. Jing, Y., et al.: Visual search at pinterest. In: Proceedings of the 21th ACM SIGKDD International Conference on Knowledge Discovery and Data Mining, pp. 1889–1898. ACM (2015)
14. Kovashka, A., Parikh, D., Grauman, K.: WhittleSearch: image search with relative attribute feedback. In: 2012 IEEE CVPR. IEEE (2012)
15. Kovashka, A., Parikh, D., Grauman, K.: WhittleSearch: interactive image search with relative attribute feedback. Int. J. Comput. Vis. **115**(2), 185–210 (2015)
16. Liu, L., Chen, J., Fieguth, P.W., Zhao, G., Chellappa, R., Pietikäinen, M.: A survey of recent advances in texture representation. CoRR abs/1801.10324 (2018). http://arxiv.org/abs/1801.10324
17. Liu, S., Ng, T.T., Sunkavalli, K., Do, M.N., Shechtman, E., Carr, N.: PatchMatch-based automatic lattice detection for near-regular textures. In: Proceedings of the IEEE International Conference on Computer Vision, pp. 181–189 (2015)
18. Loi, H., Hurtut, T., Vergne, R., Thollot, J.: Programmable 2D arrangements for element texture design. ACM Trans. Graph. **36**(4) (2017). https://doi.org/10.1145/3072959.2983617
19. Hadi Kiapour, M., Han, X., Lazebnik, S., Berg, A.C., Berg, T.L.: Where to buy it: matching street clothing photos in online shops. In: International Conference on Computer Vision (2015)
20. Ma, C., Wei, L.Y., Lefebvre, S., Tong, X.: Dynamic element textures. ACM Trans. Graph. **32**(4), 90:1–90:10 (2013). https://doi.org/10.1145/2461912.2461921
21. Ma, C., Wei, L.Y., Tong, X.: Discrete element textures. ACM Trans. Graph. **30**(4), 62:1–62:10 (2011). https://doi.org/10.1145/2010324.1964957
22. MATLAB: version R2019a. The MathWorks Inc., Natick, Massachusetts (2019)
23. Matthews, T., Nixon, M.S., Niranjan, M.: Enriching texture analysis with semantic data. In: Proceedings of the IEEE Conference on Computer Vision and Pattern Recognition, pp. 1248–1255 (2013)

24. Niknam, M., Kemke, C.: Modeling shapes and graphics concepts in an ontology. In: SHAPES (2011)
25. Smeulders, A.W., Worring, M., Santini, S., Gupta, A., Jain, R.: Content-based image retrieval at the end of the early years. IEEE Trans. Pattern Anal. Mach. Intell. **22**(12), 1349–1380 (2000)
26. Tamura, H., Mori, S., Yamawaki, T.: Textural features corresponding to visual perception. IEEE Trans. Syst. Man Cybern. **8**(6), 460–473 (1978)
27. Tremblay, J., et al.: Training deep networks with synthetic data: bridging the reality gap by domain randomization. In: Proceedings of CVPR Workshops (2018)
28. Van De Weijer, J., Schmid, C., Verbeek, J., Larlus, D.: Learning color names for real-world applications. IEEE Trans. Image Process. **18**(7), 1512–1523 (2009)
29. Velázquez, E., Martínez, I., Getzin, S., Moloney, K.A., Wiegand, T.: An evaluation of the state of spatial point pattern analysis in ecology. Ecography **39**(11), 1042–1055 (2016)
30. Yang, F., et al.: Visual search at eBay. In: Proceedings of the 23rd ACM SIGKDD International Conference on Knowledge Discovery and Data Mining, pp. 2101–2110. ACM (2017)
31. Zhao, P., Quan, L.: Translation symmetry detection in a fronto-parallel view. In: CVPR 2011, pp. 1009–1016. IEEE (2011)

Multimedia

An Efficient Approximate kNN Graph Method for Diffusion on Image Retrieval

Federico Magliani[1]([✉])[iD], Kevin McGuinness[2][iD], Eva Mohedano[2],
and Andrea Prati[1][iD]

[1] IMP Lab, University of Parma, Parma, Italy
federico.magliani@studenti.unipr.it
[2] Insight Centre for Data Analytics, DCU, Dublin, Ireland

Abstract. The application of the diffusion in many computer vision and artificial intelligence projects has been shown to give excellent improvements in performance. One of the main bottlenecks of this technique is the quadratic growth of the kNN graph size due to the high-quantity of new connections between nodes in the graph, resulting in long computation times. Several strategies have been proposed to address this, but none are effective and efficient. Our novel technique, based on LSH projections, obtains the same performance as the exact kNN graph after diffusion, but in less time (approximately 18 times faster on a dataset of a hundred thousand images). The proposed method was validated and compared with other state-of-the-art on several public image datasets, including Oxford5k, Paris6k, and Oxford105k.

Keywords: Content-Based Image Retrieval · Diffusion · kNN graph

1 Introduction

Content-Based Image Retrieval (CBIR) is concerned with finding the most similar images to a query in an image dataset, selected or photographed by the user. Recent improvements in features extraction through Convolutional Neural Networks (CNN) and algorithms for embedding, like the several R-MAC strategies [6,15,20], have made it possible to obtain excellent results on datasets of hundreds of thousand images in reasonable time [14]. Recently, the application of diffusion process on CBIR datasets have allowed boosting retrieval performance [11]: it permits finding more neighbour, that are close to the query on the nearest-neighbour manifold but not in the Euclidean representation space (Fig. 1). Diffusion propagates the similarities from a query point on a pairwise affinity matrix to all the dataset elements [26]. To apply this process, it is necessary to create a kNN graph of all image embeddings in the dataset. Generally, the more discriminative the embeddings are, the better the results achievable through diffusion.

Diffusion is an iterative process that simulates a random walk on the image similarity graph. It consists of walking on the graph, from the query point, with

© Springer Nature Switzerland AG 2019
E. Ricci et al. (Eds.): ICIAP 2019, LNCS 11752, pp. 537–548, 2019.
https://doi.org/10.1007/978-3-030-30645-8_49

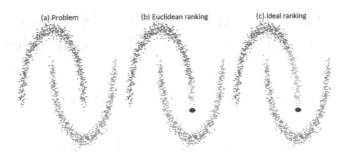

Fig. 1. In the first figure (a) two distributions of data are represented: in one distribution the points are blue-coloured and in the other the points are orange-coloured. In the second figure (b), the black point indicates the query point and the green points represent the results obtained after the execution of the retrieval exploiting the Euclidean distance. As you can see some correct results are retrieved (points belonging to the blue distribution), but also some incorrect results (points belonging to the orange distribution). Instead, the third figure (c) represents the ideal ranking for the indicated query point. This result can be easily obtained applying the diffusion process from the query point to the other elements of the dataset. Best viewed in color. (Color figure online)

the objective of finding the best path, i.e. to retrieve the neighbours of the query point. This is possible exploiting the weights of the edges of the kNN graph, which indicate the similarity between two nodes: the greater the weight, the more similar the two nodes are.

Unfortunately, this recent method leads to new challenges: understanding the data distribution to correctly set the diffusion parameters, dealing with the size of the kNN graph, which grows quadratically with the dataset size, and reducing the convergence time for the resolution of the linear system related to the diffusion mechanism.

The kNN graph is needed to apply diffusion and the number of the edges in the graph is important for the final retrieval performance. Furthermore, it is impossible to know how many and which edges the graph needs for achieving good performance before applying diffusion. Therefore, a common strategy used in previous works was a brute-force approach, i.e. the graph is created with the connections between all the possible pairs of nodes. Obviously, increasing the number of edges increases the size of the entire graph. For example, considering a dataset composed by N images, the exact or brute-force graph will have $N \cdot N$ edges and the approach will have a complexity $O(N^2)$; if $N = 100K$, the number of edges will be 10 billion.

Several methods proposed to implement an approximated method for the creation of the kNN graph, drastically reducing the computational time [1,3,19,25].

Following this idea that not all the edges are necessary for creating the kNN graph, we propose a fast approach for the creation of an approximate version of the kNN graph, based on LSH projections [9], which maintains only the useful edges to reduce computation time and memory requirements. The new graph achieves the same retrieval results as the exact kNN graph after diffusion [26] on several public image datasets, but does so more efficiently.

The main contributions of this paper are:

- An efficient algorithm based on LSH projections for the creation of an approximate kNN graph that obtains the same performance as brute-force in less time.
- Several optimizations in the implementation that reduce the computational time and memory use.
- The use of the multi-probe LSH [13] for improving diffusion performance on the kNN graph.

2   Related Work

Graphs have been used for different tasks in computer vision: applying diffusion for image retrieval [11], unsupervised fine-tuning [10], propagating labels for semi-supervised learning [4], creating manifold embeddings [24], and training classifiers exploiting the cycles found in the graph [12].

In particular, a k-Nearest Neighbor (kNN) graph is an undirected graph G denoted by $G(V, E)$, where V represents the set of nodes $V = \{v_1, v_2, \ldots, v_n)\}$ and E represents the set of edges $E = \{(e_1, e_2, \ldots, e_n)\}$. The nodes represent all the images in the dataset and the edges represent the connections between nodes. The weight of each edge determines how much the two images are similar: the higher the weight, the more similar the two images are. The weights of the edges are set using cosine similarities between embeddings.

The problem of kNN graph creation has been addressed in the literature in several ways. The simplest and naive approach is brute-force, which tends to be very slow but usually obtains the best results.

To speed up the process while retaining good retrieval accuracy, approximated kNN graphs have been used. The methods for the construction of the approximate kNN graph can be divided in two strategies: methods following the strategy of divide and conquer, and methods using local search (e.g., NN-descent [3]). Divide-and-conquer methods generally consist of two stages: subdividing the dataset in parts (divide), and creating a kNN graph for each sample followed by merging all subgraphs to form the final kNN graph (conquer).

As foreseeable, the performance and the computational time depend on the number of subdivisions. The most famous approach following the divide and conquer is based on Locality Sensitive Hashing (LSH) projections [9] for creating the approximate kNN graph [25]. The authors in [25] used a spectral decomposition of a low-rank graph matrix that needs much time because it is supervised. Chen *et al.* [1] follow the same strategy, but they apply recursive Lanczos bisection [1]. They proposed two divide steps: the overlap and the glue method. In the former, the current set is divided in two overlapping subsets, while in the latter, the current set is divided into two disjoint subsets and a third, called gluing set, is used to merge the two resulting disjoint subsets. Wang *et al.* [21] implemented an algorithm for the creation of an approximate kNN graph through the application in several iterations of the divide-and-conquer strategy. The peculiarity of the method is that the subsets of the dataset elements used during the divide phase are randomly chosen. Repeating several times this process allows to theoretically cover the entire dataset. Our approach differs from these approaches in the way the LSH projections are created. Furthermore, the strategy followed for creating the graph is different and more efficient. Moreover, as an alternative to LSH, there are several strategies for the hashing phase reported in literature [23]. They can be categorized based on the method for preserving the similarities (pairwise, multiwise or implicit) and the quantization phase.

Regarding the second strategy (local search), Dong *et al.* [3] proposed an approach called NN-descent [3], based on the idea that "a neighbour of my neighbour is my neighbour." For each image descriptor, a random kNN list is created. The algorithm starts searching random pairs on the kNN list, then it calculates the similarity between elements and finally updates the kNN list of these elements. This process continues until the number of updates is smaller than a threshold. Obviously, by increasing the number of neighbours contained in the kNN list it tends to the brute-force approach; therefore, the trade-off between the speed and accuracy performance needs to be correctly evaluated. Park *et al.* [16], Houle *et al.* [7] and Debatty *et al.* [2] proposed variations to the NN-descent, by adapting the basic approach to their specific application domains. Sieranoja *et al.* [19] proposed a solution, called Random Pair Division, that exploits both the divide and conquer and the NN-descent techniques. The division of the dataset in subsamples is executed through the random selection of two dataset descriptors: if the descriptor to be clusterized is close to the first one, it will be put in the first set, otherwise in the second one. After that, all image descriptors are clustered: if the size of each set is greater than a threshold, the subdivision process continues in the same way only for this large set. The conquer phase is executed through the application of the brute-force approach. In the end, a one-step neighbour propagation is applied for improving the final performance. It also exploits the principle of NN-descent: similar nodes that are not connected will be connected.

3   Proposed Approach: LSH kNN Graph

The proposed approach uses LSH projections to divide the global descriptors of the dataset in many subsets. We first explain LSH and then detail a fast and efficient solution for kNN graph creation for diffusion in image retrieval.

3.1   Notations and Background of LSH

Locality-Sensitive Hashing (LSH) [9] is one of the first hashing technique proposed for compression and indexing tasks. After the creation of some projection functions, it allows projection of points close to each other into the same bucket with high probability. It is defined as follows [22]: a family of hash functions $\mathcal{H}$ is called (R, cR, P_1, P_2)-sensitive if, for any two items $\mathbf{p}$ and $\mathbf{q}$, it holds that:

- if $\text{dist}(\mathbf{p}, \mathbf{q}) \leq R$, $\text{Prob}[h(\mathbf{p}) = h(\mathbf{q})] \geq P_1$
- if $\text{dist}(\mathbf{p}, \mathbf{q}) \geq cR$, $\text{Prob}[h(\mathbf{p}) = h(\mathbf{q})] \leq P_2$

with $c > 1$, $P_1 > P_2$, R is a distance threshold, and $h(\cdot)$ is the hash function. In other words, the hash function h must satisfy the property to project "similar" items (with a distance lower than the threshold R) to the same bucket with a probability higher than P_1, and have a low probability (lower than $P_2 < P_1$) to do the same for "dissimilar" items (with distance higher than $cR > R$).

The hash function used in LSH for Hamming space embedding is a scalar projection:

$$h(\mathbf{x}) = \text{sign}(\mathbf{x} \cdot \mathbf{v})$$

where $\mathbf{x}$ is the feature vector and $\mathbf{v}$ is a fixed random vector sampled from an D-dimensional isotropic Gaussian distribution $\mathcal{N}(0, I)$. The hashing process is repeated L times, with different Gaussian samples to increase the probability of satisfying the above constraints.

Subsequently, different hashing techniques may be implemented. The multi-probe LSH [13] has the objective to reduce the number of hash tables used for the projections, exploiting the fundamental principle of LSH that similar items will be projected in the same buckets or in near buckets with high probability. During the search phase, multi-probe LSH checks also the buckets near the query bucket. In the end, this approach allows to improve the final performance, but it increases the computational time.

3.2   Basic Algorithm for kNN Graph Construction

Given a dataset $\mathcal{S} = \{s_1, \ldots, s_N\}$, composed by N images, and a similarity measure $\theta : \mathcal{S} \times \mathcal{S} \to \mathbb{R}$, the kNN graph for $\mathcal{S}$ is a undirected graph G, that contains edges between the nodes i and j with the value from the similarity measure $\theta(s_i, s_j) = \theta(s_j, s_i)$. The similarity measure can be calculated in different ways related to the topic. In this case we use the cosine similarity as a metric, so the similarity is calculated through the application of the dot product between the image descriptors.

Our approach, called LSH kNN graph, follows the idea to first subdivide the entire dataset in many subsets, based on the concept of similarity between the images contained in the dataset. This process is done through the use of LSH projections and allows creation of a set of buckets $B = \{B_1, \ldots, B_N\}$ from several hash tables $L = \{L_1, \ldots, L_M\}$. The number of buckets N depends on the bits used for the projection (δ) and to the number of the hash tables (M): $N = 2^\delta \cdot M$. Each of these buckets will contain the projected elements $B_1 = \{b_{11}, \ldots, b_{1n}\}$. The result of this process represents an approximate result because it is not generally possible to project every element the dataset into the same bucket an as all its neighbours. It is therefore necessary to find a trade-off between the number of the buckets for each hash table (2^δ), modifying the bits used (δ) for the hashing, and the number of hash tables (M) used for the projection. For this first task, using a small number of buckets allows to project more data in the same bucket. It reduces the computational time for this phase, but it increases the entire computation of the overall approach. On the other hand, a high number of buckets in each hash table increases the computational time of this step, but it reduces overall computation.

For each bucket containing a subset of the dataset, a brute-force graph with edges $G_i = \{(b_{ix}, b_{iy}, \theta(b_{ix}, b_{iy})) : (b_{ix}, b_{iy}) \in B_i\}$ is constructed. Applying a brute-force construction on many subsets is faster than apply one time the brute-force on the entire dataset. In the end all the subgraphs need to be merged in the final graph $G = G_1 \cup \cdots \cup G_N$.

Unlike the usual LSH [25] based method, the proposed approach does not follow exactly the divide and conquer strategy. LSH projections are applied for dividing the dataset into subsets, but for reducing the computational time it is preferable to start creating the final graph, instead to create many approximate kNN graph and then merge them using the one-step neighbour propagation algorithm. The number of elements to sort in the kNN list and the number of similarity scores to calculate improves the quality of the final graph and the retrieval accuracy, but also reduces the computational time.

3.3 Multi-probe LSH

We also propose a multi-probe version, called multi LSH kNN graph, to reduce the number of hash tables used. Unlike the classic multi-probe LSH algorithm [13], in which the system checks neighboring buckets during the search phase, here all the elements are projected in the neighbors buckets during the projection phase, but only in the 1-neighbourhood. This represents the set of buckets differing by one bit to the analysed bucket (i.e. with Hamming distance $H_d \leq 1$). More formally, the elements obtained with the application of the multi-probe LSH are the followings:

$$B_{\text{multi-probe}} = \{b_{x1}, \ldots, b_{xp} : H_d(b_{\text{query}}, b_{xj}) \leq 1, \, b_{xj} \in B, \, 0 \leq x \leq P\}$$

Note that the number of neighbours of each bucket scales with the bits used for the projection as: $\sum_{i=0}^{l} \binom{\log_2 \delta}{i}$. Even though it increases the final retrieval performance, this approach requires more time for the kNN graph creation than the previous one. To get a good trade-off between the computational time required for the similarity measure calculations and the quality of the final graph, only a percentage γ of the elements projected on the 1-neighbour buckets are retained. The best trade-off is reached using $\gamma = 50\%$, which means that each element is also projected randomly in the half of its 1-neighbour buckets.

During the *conquer* phase, as in the previous proposed method, all the pairs of the indexes of the images found in the buckets will be connected through the calculation of the similarity measure.

4   Experimental Results

Previous works have evaluated the methods for creating approximate kNN graphs by checking the number of common edges between the approximate and the exact kNN graph. In our case the kNN graph pipelines are evaluated after the diffusion and retrieval modules in order to evaluate how effective (and efficient) are our proposals for the task in terms of retrieval accuracy when diffusion is applied. The diffusion approach and the R-MAC descriptors adopted are the same of the work of Iscen et al. [11].

4.1   Datasets

There are many different image datasets for Content-Based Image Retrieval that are used to evaluate algorithms. The most used are:

- **Oxford5k** [17] containing 5063 images, subdivided in 11 classes. All the images are used as database images and there are 55 query images, which are cropped to make the querying phase more difficult;
- **Paris6k** [18] containing 6412 images, subdivided in 12 classes. All the images are used as database images and there are 55 query images, again cropped;
- **Flickr1M** [8] containing 1 million Flickr images used for large scale evaluation. The images are divided in multiple classes and are not specifically selected for image retrieval.

The **Oxford105K dataset** is a combination of Oxford5k and 100K distractors from Flickr1M.

4.2   Evaluation Metrics

Mean Average Precision (mAP) is used on all datasets to evaluate the retrieval accuracy. We use L_2 distances to compare query images with the database ones.

4.3   Sparse Matrices for kNN Graph

It is worth emphasizing that there are a lot of null values in the affinity matrix. In fact, on Oxford5k the approximate kNN graph constructed with LSH kNN graph method has only the 0.7% of the edges of the brute-force graph. Furthermore, not all the similarity measure are useful for the diffusion process, suggesting to remove or avoid to insert edges with weight less than a threshold (th), without jeopardizing the final retrieval performance. Hence, each element of the matrix can be represented as following:

$$g_{ij} = \begin{cases} \theta(s_i, s_j) & \text{if } \theta(s_i, s_j) \geq th \\ 0 & \text{otherwise} \end{cases}$$

From our experiments, this threshold can be set to 0.3. Given the high number of null values in the affinity matrix, sparse matrices can be used to reduce the computational time and still obtain good results also on large datasets. Moreover, considering that the matrix is symmetric, only the upper or lower values of the matrix are needed:

$$g_{ij} = \begin{cases} \theta(s_i, s_j) & \text{if } j \geq i \wedge \theta(s_i, s_j) \geq th \\ 0 & \text{otherwise} \end{cases}$$

If the similarity value is missing, the row and the column are switched.

4.4   Implementation Details

Two different types of sparse matrix has been tested: Compressed Row Storage (CRS) format and Coordinate (COO) format [5]. The CRS sparse matrix is composed by three vectors: the values of the dense matrix different from zero; the column indexes of the elements contained in the values vector; and the locations of the values vector that indicate the beginning of a new row. Instead, the COO sparse matrix is composed by three vectors: a vector representing the non-zero elements, the row and the column coordinate of each value contained in the values vector. The second solution is simpler than the first to implement, but it requires more space on disk.

However, using hash tables, it happens that the same edge weight is inserted multiple times. Therefore, every time a new value is inserted in a CRS matrix, checking whether the value is already in the matrix might be a possible solution. Unfortunately, this tends to be a time consuming process. Conversely, using a COO matrix, all the values (including repeated ones) are inserted, but a sorting is performed and duplicates are removed.

4.5   Results on Oxford5k

Table 1 reports the retrieval results after diffusion application of different kNN graph techniques. Note that changing the values of LSH (δ and L) produces different results. The best configuration is $\delta = 6$ and $L = 2$ applying the multi LSH kNN graph approach. the best trade-off between the computational time for kNN graph creation and the final retrieval performance is the LSH kNN graph with $\delta = 6$ and $L = 20$. NN-descent produces good results, but it needs a lot of time for the graph creation (55 s). Furthermore, it does not obtain results comparable to the other methods.

RP-div [19] is very fast but collecting random elements from the dataset for the divide task does not give good results in retrieval after diffusion.

The method implemented by Wang *et al.* [21] obtains a different result each execution, so the reported performance is the average of ten experiments. The approach is very fast, but did not achieve the best mAP. Note also that the brute-force method is executed on GPU, instead all the other methods are executed on CPU.

Table 1. Comparison of different approaches of kNN graph creation tested on Oxford5k. * indicates that the method is a C++ re-implementation.

Method	LSH projection	kNN graph creation	mAP
LSH kNN graph ($\delta = 6, L = 20$)	0.45 s	**0.52 s**	90.95%
LSH kNN graph ($\delta = 8, L = 10$)	0.4 s	0.95 s	88.98%
Multi LSH kNN graph ($\delta = 6, L = 2$)	0.29 s	1.54 s	**91.13%**
NN-descent [3]*	–	55 s	83.81%
RP-div [19] (size = 50)*	–	1.16 s	82.68%
Wang et al. [21]*	–	1.5 s	90.60%
Brute-force	–	1.33 s	90.79%

We also perform some experiments with regional descriptors (Table 2). The use of regional descriptors demonstrates an improvement on the final performance due to high number of descriptors for each image (usually 21). In this case the total number of descriptors used for the creation of the kNN graph are approximately 100K. Note we omit testing RP-div and NN-descent here due to poor previous accuracy/computation performance.

Table 2. Comparison of different approaches of kNN graph creation tested on Oxford5k using regional R-MAC descriptors. * indicates that the method is a C++ re-implementation.

Method	LSH projection	kNN graph creation	mAP
LSH kNN graph ($\delta = 6, L = 20$)	9 s	100 s	**94.67%**
LSH kNN graph ($\delta = 8, L = 10$)	6 s	**45 s**	93.68%
Multi LSH kNN graph ($\delta = 6, L = 2$)	6 s	350 s	93.96%
Wang et al. [21]*	–	148 s	91.69%
Brute-force	–	15816 s	93.80%

4.6 Results on Paris6k

Table 3 shows the results on the Paris6k dataset, which are similar to those obtained to Oxford5k.

However, in this case, LSH kNN graph is the fastest approach and also it obtains the best retrieval performance after the application of diffusion. Multi-LSH kNN method obtains a good result, but in more time than the brute-force approach.

4.7 Results on Oxford105k

Table 4 reports results for the experiments executed on Oxford105k again RP-div and NN-descent are not tested due to poor trade-off previously obtained.

Table 3. Comparison of different approaches of kNN graph creation tested on Paris6k. * indicates that the method is a C++ re-implementation.

Method	LSH projection	kNN graph creation	mAP
LSH kNN graph ($\delta = 6, L = 20$)	1 s	0.80 s	**97.01%**
LSH kNN graph ($\delta = 8, L = 10$)	0.78 s	**0.28 s**	95.93%
Multi LSH kNN graph ($\delta = 6, L = 2$)	0.35 s	2.28 s	96.81%
NN-descent [3] (neighbours $= 50$)*	–	60.10 s	94.24%
RP-div [19] (size $= 50$)*	–	3.63 s	96.25%
Wang et al. [21]*	–	1.95 s	96.75%
Brute-force	–	1.81 s	96.83%

Increasing the dimension of the dataset illustrates the difference in accuracy and computational time between the proposed approach and brute-force. The proposed approaches obtain better results and trade-offs than other methods. In particular, LSH kNN graph ($\delta = 6$ and $L = 20$) achieves 92.50% in only 77 s for the graph creation process. The multi LSH kNN graph needs more time than the previous approach, but it reaches the best mAP on this dataset equals of 92.85%.

Table 4. Comparison of different approaches of kNN graph creation tested on Oxford105k. * indicates that the method is a C++ re-implementation.

Method	LSH projection	kNN graph creation	mAP
LSH kNN graph ($\delta = 6, L = 20$)	23 s	**77 s**	92.50%
LSH kNN graph ($\delta = 8, L = 10$)	15 s	145 s	90.79%
Multi LSH kNN graph ($\delta = 6, L = 4$)	5 s	420 s	**92.85%**
Wang et al. [21]*	–	150 s	91.00%
Brute-force	–	4733 s	91.45%

5   Conclusions

We presented an algorithm called LSH kNN graph for the creation of an approximate kNN graph exploiting LSH projections. First, the elements of the dataset are subdivided in several subsets using an unsupervised hashing function and, then, for each one of the subsets a subgraph is created applying the brute-force approach. The application of this algorithm with sparse matrices achieves very good results even on datasets that with a large number of images. The proposed methods can generate a kNN graph faster than the brute-force approach and other state-of-the-art approaches, obtaining the same or better accuracy results after diffusion. Furthermore, another version of the algorithm called multi LSH kNN graph was proposed, which uses multi-probe LSH instead of LSH for the subdivision of the elements in the subsets, increasing the quality of the final graph due to the greater number of elements found in the buckets of the hash tables. In future work, we are pursuing the distribution these approaches across several machines to allow processing even larger datasets.

Acknowledgment. This is work is partially funded by Regione Emilia Romagna under the "Piano triennale alte competenze per la ricerca, il trasferimento tecnologico e l'imprenditorialità".

This publication has emanated from research conducted with the financial support of Science Foundation Ireland (SFI) under grant number SFI/15/SIRG/3283 and SFI/12/RC/2289.

References

1. Chen, J., Fang, H.R., Saad, Y.: Fast approximate kNN graph construction for high dimensional data via recursive Lanczos bisection. J. Mach. Learn. Res. **10**(Sep), 1989–2012 (2009)
2. Debatty, T., Michiardi, P., Thonnard, O., Mees, W.: Building K-NN graphs from large text data. In: IEEE International Conference on Big Data, pp. 573–578. IEEE (2014)
3. Dong, W., Moses, C., Li, K.: Efficient K-nearest neighbor graph construction for generic similarity measures. In: Proceedings of the 20th International Conference on World Wide Web, pp. 577–586. ACM (2011)
4. Douze, M., Szlam, A., Hariharan, B., Jégou, H.: Low-shot learning with large-scale diffusion. In: Proceedings of the IEEE Conference on Computer Vision and Pattern Recognition, pp. 3349–3358 (2018)
5. Golub, G.H., Van Loan, C.F.: Matrix Computations, vol. 3. JHU press, Baltimore (2012)
6. Gordo, A., Almazan, J., Revaud, J., Larlus, D.: End-to-end learning of deep visual representations for image retrieval. Int. J. Comput. Vis. **124**(2), 237–254 (2017)
7. Houle, M.E., Ma, X., Oria, V., Sun, J.: Improving the quality of K-NN graphs for image databases through vector sparsification. In: Proceedings of International Conference on Multimedia Retrieval, p. 89. ACM (2014)
8. Huiskes, M.J., Lew, M.S.: The MIR flickr retrieval evaluation. In: Proceedings of the 1st ACM International Conference on Multimedia Information Retrieval, pp. 39–43. ACM (2008)
9. Indyk, P., Motwani, R.: Approximate nearest neighbors: towards removing the curse of dimensionality. In: Proceedings of the Thirtieth Annual ACM Symposium on Theory of Computing, pp. 604–613. ACM (1998)
10. Iscen, A., Tolias, G., Avrithis, Y., Chum, O.: Mining on manifolds: metric learning without labels. In: Proceedings of the IEEE Conference on Computer Vision and Pattern Recognition, pp. 7642–7651 (2018)
11. Iscen, A., Tolias, G., Avrithis, Y.S., Furon, T., Chum, O.: Efficient diffusion on region manifolds: recovering small objects with compact CNN representations. In: Proceedings of the IEEE Conference on Computer Vision and Pattern Recognition, vol. 1, p. 3 (2017)
12. Li, D., Hung, W.-C., Huang, J.-B., Wang, S., Ahuja, N., Yang, M.-H.: Unsupervised visual representation learning by graph-based consistent constraints. In: Leibe, B., Matas, J., Sebe, N., Welling, M. (eds.) ECCV 2016. LNCS, vol. 9908, pp. 678–694. Springer, Cham (2016). https://doi.org/10.1007/978-3-319-46493-0_41

13. Lv, Q., Josephson, W., Wang, Z., Charikar, M., Li, K.: Multi-probe LSH: efficient indexing for high-dimensional similarity search. In: Proceedings of the 33rd International Conference on Very Large Data Bases, pp. 950–961. VLDB Endowment (2007)

14. Magliani, F., Fontanini, T., Prati, A.: Landmark recognition: from small-scale to large-scale retrieval. In: Hassaballah, M., Hosny, K.M. (eds.) Recent Advances in Computer Vision. SCI, vol. 804, pp. 237–259. Springer, Cham (2019). https://doi.org/10.1007/978-3-030-03000-1_10

15. Magliani, F., Prati, A.: An accurate retrieval through R-MAC+ descriptors for landmark recognition. In: Proceedings of the 12th International Conference on Distributed Smart Cameras, p. 6. ACM (2018)

16. Park, Y., Park, S., Lee, S.G., Jung, W.: Scalable K-nearest neighbor graph construction based on greedy filtering. In: Proceedings of the 22nd International Conference on World Wide Web, pp. 227–228. ACM (2013)

17. Philbin, J., Chum, O., Isard, M., Sivic, J., Zisserman, A.: Object retrieval with large vocabularies and fast spatial matching. In: Proceedings of the IEEE Conference on Computer Vision and Pattern Recognition (2007)

18. Philbin, J., Chum, O., Isard, M., Sivic, J., Zisserman, A.: Lost in quantization: improving particular object retrieval in large scale image databases. In: Proceedings of the IEEE Conference on Computer Vision and Pattern Recognition, pp. 1–8. IEEE (2008)

19. Sieranoja, S., Fränti, P.: Fast random pair divisive construction of KNN graph using generic distance measures. In: Proceedings of the 2018 International Conference on Big Data and Computing, pp. 95–98. ACM (2018)

20. Tolias, G., Sicre, R., Jégou, H.: Particular object retrieval with integral max-pooling of CNN activations. arXiv preprint arXiv:1511.05879 (2015)

21. Wang, J., Wang, J., Zeng, G., Tu, Z., Gan, R., Li, S.: Scalable K-NN graph construction for visual descriptors. In: 2012 IEEE Conference on Computer Vision and Pattern Recognition, pp. 1106–1113. IEEE (2012)

22. Wang, J., Shen, H.T., Song, J., Ji, J.: Hashing for similarity search: a survey. arXiv preprint arXiv:1408.2927 (2014)

23. Wang, J., Zhang, T., Sebe, N., Shen, H.T., et al.: A survey on learning to hash. IEEE Trans. Pattern Anal. Mach. Intell. 40(4), 769–790 (2017)

24. Xu, J., Wang, C., Qi, C., Shi, C., Xiao, B.: Iterative manifold embedding layer learned by incomplete data for large-scale image retrieval. IEEE Trans. Multimed. 21(6), 1551–1562 (2019)

25. Zhang, Y.-M., Huang, K., Geng, G., Liu, C.-L.: Fast kNN graph construction with locality sensitive hashing. In: Blockeel, H., Kersting, K., Nijssen, S., Železný, F. (eds.) ECML PKDD 2013. LNCS (LNAI), vol. 8189, pp. 660–674. Springer, Heidelberg (2013). https://doi.org/10.1007/978-3-642-40991-2_42

26. Zhou, D., Weston, J., Gretton, A., Bousquet, O., Schölkopf, B.: Ranking on data manifolds. In: Advances in Neural Information Processing Systems, pp. 169–176 (2004)

Easing Function as a Tool of Color Correction for Display Stitching in Virtual Reality

Dariusz Sawicki[1](✉) (iD), Agnieszka Wolska[2] (iD), Mariusz Wisełka[2] (iD),
and Szymon Ordysiński[2] (iD)

[1] Warsaw University of Technology, Warsaw, Poland
Dariusz.Sawicki@ee.pw.edu.pl
[2] Central Institute for Labour Protection - National Research Institute
(CIOP-PIB), Warsaw, Poland
{agwol,marwi,szord}@ciop.pl

Abstract. For many multimedia applications, the image stitching problem is very important. We analyzed this problem for the SEMI-CAVE virtual reality installation. In this study, we aim to analyze the manner in which color changes for correcting image stitching with regard to human perception (subjective evaluation of stitching quality). We propose to use Penner's easing function for changing color of image stitching and obtain a proper perceptual transition of color. A series of experiments were conducted in the SEMI-CAVE environment. 27 participants assessed the quality of the black-to-white transition realized using 7 different Penner's functions. The participants assessed the smoothness of the transition and the occurrence of perceptual artifacts. The analysis of the experimental results showed that the InOutSine function provides the best perceptual effects. Moreover, the obtained results (ranking of functions from the best to the worst) were statistically confirmed using Chi-square analysis.

Keywords: Perception · Lateral inhibition · Easing function ·
Cave virtual reality · Image stitching

1 Introduction

Virtual reality (VR) is one of the most spectacular IT proposals of recent years. Although VR is primarily used in the entertainment industry, e.g., in computer games, it also supports serious research in many other areas. Although known for many years, one of the less popular VR solutions is cave automatic virtual environment (CAVE) [1, 2]. It has not been very popular because of the high cost and installation problems. However, SEMI-CAVE is an example of CAVE implementation, which was developed at the Central Institute for Labor Protection - National Research Institute (CIOP-PIB) [3]. The SEMI-CAVE laboratory, which is involved in interdisciplinary research on the health and safety of employees, was built as a part of Tech-Safe-Bio project [4]. Virtual cave reality allows researchers to study the impact of the physical environment on employees in different conditions. Note that such studies would not be possible on such a wide scale in real-life conditions.

© Springer Nature Switzerland AG 2019
E. Ricci et al. (Eds.): ICIAP 2019, LNCS 11752, pp. 549–559, 2019.
https://doi.org/10.1007/978-3-030-30645-8_50

The most important problem related to CAVE installation is the quality of the displayed images. It determines the correctness of immersion into the VR [5], which is inside created. A key issue for display quality is the problem of image stitching. For stitching images, when performing geometrical corrections, local shape changes are necessary so that the combination of pair of neighboring images is invisible. This problem has been known since the beginning of the Cave installation and has been practically solved now [6, 7].

A much more interesting problem is correcting luminance and color while stitching images because it forces to change the color of the displayed information. Modern hardware solutions of graphic cards, allow performing any color manipulation of pixels at the shader level [8]. In such solution color manipulation does not take up computer resources and can be performed in real-time, regardless of other operations. The problem seems trivial because the correcting the color of stitched images occurs in a large space where local, high color changes occur (related to the image content). Therefore, the results of color manipulation should not be noticeable. However, very often we can see large surfaces of almost the same color. For example, the sky (the same blue color) may occupy 1/3 of the image area and for such a situation, incorrect local color changes will be unnatural, i.e., they will interfere with the perception.

Thus, can image stitching be improved to obtain a better immersion into the virtual environment? In fact, the stitching problem is important not only in CAVE VR implementation. The problem of aligning luminance increase and color correction is found in many other multimedia applications. We perform image stitching to create panoramas in photography, computer graphics, and commercials. Therefore, selecting a method for color correction is a practical problem and worth exploring. In this study, we aim to analyze the manner in which color should be changed for correcting image stitching with regard to human perception (subjective evaluation of stitching quality) in a SEMI-CAVE environment. We propose the function for correcting color in this application, which is the most preferred by observers.

2   The Stitching Problem in SEMI-CAVE Virtual Reality

The SEMI-CAVE installation was dedicated to studying the impact of visual environment of the workplace on human psychophysiology. In this laboratory, the VR obtained allows creating different working environments in which subjects could perform specific working tasks. Thus, the large space of VR was the decisive argument for selecting the CAVE type as a VR installation. We realized our laboratory in a room that had internal projections with the following dimensions: 8.6 × 4.3 m. For displaying images, we used six projectors that were equipped with short throw optics. The projectors allowed for lens shift and keystone correction in two directions. Because of this construction, we also obtained the expected shadow-free work area. Figure 1 shows the arrangement of projectors in our laboratory, the details and basic technical aspects of the installation are reported in conference paper [3].

Both the vibrations and aging of the supporting structure, on which the projectors are mounted, and the aging of projectors influence the quality of the created images. Both geometry and color need to be improved in an effective way on a regular basis.

We have independently projected the image stitching subsystem for the correction of geometry and color. The application has been implemented at the shader level; therefore, the correction is directly executed by the graphics card processor. The details of the algorithm for geometrical correction are presented in [7]. The problem of color correction was more interesting and definitely required additional research.

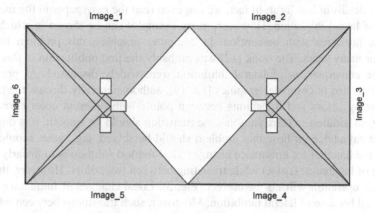

Fig. 1. SEMI-CAVE laboratory: six projectors create six images on four walls [7]

3 Perception of Local Color Changes – A Lateral Inhibition

The phenomenon of lateral inhibition occurs on the retina of the human eye [9]. The stimulated retinal neurons affect the neighboring neurons; moreover, the neuron's response depends not only on the level of luminance (color) observed but also on the luminance (color) of the neighboring points.

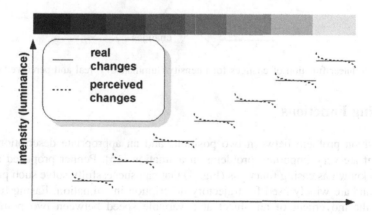

Fig. 2. The phenomenon of lateral inhibition – real and perceived changes of intensity (luminance)

Because of lateral inhibition, the eye is more sensitive to local changes in luminance (color) compared to its level, and local changes are perceptually increased [10, 11] (Fig. 2). It is worth emphasizing that the problem is not dependent on the color: lateral inhibition occurs in the same manner for each color component and for gray scale.

Lateral inhibition is very important for human perception because it allows us to recognize details in low light; in fact, we can even read the newspaper in the moonlight because of lateral inhibition. However, many examples can be shown in which lateral inhibition interferes with perception. In computer graphics, this problem has been known for many years. The book [12] was probably the first publication in this field in which the consequences of lateral inhibition were widely discussed. At present, in textbooks related to computer graphics [13, 14], authors generally discuss the problem of combining colors and transitions between points with different color coordinates. However, in addition to clarifying that the transition should be smooth, it is difficult to find practical advice on how this problem should be solved, e.g., what should be the shape of the function for luminance change? The simplest solution is to linearly change the value of luminance (color) while transiting between two colors. However, the effect of such an operation will not be correct (Fig. 3). Local changes of luminance will be emphasized because of lateral inhibition. Moreover, such transitions between white and black colors are not considered to be smooth and local artifacts can be seen.

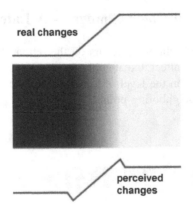

Fig. 3. The linear function of changes for intensity (luminance) – real and perceived changes

4   Easing Functions

The transition problem between two positions and an appropriate description of the movement are very important problems in animation [15]. Penner proposed a set of functions known as easing functions (Fig. 4) that can successfully solve such problems [16, 17] and are widely used for trajectory description in animation. Easing functions describe the movement of an object at a variable speed between two points. It is possible to distinguish several types of functions that have common movement features such as smooth start (Ease-In), smooth braking (Ease-Out), smooth start, and braking

(Ease-In-Out). The libraries of Qt [18] and Windows Presentation Foundation [19] provided an additional type of easing function (extended set) that has not been proposed by Penner. These functions are characterized by sudden start and sudden braking (Ease-Out-In). The approximation of easing functions [20] based on Bézier curves allows for their effective use by animators in practical applications.

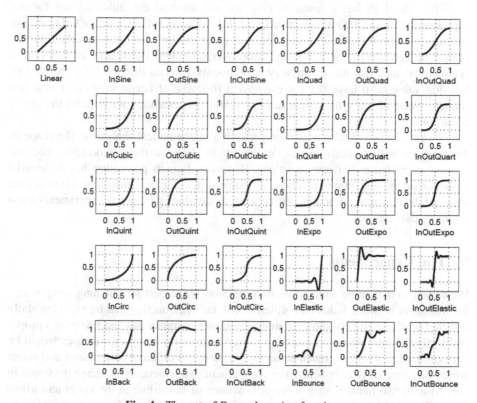

Fig. 4. The set of Penner's easing functions

Color correction requires a smooth connection of two levels of color (luminance). A good example of combining functions is Penner's functions, which are used in animation. A selected set of Penner's functions ensures smooth connections. Although the author of easing functions talks about combining the trajectory of motion, we can use these functions in a non-standard manner to combine changes in other parameters in situations where proper smoothness is required. To apply Penner's functions for color correction, we have identified a set of functions that meet the following conditions:

- The function has to be symmetrical, i.e., the smooth transition between two colors (luminance levels) should be symmetrical.
- The function should ensures smoothness and uniformity of changes, i.e., it is important that the change in color (luminance level) gives the impression of being as smooth, uniform (in increase and decrease) and gradual as possible.

- The function is not characterized by local disturbances (steps or oscillations), i.e., this condition is important primarily from the perceptual point of view. An example of local disturbing artifacts can be seen in Fig. 3. Not only are the mathematical properties of the function important but it is also important to ensure that an appropriate sensation considers lateral inhibition.

From all of Penner's functions (Fig. 4), we selected the following set for our experiments: Linear, InOutSine, InOutQuad, InOutCubic, InOutQuart, InOutQuint, and InOutExpo. The InOutBounce function is a great example of local disturbances that cannot be considered for this study. Moreover, although the InOutCirc function is symmetrical and smooth, preliminary experiments showed that the local increase of function value is so large that the eye sees it (because of lateral inhibition) as a step change. None of the symmetrical functions from the extended set fulfilled the above conditions.

For the selected functions, we can perform a mathematical analysis of the shape of the function and its derivatives. We can try to describe their smoothness and the manner of increase or decrease values. However, human perception has a decisive influence on the selection of functions for correcting color and luminance. To select the appropriate (the best) function, we decided to conduct perceptual experiments on a group of participants.

5   The Experiments

We aimed to determine which transition function is the best for stitching images, i.e., for transition between fields with different colors. The function can be experimentally selected by consecutively showing all the examples of transitions and selecting a proper (subjective) order. However, assessing different cases for many shown cases would be very difficult. It would be much easier to compare two different connections and select which one (one of two) is better. For comparison, we generated an image (example in Fig. 5) with two fields having different functions of transition: in the upper and lower field. These fields are separated by a field of step (hard) change. For each comparison, the participant had to answer three questions:

1. Which transition between black and white is better (more uniform changes or more smooth on a wider space)? – upper or lower (one of two).
2. Are the artifacts associated with the transition (luminance boost, local disturbances, or local unexpected changes) visible in the upper image? – Yes or No.
3. Are the artifacts associated with the transition (luminance boost, local disturbances, or local unexpected changes) visible in the lower image? – Yes or No.

The experiment comprised a set of comparisons. We considered seven different transitional functions. Then, we generated all sets of pairs of transitions for this selected set of functions. Because such a task is described by combination (without repetition), there are 21 different pairs in this case. In addition, these sets were repeated after changing upper with lower function in each pair. This change was done, so that the lower or upper position do not affect the result (subjectively).

Fig. 5. An example of image presented to the participant in one comparison of the experiment. In presented here image in the upper part the InOutQuint function is used, in the lower part the InOutSin function is used. The lower should be better: more space, more smooth. In the upper image the change takes place in a smaller space – it seems to be more rapid, sharper.

Finally, each participant observed 42 images (comparisons) and answered three questions in each case. After carrying out the entire set of comparisons, we summarized the winning transitions. On this basis, we determined the order of the ranking list as well as the winner of the assessment.

At the start of the test (before the first comparison), each participant had seen two teaching images. In the first image, several evidently different functions of the transition were shown. This allowed understanding the difference in transition between white and black and how the differences can be seen. In the second image, various artifacts were shown to understand the type of artifacts (local distortions) that can be found in the images.

The experiment was attended by 27 participants: 13 women and 14 men. The participants were healthy and without visual disturbances. The participants were aged between 21 and 65 years and the average age was 43.4 years.

6   The Analysis of the Results

When comparing the quality of the transition function, InOutQuad and InOutSine showed the best evaluation (Fig. 6), while InOutExpo showed the worst evaluation. To verify whether the comparison of individual functions differs in a statistically significant way, a Chi-square test for one variable was performed. The null hypothesis of this test assumes that all the functions that are compared have the same quality of color transitions. In such cases, a positive selection of individual functions would be random, i.e., all the functions would have the same number of positive ratings. However, the alternative hypothesis would say that individual functions differ in terms of the quality of color transitions, and positive evaluations will be non-systemically distributed in a systematic manner because of the quality of individual functions.

The result of the Chi-square test ($(6, N = 27) = 282.7$; $p < 0.001$) indicates that the null hypothesis should be rejected and an alternative hypothesis should be adopted.

This indicates that, depending on the evaluation of the perception of color transitions, the compared functions differs in a statistically significant manner.

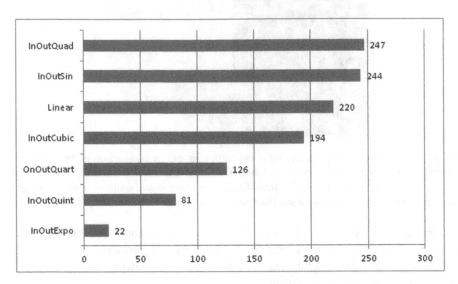

Fig. 6. The sum of the number of positive ratings (wins) of individual functions awarded by participants in consecutive comparisons. The more wins, the better the transition function

Regardless, we conducted an analysis of the recognition of artifacts. The lowest number of participant artifacts was noted for the cases of the InOutSin and InOutQuad functions, whereas the worst rated (the largest number of artifacts) was noted for the Linear function (Fig. 7).

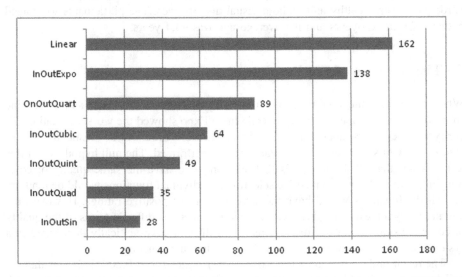

Fig. 7. The sum of the number of artifacts recognized by participants in images. The fewer number of artifacts, the better the transition function

Because of the strong impact of lateral inhibition on perceiving images, both evaluations affected the final result. Therefore, for individual transient functions, we subtracted the number of recognized artifacts from the number of wins in the comparisons. Figure 8 shows the final result after appropriate scaling (the values have been "shifted" so that there is no value less than 1).

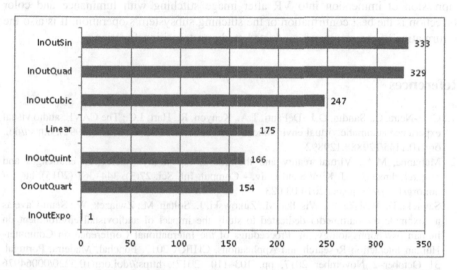

Fig. 8. The final result of the experiment (after scaling). The number of points from comparison minus number of points from artifacts' assessment. The more points, the better the transition function

The result of the Chi-square test ((6, N = 27) = 398.7; p < 0.001) confirmed that the obtained final order in the ranking of transition function is statistically significant.

7 Summary

To change the luminance (color) of stitched images, we propose using Penner's easing function. In typical applications, they are used to describe and combine trajectories of movements; however, they were very convenient and effective in an atypical application in which easing functions were used to describe changes in luminance (and colors).

To select which function describes the change in luminance (color) in the best perceptively manner, we conducted a series of experiments. In fact, 27 participants assessed the quality of transition from black to white, which was realized using seven different Penner's functions. The participants assessed the smoothness of the transition and the occurrence of artifacts. The results showed that the InOutSine function gives the best perceptual effects, the InOutQuad function is only slightly worse, and the InOutExpo function is the worst solution. An interesting result is the evaluation of the

Linear function, which is the simplest and most popular solution. It was only ranked at the fourth position in the classification but turned out to be almost twice as bad (counting the points obtained) in relation to the best solution. The results (ranking of functions from the best to the worst) were statistically confirmed using Chi-square analysis.

Thus, we implemented Penner's function in a SEMI-CAVE installation. The good impression of immersion into VR after image stitching with luminance and color correction is the best confirmation of the stitching subsystem's operation. It is also the confirmation of the results of conducted study on transition functions.

References

1. Cruz-Neira, C., Sandin, D.J., DeFanti, T.A., Kenyon, R., Hart, J.C.: The CAVE: audio visual experience automatic virtual environment. Commun. ACM **35**(6), 64–72 (1992). https://doi.org/10.1145/129888.129892
2. Muhanna, M.A.: Virtual reality and the CAVE: taxonomy, interaction challenges and research directions. J. King Saud Univ. – Comput. Inf. Sci. **27**(3), 344–361 (2015). https://doi.org/10.1016/j.jksuci.2014.03.023
3. Sawicki, D., Wolska, A., Wisełka, M., Żukowski, J., Sołtan, M., Związek, W.: Semi-Cave as an example of multimedia dedicated to study the impact of audiovisual environment on human psychophysiology. In: Proceedings of the International Conference on Computer-Human Interaction Research and Applications, CHIRA 2017, Funchal, Madeira, Portugal, 31 October–2 November 2017, pp. 103–110 (2017). https://doi.org/10.5220/00064976 01030110
4. TECH-SAFE-BIO - The Centre for Research and Development on Work Processes and Safety Engineering. http://www.ciop.pl/CIOPPortalWAR/appmanager/ciop/en?_nfpb=true&_pageLabel=P3320011430144862071 1504. Accessed 2 Apr 2019
5. Slater, M.: A Note on Presence Terminology (2003). http://www.cs.ucl.ac.uk/research/vr/Projects/Presencia/ConsortiumPublications/ucl_cs_papers/presence-terminology.htmmelsla-terJan27200391557.htm. Accessed 2 Apr 2019
6. Kim, M.J., Wang, X., Love, P.E.D., Li, H., Kang, S.C.: Virtual reality for the built environment: a critical review of recent advances. J. Inf. Technol. Constr. **18**, 279–305 (2013). http://www.itcon.org/2013/14
7. Sawicki, D., Izdebski, Ł., Wolska, A., Wisełka, M.: Geometrical picture integration in SEMI-CAVE virtual reality. In: Proceedings of the International Conference on Computer-Human Interaction Research and Applications, CHIRA 2018, Seville, Spain, 19–21 September 2018, pp. 100–107. https://doi.org/10.5220/0006922701000107
8. Bailey, M., Cunningham, S.: Graphics Shaders: Theory and Practice, 2nd edn. A K Peters/CRC Press, Boca Raton (2011)
9. Bakshi, A., Ghosh, K.: A neural model of attention and feedback for computing perceived brightness in vision (chap. 26). In: Handbook of Neural Computation, pp. 487–513. Academic Press (2017). https://doi.org/10.1016/B978-0-12-811318-9.00026-0
10. Snowden, R., Thompson, P., Troscianko, T.: Basic Vision. An Introduction to Visual Perception, Revised edn. Oxford University Press, Oxford (2012)
11. Purves, D., Lotto, R.B.: Why We See What We Do. An Empirical Theory of Vision. Sinuaer Associates Inc., Sunderland (2003)

12. Hall, R.: Illumination and Color in Computer Generated Imagery. Springer, New York (1989). https://doi.org/10.1007/978-1-4612-3526-2
13. Hughes, J.F., et al.: Computer Graphics: Principles and Practice, 3rd edn. Addison-Wesley Professional, Boston (2013)
14. Thompson, W., Fleming, R., et al.: Visual Perception from a Computer Graphics Perspective. CRC Press, Boca Raton (2012)
15. Parent, R.: Computer Animation, 3rd Revised edn. Morgan Kaufmann, Burlington (2012)
16. Penner, R.: Motion, tweening, and easing (chap. 7). In: Programming Macromedia Flash MX, pp. 191–240. McGraw-Hill/OsborneMedia (2002). http://robertpenner.com/easing/penner_chapter7_tweening.pdf. Accessed 6 Apr 2019
17. Robert Penner's Easing Functions. http://robertpenner.com/easing/. Accessed 2 Apr 2019
18. Qt Documentation. Animator QML Type. https://doc.qt.io/qt-5/qml-qtquick-animator.html. Accessed 8 Apr 2019
19. Windows Presentation Foundation. Easing Functions. https://docs.microsoft.com/en-us/dotnet/framework/wpf/graphics-multimedia/easing-functions. Accessed 8 Apr 2019
20. Izdebski, Ł., Sawicki, D.: Easing functions in the new form based on bézier curves. In: Chmielewski, L., Datta, A., Kozera, R., Wojciechowski, K. (eds.) ICCVG 2016. LNCS, vol. 9972, pp. 37–48. Springer, Cham (2016). https://doi.org/10.1007/978-3-319-46418-3_4

Hand Gestures for the Human-Car Interaction: The Briareo Dataset

Fabio Manganaro, Stefano Pini, Guido Borghi[✉], Roberto Vezzani, and Rita Cucchiara

Department of Engineering "Enzo Ferrari",
University of Modena and Reggio Emilia, Modena, Italy
{fabio.manganaro,s.pini,guido.borghi,roberto.vezzani,
rita.cucchiara}@unimore.it

Abstract. *Natural User Interfaces* can be an effective way to reduce driver's inattention during the driving activity. To this end, in this paper we propose a new dataset, called *Briareo*, specifically collected for the hand gesture recognition task in the automotive context. The dataset is acquired from an innovative point of view, exploiting different kinds of cameras, *i.e.* RGB, infrared stereo, and depth, that provide various types of images and 3D hand joints. Moreover, the dataset contains a significant amount of hand gesture samples, performed by several subjects, allowing the use of deep learning-based approaches. Finally, a framework for hand gesture segmentation and classification is presented, exploiting a method introduced to assess the quality of the proposed dataset.

Keywords: Hand gesture classification · Automotive dataset · Driver attention monitoring · Deep learning · C3D · LSTM

1 Introduction

Natural User Interfaces (NUIs), *i.e.* interfaces in which the interaction is not carried through physical devices (like mouses and keyboards), are becoming more and more important in many computer vision fields and a key component of new technological tools, since they are extremely *user-friendly* and *intuitive* [9].

Recently, NUIs are gathering attention also in the *automotive* context, where they can be used for a variety of applications in order to reduce driver inattention. In fact, they can increase the amount of time in which driver attention is focused on driving activity. Indeed, driver distraction, according to the *National Highway Traffic Safety Administration*[1] (NHTSA), is generally defined as "an activity that could divert a person's attention away from the primary task of driving", and is one of the most important causes in fatal road crashes [5].

Generally, three types of driver distraction are identified in the literature [1,2]:

---

[1] https://www.nhtsa.gov.

© Springer Nature Switzerland AG 2019
E. Ricci et al. (Eds.): ICIAP 2019, LNCS 11752, pp. 560–571, 2019.
https://doi.org/10.1007/978-3-030-30645-8_51

- **Manual Distraction:** driver's hands are not on the steering wheel for a prolonged amount of time. As a consequence, the driver is not ready to avoid road obstacles, such as cars and pedestrians;
- **Visual Distraction:** driver's eyes are not looking at the road, since they are engaged in different tasks, such as reading a newspaper or looking at the phone;
- **Cognitive Distraction:** driver's attention is not focused on the driving activity due to the *fatigue*, *i.e.* "the inability of disinclination to continue an activity, generally because the activity has been going for too long" [10], or due to bad physical conditions or the cognitive load due to external factors.

The availability of systems that can be controlled via the *Natural Language*, like vocal commands or hand gestures [3], could significantly reduce the causes of manual and visual distraction since they generally lead to a reduction of the amount of time involved in interactive activities. Besides, as reported in [12], today drivers are more engaged in secondary tasks than in the past due to the presence, for instance, of smartphones.

For these reasons, in this paper we investigate the development of a hand gesture-based interaction system, based on computer vision techniques, aiming to obtain a safer interaction between the driver and the car system. A key element in its development is the collection of a new dataset, called *Briareo*, specifically designed for the driver hand gesture classification and segmentation with deep learning-based approaches, which includes a significant amount of annotated samples.

In particular, we focus on *dynamic* hand gestures, *i.e.* each gesture is a combination of motion and one or more hand poses: thus, we neglect static hand gestures, that are out of the scope of this paper. Images have been collected from an innovative point of view, different from other perspectives proposed in the past literature: the acquisition devices are placed in the central tunnel between the driver and the passenger seats, orientated towards the car ceiling. In this way, visual occlusions produced by driver's body can be mitigated.

To collect the dataset, three main requirements about the automotive context have been taken into account [18]:

- **Light Invariance:** vision-based systems have to be reliable even in presence of dramatic light changes (generated, for instance, by the alternation between day and night, tunnels, or bad weather conditions);
- **Non-invasinevess:** driver's movements and gaze must not be impeded during the driving activity. Consequently, sensors have to be easily integrated into the car dashboards;
- **Real Time performance:** interaction systems have to quickly detect gestures and provide a fast feedback of the system;

To tackle the first requirement, we propose the use of infrared-based sensors. Moreover, we select devices that are also able to acquire *depth maps*, *i.e.* particular types of images in which each pixel corresponds to the distance between the acquisition device and that point in the scene. Recently, several infrared and depth devices with high-quality sensors and with a small form factor have been introduced, which fulfil the second requirement.

The rest of the paper is organized as follow. In the next section, related datasets and methods about hand gesture classification are analyzed. Then, in Sect. 3, the *Briareo* dataset is presented, detailing all the features and data collected. In Sect. 4, two baseline methods are proposed, in order to assess the quality of the proposed dataset and to move towards the development of a gesture-based interaction framework. Experimental results are presented in Sect. 5. Finally, Sect. 6 draws the conclusions.

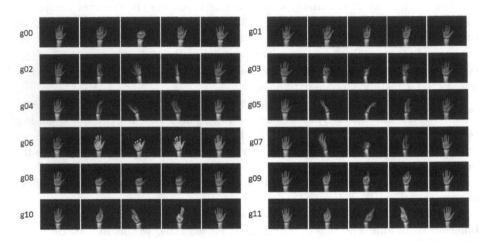

Fig. 1. Gesture classes included in the *Briareo* dataset. As shown, only *dynamic* gestures are present in the dataset. For further details, see Sect. 3.2.

2   Related Datasets

Recently, several public datasets have been presented in the literature about the driver gesture classification task [11,14,15]. These datasets propose various gesture classes, performed by multiple subjects, with diverse gesture complexity and sensors used for the acquisition part. A summary of these datasets is reported in Table 1.

The *Chalearn* dataset [6] contains a high number of subjects and samples, but it is based only on the *Italian Sign Language* and it is acquired in an indoor environment. The automotive dataset called *Turms* [1] is acquired in a real automotive context, but it is focused on driver's hand detection and tracking, then no hand gestures are present.

The dataset proposed in [11] contains both 3D hand joints information and depth maps, acquired jointly with a *Leap Motion* device and the first version of the *Microsoft Kinect*. There are 10 different gestures performed by 14 people, and each gesture is repeated for 10 times. The acquisition has been conducted in an indoor environment and the devices are frontally placed with respect to the subjects. Unfortunately, hand gestures are *static* and belong to the *American Sign Language*.

The *VIVA Hand Gesture Dataset* [15] is a dataset released for the namesake challenge, organized by the *Laboratory for Intelligent and Safe Automobiles* (LISA). This dataset has been designed to study natural human activities in confused and difficult contexts, with a variable illumination and frequent occlusions. 19 gesture classes are reported, taken from 8 different subjects, simulating real driving situations. Authors provide both RGB and depth maps acquired using the first version of the *Microsoft Kinect*. It is worth noting that users perform gestures around the infotainment area, placing the right hand on a green and flat surface to facilitate vision-based algorithms. The best gesture recognition method proposed in the challenge consists of a 3D convolutional neural network-based algorithm which has been presented by Molchanov *et al.* in [13].

Table 1. Datasets for the hand gesture classification task. We report the number of subjects and gesture classes and the types of data included: RGB images, depth maps (acquired with *Structured Light* (SL) or *Time-of-Flight* (ToF) devices), infrared images. Moreover, we report the presence of 3D hand joints (3DJ) and dynamic gestures.

Dataset	Year	#subjs	#gest	RGB	Depth	IR	3DJ	Dynamic
Unipd [11]	2014	14	10	√	SL		√	
VIVA [15]	2014	8	19	√	SL	√		√
Nvidia [14]	2015	20	25	√	SL	√		√
LMDHG [4]	2017	21	13			√	√	√
Turms [1]	2018	7	-			√		√
Briareo	2019	40	12	√	ToF	√	√	√

The *Nvidia Dynamic Hand Gesture* dataset [14] presents 25 types of gestures recorded by multiple sensors (*SoftKinetic DS235* and a *DUO 3D* stereo camera) from different points of view: acquisition devices are frontal placed and top-mounted with respect to the driver position. The acquisition has been carried out in an indoor car simulator. Users perform gestures with the right hand while the left one grasps the steering wheel. The dataset contains the recordings of 20 subjects, even if some of them contributed only partially, not performing the entire recording session. In addition, optical flow is computed on intensity images and it is publicly released.

The *Leap Motion Dynamic Hand Gesture* (LMDHG) dataset [4] contains unsegmented dynamic gestures, performed with either one or two hands. The *Leap Motion* sensor has been employed as acquisition device because its SDK is able to extract the 3D coordinates of 23 hand joints. This dataset is composed of several sequences executed by 21 participants and it contains 13 types of gestures performed randomly alongside an additional no-gesture action. Overall, 50 sequences are released, leading to a total of 608 gesture instances.

3   The Briareo Dataset

In this Section, we introduce the *Briareo* dataset, highlighting the original contributions of the proposed data collection with respect to the previous ones.

As mentioned above, this dataset contains *dynamic* hand gestures, shown in Fig. 1, acquired indoor in a real car dashboard. Furthermore, the dataset introduces an innovative point of view, not used in previous datasets: we place the acquisition devices in the central tunnel, between the driver and the passenger seat. This choice has been driven by the hypothesis that from this point of view it is possible to acquire gestures with minor visual occlusions compared to other camera positions. Moreover, in this position the acquisition devices can be easily integrated and are protected by direct sunlight, which is a critical element for infrared-based sensors.

Finally, this dataset contains a great variability in the collected data: a high number of subjects and gestures have been recorded. The great amount of annotated data allows using deep learning-based techniques. The dataset is publicly available[2].

Fig. 2. Sample infrared, RGB, and depth images from the *Briareo* dataset. Samples have been acquired with a standard RGB camera and the *Pico Flexx* device.

3.1   Acquisition Devices

Three different sensors are used in order to acquire the dataset.

Firstly, a traditional RGB camera is exploited, able to acquire data up to 30 frames per second. In order to maintain the realism of the automotive environment, no external light sources have been added: this results in dark intensity frames with low contrast, as depicted in Fig. 2. Secondly, we used a depth sensors, namely the *Pico Flexx*[3], which has the following features:

---

[2] http://imagelab.ing.unimore.it/briareo.
[3] https://pmdtec.com/picofamily/flexx.

- **Time-of-Flight (ToF):** thanks to this technology, the device is able to acquire 16-bit depth maps with a spatial resolution of 224 × 171. As reported in [16], ToF technology provides better quality and a faster frame rate than the *Structured Light* devices (*e.g.* the first version of the *Microsoft Kinect*), reducing the number of visual artefacts, like holes and missing values;
- **Form Factor:** the sensor has very limited dimensions (68 mm × 17 mm × 7.35 mm) and weight (8 g), so it can be easily integrated in the car cockpit;
- **High Framerate:** different work modalities are available for the device: selecting a limited acquisition range, it is able to acquire up to 45 frames per second. This is a crucial element in order to achieve real time performance;
- **Acquisition range:** there are two possible depth resolutions, the first one acquires objects in the range 0.5−4 m, while the second one in the range 0.1−1 m. We set the second modality: in this way, the sensor is able to correctly acquire gestures performed close to the device. Indeed, we hypothesize that a distance grater than 1 meter is useless in our acquisition setting.

Finally, we employ an infrared stereo camera, the *Leap Motion*[4], with the following features:

- **Infrared cameras:** the device has two infrared cameras with a resolution of 640 × 240 and 400 × 400 pixels for raw and rectified frames, respectively;
- **High Framerate:** up to 200 frames per second;
- **Form Factor:** this device is only 70 × 12 × 3 mm and 32 g of weight;

Moreover, this sensor is equipped with a fish-eye lens that allows to capture a 150-degree scene from very short distances. The SDK of the Leap Motion device is able to acquire, in addition to infrared images, several hand joints, together with their orientations and bone lengths, as shown in Fig. 3.

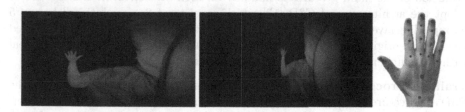

Fig. 3. Data acquired through the *Leap Motion* device: from the left, the raw and the rectified frame, and the hand joints (blue), including the fingertips (red), the palm center (green) and the wrist position (orange). (Color figure online)

---

[4] https://www.leapmotion.com.

3.2 Statistics

The *Briareo* dataset contains 12 dynamic gesture classes, designed with a view to the development of an interactive generic system, as follows: *fist* (g00), *pinch* (g01), *flip-over* (g02), *telephone* (g03), *right swipe* (g04), *left swipe* (g05), *top-down swipe* (g06), *bottom-up swipe* (g07), *thumb* (g08), *index* (g09), *clockwise rotation* (g10) and *counterclockwise rotation* (g11).

A total of 40 subjects (33 males and 7 females) have taken part to the data collection. Every subject performs each gesture 3 times, leading to a total of 120 collected sequences. Each sequence lasts at least 40 frames. At the end of this procedure, we record an additional sequence including all hand gestures in a single recording. The three cameras have been synchronized so that the frames at a certain instant depict the same scene.

The following data are released within the dataset: RGB images (traditional camera), depth maps and infrared intensities (Pico Flexx), raw and rectified infrared images (Leap Motion), 3D hand joints (Leap Motion SDK). Samples are reported in Figs. 2 and 3.

4 Proposed Baselines

In this Section, we investigate the use of two methods to tackle the gesture classification task, handling the temporal evolution of the dynamic hand gestures in two different ways: 3D convolutions and recurrent neural architecture.

4.1 3D Convolutional Network

Architecture. Taking inspiration from [14], we propose a 3D convolutional neural network to tackle the gesture classification task. Therefore, the temporal evolution of the hand gestures is handled through 3D convolutional layers. We adopt the architecture of C3D [17] which consists of 8 convolutional layers, 5 max-pooling layers and a *softmax* layer. The last 487-dimensional fully connected layer of the original architecture is replaced with a 12-dimensional layer to deal with the number of classes of the *Briareo* dataset.

Training Procedure. Input frames are resized to 112×112 to deal with the C3D architecture constraints and grouped in mini-batches of size 8. As optimizer, we exploit the Stochastic Gradient Descent (SGD) with a learning rate of 10^{-2} and a momentum of 0.5. We use the binary categorical cross-entropy as loss function. Input images are normalized so that the mean and the variance are 0 and 1, respectively. Since each gesture of the dataset has a different duration, we create fixed-length input sequences in the following way: given a single sequence, starting from the central frame (w.r.t. the whole length of the sequence) 20 contiguous frames towards the beginning and 20 towards the end are extracted and stacked to form the input of the proposed architectures.

Table 2. Inference time of the C3D model w.r.t different architectures and input types.

	RGB	Depth	Infrared
Nvidia 1080 Ti	$1.96 \pm 0.49\,\text{ms}$	$2.26 \pm 1.17\,\text{ms}$	$2.19 \pm 0.93\,\text{ms}$
Nvidia Titan X	$1.87 \pm 0.77\,\text{ms}$	$2.07 \pm 0.89\,\text{ms}$	$1.86 \pm 0.92\,\text{ms}$
CPU	$4.01 \pm 0.24\,\text{s}$	$3.89 \pm 0.24\,\text{s}$	$3.88 \pm 0.24\,\text{s}$

4.2 Long-Short Term Memory

Architecture. Differently from the previous network, here we aim to handle the temporal evolution of the hand gesture through a recurrent neural network, in particular the *Long-Short Term Memory* (LSTM) [7]. The LSTM model employed is described by the following equations:

$$I_t = \sigma(W_i x_t + U_i H_{t-1} + b_i) \tag{1}$$

$$F_t = \sigma(W_f x_t + U_f H_{t-1} + b_f) \tag{2}$$

$$O_t = \sigma(W_o x_t + U_o H_{t-1} + b_o) \tag{3}$$

$$G_t = tanh(W_c x_t + U_c H_{t-1} + b_c) \tag{4}$$

$$C_t = F_t \odot C_{t-1} + I_t \odot G_t \tag{5}$$

$$H_t = O_t \odot tanh(C_t) \tag{6}$$

in which F_t, I_t, O_t are the gates, C_t is the memory cell, G_t is the candidate memory, and H_t is the hidden state. W, U, and b are learned weights and biases, while x_t corresponds to the input at time t as defined in the previous section. Finally, the $\odot$ operator is the element-wise product.

We exploit a LSTM module with a hidden size of 256 units and 2 layers, adding a final fully connected layer with 12 units, corresponding to the number of the gesture classes.

Training Procedure. As reported in Sect. 3.1, for each frame the Leap Motion SDK gives the 3D joints of the hand and the palm center, represented with the (x, y, z) coordinates in the 3D space. A feature set is then created, including the position of each finger joint and of the palm center, along with the speed and the direction (expressed in terms of *yaw*, *pitch* and *roll* angles) of the fingertips. Data are then normalized to obtain zero mean and unit variance.

The network is then trained using as input this pre-processed data, exploiting the Adam optimizer [8] with learning rate 10^{-3}, weight decay 10^{-4}, and a batch size of 2. As loss function, we use the binary categorical cross-entropy. We empirically set the length of each training sequence equal to 40 frames.

5 Experimental Results

The following experimental results have been obtained in a *cross-subject* setting: we randomly put the recordings of 32 subjects in the train and the validation

Table 3. Results expressed in terms of accuracy and improvement of the proposed models with respect to the 12 hand gesture classes of the *Briareo* dataset.

Gesture	Gesture label	C3D			LSTM 3D Joints
		RGB	Depth	Infrared	
Fist	g0	0.542	0.708	0.750	0.875
Pinch	g1	0.833	0.875	0.958	1.000
Flip-over	g2	0.792	0.750	0.875	0.958
Telephone call	g3	0.625	0.792	1.000	1.000
Right swipe	g4	0.833	0.833	0.917	0.917
Left swipe	g5	0.833	0.917	0.792	1.000
Top-down swipe	g6	0.917	0.750	0.958	1.000
Bottom-up swipe	g7	0.750	0.833	0.875	0.917
Thumb up	g8	0.917	0.625	1.000	0.875
Point	g9	0.667	0.708	1.000	1.000
Rotation (CW)	g10	0.542	0.375	0.750	0.917
Rotation (CCW)	g11	0.417	0.958	0.635	0.875
	all	**0.722**	**0.760**	**0.875**	**0.944**
Improvement		-	+0.038	+0.153	+0.222

set and the recordings of the other 8 subjects in the test set. We maintain this division for every test here reported.

Aiming to investigate the contribution of each input modality to the final hand gesture classification accuracy, we train the C3D model separately on the three modalities, *i.e.* RGB, infrared, and depth images. Moreover, we train the proposed LSTM model on the 3D hand joints computed by the Leap Motion SDK. The overall accuracy w.r.t. each gesture and input type is reported in Table 3.

The model that analyzes RGB images obtains the worst result, due to the low brightness and contrast of the acquired images, even though some gestures (*e.g. g6* and *g8*) are easily recognized. As expected, a significant improvement is introduced when analyzing depth maps and infrared images, thanks to the higher image quality and reliability.

As shown in the right part of Table 3, the LSTM model, which analyzed 3D hand joints, achieves the best overall accuracy. However, this performance is based on a correct localization of the 3D hand joints provided by the Leap Motion SDK, limiting the applicability of this method to real world applications.

Considering the high accuracy obtained by the proposed models, we developed a reference framework for the classification of gestures. The C3D model and the infrared images have been selected to deal with both accuracy and speed, without being dependent on external software (*e.g.* the Leap Motion SDK).

The proposed framework processes input data frame by frame and a temporary buffer is maintained, through a sliding windows approach. As soon as

40 frames are stacked, the buffer is classified by the C3D model. The gesture is classified and considered valid only if the prediction confidence reaches a certain threshold, empirically set to 0.85.

In Figure 4 we report the flow chart of the proposed framework, and some screenshots of the graphical user interface, showing infrared and depth frames on the left, and the predicted gesture label on the right.

Finally, we test the inference time of the C3D model in a desktop computer equipped with an *Intel i7-6850K* (3.8 GHz) and 64 GB of memory. This test is carried out on two different GPU, namely the *Nvidia 1080 Ti* and the *Nvidia Titan X*, as well as without graphical accelerators. The model has been developed using *PyTorch*. For investigation purposes, we test the network with each input type, *i.e.* RGB, infrared, and depth (spatial resolution and data precision vary). The times required for the inference of a single frame are reported in Table 2. As it can be seen, real time performance are achieved when running the model on GPUs.

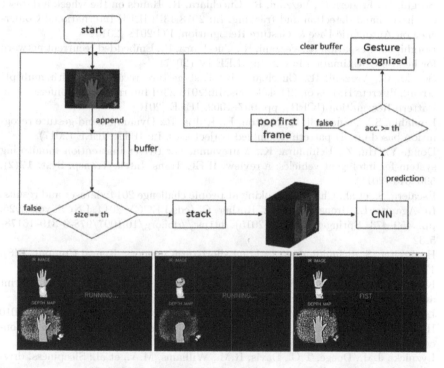

Fig. 4. From the top, the flow chart of the sliding window-based framework for the gesture segmentation and classification task. Then, sample output of the developed framework with the predicted gesture on the right.

6   Conclusions

A new dataset, called *Briareo* and designed for the classification of hand gestures in the automotive setting, has been presented. The dataset contains recording acquired from an innovative point of view with three different acquisition devices, *i.e.* RGB, depth, and infrared cameras.

A C3D-based and a LSTM-based network have been trained and tested on the proposed dataset in order to investigate the quality and the complexity of the collected images and 3D hand joints, achieving a significant accuracy and representing a challenging baseline for future work.

Finally, a real-time hand gesture recognition framework has been presented, showing the capabilities of the proposed dataset and models.

References

1. Borghi, G., Frigieri, E., Vezzani, R., Cucchiara, R.: Hands on the wheel: a dataset for driver hand detection and tracking. In: 2018 13th IEEE International Conference on Automatic Face & Gesture Recognition, FG 2018 (2018)
2. Borghi, G., Gasparini, R., Vezzani, R., Cucchiara, R.: Embedded recurrent network for head pose estimation in car. In: IEEE IV (2017)
3. Borghi, G., Vezzani, R., Cucchiara, R.: Fast gesture recognition with multiple stream discrete HMMs on 3D skeletons. In: 2016 23rd International Conference on Pattern Recognition (ICPR), pp. 997–1002. IEEE (2016)
4. Boulahia, S.Y., Anquetil, E., Multon, F., Kulpa, R.: Dynamic hand gesture recognition based on 3D pattern assembled trajectories. In: IPTA. IEEE (2017)
5. Dong, Y., Hu, Z., Uchimura, K., Murayama, N.: Driver inattention monitoring system for intelligent vehicles: a review. IEEE Trans. Intell. Transp. Syst. **12**(2), 596–614 (2011)
6. Escalera, S., et al.: ChaLearn looking at people challenge 2014: dataset and results. In: Agapito, L., Bronstein, M.M., Rother, C. (eds.) ECCV 2014. LNCS, vol. 8925, pp. 459–473. Springer, Cham (2015). https://doi.org/10.1007/978-3-319-16178-5_32
7. Hochreiter, S., Schmidhuber, J.: Long short-term memory. Neural Comput. **9**(8), 1735–1780 (1997)
8. Kingma, D.P., Ba, J.: Adam: a method for stochastic optimization. arXiv preprint arXiv:1412.6980 (2014)
9. Liu, W.: Natural user interface-next mainstream product user interface. In: 2010 IEEE 11th International Conference on Computer-Aided Industrial Design & Conceptual Design 1, vol. 1, pp. 203–205. IEEE (2010)
10. Lyznicki, J.M., Doege, T.C., Davis, R.M., Williams, M.A., et al.: Sleepiness, driving, and motor vehicle crashes. JAMA **279**(23), 1908–1913 (1998)
11. Marin, G., Dominio, F., Zanuttigh, P.: Hand gesture recognition with leap motion and kinect devices. In: 2014 IEEE ICIP, pp. 1565–1569. IEEE (2014)
12. McKnight, A.J., McKnight, A.S.: The effect of cellular phone use upon driver attention. Accid. Anal. Prev. **25**(3), 259–265 (1993)
13. Molchanov, P., Gupta, S., Kim, K., Kautz, J.: Hand gesture recognition with 3D convolutional neural networks. In: Proceedings of the IEEE Conference on Computer Vision and Pattern Recognition Workshops, pp. 1–7 (2015)

14. Molchanov, P., Yang, X., Gupta, S., Kim, K., Tyree, S., Kautz, J.: Online detection and classification of dynamic hand gestures with recurrent 3D convolutional neural network. In: Proceedings of the IEEE Conference on Computer Vision and Pattern Recognition, pp. 4207–4215 (2016)
15. Ohn-Bar, E., Trivedi, M.M.: Hand gesture recognition in real time for automotive interfaces: a multimodal vision-based approach and evaluations. IEEE Trans. Intell. Transp. Syst. **15**(6), 2368–2377 (2014)
16. Sarbolandi, H., Lefloch, D., Kolb, A.: Kinect range sensing: structured-light versus time-of-flight kinect. In: Computer Vision and Image Understanding, pp. 1–20 (2015)
17. Tran, D., Bourdev, L., Fergus, R., Torresani, L., Paluri, M.: Learning spatiotemporal features with 3D convolutional networks. In: Proceedings of the IEEE International Conference on Computer Vision (ICCV), pp. 4489–4497 (2015)
18. Venturelli, M., Borghi, G., Vezzani, R., Cucchiara, R.: From depth data to head pose estimation: a Siamese approach. In: 12th International Joint Conference on Computer Vision, Imaging and Computer Graphics Theory and Applications, VISAPP 2017 (2016)

Prediction of Social Image Popularity Dynamics

Alessandro Ortis[✉], Giovanni Maria Farinella, and Sebastiano Battiato

Department of Mathematics and Computer Science, University of Catania,
Viale A. Doria, 6, 95125 Catania, Italy
{ortis,gfarinella,battiato}@dmi.unict.it

Abstract. This paper introduces the new challenge of forecasting the engagement score reached by social images over time. The task to be addressed is hence the estimation, in advance, of the engagement score dynamic over a period of time (e.g., 30 days) by exploiting visual and social features. To this aim, we propose a benchmark dataset that consists of ∼20K Flickr images labelled with their engagement scores (i.e., views, comments and favorites) in a period of 30 days from the upload in the social platform. For each image, the dataset also includes user's and photo's social features that have been proven to have an influence on the image popularity on Flickr. We also present a method to address the aforementioned problem. The engagement score dynamic is represented as the combination of two properties related to the dynamic and the magnitude of the engagement sequence, referred as shape and scale respectively. The proposed approach models the problem as the combination of two prediction tasks, which are addressed individually. Then, the two outputs are properly combined to obtain the prediction of the whole engagement sequence. Our approach is able to forecast the daily number of views reached by a photo posted on Flickr for a period of 30 days, by exploiting features extracted from the post. This means that the prediction can be performed before posting the photo.

Keywords: Image popularity prediction · Social media engagement

1 Introduction and Motivation

One of the most promising application of social media analysis is related to social marketing campaigns. In this context, several companies are interested in the automatic analysis of the level of engagement of potential customers with respect to the different posts related to their products. The user engagement is usually measured in terms of number of views, likes or shares. This information can be further combined with web search engines and companies website visits statistics to find correlations between social advertising campaigns and their aimed outcomes. Khosla et al. [7] proposed a log-normalized popularity score that has been then commonly by the community to measure the level of

© Springer Nature Switzerland AG 2019
E. Ricci et al. (Eds.): ICIAP 2019, LNCS 11752, pp. 572–582, 2019.
https://doi.org/10.1007/978-3-030-30645-8_52

engagement of an image. Let c_i be a measure of the engagement related to a social media item i (e.g., number of likes, number of views, etc.). The popularity score of the item i is computed as:

$$score(i) = \log\left(\frac{c_i}{T_i} + 1\right) \tag{1}$$

where T_i is the number of days since the item i has been uploaded on the social platform. In order to estimate the popularity with Eq. 1, the cumulative engagement obtained by an image post until a specific day is normalized with respect to the total number of days of the post. However, the formulation of the popularity score does not take into account the dynamic of the engagement of the image post. We observe that the relative increment of the engagements over time is not constant and tends to decrease over time. Therefore, the Eq. 1 tends to penalize social media contents published in the past with respect to more recent contents, especially when the difference between the dates of the upload of different posts is large. As claimed in previous works [12], the number of views increases in the first few days, and then remains stable over time. As consequence, the popularity score computed as in Eq. 1 decreases with the oldness of an image, but this fact has not been considered in the popularity score formulation commonly used in the state of the art works. In other words, two pictures with similar engagement dynamic but very different lifetime, have to be ranked differently. The work presented in this paper proposes a new challenging task which finds very practical applications in recommendation systems and advertisement placement. A new benchmark dataset is released, consisting on a collection of ~20K Flickr images, with related user and photo meta-data and three engagement scores tracked for 30 days. The presented dataset will allow the community to perform more accurate and sophisticated analysis on social media content engagement. Moreover, the proposed framework empowers the development of systems that support the publication and promotion of social contents, by providing a forecast of the engagement dynamics. This can suggest when old contents should be replaced by new ones before they become obsolete.

2   Related Works

Many researches tried to gain insights to understand which features make an image popular for large groups of users [3,4,7–9]. The authors of [7] analysed the importance of several cues related to the image or to the social profile of the user that lead to high or low values of popularity. The selected features were used to train a Support Vector Regressor (SVR) to predict the image popularity score defined in Eq. 1. Cappallo et al. [6] addressed the popularity prediction task as a ranking problem. They used a latent-SVM with an objective function defined to preserve the ranking of the popularity scores between pairs of images. Few works have considered the evolution of the image popularity over time. In [1] the authors considered the number of likes achieved within the first hour of the post lifecycle to forecast the popularity after one day, one week or one month. The problem has been treated as a binary classification tasks (i.e., popular vs. non-popular) by thresholding the popularity scores. The paper [10] aims to predict popularity of a category (i.e., a brand) by introducing a category representation, based on user's posts daily number of likes. The time-aware task proposed in the ACM Multimedia 2017 SMP Challenge[1] aims to predict the top-k popular posts among a group of new posts, given the data related to the history of the past posts in the social platform. Differently than the SMP Challenge, in this work we propose a dataset that reports the engagement scores (i.e., number of views, comments and favorites) of all the involved images recorded on a day-to-day basis for 30 consecutive days. This allows to compute the popularity score for an arbitrary day and to perform more specific analyses on the photo lifecycle. Time aware popularity prediction methods exploit time information to define proper image representations used to infer the image popularity score as in Eq. 1 at a precise time. Indeed, most of the existing works exploit features based on the popularity achieved in the first period. Bandari et al. [2] propose a method which aims to predict popularity of items prior to their posting, however it focuses on news article (i.e., tweets) and the popularity prediction results (i.e., regression) are not satisfactory, as claimed by the authors themselves. Indeed they achieve good results by quantizing the range of popularity values and performing a classification. On the contrary we predict a temporal sequence at time zero, without any temporal hints. Differently than previous works, our approach focuses on the prediction of the whole temporal sequence of image popularity scores (30 days) with a daily granularity, at time zero (i.e., using only information known before the post is published) and without any temporal hints. We designed a regression approach with the aim to estimate the actual values of popularity, instead of quantizing the ranges of possible popularity values or distinguish between popular and non-popular posts (i.e., binary classification). This makes the task very challenging, as there is not an upper bound for the popularity score values and regression errors are considered in the whole 30 days predicted sequences.

3   Proposed Dataset

Most of the datasets on image popularity prediction are based on Flickr. However, the platform only provides the cumulative values of the engagement scores. For this reason we built and released a new dataset including multiple daily values of the engagement scores over 30 days[2]. More than $20K$ images have been downloaded and tracked considering a period of 30 days. In particular, the first day of crawling the procedure downloads a batch of the latest photos uploaded on Flickr. We run this procedure multiple times by varying the day of the week and time of download in order to avoid the introduction of bias in the dataset. All the social features related to the users, the photos and groups were collected, as well as a number of information useful to compute the engagement scores are downloaded for the following 30 days (i.e., views, comments and favorites). In

---

[1] https://social-media-prediction.github.io/PredictionChallenge/.

[2] The dataset is available at http://iplab.dmi.unict.it/popularitydynamics.

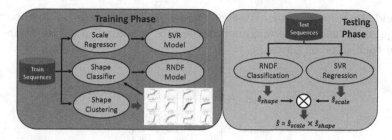

Fig. 1. The pipeline performs the estimation of two properties: the sequence engagement shape $\hat{s}_{shape}$ and scale $\hat{s}_{scale}$. The shape is estimated by exploiting a Random Forest Classifier (RNDF), whereas a Support Vector Regressor (SVR) is employed to estimate the scale.

all the experiments described in this paper, the engagement score is computed using the number of views, as it is the most used score in the state of the art. However, the other two scores are available with the dataset for further studies. In order to obtain a fine-grained sampling, the first sample of the social data related to a post is taken within the first 2 h from the time of the image upload. Then, a daily procedure takes at least 2 samples per day of the social data for each image. Several social features related to users, photos and the groups have been retrieved. In particular, for each user we recorded: the number of the user's contacts, if the user has a pro account, photo counts, mean views of the user's photos, number of groups the user is enrolled in, the average number of members and photos of the user's groups. For each picture we considered: the size of the original image, title, description, number of albums, groups the picture is shared in, the average number of members and photos of the groups in which the picture is shared in, as well as the tags associated by the user. Moreover, for each photo, the dataset includes the geographic coordinates, the date of the upload, the date of crawling, the date of when the picture has been taken, as well as the Flickr IDs of all the considered users, photos and groups[3]. We tracked a total of 21.035 photos for 30 days. Some photos have been removed by authors (or not longer accessible through the APIs) during the period of crawling. As result, there are photos that have been tracked for a longer period than others. In particular the dataset consists of: 19.213 photos tracked at least 10 days, 18.838 photos tracked at least 20 days and 17.832 photos tracked at least 30 days. In our experiments we considered the set of photos tracked for 30 days, as it represents the most challenging scenario.

4   Proposed Method

A given sequence s related to the number of views of a posted image over n days, can be formulated as the combination of two properties, namely the *sequence*

---

[3] The IDs of all the entities allow further API requests.

shape and the *sequence scale*. We define these properties as in Eq. 2. In particular, s_{scale} is defined as the maximum value of s, whereas s_{shape} is obtained by dividing each value of s by s_{scale}:

$$s = [v_0, v_1, \ldots, v_n]$$
$$s_{scale} = max\{s\} = v_n \tag{2}$$
$$s_{shape} = \left[\frac{v_0}{v_n}, \frac{v_1}{v_n}, \ldots, \frac{v_n}{v_n}\right]$$

Therefore, given s_{shape} and s_{scale}, we can obtain the sequence s as follows.

$$s = s_{shape} \times s_{scale} \tag{3}$$

The engagement sequence can be hence considered as a pair of shape and scale. The shape describes the general dynamic (i.e., trend) of the sequence in the monitored period, regardless its actual values. Moreover, sequences with similar shapes can be associated to a more general shape, named "shape prototype". The sequence scale represents the degree of popularity reached by the photo in n days. We observed that two sequences with the same shape could have very different scales, and vice-versa. To motivate this assumption, we analysed the distributions of the s_{scale} values related to sequences grouped by the assigned shape prototype (i.e., s^*_{shape}). This distribution is shown in Fig. 2. There is a huge variability of the s_{scale} values within the sequences of the same shape. This demonstrates the independent relationship between the scale and the shape of a sequence. Based on this assumption, the proposed approach performs two separate estimations for the shape and the scale of the engagement related to a period of $n = 30$ days. Then, the two results are combined to perform the estimation of the final engagement sequence associated to the photo (see Fig. 1). The shape of the training sequences are grouped with a clustering procedure during the training phase. All the sequences in the same cluster are represented by a shape prototype denoted by s^*_{shape}. The obtained shape prototypes s^*_{shape} are used as labels to train a classifier in order to predict the shape prototype to which a new sequence has to be assigned, given the set input social features. The predicted shape prototype for a new sequence is denoted by $\hat{s}_{shape}$. A Support Vector Regressor (SVR) is also trained to infer the value of s_{scale} given the social features. The output of the regressor is denoted by $\hat{s}_{scale}$. The final engagement estimation of an image post for the period of n days is obtained as $\hat{s} = \hat{s}_{shape} \times \hat{s}_{scale}$. We evaluated the proposed approach by exploiting features extracted from the user information, the photo metadata or from the visual content. Although in previous works on popularity prediction the most effective results have been obtained by considering a combination of user information and photo meta-data, some experiments [7] suggest that the semantic content of the picture also influence the prediction. For this reason we evaluated 6 visual representation extracted from the pictures by exploiting three state of the art Convolutional Neural Networks (CNN). For each architecture we extracted the last two layers of activations before the softmax, referred here as $f1$ and $f2$.

Specifically we considered a CNN specialized to classify images into 1183 categories including 978 objects and 205 places (Hybridnet [13]); a CNN trained to assign an Adjective-Noun Pair to an input image among 4342 different ANPs (DeepSentiBank [5]); and a CNN for object classification trained on 1000 categories (GoogleNet [11]).

4.1 Shape Prototyping

Considering Eq. 2, all the s_{shape} sequences have values in the range $[0, 1]$. We consider that all the sequences with the "same" dynamics will have a very similar s_{shape}. Since groups of sequences with the same shape embody instances with a common engagement trend, in the first step of our approach we try to infer a number of popularity shape prototypes representing the different groups of shapes. To this aim, we perform a K-means clustering to group the training sequences. The obtained cluster centroids represent the dynamic models for the sequences within clusters (i.e., each centroid sequence is a shape prototype). In order to select a proper number of clusters for the training sequences (i.e., number of shape prototypes), we performed clustering by considering a wide range of values for K. Then we selected the optimal K considering the Within cluster Sum of Squares (WSS) and the Between cluster Sum of Squares (BSS) indices. The best results have been obtained with $K = 50$.

4.2 Shape Prediction

The result of the shape clustering is a set of shape prototypes. Given this "dictionary" of shapes, any sequence can be assigned to a cluster by comparing its shape with respect to the prototypes. By exploiting the set of shape prototypes we labelled all the sequences in the training and testing dataset by assigning each sequence to a prototype. Then, considering the training sequences, we built a classifier that takes only the social features associated to a post, and predicts the shape (i.e., the prototype) of the corresponding sequence. In order to find the best classifier, we evaluated a pool of algorithms common used for classification tasks, as well as several variations of the social features as input. In particular, we considered the following classifiers: Random Forest (RNDF), Decision Tree (DT), k-Nearest Neighbour (kNN), SVM with RBF or linear kernel and Multilayer Perceptron (MLP). The best results have been achieved by using all the social features described in Sect. 3 as input of a RNDF classifier. Some of the considered methods required the selection of parameters (e.g., the number of neighbours K for kNN, the parameters C and γ for LSVM and RBFSVM, etc.) which we have established with a grid search method over the training data. In the proposed approach, given a new test image post, the RNDF classifier is hence used to assign a shape prototype based only on its social features.

4.3 Scale Estimation

In order to estimate the value s_{scale}, we trained a Support Vector Regressor (SVR). In particular, we consider the s_{scale} values to compute the popularity score as in Eq. 1, then the SVR is trained to predict the popularity score. After the prediction, the estimation of the number of views is obtained by inverting Eq. 1. Let $\hat{p}$ be the popularity score estimated by the SVR, the number of views is hence computed by the following equation:

$$\hat{s}_{scale} = (e^{\hat{p}} - 1) \times n \tag{4}$$

First, we evaluated the estimation performances to infer the scale by training the SVR with a single feature as input. For each experimental setting, we computed the Spearman's correlation between the predicted score and the Ground Truth. This provided a measure of correlation between the features and the value of s_{scale}. In the second stage of experiments, we trained the SVR by considering the concatenation of social features as input. The groups of features have been selected in a greedy fashion considering the performance obtained individually. We have also evaluated two approaches that exploits as input the results obtained by the SVRs trained with the single features. As these methods perform a fusion of several outputs after the prediction, they are often referred as "late fusion" strategies. In the approach named *Late Fusion 1* the outputs of the SVRs are averaged, whereas in the approach *Late Fusion 2* the outputs of the SVRs are concatenated and used to train a new SVR. Scale estimation results, in terms of Spearman's correlation, are reported in Tables 1 and 2.

5   Problem Analysis

As observed, previous works in popularity prediction simplify the task by quantizing the possible output values into two values [1,2], or by just predicting a ranking between pictures [6] rather than the actual values of popularity. Furthermore, the majority of these works predict a single score, normalized at an arbitrary age of the post, rather than the dynamic of the post popularity. The few works that aim to predict dynamics lean on the early sequence values (e.g., [1]). This makes the addressed task very challenging. In order to understand the task difficulty, we performed an ablation analysis aimed to understand how the inference of the shape and the scale affect the estimation of the whole sequence. Each experiment exploits some Ground Truth knowledge about either the scale and the shape of the sequences. Therefore, the experiment error rates can be considered as lower bounds for the proposed approach. The considered experimental settings are the following:

- **Case A:** the inferred sequence is obtained by considering both the shape of the Ground Truth (s^*_{shape}) and the Ground Truth scale value (s_{scale}). This method achieves the minimum possible error as both values are taken from the Ground Truth. The measured error is due to the clustering approximation of the sequences.
- **Case B:** in this case the shape is predicted ($\hat{s}_{shape}$), whereas the scale value is taken from the Ground Truth (s_{scale}). The measured error is due to the clustering approximation of the sequences and the error of the classification to assign the shape prototype.

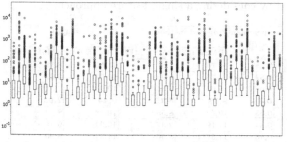
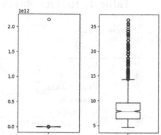

Fig. 2. Distributions of the s_{scale} values of sequences grouped by the s^*_{shape} prototypes assigned by the clustering procedure.

Fig. 3. Box-and-whisker plot of RMSE values (left) computed on a test set. Same distribution after removing the 25% highest/lowest values (right).

- **Case C:** this case combines the shape of the Ground Truth (s^*_{shape}) and the predicted scale value $(\hat{s}_{scale})$. The measured error is due to the clustering approximation of the sequences and the error in the estimation of the scale.

The mean RMSE errors, considering 10 random runs, of Case A and Case B are 4.97 and 7.51 respectively. These measures are not affected by the prediction of the scale and depend only on the clustering and shape prototyping steps. The results of Case C are affected by the scale estimation. As detailed above, the errors concerning the ablation experiments are related to either the shape and the scale estimations, depending on the definition of the prior Ground Truth knowledge. From this analysis we observed that the whole sequence estimation is more sensitive to errors in the scale prediction. Indeed, an error in the scale affects all the elements of the sequence and hence the RMSE value. Moreover, since we don't quantize the possible output values as done in previous works, there is not an upper bound for the estimated popularity scale and the predicted value could be very large with high magnitude. When the error is averaged, even a few large values could affect the final result. The left plot in Fig. 3 shows the box-and-whisker plot of the computed RMSE values for Case C. From this plot, it's clear that the mean of the RMSE errors is not a good method for the evaluation of the performance, as it is skewed by few large values. Figure 2 shows the presence of several s_{scale} values which are outliers with respect the data distribution. Indeed, the dataset includes few examples with very large scales (depicted as circles in the box-and-whisker plots). For instance, there are only 11 sequences with s_{scale} between $10k$ and $30k$ views. The presence of such few uncommon examples with very large magnitudes caused the skewness in the test error distribution observed in Fig. 3. For these reasons we considered two performance measures for the evaluation of either the proposed method and the Case C (i.e., the two methods that infer the scale of the sequences). Specifically, we considered the 25% truncated RMSE (tRMSE 0.25), also known as the interquartile mean, and the Median RMSE (RMSE MED). The interquartile mean discards an equal

Table 1. Results obtained by considering a single feature approach.

Feature source	Feature ID	Features	Spearman	Proposed method		Case C (shape)	
				tRMSE 0.25	RMSE MED	tRMSE 0.25	RMSE MED
User	0	Ispro	0,25	11,74	8,87	11,50	8,79
User	1	Contacts	0,52	10,48	8,96	10,22	8,69
User	2	PhotoCount	−0,06	11,00	9,65	10,70	9,31
User	3	MeanViews	**0,73**	**9,68**	**8,19**	**9,44**	**7,95**
User	4	GroupsCount	0,53	10,42	8,55	10,18	8,42
User	5	GroupsAvgMembers	0,44	11,19	9,37	10,91	9,11
User	6	GroupsAvgPictures	0,46	11,57	8,96	11,31	8,90
Photo	7	Size	0,05	11,03	9,45	10,72	9,18
Photo	8	Title	0,03	11,01	9,63	10,72	9,30
Photo	9	Description	0,06	10,96	9,58	10,66	9,21
Photo	10	NumSets	0,20	11,57	9,33	11,26	9,14
Photo	11	NumGroups	0,34	10,95	9,63	10,65	9,32
Photo	12	AvgGroupsMemb	0,34	10,88	9,54	10,59	9,24
Photo	13	AvgGroupPhotos	0,34	10,91	9,58	10,61	9,28
Photo	14	Tags	0,11	11,27	9,36	10,97	9,20
Visual	hybrid_f1	Hybridnet fc7	0,22	21,61	17,97	20,08	17,44
Visual	hybrid_f2	Hybridnet fc8a	0,26	13,37	11,76	12,95	11,38
Visual	senti_f1	DeepSentiBank fc7	0,25	21,16	18,27	20,60	17,82
Visual	senti_f2	DeepSentiBank fc8	0,30	16,52	14,32	15,99	13,77
Visual	google_f1	GoogleNet pool5/7 × 7_s1	0,26	13,85	12,15	13.43	11,74
Visual	google_f2	GoogleNet loss3/classifier	0,27	13,18	11,61	12,76	11,17

amount of either high and low tails of a distribution. This means that either the best and the worst 25% error values are removed from the mean computation (right plot in Fig. 3). After this process the distribution of the errors is more clear, yet it is still skewed by some outliers depicted as circles.

6   Popularity Dynamic Results

The experimental results have been obtained by averaging the output of 10 random train/test splits with a proportion of 1:9 between the number of test and training images[4]. Given an image represented by a set of social feature, the proposed approach exploits a Random Forest Classifier to predict the shape prototype $\hat{s}_{shape}$. Then an SVR is used to estimate the popularity score of the image after 30 days. This value is then transformed by using Eq. 4, in order to obtain the scale estimation $\hat{s}_{scale}$. Finally, the estimated shape $\hat{s}_{shape}$ and the estimated scale $\hat{s}_{scale}$ are combined to obtain the predicted sequence $\hat{s}$ (Fig. 1).

Tables 1 and 2 show the results for Case C and for the proposed approach in terms of tRMSE and Median RMSE at varying of the input feature used by the scale regressor (i.e., the SVR). The results obtained by feeding the SVR with a single feature are detailed in Table 1. In particular, the Spearman's correlation between the input feature and the Ground Truth popularity is reported in the fourth column. Considering the achieved Spearman's values, one can observe that the features related to the user have higher correlation values with respect to

---

[4] The same protocol has been applied during the ablation study described in Sect. 5.

Table 2. Evaluation results obtained by combining the features.

Feature ID	Feature	Spearman	Proposed method		Case C (shape)	
			tRMSE 0.25	RMSE MED	tRMSE 0.25	RMSE MED
all	concat(0–14)	0,63	9,59	7,43	9,38	7,26
user	concat(0–6)	0,66	9,86	**7,03**	9,67	6,92
photo	concat(7–14)	0,28	10,80	8,58	10,50	8,30
best_photo	concat(11, 12, 13)	0,34	10,63	9,09	10,35	8,84
user2	concat(3,4)	0,71	9,60	7,66	9,38	7,54
user3	concat(1,3,4)	0,71	9,48	7,51	9,28	7,37
user5	concat(1, 3, 4, 5, 6)	0,68	9,77	7,30	9,59	7,24
	concat(user2, best_photo)	**0,72**	9,49	7,55	9,27	7,43
	concat(user3, best_photo)	0,71	**9,37**	7,38	**9,16**	7,27
	concat(user5,best_photo)	0,69	9,48	7,28	9,28	**7,20**
	Late Fusion 1 (AVG)	0,59	10,70	9,34	10,43	9,06
	Late Fusion 2 (SVR)	0,46	11,91	8,91	11,66	8,86

the others. The other columns in Table 1 report the error rates on the estimation of the prediction of the whole sequence in terms of trimmed RMSE (tRMSE) and Median RMSE (RMSE MED) for the proposed method (columns 5 and 6) and the Case C (columns 7 and 8). The experiments pointed out that the visual features achieves higher error rates. Indeed, the popularity of a photo in terms of number of views is directly related to the capability of the user and the photo to reach as many users as possible in the social platform. Based on the results reported in Table 1, we further considered the combination of the most effective features for the estimation of the sequence scale. To this aim, we evaluated several early and late fusion strategies. The early fusion consists on creating a new input for the SVR, obtained by the concatenation of the selected features. In particular, we evaluated 10 different combinations of features. Each combination is assigned to an identifier for readability. The obtained results show that in the experiments which involve user related features, the achieved error rates are lower and similar. Indeed, the higher error rates are obtained by the combinations that do not consider user features. The best results in terms of tRMSE are obtained by combining the three best user's features (i.e., identified by the ID "user3" in Table 2) and the best photo's features (i.e., "best_photo"). Whereas the best results in terms of Median RMSE are obtained by using only the user related features (i.e., "user").

7   Conclusions and Future Works

In this paper we introduced a new challenging task of estimating the popularity dynamics of social images. To benchmark the problem, a new publicly available dataset is proposed. We also describe a method to forecast the whole sequence of views over a period of 30 days of a photo shared on Flickr, without constrains on the estimated values, nor considering the early values of the sequences. Future works can be devoted to the extension of the dataset by taking into account other social platforms, relations among the followers, as well as features inspired by human perception and sentiment analysis. Future experiments could consider the prediction of the popularity dynamics at different time scales. Also, more sophisticated approaches to define the shape prototypes could be evaluated.

References

1. Almgren, K., Lee, J., et al.: Predicting the future popularity of images on social networks. In: Proceedings of the 3rd Multidisciplinary International Social Networks Conference on SocialInformatics 2016, Data Science 2016, p. 15. ACM (2016)
2. Bandari, R., Asur, S., Huberman, B.A.: The pulse of news in social media: forecasting popularity. In: ICWSM, vol. 12, pp. 26–33 (2012)
3. Battiato, S., et al.: Organizing videos streams for clustering and estimation of popular scenes. In: Battiato, S., Gallo, G., Schettini, R., Stanco, F. (eds.) ICIAP 2017. LNCS, vol. 10484, pp. 51–61. Springer, Cham (2017). https://doi.org/10.1007/978-3-319-68560-1_5
4. Battiato, S., et al.: The social picture. In: Proceedings of the 2016 ACM on International Conference on Multimedia Retrieval, pp. 397–400. ACM (2016)
5. Borth, D., Ji, R., Chen, T., Breuel, T., Chang, S.F.: Large-scale visual sentiment ontology and detectors using adjective noun pairs. In: Proceedings of the 21st ACM International Conference on Multimedia, pp. 223–232. ACM (2013)
6. Cappallo, S., Mensink, T., Snoek, C.G.: Latent factors of visual popularity prediction. In: Proceedings of the 5th ACM on International Conference on Multimedia Retrieval, pp. 195–202. ACM (2015)
7. Khosla, A., Das Sarma, A., Hamid, R.: What makes an image popular? In: Proceedings of the 23rd International Conference on World Wide Web, pp. 867–876. ACM (2014)
8. Ortis, A., Farinella, G.M., Torrisi, G., Battiato, S.: Visual sentiment analysis based on objective text description of images. In: 2018 International Conference on Content-Based Multimedia Indexing (CBMI), pp. 1–6. IEEE (2018)
9. Ortis, A., Farinella, G.M., D'Amico, V., Addesso, L., Torrisi, G., Battiato, S.: RECfusion: automatic video curation driven by visual content popularity. In: Proceedings of the 23rd ACM International Conference on Multimedia, pp. 1179–1182. ACM (2015)
10. Overgoor, G., Mazloom, M., Worring, M., Rietveld, R., van Dolen, W.: A spatio-temporal category representation for brand popularity prediction. In: Proceedings of the 2017 ACM on International Conference on Multimedia Retrieval, pp. 233–241. ACM (2017)
11. Szegedy, C., et al.: Going deeper with convolutions. In: Proceedings of the IEEE Conference on Computer Vision and Pattern Recognition (2015)
12. Valafar, M., Rejaie, R., Willinger, W.: Beyond friendship graphs: a study of user interactions in Flickr. In: Proceedings of the 2nd ACM Workshop on Online Social Networks, pp. 25–30. ACM (2009)
13. Zhou, B., Lapedriza, A., Xiao, J., Torralba, A., Oliva, A.: Learning deep features for scene recognition using places database. In: Advances in Neural Information Processing Systems, pp. 487–495 (2014)

Detecting Sounds of Interest in Roads with Deep Networks

Pasquale Foggia[1], Alessia Saggese[1(✉)], Nicola Strisciuglio[2], Mario Vento[1], and Vincenzo Vigilante[1]

[1] Department of Information Engineering,
Electrical Engineering and Applied Mathematics (DIEM),
University of Salerno, Fisciano, Italy
{pfoggia,asaggese,mvento,vvigilante}@unisa.it
[2] Bernoulli Institute for Mathematics, Computer Science and Artificial Intelligence,
University of Groningen, Groningen, The Netherlands
n.strisciuglio@rug.nl

Abstract. Monitoring of public and private places is of great importance for security of people and is usually done by means of surveillance cameras. In this paper we propose an approach for monitoring of roads, to detect car crashes and tire skidding, based on the analysis of sound signals, which can complement or, in some cases, substitute video analytic systems. The system that we propose employs a MobileNet deep architecture, designed to efficiently run on embedded appliances and be deployed on distributed systems for road monitoring. We designed a recognition system based on analysis of audio frames and tested it on the publicly available MIVIA road events data set. The performance results that we achieved (recognition rate higher than 99%) are higher than existing methods, demonstrating that the proposed approach can be deployed on embedded devices in a distributed surveillance system.

Keywords: Audio event detection · Deep learning · MobileNet

1 Introduction

The recent needs for monitoring of cities and public environments stimulated the artificial intelligence and pattern recognition research communities to develop innovative approaches for behaviour analysis [1,6], action recognition [15,34], traffic monitoring [36], among others.

Many existing approaches are based on analysis of visual information recorded by means of surveillance cameras and are successfully employed in monitoring of private and public spaces. The use of cameras has, however, limitations that are determined by occlusions, due to objects in the scene or to the camera field of view, and varying illumination or weather conditions. For instance, algorithms have to deal with changes between daylight and night, or with fog, snow, rain, and so on. In this context, the analysis of audio information has a

© Springer Nature Switzerland AG 2019
E. Ricci et al. (Eds.): ICIAP 2019, LNCS 11752, pp. 583–592, 2019.
https://doi.org/10.1007/978-3-030-30645-8_53

complementary role to video analysis, in that the two data modalities can be employed together to increase the reliability of the recognition and surveillance systems. In some cases, such as public toilets for privacy issues, audio analytic systems can be deployed as substitute of video analytic systems. In very large deposit areas or along big roads, the use of microphones instead of cameras can have positive implications on the deployment costs of a safety monitoring system. Microphones are cheaper than cameras and can cover a larger area [13]. In this work, we design a system for detection of events of interest for monitoring of safety of road environments based on efficient deep networks, which can be deployed on embedded systems.

Existing methods for audio surveillance were analyzed in a comprehensive survey paper in [11]. Early works focused on designing sets of features that could extract important information from the input audio signal, such as log-frequency filter banks [26], Mel-frequency Cepstral Coefficients [20], perceptual linear prediction coefficients [30]. In order to design a meaningful feature set, substantial knowledge about the problem at and and the characteristics of the sounds of interest was necessary. For instance, a peculiar feature of a gunshot is its abrupt increase of signal energy at high frequencies, which is recognizable as a high value of the zero crossing rate feature. Hand-engineered feature sets were used together with a classifier to perform the detection and recognition tasks. Various classifiers were proposed. In [2,9], Gaussian Mixture Model (GMM) based classifiers were deployed, while One-Class Support Vector Machines were proposed in [31]. Spectro-temporal features were also used together with various classifiers, as they are able to effectively describe frequency information in signal sub-bands during time that can be used to distinguish abnormal sounds from common background sounds [8,12]. A biologically-inspired time-frequency representation, called Gammatonegram, was modeled in [29] from measurements performed on the cochlea membrane of the auditory system and subsequently used in [14] for detection of sound of interest with an AdaBoost classifier.

More recently, research was focused on learning suitable representations directly from training data, as engineering robust feature sets requires a broad, not always available, knowledge of the places and sounds of interest, and is not scalable to dynamic environments. Methods for learning representations based on the bag-of-words approach were proposed [3,7,28]. Systems tailored for surveillance applications were subsequently proposed [17], with variants based on non-negative matrix factorization [19] or sparse coding [23]. Applications of these methods to road environments were studied in [13,16] and to changing scenarios in [33]. Biologically-inspired feature extractors, named COPE (Combination of Peaks of Energy), were proposed and are able to learn robust sound representation from single prototype samples [38,39]. Convolutional Networks (CNNs) and Deep learning approaches were more recently proposed to learn effective, hierarchical representations of the sounds of interest jointly with a classification model [4]. The representation power of CNNs and deep networks is a key factor for their success and use in sound event detection [10,21,24].

The recognition method that we propose in this work is based on the convolutional architecture of MobileNet [22,35], thought to be efficient enough to run on embedded and mobile systems, trained to detect events of interest for road monitoring in time-frequency representations of the input audio signal. We report the results of experiments that we performed on the MIVIA road events data set [13], and compare them with those reported by other existing methods. We show that the proposed system achieves good performance, maintaining computational requirements that are feasible for the deployment on embedded devices in a surveillance and monitoring system. Furthermore, differently from other existing deep learning based approaches, is robust enough even if the amount of data for training is not so high.

The rest of the paper is organized as follows. In Sect. 2, we describe the architecture of the proposed method. In Sect. 3.1 we present the data set used for the experiments, while in Sect. 3.2 we report the results that we achieved and compare them with those of other existing approaches. Finally, we draw conclusions in Sect. 4.

2   The Proposed Method

In order to detect sounds with very short duration (like the ones that may arise on the road), we segment the audio stream in consecutive *audio frames* by means of a 3 s mobile Hamming windows. Furthermore, in order to also have the possibility to detect those events that may occur on the border of the windows, a 66% overlap between two consecutive windows has been introduced.

Given a single audio-frame, we employ a time-frequency based representation, which has been widely employed by the scientific community, due to the high representational power; indeed, it has been experimentally shown that this kind of representation generally performs better than still temporal ones (namely the raw data, encoding temporal information of the signal) [21,25]. Among the time-frequency available representations, we decided to use the most famous one, namely the spectrogram. This is a visual representation of the spectrum of frequencies of the sound based on Short-Time Fourier Transform (STFT). An example of the spectrogram for our classes of interest is reported in Fig. 1. Thanks to this choice, we can manage an audio analysis problem as it would be in practice an image analysis problem.

It implies to have the possibility to inherit the wide literature in this field related to deep learning, and in particular to Convolutional Neural Networks (CNNs), which achieved a great success in almost all the image classification tasks. Although so powerful, deep networks have not been widely used in sound event recognition problems, although achieving a notable success in other audio-based tasks, such as music classification [18], sentiment analysis [41] or sentence classification [27].

In more details, our network inherits the architecture of the well known MobileNet network [22,35], introduced so as to be particularly suited for working in real time over embedded systems. Indeed, in a recent benchmarking reporting

| (a) car crash | (b) tire skidding |

Fig. 1. Example of the spectrogram for Car crash (a) and Tire skidding (b) events of interest. X-axis represents the time (in seconds, from 0 to 3 s), while the Y-axis the frequency (in kHz, and it ranges from 0 to 16 with a linear scale).

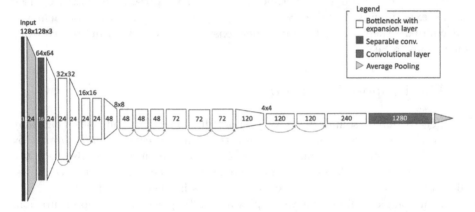

Fig. 2. Architecture of the MobileNet v2 network used in the proposed system.

the performance of several well-known deep networks applied to the problem of image recognition [5], MobileNet has proved to be a good tradeoff between the accuracy, the number of floating-point operations and the number of parameters required for training the network.

The main idea behind MobileNet lies in the fact that a convolutional layer can be split in a *depthwise* operation followed by a *pointwise* operation, without paying in terms of representational power of the layer. The main advantage before this choice is that 3×3 convolutions require 8 to 9 times less operations, with a consequent reduction in the number of parameters [22]. Having a lower number of parameter in turns also allows to reduce the number of data required for training. This is a very important and not negligible feature when dealing with sound event recognition problem, and in particular with audio analysis on the road, since the amount of data available for training is very limited.

In more details, we use MobileNet v2 [35], whose architecture is reported in Fig. 2. It is equipped with a novel layer, namely the inverted residual with linear bottleneck; this layer takes as input a low-dimensional compressed representa-

Table 1. Details of the composition of the MIVIA road events data set. The duration is expressed in seconds. BN refers to background noise, CC to car crash and TS to tire skidding.

	Events	Duration (s)
BN	-	2732
CC	200	326.3
TS	200	522.5

tion, which is expanded and then filtered with a lightweight depthwise convolution layer. In other words, the number of feature maps is increased (expansion) and then decreased (projection); data is scattered in a higher-dimensional space so that the non-linear power of ReLU activation function can be exploited without information loss.

3   Experiments

In this section we describe the dataset used in our experimentation (in Subsect. 3.1), together with the results achieved on this dataset, and compare them with the ones achieved by state of the art methodologies (in Subsect. 3.2).

3.1   Dataset

We carried out experiments on the MIVIA road events data set [13], which is publicly available for research purpose at the url http://mivia.unisa.it. The data set is composed of 57 audio clips of about one minute each, sampled at 32 KHz and with a resolution of 16 bits per sample. According to our knowledge, this is the only dataset available in the literature for the problem of sound event recognition on the road. The data set contains 400 events of interest (200 car crash and 200 tire skidding), which occur superimposed to different background sounds. The audio clips are divided in four independent folds each containing 50 events of interest per class, for cross-validation experiments. In the following we refer to car crash with *CC*, to tire skidding with *TS* and to background noise with *BN*. In Table 1, we report details about the composition of the data set.

3.2   Results and Comparison

The experimentation has been performed by a 4-folds cross validation: in order to reduce the variability on the results, three folds have been used for training and the remaining for testing. Finally, the results obtained over the four tests have been averaged and reported.

In more details, we compute the following metric:

- Recognition Rate (RR), computed as the ratio between the number of correctly classified events of interest and the total number of events.

- False Positive Rate (FPR), computed as the ratio between the number of events detected when only the background is present (false positives) and the total number of events.
- Miss Rate (MR), computed as the ratio between the number of events of interest not detected (misses) and the total number of events.
- Error Rate (ER): computed as the ratio between the number of events of interest detected but misclassified (classification errors) and the total number of events.

Furthermore, we use two different protocols, namely *frame-based* and *event-based*. According to the *frame-based* protocol, the recognition rate, the miss rate and the error rate are computed by considering the total number of audio frames, namely the total number of spectrogram images. Viceversa, in the *event-based* protocol the evaluation is not done by considering the single audio frame but the whole event. In particular, an event of interest (TS and CC), is considered correctly detected if it is identified for at least one of the consecutive windows in which it appears. Performance calculated in this second way will offer a better understanding of the perceived performance of the final system, since it accounts for the fact that, from the point of view of the user, it is sufficient to detect each event once to trigger an alarm, discarding a certain amount of irrelevant False Negatives; this protocol is widely used in literature since it makes up for groundtruth ambiguities regarding the precise start and stop time of an event.

The training of the network has been performed by a mini-batch gradient descent optimization algorithm based on the adaptive learning rate RMSprop [32]. Furthermore, a fine tuning has been performed: ImageNet dataset has been used for training the network and initializing the weights; then, a fine tuning is performed by using Mivia Audio Road dataset.

The results are reported in Table 2; the proposed solution achieve a 88.85% of recognition rate with the frame based protocol, while an impressive 99.50% of recognition rate with the event based protocol.

It is still more impressive that this is not paid in terms of false positives; indeed, we have only a 3.76% of FPR. The results are still more impressive if compared with state of the art methodologies, based both on traditional and deep learning methodologies, as shown in Table 2.

The paper proposed in [17,39] and [13], whose performance ranges from 80.25% to 94.00%, are based on traditional machine learning approaches. The improvement in this case (from about +5% to about +19%) is notable considering the reduced size of the dataset we used for the experimentation. This result, indeed, confirms that MobileNet v2 we used in our system is able to achieve good results even in presence of a limited amount of training data.

This is not the same for other deep learning based architecture, and in particular NASNet [42] and AENET [40]. According to a recent benchmarking [5], NASNet is able to reach the highest accuracy on the problem of image recognition, paying this in terms of time required for the elaboration, being extremely slow. Viceversa, AENet is based on VGG [37], which is according to the same benchmark reported above among the best tradeoff between accuracy and computational burden. Furthermore, AENet is, at the best of our knowledge, the only network proposed in the literature for sound event recognition whose network weights are freely available for benchmarking purposes. The proposed approach outperforms both AENet and NASNet, with an improvement of about $+4,5\%$ and $+5\%$ in terms of recognition rate over frame based protocol. Such results confirm the effectiveness of the proposed approach.

Table 2. Comparison of the proposed approach with other state of the art methodologies in terms of recognition rate (RR), false positive rate (FPR), miss rate (MR) and error rate (ER) applying the frame by frame and the event based protocols. For each one, we also report whether the Neural Network was trained from scratch or was fine-tuned from a pretrained network in a transfer learning fashion.

Method	Ref.	Training	Frame-based (%)				Event-based (%)			
			RR	FPR	MR	ER	RR	FPR	MR	ER
Proposed	-	fine tuning	88.85	3.76	6.95	4.20	**99.50**	3.76	0.00	0.50
COPE	[39]	from scratch	–	–	–	–	94.00	3.95	4.75	1.25
HF+BoW	[13]	from scratch	–	–	–	–	82.00	2.85	17.75	0.25
BARK+BoW	[17]	from scratch	–	–	–	–	80.25	7.69	19.00	0.75
MFCC+BoW	[17]	from scratch	–	–	–	–	80.25	10.96	21.75	3.25
NASNet	[42]	fine tuning	84.58	5.51	8.23	7.19	–	–	–	–
AENet	[40]	fine tuning	85.23	6.12	10.14	4.63	–	–	–	–

4 Conclusions

We designed a system for road monitoring and detection of hazardous events by automatic analysis of sound signals. The proposed approach is based on processing a time-frequency representation of the input sounds by means of a lightweight convolutional architecture named MobileNet; as we demonstrated, it is able to achieve high recognition results in highly noisy road environments. The low amount of trainable parameters of MobileNet makes this architecture particularly suitable for problems of road monitoring, where labeled training examples are available in limited quantity. The proposed system achieved higher performance results (event recognition rate $> 99\%$) than other existing methods on the MIVIA road events data set and qualifies to be deployed on embedded distributed surveillance systems, as it has low computational requirements.

References

1. Acampora, G., Foggia, P., Saggese, A., Vento, M.: Combining neural networks and fuzzy systems for human behavior understanding. In: 2012 IEEE Ninth International Conference on Advanced Video and Signal-Based Surveillance, pp. 88–93, September 2012. https://doi.org/10.1109/AVSS.2012.25

2. Atrey, P.K., Maddage, N.C., Kankanhalli, M.S.: Audio based event detection for multimedia surveillance. In: IEEE ICASSP, vol. 5 (2006)
3. Aucouturier, J.J., Defreville, B., Pachet, F.: The bag-of-frames approach to audio pattern recognition: a sufficient model for urban soundscapes but not for polyphonic music. J. Acoust. Soc. Am. **122**(2), 881–891 (2007)
4. Aytar, Y., Vondrick, C., Torralba, A.: SoundNet: learning sound representations from unlabeled video. In: NIPS 2016 (2016)
5. Bianco, S., Cadene, R., Celona, L., Napoletano, P.: Benchmark analysis of representative deep neural network architectures. IEEE Access 1 (2018). https://doi.org/10.1109/ACCESS.2018.2877890
6. Brun, L., Saggese, A., Vento, M.: Dynamic scene understanding for behavior analysis based on string kernels. IEEE Trans. Circ. Syst. Video Technol. **24**(10), 1669–1681 (2014). https://doi.org/10.1109/TCSVT.2014.2302521
7. Carletti, V., Foggia, P., Percannella, G., Saggese, A., Strisciuglio, N., Vento, M.: Audio surveillance using a bag of aural words classifier. In: IEEE AVSS, pp. 81–86 (2013). https://doi.org/10.1109/AVSS.2013.6636620
8. Chu, S., Narayanan, S., Kuo, C.C.J.: Environmental sound recognition with time-frequency audio features. IEEE Trans. Audio Speech Lang. Process. **17**(6), 1142–1158 (2009). https://doi.org/10.1109/TASL.2009.2017438
9. Clavel, C., Ehrette, T., Richard, G.: Events detection for an audio-based surveillance system. In: ICME, pp. 1306–1309 (2005). https://doi.org/10.1109/ICME.2005.1521669
10. Colangelo, F., Battisti, F., Carli, M., Neri, A., Calabró, F.: Enhancing audio surveillance with hierarchical recurrent neural networks. In: AVSS, pp. 1–6, August 2017. https://doi.org/10.1109/AVSS.2017.8078496
11. Crocco, M., Cristani, M., Trucco, A., Murino, V.: Audio surveillance: a systematic review. ACM Comput. Surv. **48**(4), 52:1–52:46 (2016). https://doi.org/10.1145/2871183
12. Dennis, J., Tran, H.D., Chng, E.S.: Image feature representation of the subband power distribution for robust sound event classification. IEEE Trans. Audio Speech Lang. Process. **21**(2), 367–377 (2013)
13. Foggia, P., Petkov, N., Saggese, A., Strisciuglio, N., Vento, M.: Audio surveillance of roads: a system for detecting anomalous sounds. IEEE Intell. Transp. Syst. **17**(1), 279–288 (2016). https://doi.org/10.1109/TITS.2015.2470216
14. Foggia, P., Saggese, A., Strisciuglio, N., Vento, M.: Cascade classifiers trained on gammatonegrams for reliably detecting audio events. In: IEEE International Conference on Advanced Video and Signal Based Surveillance (AVSS), pp. 50–55, August 2014
15. Foggia, P., Saggese, A., Strisciuglio, N., Vento, M.: Exploiting the deep learning paradigm for recognizing human actions. In: IEEE AVSS 2014, pp. 93–98 (2014). https://doi.org/10.1109/AVSS.2014.6918650
16. Foggia, P., Saggese, A., Strisciuglio, N., Vento, M., Petkov, N.: Car crashes detection by audio analysis in crowded roads. In: IEEE AVSS, pp. 1–6 (2015). https://doi.org/10.1109/AVSS.2015.7301731
17. Foggia, P., Petkov, N., Saggese, A., Strisciuglio, N., Vento, M.: Reliable detection of audio events in highly noisy environments. Pattern Recogn. Lett. **65**, 22–28 (2015). https://doi.org/10.1016/j.patrec.2015.06.026
18. Fu, Z., Lu, G., Ting, K.M., Zhang, D.: A survey of audio-based music classification and annotation. IEEE Trans. Multimed. **13**(2), 303–319 (2011). https://doi.org/10.1109/TMM.2010.2098858

19. Giannoulis, D., Stowell, D., Benetos, E., Rossignol, M., Lagrange, M., Plumbley, M.D.: A database and challenge for acoustic scene classification and event detection. In: EUSIPCO, pp. 1–5 (2013)
20. Guo, G., Li, S.Z.: Content-based audio classification and retrieval by support vector machines. IEEE Trans. Neural Netw. **14**(1), 209–215 (2003)
21. Hertel, L., Phan, H., Mertins, A.: Comparing time and frequency domain for audio event recognition using deep learning. In: International Joint Conference on Neural Networks (IJCNN), pp. 3407–3411 (2016)
22. Howard, A.G., et al.: MobileNets: efficient convolutional neural networks for mobile vision applications. arXiv (2017)
23. Lu, X., Tsao, Y., Matsuda, S., Hori, C.: Sparse representation based on a bag of spectral exemplars for acoustic event detection. In: IEEE ICASSP, pp. 6255–6259 (2014). https://doi.org/10.1109/ICASSP.2014.6854807
24. Medhat, F., Chesmore, D., Robinson, J.: Environmental sound recognition using masked conditional neural networks. In: Cong, G., Peng, W.-C., Zhang, W.E., Li, C., Sun, A. (eds.) ADMA 2017. LNCS (LNAI), vol. 10604, pp. 373–385. Springer, Cham (2017). https://doi.org/10.1007/978-3-319-69179-4_26
25. Mesaros, A., et al.: Detection and classification of acoustic scenes and events: Outcome of the dcase 2016 challenge. IEEE/ACM Trans. Audio Speech Lang. Process. **26**(2), 379–393 (2018). https://doi.org/10.1109/TASLP.2017.2778423
26. Nadeu, C., Macho, D., Hernando, J.: Time and frequency filtering of filter-bank energies for robust HMM speech recognition. Speech Commun. **34**, 93–114 (2001). https://doi.org/10.1016/S0167-6393(00)00048-0
27. Ouyang, X., Gu, K., Zhou, P.: Spatial pyramid pooling mechanism in 3D convolutional network for sentence-level classification. IEEE/ACM Trans. Audio Speech Lang. Process. **26**(11), 2167–2179 (2018). https://doi.org/10.1109/TASLP.2018.2852502
28. Pancoast, S., Akbacak, M.: Bag-of-audio-words approach for multimedia event classification. In: Interspeech (2012)
29. Patterson, R.D., Robinson, K., Holdsworth, J., Mckeown, D., Zhang, C., Allerhand, M.: Complex sounds and auditory images. In: Auditory Physiology and Perception, pp. 429–443 (1992)
30. Portelo, J., Bugalho, M., Trancoso, I., Neto, J., Abad, A., Serralheiro, A.: Non-speech audio event detection. In: IEEE ICASSP, pp. 1973–1976 (2009)
31. Rabaoui, A., Davy, M., Rossignol, S., Ellouze, N.: Using one-class SVMs and wavelets for audio surveillance. IEEE Trans. Inf. Forensics Secur. **3**(4), 763–775 (2008)
32. Ruder, S.: An overview of gradient descent optimization algorithms. CoRR abs/1609.04747 (2016). http://arxiv.org/abs/1609.04747
33. Saggese, A., Strisciuglio, N., Vento, M., Petkov, N.: Time-frequency analysis for audio event detection in real scenarios. In: IEEE AVSS, pp. 438–443 (2016). https://doi.org/10.1109/AVSS.2016.7738082
34. Saggese, A., Strisciuglio, N., Vento, M., Petkov, N.: Learning skeleton representations for human action recognition. Pattern Recogn. Lett. **118**, 23–31 (2019). https://doi.org/10.1016/j.patrec.2018.03.005
35. Sandler, M., Howard, A., Zhu, M., Zhmoginov, A., Chen, L.C.: Inverted residuals and linear bottlenecks: Mobile networks for classification, detection and segmentation. arXiv (2018)
36. Shirazi, M.S., Morris, B.T.: Looking at intersections: a survey of intersection monitoring, behavior and safety analysis of recent studies. IEEE Trans. Intell. Transp. Syst. **18**(1), 4–24 (2017). https://doi.org/10.1109/TITS.2016.2568920

37. Simonyan, K., Zisserman, A.: Very deep convolutional networks for large-scale image recognition. CoRR abs/1409.1556 (2014)
38. Strisciuglio, N., Vento, M., Petkov, N.: Bio-inspired filters for audio analysis. In: Amunts, K., Grandinetti, L., Lippert, T., Petkov, N. (eds.) BrainComp 2015. LNCS, vol. 10087, pp. 101–115. Springer, Cham (2016). https://doi.org/10.1007/978-3-319-50862-7_8
39. Strisciuglio, N., Vento, M., Petkov, N.: Learning representations of sound using trainable cope feature extractors. Pattern Recogn. **92**, 25–36 (2019). https://doi.org/10.1016/j.patcog.2019.03.016
40. Takahashi, N., Gygli, M., Gool, L.V.: AENet: learning deep audio features for video analysis. IEEE Trans. Multimed. **20**(3), 513–524 (2018). https://doi.org/10.1109/TMM.2017.2751969
41. Zhang, S., Zhang, S., Huang, T., Gao, W., Tian, Q.: Learning affective features with a hybrid deep model for audio-visual emotion recognition. IEEE Trans. Circ. Syst. Video Technol. **28**(10), 3030–3043 (2018). https://doi.org/10.1109/TCSVT.2017.2719043
42. Zoph, B., Vasudevan, V., Shlens, J., Le, Q.V.: Learning transferable architectures for scalable image recognition. CoRR abs/1707.07012 (2017). http://arxiv.org/abs/1707.07012

Biomedical and Assistive Technology

Geometry-Based Skin Colour Estimation for Bare Torso Surface Reconstruction

João P. Monteiro[1,3](✉) ⓘ, Hooshiar Zolfagharnasab[1,3] ⓘ,
and Hélder P. Oliveira[2,3] ⓘ

[1] Faculdade de Engenharia, Universidade do Porto, Porto, Portugal
jpsm@ieee.org
[2] Faculdade de Ciências, Universidade do Porto, Porto, Portugal
[3] Instituto de Engenharia de Sistemas e Computadores, Tecnologia e Ciência,
Porto, Portugal

Abstract. Three-dimensional imaging techniques have been endeavouring at reaching affordable ubiquity. Nevertheless, its use in clinical practice can be hampered by less than naturally looking surfaces that greatly impact its visual inspection. This work considers the task of surface reconstruction from point clouds of non-rigid scenes acquired through structured-light-based methods, wherein the reconstructed surface contains some level of imperfection to be inpainted before visualized by experts in a clinically oriented context. Appertain to the topic, the recovery of colour information for missing or damaged partial regions is considered. A local geometry-based interpolation method is proposed for the reconstruction of the bare human torso and compared against a reference differential equations based inpainting method. Widely used perceptual distance-based metrics, such as PSNR, SSIM and MS-SSIM, and the evaluation from a panel of experienced breast cancer surgeons is presented for the discussion on inpainting quality assessment.

Keywords: Applications of computer vision · Point cloud processing

1 Introduction

Among several clinically oriented applications, recent developments in Breast Cancer Conservative Treatment (BCCT) related procedures have been promoting the use of patient-specific three-dimensional (3D) surface data [15]. On that account, the main applications have been to support surgery planning, improve the objective assessment of aesthetic outcome, and facilitate physician-patient

This work is co-financed by the ERDF - European Regional Development Fund through the Norte Portugal Regional Operational Programme (NORTE 2020), and the LISBOA2020 under the PORTUGAL 2020 Partnership Agreement and through the Portuguese National Innovation Agency (ANI) as a part of project BCCT.plan: NORTE-01-0247-FEDER-017688, and also by Fundação para a Ciência e a Tecnologia (FCT) within Ph.D. grant number SFRH/BD/138823/2018.

E. Ricci et al. (Eds.): ICIAP 2019, LNCS 11752, pp. 595–606, 2019.
https://doi.org/10.1007/978-3-030-30645-8_54

communication. The potential advantages regarding the use of 3D imaging techniques includes the possibility to navigate through the patient-specific 3D surface and, an improved perception of volumetric data. Nonetheless, and despite the reported potential benefits, 3D techniques still present drawbacks regarding its use in clinical practice [17].

In this paper, we address a problem that arises from the pairwise registration of unorganized coloured point clouds (PCs) of non-rigid objects under changing illumination conditions [22], wherein the point cloud contains a considerable level of missing colour information. Within the context of a complete surface reconstruction pipeline, the main purpose of this work is to improve the visual quality of patient-specific 3D reconstructions from RGB-D data by exploring the proposed scene-specific structure approximation of breast surface for breast skin colour estimation. This approach is intended to repair the surface colour enough to avoid the presence of distracting colour artefacts while keeping the usage of resources at a minimum and not requiring any training corpus.

1.1   Related Work

3D Surface Imaging. Surface imaging of the breast has been yielding significant advances in recent years. To this end, much has contributed the advent of different 3D scanners based on laser, structured light, or digital photogrammetry. Further detail on current methods and its application to clinical practice can be found in the review by y O'Connell *et al.* [15]. Of particular relevance to this work is the observed relevancy of depth sensing devices like the Microsoft Kinect for the aforementioned context [16,25]. Its depth sensing capabilities, based on an infrared (IR) laser projector combined with a monochrome CMOS sensor, provide depth and colour information at a frame rate of up to 30 fps, thus producing sets of unorganized points, each defined by their x, y, z coordinates and associated colour.

Notwithstanding, the convenience of structured light based devices is not compromise-free. It is possible to recognize a significant presence of noise in its data. In that regard, it should be highlighted that Microsoft Kinect's depth sensor relies on the comparison of a known pattern against each new frame retrieved from its IR camera. In each frame, a specular pattern projected by Microsoft Kinect itself and deformed by real world scene is expected to be observed. Since it is an active sensor, other sources of IR light, like halogen operating room lights or even direct sunlight, can degrade the reconstructed depth images. For more detail on this topic the review by Mallick *et al.* [14] is suggested.

Colour Inpainting on PCs. Different problems can be formulated as interpolation problems aiming at computing new values for missing data in coherence with a set of known data. Motivated by applications such as image restoration, object removal, or disocclusion in image-based rendering, different inpainting techniques have recently thrived in the related fields of computer vision [9]. Furthermore, inpainting can be recognized as an il-posed inverse problem that typically implies the use of local or global priors based on the assumption that statistical properties or geometrical structures are in some way common to both known and unknown elements of data. For the case of image inpainting, its purpose refers not only to the recovery of missing or damaged parts in an image but also to the pursuit of a resulting image looking as natural as possible [3].

Recently, several partial differential equation methods have been proposed for the problem of inpainting on images, PCs [6], or manifold-valued images [1]. Appositely, Garcia [8,23] proposed to perform the estimation of missing data by exploiting Discrete Cosine Transform (DCT) to obtain the required regression equation. Although recognizing the regression equation vulnerable to the residual sum of squares (RSS) amongst the data (both available and estimated ones), Garcia proposed a smoothing coefficient to be used as compensation, to be selected by a generalized cross validation (GCV) methodology to be applied iteratively to find the best smoothing coefficient.

Inpainting Quality Assessment. As recognized in a review of inpainting quality assessment metrics by Qureshi *et al.* [19], despite considerable amount of work devoted to various aspects of inpainting techniques, the task of Image Inpainting Quality Assessment (IIQA) lends itself to current open challenges, that are further explored in the aforementioned publication. Reiterating that inpainting can be defined as the process of restoring missing pixels in a convincing and plausible way, the goal for IIQA is to evaluate the quality of the restored images. In that sense, traditional fidelity-based metrics would mainly attempt at quantifying distortions in degraded images. Notwithstanding, the process of inpainting is expected to produce final images that may be somehow different from the original ones with the introduction of new types of artefacts that may affect the perceived quality in different ways. For that matter, subjective assessment methods are reckoned as within closer proximity to perceived quality. However, these methodologies are typically time-consuming and cumbersome to conduct.

Objective methods have been proposed to predict perceived image quality through the use of mathematical tools to extract characteristic features from the images. The Peak Signal to Noise Ratio (PSNR) is a widely used fidelity metric that has been used for quality evaluation of inpainted images. Despite that, it has been demonstrated that PSNR may not necessarily correlate well with perceptual quality assessment. Being recognized as presenting an improved correlation with subjective quality perception [12], Structural Similarity Measure (SSIM) and related proposed variations, *e.g.* Multiscale Structural Similarity (MS-SSIM) [24], are full reference assessment methodologies that can be regarded as a modified distance measure between two images. Structure-based methods show a tendency to fail whenever large regions of an image are inpainted given that the larger the region to be inpainted, the greater the distance from the estimated region to the original region tends to be.

2 Materials and Methods

We proposed to tackle the patient-specific data visualization by using a geometry-based approach to estimate erroneously assigned colour of a reconstructed surface. For this purpose, a reconstruction pipeline previously presented in [4] is hereafter considered. The approach comprehends two main stages: reconstruction of the torso and geometrical colour correction. Such approach provides multiple, artefact-contaminated, unordered PCs aligned to a common reference, and is, thereby, the baseline scenario to evaluate the proposed method (Fig. 1).

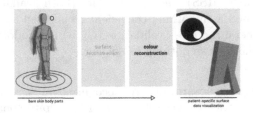

Fig. 1. Overview of the considered framework: surface shape and colour reconstruction in a clinically oriented application of patient-specific data with skin colour estimation. (Color figure online)

2.1 Reconstruction of the Torso

The surface imaging method presented in [4] appertains to the attainment of patient-specific 3D surface data from readily available off-the-shelf devices in a setting that could be widely adopted in clinical practice. An overview of the method is presented in Fig. 2. Briefly, given a sequence of RGB-D images of a patient in upright position turning about the longitudinal axis of the body, a set of poses is selected and the corresponding PCs are generated and registered using a two-step ICP-based method. Moreover, the steps that precede the point cloud generation are summarized below:

- Segmentation of the human silhouette in the depth images, performed via a discontinuity based approach, using Gabor filters followed by the Otsu's algorithm [18].
- View selection, through a rule-based approach using features from segmented silhouette [10].
- Depth-map filtering, using the segmentation of the colour image with Grab-Cut algorithm [21].

The registration of the views, on the other hand, is based on the work proposed in [4]. The output of the method is a coloured point cloud representing patient's upper torso and limbs surface that presents artefacts due to different acquisition light condition when patient is rotating.

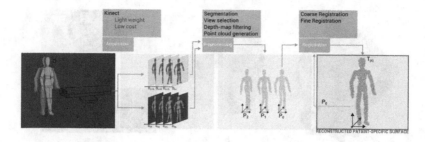

Fig. 2. Overview of the surface reconstruction method from RGB-D data, comprehending segmentation of the human silhouette, view selection from video stream, depth filtering, point cloud generation and two-step ICP registration. (Color figure online)

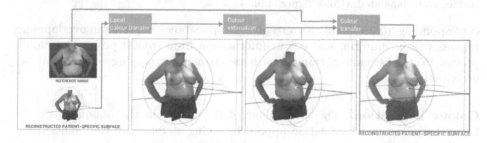

Fig. 3. Overview of the colour inconsistency correction method comprising multiple view colour transfer, inpainting and reference image based colour transfer. (Color figure online)

2.2 Geometrical Colour Correction

An overview of the three-fold geometrically informed colour correction procedure is schematised in Fig. 3. The reasoning behind this strategy is that the input data contains enough information to allow a reconstruction approach based on the smooth continuity of the local structures colour, and, that such approach could rival with a more traditional inductive, data-intensive learning one.

Local Colour Transfer. Considering the multiple PCs relating to body surface regions that partially overlap (one frontal and two oblique) registered by the aforementioned surface reconstruction method of [4], the first step of the proposed method is a straightforward proximity-based local colour transfer approach. Pertaining to the PC from the frontal pose as the target reference appearance, point correspondences to each oblique view are computed by a closest point search. The distance between two PCs, *e.g.* P and Q, is, in this matter, defined as their pointwise Euclidean minimum distance ($dist(P, Q) = min_{p \in P, q \in Q} dist(p, q)$). Then, each point belonging to any of the oblique PCs which distance to its nearest neighbour in the frontal point cloud is smaller than a small neighbourhood threshold value (<3mm) is assigned the colour of the

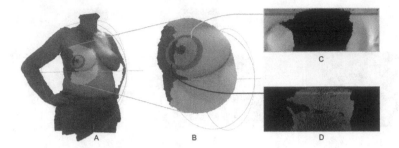

Fig. 4. Illustration of the proposed geometry-based skin-colour estimation: (A) Example input set of registered PCs; (B) Detail of region of interest; (C) Mercator projection of the breast surface from the frontal view, and (D) Mercator projection of the breast surface to be inpainted. (Color figure online)

corresponding frontal point. As a result, the appearance of points in overlapping regions will be uniform, and colour information from frontal pose point cloud prevail. Notwithstanding, transitions between non-overlapping regions will be accentuated.

Colour Estimation. The new colour of the points in the oblique views is found based on an interpolation approach, taking as reference the points from the frontal views in the same radius range (Fig. 4). To do so, a given point cloud $P = \{p_i \in \mathbb{R}^3\}_{i=1}^n$, with n points, is projected on a Mercator image by converting to spherical coordinates (r, θ, φ) each p_i with (x, y, z) coordinates (Fig. 5), considering the origin of the coordinate system at the central position of the nipple-areola complex (O'').

It follows the colour estimation on the Mercator projection space [7], using the following equation:

$$f_C(\theta) = C_L + (C_H - C_L)\frac{exp(\alpha(\theta - min_\theta)) - 1}{exp(\alpha(max_\theta - min_\theta)) - 1} \tag{1}$$

where C_L and C_H are the colour at the extremities of the strip in the frontal view; θ is the angle of the region where the colour is to be estimated; min_θ and max_θ are, respectively, the minimum and maximum angles of the region to be estimated; α is the parameter that controls the propagation of the colour between extremities, and, $f_C(\theta)$ is the new colour at a given angle θ.

Colour Transfer. For the final step, we use the information from a 2D reference image to change and improve the colour appearance of the 3D PCs, using the following equation [20]:

$$f_C(x) = \frac{\sigma_{2D}}{\sigma_k}(x - \mu_k) + \mu_{2D} \tag{2}$$

where σ_k and μ_k are respectively the mean and standard deviation of the source image (Microsoft Kinect data) and σ_{2D} and μ_{2D} the same for the target image (2D reference data).

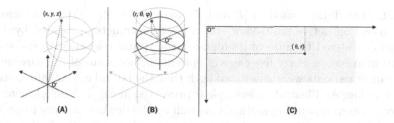

Fig. 5. Generation of Mercator image: Projection of 3D surface data (A) onto a 2D plane (C) by fitting an ellipsoid (B) to the surface and applying a Mercator map projection.

2.3   Experimental Set-Up

An experiment was conducted to evaluate the performance of the proposed geometry-based estimation method against a reference inpainting methodology by subjective assessment by experts. Four expert surgeons (all male) with normal vision were asked to report about the perceived image quality via a paired comparison test. Inpainted images were generated with two methods, *i.e.*, the reported in [23] (*Reference*) and our skin colour estimation framework (*Proposed*). The subjects had no prior knowledge on the types of images displayed (*i.e.*, whether they were original images or images that had been inpainted by using one of the considered methods). Subjects observed three image pairs generated from the same original image (*i.e.*, the considered pairs for a single image were: *Original* vs. *Reference*, *Original* vs. *Proposed*, *Reference* vs. *Proposed*. Figure 6 illustrates the test procedure. The 3-point score range for each comparison was: (1) *Left image seems more realistically looking*, (2) *Right image seems more realistically looking*, and (3) *Both images seem equally realistically looking*. The LCD monitor used for visualization was 17 inch with 1920 × 1080 pixel resolution.

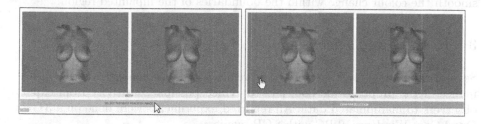

Fig. 6. Example test procedure for ranking inpainted images from pairwise comparisons by experts. For a given image pair, the user was asked to express preference according to a 3-point score: (1) *Left image seems more realistically looking than right image*; (2) *Right image seems more realistically looking than left image*, and (3) *Both images seem equally realistically looking*.

Dataset. The dataset used in [4] and [5], acquired with a dedicated scanning system based on active multi-view stereo-photogrammetry provided by 3dMD [13], was considered because of its high-accuracy, and relevancy to the specific application at hands. Forty five cases of optical surface scans of the bare torso of breast cancer patients were annotated such that the lateral colour information is mostly missing. An illustrative example is presented in Fig. 7. Besides using each of the considered inpainting methods, as well as the original colours to generate the dataset for subjective assessment by a group of experts, the background of each image was compute as the mean colour of the foreground.

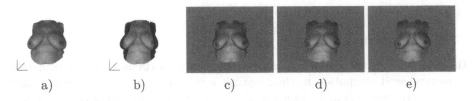

   a)   b)   c)   d)   e)

Fig. 7. Example annotation of surface data to generate dataset for evaluating inpainting: (a) surface mesh; (b) annotated mesh surface; (c) image generate from the original mesh (*Original*); (d) image generate with the reference inpainting method (*Reference*) and, (e) image generate with the proposed inpainting method (*Proposed*).

Implementation Details. The proposed inpainting method was implemented in C++ using PCL[1] and OpenCV[2] libraries ($\alpha = 0.01$). For the reference method [23], an available MATLAB implementation was used and, a preprocessing step was introduced to convert each model's PC to a voxel representation. The size of voxel was experimentally selected to be 2 mm. Each voxel represents the average colour of the points which are within the same datum, though voxels that contain a point with missing colour are tagged to be inpainted. The inpainting was performed in each channel individually. Lastly, a median filter was used to smooth the colour change within the boundaries of the inpainted region.

3   Results and Discussion

Several experiments were performed on realistic data to demonstrate the performance of the proposed method, and to evince possible sensitivity from expert observers to manipulated data. All reported experiments were done on a 3 GHz Quad-Core Windows 10 PC with 8 GB memory.

Table 1 provides the results of performance between the *Proposed* and *Reference* [23] methods and each IQA approaches considered (PSNR, SSIM and MS-SSIM). The best and worst cases identified in Table 1 of the tested inpainted images are rendered against the original data and presented in Fig. 8.

---

[1] http://www.pointclouds.org/.

[2] http://opencv.org/.

Table 1. Distance-based full-reference metrics, (PSNR, SSIM and MS-SSIM) to compare inpainted images by *Proposed* and *Reference* methods on the forty five images dataset produced from surface data originally acquired using a 3dMD system [13], and annotated to present missing colour areas.

	PSNR				SSIM				MS-SSIM			
	avg.	std.	max.	min.	avg.	std.	max.	min.	avg.	std.	max.	min.
Proposed	**35.923**	3.499	44.461	29.604	0.963	0.023		0.899	0.973	0.016	0.995	0.929
Reference	36.907	3.114	43.566	29.292	**0.967**	0.021		0.891	**0.976**	0.014		0.923

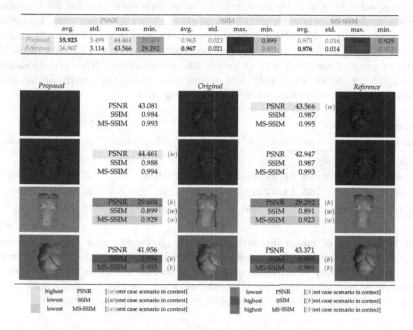

highest PSNR   [(w)orst case scenario in context]   lowest   PSNR   [(b)est case scenario in context]
lowest   SSIM   [(w)orst case scenario in context]   highest SSIM   [(b)est case scenario in context]
lowest   MS-SSIM [(w)orst case scenario in context]   highest MS-SSIM [(b)est case scenario in context]

Fig. 8. Illustrate images of cases highlighted in Table 1

From Table 1 it is possible to observe some level of inconsistency between different IQA metrics. On the one hand, considering PSNR alone, the images inpainted using the *Proposed* inpainting method seem to be, on average, closer to the original colours (*i.e.* ≈35.9 dB against ≈36.9 dB for the *Reference* method). On the other hand, the worst case scenario for the *Proposed* method (*i.e.* the highest PSNR value) was worst than the worst case scenario for the *Reference* method (*i.e.* ≈44.5 dB against ≈43.6 dB for the *Reference* method). As for the SSIM and MS-SSIM methodologies, they seem to be consistent between each other, but differently from PSNR; the *Reference* inpainting method verified the average highest score (*i.e.* most similar to original colour images), even if the difference is smaller than the standard deviation of each of the averages. Also distinctively from the results for the PSNR metric, the best case scenario, by a narrow margin, for both the SSIM and MS-SSIM metrics (*i.e.* values closer to 1) was verified to be produced by the *Proposed* inpainting method.

The results of the subjective assessment are presented in the Table 2. Similarly as in [11], the results of paired comparison were fit to the Bradley-Terry model [2] to obtain a global rank for each method (*Original, Proposed* and *Reference*) by each expert annotator (noted [a], [b], [c], [d]) and presented in Table 3.

Table 2. Paired comparison data of expressed preferences over images produced with different inpainting methods (*Reference* and *Proposed* methods) against ground-truth (*Original*) by four expert annotators ([a], [b], [c], [d]). **1** and **2** refer to the number of choices in favour of an image produced by the method in the first and the second column respectively. **X** denotes the number of no preferences expressed. Each annotator expressed preference over each of 168 image pairs. A set of image pairs comprise 56 comparisons (besides the total 45 of the dataset, 11 images were randomly chosen to be shown twice, in an uninformed way and non consecutive order) for each of the three considered pairs of methods and ground-truth (*Original* vs. *Reference*, *Original* vs. *Proposed*, *Reference* vs. *Proposed*). The subset of 69 cases that verify an unanimous agreement between annotators ([abcd]) is also presented.

Comparison outcome	1					X					2				
Annotator	[a]	[b]	[c]	[d]	[abcd]	[a]	[b]	[c]	[d]	[abcd]	[a]	[b]	[c]	[d]	[abcd]
Method 1 Method 2															
Original *Reference*	**56**	**51**	**40**	**40**	**29**	0	4	15	11	0	0	1	1	5	0
Original *Proposed*	**55**	**53**	**37**	**39**	**29**	1	2	14	13	0	0	1	5	4	0
Reference *Proposed*	3	3	2	25	0	**35**	**32**	**48**	**20**	**10**	18	21	6	11	1

Table 3. Ranking of image inpainting methods (*Reference* and *Proposed* methods) against ground-truth (*Original*) based on Bradley-Terry strength parameters Bayesian maximum a posteriori (MAP) estimates and standard errors (*s.e.*) from expressed preferences by expert annotators. The estimates are on the log scale such that its mean is zero for each of the four annotators expressed preferences data fit.

Rank	1st			2nd			3rd		
Estimate	MAP	*s.e.*		MAP	*s.e.*		MAP	*s.e.*	
Annotator Self-agreement[†]									
[a] 90% (30/33)	*Original*	2.95	0.789	*Proposed*	−1.13	0.423	*Reference*	−1.82	0.440
[b] 81% (27/33)	*Original*	1.95	0.389	*Proposed*	−0.55	0.260	*Reference*	−1.40	0.295
[c] 66% (22/33)	*Original*	1.14	0.255	*Proposed*	−0.37	0.207	*Reference*	−0.77	0.218
[d] 66% (22/33)	*Original*	0.92	0.215	*Reference*	−0.36	0.191	*Proposed*	−0.56	0.197
[abcd][§] 100% (9/9)	*Original*	3.32	1.490	*Proposed*	−1.33	0.836	*Reference*	−2.00	0.881

[†] The self-agreement was computed as the ratio between the number of matching image pairs preferences and the total number of repeated image pairs, from the paired comparison data containing 33 repeated pairs of images in the set of 168 comparisons.
[§] The subset of 69 comparisons verifying unanimous agreement between annotators, containing 9 repeated pairs of images.

4   Conclusions

A geometry-based approach to estimate colour of unorganized PCs with partially missing colour information was proposed for the problem of skin colour estimation within the context of bare torso surface reconstruction. The proposed approach was inspired on the hypothesized smooth continuity of the local structures colour over the area of interest.

Perceptual distance-based metrics, such as PSNR, SSIM and MS-SSIM, and the evaluation from a panel of experienced breast cancer surgeons in the form of ranking from the pairwise comparison test seem to suggest that images with the original colours are still perceived distinctively from the images with partial areas inpainted by either of the methods considered (*i.e. Proposed* and *Reference*). Notwithstanding, and despite inter and intra annotator variability, the proposed geometry-based skin colour estimation for bare torso surface reconstruction method seems to gain the upper-hand to the *Reference*, including in the subset of image pairs that verified unanimous agreement between annotators.

References

1. Bačák, M., Bergmann, R., Steidl, G., Weinmann, A.: A second order nonsmooth variational model for restoring manifold-valued images. SIAM J. Sci. Comput. **38**(1), A567–A597 (2016). https://doi.org/10.1137/15m101988x
2. Bradley, R.A., Terry, M.E.: Rank analysis of incomplete block designs: I. The method of paired comparisons. Biometrika **39**(3/4), 324 (1952). https://doi.org/10.2307/2334029
3. Buyssens, P., Daisy, M., Tschumperle, D., Lezoray, O.: Exemplar-based inpainting: technical review and new heuristics for better geometric reconstructions. IEEE Trans. Image Process. 1 (2015). https://doi.org/10.1109/tip.2015.2411437
4. Costa, P., Monteiro, J.P., Zolfagharnasab, H., Oliveira, H.P.: Tessellation-based coarse registration method for 3D reconstruction of the female torso. In: 2014 IEEE International Conference on Bioinformatics and Biomedicine (BIBM). IEEE (2014). https://doi.org/10.1109/bibm.2014.6999173
5. Eiben, B., et al.: Breast conserving surgery outcome prediction: a patient-specific, integrated multi-modal imaging and mechano-biological modelling framework. In: Tingberg, A., Lång, K., Timberg, P. (eds.) IWDM 2016. LNCS, vol. 9699, pp. 274–281. Springer, Cham (2016). https://doi.org/10.1007/978-3-319-41546-8_35
6. Elmoataz, A., Lozes, F., Toutain, M.: Nonlocal PDEs on graphs: from tug-of-war games to unified interpolation on images and point clouds. J. Math. Imaging Vis. **57**(3), 381–401 (2016). https://doi.org/10.1007/s10851-016-0683-3
7. Floater, M.S., Hormann, K.: Surface parameterization: a tutorial and survey. In: Dodgson, N.A., Floater, M.S., Sabin, M.A. (eds.) Advances in Multiresolution for Geometric Modelling, Mathematics and Visualization, pp. 157–186. Springer, Heidelberg (2005). https://doi.org/10.1007/3-540-26808-1_9
8. Garcia, D.: Robust smoothing of gridded data in one and higher dimensions with missing values. Comput. Stat. Data Anal. **54**(4), 1167–1178 (2010). https://doi.org/10.1016/j.csda.2009.09.020
9. Guillemot, C., Meur, O.L.: Image inpainting: overview and recent advances. IEEE Sig. Process. Mag. **31**(1), 127–144 (2014). https://doi.org/10.1109/msp.2013.2273004
10. Hachaj, T., Ogiela, M.R.: Rule-based approach to recognizing human body poses and gestures in real time. Multimed. Syst. **20**(1), 81–99 (2013). https://doi.org/10.1007/s00530-013-0332-2
11. Lai, W.S., Huang, J.B., Hu, Z., Ahuja, N., Yang, M.H.: A comparative study for single image blind deblurring. In: 2016 IEEE Conference on Computer Vision and Pattern Recognition (CVPR). IEEE (2016). https://doi.org/10.1109/cvpr.2016.188

12. Lin, W., Kuo, C.C.J.: Perceptual visual quality metrics: a survey. J. Vis. Commun. Image Represent. **22**(4), 297–312 (2011). https://doi.org/10.1016/j.jvcir.2011.01.005

13. Losken, A., Seify, H., Denson, D.D., Paredes, A.A., Carlson, G.W.: Validating three-dimensional imaging of the breast. Ann. Plast. Surg. **54**(5), 471–476 (2005). https://doi.org/10.1097/01.sap.0000155278.87790.a1

14. Mallick, T., Das, P.P., Majumdar, A.K.: Characterizations of noise in kinect depth images: a review. IEEE Sens. J. **14**(6), 1731–1740 (2014). https://doi.org/10.1109/jsen.2014.2309987

15. O'Connell, R.L., Stevens, R.J., Harris, P.A., Rusby, J.E.: Review of three-dimensional (3D) surface imaging for oncoplastic, reconstructive and aesthetic breast surgery. Breast **24**(4), 331–342 (2015). https://doi.org/10.1016/j.breast.2015.03.011

16. Oliveira, H.P., Cardoso, J.S., Magalhaes, A., Cardoso, M.J.: Methods for the aesthetic evaluation of breast cancer conservation treatment: a technological review. Curr. Med. Imaging Rev. **9**(1), 32–46 (2013). https://doi.org/10.2174/1573405611309010006

17. Oliveira, S.P., et al.: Three-dimensional planning tool for breast conserving surgery: a technological review. Crit. Rev. Biomed. Eng. (2018). https://doi.org/10.1615/critrevbiomedeng.2018028476

18. Otsu, N.: A threshold selection method from gray-level histograms. IEEE Trans. Syst. Man Cybern. **9**(1), 62–66 (1979). https://doi.org/10.1109/tsmc.1979.4310076

19. Qureshi, M.A., Deriche, M., Beghdadi, A., Amin, A.: A critical survey of state-of-the-art image inpainting quality assessment metrics. J. Vis. Commun. Image Represent. **49**, 177–191 (2017). https://doi.org/10.1016/j.jvcir.2017.09.006

20. Reinhard, E., Adhikhmin, M., Gooch, B., Shirley, P.: Color transfer between images. IEEE Comput. Grap. Appl. **21**(4), 34–41 (2001). https://doi.org/10.1109/38.946629

21. Rother, C., Kolmogorov, V., Blake, A.: GrabCut. ACM Trans. Graph. **23**(3), 309 (2004). https://doi.org/10.1145/1015706.1015720

22. Tam, G.K.L., et al.: Registration of 3D point clouds and meshes: a survey from rigid to nonrigid. IEEE Trans. Vis. Comput. Graph. **19**(7), 1199–1217 (2013). https://doi.org/10.1109/tvcg.2012.310

23. Wang, G., Garcia, D., Liu, Y., de Jeu, R., Dolman, A.J.: A three-dimensional gap filling method for large geophysical datasets: application to global satellite soil moisture observations. Environ. Model. Softw. **30**, 139–142 (2012). https://doi.org/10.1016/j.envsoft.2011.10.015

24. Wang, Z., Simoncelli, E.P., Bovik, A.C.: Multiscale structural similarity for image quality assessment. In: 37th Asilomar Conference on Signals, Systems & Computers, vol. 2, pp. 1398–1402. IEEE (2003). https://doi.org/10.1109/acssc.2003.1292216

25. Wheat, J., Choppin, S., Goyal, A.: Development and assessment of a microsoft kinect based system for imaging the breast in three dimensions. Med. Eng. Phys. **36**(6), 732–738 (2014). https://doi.org/10.1016/j.medengphy.2013.12.018

Ontology-Driven Food Category Classification in Images

Ivan Donadello[✉] and Mauro Dragoni

Fondazione Bruno Kessler, Via Sommarive 18, 38123 Trento, Italy
{donadello,dragoni}@fbk.eu

Abstract. The self-management of chronic diseases related to dietary habits includes the necessity of tracking what people eat. Most of the approaches proposed in the literature classify food pictures by labels describing the whole recipe. The main drawback of this kind of strategy is that a wrong prediction of the recipe leads to a wrong prediction of any ingredient of such a recipe. In this paper we present a multi-label food classification approach, exploiting deep neural networks, where each food picture is classified with labels describing the food categories of the ingredients in each recipe. The aim of our approach is to support the detection of food categories in order to detect which one might be dangerous for a user affected by chronic disease. Our approach relies on background knowledge where recipes, food categories, and their relatedness with chronic diseases are modeled within a state-of-the-art ontology. Experiments conducted on a new publicly released dataset demonstrated the effectiveness of the proposed approach with respect to state-of-the-art classification strategies.

Keywords: Food classification · Knowledge-based system · Food tracking · Food dataset · mHealth

1 Introduction

Chronic diseases are responsible for approximately 70% of deaths among Europe and U.S. each year and they account for about 75% of the health spending[1,2]. Such chronic diseases can be largely preventable by eating healthily, exercising regularly, avoiding (tobacco) smoking, and receiving preventive services. Prevention at every stage of life would help people stay healthy, avoid or delay the onset of diseases, and keep diseases they already have from becoming worse or debilitating; it would also help people lead productive lives and, at the end, reduce the costs of public health.

Dietary tracking is one of the pillars for the self-management of chronic diseases. One of the most common modalities for tracking eaten food is to keep a

---

[1] http://www.who.int/nmh/publications/ncd_report_full_en.pdf.
[2] https://www.cdc.gov/media/releases/2014/p0501-preventable-deaths.html.

© Springer Nature Switzerland AG 2019
E. Ricci et al. (Eds.): ICIAP 2019, LNCS 11752, pp. 607–617, 2019.
https://doi.org/10.1007/978-3-030-30645-8_55

diary of food pictures as implemented in numerous commercial applications. The use of food pictures opens the challenge of recognizing all the taken food from users' pictures. State-of-the-art approaches classify meal images according to the food they contain. However, they are not able to infer the food categories given by the recipe of that particular food. The detection of these categories is fundamental for people affected by particular diseases, such as diabetes, hypertension or obesity.

In this work, we propose a strategy based on the multi-label classification of food pictures according to the food categories contained in a specific food recipe of the Mediterranean diet. We compare this method against the (more standard) single-label classification of the food recipe and the inference of the contained food categories. Our claim is that a classification error in a single food recipe affects the majority of the inferred food categories. For example, a single-label classifier may confuse two similar pasta recipes, e.g., "Pasta with carbonara sauce" and "Pasta with cheeses" that, even if they might be aesthetically similar, they have different food categories. Indeed, the former contains cold cuts that affect people suffering of cardiovascular diseases. This can be prevented with a multi-label classification. Moreover, food categories, thanks to the use of background knowledge, can be associated with a risk level with respect to specific diseases. Within this scenario, the use of background knowledge helps for two reasons. Firstly, it gives the possibility of modeling logical relationships between food categories and risk levels with respect to specific diseases. Secondly, information collected from users can be exploited within a behavior change context to support them in changing their dietary habits through the implementation of goal-based strategies [21]. The contribution of the paper is the following:

- food pictures are classified with respect to the set of food categories contained in the food recipe. This outperforms the standard (single-label) classification of food recipes and the consequent inference of the food categories;
- background knowledge is used for inferring which are the food categories contained within each recipe together with information about the risk level of each food category with respect to a first identified set of chronic diseases;
- a new dataset of food pictures and the source code of the classification tool have been released in order to support the reproducibility of the results and to foster further research in this direction.

2   Related Work

The recognition of foods from images is the first step for the dietary tracking. This task has been studied by the Computer Vision community with techniques of image classification/segmentation and volume estimation. The first works rely on the extraction of visual features from the images and the consequent use of classifiers. The main features used are local and global features, SIFT, textons and local binary patterns [1,9,11–13,15,17]. The classifiers are k-NN classifiers, Support Vector or Kernel Machines. The works in [12,13] also developed the first food images datasets: the Food50 and Food85, with 50 and 85 labels of

Japanese foods, respectively. In [15] the authors developed the UEC FOOD-100 dataset (100 food labels), successively extended with 256 labels in UEC FOOD-256 [17]. Food-101 [1] is one of the biggest datasets having 101,000 images with 101 food labels. Here the authors mine discriminant food image parts with Random Forests and classify them with a SVM. These techniques have been used in mobile apps for food tracking, such as, Food-Log [18], DietCam [19], FoodCam [17], Snap-n-Eat [29]. They also perform an approximate estimation of the taken calories with volume estimation techniques. However, the growing availability of huge datasets and hardware resources has made Convolutional Neural Networks (CNNs) the standard technique for food classification [2,4,14, 16,22,28], thus avoiding the use of engineered features. In [2] the authors combine CNNs and Conditional Random Fields to predict both food and ingredient labels in a multi-task learning setting. They also developed one of the biggest food images dataset: the VIREO Food-172 dataset. It contains 172 food labels, 353 ingredients labels and 110,241 images. The Food524DB dataset is used in [4] for food recognition with CNNs and gathers the Food50, Food-101, UEC FOOD-256 and VIREO Food-172 datasets. It contains 524 food labels and 247,636 images.

A more fine-grained analysis of the meal is performed by estimating also the quantity of food in the dish and the consequent calories intake. The first step is the semantic segmentation of the food in the dish and the quantity computation with techniques of volume estimation. However, these techniques also require a database of foods and relatives densities. The GoCARB [5] system estimates the carbohydrates intake for people with diabetes. After a segmentation of the foods their classification is performed with SVMs. The volume estimation performs the 3D reconstruction of the food with stereo vision techniques. A density table returns the carbohydrates for each food label. A similar technique is used also in [26]. Other works exploit a known reference object (e.g., a thumb [25] or a wallet [24]) for volume computation or assume a defined shape template for a given class of foods [10]. The Im2Calories system [23] uses a CNN to predict a depth map of the food image that is used to build the 3D model of the meal. Quantity estimation can be addressed with a multi-task learning approach by defining a tailored CNN that both learns the classification of the food in the dish and the relative calories or volume. However, this interesting direction requires a dataset with the annotated calories [8] or the depth information in the images [20]. In [3] the authors use CNNs to perform semantic segmentation to estimate the leftovers in the trays in the canteens. They also developed the UNIMIB2016 dataset with 73 food labels to test their method.

Few works among those mentioned above predict food categories and match them with some nutritional facts in a database [2,5,8,25,29]. Also, they predict only one food category (e.g., pasta) for each detected food and this can be inaccurate. Indeed, a pasta dish should be avoided by a person suffering of diabetes. However, a pasta dish might have carbonara sauce, containing eggs, aged cheese and cold cuts. One, or more, of these food categories could be not suitable for people suffering of obesity, hypertension or cardiovascular diseases.

In these cases it is important to have a food recognition system that performs multi-label classification of the several food categories in the dish.

3   Background Knowledge

The use of background knowledge allows the design of intelligent systems having the purpose of going beyond the sole classification of food images. Such background knowledge, indeed, enables the possibility of exploiting logic relationships and inference capabilities for reusing the results of the food classification task in order to support users for more complex goals. For example, background knowledge can formalize specific dietary patterns that can be used to improve users' lifestyle, avoiding the rise or sharpening of chronic diseases, and to support them in changing their behaviors. Here we propose a strategy to predict food categories from food images. These categories might represent a warning for people affected by specific diseases (e.g. "Pasta" for people affected by diabetes). Our approach relies on a state-of-the-art conceptual model for the Mediterranean diet, called HeLiS, defining the dietary and physical activity domains together with entities modeling concepts concerning users' profiles and the monitoring of their activities. For the description of the conceptual model and of the methodology adopted for building it, the reader can refer to [7]. Here, the HeLiS ontology (http://w3id.org/helis) has been extended by adding, to the dietary domain, information concerning the risk level of food categories with respect to specific diseases. In this section, we limit to mention the main concepts involved into the food classification task proposed in this paper together with the ones modeled within the HeLiS ontology extension. Figure 1 shows an excerpt of the HeLiS ontology containing the concepts involved into our classification task.

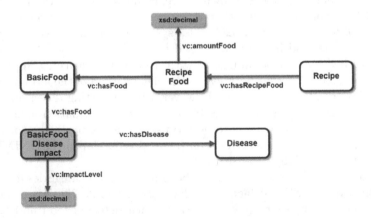

Fig. 1. Excerpt of the HeLiS ontology including the main concepts exploited for the proposed food classification approach.

Instances of the BasicFood concept describe foods for which micro-information concerning nutrients (carbohydrates, lipids, proteins, minerals, and vitamins) is available. Moreover, these instances also contain information about the category to which each BasicFood belongs to (such as Pasta, Aged Cheese, Eggs, Cold Cuts and Vegetal Oils). While instances of the Recipe concept describe the composition of complex dishes (such as Pasta with Carbonara Sauce) as a list of instances of the RecipeFood concepts. This concept reifies the relationships between each Recipe individual, the list of BasicFood it contains and the amount of each BasicFood. Besides this dual classification, instances of both BasicFood and Recipe concepts are categorized under a more fine-grained structure. Regarding the number of individuals, currently, the HeLiS ontology contains 986 individuals of type BasicFood and 4408 individuals of type Recipe.

The Disease concept models the chronic diseases supported by the system and for which information about the risk level relationship with specific BasicFood is available. Currently, we instantiated the Disease concept for the "diabetes", "kidney diseases", "cardiovascular diseases", "hypertension", and "obesity" diseases. Finally, the BasicFoodDiseaseImpact concept reifies the relationships between each Disease and BasicFood individuals and, for each reification, it contains a number representing the risk level of that BasicFood for that Disease. The risk level is represented by a numeric value ranging from 0 (no risk) to 3 (high risk) and is useful for the generation of warning messages to users in a behavioral-change system. For example, the food category Eggs has a low risk level for diabetes. Thus, the warning messages for a user suffering of diabetes will be soft if the user exceeds with the consume of eggs.

4 Multi-label Food Category Classification

Our goal is to assign every food image with a set of food category labels. These categories refer to the ingredients that compose the food recipe in the image and are provided by the HeLiS ontology. We address this problem as a multi-label image classification task where $\mathcal{X} \in \mathbb{R}^d$ is the input domain of our images and BasicFood is the set of the possible food category labels. Given an image $x \in \mathcal{X}$, we need to predict a vector $y = \{y_1, y_2, \ldots, y_K\} \subseteq$ BasicFood where y_i is the i-th food category label associated to x. Up to our knowledge, state-of-the-art methods in food image recognition do not exploit multi-label classification. They classify images according to only one single label taken from Recipe. Therefore, we exploit two methods: (i) a direct multi-label classification of the food categories with a CNN and (ii) a single-label image classification of the food recipes (e.g., Pasta with Carbonara Sauce) with a CNN and then the logical inference of all its food categories (i.e., Pasta, Eggs, etc.) through the RecipeFood concept.

4.1 Methods

Current methods in image classification use supervised deep learning techniques based on CNNs. These are able to learn the salient features of an image in order to classify it according to some training examples. Many CNNs have been developed exploiting several combinations of the hidden layers (convolutions, poolings, activations) in order to address the main challenges of the visual recognition. In both methods (i) and (ii) we separately train (on the dataset in Sect. 5.1) one of the most performing CNN, the Inception-V3 [27]. This network presents convolutional filters of multiple sizes operating at the same level. This makes the network "wider" and able to better detect the salient parts of an image both locally and globally. Finally, the network has a standard fully-connected layer for predicting the classes.

Direct Multi-label Classification. For this task we train the Inception-V3 for directly learning the vector y of the food categories in BasicFood. We use a sigmoid as activation function of the last fully-connected layer and binary cross entropy as loss function. This is a standard setting for multi-label classification.

Single-Label Classification and Inference. Another method to classify the food categories in a meal image consists in: (i) classifying an input image with a CNN according to the food label it contains (e.g., Pasta with Carbonara Sauce). This is the standard multiclass classification where one image is classified with only one food label among many classes. (ii) Inferring the food category labels from the food label by using the concepts and properties of HeLiS. In our example, the detection of Pasta with Carbonara Sauce implies the presence of these food categories: Pasta, Eggs, Aged cheese, Vegetal Oils and Cold cuts. More formally, let CNN an Inception-V3 trained to multiclassify food labels in Recipe. Here the activation function of the last fully-connected layer is a softmax and the loss function is a categorical cross entropy. Thus $CNN(x) = \langle s_1, s_2, \ldots, s_n \rangle$ with $s_i \in \mathbb{R}$ is the classification score of the network for the label $l_i \in$ Recipe. Let $l^* \in$ Recipe be the label with highest score in $CNN(x)$, then the food category labels vector y is defined as:

$$y = \{y_i \in \texttt{BasicFood} \mid \exists w \in \texttt{RecipeFood} : \texttt{hasFood}(w, y_i) \land$$
$$\texttt{hasRecipeFood}(l^*, w)\} \quad (1)$$

5 Experiments

Here we compare the multi-label and single-label plus inference methods for the food category classification from meal images. Our claim is that a classification error in a single food recipe affects the majority of the inferred food categories leading to inaccurate results. The dataset and the tool are publicly available at https://github.com/ivanDonadello/Food-Categories-Classification.

5.1 The Food and Food Categories (FFoCat) Dataset

The HeLiS ontology contains the food and food category concepts (Sect. 3) exploited in the multi-label classification. We build a new dataset from these concepts. We sample some of the most common recipes in Recipe and use them as food labels. The food categories are then automatically retrieved from `BasicFood` with a SPARQL query. Examples of food labels are `Pasta with Carbonara Sauce` and `Baked Sea Bream`. Their associated food categories are `Pasta, Aged Cheese, Vegetal Oils, Eggs, Cold Cuts` and `Fresh Fish, Vegetal Oils`, respectively. We collect 156 labels for foods and 51 for food categories. We scrape the Web using Google Images as search engine to download all the images related to the food labels. Then, we manually clean the dataset resulting in 58,962 images with 47,108 images for the training set and 11,854 images for the test set (80–20 ratio of splitting). The dataset is affected by some natural imbalance, indeed the food categories present a long-tail distribution: only few food categories labels have the majority of the examples. On the contrary, many food categories labels have few examples. This makes the food classification challenging.

5.2   Experimental Settings

For both multi and single-label we train the Inception-V3 network from scratch on the FFoCat training set (with different loss functions) to find the best set of weights. The fine tuning using a pre-trained Inception-V3 did not perform sufficiently. We resized the images to 299×299 pixels and perform data augmentation by using rotations, width and height shifts, shearing, zooming and horizontal flipping. We run 100 epochs of training with a batch size of 16 and a learning rate of 10^{-6}. We adopt the early stopping criterion to prevent overfitting. The training has been performed with the Keras framework (TensorFlow as backend) on a PC equipped with a NVIDIA GeForce GTX 1080 Ti. We obtain the 93.43% and the 41.02% of accuracy for the multi and single-label classification tasks.

5.3   Metrics

As performance metric we use the mean average precision (MAP) that summarizes the classifier precision-recall curve. This is computed by listing the obtained classification scores of the food/food categories for all the test set pictures. We threshold this list at multiple values in $[0, 1]$ and the predictions are the set of labels with score higher than the threshold. The MAP is $\sum_{i=1}^{n}(R_n - R_{n-1})P_n$, i.e., the weighted mean of precision P_n achieved at each threshold level n. The weight is the increase of the recall in the previous threshold: $R_n - R_{n-1}$. The macro AP is the average of the AP over the classes, the micro instead considers each entry of the predictions as a label. We prefer MAP instead of accuracy as the latter can give misleading results for sparse vectors. Indeed, Accuracy = (TP+TN)/(TP+TN+FP+FN) with TP (TN) the true positives (negatives) and FP (FN) the false positives (negatives). Therefore, a classifier returning a zero vector y for the 51 food categories achieves an accuracy of 92%.

5.4   Results and Discussions

Given an (set of) input image(s) x, the computing of the precision-recall curve requires the predicted vector y of food category labels and a score associated to each label in y. In the multi-label method this score is directly returned by the Inception-V3 network. In the single-label and inference method this score needs to be computed. We tested two strategies: (i) we perform *exact inference* of the food categories from HeLiS and assign the value 1 to the scores of each $y_i \in y$; (ii) the food categories labels inherit the *uncertainty* returned by the CNN. The score of each y_i is the value s_i returned by $CNN(x)$. Table 1 reports the results.

Table 1. The multi-label classification of food categories outperforms in average precision (AP) the methods based on single-label classification and logical inference.

Method	Micro-AP (%)	Macro-AP (%)
Multi-label	**76.28**	**49.81**
Single-class exact	50.74	31.82
Single-class uncert.	60.51	42.73

The direct multi-label model outperforms the single-label models of approximately 26 and 16 points of micro-AP and 21 and 8 points of macro-AP, respectively. The micro-AP is always better than the macro-AP as it is sensible to the mentioned imbalance of the data. Moreover, the precision-recall curve (Fig. 2) of the direct multi-label model is always above the other models. This confirm our claim that errors in the single recipe classification propagate to the majority of the food categories the recipe contains. That is, the inferred food categories will be wrong because the recipe classification is wrong. On the other hand, errors in the direct multi-label classification will affect only few food categories. Good performance in dietary-tracking systems are important especially if the predictions

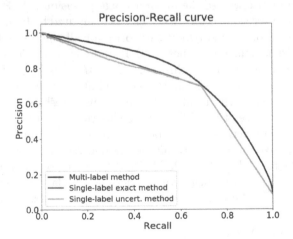

Fig. 2. The multi-label classification of food categories outperforms in average precision (AP) the methods based on single-label classification and logical inference.

are used in a behavioural-change system for generating proper user feedback. Indeed, the misclassification of a meal could generate wrong warning messages or even no message to users. To this aim, we also perform a qualitative comparison of the methods using testing images, see Fig. 3. The top-left meal of Fig. 3 contains a `Pasta with Garlic, Oil and Chili Peppers` that is misclassified by the single-label method with a `Pasta with Carbonara Sauce`, thus inferring wrong `Eggs` and `Cold Cuts`. In this case, for example, the intake of `Cold Cuts` could violate a dietary restriction (e.g., to consume no more than two portions of cold cuts in a week) with the consequent generation of an erroneous warning message for a user that should avoid the excessive intake of `ColdCuts`. Here, the multi-label method classifies all the categories correctly. The top-right image contains a `Vegetable Pie`, the single-label method misclassifies it and infers the wrong category of `Pizza Bread`, whereas the multi-label method is more precise. The low-left image contains `Backed Potatoes` and the single-label classification classifies it as `Backed Pumpkin` thus missing the category of `Fresh Starchy Vegetables`. This category is retrieved by the multi-label method that, within a behavioural-change system, can trigger the generation of a warning message for people affected by, for example, diabetes. Regarding the last low-right image, the single-label classification and inference method wrongly classifies the input image as `Tomato and Ricotta Cheese Pasta`, thus containing `FreshCheese` instead of `Eggs` and `TomatoSauces` instead of `ColdCuts`. In this case, no warning message will be generated for a user that should avoid `ColdCuts` and has already violated the consequent restriction in the last few days.

Fig. 3. Example images leading to wrong user messages with the multi-class model.

6   Conclusions

This paper discusses a multi-label food classification strategy for classifying food pictures based on the food categories contained in the recipe instead of the recipe itself. The aim of the proposed approach is to detect food categories having a high risk level for people affected by specific chronic diseases. The proposed strategy relies on the use of background knowledge exploited for inferring food categories from a recipe and their links with the risk level associated with each chronic disease. Moreover, we provide a new dataset containing 58,962 annotated images. Results demonstrated the effectiveness of the proposed classification strategy. Moreover, our proposal outperforms a more standard method based on single-image classification and inference of the food categories.

Future work will focus on designing multi-task learning algorithms for the joint prediction of both foods and food categories. In addition, we want to further exploit the combination of deep learning with ontologies by using constraints-based methods, such as Logic Tensor Networks [6], already applied to image classification tasks. Both these directions will be tested on bigger and standard image datasets containing food and food categories, such as VIREO FOOD-172 [2]. Finally, the proposed strategy opens also the possibility of being integrated into intelligent systems implementing behavior change policies for supporting users in adopting healthy lifestyles.

References

1. Bossard, L., Guillaumin, M., Van Gool, L.: Food-101 – mining discriminative components with random forests. In: Fleet, D., Pajdla, T., Schiele, B., Tuytelaars, T. (eds.) ECCV 2014. LNCS, vol. 8694, pp. 446–461. Springer, Cham (2014). https://doi.org/10.1007/978-3-319-10599-4_29
2. Chen, J., Ngo, C.: Deep-based ingredient recognition for cooking recipe retrieval. In: ACM Multimedia, pp. 32–41. ACM (2016)
3. Ciocca, G., Napoletano, P., Schettini, R.: Food recognition: a new dataset, experiments, and results. IEEE J. Biomed. Health Inform. **21**(3), 588–598 (2017)
4. Ciocca, G., Napoletano, P., Schettini, R.: Learning CNN-based features for retrieval of food images. In: Battiato, S., Farinella, G.M., Leo, M., Gallo, G. (eds.) ICIAP 2017. LNCS, vol. 10590, pp. 426–434. Springer, Cham (2017). https://doi.org/10.1007/978-3-319-70742-6_41
5. Dehais, J., Anthimopoulos, M., Shevchik, S., Mougiakakou, S.G.: Two-view 3D reconstruction for food volume estimation. IEEE Trans. Multimed. **19**(5), 1090–1099 (2017)
6. Donadello, I., Serafini, L., d'Avila Garcez, A.S.: Logic tensor networks for semantic image interpretation. In: IJCAI, pp. 1596–1602 (2017). ijcai.org
7. Dragoni, M., Bailoni, T., Maimone, R., Eccher, C.: HeLiS: an ontology for supporting healthy lifestyles. In: Vrandečić, D., et al. (eds.) ISWC 2018. LNCS, vol. 11137, pp. 53–69. Springer, Cham (2018). https://doi.org/10.1007/978-3-030-00668-6_4
8. Ege, T., Yanai, K.: Image-based food calorie estimation using knowledge on food categories, ingredients and cooking directions. In: ACM Multimedia (Thematic Workshops), pp. 367–375. ACM (2017)
9. Farinella, G.M., Moltisanti, M., Battiato, S.: Classifying food images represented as bag of textons. In: ICIP, pp. 5212–5216. IEEE (2014)
10. He, Y., Xu, C., Khanna, N., Boushey, C.J., Delp, E.J.: Food image analysis: segmentation, identification and weight estimation. In: ICME, pp. 1–6. IEEE Computer Society (2013)
11. He, Y., Xu, C., Khanna, N., Boushey, C.J., Delp, E.J.: Analysis of food images: features and classification. In: 2014 IEEE International Conference on Image Processing (ICIP), pp. 2744–2748. IEEE (2014)

12. Hoashi, H., Joutou, T., Yanai, K.: Image recognition of 85 food categories by feature fusion. In: ISM, pp. 296–301. IEEE Computer Society (2010)
13. Joutou, T., Yanai, K.: A food image recognition system with multiple kernel learning. In: ICIP, pp. 285–288. IEEE (2009)
14. Kagaya, H., Aizawa, K., Ogawa, M.: Food detection and recognition using convolutional neural network. In: ACM Multimedia, pp. 1085–1088. ACM (2014)
15. Kawano, Y., Yanai, K.: Real-time mobile food recognition system. In: CVPR Workshops, pp. 1–7. IEEE Computer Society (2013)
16. Kawano, Y., Yanai, K.: Food image recognition with deep convolutional features. In: UbiComp Adjunct, pp. 589–593. ACM (2014)
17. Kawano, Y., Yanai, K.: FoodCam-256: a large-scale real-time mobile food recognition system employing high-dimensional features and compression of classifier weights. In: ACM Multimedia, pp. 761–762. ACM (2014)
18. Kitamura, K., Yamasaki, T., Aizawa, K.: FoodLog: capture, analysis and retrieval of personal food images via web. In: CEA@ACM Multimedia, pp. 23–30. ACM (2009)
19. Kong, F., Tan, J.: DietCam: automatic dietary assessment with mobile camera phones. Pervasive Mob. Comput. 8(1), 147–163 (2012)
20. Lu, Y., Allegra, D., Anthimopoulos, M., Stanco, F., Farinella, G.M., Mougiakakou, S.G.: A multi-task learning approach for meal assessment. In: MADiMa@IJCAI, pp. 46–52. ACM (2018)
21. Maimone, R., Guerini, M., Dragoni, M., Bailoni, T., Eccher, C.: PerKApp: a general purpose persuasion architecture for healthy lifestyles. J. Biomed. Inform. 82, 70–87 (2018)
22. Mezgec, S., Koroušić Seljak, B.: NutriNet: a deep learning food and drink image recognition system for dietary assessment. Nutrients 9(7), 657 (2017)
23. Myers, A., et al.: Im2Calories: towards an automated mobile vision food diary. In: ICCV, pp. 1233–1241. IEEE Computer Society (2015)
24. Okamoto, K., Yanai, K.: An automatic calorie estimation system of food images on a smartphone. In: MADiMa@ACM Multimedia, pp. 63–70. ACM (2016)
25. Pouladzadeh, P., Shirmohammadi, S., Almaghrabi, R.: Measuring calorie and nutrition from food image. IEEE Trans. Instrum. Meas. 63(8), 1947–1956 (2014)
26. Puri, M., Zhu, Z., Yu, Q., Divakaran, A., Sawhney, H.S.: Recognition and volume estimation of food intake using a mobile device. In: WACV, pp. 1–8. IEEE Computer Society (2009)
27. Szegedy, C., Vanhoucke, V., Ioffe, S., Shlens, J., Wojna, Z.: Rethinking the inception architecture for computer vision. In: CVPR, pp. 2818–2826. IEEE Computer Society (2016)
28. Zhang, W., Zhao, D., Gong, W., Li, Z., Lu, Q., Yang, S.: Food image recognition with convolutional neural networks. In: UIC/ATC/ScalCom, pp. 690–693. IEEE Computer Society (2015)
29. Zhang, W., Yu, Q., Siddiquie, B., Divakaran, A., Sawhney, H.: "Snap-n-Eat" food recognition and nutrition estimation on a smartphone. J. Diab. Sci. Technol. 9(3), 525–533 (2015)

Real-Time Neurodegenerative Disease Video Classification with Severity Prediction

Vincenzo Dentamaro[1]([✉]) [iD], Donato Impedovo[2] [iD],
and Giuseppe Pirlo[2]

[1] Georgia Institute of Technology, Atlanta, GA 30332, USA
vincenzo@gatech.edu
[2] Dipartimento di Informatica, Università degli studi di Bari, 70121 Bari, Italy
{donato.impedovo, giuseppe.pirlo}@uniba.it

Abstract. In this paper, an automatic diagnosis system for neurodegenerative diseases is presented. Starting with an existing neurodegenerative diseases gait dataset, namely the NDDGD dataset, classification and regression algorithms have been trained, with the inter-patient dataset separation scheme (walking patterns used for training and testing, belong to different people), and integrated within a larger automatic diagnosis system which make use of videos in input or real-time streaming from cameras for predicting the neurodegenerative disease, if present, and its stage. The proposed system is capable of predicting among 3 neurodegenerative diseases, namely: amyotrophic lateral sclerosis disease (ALS), Parkinson's disease (PD), Huntington's disease (HUN) and differentiate among the severity (stage) level of the disease, if found.

The system makes use of common cameras for the 2D pose estimation and features engineering. The system can be easily deployed in hospitals and houses in order to help physicians with the diagnosis. When used in conjunction with physicians, this system can be a valuable tool for neurodegenerative diseases prediction.

Keywords: NDDGD dataset · Neuro degenerative diseases · Pose estimation · Parkinson · ALS · Huntington

1 Introduction

Neurodegenerative diseases are incurable and afflict humanity. A timely diagnosis could help the physician to slow down the progress of the disease thus improving the quality of the rest of life. To date, the diagnosis of these diseases is long and expensive, and understanding the first symptoms is a complex activity. Neurodegenerative diseases result in a behavioral, cognitive and execution functionalities degradation. Some Computer Aided Diagnosis (CAD) tools have been proposed based on behavioral biometrics and from a pure pattern recognition perspective [1] as for example handwriting [2, 3] by inspecting various aspects of the neuromuscular system [4], but also velocity-based models [5]. A more comprehensive review is treated in [1] and [6]. Motions problems are related to these diseases ant to their severity. Changes in behavioral biometrics can be a prominent biomarker. In fact, human movements are

© Springer Nature Switzerland AG 2019
E. Ricci et al. (Eds.): ICIAP 2019, LNCS 11752, pp. 618–628, 2019.
https://doi.org/10.1007/978-3-030-30645-8_56

complex activities which involve cognitive, kinesthetic and perceptual-motor components [6]: their evolution can be adopted for diseases evaluation by using several kind
of inertial sensors [7] with the aim to perform real-time gait monitoring for different
kind of pathologies, such as Parkinson's disease [8].

Among the other biometrics, a crucial role is played by gait. This activity is
fundamental in the life of humans and it is carried out from the first years of life,
although it requires the use of many resources of the nervous system to bring it to
completion. In fact, neurodegenerative diseases tend to destroy various parts of the
nervous system depending on which disease is contracted, bringing, in addition, various disorders manifested while walking. Of particular interest is the application
commercially available inertial sensors to the gait analysis [9]. Those sensors are very
effective, as shown in [10].

In this work, starting with the existing NDDGD [11, 12] neurodegenerative diseases gait dataset, several classification and regression algorithms have been trained
and tested with an inter-patient separation scheme and later integrated within a larger
automatic diagnosis system which make use of videos in input or real-time streaming
from cameras for predicting the neurodegenerative disease, if present, and its stage. The
proposed system is capable of predicting among 3 neurodegenerative diseases and
differentiate among the severity (stage) level of the disease, if found. This is an early
exploratory analysis on inter-patient separation scheme used for neurodegenerative
disease prediction. This separation scheme is very popular on practical computer aided
diagnosis system, where the models are trained and tested over disease patterns of
different people, and thus enable the application of these systems outside the mere
laboratory research, with concrete applications in hospitals and specialized centers.

Thus, this system, is a valuable tool for training physicians and neurologists who
need to compare their results with the results obtained by our system for assessing the
right disease and its stage.

The use of common cameras for the 2D pose estimation and features engineering is
twofold: its cheap compared to depth cameras or 3D tracking wearable sensors, can
easily be deployed in every hospital and even in houses and it doesn't require the
patient to wear anything, thus avoiding problems linked to forgetfulness and rejection.

The paper is organized as follows. Section 2 contains a brief description of the
treated diseases as well an introduction on gait analysis, Sect. 3 describes the dataset
used and related works, Sect. 4 discusses the architecture of the proposed system,
Sect. 5 discusses the algorithms used and results. Section 6 contains conclusions and
future work.

2 Diseases and Gait Cycle Analysis

Neurodegenerative diseases show long neuronal cells leak that turns in some physical
disorders during walking. Some of most known and serious neurodegenerative diseases
are Parkinson's (PD), amyotrophic lateral sclerosis disease (ALS), Alzheimer's (AD),
Huntington Chorea (HUN) and Dementias (DD).

In PD patients, slowness of automatic movements is detected as well as balance. The main physical motor symptoms are rigidity with hypertonia, bradykinesia and, in a deep stage, lack of balance and akinesia [13].

ALS is a disorder with no etiology, and its symptom is an evolutionary muscular atrophy, decrease in strength as well as phonation and chewing disorders [14].

In AD the neuronal lack causes serious damages in terms of short-term memory comprehension capability as well as normal life. Alzheimer's disease is characterized by uncoordinated movements, erect standing and walking, facial grimaces, dysarthria, dysphagia, alteration of breathing and hyperkinesia accentuated by emotions [15].

DD represent a group of typical, but not exclusive, neurodegenerative diseases of old age, with irreversible loss or reduction of intellectual abilities. However, the disease itself can be found only when clinical evidences appear [16].

The HUN is a hereditary disease in which cognitive and motor skills are particularly compromised. The first clues are mood changes, memory loss, dementia, difficulty in walking, language and swallowing, depression and, in last stages, suicide [16].

In this work, according to [17], the gait cycle is considered to be constituted by the following eight phases:

- Initial contact (IC): when the foot touches the ground;
- Loading response (LR): when the other foot is lifted for the swinging;
- Mid Stance (MS): the swinging foot exceeds the foot that acts as a lever;
- Terminal stance (TS): the right foot's heel moves vertically until the left foot touches the ground;
- Pre-swing (PS): now the left foot acts as a lever allowing the right foot to walk in;
- Initial Swing: the hip, knee, and ankle are flexed to begin advancement of the limb forward and create clearance of the foot over the ground.
- Mid-swing (MS): the left leg's tibia is vertical so that right leg can overcome it;
- Terminal swing (TS): the progress of the limbs is completed when the right leg moves in front of the left thigh and the right foot touches the ground, going back to the IC phase.

3   Dataset and Related Works

3.1   Dataset

There is not a large amount of publicly available dataset related to gait and neuro-muscular diseases. The most used is, probably, the Gait Dynamics in Neuro-Degenerative Disease Data Base (NDDGD) [11, 12]. It includes 15 patients with Parkinson's disease, 20 patients with Huntington's disease, and 13 patients with amyotrophic lateral sclerosis. In addition, 16 healthy control subjects are also included. The raw data were obtained using force-sensitive resistors, with the output roughly proportional to the force under the foot. The dataset contains the features listed in Table 1:

Table 1. Features of NDDGD dataset

1	Elapsed time (sec)
2	Left stride interval (sec)
3	Right stride interval (sec)
4	Left swing interval (sec)
5	Right swing interval (sec)
6	Left swing interval (% of stride)
7	Right swing interval (% of stride)
8	Left stance interval (sec)
9	Right stance interval (sec)
10	Left stance interval (% of stride)
11	Right stance interval (% of stride)
12	Double support interval (sec)
13	Double support interval (% of stride)

The dataset also includes clinical information for each subject, including age, gender, height, weight, walking speed, and a measure of disease severity or duration. For the subjects with Parkinson's disease, this is the Hohn and Yahr score is reported.

Gait recognition has been performed in several ways: with infrared sensors [18] or from b/w images by extracting the silhouette [19], with inertial sensors, UWB sensors and much more.

3.2 Related Works

Zheng et al. [20] investigated three supervised learning algorithms (SVM, Kstar and Random Forest) with a reduced set of features for the aim of ALS, HD and PD classification. Feature selection has been also performed by authors of [21]. In this case Recursive Feature Elimination (RFE) was adopted to select the top 5 features, successively Random Forest and Bagging CART were adopted to obtain, respectively, 96.93% and 97.43% of accuracy.

Ye et al. [22] observed that patients' gait dynamic is non-linear, so that they proposed an Adaptive Neuro-Fuzzy Inference System (ANFIS) able to combine neural network adaptive capabilities and the fuzzy logic approach. Also in this case a reduced set of features is adopted: left stride interval, right stride interval, left stance interval, right stance interval, and double support interval. Tests are performed discriminating each patient group from the HC within a binary task. Accuracy ranges from 90 to 94%. At the same time, standard classifiers have been adopted observing comparable results to those obtained by authors.

In [23] authors used different feature selection methods gaining a final accuracy of 93% on a similar schema proposed in [22]. In [24] authors used Gaussian radial basis function and SVM to predict Parkinson's disease patterns from human gait with accuracy of 83.3%.

In [25] authors developed a FPGA which is capable of correctly recognize health and unhealthy patterns from gait analysis and perform classification with accuracy of 93.8%, 89.1%, 94% and 93.3%, respectively for ALS, HD, PD, and healthy person.

Differently from the previously mentioned works, here an inter-patient data scheme is used [26], more specifically gaits of different people are used to predict the health status of others. More specifically, patients for training and testing are chosen randomly, as it will be described later in Sect. 5, but each patient and his/her signals will be exclusively used in training or testing, not both.

4   System Architecture

4.1   Classification and Regression Models

In the proposed schema there are 4 different models: the first is a multi-class classification model which predicts if the instance to evaluate belongs to ALS, HUN, PD or is a HC. As it will be shown later, this model predicts probabilities for an instance to fall into one of the four classes. Than for each class, except for HC, a regression model is used.

The regression model was previously trained separately on its subset of instances belonging to the same class, separated in training set and test set respecting the inter-patient scheme previously described. It is used to predict the severity/duration of the disease.

The multi-class classification model outputs a probability of the instance belonging to a specific class. If the class is a disease, the system specifies the top two disease (ranking probabilities), otherwise the system just outputs that the instance belongs to a healthy person. If the classified instance is evaluated to belong to a disease class, the system uses the previously trained regression model for that disease and use it to predict the severity or duration (in months) of the disease. At the end the system outputs the top two classes found and their severity/duration if applicable.

4.2   Video Real-Time Classification and Severity Prediction

The 4 models developed at previous step are then integrated into a bigger system that allows for real-time video neuro-degenerative disease classification and severity prediction. The following steps are performed [27]:

- Frame extraction: video input is acquired from the recording device in real-time and frames are extracted for further processing.
- Skeleton calculation: a skeleton extraction process is performed, i.e. the individual's "skeleton" is obtained for the acquisition of the most important points, such as the hips, knees, feet, shoulders and head. The angle of the head is then obtained to differentiate the right side from the left.
- Gait feature extraction: the data previously extracted from the image are analyzed to extract the gait features.
- Gait classification and severity prediction: the results of the previous phase are inserted in the classifier that will return the class to which the analyzed data belongs.

The classifier will be able to distinguish a healthy gait from a patient and give information on the disease that has been identified in that dataset.

Skeleton Calculation with Pose Estimation

OpenPose [28] has been used for pose estimation. The algorithm here used was designed to find the key points of a person (shoulders, head, arms, hips, knees and ankles) in 2D images [27]. The algorithm learns jointly, both the positions of the parts of the body and their association through two branches of the same forecasting process. The model was trained on over 25,000 images of the MPII database [29] (multi person database).

The model receives a color image of any size as input and produces, as output, a list with the 2D coordinates in terms of pixels of the key points of the person in the image.

Gait Feature Extraction

The coordinates and time stamp within each frame, for the right and left ankle, are used to estimate all the features present in the NDGGD Database and shown in Table 1.

Gait feature extraction is performed in two steps: elimination of position errors, identification and feature engineering. Since the analyzed patients, with a neurodegenerative disease, all showed a shuffling walk, that is the behavior to crawl feet on the ground without lifting them, only the x-coordinate have been considered.

The pose estimation process introduces some errors. For example, in the stance phase, in which the foot is stopped on the ground, the x-axis data of the shin should return with a series of identical values. However, there may be variations in the series that are due to the swing phase (the one in which the foot is moving). Moreover, the right ankle is frequently mixed with the left ankle. To remove these errors, a threshold time was set at 0.15 s to consider a stance phase (roughly 4 consecutive frames). Values affected by the described errors are forced to those of the series to which they are considered to belong. Technically a forward fill procedure was applied.

In this way, stances phases are identified as a series of identical values. Successively, swing phases are those between two phase of stance.

The phases of double support are the phases in which both steps are in stance and finally the stride is the sum of a stance and the next swing. Time duration of the aforementioned phases are calculated by using the timestamp of each frame. The result of this process is a new unlabeled instance with same features of NDDGD database as in Table 1.

All features have been normalized with Z-Score (using standard deviation and mean computed on training set) and fed into the classification engine for disease prediction and its severity/duration.

5 Performance Comparison

The training/testing splitting process of the dataset has been realized according to a probability value P_r taken from a uniform distribution D at random. If such value $P_r < 0.35$, the entire file corresponding to all the instances computed from that particular person, are entered in the test set, otherwise they enter in the training set. The same training set/test set split is than used for training the regression models of each disease class.

The dataset is almost balanced if each disease class is compared against the control class, but in case of multi-class classification, a class balancing is required. For class balancing, LICIC [30] has been used with linear kernel and a components ratio of 0.6.

The data is normalized with z-score and all tests are executed with 10-fold cross validation technique.

Table 2 reports prediction accuracies. As can be easily observed, multi-class classification on the inter-patient scheme on this dataset, is not a trivial problem.

Table 2. Multi-class classification accuracies with LICIC balancing

Algorithm	Cross val accuracy	Prediction accuracy
Adaboost over DecisionTree with 100 trees and max depth 100	0.8067	0.4459
Random forest 100 estimators and max depth 100	0.8045	0.4674
K-Nearest Neighbors with K = 21	0.725	0.4341
Neural Network 2 hidden layers with 8 neuron and 4 neurons, Adam as solver	0.6949	0.4674

All models' parameters have been selected with grid search technique and the parameters with better cross validation accuracies have been selected.

All the algorithms used have accuracies < 0.5. Figure 1 shows that the classification algorithm makes errors in all the classes, which means that, for the inter-patient scheme, the data distribution over classes in the training set is not representative of the real data distribution. This result is related to the fact that time features are not very representative of the particular walk pattern of a certain disease, since almost all diseases share similar time features patterns.

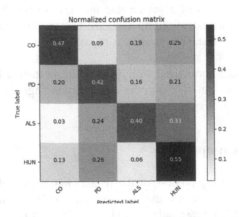

Fig. 1. Confusion matrix for Neural Network with LICIC

Successively a binary classification has been considered by testing each disease vs the control class. In this case, Neural Networks with two hidden layers, with respectively 8 and 4 neurons, has been used.

Table 3 shows the various accuracies obtained when performing binary classification. In each classification task, the training set has been balanced with LICIC. The results show that the system achieves almost 80% of accuracy when predicting ALS vs healthy control people, follows Parkinson VS healthy control people with about 71% of accuracy and finally Huntington vs healthy control people with 69% of accuracy.

Table 3. Accuracies for Neural Network over different tasks

Task	Cross validation accuracy	Prediction accuracy
Parkinson vs control	0.8682	0.7093
ALS vs control	0.9621	0.8012
Huntington vs control	0.8373	0.6859

Table 4 shows the RMSE errors when performing the prediction of severity/duration.

Table 4. RMSE errors with best performing algorithm with respect to disease class.

Task	Best performing algorithm	RMSE
Parkinson severity prediction	NN with 8 neurons in one single hidden layer	0.973
ALS duration (months)	Random forest with 10 trees and max depth 4	15.517
Huntington severity	Random forest with 10 trees and 4 as max depth	4.259

As it is possible to note, an accurate prediction of the duration (in months) for the ALS produces an error of about 15 months. Parkinson severity is quite appreciable, HUN severity, being a sum, has an appreciable deviation of 4.26 HUN score. Values are not extremely accurate, but, keeping into consideration the deviations, will help the physician with the diagnosis.

To recapitulate, feed forward neural network with two hidden layers with 8 and 4 neurons per hidden layer, is the architecture that provides the best generalization accuracy when performing binary classification as shown in Table 3. Instead for the severity/duration prediction, each task has its own best model: for Parkinson severity prediction, a feedforward neural network with one single hidden layer and 8 neurons achieved the lowest RMSE error. For ALS duration and Huntington disease, the random forest regressor with 10 trees and a max depth of 4 is the model who achieved the lowest RMSE in both tasks.

Real-Time Video Disease Classification

Because of the limitations in multi-class classification, during the real-time test phase with video cameras, it has been decided to show the first two most confident classified diseases with their respective severity/duration prediction. The multi-class classification algorithm selected, the Neural Network, instead of outputting a single class, it outputs the probabilities that the testing instance belongs to each class (PD, HUN, ALS; CO), the first two classes with highest ratio (sorted in descending order) are shown and for each class, the severity/duration value is predicted and showed.

The multi-class classification keeping the first two most probable classes showed a cross validation accuracy of 0.9620 and an overall accuracy of 0.7637 by using the same Neural Network as specified previously, as the same inter-patient scheme. The accuracies over all classes can be seen in the confusion matrix represented in Fig. 2.

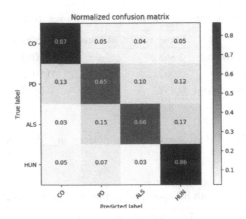

Fig. 2. Confusion matrix for Neural Network with LICIC and two most probable classes

By using the limited amount of videos available on internet showing Parkinsonian patients and Alzheimer's patients gait, the system was capable of correctly recognizing the right disease, within the top two most probable classes, in the majority of gaits.

6   Conclusions and Future Work

A real-time system for neurodegenerative diseases classification and severity/duration prediction has been here presented. When using the inter-patient dataset separation scheme, suitable for medical purposes, features present in NDDGD dataset are not representative of the particular pattern able to accurately discriminate a specific neurodegenerative disease from others in a multi-class classification scenario. It has been observed that almost all neurodegenerative diseases exhibit similar temporal features patterns. For this reason, class belonging probabilities have been computed to show the two most probable classes, with their respective severity/duration maturity (and a confidence level: the RMSE). In a future work, other features as well as stability medals [31] and zoning techniques [32] will be evaluated in an inter-patient separation scheme.

Acknowledgments. This work is within the BESIDE project (no. YJTGRA7) funded by the Regione Puglia POR Puglia FESR - FSE 2014-2020. Fondo Europeo Sviluppo Regionale. Azione 1.6 - Avviso pubblico "InnoNetwork".

References

1. Impedovo, D., Pirlo, G.: Dynamic handwriting analysis for the assessment of neurodegenerative diseases: a pattern recognition perspective. IEEE Rev. Biomed. Eng. **12**, 209–220 (2019)
2. Pirlo, G., Diaz, M., Ferrer, M.A., Impedovo, D., Occhionero, F., Zurlo, U.: Early diagnosis of neurodegenerative diseases by handwritten signature analysis. In: Murino, V., Puppo, E., Sona, D., Cristani, M., Sansone, C. (eds.) ICIAP 2015. LNCS, vol. 9281, pp. 290–297. Springer, Cham (2015). https://doi.org/10.1007/978-3-319-23222-5_36
3. Ubul, K., Tursun, G., Aysa, A., Impedovo, D., Pirlo, G., Yibulayin, T.: Script identification of multi-script documents: a survey. IEEE Access **5**, 6546–6559 (2017). 7890400
4. Impedovo, D., et al.: Writing generation model for health care neuromuscular system investigation. In: Formenti, E., Tagliaferri, R., Wit, E. (eds.) CIBB 2013. LNCS, vol. 8452, pp. 137–148. Springer, Cham (2014). https://doi.org/10.1007/978-3-319-09042-9_10
5. Impedovo, D.: Velocity-based signal features for the assessment of Parkinsonian handwriting. IEEE Sig. Process. Lett. **26**(4), 632–636 (2019)
6. De Stefano, C., Fontanella, F., Impedovo, D., Pirlo, G., Scotto di Freca, A.: Handwriting analysis to support neurodegenerative diseases diagnosis: a review. Pattern Recogn. Lett. **121**, 37–45 (2019)
7. Sant' Anna, A., Wickström, N., Eklund, H., Zügner, R., Tranberg, R.: Assessment of gait symmetry and gait normality using inertial sensors: in-lab and in-situ evaluation. In: Gabriel, J., et al. (eds.) BIOSTEC 2012. CCIS, vol. 357, pp. 239–254. Springer, Heidelberg (2013). https://doi.org/10.1007/978-3-642-38256-7_16
8. Tay, A., et al.: Real-time gait monitoring for Parkinson disease. In: 10th IEEE International Conference on Control and Automation (ICCA), pp. 1796–1801 (2013)
9. Zhang, J.T., Novak, A.C., Brouwer, B., Li, Q.: Concurrent validation of Xsens MVN measurement of lower limb joint angular kinematics. Physiol. Meas. **34**(8), 63–69 (2013)
10. Howcroft, J., Kofman, J., Lemaire, E.D.: Review of fall risk assessment in geriatric populations using inertial sensors. J. Neuroeng. Rehabil. **10**(1), 91 (2013)
11. Hausdorff, J.M., Lertratanakul, A., Cudkowicz, M.E., Peterson, A.L., Kaliton, D., Goldberger, A.L.: Dynamic markers of altered gait rhythm in amyotrophic lateral sclerosis. J. Appl. Physiol. **88**(6), 2045–2053 (2000)
12. Hausdorff, J.M., et al.: Altered fractal dynamics of gait: reduced stride-interval correlations with aging and Huntington's disease. Appl. Physiol. **82**(1), 262–269 (1997)
13. Goldenberg, M.M.: Medical management of Parkinson's disease. Pharm. Ther. **33**(10), 590 (2008)
14. Krivickas, L.S.: Amyotrophic lateral sclerosis and other motor neuron diseases. Phys. Med. Rehabil. Clin. **14**(2), 327–345 (2003)
15. Kaufman, D., Geyer, H., Milstein, M.: Kaufman's Clinical Neurology for Psychiatrists. E-Book. Elsevier Health Sciences, Amsterdam (2016)
16. Rosenblatt, A., Neal, G., Mance, M.A., Paulsen, J.: A Physician's Guide to the Management of Huntington's Disease. Huntington's Disease Society of America, New York (1999)
17. Kharb, A., Saini, V., Jain, Y.K., Dhiman, S.: A review of gait cycle and its parameters. IJCEM Int. J. Comput. Eng. Manag. **13**, 78–83 (2011)
18. Xue, Z., Ming, D., Song, W., Wan, B., Jin, S.: Infrared gait recognition based on wavelet transform and support vector machine. Pattern Recogn. **43**(8), 2904–2910 (2010)
19. Liu, Z., Sudeep, S.: Simplest representation yet for gait recognition: averaged silhouette. In: Proceedings of the 17th International Conference on Pattern Recognition, ICPR 2004, vol. 4. IEEE (2004)

20. Zheng, H., Yang, M., Wang, H., McClean, S.: Machine learning and statistical approaches to support the discrimination of neuro-degenerative diseases based on gait analysis. In: McClean, S., Millard, P., El-Darzi, E., Nugent, C. (eds.) Intelligent Patient Management. SCI, vol. 189, pp. 57–70. Springer, Heidelberg (2009). https://doi.org/10.1007/978-3-642-00179-6_4

21. Makhdoomi, N.A., Gunawan, T.S., Habaebi, M.H.: Human gait recognition and classification using similarity index for various conditions. In: IOP Conference Series: Materials Science and Engineering, vol. 53, no. 1. IOP Publishing (2013)

22. Ye, Q., Yi, X., Yao, Z.: Classification of gait patterns in patients with neurodegenerative disease using adaptive neuro-fuzzy inference system. Comput. Math. Methods Med. **2018**, 8 (2018). 9831252

23. Yang, M., Zheng, H., Wang, H., McClean, S.: Feature selection and construction for the discrimination of neurodegenerative diseases based on gait analysis. In: 2009 3rd International Conference on Pervasive Computing Technologies for Healthcare, pp. 1–7 (2009)

24. Shetty, S., Rao, Y.S.: SVM based machine learning approach to identify Parkinson's disease using gait analysis. In: 2016 International Conference on Inventive Computation Technologies (ICICT), pp. 1–5 (2016)

25. Saadeh, W., Altaf, M.A.B., Butt, S.A.: A wearable neuro-degenerative diseases detection system based on gait dynamics. In: 2017 IFIP/IEEE International Conference on Very Large Scale Integration, Abu Dhabi, pp. 1–6 (2017)

26. Dentamaro, V., Impedovo, D., Pirlo, G.: A new ConvNet architecture for heartbeat classification. In: Proceedings of the ICPRAI, Montréal, QC, Canada (2018)

27. Ajay, J., Song, C., Wang, A., Langan, J., Li, Z., Xu, W.: A pervasive and sensor-free deep learning system for Parkinsonian gait analysis. In: 2018 IEEE EMBS International Conference on Biomedical & Health Informatics (BHI), Las Vegas, NV, pp. 108–111 (2018)

28. Cao, Z., Hidalgo, G., Simon, T., Wei, S.E., Sheikh, Y.: OpenPose: realtime multi-person 2D pose estimation using part affinity fields. arXiv preprint arXiv:1812.08008 (2018)

29. Andriluka, M., Pishchulin, L., Gehler, P., Schiele, B.: 2D human pose estimation: New benchmark and state of the art analysis. In: Proceedings of the IEEE Conference on Computer Vision and Pattern Recognition, Columbus, OH, pp. 3686–3693 (2014)

30. Dentamaro, V., Impedovo, D., Pirlo, G.: LICIC: less important components for imbalanced multiclass classification. Information **9**(12), 317 (2018)

31. Pirlo, G., Impedovo, D.: On the measurement of local stability of handwriting: an application to static signature verification. In: 2010 IEEE Workshop on Biometric Measurements and Systems for Security and Medical Applications, Taranto, pp. 41–44 (2010)

32. Pirlo, G., Impedovo, D.: Adaptive membership functions for handwritten character recognition by voronoi-based image zoning. IEEE Trans. Image Process. **21**(9), 3827–3837 (2012)

Learning to Rank Food Images

Dario Allegra[1]([✉]), Daniela Erba[2], Giovanni Maria Farinella[1],
Giovanni Grazioso[2], Paolo Danilo Maci[1], Filippo Stanco[1],
and Valeria Tomaselli[3]

[1] University of Catania, Catania, Italy
{allegra,gfarinella,fstanco}@dmi.unict.it
[2] University of Milan, Milan, Italy
{daniela.erba,giovanni.grazioso}@unimi.it
[3] STMicroelectronics, Catania, Italy
valeria.tomaselli@st.com

Abstract. In the last decade food understanding has become a very attractive topic. This has implied the growing demand of Computer Vision algorithms for automatic diet assessment to treat or prevent food related diseases. However, the intrinsic variability of food, makes the research in this field incredibly challenging. Although many papers about classification or recognition of food images have been published in recent years, the literature lacks of works which address volume and calories estimation problem. Since an ideal food understanding engine should be able to provide information about nutritional values, the knowledge of the volume is essential. Differently from the state-of-art works, in this paper we address the problem of volume estimation through Learning to Rank algorithms. Our idea is to work with a predefined set of possible portion size and exploit a ranking approach based on Support Vector Machine (SVM) to sort food images according to the volume. At the best of our knowledge, this is the first work where food volume analysis is treated as a raking problem. To validate the proposed methodology we introduce a new dataset of 99 food images related to 11 food plates. Each food image belongs to one over three possible portion size (i.e., small, medium, large). Then, we provide a baseline experiment to assess the problem of learning to rank food images by using three different image descriptors based on Bag of Visual Words, GoogleNet and MobileNet. Experimental results, confirm that the exploited paradigm obtain good performances and that a ranking function for food volume analysis can be successfully learnt.

Keywords: Learning to rank · Ranking SVM · Food volume · Diet monitoring

1 Introduction

Nowadays, people tend to ignore the impact that the food may have in their life. Unfortunately, an inadequate nutrition is one of the main causes of many

E. Ricci et al. (Eds.): ICIAP 2019, LNCS 11752, pp. 629–639, 2019.
https://doi.org/10.1007/978-3-030-30645-8_57

chronic diseases such as obesity, diabetes, cancer, osteoporosis, dental diseases and cardiovascular problems [1,26]. Also, people ignoring healthy diet can incur in malnutrition problems.

Malnutrition can be defined as "any nutritional imbalance" that comprises over and under-nutrition and mainly involves elderly people, even in developed countries. The inadequate nutrition has been documented either in institutionalised as well as in free living elderly and exerts negative effects on health outcomes. The prevalence of malnutrition was estimated as 14% in older population. Moreover, the 28–45% of older people, recently moved to care homes or hospitals, were malnourished on admission [10]. This situation has serious consequences for individuals as well as for society, including the increasing risk for morbidity, mortality and consequently for social cost. However, nutrition screening of older adults is extremely difficult: some of the screening methods can be self-reported, with possible misreports, others can be only administered by trained clinicians, while the biochemical markers are time consuming and expensive to use.

In recent years, these facts led Computer Vision researchers to develop new solutions for automatically collected information during food intake in the context of people diet monitoring [3,20,23,30]. Nevertheless, the intrinsic food variability in colour and shapes, as well as the great assortment of ingredients, makes very challenging the development of an efficient and effective food understanding engine. Ideally, a comprehensive system should be able to detect food dish, recognise the ingredients, estimate the volume and finally provide nutritional values. In the last decade, the spread of annotated datasets of food images [5,11–13,16,19,22,24,29] coupled with the massive use of learned based feature, have led promising performance for food detection and recognition tasks. On the contrary, quantity estimation studies have suffered the lack of proper datasets. Since 3D information have to be inferred for a correct volume estimation, in a totally unsupervised environment with no spatial references, it results in a extremely challenging problem [2,6–8,18,23,25].

However, in order to simplify patients diet monitoring, the current practice in healthcare facilities is to serve a set of standard food portions (e.g., small, medium, large). In this context, it is not necessary to estimate the exact amount of food in the dish, and the problem can be addressed using ranking strategies. In other words, given two images I_1 and I_2, one looks for a function $rank(\cdot)$ such that $rank(I_1) < rank(I_2)$ if the food amount depicted in I_1 is lower then the food amount depicted in I_2. With this idea in mind, and inspired by [21], we investigate the use of Learning to Rank algorithms [17] to sort food images according to the portion size.

To this aim, we introduce a new annotated dataset of 99 images and provide a baseline by using Ranking SVM [14] with three different kinds of visual features, i.e. Bag of words, GoogleNet features [27,28] and MobileNet features [15]. Although Learning to Rank have been successfully used in Information Retrieval, Natural Language Processing and Data Mining [17], at the best of our knowledge this is the first time it is employed for food amount ranking. Hence, the novel contributions of this work is two-fold:

- a new annotated dataset to face food ranking problem with respect to the portion size;
- the assessment of Ranking SVM [21] to learn a ranking function with different visual features.

The paper is organized as following. In Sect. 2 we report the related works in the field. In Sect. 3 we focus on the contribution of this work by detailing the proposed dataset and the considering a Learning to Rank approach. Section 4 describes the experimental settings and reports results. Section 5 summarise conclusions.

2   Related Works

Several works related to food understanding are available in literature. Most of them focus on food detection, recognition and classification and are motivated by the increasing demand of assistive technologies for diet monitoring [3,20,23,30]. In 2009, Puri et al. [23] proposed a system for food recognition and volume estimation. The classifier was obtained as a linear combination of multiple weak SVM classifiers trained on texture features. The volume was inferred by using RANSAC and dense stereo matching for depth map construction. In [8], Dehais et al. employed stereo pairs to compute disparity map and build a dense points cloud which is aligned to the table plane. This framework was designed to work by using a reference card placed on the table. By assuming the different food items in the plate are already segmented, each segment is projected on the 3D space for volume computation. In 2013, Chen et al. [6] presented a method for volume estimation from single view image. The approach requires a specific shape model for each food category and a calibrated reference marker. In 2017, Dehais et al. [7] proposed to estimate volume of multi-food meals with unconstrained 3D shape using stereo vision. The approach required two meals image of food placed inside elliptical plate, a credit card sized reference next to the plate and a segmentation map. Allegra et al. [2], proposed to use RGB-D images and supervised learning to perform depth estimation. The authors performed semantic segmentation by using U-Net and then they used a modified version of the CNN in [9] for depth inference from single RGB input. In 2018, Lu et al. [18] presented a Multi-Tasking Learning approach to estimate volume of food items from single RGB image. The proposed CNN architecture is composed by multiple modules. The first one is a feature extraction module and it is composed by ResNet50 and Feature Pyramid Network (FPN). The second module is the depth prediction net, which is mainly based on an encoder-decoder design architecture with skip connections and multi-scale side predictions. Semantic segmentation is performed by a Region Proposal Network (RPN) and a recognition net. The output of RPN is used to provide a food candidate mask and then the final volume was obtained through a CNN regressor.

Unlike the previous works, in this paper we propose to address food amount estimation as a raking problem. We neither perform depth estimation nor other

3D reconstruction steps since we operate in a context with a set of fixed food portions (small, medium and large portions served at the canteen of the University). Ranking is one of the fundamental problems in information retrievals. Given a query q and a collection of documents D that match the query, ranking consists of sorting the documents according to some criterion. Learning to Rank (LTR) refers to machine learning strategies for training a model for a ranking task [17]. Specifically, we use LTR to train a model for a ranking task which lies in sorting RGB food images according to the relative visual attribute "portion size". The concept of relative attribute was introduced in [21] by Parikh and Grauman. Their aim was to provide a way to estimate the degree of an attribute give an image. Hence, differently than predicting the presence of an attribute, a relative attribute indicates the strength of an attribute in an image with respect to other images.

3   Materials and Methods

The main contribution of this paper lies in using Rankig SVM to train a model for ranking food images according to the portion size. Additionally, for validation purpose, we introduce a new dataset whose details are described in the following section. The dataset is publicly available for research purposes[1]. In order to provide a baseline, we perform a comparison between three different kinds of image descriptors which we exploit with Rankig SVM: Bag of Words [4], GoogleNet features [28] and MobileNet features [15].

3.1   Proposed Dataset

The proposed dataset consists of 99 RGB images belonging to 11 different classes (es. "insalata orzo e verdura", "cordon bleu", "fusilli alla crudaiola", etc.). Each image is associated to one portion size among three possible portion sizes: small, medium and large. For each class we collected 9 images corresponding to 3 images for each portion size. Moreover, in order to introduce variability, during acquisition we have used plates with two different diameters: 18cm (small plate) and 22.8cm (large plate). All the acquisition have been performed by a standard RGB camera fixed in a support and a centered top view with respect to the plate. In Fig. 1 are shown some examples of images belonging to the proposed dataset. At the best of our knowledge, state-of-art datasets are not suitable to test LTR approaches. Hence, differently from them, the proposed dataset includes multiple portion sizes for each dish to properly test LTR methods. To promote new task of ranking food images and to make repeatable our experiments, the proposed dataset is publicly available.

---

[1] Dataset Page: http://iplab.dmi.unict.it/foodLTR/.

3.2 Ranking SVM

Ranking SVM is a popular rank method proposed by Herbrich et al. [14]. The idea behind Ranking SVM is to transform ranking into pairwise classification and employ the standard SVM strategy to perform the learning task according to one specific attribute. Given the image descriptor $\mathbf{x}_i \in \mathbb{R}^n$ of the image I_i, the final aim is to find a ranking function $r_m(\cdot)$:

$$r_m(\mathbf{x}_i) = \mathbf{w}_m^T \mathbf{x}_i \tag{1}$$

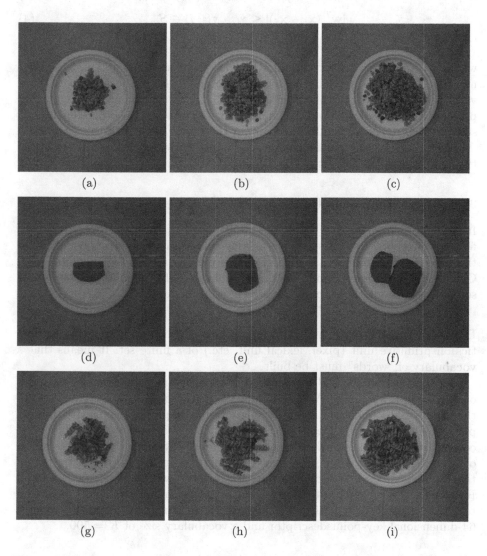

(a)   (b)   (c)

(d)   (e)   (f)

(g)   (h)   (i)

Fig. 1. Examples of three different food classes within the dataset (rows) and related portion sizes: small (first column) medium (second column) large (third column).

such that $r_m(\mathbf{x}_i) \geq r_m(\mathbf{x}_j)$ if and only if the strength of the attribute in I_i is higher than the strength of the attribute in the image I_j.

Hence, more formally, Ranking SVM is defined as the following constrained optimization problem:

$$\text{minimize} \quad \frac{1}{2}\|\mathbf{w}_m^T\|_2^2 + C\left(\sum \xi_{ij}^2 + \sum \gamma_{ij}^2\right) \tag{2}$$

subject to:

$$|\mathbf{w}_m^T(\mathbf{x}_i - \mathbf{x}_j)| \geq 1 - \xi_{ij} \quad \forall (i,j) \in O_m \tag{3}$$

$$|\mathbf{w}_m^T(\mathbf{x}_i - \mathbf{x}_j)| \leq \gamma_{ij} \quad \forall (i,j) \in S_m \tag{4}$$

$$\xi_{ij} \geq 0 \quad \gamma_{ij} \geq 0 \tag{5}$$

where ξ_{ij} and γ_{ij} are slack variables to relax the constrains and control SVM margins; $C > 0$ is a regularization parameters to limit the growth of slack variables; O_m is the set of the ordered pair (i,j) such that image I_i has a higher presence of the attribute than the image I_j; S_m is the set of the ordered pair (i,j) such that the images I_i and I_j have about the same presence of the attribute.

Hence, during the training phase, one has to provide the descriptors of the training images and the set O_m and S_m.

3.3   Image Representation

In order to apply Ranking SVM, each RGB image I_i has to be described by a feature vector $\mathbf{x}_i$. In this study we employ three difference strategies to build the descriptor $\mathbf{x}_i$, namely the Bag of Words paradigm with SURF, pre-trained GoogLeNet Inception *v3* and pre-trained MobileNet. In the following, we report some details about the employed representation models.

Bag of Visual Words. All BoW approaches are based on frequency statistics on primitive unit (pixel, lexical unit, etc.) of a finite set. It means that a vocabulary of "words" must be built.

The general idea behind this method is to represent an image as a histogram of visual words frequency. As first step, key-point descriptors are extracted from the images. Subsequently, a clustering algorithm is employed to quantize the key-points feature space by identifying K centroids to be used as a vocabulary V composed by K visual words. Then, the final representation of an image consists of a normalised histogram H, where the bin H_i is related to the frequency of the visual word $v_i \in V$. For experimental purpose, we have used Speeded Up Robust Features (SURF) [4] for key-points extraction, and K-Means algorithm to create a vocabulary with a specific size K. In our experiments we adopt a 64-dimensional key-point descriptor and a vocabulary size of $K = 500$.

GoogLeNet Inception V3. GoogLeNet Inception *v3* [28] is a Convolutional Neural Network (CNN) pre-trained on ImageNet. Its architecture consists of 42 layers. Differently from the previous version [27], in *v3* the computational burden is limited, but the effectiveness in term of accuracy is unaltered. This is realized by replacing 5×5 convolutions with 3×3 convolutions and by employing factorization methods. In this work, we used pre-trained GoogLeNet Inception *v3* to extract visual features from food images, so the last layer is removed and a Global Average Pooling layer is placed to get a 2048-dimensions feature vector.

MobileNet. MobileNet [15] is based on a streamlined architecture that employs depthwise separable convolution to build light and efficient deep neural networks. Depthwise separable convolution is a form of factorized convolutions which replaces a standard convolution with both, depthwise convolution and a 1×1 convolution called pointwise. This makes MobileNet suitable for low-powerful devices. To extract visual features for our experiments, we used a MobileNet pre-trained on ImageNet. The architecture consists of 28 layers, but we remove the last one and use Global Average Pooling to get a 256-dimensions descriptor.

4   Experiments and Results

To assess the proposed approach, we employ three-fold cross validation method. Hence, we run three times the experiments by using 66 images for training purpose and 33 for testing. Finally, we average the results. Note that test set always includes 1 small, 1 medium and 1 large portion image for each of the 11 classes. Moreover, all the images are resized to 250×250 pixels. In training phase we consider all the possible pairs in order to define O_m and S_m (see Sect. 3.2), whereas in test phase we validate the method by considering the ordering inferred for images triplets. For a proper quantitative evaluation we use two different evaluation measures, i.e. accuracy and Hamming distance, that are detailed in the next sections.

4.1   Training Phase

Training Ranking SVM model requires to build the set O_m and S_m described in Sect. 3.2. The number of all possible pairs (i, j) can be easily computed as $\binom{66}{2}$, hence $|O_m| + |S_m| = 2145$. Moreover, since S_m includes all the pairs related to the images with the same degree of the considered attribute (i.e, portion size), we have that $|S_m| = 3 \times \binom{22}{2} = 693$. The rest of 1452 pairs belong to O_m. We would like to highlight that although 66 images could be considered a limited number of data for training purpose, the actual training data for Ranking SVM lie in the pairs in $O_m \cup S_m$, i.e. 2145.

4.2   Testing Phase

Since in this work we want to distinguish between three different portion size, we decide to evaluate the proposed method by considering images triplets.

Hence, we use the $\binom{33}{3} = 5456$ possible triplets as testing samples. For each images triplet $\{I_s, I_p, I_q\}$ and the related descriptors $\{\mathbf{x}_s, \mathbf{x}_p, \mathbf{x}_q\}$, we compared the ground truth ranking $r^*(\cdot)$ (which we can compute using labels: small, medium, large) with respect to the one inferred through Ranking SVM approach, i.e. $r_m(\cdot)$.

4.3   Evaluation Measures

To quantitatively evaluate the performances of a learned ranking function $r_m(\cdot)$, we used two different measures: accuracy and Hamming distance. In this context, the accuracy is related to the number of correctly sorted triplets over the total number of tested triplets. More formally, we define the accuracy of the ranking function $r_m(\cdot)$:

$$acc = \sum_{k=1}^{M} \left(\frac{\delta_k}{M} \right) \tag{6}$$

where M is the number of testing triplets. Given the ground truth ranking values $\{r^*(\mathbf{x}_s^k), r^*(\mathbf{x}_p^k), r^*(\mathbf{x}_q^k)\}$ related to the k-th triplet $\{I_s^k, I_p^k, I_q^k\}$, and assuming a ranking order $r^*(\mathbf{x}_s) \leq r^*(\mathbf{x}_p) \leq r^*(\mathbf{x}_q)$, the value of δ_k is defined as following:

$$\delta_k = \begin{cases} 1 & \text{if} \quad r_m(\mathbf{x}_s) \leq r_m(\mathbf{x}_p) \leq r_m(\mathbf{x}_q) \\ 0 & \text{otherwise} \end{cases} \tag{7}$$

In a nutshell, we can say that $\delta_k = 1$ if the ground truth ranking order and the inferred ranking order agrees on a triplet.

Differently, Hamming distance evaluates the specific mismatching between the elements of the ground truth sorted triplet and the elements of the predicted one. Moreover, we assign a higher penalty if the mismatching occurs between a small portion and a large portion. For the sake of formalism, we define an ordered triplet as $\mathbf{T} = (I_s, I_p, I_q)$ and a function $label : \mathbb{I} \to \{1, 2, 3\}$:

$$label(I) = \begin{cases} 1 & \text{if image } I \text{ depicts a small portion} \\ 2 & \text{if image } I \text{ depicts a medium portion} \\ 3 & \text{if image } I \text{ depicts a large portion} \end{cases} \tag{8}$$

Then, if $\mathbf{T}^*$ is a correctly ordered triplet and $\mathbf{T}_m$ is the predicted one, hamming distance between $\mathbf{T}*$ and $\mathbf{T}_m$ is defined as:

$$hd(\mathbf{T}^*, \mathbf{T}_m) = \sum_{k=1}^{3} |label(T_k^*) - label(T_{mk})| \tag{9}$$

where T_k is the k-th images in the ordered triplet. In our experimental settings, Hamming distance is computed for all the testing triplets and then the average is considered.

Table 1. Experimental results

	BoW	GoogLeNet	MobileNet
Accuracy	83.45%	87.84%	94.05%
Hamming dist.	0.2963	0.2440	0.1193

4.4 Results

To benchmark the dataset and validate the proposed approach we perform test with BoW, GoogLeNet and MobileNet features on 5456 triplets. Experimental results in terms of both accuracy and Hamming distance are reported in Table 1.

Considering the evaluation in terms of accuracy, Ranking SVM on food images achieves best results when deep learning based features are used to represent images. This result is not surprising, since deep learning features tend to be more descriptive than the classic ones, even without fine-tuning. Specifically, MobileNet representation performed better than GoogLeNet in our experiments (94.05% vs 87.84%).

The performance in terms of Hamming distance follow the same trend. Since it measures the error degree, MobileNet presents the lowest average Hamming distance. For a better understanding of the values report in Table 1, we want to remark that, according the description given in Sect. 4.3, the higher value (i.e., the maximum error) for Hamming distance is 4. For example, it can be obtained if we compare to ordered triplet with labels $(1, 2, 3)$ and $(3, 2, 1)$ respectively.

5 Conclusion

The work presented in this paper is motivated by the massive demand for automatic systems for food intake monitoring. In a context where a predefined set of portion size are available, we proposed a novel approach for food portion sorting based on Learning to Rank algorithms. This allows to face the problem by avoiding depth and 3D estimation as in literature works which operate in less-constrained environments. To validate the proposed method, we introduce a new dataset of 99 images, which includes 11 categories and three distinct food portions, namely small, medium and large. Experiments have been performed with three different image descriptors based on Bags of Words, GoogleNet and MobileNet and with the LTR algorithm Ranking SVM. Results show that the evaluated method gives the opportunity for future extensions and industrial applications. Currently, we are planning to extend the dataset by performing new acquisitions in real healthcare facilities under the supervision of nutritionists.

Acknowledgments. We acknowledge Laser Consortium (Monza) for supporting the acquisition of food images used in this work.

References

1. Diet, nutrition and the prevention of chronic diseases. Technical report. WHO Technical Report Series - 916, Report of a Joint WHO/FAO Expert Consultation, January 2002
2. Allegra, D., et al.: A multimedia database for automatic meal assessment systems. In: Battiato, S., Farinella, G.M., Leo, M., Gallo, G. (eds.) ICIAP 2017. LNCS, vol. 10590, pp. 471–478. Springer, Cham (2017). https://doi.org/10.1007/978-3-319-70742-6_46
3. Arab, L., Estrin, D., Kim, D.H., Burke, J., Goldman, J.: Feasibility testing of an automated image-capture method to aid dietary recall. Eur. J. Clin. Nutr. **65**, 1156–1162 (2011)
4. Bay, H., Tuytelaars, T., Van Gool, L.: SURF: speeded up robust features. In: Leonardis, A., Bischof, H., Pinz, A. (eds.) ECCV 2006. LNCS, vol. 3951, pp. 404–417. Springer, Heidelberg (2006). https://doi.org/10.1007/11744023_32
5. Bossard, L., Guillaumin, M., Van Gool, L.: Food-101 – mining discriminative components with random forests. In: Fleet, D., Pajdla, T., Schiele, B., Tuytelaars, T. (eds.) ECCV 2014. LNCS, vol. 8694, pp. 446–461. Springer, Cham (2014). https://doi.org/10.1007/978-3-319-10599-4_29
6. Chen, H.C., et al.: Model-based measurement of food portion size for image-based dietary assessment using 3D/2D registration. Meas. Sci. Technol. **24**(10), 105701 (2013)
7. Dehais, J., Anthimopoulos, M., Shevchik, S., Mougiakakou, S.: Two-view 3D reconstruction for food volume estimation. IEEE Trans. Multimed. **19**, 1090–1099 (2017)
8. Dehais, J., Shevchik, S., Diem, P., Mougiakakou, S.G.: Food volume computation for self dietary assessment applications. In: International Conference on Bioinformatics and Bioengineering, November 2013
9. Eigen, D., Puhrsch, C., Fergus, R.: Depth map prediction from a single image using a multi-scale deep network. In: Neural Information Processing Systems, vol. 3, pp. 2366–2374, January 2014
10. Elia, M., Stratton, R.J.: Geographical inequalities in nutrient status and risk of malnutrition among English people aged 65 y and older. Nutrition **21**(11), 1100–1106 (2005)
11. Farinella, G.M., Allegra, D., Moltisanti, M., Stanco, F., Battiato, S.: Retrieval and classification of food images. Comput. Biol. Med. **77**, 23–39 (2016)
12. Farinella, G.M., Allegra, D., Stanco, F.: A benchmark dataset to study the representation of food images. In: Agapito, L., Bronstein, M.M., Rother, C. (eds.) ECCV 2014. LNCS, vol. 8927, pp. 584–599. Springer, Cham (2015). https://doi.org/10.1007/978-3-319-16199-0_41
13. Farinella, G.M., Allegra, D., Stanco, F., Battiato, S.: On the exploitation of one class classification to distinguish food vs non-food images. In: Murino, V., Puppo, E., Sona, D., Cristani, M., Sansone, C. (eds.) ICIAP 2015. LNCS, vol. 9281, pp. 375–383. Springer, Cham (2015). https://doi.org/10.1007/978-3-319-23222-5_46
14. Herbrich, R., Graepel, T., Obermayer, K.: Large margin rank boundaries for ordinal regression. In: Bartlett, P.J., Schölkopf, B., Schuurmans, D., Smola, A.J. (eds.) Advances in Large Margin Classifiers, vol. 88, pp. 115–132. MIT Press, Cambridge (2000)
15. Howard, A.G., et al.: MobileNets: efficient convolutional neural networks for mobile vision applications. CoRR abs/1704.04861 (2017)

16. Kawano, Y., Yanai, K.: Automatic expansion of a food image dataset leveraging existing categories with domain adaptation. In: Agapito, L., Bronstein, M.M., Rother, C. (eds.) ECCV 2014. LNCS, vol. 8927, pp. 3–17. Springer, Cham (2015). https://doi.org/10.1007/978-3-319-16199-0_1

17. Li, H.: A short introduction to learning to rank. IEICE Trans. Inf. Syst. **94-D**, 1854–1862 (2011)

18. Lu, Y., Allegra, D., Anthimopoulos, M., Stanco, F., Farinella, G.M., Mougiakakou, S.: A multi-task learning approach for meal assessment. In: Joint Workshop on Multimedia for Cooking and Eating Activities and Multimedia Assisted Dietary Management, pp. 46–52 (2018)

19. Matsuda, Y., Hoashi, H., Yanai, K.: Recognition of multiple-food images by detecting candidate regions. In: International Conference on Multimedia and Expo, pp. 25–30, July 2012

20. O'Loughlin, G., et al.: Using a wearable camera to increase the accuracy of dietary analysis. Am. J. Prev. Med. **44**, 297–301 (2013)

21. Parikh, D., Grauman, K.: Relative attributes. In: International Conference on Computer Vision, pp. 503–510 (2011)

22. Pouladzadeh, P., Yassine, A., Shirmohammadi, S.: FooDD: food detection dataset for calorie measurement using food images. In: Murino, V., Puppo, E., Sona, D., Cristani, M., Sansone, C. (eds.) ICIAP 2015. LNCS, vol. 9281, pp. 441–448. Springer, Cham (2015). https://doi.org/10.1007/978-3-319-23222-5_54

23. Puri, M., Zhu, Z., Yu, Q., Divakaran, A., Sawhney, H.: Recognition and volume estimation of food intake using a mobile device. In: Workshop on Applications of Computer Vision, December 2009

24. Ragusa, F., Furnari, A., Farinella, G.M.: Understanding food images to recommend utensils during meals. In: Battiato, S., Farinella, G.M., Leo, M., Gallo, G. (eds.) ICIAP 2017. LNCS, vol. 10590, pp. 419–425. Springer, Cham (2017). https://doi.org/10.1007/978-3-319-70742-6_40

25. Rhyner, D., et al.: Carbohydrate estimation by a mobile phone-based system versus self-estimations of individuals with type 1 diabetes mellitus: a comparative study. J. Med. Internet Res. **18**, e101 (2016)

26. Suthumchai, N., Thongsukh, S., Yusuksataporn, P., Tangsripairoj, S.: FoodForCare: an Android application for self-care with healthy food. In: International Student Project Conference (ICT-ISPC), pp. 89–92, May 2016

27. Szegedy, C., et al.: Going deeper with convolutions. In: Computer Vision and Pattern Recognition, pp. 1–9, June 2015

28. Szegedy, C., Vanhoucke, V., Ioffe, S., Shlens, J., Wojna, Z.: Rethinking the inception architecture for computer vision. In: Computer Vision and Pattern Recognition, pp. 2818–2826 (2016)

29. Xin, W., Kumar, D., Thome, N., Cord, M., Precioso, F.: Recipe recognition with large multimodal food dataset. In: International Conference on Multimedia Expo Workshops, pp. 1–6, July 2015

30. Zhu, F., et al.: The use of mobile devices in aiding dietary assessment and evaluation. IEEE J. Sel. Top. Sig. Process. **4**, 756–766 (2010)

Analysis of Dynamic Brain Connectivity Through Geodesic Clustering

A. Yamin[1,2(✉)], M. Dayan[1,3], L. Squarcina[4], P. Brambilla[5],
V. Murino[1,6], V. Diwadkar[7], and D. Sona[1,8]

[1] Pattern Analysis and Computer Vision, Istituto Italiano di Tecnologia,
Genoa, Italy
{muhammad.yamin, diego.sona}@iit.it
[2] Department of Electrical, Electronics and Telecommunication Engineering
and Naval Architecture, Università degli Studi di Genova, Genoa, Italy
[3] Human Neuroscience Platform, Foundation Campus Biotech Geneva, Geneva,
Switzerland
[4] Scientific Institute IRCCS "E. Medea", Bosisio Parini, Italy
[5] Fondazione IRCCS Ca' Granda Ospedale Maggiore Policlinico,
Università di Milano, Milan, Italy
[6] Department of Computer Science, Università di Verona, Verona, Italy
[7] Department of Psychiatry and Behavioral Neuroscience,
Wayne State University, Detroit, USA
[8] Neuroinformatics Laboratory, Fondazione Bruno Kessler, Trento, Italy

Abstract. Analysis of dynamic functional connectivity allows for studying the time variant behavior of brain connectivity during specific tasks or at rest. There is, however, a debate around the significance of studies analyzing the dynamic connectivity, as it is usually estimated using short subsequences of the entire time-series. Therefore, a question that naturally arises is whether the dynamic connectivity information is robust enough to compare connectivity matrices. In this paper we investigate the importance of the choice of metric on the space of graphs to answer this question, using a dataset of twins under the assumption that twins connectivity is more similar than in any other pair of unrelated subjects. Specifically, the problem was formulated as a classification task between twin and non-twin pairs. The approach described in the paper relies on geodesic clustering of dynamic connectivity matrices to find a subset of brain states, which were then used to encode the pairwise connectivity similarities between subjects. Experiments were performed to compare the use of Euclidean distance in a vectorial space and a geodesic distance in the Riemannian space of symmetric positive definite matrices. We showed that the geodesic distance provided a better classification of twins subjects, suggesting this use of this distance can robustly compare dynamic connectivity matrices.

Keywords: Dynamic functional connectivity · Geodesic clustering ·
Connectomes · Task-based fMRI · SVM · Symmetric positive definite matrices

© Springer Nature Switzerland AG 2019
E. Ricci et al. (Eds.): ICIAP 2019, LNCS 11752, pp. 640–648, 2019.
https://doi.org/10.1007/978-3-030-30645-8_58

1 Introduction

Connectomics is a relatively recent field of research in neuroimaging, which allows neuroscientists to inspect the association between different regions in the brain. Analysis of functional connectivity (FC) using time series extracted from functional magnetic resonance imaging (fMRI) has allowed new advances in the understanding of the connectivity organization of the human brain. In recent decades, FC has been widely used to examine the functional organization of brain network in many psychiatric and neurodegenerative diseases. In most cases, FC is defined as temporal covariance or correlation of BOLD activity between different brain regions [1]. Dynamic functional connectivity (DFC) is a new approach allowing studying how brain connectivity is modulated in time. Analysis of DFC is usually based on the study of a time series of connectivity matrices obtained with a sliding window approach, in which the overall time-series signal is divided into overlapping segments, which are used to estimate the time-dependent correlation/covariance of brain activity [2, 3]. Recent studies suggest that uncontrolled but reoccurring patterns of brain connectivity among intrinsic network can be captured during task or rest by examining the dynamic behavior of FC [2, 4]

Many methods have been proposed to examine DFC. In [5, 6] authors proposed an approach based on singular value decomposition and dictionary learning to investigate the DFC patterns. In [5], estimation of eigen-connectivity and extraction of its temporal weights has been proposed. Clustering of DFC matrices with k-means and independent component analysis have been proposed in [2] suggesting that clusters are brain states representing specific patterns of brain connectivity. In [7], a framework similar to [2] using temporal independent component analysis (TICA) instead of clustering is proposed to compute the states, which are maximally mutually temporally independent. Moreover, as suggested by [8, 9] states can also be computed by clustering dynamically derived graph metrics or some higher-level information e.g. computing similarity vectors between different independent vector analysis (IVA) components [10] instead of DFC matrices.

Almost all MRI studies on DFC are based on resting state fMRI. In this paper, on the contrary, we have investigated task-based fMRI, which encourages the identification of integration mechanism between specific task-related brain regions and is useful to identify task-related networks in brain connectivity [11, 12]. Specifically, we used a task-based fMRI dataset acquired on twins [13], to investigate the effect of genetic heritability on the dynamics of functional brain networks. The main purpose of this study is to evaluate if there are DFC patterns shared among twins, allowing discriminating twin pairs from unrelated pairs. In our previous study [13], we have shown that differentiation between two groups was measurable when using the graph Laplacian representation of non-dynamic FC matrices, which transforms the representation of data into the smoothed space of positive semi-definite matrices [14]. A Fréchet metric on this space was then used to measure the similarity between networks [13]. In [15] we have further extended the use of graph Laplacian and Fréchet metric to classify between MZ & DZ twin pairs using DFC matrices. To this aim we computed the distance between each pair of DFC matrices and the vector representation of the sequence of distances was then used by a linear SVM for classification.

In this paper, we want to investigate the DFC analysis exploiting the concept of brain states. To perform this investigation, we exploited the similarity of DFC patterns associated with the brain states of the two groups (twins and non-twins). To this aim, we clustered the DFC matrices into reference states and then we used a compact representation to perform a classification.

Some recent approaches suggest similar FC analysis, e.g., in [16] SVMs were used to discriminate traumatic brain injury after encoding DFC with k-means clustering. Similarly, in [17] enhanced FC variability was used to classify autism spectrum disorder from healthy controls. All above methods, exploiting clustering to generate a set of reference states, are based on similarities computed in a vectorial space. Using metrics on the vectorial space – like the Euclidean distance frequently used in k-means – is sub-optimal [15]. We know however, that FC matrices can be managed to form a manifold of positive definite matrices, and a more appropriate choice of similarity is to use a geodesic metric defined on the smooth manifold. Therefore, in our approach we used a geodesic metric both to cluster the matrices with k-means and to extract the features to be used by the classifier.

We made some experiments both using the Euclidean metric in a vectorial space and a geodesic metric (Log Euclidean distance) on the Riemannian space of symmetric positive definite matrices. The results suggest that using a proper geodesic distance is much more valuable in describing the similarity between graphs, allowing a better clustering of graphs and, for our specific task, resulting in a much higher classification accuracy when compared to a method based on simple Euclidean distance.

In the following Sect. 2 we will describe the data and the processing methods used to estimate the DFC with graphical LASSO, to cluster the graphs using geodesic metric within k-means, and to encode the subject pairs building the features with the geodesic metric. In Sect. 3 we will provide the results of all experiments, and a brief discussion with some concluding remarks will be given in Sect. 4.

2 Materials and Methods

2.1 Data Acquisition and Pre-processing

A total of 26 subjects, corresponding to 13 twin pairs (7 monozygotic, 6 dizygotic,) were recruited from the population-based Italian Twin Registry. fMRI data was acquired on a 3-Tesla MR imaging unit Siemens Allegra system (Siemens, Erlangen, Germany) with a standard head coil. T2*-weighted images were acquired using a gradient-echo EPI-BOLD pulse sequence (TR: 2000 ms; TE: 30 ms; flip angle 75°; FOV: 92 × 192; 31 axial slices; thickness: 3 mm; in-plane: 3 mm^2; matrix: 64 × 64). High-resolution MPRAGE T1-weighted structural images were acquired in the same session (TR: 2300 ms; TE: 3.93 ms; flip angle 12°; FOV: 256 × 256; 160 axial slices; slice thickness: 1 mm; matrix 256 × 256). In our experiment, fMRI data were collected with right and left hand consecutively in two separate scans by using traditional Poffenberger paradigm [18], the task protocol was well synchronized for all subjects, allowing the comparison of BOLD signal across different subjects. fMRI pre-processing was done including realignment, time slice correction, motion correction and normalization. Mean time-series of each region, defined using the Automated Anatomical Labeling atlas [19] (90 ROI Cerebrum only), were then extracted from processed fMRI. For further details of the processing pipeline refers to [13].

2.2   Dynamic Functional Connectivity Estimation

Given N the number of regions in the atlas (in our case AAL is made by $N = 90$) we estimated the $N \times N$ covariance matrices $\sum_i(w)$, for all subject $i = 1 \ldots M$, (M is total number of subjects) and for all sliding windows $w = 1 \ldots W$ over the fMRI time-series (W is the total number of windows). In our experiments we used a sliding window of size $\Delta t = 30$ TR (60 s) and a step size of 4 TR (8 s) [14]. This resulted in $W = 83$ DFC matrices $\sum_i$ describing the modulation of connectivity along the entire recorded sequence. Due to the relatively small windows size, the estimation of the covariance matrices might be unstable and heavily affected by the limited amount of information. To overcome this issue a more robust estimate of the covariance with small data can be obtained from the estimate of a sparse version of the inverse of the covariance matrix $\sum_i^{-1}(w)$ [20–22]. This sparse precision matrix can be obtained regularizing the estimated parameters with the graphical LASSO as described in [23]. This method has proven to be very effective when there are limited number of observations at each node [2, 24], such as in our case where we have small intervals of fMRI scan.

The covariance matrices are always guaranteed to be symmetric positive semi-definite, however, in real applications they are frequently also symmetric positive definite (SPD). If some matrices are not SPD we can apply a small regularization ($\sum_i = \sum_i + \lambda I$) making them SPD. In this way they form a Riemannian manifold of SPD matrices [24] which enable us to analyze the DFC matrices on the manifold instead of using the vector space [13, 25]. To take full advantage of the manifold structure of SPD matrices, it is essential to consider a geodesic distance, which measure the shortest path between two points (two matrices in our case) along the smooth and curved manifold [13]. There are some possible alternative geodesic distances on the Riemannian manifold of SPD matrices [25, 26], we decided to adopt the Log-Euclidean distance, which is simple, and fast to compute:

$$d_L(\Sigma_i, \Sigma_j) = \| \log(\Sigma_i) - \log(\Sigma_j) \|, \tag{1}$$

where $\sum_i \sum_j$ are two DFC matrices.

As described in our previous work [13], there is no effect of task (left and right hand) between the two groups. So, for each subject we averaged the DFC matrices across tasks by using geodesic mean (see Eq. 2) [27] so that the geometric nature of matrices is maintained.

2.3 Dynamic States and Geodesic Clustering Analysis

In order to define a set of states describing intrinsic brain network patterns, we have used geodesic k-means clustering on SPD matrices [28] to associate a state to each cluster. To initialize the cluster centroids, we first selected a set of exemplar matrices [2] from the data (8 matrices per subject in our case) maximizing the distance from the rest of the exemplars of the same subject. The geodesic k-means was then applied on the set of exemplars to obtain the initial centroids, which were then refined running again the geodesic k-means on all DFC matrices of all subjects. In order to run the geodesic k-means, we used the Log-Euclidean distance [25] as defined in Eq. (1) for which the mean of multiple covariance matrices can be computed in a closed form:

$$\Sigma_L = \exp\{\arg\inf_\Sigma \sum_{i=1}^n \|\log \Sigma_i - \log \Sigma\|^2\} = \exp\left\{\frac{1}{n}\sum_{i=1}^n \log \Sigma_i\right\}, \tag{2}$$

In order to choose the optimal number K of clusters we used two criteria. The first criterion was based on the minimization of the Sum of Squared Error (SSE):

$$SSE = \sum_{i=1}^K \sum_{\Sigma \in C_i} d^2(m_i, \Sigma) \tag{3}$$

where Σ is a DFC matrix associated to cluster C_i and m_i is the corresponding centroid.

The second criterion was based on the necessity of having in any cluster some matrices for all subjects, due to the encoding framework explained below. We, therefore, computed the SSE by using Eq. (3) ranging over a number of clusters $(K = 2 \ldots 10)$. In our case the best solution fulfilling with the two criteria resulted to be with K = 2. This result also supports the hypothesis that in a task-based fMRI there appears at least two macro states, one is a task-related state and the second one is a no-task state.

2.4 Feature Extraction and Classification

The working hypothesis is that dynamic connectivity between twin pairs would be more similar than between un-related pairs, and based on this we can classify pairs either as twins or as unrelated. Therefore, we need to encode the subject's similarity taking into account the brain state. To this aim, subjects' representatives were computed for all clusters. More specifically, the subset of all DFC matrices of a subject associated to a cluster were averaged with a geodesic mean creating a subject representative for that cluster. In this way, a subject has a representative for each cluster.

At this point, we could compute the features characterizing the similarity between the subjects. For each pair of subjects we measured the inter-subject geodesic distance between the two subject representatives of each cluster. In addition, we computed the geodesic distance of each subject representative from the cluster centroids. Therefore, for each pair of subjects (twins or unrelated) there are 3 distances per cluster (features) and in our experiments the data representation included a total of 6 features because we have K = 2 clusters.

In our data set, we have 13 twin pairs, corresponding to 26 subjects that can be recombined to form 312 unrelated pairs. In short, we have a dataset composed of 13 samples from the twin's class and 312 samples from the unrelated class. Due to the high unbalanced dataset, we opted to use the weighted SVM [29] with three cross-fold validation. To this aim, we divided our data into 3 chunks randomly selecting the samples while maintaining the proportion between the classes (each fold was composed by 104 samples from the unrelated pairs and 4 from twin's pairs). For statistical purpose, we repeated 100 times this cross-validation procedure with the randomized selection of folds. We evaluated the results in terms of average accuracy, precision, recall, F1 score and confusion matrix.

In all our experiments, all distances between graphs and means of graphs were computed using the Log-Euclidean distance Eq. (1) and the corresponding geodesic mean Eq. (2) respectively. However, for the sake of comparison we performed identical experiments using the Euclidean distance and the corresponding Euclidian mean.

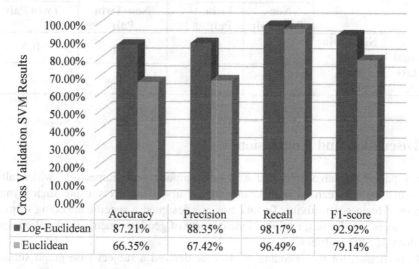

Fig. 1. Comparison of average performance of classification with weighted linear SVM classifier with Log-Euclidean distance (blue bars) and with Euclidean distance (orange bars). (Color figure online)

3   Results

Figure 1 shows the results of classification with the weighted SVM when using the Log-Euclidean distance (blue bars) and the Euclidean distance (red bars). It can be observed that using the geodesic metric to describe the data considerably boosts the performance during classification, i.e., during the exploitation of the encodings. In particular, the accuracy with "geodesic encoding", 87.21%, is much higher than the

"Euclidean encoding" accuracy, 66.35%. Similar differences can be observed for the precision (88.35% versus 67.42%) and F1 score (92.92% versus 79.14%). Higher and similar recall for both metrics could be due to the higher unbalance in the classes. The embed table in Fig. 1 summarizes these results.

The mean confusion matrix for both distance metrics is given in Table 1. It can be observed that when using geodesic distance during the data encoding the rate of correctly classified pairs is much better than using Euclidean distance. These results strongly support the fact that the use of Euclidean metric on symmetric positive definite matrices is suboptimal. Hence, a better way to compare and process the undirected weighted graphs described by SPD is to use a geodesic distance on the Riemannian space.

Table 1. Average confusion matrix showing the performance of classification when using the Log-Euclidean distance or the Euclidean distance

Log-Euclidean Distance Confusion Matrix				Euclidean Distance Confusion Matrix	
		Predicted Class		Predicted Class	
		Non-Twin Pair	Twin Pair	Non-Twin Pair	Twin Pair
Actual Class	Non-Twin Pair	275	37	210	102
	Twin Pair	4	9	8	5

4 Discussion and Conclusion

In this paper, we have presented a novel computational framework, which allows distinguishing between twins and unrelated pairs of subjects using their dynamic functional brain connectivity. To this aim, we designed a specific encoding of graphs into subjects' similarities, exploiting the concept of geodesic metric on the Riemannian manifold of SPD matrices.

In particular, for the encoding of data we derived a subject-wise graph similarity representation exploiting a geodesic k-means clustering. Indeed, the algorithm uses the Log-Euclidean metric on the space of functional brain graphs. Once the clusters were generated, the Log-Euclidean metric was also used to calculate the similarity of two subjects in terms of distance between subjects and distance from cluster centroid. These distances were used as features for the data representation. Due to the highly unbalanced dataset to solve the classification task we used the weighted SVM.

In order to evaluate whether, beyond having a good estimation of covariance matrices, it is important to use metrics working on the space of data, we made an identical experiment using the Euclidean distance in place of the geodesic distance. The results of our study clearly demonstrate that use of Euclidean distance is not the best choice, as it is not properly managing the complex structure of graphs, indeed the classification performance is boosted when using the geodesic distance.

This study also reveals that a careful encoding of the dynamic functional connectivity allows a clear distinction of twin pairs from non-twin pairs.

Acknowledgement. The authors acknowledge Cigdem Beyan and Muhammad Shahid for the helpful discussions.

References

1. Friston, K.J., Frith, C.D., Liddle, P.F., Frackowiak, R.S.J.: Functional connectivity: the principal-component analysis of large (PET) data sets. J. Cereb. Blood Flow Metab. **13**, 5 (1993). https://doi.org/10.1038/jcbfm.1993.4
2. Allen, E.A., Damaraju, E., Plis, S.M., Erhardt, E.B., Eichele, T., Calhoun, V.D.: Tracking whole-brain connectivity dynamics in the resting state. Cereb. Cortex **24**(3), 663–676 (2014)
3. Chang, C., Liu, Z., Chen, M.C., Liu, X., Duyn, J.H.: EEG correlates of time-varying BOLD functional connectivity. NeuroImage **72**(15), 227–236 (2013)
4. Sakoğlu, Ü., Pearlson, G.D., Kiehl, K.A., Wang, Y.M., Michael, A.M., Calhoun, V.D.: A method for evaluating dynamic functional network connectivity and task-modulation: application to schizophrenia. MAGMA **23**, 351–366 (2010). https://doi.org/10.1007/s10334-010-0197-8
5. Leonardi, N., et al.: Principal components of functional connectivity: a new approach to study dynamic brain connectivity during rest. NeuroImage **83**, 937–950 (2013)
6. Leonardi, N., Shirer, W., Greicius, M., Van De Ville, D.: Disentangling dynamic networks: separated and joint expressions of functional connectivity patterns in time. Hum. Brain Mapp. **35**(12), 5984–5995 (2014)
7. Yaesoubi, M., Miller, R.L., Calhoun, V.D.: Mutually temporally independent connectivity patterns: a new framework to study the dynamics of brain connectivity at rest with application to explain group difference based on gender. NeuroImage **107**, 85–94 (2015)
8. Li, X., et al.: Dynamic functional connectomics signatures for characterization and differentiation of PTSD patients. Hum. Brain Mapp. **35**, 1761–1778 (2014)
9. Chiang, S., et al.: Time-dependence of graph theory metrics in functional connectivity analysis. NeuroImage **125**, 601–615 (2016)
10. Ma, S., Calhoun, V.D., Phlypo, R., Adal, T.: Dynamic changes of spatial functional network connectivity in healthy individuals and schizophrenia patients using independent vector analysis. NeuroImage **90**, 196–206 (2014)
11. Varoquaux, G., Craddock, R.C.: Learning and comparing functional connectomes across subjects. NeuroImage **80**, 405–415 (2013)
12. Richiardi, J., Eryilmaz, H.I., Schwartz, S., Vuilleumier, P.: Decoding brain states from fMRI connectivity graphs. NeuroImage **56**(2), 616–626 (2011)
13. Yamin, A., et al.: Comparison of brain connectomes using geodesic distance on manifold: a twin's study. In: International Symposium on Biomedical Imaging 2019, Venice, 8–11 April 2019
14. Li, K., Guo, L., Nie, J., Li, G., Liu, T.: Review of methods for functional brain connectivity detection using fMRI. Comput. Med. Imaging Graph. **33**(2), 131–139 (2009)
15. Yamin, A., et al.: Investigating the impact of genetic background on brain dynamic functional connectivity through machine learning: a twins study. In: IEEE-EMBS International Conference on Biomedical and Health Informatics, Chicago, IL, USA, 19–22 May 2019

16. Victor, M.V., Andrew, R.M., Kent, A.K., Vince, D.C.: Dynamic functional network connectivity discriminates mild traumatic brain injury through machine learning. Neuroimage: Clin. **19**, 30–37 (2018)
17. Tejwani, R., Liska, A., You, H.: Autism Classification Using Brain Functional Connectivity Dynamics and Machine Learning (2019). https://arxiv.org/pdf/1712.08041.pdf
18. Poffenberger, A.T.: Reaction Time to Retinal Stimulation, with Special Reference to the Time Lost in Conduction Through Nerve Centers. The Science Press, New York (1912)
19. Tzourio-Mazoyer, N., et al.: Automated anatomical labeling of activations in SPM using a macroscopic anatomical parcellation of the MNI MRI single-subject brain. Neuroimage **15**, 273–289 (2002)
20. Marrelec, G., et al.: Partial correlation for functional brain interactivity investigation in functional MRI. Neuroimage **32**, 228–237 (2006)
21. Varoquaux, G., Gramfort, A., Poline, J.B., Thirion, B., Zemel, R, Shawe-Taylor, J.: Brain covariance selection: better individual functional connectivity models using population prior. In: Advances in Neural Information Processing Systems, Vancouver, Canada (2010)
22. Smith, S.M., et al.: Network modelling methods for FMRI. Neuroimage **54**, 875–891 (2011)
23. Friedman, J., Hastie, T., Tibshirani, R.: Sparse inverse covariance estimation with the graphical lasso. Biostatistics **9**(3), 432–441 (2008). https://doi.org/10.1093/biostatistics/kxm045
24. Rashid, B., Damaraju, E., Pearlson, G.D., Calhoun, V.D.: Dynamic connectivity states estimated from resting fMRI identify differences among Schizophrenia, bipolar disorder, and healthy control subjects. Front. Hum. Neurosci. **8**, 897 (2014). https://doi.org/10.3389/fnhum.2014.00897
25. Dodero, L., Minh, H.Q., Biagio, M.S., Murino, V., Sona, D.: Kernel-based classification for brain connectivity graphs on the Riemannian manifold of positive definite matrices. In: ISBI 2015, 16–19 April 2015
26. Dodero, L., Sambataro, F., Murino, V., Sona, D.: Kernel-based analysis of functional brain connectivity on Grassmann manifold. In: Navab, N., Hornegger, J., Wells, W., Frangi, A. (eds.) MICCAI 2015. LNCS, vol. 9351, pp. 604–611. Springer, Cham (2015). https://doi.org/10.1007/978-3-319-24574-4_72
27. Dryden, I.L., Koloydenko, A., Zhou, D.: Non-Euclidean statistics for covariance matrices, with applications to diffusion tensor imaging. Ann. Appl. Stat. **3**(3), 1102–1123 (2009)
28. Lee, H., Ahn, H.-J., Kim, K.-R., Kim, P., Koo, J.-Y.: Geodesic clustering for covariance matrices. Commun. Stat. Appl. Methods **22**, 321–331 (2015). https://doi.org/10.5351/CSAM.2015.22.4.321
29. Yang, X., Song, Q., Cao, A.: Weighted support vector machine for data classification. In: Proceedings of 2005 IEEE International Joint Conference on Neural Networks, Montreal, Quebec, vol. 2, pp. 859–864 (2005). https://doi.org/10.1109/IJCNN.2005.1555965

ActiVis: Mobile Object Detection and Active Guidance for People with Visual Impairments

J. C. Lock[1]([⊠]), A. G. Tramontano[2], S. Ghidoni[2], and N. Bellotto[1]

[1] School of Computer Science, University of Lincoln, Lincoln, UK
jaycee.lock@gmail.com
[2] Department of Information Engineering, University of Padova, Padua, Italy

Abstract. The ActiVis project aims to deliver a mobile system that is able to guide a person with visual impairments towards a target object or area in an unknown indoor environment. For this, it uses new developments in object detection, mobile computing, action generation and human-computer interfacing to interpret the user's surroundings and present effective guidance directions. Our approach to direction generation uses a Partially Observable Markov Decision Process (POMDP) to track the system's state and output the optimal location to be investigated. This system includes an object detector and an audio-based guidance interface to provide a complete active search pipeline. The ActiVis system was evaluated in a set of experiments showing better performance than a simpler unguided case.

Keywords: Active vision · Vision impairment · Object detection

1 Introduction

There are an estimated half a billion people that live with mild to severe vision impairment or total blindness and this number is expected to significantly rise with an ageing population [7]. There has been a rise interest from industrial partners in utilising modern technology to make their products more accessible, and improvements in modern computing power and image processing capabilities have made this easier. This work is part of the ActiVis[1] project, which aims to enable people with vision impairments to independently navigate and find objects within an unknown indoor environment using only a mobile phone and its camera. Our solution is inspired by active vision research [3], but it replaces the electro-mechanical servo typically found in active vision systems with a user's arm and hand, as pictured in Fig. 1. This paper expands upon concepts proposed in [4,14] and extends the concept presented in [15] with a fully working system.

ActiVis uses the camera's current and previous image data as input and leverages its understanding of inter-object spatial relationships to determine the

---

[1] http://lcas.github.io/ActiVis.

© Springer Nature Switzerland AG 2019
E. Ricci et al. (Eds.): ICIAP 2019, LNCS 11752, pp. 649–660, 2019.
https://doi.org/10.1007/978-3-030-30645-8_59

Fig. 1. The system in use during an experiment with a blindfolded participant.

best navigation action to find the target object. For this, we expanded upon our previous work and implemented a Partially Observable Markov Decision Process (POMDP) on a mobile phone that generates real-time navigation instructions for the user. The current paper includes the following main contributions:

- a new controller that enables object search and guidance on a mobile phone;
- a complete system pipeline that includes audio interface, object detection and human control;
- experiments that evaluate the efficacy of the proposed system.

Section 2 discusses relevant previous work, followed by a description of the active vision system and controller in Sect. 3. The experiments and their results are discussed in Sects. 4 and 5. The paper is concluded in Sect. 6.

2 Previous Work

Early attempts to solve this guidance problem used markers encoded with object or environmental information and a smartphone that scans the environment for these simple patterns [9,16]. The device uses audio feedback to read out the embedded information or guide the user towards the markers. While improvements to feature detectors have made it viable to replace markers with real objects [18], an alternative guidance approach is proposed in VizWiz [5] which uses a Mechanical Turk worker to manually locate and guide towards the desired object within a user-provided picture.

The issue with a marker-based approach is that it requires significant effort to place and maintain them in an environment, which is remedied by markerless systems. However, both of these methods use passive guidance approaches that rely on the user placing the desired marker/object within the camera's view by themselves before any guidance is provided. VizWiz [5] can leverage a human's understanding of the environment to guide a user to the correct location, but there is significant lag and a reliance on a good internet connection and remote worker being available. Previous work on the ActiVis system [15] addressed the

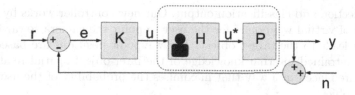

Fig. 2. The system control loop including a human and the controller.

passive guidance issue by implementing a Markov Decision Process (MDP) that gives the user pointing instructions to find an out-of-view object, showing that this is a viable method for object search. However, that work used QR-codes to simulate real objects and on-screen prompts to present the guidance instructions. In this paper we expand the control model, replacing the QR-codes with real objects and providing audio guidance, thereby implementing a complete object detection and guidance pipeline for people with vision impairments.

Object detectors can be broadly classified in two-stage models, which use an external algorithm to select regions of interest where to perform object inference [19], and single-stage models, which generate multiple windows of different sizes and checks each window for any objects. Between these two classes, there is a speed-accuracy trade-off, where the two-stage models typically produce more accurate results, but are slower and require more computing resources [12]. On the other hand, single-stage models, such as SSD and MobileNet [2,13], produce less accurate results but require significantly less parameters and FLOPS to perform object inference than the two-stage models.

3 Active Vision System

A complete system diagram for ActiVis is given in Fig. 2. This diagram shows a typical feedback control loop that generates a control signal to minimise some error signal, e, and drive the output to some reference, r. In our case, the system incorporates a human within the loop; r is the target object and y is the actual observation of the mobile device's camera.

Adding a human into the loop requires an additional block, H, representing a human that receives a control signal, u, from the controller, K. However, the challenge is that a person may interpret u in some unpredictable way, resulting in the signal u^* that points the camera, P, to a new object observation, y. It is therefore important to design K to be robust enough to accommodate different user habits and limitations, to ensure that u^* tracks u as closely as possible. The object detector's classification error, n, is added to the feedback loop as a noise signal that affects K's output.

In our previous work [15], we assumed a perfect object classifier and solved the problem using an MDP. In this paper we remove that assumption and replace the MDP with a POMDP-based controller that can handle uncertainties in the object detection and classification output. Our new controller works by generating a trail of virtual waypoints for the user to point the camera towards, which eventually leads to the target object. The waypoint positions are based on the model's pre-trained internal knowledge of the inter-object spatial relationships and they are placed in a way that maximises the probability of the user finding the target object.

3.1   Controller Design

A POMDP is an extension to a MDP that handles cases where the state is not directly observable, allowing it to be used in more realistic scenarios. The implication, however, is that a POMDP-based agent does not know its state at any point in time, but must infer it based on the known model parameters and sensor accuracy, which in our case is the object detector's accuracy. This state inference relies on a so-called *belief meta-state*, which is updated with additional observations to reflect the likelihood that the agent is in any given state. The belief state is fully observable by the agent and is used to infer the mobile device's current state and generate the next action.

A POMDP model is described by the 8-tuple $(\mathbf{S}, \mathbf{A}, \mathbf{T}, \mathbf{R}, \mathbf{\Omega}, \mathbf{O}, \mathbf{b}, \gamma)$, where $\mathbf{S}$ represents a finite set of discrete states, $\mathbf{A}$ is a set of discrete actions, $\mathbf{T}$ is a matrix containing the probabilities of transitioning from state s to state s' (where $s, s' \in \mathbf{S}$) after executing action a (where $a \in \mathbf{A}$), and $\mathbf{R}$ is the reward the agent receives for executing a and reaching s'. $\mathbf{\Omega}$ is the set of possible state observations, while the matrix $\mathbf{O}$ contains the probabilities of making observation $o \in \mathbf{\Omega}$ when in s after executing a. Finally, $\mathbf{b}$ is the belief vector containing the state probability distribution and γ is a discount factor that prioritises long-term over short-term rewards, which affects the model's convergence rate.

Parameters. The state is given by $s = \langle u, n, v \rangle$, where u is the object within view, n is the number of search steps taken during the search and v is a binary variable indicating whether a waypoint has been visited before. The possible actions that dictate the location where the mobile device will generate the next waypoint are given by $\mathbf{A} = \{\text{UP, DOWN, LEFT, RIGHT}\}$. $\mathbf{T}$ was determined by extracting the inter-object spatial relationships for a limited number of objects, in terms of the actions $\mathbf{A}$, from the OpenImages [10] dataset. For example, by iterating over the images containing the objects of interest, we can see that the object 'monitor' is located above (i.e. UP) the object 'keyboard' in 16% of the images containing both objects (see Fig. 3). The transition function for this case is $t(s, a, s') = t(\text{keyboard}, \text{UP}, \text{monitor}) = 0.16$.

The reward function encourages the device controller to search for the target object by giving a substantial reward if the object is found, while penalising the controller for every action that does not result in a successful object detection. Furthermore, additional penalties are given if the controller generates a waypoint in an area it has explored before ($v = \text{true}$) or when it exceeds some search-length threshold denoted by $n_{\max}$. The reward values were empirically

Fig. 3. Images from the OpenImage dataset [10] containing some typical objects.

determined starting from the implementation of our previous MDP model [15], the rewards of which are summarised in Table 1 together with the new ones. The penalty given for every waypoint generated that does not lead to the target was significantly increased for this model to offset the delay before large penalties are introduced and increase the model's urgency.

Table 1. The reward function for the POMDP.

Reward condition	POMDP	MDP [15]
$r(o = o_{target})$	10000	10000
$r(v = \text{true})$	-75	-10
$r(n > n_{\max})$	-75	-10
otherwise $r(\cdot)$	-100	-1

The state observations are identical to the states that the mobile device can enter into. In this case, however, uncertainty is introduced into the observation by the object detector. Instead, the previous search locations and search time are fully observable, since they can be tracked by the mobile device. **O** therefore only contains the classification/misclassification probabilities of the object detector. These values were found by performing a set of classification tests with the object detector and generating a confusion matrix to populate **O**.

Training. We encoded 15+1 objects into the current system, including a 'nothing' item in case the detector does not see anything of interest:

$$\mathbf{U} = \{nothing, monitor, keyboard, mouse, desk, laptop, mug, window,$$
$$lamp, backpack, chair, couch, plant, telephone, whiteboard, door\}.$$

We set $n_{\max}$ to 11 waypoints, after which the agent gets penalised for every additional waypoint it generates that does not lead to the target object. This results in a total of 352 reachable states ($n_{states} = 16 \times 11 \times 2$), with any state containing the target object acting as a terminal state.

The POMDP model is trained to generate a policy that contains the optimal belief-action mapping, which the controller can use to produce the optimal waypoint locations. This is done by the model exploring the entire state-action-observation space and optimising the policy to maximise its long-term cumulative reward. However, **b** is a vector of continuous probability distributions with infinite combinations, making POMDPs time-consuming or even impossible to solve exactly. This was the case for our moderately-sized state space, so we opted for an approximate method instead, using the Point-Based Value Iteration (PBVI) algorithm [17] implemented in the AI-Toolbox library[2]. The PBVI algorithm speeds up the training process by selecting a smaller subset of representative belief points from **b** and tracking these points only. Using the PBVI algorithm, we generated a total of 15 policies, one for each target object.

3.2 Guidance System Implementation

We implemented the object detector and the POMDP controller in an Android app and combined it with an audio interface that provides non-visual guidance instructions. We use non-intrusive bone-conducting headphones to transmit the audio signals to the user without blocking other ambient sounds. The app runs in real-time on an Asus ZenPhone AR with Android 7.0 and ARCore[3] enabled.

Audio Interface. To describe the waypoints' pan and tilt positions, we implemented an improved version of the interface described in [4] that uses a spatialised audio signal. However, since our headphones bypass the ear's pinnae that allow a person to localise the height [20], we spatialise the audio in the pan dimension only. To convey the tilt angle, we instead exploit a human's natural association of high and low sound sources with a high and low sound frequency, respectively [6], and adjust the sound source's pitch accordingly. A similar approach was used in [22].

Object Detector. To recognise objects we used SSD-Lite, which is a single-stage object detection and classification network based on the SSD architecture that implements MobileNetV2 [21]. This is a lightweight model that requires relatively little memory to perform inference tasks, making it suitable for mobile platforms. This model achieves a mean average precision (mAP) of 0.22 with 4.3M parameters and 0.8B FLOPS on the COCO dataset [11]. The full SSD model achieves a slightly higher mAP (0.25), but with significantly more parameters (34.3M) and FLOPS (34.36B).

The network was trained with a maximum of 10,000 object samples for each class in **U**, taken from the OpenImages dataset [10], with a 60-20-20% split

---

[2] http://github.com/Svalorzen/AI-Toolbox.

[3] http://developers.google.com/ar/.

for training, validation and testing respectively. We set a relatively high confidence threshold of 0.7 to reduce the likelihood of false-positives. Training for 120 epochs, with 1000 iterations each, we achieved a mAP of 0.16 on this dataset and produced a TensorFlow Lite model that is Android-compatible. We used this model to finally implement our SSD-Lite object detector on the mobile device.

Waypoint Generation. To search the target object, the system uses the policy file from the POMDP training process, which defines the best location of next waypoint based on the device's current state. This state is tracked by the device throughout the app's runtime by performing object detection and recording the previous search locations and waypoint positions. The latter are obtained by discretising the world into a 6×6 grid, where each cell represents a $35°$ rotation, and setting the relevant grid unit's v value when visited. This setup gives the state access to perfectly observable n and v parameters, while the observation u is generated by the object detector. When the device makes a new observation, either because the user rotates the device past $35°$ or sees a new object, the device triggers the controller to generate a new waypoint location. The controller uses o to update b and queries the policy for the best location to place the new waypoint. The policy output is an action from $\mathbf{A}$ that indicates the next adjacent grid square to place the waypoint, e.g. an 'UP' output would result in a waypoint being placed one grid square above the current view.

4   Experiment Design

To evaluate the guidance system's effectiveness, we designed a set of experiments to measure its performance in driving a user towards a target object within a static environment. We conducted an additional set of experiments with an alternative system that relies on a user's intuition and prior knowledge to generate actions instead, to act as a baseline measurement for our system's results.

Both experiment environments and the object placements within them were modelled on a typical office and care was taken to ensure that both environments were unique in layout and object placement, though some cross-experiment occurrences appear with the larger, more static objects (e.g. door, desk). Also, to minimise any cross-experiment learning effects, two different sets of objects were used for each experiment. If any (medium-small) objects occurred in both experiments, they were placed at different positions. In particular, the objects in the guided case experiment are $\mathbf{U}_g = \{door, desk, chair, whiteboard, mouse, laptop, backpack, mug\}$, while the objects in the unguided case are $\mathbf{U}_{ug} = \{door, desk, chair, whiteboard, mouse, monitor, telephone, keyboard\}$.

We recruited 10 participants (8 male, 2 female; average age 29.2 years) for the experiments, including 2 legally blind participants. The other 8 participants were blindfolded. A time limit of 45 s was set for each experiment run, which ended either by finding the target object or reaching the time limit. There was one experiment run per target in each respective environment, giving 8 experiment runs for each the of guided and unguided cases.

4.1   Unguided Case

For this experiment, the mobile camera and object detector acts as the participants' eyes and informs them about the objects within the camera's view. It is then up to the participant to exploit their prior knowledge and intuition to manipulate the camera and find the target object. In this case, the human acts as both the controller and the actuator. Similar to other commercially available applications, such as SeeingAI[4] and TapTapSee[5], the unguided version of our app only reads out the objects upon the user's request by tapping on the screen. When the target object comes within the camera's view and is correctly detected, the device vibrates to inform the participant.

4.2   Guided Case

In this experiment, we evaluate the performance of the guidance system in an object search task, where the perception and control tasks are performed by the guidance system and the participant acts as the actuator, interpreting control signals and outputting actuation forces on the camera sensor (see Fig. 2). To reduce the possibility of the participants ignoring the guidance instructions to find the target object by themselves, they were not told which objects they were actually looking for. This also helped to focus on the performance measurement of the guidance system only, isolating it from external factors such as user common-sense or other biases. A new run then started with the experiment staff selecting the (unknown) target object for the user.

5   Results

5.1   Target Acquisition

As in [15], we use the target acquisition rate (TAR) to compute the proportion of objects that the participants found during an experiment. For example, a TAR of 0.5 indicates that a participant found the target object in 50% of the searches. Taking each participant's TAR as a datum, the unguided case produced a higher average TAR (0.54 vs. 0.46), meaning that the participants found 8% more objects without guidance instructions. However, the Kruskal-Wallis (KW) test for non-normal data shows that statistically there is no significant difference between these results ($p_{kw} = 0.16$), meaning we cannot conclude which experiment produced the best TAR. All the experiment results are summarised in Table 2.

---

[4] http://www.microsoft.com/en-us/ai/seeing-ai.
[5] http://taptapseeapp.com.

5.2   Time to Target

The time it takes to find a target object is an important indicator of system performance, where less time indicates a shorter search time and increased performance. The data for the search times in the guided and unguided experiments are shown in Fig. 4. It can be seen that the guidance system reduced the overall time to find each target object. This is confirmed by the data that show an average search time of 12.5 s for the guided experiment and 17.2 s for the unguided case ($p_{kw} = 0.045$), an improvement of around 27%. These results compare also favourably with those obtained in our previous version of the system [15], where an average time-to-target of 34 s was recorded. However, it should be noted that the system implementation and experimental design in the current paper are significantly different from our previous work, so this comparison is interesting but not indicative of any major improvement.

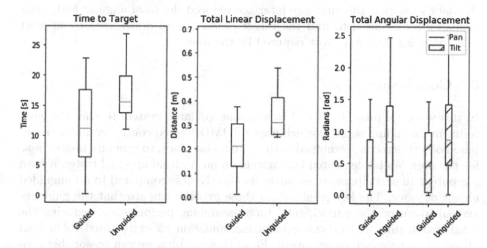

Fig. 4. A set of boxplots comparing the total linear and angular displacements, as well as the time to target for each experiment.

Table 2. A summary of the experiment results.

	Guided	Unguided	KW statistic
TAR [%]	46 ± 13	54 ± 15	0.16
Time to target [s]	12.5 ± 11.9	17.2 ± 11.5	0.045
Pan angle displacement [rad]	0.68 ± 1.1	0.99 ± 1.2	0.029
Tilt angle displacement [rad]	0.68 ± 1.1	1.04 ± 1.2	0.011
Linear displacement [rad]	0.23 ± 0.22	0.36 ± 0.22	0.012

5.3 Movement

Finally, to give an indication of the effort required to find each target, we look at the mobile device's displacement data. In this case, less device displacement is desirable, since it implies less physical exertion was demanded from the user. The device displacement was measured in both linear (x, y, z) and angular (pan, tilt) dimensions. Integrating these data, we obtain the total absolute displacement in each dimension. These results are plotted in Fig. 4.

The boxplots for the total angular displacement show a consistent reduction in radians in the guided case for both the pan (0.68 rad vs. 0.99 rad, $p_{kw} = 0.029$) and tilt dimensions (0.68 rad vs. 1.05 rad, $p_{kw} = 0.011$). The guidance system therefore reduces the total angular displacement to find the objects by 31% and 35% for the pan and tilt dimensions, respectively. The total linear displacement is also reduced when using the guidance interface by approximately 36% (0.23 m vs. 0.36 m, $p_{kw} = 0.012$). These results are summarised in Table 2. To conclude, the data show that the guidance interface reduced the total angular and linear displacement required to find the target objects in all dimensions by at least 31%, reducing the total effort required by the user.

6 Conclusion

In this work, we presented ActiVis, a mobile guidance system to scan the environment for finding objects, which uses a POMDP-based controller and a vision-based object detector, combined with an audio interface, to generate instructions for the user. We implemented this system on an Android app and tested it with a group of 10 participants to evaluate its effectiveness compared to an unguided object detector. The key results from these experiments are that the guidance system improved the participants' target-searching performance, reducing the total search time and overall camera manipulation effort required to find an object in an unknown environment. From these results, we can reasonably conclude that our new active search approach is potentially useful for similar mobile applications to help people with visual impairments.

The system can benefit from future work that focuses on improving the flexibility and usability of the system. New datasets that include the 3D positions of the objects and camera, similar to what has been done in robotics [1] but with a more diverse set of real scenes, would make it possible to train our model with more accurate transition and observation models and possibly extend it to be able to cope with depth. The usability of the system can potentially be improved with a more sophisticated audio interface and adding adaptive control algorithms that change the interface's behaviour based on the user performance over time [8].

Acknowledgements. This research is partly supported by a Google Faculty Research Award. We would like to thank the Voluntary Centre Services UK for their help in facilitating the experiments with people with limited vision.

References

1. Ammirato, P., Poirson, P., Park, E., Kosecka, J., Berg, A.C.: A dataset for developing and benchmarking active vision. In: Proceedings of ICRA. IEEE (2017)
2. Howard, A.G., et al.: MobileNets: efficient convolutional neural networks for mobile vision applications. CoRR (2017)
3. Bajcsy, R., Aloimonos, Y., Tsotsos, J.K.: Revisiting active perception. Auton. Robots **42**, 1–20 (2017)
4. Bellotto, N.: A multimodal smartphone interface for active perception by visually impaired. In: SMC International Workshop on Human Machine Systems, Cyborgs and Enhancing Devices. IEEE (2013)
5. Bigham, J.P., Jayant, C., Miller, A., White, B., Yeh, T.: VizWiz:: LocateIt - enabling blind people to locate objects in their environment. In: Proceedings of CVPR Workshops, pp. 65–72. IEEE (2010)
6. Blauert, J.: Spatial Hearing: The Psychophysics of Human Sound Localization. MIT Press, Cambridge (1997)
7. Bourne, R.R., et al.: Magnitude, temporal trends, and projections of the global prevalence of blindness and distance and near vision impairment: a systematic review and meta-analysis. Lancet Global Health **5**, 888–897 (2017)
8. Gallina, P., Bellotto, N., Di Luca, M.: Progressive co-adaptation in human-machine interaction. In: International Conference on Informatics in Control, pp. 2362–2368 (2015)
9. Gude, R., Østerby, M., Soltveit, S.: Blind navigation and object recognition. Laboratory for Computational Stochastics, University of Aarhus, Denmark (2013)
10. Kuznetsova, A., et al.: The Open Images Dataset V4: unified image classification, object detection, and visual relationship detection at scale. CoRR (2018)
11. Li, Y., Li, J., Lin, W., Li, J.: Tiny-DSOD: lightweight object detection for resource-restricted usages. In: Proceedings of BMVC (2018)
12. Liu, L., et al.: Deep learning for generic object detection: a survey. CoRR (2018)
13. Liu, W., et al.: SSD: single shot multibox detector. In: Leibe, B., Matas, J., Sebe, N., Welling, M. (eds.) ECCV 2016. LNCS, vol. 9905, pp. 21–37. Springer, Cham (2016). https://doi.org/10.1007/978-3-319-46448-0_2
14. Lock, J.C., Cielniak, G., Bellotto, N.: Portable navigations system with adaptive multimodal interface for the blind. In: AAAI Spring Symposium - Designing the User Experience of Machine Learning Systems (2017)
15. Lock, J.C., Cielniak, G., Bellotto, N.: Active object search with a mobile device for people with visual impairments. In: Proceedings of the 14th International Joint Conference on Computer Vision Theory and Applications, pp. 476–485 (2019)
16. Manduchi, R.: Mobile vision as assistive technology for the blind: an experimental study. In: Miesenberger, K., Karshmer, A., Penaz, P., Zagler, W. (eds.) ICCHP 2012. LNCS, vol. 7383, pp. 9–16. Springer, Heidelberg (2012). https://doi.org/10.1007/978-3-642-31534-3_2
17. Pineau, J., Gordon, G., Thrun, S., et al.: Point-based value iteration: an anytime algorithm for POMDPs. In: International Joint Conference on Artificial Intelligence Organization, pp. 1025–1032 (2003)
18. Redmon, J., Divvala, S., Girshick, R., Farhadi, A.: You only look once: unified, real-time object detection. In: Proceedings of CVPR, pp. 779–788. IEEE (2016)
19. Ren, S., He, K., Girshick, R.B., Sun, J.: Faster R-CNN: towards real-time object detection with region proposal networks. Trans. Pattern Anal. Mach. Intell. **39**, 1137–1149 (2015)

20. Roffler, S.K., Butler, R.A.: Factors that influence the localization of soundin the vertical plane. J. Acoust. Soc. Am. **43**, 1255–1259 (1968)
21. Sandler, M.B., Howard, A.G., Zhu, M., Zhmoginov, A., Chen, L.C.: MobileNetV2: inverted residuals and linear bottlenecks. In: Proceedings of CVPR, pp. 4510–4520 (2018)
22. Schauerte, B., Martinez, M., Constantinescu, A., Stiefelhagen, R.: An assistive vision system for the blind that helps find lost things. In: Miesenberger, K., Karshmer, A., Penaz, P., Zagler, W. (eds.) ICCHP 2012. LNCS, vol. 7383, pp. 566–572. Springer, Heidelberg (2012). https://doi.org/10.1007/978-3-642-31534-3_83

3TP-CNN: Radiomics and Deep Learning for Lesions Classification in DCE-MRI

Michela Gravina, Stefano Marrone[✉], Gabriele Piantadosi, Mario Sansone, and Carlo Sansone

DIETI - University of Naples Federico II, Naples, Italy
mi.gravina@studenti.unina.it
{stefano.marrone,gabriele.piantadosi,mario.sansone,
carlo.sansone}@unina.it

Abstract. Dynamic Contrast Enhanced-Magnetic Resonance Imaging (DCE-MRI) is a diagnostic method for the detection and diagnosis of breast cancer. Requiring the acquisition of images before and after the injection of a paramagnetic contrast agent, it provides a large amount of data that can hardly be analyzed without the use of a Computer Aided Diagnosis (CAD) system, whose aim is to support radiologists in the interpretation of medical images. Among the major issues in developing a CAD for the breast DCE-MRI there is the lesion diagnosis, namely the classification of lesioned tissues according to the tumour aggressiveness. Several studies have been conducted so far to explore the applicability of Deep Learning (DL) approaches to the automatic breast lesions classification. However, we argue that solutions only relying on DL are not so effective since past learned experience in the radiomics field should also be kept in mind to better exploit the dynamics of contrast agent and its effect on the acquired images. To this aim, we propose an approach that exploits the well-known Three Time Points (3TP) idea to select the specific time points that best highlight the tissues under analysis. Our findings show that promising results can then be obtained by using transfer learning, resulting in an approach that is able to outperform both the classical (non-deep) and some very recent deep proposals.

Keywords: Deep learning · CNN · 3TP · DCE-MRI · Breast · Cancer · Lesion classification

1 Introduction

The breast cancer worldwide number of cases has significantly increased since the 1970s. This phenomenon is partly due to modern lifestyles, with recent studies showing that tumours are mostly an environmental rather than a genetic disease, being the results of factors like pollution, smoking, nutrition, radiation, stress, and traumas. Tumours grow and expand without evident signs, coming out with symptoms only at an advanced stage of the disease. For this reason, early detection is the key factor to improve breast neoplasm prognosis.

© Springer Nature Switzerland AG 2019
E. Ricci et al. (Eds.): ICIAP 2019, LNCS 11752, pp. 661–671, 2019.
https://doi.org/10.1007/978-3-030-30645-8_60

In recent years, Dynamic Contrast Enhanced-Magnetic Resonance Imaging (DCE-MRI) has demonstrated great potential in screening different tumours tissues, gaining increasing popularity as an important complementary diagnostic methodology for early detection of breast cancer [9]. It involves the intravenous injection of a contrast agent (CA) in order to highlight both the physiological and morphological characteristics of the tissue. The contrast agent is a paramagnetic or super-paramagnetic substance (such as Gadolinium-based), characterized by a specific absorption time that, spreading with different speed in function of the tissue vascularization, allows to highlight the damaged tissues with respect to the surrounding healthy ones.

A DCE-MRI study consists of MRI images taken before (pre-contrast series) and after (post-contrast series) the intravenous injection of the contrast agent, involving the acquisition of 3D volumes at different times, thus resulting in a 4D volume (Fig. 1a) with 3 spatial dimensions (x, y, z) and one temporal dimension. Each DCE-MRI voxel (a pixel in three-dimensional space) is associated with a Time Intensity Curve (TIC) which reflects the absorption and the release of the contrast agent (Fig. 1b), following the vascularisation characteristics of the tissue under analysis [14].

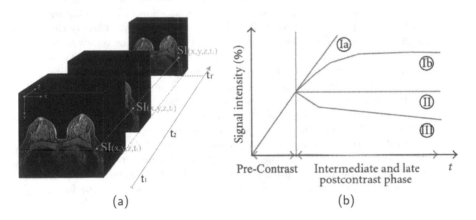

(a)   (b)

Fig. 1. DCE-MRI and Time Intensity Curves. (a) A representation of the four dimensions (3 spatial + 1 temporal) of a typical breast DCE-MRI scan; (b) some examples of Time Intensity Curves: *Type I* corresponds to a straight (Ia) or curved (Ib) line where the contrast absorption continues over the entire dynamic study (typical of healthy tissues or benign neoplasms); *Type II* represents a plateau curve with a sharp bend after the initial upstroke (typical of probably malignant lesions); finally, *Type III* shows a washout time course (typical of malignant lesions).

Although a visual assessment of the lesion malignity could be performed by analyzing the TIC, lesion diagnosis is a hard and time-consuming task because (i) real curves are much noisier than the illustrative ones and (ii) the involved amount of data is so huge that it can hardly be inspected without the use of a Computer Aided Detection/Diagnosis (CAD) system. Focusing on the automatic

CAD system, lesion diagnosis can be considered as the binary classification task of distinguishing between benign and malignant tumours.

Performing lesion diagnosis by means of a classifier model requires to extract the features that best suite the task and, to this aim, newer hand-crafted features are continuously proposed by domain experts. In the last years, Deep Learning (DL) based approaches have gained popularity in many pattern recognition tasks, with Convolutional Neural Networks (CNNs) - artificial neural networks consisting in different convolutional layers stacked to form a deep architecture able to automatically learn a compact hierarchical representation of the input - performing particularly well on images. Although this characteristic suggests exploring CNNs also for biomedical images processing, accordingly to the radiomics point of view (medical images are more than pictures [5]) *our idea is that the underlying physiological characteristics of DCE-MR images should also be taken into account in order to effectively exploit all the available information.*

In 1997 the study conducted by Degani [2] proved that it is possible to effectively analyze DCE-MRI data considering only volumes at very specific time points (3TP method), bringing a huge contribution to the research in the radiomics field. Despite this, literature works do not seem to consider this methodology, with authors mostly using deep learning approaches to extract the features that best contribute to task solution.

In this work, *we want to join the radiomics methodology and CNNs*, in order to exploit the medical experience and the deep learning capabilities for the automatic breast lesion classification task in DCE-MRI. To this aim *we propose 3TP-CNN, a methodology that guides the choice of DCE-MRI volume to feed to CNNs,* exploring, as a case of study, the breast DCE-MRI. Finally, since the amount of available training data is usually small, we propose to fine-tune a pre-trained CNN after a replication-based data augmentation stage that demonstrated to be effective when dealing with biomedical images.

The rest of the paper is organized as follows: Sect. 2 introduces the proposed approach, the dataset used and the experimental setup; Sect. 3 reports the obtained results, comparing them with those obtained by some competitors; finally, Sect. 4, discusses those results and provides some conclusions.

2   3TP-CNN for Lesions Diagnosis

Lesion diagnosis consists in classifying Regions of Interest (ROIs) according to the aggressiveness of the included tumour. The task can be addressed as the binary classification problem of distinguishing between malignant and benign lesions. To this aim, most literature proposals rely on hand-crafted features to describe ROI characteristics such as the TIC behaviour (**Dynamics Features**), the lesion's texture (**Textural Features**) or shape (**Morphological features**), etc. The works so far proposed mostly exploit the DCE-MRI volumes in three way: by using all the available time series [11], by searching the best combination of acquisitions [6] or by arbitrarily fixing one of them [1]. Although all these approaches show interesting performances, the main limitation is that their applicability is strongly affected by the dataset characteristics.

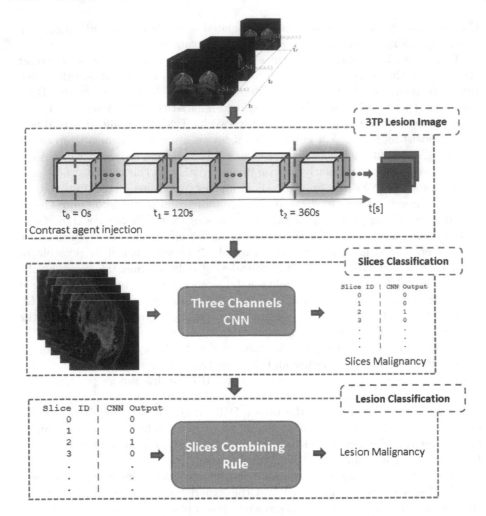

Fig. 2. The proposed 3TP-CNN classification schema: the first block shows the 3TP lesions image extraction step generating a 3-channels images for each lesion by considering the time points suggested in [2]; in the second block, each slice is classified separately; finally, in the third block, a unique label for each lesion is computed by combining the results of all its slices.

To overcome this limitation, in this paper we propose to exploits the well-known Three Time Points (3TP) [2] approach to select the specific time points that best highlight the contrast agent absorption and then fine-tune a pre-trained CNN for the actual slice-by-slice classification. In particular, we propose to extract slices along the projection having the higher resolution, considering the different acquisitions of the same slice along time as different channels within the same image that we will feed to the CNN. This allows to perform the classification on images always related to the same physiological characteristics of the tissues under analysis, making our approach independent from the acquisition protocol. To the best of our knowledge, this is the first work that exploits the 3TP-method for lesion diagnosis in DCE-MRI. The proposed approach consists in three main steps (Fig. 2):

- **3TP Lesion Image** extraction, in which for each slice containing a lesion, a 3-channels image is created by stacking the three instances acquired at the three time points suggested by Degani et al. [2]
- **Slice Classification**, during which each slice is classified as malignant or benign
- **Lesion Classification**, in which each lesion is classified by combining results of all its slices, producing a unique label for each lesion

2.1 3TP Lesion Image Extraction

As aforementioned in Sect. 1, a DCE-MRI is a 4D volume having 3 spatial dimensions and a temporal one that represents the acquisition of 3D volumes over time. Starting from it, we propose to extract 3TP images by cutting the sequence of 3D volumes along the axis having the highest resolution. This process generates a set of 3D volumes, each representing the same section (slice) of the tissue seen at different temporal instants. These volumes are extracted only for slices containing a lesion. This is made possible by the lesion segmentation module (one of the stages of a typical CAD system [12]) that localizes the lesion by identifying the Region of Interest (ROI), namely a binary mask that bounds the portion of the tissue within the lesion is.

Each 3D volume can be interpreted as a multi-channel image (since made of slices referring to the very same portion of the tissue) whose number of channels depends on the temporal instants considered during the extraction procedure. In this work we propose to fix the considered number of temporal instant by taking into account the 3TP method proposed by Degani [2], according to which the lesion classification can be improved by taking contrast enhanced images (DCE-MRI) at three time points identified by the time (in seconds) passed after the contrast agent injection. Only three time points are taken into account: a pre-contrast one (t_0), one 2 min after the contrast agent injection $(t_1$, corresponding to the pick of contrast agent levels in tissues) and one 6 min after contrast agent injection $(t_2$, corresponding to the end of the CA washout). For each slice, the resulting 3TP image is a 3-channel image composed of the same slice extracted by the tree volumes acquired at the time instance nearest to t_0, t_1 and t_2 (firt block of Fig. 2).

The obtained images are further pre-processed by extracting only the portion of the data within a squared box centered in the lesion centre and having size 1.5 times the maximum diameter of the lesion itself. Image values are then normalized between 0 and 1, ensuring that, in the next stage, the CNN operates on images having the same scale across different lesions. Finally, all the images are resized to match the input layer size for the used CNN.

2.2 Slices Classification

In order to assess the malignancy of each 3TP image, we propose to fine-tune a CNN pre-trained on ImageNet [3]. It is worth noticing that we do not fix any CNN, as long as it has a 3-channels input layer. We propose to exploit fine-tuning since biomedical images datasets do not usually gather a proper amount of data to effectively train a big CNN from scratch.

Despite the use of fine-tuning, the training procedure could still not be able to properly learn images characteristics since the images could not be enough even for a fine-tuning and because classes are usually very unbalanced. The small size is mostly due to the small number of patients involved in DCE-MRI programs, while the dataset unbalance is because the sizes of malignant and benign lesions are usually very different, resulting in different number of slices per lesion type.

As a consequence, both a data augmentation and a balancing phase are needed. In this work, two variants of data augmentation are explored. The first consists in the application of random rotation and flipping, while the second simply consists in replicating the data (slice replication). In both variants, the dataset is balanced by replicating some randomly chosen slices belonging to the minority class.

2.3 Lesion Classification

At the end of the previous stage, each lesion is associated with a probability of being a malignant or a benign one. However, since the final aim of the work is to classify each lesion, as a final step we combine the classes of all the slices from a given lesion into a single class. In this work, among all the possible combining strategies (CS) we considered:

- **Majority voting (MV)**, in which the class of the lesion is the most common class over all its slices
- **Weighted Majority(WMV)**, that acts as MV, but in which each slice contribution is weighted by its probability
- **Biggest Slice(BS)**, in which the lesion is associated with the class of the slice containing the biggest portion of the lesion

2.4 Experimental Setup

The proposed approach is general and can be applied to the classification of lesions of different organs and by using different DCE-MRI protocols. The same goes for the CNN used for the slice classification and on the other hyperparameters. The experiments have been carried out using Pytorch, evaluating the code on a physical server hosted in our university HPC center[1] equipped with 2 × Intel(R) Xeon(R) Intel(R) 2.13 GHz CPUs (4 cores), 32 GB RAM and an Nvidia Titan XP GPU (Pascal family) with 12 GB GRAM. Slice extraction step and non-deep competitors approaches (Sect. 2.4) have been implemented in MAT-LAB.

---

[1] http://www.scope.unina.it.

Dataset. In this work, we will focus on the breast lesion diagnosis. The dataset is constituted of 39 women breast DCE-MRI (average age 50 years, in range 31–74) with benign or malignant lesions histopathologically proven: 36 lesions were malignant and 22 were benign. All patients underwent imaging with a 1.6 T scanner (SymphonyTim, Siemens Medical System, Erlangen, Germany) equipped with breast coil. DCE T1-weighted FLASH 3D axial fat-saturated images were acquired (TR/TE: 5.08/2.39 ms; flip angle: 15°; matrix: 384×384; thickness: 1.6 mm; acquisition time: 110 s; 128 slices spanning entire breast volume). One series (t_0) was acquired before and 8 series (t_1–t_8) after intravenous injection of a positive paramagnetic contrast agent (gadolinium-diethylene-triamine penta-acetic acid, Gd-DOTA, Dotarem, Guerbet, Roissy CdG Cedex, France).

An experienced radiologist delineated suspect ROIs using original and *subtractive* image series, defined by subtracting t_0 series from the t_1 series. The manual segmentation stage was performed in Osirix [13], that allows the user to define ROIs at a sub-pixel level.

Related Works. In this work, we consider two classical (non-deep) and two deep learning based works proposed in the literature to compare with the performance of our approach. Fusco et al. [4] propose to use both Dynamic and Morphological features, combining them by using a Multiple Classifier System, in order to take into account the contrast agent concentration and the lesion shape. Piantadosi et al. [11] propose to use Local Binary Patterns on Three Orthogonal Planes (LBP-TOP) descriptor to provide a set of feature by thresholding the neighbourhood of each pixel and considers the result as a binary number. As threshold, the luminance value of the pixel in the centre of the neighbourhood is considered. In [1], Antropova et al. explore the use of a CNN (AlexNet, pre-trained on ImageNet) as feature extractor and then use an SVM for the actual classification. To match the 3-channels input layer, the authors propose to replicate slices extracted from the second post-contrast series. Finally, Haarburger et al. [6] proposed the fine-tuning of a ResNet34 [7] CNN. To match the 3-channels input layer, the authors propose to perform a grid-search among all the possible combinations of time series.

3 Results

The protocol considered in this work has the axial slice as the one having the higher resolution, therefore we extracted the 3TP images along this plane. Performance is evaluated using a 10-fold cross-validation. Since the classification stage is performed slice-by-slice, it is very important to perform a patient-based instead of a slice-based cross-validation, in order to reliably compare different models by avoiding mixing intra-patient slices in the evaluation phase. Slices were replicated three times (obtaining a training dataset 3 times bigger than the original one). As CNN we used AlexNet [8] since in our previous investigations [10] it has shown the best trade-off between classification performance and training time. Performances are evaluated in terms of Accuracy (ACC), Sensitivity (SEN), Specificity (SPE), F1-Score (F1) and Area under ROC curve (AUC).

Tables 1 and 2 compare the proposed approach varying the model parameters, such as batch size, combining strategy and data augmentation in order to find their best configuration. The fine-tuning of AlexNet has been performed replacing the last fully connected layers. The best result was achieved by using a learning rate of 10^{-5}.

Table 3 compares our best configuration with some literature proposal (Sect. 2.4) and with our proposal without the use of 3TP images as input (1TP AlexNet with Slice Replication) to assess how the 3TP approach affects the performance. The same parameters configuration of our best model was used, but only the second post-contrast series from the 4D DCE-MRI data was taken. It is worth noticing that, since Antropova et al. [1] do not provide enough information about the SVM hyper-parameters settings, we performed an optimization of the classification stage: the best results were obtained by using an SVM with a polynomial kernel of degree equal to 1 and $C = 1$. Majority voting (MV) is considered as combining strategy.

Table 1. Comparing different 3TP-AlexNet training modalities, by varying the slice combining rule and batch size.

	Batch Size	CS	ACC	SPE	SEN	F1	AUC
3TP AlexNet	1	MV	69.23%	50.00%	85.71%	75.00%	67.86%
		BS	69.23%	**55.56%**	80.95%	73.91%	70.5%
		WMV	66.67%	44.44%	85.71%	73.47%	75.13%
	4	MV	69.23%	44.44%	**90.48%**	76,00%	67.46%
		BS	66.67%	44.44%	85.71%	73.47%	72.75%
		WMV	69.23%	44.44%	**90.48%**	76.00%	78.31%
	8	MV	69.23%	50.00%	85.71%	75.00%	67.86%
		BS	66.67%	50.00%	80.95%	72.34%	72.09%
		WMV	69.23%	50.00%	85.71%	75,00%	**78.84%**
	16	MV	**71.79%**	**55.56%**	85.71%	**76.6%**	70.63%
		BS	69.23%	50,00%	85.71%	75,00%	66.8%
		WMV	69.23%	50,00%	85.71%	75,00%	77.25%

Table 2. Comparing different 3TP-AlexNet Slice Replication training modalities, by varying the slice combining rule and batch size.

	Batch Size	CS	ACC	SPE	SEN	F1	AUC
3TP AlexNet with Slice Replication	1	MV	71.79%	55.56%	**85.71%**	76.6%	70.63%
		BS	**74.36%**	61.11%	**85.71%**	**78.26%**	**81.48%**
		WMV	69.23%	50.00%	**85.71%**	75.00%	79.37%
	4	MV	71.79%	61.11%	80.95%	75.56%	71.03%
		BS	66.67%	50,00%	80.95%	72.34%	79.23%
		WMV	71.79%	61.11%	80.95%	75.56%	76.98%
	8	MV	69.23%	61.11%	76.19%	72.73%	68.65%
		BS	71.79%	**66.67%**	76.19%	74.42%	73.68%
		WMV	69.23%	61.11%	76.19%	72.73%	77.51%
	16	MV	64.1%	44.44%	80.95%	70.83%	62.7%
		BS	71.79%	55.56%	**85.71%**	76.6%	74.34%
		WMV	64.1%	44.44%	80.95%	70.83%	74.87%

Table 3. Comparison of the best results obtained by our approach with those achieved by other state-of-the-art approaches and with the results obtained without exploiting the 3TP idea.

Methodology	ACC	SPE	SEN	F1	AUC
3TP-AlexNet with Slice Replication	**74.36%**	**61.11%**	**85.71%**	**78.26%**	**81.48%**
1TP AlexNet with Slice Replication	66.67%	50.00%	80.95%	72.34%	75.93%
ResNet34 (Haarburger et al.) [6]	58.97%	33.33%	80.95%	68.00%	79.89%
AlexNet & SVM (Antropova et al.) [1]	64.10%	38.89%	**85.71%**	72.00%	62.30%
LBP-TOP (Piantadosi et al.) [11]	50.10%	48.72%	51.28%	52.53%	71.83%
Dyn.& Morph.+ MCS(Fusco et al.) [4]	62.07%	31.82%	80.56%	72.50%	56.19%

4 Discussion and Conclusions

The aim of this paper was to investigate automatic lesion malignancy classification in DCE-MRI proposing a solution that joined the radiomics methodology and Convolutional Neural Networks (CNNs), in order to exploit the medical experience and the deep learning capabilities. For this reason, Three Time Points approach (3TP), exploited in Slice extraction step, was applied in order to highlight contrast agent absorption that is decisive in the discrimination between malignant and benign lesions. In our opinion, the past learned experience should always be taken into account because it could provide information that may improve classifier performance. As a case of study, breast DCE-MRI was considered.

Results presented in Tables 1 and 2 compare all the CNN-based approaches obtained by varying the slice combining strategies and batch size. 3TP-AlexNet Slice Replication with a batch size equal to 1 reaches the best results. The most effective slice combining technique is to consider as lesion class the one predicted by the slice containing the biggest ROI. This is reasonable since the biggest ROI in a lesion is likely to bring the majority of the lesion malignancy information.

Table 3 compares our best approach with some methods proposed in the literature, showing that our proposal is able to outperform both the classical (non-deep) approaches and the deep proposals. Haarburger et al. [6] defined the best set of contrast images exploring all the combination of the images provided by the acquisition protocol, while, in our case, the set of contrast images that should be considered is suggested by medical knowledge. This implies that our proposal can be applied for all protocols involving at least 3 acquisitions: the only constraint is the need to have acquisitions close to the times suggested by Degani. Furthermore, Table 3 shows the significant impact that the 3TP method had on system performance, reporting the results obtained by the implementation of a methodology that does not exploit the 3TP method.

The obtained results confirm our idea of exploiting past learned experience in order to provide the network with the medical knowledge that contributes to lesion diagnosis. In addition, it is worth noting that our methodology is not only independent of the protocol, but also of the CNN used for lesion classification: in fact, the choice of AlexNet [8] is only a case-of-study choice.

Since contrast agent absorption is decisive for lesion diagnosis, future work will focus on exploring approaches that are able to further enhance the temporal dynamics of the acquired signal, reflecting the absorption and release of contrast agent. We argue that when performing lesion diagnosis by means of a classifier system, performance depends on the dynamic or spatio-temporal information coming from DCE-MRI data rather than on the CNN used for classification.

Acknowledgments. The authors gratefully acknowledge the support of NVIDIA Corporation with the donation of the Titan Xp GPU used for this research, the availability of the Calculation Centre SCoPE of the University of Naples Federico II and his staff. The authors also thanks Dr. Antonella Petrillo, Head of Division of Radiology and PhD Roberta Fusco, Department of Diagnostic Imaging, Radiant and Metabolic Therapy, "Istituto Nazionale dei Tumori Fondazione G. Pascale", Naples, Italy, for providing data. This work is part of the "Synergy-net: Research and Digital Solutions against Cancer" project (funded in the framework of the POR Campania FESR 2014-2020 - CUP B61C17000090007).

References

1. Antropova, N., Huynh, B., Giger, M.: SU-D-207B-06: predicting breast cancer malignancy on DCE-MRI data using pre-trained convolutional neural networks. Med. Phys. **43**(6), 3349–3350 (2016). https://doi.org/10.1118/1.4955674. http://www.ncbi.nlm.nih.gov/pubmed/28048384
2. Degani, H., Gusis, V., Weinstein, D., Fields, S., Strano, S.: Mapping pathophysiological features of breast tumors by MRI at high spatial resolution. Nature Med. **3**(7), 780–782 (1997)
3. Deng, J., Dong, W., Socher, R., Li, L.J., Li, K., Fei-Fei, L.: ImageNet: a large-scale hierarchical image database. In: IEEE Conference on Computer Vision and Pattern Recognition 2009, CVPR 2009, pp. 248–255. IEEE (2009)
4. Fusco, R., Sansone, M., Petrillo, A., Sansone, C.: A multiple classifier system for classification of breast lesions using dynamic and morphological features in DCE-MRI. In: Gimel'farb, G., et al. (eds.) Structural, Syntactic, and Statistical Pattern Recognition, pp. 684–692. Springer, Heidelberg (2012). https://doi.org/10.1007/978-3-642-34166-3_75
5. Gillies, R.J., Kinahan, P.E., Hricak, H.: Radiomics: images are more than pictures, they are data. Radiology **278**(2), 563–577 (2015)
6. Haarburger, C., et al.: Transfer learning for breast cancer malignancy classification based on dynamic contrast-enhanced MR images. Bildverarbeitung für die Medizin 2018. I, pp. 216–221. Springer, Heidelberg (2018). https://doi.org/10.1007/978-3-662-56537-7_61
7. He, K., Zhang, X., Ren, S., Sun, J.: Deep residual learning for image recognition. In: The IEEE Conference on Computer Vision and Pattern Recognition (CVPR), June 2016
8. Krizhevsky, A., Sutskever, I., Hinton, G.E.: ImageNet classification with deep convolutional neural networks. In: Pereira, F., Burges, C.J.C., Bottou, L., Weinberger, K.Q. (eds.) Advances in Neural Information Processing Systems 25, pp. 1097–1105. Curran Associates, Inc. (2012)

9. Lehman, C.D., et al.: MRI evaluation of the contralateral breast in women with recently diagnosed breast cancer. N. Engl. J. Med. **356**(13), 1295–1303 (2007). pMID: 17392300

10. Marrone, S., Piantadosi, G., Fusco, R., Petrillo, A., Sansone, M., Sansone, C.: An investigation of deep learning for lesions malignancy classification in breast DCE-MRI. In: Battiato, S., Gallo, G., Schettini, R., Stanco, F. (eds.) ICIAP 2017. LNCS, vol. 10485, pp. 479–489. Springer, Cham (2017). https://doi.org/10.1007/978-3-319-68548-9_44

11. Piantadosi, G., Fusco, R., Petrillo, A., Sansone, M., Sansone, C.: LBP-TOP for volume lesion classification in breast DCE-MRI. In: Murino, V., Puppo, E. (eds.) ICIAP 2015. LNCS, vol. 9279, pp. 647–657. Springer, Cham (2015). https://doi.org/10.1007/978-3-319-23231-7_58

12. Piantadosi, G., Marrone, S., Fusco, R., Sansone, M., Sansone, C.: Comprehensive computer-aided diagnosis for breast t1-weighted dce-mri through quantitative dynamical features and spatio-temporal local binary patterns. IET Comput. Vis. **12**(7), 1007–1017 (2018)

13. Rosset, A., Spadola, L., Ratib, O.: OsiriX: an open-source software for navigating in multidimensional DICOM images. J. Digit. Imaging **17**, 205–216 (2004)

14. Tofts, P.S.: T1-weighted DCE imaging concepts: modelling, acquisition and analysis. Magneton Flash Siemens **3**, 30–39 (2010)

On Generative Modeling of Cell Shape Using 3D GANs

David Wiesner[(✉)], Tereza Nečasová, and David Svoboda

Centre for Biomedical Image Analysis, Faculty of Informatics,
Masaryk Univesity, Brno, Czech Republic
davidw@mail.muni.cz

Abstract. The ongoing advancement of deep-learning generative models, showing great interest of the scientific community since the introduction of the generative adversarial networks (GAN), paved the way for generation of realistic data. The utilization of deep learning for the generation of realistic biomedical images allows one to alleviate the constraints of the parametric models, limited by the employed mathematical approximations. Building further upon the laid foundation, the 3D GAN added another dimension, allowing generation of fully 3D volumetric data. In this paper, we present an approach to generating fully 3D volumetric cell masks using GANs. Presented model is able to generate high-quality cell masks with variability matching the real data. Required modifications of the proposed model are presented along with the training dataset, based on 385 real cells captured using the fluorescence microscope. Furthermore, the statistical validation is also presented, allowing to quantitatively assess the quality of data generated by the proposed model.

Keywords: Image-based simulations · 3D GAN · Training stability · Microscopy data · Digital cell shape

1 Introduction

The field of generative image modeling, led by the models based on generative adversarial networks (GAN) [5], has advanced substantially in recent years [2,20]. The ability to capture important features directly from training data allows the generation of realistically looking images without the need of employing vast amounts of parameters or feature extraction. During the training, two networks, generator and discriminator, compete in an non-cooperative game. The model is able to properly learn only if the training dynamics between both networks is maintained so that neither of them is much stronger that the other, i.e. neither network wins the game. This makes the training very sensitive to model architecture and optimization parameters [8].

The adaptation of convolutional network architectures [7] for GANs (DCGAN) [11] allowed the generation of images with much higher resolution.

© Springer Nature Switzerland AG 2019
E. Ricci et al. (Eds.): ICIAP 2019, LNCS 11752, pp. 672–682, 2019.
https://doi.org/10.1007/978-3-030-30645-8_61

The fully connected layers were replaced by the convolutional layers, which led to dramatic reduction in size of the models. Furthermore, the 3D ShapeNets [19] adapted the convolutional architecture, used previously for 2D images, to fully 3D, allowing the classification and retrieval of volumetric data. The 3D convolutional architecture of ShapeNets was subsequently adapted for generative modeling in 3D GAN [18], allowing the generation of volumetric data. The utilization of GANs in the field of biomedical image generation demonstrated their ability to generate realistic looking cellular specimens in 2D (CytoGAN) [4]. However, the generation of 3D volumetric cellular data via deep networks has not yet been thoroughly explored.

The validation of automated bioimage analysis algorithms relies on the good testing data, consisting of images containing specimens and accompanying ground truth. As the manual annotation of image data acquired using real microscopes is often infeasible [3], there is an ongoing development of simulators generating synthetic cellular specimens to produce suitable testing datasets [16]. The generation of synthetic cellular specimens in 3D is often based on parametric models [16]. Parametric models limit the variability of the data by imposing various mathematical approximations, simplifying the real biological processes.

To overcome these limitations, we present a deep-learning based model to generate realistic 3D volumetric cell masks. Our method improves upon the cell shape generation using a parametric model [15] by employing 3D GANs. To achieve good data variability, the training dataset for the generative model, based on 385 volumetric images of cells acquired using the fluorescence microscope, was subsequently augmented to obtain 1155 images. As the 3D GAN model with optimization parameters presented in the original paper [18] was not exhibiting a good convergence on this dataset, we discuss learning stabilization, and present necessary alterations to stabilize the process of generating resulting volumetric cell masks. We also present the statistical validation of the generated data, as the good convergence of the model is not sufficient to guarantee good coverage of the features contained in the real data.

2 Method

2.1 Data Preparation

The data preparation is an important preliminary step toward generating statistically plausible data. It needs to be done properly to allow modeling of the real data distribution as closely as possible. The initial dataset consisted of 385 fully 3D images of individual human leukemia cells (HL60) stained with DAPI, which were captured using a fluorescence microscope (Fig. 1). The utilized microscope was Zeiss Axiovert 200M with alpha Plan-Fluar objective ($100\times/1.45$ NA), Yokogawa CSU-10 confocal unit and Andor iXon 887 back illuminated EM CCD camera. However, this dataset could not be fed directly to the neural network, as it needed the preprocessing pass (Fig. 2) due to uneven size of the captured images and noise introduced by the CCD camera. Reducing the need of manual

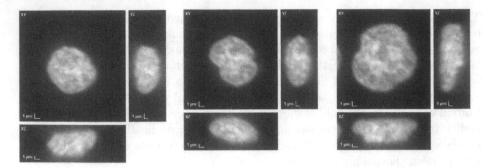

Fig. 1. Example of the volumetric images of human leukemia cells (HL60) stained with DAPI from the real specimens acquired using the optical microscope Zeiss Axiovert 200M with alpha Plan-Fluar objective (100×/1.45 NA), Yokogawa CSU-10 confocal unit and Andor iXon 887 back illuminated EM CCD camera. The visualization shows maximum intensity projections along the particular axes.

human intervention during this task was important, as going through the whole dataset by hand is very time-consuming and an error-prone process.

As the dataset consists of 3D volumetric images, the preprocessing has to consider all three dimensions. In the first step, the high-frequency noise is filtered by a 3D median filter with $3 \times 3 \times 3$ convolution kernel, emphasizing a smooth coherent structure of captured cells. Furthermore, as the images may be of varying size, the proper scaling and resampling must be done to make the dataset consistent with the input dimensions of the network, i.e. $64 \times 64 \times 64$. To achieve this, all images in the dataset were resampled using Lanczos filtering algorithm. The Lanczos algorithm uses the sinc functions, instead of simple linear or cubic interpolation, allowing to produce more detailed cell images.

At this point, the resulting filtered 3D cell images of size $64 \times 64 \times 64$ had to be converted into binary masks which represent the real-life cell shapes fed to the neural network. All volumetric images are processed by thresholding algorithm using Otsu method [10]. However, the results of the thresholding algorithm may not always be perfect.

The noise and small inaccuracies are very common in the resulting raw 3D masks. Moreover, some of the masks also contained cut-off parts of the cells in the image corners (as can be seen in Fig. 1). To mitigate this, we used a morphological erosion with a spherical structuring element of radius 3, followed by removal of smaller 26-connected components, and dilation with a spherical structuring element of radius 3. This sequence of operations resulted in removal of all objects, except the largest one, from the mask, producing filtered 3D mask containing exactly one cell.

Finally, all 385 filtered masks were augmented to further extend the data. The employed 3D affine geometric transformations were the rotation around the x axis and the reflection over axes x, y, and z. The resulting augmented training dataset contained 1155 binary cell masks.

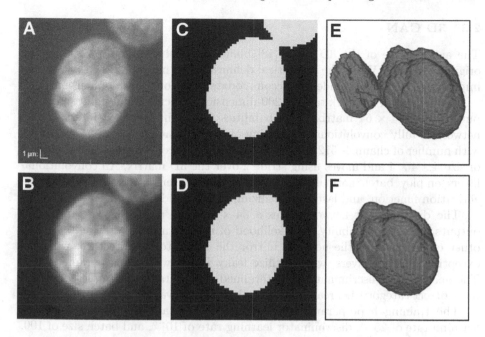

Fig. 2. Preparation of training data consisting of volumetric cell masks for 3D GAN model. Images A to D are maximum intensity projections of axis XY, images E and F are 3D visualizations of the data shown in C and D. Images D and F show the final form of training data which was used to train the model. **(A)** Real human leukemia cells captured using fluorescence microscope. **(B)** Median filtering with $3 \times 3 \times 3$ kernel and Lanczos resampling to size $64 \times 64 \times 64$ voxels. **(C, E)** Thresholding using Otsu algorithm. **(D, F)** Erosion using a spherical structuring element with radius 3, followed by removal of smaller 26-connected components, and dilation with a spherical structuring element with radius 3.

2.2 Original GAN

The Generative Adversarial Network (GAN) [5] model consists of two neural networks, generator and discriminator, which are competing against each other in the minimax game. The generator, given the vectors of random samples as the input, tries to mimic the training data distribution and convince the discriminator that the generated data comes from the training set. Discriminator, posing as the generator's adversary, tries to distinguish between the real training data and the synthetic data generated by the generator network. The minimax objective function, defining loss for both networks, is given as

$$\min_{\theta_g} \max_{\theta_d} \left[\mathbb{E}_{x \sim p_{data}} \log(D_{\theta_d}(x)) + \mathbb{E}_{z \sim p_{noise}} \log(1 - D_{\theta_d}(G_{\theta_g}(z))) \right],$$

where sample x comes from a real data distribution p_{data}, and a sample z is random vector from a noise distribution p_{noise}. The generator G with weights θ_g outputs the synthetic image. The discriminator D with weights θ_d outputs the probability that the data comes from the real distribution p_{data}.

2.3   3D GAN

The architecture of the 3D GAN [18] builds upon the foundation set by the original GAN [5]. While the theoretical definition was not modified, the network implementation was extended to accommodate additional data dimension.

The generator network takes a 200-dimensional vector as an input, and outputs a $64 \times 64 \times 64$ matrix of probabilities falling in the $[0, 1]$ interval. The network is fully convolutional, consisting of five volumetric convolutional layers with number of channels 512, 256, 128, 64, 1. The 3D convolution utilizes kernels of size $4 \times 4 \times 4$ and moves using stride 2 over the 3D matrix. All convolutional layers employ batch normalization, with hidden layers utilizing ReLU as the activation function, and last layer utilizing the sigmoid function.

The discriminator network takes a $64 \times 64 \times 64$ matrix as an input, and outputs a single probability, i.e. likelihood of real data, in the range $[0, 1]$. The other components of the network mirror the generator architecture, with the exception of inner layers, which utilize leaky ReLU with slope parameter 0.2. The accuracy of discriminator is determined by the ratio of samples classified into correct category, i.e. real or generated, assuming values in the $[0, 1]$ interval.

The training hyperparameters published in [18] are as follows: Generator learning rate of 25^{-4}, discriminator learning rate of 10^{-5}, and batch size of 100. The ADAM with $\beta = 0.5$ was chosen as the optimization algorithm, performing adaptive gradient descent and adjusting the weights of both networks. The training cycle runs in an alternating manner for both networks. However, as the discriminator typically learns faster than the generator, the training of the discriminator network is skipped if the discriminator accuracy exceeds 0.8.

2.4   Stabilizing the 3D GAN

The evolution of the loss of generator and discriminator networks, along with the discriminator accuracy, during training is a crucial indicator of the convergence of a model. If the network is learning properly, the losses of both networks are converging toward a stable value, and the discriminator accuracy is 0.5, i.e. the discriminator is not able to tell apart the real and generated data. The GAN models suffer from an inclination toward training instability [8], where discriminator often learns much faster than the generator.

However, a good convergence does not guarantee that the generator network learns the target distribution properly. The GAN networks are prone to mode collapse, which is a state, where generator learns to fool the discriminator by outputting virtually identical samples, i.e. one data modality. As the target distribution is often multimodal, this severely limits the scope of generated data distribution. The statistical analysis of the data, investigating, among other properties, whether the model exhibits mode collapse, is presented in subsequent sections of this text.

Among the considered methods, aiming to stabilize training and counteract the mode collapse problem in this paper, was the feature matching [12], Wasserstein GAN (WGAN) [1], and Wasserstein GAN with gradient penalty

(WGAN-GP, 3D-IWGAN) [6,13]. The feature matching method uses the L2 distance to measure the statistical difference between real and generated data and incorporates it into the objective function. The WGAN measures the difference between distributions using the Wasserstein metric, where the generator and discriminator are stripped of the sigmoid functions in the last layers and output real numbers instead of probabilities, and the weights of discriminator are clipped to satisfy the Lipschitz constraint. The WGAN-GP improves further on the proposed model and exchanges the weight clipping for gradient penalization, yielding better results.

These methods, and the WGAN-GP in particular, exhibited better convergence during training. However, they did not offer a significant improvement for this particular use-case, as the generated samples showed inadequate quality when observed visually, despite the increased training stability.

2.5 Resulting Model

The resulting stabilized model uses hyperbolic tangent, instead of sigmoid function, as a nonlinearity in the last layer of the generator network, and a batch size of 64. The random noise vector given to the generator is sampled from the normal distribution with standard deviation 0.33, rather than from uniform distribution over $[0, 1]$. The loss functions of generator and discriminator were altered to compute a sigmoid cross entropy, i.e.

$$Loss_G = -\mathbb{E}_{z \sim p_{noise}} \log(\sigma(D_{\theta_d}(G_{\theta_g}(z)))) \tag{1}$$

$$Loss_D = -\mathbb{E}_{x \sim p_{data}} \log(\sigma(D_{\theta_d}(x))) - \mathbb{E}_{z \sim p_{noise}} \log(1 - \sigma(D_{\theta_d}(G_{\theta_g}(z)))) \tag{2}$$

with

$$\sigma(x) = \frac{1}{1 + \epsilon^{-x}} \in (0, 1).$$

Both loss functions are minimized by the ADAM optimizer with the same parameters as the original 3D GAN.

3 Results

3.1 Training the Model and Generating the Masks

The computational server used for the training of resulting 3D GAN model with altered loss functions (1), (2) was equipped with dual AMD EPYC 7351 16-core processors, presenting total number of 64 virtual processors, accompanied by 512 GB RAM and NVIDIA Quadro P6000 GPU with 24 GB memory. The model was trained for 1000 epochs, with whole process taking approximately 3 h.

The trained model was subsequently used for generation of the synthetic dataset of 1155 3D binary images of cell masks. The binary masks, generated by the trained model, occasionally exhibited a subtle noise, represented by small disconnected structures. This is a behavior, which is also mentioned in the original 3D GAN paper [1]. Image processing, employing common morphological operations, was used to mitigate the issue and filter this noise out.

The whole process, including the generation of synthetic data by the 3D GAN model, has very light requirements on computational resources. The whole generation procedure, along with the mask refinement, was done in approximately 5 min. This demonstrates the ability to generate virtually unlimited amounts of data in a very short time.

The whole generated dataset was subsequently submitted to the statistical validation, i.e. none of the generated masks were excluded.

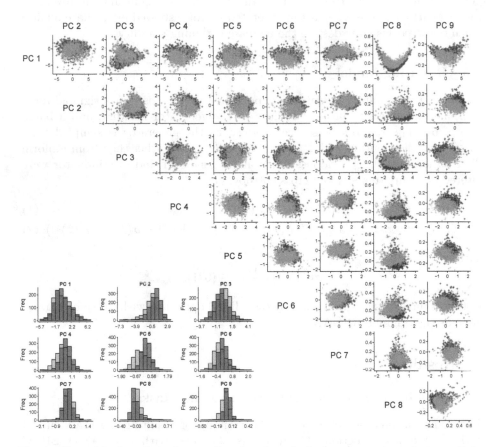

Fig. 3. The validation of synthetic cells using the principal component analysis applied to the nine morphological descriptors. The images of real (yellow) and synthetic (blue) datasets are represented as datapoints in multidimensional transformed feature space. The topright corner plots the distribution of the points in the subspaces given by each pair of the principal components (PCs). The bottomleft corner includes histograms of the distribution in each component in real (yellow) and synthetic (blue) data separately. The better the overlap of the cluster of datapoints or histograms, the closer the resulted images to the real images are from the variability point of view. (Color figure online)

3.2   Validation

The good behavior of the 3D GAN model during training, signified by the continuous and steady convergence of generator and discriminator loss functions, along with the balanced discriminator accuracy, does not guarantee a good coverage of the variability in the real dataset by the generator. Therefore, the external validation of the plausibility of the resulted synthetic data is required as well.

Besides inspecting the generated images visually, the synthetic data has been compared to the real data to quantitatively ensure rigidity and correctness of the proposed model. The automated analysis routine was developed, producing nine morphological measurements possibly to use for comparison of real and synthetic dataset. The computed descriptors on the individual binary masks were volume of object, surface of object, roundness, object radius (minimum, maximum, and mean), elongation (major and minor), and rectangularity. The employed morphological measurements were extracted from full 3D cell masks.

Following the protocol described in [9], the principal component analysis was applied to all descriptors for all 2310 images (1155 real and 1155 synthetic). This way the original nine-dimensional feature space of the descriptors was transformed and the majority of information was pushed into the first components. Consequently, the Jaccard index was computed over the two ellipsoids enveloping the clusters of datapoints in the feature space composed by the first three principal components.

The matrix plot of all components is shown in Fig. 3 (topright corner). In each plot the values of components are plotted against each other. The color is respective to the particular set of images, i.e. yellow for the real data, and blue for synthetic data. The better the cluster of synthetic datapoints fits the cluster of real datapoints, the closer the resulted images to the real images are from the variability point of view. Since the majority of information (83.0%) is in the three main components, the overlap of the blue and yellow cluster is important especially in the three topleft figures (PC1 against PC2, PC1 against PC3, PC2 against PC3). The Jaccard index of the ellipsoids created in this feature subspace is 0.651. One can see the overlap of blue and yellow clusters also in the other components despite they are much less informative.

The bottomleft corner of Fig. 3 includes the histograms showing the distribution of each component separately in the real (yellow) and synthetic (blue) image data. The histograms also show the high similarity in distribution of both samples because they mostly overlap. The distributions correspondence of principal components in real and synthetic datasets was tested in the first three principal components using the Kolmogorov-Smirnov test. The first principal component, yielding over 46% of the overall variability, were found to have no statistical difference between the real and synthetic group of images (p-value > 0.05). However, the test of the other components rejected the null hypothesis about the equal probability distributions (p-value < 0.001).

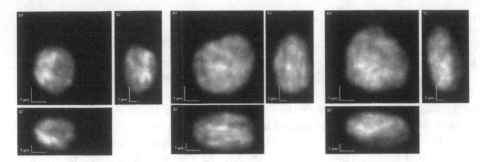

Fig. 4. Example of the volumetric images of human leukemia cells (HL60) stained with Hoescht simulated in the MitoGen [14] framework using the refined data generated by the resulting generative model. The visualization shows maximum intensity projections along the particular axes. The simulation was done using virtual microscope Zeiss S100, with objective Zeiss 63x/1.40 Oil, confocal unit Atto CARV, and virtual camera Micromax 1300-YHS.

3.3   Application

To demonstrate the use of the generated dataset, we used the well-established MitoGen [14] framework to generate synthetic cell specimens from the obtained masks (Fig. 4).

The MitoGen framework is used by participants and organizers of the Cell Tracking Challenge (CTC, http://celltrackingchallenge.net) [17]. The parameter-driven approach of generating cell shapes in MitoGen considerably limits the variability of the data by imposing a mathematical approximation. By using the masks generated by the proposed model as a basis for the cell simulation, we were able to generate synthetic cells with shapes exhibiting feature distribution similar to the real world specimens.

Comment. To further investigate the similarity among the real images, images generated using GANs, and images synthesized by original MitoGen, the principal component analysis over these three datasets was computed in the same manner as described in Sect. 3.2. The corresponding Jaccard index comparing the real data and data from GANs in the resulting feature space of all three datasets yielded 0.718. The Jaccard index evaluated from real data and data synthesized from MitoGen was 0.223 (in the same feature space). Despite the visually similar images from MitoGen, the images from GANs covered the variability of the real images more effectively.

4   Conclusion

We presented the semi-automated method to generate synthetic fully 3D cell masks from volumetric images of real cells. We have covered all steps involved in the process, i.e. the preparation of training dataset, the training stabilization of the deep generative model, and the validation of the data. We have also demonstrated the generation of statistically plausible synthetic cells using the generated binary masks.

The proposed generative model, using altered loss function and different noise vector distribution, exhibits better stability on given HL60 dataset than the original 3D GAN. Furthermore, the conducted statistical validation shows good coverage of the target distribution by the generator based on the evaluation results.

The achieved results testify the great learning capacity of GANs. The possible direction of future work includes generation of samples with higher resolution than original $64 \times 64 \times 64$, which will also require further training stability considerations. Besides the increased resolution, the addition of another dimension would be also considerable improvement, allowing the generation of 3D time-lapse sequences, making the generated image data effectively 4D. Furthermore, the results of the Kolmogorov-Smirnov test indicate possibilities for further improvements in generating synthetic data matching the real distribution.

The source codes, along with the trained model, are publicly available on https://cbia.fi.muni.cz/research/simulations/gan.

Acknowledgement. This work was supported by the Czech Science Foundation (Grant No. GA17-05048S). We gratefully acknowledge the support of the NVIDIA Corporation and their donation of the Quadro P6000 GPU used for this research.

References

1. Arjovsky, M., Chintala, S., Bottou, L.: Wasserstein generative adversarial networks. In: Proceedings of the 34th International Conference on Machine Learning. Proceedings of Machine Learning Research, vol. 70, pp. 214–223. PMLR, International Convention Centre, Sydney, Australia, 06–11 August 2017
2. Brock, A., Donahue, J., Simonyan, K.: Large scale GAN training for high fidelity natural image synthesis. arXiv preprint arXiv:1809.11096 (2018)
3. Coutu, D.L., Schroeder, T.: Probing cellular processes by long-term live imaging-historic problems and current solutions. J. Cell Sci. **126**(17), 3805–3815 (2013)
4. Goldsborough, P., Pawlowski, N., Caicedo, J.C., Singh, S., Carpenter, A.: Cyto-GAN: Generative modeling of cell images. bioRxiv, p. 227645 (2017)
5. Goodfellow, I., et al.: Generative adversarial nets. In: Advances in Neural Information Processing Systems, vol. 27, pp. 2672–2680. Curran Associates, Inc. (2014)
6. Gulrajani, I., Ahmed, F., Arjovsky, M., Dumoulin, V., Courville, A.C.: Improved training of wasserstein GANs. In: Advances in Neural Information Processing Systems vol. 30, pp. 5767–5777. Curran Associates, Inc. (2017)
7. Lee, H., Grosse, R., Ranganath, R., Ng, A.Y.: Convolutional deep belief networks for scalable unsupervised learning of hierarchical representations. In: Proceedings of the 26th Annual International Conference on Machine Learning, ICML 2009, pp. 609–616. ACM, New York (2009)
8. Mescheder, L., Geiger, A., Nowozin, S.: Which training methods for GANs do actually converge? In: International Conference on Machine learning (ICML) (2018)

9. Nečasová, T., Svoboda, D.: Visual and quantitative comparison of real and simulated biomedical image data. In: Leal-Taixé, L., Roth, S. (eds.) Computer Vision – ECCV 2018 Workshops. LNCS, vol. 11134, pp. 385–394. Springer, Cham (2019). https://doi.org/10.1007/978-3-030-11024-6_28

10. Otsu, N.: A threshold selection method from gray-level histograms. IEEE Transact. Syst. Man Cybern. **9**(1), 62–66 (1979)

11. Radford, A., Metz, L., Chintala, S.: Unsupervised representation learning with deep convolutional generative adversarial networks. arXiv preprint arXiv:1511.06434 (2015)

12. Salimans, T., Goodfellow, I., Zaremba, W., Cheung, V., Radford, A., Chen, X.: Improved techniques for training GANs. In: Advances in neural information processing systems, pp. 2234–2242 (2016)

13. Smith, E., Meger, D.: Improved adversarial systems for 3D object generation and reconstruction. arXiv preprint arXiv:1707.09557 (2017)

14. Svoboda, D., Ulman, V.: MitoGen: a framework for generating 3D synthetic time-lapse sequences of cell populations in fluorescence microscopy. IEEE Transact. Med. Imaging **36**(1), 310–321 (2017)

15. Svoboda, D., Kozubek, M., Stejskal, S.: Generation of digital phantoms of cell nuclei and simulation of image formation in 3D image cytometry. Cytometry Part A J. Int. Soc. Adv. Cytometry **75**(6), 494–509 (2009)

16. Ulman, V., Svoboda, D., Nykter, M., Kozubek, M., Ruusuvuori, P.: Virtual cell imaging: a review on simulation methods employed in image cytometry. Cytometry Part A **89**(12), 1057–1072 (2016)

17. Ulman, V., et al.: An objective comparison of cell-tracking algorithms. Nat. Methods **14**(12), 1141 (2017)

18. Wu, J., Zhang, C., Xue, T., Freeman, B., Tenenbaum, J.: Learning a probabilistic latent space of object shapes via 3D generative-adversarial modeling. In: Advances in Neural Information Processing Systems, vol. 29, pp. 82–90. Curran Associates, Inc. (2016)

19. Wu, Z., et al.: 3D ShapeNets: A deep representation for volumetric shapes. In: Proceedings of the IEEE conference on computer vision and pattern recognition, pp. 1912–1920 (2015)

20. Xiong, W., Luo, W., Ma, L., Liu, W., Luo, J.: Learning to generate time-lapse videos using multi-stage dynamic generative adversarial networks. In: Proceedings of the IEEE Conference on Computer Vision and Pattern Recognition. pp. 2364–2373 (2018)

Using Handwriting Features
to Characterize Cognitive Impairment

Nicole Dalia Cilia, Claudio De Stefano, Francesco Fontanella^(✉),
Mario Molinara, and Alessandra Scotto Di Freca

Department of Electrical and Information Engineering (DIEI),
University of Cassino and Southern Lazio,
Via G. Di Biasio, 43, 03043 Cassino, FR, Italy
{nicoledalia.cilia,destefano,fontanella,m.molinara,a.scotto}@unicas.it

Abstract. Cognitive impairments affect skills such as communication,
understanding or memory and they may be a short-term problem or
a permanent condition. Among the diseases involving cognitive impairments, neurodegenerative ones are the most common and affect millions
of people worldwide. Handwriting is one of the daily activities affected by
these kinds of impairments, and its anomalies are already used as diagnosis sign, e.g. micrographia in Parkinson's patients. Nowadays, many
studies have been conducted to investigate how cognitive impairments
affect handwriting, but few of them have used classification algorithms
as a tool to support the diagnosis of these diseases. Moreover, almost all
of these studies have involved a few dozens of subjects. In this paper,
we present a study in which the handwriting of more than one hundred
subjects has been recorded while they were performing some elementary
tasks, such as the copy of simple words or the drawing of elementary
forms. As for the features, we used those related to the handwriting
movements. The results seem to confirm that handwriting analysis can
be used to develop machine learning tools to support the diagnosis of
cognitive impairments.

Keywords: Handwriting · Classification algorithms ·
Cognitive impairments

1 Introduction

Cognitive impairments may be caused by a large group of neurological disorders
with heterogeneous clinical and pathological expressions. They are defined as
cognitive decline greater than expected for an individual's age and education
level but that does not interfere notably with activities of daily life. Cognitive
impairment symptoms can remain stable or even disappear, but for more than
half of the cases they evolve into a dementia disease [6]. Cognitive impairment

This work is supported by the Italian Ministry of Education, University and Research
(MIUR) within the PRIN2015-HAND project.

E. Ricci et al. (Eds.): ICIAP 2019, LNCS 11752, pp. 683–693, 2019.
https://doi.org/10.1007/978-3-030-30645-8_62

can thus be regarded as a risk state for dementia, and its identification could lead to the prevention of a dementia disease. Moreover, the amnestic subtype of cognitive impairments has a high risk of progression to Alzheimer's disease, and it could constitute a prodromal stage of this disorder. To date, cognitive impairments are diagnosed by physicians. However, in the cases in which it is difficult to confirm the diagnosis, biomarker tests such as brain imaging and cerebrospinal fluid tests may be performed to determine if the patient's cognitive impairment is due to Alzheimer's.

Among the daily activities affected by cognitive impairments, there is certainly the handwriting, which is based on cognitive and perceptive-motor skills [21]. Deterioration in writing skills had already emerged in the first diagnosis of Alzheimer's disease (AD) in 1907 [11]. In recent decades, however, researchers have more accurately discovered that the handwriting of Alzheimer's patients shows alterations in spatial organization and poor control of movement [13]. Several studies have also been published to study the effectiveness of handwriting analysis as a tool for diagnosis and monitoring of Parkinson's disease (PD) [20]. Recently, it has been also observed that some aspects of the writing process are more vulnerable than others and may present diagnostic signs. For example, during the clinical course of AD, dysgraphia occurs both during the initial phase and in the subsequent phase of the progression of the disorder. However, most of the studies which analyze the effects of cognitive impairments on handwriting published so far have been conducted in the medical field, where typically statistical tools, e.g. ANOVA analysis, are used to investigate the relationship between the disease and each of the variables taken into account [8,12,16,18,23]. On the contrary, very few studies have been published that use classification algorithms to analyze people's handwriting to detect those affected by cognitive impairments. Moreover, almost all of these studies have involved few dozens of subjects, thus limiting the effectiveness of classification algorithms, such as neural networks, SVMs and decision trees [7,22]. To try to overcome this problem, we proposed [3] a protocol consisting of twenty-five handwriting tasks (copy, reverse copy, free writing, drawing, etc.) to investigate how cognitive impairments affect the different motor and cognitive skills involved in the handwriting process.

In this paper, we present the results of a preliminary study in which we have considered nine of the tasks included in the above-mentioned protocol, with the aim to characterize the handwriting of patients affected by cognitive impairments. We collected the data produced by 130 subjects, by using a graphic tablet. From these data, we extracted the most common features used in the literature [5], both on-air and on-paper. As for the classification algorithms, we considered four well-known and widely-used classifiers and we characterized their performance in terms of recognition rate and false negative rate. The achieved results confirm our hypothesis that handwriting analysis can be used to develop machine learning tools to support the diagnosis of cognitive impairments. The paper is organized as follows: Sect. 2 describes the data collection, the protocol developed to collect traits of patients and shows the feature extraction method.

Section 3 displays the experiments and presents the results obtained. We conclude our paper in Sect. 4 with some future work perspectives.

2 Data Collection and Protocol

In the following subsections, the dataset collection procedure, the protocol designed for collecting handwriting samples, the segmentation and feature extraction methods, are detailed.

2.1 Data Collection

The 130 subjects who participated to the experiments, namely 68 AD patients and 62 healthy controls, were recruited with the support of the geriatric ward, Alzheimer unit, of the "Federico II" hospital in Naples. As concerns the recruiting criteria, we took into account clinical tests (such as PET, TAC and enzymatic analyses) and standard cognitive tests (such as MMSE). In these tests, the cognitive skills of the examined subject were assessed by using questionnaires including questions and problems in many areas, which range from orientation to time and place, to registration recall. As for the healthy controls, in order to have a fair comparison, demographic as well as educational characteristics were considered and matched with the patient group. Finally, for both patients and controls, it was necessary to check whether they were on therapy or not, excluding those who used psychotropic drugs or any other drug that could influence their cognitive abilities. As regards the dataset employed it is slightly unbalanced by the total number of patients and controls (68 - 62) and by the average age within each group (73, 16 - 63, 67). This is due to the difficulty in recruiting young patients. However we preferred not to use a subset of subjects because, although the results may be affected by these features, the aim of the work, as will be discussed further below, is to evaluate the contribution of three groups of features extracted from the handwriting (on paper - on air and all features, for more details see Sect. 2.3).

The data were collected by using a graphic tablet, which allowed the recording of pen movements during the handwriting process. During the trial, images and sound stimuli are also provided to the subject to guide the execution of the tasks. Moreover, the white sheets on which subjects are supposed to write contain the instructions of the tasks and the letters/words/phrases to be copied. Finally, the subjects were also asked to follow the indications provided by the experimenter.

2.2 The Protocol

The proposed has been defined with the aim of recording the dynamics of the handwriting, in order to investigate whether there are specific features that allow us to distinguish subjects affected by the above mentioned diseases from healthy ones. The nine tasks considered for this study are selected from a larger experimental protocol presented in [3], and they are arranged in increasing order of difficulty, in terms of the cognitive functions required. The goal of these tasks is to test the patients' abilities in repeating complex graphic gestures, which have a semantic meaning, such as letters and words of different lengths and with different spatial organizations. The tasks have been selected according to the literature, which suggests that:

(i) graphical tasks and free spaces allow the assessment of the spatial organization skills of the patient;
(ii) the copy and dictation tasks allow to compare the variations of the writing respect to different stimuli (visual or sound);
(iii) tasks involving different pen-ups allow the analysis of air movements, which it is known to be altered in the AD patients;
(iv) tasks involving different graphic arrangements, e.g. words with ascenders and/or descendants, or complex graphic shapes, allow testing fine motor control capabilities.

Furthermore, in order to evaluate patient responses under different fatigue conditions, these tasks should be provided by varying their intensity and duration.

(1) As in [22] or in [11], in the first task the subjects must copy three letters which have different graphic composition and presented ascender and descender in the stroke.
(2) The second task consists in copying four letters on adjacent rows. The aim of the cues is to test the spatial organization abilities of the subject [15].
(3–4) The tasks 3 and 4 require the participants to write continuously for four times, in cursive, a single letter and a bigram, respectively [10,19]. These letters have been chosen because they can be done with a single continuous stroke and contain ascenders, descenders and loops. These characteristics allow the testing of the motion control alternation.
(5–8) The tasks 5, 6, 7 and 8 imply word copying, which is the most explored activity in the analysis of handwriting for individuals with cognitive impairment [10,14,22]. Moreover, to observe the variation of the spatial organization, we have introduced a copy of the same word without or with a cue.
(9) In the ninth task, subjects are asked to write, above a line (the cue), a simple phrase, dictated them by the experimenter. The phrase has a complete meaning, and describes an action easy to memorize. As in [8], the hypothesis is that the movements can be modified because of the lack of visualization of the stimulus.

2.3   Segmentation and Feature Extraction

The features extracted during the handwriting process have been exploited to investigate the presence of cognitive impairment in the examined subjects. We used the MovAlyzer tool ([9]) to process the handwritten trace, considering both on-paper and on-air traits and then segmenting them in elementary strokes.

The feature values were computed for each stroke and averaged over all the strokes relative to a single task: we considered for each feature both the mean value and the maximum value for that task. Note that, as suggested in [22], we have separately computed the features over on-paper and on-air traits, since the literature shows significant differences in motor performance in these two conditions. As for the features, we used those related to subject handwriting movements such as, for example, velocity, acceleration and jerk. Moreover, we also taken into account the age of and level of education of the subjects.

Finally, as detailed below, we have merged all tasks in a single dataset, adding the information identifying each specific task.

3   Experiments and Results

Three different groups of data were considered in the experiments: the data obtained by selecting only on-air features, those obtained by selecting only on-paper features and those relative to the use of both types of features. The data were produced by 130 subjects, each performing the 9 tasks illustrated in Subsect. 2.2. As for the classification stage, we used four different classification schemes included in Weka tool: The Random Forest (RF), the Decision Tree (DT) [17], the Neural Network (NN), and the Support Vector Machines (SVM). The classifiers used by the Random Forest are 100 Random Trees (for more details see [1]). For the Neural Network classifier the number of hidden nodes are equal to (number of features + number of classes)/2. Finally, RBF kernel is used with parameter γ equal to 0.5 for SVM classifier ([2]). For all of them, 500 iterations for the training phase were performed and a 5 fold validation strategy was considered.

Being, in this preliminary study, the dataset still unbalanced by age and education, the results could be biased by such not uniform distribution of these features: we discussed this point in Subsect. 2.1. Thus, we performed a further set of experiments discarding such features.

The tables shown below summarize the values of Recognition Rate (RR) and False Negative Rate (FNR) for each task. In each table, the first column reports the types of features used, the second one the classifier employed, while the following columns report, for each task, the value of RR and FNR, respectively. Finally, the last two columns respectively show RR and FNR obtained without considering age and education (column labeled as "Reduced" in all the tables).

It is worth noticing that the false negative rate is very relevant in medical diagnosis applications, since it characterizes the ability to keep as low as possible the number of subjects affected by cognitive impairments, which are discarded by the system, thus allowing their inclusion in the appropriate therapeutic pathway.

The preliminary results are very promising and seem to encourage the use of classification systems based on these features for supporting cognitive impairment diagnoses. From the tables shown below (Tables 1, 2, 3, 4, and 5) we can point out that: firstly, for each task the maximum value (in bold) of RR is over 70%, reaching peaks in some tasks, such as the fifth one, exhibiting values of

Table 1. Classification results of tasks 1 and 2.

Features	Classifier	Task 1				Task 2			
		All		Reduced		All		Reduced	
		RR	FNR	RR	FNR	RR	FNR	RR	FNR
All	RF	71.96	28.79	66.66	42.42	66.41	33.82	70.14	35.29
	DT	66.66	19.70	62.12	45.45	66.41	36.76	64.17	47.06
	NN	68.94	36.36	**71.21**	42.42	68.94	36.76	64.92	44.12
	SVM	74.24	28.79	67.42	52.51	**74.24**	27.27	67.16	54.41
On paper	RF	72.72	28.79	66.66	40.91	72.38	23.53	69.40	36.76
	DT	65.90	27.27	62.87	40.91	67.16	36.76	66.41	51.17
	NN	70.25	32.35	66.66	54.55	69.40	36.76	**71.64**	36.76
	SVM	**75.24**	22.73	65.90	54.55	71.64	23.53	70.14	51.47
On air	RF	71.21	22.73	53.03	48.48	60.44	33.82	44.77	64.71
	DT	68.18	18.18	50.00	72.72	70.89	**8.82**	50.74	0.0
	NN	62.12	36.76	62.12	60.61	63.42	8.82	47.01	64.71
	SVM	71.21	18.18	54.54	80.30	69.40	20.59	44.02	50.00

Table 2. Classification results of tasks 3 and 4.

Features	Classifier	Task 3				Task 4			
		All		Reduced		All		Reduced	
		RR	FNR	RR	FNR	RR	FNR	RR	FNR
All	RF	**69.09**	44.90	**70.00**	44.90	**71.42**	36.00	65.71	42.00
	DT	61.81	40.82	58.18	69.39	63.81	30.00	**67.61**	44.00
	NN	68.94	36.36	69.09	38.78	57.14	50.00	59.04	54.00
	SVM	65.45	53.06	64.54	67.35	70.47	32.00	65.71	48.00
On paper	RF	68.18	44.90	62.72	55.10	66.66	38.00	65.70	44.00
	DT	63.63	30.61	60.00	79.59	67.62	34.00	65.71	42.00
	NN	64.54	48.98	64.54	48.98	62.85	42.00	61.90	48.00
	SVM	67.27	51.01	63.63	77.55	68.57	28.00	61.90	58.00
On air	RF	67.27	44.90	61.81	51.02	61.90	42.00	60.00	52.00
	DT	66.36	22.45	57.27	77.55	63.80	18.00	53.33	74.00
	NN	66.36	42.86	60.00	71.43	60.95	50.00	63.80	30.00
	SVM	62.72	44.90	56.26	91.89	**71.42**	18.00	56.19	66.00

about 76%. Secondly, we can observe that, on average, the Random Forest classifier provides higher classification rates. This result is in good accordance with the theory, considering that the Random Forest is an ensemble of classifiers. However, as reported in the last column, FNR is lower using DT classifier. In

Table 3. Classification results of tasks 5 and 6.

Features	Classifier	Task 5				Task 6			
		All		Reduced		All		Reduced	
		RR	FNR	RR	FNR	RR	FNR	RR	FNR
All	RF	75.67	25.45	70.27	30.91	69.29	39.22	69.29	43.14
	DT	66.66	38.18	55.85	52.73	64.91	41.18	63.15	58.82
	NN	73.87	27.27	64.86	40.00	66.66	29.41	65.78	41.18
	SVM	**76.57**	27.27	**72.02**	40.00	70.17	41.18	**70.17**	58.98
On paper	RF	**76.57**	23.64	64.86	36.36	68.41	43.14	62.28	47.06
	DT	67.56	41.82	64.86	41.82	71.93	21.57	63.15	60.78
	NN	72.07	30.91	71.17	36.36	**73.68**	25.49	63.15	49.02
	SVM	73.87	32.73	71.17	43.64	**73.68**	39.22	66.33	50.98
On air	RF	64.68	34.55	57.65	45.45	64.03	45.10	54.38	58.82
	DT	61.26	38.18	59.45	65.45	63.15	39.22	50.00	88.24
	NN	67.56	32.73	66.66	36.36	64.03	41.18	53.50	68.63
	SVM	67.56	32.7	61.26	67.27	72.80	25.49	55.26	96.08

Table 4. Classification results of tasks 7 and 8.

Features	Classifier	Task 7				Task 8			
		All		Reduced		All		Reduced	
		RR	FNR	RR	FNR	RR	FNR	RR	FNR
All	RF	63.63	38.46	56.36	51.92	70.43	36.54	66.08	38.46
	DT	53.63	59.62	63.23	62.72	69.56	38.46	**69.56**	42.31
	NN	64.54	34.62	58.18	40.38	67.82	38.46	63.47	48.08
	SVM	68.18	34.62	**63.63**	55.77	65.21	38.46	**69.56**	50.00
On paper	RF	**64.54**	38.46	59.98	48.08	68.69	38.46	64.34	55.77
	DT	62.72	40.38	**63.63**	75.00	66.95	38.46	59.13	51.92
	NN	63.63	42.31	59.09	55.77	66.95	30.77	60.86	53.85
	SVN	67.27	30.77	60.90	65.38	70.43	34.62	65.21	61.54
On air	RF	63.63	38.46	41.81	63.46	**72.17**	30.77	62.60	51.92
	DT	62.72	21.15	51.81	96.15	67.82	34.62	60.68	73.08
	NN	64.54	36.54	43.63	80.77	70.43	28.85	60.00	48.08
	SVM	**70.00**	23.08	56.36	86.54	68.69	32.69	59.13	80.77

particular, the lower value of FNR occurs considering the on-paper traits of the second task, with a value of 8.82%.

Finally, Table 6 shows the results obtained by merging, for each subject, the features derived from the whole set of tasks. For the sake of comparison, three groups of data were generated using the same criteria as in the previous set

Table 5. Classification results of task 9.

Features	Classifier	Task 9			
		All		Reduced	
		RR	FNR	RR	FNR
All	RF	**72.30**	34.85	**71.53**	34.92
	DT	66.92	31.75	57.69	60.23
	NN	66.92	34.92	69.23	34.92
	SVM	**73.07**	26.98	**71.53**	44.44
On paper	RF	70.00	26.98	64.61	42.86
	DT	67.69	12.70	61.53	61.90
	NN	69.23	28.57	68.46	47.62
	SVM	**73.07**	23.81	51.53	49.21
On air	RF	70.00	34.92	56.92	47.62
	DT	69.23	33.33	50.00	66.67
	NN	66.92	34.92	50.00	69.84
	SVM	67.69	30.16	51.53	87.30

Table 6. Classification results of all tasks.

Features	Classifier	All Tasks			
		All		Reduced	
		RR	FNR	RR	FNR
All	RF	93.19	11.07	**72.66**	36.69
	DT	89.82	7.51	69.75	45.26
	NN	75.96	32.41	71.07	48.02
	SVM	74.74	28.66	69.57	45.85
On paper	RF	**94.53**	16.80	58.62	49.01
	DT	84.64	**6.32**	54.48	49.21
	NN	78.03	33.00	58.72	54.35
	SVM	74.93	26.68	56.55	49.60
On air	RF	93.12	10.28	70.03	38.93
	DT	90.20	8.70	68.61	80.63
	NN	70.97	24.70	67.58	72.92
	SVM	70.40	24.11	67.67	84.39

of experiments (on-air, on-paper and both features). Furthermore, to avoid the above-mentioned bias, we excluded age and education features as in the previous case. Using these datasets, we repeated all the classification experiments: the results indicate an increase in the overall performance, showing higher recognition rates and lower false negative rates. In particular, the best value is obtained using RF classifier with on-paper features. The FNR is always very low, reaching the minimum value using DT with on paper. The exclusion of features related to age and education does not show particularly encouraging results.

Although the best performing group of features is on-paper, if we reduce the dataset excluding age and education features (Reduced Condition), the performance drops drastically. However, it is noteworthy that this does not happen using all-features condition. This leads us to claim that the on-air features have the greatest weight in the classification of patients, and that the on-paper features contribute very little in increasing the RR of the classification. If we consider all the tasks, in fact, the RR obtained with all-features differs by just two percentage points compared to that obtained with only on-air features. On the other hand, a similar argument does not apply to the classification values obtained on single tasks, in which the general performances are good also in the reduced condition, in most cases using on-paper or all-features, and do not differ significantly from the all-features classification values.

4 Conclusions and Future Works

In this paper, we presented a novel solution for the early diagnosis of Alzheimer's disease by analyzing features extracted from handwriting. The preliminary results obtained are encouraging and the work is in progress to increase general performance.

To date, this work represents the state of art of diagnosing of AD by means of machine learning techniques with a so large dataset. Nonetheless, for the future works we will try to better balance the data recruiting both young patients and aged healthy controls in order to make the dataset homogeneous, as much as possible, in terms of employed features. We will also try to investigate feature selection techniques to detect most informative features, for better explaining the relevance of each feature in the classification process. Finally, we will try to aggregate the tasks of all classifiers, combining the results of them [4]. In other terms, we will combine the results of the four classifiers taken into account, trained on one of nine tasks, and we will introduce a reject option to improve classification reliability (reducing the risk of false negative).

References

1. Breiman, L.: Random forests. Mach. Learn. **45**(1), 5–32 (2001)
2. Chang, C.C., Lin, C.J.: LIBSVM - a library for support vector machines, the Weka classifier works with version 2.82 of LIBSVM (2001)
3. Cilia, N.D., De Stefano, C., Fontanella, F., di Freca, A.S.: An experimental protocol to support cognitive impairment diagnosis by using handwriting analysis. Proc. Comput. Sci. **141**, 466–471 (2018)
4. De Stefano, C., D'Elia, C., Di Freca, A., Marcelli, A.: Classifier combination by bayesian networks for handwriting recognition. Int. J. Pattern Recognit Artif Intell. **23**(5), 887–905 (2009)

5. De Stefano, C., Fontanella, F., Impedovo, D., Pirlo, G., di Freca, A.S.: Handwriting analysis to support neurodegenerative diseases diagnosis: a review. Pattern Recognit. Lett. **121**, 37–45 (2018)
6. Elbaz, A., Carcaillon, L., Kab, S., Moisan, F.: Epidemiology of parkinson's disease. Revue Neurologique **172**(1), 14–26 (2016)
7. Garre-Olmo, J., Faundez-Zanuy, M., de Ipiña, K.L., Calvo-Perxas, L., Turro-Garriga, O.: Kinematic and pressure features of handwriting and drawing: Preliminary results between patients with mild cognitive impairment, alzheimer disease and healthy controls. Curr. Alzheimer Res. **14**, 1–9 (2017)
8. Hayashi, A., et al.: Neural substrates for writing impairments in japanese patients with mild alzheimer's disease: a spect study. Neuropsychologia **49**(7), 1962–1968 (2011)
9. Teulings, H.L., Van Gemmert, A.E.: Proceedings of the 11th Conference of the International Graphonomics Society. Scottsdale, Arizona pp. 1149–1168 (2003)
10. Impedovo, D., Pirlo, G.: Dynamic handwriting analysis for the assessment of neurodegenerative diseases: a pattern recognition perspective. IEEE Rev. Biomed. Eng. **12**, 1–13 (2018)
11. Lambert, J., Giffard, B., Nore, F., de la Sayette, V., Pasquier, F., Eustache, F.: Central and peripheral agraphia in alzheimer's disease: From the case of auguste D. to a cognitive neuropsychology approach. Cortex **43**(7), 935–951 (2007)
12. Müller, S., Preische, O., Heymann, P., Elbing, U., Laske, C.: Diagnostic value of a tablet-based drawing task for discrimination of patients in the early course of alzheimer's disease from healthy individuals. J. Alzheimer's Dis. **55**(4), 1463–1469 (2017)
13. Neils-Strunjas, J., Groves-Wright, K., Mashima, P., Harnish, S.: Dysgraphia in Alzheimer's disease: a review for clinical and research purposes. J. Speech Lang. Hear. Res. **49**(6), 1313–1330 (2006)
14. Onofri, E., Mercuri, M., Archer, T., Ricciardi, M.R., Massoni, F., Ricci, S.: Effect of cognitive fluctuation on handwriting in Alzheimer's patient: a case study. Acta Medica Mediterr. **3**, 751 (2015)
15. Onofri, E., Mercuri, M., Salesi, M., Ricciardi, M., Archer, T.: Dysgraphia in relation to cognitive performance in patients with Alzheimer's disease. J. Intellect. Disabil. Diagn. Treat. **1**, 113–124 (2013)
16. de Paula, J.J., Albuquerque, M.R., Lage, G.M., Bicalho, M.A., Romano-Silva, M.A., Malloy-Diniz, L.F.: Impairment of fine motor dexterity in mild cognitive impairment and Alzheimer's disease dementia: association with activities of daily living. Revista Brasileira de Psiquiatria **38**, 235–238 (2016)
17. Quinlan, J.R.: C4.5: Programs for Machine Learning (Morgan Kaufmann Series in Machine Learning). Morgan Kaufmann, San Francisco (1993)
18. Schröter, A., Mergl, R., Bürger, K., Hampel, H., Möller, H.J., Hegerl, U.: Kinematic analysis of handwriting movements in patients with Alzheimer's disease, mild cognitive impairment, depression and healthy subjects. Dement. Geriatr. Cogn. Disord. **15**(3), 132–142 (2003)
19. Slavin, M.J., Phillips, J.G., Bradshaw, J.L., Hall, K.A., Presnell, I.: Consistency of handwriting movements in dementia of the Alzheimer's type: a comparison with Huntington's and Parkinson's diseases. J. Int. Neuropsychol. Soc. **5**(1), 20–25 (1999)
20. Smits, E.J., et al.: Standardized handwriting to assess Bradykinesia, Micrographia and tremor in Parkinson's disease. PLoS ONE **9**(5), e97614 (2014)

21. Tseng, M.H., Cermak, S.A.: The influence of ergonomic factors and perceptual-motor abilities on handwriting performance. Am. J. Occup. Ther. **47**(10), 919–926 (1993)
22. Werner, P., Rosenblum, S., Bar-On, G., Heinik, J., Korczyn, A.: Handwriting process variables discriminating mild Alzheimer's disease and mild cognitive impairment. J. Gerontol. Psychol. Sci. **61**(4), 228–236 (2006)
23. Yan, J.H., Rountree, S., Massman, P., Doody, R.S., Li, H.: Alzheimer's disease and mild cognitive impairment deteriorate fine movement control. J. Psychiatr. Res. **42**(14), 1203–1212 (2008)

Preliminary Experiment of the Interactive Registration of a Trocar for Thoracoscopy with HoloLens Headset

Christophe Lohou[1]([✉]) [iD], Bruno Miguel[1,2], and Kasra Azarnoush[2]

[1] Université Clermont Auvergne, CNRS, SIGMA Clermont, Institut Pascal,
63000 Clermont-Ferrand, France
christophe.lohou@uca.fr
[2] Université Clermont Auvergne, CHU Clermont-Ferrand, CNRS, SIGMA Clermont,
Institut Pascal, 63000 Clermont-Ferrand, France

Abstract. During surgical procedures, it may be necessary to insert one or several trocars between the patient's ribs. This is the case, for example, with mini-invasive cardiac surgery to replace one or several heart valves assisted by 3D thoracoscopy: a trocar must be inserted before the camera is introduced.

Most systems that provide visual assistance are complex and expensive. They are based either on robotics or magnetic tracking, and allow to track a precise positioning of surgical instruments and to provide an augmented visualization on a screen inside the operating room. Nevertheless, few operating rooms for this type of intervention own this type of hardware and most surgeons place and insert a trocar without visual assistance.

In this paper, we have proposed a first software prototype of trocar guidance which exploits the mixed reality framework through the use of the Microsoft HoloLens headset. The surgeon first defines the position and direction of insertion using the CT scan in order to minimize the risk of damaging the patient's internal organs during the trocar insertion then an interactive registration may help him or her during the intervention. In this article, we describe the sequence of computing steps and the first obtained results about such kind of interactive registration.

Keywords: Mixed reality · Interactive registration · Cardiac surgery · HoloLens

1 Context

1.1 Mixed Reality

Microsoft HoloLens headsets [1] were recently released in France (December 2016). Such a headset uses several different sensors. It is a self-contained computer with Wi-Fi connectivity. These headsets have a semi-transparent visor on

© Springer Nature Switzerland AG 2019
E. Ricci et al. (Eds.): ICIAP 2019, LNCS 11752, pp. 694–703, 2019.
https://doi.org/10.1007/978-3-030-30645-8_63

Fig. 1. HoloLens headset and user view [2].

which 3D objects, called *holograms*, are projected; therefore, these holograms are superimposed on the user's environment through the visor. A user can interact with these objects by headset-recognized gestures if the developed application has intended it (for example: aiming at an object to select it, then pinching the fingers and moving the hand to move this object), see Fig. 1. Moreover, the headset also scans the environment, and holograms can interact with it. Unity framework [3] with the appropriate software library MixedRealityToolkit-Unity (MRTK) [4], allow us to design interactive 3D graphics applications that can be deployed in this type of hardware (nevertheless with Unity and C#programming language skills). To design such an application, we must plan both the content to be displayed and all possible user's interactions with the environment. More precisely, 3D content must be modeled with a 3D modeler software (for example, Blender [5]), then it must be imported inside the Unity application to be arranged in a 3D scene; then chosen interactions must be encoded (C#scripts in Visual Studio [6]). When the implementation of the application is finished inside Unity, we may deploy it in the HoloLens headset.

1.2 Medical Context

During surgical procedures, it may be necessary to insert one or several trocars between the patient's ribs. This is the case, for example, with mini-invasive cardiac surgery to replace one or several heart valves assisted by 3D thoracoscopy: a trocar must be inserted before the camera is introduced. Most systems that provide visual assistance to trocar placement are complex and expensive. They are based either on robotics or magnetic tracking, and allow to track a precise positioning of surgical instruments and to provide an augmented visualization on a screen inside the operating room. Nevertheless, few operating rooms for this type of intervention own this type of hardware and most surgeons place and insert a trocar without visual assistance.

Minimally Invasive Surgeries (MIS). A large number of surgical techniques have evolved to minimally invasive surgical techniques (or MIS). One of the best known of MIS is laparoscopy in gynecology. Rather than making large openings

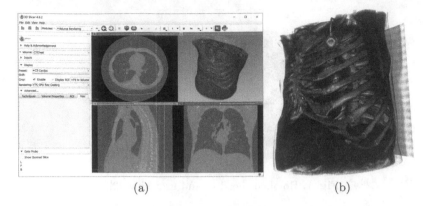

(a)   (b)

Fig. 2. CT-scan (CTChest sample – Slicer 3D [7], volume-rendering cardiac setting), volume-rendering MR generic in MITK [8].

in the patient, several mini-incisions are made. These techniques lead to faster recovery and shorter hospitalizations. The counterpart is that the surgeon no longer has a direct vision of the organs he has to handle. Some of these techniques require the use of trocars and in most cases, no visual assistance is offered.

About Incisions with Trocar. Many techniques for trocar insertion rely on the skills of clinicians (positioning relative to anatomical landmarks on the patient ...), and do not use visual assistance. In other words, trocars are often blind-inserted. See for example, the recent study about the initial placement of a trocar without any visual assistance in case of bariatric surgery [9]. Some clinicians have begun to study the impact of trocar placement, trocar diameter, hole size compared with subsequent intervention, healing, see for example a study in the case of chest surgery [10], laparoscopy [11].

We can find studies on the placement of trocar for minimally invasive surgery in the case of laparoscopy (measure of kinetic aspects of trocar insertion [12]), and with a surgical robot [13], see also the recent use of machine learning [14].

Minimally Invasive Cardiac Surgeries (MICS). In [15], authors review the evolution of various open heart cardiac surgery procedures (full sternotomy) to minimally invasive cardiac surgeries (MICS), these techniques were initiated following the growing interest of laparoscopic surgery. It is described the interest to avoid opening the thorax, to perform an extracorporeal circulation and to make instead some incisions for specific procedures (mini-thoracotomy) and if it is recommended for patients. These new approaches aim to reduce the complications associated with sternotomy, postoperative pain, and lead, as said before, to faster recovery and shorter hospitalizations.

For some centers that are equipped, some mitral valve replacement are assisted by video [16] or robot [17], see also [18].

Mixed Reality. In [19], the authors exploit HoloLens interactive commands for visualization (with no registration) of a 3D model of myocardial scar. In

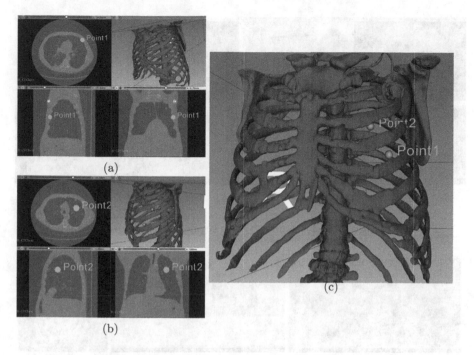

Fig. 3. Two points are marked in the CT-scan.

[20], a manual registration is made to superimpose 3D models (vascular tree) onto patient's body, as it is the case for our experiment. We believe that this application is exploited rather for the visualization of data than for a precise registration (see wireframed box in Fig. 3 of [20], outside the patient's body). In [21,22], a project superimpose a patient's vascular tree by registering it with an electromagnetic tracking system, several additional data are also displayed (orthogonal views of CT and angioscopies). In [23], we find the same guidance system for the alignment of a guide hole drilling guide (position and orientation) in case of hip surgery. The system requires a robotic arm, an additional camera and markers for guidance.

Our Motivation. We have proposed a first software prototype of trocar guidance which exploits the mixed reality framework through the use of the Microsoft HoloLens headset. The surgeon first defines the position and direction of insertion using the CT scan in order to minimize the risk of damaging the patient's internal organs during the trocar insertion then an interactive registration may help him or her during the intervention.

In this article, we describe the sequence of computing steps and the first obtained results about such kind of interactive registration.

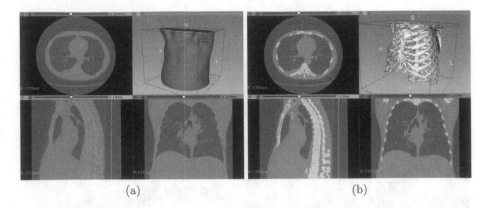

(a)   (b)

Fig. 4. (a) Torso and (b) ribs segmentation (Slicer).

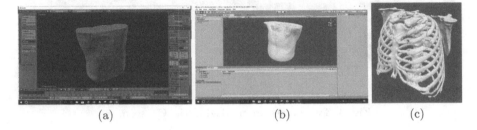

(a)   (b)   (c)

Fig. 5. (a) Torso mesh decimation (Blender), (b) torso and (c) ribs import into Unity.

2   Our Software Prototype

2.1   Preoperative Phase

The objective is to achieve a centered incision between a pair of patient's ribs, while not damaging internal organs. The surgeon identifies in the patient's CT-scan, Fig. 2, how he or she wishes to insert the trocar (position and orientation), by defining two points in the CT, Fig. 3. More precisely, the surgeon scrolls through the sections of the CT-scan, positions the first point on the patient's surface between two ribs which corresponds to the insertion point of the trocar (Point1 in Figs. 3(a) and (c)), then positions the second point inside the patient's body, in order to avoid damaging the patient's organs when the trocar will be inserted (Point2 in Figs. 3(b) and (c)). In this way, he or she defines a virtual trocar, or the pair (position, orientation) of a virtual trocar, that will later assist him or her when inserting the actual trocar.

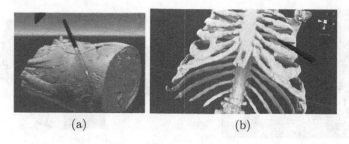

(a)   (b)

Fig. 6. Several possibilities of visualization of the 3D model of the virtual trocar (in red) according to torso and ribs transparency. (Color figure online)

2.2 Preparation of the Application to Be Transferred into the Headset

Our application must be embedded inside the HoloLens headset. Patient-specific data (torso, ribs, position/orientation of a virtual trocar) must be available into the headset to help the surgeon during the surgical procedure.

Here are the steps that the surgeon (or one of his or her assistants) must perform to design this digital content:

- (Step 1) to segment torso (Fig. 4(a)) and ribs (Fig. 4(b)) in Slicer software;
- (Step 2) to import the torso mesh into Blender software, and to decimate the torso mesh (in order to reduce the data volume to be projected on the visor's headset) (Fig. 5(a));
- (Step 3) to import of both the torso (Fig. 5(b)) and ribs (Fig. 5(c)) in our Unity application respecting the spacing parameters of the DICOM file of the patient's CT-scan. Then, our application computes the modeling of a 3D virtual trocar (in red) by using the two points previously marked by the surgeon (Fig. 6);
- (Step 4) to deploy the application (with these data) inside the HoloLens headset. Note that it is also possible to transfer data to the application embedded inside HoloLens through the cloud, and not to deploy for each patient.

2.3 Our Embedded Software Inside Hololens Headset

Our application will propose to the user to interactively register patient's data on the actual patient in the operating room. Details about this interactive registration are given in the next section.

3 Interactive Registration

3.1 3D Model to Be Registered

It seems difficult to directly align the 3D model of the patient's torso with the actual patient's torso. Therefore, we have chosen to define an intermediate 3D

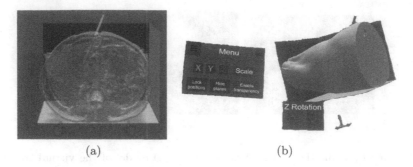

(a)   (b)

Fig. 7. (a) Intermediate model for the interactive registration, (b) possibility to translate and to orient the intermediate model with the menu of our embedded application. (Color figure online)

model that will be registered onto the patient. This 3D intermediate model is constituted in this way: its origin corresponds with the origin of the DICOM file (in other words it corresponds to the CT-scan with the appropriate scales/spacing according to the CT-scan resolution), it contains the torso, the ribs, the two previously defined points. We also add three planes to this intermediate model (Fig. 7(a)):

- the first plane (green plane) is the plane of the back of the patient which corresponds to the surface of the table,
- the second plane (blue plane) is the one that corresponds to a virtual plane passing through the patient's shoulders, thus the CT-scan must record this area,
- the third plane (red plane) corresponds to the virtual plane between the patient's torso and his left arm.

3.2   Registration Procedure

Our application is designed in such a way that this 3D intermediate model can be translated or orientated (Fig. 7(b)). In this way, the user of this application can position the intermediate model so as to first match it (translation and orientation) with the intervention table (green plane), then moves (translation and orientation) the model in such a way that it corresponds with the plane of the patient's shoulders (blue plane), finally translates the model so that the red plane is between the torso and the patient's left arm.

In practice, once this first rough registration of the intermediate model is made, it may be interesting not to display it longer, and to reveal only the torso and ribs (when the torso is totally transparent). Note that it is also possible to orient the first plane if the patient's back is not fully over the table (this is the case for some surgical procedures).

Fig. 8. View through the headset by the surgeon: it is difficult to see the trocar due to the 3D models projection.

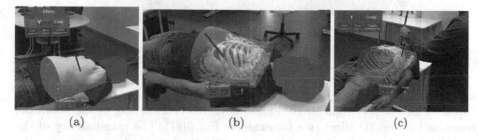

(a)   (b)   (c)

Fig. 9. View through the headset by one surgeon's assistant. (Color figure online)

4   Results

4.1   Intraoperative Step

Different difficulties occur: a minimum distance (80 cm) from the helmet's wearer to the first 3D object to be visualized is required, we modified it (near clipping plane property in an appropriate script of MRTK library). If the surgeon wears the helmet, it is very difficult for him or her to see the trocar even by adjusting the transparency of the models, Fig. 8. Therefore, one of his or her assistants must wear the headset and will help the surgeon to position the real trocar according to the materialization of the virtual trocar on the visor of the headset.

The assistant must first interactively register the intermediate model with the procedure described in the previous section. Then, he or she can remove the intermediate model and only see the 3d models of torso and trocar (Fig. 9(a)), or the set of torso in transparency, ribs and trocar (Fig. 9(b)) to better fit the interactive registration. Then, the assistant can begin guiding the surgeon in such a way that he or she first positions the tip of the trocar and then directs it (according to the virtual trocar in red) (Fig. 9(c)). The assistant must move around the surgeon to give the best fitting, Fig. 10.

4.2   First Results

Although this approach provides information that surgeons do not currently have, it is rather difficult to make a realignment with 3D data: the assistant

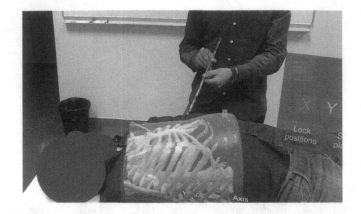

Fig. 10. View through the headset by the surgeon's assistant. Trocar alignment.

must move many times to find the best fitting of position and orientation of the trocar, which is very difficult to do due both to the crowding of the operating room and of the 3D effect (see for example Fig. 9(c)). The transparency of the model has to be adapted many times in order to be able to superimpose the plans of the intermediate model or finally only the torso at best on the patient.

4.3   Future Works

In this paper, we study a first proof of feasibility to use HoloLens to assist cardiac surgeons to position trocar and it is difficult to evaluate any positioning or orientation accuracy. Although the order of magnitude is relatively large (a 4 to 5 cm space between ribs), it remains difficult to perform a precise interactive placement of the trocar.

We continue our work in order to facilitate the registration procedure by using a marker-based functionality recently provided by Unity (Vuforia library [24]).

Acknowledgements. Authors would like to thank Arthur Jacquin, student in DUT Informatique Graphique at IUT de Clermont-Ferrand (Le Puy-en-Velay) for the software design. This project has benefited a french national grant: PEPS INSIS CNRS "Sciences de l'Ingénierie pour la Santé pour accompagner des projets translationnels", 2017, Projet AVACM (Assistance Visuelles Augmentée lors de Consultations Médicales). Thanks to Professors Rositi and Appadoo, IUT de Clermont-Ferrand (Le Puy-en-Velay), during experiments and for pictures.

References

1. HoloLens. https://www.microsoft.com/en-us/hololens
2. Rositi, H., et al. Presentation of a software application in mixed reality with HoloLens headset, for a nutrition workshop. In preparation

3. Unity framework. https://unity3d.com/
4. MixedRealityToolkit-Unity library. https://github.com/microsoft/MixedRealityToolkit-Unity
5. Blender modeler. https://www.blender.org/
6. Visual Studio. https://visualstudio.microsoft.com/vs/enterprise/
7. Slicer software. https://www.slicer.org/
8. MITK software. https://www.mitk.org/
9. Clapp, B.: Optimal initial trocar placement for morbidity obese patients. J. Soc. Laparoendosc. Surg. **22**(4), e2017.00101 (2018)
10. Migliore, M.: Efficacy and safety of single-trocar technique for minimally invasive surgery of the chest in the treatment of noncomplex pleural disease. J. Thorac. Cardiovasc. Surg. **126**, 1618–1623 (2003)
11. Alkatout, I., Mettler, L., Maass, N., Noé, G.-K., Elessawy, M.: Abdominal anatomy in the context of port placement and trocars. J. Turk. Ger. Gynecol. Assoc. **16**(4), 241–251 (2015)
12. Kodera, Y.: Measurement of inserting motion of bladeless trocar at real surgery for development of a virtual training system for initial trocar placement in laparoscopic surgery. Hepatogastroenterology **58**, 854–858 (2011)
13. Wörn, H., Weede, O.: Optimizing the setup configuration for manual and robotic assisted minimally invasive surgery. In: World Congress on Medical Physics and Biomedical Engineering, pp. 55–58, Munich, Germany (2009)
14. Yu, L., Yu, X., Chen, X., Zhang, F.: Laparoscope arm automatic positioning for robot-assisted surgery based on reinforcement learning. Mech. Sci. **10**, 119–131 (2019)
15. Iribarne, A., et al.: The golden age of minimally invasive cardiothoracic surgery: current and future perspectives. Future Cardiol. **7**(3), 333–346 (2011)
16. Obadia, J.-F.: Chirurgie cardiaque mini-invasive assitée par vidéothoracoscopie. EMC, Techniques Chirurgicales - Thorax, pp. 42–519 (2010)
17. Konietschke, R., Weiss, H., Ortmaier, T., Hirzinger, G.: A preoperative planning procedure for robotically assisted minimally invasive interventions, CURAC 2004, Computer- und Roboterassistierte Chirurgie, Munich (2004)
18. Czesla, M., Kattner, S., Balan, R., Massoudy, P.: Evolution of a minimally invasive mitral valve program. J. Visualized Surg. **2**, 169 (2016)
19. Jang, J., Tschabrunn, C.M., Barkagan, M., Anter, E., Menze, B., Nezafat, R.: Three-dimensional holographic visualization of high-resolution myocardial scar on HoloLens. PLoS ONE **13**(10), e0205188 (2018)
20. Pratt, P., et al.: Through the HoloLens looking glass: augmented reality for extremity reconstruction surgery using 3D vascular models with perforating vessels. Eur. Radiol. Exp. **2**(1), 2 (2018)
21. Kuhlemann, I., Kleemann, M., Jauer, P., Schweikard, A., Ernst, F.: Towards X-ray free endovascular interventions using HoloLens for on-line holographic visualization. Healthc. Technol. Lett. **4**(5), 184–187 (2017)
22. Garcia-Vasquez, V., et al.: Navigation and visualisation with HoloLens in endovascular aortic repair. Innov. Surg. Sci. **3**(3), 167–177 (2018)
23. Liu, H., Auvinet, E., Giles, J., y Baena, F.R.: Augmented reality based navigation for computer assisted hip resurfacing: a proof of concept study. Ann. Biomed. Eng. **46**(10), 1595–1605 (2018)
24. Vuforia. https://www.vuforia.com

Digital Forensics

Lightweight Deep Learning Pipeline for Detection, Segmentation and Classification of Breast Cancer Anomalies

Hugo S. Oliveira[1]([✉]), João F. Teixeira[2,3], and Hélder P. Oliveira[1,3]

[1] Faculty of Sciences, University of Porto, Porto, Portugal
hugo.soares@fe.up.pt
[2] Faculty of Engineering, University of Porto, Porto, Portugal
[3] INESC TEC, Porto, Portugal

Abstract. The small amount of public available medical images hinders the use of deep learning techniques for mammogram automatic diagnosis. Deep learning methods require large annotated training sets to be effective, however medical datasets are costly to obtain and suffer from large variability. In this work, a lightweight deep learning pipeline to detect, segment and classify anomalies in mammogram images is presented. First, data augmentation using the ground-truth annotation is performed and used by a cascade segmentation and classification methods.

Results are obtained using the INbreast public database in the context of lesion detection and BI-RADS classification. Moreover, a pre-trained Convolutional Neural Network using ResNet50 is modified to generate the lesion regions proposals followed by a false positive reduction and contour refinement stages while a pre-trained VGG16 network is fine-tuned to classify mammograms.

The detection and segmentation stage results show that the cascade configuration achieves a DICE of 0.83 without massive training while the multi-class classification exhibits an MAE of 0.58 with data augmentation.

Keywords: Lesion detection · Segmentation · Classification · Deep learning

1 Introduction

Breast cancer is considered a massive health problem worldwide being accountable for 15% of cancer deaths among females between 40 and 55 years of age. Despite this fact, the most effective form to reduce the mortality rate its early diagnosis [7]. The majority of the early diagnoses are still manual, achieving a sensitivity of 84% and sensibility of 91% [6]. To improve the accuracy of this manual interpretation, a double reading by another clinical expert or Computer Aided Detection (CAD) system is put in place. CAD systems are useful in

© Springer Nature Switzerland AG 2019
E. Ricci et al. (Eds.): ICIAP 2019, LNCS 11752, pp. 707–715, 2019.
https://doi.org/10.1007/978-3-030-30645-8_64

the detection, segmentation, and classification of lesions. Mammograms lesions namely breast masses commonly exhibit low signal-to-noise ratio, inconsistent appearance, and irregular shape, hampering its correct segmentation and classification [11]. The major drawback of CAD systems are the large number of False Positives (FP), while missing large portions of True Positives (TP) [9]. Recently, Deep Learning (DL) based strategies increased segmentation and classification performance. A particular advantage of DL models is their ability to automatically learn a rich hierarchy of key representative features automatically, enabled to aid the expert interpretation of the breast mammogram images. Nevertheless, DL models are trained on datasets, and need to be adapted to work in the imaging domain where the number of annotated datasets is much smaller.

Mammogram diagnosis commonly encompasses lesion detection, segmentation and classification steps. Robust lesion segmentation plays a vital in mammogram diagnosis, due to the association between the lesion shape irregularities and the probability of cancer [6]. Ground Truth (GT) annotations tend to be limited among the different databases, making the design of a robust mass segmentation algorithm challenging. To address this problematic, a large number of methods have been proposed, ranging from level set approaches [10], up to ones based in Shortest Path (SP) [3] procedures. Concerning DL models, Dhungel in [4] makes use of Convolutional Neural Networks (CNN) and deep belief networks as potential functions in structured prediction models to segment and classify breast masses. The work is based on multi-scale Deep Belief Nets (m-DBN) and Gaussian Mixture Model (GMM) for candidate generation followed by a FP reduction step, based on the features provided by two CNN, and used by an SVM classifier finalized with a Random Forest (RF) for final candidate selection. Dhungel in [5] extends his previous work by adding a hypothesis refinement based on Bayesian Optimization and Level Set method for final contour refinement, while for mass classification, a CNN model trained in two stages is used to determine mass malignancy.

With the goal to obtain a lightweight deep learning pipeline to robustly detect, segment and classify mammogram image anomalies, we evaluate the potentialities of transfer learning techniques by reusing pre-trained DL models to facilitate training and circumvent the small annotated datasets problematic. CNN has the advantage of automatically learn representative features, contrary to the hand-crafted ones that may be less representative. For the task, an augmentation, segmentation, and classification techniques are proposed and evaluated on INbreast dataset [8]. The segmentation component consists in a cascade of methods for semantic segmentation, formed by an initial region proposal stage, a CNN classifier, for FP reduction, and a final graph-based segmentation method, for lesion contour refinement. Regarding multi-class classification, a pre-trained CNN is employed with the last layers reconfigured and fine-tuned to our training data to predict the Breast Imaging Reporting And Data System (BI-RADS) level. The accuracy of the segmentation and BI-RADS classification methods are compared against GT annotations using the following measures: True Positive rate (TPr), FP for detection, Dice Coefficient (DC) for segmentation and Mean Absolute Error (MAE) for classification. The results show that the system correlates well with the GT annotations and is able to detect 85% of the masses at three FP, with a DC of 83%, achieving an final MAE of 0.524 for classification without extensive training.

2 Proposed Framework and Experiments

The proposed work is divided into three main stages: first the dataset construction and corresponding data augmentation techniques, secondly the cascade segmentation procedure and third the mammogram malignancy prediction. Common data augmentation consist in images rotations and mirroring during training. In order to increase the robustness of the models, we encompass image transformation by the use of affine transformations, enabling a training set with n images be increased to $n \times (n - 1)$ images by applying a single affine transformation. The dataset is constructed by cropping breast regions from original mammograms and images are zero padding until the $2^{11} \times 2^{11}$ size. Translations, rotations, shear and zoom transformations where employed to increase training set. Considering that BI-RADS 6 that corresponds to biopsied cases with fewer examples and BI-RADS 5 to highly suggestive of malignancy with a lower number of cases, we merged both classes into a single one (56). Dataset augmentation, encompasses only rotations, mirroring, and affine transformation with an maximum of 20% of deformation to maintain lesion contour appearance. Table 1 summarizes the training set with examples in Fig. 1.

To tune the ResNet50 for the segmentation task, the training set encompasses 40 patch samples from mass region box with a 0.9 overlap and 40 from breast region. The main objective is for models to learn the difference between masses and background. All initial images are subject to background removal and breast region is cropped and scaled until it reaches one of the minor axis length (x or y) of the original image. After this process images are then resized to 1/4 enabling to encompass the largest mass lesions inside a 224×224 box size to fit network input (Fig. 2), with the smaller mass lesion contour occupying a minimum 35×35 pixels box, crucial to maintaining relevant lesion features. Final dataset contains 44800 patch images from both classes.

Table 1. Dataset size for BI-RADS classification.

Data	1	2	3	4	56	Total
Original	67	220	23	43	57	410
Train 75%	50	165	17	32	43	307
Test 25%	17	55	6	10	15	101
Train Aug (A)	250	825	85	160	215	1535
Train Aug (A+T)	750	2475	255	480	645	4605
Train Aug (A+Af+R+T+M+Z)	19800	2040	3840	4440	2200	32320

A - Angle, Af - Affine, T - Translation, M - Mirror, R - Rotation, Z - Zoom

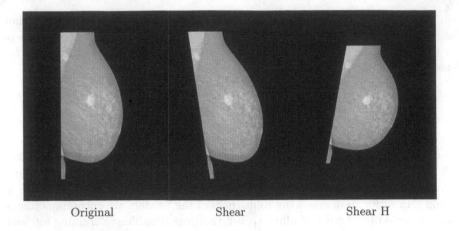

Original   Shear   Shear H

Fig. 1. Example of the constructed dataset (without mirroring).

For mass detection and segmentation, the first stage *(Resnet)* corresponds to the generation of the initial region candidates (Fig. 2), accomplished by the reuse a pre-existing CNN architecture trained in Imagenet[1], namely a ResNet50 with the final layer modified for to distinguish between mass/background images. The model is then re-trained on our sampled images patches. The choice of ResNet50 relies on the fact is composed of convolutional layers and a final global averaging pool layer, making this network suitable to compute Class Activation Maps (CAM)[2] directly without further training. The final model is then used to generate the region's proposals by sliding the image input model on larger images and attain the CAM. Regions similar to mass lesions exhibit higher activation's values, suggesting that the particular area may correspond to a Region of Interest (ROI). From CAM, square mass images candidates are taken from regions that present a CAM above the threshold T.

Since a higher number of regions may correspond to background areas, a second stage, the **FP** reduction consisting in a CNN classifier using a VGG architecture is trained using the same patch lesion/background dataset to classify the initial region's proposals as mass/background, enabling to discard FP detection's while attaining TP ones.

The third and final module of the segmentation component, the contour refinement **(Ref)**, operates only on positively identified regions. This stage consists of a SP operating in Cartesian Coordinates proposed by [3] to determine the outside boundary of convex objects. SP operating in the Cartesian Coordinates benefit from the fact that the graph is generated from the image on its original form, avoiding deformations associated with image transformations. An inverse cost function centered on the object is modulated to avoid small

---

[1] https://image-net.org/.

[2] https://jacobgil.github.io/deeplearning/class-activation-maps.

inner paths collapsing over the seed point being naturally favored when using Cartesian Coordinates.

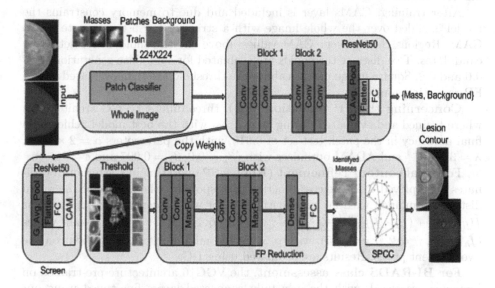

Fig. 2. Region proposal + FP reduction + contour refinement.

For BI-RADS determination, a pre-trained CNN is used, namely the VGG16 architecture trained on Imagenet. This choice is supported by the simplicity of VGG16 combined with good performance in medical context images. Since VGG16 has an input size of 224×224 with 3 channels being able to identify 1000 different classes, we resize our images dataset and replicate gray image channel among the 3 channels to fit network input and redefine to output layer to our 5 BI-RADS class problem. Table 1 summarizes the constructed dataset. Lower classes correspond to the normal cases that are the most common the population.

Both segmentation and classification performance is evaluated on INbreast [8] database. All the models are trained using two non-overlapping subsets with a 75% random split for training and testing. 5-fold cross-validation was used to determine the best parameters.

The initial region proposal (Resnet), the ResNet50 learning rate was set to $\alpha = 3 \times 10^{-3}$, $\lambda = 4 \times 10^{-4}$ and ADAM was the selected optimizer with ($\beta_1 = 0.9, \beta_2 = 0.995$ and $\epsilon = 10^{-6}$, trained for 30 epochs using the lesion/background images setting the batch size to 32. Only the new added layers are fine-tuned in the initial phase. Then, different parts of the network, deeper, middle and shallow layers where unfrozen individually and retrained during 10 epochs each, with learning rates set to 4×10^{-3} for deeper layers, 3×10^{-4} for middle layers and 3×10^{-5} for shallow layers. This retrain strategy relies in the fact that low level features do not vary as much as high level features among different datasets.

After training, CAMs layer is included and due to memory constrains the model is slided over the whole image with a stride of $l = 5$ to generate image CAM. Regions that present CAM values above the threshold T are set to be candidates. Two distinct thresholds are evaluated for candidate generation, $T = 0.6$ and 0.8. Square image patches above the threshold are then evaluated by the FP reduction stage.

Concerning the FP reduction (FP), three different VGG architectures where trained and evaluated during 40 epochs, with the best model achieving a final accuracy in the patch test set of 0.915, with the parameters $\alpha = 2 \times 10^{-5}$, $\lambda = 3 \times 10^{-4}$ and ADAM optimizer with ($\beta_1 = 0.9, \beta_2 = 0.997$ and $\epsilon = 10^{-6}$).

For final contour refinement (Ref), a SP operating in Cartesian Coordinates is employed with the cost function corresponding the inverse of the radial distance combined with an exponential law for weight generation expressed as $\hat{f}(g) = f_l + (f_h - f_l) \frac{\exp((255-g) \cdot \beta) - 1}{\exp(255 \cdot \beta) - 1}$, with $f_h, f_l, \beta \in \mathbb{R}$ set to be constant values ($f_h = 30, f_l = 2, \beta = 0.025$), with g being the minimum of the gradient on the two incident pixels. Results are evaluated using DC.

For BI-RADS class assessment, the VGG16 architecture pre-trained on Imagenet was used, with the new fully connected layers fine-tuned using our training data composed full breast images resized to fit network input. Initial training parameters where $\alpha = 2 \times 10^{-2}$, $\lambda = 1 \times 10^{-4}$ and ADAM as the optimizer with ($\beta_1 = 0.9, \beta_2 = 0.995$ and $\epsilon = 10^{-6}$). After training the final layer, we employ the same strategy used in the ResNet50 to retrain the deeper, middle and shallow layers of the network during 10 epochs also. The learning rates for deeper layers was set to 4×10^{-3}, 4×10^{-4} for middle layers and 4×10^{-5} for shallow layers. Results are evaluated using the MAE.

3   Results

Results are divided into two main components: segmentation and classification. Results on each stage of the segmentation cascade are compared with a State-of-the-art (SotA) method proposed by [5], that uses a Conditional Random Field (CRF) model with active contour refinement, and a manual approach proposed by Brake [1], listed in Table 2. The **method** column lists SotA works and the stages of the segmentation cascade, with a example of the segmentation stages exhibited on Fig. 3.

Several observations can be drawn from the segmentation stage:

- **Effect of the threshold T:** The region proposal stage presented an higher FP number and sensitivity of 10(1.8) and 0.85(0.1) respectively) when using a lower T.
- **Effect of the FP Reduction:** Some of the TP where rejected due to center shift initial detection, misleading the classifier.

Table 2. Performance evaluation of lesion region proposal + classifier + contour refinement. Results *mean(std)*.

Method	# FP	TP_r	DICE
Dhungel [5]	1.00(-)	0.90(-)	0.85(0.02)
ResNet ($T = 0.6$)	10(1.8)	0.86(0.09)	0.72(0.08)
ResNet ($T = 0.8$)	8(1.7)	0.83(0.10)	0.68(0.07)
Res.+FP+Ref ($T = 0.6$)	3(0.20)	0.85(0.07)	**0.83(0.10)**
Res.+FP+Ref ($T = 0.8$)	2(0.11)	0.76(0.07)	0.70(0.13)
Brake [1] (Man)			0.820(-)

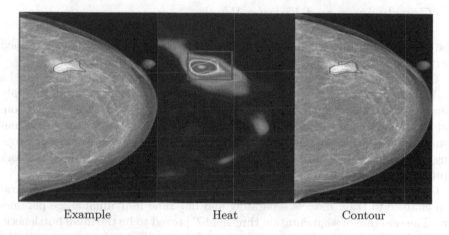

Example	Heat	Contour

Fig. 3. Pairwise comparison between mammogram image and heatmaps (Blue - GT, Red - Detection). SP operate only on positive identified patches. (Color figure online)

– **Contour Refinement:** The SP exhibited similar accuracy when compared with the original work due to the similarities on the datasets Full Field Digital Mammography (FFDM).

Concerning the BI-RADS classifier, results are summarized in Table 3. The listed SotA method consist in Maximal-Coupled Learning using the GT annotation masks to extract features for BI-RADS classification [2].

Table 3. Attained accuracy in the test set, *mean(std)*.

Data	MAE
SotA - (Manual) Max. Coupled Learn. [2]	0.190(-)
Using Train Aug (A)	1.343(0.503)
Using Train Aug (A+Af+R+T+M+Z)	**0.584(0.011)**

Several observations can be drawn from the classification stage:

- **Effect of the data augmentation:** The affine data augmentation technique outperformed the simple rotation and mirroring of the images.
- **Effect of the image resizing:** Small calcifications that are associated with high malignancy level cannot be detected by the model and mislead the final BI-RADS level prediction.
- **Effect of pre-trained networks:** The use of pre-trained networks enabled to reuse the convolutional layers as robust feature extractor to generate a robust model without massive training data.

4   Conclusions and Future Work

The present work concerns the creation of a lightweight DL pipeline easily trained for detection, segmentation and classification of mammogram images.

Data augmentation without altering lesion shape appearance proved to be vital, enabling to generate a vast dataset improving model generalization. Only affine transformations such as zoom, shear with a maximum of 20%, translation, and rotation were considered. Shear with larger percentages and elastic deformation must be considered and asses their impact in classifier performance. Cropping and scaling enabled to create a dataset suitable to fit pre-trained network input without losing to much detail on smaller mass lesions.

Concerning the segmentation stage, the formulation of a cascade configuration enabled to train models separately and fine-tune individual stage parameters. The selection of segmentation threshold T proved to be the main bottleneck, with higher T values leading to a rejection of some of TP lesions that exhibited lower probability. Integrating both stages into a single one by using a Faster R-CNN architecture and fine-tune to our dataset can attenuate this problem. Contour refinement enabled to refine the lesion segmentation in great detail.

The BI-RADS level classification benefit from the use of a pre-trained network, enabling to obtain a robust classifier without extensive data and training time. However, BI-RADS report to the higher level must be carefully analyzed. While our approach does not beat the SotA, its prediction uses only images without using any GT contour annotation for feature extraction. Overhall, the reuse of pre-trained models enabled the creation of a well performing pipeline without extensive data and training.

Acknowledgments. This work is co-financed by the ERDF - European Regional Development Fund through the Norte Portugal Regional Operational Programme (NORTE 2020), and the LISBOA2020 under the PORTUGAL 2020 Partnership Agreement and through the Portuguese National Innovation Agency (ANI) as a part of project BCCT.plan: NORTE-01-0247-FEDER-017688, and also by Fundação para a Ciência e a Tecnologia (FCT) within Ph.D. grant number SFRH/BD/135834/2018.

References

1. te Brake, G.M., Karssemeijer, N., Hendriks, J.H.: An automatic method to discriminate malignant masses from normal tissue in digital mammograms. Phys. Med. Biol. **45**, 2843–2857 (2000)
2. Cardoso, J.S., Domingues, I.: Max-coupled learning: application to breast cancer. In: 2011 10th International Conference on Machine Learning and Applications and Workshops (2011)
3. Cardoso, J.S., Domingues, I., Oliveira, H.P.: Closed shortest path in the original coordinates with an application to breast cancer. Int. J. Pattern Recognit. Artif. Intell. (2015)
4. Dhungel, N., Carneiro, G., Bradley, A.P.: Automated mass detection in mammograms using cascaded deep learning and random forests. In: International Conference on Digital Image Computing: Techniques and Applications (2015)
5. Dhungel, N., Carneiro, G., Bradley, A.P.: A deep learning approach for the analysis of masses in mammograms with minimal user intervention. Med. Image Anal. **37**, 114–128 (2017)
6. Giger, M.L.: Medical imaging and computers in the diagnosis of breast cancer. In: Photonic Innovations and Solutions for Complex Environments and Systems (PISCES) II. International Society for Optics and Photonics (2014)
7. Hela, B., Hela, M., Kamel, H., Sana, B., Najla, M.: Breast cancer detection: a review on mammograms analysis techniques. In: 10th International Multi-Conferences on Systems, Signals Devices (SSD 2013) (2013)
8. Moreira, I.C., Amaral, I., Domingues, I., Cardoso, A., Cardoso, M.J., Cardoso, J.S.: INbreast: toward a full-field digital mammographic database. Acad. Radiol. **19**, 236–248 (2012)
9. Oliver, A., et al.: A review of automatic mass detection and segmentation in mammographic images. Med. Image Anal. **14**, 87–110 (2010)
10. Rahmati, P., Adler, A., Hamarneh, G.: Mammography segmentation with maximum likelihood active contours. Med. Image Anal. **16**, 1167–1186 (2012)
11. Tang, J., Rangayyan, R.M., Xu, J., El Naqa, I., Yang, Y.: Computer-aided detection and diagnosis of breast cancer with mammography: recent advances. IEEE Trans. Inf. Technol. Biomed. **13**, 236–251 (2009)

1-D DCT Domain Analysis for JPEG Double Compression Detection

Oliver Giudice[1], Francesco Guarnera[1(✉)], Antonino Paratore[2],
and Sebastiano Battiato[1]

[1] Image Processing Laboratory, University of Catania, Catania, Italy
{giudice,battiato}@dmi.unict.it, francesco.guarnera@unict.it
[2] iCTLab s.r.l., Spin-off of University of Catania, Catania, Italy
antonino.paratore@ictlab.srl
http://www.ictlab.srl

Abstract. The authenticity of an evidence is a necessary and crucial requirement in forensic investigations and trials, expecially when it comes to digital evidences. In order to demonstrate the authenticity of a (digital) image, different techniques have been proposed in the last years which take advantage of some kinds of detectable anomalies on double or multiple compressed JPEG images. In this article, we present an in-depth analysis in the DCT Domain of an image exploiting the "first-digits" statistics after 1D-DCT transformation. The insights thus obtained were used to build a simple and explainable classifier able to detect doubly compressed JPEG images; this approach seems to outperform much more complex techniques in the state-of-the-art.

Keywords: DQD · Image forensics · DCT coefficients

1 Introduction

The total number of digital images acquired, stored or shared all over the world is unimaginable and constantly growing due to the spread of social networks. Simultaneously, the importance of proving the authenticity of digital data is increasing. If an image is involved in a forensic investigation it is mandatory to demonstrate the originality or integrity for the image itself. The difference between the integrity and the authenticity of an image is the following: the process to demonstrate the integrity of an image is related to the certainty that the image was acquired, stored in an image file and never edited again; if the image was successively transformed but its meaning didn't change we can define the image authentic although it lost the integrity. Most of the times the image is acquired and stored by devices such as digital camera or smartphone directly in JPEG compressed format. If an already-acquired image is opened, manipulated in some way and then saved into another image file, this last one is different from the original thus it lost its integrity. Consequently, according to the last definition all the images on social networks can be considered without integrity but

© Springer Nature Switzerland AG 2019
E. Ricci et al. (Eds.): ICIAP 2019, LNCS 11752, pp. 716–726, 2019.
https://doi.org/10.1007/978-3-030-30645-8_65

nothing can be said about authenticity. Thus the Double Compression Detection in an image is the first step for any digital forensics image analysis: if no double compression is detected, the integrity of the image has not been lost, it is authentic and no further analyses are needed, otherwise additional analysis like tampering or copy-move-forge detection should be carried out [3]. Given that the alteration of an image involves a multiple JPEG compression process, it is possible to detect some traces of this on the image itself. These traces are strictly related to the JPEG algorithm and the compression parameters used each time the image was saved and stored in a JPEG image file. State-of-the-art already demonstrated that the most important piece of information of a digital image is hidden in the DCT domain. This piece of information has to be discovered and correctly represented in a mathematical form. Thus it can be employed for many automated image processing tasks [2,4,5,11,26] like object recognition, scene recognition or image forensics. In this paper, in order to find a new technique for the Double Compression Detection problem, the DCT domain of single and double compressed JPEG images was investigated and interesting insights were detected in the first digits statistics of elements in 1-D DCT transformed 8×8 blocks of an image. This is the main contribution of this paper. The discovered insights are very interesting in terms of their simplicity and might open new research paths. Their potential was also demonstrated by exploiting them as features for a simple Machine Learning classifier for double compressed image detection and by comparison with state-of-the-art. The remainder of this paper is organized as follows. In Sect. 2 a brief background of JPEG compression algorithm and properties useful to better understand this paper will be presented. Then, in Sect. 3 the state-of-the-art of double compression detection methods will be discussed. Section 4 will describe the employed datasets on which the investigation in the DCT domain described in Sect. 5 was carried out. Section 6 demonstrates the usability of the discovered insights in an automated classifier and Sect. 7 shows and discusses the achieved results with comparisons with state-of-the-art methods. Finally Sect. 8 concludes this paper with some ideas for further works.

2   JPEG Compression and Double Compression

The JPEG compression is probably the most well-known method for image's compression. In brief, starting from a RAW color image, the main steps of the JPEG algorithm are the following: at first the luminance component is separated from the chrominance one converting the input image from the RGB to $YCbCr$. After that the image is partitioned into 8×8 non overlapping blocks and the corresponding values are converted from unsigned integer, in the range $[0, 255]$, to signed values belonging to the range $[-128, 127]$. At this point a 2-D DCT transform is applied to each block, followed by a *Quantization*, using for each DCT coefficient of the 8×8 non-overlapping block a corresponding integer value defined in a Quantization Table. The elements in the Quantization Table are related to the so called Quality Factor (QF) which defines the level of compression and reduction of information obtainable by JPEG. The quantized coefficients obtained are then rounded and the results of the ratio between the original DCT coefficients and the corresponding quantized ones, are then transformed into a data stream furtherly encoded by entropic compression. The entire process is lossy and this lossy behaviour leaves traces on images that can be exploited to predict if an image has gone through the JPEG algorithm. It is easy to note that the principal step in the JPEG algorithm which mainly reduces the information (and the size) in an image is the quantization step. Thus most of papers talk about *Double Quantization Detection* (DQD). The quantization step is driven in its outcome by the QF. Then for each compression a $QF - n$ is defined where n is how many times the image have gone through a JPEG compression process.

3   Related Works

Many DQD techniques have been proposed in literature during the last years. At first, Fan and De Queiroz [9,10], described an approach able to discriminate between images not compressed and JPEG compressed ones, independently from the number of compressions performed. They exploited the banal insight that if an image has never been previously JPEG-compressed, then the pixel differences across 8×8 block boundaries should not be noticeable.

The first attempt on detecting single vs. double JPEG compression was presented in [12] where the authors demonstrated that the distribution probability of the first digits law of the DCT coefficients in original JPEG images (single-compressed) follows a Benford-like logarithmic law ([14]). In [17] the authors furtherly analyzed the first digit distribution of each sub-band of DCT coefficients independently, while [15] extended the Benford-like law including the *zero* in the first digit distribution. Machine Learning classification technique were introduced by the works of [6] (inspired by [20]), and [8], which is itself a refinement of [7]. In [32] the authors built probability maps upon JPEG DCT coefficients, exploiting PCA for dimensional reduction and SVMs for classification. Pasquini et al. [22], proposed a binary decision test, based on the Benford-Fourier theory and improved it in [23] or even more [24] to face also multi (up to three) JPEG compressions and finally refining it in [25] with the introduction of features from images analysed in the spatial domain. On the other hand in [31] the authors created a new feature called *factor histogram* describing the distribution of the factors related to quantized DCT coefficients.

With the widespread of machine learning techniques and specifically Convolutional Neural Networks (CNN), new methods have been proposed for the DQD problem [1,18,21,28,29]. CNNs have demonstrated to be incredibly powerful in finding invisible correlation in data, specifically on images, but they are also very intensive in terms of computational costs, prone to overfitting and strictly related to the dataset on which they trained. Moreover, most of the predicted outcomes are not explainable and unpredictable making the use of CNNs uneffective in forensics. However, Li et al. [19] and Wang et al. [30] proposed new

DQD techniques able to outperform even CNNs. They are based on the statistics between adjacent DCT coefficients in 8×8 blocks of an image. In particular [19] rearranged the 8×8 blocks in 1×64 blocks thus extracting adjacent elements statistics as a feature vector for a SVM classifier, while [30] processed adjacent elements by means of a Markov Model, thus building a new feature vector for a SVM binary classifier.

4   Dataset

The aim of this paper is to investigate images in the DCT domain in order to find insights or a technique that works for the DQD task opening new research paths and outperforming the state-of-the-art. To this aim the analysis were perfomed on different datasets. The first one, is synthetic and constructed starting from the UCID dataset [27] employs standard-tables (with non standard tables ones only for same QF1-QF2), so it will be called UCID-derived. It is composed by 500 random images compressed twice into new JPEG images in order to cover many combination of QF1-QF2 as described below:

$$QF1_n n \in [100/95/90/.......\/50] \tag{1}$$

$$QF2_m m \in [100/95/90/.......\/50] \tag{2}$$

This process created 121 sets of 500 images for each couple of Quality Factors *QF1-QF2* The second dataset is the dataset presented in Giudice et al. [13] which contains images downloaded from social networks and the corresponding original ones. This last dataset employs completely non-standard tables, and is useful to evaluate all considerations and techniques *in the wild* with image coming from everyday usage: indeed images downloadable from Social Networks are double (or multiple) compressed. Being in the wild the dataset presents many combinations of QF1-QF2 most of them are estimable but not known a priori.

5   Investigating the DCT Domain

An evaluation of those studies based on the first digit statistics w.r.t. the Benford's Law ([12,17] and [15]) was carried out on images, taken in the wild from social networks taken from the dataset presented in [13]. Figure 1a shows the normalized histogram of the First Digit statistics obtained for single and double compressed images w.r.t. the Benford's Law in which all curves are perfectly overlapping. This demonstrates that all those approaches work only on specific conditions and are not effective in the wild. The main problem of [12,17] and [15], is that they compute statistics from all the 63 numbers obtained after the 2-D DCT transformation, in each 8×8 block. In this way components related to many frequencies are "mixed" altogether averaging everything. Indeed, taking into account the first digit statistics of just one coefficient is also almost ineffective, as shown in Fig. 1b: the curves obtained on single and double compressed images are overlapping and also are both separating from the Benford's law. The

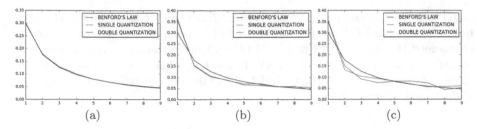

Fig. 1. First Digit distribution on images. (a) shows the Benford's law (blue) and the first digit distribution averaged on all 64 elements of 2-D DCT transformed 8 × 8 blocks. The green line shows the single compressed distribution while the red one the distribution obtained from double compressed images. The three curves are fully overlapped. Better separation is obtainable by computing the first digit statistics on only one element of the 8 × 8 block, as shown in (b) or by computing it after 1-D DCT transform (c). This last distributions while being easily and visibly separable differs from the Benford's law. (Color figure online)

separation, of the two curves, can be obtained by evaluating a 1D-DCT transformation on the 8 × 8 blocks. In this way a directional DCT is computed (through the vertical or horizontal direction) and the first digit statistics for single and double compressed images become separable as shown in Fig. 1c. Having two separate histograms means that the distribution is a good feature to be exploited for the DQD problem. Figure 1c shows the statistics obtained on the best element w.r.t. the separation of the two curves: not all elements showed a good separation, thus a further analysis was carried out on 8 × 8 blocks transformed through both 1-D DCT (in both directions) and 2-D DCT. Figure 2 shows the heatmaps for the three analysis, for each of the 64 elements in a 8 × 8 block. Each element (i, j) in the three heatmaps is represented in terms of the obtained cosine distance between the first digit statistics between the single and the double compressed image obtained on (i, j). The distance value is averaged through all images on the social network images dataset [13]. In particular, Fig. 2a, as already stated for Fig. 1b, shows that 2D-DCT produce not very separable histograms (black color means low distance values), while Figs. 2b and 2c show that both directions of 1D-DCT achieve a very good separation. Specifically, the best separation in terms of distance values is obtained on elements in the bottom part of the 8 × 8 block for vertical 1-D DCT and in the right part of the 8 × 8 block in the horizontal 1-D DCT. The 1-D DCT transform in conjunction with the first digit statistics is able to produce a good histogram separation for single and double compressed images, but those curves as shown in Fig. 1c do not follow the Benford's Law, thus a new law should be used to detect double compressed images. To this aim a novel classification technique was experimented and will be presented in the next section.

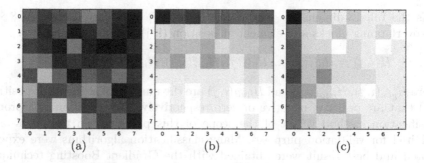

Fig. 2. Heatmap representation of cosine distance values between the first digit statistics obtained for single and double compressed image. The distance is computed for each element inside the 8 × 8 block. Black values means distance equal to zero. (a) shows the distance values obtained after 2-D DCT transform while values obtained after 1-D DCT trasform are shown in (b) w.r.t. vertical direction and (c) horizontal one.

6 Validation Through Automated DQD Technique

The insights obtained through the investigation carried out and described in this paper suggested a simple computational approach, together with visible statistics that allow to detect double compressed images. In order to evaluate if this feature can be exploited to correctly detect double compressed images, a test on many samples has to be carried out. Thus, a classification technique was built in order to model the new law, that was demonstrated to be different from the Benford's one, able to automatically detect double compressed images. The DQD law is modelled on top of all the explainable insights described in Sect. 5 and takes into account a feature vector that not only contains the statistics of all the first digits (including 0), but also the signs statistics (positive or negative) of the elements. Thus, a 13-dimensional feature vector was obtained for each of the 64 elements of the 8 × 8 blocks processed with the 1-D DCT transformation.

In a more formal representation, given a JPEG image I, it is possible to divide it into N non-overlapping 8 × 8 pixels blocks B_n with $n \in [0, N-1]$, and with each B_n containing 64 elements $B_n(i,j)$ with $i,j \in [0,7]$. Given the first digit function definition as follows:

$$FirstDigit_d(x) = \begin{cases} 1 & \text{if } x \text{ has a value with the first digit equal to } d \\ 0 & \text{otherwise} \end{cases} \tag{3}$$

Starting from an element at position (i, j) in the 8 × 8 block it is possible to compute the first digit and signs statistics, for all $n \in [0, N-1]$ as follows:

$$H_d(i,j) = \sum_n FirstDigit_d(B_n(i,j)) \tag{4}$$

Thus the full 13-dimensions feature vector $H(i,j)$ for image I with N 8×8 non-overlapping blocks and element at position (i, j) is defined as follows:

$$H(i,j) = H_0(i,j), ..., H_9(i,j), H_{pos}(i,j), H_{neg}(i,j), H_{null}(i,j) \tag{5}$$

where $H_{pos}(i,j)$, $H_{neg}(i,j)$ and $H_{null}(i,j)$ are the number of elements at position (i, j) that are positive, negative or zero respectively. The selection of a proper classification method is out of the scope of this paper, given that it is only exploited for validation purposes. Many classification algorithms were experimented and best result were obtained with the Gradient Boosting technique. The Gradient Boosting (GBoost) technique was employed to train 64 different classifiers $C(i,j)$ for each element in the 8×8 block. As expected, best results were obtained w.r.t. highest frequency components among the elements of the 8×8 block transformed through any of the two 1-D DCT transforms. This was expected as already visually-described by distance values of histogram curves shown in Fig. 2.

7   Experimental Results

The experimental phase was carried out by training and then testing the images from the two datasets described in Sect. 4. The UCID-derived image dataset were divided into two sets: training set and test set. The training set was used to train the 64 classifiers (one for each element of the 8×8 block) and the test set was employed to compute the accuracy measurements. The test was repeated by means of 5-fold Cross Validation and the results reported in this paper are the average accuracy measurements among all runs. In Table 1 the obtained accuracy measurements are shown and compared with the most recent state-of-the-art techniques for each couple of QF1-QF2. In almost all the different cases the proposed technique outperforms the current methods described in literature. Moreover, the proposed technique is able to detect double compression in images with $QF1 = QF2$, as it was investigated by Huang et al. [16] only. The selection of the best element among the 64 available is very important: the accuracy reported in Table 1 for the proposed technique is the average obtained from all the 8 elements taken in the last row or column w.r.t. the direction of the 1-D DCT, as already stated before. A further improvement could be possible with a better and automated element selection method.

Finally, another test was carried out on images taken in the wild from the social network dataset [13]. Results are reported in Table 2 for 1-D DCT on vertical and horizontal directions. The best accuracy level is reported to be of 95% and demonstrates the effectiveness of the technique. Values for the first row and column are not reported being related to low frequency components that have no discriminative information.

Table 1. Results in terms of best accuracy obtained on the same UCID-derived dataset, between the best methods in the state-of-the-art compared to the proposed approach w.r.t. QF1-QF2 couples.

QF1/QF2		50	60	70	80	90
50	1D-DCT GBoost	**0.72**	**1.00**	**1.00**	**1.00**	0.92
	[30]	–	–	–	–	–
	[19]	–	0.9976	0.9992	0.9995	**0.9998**
60	1D-DCT GBoost	0.96	**0.68**	**1.0**	0.96	0.92
	[30]	–	–	–	–	–
	[19]	**0.98**	-	0.9988	**0.9992**	**0.9998**
70	1D-DCT GBoost	**1.0**	**1.0**	**0.76**	**1.0**	0.88
	[30]	–	–	0.47	**1.0**	**1.0**
	[19]	0.9918	0.991	–	0.9988	0.9993
80	1D-DCT GBoost	**1.0**	**1.0**	**1.0**	0.76	0.92
	[30]	–	–	0.98	**0.96**	0.99
	[19]	0.9843	0.9929	0.9936	–	**0.9993**
90	1D-DCT GBoost	**1.0**	**1.0**	**1.0**	**1.0**	0.76
	[30]	–	–	0.96	0.99	**0.91**
	[19]	0.9462	0.9695	0.9784	0.9961	–

Table 2. Accuracy results obtained for each coefficient on Giudice et al. [13] dataset. Best accuracy results come from elements in the last row and column for 1-D DCT on vertical and horizontal directions respectively and confirm the heatmaps described in Fig. 2b and c.

		Vertical									Horizontal						
	0	1	2	3	4	5	6	7		0	1	2	3	4	5	6	7
0	–	–	–	–	–	–	–	–	0	–	0.6	0.8	0.75	0.8	0.85	0.8	0.95
1	0.85	0.75	0.7	0.8	0.8	0.6	0.6	0.6	1	–	0.5	0.75	0.65	0.85	0.7	0.85	0.9
2	0.8	0.75	0.65	0.75	0.8	0.8	0.6	0.8	2	–	0.75	0.8	0.65	0.85	0.8	0.8	0.8
3	0.8	0.75	0.7	0.8	0.75	0.8	0.8	0.75	3	–	0.7	0.75	0.75	0.85	0.8	0.9	0.8
4	0.85	0.75	0.8	0.8	0.9	0.8	0.65	0.9	4	–	0.7	0.7	0.55	0.85	0.8	0.75	0.85
5	0.85	0.85	0.85	0.8	0.9	0.75	0.7	0.9	5	–	0.65	0.75	0.8	0.85	0.7	0.85	0.85
6	0.85	0.85	0.8	0.75	0.8	0.85	0.9	0.8	6	–	0.8	0.75	0.65	0.8	0.75	0.85	0.85
7	0.9	0.85	0.85	0.95	0.9	0.95	0.95	0.9	7	–	0.65	0.8	0.7	0.8	0.9	0.9	0.95

8   Conclusions and Future Works

In this paper an in-depth analysis of the elements in 8×8 blocks of a JPEG image was carried out in the DCT domain with the aim of finding useful information to be exploited in the Double Quantization Detection problem. Through the analyses, the first digit statistics was employed with discriminative results in the highest frequency components (the last row or the last column) in the 1D-DCT transformed 8×8 blocks. Thus the first digit statistics was encoded as a feature for a simple Gradient Boost Classifier in order to be able to evaluate the detection effectiveness on synthetic couples of double compressed images and on images taken in the wild. Results demonstrated to outperform state-of-the-art methods in terms of accuracy, easiness, explainability and fastness of the technique.

Further investigation will be devoted to the formalization of the underlying mathematical law in order to build a self-explainable DQD technique; moreover it could be possible to exploit 1-D DCT Domain Analysis in order to detect tampered region in JPEG images.

References

1. Barni, M.: Aligned and non-aligned double JPEG detection using convolutional neural networks. J. Vis. Commun. Image Represent. **49**, 153–163 (2017)
2. Battiato, S., Farinella, G.M., Gallo, G., Giudice, O.: On-board monitoring system for road traffic safety analysis. Comput. Ind. **98**, 208–217 (2018)
3. Battiato, S., Giudice, O., Paratore, A.: Multimedia forensics: discovering the history of multimedia contents. In: Proceedings of the 17th International Conference on Computer Systems and Technologies 2016, pp. 5–16. ACM (2016)
4. Battiato, S., Mancuso, M., Bosco, A., Guarnera, M.: Psychovisual and statistical optimization of quantization tables for DCT compression engines. In: Proceedings 11th International Conference on Image Analysis and Processing, pp. 602–606. IEEE (2001)
5. Battiato, S., Messina, G.: Digital forgery estimation into DCT domain: a critical analysis. In: Proceedings of the First ACM workshop on Multimedia in forensics, pp. 37–42. ACM (2009)
6. Bianchi, T., De Rosa, A., Piva, A.: Improved DCT coefficient analysis for forgery localization in JPEG images. In: International Conference on Acoustics Speech and Signal Processing. ICASSP, pp. 2444–2447 (2011)
7. Bianchi, T., Piva, A.: Detection of non-aligned double JPEG compression with estimation of primary compression parameters. In: 18th IEEE International Conference on Image Processing, ICIP, pp. 1929–1932 (2011)
8. Bianchi, T., Piva, A.: Image forgery localization via block-grained analysis of JPEG artifacts. IEEE Transact. Inf. Forensics Secur. **7**(3), 1003–1017 (2012)
9. Fan, Z., de Queiroz Ricardo, L.: Maximum likelihood estimation of JPEG quantization table in the identification of bitmap compression history. In: Proceedings of the International Conference on Image Processing, vol. 1, pp. 948–951. (2000)
10. Fan, Z., de Queiroz, R.L.: Identification of bitmap compression history: JPEG detection and quantizer estimation. IEEE Transact. Image Process. **12**(2), 230–235 (2003)
11. Farinella, G.M., Ravì, D., Tomaselli, V., Guarnera, M., Battiato, S.: Representing scenes for real-time context classification on mobile devices. Pattern Recogn. **48**(4), 1086–1100 (2015)
12. Fu, D., Shi, Y., Su, W.: A generalized Benford's law for JPEG coefficients and its applications in image forensics. In: Security, Steganography, and Watermarking of Multimedia Contents IX, vol. 6505, p. 65051L. International Society for Optics and Photonics (2007)

13. Giudice, O., Paratore, A., Moltisanti, M., Battiato, S.: A classification engine for image ballistics of social data. In: Battiato, S., Gallo, G., Schettini, R., Stanco, F. (eds.) ICIAP 2017. LNCS, vol. 10485, pp. 625–636. Springer, Cham (2017). https://doi.org/10.1007/978-3-319-68548-9_57

14. Hill, T.: A statistical derivation of the significant-digit law. Stat. Sci. **10**, 354–363 (1995)

15. Hou, W., Ji, Z., Jin, X., Li, X.: Double JPEG compression detection base on extended first digit features of DCT coefficients. Int. J. Inf. Educ. Technol. **3**(5), 512–515 (2013)

16. Huang, F., Huang, J., Shi, Y.Q.: Detecting double JPEG compression with the same quantization matrix. IEEE Transact. Inf. Forensics Secur. **5**(4), 848–856 (2010)

17. Li, B., Shi, Y.Q., Huang, J.: Detecting doubly compressed JPEG images by using mode based first digit features. IEEE **10**, 730–735 (2008)

18. Li, B., Luo, H., Zhang, H., Tan, S., Ji, Z.: A multi-branch convolutional neural network for detecting double JPEG compression. arXiv preprint arXiv:1710.05477 (2017)

19. Li, J., Lu, W., Weng, J., Mao, Y., Li, G.: Double JPEG compression detection based on block statistics. Multimedia Tools Appl. **77**(24), 31895–31910 (2018)

20. Lin, Z.: Automatic and fine-grained tampered JPEG image detection via DCT coefficient analysis. Pattern Recogn. **42**(11), 2492–2501 (2009)

21. Park, J., Cho, D., Ahn, W., Lee, H.K.: Double JPEG detection in mixed JPEG quality factors using deep convolutional neural network. In: The European Conference on Computer Vision (ECCV), September 2018

22. Pasquini, C., Boato, G., Perez-Gonzalez, F.: A benford-fourier JPEG compression detector. In: IEEE International Conference on Image Processing, ICIP, pp. 5322–5326 (2014)

23. Pasquini, C., Boato, G., Perez-Gonzalez, F.: Multiple JPEG compression detection by means of benford-fourier coefficients. In: IEEE International Workshop on Information Forensics and Security (WIFS), pp. 113–118 (2014)

24. Pasquini, C., Bohme, R.: Towards a theory of jpeg block convergence. In: 2018 25th IEEE International Conference on Image Processing (ICIP), pp. 550–554. IEEE (2018)

25. Pasquini, C., Schöttle, P., Böhme, R., Boato, G., Pèrez-Gonzàlez, F.: Forensics of high quality and nearly identical JPEG image recompression. In: Proceedings of the 4th ACM Workshop on Information Hiding and Multimedia Security, pp. 11–21. ACM (2016)

26. Ravì, D., Bober, M., Farinella, G.M., Guarnera, M., Battiato, S.: Semantic segmentation of images exploiting DCT based features and random forest. Pattern Recogn. **52**, 260–273 (2016)

27. Schaefer, G., Stich, M.: UCID: An uncompressed color image database. In: Storage and Retrieval Methods and Applications for Multimedia 2004, vol. 5307, pp. 472–481. International Society for Optics and Photonics (2003)

28. Uricchio, T., Ballan, L., Roberto Caldelli, I., et al.: Localization of JPEG double compression through multi-domain convolutional neural networks. In: Proceedings of the IEEE Conference on Computer Vision and Pattern Recognition Workshops, pp. 53–59 (2017)

29. Wang, Q., Zhang, R.: Double JPEG compression forensics based on a convolutional neural network. EURASIP J. Inf. Secur. **2016**(1), 23 (2016)

30. Wang, Z.F., Zhu, L., Min, Q.S., Zeng, C.Y.: Double compression detection based on feature fusion. In: 2017 International Conference on Machine Learning and Cybernetics (ICMLC), vol. 2, pp. 379–384. IEEE (2017)
31. Yang, J., Zhua, G., Huang, J.: Detecting doubly compressed JPEG images by factor histogram. In: Asia Pacific Signal and Information Processing Association - Annual Summit and Conference (APSIPA ASC) (2011)
32. Yang, P., Ni, R., Zhao, Y.: Double JPEG compression detection by exploring the correlations in DCT domain. In: 2018 Asia-Pacific Signal and Information Processing Association Annual Summit and Conference (APSIPA ASC), pp. 728–732. IEEE (2018)

Image Processing for Cultural Heritage

Artpedia: A New Visual-Semantic Dataset with Visual and Contextual Sentences in the Artistic Domain

Matteo Stefanini⬡, Marcella Cornia⬡, Lorenzo Baraldi$^{(\boxtimes)}$⬡,
Massimiliano Corsini⬡, and Rita Cucchiara⬡

University of Modena and Reggio Emilia, Modena, Italy
{matteo.stefanini,marcella.cornia,lorenzo.baraldi,
massimiliano.corsini,rita.cucchiara}@unimore.it

Abstract. As vision and language techniques are widely applied to real-istic images, there is a growing interest in designing visual-semantic mod-els suitable for more complex and challenging scenarios. In this paper, we address the problem of cross-modal retrieval of images and sentences coming from the artistic domain. To this aim, we collect and manu-ally annotate the *Artpedia* dataset that contains paintings and textual sentences describing both the visual content of the paintings and other contextual information. Thus, the problem is not only to match images and sentences, but also to identify which sentences actually describe the visual content of a given image. To this end, we devise a visual-semantic model that jointly addresses these two challenges by exploiting the latent alignment between visual and textual chunks. Experimental evaluations, obtained by comparing our model to different baselines, demonstrate the effectiveness of our solution and highlight the challenges of the proposed dataset. The Artpedia dataset is publicly available at: http://aimagelab. ing.unimore.it/artpedia.

Keywords: Cross-modal retrieval · Visual-semantic models · Cultural heritage

1 Introduction

The integration of vision and language has recently gained a lot of attention from both computer vision and NLP communities. As humans, we can seamlessly connect what we visually see or imagine and what we hear or say, therefore building effective bridges between our ability to see and our ability to express ourselves in a common language. In the effort of artificially replicating these connections, new algorithms and architectures have recently emerged for image and video captioning [1,5,16] and for visual-semantic retrieval [7,13,15]. The former architectures combine vision and language in a generative flavour on the textual side, and in the latter common spaces are built to integrate the two domains and retrieve textual elements given visual queries, and vice versa.

© Springer Nature Switzerland AG 2019
E. Ricci et al. (Eds.): ICIAP 2019, LNCS 11752, pp. 729–740, 2019.
https://doi.org/10.1007/978-3-030-30645-8_66

While the standard objective in visual-semantic retrieval is that of associating images and *visual sentences* (*i.e.* sentences that visually describe something), the variety of sentences which can be found in textual corpora is definitely larger, and also contains sentences which do not describe the visual content of a scene. Here, we go a step beyond and extend the task of visual-semantic retrieval to a setting in which the textual domain does not exclusively contain visual sentences, and explore the task of identifying relevant visual sentences given image queries. As such, the task establishes two challenges, the first one being that of understanding whether the sentence has a visually relevant content, and the second being that of associating elements between the two domains.

Further, we also address a second shortcoming of most visual-semantic works, *i.e.* that of dealing with photo-realistic images and simple texts. As there is a growing need of extending these algorithms to less general semantic and visual domains, we both increase the complexity on the visual and on the semantic side. To create an environment where all the aforementioned challenges live together, we focus on the case of artistic data—which surely advertise more complex and unusual visual and semantic features, and propose a new dataset with *visual* and *contextual* sentences for each visual item. In short, visual sentences deal with the visual appearance of the item, contextual ones describe either the item or its context without dealing with its visual appearance.

We also design and evaluate a model for jointly associating visual and textual elements, and identifying visual textual samples as opposed to contextual ones. Taking inspiration from state of the art models for visual-semantic retrieval, we test both traditional approaches, based on global feature vectors, and approaches that model the latent alignment between visual and textual chunks.

The rest of this paper is organized as follows: after briefly reviewing the related literature in Sect. 2, we present the *Artpedia* dataset in Sect. 3. Further, in Sect. 4 we propose our model for bringing visual and contextual sentences in visual-semantic retrieval, which is subsequently evaluated together with different baselines in Sect. 5.

2   Related Work

In this section, we first give an overview of cross-modal retrieval models. Then, we review computer vision works related to the cultural heritage domain with a focus on other relevant datasets for art understanding.

2.1   Cross-Modal Retrieval

Cross-modal retrieval is one of the core challenges in computer vision and multimedia communities and consists in the retrieval of visual items given textual queries, and vice versa. In this context, several cross-modal retrieval models have been proposed [7,13,15], with the objective of minimizing the distance of matching image-text pairs and, on the contrary, maximizing that of non-matching elements. Among them, Faghri *et al.* [7] introduced a simple modification of

Table 1. Overview of the most relevant datasets containing artistic images.

Dataset	# Images	# Sentences	Manually annotated	Task
Wikipaintings [12]	85,000	–	✗	Classification
Art500k [18]	554,198	–	✗	Classification and retrieval
Brueghel [21]	1,587	–	✓	Near duplicate detection
SemArt [8]	21,383	21,383	✗	Visual-semantic retrieval
EsteArtworks [3]	553	1,278	✓	Visual-semantic retrieval
BibleVSA [2]	2,282	2,271	✓	Visual-semantic retrieval
Artpedia	2,930	28,212	✓	Visual-semantic retrieval (with contextual sentences)

standard loss functions based on the use of hard negatives that has been demonstrated to be effective in improving the performance of cross-modal retrieval and has been widely adopted by several subsequent methods [6,10,11,15].

Inspired by the use of multiple image descriptors to improve related visual-semantic tasks [1,25], Lee *et al.* [15] have recently proposed to match images and corresponding descriptions by inferring a latent correspondence between image regions and single words of the caption. In this work, we exploit a similar attentive mechanism to match each painting with the sentences that actually describe the visual content of the painting itself, and we demonstrate the effectiveness of using multiple image regions in place of a single image descriptor also for visual-semantic artistic data.

2.2 Computer Vision for Cultural Heritage

In the last years, several efforts have been done to apply computer vision techniques to the cultural heritage domain resulting in different works and applications ranging from generative models to classification and retrieval solutions. On the generative and synthesis side, up-and-coming results have been obtained by style transfer models that aim to transfer the style of a painting to a real photo [9] and, on the contrary, create a realistic representation of a given painting [23,24].

On a different note, several large-scale art datasets have been proposed to foster researches on this domain, with a particular focus on style and genre recognition [12,18]. For a comprehensive analysis, Table 1 shows a summary of the most relevant dataset related to the cultural heritage domain. To the best of our knowledge, there is a limited bunch of works that address the problem of retrieving artistic images from textual descriptions, and vice versa [2,3,8]. While [2,3] take the problem in a semi-supervised way by exploiting the knowledge from large-scale datasets containing realistic images, [8] uses additional metadata such as title, author, genre, and period of the paintings to match images and text. In this paper, we instead propose a visual-semantic model capable of discriminating *visual* and *contextual* sentences for each considered painting and, at the same time, associating the corresponding visual and textual elements.

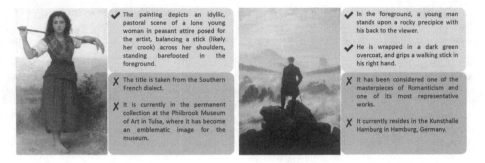

Fig. 1. Sample paintings from our Artpedia dataset with corresponding visual (green boxes) and contextual (red boxes) sentences. (Color figure online)

3   The Artpedia Dataset

To foster the research on the development of visual-semantic algorithms which deal with contextual sentences, we propose a novel dataset with visual and contextual sentences describing real paintings. *Artpedia* contains a collection of 2,930 painting images, each associated to a variable number of textual descriptions. Each sentence is labelled either as a *visual* sentence or as a *contextual* sentence, if does not describe the visual content of the artwork. Contextual sentences can describe the historical context of the artwork, its author, the artistic influence or the place where the painting is exhibited. As in standard cross-modal datasets, the association between sentences and painting is also provided. A sample of the dataset and its annotations is shown in Fig. 1.

As the name suggests, the dataset has been collected by crawling Wikipedia pages. To this aim, our crawling strategy followed the Wikipedia category hierarchy by navigating all categories containing paintings between the 13th and the 21th century. We then extracted the textual descriptions taking into account all the summaries of each Wikipedia page and the description section whenever present. Finally, we split the text into sentences using the spaCy NLP toolbox[1] and manually annotated each sentence either as visual or contextual. As an additional product of the crawling procedure, we also release the title and the year of each painting, together with the URL of each image.

Overall, Artpedia contains a total of 28,212 sentences, 9,173 labelled as visual sentences and the remaining 19,039 as contextual sentences. On average, each painting is associated with 3.1 visual and 6.5 contextual sentences. The mean length of the textual items is 21.5 words, considerably longer than those of standard image captioning datasets. For a comprehensive analysis of the visual and semantic content of our Artpedia dataset, we report in Fig. 2 the distribution of paintings over the given range of centuries, the distribution of sentence lengths, and the most common object classes obtained by running a pre-trained object detector [14,20].

---

[1] https://spacy.io/.

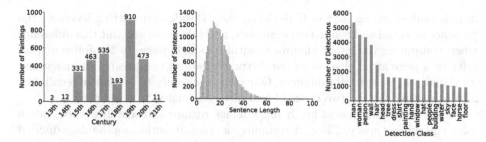

Fig. 2. Analyses on our Artpedia dataset. From left to right, we report the painting distribution over centuries, the sentence lengths distribution, and the most common detection classes.

Table 2. Number of paintings, visual and contextual sentences for each Artpedia split.

	Training	Validation	Test
Paintings	2,252	339	339
Visual sentences	7,109	1,036	1,028
Contextual sentences	14,822	2,134	2,083

With respect to other visual-semantic datasets containing artistic images (reported in Table 1), Artpedia provides a larger number of sentences, divided into visual and contextual through a manual annotation procedure. Moreover, to the best of our knowledge, this is the only dataset that contains two types of artistic sentences describing both the visual content of the paintings and other contextual information. For this reason, we devise a visual-semantic model capable of jointly discriminating between visual and contextual sentences of the same painting, and identifying which visual descriptions from a subset of textual elements (*i.e.* a subset of visual descriptions from different paintings) are associated to a specific painting.

To allow the training of our model and foster researches on this domain, we also provide training, validation and test splits obtained by proportionally dividing the number of paintings. Splits have been obtained with the constraint of balancing the distributions over centuries and the number of visual sentences to maintain relevant statistics across the subsets. Table 2 reports the number of paintings for each split along with the corresponding number of visual and contextual sentences.

4 Aligning Visual and Contextual Sentences with Images

Cross-modal retrieval is characterized by two main tasks: when the query is a textual sentence, the objective is to retrieve the most relevant images, while with an image as a query, the objective is to retrieve the most relevant sentences. The goal is to maximize recall at K, the fraction of queries for which the most relevant item is ranked among the top K retrieved ones. Besides, our setting leverages the presence of visual and contextual sentences, and takes into account this difference when computing the latent alignment within a single page. In the following, we refer to a page as an element of our Artpedia dataset comprising an image and its visual and contextual sentences. Our goal is not only to maximize recall, but also to distinguish the two types of sentences associated to a painting.

In a nutshell, our model firstly maps image regions and sentence words into a joint embedding space. Then, it computes a cross-attention mechanism divided in two branches, where one attends to words with respect to each image region, while the other attends to image regions with respect to each word. This mechanism computes a similarity score for each branch between an image and a sentence. During training, the similarity score is used to minimize two loss functions: our intra-page loss, which strives to rank the sentences associated to a single image, bringing near its visual sentences and pushing away its contextual ones, and the inter-page triplet ranking loss that takes into account all images and their visual sentences as in standard cross-modal retrieval settings.

4.1 Similarity Function

As mentioned before, the similarity is computed with a cross-attention mechanism that comprises two distinct branches: image-to-text and text-to-image attention, inspired by [15,25]. Since the two branches are similar, diversified only by the input order, we only describe the first one.

Firstly, given an image I, we extract salient regions such that each of them encodes an object or other entities, and project them into the joint embedding space, obtaining a final set of regions $\{v_1, \ldots, v_k\}, v_i \in \mathbb{R}^D$. Also, given a sentence T composed of n words, encoded with a word embedding strategy, we project each word into the joint embedding space thus obtaining a vector $e_j \in \mathbb{R}^D$ for each word j. Therefore, given an image I with k detected regions and a sentence T with n words, we compute the similarity matrix for all possible region-word pairs:

$$s_{ij} = v_i^\top e_j \quad i \in [1, k], j \in [1, n] \tag{1}$$

where s_{ij} represents the similarity between the region i and the word j. Since region and word features are ℓ_2 normalized, this product corresponds to a cosine similarity.

To attend words with respect to each image region, we compute a sentence-context vector for each region. The sentence-context vector a_i is a weighted representation of the sentence with respect to the region i of the image, where the similarities between the region i and the sentence words are used to weight each word as follows:

$$a_i = \sum_{j=1}^{n} \alpha_{ij} e_j \tag{2}$$

where

$$\alpha_{ij} = \frac{\exp\left(\lambda_s s_{ij}\right)}{\sum_{j=1}^{n} \exp\left(\lambda_s s_{ij}\right)} \tag{3}$$

and λ_s is a temperature parameter [4].

Finally, to evaluate the similarity of each image region given the sentence-context, we compute the cosine similarity between the attended sentence vector a_i and each image region feature v_i:

$$R\left(v_i, a_i\right) = \frac{v_i^\top a_i}{\|a_i\|} \tag{4}$$

To summarize the similarity between an image I and a sentence T, we employ average pooling between all image regions and the sentence-context vector:

$$R_{AVG}(I, T) = \frac{\sum_{i=1}^{k} R\left(v_i, a_i\right)}{k} \tag{5}$$

Likewise, the other branch follows the same procedure but swapping image regions and sentence words, computing a region-context vector for each sentence word, evaluating their cosine similarities and summarizing the final branch score in the same way. Finally, by averaging the similarity scores of the two branches, we obtain the final similarity score $S(I, T)$ between an image I and a sentence T.

4.2 Training

Intra-page Loss. With the objective of correctly ranking visual and contextual sentences of a given image, we propose an intra-page loss function that learns the latent alignment between an image and its corresponding visual sentences within a single page of the dataset. Given an image I, a visual sentence T_V and a contextual sentence T_C, our intra-page loss is computed by taking into account the similarity score $S(I, T_V)$ between the image and the visual sentence and the similarity score $S(I, T_C)$ between the image and the contextual one:

$$L_{intra}(I, T_V, T_C) = [\alpha - S(I, T_V) + S(I, T_C)]_+ \tag{6}$$

where $[x]_+ = max(x, 0)$ and α is the margin. Note that, since this loss function is computed within a single page, both considered visual and contextual sentence are taken within the sentences of the given image I.

Inter-page Triplet Ranking Loss. Since our final objective is not only to identify visual and contextual sentences of the same image, but also to associate matching image-visual sentence pairs within the entire dataset, we define an inter-page triplet ranking loss, which is typical of cross-modal retrieval methods.

As proposed in [7], we focus solely on the hardest negatives in the mini-batch. So that, our final inter-page triplet ranking loss with margin α is defined as follows:

$$L_{inter}(I, T) = \max_{\hat{T}} \left[\alpha - S(I, T) + S(I, \hat{T})\right]_+ + \max_{\hat{I}} \left[\alpha - S(I, T) + S(\hat{I}, T)\right]_+ \tag{7}$$

where only the hardest negative sentences $\hat{T}$ or hardest negative images $\hat{I}$ for each positive pair $S(I, T)$ are taken into account. In our case, a negative sentence $\hat{T}$ is a visual sentence of another image. Since this loss function aims to associate images and visual sentences of the entire dataset, contextual sentences are only used by our intra-page loss.

Final Training Objective. The final training loss is obtained by a linear combination of the two loss functions, *i.e.* $L = \lambda_w L_{inter} + (1 - \lambda_w) L_{intra}$, where $\lambda_w \in [0, 1]$ is a parameter that weights the contribution of the two losses. When λ_w is equal to 0, the training procedure only minimizes our intra-page loss, whilst when λ_w is equal to 1, all the attention is given to the inter-page triplet ranking loss.

5   Experimental Evaluation

In this section, we experimentally evaluate the effectiveness of our approach by comparing it with different baselines. First, we provide all implementation details used in our experiments.

5.1   Implementation Details

To encode image regions, we use Faster R-CNN [20] trained on Visual Genome [1, 14], thus obtaining 2048-dimensional feature vectors. For each image, we exploit the top 20 detected regions with the highest class confidence scores. To project regions into the visual-semantic embedding space, we use a fully connected layer with a size of 512.

For the textual counterpart, we compare GloVe [19] with word embeddings learned from scratch. In both cases, the word embedding size is set to 300. Then, with the aim of capturing the semantic context of the sentence, we employ a bi-directional GRU with a size of 512, so that given a sentence with n words, the bi-directional GRU captures the context reading forward from word 1 to n and reading backwards from word n to 1, averaging the two hidden states to obtain the final embedding vector for each word.

To train our model, we use the Adam optimizer with an initial learning rate of 10^{-6} decreased by a factor of 10 after 15 epochs. In all our experiments, we use a batch size of 128 and clip the gradients at 2. Finally, the margin α and the temperature parameter λ_s are respectively set to 0.2 and 6.

5.2   Baselines

To evaluate our solution, we build different baselines to quantify both the effectiveness of using a cross-attention model and that of our intra-page loss. To this aim, we first exploit global features to encode images and sentences in place of multiple feature vectors for each image or sentence. In particular, to encode images, we extract 2048-dimensional feature vectors from the average pooling layer of a ResNet-152, while, to encode sentences, we feed word embeddings

Table 3. Intra-page results in terms of Average Precision (AP).

Model	Word embedding	AP
Global features with BCE loss	Learned	39.3
Global features with BCE loss	GloVe	40.8
Global features with intra-page loss	Learned	52.8
Global features with intra-page loss	GloVe	**55.3**
Cross-attention with BCE loss	Learned	42.6
Cross-attention with BCE loss	GloVe	41.7
Cross-attention with intra-page loss	Learned	86.3
Cross-attention with intra-page loss	GloVe	**88.5**

through a bi-directional GRU network and average the outputs of the last hidden state in both directions. After projecting both images and sentences into a common embedding space, the final similarity score between an image and a sentence is given by the cosine similarity between the two ℓ_2-normalized embedding vectors.

Furthermore, we compare the proposed intra-page loss function with respect to binary cross-entropy. Therefore, visual and contextual sentences are not projected into the same embedding space, but fed through a binary classification branch. In practice, each sentence is classified either as visual or contextual by concatenating the image and sentence embeddings and feeding them through two fully connected layers of size 512 and 1, respectively. For the cross-attention model, the image embedding is obtained by averaging the image region embedding vectors, while the sentence embedding is obtained by averaging the last hidden states of the bi-directional GRU in the two directions.

For both baselines, all other hyper-parameters and training details are the same as those used in our complete model.

5.3 Cross-Modal Retrieval Results

We first evaluate the effectiveness of our model to identify and distinguish visual sentences with respect to contextual ones. Table 3 shows the results on the Artpedia test set in terms of average precision (AP). In particular, the results are obtained by training the models with λ_w equal to 0 (*i.e.* by only minimizing the intra-page loss or binary cross-entropy). As it can be seen, our intra-page loss function always obtains better performance with respect to the binary cross-entropy baseline either when exploiting global features to embed images and sentences or when using the cross-attention approach described in Sect. 4. Regarding the word embedding strategy, GloVe vectors achieve better results with respect to word embeddings learned from scratch, probably due to the presence of peculiar words, typical of the artistic domain.

In Table 4, we show the performance of our complete model trained with various λ_w weights to differently balance the contribution of the two loss func-

Table 4. Cross-modal retrieval results with a different number N of retrievable items and with respect to different λ_w weights.

Model	Word emb.	λ_w	AP	N = 10 Img-to-Text		Text-to-Img		N = 50 Img-to-Text		Text-to-Img		N = 100 Img-to-Text		Text-to-Img	
				R@1	R@5	R@1	R@5	R@1	R@5	R@1	R@5	R@1	R@5	R@1	R@5
Global	Learned	0.25	44.9	9.4	36.3	7.6	50.0	2.4	8.3	1.3	8.9	0.6	5.0	0.5	3.6
Global	GloVe		43.1	12.4	35.4	8.5	48.7	2.7	9.1	2.2	11.1	0.6	5.3	1.8	5.5
X-Attn	Learned		85.9	15.3	40.4	17.5	61.9	2.7	13.3	4.2	16.7	2.1	8.0	2.2	9.0
X-Attn	GloVe		**88.2**	**19.8**	**44.0**	**22.7**	**69.6**	**8.6**	**22.1**	**6.1**	**23.6**	**4.4**	**15.9**	**4.0**	**14.8**
Global	Learned	0.50	50.2	9.4	38.1	9.9	50.7	1.8	10.0	2.0	10.5	0.6	6.2	1.1	5.1
Global	GloVe		46.0	8.8	37.2	9.8	48.9	1.2	10.0	2.0	10.1	1.8	4.1	1.0	4.4
X-Attn	Learned		85.2	11.5	40.1	17.4	61.0	3.2	13.6	3.8	18.7	1.2	7.7	2.4	9.9
X-Attn	GloVe		**87.5**	**26.3**	**54.3**	**21.2**	**69.7**	**8.8**	**27.7**	**7.5**	**22.9**	**6.2**	**18.6**	**4.1**	**14.1**
Global	Learned	0.75	53.4	10.6	38.3	10.4	50.0	2.4	10.6	2.3	11.6	1.5	5.6	1.4	6.2
Global	GloVe		44.9	10.9	34.2	8.9	47.7	1.8	8.6	1.8	9.3	0.9	4.4	0.7	4.6
X-Attn	Learned		84.6	10.9	37.5	18.5	64.3	2.7	10.0	5.1	20.1	1.2	7.1	2.9	11.4
X-Attn	GloVe		**86.5**	**29.5**	**57.2**	**23.7**	**71.2**	**13.6**	**31.9**	**5.8**	**23.1**	**8.6**	**22.7**	**4.1**	**13.6**

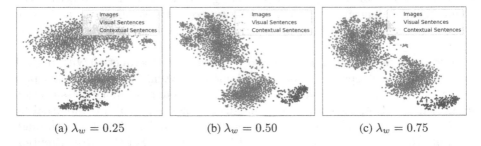

(a) $\lambda_w = 0.25$ (b) $\lambda_w = 0.50$ (c) $\lambda_w = 0.75$

Fig. 3. Comparison between visual-semantic embedding spaces obtained by training the model with different λ_w weights. Visualizations are obtained by running the t-SNE algorithm [17] on top of embedding vectors representing images and sentences (both visual and contextual).

tions. In this case, the goal is not only to correctly distinguish between visual and contextual sentences of a given image, but also to find the corresponding visual sentences from a subset of other textual elements (*i.e.* visual sentences of different images). Results are reported in terms of recall@K ($K = 1, 5$) using a different number N of items from which perform retrieval. In details, given an image as a query, the retrieval of a textual element is performed from a subset of visual sentences of N different images (*i.e.* the visual sentences of the query and those of other $N - 1$ randomly selected images). Instead, given a textual query, the retrieval of an image is performed from a subset of N different images (*i.e.* the image linked to the query and other $N - 1$ randomly selected images from the Artpedia test set). We also report the results of identifying visual sentences with respect to contextual ones in terms of average precision. As it can be noticed, by increasing the λ_w weight, we obtain an increment of recall metrics with a slight drop of average precision values, in almost all considered combinations of features and word embeddings. Also in this case, the cross-attention mechanism and the GloVe word embeddings achieve better results than global features and learned word embeddings.

Finally, Fig. 3 shows learned embedding spaces using the best model (*i.e.* cross-attention with GloVe word embeddings) using different λ_w weights. Since in this case images and sentences are composed of an embedding vector for each image region and word of the sentence, we represent each image or sentence by summing the ℓ_2-normalized embedding vectors of its image regions or words, and ℓ_2-normalized again the result. This strategy has been largely used in image and video retrieval works, and is known for preserving the information of the original vectors into a compact representation with fixed dimensionality [22]. To get a suitable two-dimensional representation out of a 512-dimensional space, we run the t-SNE algorithm [17], which iteratively finds a non-linear projection which preserves pairwise distances from the original space. As it can be observed, the higher the λ_w weight, the greater the distance between images and visual sentences in the embedding space, thus confirming the drop of average precision values when decreasing the importance of our intra-page loss during training.

6   Conclusion

In this paper, we have addressed the problem of cross-modal retrieval of images and sentences coming from the artistic domain. To this aim, we have collected and manually annotated a new visual-semantic dataset with visual and contextual sentences for each collected painting. Further, we have designed and evaluated a cross-modal retrieval model that jointly associates visual and textual elements, and discriminates between visual and contextual sentences of the same image. Experimental evaluations conducted with respect to different baselines have shown promising results and have demonstrated the effectiveness of our solution on both considered visual-semantic retrieval tasks.

References

1. Anderson, P., et al.: Bottom-up and top-down attention for image captioning and visual question answering. In: CVPR (2018)
2. Baraldi, L., Cornia, M., Grana, C., Cucchiara, R.: Aligning text and document illustrations: towards visually explainable digital humanities. In: ICPR (2018)
3. Carraggi, A., Cornia, M., Baraldi, L., Cucchiara, R.: Visual-semantic alignment across domains using a semi-supervised approach. In: Leal-Taixé, L., Roth, S. (eds.) ECCV 2018. LNCS, vol. 11134, pp. 625–640. Springer, Cham (2019). https://doi.org/10.1007/978-3-030-11024-6_47
4. Chorowski, J.K., Bahdanau, D., Serdyuk, D., Cho, K., Bengio, Y.: Attention-based models for speech recognition. In: NeurIPS (2015)
5. Cornia, M., Baraldi, L., Cucchiara, R.: Show, control and tell: a framework for generating controllable and grounded captions. In: CVPR (2019)
6. Engilberge, M., Chevallier, L., Pérez, P., Cord, M.: Finding beans in burgers: deep semantic-visual embedding with localization. In: CVPR (2018)

7. Faghri, F., Fleet, D.J., Kiros, J.R., Fidler, S.: VSE++: improving visual-semantic embeddings with hard negatives. In: BMVC (2018)

8. Garcia, N., Vogiatzis, G.: How to read paintings: semantic art understanding with multi-modal retrieval. In: Leal-Taixé, L., Roth, S. (eds.) ECCV 2018. LNCS, vol. 11130, pp. 676–691. Springer, Cham (2019). https://doi.org/10.1007/978-3-030-11012-3_52

9. Gatys, L.A., Ecker, A.S., Bethge, M.: Image style transfer using convolutional neural networks. In: CVPR (2016)

10. Gu, J., Cai, J., Joty, S.R., Niu, L., Wang, G.: Look, imagine and match: improving textual-visual cross-modal retrieval with generative models. In: CVPR (2018)

11. Huang, Y., Wu, Q., Song, C., Wang, L.: Learning semantic concepts and order for image and sentence matching. In: CVPR (2018)

12. Karayev, S., et al.: Recognizing image style. In: BMVC (2014)

13. Kiros, R., Salakhutdinov, R., Zemel, R.S.: Unifying visual-semantic embeddings with multimodal neural language models. In: NeurIPS Workshops (2014)

14. Krishna, R., et al.: Visual genome: connecting language and vision using crowd-sourced dense image annotations. Int. J. Comput. Vision 123(1), 32–73 (2017)

15. Lee, K.-H., Chen, X., Hua, G., Hu, H., He, X.: Stacked cross attention for image-text matching. In: Ferrari, V., Hebert, M., Sminchisescu, C., Weiss, Y. (eds.) ECCV 2018. LNCS, vol. 11208, pp. 212–228. Springer, Cham (2018). https://doi.org/10.1007/978-3-030-01225-0_13

16. Lu, J., Yang, J., Batra, D., Parikh, D.: Neural baby talk. In: CVPR (2018)

17. Van der Maaten, L., Hinton, G.: Visualizing data using t-SNE. J. Mach. Learn. Res. 9(Nov), 2579–2605 (2008)

18. Mao, H., Cheung, M., She, J.: DeepArt: learning joint representations of visual arts. In: ACM Multimedia (2017)

19. Pennington, J., Socher, R., Manning, C.: Glove: global vectors for word representation. In: EMNLP (2014)

20. Ren, S., He, K., Girshick, R., Sun, J.: Faster R-CNN: towards real-time object detection with region proposal networks. In: NeurIPS (2015)

21. Shen, X., Efros, A.A., Mathieu, A.: Discovering visual patterns in art collections with spatially-consistent feature learning. In: CVPR (2019)

22. Tolias, G., Sicre, R., Jégou, H.: Particular object retrieval with integral max-pooling of CNN activations. In: ICLR (2016)

23. Tomei, M., Baraldi, L., Cornia, M., Cucchiara, R.: What was Monet seeing while painting? Translating artworks to photo-realistic images. In: Leal-Taixé, L., Roth, S. (eds.) ECCV 2018. LNCS, vol. 11130, pp. 601–616. Springer, Cham (2019). https://doi.org/10.1007/978-3-030-11012-3_46

24. Tomei, M., Cornia, M., Baraldi, L., Cucchiara, R.: Art2Real: unfolding the reality of artworks via semantically-aware image-to-image translation. In: CVPR (2019)

25. Xu, T., et al.: AttnGAN: fine-grained text to image generation with attentional generative adversarial networks. In: CVPR (2018)

Image-to-Image Translation to Unfold the Reality of Artworks: An Empirical Analysis

Matteo Tomei[ID], Marcella Cornia[ID], Lorenzo Baraldi[(✉)][ID], and Rita Cucchiara[ID]

University of Modena and Reggio Emilia, Modena, Italy
{matteo.tomei,marcella.cornia,lorenzo.baraldi,rita.cucchiara}@unimore.it

Abstract. State-of-the-art Computer Vision pipelines show poor performances on artworks and data coming from the artistic domain, thus limiting the applicability of current architectures to the automatic understanding of the cultural heritage. This is mainly due to the difference in texture and low-level feature distribution between artistic and real images, on which state-of-the-art approaches are usually trained. To enhance the applicability of pre-trained architectures on artistic data, we have recently proposed an unpaired domain translation approach which can translate artworks to photo-realistic visualizations. Our approach leverages semantically-aware memory banks of real patches, which are used to drive the generation of the translated image while improving its realism. In this paper, we provide additional analyses and experimental results which demonstrate the effectiveness of our approach. In particular, we evaluate the quality of generated results in the case of the translation of landscapes, portraits and of paintings coming from four different styles using automatic distance metrics. Also, we analyze the response of pre-trained architecture for classification, detection and segmentation both in terms of feature distribution and entropy of prediction, and show that our approach effectively reduces the domain shift of paintings. As an additional contribution, we also provide a qualitative analysis of the reduction of the domain shift for detection, segmentation and image captioning.

Keywords: Image-to-image translation · Cultural heritage

1 Introduction

Although our society has inherited a huge patrimony of artworks, Computer Vision techniques are usually conceived for realistic images and are rarely applied to visual data coming from the artistic domain, regardless of the potential benefits of having architectures capable of understanding our cultural heritage.

As most of the recent computer vision achievements have relied on learning low-level and high-level features from images depicting the real world, it

© Springer Nature Switzerland AG 2019
E. Ricci et al. (Eds.): ICIAP 2019, LNCS 11752, pp. 741–752, 2019.
https://doi.org/10.1007/978-3-030-30645-8_67

Landscapes   Portraits
VGG-19 [23]   ResNet-101 [8]   VGG-19 [23]   ResNet-101 [8]

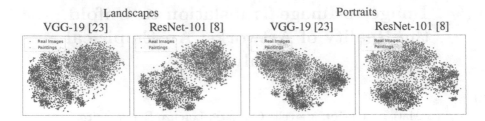

Fig. 1. Domain shift visualization between paintings and real images when applying existing computer vision models. Visualization is obtained by extracting visual features from both real and artistic images (last layer before classification) and by running the t-SNE algorithm [19] on top of that to obtain a 2-d visualization. Details on data collection are reported in Sect. 3.1.

is also not straightforward to apply pre-trained architectures to the domain of artworks and paintings, whose texture and low-level features are different from those of the real world [2,22,24]. An example of the resulting effect is shown in Fig. 1, where we plot the activations of two pre-trained image classification architectures (respectively, VGG-19 [23] and ResNet-101 [8]) on real images and paintings, belonging to the categories of landscapes and portraits. As it can be seen, even though real and artistic images belong to the same semantic classes, their predicted feature distributions remain separate, clearly highlighting the difficulty of the two pre-trained networks to deal with artistic data.

It shall be noted, on the other side, that it is not feasible to re-train state-of-the-art architectures on artistic data, as no large annotated datasets exist in the cultural heritage domain. To address this domain-shift problem while still exploiting the knowledge learned in pre-trained architectures, we have recently proposed a pixel-level domain translation architecture [25], that can map paintings to photo-realistic visualizations by generating translation images which look realistic while preserving the semantic content of the painting. The problem is one of unpaired domain translation, as no annotated pairing exists, *i.e.* photo realistic visualizations of paintings are rarely available – an when they are, they usually come in limited number. Therefore, the translation is learned by recovering a latent alignment between two unpaired sets: that of paintings and that of real images. The proposed solution is based on a generative cycle-consistent architecture, endowed with multi-scale memory banks which are in charge of memorizing and recovering the details of realistic images, in a semantically consistent way. As a result, generated images look more realistic from a qualitative point of view. Also, they are closer to real images in the feature space of pre-trained architectures, leading to reduced prediction errors without the need of re-training state-of-the-art approaches.

In this paper, after a brief description of our architecture, we provide additional analyses and experimental results to showcase the effectiveness of our approach. Firstly, we evaluate the quality of the generated images in the case of the translation of landscapes, portraits and four different artistic styles, in comparison with other state-of-the-art unpaired translation approaches. Further, we investigate the response of pre-trained architectures for classification, detection and semantic segmentation. As results will show, our approach reduces the entropy of prediction and produces images which are close in feature space to real images. Finally, we conduct a qualitative analysis of the reduction in domain shift, by testing with pre-trained detection, segmentation and captioning networks.

2 Semantically-Aware Image-to-Image Translation

In order to make state-of-the-art computer vision techniques suitable for understanding artistic data, we have not proposed a new specific architecture for this kind of data, but adopted instead a more general solution which fits available data to existing methods. The data adaptation approach we follow consists in the transformation of a painting to a photo-realistic visualization preserving the content and the overall appearance. This is done through generative models [6] equipped with a cycle-consistent constraint [26] and a semantic knowledge of the scene.

2.1 Cycle-Consistency

Early results of translations between paintings and reality have been shown in Zhu *et al.* [26], on a limited number of artistic settings. In a nutshell, their architecture consists of two Generative Adversarial Networks [6], one taking real photos as input and trained to generate fake paintings, and the other taking real paintings as input and trained to generate fake photos. When a new (realistic or artistic) image is synthesized by a generator, it is brought back to its original domain by the other generator and the resulting distance with the original image becomes the cycle-consistency objective to minimize. Formally, being x a sample from the artistic domain X, y a sample from the realistic domain Y, G and F two functions mapping images from X to Y and from Y to X respectively, the cycle-consistency imposes that $F(G(x)) \approx x$ and that $G(F(y)) \approx y$.

Since our objective is that of generating realistic images, rather than style-transferred version of real images, we focused on the first constraint. We noticed, however, that the adversarial objectives and cycle-consistency loss proposed in [26], alone, often fail to preserve semantic consistency and to produce realistic details.

2.2 Semantic-Consistency and Realistic Details

Our first exploration regarded the possibility of constraining our baseline to produce photo-realistic details at multiple scales, and not only an overall plausible image. Our main intuition was that the realism, at sufficiently small scales, can be obtained from existing real details, recovered from previously extracted patches coming from the realistic domain. Following this line, in a preliminary work [24] we reached better results with respect to the Cycle-GAN baseline. Later, we further improved the realism of the generation by considering patches as members of specific semantic classes and trying to preserve this membership during the generation [25].

Memory Banks. Considering details as fixed-size square patches, we model the distribution of realistic details as a set of memory banks, each containing a number of patches obtained from available real photos (*i.e.* from domain Y). Each memory bank $\boldsymbol{B}^c$ contains only RGB patches belonging to a specific semantic class c, as predicted by the weakly-supervised model by Hu *et al.* [10], leading to as many memory banks as the number of different classes found in Y, plus a background class. Patches are extracted in a sliding window manner, with specific sizes and strides.

Since we want the semantic content of an image to be the same before and after the generation, we also need to keep the semantic segmentation masks of source images, *i.e.* images coming from domain X. In the following, a mask of class c, from source image x, will be denoted as $\boldsymbol{M}_x^c$.

Semantically-Consistent Generation. In order to make the generator $G(x)$ aware of the semantic content of its input artistic image, we exploit masks $\boldsymbol{M}_x^c$. They let us split the content of the source image x (and therefore of its translation $G(x)$) according to the semantic classes composing the scene. During training, when a translated image $G(x)$ is generated, each of its regions belonging to a specific class is split into patches as well. We developed a matching strategy to pair generated patches of class c with their most-similar real patches belonging to memory bank $\boldsymbol{B}^c$, and we adopted the contextual loss [20] to maximize this similarity. Since the goal of our work is to enhance the performance of existing architectures on artistic data, the exploitation of semantic masks computed on paintings would create a chicken-egg problem. To overcome this limitation, we regularly update masks from the painting x, $\boldsymbol{M}_x^c$, with masks from the generated image $G(x)$, $\boldsymbol{M}_{G(x)}^c$, as the training proceeds.

Patch-Similarity Driven Generation. Being $\boldsymbol{K}^c$ the set of generated patches from regions of $G(x)$ belonging to class c, we compute the cosine similarity between all patches in $\boldsymbol{K}^c$ and all patches in $\boldsymbol{B}^c$ and perform a row-wise softmax normalization to the pairwise similarity matrix. The result is an affinity matrix A_{ij}^c, where i indexes $\boldsymbol{K}^c$ and j indexes $\boldsymbol{B}^c$. Repeating this operation for each mask found in $G(x)$, we obtain a number of affinity matrices equal to the number of semantic classes in $G(x)$. The contextual loss [20] is in charge of minimizing the distance between pairs of similar patches:

$$\mathcal{L}_{CX}^c(\boldsymbol{K}^c, \boldsymbol{B}^c) = -\log\left(\frac{1}{N_K^c}\left(\sum_i \max_j A_{ij}^c\right)\right), \tag{1}$$

with N_K^c denoting the cardinality of $\boldsymbol{K}^c$. The complete contextual objective is the summation of Eq. 1 computed for each class c found in $G(x)$, *i.e.* with different affinity matrices A_{ij}^c:

$$\mathcal{L}_{CX}(\boldsymbol{K}, \boldsymbol{B}) = \sum_c -\log\left(\frac{1}{N_K^c}\left(\sum_i \max_j \boldsymbol{A}_{ij}^c\right)\right). \tag{2}$$

All the previous discussed operations are repeated considering patches extracted with different size and stride values, using scale-specific memory banks and leading to scale-specific affinity matrices. The overall multi-scale contextual loss is the sum of scale-specific contextual losses:

$$\mathcal{L}_{CXMS}(\boldsymbol{K}, \boldsymbol{B}) = \sum_s \mathcal{L}_{CX}^s(\boldsymbol{K}, \boldsymbol{B}). \tag{3}$$

Our final loss is the composition of adversarial, cycle-consistent and contextual losses, as follows:

$$\mathcal{L}(G, F, D_X, D_Y, \boldsymbol{K}, \boldsymbol{B}) = \mathcal{L}_{GAN}(G, D_Y, X, Y) + \mathcal{L}_{GAN}(F, D_X, Y, X) \\ + \mathcal{L}_{CYC}(G, F) + \lambda\mathcal{L}_{CXMS}(\boldsymbol{K}, \boldsymbol{B}) \tag{4}$$

where $\mathcal{L}_{GAN}$ and $\mathcal{L}_{CYC}$ are, respectively, the adversarial and cycle-consistency losses mentioned in Sect. 2.1, and λ controls the contextual loss importance.

Table 1. Evaluation in terms of Kernel Inception Distance $\times 100 \pm$ std. $\times 100$ [3]. Note that results on style-specific settings are obtained from models trained on the generic landscape setting.

Method	Landscapes	Portraits	Expressionism	Impressionism	Realism	Romanticism
Original paintings	6.17 ± 0.48	5.10 ± 0.55	8.16 ± 0.50	8.43 ± 0.47	7.57 ± 0.47	5.68 ± 0.39
Style-transferred reals	8.50 ± 0.56	4.67 ± 0.57	10.16 ± 0.53	10.49 ± 0.58	10.06 ± 0.46	9.20 ± 0.51
UNIT [18]	5.70 ± 0.42	3.23 ± 0.40	7.07 ± 0.41	7.76 ± 0.52	8.05 ± 0.52	7.47 ± 0.52
Cycle-GAN [26]	2.61 ± 0.30	$\mathbf{2.66 \pm 0.33}$	4.03 ± 0.36	4.04 ± 4.33	4.04 ± 0.44	3.48 ± 0.39
Ours	$\mathbf{2.18 \pm 0.37}$	3.20 ± 0.42	$\mathbf{3.52 \pm 0.34}$	$\mathbf{3.30 \pm 0.37}$	$\mathbf{2.95 \pm 0.35}$	$\mathbf{2.80 \pm 0.35}$

3 Experimental Evaluation

3.1 Datasets

Our artistic datasets all come from Wikiart[1]. Besides generic landscape artworks, we also collected four sets of paintings considering different artistic styles (*i.e.* expressionism, impressionism, realism, and romanticism). To validate our model under a different setting, we used a set of generic portraits as additional dataset. The training of the model was performed by using two sets of real images, one depicting real landscapes, while the other representing real people photos. The size of each considered set of images is, respectively, landscape paintings: 2044, portraits: 1714, expressionism: 145, impressionism: 852, realism: 310, romanticism: 256, real landscape photographs: 2048, real people photographs: 2048. Due to the limited size of the style-specific sets of paintings, we only used them to validate the generalization capabilities of our model on unseen landscape images.

---

[1] https://www.wikiart.org/.

Table 2. Mean entropy values of images generated through our method and competitors. Results are reported for different computer vision tasks, *i.e.* classification (VGG-19, ResNet-101), segmentation (Mask^X R-CNN), and detection (Faster R-CNN).

Method	VGG-19	ResNet-101	Mask^X R-CNN	Faster R-CNN
Real photos	4.13	3.81	0.63	2.03
Original paintings	6.10	5.35	0.68	2.33
Style-transferred reals	6.20	5.63	0.69	2.65
UNIT [18]	5.14	5.15	0.68	2.31
Cycle-GAN [26]	5.00	4.95	**0.66**	2.23
Ours	**4.72**	**4.74**	**0.66**	**2.21**

3.2   Implementation Details

Our generative networks are inspired by Johnson *et al.* [12], with two stride-2 convolutions, several residual blocks and two stride-1/2 convolutions. Our discriminators are PatchGANs [11,15,16]. Memory banks patches were obtained from the two sets of real images (*i.e.* real landscape photographs and real people photographs). Paintings masks were updated with generated images masks every 20 epochs, starting from epoch 40. Three patch scales were adopted for the multi-scale version of the model: 4×4 with stride 4, 8×8 with stride 5 and 16×16 with stride 6. The chosen value for λ in Eq. 4 was 0.1. Weights were initialized from a Gaussian distribution with 0 mean and standard deviation 0.02. We trained our model for 300 epochs using Adam optimizer [13] with a batch size of 1. A constant learning rate of 0.0002 was used for the first 100 epochs, making it linearly decay to zero over the next 200 epochs. To reduce training time, an early stopping technique was adopted: if the Fréchet Inception Distance [9] did not decrease for 30 consecutive epochs, the training was stopped.

3.3   Visual Quality Evaluation

A quantitative evaluation of the realism of images generated by our method can be performed through a similarity measure between fake images and target distribution samples representations in the Inception architecture. We adopt the Kernel Inception Distance (KID) [3], which measures the squared Maximum Mean Discrepancy between Inception representations. Compared to the Fréchet Inception Distance [9], the KID metric results to be more reliable especially when it is computed over fewer test images than the dimensionality of the Inception features. Table 1 shows KID values computed between the representations of generated and real images, for different settings. Following the original paper [3], the final KID values were averaged over 100 different splits of size 100, randomly sampled from each setting. As it can be seen, our semantic-aware architecture is able to lower the KID in almost all the settings. Our KID values are compared with those from Cycle-GAN [26] and UNIT [18], which we trained on

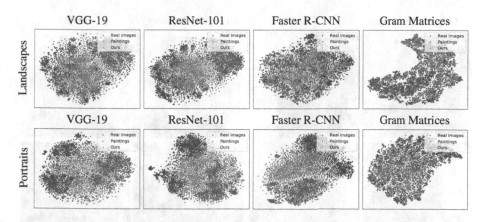

Fig. 2. Distribution of different types of features extracted from landscape and portrait images. We report feature distributions coming from VGG-19 and ResNet-101 for classification, Faster R-CNN for detection, and Gram matrices which encode image textures.

datasets discussed in Sect. 3.1 adopting original authors' implementations. The style-transferred reals row reports the KID values of images obtained through Gatys *et al.* [4] method, considering real photos as content images and randomly sampled paintings (from a specific artistic setting) as style images. The style-specific columns of Table 1 report KID values on expressionism, impressionism, realism and romanticism computed using the models trained on generic landscapes.

3.4 Entropy Analysis

The analysis of the output probabilities from a model can be helpful to evaluate its level of uncertainty about its input. Specifically, we can compute the entropy value of a specific model on a given image, based on its output probabilities. Averaging the entropy values computed on all the images from a given setting, we can determine how much a model is uncertain about its scores on this setting: with an high entropy value, the model will have an high level of uncertainty. Table 2 shows average entropy values of different existing models on original paintings, real photos and images generated through our model and competitors. As it can be noticed, our model brings to the lowest mean entropy in all the considered tasks, *i.e.* classification (VGG-19 [23], ResNet-101 [8]), semantic segmentation (Mask^X R-CNN [10]) and detection (Faster R-CNN [21]). The entropy was computed by averaging image entropy for classification, pixel entropy for segmentation and bounding box entropy for detection, on the landscapes and portraits settings.

Original Painting   Ours   Original Painting   Ours

Fig. 3. Segmentation results on original portraits and their translated versions. Our method leads to improved segmentation performance of existing models on artistic data.

3.5   Feature Distributions Visualization

As mentioned in Sect. 1, there is a strong domain gap between real images and paintings, especially when considering distributions of features coming from a CNN. To verify the reduction of this domain gap, Fig. 2 shows the distributions of different types of features extracted from images generated by our model, their artistic versions, and real images. We compare feature distributions coming from two classification models (*i.e.* VGG-19 [23], ResNet-101 [8]) and from an object detection network (*i.e.* Faster R-CNN [21]). We also include feature distributions representing Gram matrices [5] which encode image styles and textures. To represent each image, we extracted a visual feature vector coming either from the *fc7* layer of a VGG-19 or the average pooling layer of a ResNet-101. In the case of the detection network, we extracted a set of feature vectors from Faster R-CNN trained on Visual Genome [14], representing the detected image regions which were averaged to obtain a single visual descriptor for each image. To compute Gram matrices, we extracted features from the *fc3* layer of a VGG-19. Given these n-dimensional representations of each image (with n equal to 2048 for ResNet-101 and Faster R-CNN, and 4096 for VGG-19 and the Gram matrices), we projected them into a 2-dimensional space by using the t-SNE algorithm [19]. As it can be seen, the distributions of our generated images are closer to the distributions of real images than to those of paintings, thus confirming the reduction of the domain shift between real and artistic images in almost all considered settings.

Original Painting   Ours   Original Painting   Ours

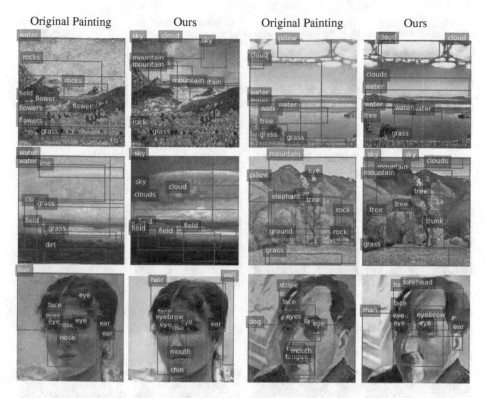

Fig. 4. Detection results on original paintings and their translated versions. Our model leads to improved results of existing detection models on the artistic domain.

4 Reducing the Domain Shift: A Qualitative Analysis

The scarcity of annotated artistic datasets does not allow to use standard quantitative evaluation metrics for computer vision models on our data. We can numerically assess the quality of the generation, but we cannot systematically evaluate if a pre-trained segmentation model, for example, works better on our generated images with respect to the original paintings. For this reason we show, through a number of qualitative examples, that a fake-realistic image generated by our architecture is easily understandable by state-of-the-art models, unlike its original painted version. Figure 3 shows painting-generated image pairs which are both given as input to Mask R-CNN [7] pre-trained on COCO [17]: besides improving the score for well-labeled masks, we are also able to reduce the number of false positives (top-left and bottom-right) and false negatives (bottom-left). Figure 4 illustrates bounding boxes predicted by Faster R-CNN [21] pre-trained on Visual Genome [14]: again we demonstrate improved results, detecting true clouds instead of pillows (top-right) or true sky instead of water (top-left and middle-left). Finally, Fig. 5 presents sentences generated by the captioning approach of [1] on paintings and fake generated photos. As it can be observed,

Original Painting	Ours	Original Painting	Ours

A close up of a bear on a body of water.

A body of water with a mountain in the background.

A painting of a forest with a sky background.

A view of a forest with a cloudy sky.

A large body of water with a boat in the background.

A large body of water with a sunset in the background.

A body of water with a body of water.

A body of water surrounded by a city.

A dog that is looking into the camera.

A close up of a person wearing a hat.

A close up of a person wearing a tie.

A close up of a person wearing glasses.

Fig. 5. Image captioning results on original paintings and their realistic versions generated by our model. Textual descriptions of realistic images are in general more detailed and consistent with the subject depicted in the scene.

textual descriptions become more accurate and aligned with the depicted scene after using our translation approach. Also, we observe a reduction in the number of hallucinations (*e.g.* a *boat* in the middle-left example, a *dog* in the bottom-left example). These observations justify and motivate our work, which is an attempt to enlarge the computer vision field to the still unexplored artistic domain.

5   Conclusion

We have presented an unpaired image-to-image translation approach which can translate paintings to photo-realistic visualizations. Our work is motivated by the poor performance of pre-trained architectures on artistic data, and by need of Computer Vision pipelines capable of understanding the cultural heritage. The presented approach is based on a cycle-consistent translation framework endowed with multi-scale memory banks of patches, so that generated patches are constrained to be similar to real ones. Further, it also includes a semantic-aware strategy so to impose the semantic correctness of generated patches. In this paper, we have conducted additional experiments and evaluations: firstly, we have assessed the visual quality of generated images, in the case of landscapes, portraits and paintings from different styles. Further, we have investigated the response of pre-trained architectures in terms of entropy of prediction and feature distribution. Results have confirmed that our approach is able to generate images which look realistic both from a qualitative point of view and in terms of the predictions given by pre-trained architectures. Finally, as an additional contribution we have presented some qualitative predictions given by detection, segmentation and captioning networks on images generated by our approach.

References

1. Anderson, P., et al.: Bottom-up and top-down attention for image captioning and visual question answering. In: Proceedings of the IEEE Conference on Computer Vision and Pattern Recognition (2018)
2. Baraldi, L., Cornia, M., Grana, C., Cucchiara, R.: Aligning text and document illustrations: towards visually explainable digital humanities. In: Proceedings of the International Conference on Pattern Recognition (2018)
3. Bińkowski, M., Sutherland, D.J., Arbel, M., Gretton, A.: Demystifying MMD GANs. In: Proceedings of the International Conference on Learning Representations (2018)
4. Gatys, L.A., Ecker, A.S., Bethge, M.: A neural algorithm of artistic style. arXiv preprint arXiv:1508.06576 (2015)
5. Gatys, L.A., Ecker, A.S., Bethge, M.: Image style transfer using convolutional neural networks. In: Proceedings of the IEEE Conference on Computer Vision and Pattern Recognition (2016)
6. Goodfellow, I., et al.: Generative adversarial nets. In: Advances in Neural Information Processing Systems (2014)
7. He, K., Gkioxari, G., Dollár, P., Girshick, R.: Mask R-CNN. In: Proceedings of the International Conference on Computer Vision (2017)
8. He, K., Zhang, X., Ren, S., Sun, J.: Deep residual learning for image recognition. In: Proceedings of the IEEE Conference on Computer Vision and Pattern Recognition (2016)
9. Heusel, M., Ramsauer, H., Unterthiner, T., Nessler, B., Klambauer, G., Hochreiter, S.: GANs trained by a two time-scale update rule converge to a Nash equilibrium. In: Advances in Neural Information Processing Systems (2017)
10. Hu, R., Dollár, P., He, K., Darrell, T., Girshick, R.: Learning to segment every thing. In: Proceedings of the IEEE Conference on Computer Vision and Pattern Recognition (2018)
11. Isola, P., Zhu, J.Y., Zhou, T., Efros, A.A.: Image-to-image translation with conditional adversarial networks. In: Proceedings of the IEEE Conference on Computer Vision and Pattern Recognition (2017)
12. Johnson, J., Alahi, A., Fei-Fei, L.: Perceptual losses for real-time style transfer and super-resolution. In: Proceedings of the European Conference on Computer Vision (2016)

13. Kingma, D.P., Ba, J.: Adam: a method for stochastic optimization. In: Proceedings of the International Conference on Learning Representations (2015)
14. Krishna, R., et al.: Visual genome: connecting language and vision using crowd-sourced dense image annotations. Int. J. Comput. Vis. **123**(1), 32–73 (2017)
15. Ledig, C., et al.: Photo-realistic single image super-resolution using a generative adversarial network. In: Proceedings of the IEEE Conference on Computer Vision and Pattern Recognition (2017)
16. Li, C., Wand, M.: Precomputed real-time texture synthesis with Markovian generative adversarial networks. In: Leibe, B., Matas, J., Sebe, N., Welling, M. (eds.) ECCV 2016. LNCS, vol. 9907, pp. 702–716. Springer, Cham (2016). https://doi.org/10.1007/978-3-319-46487-9_43
17. Lin, T.Y., et al.: Microsoft COCO: common objects in context. In: Fleet, D., Pajdla, T., Schiele, B., Tuytelaars, T. (eds.) ECCV 2014. LNCS, vol. 8693, pp. 740–755. Springer, Cham (2014). https://doi.org/10.1007/978-3-319-10602-1_48
18. Liu, M.Y., Breuel, T., Kautz, J.: Unsupervised image-to-image translation networks. In: Advances in Neural Information Processing Systems (2017)
19. Van der Maaten, L., Hinton, G.: Visualizing data using t-SNE. J. Mach. Learn. Res. **9**(Nov), 2579–2605 (2008)
20. Mechrez, R., Talmi, I., Shama, F., Zelnik-Manor, L.: Learning to maintain natural image statistics. arXiv preprint arXiv:1803.04626 (2018)
21. Ren, S., He, K., Girshick, R., Sun, J.: Faster R-CNN: towards real-time object detection with region proposal networks. IEEE Trans. Pattern Anal. Mach. Intell. **39**(6), 1137–1149 (2017)
22. Shen, X., Efros, A.A., Mathieu, A.: Discovering visual patterns in art collections with spatially-consistent feature learning. In: Proceedings of the IEEE Conference on Computer Vision and Pattern Recognition (2019)
23. Simonyan, K., Zisserman, A.: Very deep convolutional networks for large-scale image recognition. In: Proceedings of the International Conference on Learning Representations (2015)
24. Tomei, M., Baraldi, L., Cornia, M., Cucchiara, R.: What was Monet seeing while painting? Translating artworks to photo-realistic images. In: Leal-Taixé, L., Roth, S. (eds.) ECCV 2018. LNCS, vol. 11130, pp. 601–616. Springer, Cham (2019). https://doi.org/10.1007/978-3-030-11012-3_46
25. Tomei, M., Cornia, M., Baraldi, L., Cucchiara, R.: Art2Real: unfolding the reality of artworks via semantically-aware image-to-image translation. In: Proceedings of the IEEE Conference on Computer Vision and Pattern Recognition (2019)
26. Zhu, J.Y., Park, T., Isola, P., Efros, A.A.: Unpaired image-to-image translation using cycle-consistent adversarial networks. In: Proceedings of the International Conference on Computer Vision (2017)

VEDI: Vision Exploitation for Data Interpretation

G. M. Farinella[1,2]([⊠]), G. Signorello[2], S. Battiato[1], A. Furnari[1], F. Ragusa[1],
R. Leonardi[1], E. Ragusa[3], E. Scuderi[3], A. Lopes[3], L. Santo[3],
and M. Samarotto[3]

[1] IPLAB - Department of Mathematics and Computer Science,
University of Catania, Catania, Italy
gfarinella@dmi.unict.it
[2] CUTGANA, University of Catania, Catania, Italy
[3] Xenia Gestione Documentale s.r.l. - Xenia Progetti s.r.l., Acicastello, Italy

Abstract. We present VEDI (Vision Exploitation for Data Interpretation), an integrated system to jointly assist the visitors of cultural sites and provide meaningful statistics about the visits to the managers of the sites. To address both goals, VEDI includes a wearable assistant (implemented through a wearable device such as HoloLens) which leverages Computer Vision algorithms to understand where the user is and what they are paying attention to. At the visitor's end, such information is leveraged to augment the visit by displaying additional information on the observed points of interest, helping the visitors to navigate the site and suggesting what to see next. Concurrently, a back-end extracts high-level behavioral information from the captured video content which is used to provide the site manager with meaningful statistics and performance indexes on the cultural site. Experiments show that VEDI achieves good results on both the indoor and outdoor cultural sites considered for the experimentation.

Keywords: First person vision · Egocentric vision ·
AI for cultural sites

1 Introduction

Cultural sites are visited everyday by many visitors. This foster the interest developing technologies able to assist the visitor by automatically providing information related to the environment (e.g., the visitor's location in the site) or the observed points of interest (e.g., details on the observed points of interest). Also, for site managers, it is important to understand the behavior of visitors (e.g., inferring what they have seen and where they have been) to measure the performance of the cultural site and improve its services. Most cultural sites currently support their visitors through printed material, audio guides, panels and catalogs, whereas behavioral information is collected from visitors through

© Springer Nature Switzerland AG 2019
E. Ricci et al. (Eds.): ICIAP 2019, LNCS 11752, pp. 753–763, 2019.
https://doi.org/10.1007/978-3-030-30645-8_68

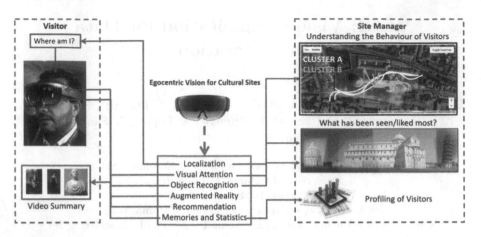

Fig. 1. A scheme of the services provided by VEDI.

surveys. While these classic methodologies are widely employed in cultural sites, they suffer from several limitations. For instance, audio guides and informative panels require the visitor to constantly switch their attention between the cultural site and the supporting media, wheres collecting behavioral information through surveys usually requires time and does not easily scale to large numbers of visitors.

In this paper, we present VEDI (Vision Exploitation for Data Interpretation), an integrated system which includes a wearable device capable of supporting the visitors of cultural sites, as well as a back-end to analyze the visual information collected by the wearable system and infer behavioral information useful for the site manager. To achieve the aforementioned goals, VEDI implements algorithms to localize visitors in the cultural site and recognize the points of interest observed during the visits from the visitors' point of view. The inferred information is then used to provide the following services: (1) a "Where am I?" service which informs the visitor on their location in the site during their visit; (2) a service to provide the visitor with additional information on the observed points of interest using Augmented Reality; (3) a service to estimate the visitors' attention during the visits (e.g., what has been seen most, which places have been most visited). The obtained information can be used by the site manager to profile the visitors and gain insights into the quality of the provided services; (4) a recommendation system to suggest visitors what to see next based on their current location and history of observed points of interest; (5) a system to generate a video summary of each visit, which can be given to the visitor as a "digital memory". Figure 1 shows a scheme of the services offered by VEDI to visitors and cultural site mangers.

The proposed system has been tested in two cultural sites: "Monastero dei Benedettini" and "Orto Botanico". The former is an indoor environment in which we have considered 9 different contexts and 57 points of interest. The latter is an outdoor site composed by 9 different areas, each including plants belonging to different families (we consider 16 plants as points of interest for the experimentation). Experiments show that the proposed VEDI system achieves good performance in the tasks of visitor localization and point of interest recognition on the considered cultural sites.

The remainder of the paper is organized as follows. Section 2 reports the related work. Section 3 presents the collected and publicly available datasets. Section 4 describes the architecture of VEDI and discusses the services provided by the system. Section 5 reports the experimental results, whereas Sect. 6 concludes the paper.

2 Related Work

Augmented Cultural Experience with Wearable and Mobile Devices. Different works investigated the use of wearable and mobile devices for augmented cultural experience [3]. Among the most notable works, the authors of [1] exploited gesture recognition to enable interaction between users and artworks. In [17] a system to support the visitors of natural sites through multimodal navigation of multimedia contents was proposed. In [6] it was suggested to analyze georeferenced images through Visual Analytics tools to identify trends, patterns and relationships among images collected from social media. Differently from the aforementioned works, the proposed VEDI has been designed to both support the visitors of cultural sites and provide useful behavioral information to the site manager.

User Localization form Wearable Devices. Beside classic approaches to scene understanding [2], previous works have investigated method to achieve localization from egocentric images. In [18], a system to perform room-based localization and scene recognition from a wearable camera has been introduced. The authors of [7] proposed a system to infer the 6 Degrees of Freedom pose of a camera directly from egocentric images. The authors of [19] presented an approach to perform world-scale photo gelolocation using Convolutional Neural Networks. The authors of [4,5] proposed an approach to perform room-based localization from few training data. The approach has later been applied in the context of a cultural site in [12]. The authors of [9] exploited egocentric images and GPS to address outdoor localization. In [14] it was presented an approach to perform large scale image-based localization based on direct 2D-to-3D matching.

Object Detection/Recognition in Cultural Sites. Our work is related to previous investigations using object detection to estimate the attention of visitors in a cultural site. The authors of [10] investigated the use of Fully Convlutional Networks to perform egocentric image classification and object deteciton in a museum. The authors of [15] presented a system to detect artworks and analyze audio activity to implement a smart audio guide with a smartphone. The proposed VEDI system leverages state of the art object detectors to recognize the points of interest observed by the visitors of a cultural site. Specifically, our system relies on the YOLOv3 object detector [13].

Behavioural Analysis of the Visitors of a Cultural Site. Previous works
have investigated approaches for the behavioral analysis of the visitors of a cultural site. In particular, the authors of [16] have proposed empirically grounded
models of individual and collective spatial behavior, whereas an accurate analysis of the behaviours of the visitors of an exhibition has been addressed in [8].
The proposed system tackles behavioral analysis by classifying visitors into four
different profiles.

3   Experimental Cultural Sites and Datasets

Our system has been tested in two real cultural sites: "Monastero dei Benedettini" [1], which is an indoor environment, and "Orto Botanico" [2], which is a outdoor
natural site. Specifically, we have collected and labeled different datasets of egocentric videos useful to drive the design of context-based localization algorithms
and point of interest recognition algorithms. The datasets are also useful to
and assess the performances of algorithms in both indoor and outdoor environments. The collected datasets, which are described in the following, are publicly
available for research purposes at the following URL: http://iplab.dmi.unict.it/
VEDI_project.

UNICT-VEDI. This dataset has been originally introduced in [12] to address
context-based visitors localization and subsequently extended in [11] to study the
problem of point of interest recognition. The dataset consists of several videos
acquired using two wearable devices: HoloLens and GoPro Hero 4. The videos
have been temporally annotated to indicate in each frame (1) the location of
the visitor (the room in which they are located) and (2) the "point of interest"
observed by the visitor (e.g., a painting, a statue or an architectural element).
The dataset comprises a total of 9 environments and 57 points of interest. We
also provide bounding box annotations for about 1000 frames for each of the 57
points of interest. This amounts to a total of 54248 frames labeled with bounding
boxes in the whole dataset (see the Fig. 2).

EgoNature. This dataset has been collected in the natural site "Orto Botanico"
to test context-based localization. In particular, the dataset contains 9 contexts,
which are 9 areas of the site relevant for the visitors. Egocentric videos have
been acquired using a Pupil 3D Eye Tracker headset coupled with a smartphone
(Honor 9) to collect GPS locations which are later synced to the videos. More
details are available in [9].

UNICT-VEDI_Succulente. This dataset has been collected in the natural site
"Orto Botanico" to perform point of interest recognition. It includes 16 points
of interest representing plants belonging to following families: (1) Apocynaceae,
(2) Bombacaceae, (3) Cactaceae, (4) Crassulaceae, (5) Euphorbiaceae, (6) Lami-
aceae, (7) Liliaceae. For each frame, we have annotated the plant depicted in the

---

[1] http://monasterodeibenedettini.it.

[2] http://ortobotanico.unict.it/.

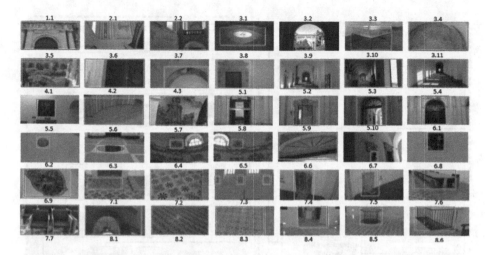

Fig. 2. Some examples from UNICT-VEDI along with bounding box annotations.

Fig. 3. Examples of the 16 plants belonging to the UNICT-VEDI_Succulente dataset.

image. The dataset contains 36, 728 labeled images. Figure 3 shows some images of the points of interest present in the dataset.

4   Architecture and Services

In this Section, we first discuss the general architecture of VEDI (Sect. 4.1), then present the services implemented by the system (Sect. 4.2).

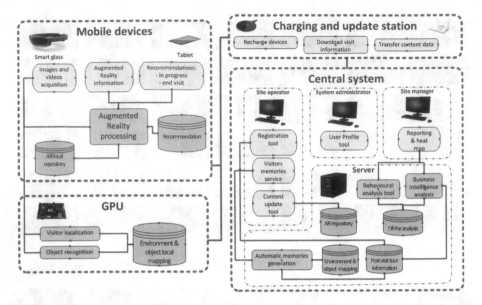

Fig. 4. The VEDI system is made up of 4 components: (1) Mobile devices, (2) GPU, (3) Charging and update station, (4) Central system.

4.1   Architecture

Figure 4 illustrates the high level architecture of the proposed VEDI system, which is made up of the following components:

- **Mobile devices:** mobile devices such as smart glasses and tablets are provided to the visitors of the cultural site. These devices are used to both acquire images and video from the point of view of the visitors, as well as to provide additional information or recommendations to the visitor through Augmented Reality;
- **Graphic Processing Unit (GPU):** directly connected to the wearable device, it is used to provide additional computational power in order to to process egocentric video and address visitor localization and object recognition;
- **Charging and update station:** used at the end of the visit to recharge the wearable devices, transfer the information collected during the visit (e.g., video) to the central system, and update the contents (e.g., 3D models) provided during the visit;
- **Central system:** handles system management, processes and store all data collected by the wearable devices. The central system comprises a *Server*, which includes components to handle the egocentric data collected during the visits and analyze it for behavioral analysis, business intelligence analysis and automatic generation of digital video memories to be provided to the visitors. Moreover, the following actors take part to the central system:

- *System administrator:* can access all system functions, define user profiles (site operator, site manager) and enable/disable specific functions;
- *Site operator:* can access the following functions: (1) "registration tool", which allows to associate their identity to the assigned mobile device id; (2) "visitors memories service", which automatically generates a video containing the salient moments of each visit to be sent to the user, post-card or other digital gadgets representing objects observed during the visit; (3) "content update tool" which allows to update the contents stored in the AR repository;
- *Site manager:* can use the "Reporting & Head-Map" tool to visualize performance indexes and statistic indicators generated after normalization, aggregation and management of data, as well as all behavioral information periodically extracted by the system using dedicated algorithms.

4.2 Services

This Section presents the services implemented by VEDI. Demo videos of the different services are available at the following URL: http://iplab.dmi.unict.it/VEDI_project/#video.

Localization and Points of Interest Recognition: Given the different nature of indoor and outdoor contexts, visitors localization and point of interest recognition are carried out using different algorithms. In indoor contexts (e.g., the *UNICT-VEDI* dataset), the system performs context-based localization of visitors by processing the acquired egocentric video with a multi-stage localization algorithm which we describe in details in [12]. The recognition of the points of interest observed by visitors is carried out using an approach based on a Yolov3 object detector [13], which is detailed in [11]. In the *outdoor contexts* (i.e., the *EgoNature* and *UNICT-VEDI_Succulente* datasets), we perform context-based localization by fusing GPS measurements and egocentric images by means of the multi-modal localization algorithm described in [9]. Recognition of points of interest is addressed in *UNICT-VEDI_succulente* as a classification problem, by fine-tuning an AlexNet CNN to discriminate between images belonging to the 16 different points of interest.

Augmented Reality. The AR GUI is triggered when a point of interest is recognized and observed for a significant amount of time. This leaves to the visitor the decision on which "augmented" information they are interested in. To reach this goal, the user interface has been designed according to the following three features:

1. The user interaction panel used to choose the multimedia contents of interest should not remain constantly in front of the visitor;
2. The GUI has been designed relying on the use of transparency to never completely impede the visibility of the external world;
3. The area engaged by the interface is designed to be as small as possible.

  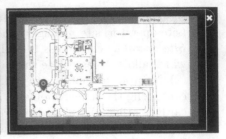

Fig. 5. AR GUI examples. From left to right: additional information on the observed point of interest, a 3D model shown to the visitor, a map showing the position of the visitor in the cultural site.

See Fig. 5 for same examples of the AR GUI.

Behavior Analysis and Visual Analytics. To study the behavior of visitors, we compute the following indicators for each cultural site:

- Attraction index: ratio between the number of visitors observing a given point of interest and total number of visitors;
- Retention index: measuring the average time spent in front of an information-communication element (e.g., a panel, a video, a caption, etc.);
- Usage times: times of use (for the overall visit, for specific sections, for types of users);
- Sweep Rate Index (SRI): the ratio between the total size of the exposure, in square meters, and the average time spent by visitors within the exposure itself;
- Diligent Visitor Index (DVI): the percentage of visitors who stopped in front of more than half of the points of interest of the cultural site.

Data Visualization. The VEDI platform is engineered to provide the managers of cultural sites with utilities and tools to create awareness on the visitors' behavior. Cultural site manager can explore visitors' behavioral data and have insights on the characteristics of each class of visitors (e.g., male-female, young-adult, low-high education, local-alien) through specific data report. This is done relying on the output of the localization and point of interest recognition algorithms discussed in the previous paragraphs. The data visualization tools offer the site manager a way to assess in which areas the visitors spend more time and the most followed routes inside the building (see Fig. 6). Finally, VEDI assists the managers by providing internationally known key performance indexes such as "Attraction Index", "Sweep Rate Index" and "Diligent Visitors Index" to benchmark the performances of the considered cultural site against similar sites.

Memories. This service allows to automatically generate a video summary of a visit by taking into account (1) semantic information about locations and observed points of interest obtained using the localization and point of interest recognition algorithms, (2) meta-data (e.g., photos, descriptions) on the site, contexts and points of interest.

Fig. 6. An example of data visualization, where a heat map is used to demonstrate the behavior of the visitors.

5 Experimental Results

We tested our system to assess the performances of localization and point of interest recognition systems, which are at the core of VEDI. Table 1(a) reports the results of the context-based localization system on UNICT-VEDI. Following [12], we evaluate our system using a frame-based mean F_1 score (mFF_1), which is the mean F_1 scores across classes computed over frames, as well as a segment-based F_1 score $(mASF_1)$, which is the mean average F_1 score, when the system is used to retrieve video segments (please see [12] for more details on the evaluation measures). As can be seen, the proposed approach achieves usable results with videos acquired using both HoloLens and GoPro considering all evaluation measures.

Table 1(b) compares the proposed approach for point of interest recognition [11] based on a Yolov3 object detector with respect to the following baseline: (1) 57-POI - the localization method proposed in [11] adapted for point of interest recognition, (2) 57-POI-N, as in 57-POI but training using both positive and negative frames (i.e., frames in which no point of interest is observed), (3) 9-Classifiers, the combination of 9 context-specific 57-POI point of interest recognition methods with the localization system proposed in [11]. It should be noted that $9 - Classifier$ is computational expensive both at training and test time due to the need to train context-specific recognition systems. All results are evaluated using mean frame-based F_1 score. Results confirm that the proposed approach allows to obtain good performances comparable with 9-Classifiers using a context-generic recognition system at a lower computational cost.

Table 1(c) reports the results of different variants of the proposed system for context-based outdoor localization which uses both egocentric images and GPS. Localization results are measured using frame-based accuracy. The time required to process and localize a single image in CPU is reported in milliseconds (ms). All methods use a variant of SqueezeNet to process images and a Decision Tree (DCT) to process GPS. SqueezeNet-n modeles denote a simplified (and hence faster) SqueezeNet architecture which considers only the n convolutional layers.

All methods obtain good results. Considerably faster inference is obtained using SqueezeNet-6 + DCT.

Table 1. The results obtained by VEDI system in the fundamental tasks of localization (a and c) and point of interest recognition (b).

	HoloLens	GoPro
mFF_1	0.82	0.81
$mASF_1$	0.71	0.71

(a)

Method	F_1 score
57-POI	0.59
57-POI-N	0.62
9-Classifiers	0.66
Proposed	0.68

(b)

Method	Accuracy	Time (ms)
SqueezeNet-6 + DCT	0.86	4.7
SqueezeNet-9 + DCT	0.86	6.09
SqueezeNet-11 + DCT	0.86	6.60
SqueezeNet + DCT	0.91	22.9

(c)

Regarding to the outdoor point of interest recognition system based on AlexNet, it achieves a mean F_1 score of 89.02% on the UNICT-VEDI_Succulente dataset when discriminating among the 16 considered points of interest.

6   Conclusion

We have presented VEDI, an integrated wearable system to assist the visitors of cultural sites by providing additional information on the observed points of view during their visits, as well as the site managers by automatically inferring useful performance indicators and behavioral information on the cultural sites. Experiments on two cultural sites highlight the good performance achieved by the proposed approach in the fundamental tasks of localizing visitors and recognizing points of interest.

Acknowledgment. This research is supported by PON MISE - Horizon 2020, Project VEDI - Vision Exploitation for Data Interpretation, Prog. n. F/050457/02/X32 - CUP: B68I17000800008 - COR: 128032, and Piano della Ricerca 2016-2018 linea di Intervento 2 of DMI of the University of Catania.

References

1. Baraldi, L., Paci, F., Serra, G., Benini, L., Cucchiara, R.: Gesture recognition using wearable vision sensors to enhance visitors' museum experiences. IEEE Sens. J. **15**, 2705–2714 (2015)
2. Battiato, S., Farinella, G.M., Gallo, G., Ravì, D.: Scene categorization using bag of textons on spatial hierarchy. In: International Conference on Image Processing, pp. 2536–2539. IEEE (2008)
3. Cucchiara, R., Del Bimbo, A.: Visions for augmented cultural heritage experience. IEEE Multimedia **21**(1), 74–82 (2014)
4. Furnari, A., Battiato, S., Farinella, G.M.: Personal-location-based temporal segmentation of egocentric video for lifelogging applications. J. Vis. Commun. Image Represent. **52**, 1–12 (2018)

5. Furnari, A., Farinella, G.M., Battiato, S.: Recognizing personal locations from egocentric videos. IEEE Transact. Hum. Mach. Syst. **47**, 6–18 (2017)
6. Gallo, G., Signorello, G., Farinella, G., Torrisi, A.: Exploiting social images to understand tourist behaviour. In: ICIAP, pp. 707–717 (2017)
7. Kendall, A., Grimes, M., Cipolla, R.: Posenet: A convolutional network for real-time 6-dof camera relocalization. In: ICCV, pp. 2938–2946 (2015)
8. Levasseur, M., Veron, E.: Ethnographie d'une exposition. Histoires d'expo, Peuple et culture, pp. 29–32 (1983)
9. Milotta, F.L.M., Furnari, A., Battiato, S., Salvo, M.D., Signorello, G., Farinella, G.M.: Visitors localization in natural sites exploiting egoVision and GPS. In: International Conference on Computer Vision Theory and Applications (2019)
10. Portaz, M., Kohl, M., Quénot, G., Chevallet, J.P.: Fully convolutional network and region proposal for instance identification with egocentric vision. In: IEEE Conference on Computer Vision and Pattern Recognition, pp. 2383–2391 (2017)
11. Ragusa, F., Furnari, A., Battiato, S., Signorello, G., Farinella, G.M.: Egocentric point of interest recognition in cultural sites. In: VISAPP (2019)
12. Ragusa, F., Furnari, A., Battiato, S., Signorello, G., Farinella, G.M.: Egocentric visitors localization in cultural sites. ACM J. Comput. Cult. Heritage **12**, 11 (2019)
13. Redmon, J., Farhadi, A.: Yolov3: an incremental improvement. CoRR abs/1804.02767, http://arxiv.org/abs/1804.02767 (2018)
14. Sattler, T., Leibe, B., Kobbelt, L.: Efficient & effective prioritized matching for large-scale image-based localization. PAMI **39**, 1744–1756 (2017)
15. Seidenari, L., Baecchi, C., Uricchio, T., Ferracani, A., Bertini, M., Bimbo, A.D.: Deep artwork detection and retrieval for automatic context-aware audio guides. TOMM **13**(3s), 35 (2017)
16. Shell, D.A., et al.: Spatial behavior of individuals and groups: preliminary findings from a museum scenario. In: IROS 2007 Workshops (2007)
17. Signorello, G., Farinella, G.M., Gallo, G., Santo, L., Lopes, A., Scuderi, E.: Exploring protected nature through multimodal navigation of multimedia contents. In: ACIVS, pp. 841–852 (2015)
18. Torralba, A., Murphy, K.P., Freeman, W.T., Rubin, M.A.: Context-based vision system for place and object recognition. In: Proceedings of Ninth IEEE International Conference on Computer Vision, 2003, pp. 273–280. IEEE (2003)
19. Weyand, T., Kostrikov, I., Philbin, J.: PlaNet - photo geolocation with convolutional neural networks. In: Leibe, B., Matas, J., Sebe, N., Welling, M. (eds.) ECCV 2016. LNCS, vol. 9912, pp. 37–55. Springer, Cham (2016). https://doi.org/10.1007/978-3-319-46484-8_3

Author Index

Printed in the United States
By Bookmasters